SPECIALIST

MICROSOFT® OFFICE 2003

NITA RUTKOSKY

Pierce College at Puyallup
Puyallup, Washington

Project Editor	Sonja Brown
Developmental Editors	Courtney Kost, James Patterson
Senior Designer	Leslie Anderson
Technical Reviewer	Desiree Faulkner
Cover Designer	Jennifer Wreisner
Copyeditor	Susan Capecchi
Desktop Production Specialists	Lisa Beller, Erica Tava, and Desktop Solutions
Proofreaders	Joy McComb, Kathryn Savoie
Indexer	Nancy Fulton
Photo Researcher	Paul Spencer

Publishing Team—George Provol, Publisher; Janice Johnson, Director of Product Development and Instructional Design; Tony Galvin, Acquisitions Editor; Lori Landwer, Marketing Manager; Shelley Clubb, Electronic Design and Production Manager

Acknowledgments—The author and editors wish to thank the following instructors for their technical and academic contributions:

- Kay M. Newton, Commonwealth Business College, Michigan City, IN, for testing the Word 2003 exercises and assessing instruction
- Susan Lynn Bowen, Valdosta Technical College, Valdosta, GA, for testing the Excel 2003, Access 2003, and PowerPoint 2003 exercises and assessing instruction
- Ann Lewis, Ivy Tech State College, Evansville, IN, for creating the Chapter Challenge exercises for Word 2003, Excel 2003, Access 2003, and PowerPoint 2003
- Denise Seguin, Fanshawe College, London, Ontario, Canada, for writing the introductions to Word 2003, Excel 2003, Access 2003, and PowerPoint 2003

Photo Credits
Word 2003: S1, Jose Luis Pelaez, Inc./CORBIS; S2 (counterclockwise from left), Steve Chenn/CORBIS, Left Lane Productions/CORBIS, CORBIS; S3, Jose Luis Pelaez, Inc./CORBIS; S4, Ariel Skelley /CORBIS.
Excel 2003: S1 (top to bottom) Owaki – Kulla/CORBIS, CORBIS, Rob Lewine/CORBIS; S2, AFP/CORBIS; S3, Jose Luis Pelaez, Inc./CORBIS; S4, LWA-JDC/CORBIS.
Access 2003: S1 (counterclockwise from top), William Gottlieb/CORBIS; CORBIS; CORBIS; Will & Deni McIntyre/CORBIS.
PowerPoint 2003: S1, Rob Lewine/CORBIS, CORBIS; S2, T. Kevin Smyth/CORBIS.

Library of Congress Cataloging-in-Publication Data

Rutkosky, Nita Hewitt.
Microsoft Office 2003: specialist certification / Nita Rutkosky.
p. cm. — (Benchmark series)
Includes index.
ISBN 0-7638-2053-9
1. Microsoft Office. 2. Business--Computer programs. 3. Electronic data processing personnel--Certification. 4. Microsoft software--Examinations--Study guides. I. Title. II. Benchmark series (Saint Paul, Minn.)

HF5548.4.M525R8685 2004
005.36—dc22

2003061555

Text: ISBN 0-7638-2053-9
Product Number 05620

Published by **EMC**Paradigm
875 Montreal Way
St. Paul, MN 55102

(800) 535-6865
E-mail: educate@emcp.com
Web site: www.emcp.com

Printed in the United States of America
10 9 8 7 6 5 4 3

CONTENTS

**These activities appear at the end of every chapter.*

WELCOME

You are about to begin working with a textbook that is part of the Benchmark Office 2003 Series. The word *Benchmark* in the title holds a special significance in terms of *what* you will learn and *how* you will learn. *Benchmark*, according to *Webster's Dictionary*, means "something that serves as a standard by which others may be measured or judged." In this text, you will learn the Microsoft Office Specialist skills required for certification on the Specialist and/or Expert level of one or more major applications within the Office 2003 suite. These skills are benchmarks by which you will be evaluated, should you choose to take one or more certification exams.

The design and teaching approach of this textbook also serve as a benchmark for instructional materials on software programs. Features and commands are presented in a clear, straightforward way, and each short section of instruction is followed by an exercise that lets you practice using the new feature. Gradually, as you move through each chapter, you will build your skills to the point of mastery. At the end of a chapter, you are offered the opportunity to demonstrate your newly acquired competencies—to prove you have met the benchmarks for using the Office suite or an individual program. At the completion of the text, you are well on your way to becoming a successful computer user.

EMC/Paradigm's Office 2003 Benchmark Series includes textbooks on Office 2003, Word 2003, Excel 2003, Access 2003, and PowerPoint 2003. Each book includes a Student CD, which contains documents and files required for completing the exercises. A CD icon and folder name displayed on the opening page of each chapter indicates that you need to copy a folder of files from the CD before beginning the chapter exercises. *(See the inside back cover for instructions on copying a folder.)*

Introducing Microsoft Office 2003

Microsoft Office 2003 is a suite of programs designed to improve productivity and efficiency in workplace, school, and home settings. A suite is a group of programs that are sold as a package and are designed to be used together, making it possible to exchange files among the programs. The major applications included in Office are Word, a word processing program; Excel, a spreadsheet program; Access, a database management program; and PowerPoint, a slide presentation program.

Using the Office suite offers significant advantages over working with individual programs developed by different software vendors. The programs in the Office suite use similar toolbars, buttons, icons, and menus, which means that once you learn the basic features of one program, you can use those same features in the other programs. This easy transfer of knowledge decreases the learning time and allows you to concentrate on the unique commands and options within each program. The compatibility of the programs creates seamless integration of data within and between programs and lets the operator use the program most appropriate for the required tasks.

New Features in Office 2003

Users of previous editions of Office will find that the essential features that have made Office popular still form the heart of the suite. New enhancements include improved templates for both business and personal use. The Smart Tags introduced in Office XP also have been enhanced in Office 2003 with special customization options. One of the most far-reaching changes is the introduction of XML (eXtensible Markup Language) capabilities. Some elements of this technology were essentially hidden behind the scenes in Office XP. Now XML has been brought to the forefront. XML enables data to be used more flexibly and stored regardless of the computer platform. It can be used between different languages, countries, and across the Internet. XML heralds a revolution in data exchange. At the same time, it makes efficient and effective use of internal data within a business.

Structure of the Benchmark Textbooks

Users of the Specialist Certification texts and the complete application textbooks may begin their course with an overview of computer hardware and software, offered in the *Getting Started* section at the beginning of the book. Your instructor may also ask you to complete the *Windows XP* and the *Internet Explorer* sections so you become familiar with the computer's operating system and the essential tools for using the Internet.

Instruction on the major programs within the Office suite is presented in units of four chapters each. Both the Specialist and Expert levels contain two units, which culminate with performance assessments to check your knowledge and skills. Each chapter contains the following sections:

- performance objectives that identify specifically what you are expected to learn
- instructional text that introduces and explains new concepts and features
- step-by-step, hands-on exercises following each section of instruction
- a chapter summary
- a knowledge self-check called Concepts Check
- skill assessment exercises called Skills Check
- a case study exercise called Chapter Challenge

Exercises offered at the end of units provide writing and research opportunities that will strengthen your performance in other college courses as well as on the job. The final activities simulate interesting projects you could encounter in the workplace.

Benchmark Series Ancillaries

The Benchmark Series includes some important resources that will help you succeed in your computer applications courses:

Snap Training and Assessment

A Web-based program designed to optimize skill-based learning for all of the programs of Microsoft Office 2003, Snap is comprised of:

- a learning management system that creates a virtual classroom on the Web, allowing the instructor to schedule tutorials and tests and to employ an electronic gradebook;
- over 200 interactive, multimedia tutorials, aligned to textbook chapters, that can be used for direct instruction or remediation;
- a test bank of over 1,800 performance skill items that simulate the operation of Microsoft Office and allow the instructor to assign pretests, to administer chapter posttests, and to create practice tests to help students prepare for Microsoft Office Specialist certification exams; and
- over 6,000 concept items that can be used in combined concepts/application courses to monitor student understanding of technical and computer literacy knowledge.

Instructor's Guide on CD-ROM

Included on the CD are suggested syllabi and grading plans, hints for completing exercises, teaching overviews for each chapter, exercise model answers in PDF and live program formats, the student data files, PowerPoint presentations, supplementary assessments, and tests.

Online Resource Center

Internet Resource Centers hosted by EMC/Paradigm provide additional material for students and instructors using the Benchmark books. Online you will find Web links, updates to textbooks, study tips, quizzes and assignments, and supplementary projects.

Class Connection

Available for both WebCT and Blackboard, EMC/Paradigm's Class Connection is a course management tool for traditional and distance learning.

What does this logo mean?

It means this courseware has been approved by the Microsoft® Office Specialist program to be among the finest available for learning Microsoft Word 2003, Microsoft Excel 2003, Microsoft Access 2003, and Microsoft PowerPoint 2003. It also means that upon completion of this courseware, you may be prepared to take exams for Microsoft Office Specialist qualification.

What is a Microsoft Office Specialist?

A Microsoft Office Specialist is an individual who has passed exams for certifying his or her skills in one or more of the Microsoft Office desktop applications such as Microsoft Word, Microsoft Excel, Microsoft PowerPoint, Microsoft Outlook, Microsoft Access, or Microsoft Project. The Microsoft Office Specialist Program typically offers certification exams at the Specialist and Expert skill levels. The Microsoft Office Specialist program is the only program in the world approved by Microsoft for testing proficiency in Microsoft Office desktop applications and Microsoft Project. This testing program can be a valuable asset in any job search or career advancement.

More Information

- To learn more about becoming a Microsoft Office Specialist, visit www.microsoft.com/officespecialist.
- To learn about other Microsoft Office Specialist approved courseware from EMC/Paradigm Publishing, visit www.emcp.com.

The availability of Microsoft Office Specialist certification exams varies by application, application version, and language. Visit www.microsoft.com/officespecialist for information on exam availability.

OFFICE 2003

GETTING STARTED IN OFFICE 2003

In this textbook, you will learn to operate several microcomputer application programs that combine to make an application "suite." This suite of programs is called Microsoft Office 2003. The programs you will learn to operate are the ***software***, which include instructions telling the computer what to do. Some of the software programs in the suite include a word processing program called *Word*, a spreadsheet program called *Excel*, a presentation program called *PowerPoint*, and a database program called *Access*.

Identifying Computer Hardware

The computer equipment you will use to operate the suite of programs is referred to as ***hardware***. You will need access to a microcomputer system that should consist of the CPU, monitor, keyboard, printer, disk drives, and mouse. If you are not sure what equipment you will be operating, check with your instructor. The computer system displayed in Figure G.1 consists of six components. Each component is discussed separately in the material that follows.

FIGURE G.1 ***Microcomputer System***

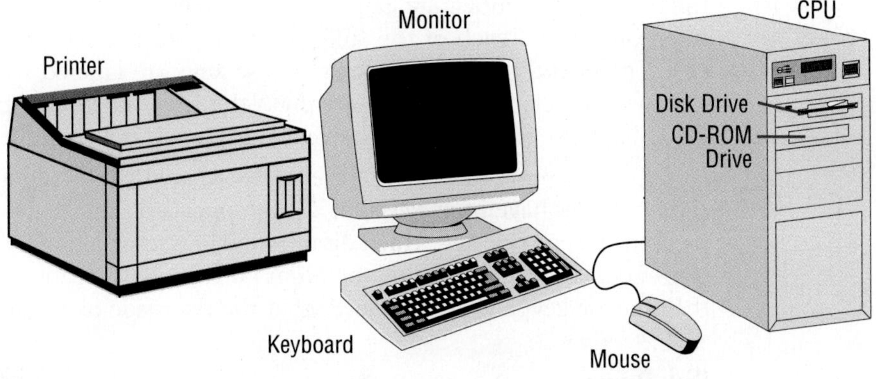

CPU

CPU stands for Central Processing Unit and it is the intelligence of the computer. All the processing occurs in the CPU. Silicon chips, which contain miniaturized circuitry, are placed on boards that are plugged into slots within the CPU. Whenever an instruction is given to the computer, that instruction is processed through circuitry in the CPU.

Monitor

The monitor is a piece of equipment that looks like a television screen. It displays the information of a program and the text being input at the keyboard. The quality of display for monitors varies depending on the type of monitor and the level of resolution. Monitors can also vary in size—generally from 14-inch size up to 21-inch size or larger.

Keyboard

The keyboard is used to input information into the computer. Keyboards for microcomputers vary in the number and location of the keys. Microcomputers have the alphabetic and numeric keys in the same location as the keys on a typewriter. The symbol keys, however, may be placed in a variety of locations, depending on the manufacturer. In addition to letters, numbers, and symbols, most microcomputer keyboards contain function keys, arrow keys, and a numeric keypad. Figure G.2 shows an enhanced keyboard.

FIGURE G.2 ***Microcomputer Enhanced Keyboard***

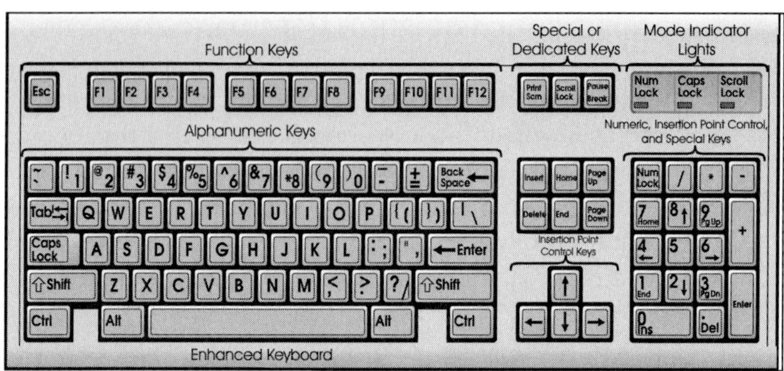

The 12 keys at the top of the enhanced keyboard, labeled with the letter F followed by a number, are called ***function keys***. These keys can be used to perform functions within each of the suite programs. To the right of the regular keys is a group of ***special*** or ***dedicated keys***. These keys are labeled with specific functions that will be performed when you press the key. Below the special keys are arrow keys. These keys are used to move the insertion point in the document screen.

In the upper right corner of the keyboard are three mode indicator lights. When certain modes have been selected, a light appears on the keyboard. For example, if you press the Caps Lock key, which disables the lowercase alphabet, a light appears next to Caps Lock. Similarly, pressing the Num Lock key will disable the special functions on the numeric keypad, which is located at the right side of the keyboard.

Disk Drives

Depending on the computer system you are using, Microsoft Office 2003 is installed on a hard drive or as part of a network system. Whether you are using

Office on a hard drive or network system, you will need to have available a CD drive and a floppy disk drive or other storage media. You will insert the CD (compact disk) that accompanies this textbook in the CD drive and then copy folders from the CD to a disk in the floppy disk drive. You will also save documents you complete at the computer to folders on your disk in the floppy drive.

Printer

When you create a document in Word, it is considered ***soft copy***. If you want a ***hard copy*** of a document, you need to print it. To print documents you will need to access a printer, which will probably be either a laser printer or an ink-jet printer. A laser printer uses a laser beam combined with heat and pressure to print documents, while an ink-jet printer prints a document by spraying a fine mist of ink on the page.

Mouse

Many functions in the suite of programs are designed to operate more efficiently with a ***mouse***. A mouse is an input device that sits on a flat surface next to the computer. A mouse can be operated with the left or the right hand. Moving the mouse on the flat surface causes a corresponding mouse pointer to move on the screen. Figure G.1 shows an illustration of a mouse.

Using the Mouse

The programs in the Microsoft Office suite can be operated using a keyboard or they can be operated with the keyboard and a mouse. The mouse may have two or three buttons on top, which are tapped to execute specific functions and commands. To use the mouse, rest it on a flat surface or a mouse pad. Put your hand over it with your palm resting on top of the mouse and your wrist resting on the table surface. As you move the mouse on the flat surface, a corresponding pointer moves on the screen.

When using the mouse, there are four terms you should understand—point, click, double-click, and drag. When operating the mouse, you may need to ***point*** to a specific command, button, or icon. Point means to position the mouse pointer on the desired item. With the mouse pointer positioned on the desired item, you may need to ***click*** a button on the mouse. Click means quickly tapping a button on the mouse once. To complete two steps at one time, such as choosing and then executing a function, ***double-click*** a mouse button. Double-click means to tap the left mouse button twice in quick succession. The term ***drag*** means to press and hold the left mouse button, move the mouse pointer to a specific location, and then release the button.

Using the Mouse Pointer

The mouse pointer will change appearance depending on the function being performed or where the pointer is positioned. The mouse pointer may appear as one of the following images:

The mouse pointer appears as an I-beam (called the ***I-beam pointer***) in the document screen and can be used to move the insertion point or select text.

The mouse pointer appears as an arrow pointing up and to the left (called the ***arrow pointer***) when it is moved to the Title bar, Menu bar, or one of the toolbars at the top of the screen or when a dialog box is displayed. For example, to open a

new document with the mouse, you would move the I-beam pointer to the File option on the Menu bar. When the I-beam pointer is moved to the Menu bar, it turns into an arrow pointer. To make a selection, position the tip of the arrow pointer on the File option, and then click the left mouse button. At the drop-down menu that displays, make selections by positioning the arrow pointer on the desired option and then clicking the left mouse button.

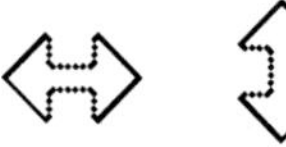

The mouse pointer becomes a double-headed arrow (either pointing left and right, pointing up and down, or pointing diagonally) when performing certain functions such as changing the size of an object.

In certain situations, such as moving an object or image, the mouse pointer becomes a four-headed arrow. The four-headed arrow means that you can move the object left, right, up, or down.

When a request is being processed or when a program is being loaded, the mouse pointer may appear with an hourglass beside it. The hourglass image means "please wait." When the process is completed, the hourglass image is removed.

The mouse pointer displays as a hand with a pointing index finger in certain functions such as Help and indicates that more information is available about the item.

Choosing Commands

Once a program is open, several methods can be used in the program to choose commands. A command is an instruction that tells the program to do something. You can choose a command with one of the following methods:

- Click a toolbar button with the mouse
- Choose a command from a menu
- Use shortcut keys
- Use a shortcut menu

Choosing Commands on Toolbars

When a program such as Word or PowerPoint is open, several toolbars containing buttons for common tasks are available. In many of the suite programs, two toolbars are visible on the screen. One toolbar is called the Standard toolbar; the other is referred to as the Formatting toolbar. To choose a command from a toolbar, position the tip of the arrow pointer on a button, and then click the left mouse button. For example, to print the file currently displayed in the screen, position the tip of the arrow pointer on the Print button on the Standard toolbar, and then click the left mouse button.

Choosing Commands on the Menu Bar

Each of the suite programs contains a Menu bar that displays toward the top of the screen. This Menu bar contains a variety of options you can use to perform functions and commands on data. Functions are grouped logically into options, which display on the Menu bar. For example, features to work with files are grouped in the File option. Either the mouse or the keyboard can be used to make choices from the Menu bar or make a choice at a dialog box.

To use the mouse to make a choice from the Menu bar, move the I-beam pointer to the Menu bar. This causes the I-beam pointer to display as an arrow pointer. Position the tip of the arrow pointer on the desired option, and then click the left mouse button.

To use the keyboard, press the Alt key to make the Menu bar active. Options on the Menu bar display with an underline below one of the letters. To choose an option from the Menu bar, type the underlined letter of the desired option, or move the insertion point with the Left or Right Arrow keys to the option desired, and then press Enter. This causes a drop-down menu to display.

For example, to display the File drop-down menu in Word as shown in Figure G.3 using the mouse, position the arrow pointer on File on the Menu bar, and then click the left mouse button. To display the File drop-down menu with the keyboard, press the Alt key, and then type the letter F for File.

FIGURE G.3 ***Word File Drop-Down Menu***

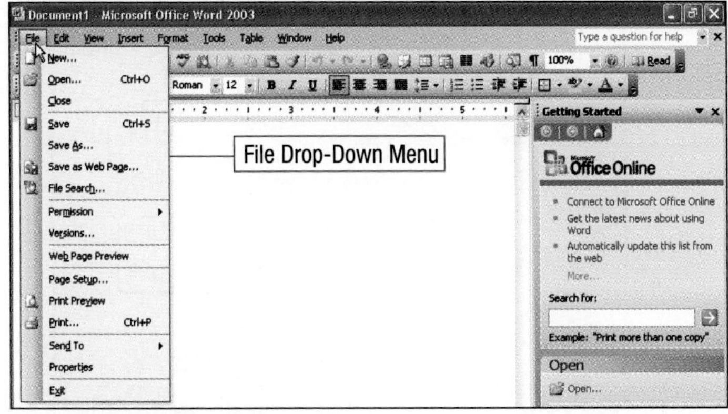

Choosing Commands from Drop-Down Menus

To choose a command from a drop-down menu with the mouse, position the arrow pointer on the desired option, and then click the left mouse button. At the drop-down menu that displays, move the arrow pointer down the menu to the desired option, and then click the left mouse button.

To make a selection from the drop-down menu with the keyboard, type the underlined letter of the desired option. Once the drop-down menu displays, you do not need to hold down the Alt key with the underlined letter. If you want to close a drop-down menu without making a choice, click in the screen outside the drop-down menu, or press the Esc key twice.

If an option can be accessed by clicking a button on a toolbar, the button is displayed preceding the option in the drop-down menu. For example, buttons display before the New, Open, Save, Save as Web Page, File Search, Print Preview, and Print options at the File drop-down menu (see Figure G.3).

Some menu options may be gray shaded (dimmed). When an option is dimmed, that option is currently not available. For example, if you choose the Table option on the Menu bar, the Table drop-down menu displays with dimmed options including Merge Cells, Split Cells, and Split Table.

Some menu options are preceded by a check mark. The check mark indicates that the option is currently active. To make an option inactive (turn it off) using the mouse, position the arrow pointer on the option, and then click the left mouse button. To make an option inactive with the keyboard, type the underlined letter of the option.

If an option from a drop-down menu displays followed by an ellipsis (...), a dialog box will display when that option is chosen. A dialog box provides a variety of options to let you specify how a command is to be carried out. For example, if you choose File and then Print from the PowerPoint Menu bar, the Print dialog box displays as shown in Figure G.4.

FIGURE G.4 **PowerPoint Print Dialog Box**

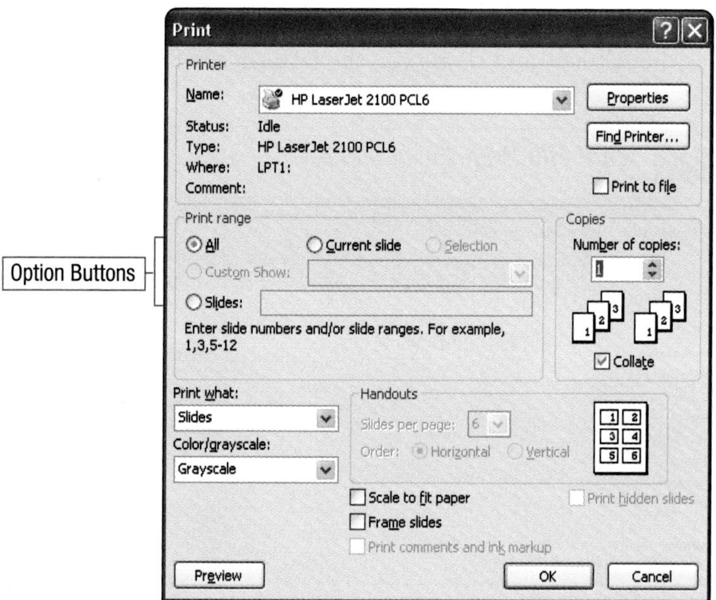

Or, if you choose Format and then Font from the Word Menu bar, the Font dialog box displays as shown in Figure G.5.

FIGURE G.5 **Word Font Dialog Box**

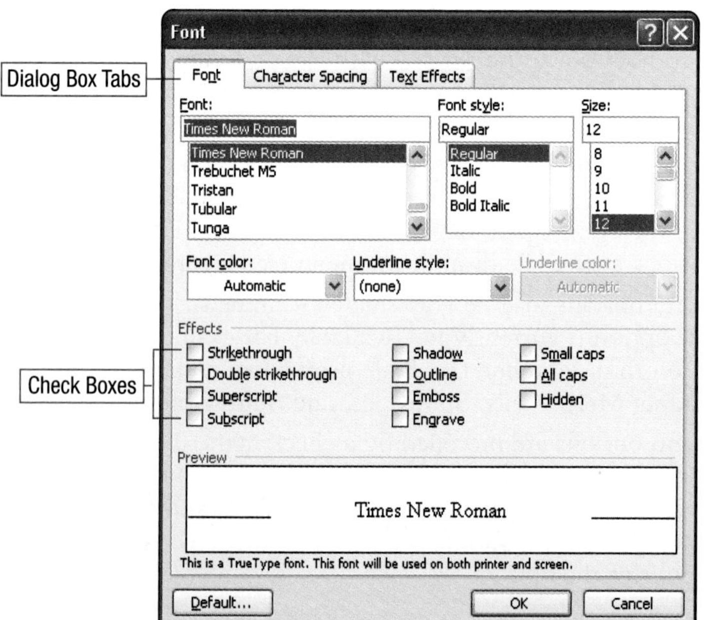

Some dialog boxes provide a set of options. These options are contained on separate tabs. For example, the Font dialog box shown in Figure G.5 contains a tab at the top of the dialog box with the word Font on it. Two other tabs display to the right of the Font tab—Character Spacing and Text Effects. The tab that displays in the front is the active tab. To make a tab active using the mouse, position the arrow pointer on the desired tab, and then click the left mouse button. If you are using the keyboard, press Ctrl + Tab or press Alt + the underlined letter on the desired tab. For example, to change the tab to Character Spacing in the Font dialog box, click Character Spacing, or press Ctrl + Tab, or press Alt + R.

To choose options from a dialog box with the mouse, position the arrow pointer on the desired option, and then click the left mouse button. If you are using the keyboard, press the Tab key to move the insertion point forward from option to option. Press Shift + Tab to move the insertion point backward from option to option. You can also hold down the Alt key and then press the underlined letter of the desired option. When an option is selected, it displays either in reverse video (white letters on a dark background) or surrounded by a dashed box called a ***marquee***.

A dialog box contains one or more of the following elements: text boxes, list boxes, check boxes, option buttons, spin boxes, and command buttons.

Text Boxes

Some options in a dialog box require text to be entered. For example, the boxes below the *Find what* and *Replace with* options at the Excel Find and Replace dialog box shown in Figure G.6 are text boxes. In a text box, you type text or edit existing text. Edit text in a text box in the same manner as normal text. Use the Left and Right Arrow keys on the keyboard to move the insertion point without deleting text and use the Delete key or Backspace key to delete text.

FIGURE G.6 ***Excel Find and Replace Dialog Box***

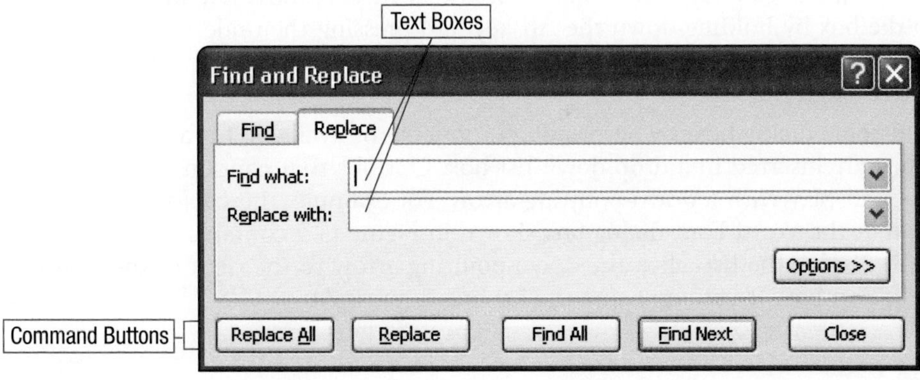

List Boxes

Some dialog boxes such as the Access Open dialog box shown in Figure G.7 may contain a list box. The list of files below the *Look in* option is contained in a list box. To make a selection from a list box with the mouse, move the arrow pointer to the desired option, and then click the left mouse button.

FIGURE

G.7 Access Open Dialog Box

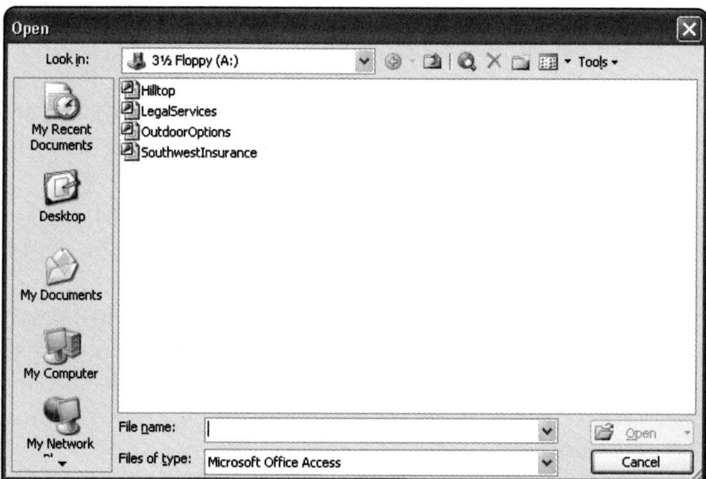

Some list boxes may contain a scroll bar. This scroll bar will display at the right side of the list box (a vertical scroll bar) or at the bottom of the list box (a horizontal scroll bar). Either a vertical scroll bar or a horizontal scroll bar can be used to move through the list if the list is longer than the box. To move down through a list on a vertical scroll bar, position the arrow pointer on the down scroll triangle and hold down the left mouse button. To scroll up through the list in a vertical scroll bar, position the arrow pointer on the up-pointing arrow and hold down the left mouse button. You can also move the arrow pointer above the scroll box and click the left mouse button to scroll up the list or move the arrow pointer below the scroll box and click the left mouse button to move down the list. To move through a list with a horizontal scroll bar, click the left-pointing arrow to scroll to the left of the list or click the right-pointing arrow to scroll to the right of the list.

To make a selection from a list using the keyboard, move the insertion point into the box by holding down the Alt key and pressing the underlined letter of the desired option. Press the Up and/or Down Arrow keys on the keyboard to move through the list.

In some dialog boxes where enough room is not available for a list box, lists of options are inserted in a drop-down list box. Options that contain a drop-down list box display with a down-pointing arrow. For example, the *Underline style* option at the Word Font dialog box shown in Figure G.5 contains a drop-down list. To display the list, click the down-pointing arrow to the right of the *Underline style* option box. If you are using the keyboard, press Alt + U.

Check Boxes

Some dialog boxes contain options preceded by a box. A check mark may or may not appear in the box. The Word Font dialog box shown in Figure G.5 displays a variety of check boxes within the *Effects* section. If a check mark appears in the box, the option is active (turned on). If there is no check mark in the check box, the option is inactive (turned off).

Any number of check boxes can be active. For example, in the Word Font dialog box, you can insert a check mark in any or all of the boxes in the *Effects* section and these options will be active.

To make a check box active or inactive with the mouse, position the tip of the arrow pointer in the check box, and then click the left mouse button. If you are using the keyboard, press Alt + the underlined letter of the desired option.

Option Buttons

In the PowerPoint Print dialog box shown in Figure G.4, the options in the *Print range* section are preceded by option buttons. Only one option button can be selected at any time. When an option button is selected, a green circle displays in the button.

To select an option button with the mouse, position the tip of the arrow pointer inside the option button, and then click the left mouse button. To make a selection with the keyboard, hold down the Alt key, and then press the underlined letter of the desired option.

Spin Boxes

Some options in a dialog box contain measurements or numbers that can be increased or decreased. These options are generally located in a spin box. For example, the Word Paragraph dialog box shown in Figure G.8 contains spin boxes located after the *Left*, *Right*, *Before*, and *After* options. To increase a number in a spin box, position the tip of the arrow pointer on the up-pointing arrow to the right of the desired option, and then click the left mouse button. To decrease the number, click the down-pointing arrow. If you are using the keyboard, press Alt + the underlined letter of the desired option, and then press the Up Arrow key to increase the number or the Down Arrow key to decrease the number.

FIGURE G.8 ***Word Paragraph Dialog Box***

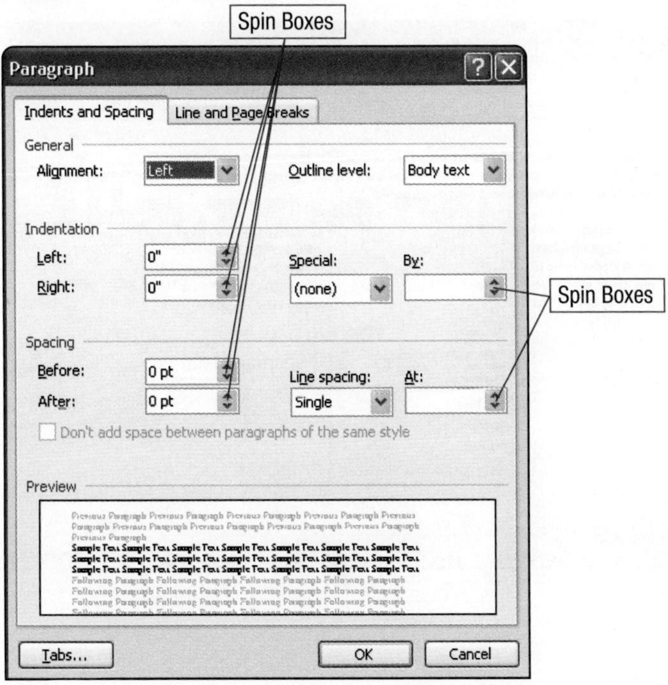

Command Buttons

In the Excel Find and Replace dialog box shown in Figure G.6, the boxes along the bottom of the dialog box are called ***command buttons***. A command button is used to execute or cancel a command. Some command buttons display with an ellipsis (...). A command button that displays with an ellipsis will open another dialog box. To choose a command button with the mouse, position the arrow pointer on the desired button, and then click the left mouse button. To choose a command button with the keyboard, press the Tab key until the desired command button contains the marquee, and then press the Enter key.

Choosing Commands with Shortcut Keys

At the left side of a drop-down menu is a list of options. At the right side, shortcut keys for specific options may display. For example, the shortcut keys to save a document are Ctrl + S and are displayed to the right of the Save option at the File drop-down menu shown in Figure G.3. To use shortcut keys to choose a command, hold down the Ctrl key, type the letter for the command, and then release the Ctrl key.

Choosing Commands with Shortcut Menus

The software programs in the suite include menus that contain commands related to the item with which you are working. A shortcut menu appears right where you are working in the document. To display a shortcut menu, click the *right* mouse button or press Shift + F10.

For example, if the insertion point is positioned in a paragraph of text in a Word document, clicking the *right* mouse button or pressing Shift + F10 will cause the shortcut menu shown in Figure G.9 to display in the document screen.

FIGURE G.9 ***Word Shortcut Menu***

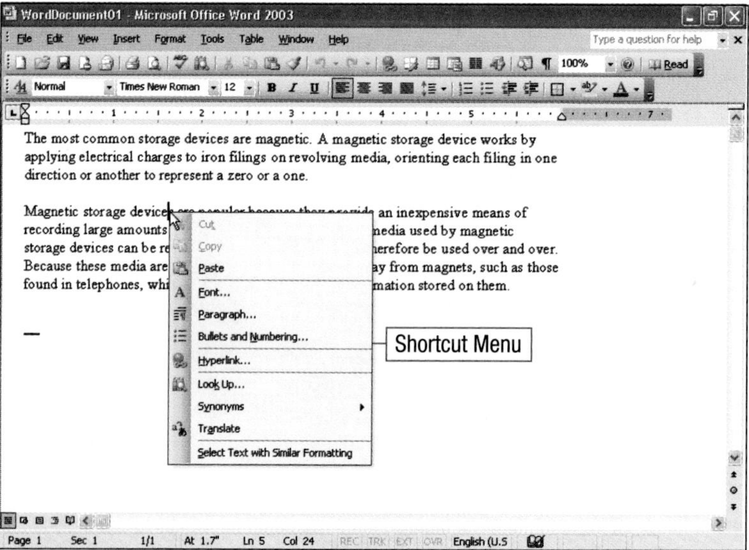

To select an option from a shortcut menu with the mouse, click the desired option. If you are using the keyboard, press the Up or Down Arrow key until the desired option is selected, and then press the Enter key. To close a shortcut menu without choosing an option, click anywhere outside the shortcut menu or press the Esc key.

Working with Multiple Programs

As you learn the various programs in the Microsoft Office suite, you will notice how executing commands in each is very similar. For example, the steps to save, close, and print are virtually the same whether you are working in Word, Excel, or PowerPoint. This consistency between programs greatly enhances a user's ability to easily transfer knowledge learned in one program to another within the suite.

Another appeal of Microsoft Office is the ability to have more than one program open at the same time. For example, you can open Word, create a document, and then open Excel, create a spreadsheet, and copy the spreadsheet into Word.

When a program is open, the name of the program, followed by the file name, displays in a button on the Taskbar. When another program is opened, the program name and file name display in a button that is positioned to the right of the first program button. Figure G.10 shows the Taskbar with Word, Excel, and PowerPoint open. To move from one program to another, all you need to do is click the button on the Taskbar representing the desired program file.

FIGURE G.10 ***Taskbar with Word, Excel, and PowerPoint Open***

Completing Computer Exercises

Some computer exercises in this textbook require that you open an existing file. Exercise files are saved on the Student CD that accompanies this textbook. The files you need for each chapter are saved in individual folders. Before beginning a chapter, copy the necessary folder from the CD to a preformatted data disk. After completing exercises in a chapter, delete the chapter folder before copying the next chapter folder. (Check with your instructor before deleting a folder.)

The Student CD also contains model answers in PDF format for the exercises *within* (but not at the end of) each chapter so you can check your work. To access the PDF files, you will need to have Adobe Acrobat Reader installed on your computer's hard drive. The program and installation instructions are included on the Student CD in the AdobeAcrobatReader folder.

Copying a Folder

As you begin working in a chapter, copy the chapter folder from the CD to your disk. (Not every chapter contains a folder on the CD. For example, when completing exercises in the Access chapters, you will copy individual database files rather than individual chapter folders. Copy the chapter folder from the CD to your disk using the My Computer window by completing the following steps:

1. Insert the CD that accompanies this textbook in the CD drive.
2. Insert a formatted 3.5-inch disk in the disk drive.
3. At the Windows XP desktop, open the My Computer window by clicking the Start button and then clicking My Computer at the Start menu.
4. Double-click the CD drive in the contents pane (probably displays as *OFFICE2003_BENCH* followed by the drive letter).
5. Double-click the desired program folder name in the contents pane. (For example, if you are copying a folder for a Specialist Word chapter, double-click the *Word2003Specialist* folder.)
6. Click once on the desired chapter subfolder name to select it.
7. Click the Copy this folder hyperlink in the *File and Folder Tasks* section of the task pane.
8. At the Copy Items dialog box, click *3½ Floppy (A:)* in the list box and then click the Copy button.
9. After the folder is copied to your disk, close the My Computer window by clicking the Close button (white X on red background) that displays in the upper right corner of the window.

Deleting a Folder

Before copying a chapter folder onto your disk, delete any previous chapter folders. Do this in the My Computer window by completing the following steps:

1. Insert your disk in the disk drive.
2. At the Windows XP desktop, open the My Computer window by clicking the Start button and then clicking My Computer at the Start menu.
3. Double-click *3½ Floppy (A:)* in the contents pane.
4. Click the chapter folder in the list box.
5. Click the Delete this folder hyperlink in the *File and Folder Tasks* section of the task pane.
6. At the message asking if you want to remove the folder and all its contents, click the Yes button.
7. If a message displays asking if you want to delete a read-only file, click the Yes to All button.
8. Close the My Computer window by clicking the Close button (white X on red background) that displays in the upper right corner of the window.

Viewing or Printing the Exercise Model Answers

If you want to access the PDF model answer files, first make sure that Adobe Acrobat Reader is installed on your hard drive. (If it is not, installation instructions and the program file are available within the AdobeAcrobatReader folder on the Student CD.) Double-click the ExerciseModelAnswers(PDF) folder, double-click the desired chapter subfolder name, and double-click the appropriate file name to open the file. You can view and/or print the file to compare it with your own completed exercise file.

OFFICE 2003

USING WINDOWS XP

A computer requires an operating system to provide necessary instructions on a multitude of processes including loading programs, managing data, directing the flow of information to peripheral equipment, and displaying information. Windows XP Professional is an operating system that provides functions of this type (along with much more) in a graphical environment. Windows is referred to as a ***graphical user interface*** (GUI—pronounced *gooey*) that provides a visual display of information with features such as icons (pictures) and buttons. In this introduction you will learn the basic features of Windows XP.

Historically, Microsoft has produced two editions of Windows—one edition for individual users (on desktop and laptop computers) and another edition for servers (on computers that provide service over networks). Windows XP is an upgrade and a merging of these two Windows editions and is available in two versions. The Windows XP Home Edition is designed for home use and Windows XP Professional is designed for small office and workstation use. Whether you are using Windows XP Home Edition or Windows XP Professional, you will be able to complete the steps in the exercises in this introduction.

Before using one of the software programs in the Microsoft Office suite, you will need to start the Windows XP operating system. To do this, turn on the computer. Depending on your computer equipment configuration, you may also need to turn on the monitor and printer. If you are using a computer that is part of a network system or if your computer is set up for multiple users, a screen will display showing the user accounts defined for your computer system. At this screen, click your user account name and, if necessary, type your password and then press the Enter key. The Windows XP operating system will start and, after a few moments, the desktop will display as shown in Figure W.1. (Your desktop may vary from what you see in Figure W.1.)

FIGURE W.1 *Windows XP Desktop*

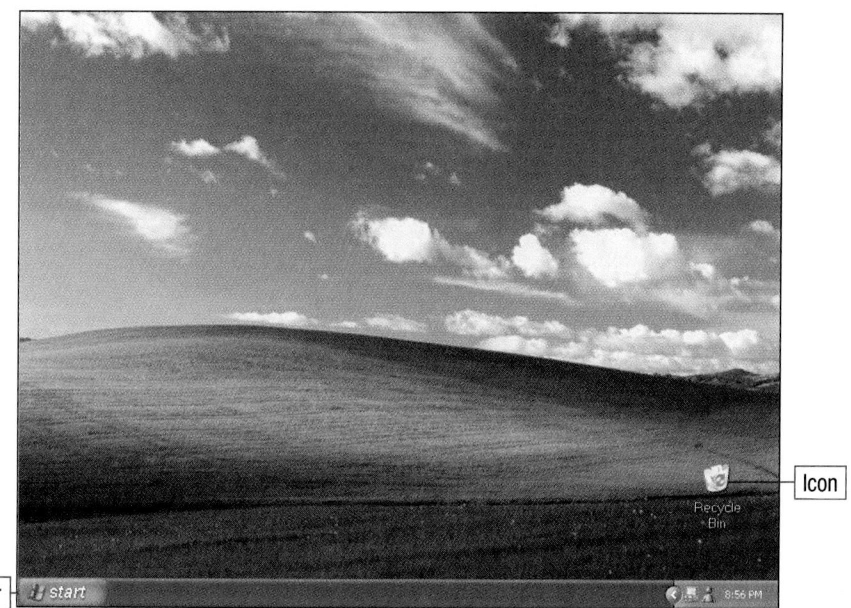

Exploring the Desktop

When Windows XP is loaded, the main portion of the screen is called the ***desktop***. Think of the desktop in Windows as the top of a desk in an office. A business person places necessary tools—such as pencils, pens, paper, files, calculator—on the desktop to perform functions. Like the tools that are located on a desk, the desktop contains tools for operating the computer. These tools are logically grouped and placed in dialog boxes or panels that can be displayed using icons on the desktop. The desktop contains a variety of features for using your computer and software programs installed on the computer. The features available on the desktop are represented by icons and buttons.

Using Icons

Icons are visual symbols that represent programs, files, or folders. Figure W.1 identifies the *Recycle Bin* icon located on the Windows XP desktop. The Windows XP desktop on your computer may contain additional icons. Programs that have been installed on your computer may be represented by an icon on the desktop. Also, icons may display on your desktop representing files or folders. Double-click an icon and the program, file, or folder it represents opens on the desktop.

Using the Taskbar

The bar that displays at the bottom of the desktop (see Figure W.1) is called the ***Taskbar***. The Taskbar, shown in Figure W.2, contains the Start button, a section that displays task buttons representing open programs, and the notification area.

FIGURE W.2 ***Windows XP Taskbar***

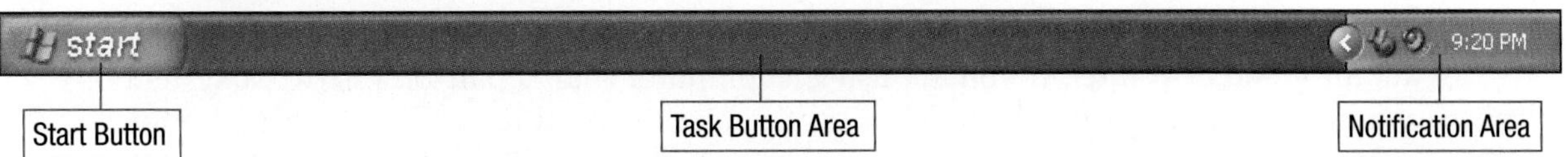

Click the Start button, located at the left side of the Taskbar, and the Start menu displays as shown in Figure W.3 (your Start menu may vary). You can also display the Start menu by pressing the Windows key on your keyboard or by pressing Ctrl + Esc. The left column of the Start menu contains pinned programs, which are programs that always appear in that particular location on the Start menu, and links to the most recently and frequently used programs. The right column contains links to folders, the Control Panel, online help, and the search feature.

FIGURE W.3 ***Start Menu***

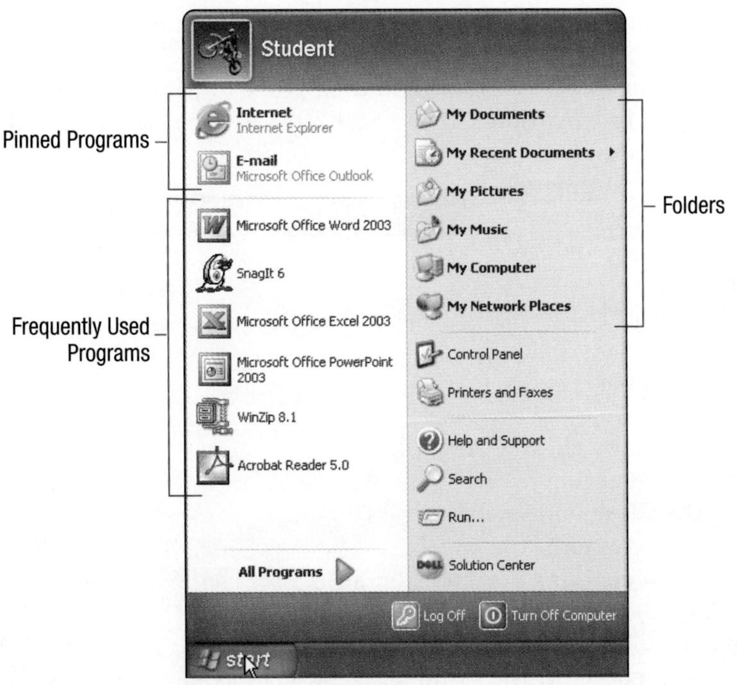

To choose an option from the Start menu, drag the arrow pointer to the desired option (referred to as ***pointing***), and then click the left mouse button. Pointing to options at the Start menu followed by a right-pointing arrow will cause a side menu to display with additional options. When a program is open, a task button representing the program appears on the Taskbar. If multiple programs are open, each program will appear as a task button on the Taskbar (a few specialized tools may not).

exercise 1

OPENING PROGRAMS AND SWITCHING BETWEEN PROGRAMS

1. Open Windows XP. (To do this, turn on the computer and, if necessary, turn on the monitor and/or printer. If you are using a computer that is part of a network system or if your computer is set up for multiple users, you may need to click your user account name and, if necessary, type your password and then press the Enter key. Check with your instructor to determine if you need to complete any additional steps.)
2. When the Windows XP desktop displays, open Microsoft Word by completing the following steps:
   a. Position the arrow pointer on the Start button on the Taskbar and then click the left mouse button.
   b. At the Start menu, point to All Programs (a side menu displays) and then point to Microsoft Office (another side menu displays).
   c. Drag the arrow pointer to Microsoft Office Word 2003 in the side menu and then click the left mouse button.
   d. When the Microsoft Word program is open, notice that a task button representing Word displays on the Taskbar.
3. Open Microsoft Excel by completing the following steps:
   a. Position the arrow pointer on the Start button on the Taskbar and then click the left mouse button.
   b. At the Start menu, point to All Programs and then point to Microsoft Office.
   c. Drag the arrow pointer to Microsoft Office Excel 2003 in the side menu and then click the left mouse button.
   d. When the Microsoft Excel program is open, notice that a task button representing Excel displays on the Taskbar to the right of the task button representing Word.

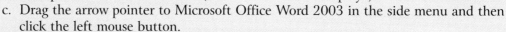

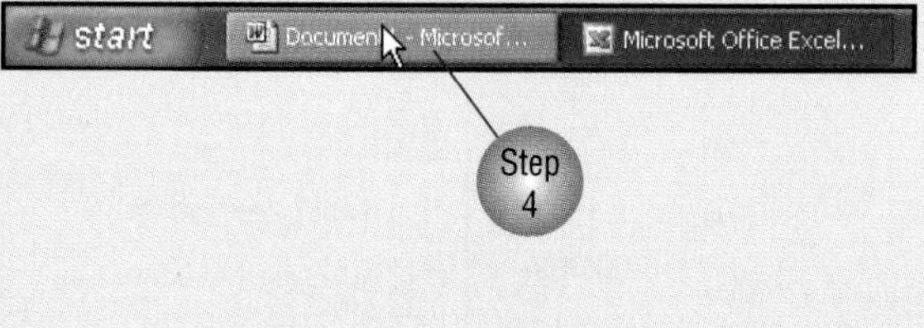

4. Switch to the Word program by clicking the task button on the Taskbar representing Word.
5. Switch to the Excel program by clicking the task button on the Taskbar representing Excel.
6. Exit Excel by clicking the Close button that displays in the upper right corner of the Excel window. (The Close button contains a white *X* on a red background.)
7. Exit Word by clicking the Close button that displays in the upper right corner of the Word window.

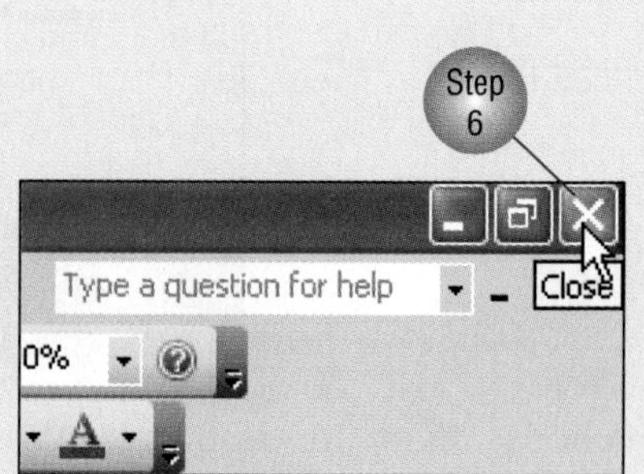

Exploring the Notification Area

The notification area is located at the right side of the Taskbar and contains the system clock along with small icons representing specialized programs that run in the background. Position the arrow pointer over the current time in the notification area of the Taskbar and today's date displays in a small yellow box above the time. Double-click the current time displayed on the Taskbar and the Date and Time Properties dialog box displays as shown in Figure W.4.

FIGURE W.4 **Date and Time Properties Dialog Box**

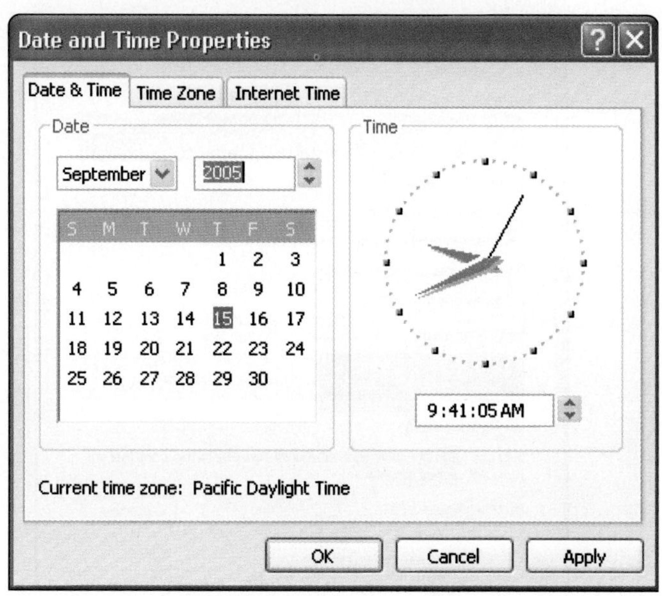

Change the date with options in the *Date* section of the dialog box. For example, to change the month, click the down-pointing arrow at the right side of the option box containing the current month and then click the desired month at the drop-down list. Change the year by clicking the up- or down-pointing arrow at the right side of the option box containing the current year until the desired year displays. To change the day, click the desired day in the monthly calendar that displays in the dialog box. To change the time, double-click either the hour, minute, or seconds and then type the appropriate time or use the up- and down-pointing arrows to adjust the time.

Some programs, when installed, will add an icon to the notification area of the Taskbar. Display the name of the icon by positioning the mouse pointer on the icon and, after approximately one second, the icon label displays in a small yellow box. Some icons may display information in the yellow box rather than the icon label. If more icons have been inserted in the notification area than can be viewed at one time, a left-pointing arrow button displays at the left side of the notification area. Click this left-pointing arrow button and the remaining icons display.

Setting Taskbar Properties

By default, the Taskbar is locked in its current position and size. You can change this default setting, along with other default settings, with options at the Taskbar and Start Menu Properties dialog box, shown in Figure W.5. To display this dialog box, position the arrow pointer on any empty spot on the Taskbar, and then click the *right* mouse button. At the shortcut menu that displays, click Properties.

FIGURE W.5 **Taskbar and Start Menu Properties Dialog Box**

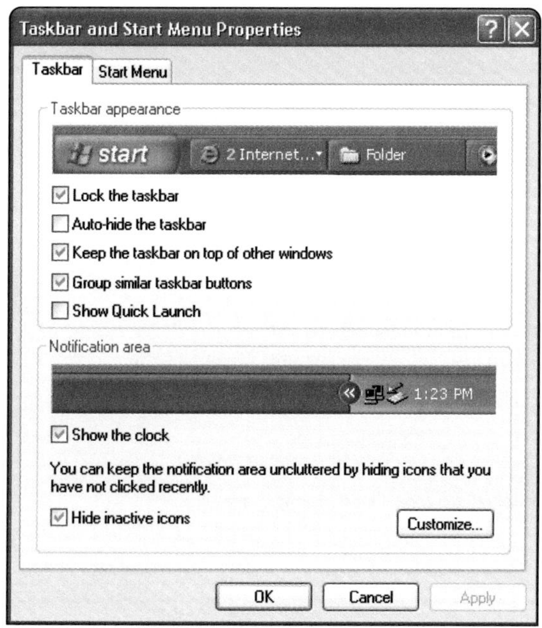

Each property is controlled by a check box. Property options containing a check mark are active. Click the option to remove the check mark and make the option inactive. If an option is inactive, clicking the option will insert a check mark in the check box and turn on the option (make it active).

exercise 2 CHANGING TASKBAR PROPERTIES

1. Make sure Windows XP is open and the desktop displays.
2. Hide the Taskbar and remove the display of the clock by completing the following steps:
   a. Position the arrow pointer on any empty area on the Taskbar and then click the *right* mouse button.
   b. At the shortcut menu that displays, click Properties.
   c. At the Taskbar and Start Menu Properties dialog box, click *Auto-hide the taskbar*. (This inserts a check mark in the check box.)
   d. Click *Show the clock*. (This removes the check mark from the check box.)

e. Click the Apply button.
f. Click OK to close the dialog box.

3. Display the Taskbar by positioning the mouse pointer at the bottom of the screen. When the Taskbar displays, notice that the time no longer displays at the right side of the Taskbar.
4. Return to the default settings for the Taskbar by completing the following steps:
   a. With the Taskbar displayed (if it does not display, position the mouse pointer at the bottom of the desktop), position the arrow pointer on any empty area on the Taskbar and then click the *right* mouse button.
   b. At the shortcut menu that displays, click Properties.
   c. At the Taskbar and Start Menu Properties dialog box, click *Auto-hide the taskbar*. (This removes the check mark from the check box.)
   d. Click *Show the clock*. (This inserts a check mark in the check box.)
   e. Click the Apply button.
   f. Click OK to close the dialog box.

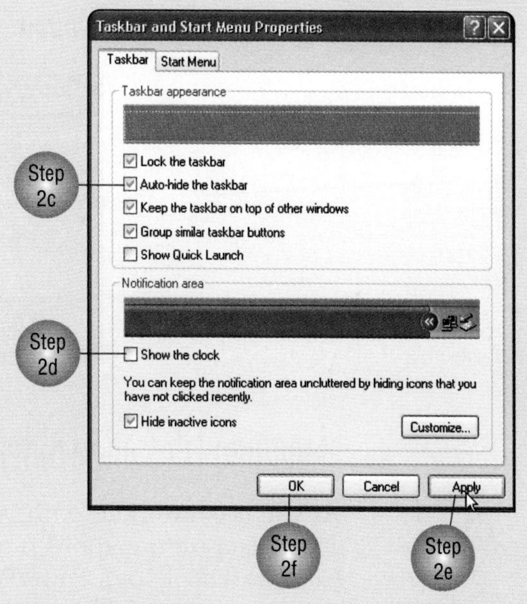

Turning Off the Computer

When you are finished working with your computer, you can choose to shut down the computer completely, shut down and then restart the computer, put the computer on standby, or tell the computer to hibernate. Do not turn off your computer until your screen goes blank. Important data is stored in memory while Windows XP is running and this data needs to be written to the hard drive before turning off the computer.

To shut down your computer, click the Start button on the Taskbar and then click *Turn Off Computer* at the Start menu. At the Turn off computer window, shown in Figure W.6, click the *Stand By* option and the computer switches to a low power state causing some devices such as the monitor and hard disks to turn off. With these devices off, the computer uses less power. Stand By is particularly useful for saving battery power for portable computers. Tell the computer to "hibernate" by holding down the Shift key while clicking the *Stand By* option. In hibernate mode, the computer saves everything in memory on disk, turns off the monitor and hard disk, and then turns off the computer. Click the *Turn Off* option if you want to shut down Windows XP and turn off all power to the computer. Click the *Restart* option if you want to restart the computer and restore the desktop exactly as you left it. You can generally restore your desktop from either standby or hibernate by pressing once on the computer's power button. Usually, bringing a computer out of hibernation takes a little longer than bringing a computer out of standby.

FIGURE W.6 ***Turn Off Computer Window***

Managing Files and Folders

As you begin working with programs in Windows XP, you will create files in which data (information) is saved. A file might contain a Word document, an Excel workbook, or a PowerPoint presentation. As you begin creating files, consider creating folders into which those files will be stored. File management tasks such as creating a folder and copying and moving files and folders can be completed at the My Computer window. To display the My Computer window shown in Figure W.7, click the Start button on the Taskbar and then click My Computer. The various components of the My Computer window are identified in Figure W.7.

FIGURE W.7 ***My Computer Window***

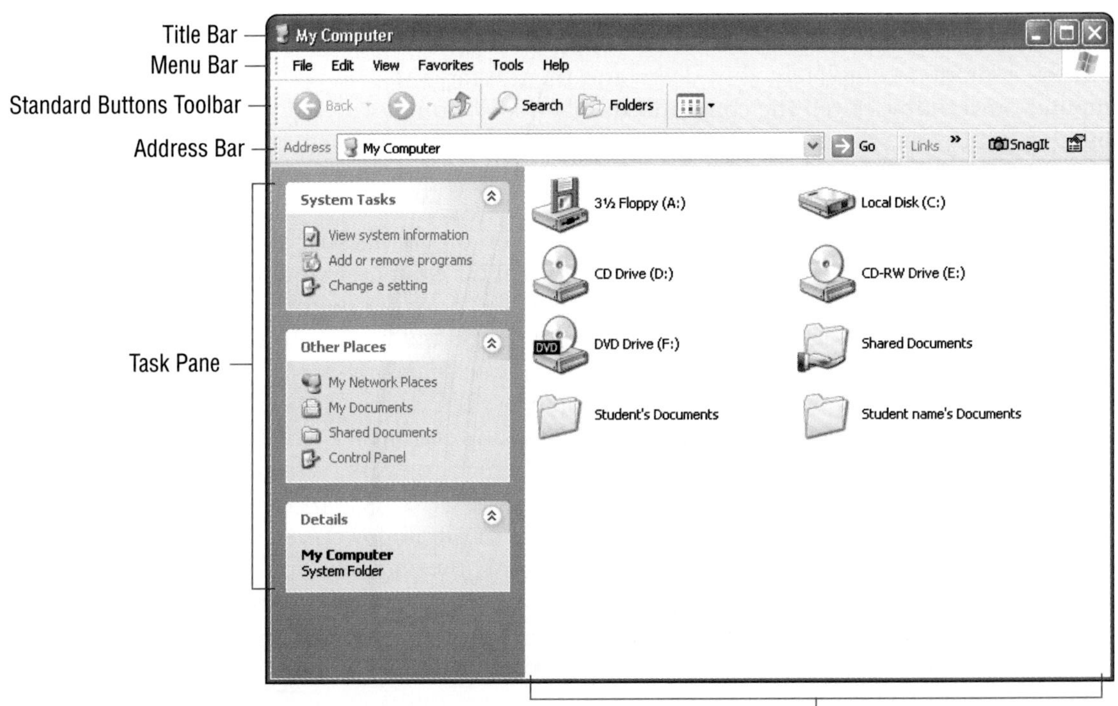

Copying, Moving, and Deleting Files/Folders

File and folder management activities might include copying and moving files or folders from a folder or drive to another or deleting files or folders. The My Computer window offers a variety of methods for copying, moving, and deleting files/folders. You can use options in the task pane, drop-down menu options, or shortcut menu options. This section will provide you with the steps for copying, moving, and deleting files/folders using options in the task pane.

To copy a file/folder to another folder or drive, first display the file in the contents pane by identifying the location of the file. If the file is located in the My Documents folder, click the My Documents hyperlink in the *Other Places* section of the task pane. If the file is located on the hard drive, double-click the desired drive in the contents pane and if the file is located on a floppy disk or CD, double-click the desired drive letter or CD letter. Next, click the folder or file name in the contents pane that you want to copy. This changes the options in the task pane to include management options such as renaming, moving, copying, and deleting folders or files. Click the Copy this folder (or Copy this file) hyperlink in the task pane and the Copy Items dialog box displays as shown in Figure W.8. At the Copy Items dialog box, click the desired folder or drive and then click the Copy button.

FIGURE W.8 ***Copy Items Dialog Box***

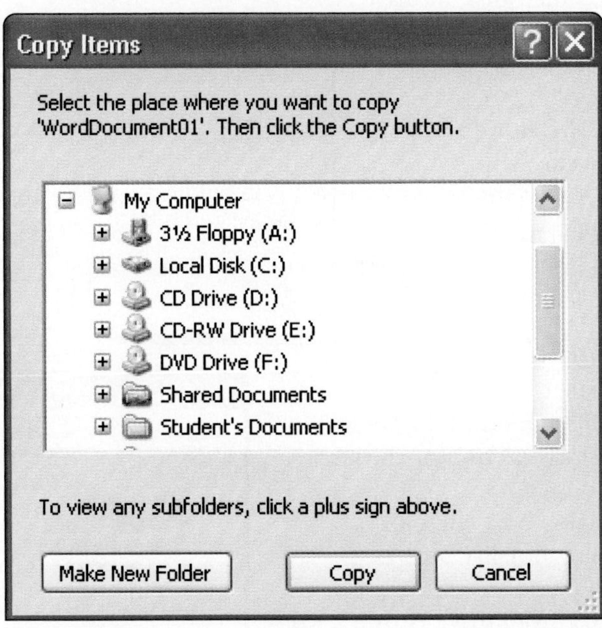

To move a file or folder to another folder or drive, select the file or folder and then click the Move this folder (or Move this file) hyperlink. At the Move Items dialog box, specify the location, and then click the Move button. Copying a file or folder leaves the file or folder in the original location and saves a copy at the new location, while moving removes the file or folder from the original location and moves it to the new location.

You can easily remove (delete) a file or folder from the My Computer window. To delete a file or folder, click the file or folder in the contents pane, and then click the Delete this folder (or Delete this file) hyperlink in the task pane. At the dialog box asking you to confirm the deletion, click Yes. A deleted file or folder is sent to the Recycle Bin. You will learn more about the Recycle Bin in the next section.

In Exercise 3, you will insert the CD that accompanies this book into the CD drive. When the CD is inserted, the drive may automatically activate and a dialog box may display on the screen telling you that the disk or device contains more than one type of content and asking what you want Windows to do. If this dialog box displays, click Cancel to remove the dialog box.

exercise 3

COPYING A FILE AND FOLDER AND DELETING A FILE

1. At the Windows XP desktop, insert the CD that accompanies this textbook into the CD drive. If a dialog box displays telling you that the disk or device contains more than one type of content and asking what you want Windows to do, click Cancel.
2. At the Windows XP desktop, open the My Computer window by clicking the Start button on the Taskbar and then clicking My Computer at the Start menu.
3. Copy a file from the CD that accompanies this textbook to a disk in drive A by completing the following steps:
   a. Insert a formatted 3.5-inch disk in drive A.
   b. In the contents pane, double-click the name of the drive containing the CD (probably displays as OFFICE2003_BENCH followed by a drive letter). (Make sure you double-click because you want the contents of the CD to display in the contents pane.)
   c. Double-click the *Windows* folder in the contents pane.
   d. Click ***WordDocument01*** in the contents pane to select it.
   e. Click the Copy this file hyperlink located in the *File and Folder Tasks* section of the task pane.
   f. At the Copy Items dialog box, click *3½ Floppy (A:)* in the dialog box list box.
   g. Click the Copy button.
4. Delete **WordDocument01** from drive A by completing the following steps:
   a. Click the My Computer hyperlink located in the *Other Places* section of the task pane.
   b. Double-click *3½ Floppy (A:)* in the contents pane.

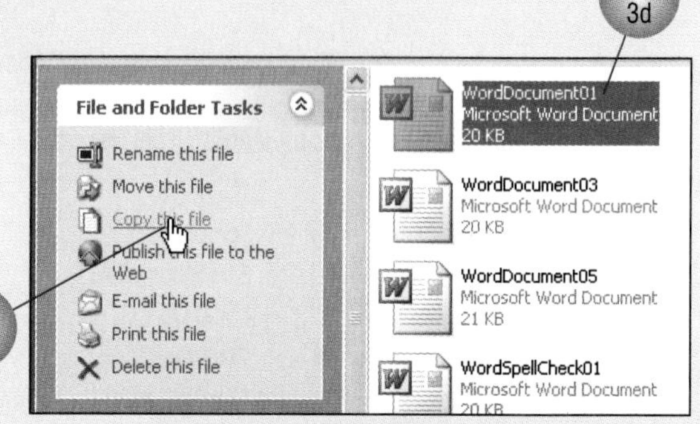

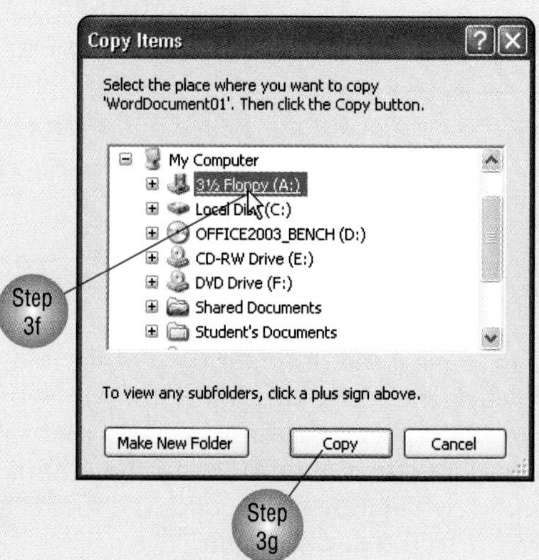

c. Click ***WordDocument01***.
d. Click the Delete this file hyperlink in the *File and Folder Tasks* section of the task pane.
e. At the message asking you to confirm the deletion, click Yes.

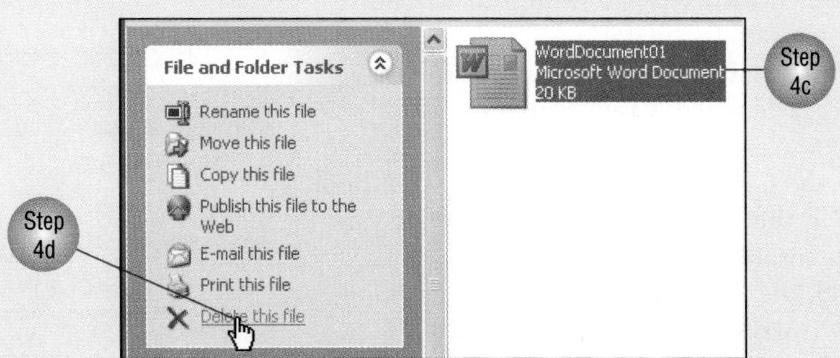

5. Copy the Windows folder from the CD drive to the disk in drive A by completing the following steps:
   a. Click the My Computer hyperlink in the *Other Places* section of the task pane.
   b. In the contents pane, double-click the name of the drive containing the CD (probably displays as OFFICE2003_BENCH followed by a drive letter).
   c. Click the *Windows* folder in the contents pane to select it.
   d. Click the Copy this folder hyperlink in the *File and Folder Tasks* section of the task pane.
   e. At the Copy Items dialog box, click *3½ Floppy (A:)* in the list box.
   f. Click the Copy button.
6. Close window by clicking the Close button (contains a white *X* on a red background) located in the upper right corner of the window. (You can also close the window by clicking File on the Menu bar and then clicking Close at the drop-down menu.)

Selecting Files/Folders

You can move, copy, or delete more than one file or folder at the same time. Before moving, copying, or deleting files/folders, select the desired files or folders. Selecting files/folders is easier when you change the display in the contents pane to List or Details. To change the display, open the My Computer window and then click the Views button on the Standard Buttons toolbar. At the drop-down list that displays, click the *List* option or the *Details* option.

To move adjacent files/folders, click the first file or folder and then hold down the Shift key and click the last file or folder. This selects and highlights all files/folders from the first file/folder you clicked to the last file/folder you clicked. With the adjacent files/folders selected, click the Move the selected items hyperlink in the *File and Folder Tasks* section of the task pane, and then specify the desired location at the Move Items dialog box. To select nonadjacent files/folders, click the first file/folder to select it, hold down the Ctrl key and then click any other files/folders you want to move or copy.

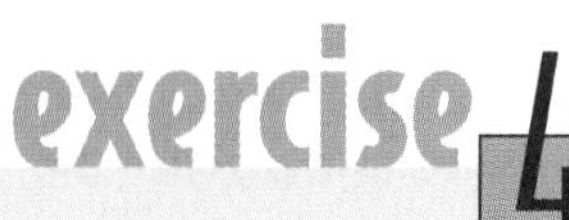

exercise 4 COPYING AND DELETING FILES

1. At the Windows XP desktop, open the My Computer window by clicking the Start button and then clicking My Computer at the Start menu.
2. Copy files from the CD that accompanies this textbook to a disk in drive A by completing the following steps:
   a. Make sure the CD that accompanies this textbook is inserted in the CD drive and a formatted 3.5-inch disk is inserted in drive A.
   b. Double-click the CD drive in the contents pane (probably displays as OFFICE2003_BENCH followed by the drive letter).
   c. Double-click the *Windows* folder in the contents pane.
   d. Change the display to Details by clicking the Views button on the Standard Buttons toolbar and then clicking *Details* at the drop-down list.
   e. Position the arrow pointer on **WordDocument01** in the contents pane and then click the left mouse button.
   f. Hold down the Shift key, click ***WordDocument05***, and then release the Shift key. (This selects **WordDocument01, WordDocument02, WordDocument03, WordDocument04**, and **WordDocument05**.)
   g. Click the Copy the selected items hyperlink in the *File and Folder Tasks* section of the task pane.
   h. At the Copy Items dialog box, click *3½ Floppy (A:)* in the list box and then click the Copy button.

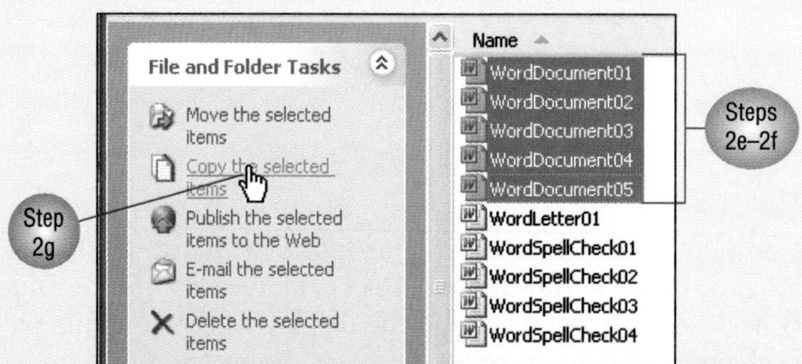

3. Display the files and folder saved on the disk in drive A by completing the following steps:
   a. Click the My Computer hyperlink in the *Other Places* section of the task pane.
   b. Double-click *3½ Floppy (A:)* in the contents pane.
4. Delete the files from drive A that you just copied by completing the following steps:
   a. Change the view by clicking the Views button on the Standard Buttons toolbar and then clicking *List* at the drop-down list.
   b. Click ***WordDocument01*** in the contents pane.

c. Hold down the Shift key, click ***WordDocument05***, and then release the Shift key. (This selects **WordDocument01**, **WordDocument02**, **WordDocument03**, **WordDocument04**, and **WordDocument05**.)
d. Click the Delete the selected items hyperlink in the *File and Folder Tasks* section of the task pane.
e. At the message asking you to confirm the deletion, click Yes.

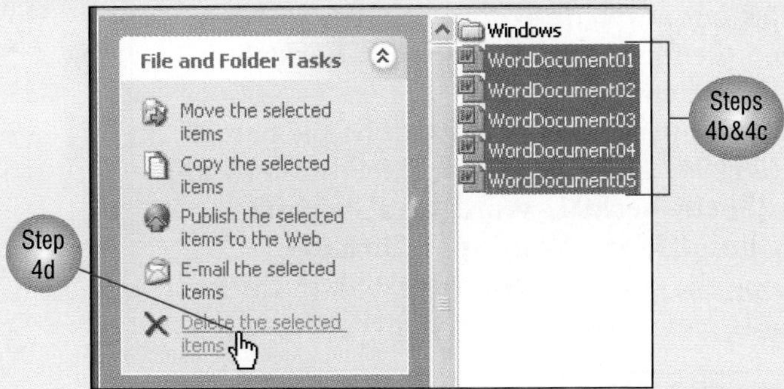

5. Close the window by clicking the Close button (white *X* on red background) that displays in the upper right corner of the window.

Manipulating and Creating Folders

As you begin working with and creating a number of files, consider creating folders in which you can logically group the files. To create a folder, display the My Computer window and then display in the contents pane the drive or disk on which you want to create the folder. Click the File option on the Menu bar, point to New, and then click Folder at the side menu. This inserts a folder icon in the contents pane and names the folder *New Folder*. Type the desired name for the new folder and then press Enter.

exercise 5

CREATING A NEW FOLDER

1. At the Windows XP desktop, open the My Computer window.
2. Create a new folder by completing the following steps:
   a. Make sure your disk is inserted in drive A (this disk contains the Windows folder you copied in Exercise 3).
   b. Double-click *3½ Floppy (A:)* in the contents pane.
   c. Double-click the *Windows* folder in the contents pane. (This opens the folder.)
   d. Click File on the Menu bar, point to New, and then click Folder.

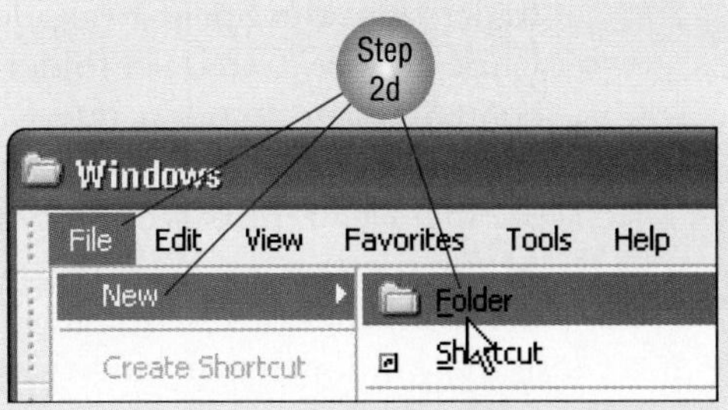

e. Type **SpellCheckFiles** and then press Enter. (This changes the name from *New Folder* to *SpellCheckFiles*.)

3. Copy **WordSpellCheck01**, **WordSpellCheck02**, **WordSpellCheck03**, and **WordSpellCheck04** into the SpellCheckFiles folder you just created by completing the following steps:
   a. Click the Views button on the Standard Buttons toolbar and then click *List* at the drop-down list.
   b. Click once on the file named **WordSpellCheck01** located in the contents pane.
   c. Hold down the Shift key, click once on the file named ***WordSpellCheck04***, and then release the Shift key. (This selects **WordSpellCheck01**, **WordSpellCheck02**, **WordSpellCheck03**, and **WordSpellCheck04**.)
   d. Click the Copy the selected items hyperlink in the *File and Folder Tasks* section of the task pane.

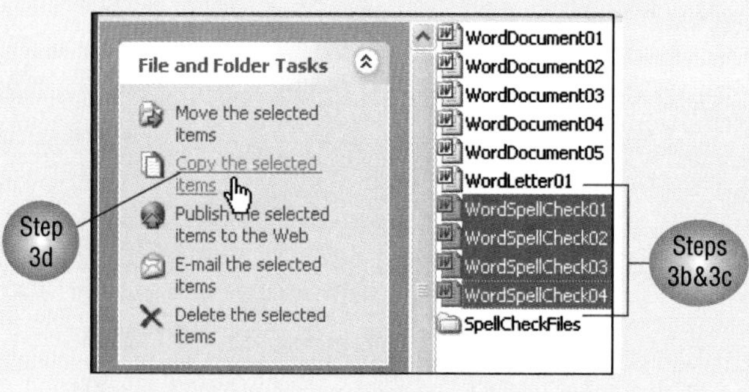

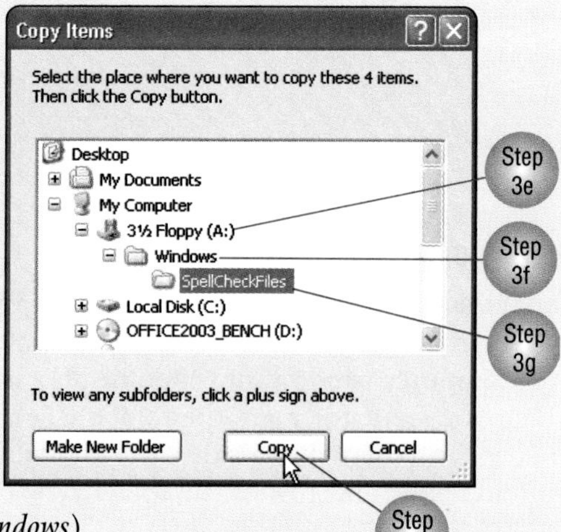

   e. At the Copy Items dialog box, click *3½ Floppy (A:)* in the list box.
   f. Click *Windows* (below *3½ Floppy (A:)*) in the list box.
   g. Click *SpellCheckFiles* in the list box (below *Windows*).
   h. Click the Copy button.
4. Display the files you just copied by double-clicking the *SpellCheckFiles* folder in the contents pane.
5. Delete the SpellCheckFiles folder and its contents by completing the following steps:
   a. Click the Up button on the Standard Buttons toolbar. (This displays the contents of the Windows folder which is up one folder from the SpellCheckFiles folders.)
   b. Click the *SpellCheckFiles* folder in the contents pane to select it.
   c. Click the Delete this folder hyperlink in the *File and Folder Tasks* section of the task pane.
   d. At the message asking you to confirm the deletion, click Yes.
6. Close the window by clicking the Close button located in the upper right corner of the window.

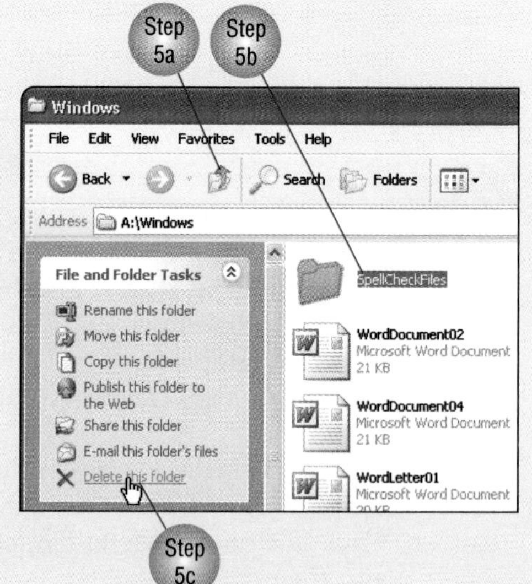

Using the Recycle Bin

Deleting the wrong file can be a disaster but Windows XP helps protect your work with the Recycle Bin. The Recycle Bin acts just like an office wastepaper basket; you can "throw away" (delete) unwanted files, but you can "reach in" (restore) to the Recycle Bin and take out a file if you threw it away by accident.

Deleting Files to the Recycle Bin

A file/folder or selected files/folders deleted from the hard drive are automatically sent to the Recycle Bin. Files/folders deleted from a disk are deleted permanently. (Recovery programs are available, however, that will help you recover deleted text. If you accidentally delete a file/folder from a disk, do not do anything more with the disk until you can run a recovery program.)

One method for deleting files is to display the My Computer window and then display in the contents pane the file(s) and/or folder(s) you want deleted. Click the file or folder or select multiple files or folders and then click the appropriate delete option in the task pane. At the message asking you to confirm the deletion, click Yes.

Another method for deleting a file is to drag the file to the *Recycle Bin* icon on the desktop. Drag a file icon to the Recycle Bin until the *Recycle Bin* icon is selected (displays with a blue background) and then release the mouse button. This drops the file you are dragging into the Recycle Bin.

Recovering Files from the Recycle Bin

You can easily restore a deleted file from the Recycle Bin. To restore a file, double-click the *Recycle Bin* icon on the desktop. This opens the Recycle Bin window shown in Figure W.9. (The contents of the Recycle Bin will vary.)

FIGURE W.9 ***Recycle Bin Window***

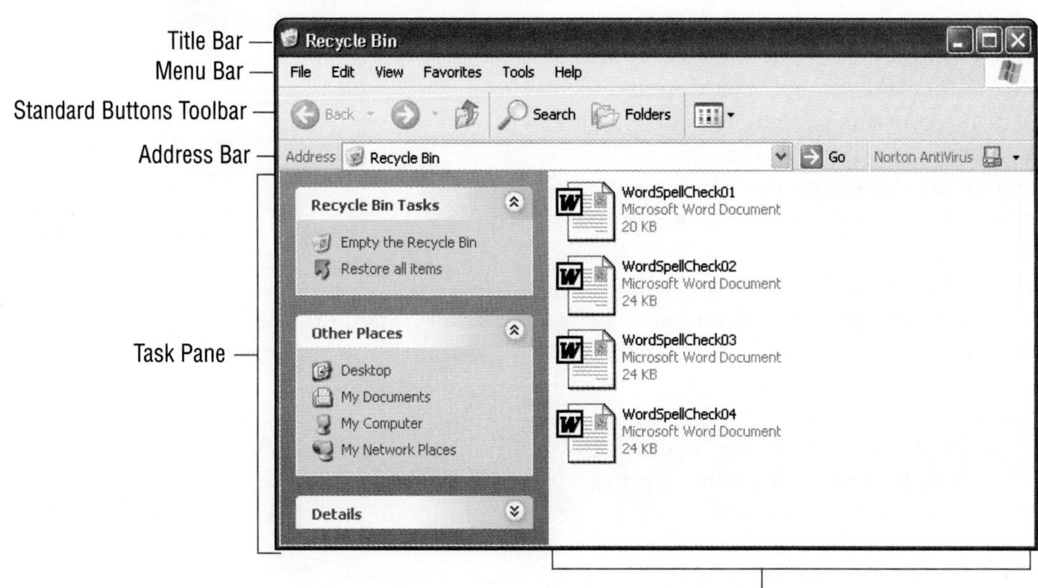

To restore a file, click the file you want restored, and then click the Restore this item hyperlink in the *Recycle Bin Tasks* section of the task pane. This removes the file from the Recycle Bin and returns it to its original location. You can also restore a file by positioning the arrow pointer on the file, clicking the *right* mouse button, and then clicking Restore at the shortcut menu.

exercise 6 DELETING FILES TO AND RECOVERING FILES FROM THE RECYCLE BIN

(Before completing this exercise, check with your instructor to determine if you can copy files to the hard drive.)

1. At the Windows XP desktop, open the My Computer window.
2. Copy files from your disk in drive A to the My Documents folder on your hard drive by completing the following steps:
   a. Make sure your disk containing the Windows folder is inserted in drive A.
   b. Double-click *3½ Floppy (A:)* in the contents pane.
   c. Double-click the *Windows* folder in the contents pane.
   d. Click the Views button on the Standard Buttons toolbar and then click *List* at the drop-down list.
   e. Position the arrow pointer on **WordSpellCheck01** and then click the left mouse button.
   f. Hold down the Shift key, click ***WordSpellCheck04***, and then release the Shift key.
   g. Click the Copy the selected items hyperlink in the *File and Folder Tasks* section of the task pane.
   h. At the Copy Items dialog box, click *My Documents* in the list box.
   i. Click the Copy button.

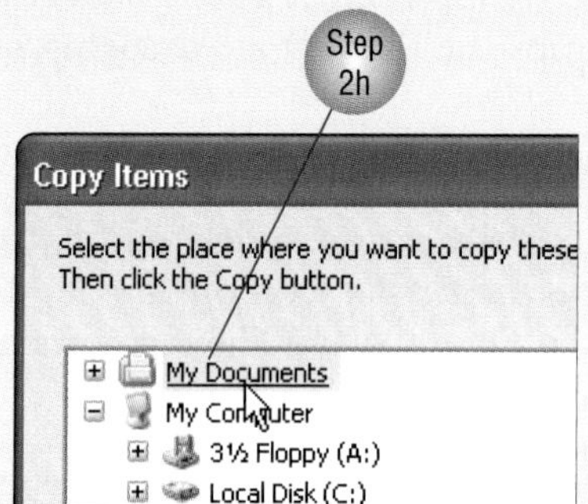

3. Click the My Documents hyperlink in the *Other Places* section of the task pane. (The files you copied, **WordSpellCheck01** through **WordSpellCheck04**, will display in the contents pane in alphabetical order.)

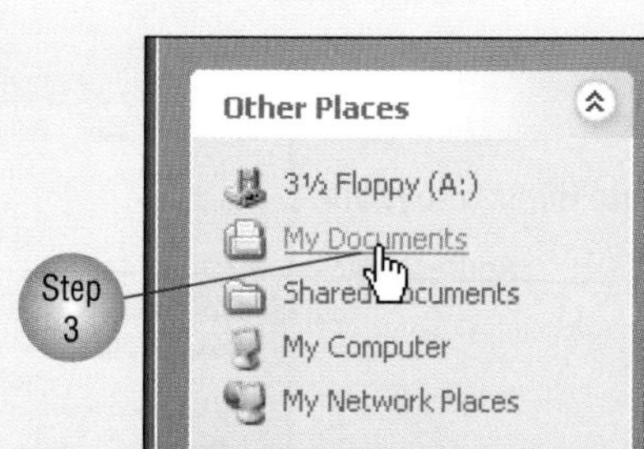

4. Delete **WordSpellCheck01** through **WordSpellCheck04** from the My Documents folder and send them to the Recycle Bin by completing the following steps:
   a. Select **WordSpellCheck01** through **WordSpellCheck04** in the contents pane. (If these files are not visible, you will need to scroll down the list of files.)
   b. Click the Delete the selected items hyperlink in the *File and Folder Tasks* section of the task pane.
   c. At the message asking you to confirm the deletion to the Recycle Bin, click Yes.
5. Click the Close button to close the window.
6. At the desktop, display the contents of the Recycle Bin by double-clicking the *Recycle Bin* icon.

7. At the Recycle Bin window, restore **WordSpellCheck01** through **WordSpellCheck04** to the My Documents folder by completing the following steps:
   a. Select **WordSpellCheck01** through **WordSpellCheck04** in the contents pane of the Recycle Bin window. (If these files are not visible, you will need to scroll down the list of files.)
   b. With the files selected, click the Restore the selected items hyperlink in the *Recycle Bin Tasks* section of the task pane.

8. Close the Recycle Bin window by clicking the Close button located in the upper right corner of the window.
9. Display the My Computer window.
10. Click the My Documents hyperlink in the *Other Places* section of the task pane.
11. Delete the files you restored by completing the following steps:
    a. Select **WordSpellCheck01** through **WordSpellCheck04** in the contents pane. (If these files are not visible, you will need to scroll down the list of files. These are the files you recovered from the Recycle Bin.)
    b. Click the Delete the selected items hyperlink in the *File and Folder Tasks* section of the task pane.
    c. At the message asking you to confirm the deletion, click Yes.
12. Close the window.

Emptying the Recycle Bin

Just like a wastepaper basket, the Recycle Bin can get full. To empty the Recycle Bin, position the arrow pointer on the *Recycle Bin* icon on the desktop and then click the *right* mouse button. At the shortcut menu that displays, click Empty Recycle Bin. At the message asking you to confirm the deletion, click Yes. You can also empty the Recycle Bin by double-clicking the *Recycle Bin* icon. At the Recycle Bin window, click the Empty the Recycle Bin hyperlink in the *Recycle Bin Tasks* section of the task pane. At the message asking you to confirm the deletion, click Yes. (You can also empty the Recycle Bin by clicking File on the Menu bar and then clicking Empty Recycle Bin at the drop-down menu.)

Emptying the Recycle Bin deletes all files/folders. You can delete a specific file/folder from the Recycle Bin (rather than all files/folders). To do this, double-click the *Recycle Bin* icon on the desktop. At the Recycle Bin window, select the file/folder or files/folders you want to delete. Click File on the Menu bar and then click Delete at the drop-down menu. (You can also right-click a selected file/folder and then click Delete at the shortcut menu.) At the message asking you to confirm the deletion, click Yes.

exercise 7 EMPTYING THE RECYCLE BIN

(Before completing this exercise, check with your instructor to determine if you can delete files/folders from the Recycle Bin.)

1. At the Windows XP desktop, double-click the *Recycle Bin* icon.
2. At the Recycle Bin window, empty the contents of the Recycle Bin by completing the following steps:
   a. Click the Empty the Recycle Bin hyperlink in the *Recycle Bin Tasks* section of the task pane.
   b. At the message asking you to confirm the deletion, click Yes.
3. Close the Recycle Bin window by clicking the Close button located in the upper right corner of the window.

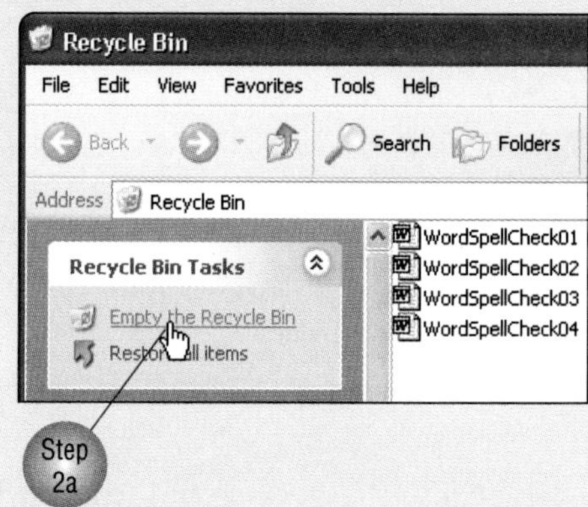

Step 2a

When the Recycle Bin is emptied, the files cannot be recovered by the Recycle Bin or by Windows XP. If you have to recover a file, you will need to use a file recovery program such as Norton Utilities. These utilities are separate programs, but might be worth their cost if you ever need them.

Creating a Shortcut

If you use a file or program on a consistent basis, consider creating a shortcut to the file or program. A shortcut is a specialized icon that represents very small files that point the operating system to the actual item, whether it is a file, a folder, or an application. For example, in Figure W.10, the *Shortcut to PracticeDocument* icon represents a path to a specific file in the Word 2003 program. The icon is not the actual file but a path to the file. Double-click the shortcut icon and Windows XP opens the Word 2003 program and also opens the file named PracticeDocument.

FIGURE W.10 ***PracticeDocument Shortcut Icon***

One method for creating a shortcut is to display the My Computer window and then display the drive or folder where the file is located. Right-click the desired file, point to Send To, and then click Desktop (create shortcut). You can easily delete a shortcut icon from the desktop by dragging the shortcut icon to the *Recycle Bin* icon. This deletes the shortcut icon but does not delete the file to which the shortcut pointed.

exercise 8

CREATING A SHORTCUT

1. At the Windows XP desktop, display the My Computer window.
2. Make sure your disk is inserted in drive A.
3. Double-click *3½ Floppy (A:)* in the contents pane.
4. Double-click the *Windows* folder in the contents pane.
5. Change the display of files to a list by clicking the Views button on the Standard Buttons toolbar and then clicking *List* at the drop-down list.
6. Create a shortcut to the file named **WordLetter01** by right-clicking on ***WordLetter01***, pointing to Send To, and then clicking Desktop (create shortcut).

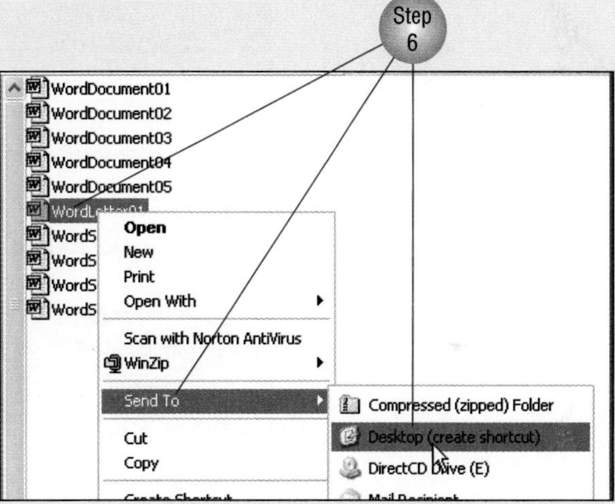

7. Close the My Computer window by clicking the Close button located in the upper right corner of the window.
8. Open Word 2003 and the file named **WordLetter01** by double-clicking the **WordLetter01** shortcut icon on the desktop.
9. After viewing the file in Word, exit Word by clicking the Close button that displays in the upper right corner of the window.
10. Delete the **WordLetter01** shortcut icon by completing the following steps:
    a. At the desktop, position the mouse pointer on the **WordLetter01** shortcut icon.
    b. Hold down the left mouse button, drag the icon on top of the *Recycle Bin* icon, and then release the mouse button.

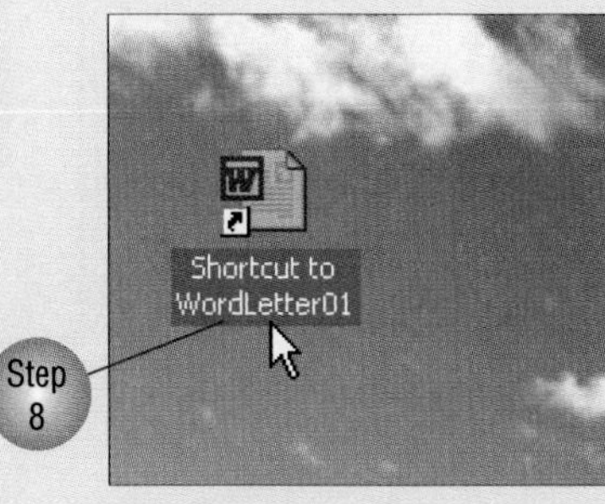

Customizing the Desktop

You can customize the Windows XP desktop to fit your particular needs and preferences. For example, you can choose a different theme, change the desktop background, add a screen saver, and apply a different appearance to windows, dialog boxes, and menus. To customize the desktop, position the arrow pointer on any empty location on the desktop and then click the *right* mouse button. At the shortcut menu that displays, click Properties. This displays the Display Properties dialog box with the Themes tab selected as shown in Figure W.11.

FIGURE W.11 ***Display Properties Dialog Box with Themes Tab Selected***

Changing the Theme

A Windows XP theme specifies a variety of formatting such as fonts, sounds, icons, colors, mouse pointers, background, and screen saver. Windows XP contains two themes—Windows XP (the default) and Windows Classic (which appears like earlier versions of Windows). Other themes are available as downloads from the Microsoft Web site. Change the theme with the *Theme* option at the Display Properties dialog box with the Themes tab selected.

Changing the Desktop

With options at the Display Properties dialog box with the Desktop tab selected, as shown in Figure W.12, you can choose a different desktop background and customize the desktop. Click any option in the *Background* list box and preview the results in the preview screen. With the *Position* option, you can specify that the background image is centered, tiled, or stretched on the desktop. Use the *Color* option to change the background color and click the Browse button to choose a background image from another location or Web site.

FIGURE W.12 ***Display Properties Dialog Box with Desktop Tab Selected***

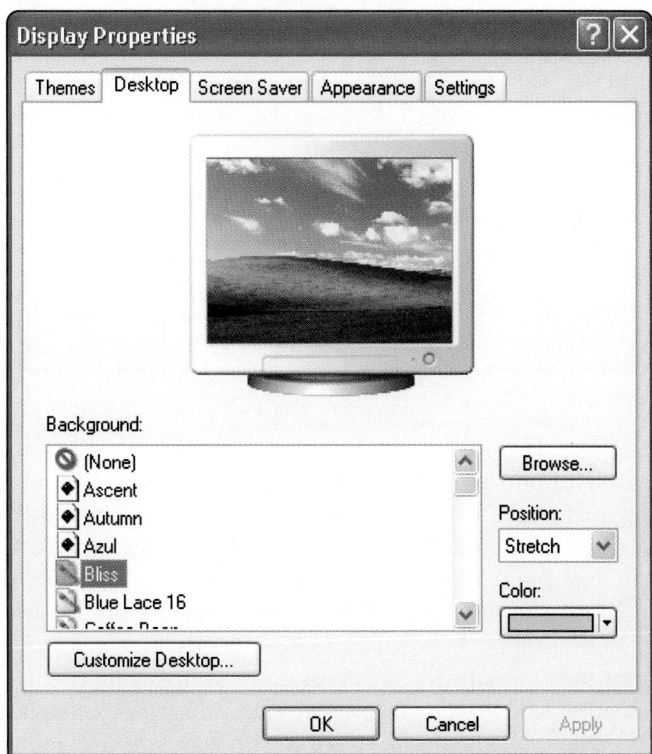

Adding a Screen Saver

If your computer sits idle for periods of time, consider adding a screen saver. A screen saver is a pattern that changes constantly, thus eliminating the problem of an image staying on the screen too long. To add a screen saver, display the Display Properties dialog box and then click the Screen Saver tab. This displays the dialog box as shown in Figure W.13.

FIGURE

W.13 ***Display Properties Dialog Box with Screen Saver Tab Selected***

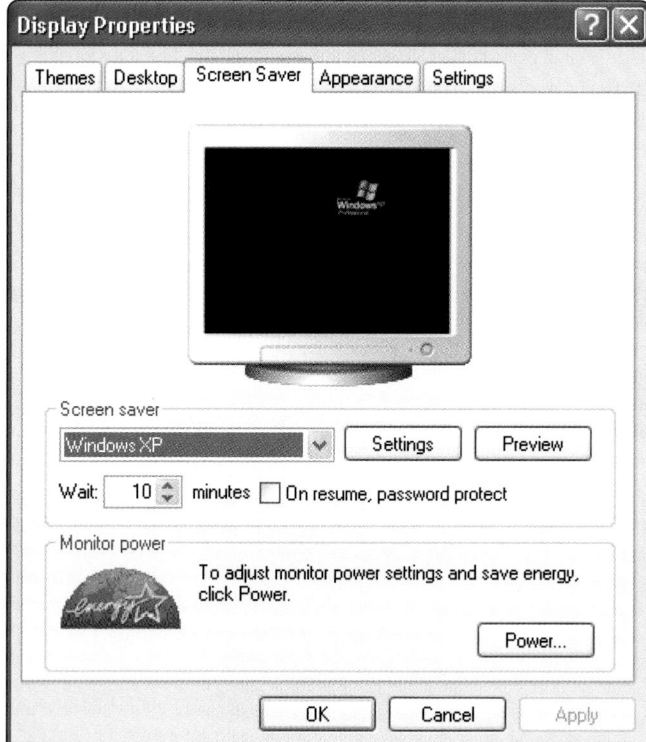

Click the down-pointing arrow at the right side of the *Screen saver* option box to display a list of installed screen savers. Click a screen saver and a preview displays in the monitor located toward the top of the dialog box. Click the Preview button and the dialog box is hidden and the screen saver displays on your monitor. Move the mouse or click a button on the mouse and the dialog box will reappear.

If your computer's hardware is Energy Star compatible, the *Monitor power* section is enabled. Click the Power button and a dialog box displays with options for choosing a power scheme appropriate to the way you use your computer. The dialog box also includes options for specifying how long the computer can be left unused before the monitor and hard disk are turned off and the system goes to standby or hibernate mode.

Changing Colors

Click the Appearance tab at the Display Properties dialog box and the dialog box displays as shown in Figure W.14. At this dialog box, you can change the desktop scheme. Schemes are predefined collections of colors used in windows, menus, title bars, and system fonts. Windows XP loads with the Windows XP style color scheme. Choose a different scheme with the *Windows and buttons* option and choose a specific color with the *Color scheme* option.

FIGURE W.14 *Display Properties Dialog Box with Appearance Tab Selected*

Changing Settings

Click the Settings tab at the Display Properties dialog box and the dialog box displays as shown in Figure W.15. At this dialog box, you can set color and screen resolution.

FIGURE W.15 *Display Properties Dialog Box with Settings Tab Selected*

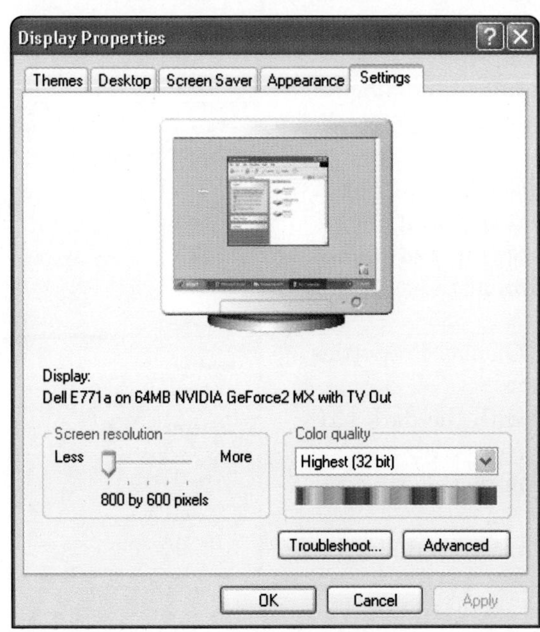

The *Color quality* option determines how many colors your monitor displays. The more colors that are shown, the more realistic the images will appear. However, a lot of computer memory is required to show thousands of colors. Your exact choice is determined by the specific hardware you are using. The *Screen resolution* slide bar sets the screen's resolution. The higher the number, the more you can fit onto your screen. Again, your actual values depend on your particular hardware.

exercise 9

CUSTOMIZING THE DESKTOP

(Before completing this exercise, check with your instructor to determine if you can customize the desktop.)

1. At the Windows XP desktop, display the Display Properties dialog box by positioning the arrow pointer on an empty location on the desktop, clicking the *right* mouse button, and then clicking Properties at the shortcut menu.

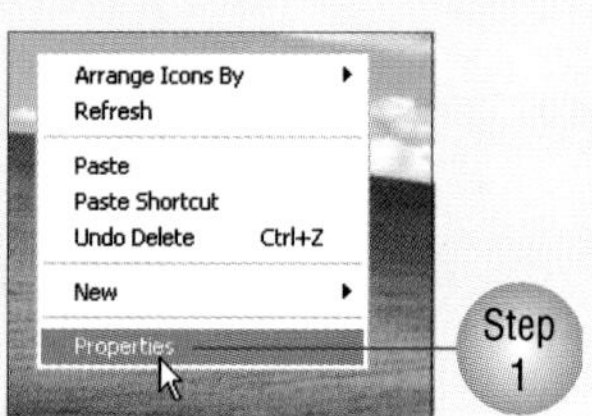

2. At the Display Properties dialog box, change the desktop background by completing the following steps:
   a. Click the Desktop tab.
   b. If a background is selected in the *Background* list box (other than the *(None)* option), make a note of this background name.
   c. Click *Blue Lace 16* in the *Background* list box. (If this option is not available, choose another background.)
   d. Make sure *Tile* is selected in the *Position* list box.
   e. Click OK to close the dialog box.

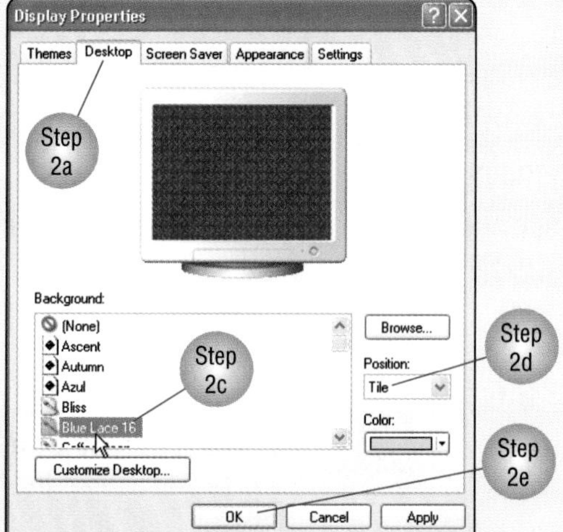

3. After viewing the desktop with the Blue Lace 16 background, remove the background image and change the background color by completing the following steps:
   a. Display the Display Properties dialog box.
   b. At the Display Properties dialog box, click the Desktop tab.
   c. Click *(None)* in the *Background* list box.
   d. Click the down-pointing arrow at the right side of the *Color* option and then click the dark red option at the color palette.
   e. Click OK to close the Display Properties dialog box.

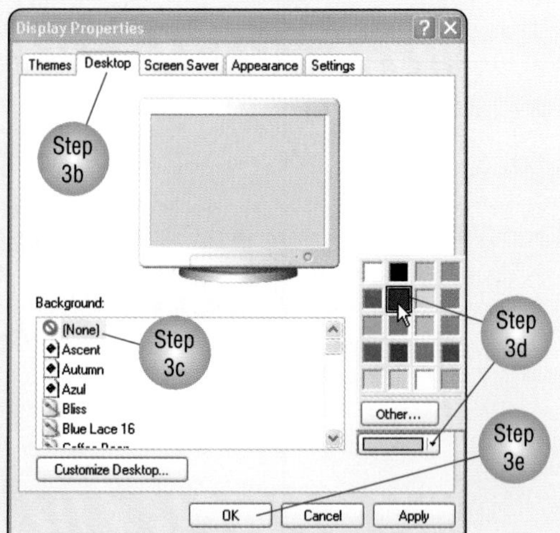

4. After viewing the desktop with the dark red background color, add a screen saver and change the wait time by completing the following steps:
   a. Display the Display Properties dialog box.

b. At the Display Properties dialog box, click the Screen Saver tab. (If a screen saver is already selected in the *Screen saver* option box, make a note of this screen saver name.)
c. Click the down-pointing arrow at the right side of the *Screen saver* option box.
d. At the drop-down list that displays, click a screen saver that interests you. (A preview of the screen saver displays in the screen located toward the top of the dialog box.)
e. Click a few other screen savers to see how they will display on the monitor.
f. Click OK to close the Display Properties dialog box. (At the desktop the screen saver will display, by default, after the monitor has sat idle for one minute.)

5. Return all settings back to the default by completing the following steps:
   a. Display the Display Properties dialog box.
   b. Click the Desktop tab.
   c. If a background and color were selected when you began this exercise, click that background name in the *Background* list box and change the color back to the original color.
   d. Click the Screen Saver tab.
   e. At the Display Properties dialog box with the Screen Saver tab selected, click the down-pointing arrow at the right side of the *Screen saver* option box, and then click *(None)*. (If a screen saver was selected before completing this exercise, return to that screen saver.)
   f. Click OK to close the Display Properties dialog box.

Exploring Windows XP Help and Support

Windows XP includes an on-screen reference guide providing information, explanations, and interactive help on learning Windows features. The on-screen reference guide contains complex files with hypertext used to access additional information by clicking a word or phrase.

Using the Help and Support Center Window

Display the Help and Support Center window shown in Figure W.16 by clicking the Start button on the Taskbar and then clicking Help and Support at the Start menu. The appearance of your Help and Support Center window may vary slightly from what you see in Figure W.16.

If you want to learn about a topic listed in the *Pick a Help topic* section of the window, click the desired topic and information about the topic displays in the window. Use the other options in the Help and Support Center window to get assistance or support from a remote computer or Windows XP newsgroups, pick a specific task, or learn about the additional help features. If you want help on a specific topic and do not see that topic listed in the *Pick a Help topic* section of the window, click inside the *Search* text box (generally located toward the top of the window), type the desired topic, and then press Enter or click the Start searching button (white arrow on a green background).

FIGURE W.16 ***Help and Support Center Window***

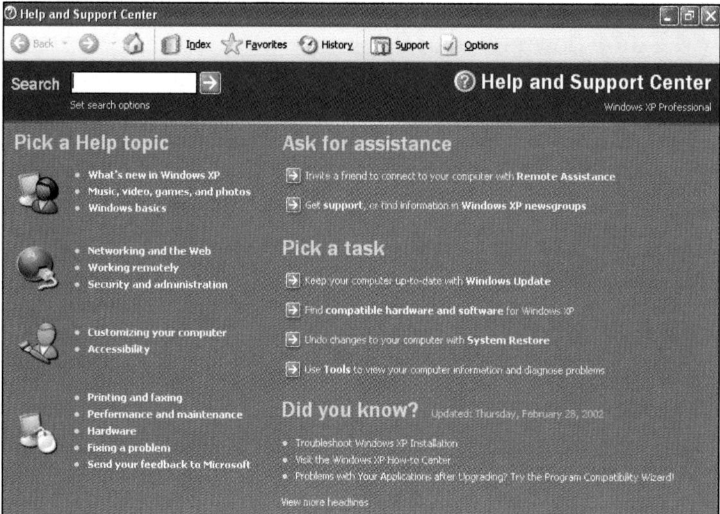

exercise 10

CUSTOMIZING THE DESKTOP

1. At the Windows XP desktop, use the Help and Support feature to learn about new Windows XP features by completing the following steps:
   a. Click the Start button on the Taskbar and then click Help and Support at the Start menu.
   b. At the Help and Support Center window, click the What's new in Windows XP hyperlink located in the *Pick a Help topic* section of the window.

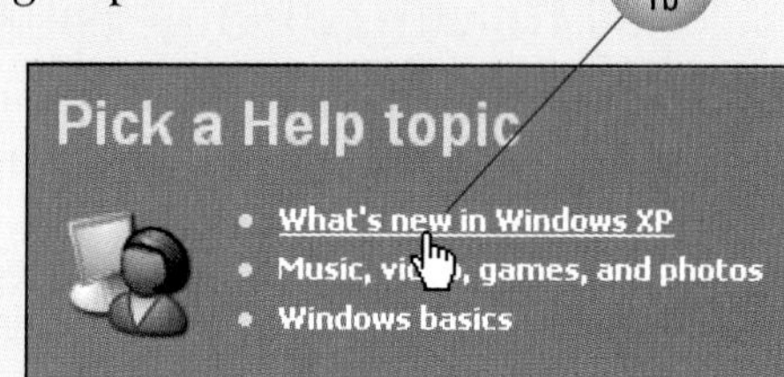

   c. Click the What's new topics hyperlink located in the *What's new in Windows XP* section of the window. (This displays a list of Help options at the right side of the window.)
   d. Click the What's new in Windows XP hyperlink located at the right side of the window below the subheading *Overviews, Articles, and Tutorials*.
   e. Read the information about Windows XP that displays at the right side of the window.
   f. Print the information by completing the following steps:
      1) Click the Print button located on the toolbar that displays above the information titled *What's new in Windows XP Professional.*
      2) At the Print dialog box, make sure the correct printer is selected and then click the Print button.

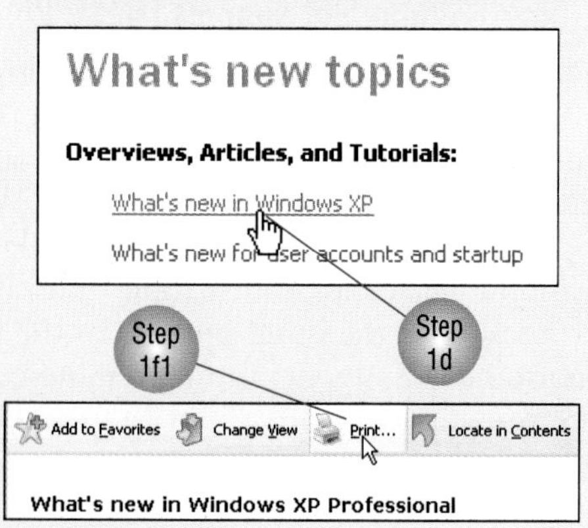

2. Return to the opening Help and Support Center window by clicking the Home button located on the Help and Support Center toolbar.
3. Use the *Search* text box to search for information on deleting files by completing the following steps:

a. Click in the *Search* text box located toward the top of the Help and Support Center window.
b. Type **deleting files** and then press Enter.
c. Click the Delete a file or folder hyperlink that displays in the *Search Results* section of the window (below the *Pick a task* subheading).
d. Read the information about deleting a file or folder that displays at the right side of the window and then print the information by clicking the Print button on the toolbar and then clicking the Print button at the Print dialog box.
e. Click the Delete or restore files in the Recycle Bin hyperlink that displays in the *Search Results* section of the window.
f. Read the information that displays at the right side of the window about deleting and restoring files in the Recycle Bin and then print the information.

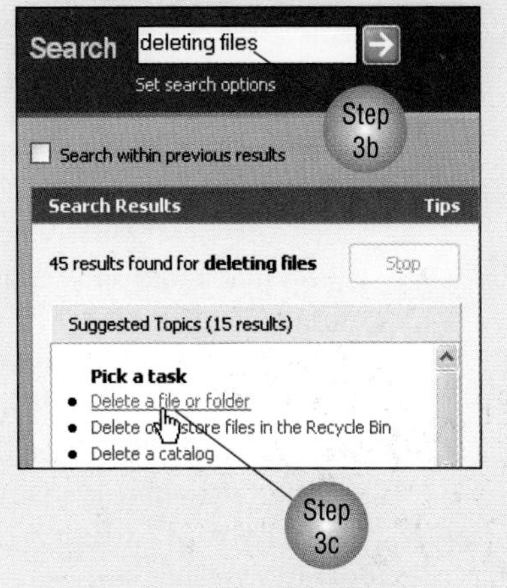

4. Close the Help and Support Center window by clicking the Close button located in the upper right corner of the window.

Displaying an Index of Help and Support Topics

Display a list of help topics available by clicking the Index button on the Help and Support Center window toolbar. This displays an index of help topics at the left side of the window as shown in Figure W.17. Scroll through this list until the desired topic displays and then double-click the topic. Information about the selected topic displays at the right side of the window. If you are looking for a specific topic or keyword, click in the *Type in the keyword to find* text box, type the desired topic or keyword, and then press Enter.

FIGURE W.17 **Help and Support Center Window with Index Displayed**

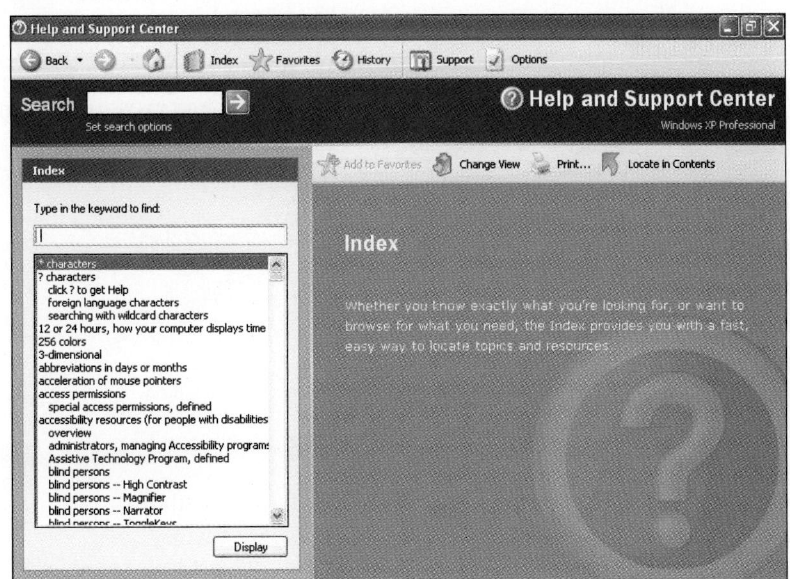

exercise 11

USING THE INDEX TO SEARCH FOR INFORMATION

1. At the Windows XP desktop, use the Index to display information on accessing programs by completing the following steps:
   a. Click the Start button on the Taskbar and then click Help and Support at the Start menu.
   b. Click the Index button on the Help and Support Center window toolbar.
   c. Scroll down the list of Index topics until *accessing programs* is visible and then double-click the subheading *overview* that displays below *accessing programs*.
   d. Read the information that displays at the right side of the window and then print the information.

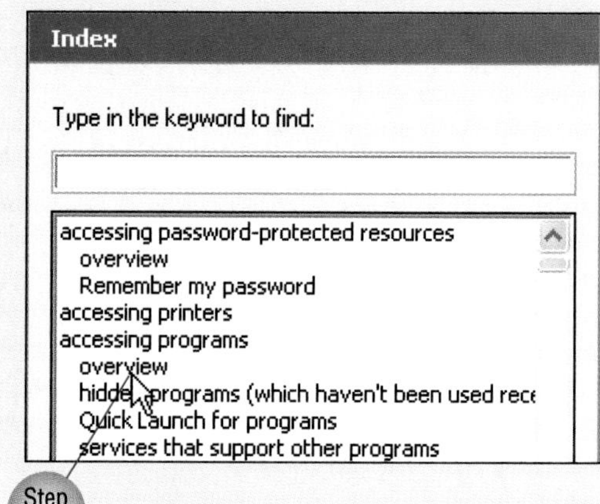

2. Find information on adding a shortcut to the desktop by completing the following steps:
   a. Select and delete the text *overview* that displays in the *Type in the keyword to find* text box and then type **shortcuts**.
   b. Double-click the subheading *for specific programs* that displays below the *shortcuts* heading.
   c. Read the information that displays at the right side of the window and then print the information.
3. Close the Help and Support Center window by clicking the Close button located in the upper right corner of the window.

OFFICE 2003

BROWSING THE INTERNET USING INTERNET EXPLORER

Microsoft Internet Explorer is a Web browser program with options and features for displaying sites as well as navigating and searching for information on the Internet. The ***Internet*** is a network of computers connected around the world. Users access the Internet for several purposes: to communicate using e-mail, to subscribe to news groups, to transfer files, to socialize with other users around the globe in "chat" rooms, and largely to access virtually any kind of information imaginable.

Using the Internet, people can access a phenomenal amount of information for private or public use. To use the Internet, three things are generally required: an Internet Service Provider (ISP), a program to browse the Web (called a ***Web browser***), and a ***search engine***. In this section, you will learn how to use the Internet Explorer Web browser to browse Web sites, search for specific sites, and download a Web page and image.

Browsing the Internet

You will use the Microsoft Internet Explorer Web browser to locate information on the Internet. Uniform Resource Locators, referred to as URLs, are the method used to identify locations on the Internet. The steps for browsing the Internet vary but generally include: opening Internet Explorer, typing the URL for the desired site, navigating the various pages of the site, printing Web pages, and then closing Internet Explorer.

To launch Internet Explorer, double-click the *Internet Explorer* icon on the Windows desktop. Figure IE.1 identifies the elements of the Internet Explorer, version 6, window. The Web page that displays in your Internet Explorer window may vary from what you see in Figure IE.1.

FIGURE

IE.1 ***Internet Explorer Window***

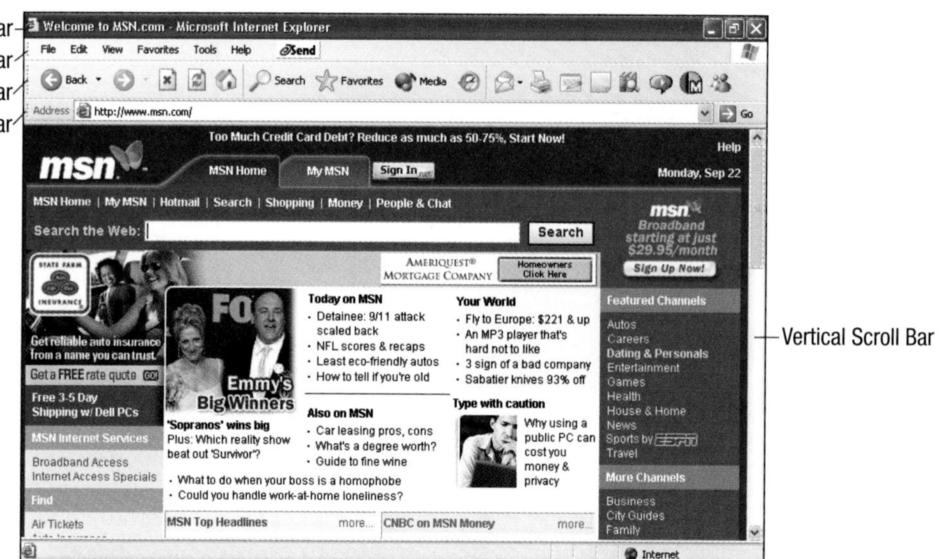

If you know the URL for the desired Web site, click in the Address bar, type the URL, and then press Enter. In a few moments, the Web site opening page displays in the Internet Explorer window. URLs (Uniform Resource Locators) are the method used to identify locations on the Internet. The format of a URL is *http://server-name.path*. The first part of the URL, *http*, stands for HyperText Transfer Protocol, which is the protocol or language used to transfer data within the World Wide Web. The colon and slashes separate the protocol from the server name. The server name is the second component of the URL. For example, in the URL http://www.microsoft.com, the server name is *microsoft*. The last part of the URL specifies the domain to which the server belongs. For example, *.com* refers to "commercial" and establishes that the URL is a commercial company. Other examples of domains include *.edu* for "educational," *.gov* for "government," and *.mil* for "military."

exercise 1

BROWSING THE INTERNET WITH INTERNET EXPLORER

1. Make sure you are connected to the Internet through an Internet Service Provider and that the Windows desktop displays. (Check with your instructor to determine if you need to complete steps for accessing the Internet.)
2. Launch Microsoft Internet Explorer by double-clicking the *Internet Explorer* icon located on the Windows desktop.
3. At the Internet Explorer window, explore the Web site for Yosemite National Park by completing the following steps:
   a. Click in the Address bar, type **www.nps.gov/yose** and then press Enter.

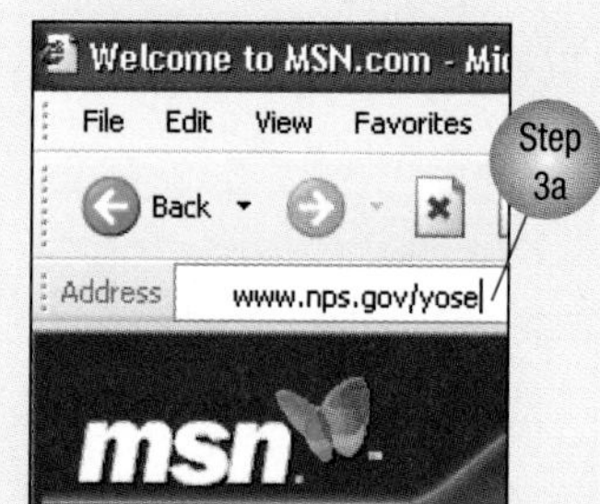

b. Scroll down the Web site home page for Yosemite National Park by clicking the down-pointing arrow on the vertical scroll bar located at the right side of the Internet Explorer window.

c. Print the Web site home page by clicking the Print button located on the Internet Explorer toolbar.

4. Explore the Web site for Glacier National Park by completing the following steps:
   a. Click in the Address bar, type **www.nps.gov/glac** and then press Enter.
   b. Print the Web site home page by clicking the Print button located on the Internet Explorer toolbar.

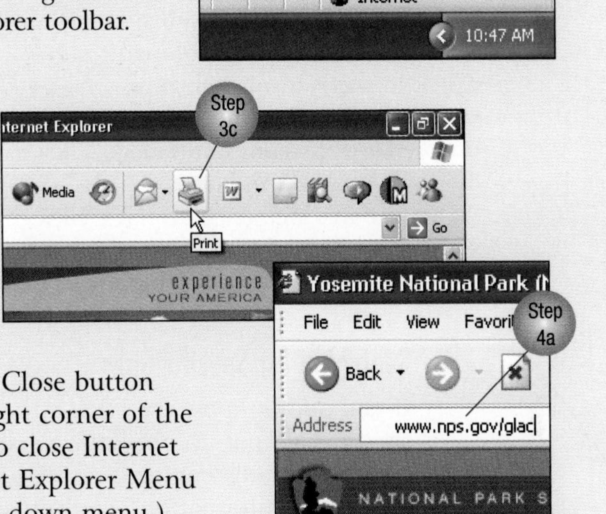

5. Close Internet Explorer by clicking the Close button (contains an *X*) located in the upper right corner of the Internet Explorer window. (You can also close Internet Explorer by clicking File on the Internet Explorer Menu bar and then clicking Close at the drop-down menu.)

Navigating Using Hyperlinks

Most Web pages contain "hyperlinks" that you click to connect to another page within the Web site or to another site on the Internet. Hyperlinks may display in a Web page as underlined text in a specific color or as images or icons. To use a hyperlink, position the mouse pointer on the desired hyperlink until the mouse pointer turns into a hand, and then click the left mouse button. Use hyperlinks to navigate within and between sites on the Internet. The Internet Explorer toolbar contains a Back button that, when clicked, will take you back to the previous Web page. If you click the Back button and then want to go back to the previous page, click the Forward button. By clicking the Back button, you can back your way out of hyperlinks and return to the Web site home page.

exercise 2

VISITING WEB SITES AND NAVIGATING USING HYPERLINKS

1. Make sure you are connected to the Internet and then double-click the *Internet Explorer* icon on the Windows desktop.
2. At the Internet Explorer window, display the White House Web page and navigate in the page by completing the following steps:
   a. Click in the Address bar, type **whitehouse.gov** and then press Enter.
   b. At the White House home Web page, position the mouse pointer on a hyperlink that interests you until the pointer turns into a hand, and then click the left mouse button.
   c. At the Web page, click the Back button. (This returns you to the White House home page.)

d. At the White House home Web page, click the Forward button to return to the previous Web page.

e. Print the Web page by clicking the Print button on the Internet Explorer toolbar.

3. Display the Amazon.com Web site and navigate in the site by completing the following steps:

a. Click in the Address bar, type www.amazon.com and then press Enter.

b. At the Amazon.com home page, click a hyperlink related to books.

c. When a book Web page displays, click the Print button on the Internet Explorer toolbar.

4. Close Internet Explorer by clicking the Close button (contains an *X*) located in the upper right corner of the Internet Explorer window.

Searching for Specific Sites

If you do not know the URL for a specific site or you want to find information on the Internet but do not know what site to visit, complete a search with a search engine. A search engine is a software program created to search quickly and easily for desired information. A variety of search engines are available on the Internet, each offering the opportunity to search for specific information. One method for searching for information is to click the Search button on the Internet Explorer toolbar. This displays a Search Companion task pane, as shown in figure IE.2 (your task pane may vary) with options for completing a search. Another method for completing a search is to visit the Web site home page for a search engine and use options at the site.

FIGURE IE.2 ***Internet Explorer Search Companion Task Pane***

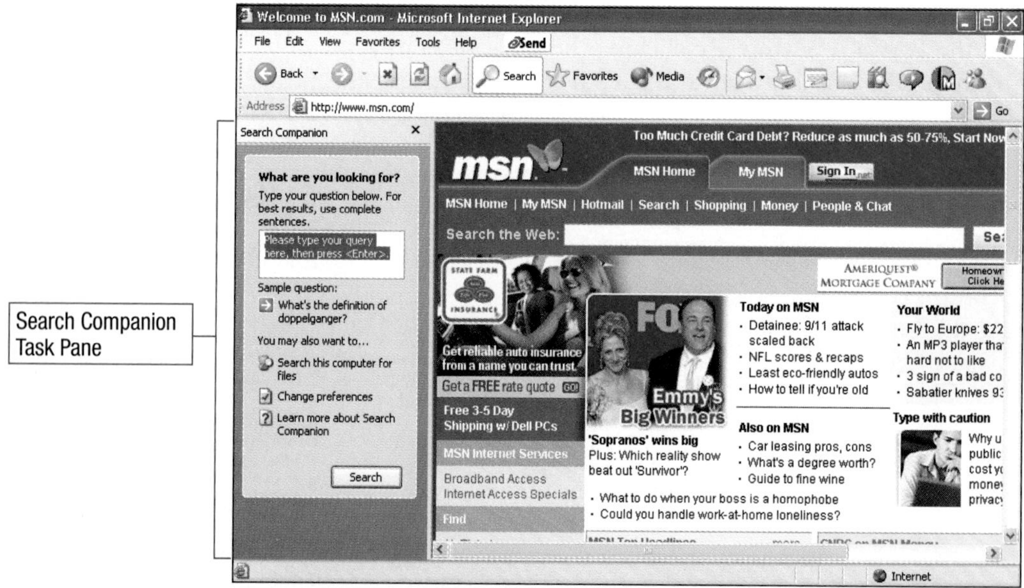

exercise 3

SEARCHING FOR SPECIFIC SITES ON THE WEB

1. Make sure you are connected to the Internet and then double-click the *Internet Explorer* icon on the Windows desktop.
2. At the Internet Explorer window, search for sites on bluegrass music by completing the following steps:
   a. Click the Search button on the Internet Explorer toolbar. (This displays the Search Companion task pane at the left side of the window.)
   b. Type **Bluegrass music** in the *What are you looking for?* text box and then press Enter.
   c. When a list of sites displays in the Search Companion task pane, click a site that interests you.
   d. When the Web site home page displays, click the Print button.

3. Click the Search button on the Internet Explorer toolbar to remove the Search Companion task pane.
4. Use the Yahoo search engine to find sites on bluegrass music by completing the following steps:
   a. Click in the Address bar, type **www.yahoo.com** and then press Enter.
   b. At the Yahoo Web site, click in the search text box, type **Bluegrass music** and then press Enter. (Notice that the sites displayed vary from the sites displayed in the earlier search.)
   c. Click hyperlinks until a Web site displays that interests you.
   d. When the site displays, click the Print button on the Internet Explorer toolbar.
5. Use the Google search engine to find sites on jazz music by completing the following steps:
   a. Click in the Address bar, type **www.Google.com** and then press Enter.
   b. When the Google Web site home page displays, click in the search text box, type **Jazz music** and then press Enter.
   c. Click a site that interests you.
   d. When the Web site home page displays, click the Print button on the Internet Explorer toolbar.

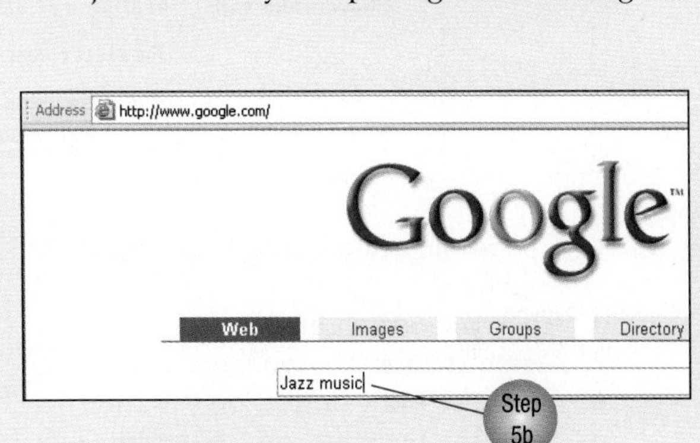

6. Close Internet Explorer.

Completing Advanced Searches for Specific Sites

The Internet contains a phenomenal amount of information. Depending on what you are searching for on the Internet and the search engine you use, some searches can result in several thousand "hits" (sites). Wading through a large number of sites can be very time-consuming and counterproductive. Narrowing a search to very specific criteria can greatly reduce the number of hits for a search. To narrow a search, use the advanced search options offered by the search engine.

exercise 4 NARROWING A SEARCH

1. Make sure you are connected to the Internet and then double-click the *Internet Explorer* icon on the Windows desktop.
2. Search for sites on skydiving in Oregon by completing the following steps:
   a. Click in the Address bar and then type **www.yahoo.com**.
   b. At the Yahoo Web site home page, click an advanced search hyperlink (this hyperlink may display as Advanced or Advanced search).
   c. At the advanced search page, click in the search text box specifying that you want all words you type to appear in the Web page (this text box may display as "all of these words").
   d. Type **skydiving Oregon tandem static line**. (This limits the search to Web pages containing all of the words typed in the search text box.)

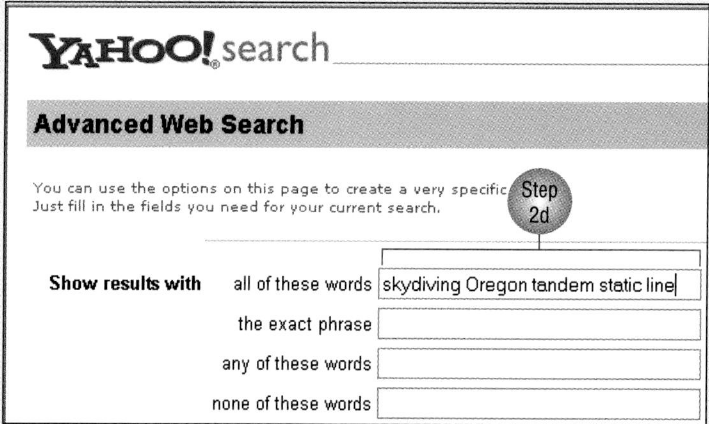

   e. Choose any other options at the advanced search Web page that will narrow your search.
   f. Click the Search button.
   g. When the list of Web sites displays, click a hyperlink that interests you.
   h. Click the Print button on the Internet Explorer toolbar to print the Web page.
   i. Click the Back button on the Internet Explorer toolbar until the Yahoo Search Options page displays.
3. Close Internet Explorer.

Downloading Images, Text, and Web Pages from the Internet

The image(s) and/or text that display when you open a Web page as well as the Web page itself can be saved as a separate file. This separate file can be viewed, printed, or inserted in another file. The information you want to save in a separate file is downloaded from the Internet by Internet Explorer and saved in a folder of your choosing with the name you specify. Copyright laws protect much of the information on the Internet. Before using information downloaded from the Internet, check the site for restrictions. If you do use information, make sure you properly cite the source.

exercise 5

DOWNLOADING IMAGES AND WEB PAGES

1. Make sure you are connected to the Internet and then double-click the *Internet Explorer* icon on the Windows desktop.
2. Download a Web page and image from Banff National Park by completing the following steps:
   a. Use a search engine of your choosing to search for the Banff National Park Web site.
   b. From the list of sites that displays, choose a site that contains information about Banff National Park and at least one image of the park.
   c. Insert a formatted disk in drive A. (Check with your instructor to determine if you should save the Web page on a disk or save it into a folder on the hard drive or network.)
   d. Save the Web page as a separate file by clicking File on the Internet Explorer Menu bar and then clicking Save As at the drop-down menu.
   e. At the Save Web Page dialog box, click the down-pointing arrow at the right side of the *Save in* option and then click *3½ Floppy (A:)* at the drop-down list. (This step may vary depending on where your instructor wants you to save the Web page.)
   f. Click in the *File name* text box (this selects the text inside the box), type **BanffWebPage** and then press Enter.
3. Save the image as a separate file by completing the following steps:
   a. Right-click the image of the park. (The image that displays may vary from what you see to the right.)
   b. At the shortcut menu that displays, click Save Picture As.

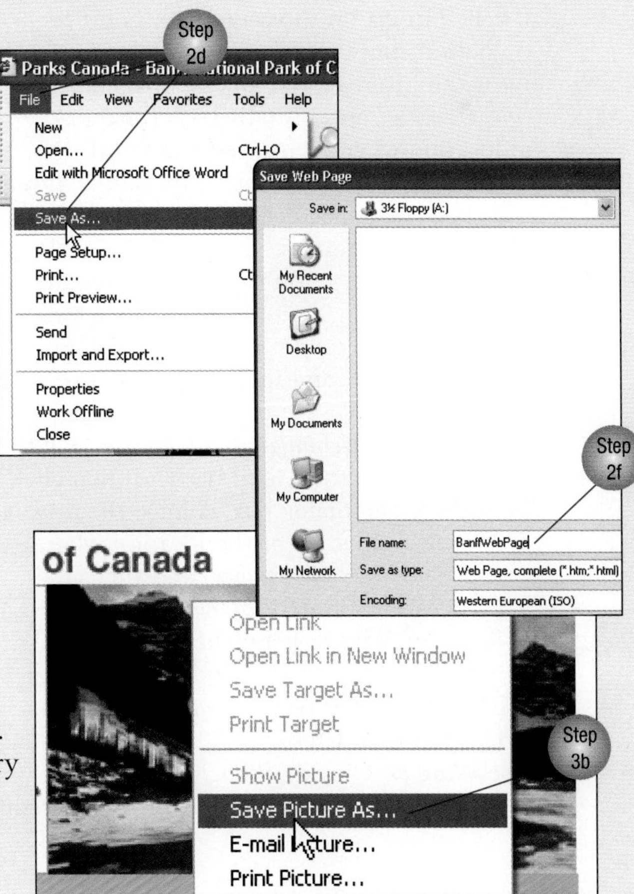

c. At the Save Picture dialog box, change the *Save in* option to drive A (or the location specified by your instructor).
d. Click in the *File name* text box, type **BanffImage** and then press Enter.

4. Close Internet Explorer.

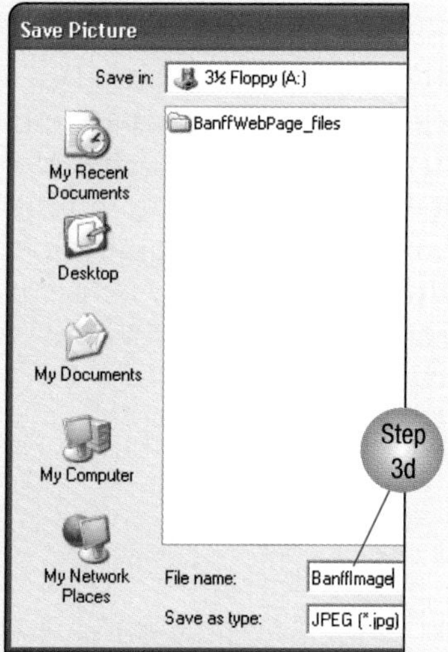

OPTIONAL **exercise**

OPENING THE SAVED WEB PAGE AND IMAGE IN A WORD DOCUMENT

1. Open Microsoft Word by clicking the Start button on the Taskbar, pointing to *All Programs*, pointing to *Microsoft Office*, and then clicking *Microsoft Office Word 2003*.
2. With Microsoft Word open, insert the image in a document by completing the following steps:
   a. Click Insert on the Menu bar, point to Picture, and then click From File.
   b. At the Insert Picture dialog box, change the *Look in* option to drive A (or the location where you saved the Banff image) and then double-click ***BanffImage***.
   c. When the image displays in the Word document, print the document by clicking the Print button on the Word Standard toolbar.
   d. Close the document by clicking File on the Menu bar and then clicking Close at the drop-down menu. At the message asking if you want to save the changes, click No.

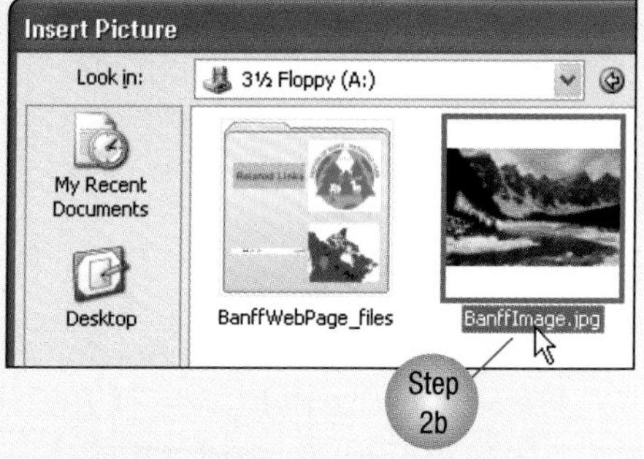

3. Open the ***BanffWebPage*** file by completing the following steps:
   a. Click File on the Menu bar and then click Open at the drop-down menu.
   b. At the Open dialog box, change the *Look in* option to drive A (or the location where you saved the Web page), and then double-click ***BanffWebPage***.
   c. Print the Web page by clicking the Print button on the Word Standard toolbar.
   d. Close the **BanffWebPage** file by clicking File and then Close.
4. Close Word by clicking the Close button (contains an *X*) that displays in the upper right corner of the screen.

SPECIALIST

MICROSOFT® WORD

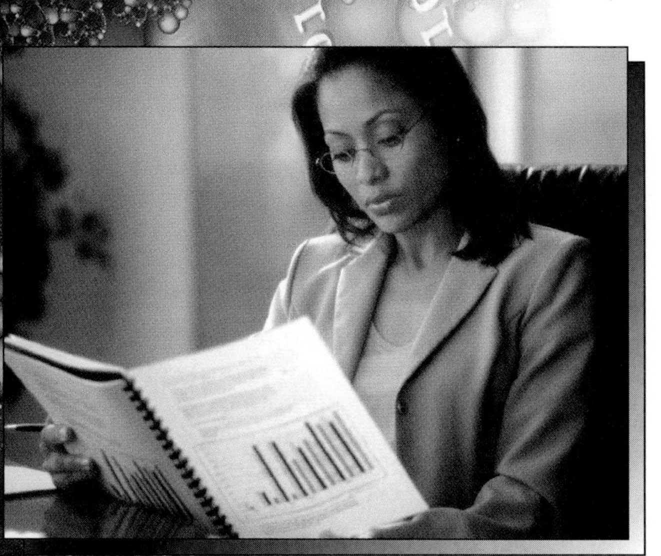

Communicating and managing information are needs that drive our entire economy. With Microsoft Word 2003, individuals and companies are in a better position than ever before to organize, analyze, and present information using word processing software.

Organizing Information

Given the enormous wealth of information available on the Internet, finding information on a particular topic is not difficult. What is challenging, though, is organizing the information so it is manageable. Word 2003 offers tools for both locating and organizing information. The Research task pane, available from the Tools menu, allows you to search the Internet, the Microsoft Encarta Encyclopedia, and other sources. Once you have found the information you need, you can organize it into topics and subtopics using the Outline view—document planning made easy!

Arranging text in charts or tables can help readers interpret complex information much more quickly. For example, which is easier to understand: paragraphs of text identifying various stocks, their type, and their prices—or a table of the same information with columns for Stock, Stock Type, and Price? With Word's Table feature, you can create tables from scratch or convert existing data into a table style of your choosing.

SPECIALIST

Making WORD Work for YOU!

Netiquette: What is considered good behavior online?

Distance conveys a degree of anonymity, and as a result, many people feel less inhibited in online situation... ...yday lives. This lessening of inhibitions sometimes leads people to dr... ...ndards of decorum when communicating online. In response, good cy... ...veloped, over the years, an informal set of guidelines for onl... Netiquette. Netiquette can be summarized by three simple precepts: ...e is a human being on the other end of your ...ng with respect, and do not transmit any message ...municate f...

conveys
convoys
Ignore All
Add to Dictionary
Paste

...out others.
writing wi... ...nts or rece...

- Be truthful. ... be someo...
- Be brief. Receiving and reading messag...
- Use titles that accurately and concisely ... postings.

Right-click to choose correct spelling from suggestions list.

Red wavy underlines mark potential spelling errors while green marks sentences with potential grammatical corrections needed.

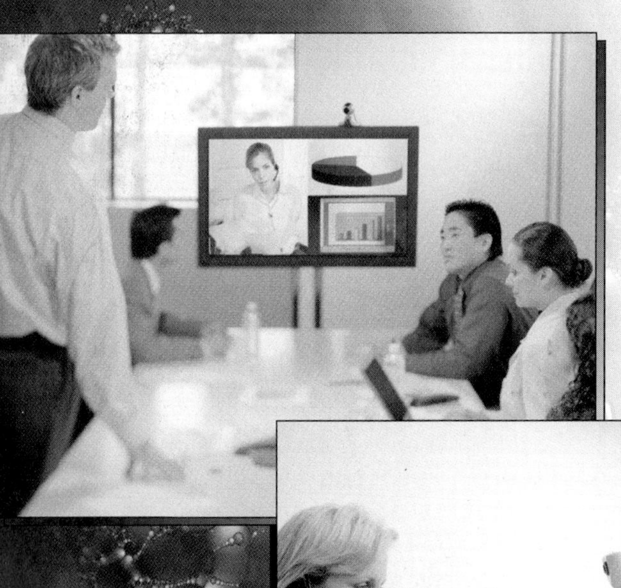

Analyzing Information

Word's Spelling, Grammar, and Thesaurus provide a set of writing tools that help you fine-tune your documents. The program marks words as you type so that you can immediately see if a word or sentence needs correction. Customize the AutoCorrect options so that Word is personalized to suit your needs by automatically changing formatting or substituting text you type with other words or phrases. Using the Word Count feature, you can display with one click an analysis of how many words, lines, paragraphs, and pages you have written.

In today's global workplace, it is very common for two or more people to collaborate on a report or proposal, often with vast geographical distances between the collaborators. Word's ability to route a document, track changes, insert and delete comments, and accept and reject changes made by multiple authors streamlines a project and helps participants capitalize on the benefits of teamwork.

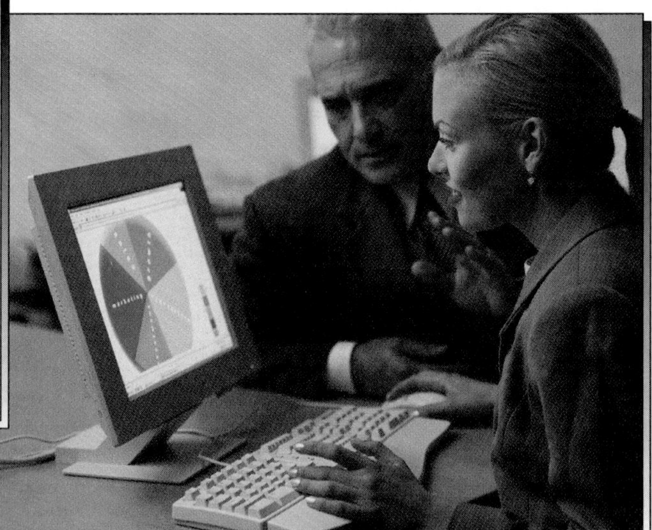

Presenting Information

Word simplifies the task of creating, editing, and formatting text so that you can concentrate on the message rather than the process. Rich text enhancements give you the capability to create visually stimulating documents. Inserting pictures, drawings, and charts is just a few mouse clicks away.

A Web presence for many businesses is often the point of first contact for external stakeholders. Apply a colorful theme to a document in just a few steps to generate an impressive Web page without having to learn programming code. You can preview the page within a browser window before saving to verify how it will look on the Web. Save the document as a Web page and Word automatically generates the corresponding tags and formatting codes that tell the browser how to display the page.

When you are nearing the completion of your studies and getting ready to enter the workforce, consider using the Resume Wizard to help sell your capabilities to prospective employers. The Resume Wizard guides you through the process of generating a professional-looking resume by stepping you through choices of layout, format, and headings. Once the Resume Wizard is finished, all you need to do is enter the text in each section. Be sure to note in your resume that you are Word 2003 proficient.

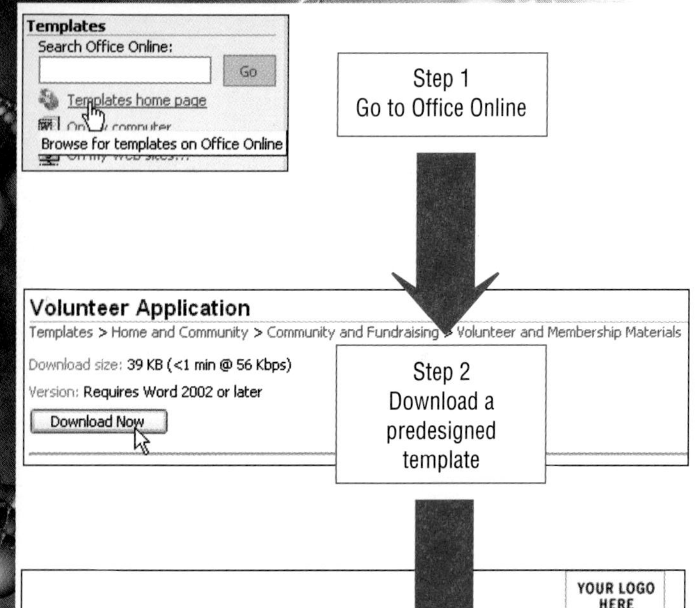

Go to Office Online and download a template to help you write your cover letter to send with your resume. After the interview, use another template to help you write a thank-you letter. With Word 2003, you can download templates for every imaginable need. Templates provide the formatting and standard text so that all you need to do in most cases is fill in the blanks.

Learning Word is an essential skill for today's employee. Microsoft Word 2003 is an easy-to-use program that will have you creating, editing, and formatting documents in no time—like a pro. You have our word.

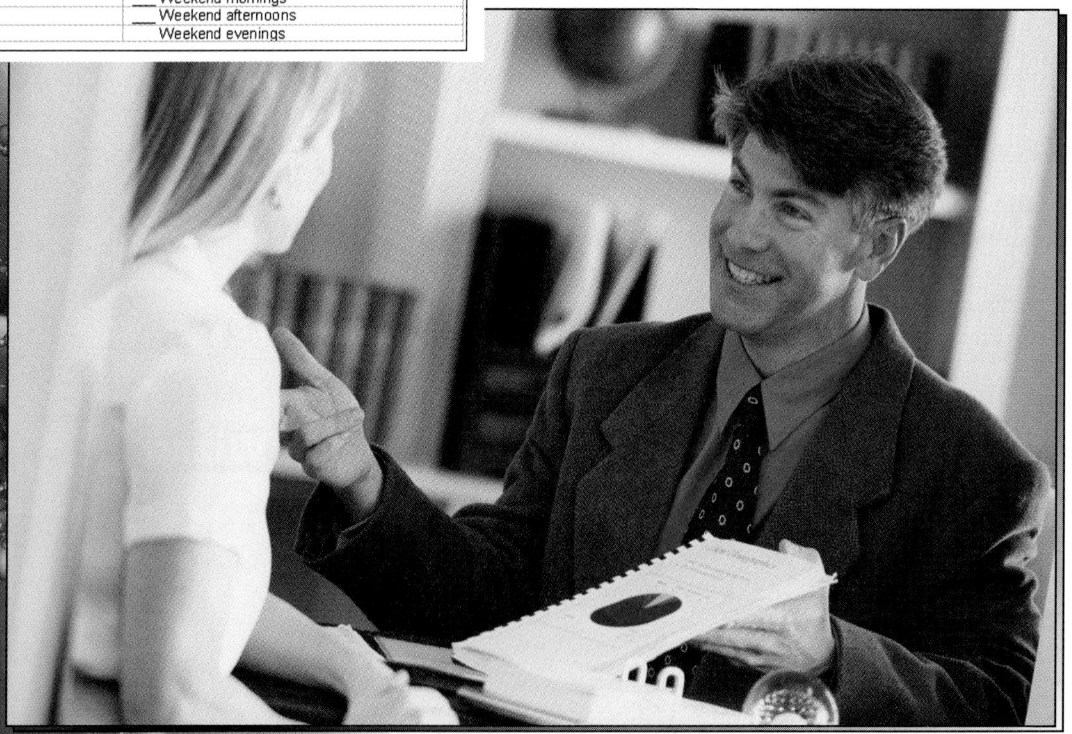

SPECIALIST

MICROSOFT®

WORD

Unit 1: Editing and Formatting Documents

- Creating, Printing, and Editing Word Documents
- Formatting Characters and Using Help
- Formatting Paragraphs
- Formatting Documents

Benchmark MICROSOFT® WORD 2003

MICROSOFT OFFICE SPECIALIST SKILLS—UNIT 1

Reference No.	Skill	Pages
WW03S-1	**Creating Content**	
WW03S-1-1	Insert and edit text, symbols and special characters	
	Insert and delete text	S23-S24
	Insert special symbols and characters	S47-S51
	Insert hidden text	S40-S41
	Check spelling in a document	S127-S131
	Check grammar in a document	S132
	Use Thesaurus to find synonyms and antonyms for specific words	S136-S139
WW03S-1-2	Insert frequently used and pre-defined text	
	Insert date and time	S52-S54
	Add words to and delete words from AutoCorrect	S134-S136
WW03S-1-3	Navigate to specific content	
	Move insertion point within a document	S19-S23
	Scroll within a document	S19-S22
WW03S-2	**Organizing Content**	
WW03S-2-2	Create bulleted lists, numbered lists and outlines	
	Create numbered and bulleted paragraphs	S73-S81
WW03S-3	**Formatting Content**	
WW03S-3-1	Format text	
	Change font, font style, font size	S37-S42
	Highlight text	S51, S53
	Apply text effects	S40-S42
	Adjust character spacing	S43-S45
	Change case of text	S48-S50
WW03S-3-2	Format paragraphs	
	Apply borders and shading	S86-S89
	Indent text	S70-S73
	Change line spacing	S81-S82
	Change alignment of text	S66-S69
	Set, move, delete, and clear tabs	S90-S97
WW03S-3-3	Apply and format columns	
	Create and format text in columns	S121-S127
WW03S-3-5	Modify document layout and page setup	
	Insert and delete a hard page break	S109-S111
	Insert and delete a hard section break	S111-S113
	Change margins	S107-S109
	Change page orientation	S108-S109
WW03S-5	**Formatting and Managing Documents**	
WW03S-5-2	Review and modify document properties	
	Display word, paragraph, and character counts	S133-S134
WW03S-5-6	Preview documents and Web pages	
	Preview a document	S110-S111
WW03S-5-7	Change and organize document views and windows	
	Reveal formatting	S83-S85
	Comparing formatting	S85-S86
	Reveal hidden text	S40
	View and navigate in a document in Reading layout	S115-S118
	Change documents views	S106, S108
	Change document zoom	S113-S115
	Display full screen	S114-S115
	Show/hide white space	S106

CHAPTER 1

CREATING, PRINTING, AND EDITING WORD DOCUMENTS

PERFORMANCE OBJECTIVES

Upon successful completion of Chapter 1, you will be able to:

- **Open Microsoft Word**
- **Create, save, name, print, open, and close a Word document**
- **Exit Word and Windows**
- **Edit a document**
- **Move the insertion point within a document**
- **Scroll within a document**
- **Select text in a document**
- **Use the Undo and Redo buttons**

Chapter01S

WORD

In this chapter, you will learn to create, save, print, open, close, and edit a Word document. Before continuing, make sure you read the *Getting Started* section presented at the beginning of this book. This section contains information about computer hardware and software, using the mouse, executing commands, and exploring Help files.

Opening Microsoft Word

Microsoft Office 2003 contains a word processing program named Word that you can use to create, save, edit, and print documents. The steps to open Word may vary depending on your system setup. Generally, to open Word, you would complete the following steps:

start

Start

1. Turn on the monitor and the CPU. (Depending on your system, you may also need to turn on the printer.)
2. After a few moments, Windows displays. At the Windows screen, position the arrow pointer on the Start button on the Taskbar (located at the bottom left side of the screen), and then click the left mouse button. This causes a pop-up menu to display.

QUICK STEPS

Open Word

1. Click Start button.
2. Point to All Programs, Microsoft Office.
3. Click Microsoft Office Word 2003.

3. Point to All Programs. (To do this, move the arrow pointer up until All Programs is selected—do not click the mouse button.) This causes a side menu to display to the right of the first pop-up menu.
4. Point to Microsoft Office. (This causes another side menu to display.)
5. Click Microsoft Office Word 2003.

HINT

To avoid opening the same program twice, use the Taskbar to see which programs are open.

Creating a Word Document

When Microsoft Word is open, a clear document screen displays as shown in Figure 1.1. The features of the document screen are described in Table 1.1. (The Standard and Formatting toolbars at your clear document screen may appear on the same line. The two toolbars have been separated for Figure 1.1.)

FIGURE 1.1 ***Clear Document Screen***

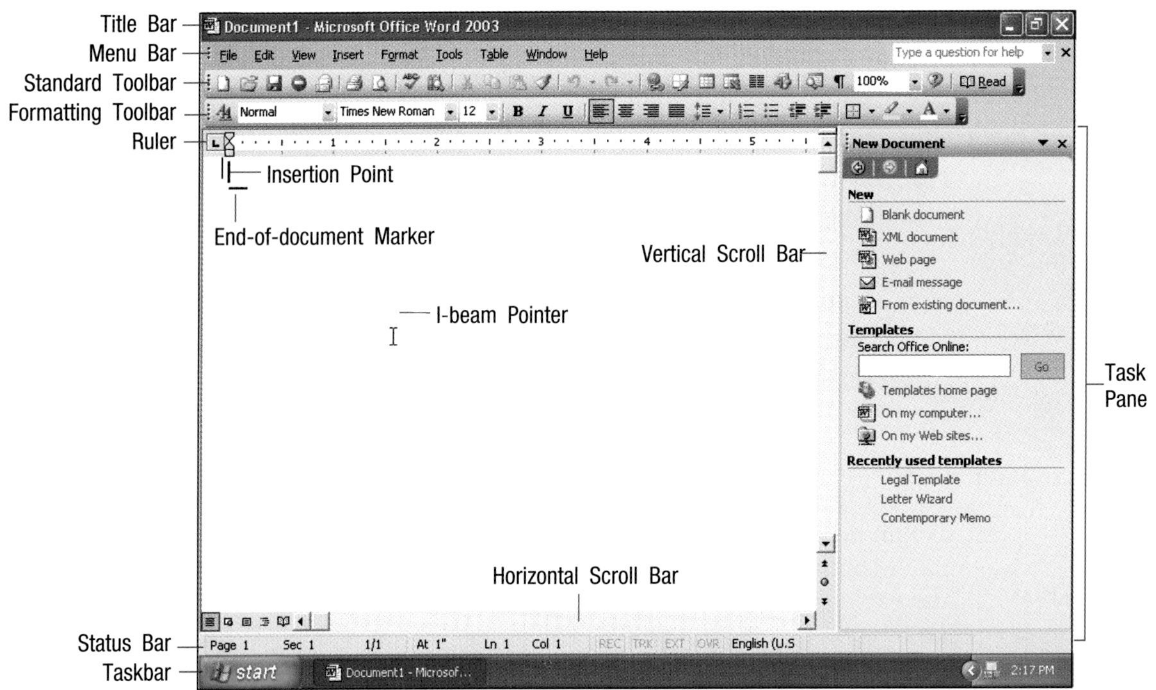

TABLE 1.1 ***Microsoft Word Screen Features***

Feature	***Description***
End-of-document Marker	The end-of-document marker indicates the end of the document.
Formatting Toolbar	The Formatting toolbar contains buttons that can quickly apply formatting to text in a document such as bold, italics, and underlining. Position the arrow pointer on a button on the Formatting toolbar and a ScreenTip displays with the button name.
I-beam Pointer	The I-beam pointer is one way the mouse pointer appears on the screen. It can be used to move the insertion point or to select text.

Insertion Point	The insertion point indicates the location where the next character entered at the keyboard will appear.
Menu Bar	The Menu bar contains a list of options to manage and customize documents. Word functions and features are grouped into menu options. For example, functions to save, close, or open a new document are contained in the File option on the Menu bar. (Buttons for some common features display at the left side of menus and shortcut commands to some features display at the right.) The *Ask a Question* text box displays at the right side of the Menu bar. Click in the text box, type a help question, press Enter, and related topics display in the Search Results task pane.
Ruler	Set margins, indents, and tabs with the Ruler.
Scroll Bars	Use the scroll bars to view various part of the document.
Standard Toolbar	The Standard toolbar contains buttons that are shortcuts for the most popular commands. For example, buttons are available for opening and saving a document. Position the arrow pointer on a button on the Standard toolbar and a ScreenTip displays with the name of the button.
Status Bar	The Status bar displays information about the text in the document and whether certain working modes are active. The Status bar also displays the current location of the insertion point by page number, section number, line measurement, line count, and column position. At the right side of the Status bar, working modes display. When a working mode is dim, it is inactive. When a working mode is active, it displays in black.
Taskbar	The Taskbar displays at the bottom of the screen. Information on the Taskbar was presented in the *Getting Started* section.
Task Pane	The task pane presents commands and options to help you perform actions in a document and it stays open, allowing you to work in your document and the task pane at the same time. The name of the task pane and the features contained in the task pane change depending on the actions being performed.
Title Bar	The document name displays at the left side of the Title bar followed by the program name (such as *Microsoft Office Word 2003*).

At a clear document screen, type the information to create a document. A document is any information you choose, for instance, a letter, memo, report, term paper, table, and so on. Some things to consider when typing text are:

- **Word Wrap:** As you type text to create a document, you do not need to press the Enter key at the end of each line because Word wraps text to the next line. A word is wrapped to the next line if it begins before the right margin and continues past the right margin. The only times you need to press Enter are to end a paragraph, create a blank line, or end a short line.

HINT

A book icon displays in the Status bar. A check mark on the book indicates no spelling errors detected in the document by the spell checker, while an *X* in the book indicates errors. Double-click the book icon to move to the next error.

- **AutoCorrect:** Word contains a feature that automatically corrects certain words as they are being typed. For example, if you type the word *adn* instead of *and*, Word automatically corrects it when you press the spacebar after the word.
- **Automatic Spell Checker:** By default, Word will automatically insert a red wavy line below words that are not contained in the Spelling dictionary or automatically corrected by AutoCorrect. This may include misspelled words, proper names, some terminology, and some foreign words. If you type a word not recognized by the Spelling dictionary, Word inserts a red wavy line below the word. If the word is correct, you can leave it as written. If, however, the word is incorrect, you have two choices—you can backspace over the word using the Backspace key and then type it correctly, or you can position the I-beam pointer on the word, click the *right* mouse button, and then click the correct spelling in the shortcut menu.
- **Automatic Grammar Checker:** Word includes an automatic grammar checker. If the grammar checker detects a sentence containing a grammatical error, a green wavy line is inserted below the sentence. At this point, leave the green wavy line. (You will learn more about the grammar checker in Chapter 4.)
- **Spacing after Punctuation:** Typically, Word uses Times New Roman as the default typeface. Times New Roman is a proportional typeface. (You will learn more about typefaces in Chapter 2.) When typing text in a proportional typeface, space once (rather than twice) after end-of-sentence punctuation such as a period, question mark, or exclamation point, and after a colon. Proportional typeface is set closer together, and extra white space at the end of a sentence or after a colon is not needed.
- **Smart Tags:** Using a smart tag, you can perform actions in Word that you would normally need to open another program to perform. For example, if you type a date, Word inserts a purple dotted line below the date, indicating a smart tag. Position the mouse pointer on the date and a smart tag icon displays. Click the icon and then choose an action from the pop-up menu such as scheduling a meeting in Outlook.
- **Option Buttons:** As you insert and edit text in a document, you may notice an option button popping up in your text. The name and appearance of this option button varies depending on the action. If a word you type is corrected by AutoCorrect, if you create an automatic list, or if autoformatting is applied to text, the AutoCorrect Options button appears. Click this button to undo the specific automatic action. If you paste text in a document, the Paste Options button appears near the text. Click this button to display options for controlling how the pasted text is formatted.

Saving a Document

Save a document approximately every 15 minutes or when interrupted.

When you have created a document, the information will need to be saved on your disk. A variety of methods can be used to save a document. You can save by clicking the Save button on the Standard toolbar; by clicking File and then Save; or with the shortcut command, Ctrl + S. For many features in this textbook, instructions for using the mouse will be emphasized. (For information on using the keyboard, refer to the "Choosing Commands" section in *Getting Started*.) To save a document with the Save button on the Standard toolbar, you would complete the following steps:

Save

1. Position the arrow pointer on the Save button (the third button from the left) on the Standard toolbar and then click the left mouse button.

2. At the Save As dialog box shown in Figure 1.2, type the name of the document.
3. Click the Save button located in the lower right corner of the dialog box.

Save a Document
1. Click Save button.
2. Type document name.
3. Click Save button.

You can also display the Save As dialog box by clicking File on the Menu bar and then clicking Save As at the drop-down menu.

FIGURE 1.2 ***Save As Dialog Box***

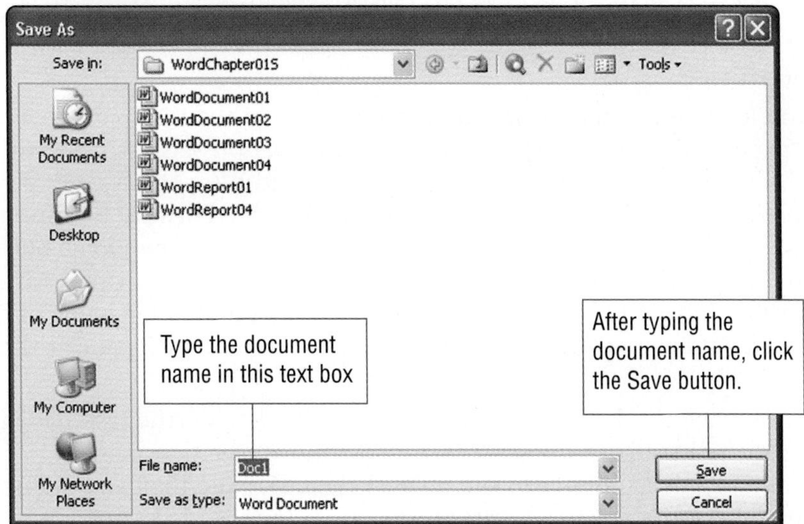

Naming a Document

Document names created in Word and other suite applications can be up to 255 characters in length, including drive letter and any folder names, and may include spaces. File names cannot include any of the following characters:

forward slash (/)	question mark (?)
backslash (\)	quotation mark (")
greater than sign (>)	colon (:)
less than sign (<)	semicolon (;)
asterisk (*)	pipe symbol (|)

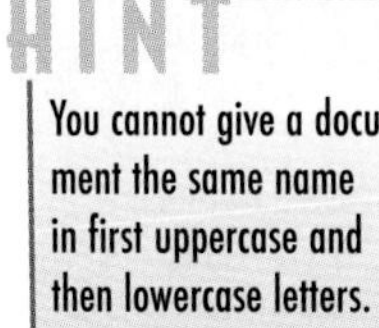

You cannot give a document the same name in first uppercase and then lowercase letters.

Canceling a Command

If a drop-down menu is displayed in the document screen, it can be removed with the mouse by positioning the I-beam pointer in the document screen (outside the drop-down menu), and then clicking the left mouse button. If you are using the keyboard, press the Alt key. You can also press the Esc key twice. The first time you press Esc, the drop-down menu is removed but the menu option on the Menu bar is still selected. The second time you press Esc, the option on the Menu bar is no longer selected.

Several methods can be used to remove a dialog box from the document screen. To remove a dialog box with the mouse, click the Cancel button or Close button. You can also click the Close button located in the upper right corner of the dialog box containing the *X*. A dialog box can be removed from the document screen with the keyboard by pressing the Esc key.

Turning On/Off and Maneuvering in the Task Pane

When you first open Microsoft Word, the Getting Started task pane displays at the right side of the screen. With options in the Getting Started task pane, you can open a specific document, create a new document, or search for specific information about Office. Depending on the actions you are performing, the task pane may be removed from the screen. For example, if you click the New Blank Document button on the Standard toolbar, a blank document displays and the task pane is removed. You can control whether the display of the task pane is on or off by clicking View and then Task Pane. You can also close the task pane by clicking the Close button (contains an *X*) located in the upper right corner of the task pane.

As you learn more features in Word, the options in the task pane as well as the task pane name may change. Maneuver within various task panes with buttons on the task pane toolbar. Click the Back button (contains a left arrow) on the toolbar to display the previous task pane or click the Forward button (contains a right arrow) to display the next task pane. Click the Home button to return to the Getting Started task pane. You can also maneuver within various task panes by clicking the Other Task Panes button (contains the name of the task pane and a down arrow) and then clicking the desired task pane at the drop-down list.

The task pane can be docked and undocked. By default, the task pane is docked at the right side of the screen. Undock (move) the task pane by positioning the mouse pointer to the right of the task pane toolbar, holding down the left mouse button (mouse pointer turns into a four-headed arrow), and then dragging the task pane to the desired location. If you undock the task pane, you can dock it back at the right side of the screen by double-clicking to the right of the task pane toolbar.

Closing a Document

Close a Document
Click File, Close.
OR
Click Close Window button.

Close Window

When a document is saved with the Save or Save As options, the document is saved and remains in the document screen. To remove the document from the screen, click File and then Close, or click the Close Window button (contains an *X*) located at the far right side of the Menu bar (immediately right of the *Ask a Question* text box). The Title bar also contains a Close button. Clicking the Close button on the Title bar will close the document and also exit Word. Clicking the Close Window button at the right side of the Menu bar will close only the document. When you close a document, the document is removed and a blank screen displays. At this screen, you can open a previously saved document, create a new document, or exit the Word program.

Printing a Document

Print

Print a Document
Click Print button.
OR
1. Click File, Print.
2. Click OK.

Many of the computer exercises you will be creating will need to be printed. A document printed on paper is referred to as ***hard copy*** and a document displayed on the screen is considered ***soft copy***. A document can be sent immediately to the printer by clicking the Print button on the Standard toolbar or through the Print dialog box. Display the Print dialog box by clicking File and then Print. At the Print dialog box, click the OK button to send the document to the printer.

Exiting Word and Windows

When you are finished working with Word and have saved all necessary information, exit Word by clicking File and then Exit. You can also exit the Word program by clicking the Close button located at the right side of the Title bar. (The Close button contains an *X*.) After exiting Word, you may also need to exit the Windows program.

HINT

Save any open documents before exiting Word.

Close

QUICK STEPS

Exit Word
Click File, Exit.
OR
Click Close button.

Completing Computer Exercises

At the end of sections within chapters and at the end of chapters, you will be completing hands-on exercises at the computer. These exercises will provide you with the opportunity to practice the presented functions and commands. The skill assessment exercises at the end of each chapter include general directions. If you do not remember how to perform a particular function, refer to the text in the chapter.

Copying Data Documents

In several exercises in each chapter, you will be opening documents provided with this textbook. Before beginning each chapter, copy the chapter folder from the CD that accompanies this textbook to a floppy disk (or other location). Detailed steps on how to copy a folder from the CD to your floppy disk are presented in the *Getting Started* section. Abbreviated steps are printed on the inside of the back cover of this textbook.

Changing the Default Folder

In this chapter and the remaining chapters in the textbook, you will be saving documents. More than likely, you will want to save documents onto a disk. You will also be opening documents that have been saved on your disk.

To save documents on and open documents from your disk, you will need to specify the drive where your disk is located as the default folder. Once you specify the drive where your disk is located, Word uses this as the default folder until you exit the Word program. The next time you open Word, you will again need to specify the drive where your disk is located. You only need to change the default folder once each time you enter the Word program.

You can change the default folder at the Open dialog box or the Save As dialog box. To change the folder to the WordChapter01S folder on the disk in drive A at the Open dialog box, you would complete the following steps:

1. Click the Open button on the Standard toolbar (the second button from the left); or click File and then Open.
2. At the Open dialog box, click the down-pointing arrow at the right side of the *Look in* option.
3. From the drop-down list that displays, click *3½ Floppy (A:)*.
4. Double-click *WordChapter01S* that displays in the list box.
5. Click the Cancel button in the lower right corner of the dialog box.

If you want to change the default folder permanently, make the change at the Options dialog box with the File Locations tab selected. To permanently change the default folder to drive A, you would complete these steps:

1. At a clear document screen, click Tools and then Options.
2. At the Options dialog box, click the File Locations tab.
3. At the Options dialog box with the File Locations tab selected, make sure *Documents* is selected in the *File types* list box and then click the Modify button.
4. At the Modify Location dialog box shown in Figure 1.3, click the down-pointing arrow at the right side of the *Look in* list box, and then click *3½ Floppy (A:)*.
5. Click the OK button.

FIGURE 1.3 **Modify Location Dialog Box**

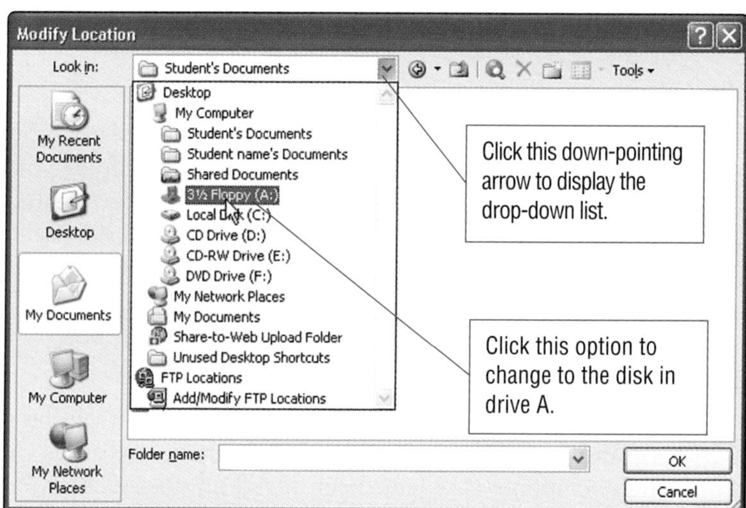

Changing the Default Type Size

QUICK STEPS

Change Default Type Size

1. Click Format, Font.
2. Click desired size in *Size* list box.
3. Click Default button.
4. Click Yes.

Typically, Word uses 12-point Times New Roman as the default font. (You will learn more about fonts in Chapter 2.) Exercises in this and other chapters will generally display text in 12-point size. If the system you are operating uses a point size other than 12, you can change the default type size to 12 by completing the following steps:

1. Click Format and then Font.
2. At the Font dialog box, click *12* in the *Size* list box.
3. Click the Default command button located in the lower left corner of the dialog box.
4. At the message box asking if you want to change the default font, click Yes.

Once the default type size has been changed in this manner, the new type size will be in effect each time you open the Word program. You only need to change the default once. Text in exercise figures in this textbook is set in a typeface other than Times New Roman, so when you type text, your line breaks may vary from the exercise figure.

(Note: Before completing Exercise 1, copy to your disk the WordChapter01S subfolder from the Word2003Specialist folder on the CD that accompanies this textbook. Steps on how to copy a folder are presented on the inside of the back cover of this textbook. Do this every time you start a chapter's exercises.)

exercise 1

CREATING AND PRINTING A DOCUMENT

1. Follow the instructions in this chapter to open Windows and then Word.
2. At the clear document screen, change to the default folder where your disk is located by completing the following steps. (If the default folder has been changed permanently, these steps are not necessary. Check with your instructor before changing the default folder.)
   a. Click the Open button on the Standard toolbar.
   b. At the Open dialog box, click the down-pointing arrow to the right of the *Look in* option.
   c. From the drop-down list that displays, click *3½ Floppy (A:)* (this may vary depending on your system).
   d. Double-click the *WordChapter01S* folder name that displays in the list box.

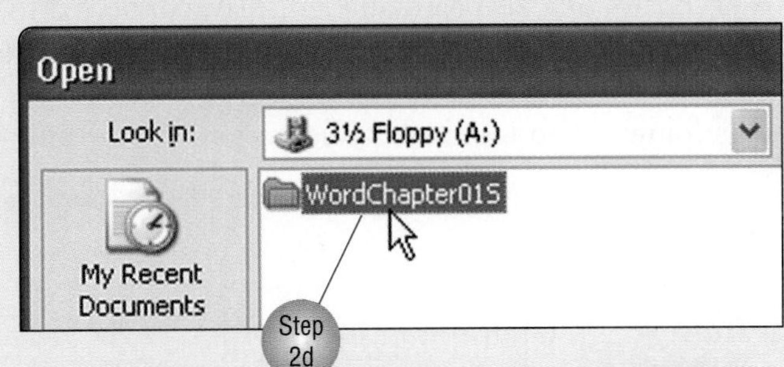

   e. Click the Cancel command button located in the lower right corner of the dialog box.
3. At the document screen, make sure that 12-point Times New Roman is the default font. (If not, change the default type size to *12* following the directions listed in the "Changing the Default Type Size" section of this chapter, or check with your instructor.)
4. Type the text in Figure 1.4. If you make a mistake while typing and the spell checker inserts a red wavy line, backspace over the incorrect word using the Backspace key, and then retype the correct word. Ignore any green wavy lines inserted by Word. (Do not worry about making a lot of corrections—you will learn more about editing a document later in this chapter.) Remember to space only once after end-of-sentence punctuation when typing the text.
5. When you are done typing the text, save the document and name it **swc1x01** (for Specialist Word, Chapter 1, Exercise 1) by completing the following steps:
   a. Click the Save button on the Standard toolbar.
   b. At the Save As dialog box, type swc1x01. (Type a zero when naming documents, not the letter O. In this textbook, the zero, *0*, displays thinner than the letter O. As you type *swc1x01,* the selected text in the *File name* text box is automatically deleted and replaced with the text you type.)
   c. Press the Enter key or click the Save button located in the lower right corner of the dialog box.

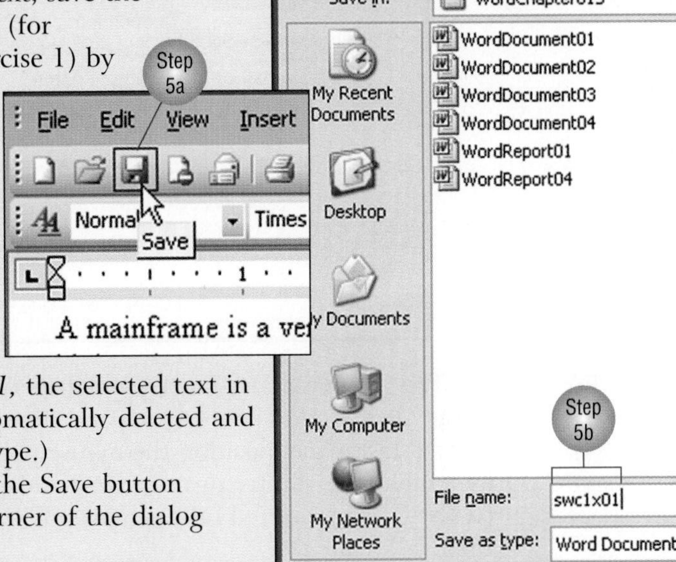

6. Print the document by clicking the Print button on the Standard toolbar.
7. Close **swc1x01** by clicking File and then Close or by clicking the Close button located at the far right side of the Menu bar. (This displays a blank screen, rather than a clear screen.)

FIGURE 1.4 **Exercise 1**

A mainframe is a very large computer used, most often in a large organization, to handle high-volume processing. A typical use of a mainframe computer would be to process the financial transactions and maintain the accounts of a large bank.

A keyboard, or a keyboard and a display, connected to a mainframe or other computer is referred to as a dumb terminal. A dumb terminal is generally used to input raw information and takes its name from the fact that it has no processor of its own. In the early days of computers, the mainframe/dumb terminal configuration was the only one available for computing.

QUICK STEPS

Open a Document
1. Click Open button.
2. Double-click document name.

Opening a Document

When a document has been saved and closed, it can be opened at the Open dialog box shown in Figure 1.5. To display this dialog box, click the Open button on the Standard toolbar or click File and then Open. At the Open dialog box, double-click the document name.

FIGURE 1.5 **Open Dialog Box**

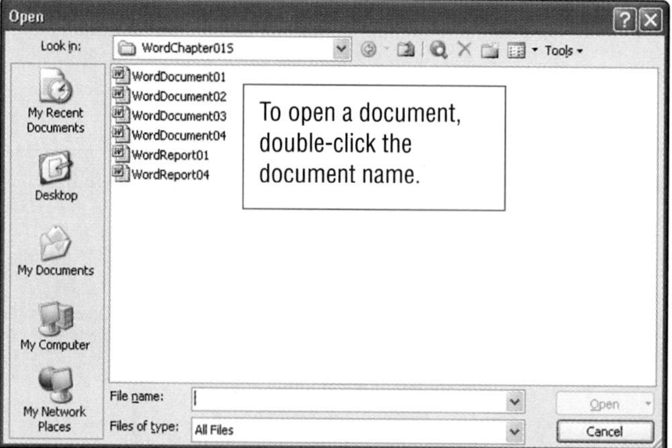

Open

The Getting Started task pane displays the most recently opened documents in the *Open* section of the task pane. To open a document from the Getting Started task pane, position the mouse pointer on the desired document name hyperlink (the pointer turns into a hand), and then click the left mouse button. (If the Getting Started task pane is not visible, display it by clicking View and then Task Pane.)

Creating a New Document

When you close a document, a blank screen displays. If you want to create a new document, display a clear document screen. To do this, click the New Blank Document button on the Standard toolbar (the first button) or click the Create a new document hyperlink in the Getting Started task pane. This displays the New Document task pane. At this task pane, click the Blank document hyperlink.

exercise 2

CREATING AND PRINTING A NEW DOCUMENT

1. At a blank screen, create a new document by clicking the New Blank Document button on the Standard toolbar (the first button from the left).
2. At the clear document screen, type the information shown in Figure 1.6. (Correct any errors highlighted by the spell checker as they occur and remember to space once after end-of-sentence punctuation. Ignore any green wavy lines inserted by Word.)
3. Save the document and name it **swc1x02** by completing the following steps:
   a. Click the Save button on the Standard toolbar.
   b. At the Save As dialog box, type swc1x02.
   c. Click the Save button or press Enter.
4. Print the document by completing the following steps:
   a. Click File and then Print.
   b. At the Print dialog box, click OK (located in the lower right corner of the dialog box).
5. Close the document by clicking File and then Close or clicking the Close button located at the right side of the Menu bar.

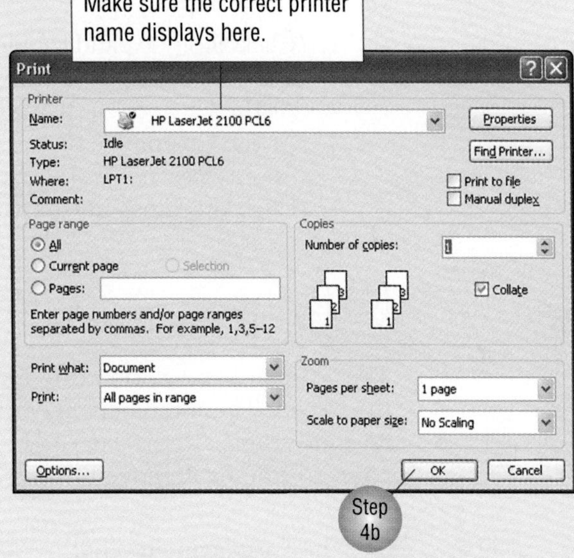

FIGURE 1.6 *Exercise 2*

A workstation is a desktop computer powerful enough to rival the performance of a minicomputer or, in some cases, of a small mainframe. Workstations are used widely for scientific, engineering, and research applications.

A personal computer, or PC, is a desktop computer that is less powerful than a workstation. As personal computers have become more powerful, the distinction between them and workstations has blurred. During the 1980s and early 1990s, networked personal computers took over many of the functions previously performed by mainframes and minis.

Expanding Drop-Down Menus

Microsoft Word personalizes menus and toolbars as you work. When you click an option on the Menu bar, only the most popular options display (considered first-rank options). This is referred to as an ***adaptive menu***. To expand the drop-down menu and display the full set of options (first-rank options as well as second-rank options), click the down arrows that display at the bottom of the drop-down menu. A drop-down menu will also expand if you click an option on the Menu bar and then pause on the menu for a few seconds. Second-rank options on the expanded drop-down menu display in gray. If you choose a second-rank option, it is promoted and becomes a first-rank option the next time the drop-down menu is displayed.

If you want all menu options displayed when you click an option on the Menu bar, turn off the adaptive menu feature. To do this, you would complete the following steps:

1. Click Tools, expand the drop-down menu by clicking the down-pointing arrows that display at the bottom of the menu, and then click Customize.
2. At the Customize dialog box, click the Options tab.
3. At the Customize dialog box with the Options tab selected, click in the *Always show full menus* check box to insert a check mark.
4. Click the Close button to close the dialog box.

Displaying Toolbars

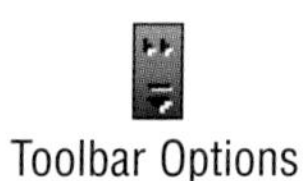
Toolbar Options

The Standard and Formatting toolbars display below the Menu bar at the top of the screen. These toolbars may display side by side with only a portion of the buttons visible. To display the hidden buttons, click the Toolbar Options button, point to Add or Remove Buttons, point to toolbar name, and a palette of buttons displays.

The Formatting toolbar in the figures in this textbook displays immediately below the Standard toolbar. With this display, more buttons on the toolbars are visible. To display the Formatting toolbar below the Standard toolbar, complete the following steps:

1. Click Tools and then Customize.
2. At the Customize dialog box, click the Options tab. (Skip this step if the Options tab is already selected.)
3. Click the *Show Standard and Formatting toolbars on two rows* option to insert a check mark in the check box.
4. Click the Close button to close the dialog box.

The display of the Standard and Formatting toolbars (as well as other toolbars) can be turned on or off. To do this, position the mouse pointer anywhere on a toolbar, and then click the *right* mouse button. At the drop-down menu that displays, click the toolbar name you want turned on or off. You can also turn on or off the display of a toolbar by clicking View on the Menu bar, pointing to Toolbars, and then clicking the toolbar name.

Editing a Document

Many documents that are created need to have changes made to them. These changes may include adding text, called ***inserting***, or removing text, called ***deleting***. To insert or delete text, you need to be able to move the insertion point to specific locations in a document without erasing the text through which it passes. To move the insertion point without interfering with text, you can use the mouse, the keyboard, or the mouse combined with the keyboard.

Moving the Insertion Point with the Mouse

The mouse can be used to move the insertion point quickly to specific locations in the document. To do this, position the I-beam pointer where you want the insertion point located, and then click the left mouse button.

Scrolling with the Mouse

In addition to moving the insertion point to a specific location, the mouse can be used to move the display of text in the document screen. Scrolling in a document changes the text displayed but does not move the insertion point. If you want to move the insertion point to a new location in a document, scroll to the location, position the I-beam pointer in the desired location, and then click the left mouse button.

You can use the mouse with the ***horizontal scroll bar*** and/or the ***vertical scroll bar*** to scroll through text in a document. The horizontal scroll bar displays toward the bottom of the Word screen and the vertical scroll bar displays at the right side. Figure 1.7 displays the Word screen with the scroll bars and scroll boxes identified.

FIGURE 1.7 ***Scroll Bars***

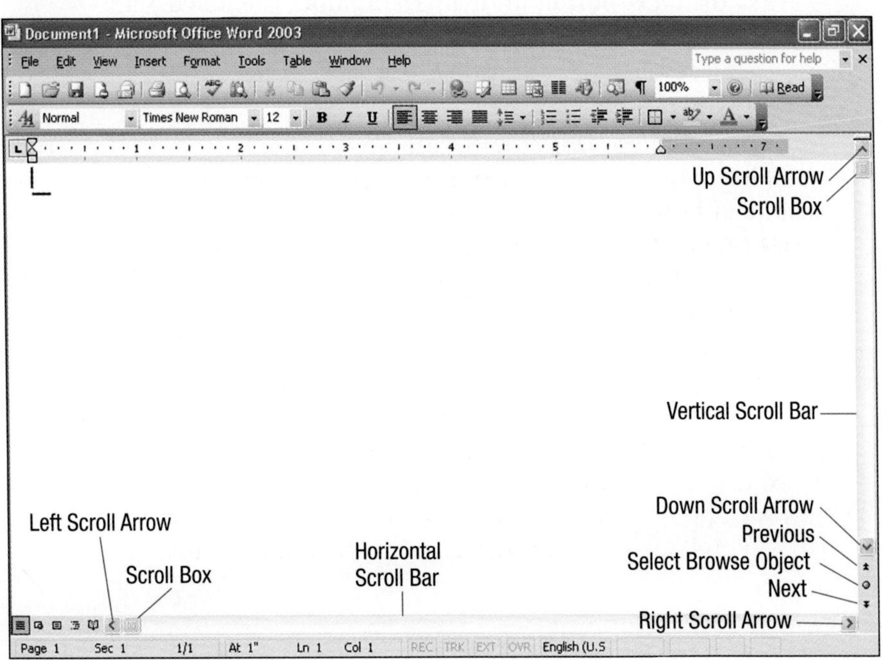

Click a scroll arrow to scroll the text in the document the direction indicated on the arrow. The horizontal and vertical scroll bars each contain a scroll box. A scroll box indicates the location of the text in the document screen in relation to the remainder of the document. To scroll up one screen at a time, position the arrow pointer above the scroll box (but below the up scroll arrow) on the vertical scroll bar, and then click the left mouse button. Position the arrow pointer below the scroll box and click the left button to scroll down a screen. If you hold down the left mouse button, the action becomes continuous. You can also position the arrow pointer on the scroll box, hold down the left mouse button, and then drag the scroll box along the scroll bar to reposition text in the document screen.

As you drag the scroll box along the vertical scroll bar in a longer document, page numbers display at the right side of the document screen in a yellow box. (You will notice this when completing Exercise 3.)

Moving the Insertion Point to a Specific Page

Along with scrolling options, Word also contains navigation buttons for moving the insertion point to a specific location. Navigation buttons are shown in Figure 1.7 and include the Previous button, the Select Browse Object button, and the Next button. The full names of and the task completed by the Previous and Next buttons vary depending on the last navigation completed. Click the Select Browse Object button and a palette of browsing choices displays. You will learn more about the Select Browse Object button in the next section.

Word includes a Go To option that you can use to move the insertion point to a specific page within a document. To move the insertion point to a specific page, you would complete the following steps:

1. Click Edit and then click Go To; or, double-click the page number at the left side of the Status bar.
2. At the Find and Replace dialog box with the Go To tab selected, type the page number.
3. Click the Go To button or press Enter. (The Go To button displays as the Next button until a page number is entered.)
4. Click the Close button to close the Find and Replace dialog box.

Browsing in a Document

Select Browse Object

The Select Browse Object button located at the bottom of the vertical scroll bar contains options for browsing through a document. Click this button and a palette of browsing choices displays. Use the options on the palette to move the insertion point to various features in a Word document. Position the arrow pointer on an option in the palette and the option name displays below the options. The options on the palette and the location of the options vary depending on the last function performed.

exercise 3

SCROLLING, BROWSING, AND MOVING THE INSERTION POINT IN A DOCUMENT

1. At a clear document screen, open **WordReport04**. (This document is located in the WordChapter01S folder you copied to your disk.)
2. Position the I-beam pointer at the beginning of the first paragraph and then click the left mouse button. (This moves the insertion point to the location of the I-beam pointer.)
3. Position the mouse pointer on the down scroll arrow on the vertical scroll bar and then click the left mouse button several times. (This scrolls down lines of text in the document.) With the mouse pointer on the down scroll arrow, hold down the left mouse button and keep it down until the end of the document displays.
4. Position the mouse pointer on the up scroll arrow and hold down the left mouse button until the beginning of the document displays.
5. Position the mouse pointer below the scroll box and then click the left mouse button. Continue clicking the mouse button (with the mouse pointer positioned below the scroll box) until the end of the document displays.
6. Position the mouse pointer on the scroll box in the vertical scroll bar. Hold down the left mouse button, drag the scroll box to the top of the vertical scroll bar, and then release the mouse button. (Notice that the document page numbers display in a yellow box at the right side of the document screen.)
7. Click on the title at the beginning of the document. (This moves the insertion point to the location of the mouse pointer.)
8. Move the insertion point to page 4 by completing the following steps:
   a. Click Edit and then Go To, or double-click the page number at the left side of the Status bar.
   b. At the Find and Replace dialog box with the Go To tab selected, make sure *Page* is selected in the *Go to what* list box, and then type 4 in the *Enter page number* text box.
   c. Click the Go To button or press Enter.
   d. Click the Close button to close the Find and Replace dialog box.
9. Click the Previous Page button located immediately above the Select Browse Object button on the vertical scroll bar. (This moves the insertion point to page 3.)
10. Click the Previous Page button again. (This moves the insertion point to page 2.)
11. Click twice on the Next Page button located immediately below the Select Browse Object button on the vertical scroll bar. (This moves the insertion point to the beginning of page 4.)

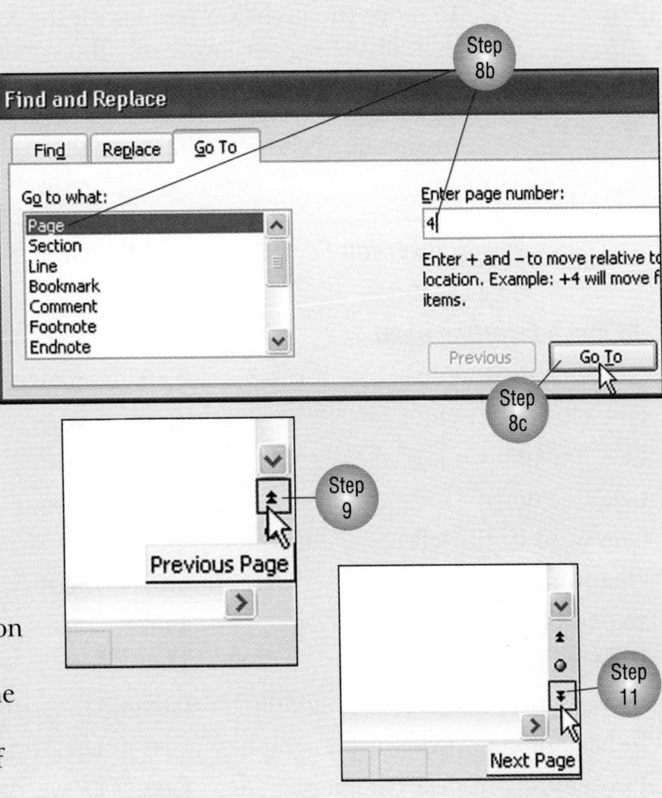

12. Move the insertion point to page 1 by completing the following steps:
    a. Click the Select Browse Object button located toward the bottom of the vertical scroll bar.
    b. At the palette of browsing choices, click the first choice in the second row (*Go To*). (The location of the *Go To* option may vary.)
    c. At the Find and Replace dialog box with the Go To tab selected, press the Delete key to delete the *4* in the Enter page number text box, and then type 1.
    d. Click the Go To button or press Enter.
    e. Click the Close button to close the Find and Replace dialog box.
13. Move to the beginning of page 2 by completing the following steps:
    a. Click the Select Browse Object button.
    b. At the palette of browsing choices, click the last choice in the top row (*Browse by Page*). (This moves the insertion point to page 2.)
    c. Click the Select Browse Object button again and then click the last choice in the top row (*Browse by Page*). (This moves the insertion point to page 3.)
14. Close **WordReport04**.

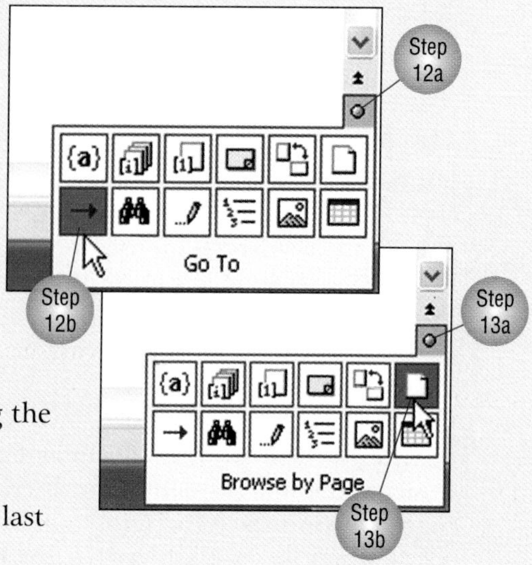

Moving the Insertion Point with the Keyboard

To move the insertion point with the keyboard, use the arrow keys located to the right of the regular keyboard. You can also use the arrow keys on the numeric keypad. If you use these keys, make sure Num Lock is off. Use the arrow keys together with other keys to move the insertion point to various locations in the document as shown in Table 1.2.

TABLE 1.2 ***Insertion Point Movement Commands***

To move insertion point	*Press*
One character left	Left Arrow
One character right	Right Arrow
One line up	Up Arrow
One line down	Down Arrow
One word to the left	Ctrl + Left Arrow
One word to the right	Ctrl + Right Arrow
To end of a line	End
To beginning of a line	Home
To beginning of current paragraph	Ctrl + Up Arrow
To beginning of previous paragraph	Ctrl + Up Arrow twice
To beginning of next paragraph	Ctrl + Down Arrow

Up one screen	Page Up
Down one screen	Page Down
To top of previous page	Ctrl + Page Up
To top of next page	Ctrl + Page Down
To beginning of document	Ctrl + Home
To end of document	Ctrl + End

When moving the insertion point, Word considers a word to be any series of characters between spaces. A paragraph is any text that is followed by a stroke of the Enter key. A page is text that is separated by a soft or hard page break. If you open a previously saved document, you can move the insertion point to where the insertion point was last located when the document was closed by pressing Shift + F5.

exercise 4 MOVING THE INSERTION POINT USING THE KEYBOARD

1. Open **WordReport01**. (This document is located in the WordChapter01S folder you copied to your disk.)
2. Press the Right Arrow key to move the insertion point to the next character to the right. Continue pressing the Right Arrow key until the insertion point is positioned at the end of the first paragraph.
3. Press Ctrl + Right Arrow key to move the insertion point to the next word to the right. Continue pressing Ctrl + Right Arrow until the insertion point is positioned on the last word of the second paragraph.
4. Press Ctrl + Left Arrow key until the insertion point is positioned at the beginning of the document.
5. Press the End key to move the insertion point to the end of the title.
6. Press the Home key to move the insertion point to the beginning of the title.
7. Press Ctrl + Page Down to position the insertion point at the beginning of page 2.
8. Press Ctrl + Page Up to position the insertion point at the beginning of page 1 (the beginning of the document).
9. Press Ctrl + End to move the insertion point to the end of the document.
10. Press Ctrl + Home to move the insertion point to the beginning of the document.
11. Close **WordReport01**.

Inserting and Deleting Text

Once you have created a document, you may want to insert information you forgot or have since decided to include. At the default document screen, Word moves existing characters to the right as you type additional text. If you want to type over something, switch to the Overtype mode. You can do this by pressing the Insert key or by double-clicking the OVR mode button on the Status bar. When Overtype is on, the OVR mode button displays in black. To turn off Overtype, press the Insert key or double-click the OVR mode button.

When you edit a document, you may want to delete (remove) text. Commands for deleting text are presented in Table 1.3.

HINT

If you type a character that takes the place of an existing character, deactivate the Overtype mode by pressing the Insert key or double-clicking the OVR button on the Status bar.

TABLE

1.3 Deletion Commands

To delete	Press
Character right of insertion point	Delete key
Character left of insertion point	Backspace key
Text from insertion point to beginning of word	Ctrl + Backspace
Text from insertion point to end of word	Ctrl + Delete

Saving a Document with Save As

QUICK STEPS

Save a Document with Save As
1. Click File, Save As.
2. Type document name.
3. Click Save button.

Earlier in this chapter, you learned to save a document with the Save button on the Standard toolbar or the Save option from the File drop-down menu. The File drop-down menu also contains a Save As option. The Save As option is used to save a previously created document with a new name. For example, suppose you create and save a document named MarketFunds, and then open it later. If you save the document again with the Save button on the Standard toolbar or the Save option from the File drop-down menu, Word will save the document with the same name. You will not be prompted to type a name for the document. If you open the document named MarketFunds, make some changes to it, and then want to save it with a new name, you must use the Save As option.

exercise 5

EDITING AND SAVING A DOCUMENT

1. Open **WordDocument01**. (This document is located in the WordChapter01S folder you copied to your disk.)
2. Save the document with the name **swc1x05** by completing the following steps:
   a. Click File and then Save As.
   b. At the Save As dialog box, type swc1x05.
   c. Click the Save button or press Enter.
3. Make the following changes to the document:
   a. Change the word *works* in the second sentence of the first paragraph to *operates*.
   b. Delete the words *means of* in the first sentence of the second paragraph and insert the words *method for*.
   c. Delete the word *Furthermore* and the comma and space following it that begins the second sentence of the second paragraph. Capitalize the *t* in *the* that now begins the second sentence.
   d. Delete the word *therefore* in the second sentence of the second paragraph.
   e. Delete the words *over and over* in the second sentence of the second paragraph and insert the words *again and again*.
   f. Delete the words *which can wreak havoc with the information stored on them* located at the end of the last sentence of the document.
   g. Delete the comma located immediately following the word *telephones* and then, if necessary, insert a period.
4. Save the document again with the same name (**swc1x05**) by clicking the Save button on the Standard toolbar or by clicking File and then Save.
5. Print and then close **swc1x05**.

Selecting Text

The mouse and/or keyboard can be used to select a specific amount of text. Once selected, you can delete the text or perform other Word functions involving the selected text. When text is selected, it displays as white text on a black background as shown in Figure 1.8.

FIGURE 1.8 ***Selected Text***

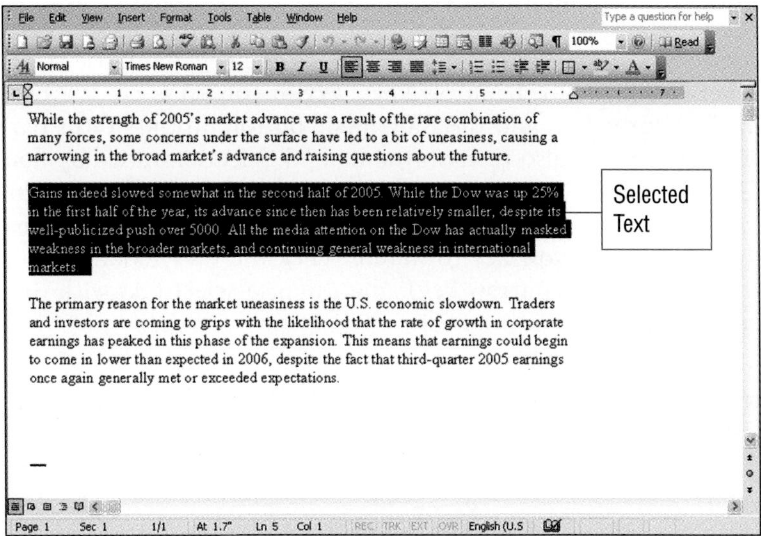

Selecting Text with the Mouse

You can use the mouse to select a word, line, sentence, paragraph, or the entire document. Table 1.4 indicates the steps to follow to select various amounts of text. To select specific amounts of text such as a line, the instructions in the table tell you to click in the selection bar. The selection bar is the space at the left side of the document screen between the left edge of the screen and the text. When the mouse pointer is positioned in the selection bar, the pointer turns into an arrow pointing up and to the right (instead of up and to the left).

TABLE 1.4 ***Selecting with the Mouse***

To select	***Complete these steps using the mouse***
A word	Double-click the word.
A line of text	Click in the selection bar to the left of the line.
Multiple lines of text	Drag in the selection bar to the left of the lines.
A sentence	Hold down the Ctrl key, then click anywhere in the sentence.
A paragraph	Double-click in the selection bar next to the paragraph or triple-click anywhere in the paragraph.
Multiple paragraphs	Drag in the selection bar.
An entire document	Triple-click in the selection bar.

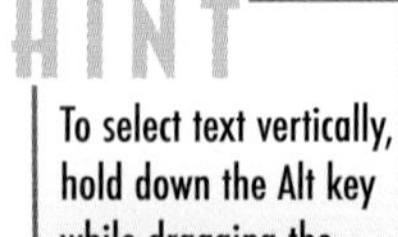

To select text vertically, hold down the Alt key while dragging the mouse.

To select an amount of text other than a word, sentence, or paragraph, position the I-beam pointer on the first character of the text to be selected, hold down the left mouse button, drag the I-beam pointer to the last character of the text to be selected, and then release the mouse button. You can also select all text between the current insertion point and the I-beam pointer. To do this, position the insertion point where you want the selection to begin, hold down the Shift key, click the I-beam pointer at the end of the selection, and then release the Shift key. To cancel a selection using the mouse, click anywhere in the document screen outside the selected text.

Selecting Text with the Keyboard

If text is selected, any character you type replaces the selected text.

To select a specific amount of text using the keyboard, use the Extend Selection key, F8, along with the arrow keys. When you press F8, the Extend Selection mode is turned on and the EXT mode button on the Status bar displays in black letters. (You can also turn on the Extend Selection mode by double-clicking the EXT mode button on the Status bar.) As you move the insertion point through text, the text is selected. If you want to cancel the selection, press the Esc key, and then press any arrow key (or double-click the EXT mode button on the Status bar and then press any arrow key). You can also select text with the commands shown in Table 1.5.

TABLE 1.5 ***Selecting with the Keyboard***

To select	*Press*
One character to right	Shift + Right Arrow
One character to left	Shift + Left Arrow
To end of word	Ctrl + Shift + Right Arrow
To beginning of word	Ctrl + Shift + Left Arrow
To end of line	Shift + End
To beginning of line	Shift + Home
One line up	Shift + Up Arrow
One line down	Shift + Down Arrow
To beginning of paragraph	Ctrl + Shift + Up Srrow
To end of paragraph	Ctrl + Shift + Down Arrow
One screen up	Shift + Page Up
One screen down	Shift + Page Down
To end of document	Ctrl + Shift + End
To beginning of document	Ctrl + Shift + Home
Entire document	Ctrl + A or click Edit, Select All

exercise 6

SELECTING AND DELETING TEXT

1. Open **WordDocument02**. (This document is located in the WordChapter01S folder you copied to your disk.)
2. Save the document with Save As and name it **swc1x06**.
3. Select the words *and use no cabling at all* and the period that follows located at the end of the last sentence in the first paragraph, and then press the Delete key.
4. Insert a period immediately following the word *signal*.
5. Delete the heading line containing the text *QWERTY Keyboard* and the blank line below it using the Extend key, F8, by completing the following steps:
   a. Position the insertion point immediately before the *Q* in *QWERTY*.
   b. Press F8 to turn on Extend Selection.
   c. Press the Down Arrow key twice. (This selects the heading and the blank line below it.)
   d. Press the Delete key.
6. Complete steps similar to those in Step 5 to delete the heading line containing the text *DVORAK Keyboard* and the blank line below it.
7. Begin a new paragraph with the sentence that reads *Keyboards have different physical appearances.* by completing the following steps:
   a. Position the insertion point immediately left of the *K* in *Keyboards* (the first word of the fifth sentence in the last paragraph).
   b. Press the Enter key twice.
8. Delete the last sentence in the last paragraph using the mouse by completing the following steps:
   a. Position the I-beam pointer anywhere in the sentence that begins *All keyboards have modifier keys....*
   b. Hold down the Ctrl key and then click the left mouse button.
   c. Press the Delete key.
9. Delete the last paragraph by completing the following steps:
   a. Position the I-beam pointer anywhere in the last paragraph (the paragraph that begins *Keyboards have different physical appearances...*).
   b. Triple-click the left mouse button.
   c. Press the Delete key.
10. Save, print, and then close **swc1x06**.

Using the Undo and Redo Buttons

Undo

Redo

If you make a mistake and delete text that you did not intend to delete, or if you change your mind after deleting text and want to retrieve it, you can use the Undo or Redo buttons on the Standard toolbar. For example, if you type text and then click the Undo button, the text will be removed. Word removes text to the beginning of the document or up to the point where text had been previously deleted. You can undo text or commands. For example, if you add formatting such as bolding to text and then click the Undo button, the bolding is removed.

If you use the Undo button and then decide you do not want to reverse the original action, click the Redo button. For example, if you select and underline text, and then decide to remove underlining, click the Undo button. If you then decide you want the underlining back on, click the Redo button. Many Word actions can be undone or redone. Some actions, however, such as printing and saving cannot be undone or redone.

In addition to the Undo and Redo buttons on the Standard toolbar, you can use options from the Edit drop-down menu to undo and redo actions. The first option at the Edit drop-down menu will vary depending on the last action completed. For example, if you click the Numbering button on the Formatting toolbar, and then click Edit on the Menu bar, the first option displays as Undo Number Default. If you decide you do not want the numbering option on, click the Undo Number Default option at the Edit drop-down menu. You can also just click the Undo button on the Standard toolbar.

HINT
You cannot undo a save.

Word maintains actions in temporary memory. If you want to undo an action performed earlier, click the down-pointing arrow to the right of the Undo button. This causes a drop-down list to display as shown in Figure 1.9.

FIGURE 1.9 ***Undo Drop-Down List***

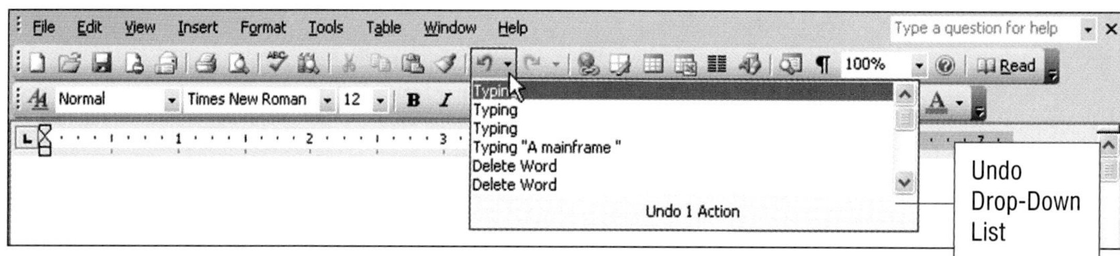

To make a selection from this drop-down list, click the desired action. Any actions preceding a chosen action are also undone. You can do the same with the actions in the Redo drop-down list. To display the Redo drop-down list, click the down-pointing arrow to the right of the Redo button. To redo an action, click the desired action. Any actions preceding the chosen action are also redone. Multiple actions must be undone or redone in sequence.

exercise 7

DELETING AND RESTORING TEXT WITH THE UNDO BUTTON

1. Open **WordDocument01**. (This document is located in the WordChapter01S folder you copied to your disk.)
2. Save the document with Save As and name it **swc1x07**.
3. Move the insertion point to the end of the document. Press the Backspace key until the last three words of the document (*stored on them.*) are deleted. Be sure to delete the space before *stored*.
4. Undo the deletion by clicking the Undo button on the Standard toolbar.
5. Redo the deletion by clicking the Redo button on the Standard toolbar.
6. Type a period after the word *information* to end the sentence.
7. Select the first sentence in the first paragraph (the sentence that begins, *The most common storage...)* and then delete it.
8. Select the second paragraph in the document and then delete it.

9. Undo the two deletions by completing the following steps:
   a. Click the down-pointing arrow to the right of the Undo button.
   b. Click the <u>second</u> *Clear* listed in the drop-down menu. (This will redisplay the first sentence in the first paragraph and the second paragraph. The sentence will be selected.)

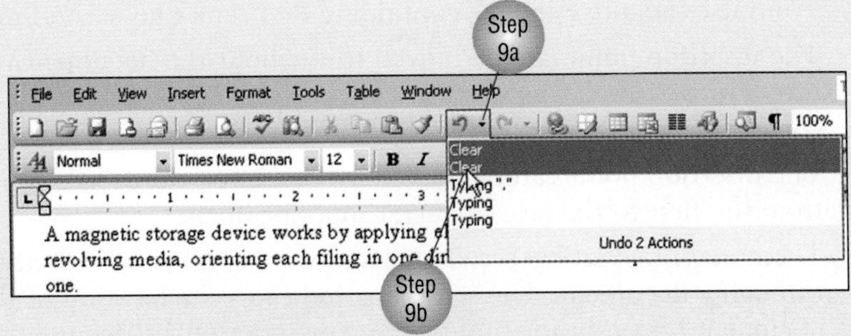

10. With the first sentence of the first paragraph selected, press the Delete key.
11. Save, print, and then close **swc1x07**.

CHAPTER summary

- Open Microsoft Word by clicking the Start button on the Taskbar, pointing to All Programs, pointing to Microsoft Office, and then clicking Microsoft Office Word 2003.
- A clear document screen contains a number of features that are described in Table 1.1.
- Word automatically wraps text to the next line as you type information. Press the Enter key only to end a paragraph, create a blank line, or end a short line.
- Word contains a feature named AutoCorrect that automatically corrects certain words as they are typed.
- When typing text, the Spell Checker feature automatically inserts a red wavy line below words not contained in the Spelling dictionary, and the automatic grammar checker inserts a green wavy line below a sentence containing a grammatical error.
- Document names can contain a maximum of 255 characters, including the drive letter and folder names, and may include spaces.
- Drop-down menus and dialog boxes can be removed from the editing window with the mouse or keyboard.
- Close a document by clicking File and then Close or clicking the Close button located at the right side of the Menu bar.
- To print a document, open the document and then click the Print button on the Standard toolbar or click File, Print, and then OK.
- Save all needed documents before exiting Word and Windows.
- Change the default folder at the Open dialog box or the Save As dialog box, or change it permanently at the Options dialog box with the File Locations tab selected.
- Open a document by displaying the Open dialog box and then double-clicking the desired document name.

- Display a clear document screen by clicking the New Blank Document button on the Standard toolbar or by clicking the Create a new document hyperlink and then clicking the Blank document hyperlink at the New Document task pane.
- The display of toolbars can be turned on or off and toolbars can be moved to different locations on the screen.
- Word uses adaptive menus containing first-rank and second-rank options.
- The insertion point can be moved throughout the document without interfering with text by using the mouse, the keyboard, or the mouse combined with the keyboard.
- The insertion point can be moved by character, word, screen, or page, and from the first to the last character in a document.
- The horizontal/vertical scroll bars and the mouse can be used to scroll through a document. The scroll box indicates the location of the text in the document screen in relation to the remainder of the document.
- Click the Select Browse Object button located at the bottom of the vertical scroll bar to display options for browsing through a document.
- Switch to Overtype mode if you want to type over something. When Overtype is on, the OVR mode button in the Status bar displays in black.
- Text can be deleted by character, word, line, several lines, or partial page using specific keys or by selecting text using the mouse or the keyboard.
- A specific amount of text can be selected using the mouse or the keyboard. That text can then be deleted or manipulated in other ways using Word functions.
- Use the selection bar, the space at the left side of the document screen between the left edge of the screen and text, to select specific units of text such as a line.
- Use the Undo button on the Standard toolbar if you change your mind after typing, deleting, or formatting text and want to undo the deleting or formatting. Use the Redo button to redo something that had been undone with the Undo button.

FEATURES summary

FEATURE	BUTTON	MENU	KEYBOARD
Open Word		Start button, All Programs, Microsoft Office, Microsoft Office Word 2003	
Save As dialog box		File, Save; or File, Save As	Ctrl + S
Close document		File, Close	
Print document			
Print dialog box		File, Print	Ctrl + P
Exit Word		File, Exit	

FEATURE	BUTTON	MENU	KEYBOARD
Options dialog box		Tools, Options	
Font dialog box		Format, Font	
Open dialog box		File, Open	Ctrl + O
New blank document		File, New, Blank document hyperlink	Ctrl + N
Customize dialog box		Tools, Customize	
Find and Replace dialog box with Go To tab selected		Edit, Go To	Ctrl + G
Undo		Edit, Undo	Ctrl + Z
Redo		Edit, Redo	Ctrl + Y

CONCEPTS check

Matching: On a blank sheet of paper, provide the correct letter or letters that match each definition.

- A ButtonTip
- B Formatting toolbar
- C Grammar checker
- D Horizontal scroll bar
- E Menu bar
- F Save As
- G ScreenTip
- H Scrolling
- I Spell checker
- J Standard toolbar
- K Status bar
- L Task pane
- M Title bar
- N Vertical scroll bar

1. This toolbar contains buttons for working with documents such as the Open button and the Save button.
2. This toolbar contains buttons for modifying the appearance of a document such as bold, italics, and underline.
3. This displays below the horizontal scroll bar and shows the current location of the insertion point.
4. This displays along the right side of the document screen (immediately left of the task pane) and is used to view various sections of a document.
5. Doing this in a document changes the text displayed but does not move the insertion point.
6. This displays at the top of the Word screen and displays the name of the currently open document.
7. This feature presents commands and options to help you perform actions in a document.
8. This appears after approximately one second when the mouse pointer is positioned on a button on a toolbar.
9. Use this option to save a previously created document with a new name.
10. This feature inserts a red wavy line below words not contained in the Spelling dictionary.

Completion: On a blank sheet of paper, indicate the correct term, command, or number for each description.

1. This displays in the document screen as a blinking vertical line.
2. This is the second line of the Word screen and contains a list of options that are used to customize a Word document.
3. At a blank screen, click this button on the Standard toolbar to open a new blank document.
4. Use this keyboard command to move the insertion point to the beginning of the previous page.
5. When Overtype is on, this mode button displays in black on the Status bar.
6. Press this key on the keyboard to delete the character left of the insertion point.
7. Complete these steps using the mouse to select one word.
8. Use this keyboard command to select text to the end of the line.
9. If you click this button on the Standard toolbar, text you just typed will be removed.
10. Use this keyboard command to move the insertion point to the end of the document.
11. Use this keyboard command to select text to the end of the paragraph.
12. To select various amounts of text using the mouse, you can click on this bar.

SKILLS check

Assessment 1

1. Open Windows and then Word.
2. At the clear document screen, change the default folder to the drive where your disk is located, and then double-click the WordChapter01S folder.
3. At the clear document screen, type the text in Figure 1.10. (Correct any errors highlighted by the spell checker as they occur and remember to space once after end-of-sentence punctuation.)
4. Save the document and name it **swc1sc01**.
5. Print and then close **swc1sc01**.

FIGURE 1.10 ***Assessment 1***

The primary storage medium used with most personal computers today is the hard drive. Typically, a person uses a hard drive to store the computer's operating system, application programs, fonts, and data files created with the application programs.

Hard drives have large storage capacities, up to several gigabytes. However large or small a hard drive is, at least 10 to 15 percent of its total capacity should be left free. If the hard drive becomes too full, the computer user is likely to experience various difficulties, such as printing problems caused by an inability to spool, or write temporarily to the drive, files that are to be printed.

Assessment 2

1. Open **WordDocument03**.
2. Save the document with Save As and name it **swc1sc02**.
3. Delete the word *rare* in the first sentence of the first paragraph.
4. Delete % in the second sentence of the second paragraph, press the spacebar once, and then type percent.
5. Delete the word *actually* in the last sentence of the second paragraph.
6. Delete the word *general* in the last sentence of the second paragraph.
7. Change the word *primary* in the first sentence of the third paragraph to *main*.
8. Delete the words *in this phase of the expansion* in the second sentence of the third paragraph.
9. Join the first and second paragraphs.
10. Save, print, and then close **swc1sc02**.

Assessment 3

1. Open **WordDocument04**.
2. Save the document with Save As and name it **swc1sc03**.
3. Delete the words *the ongoing* in the first sentence of the first paragraph.
4. Delete the last sentence in the first paragraph.
5. Delete the words *(last year's market catalyst)* in the second sentence of the second paragraph.
6. Change the word *Moreover* in the first sentence of the third paragraph to *Additionally*.
7. Insert the word *rapid* after *earlier* in the first sentence of the third paragraph.
8. Change the word *a* in the second sentence of the third paragraph to *an important*.
9. Change the word *Plus* in the last sentence of the third paragraph to *Second*.
10. Save, print, and then close **swc1sc03**.

Assessment 4

1. At a clear document screen, compose a paragraph explaining when you would use the Save As command when saving a document rather than the Save command, and the advantages to Save As.
2. Save the document and name it **swc1sc04**.
3. Print and then close **swc1sc04**.

CHAPTER challenge

You are the office assistant in the Business Division of a local community college. Several of the faculty in your division have requested that rewritable CD drives be installed in their computers. You have been asked by the division chair to look into this request. Use the Internet to research three different CD vendors. Find information on product specifications, prices, and features that might be considered advantages or disadvantages.

To summarize and present the information to your division chair, you decide to use the Contemporary Memo template from the general templates in Word. Use the Help feature to learn more about using templates when creating a new document. Include the information obtained in the first part of the Chapter Challenge in the body of the memo. Add a short paragraph that explains which product you would recommend buying and why. Save and print the memo.

The division chair is out of the office for a couple a days, but is checking her e-mail each day. She has requested that you send a copy of your memo for her to review. Send an e-mail to the division chair (your professor) with the memo you created in the second part of the Chapter Challenge attached. Print a copy of your e-mail message.

CHAPTER 2

FORMATTING CHARACTERS AND USING HELP

PERFORMANCE OBJECTIVES

Upon successful completion of Chapter 2, you will be able to:

- **Apply bold, italic, and underlining formatting**
- **Change the font and apply font effects**
- **Adjust character spacing and animate text**
- **Automate formatting with Format Painter**
- **Insert special symbols in a document and create ordinals**
- **Change text case**
- **Use AutoComplete**
- **Highlight text**
- **Insert the date and time**
- **Use the Help feature**

As you work with Word, you will learn a number of commands and procedures that affect how the document appears when printed. The appearance of a document in the document screen and how it looks when printed is called the ***format***. Formatting can include such elements as bolding, italicizing, and underlining characters; applying font, font size, font style, and special effects to text; and inserting special symbols. Microsoft Word contains an on-screen reference manual containing information on features and commands for each program within the suite. In this chapter, you will learn to use the Help feature to display information about Word.

Formatting Characters

Formatting a document can include adding enhancements to characters such as bolding, underlining, and italicizing. A variety of formatting options is displayed in Table 2.1. Bolding is typically used to highlight new terms or to draw attention to certain information. Italics serve to emphasize a word or to indicate a title of a book, a movie, or a play. Underlining can be used for emphasis or to indicate an e-mail address.

TABLE 2.1 **Character Formatting**

Formatting	Method
Uppercase letters	Press the Caps Lock key.
Bold	Press Ctrl + B or click Bold button on Formatting toolbar.
Underline	Press Ctrl + U or click Underline button on Formatting toolbar.
Italics	Press Ctrl + I or click Italic button on Formatting toolbar.

B
Bold

I
Italic

U
Underline

More than one type of character formatting can be applied to the same text. For example, you can bold and underline the same text, as shown in Figure 2.1. If formatting is applied to text, it can be removed by selecting the text and then clicking the appropriate button on the Formatting toolbar or pressing the shortcut command. For example, to remove underlining from text, you would select the text from which you want the underlining removed, and then click the Underline button on the Formatting toolbar or press Ctrl + U.

All character formatting can be removed from selected text with the shortcut command, Ctrl + spacebar. This removes *all* character formatting. For example, if bold and italics are applied to text, selecting the text and then pressing Ctrl + spacebar will remove both bold and italics.

(Note: Before completing computer exercises, delete the WordChapter01S folder on your disk. Next, copy to your disk the WordChapter02S subfolder from the Word2003Specialist folder on the CD that accompanies this textbook and then make WordChapter02S the active folder.)

exercise 1

APPLYING CHARACTER FORMATTING TO TEXT AS IT IS TYPED

1. At a clear document screen, type the document shown in Figure 2.1. When typing the text in bold, click the Bold button on the Formatting toolbar, type the text, and then click the Bold button again. Complete similar steps to underline and italicize the text in the document.
2. Save the document and name it **swc2x01a**.
3. Print **swc2x01a**.
4. With the document still open, remove underlining from the title by completing the following steps:
   a. Select the title *COMPUTER MOTHERBOARD*.
   b. Click the Underline button on the Formatting toolbar.
5. Add underlining to the bolded word *Buses* (do not underline the colon).
6. Select and then underline each of the other bolded words that begin the remaining paragraphs *(System Clock, Microprocessor, Read-only Memory, Expansion Slots)*.
7. Save the document with Save As and name it **swc2x01b**.
8. Print and then close **swc2x01b**.

FIGURE 2.1 **Exercise 1**

COMPUTER MOTHERBOARD

The main circuit board in a computer is called the *motherboard.* The motherboard is a thin sheet of fiberglass or other material with electrical pathways, called *traces*, etched onto it. These traces connect components that are soldered to the motherboard or attached to it by various connectors. Many components are found on the motherboard, including the following:

Buses: The electronic connections that allow communication between components in the computer are referred to as buses.

System Clock: A system clock synchronizes the computer's activities.

Microprocessor: The microprocessor, also called the *processor*, processes data and controls the functions of the computer.

Read-only Memory: The read-only memory (ROM) chip contains the computer's permanent memory in which various instructions are stored.

Expansion Slots: Use expansion slots to add various capabilities to a computer such as the ability to access files over a network or digitize sound or video.

Changing Fonts

Word applies a default font to text in a document. You may want to change this default to some other font for such reasons as changing the mood of a document, enhancing the visual appeal, and increasing the readability of the text.

Methods for changing the font include:

- using the Font dialog box (click Format, Font)
- using the Font button on the Formatting toolbar (click the down-pointing arrow at the right side of the Font button)

To choose an effective font for a particular document, it is helpful to understand the components of a font and the characteristics that make certain fonts suitable for headlines and short blocks of type and other fonts appropriate for reports and similar documents requiring extensive reading.

A font consists of three elements—typeface, type size, and typestyle. A ***typeface*** is a set of characters with a common design and shape. (Word refers to typeface as ***font***.) Typefaces may be decorative or plain and are either ***monospaced*** or ***proportional***. A monospaced typeface allots the same amount of horizontal space for each character. Courier is an example of a monospaced typeface. Proportional typefaces allot a varying amount of space for each character. The

HINT
Use a serif typeface for text-intensive documents.

space allotted is based on the width of the character. For example, the lowercase *i* will take up less space than the uppercase *M*.

Proportional typefaces are divided into two main categories: ***serif*** and ***sans serif***. A serif is a small line at the end of a character stroke. Traditionally, a serif typeface is used with documents that are text intensive (documents that are mainly text) because the serifs help move the reader's eyes across the page. A sans serif typeface does not have serifs (*sans* is French for *without*). Sans serif typefaces are often used for headlines and advertisements that are not text intensive. Table 2.2 shows examples of serif and sans serif typefaces.

As mentioned earlier in Chapter 1, space once after end-of-sentence punctuation and after a colon when text is set in a proportional typeface. Proportional typeface is set closer together and extra white space at the end of a sentence or after a colon is not needed.

TABLE 2.2 ***Serif and Sans Serif Typefaces***

Serif Typefaces	***Sans Serif Typefaces***
Bookman Old Style	Arial
Garamond	Eurostile
Goudy Old Style	**Haettenschweiler**
Modern No. 20	**Impact**
Rockwell	Lucida Sans
Times New Roman	Tahoma

Type size is generally set using the system developed for proportional type. The size of proportional type is measured vertically in units called ***points***. A point is approximately 1/72 of an inch. The higher the point size, the larger the characters.

Change Font

1. Click Format, Font.
2. Choose desired font, font size, and font color.
3. Click OK.

OR

Click Font, Font Size, and/or Font Color button.

Within a typeface, characters may have a varying style. Typestyles are divided into four main categories: regular (for some typefaces, this may be referred to as *normal*, *light*, *black*, *medium*, or *roman*), bold, italic, and bold italic.

Using the Font Dialog Box

Available fonts display in the *Font* list box at the Font dialog box. To display the Font dialog box, shown in Figure 2.2, click Format and then Font. You can also display the Font dialog box with a shortcut menu. To do this, position the I-beam pointer anywhere within the document screen, click the *right* mouse button, and then click the left mouse button on Font.

At the Font dialog box, click either the up- or down-pointing arrow at the right side of the *Font* list box to scroll through the list of available typefaces. As each font in the list is highlighted, the *Preview* area displays a sample of the font. Click the desired font and then click OK or press Enter. To change the font of a document on screen or previously saved as a file, you must first select the entire document and then proceed with the steps at the Font dialog box.

FIGURE 2.2 **Font Dialog Box**

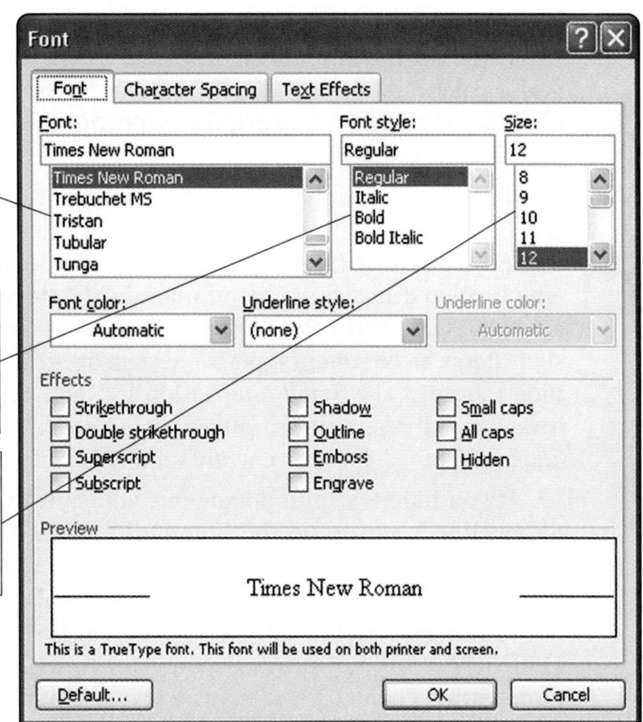

exercise 2

CHANGING THE FONT AT THE FONT DIALOG BOX

1. Open **WordDocument01**.
2. Save the document with Save As and name it **swc2x02**.
3. Change the typeface to 13-point Bookman Old Style italic by completing the following steps:
   a. Select the entire document. ***(Hint: To select the entire document press Ctrl + A or click Edit and then Select All.)***
   b. Display the Font dialog box by clicking Format and then Font.
   c. At the Font dialog box, click the up-pointing arrow at the right side of the *Font* list box until *Bookman Old Style* displays, and then click *Bookman Old Style*. (If Bookman Old Style is not available, choose another serif typeface such as Century or Garamond.)
   d. Click *Italic* in the *Font style* list box.
   e. Change the *Size* option to *13* by selecting the *12* displayed in the *Size* text box and then typing 13.
   f. Click OK or press Enter.
4. At the document screen, deselect the text by clicking anywhere in the document screen outside the selected text.
5. Save, print, and then close **swc2x02**.

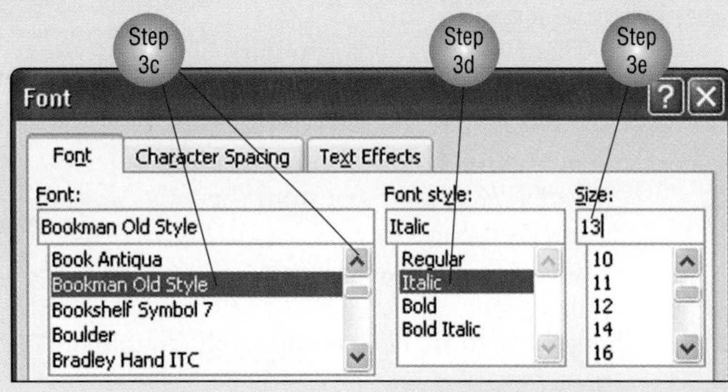

The Font dialog box contains a variety of underlining options. Click the down-pointing arrow at the right side of the *Underline style* option box and a drop-down list of underlining styles displays containing options such as a double line, thick line, dashed line, and so forth.

Click the down-pointing arrow at the right side of the *Font color* option box and a palette of choices displays. Position the arrow pointer on a color and after one second a yellow box displays with the color name. Use this option to change the color of selected text.

Apply Effect
1. Click Format, Font.
2. Click desired effect.
3. Click OK.

The *Effects* section of the Font dialog box contains a variety of options that can be used to create different character styles. For example, you can strikethrough text (which has a practical application for some legal documents in which deleted text must be retained in the document), or create superscript and subscript text. With the *Hidden* option from the Font dialog box, you can include such items as comments, personal messages, or questions in a document and then hide the text. The *Small caps* option lets you print small capital letters. This works for some printers, but not all. Additional effects include *Double strikethrough*, *Shadow*, *Outline*, *Emboss*, *Engrave*, and *All caps*.

Show/Hide ¶

If you hide text in a document, you can display the text by clicking the Show/Hide ¶ button on the Standard toolbar. With the Show/Hide ¶ button active, nonprinting characters display in the document. These nonprinting characters include paragraph and tab symbols as well as spacing characters. With nonprinting characters turned on, hidden text displays with a dotted underline. Hidden text will not print. If you want to redisplay hidden text, turn on nonprinting characters, select the text, display the Font dialog box, and then remove the check mark from the *Hidden* option.

exercise 3

CHANGING THE FONT AND FONT EFFECTS AND HIDING TEXT

1. Open **WordContract01**.
2. Save the document with Save As and name it **swc2x03**.
3. Change the font and text color by completing the following steps:
   a. Select the entire document.
   b. Display the Font dialog box.
   c. Change the font to 11-point Bookman Old Style. (If Bookman Old Style is not available, consider using another serif typeface such as Century, Century Schoolbook, or Garamond.)
   d. Change the text color to dark blue by clicking the down-pointing arrow at the right side of the *Font color* option box, and then clicking *Dark Blue* (third color from the *right* in the top row).
   e. Click OK to close the Font dialog box.
4. Change text to small caps and apply double underlining by completing the following steps:

a. Select the text *Transfers and Moving Expenses*.
b. Display the Font dialog box.
c. Click the *Small caps* option in the *Effects* section. (This inserts a check mark in the check box.)
d. Click the down-pointing arrow at the right side of the *Underline style* option box and then click the double-line option at the drop-down list.
e. Click OK to close the Font dialog box.

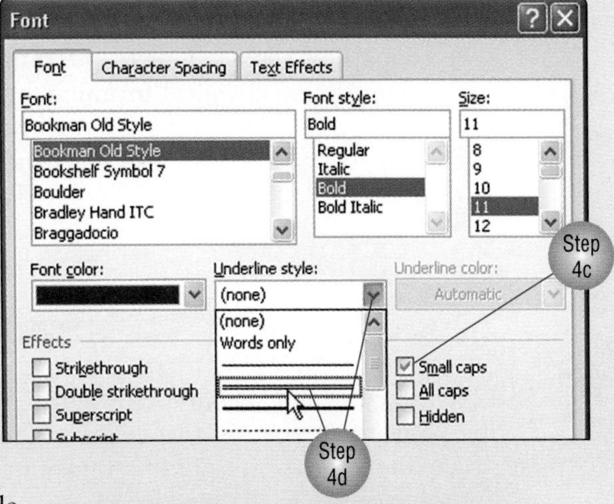

5. Follow similar steps as those in Steps 4a through 4e to apply small caps and double underlining to the heading *Sick Leave*.
6. Apply a thick underline to the text *4,000* by completing the following steps:
   a. Select *4,000*. (This text is located in the third paragraph in the *Transfers and Moving Expenses* section.)
   b. Display the Font dialog box.
   c. Click the down-pointing arrow at the right side of the *Underline style* option box and then click the thick-line option that displays below the double-line option.
   d. Click OK to close the Font dialog box.

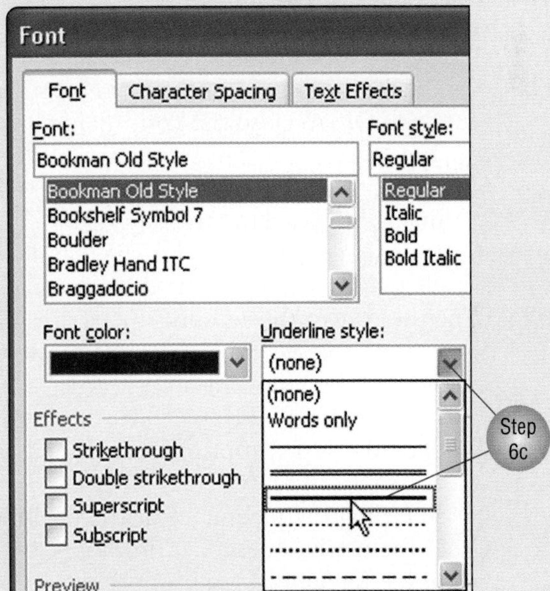

7. Hide text by completing the following steps:
   a. Select the fifth paragraph in the *Transfers and Moving Expenses* section.
   b. Display the Font dialog box, click the *Hidden* option in the *Effects* section (this inserts a check mark), and then close the Font dialog box.

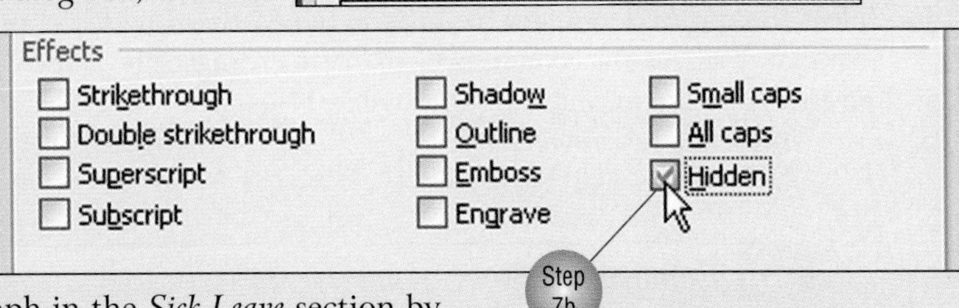

8. Hide the third paragraph in the *Sick Leave* section by completing steps similar to those in Step 6.
9. Display the hidden text by clicking the Show/Hide ¶ button on the Standard toolbar. (The hidden text is now visible and displays with a dotted underline.)
10. Redisplay the third paragraph by completing the following steps:
    a. Select the third paragraph of text in the *Sick Leave* section.
    b. Display the Font dialog box, click the *Hidden* option to remove the check mark, and then close the Font dialog box.
11. Click the Show/Hide ¶ button to turn off the display of nonprinting characters.
12. Save, print, and then close **swc2x03**. (The hidden paragraph in the *Transfers and Moving Expenses* section does not print.)

Superscript text is raised slightly above the text line and subscripted text is lowered slightly below the text line. Use superscript text for some mathematical equations such as four to the third power (written as 4^3) and use subscript text to create some chemical formulas such as H_2O. Create superscript text with the *Superscript* effect and subscript with the *Subscript* effect at the Font dialog box. Superscript text can also be created with the shortcut command Ctrl + Shift + =, and subscript text can be created with the shortcut command Ctrl + =.

exercise 4

APPLYING SUPERSCRIPT EFFECT TO TEXT AND CHANGING THE FONT

1. At a clear document screen, type the text shown in Figure 2.3 to the first superscript number and then create the first superscript number by completing the following steps:
   a. Display the Font dialog box.
   b. At the Font dialog box, click the *Superscript* check box located in the *Effects* section.
   c. Click OK to close the Font dialog box.
   d. Type the superscript number.
   e. Turn off Superscript by displaying the Font dialog box, clicking the *Superscript* check box (this removes the check mark), and then clicking OK to close the dialog box.
2. Type the text to the second superscript number and then create the second superscript number by completing the following steps:
   a. Press Ctrl + Shift + =.
   b. Type the superscript number.
   c. Press Ctrl + Shift + =.
3. Finish typing the remainder of the document using either the method described in Step 1 or Step 2 to create the remaining superscript text.
4. Select the entire document and then change the font to 12-point Bookman Old Style (or a similar serif typeface such as Century, Century Schoolbook or Garamond).
5. Save the document and name it **swc2x04**.
6. Print and then close **swc2x04**.

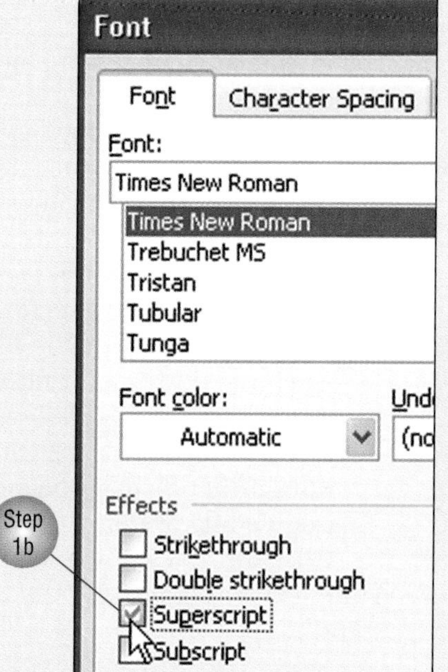

FIGURE 2.3 **Exercise 4**

The Chinese abacus consists of pebbles strung on rods inside a frame. The columns represent decimal places (ones place, tens place, hundreds place, and so on). Pebbles in the upper part of an abacus correspond to 5×10^0, or 5, for the first column; 5×10^1, or 50, for the second column; 5×10^2, or 500, for the third column; and so on. Pebbles in the lower part correspond to 1×10^0, or 1, for the first column; 1×10^1, or 10, for the second column; 1×10^2, or 100, for the third column; and so on.

Adjusting Character Spacing

Each typeface is designed with a specific amount of space between characters. This character spacing can be changed with options at the Font dialog box with the Character Spacing tab selected as shown in Figure 2.4. To display this dialog box, click Format and then Font. At the Font dialog box, click the Character Spacing tab.

FIGURE 2.4 ***Font Dialog Box with Character Spacing Tab Selected***

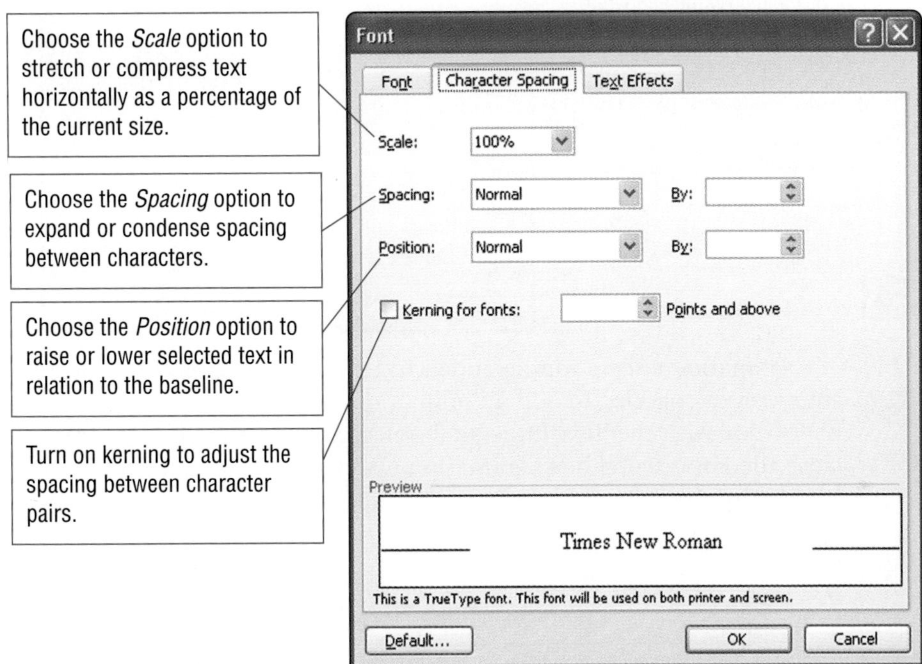
Choose the *Scale* option to stretch or compress text horizontally as a percentage of the current size.
Choose the *Spacing* option to expand or condense spacing between characters.
Choose the *Position* option to raise or lower selected text in relation to the baseline.
Turn on kerning to adjust the spacing between character pairs.
Font
Font
Character Spacing
Text Effects
Scale:
100%
Spacing:
Normal
By:
Position:
Normal
By:
Kerning for fonts:
Points and above
Preview
Times New Roman
This is a TrueType font. This font will be used on both printer and screen.
Default...
OK
Cancel

Choose the *Scale* option to stretch or compress text horizontally as a percentage of the current size. You can choose a percentage from 1 to 600. Expand or condense the spacing between characters with the *Spacing* option. Choose either the *Expanded* or *Condensed* option and then enter the desired percentage amount in the *By* text box. Raise or lower selected text in relation to the baseline with the *Position* option. Choose either the *Raised* or *Lowered* option and then enter the percentage amount in the *By* text box.

Kerning is a term that refers to the adjustment of spacing between certain character combinations. Kerning provides text with a more evenly spaced look and works only with TrueType or Adobe Type fonts. Turn on automatic kerning by inserting a check mark in the *Kerning for fonts* check box. Specify the beginning point size that you want kerned in the *Points and above* text box.

QUICK STEPS

Adjust Character Spacing
1. Click Format, Font.
2. Click Character Spacing tab.
3. Change desired option.
4. Click OK.

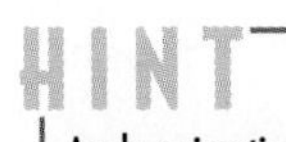
HINT

Apply animation text effects to documents that will be viewed on-screen.

Animating Text

Animation effects can be added to text at the Font dialog box with the Text Effects tab selected. To display this dialog box, shown in Figure 2.5, click Format and then Font. At the Font dialog box, click the Text Effects tab.

FIGURE 2.5 ***Font Dialog Box with Text Effects Tab Selected***

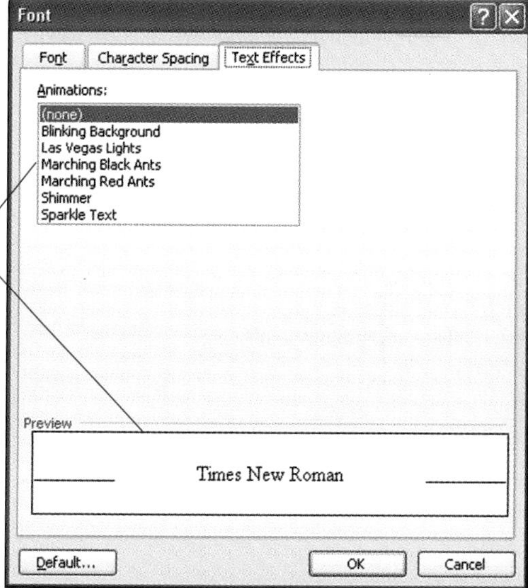

Choose an animation in this list box and view the animation effect in the Preview box.

Animate Text
1. Click Format, Font.
2. Click Text Effects tab.
3. Click desired animation.
4. Click OK.

Animation effects can be added to text, such as a blinking background, a shimmer, or sparkle. To add an animation effect, select the text, display the Font dialog box with the Text Effects tab selected, click the desired effect, and then close the Font dialog box. Animation effects added to text display in the screen but do not print.

exercise 5 ADJUSTING CHARACTER SPACING AND KERNING AND ANIMATING TEXT

1. Open **WordDocument02**.
2. Save the document with Save As and name it **swc2x05**.
3. Adjust character spacing and turn on kerning by completing the following steps:
   a. Select the entire document.
   b. Display the Font dialog box.
   c. At the Font dialog box, click the Character Spacing tab.
   d. At the Font dialog box with the Character Spacing tab selected, click the down-pointing arrow at the right side of the *Spacing* option, and then click *Expanded* at the drop-down list. (This inserts *1 pt* in the *By* text box.)
   e. Click in the *Kerning for fonts* check box. (This inserts a check mark in the check box and also inserts *12* in the *Points and above* text box.)
   f. Click OK to close the dialog box.
   g. Deselect the text.

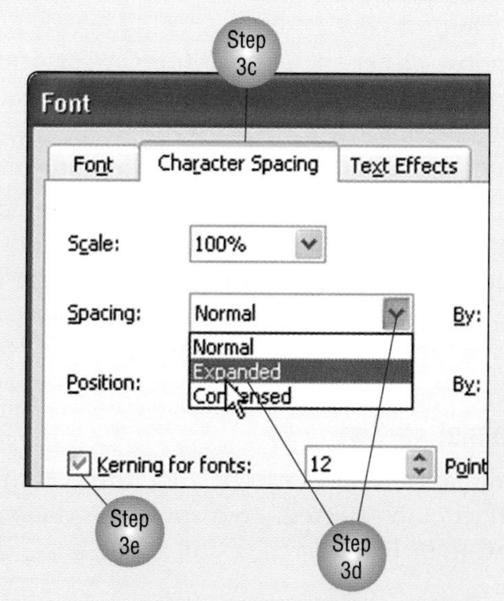

4. Save and then print **swc2x05**.
5. With **swc2x05** still open, compress text horizontally by completing the following steps:
    a. Select the entire document.
    b. Display the Font dialog box with the Character Spacing tab selected.
    c. Click the down-pointing arrow at the right side of the *Spacing* option, and then click *Normal* at the drop-down list.
    d. Select *100%* in the *Scale* option text box and then type 97. (This compresses text to 97 percent of the original horizontal spacing.)
    e. Click OK to close the dialog box.
    f. Deselect the text.
6. Add a blinking background to the title of the document by completing the following steps:
    a. Select the title *COMPUTER KEYBOARDS*.
    b. Display the Font dialog box.
    c. At the Font dialog box, click the Text Effects tab.
    d. Click the *Blinking Background* option in the list box.
    e. Click OK to close the dialog box.
7. Save, print, and then close **swc2x05**. (The animation effect does not print.)

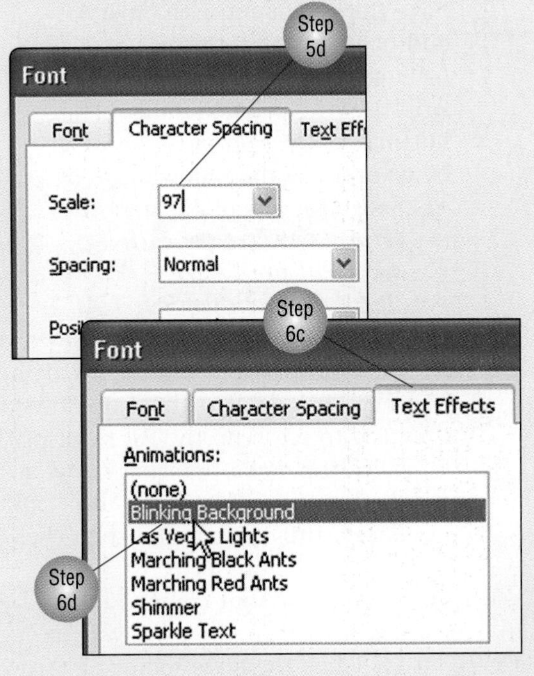

Changing Font and Font Effects Using Buttons

In addition to using the Font dialog box to select a typeface, you can use the Font button on the Formatting toolbar. The Font button displays a font name followed by a down arrow. For example, if your default typeface is Times New Roman, that name displays in the Font button. If you click the down-pointing arrow at the right side of the Font button, a drop-down list displays. Click the desired typeface at this drop-down list.

Font

Font size can be changed with options from the Font Size button on the Formatting toolbar. The Font Size button contains the current point size followed by a down arrow. To change the type size with the Font Size button, click the down-pointing arrow at the right side of the Font Size button, and then click the desired size at the drop-down list.

Font Size

The Formatting toolbar also contains a Font Color button to change the color of selected text. Click the Font Color button and the selected text changes to the color that displays on the button (below the *A*). To choose a different color, click the down-pointing arrow at the right side of the button and then click the desired color at the palette of color choices.

Font Color

exercise 6

CHANGING THE FONT TYPEFACE, SIZE, AND COLOR USING BUTTONS

1. Open **WordDocument02**.
2. Save the document with Save As and name it **swc2x06**.
3. Change the typeface to 14-point Arial and the color to indigo using buttons on the Formatting toolbar by completing the following steps:
   a. Select the entire document. ***(Hint: To select the entire document press Ctrl + A or click Edit and then Select All.)***
   b. Click the down-pointing arrow at the right side of the Font button on the Formatting toolbar and then click *Arial* at the drop-down list. (You may need to scroll up the list to display *Arial*.)
   c. Click the down-pointing arrow at the right side of the Font Size button on the Formatting toolbar and then click *14* at the drop-down list.
   d. Change the font color to indigo by completing the following steps:
      1) Click the down-pointing arrow at the right side of the Font Color button (located towards the right side of the Formatting toolbar).
      2) At the palette of color choices that displays, click *Indigo* (second color choice from the *right* in the top row).
4. Deselect the text to see what it looks like set in 14-point Arial and in indigo.
5. Save, print, and then close **swc2x06**.

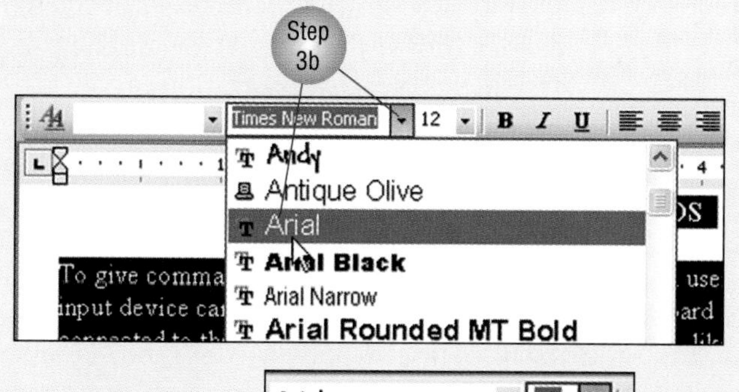

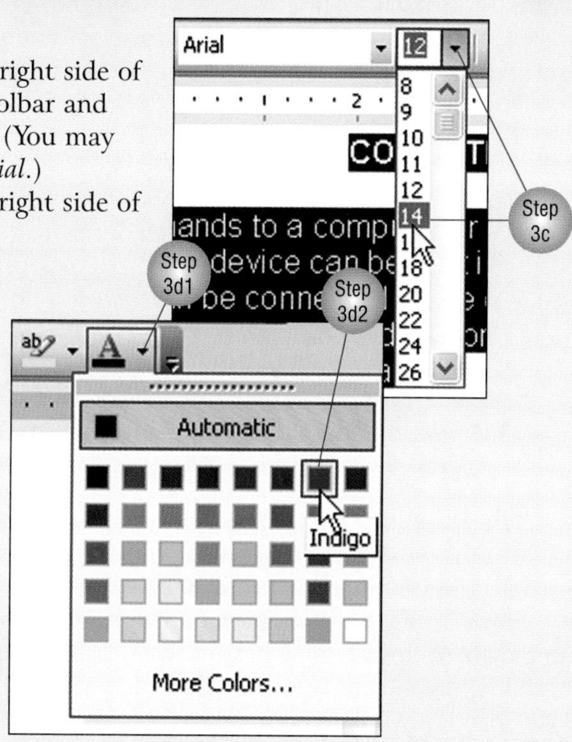

Formatting with Format Painter

HINT
You can also turn off Format Painter by pressing the Esc key.

The Standard toolbar contains a button that can be used to copy character formatting to different locations in the document. This button is called the Format Painter and displays on the Standard toolbar as a paintbrush. To use the Format Painter button, position the insertion point on a character containing the desired character formatting, click the Format Painter button, and then select text to which you want the character formatting applied.

When you click the Format Painter button, the mouse I-beam pointer displays with a paintbrush attached. If you want to apply character formatting a single time, click the Format Painter button once. If, however, you want to apply the character formatting in more than one location in the document, double-click the Format Painter button. If you have double-clicked the Format Painter button, turn off the feature by clicking the Format Painter button once.

Format with Format Painter
1. Format text.
2. Double-click Format Painter button.
3. Select text.
4. Click Format Painter button.

Inserting Symbols and Special Characters

Many of the typefaces (fonts) include special symbols such as bullets, publishing symbols, and letters with special punctuation (such as É, ö, and ñ). To insert a symbol, display the Symbol dialog box with the Symbols tab selected as shown in Figure 2.6 by clicking Insert and then Symbol. At the Symbol dialog box, double-click the desired symbol, and then click Close; or click the desired symbol, click Insert, and then click Close.

Insert Symbol
1. Click Insert, Symbol.
2. Choose desired font.
3. Double-click symbol.
4. Click Close.

FIGURE 2.6 **Symbol Dialog Box with Symbols Tab Selected**

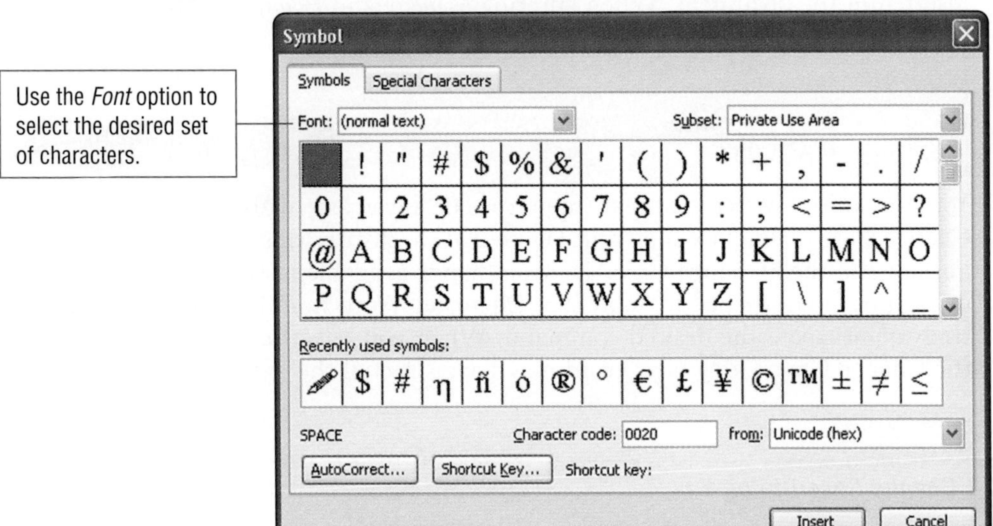

Changing the Font for Symbols

At the Symbol dialog box with the Symbols tab selected, you can change the font with the *Font* option. When you change the font, different symbols display in the dialog box. To change the font, display the Symbol dialog box with the Symbols tab selected, click the down-pointing arrow to the right of the *Font* option box, and then click the desired font at the drop-down list.

Create attractive bullets that relate to the theme of a document with symbols available at the Symbol dialog box.

HINT

Turn off formatting of ordinal numbers by removing the check mark from the *Ordinals (1st) with superscript* option at the AutoCorrect dialog box with the AutoFormat As You Type tab selected.

Inserting Special Characters

Click the Special Characters tab at the Symbol dialog box and a list of special characters displays along with shortcut keys to create the special character. To insert a special character, display the Symbol dialog box with the Special Characters tab selected, double-click the desired character, and then click the Close button.

Creating Ordinals

Word automatically formats ordinal numbers. For example, if you type *1st* and then press the spacebar, Word will correct it to *1*st. Word automatically changes the font size of the *st* and formats the letters as superscript text. This automatic feature will change other ordinal numbers such as 2nd, 3rd, 4th, and so forth.

HINT

You can turn off AutoComplete suggestions by removing the check mark from the *Show AutoComplete suggestions* check box at the AutoCorrect dialog box with the AutoText tab selected.

Using AutoComplete

Microsoft Word and other Office applications include an AutoComplete feature that inserts an entire item when you type a few identifying characters and then press Enter or F3. For example, type the letters *Wedn* and *Wednesday* displays in a ScreenTip above the letters. Press the Enter key or press F3 and *Wednesday* is inserted in the document. When entering *Monday* and *Friday* in Exercise 7, type the first four characters and then press the Enter key.

Changing Text Case

You can control the case of text (uppercase or lowercase) with options at the Change Case dialog box shown in Figure 2.7. To display this dialog box, click Format and then Change Case. The commands available at the Change Case dialog box are described in Table 2.3. Microsoft Word is an intuitive program and tries to anticipate the desired command. When you select text and then display the Change Case dialog box, Word may have selected the desired option.

FIGURE 2.7 **Change Case Dialog Box**

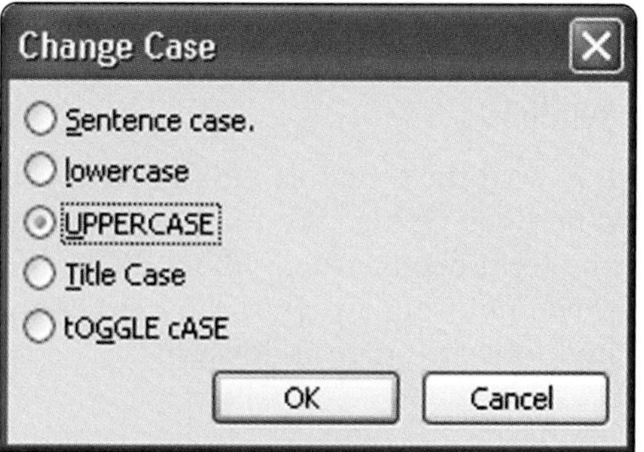

TABLE

2.3 Change Case Dialog Box Options

Option	***Action that occurs***
Sentence case.	First letter of the first word of each selected sentence is capitalized
lowercase	All selected text is changed to lowercase letters
UPPERCASE	All selected text is changed to uppercase letters
Title Case	First letter of each word in selected text is capitalized
tOGGLE cASE	All uppercase letters in selected text are changed to lowercase letters and all lowercase letters changed to uppercase letters

exercise 7 CREATING SPECIAL SYMBOLS, CHANGING CASES, AND USING FORMAT PAINTER

1. At a clear document screen, type the text in Figure 2.8 to the point where the ® symbol is to be inserted and then complete the following steps:
   a. Click Insert and then Symbol.
   b. At the Symbol dialog box, click the Special Characters tab.
   c. Double-click the ® symbol.
   d. Click the Close button.
2. Type the text to the point where the ó symbol is to be inserted and then complete the following steps:
   a. Click Insert and then Symbol.
   b. At the Symbol dialog box, click the Symbols tab.
   c. Click the down-pointing arrow at the right side of the *Font* option box, and then click *(normal text)* at the drop-down list. (You may need to scroll up to see this option. Skip this step if *(normal text)* is already selected.)
   d. Scroll through the list of symbols until the ó symbol displays (third symbol from the left in the twelfth row) and then double-click the ó symbol.
   e. Click the Close button.

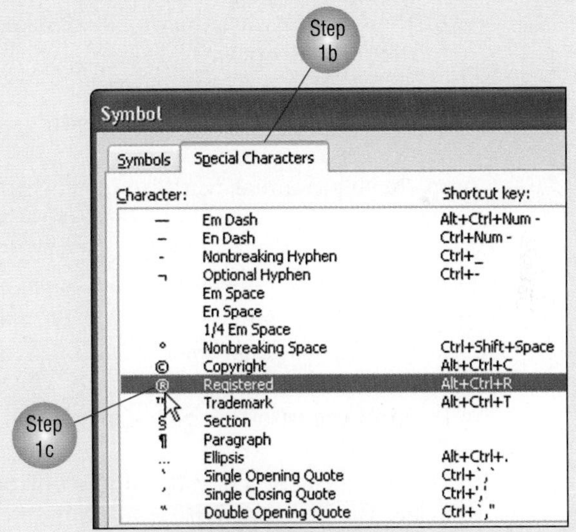

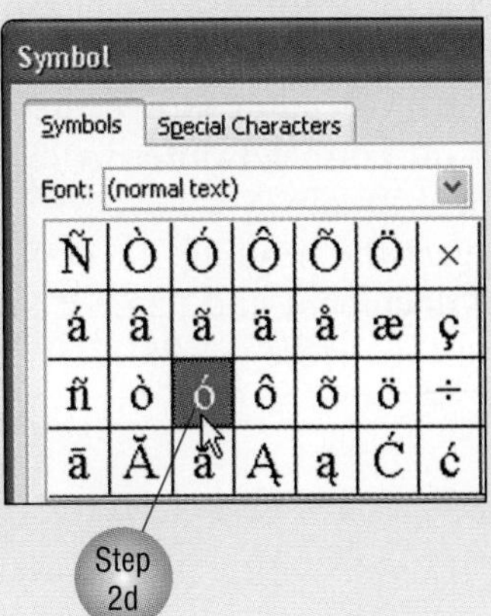

3. Type the text to the point where the ñ symbol is to be inserted and then complete the following steps:
   a. Click Insert and then Symbol.
   b. At the Symbol dialog box, make sure the *Font* option displays as *(normal text)*, and then double-click the ñ symbol (first symbol from the left in the twelfth row).
   c. Click the Close button.
   d. Repeat these steps when you type the other occurrences of *Viña*.

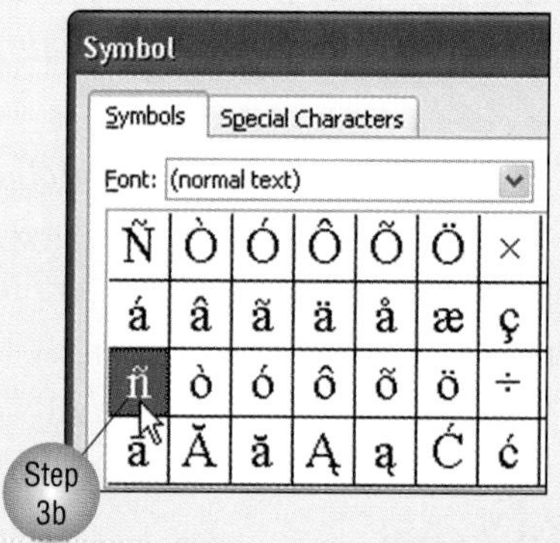

4. Type the remainder of the text in Figure 2.8. (Word will automatically change the formatting of the ordinal numbers [1st, 2nd, and 3rd].)
5. Change the case of the headings by completing the following steps:
   a. Select the heading *NEW OPTIONS IN RETIREMENT*.
   b. Click Format and then Change Case.
   c. At the Change Case dialog box, click the Title Case option.
   d. Click OK.
   e. Edit the word *In* in the first heading so the *I* is lowercase.

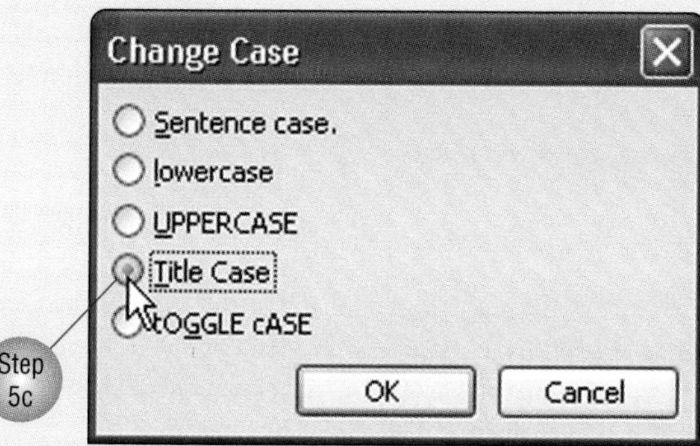

6. Complete steps similar to those in 5a through 5d to change to title case for the remaining headings (*RETIREMENT PLANS*, *TELEPHONE SERVICE IMPROVEMENTS*, *FASTER CASH WITHDRAWALS*, and *NEW FINANCIAL CONSULTANTS*).
7. Apply formatting to headings using Format Painter by completing the following steps:
   a. Select the heading *New Options in Retirement*, change the font to 14-point Arial bold, and then deselect the text.
   b. Position the insertion point on any character in the heading *New Options in Retirement*.
   c. Double-click the Format Painter button on the Standard toolbar.
   d. Select the heading *Retirement Plans*.
   e. Select the heading *Telephone Service Improvements*.
   f. Select the heading *Faster Cash Withdrawals*.
   g. Select the heading *New Financial Consultants*.
   h. Turn off Format Painter by clicking once on the Format Painter button on the Standard toolbar.
   i. Deselect the heading.
8. Save the document and name it **swc2x07**.
9. Print and then close **swc2x07**.

FIGURE 2.8 **Exercise 7**

NEW OPTIONS IN RETIREMENT
"You can now change the source of your annuity income from any MIRA® account to any other MIRA account," states Concepción Viña, Fund Manager for retirement accounts. In addition, Viña states that retirees receiving annuity income through the graduated payment method can now switch to the standard payment method.

RETIREMENT PLANS
MIRA accounts offer a three-tiered system for retirement benefits. The 1st plan is structured for those 50 years and older. If you are between the age of 35 and 49, the 2nd plan is designed for you and if you are under 35, the 3rd plan can meet your retirement needs.

TELEPHONE SERVICE IMPROVEMENTS
Access to your accumulation is now available 24 hours a day, 7 days a week through the Automated Telephone Service. You can use this service to find out your last premium paid, set up future accumulation transfers, and make multiple transfers in the same call.

FASTER CASH WITHDRAWALS
You can get cash from a supplemental retirement annuity or a preferred personal annuity. "Often, this cash can be available the next business day," states Viña.

NEW FINANCIAL CONSULTANTS
Beginning March 1, financial specialists will be available to talk to customers in person or on the telephone Monday through Friday from 9:00 a.m. to 4:30 p.m.

Highlighting Text

As people read information in books, magazines, periodicals, papers, and so forth, they may highlight important information with a highlighting pen. A highlighting pen creates a colored background through which the text can be read. This colored background draws the reader's eyes to the specific text.

Word provides a button on the Formatting toolbar that lets you highlight text in a document using the mouse. With this highlighting feature, you can select and highlight specific text in a document with a variety of colors. To use this feature, click the Highlight button on the Formatting toolbar, and then select the desired text using the mouse. When the Highlight button is activated, the I-beam pointer displays with a pen attached. Continue selecting text you want highlighted and when completed, click once on the Highlight button to deactivate it.

The default highlighting color is yellow. You can change this color by clicking the down-pointing arrow to the right of the Highlight button, and then clicking the desired color at a drop-down palette. This changes the color of the small rectangle below the pen on the Highlight button. If you are using a noncolor printer, highlighted text will print with a gray background. To remove highlighting from text, change the highlighting color to *None*, activate the Highlight button, and then select the highlighted text.

HINT
Temporarily hide all highlighting by displaying the Options dialog box with the View tab selected, removing the check mark from the *Highlight* option, and then closing the dialog box.

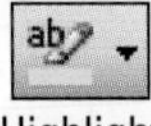
Highlight

Highlight Text
1. Click Highlight button.
2. Select text.
3. Click Highlight button.

Inserting the Date and Time

Insert the current date and/or time in a document with shortcut commands or with options at the Date and Time dialog box shown in Figure 2.9. To display the Date and Time dialog box, click Insert and then Date and Time. The Date and Time dialog box contains a list of date and time options in the *Available formats* list box. Click the desired date or time format and then click OK.

FIGURE 2.9 ***Date and Time Dialog Box***

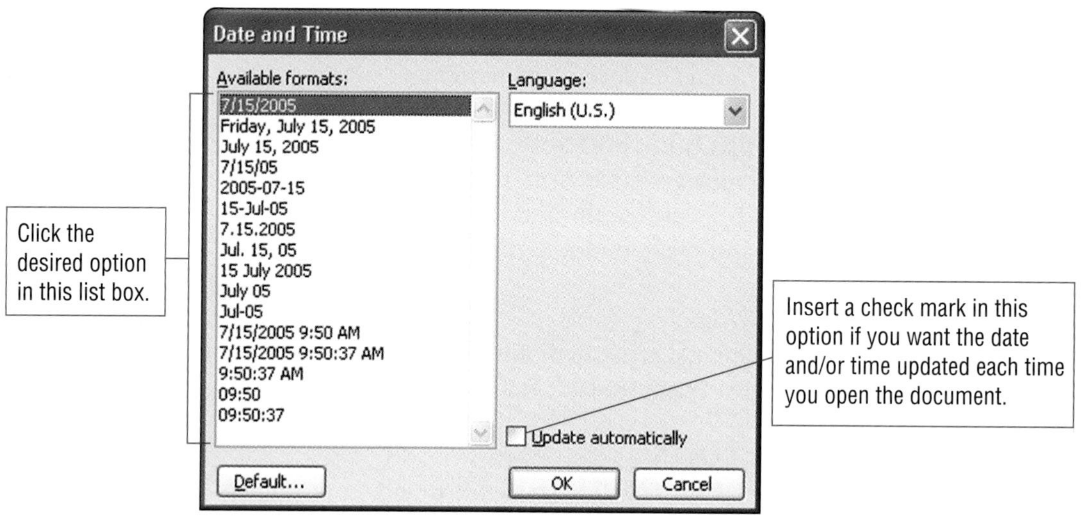

Insert Date and Time
1. Click Insert, Date and Time.
2. Click option in list box.
3. Click OK.

If the *Update automatically* option at the Date and Time dialog box does not contain a check mark, the date and/or time are inserted in the document as normal text that can be edited in the normal manner. The date and/or time can also be inserted in a document as a field. The advantage to inserting the date or time as a field is that the field can be updated with the Update Field key, F9. To insert the date and/or time as a field, insert a check mark in the *Update automatically* check box at the Date and Time dialog box. You can also insert the date as a field in a document using the shortcut command Alt + Shift + D, and insert the time as a field by pressing Alt + Shift + T. To update a date or time inserted as a field, click the date or time and then press the Update Field key, F9.

exercise 8 INSERTING THE DATE AND TIME AND HIGHLIGHTING TEXT

1. Open **WordDocument04**.
2. Save the document with Save As and name it **swc2x08**.
3. Select the entire document and then change to a serif typeface of your choosing (other than Times New Roman) and then deselect the text.

4. Highlight text in the document by completing the following steps:
   a. Click the Highlight button on the Formatting toolbar.
   b. Select the sentence *While an agreement would be positive for the financial markets, the uncertainty surrounding the budget discussion is a lingering concern.* that displays in the first paragraph.

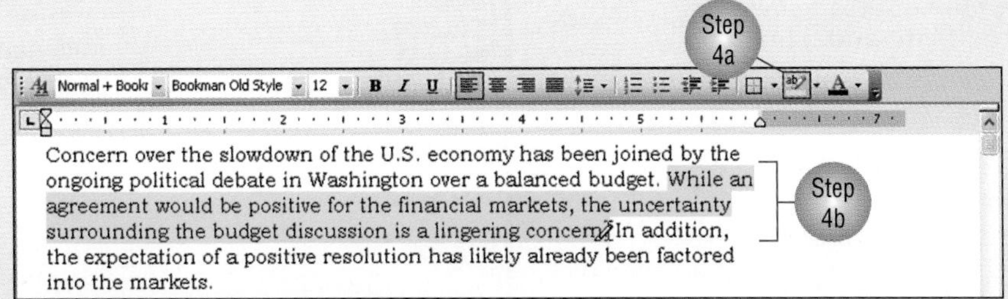

   c. Click the Highlight button to deactivate it.
5. Change the highlighting color and then highlight text in the document by completing the following steps:
   a. Click the down-pointing arrow to the right of the Highlight button on the Formatting toolbar.
   b. From the drop-down list of colors, click the Turquoise color.
   c. Select the sentence *While the sign of healthy cyclical rotation to other sections such as financial services and consumer non-durables has been noticed, no group has yet emerged as a clear leader.* that displays at the end of the second paragraph.
   d. Click the Highlight button to deactivate it.
6. Save and then print **swc2x08**.
7. Remove highighting from text in the document by completing the following steps:
   a. Click the down-pointing arrow to the right of the Highlight button on the Formatting toolbar.
   b. From the drop-down list that displays, click *None* (ScreenTip displays with *No Highlight*).
   c. Select the sentence *While an agreement would be positive for the financial markets, the uncertainty surrounding the budget discussion is a lingering concern.* that displays in the first paragraph.
   d. Return the highlight color to yellow.
   e. Click the Highlight button to deactivate it.

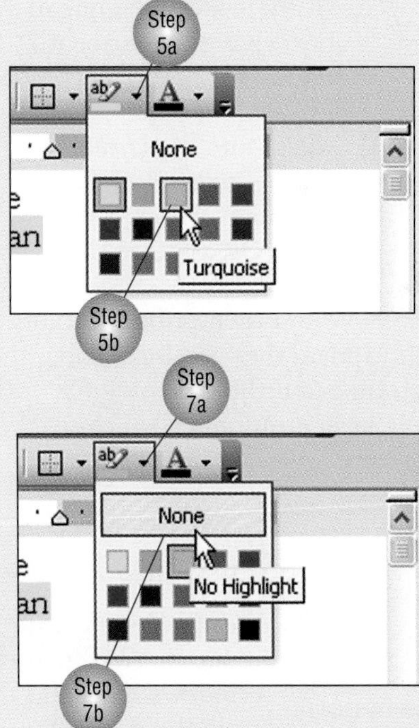

8. Insert the date and time by completing the following steps:
   a. Move the insertion point to the end of the document (at the beginning of a blank line).
   b. Type Date: and then press the spacebar once.
   c. Press Alt + Shift + D. (This inserts the current date.)
   d. Press the Enter key.
   e. Type Time: and then press the spacebar once.
   f. Press Alt + Shift + T. (This inserts the current time.)

9. Save and then print **swc2x08**.
10. Change the current date format by completing the following steps:
    a. Delete the current date.
    b. Click Insert and then Date and Time.
    c. At the Date and Time dialog box, click the fourth option in the *Available formats* list box.
    d. Click in the *Update automatically* check box to insert a check mark.
    e. Click OK to close the dialog box.
11. Change the current time format by completing the following steps:
    a. Delete the current time.
    b. Click Insert and then Date and Time.
    c. At the Date and Time dialog box, click the fourteenth option in the *Available formats* list box.
    d. Make sure the *Update automatically* check box contains a check mark.
    e. Click OK to close the dialog box.
12. Save and then print **swc2x08**.
13. Update the time by clicking the time and then pressing F9.
14. Save, print, and then close **swc2x08**.

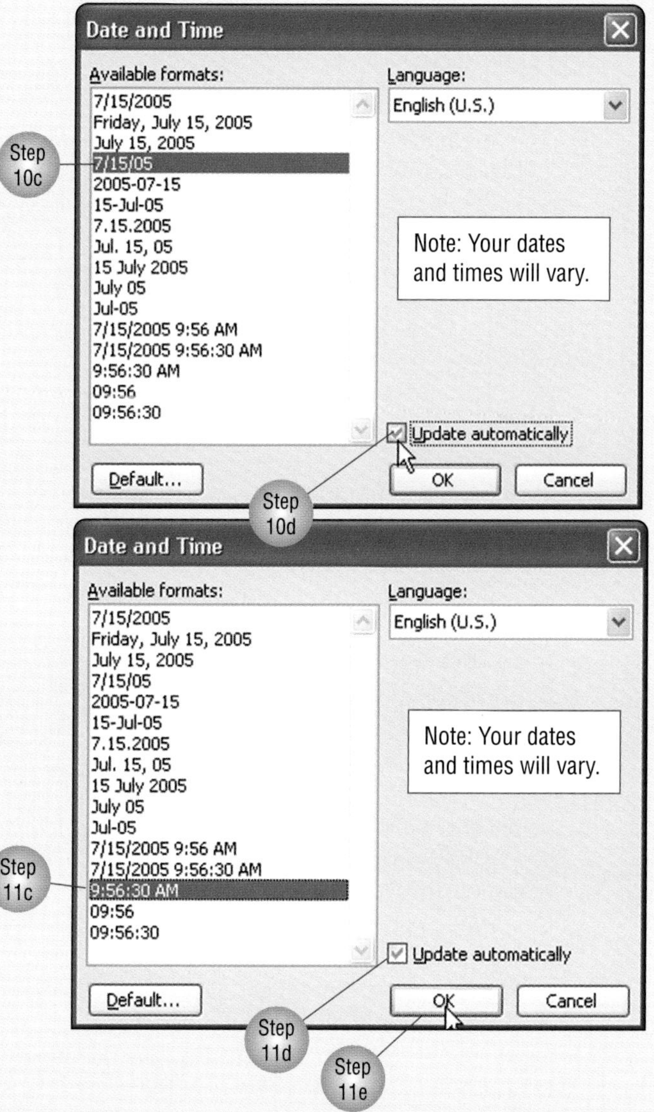

Using Help

Ask a Question

Word's Help feature is an on-screen reference manual containing information about all Word features and commands. Word's Help feature is similar to the Windows Help and the Help features in Excel, PowerPoint, and Access. Get help using the *Ask a Question* text box on the Menu bar or the Word Help task pane.

QUICK STEPS

Use *Ask a Question* Text Box
1. Click in *Ask a Question* text box.
2. Type help question.
3. Press Enter.

Getting Help Using the Ask a Question Text Box

Click the text inside the *Ask a Question* text box located at the right side of the Menu bar (this removes the text), type a help question, and then press Enter. A list of topics matching keywords in your question displays in the Search Results task pane. Click the desired topic in the Search Results task pane list box and a Microsoft Office Word Help window displays with information about the topic.

exercise 9

GETTING HELP USING THE *ASK A QUESTION* TEXT BOX

1. At a clear document screen, click the text inside the *Ask a Question* text box located at the right side of the Menu bar.
2. Type **How do I select text?**.
3. Press the Enter key. (This displays the Search Results task pane with a list of topics related to selecting.)
4. Click the Select text and graphics hyperlink in the results list box in the Search Results task pane. (This displays the Microsoft Office Word Help window with information about selecting and additional hyperlink options.)
5. In the Microsoft Office Word Help window, click the Select text by using the keyboard hyperlink. (You will need to scroll down the window to display this hyperlink.)
6. Read the information that displays in the Microsoft Office Word Help window on selecting using the keyboard.
7. Close the Microsoft Office Word Help window by clicking the Close button (contains an *X*) located in the upper right corner of the window.
8. Close the Search Results task pane by clicking the Close button (contains an *X*) located in the upper right corner of the task pane.

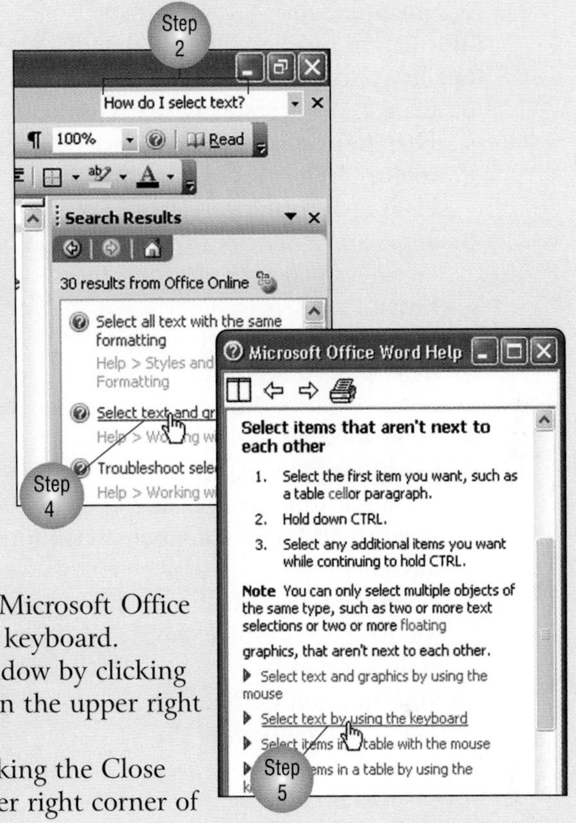

Displaying the Word Help Task Pane

You can type a question in the *Ask a Question* list box or type a question or topic in the Word Help task pane. Display this task pane by clicking the Microsoft Office Word Help button on the Standard toolbar or by clicking Help on the Menu bar and then clicking Microsoft Office Word Help at the drop-down menu.

In the Word Help task pane, type a topic, feature, or question in the *Search for* text box and then press Enter or click the Start searching button (button containing white arrow on green background).Topics related to the topic, feature, or question display in the Search Results task pane. Click a topic in the results list box and information about that topic displays in the Microsoft Office Word Help window. If the window contains a Show All hyperlink in the upper right corner, click this hyperlink and the information expands to show all help information related to the topic. When you click the Show All hyperlink, it becomes the Hide All hyperlink.

(Note: If the Office Assistant displays when you click the Microsoft Office Word Help button, turn off the display of the Office Assistant. To do this, click the Options button in the yellow box above the Office Assistant. At the Office Assistant dialog box, click the* Use the Office Assistant *option to remove the check mark from the check box, and then click OK.)

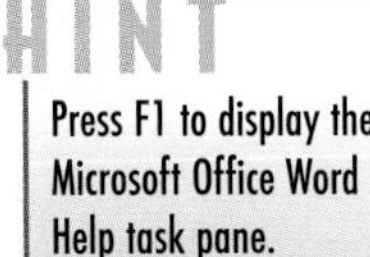

HINT
Press F1 to display the Microsoft Office Word Help task pane.

Microsoft Office Word Help

Use Help Feature
1. Click Help, Microsoft Office Word Help.
2. Type topic, feature, or question.
3. Press Enter.
4. Click desired hyperlink in Search Results task pane.

exercise 10

GETTING HELP

1. At a clear document screen, display information on changing the default font by completing the following steps:
   a. Click the Microsoft Office Word Help button on the Standard toolbar. (This displays the Word Help task pane.)
   b. Type **changing default font** in the *Search for* text box and then press Enter.
   c. Click the <u>Set the default font</u> hyperlink in the results list box. (This displays the Microsoft Office Word Help window.)
   d. Click the <u>Show All</u> hyperlink that displays in the upper right corner of the window.
   e. Read the information about setting the default font.
   f. Click the Close button to close the Microsoft Office Word Help window.

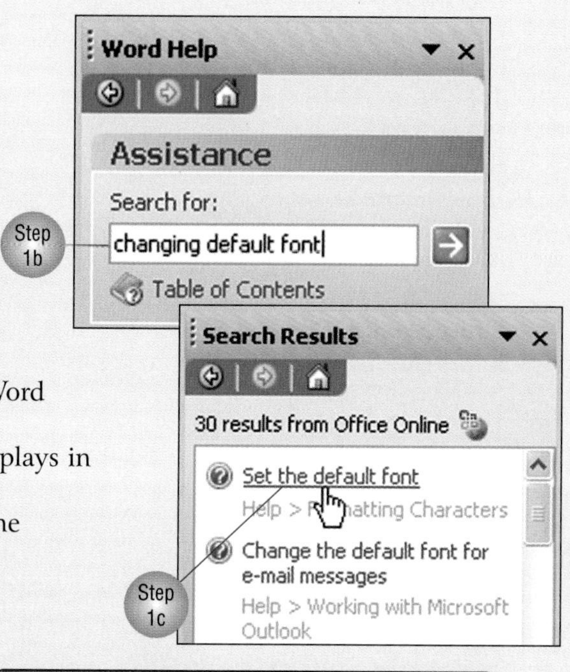

2. Find information on opening a document by completing the following steps:
   a. Click Help and then Microsoft Office Word Help.
   b. Select any text that displays in the *Search for* text box, type **open a document** and then press Enter.
   c. Click the <u>Open a file</u> hyperlink.
   d. Click the <u>Show All</u> hyperlink in the upper right corner of the Microsoft Office Word Help window and then read the information on opening a file.
   e. Click the Print button located towards the top of the Microsoft Office Word Help window to print the information. At the Print dialog box, click the Print button.
3. Close the Microsoft Office Word Help window.
4. Close the Search Results task pane.

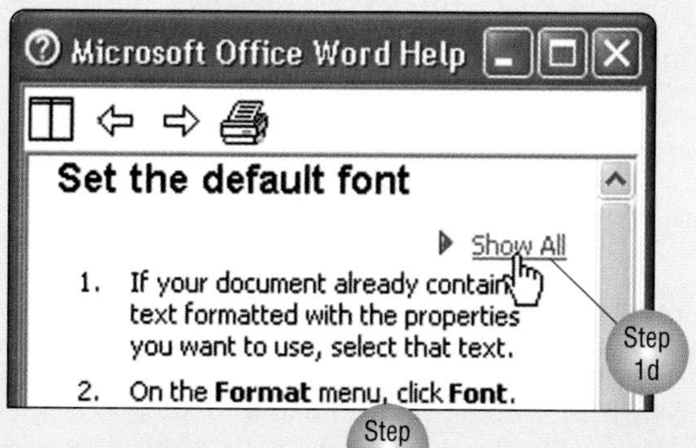

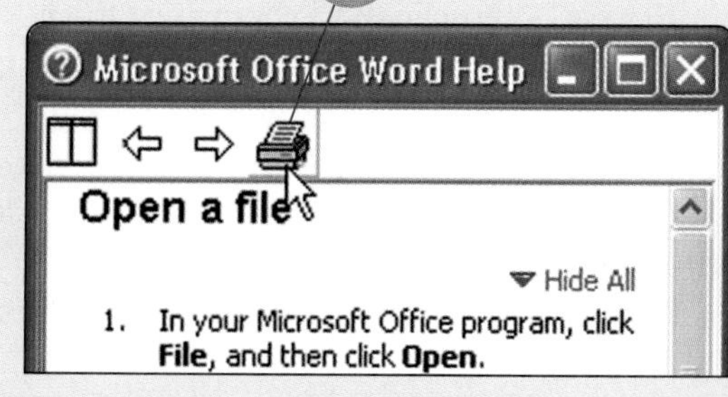

Using Additional Help Features

Click the Help option on the Menu bar and a variety of help features are available. Click the Show the Office Assistant option and the Office Assistant displays. Type a question in the Office Assistant help box and then press the Enter key or click the Search button. The Office Assistant searches for the help files and displays related topics in a list box. Click the desired hyperlink in the list box and the Microsoft Office Word Help window displays with information on the topic. This feature must be installed before it can be used.

Click Microsoft Office Online at the Help drop-down menu and you are connected to the Microsoft Office Web site. From this site, you can get answers to the most frequently asked questions about Word. You can also get up-to-date tips, templates, clip art, and Help files. Click the Contact Us option and information displays on product and services offered by Microsoft.

If you have been a WordPerfect user and would like information on how to carry out a command in Word, click Help, and then click WordPerfect Help.

Keep current on updates offered by Microsoft by clicking the Check for Updates option at the Help drop-down menu. If your computer is connected to the Internet, the Microsoft Web site displays with information on updates to Office. Office contains a self-repairing feature that will find and fix errors in Office files. To run this feature, click Help, and then click Detect and Repair. This displays the Detect and Repair dialog box with a message telling you that during the process you may be asked to provide the installation source and exit or open applications. Click the Start button to begin the detect and repair process. Click the Activate Product option if you need to activate your version of Office and click the Customer Feedback Options to display information on the Customer Experience Improvement Program.

The last option at the Help drop-down menu, About Microsoft Office Word, displays information such as the release date, license number, and system information. You can also display information about Microsoft's technical support such as a listing of support telephone numbers.

HINT

Click Help, About Microsoft Office Word, and then click the System Info button to display information about your computer such as your processor type, operating system, memory, and hard disk space.

exercise 11

DISPLAYING SYSTEM INFORMATION

1. Read information about Word by clicking Help and then About Microsoft Office Word.
2. At the About Microsoft Office Word dialog box, click the Tech Support button located in the lower right corner of the dialog box.
3. Read the information that displays and then click the Close button that displays in the upper right corner of the dialog box (contains an *X*).
4. At the About Microsoft Office Word dialog box, click the System Info button that displays in the lower right corner of the dialog box.
5. At the system information window, read the information that displays, and then close the window by clicking the Close button (contains an *X*) located in the upper right corner of the window.

Using ScreenTips

Word includes a ScreenTips feature that is available in some dialog boxes and displays in the upper right corner of the dialog box as a button containing a question mark. If you position the mouse pointer on the button, after approximately one second the word *Help* displays in a yellow box. To use the ScreenTips feature, click the ScreenTips button and the Microsoft Office Word Help window displays with information about the dialog box.

CHAPTER summary

- The appearance of a document in the document screen and when printed is called the format.
- Text can be bolded, italicized, and underlined with buttons on the Formatting toolbar or with shortcut commands. Do this as text is typed or apply the features later by selecting the text and then choosing the desired feature.
- You can remove all character formatting from selected text by pressing Ctrl + spacebar.
- A font consists of three parts: typeface, type size, and typestyle.
- Change the font at the Font dialog box or use the Font and Font Size buttons on the Formatting toolbar.
- The *Effects* section of the Font dialog box contains a variety of options that can be used to create different character styles.
- Use the *Hidden* option in the *Effects* section of the Font dialog box to hide text in a document. Display hidden text by clicking the Show/Hide ¶ button on the Standard toolbar.
- Adjust character spacing with options at the Font dialog box with the Character Spacing tab selected.
- Add animation effects to text with options at the Font dialog box with the Text Effects tab selected.
- Use the Font and Font Size buttons on the Formatting toolbar to change the font and font size of text in the document. Use the Font Color button to change text color.
- Use the Format Painter button on the Standard toolbar to copy character formatting already applied to text to different locations in the document.
- Many of the typefaces (fonts) include special symbols such as bullets and publishing symbols. Insert a symbol in a document at the Symbol dialog box.
- Control the case of text with options at the Change Case dialog box.
- The AutoComplete feature inserts an entire item when you type a few identifying characters.
- Insert the current date and/or time with options at the Date and Time dialog box or with shortcut commands. If the date or time is inserted as a field, update the field with the Update Field key, F9.
- Highlight text in a document by clicking the Highlight button on the Formatting toolbar and then selecting the text. A variety of highlighting colors is available.
- Word's Help feature is an on-screen reference manual containing information about all Word features and commands.

- Get help by typing a question in the *Ask a Question* text box located at the right side of the Menu bar.
- Display the Word Help task pane by clicking the Microsoft Office Word Help button on the Standard toolbar or by clicking Help and then Microsoft Office Word Help.
- Additional options from the Help drop-down menu include—Show the Office Assistant, Microsoft Office Online, Contact Us, WordPerfect Help, Check for Updates, Detect and Repair, Activate Product, Customer Feedback Options, and About Microsoft Office Word.
- Use the ScreenTips button in any dialog box to read information about the dialog box.

FEATURES summary

FEATURE	BUTTON	MENU	KEYBOARD
Uppercase function			Caps Lock key
Bold	B		Ctrl + B
Italic	I		Ctrl + I
Underline	U		Ctrl + U
Remove character formatting			Ctrl + spacebar
Font dialog box		Format, Font	
Display nonprinting characters	¶		
Format Painter			
Symbol dialog box		Insert, Symbol	
Change Case dialog box		Format, Change Case	
Date and Time dialog box		Insert, Date and Time	
Insert date			Alt + Shift + D
Insert time			Alt + Shift + T
Update date or time field			F9
Highlight	ab		
Microsoft Word Help		Help, Microsoft Word Help	F1

CONCEPTS check

Completion: On a blank sheet of paper, indicate the correct term, symbol, or command for each item.

1. Press these keys on the keyboard to bold selected text.
2. A font consists of three elements—a typeface, a type size, and this.
3. Click this button on the Standard toolbar to display hidden text (and nonprinting characters).
4. This keyboard command removes all character formatting from selected text.
5. This term refers to text that is lowered slightly below the regular text line.
6. Change character spacing with options at this dialog box with the Character Spacing tab selected.
7. This term refers to the adjustment of spacing between certain character combinations.
8. To use the Format Painter to apply formatting to several locations in a document, do this to the Format Painter button.
9. The number 2nd is referred to as this.
10. This feature inserts an entire item when you type a few identifying characters and then press Enter or F3.
11. The Highlight button is located on this toolbar.
12. This is the shortcut command to insert the current date.
13. This is the Update Field key.
14. Use this text box on the Menu bar to get help from the Word Help feature.
15. List the steps you would complete to insert the symbol ✂ into a document. ***(Hint: The ✂ symbol is located in the Wingdings font.)***

SKILLS check

Assessment 1

1. At a clear document screen, type the document shown in Figure 2.10. Bold, italicize, and underline the text as shown.
2. Select the heading *Rates Reduced* and change to small caps.
3. Save the document and name it **swc2sc01**.
4. Print and then close **swc2sc01**.

FIGURE

2.10 ***Assessment 1***

Rates Reduced

As a result of anticipated lower claims costs and other expected cost savings, premiums for LongLife insurance policies have been reduced, **effective Tuesday, February 1, 2005**. The new, lower premiums will apply to both existing and new policies. Policy benefits will remain the same.

The actual rate of reduction will vary depending on the policyholder's age and plan option. If you are between the ages of 35 and 49 and are enrolled in the 1st plan with a *periodic* inflation option, your premium reduction will be between 13 and 32 percent! Premiums of a colleague in the same age bracket with an *automatic* inflation option will be reduced by between 5 and 29 percent! Reductions may be higher or lower in the 2nd plan and 3rd plan.

Assessment 2

1. Open **WordDocument03**.
2. Save the document with Save As and name it **swc2sc02**.
3. Add a title to the document by completing the following steps:
   a. With the insertion point positioned immediately left of the first character in the document, press the Enter key twice.
   b. Press the Up Arrow key twice. (This moves the insertion point to the beginning blank line.)
   c. Click the Bold button.
   d. Type **ECONOMIC GAINS**.
4. Select and then bold the following text in the document:
   a. *25%* (located in the second paragraph)
   b. *5000* (located in the second paragraph)
   c. *economic slowdown* (located in the third paragraph)
5. Select and then italicize the following text in the document:
   a. *strength* (located in the first paragraph)
   b. *second half of 2005* (located in the second paragraph)
   c. *third-quarter 2005 earnings* (located in the third paragraph)
6. Deselect the text.
7. Select and then hide the last sentence in the second paragraph (the sentence that begins *All the media attention on the Dow...*).
8. Select and then hide the last sentence in the third paragraph (the sentence that begins *This means that earnings could begin...*).
9. Turn on the display of nonprinting characters, unhide the sentence you hid in the second paragraph (the sentence that begins *All the media attention on the Dow...*), and then turn off the display of nonprinting characters.
10. Save, print, and then close **swc2sc02**.

Assessment 3

1. Open **WordReport03**.
2. Save the document with Save As and name it **swc2sc03**.
3. Select the entire document and then change the font to 12-point Garamond (or a similar serif typeface).
4. Select the title *NETWORK TOPOLOGIES* and then change the font to 18-point Tahoma bold (or a similar sans serif typeface).
5. Select the heading *Linear Bus Networks* and then change the font to 14-point Tahoma bold.
6. Use Format Painter to change the formatting to 14-point Tahoma bold for the remaining two headings, *Star Networks* and *Ring Networks*.
7. Save, print, and then close **swc2sc03**.

Assessment 4

1. Open **WordDocument05**.
2. Save the document with Save As and name it **swc2sc04**.
3. Select the entire document and then change the font to 12-point Century (or a similar serif typeface), and then deselect the text.
4. Select the title *ARE YOU PREPARING FOR RETIREMENT?* and then change the font to 14-point Century bold (or the serif typeface you chose in Step 3).
5. Move the insertion point to the end of the document and then type the following text:

   The Growth Account® is a registered trademark of McCormack Funds.
   Edited by Anya Volochĕk

6. Save, print, and then close **swc2sc04**.

Assessment 5

1. Open **WordDocument02**.
2. Save the document with Save As and name it **swc2sc05**.
3. Select the entire document and then change to a serif typeface of your choosing (other than Times New Roman), and then deselect the text.
4. Select the title *COMPUTER KEYBOARDS* and then change the font size to 14 points.
5. Move the insertion point to the end of the document and then insert the current date.
6. Press the Enter key and then insert the current time.
7. Highlight the second sentence in the paragraph immediately below the *QWERTY Keyboard* heading.
8. Highlight the second sentence in the paragraph immediately below the *DVORAK Keyboard* heading.
9. Highlight the last sentence in the paragraph immediately below the *DVORAK Keyboard* heading.
10. Save, print, and then close **swc2sc05**.

Assessment 6

1. Use the Help feature to find information on AutoCorrect. ***(Hint: Click in the*** **Ask a Question** ***text box, type*** *What changes will AutoCorrect make?*, ***and then press Enter. Click the <u>About automatic corrections</u> link at the Search Results task pane.)*** At the Help window, click the *<u>Show All</u>* hyperlink located in the upper right corner of the window. Print the information by clicking the Print button on the Help window toolbar. Click OK at the Print

dialog box. Display the AutoCorrect dialog box with the AutoCorrect tab selected. (To do this, click Tools, AutoCorrect Options, and then click the AutoCorrect tab.) Look at what options AutoCorrect automatically corrects in a document.

2. After reading about and experimenting with the AutoCorrect feature, write a description of the feature that includes the following:
   a. Create a title for the description that is typed in all capital letters and is bolded.
   b. Include the steps required to display the dialog box where you can make changes to AutoCorrect.
   c. Include at least three changes that Word can make automatically.
3. Save the completed description and name it **swc2sc06**.
4. Print and then close **swc2sc06**.

CHAPTER challenge

You are the assistant editor for the newspaper on your campus. You have been asked by the senior editor to write a short paragraph describing an upcoming student event that will be featured in the first issue of the newspaper. Effectively use at least three different types of formatting described in this chapter. Save and then print the file.

The senior editor has suggested that you use a font not found in the list of fonts on your computer. Use the Help feature to learn about downloading and installing fonts from other sources. Locate a new font, download it to your computer, and then apply it to the paragraph. Since the senior editor may not have the new font on his computer, you want to ensure that your document with the new font will look the same on your editor's computer. Use the Help feature to learn about embedding fonts in a document and then embed the new font as you save your document. Print the document.

The senior editor would also like to post your paragraph to the college's Web site. Add an appropriate title at the beginning of your paragraph that displays with animated text. Prepare the file to be posted on the Web site by saving it as a Web page. Print the document.

CHAPTER 3

FORMATTING PARAGRAPHS

PERFORMANCE OBJECTIVES

Upon successful completion of Chapter 3, you will be able to:

- **Change the alignment of text in paragraphs**
- **Change spacing before and after paragraphs**
- **Indent text in paragraphs**
- **Create numbered and bulleted paragraphs**
- **Change line spacing in a document**
- **Repeat the last action**
- **Reveal and compare formatting**
- **Apply borders and shading to paragraphs**
- **Set, clear, and move tabs on the Ruler and at the Tabs dialog box**

Various formatting options and features can be applied to text in paragraphs. In this chapter, you will learn about paragraph formatting features such as aligning text, spacing before and after paragraphs, indenting text, creating numbered and bulleted paragraphs, changing line spacing, applying borders and shading, and manipulating tabs. You will also learn how to display and compare formatting applied to text at the Reveal Formatting task pane.

Formatting Paragraphs

Formatting such as changing alignment, indenting text, inserting bullets and numbers, and line spacing can be applied to paragraphs. In Word, a paragraph is any amount of text followed by a paragraph mark. A paragraph mark is inserted in a document each time the Enter key is pressed. Display paragraphs marks and other nonprinting characters by clicking the Show/Hide ¶ button on the Standard toolbar (as you learned in Chapter 2). If you want to remove paragraph formatting from text, delete the paragraph mark.

Show/Hide

Changing the Alignment of Text in Paragraphs

By default, paragraphs in a Word document are aligned at the left margin and ragged at the right margin. Change this default alignment with buttons on the Formatting toolbar or with shortcut commands as shown in Table 3.1.

TABLE 3.1 **Paragraph Alignment Buttons and Commands**

To align text	*Button Shortcut*	*Command*
At the left margin		Ctrl + L
Between margins		Ctrl + E
At the right margin		Ctrl + R
At the left and right margins		Ctrl + J

You can change the alignment of text in paragraphs before you type the text or change the alignment of existing text. If you change the alignment before typing text, the alignment formatting is inserted in the paragraph mark. As you type text and press Enter, the paragraph formatting is continued. For example, if you press Ctrl + E to turn on center aligning, type text for the first paragraph, and then press Enter, the center alignment formatting is still active and the insertion point displays centered between the left and right margins.

Aign Left

To return paragraph alignment to the default (left-aligned), click the Align Left button on the Formatting toolbar or press Ctrl + L. You can also return all paragraph formatting to the default by pressing Ctrl + Q. This shortcut command returns all paragraph formatting (not just alignment) to the default settings.

To change the alignment of existing text in a paragraph, position the insertion point anywhere within the paragraph. The entire paragraph does not have to be selected. To change the alignment of several adjacent paragraphs in a document, select a portion of the first paragraph through a portion of the last paragraph. Only a portion of the first and last paragraphs needs to be selected.

HINT

Align text in a document so the message of the document can be followed and the page is attractive.

(Note: Before completing computer exercises, delete the WordChapter02S folder on your disk. Next, copy to your disk the WordChapter03S subfolder from the Word2003Specialist folder on the CD that accompanies this textbook and then make WordChapter03S the active folder.)

exercise 1

CHANGING PARAGRAPH ALIGNMENT TO CENTERED

1. At a clear document screen, turn on the display of nonprinting characters by clicking the Show/Hide ¶ button on the Standard toolbar.
2. If the task pane is visible, turn off the display of the task pane by clicking View and then Task Pane.
3. Type the text shown in Figure 3.1. (If formatting is automatically applied to your text when you press the Enter key twice after typing the first line of text, the automatic formatting of headings is turned on. You can either press the Backspace key once to remove the automatic formatting or you can turn off the heading formatting. To do this, click Tools and then AutoCorrect Options. At the AutoCorrect dialog box, click the AutoFormat As You Type tab, remove the check mark from the *Built-in Heading styles* option, and then click OK.)
4. Make the following changes to the document:
   a. Select the entire document.
   b. With the entire document selected, change the font to 16-point Arial bold and the font color to blue.
   c. With the entire document still selected, change the alignment of paragraphs to centered by clicking the Center button on the Formatting toolbar.
   d. Deselect the text by clicking in the document screen outside the selected text.

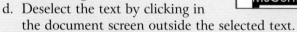

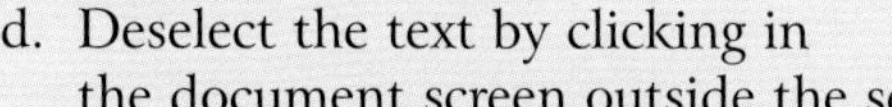

Step 4c

5. Click the Show/Hide ¶ button on the Standard toolbar to turn off the display of nonprinting characters.
6. Save the document and name it **swc3x01**.
7. Print and then close **swc3x01**.

FIGURE 3.1 ***Exercise 1***

McCORMACK FUNDS

McCormack LifeLine Trust Annuities Seminar

Thursday, March 17

8:30 a.m. to 11:30 a.m.

Conference Room C

exercise 2

CHANGING PARAGRAPH ALIGNMENT TO JUSTIFIED

1. Open **WordDocument03**.
2. Save the document with Save As and name it **swc3x02**.
3. Change the alignment of the text in paragraphs to justified by selecting the entire document and then clicking the Justify button on the Formatting toolbar.
4. Deselect the text.
5. Save, print, and then close **swc3x02**.

QUICK STEPS

Change Paragraph Alignment
Click desired alignment button on Formatting toolbar.
OR
1. Click Format, Paragraph.
2. Click *Alignment* option down-pointing arrow.
3. Click desired alignment.
4. Click OK.

Change Paragraph Spacing
1. Click Format, Paragraph.
2. Insert measurement in *Before* and/or *After* text box.
3. Click OK.

Changing Alignment at the Paragraph Dialog Box

Paragraph alignment can also be changed at the Paragraph dialog box with the Indents and Spacing tab selected as shown in Figure 3.2. To change the alignment of text in a paragraph, display the Paragraph dialog box by clicking Format and then Paragraph. At the Paragraph dialog box with the Indents and Spacing tab selected, click the down-pointing arrow at the right of the *Alignment* option box. From the drop-down list that displays, click an alignment option, and then click OK.

Spacing before and after Paragraphs

Spacing before and after paragraphs in a document can be increased or decreased with options at the Paragraph dialog box. To increase or decrease spacing before a paragraph, display the Paragraph dialog box, select the current measurement in the *Before* text box (in the *Spacing* section), and then type a new measurement. Complete similar steps to increase or decrease spacing after paragraphs except choose the *After* option. You can also click the up- or down-pointing arrows to the right of the *Before* or *After* options to increase or decrease the measurement. Word uses a point measurement for spacing before and after paragraphs. Enter or display a higher point measurement to increase the spacing, or enter or display a lower point measurement to decrease the spacing.

FIGURE

3.2 Paragraph Dialog Box with Indents and Spacing Tab Selected

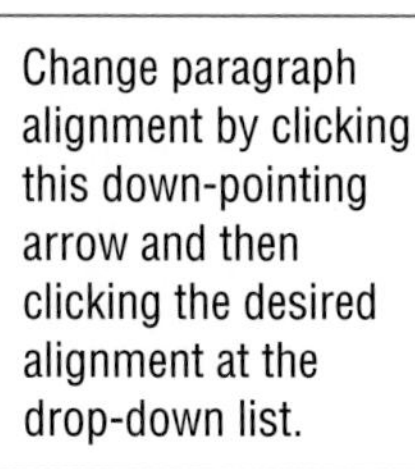

Change paragraph alignment by clicking this down-pointing arrow and then clicking the desired alignment at the drop-down list.

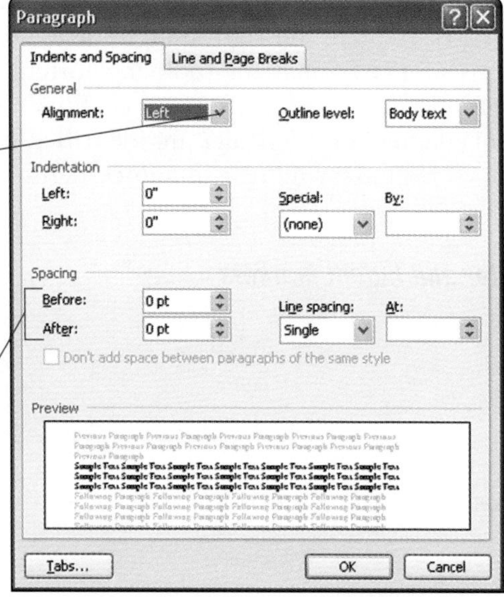

exercise 3

CHANGING SPACING BEFORE PARAGRAPHS

1. Open **WordList01**.
2. Save the document with Save As and name it **swc3x03**.
3. Select the entire document and then change the font to 12-point Bookman Old Style (or a similar serif typeface).
4. Select the title *LIFETIME REAL ESTATE ACCOUNT* and then change the font to 14-point Arial bold.
5. Center-align text and add 6 points of spacing before certain paragraphs by completing the following steps:
   a. Select from *Investment Practices of the Account* through *Expense Deductions*.
   b. With the text selected, click Format and then Paragraph. (This displays the Paragraph dialog box.)
   c. At the Paragraph dialog box, click the down-pointing arrow at the right of the *Alignment* option box, and then click *Centered*.
   d. Click once on the up-pointing arrow at the right side of the *Before* option (in the *Spacing* section). (This changes the measurement in the text box to *6 pt*.)
   e. Click OK to close the dialog box.
6. Save, print, and then close **swc3x03**.

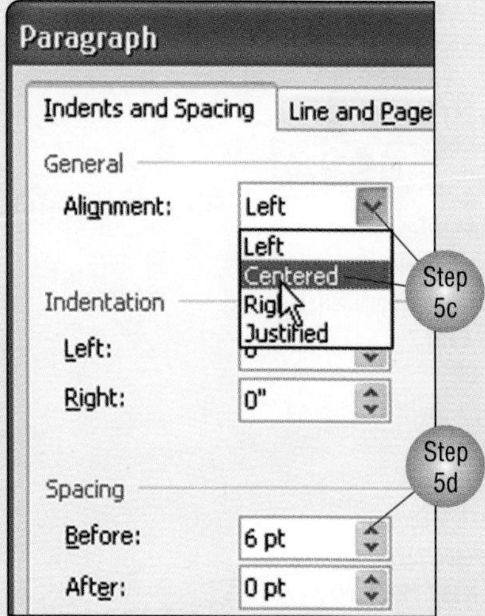

Indenting Text in Paragraphs

Alignment

By now you are familiar with the word wrap feature of Word, which ends lines and wraps the insertion point to the next line. To indent text from the left margin, or the left and right margin or to create numbered items, use indent buttons on the Formatting toolbar, shortcut commands, options from the Paragraph dialog box, markers on the Ruler, or the Alignment button on the Ruler. Indent markers on the Ruler are identified in Figure 3.3. Refer to Table 3.2 for methods for indenting text in a document.

FIGURE 3.3 ***Ruler and Indent Markers***

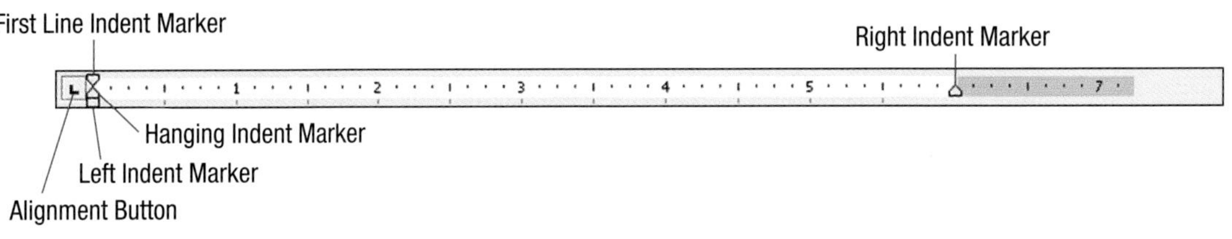

TABLE 3.2 ***Methods for Indenting Text***

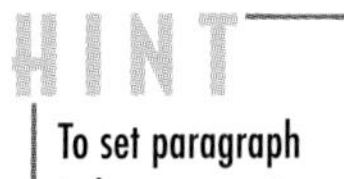

HINT

To set paragraph indents at precise measurements, use options at the Paragraph dialog box.

QUICK STEPS

Indent Text in Paragraph
Drag indent marker(s) on Ruler.
OR
Press shortcut command keys.
OR
1. Click Format, Paragraph.
2. Insert measurement in *Left*, *Right*, and/or *By* text box.
3. Click OK.

Indent	***Methods for Indenting***
First line of paragraph	• Press the Tab key. • Display Paragraph dialog box, click down arrow to the right of the *Special* option box, click *First line*, and then click OK. • Drag the First Line Indent marker on the Ruler. • Click the Alignment button located at the left side of the Ruler until the First Line Indent button displays and then click on the Ruler at the desired location.
Text from left margin	• Click the Increase Indent button on the Formatting toolbar to increase indent or click the Decrease Indent button to decrease the indent. • Press Ctrl + M to increase indent or press Ctrl + Shift + M to decrease indent. • Display the Paragraph dialog box, type the desired indent measurement in the *Left* text box, and then click OK. • Drag the Left Indent marker on the Ruler.
Text from left and right margins	• Display the Paragraph dialog box, type the desired indent measurement in the *Left* text box and the *Right* text box, and then click OK. • Drag the Left Indent marker and the Right Indent marker on the Ruler.

All lines of text except the first (called a hanging indent)	• Press Ctrl + T. (Press Ctrl + Shift + T to remove hanging indent.) • Display the Paragraph dialog box, click the down-pointing arrow to the right of the *Special* option box, click *Hanging*, and then click OK. • Click the Alignment button located at the left side of the Ruler until the Hanging Indent button displays and then click on the Ruler at the desired location.

Indents can be set on the Ruler using the Left Indent marker, the Right Indent marker, First Line Indent marker, and Hanging Indent marker. A first line indent and a hanging indent can also be set on the Ruler using the Alignment button. The Alignment button displays at the left side of the Ruler. Click this button to display the desired alignment (such as First Line Indent and Hanging Indent) and then click on the Ruler at the location where you want to set the indent.

exercise 4

INDENTING THE FIRST LINE OF PARAGRAPHS USING THE FIRST LINE INDENT BUTTON

1. Open **WordDocument03**.
2. Save the document with Save As and name it **swc3x04**.
3. Indent the first line of each paragraph .25 inch by completing the following steps:
   a. Select the entire document.
   b. Click the Alignment button located at the left side of the Ruler until the First Line Indent button displays.
   c. Click on the .25-inch mark on the Ruler.
   d. Deselect the text.
4. Save, print, and then close **swc3x04**.

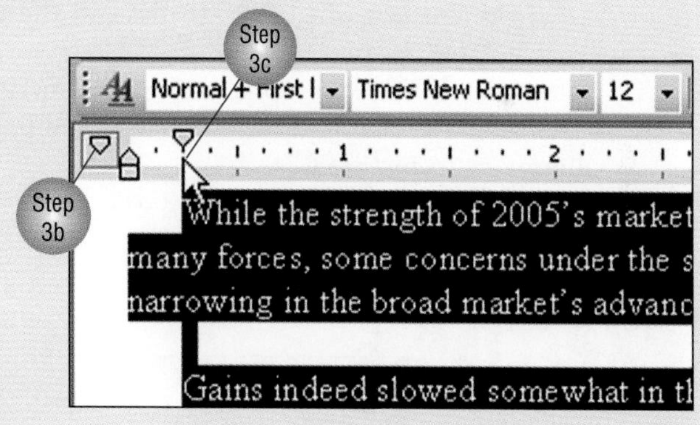

exercise 5

INDENTING TEXT FROM THE LEFT AND RIGHT MARGINS

1. Open **WordDocument07**.
2. Save the document with Save As and name it **swc3x05**.
3. Indent the second paragraph of the document from the left and right margins by completing the following steps:
   a. Make sure the Ruler is displayed.
   b. Position the insertion point anywhere in the second paragraph (begins with *I deeply care about...*).

c. Position the arrow pointer on the Left Indent marker on the Ruler, hold down the left mouse button, drag the marker to the .5-inch mark on the Ruler, and then release the mouse button.

d. Position the arrow pointer on the Right Indent marker on the Ruler, hold down the left mouse button, drag the marker to the 5.5-inch mark on the Ruler, and then release the mouse button.

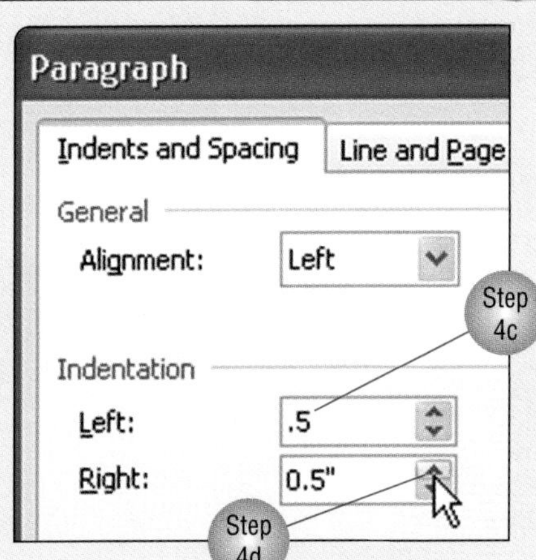

4. Indent the fourth paragraph in the document from the left and right margins by completing the following steps:
   a. Position the insertion point anywhere within the fourth paragraph (begins with *I plan to increase…*).
   b. Click Format and then Paragraph.
   c. At the Paragraph dialog box with the Indents and Spacing tab selected, select the *0"* in the *Left* text box, and then type .5.
   d. Click the up-pointing arrow at the right of the *Right* text box until *0.5"* displays in the text box.
   e. Click OK or press Enter.
5. Select all of the paragraphs in the document (excluding the title) and then change the paragraph alignment to justified.
6. Save, print, and then close **swc3x05**.

exercise 6

CREATING HANGING PARAGRAPHS

1. Open **WordBibliography**.
2. Save the document with Save As and name it **swc3x06**.
3. Create a hanging indent for the first two paragraphs by completing the following steps:
   a. Select at least a portion of the first and second paragraphs.
   b. Position the arrow pointer on the Hanging Indent marker on the Ruler, hold down the left mouse button, drag the marker to the .5-inch mark on the Ruler, and then release the mouse button.

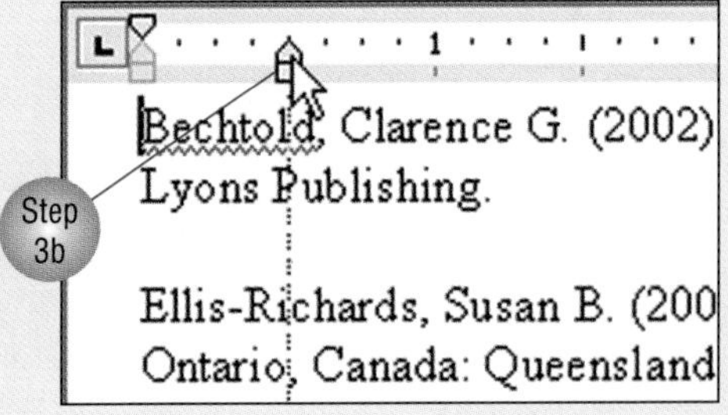

4. Create a hanging indent for the third paragraph by completing the following steps:
   a. Position the insertion point anywhere in the third paragraph.

b. Click the Alignment button located at the left side of the Ruler until the Hanging Indent button displays.
c. Click on the .5-inch mark on the Ruler.

5. Create a hanging indent for the fourth paragraph by completing the following steps:
   a. Position the insertion point anywhere in the fourth paragraph.
   b. Press Ctrl + T.
6. Create a hanging indent for the fifth paragraph by completing the following steps:
   a. Position the insertion point somewhere in the fifth paragraph.
   b. Click Format and then Paragraph.
   c. At the Paragraph dialog box with the Indents and Spacing tab selected, click the down-pointing arrow to the right of the *Special* option box, and then click *Hanging* at the drop-down list.
   d. Click OK or press Enter.
7. Select the entire document and then change to a serif typeface (other than Times New Roman) in 12-point size.
8. Save, print, and then close **swc3x06**.

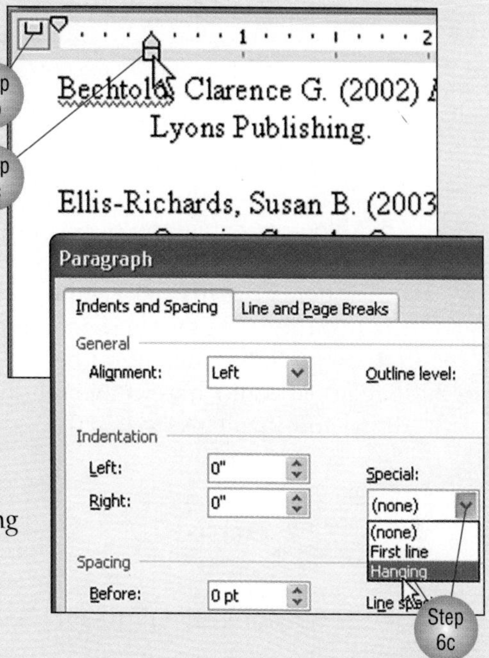

Creating Numbered and Bulleted Paragraphs

If you type *1.*, press the spacebar, type a paragraph of text, and then press Enter, Word will indent the number approximately .25 inch and then hang indent the text in the paragraph approximately .5 inch from the left margin. Additionally, the number 2. will be inserted .25 inch from the left margin at the beginning of the next paragraph. (If the automatic numbering feature is not activated, you can turn it on by clicking Tools and then AutoCorrect Options. At the AutoCorrect dialog box, click the AutoFormat As You Type tab. Click in the *Automatic numbered lists* check box to insert a check mark and then click OK.) Continue typing numbered items and Word will insert the next number in the list. To turn off numbering, press the Enter key twice or click the Numbering button on the Formatting toolbar. You can also remove all paragraph formatting from a paragraph, including automatic numbering, by pressing Ctrl + Q.

If you press Enter twice between numbered paragraphs, the automatic number is removed. To turn it back on, type the next number in the list (and the period) followed by a space, type the paragraph of text, and then press Enter. Word will automatically indent the number and hang indent the text.

When the AutoFormat feature inserts numbering and indents text, the AutoCorrect Options button displays. Click this button and a drop-down list displays with options for undoing and/or stopping the automatic numbering. An AutoCorrect Options button also displays when AutoFormat inserts automatic bulleting in a document.

HINT

If the automatic bullets or numbering feature is on, press Shift + Enter to insert a line break without inserting a bullet or number.

QUICK STEPS

Create Numbered Paragraphs
Click Numbering button on Formatting toolbar.
OR
1. Type 1.
2. Press spacebar.
3. Type text.
4. Press Enter.

OR
1. Select text.
2. Click Format, Bullets and Numbering.
3. Click Numbered tab.
4. Click numbering option.
5. Click OK.

exercise 7 CREATING NUMBERED PARAGRAPHS

1. At a clear document screen, type the text shown in Figure 3.4. When typing the numbered paragraph, complete the following steps:
   a. Type 1. and then press the spacebar.
   b. Type the paragraph of text and then press Enter. (This moves the insertion point down to the next line, inserts *2.* indented .25 inch from the left margin, and also indents the first paragraph of text approximately .5 inch from the left margin.)
   c. Continue typing the remaining text. (Remember, you do not need to type the paragraph number and period—these are automatically inserted.)
2. Save the document and name it **swc3x07**.
3. Print and then close **swc3x07**.

FIGURE 3.4 ***Exercise 7***

FREQUENTLY ASKED QUESTIONS

1. What influence did the Jacquard loom have on the subsequent development of computers?
2. Why is Charles Babbage known as the "father of the computer"?
3. What is a transistor, and what effect did its invention have on electronics in general and on computers in particular?
4. What are the main components of a computer, and what do they do?
5. How do computers encode information?
6. What is the motherboard of a computer, and what does it contain?
7. What are the main types of memory in a computer, and how do they differ from one another?
8. What are the major types of printers, and how do they differ from one another?

Turn Off Automatic Numbering
1. Click Tools, AutoCorrect Options.
2. Click AutoFormat As You Type tab.
3. Click *Automatic numbered lists* check box.
4. Click OK.

If you do not want automatic numbering in a document, turn off the feature at the AutoCorrect dialog box with the AutoFormat As You Type tab selected. To display this dialog box, click Tools and then AutoCorrect Options. At the AutoCorrect dialog box, click the AutoFormat As You Type tab. To turn off automatic numbering, remove the check mark from the *Automatic numbered lists* check box.

You can also automate the creation of numbered paragraphs with the Numbering button on the Formatting toolbar. To use this button, type the text (do not type the number) for each paragraph to be numbered, select the paragraphs to be numbered, and then click the Numbering button on the Formatting toolbar.

In addition to automatically numbering paragraphs, you can also create bulleted paragraphs. (If this feature is not activated, you can turn it on by clicking Tools and then AutoCorrect Options. At the AutoCorrect dialog box, click the AutoFormat As You Type tab. Click in the *Automatic bulleted lists* check box to insert a check mark, and then click OK.)

Figure 3.5 shows an example of bulleted paragraphs. Bulleted lists with hanging indents are automatically created when a paragraph begins with the symbol *, >, or -. Type one of the symbols, press the spacebar, type text, and then press Enter. A bullet indented .25 inch from the left margin is inserted and the text following the bullet is indented .5 inch. The type of bullet inserted depends on the type of character entered. For example, if you use the asterisk (*) symbol, a round bullet is inserted. An arrow bullet is inserted if the greater than symbol (>) is used.

FIGURE 3.5 ***Bulleted Paragraphs***

- This is a paragraph preceded by a bullet. A bullet is used to indicate a list of items or topics.
- This is another paragraph preceded by a bullet. Bulleted paragraphs can be easily created by typing certain symbols before the text or with the Bullets button on the Formatting toolbar.

exercise 8 CREATING BULLETS

1. Bold and center the title in uppercase letters as shown in Figure 3.6.
2. Type the first paragraph in the figure and then create the bulleted paragraphs by completing the following steps:
   a. With the insertion point positioned at the left margin of the first paragraph to contain a bullet, type the greater than symbol (>).
   b. Press the spacebar once.
   c. Type the text of the first bulleted paragraph (the text that begins *Loads during start-up...*).
   d. Press the Enter key once and then continue typing the text after the bullets.
3. After typing the last bulleted paragraph, press the Enter key twice (this turns off bullets), and then type the last paragraph shown in the figure.
4. Save the document and name it **swc3x08**.
5. Print and then close **swc3x08**.

FIGURE 3.6 **Exercise 8**

COMPUTER OPERATING SYSTEM

The most important piece of software used on a personal computer system is its *operating system*, or OS. The OS performs a number of interdependent functions such as the following:

- ➢ Loads during start-up, recognizes the CPU and devices connected to it, such as keyboards, monitors, hard drives, and floppy disk drives
- ➢ Manages the operations of the CPU and of devices connected to it
- ➢ Creates a *user interface*, an environment displayed on the computer screen with which the user interacts when working at the computer
- ➢ Creates and updates a file system, or *directory*, for each storage device that is attached to the computer; this directory shows the location of each file on each storage device and thus enables the user to access programs and documents
- ➢ Supports operations performed from within other programs, such as opening and closing programs, calling resources such as fonts and sounds, and saving and printing documents

Without an OS, a computer is just a paperweight. The OS brings the system to life and gives the system its character. When a person starts a computer, instructions built into the machine's ROM look for an OS, first on any disk inserted into a floppy disk drive at start-up and then on the system's primary hard drive. When found, the OS is loaded, in part, into the computer's RAM, where it remains until the computer is turned off.

Bullets

Numbers can be applied to existing text by selecting the text and then clicking the Numbering button on the Formatting toolbar. Insert bullets to selected text by clicking the Bullets button on the Formatting toolbar.

exercise 9

USING THE BULLETS AND NUMBERING BUTTONS

1. Open **WordList01**.
2. Save the document with Save As and name it **swc3x09**.
3. Add bullets to text by completing the following steps:
   a. Select text from *Investment Practices of the Account* through *Expense Deductions*.
   b. Click the Bullets button on the Formatting toolbar.
   c. Deselect the text.
4. Save and print **swc3x09**.
5. With the document still open, change the bullets to numbers by completing the following steps:
   a. Select text from *Investment Practices of the Account* through *Expense Deductions*.
   b. Click the Numbering button on the Formatting toolbar.
   c. Deselect the text.
6. Save, print, and then close **swc3x09**.

Applying Bullets and Numbering Using the Bullets and Numbering Dialog Box

In addition to the Bullets button on the Formatting toolbar, you can use options from the Bullets and Numbering dialog box to number paragraphs or insert bullets. To display this dialog box, click Format and then Bullets and Numbering. The Bullets and Numbering dialog box contains four tabs: Bulleted, Numbered, Outline Numbered, and List Styles. Select the Bulleted tab if you want to insert bullets before selected paragraphs and select the Numbered tab to insert numbers. At the Bullets and Numbering dialog box with the Outline Numbered tab displayed, you can specify the type of numbering for paragraphs at the left margin, first tab setting, second tab setting, and so on. (The options that display with *Heading 1*, *Heading 2*, or *Heading 3* are not available unless the text to be numbered has been formatted with a Heading style.)

Create Bulleted Paragraphs
Click Bullets button on Formatting toolbar.
OR
1. Type *, >, or - symbol.
2. Press spacebar.
3. Type text.
4. Press Enter.

OR
1. Select text.
2. Click Format, Bullets and Numbering.
3. Click Bulleted tab.
4. Click bullet option.
5. Click OK.

exercise 10 NUMBERING PARAGRAPHS USING THE BULLETS AND NUMBERING DIALOG BOX

1. Open **WordList01**.
2. Save the document with Save As and name it **swc3x10**.
3. Number the paragraphs in the document using the Bullets and Numbering dialog box by completing the following steps:
   a. Select the paragraphs in the document *excluding* the title and the blank lines below the title.
   b. Click Format and then Bullets and Numbering.
   c. At the Bullets and Numbering dialog box, click the Numbered tab.
   d. Click the third numbering option box in the top row.
   e. Click OK or press Enter.

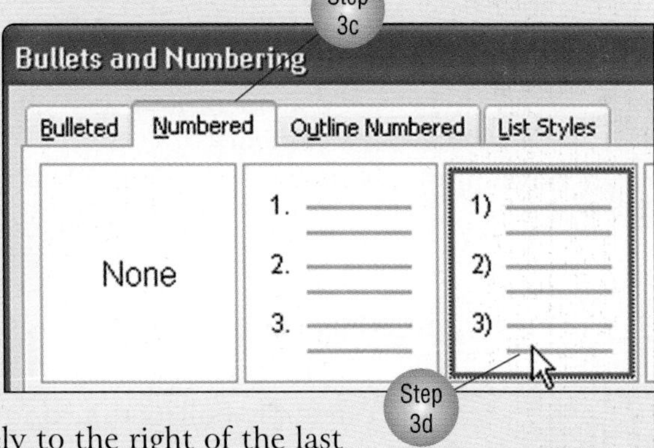

4. Add *Annuity Contracts* between paragraphs 3 and 4 by completing the following steps:
   a. Position the insertion point immediately to the right of the last letter in *Role of Account*.
   b. Press Enter. (This moves the insertion point below the previous paragraph.)
   c. Type **Annuity Contracts**.
5. Select and then delete *Investment Practices of the Account* (paragraph 1).
6. Select the entire document and then change to a sans serif typeface of your choosing in 12-point size.
7. Save, print, and then close **swc3x10**.

exercise 11

CREATING AN OUTLINE NUMBERED LIST

1. Open **WordAgenda01**.
2. Save the document with Save As and name it **swc3x11**.
3. Apply outline numbering to the document by completing the following steps:
   a. Select the paragraphs in the document *excluding* the title, subtitle, and blank lines below the subtitle.
   b. Click Format and then Bullets and Numbering.
   c. At the Bullets and Numbering dialog box, click the Outline Numbered tab.
   d. Click the second option from the left in the top row.
   e. Click OK or press Enter to close the dialog box.
   f. Deselect the text.

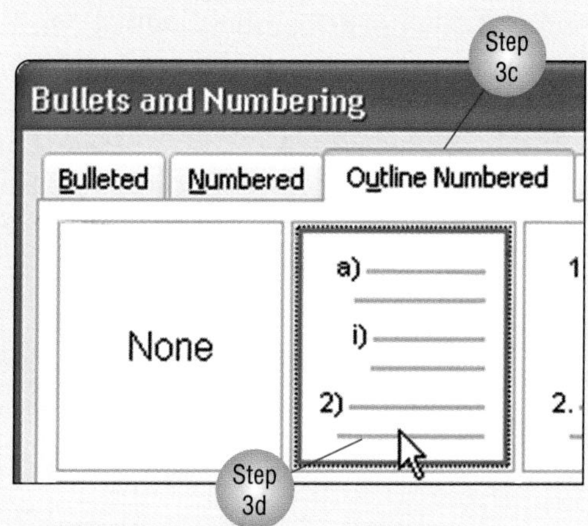

4. Save and then print **swc3x11**.
5. With the document still open, make the following changes:
   a. Delete *Sponsors* in the *Education* section.
   b. Move the insertion point immediately right of the last letter in *Personal Lines* (in the *Sales and Marketing* section), press the Enter key, and then type **Production Report**.
6. Select the entire document and then change to a serif typeface of your choosing (other than Times New Roman).
7. Save, print, and then close **swc3x11**.

Inserting Custom Bullets

HINT
Choose a custom bullet that matches the theme or mood of the document.

You can apply bullets to text in a document with options at the Bullets and Numbering dialog box with the Bulleted tab selected. Along with the bullets that display at this dialog box, you can also choose a customized bullet such as a character or picture. To choose a custom bullet, display the Bullets and Numbering dialog box with the Bulleted tab selected, click one of the bullets that display (the new custom bullet will replace the selected bullet), and then click the Customize button. This displays the Customize Bulleted List dialog box shown in Figure 3.7.

FIGURE

3.7 *Customize Bulleted List Dialog Box*

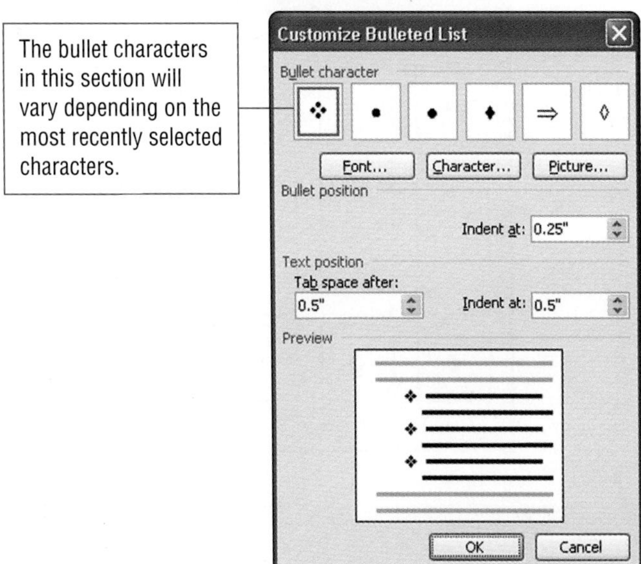

You can choose a specific bullet from a variety of fonts. To display the available list of fonts, click the Font button at the Customize Bulleted List dialog box. At the Font dialog box that displays, select the desired font in the *Font* list box, and then click OK to close the dialog box. At the Customize Bulleted List dialog box, click the Character button, and symbols display that are available from the font you selected.

Click the Picture button at the Customize Bulleted List dialog box and the Picture Bullet dialog box displays similar to the dialog box in Figure 3.8. Click the desired picture bullet in the list box and then click OK. This displays the Customize Bulleted List dialog box and the picture bullet you selected displays in the *Bullet character* section. With the picture bullet selected in the Customize Bulleted List dialog box (selected picture bullet displays surrounded by a blue border), click the OK button.

If you choose a custom or picture bullet, you can reset the bullet back to the default. To do this, display the Bullets and Numbering dialog box with the Bulleted tab selected. Click the custom or picture bullet and then click the Reset button. At the message asking if you want to reset the gallery position to the default setting, click Yes.

QUICK STEPS

Insert a Custom Bullet

1. Click Format, Bullets and Numbering.
2. Click Bulleted tab.
3. Click bullet option.
4. Click Customize button.
5. Click Character button.
6. Click desired symbol.
7. Click OK.
8. Click OK.

QUICK STEPS

Insert a Picture Bullet

1. Click Format, Bullets and Numbering.
2. Click Bulleted tab.
3. Click bullet option.
4. Click Customize button.
5. Click Picture button.
6. Click desired picture bullet.
7. Click OK.
8. Click OK.

FIGURE **3.8** ***Picture Bullet Dialog Box***

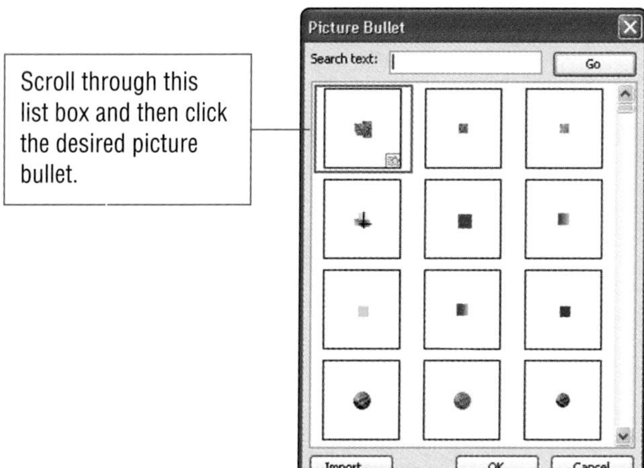

exercise 12

INSERTING A CUSTOM AND A PICTURE BULLET

1. Open **WordList02**.
2. Save the document with Save As and name it **swc3x12**.
3. Apply a character bullet to text by completing the following steps:
   a. Select the text in the document from the line *The First Mortgage Account* through the line *Expense Deductions*.
   b. Click Format and then Bullets and Numbering.
   c. At the Bullets and Numbering dialog box, click the Bulleted tab.
   d. Click the second bullet option from the left in the bottom row and then click the Customize button.
   e. At the Customize Bulleted List dialog box, click the Character button.
   f. At the Symbol dialog box, click the down-pointing arrow at the right side of the *Font* list box and then click *Times New Roman* at the drop-down list. (You may need to scroll up or down the list to display the *Times New Roman* option.)
   g. Click once on the dollar sign (located in the fifth box from the left in the top row).
   h. Click OK.
   i. At the Customize Bulleted List dialog box, make sure the dollar sign is selected in the *Bullet character* section, and then click OK.
   j. At the document, deselect the text.
4. Save and then print **swc3x12**.

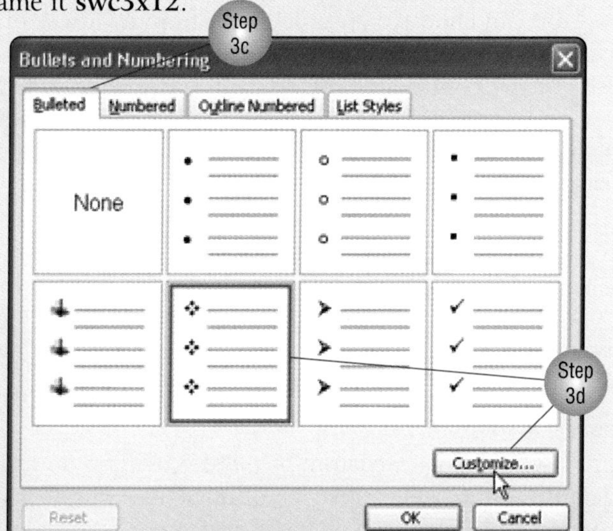

5. Insert picture bullets in the document by completing the following steps:
   a. Select the bulleted text.
   b. Click Format and then Bullets and Numbering.
   c. At the Bullets and Numbering dialog box with the Bulleted tab selected, click the first bullet option from the left in the bottom row.
   d. Click the Customize button.
   e. Click the Picture button.
   f. At the Picture Bullet dialog box, click a picture bullet of your choosing, and then click OK.
   g. At the Customize Bulleted List dialog box, make sure the picture bullet is selected in the *Bullet character* section, and then click OK.
   h. At the document, deselect the text.
6. Save and then print **swc3x12**.
7. Reset the bullets in the Bullets and Numbering dialog box by completing the following steps:
   a. Move the insertion point to the end of the document (on a blank line).
   b. Display the Bullets and Numbering dialog box with the Bulleted tab selected.
   c. Click the dollar sign bullet you inserted in Step 3 and then click the Reset button.
   d. At the message asking if you want to reset the gallery position to the default, click Yes.
   e. Click the picture bullet you inserted in Step 5 and then click the Reset button.
   f. At the message asking if you want to reset the gallery position to the default, click Yes.
   g. Click the *None* bullet option (first option from the left in the top row) and then click OK.
8. Save and then close **swc3x12**.

Changing Line Spacing

By default, the word wrap feature single-spaces text. Occasions may occur when you want to change to another line spacing, such as line and a half or double. Line spacing can be changed using the Line Spacing button on the Formatting toolbar, with shortcut commands, or with options from the Paragraph dialog box. Table 3.3 illustrates the shortcut commands to change line spacing.

Line spacing can also be changed at the Paragraph dialog box. At the Paragraph dialog box, you can change line spacing with the *Line spacing* option or the *At* option. If you click the down-pointing arrow to the right of the *Line spacing* option box at the Paragraph dialog box, a drop-down list displays with a variety of spacing options. For example, to change the line spacing to double you would click *Double* at the drop-down list. You can type a specific line spacing measurement in the *At* text box at the Paragraph dialog box. For example, to change the line spacing to double, type 2 in the *At* text box.

QUICK STEPS

Change Line Spacing
Click Line Spacing button on Formatting toolbar.
OR
Press shortcut command keys.
OR
1. Click Format, Paragraph.
2. Click *Line spacing* option down-pointing arrow.
3. Click desired line spacing option.
4. Click OK.

OR
1. Click Format, Paragraph.
2. Type line measurement in *At* text box.
3. Click OK.

TABLE

3.3 Line Spacing Shortcut Commands

Press	To change line spacing to
Ctrl + 1	Single spacing
Ctrl + 2	Double spacing
Ctrl + 5	1.5-line spacing

exercise 13

CHANGING LINE SPACING

1. Open **WordDocument04**.
2. Save the document with Save As and name it **swc3x13**.
3. Change the line spacing for all paragraphs to 1.5-line spacing by completing the following steps:
   a. Select the entire document.
   b. Click the down-pointing arrow at the right side of the Line Spacing button and then click *1.5* at the drop-down list.
   c. Click outside the selected text to deselect it.
4. Save and then print **swc3x13**.
5. Change the line spacing to double using the Paragraph dialog box by completing the following steps:
   a. Select the entire document.
   b. Click Format and then Paragraph.
   c. At the Paragraph dialog box, make sure the Indents and Spacing tab is selected, and then click the down-pointing arrow to the right of the *Line spacing* option box (this box contains the text *1.5 lines*).
   d. From the drop-down list that displays, click *Double*.
   e. Click OK to close the dialog box.
   f. Click outside the selected text to deselect it.

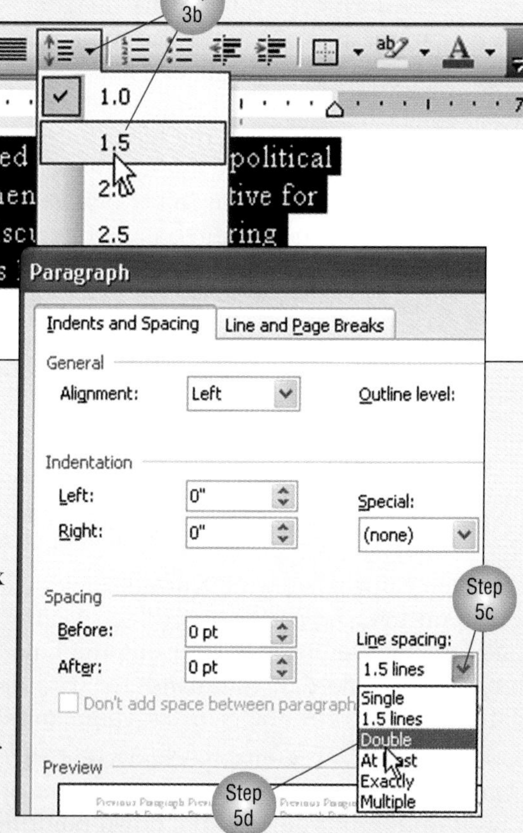

6. Save and then print **swc3x13**.
7. With **swc3x13** still open, change the line spacing to 1.3 by completing the following steps:
   a. Select the entire document.
   b. Click Format and then Paragraph.
   c. At the Paragraph dialog box, make sure the Indents and Spacing tab is selected.
   d. Click in the *At* text box and then type 1.3.
   e. Click OK to close the dialog box.
   f. Click outside the text to deselect it.
8. Save, print, and then close **swc3x13**.

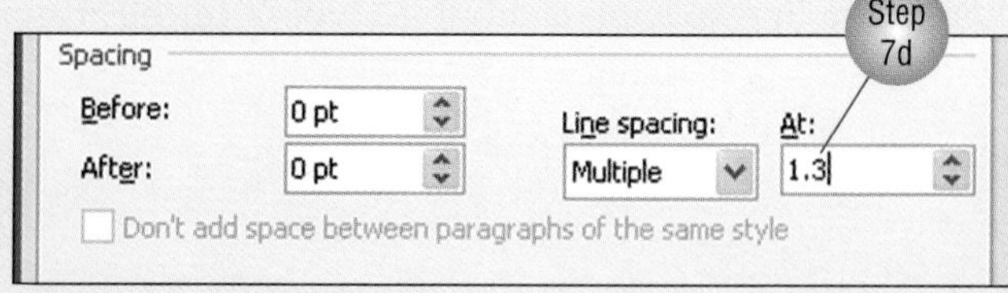

Repeating the Last Action

Use the Format Painter feature to copy character formatting to different locations in a document. If you want to apply other types of formatting, such as paragraph formatting, to a document, consider using the Repeat command. To use the Repeat command, apply the desired formatting, move the insertion point to the next location where you want the formatting applied, click Edit and then Repeat; or press Ctrl + Y; or press F4.

QUICK STEPS

Repeat Last Action
Click Edit, Repeat
OR
press Ctrl + Y
OR
press F4.

Revealing Formatting

Display formatting applied to a document or specific text in a document at the Reveal Formatting task pane. Display this task pane, shown in Figure 3.9, by clicking Format and then Reveal Formatting. You can also display the task pane by pressing Shift + F1. The Reveal Formatting task pane displays font, paragraph, and section formatting applied to text where the insertion point is positioned or to selected text.

Display Reveal Formatting Task Pane
Press Shift + F1.
OR
Click Format, Reveal Formatting.

FIGURE 3.9 ***Reveal Formatting Task Pane***

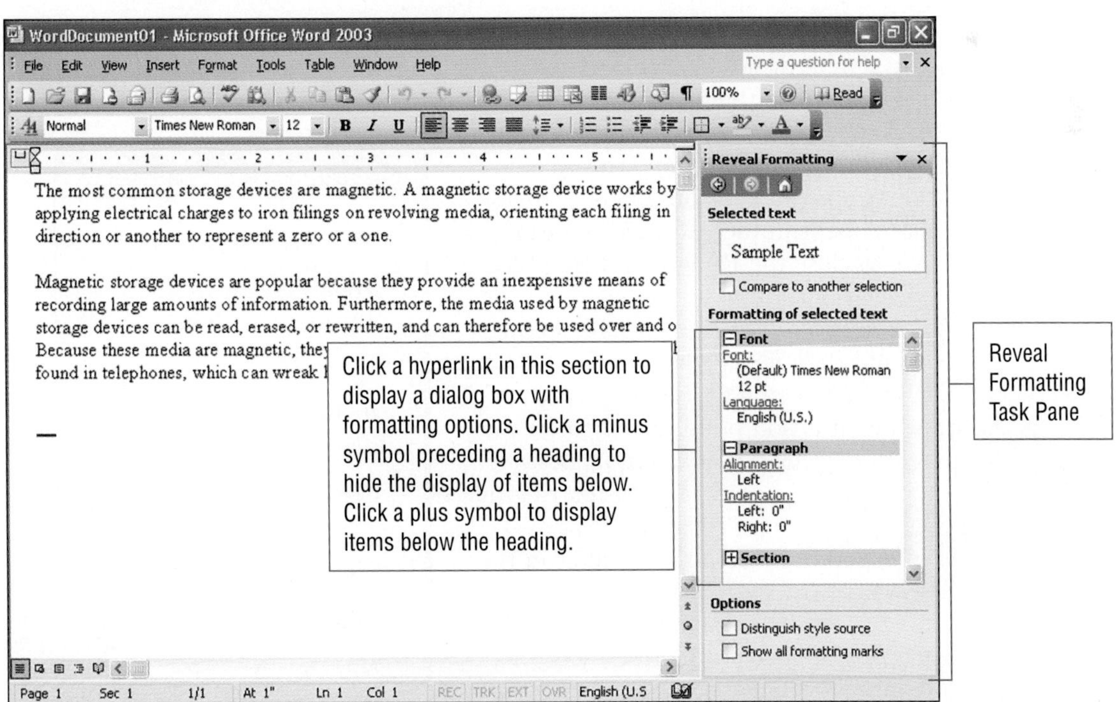

Generally, a minus symbol precedes *Font* and *Paragraph* and a plus symbol precedes *Section* in the *Formatting of selected text* section of the Reveal Formatting task pane. Click the minus symbol to hide any items below a heading and click the plus symbol to reveal items. For example, click the plus symbol preceding the Section heading and several items display below the heading including information on margins, layout, and paper.

Some items below headings in the *Formatting of selected text* section of the Reveal Formatting task pane are hyperlinks. For example, click the Font hyperlink and the Font dialog box displays. Click the Alignment or Indentation hyperlink in the Reveal Formatting task pane and the Paragraph dialog box displays. Use these hyperlinks to make changes to the document formatting.

exercise 14 FORMATTING USING THE REPEAT COMMAND AND REVEALING FORMATTING

1. Open **WordReport01**.
2. Save the document with Save As and name it **swc3x14**.
3. Select the entire document, change the typeface to Garamond (or a similar serif typeface), change the line spacing to single, and then deselect the text.
4. Bold the headings *Early Painting and Drawing Programs*, *Developments in Painting and Drawing Programs*, and *Painting and Drawing Programs Today*.
5. Apply paragraph formatting and repeat the formatting by completing the following steps:
   a. Position the insertion point anywhere in the heading *Early Painting and Drawing Programs*.
   b. Click Format and then Paragraph.
   c. At the Paragraph dialog box, click twice on the up-pointing arrow at the right side of the *Before* option (in the *Spacing* section). (This changes the measurement in the text box to *12 pt*.)
   d. Click once on the up-pointing arrow at the right side of the *After* option. (This changes the measurement in the text box to *6 pt*.)
   e. Click OK to close the Paragraph dialog box.
   f. Position the insertion point anywhere in the heading *Developments in Painting and Drawing Programs* and then repeat the paragraph formatting by pressing Ctrl + Y.
   g. Position the insertion point anywhere in the heading *Painting and Drawing Programs Today* and then repeat the paragraph formatting by pressing F4.

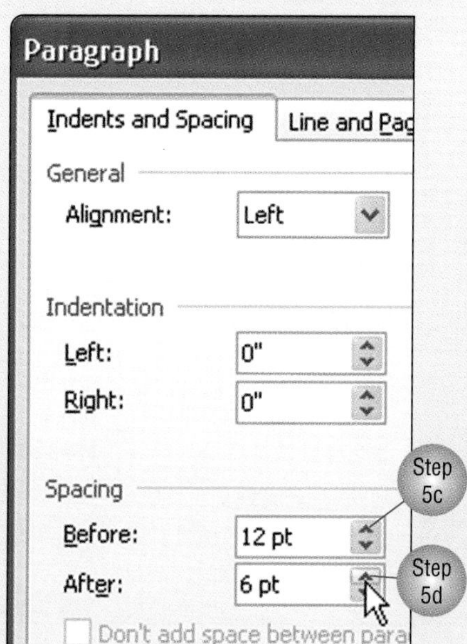

6. Move the insertion point to any character in the title *GRAPHICS SOFTWARE* and then insert 12 points of space after the paragraph.
7. Reveal formatting applied to the title by completing the following steps:
   a. Click anywhere in the title *GRAPHICS SOFTWARE*.
   b. Click Format and then Reveal Formatting. (This displays the Reveal Formatting task pane with information on the formatting applied to the title.)

c. Click anywhere in the first paragraph of text in the document. (Notice the formatting applied to the paragraph.)
d. Click anywhere in the heading *Early Painting and Drawing Programs* and notice the formatting applied to the paragraph.
e. Close the Reveal Formatting task pane by clicking the Close button located in the upper right corner of the task pane.
8. Save, print, and then close **swc3x14**.

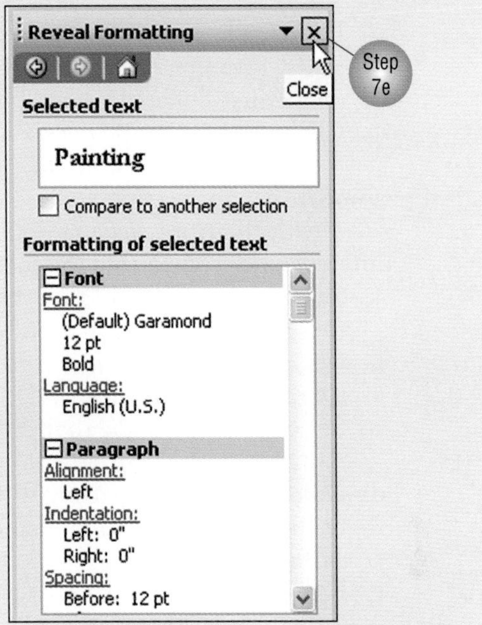

Comparing Formatting

Along with displaying formatting applied to text, the Reveal Formatting task pane can be used to compare formatting of two text selections to determine what formatting is different. To compare formatting, display the Reveal Formatting task pane and then select the first instance of formatting to be compared. Click the *Compare to another selection* check box to insert a check mark and then select the second instance of formatting to compare. Any differences between the two selections will display in the *Formatting differences* list box.

Compare Formatting
1. Display Reveal Formatting task pane.
2. Click or select text.
3. Click *Compare to another selection* check box.
4. Click or select text.

exercise 15 — COMPARING FORMATTING

1. Open **WordQuiz02**.
2. Save the document with Save As and name it **swc3x15**.
3. Compare the first bulleted paragraph with the second bulleted paragraph to determine the formatting difference by completing the following steps:
   a. Display the Reveal Formatting task pane.
   b. Select the first bulleted paragraph (the paragraph that begins *Computers currently offer both...*).
   c. Click the *Compare to another selection* check box to insert a check mark.
   d. Select the second bulleted paragraph (the paragraph that begins *Picture yourself working in the...*).
   e. Determine the formatting differences by reading the information in the *Formatting differences* list box. (The *Formatting differences* list box displays *12 pt -> 11 pt* below the Font: hyperlink, indicating that the difference is point size.)

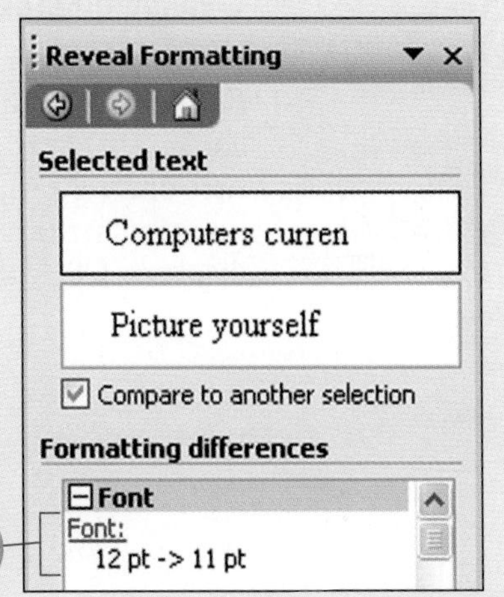

f. Format the second bulleted paragraph so it is set in 12-point size (to match the formatting of the first bulleted paragraph).
g. Click the *Compare to another selection* check box to remove the check mark.

4. Compare the formatting applied to the word *visual* with the word *audio* to determine the differences by completing the following steps:
   a. Select the word *visual* that displays in the first sentence of the first bulleted paragraph.
   b. Click the *Compare to another selection* check box to insert a check mark.
   c. Select the word *audio* that displays in the first sentence of the first bulleted paragraph.
   d. Determine the formatting differences by reading the information in the *Formatting differences* list box.
   e. Format the word *audio* so it matches the formatting of the word *visual*.
   f. Click the *Compare to another selection* check box to remove the check mark.
   g. Close the Reveal Formatting task pane.
5. Save, print, and then close **swc3x15**.

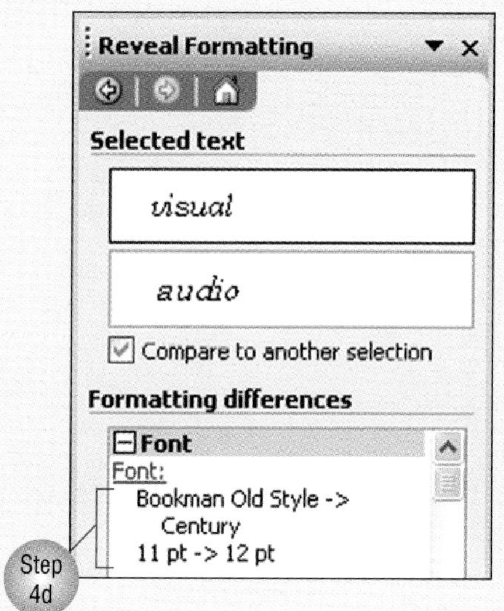

Applying Borders and Shading

QUICK STEPS

Apply Border
Click Border button on Formatting toolbar.
OR
1. Click Format, Borders and Shading.
2. Click Borders tab.
3. Specify border options.
4. Click OK.

Every paragraph you create in Word contains an invisible frame. You can add a border that appears around this frame. Add a border to specific sides of the paragraph or to all sides. You can customize the type of border line and thickness of the line as well as add shading and fill to the border. When a border is added to a paragraph of text, the border expands and contracts as text is inserted or deleted from the paragraph. You can create a border around a single paragraph or a border around selected paragraphs.

Creating a Border with the Border Button

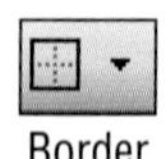
Border

One method for creating a border is to use options from the Border button on the Formatting toolbar. The name of the button changes depending on the border choice that was previously selected at the button drop-down palette. When you first open Word, the button name displays as Outside Border. Click the down-pointing arrow at the right side of the button and a palette of border choices displays. Click the option that will insert the desired border.

exercise 16

ADDING BORDERS TO PARAGRAPHS OF TEXT

1. Open **WordDocument03**.
2. Save the document with Save As and name it **swc3x16**.
3. Create a border around the first paragraph by completing the following steps:
   a. Position the insertion point anywhere in the first paragraph.
   b. Position the mouse pointer on the Border button on the Formatting toolbar and wait for the ScreenTip to display. Make sure the ScreenTip displays as *Outside Border* and then click the button. (If this is not the name for the button, click the down-pointing arrow at the right side of the button and then click the *Outside Border* option [first option in the top row].)

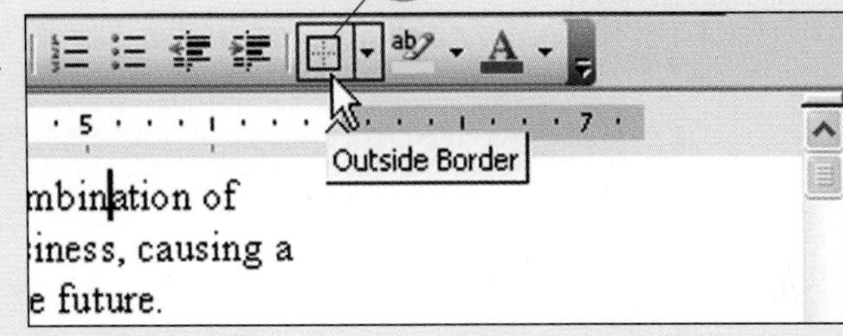

4. Complete steps similar to those in Step 3 to add a border to the second paragraph.
5. Complete steps similar to those in Step 3 to add a border to the third paragraph.
6. Save and then print **swc3x16**.
7. With the document still open, remove the borders by completing the following steps:
   a. Select the three paragraphs in the document. (You do not have to select all of the text in the first and last paragraphs, just a portion.)
   b. Click the down-pointing arrow at the right side of the Border button on the Formatting toolbar and then click the *No Border* option (second option from the left in the bottom row). (This removes the borders from the three paragraphs.)
   c. Deselect the text.

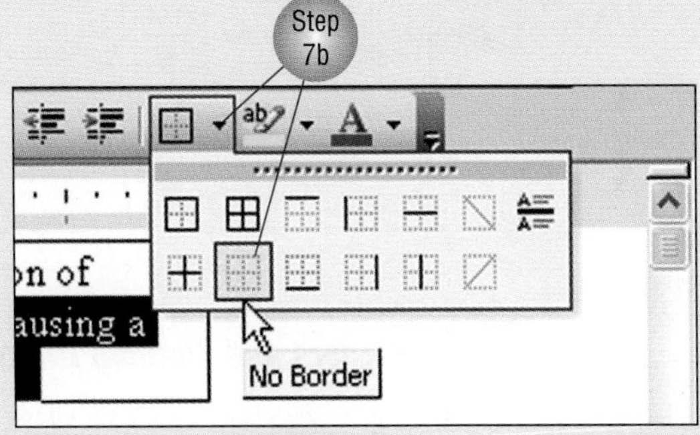

8. Add a border around and between the paragraphs by completing the following steps:
   a. Select from the middle of the first paragraph to somewhere in the middle of the third paragraph.
   b. Click the down-pointing arrow at the right side of the Border button and then click the *All Borders* option (second option from the left in the top row).
   c. Deselect the text.

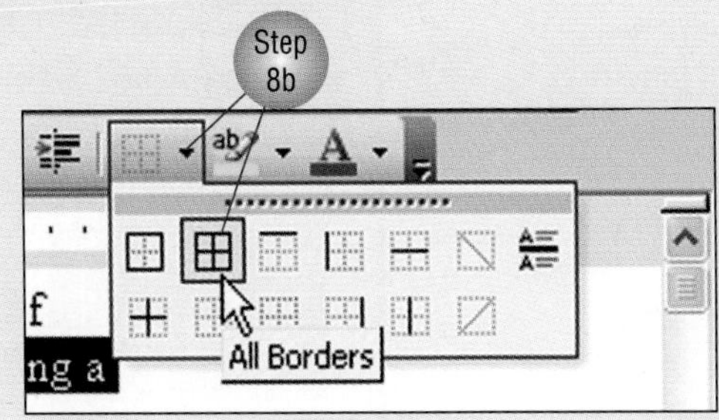

9. Save, print, and then close **swc3x16**.

Apply Shading
1. Click Format, Borders and Shading.
2. Click Shading tab.
3. Specify shading options.
4. Click OK.

Adding Borders and Shading

If you want to customize the line creating the border or add shading, use options from the Borders and Shading dialog box. To display this dialog box, shown in Figure 3.10, click Format and then Borders and Shading. Add a fill color and/or pattern to a paragraph or selected paragraphs with options at the Borders and Shading dialog box with the Shading tab selected as shown in Figure 3.11.

FIGURE 3.10 **Borders and Shading Dialog Box with the Borders Tab Selected**

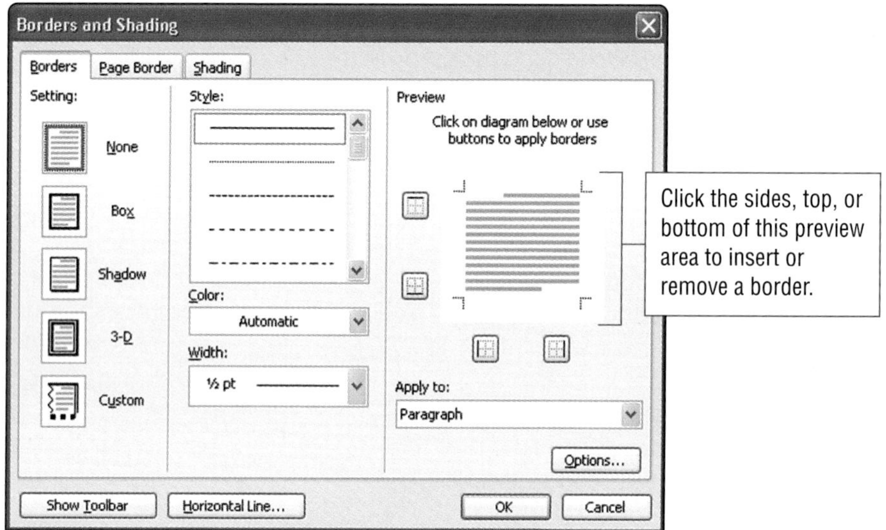

FIGURE 3.11 **Borders and Shading Dialog Box with the Shading Tab Selected**

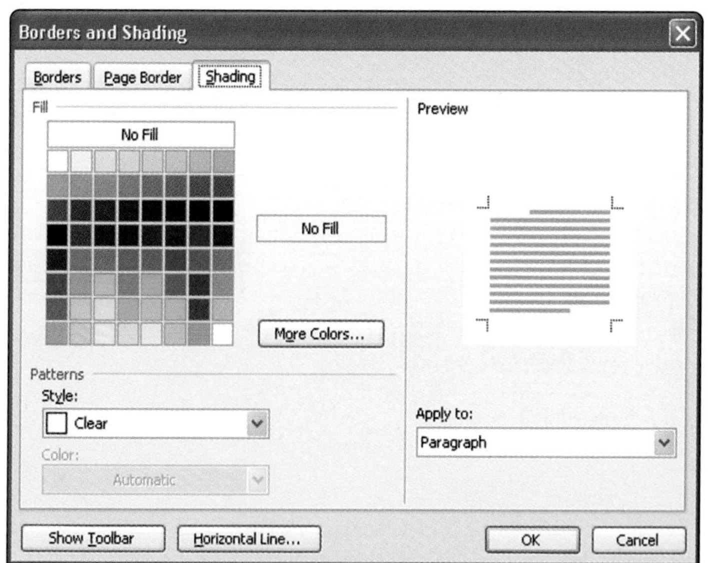

exercise 17

APPLYING BORDERS AND SHADING TO PARAGRAPHS OF TEXT

1. Open **WordDocument04**.
2. Save the document with Save As and name it **swc3x17**.
3. Create a border and apply shading to the paragraphs in the document by completing the following steps:
   a. Select all paragraphs in the document.
   b. Click Format and then Borders and Shading.
   c. At the Borders and Shading dialog box with the Borders tab selected, click the *Box* option located in the *Setting* section.
   d. Click the down-pointing arrow at the right side of the *Width* option box and then click *3 pt* at the drop-down list.
   e. Click the down-pointing arrow at the right side of the *Color* option and then click the Sea Green color (fourth color from the left in the third row) at the color palette.
   f. Click the Shading tab.
   g. Click the light turquoise color in the *Fill* section (fifth color from the left in the bottom row).
   h. Click the down-pointing arrow at the right side of the *Style* list box and then click *5%* at the drop-down list.
   i. Click OK to close the dialog box.
4. Deselect the text.
5. Save, print, and then close **swc3x17**.

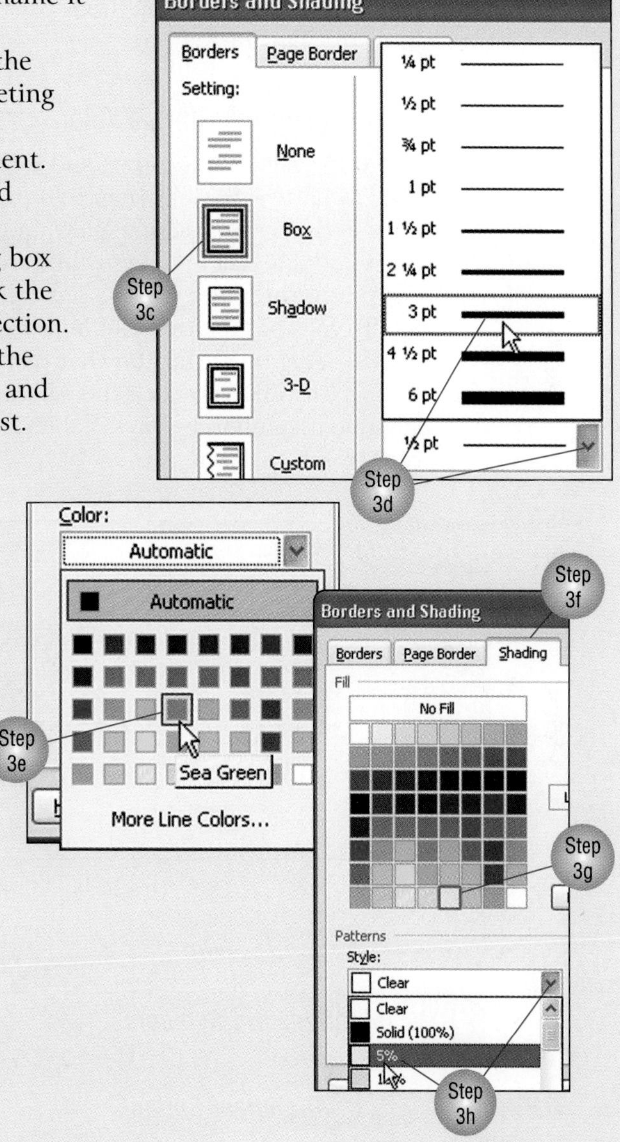

Manipulating Tabs

When you work with a document, Word offers a variety of default settings such as margins and line spacing. One of these defaults is a left tab set every .5 inch. In some situations, these default tabs are appropriate; in others, you may want to create your own. Two methods exist for setting tabs. Tabs can be set on the Ruler or at the Tabs dialog box.

Manipulating Tabs on the Ruler

Use the Ruler to set, move, and delete tabs. By default, the Ruler displays below the Formatting toolbar as shown in Figure 3.12. If the Ruler is not displayed, turn on the display by clicking View and then Ruler. The Ruler displays left tabs set every .5 inch. These default tabs are indicated by tiny vertical lines along the bottom of the Ruler. With a left tab, text aligns at the left edge of the tab. The other types of tabs that can be set on the Ruler are center, right, decimal, and bar. Use the Alignment button that displays at the left side of the Ruler to specify tabs. Each time you click the Alignment button, a different tab or paragraph alignment symbol displays. Table 3.4 shows the tab alignment button and what type of tab each will set.

FIGURE 3.12 **Ruler**

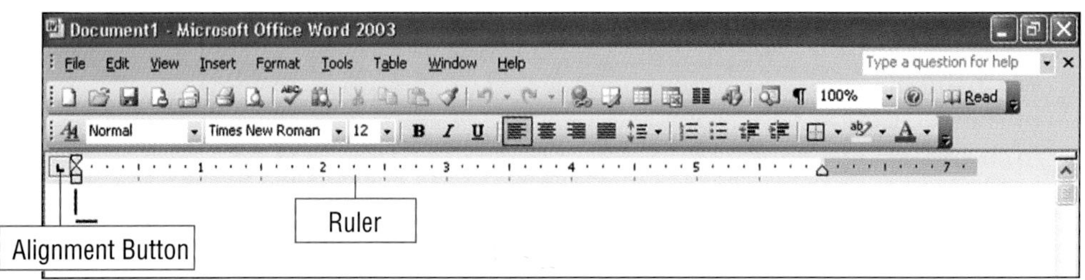

TABLE 3.4 **Tab Alignment Symbols**

Alignment Button	Type of Tab
L	Left tab
⊥	Center tab
⅃	Right tab
⊥.	Decimal tab
I	Bar tab

Setting Tabs

To set a left tab on the Ruler, make sure the left alignment symbol (see Table 3.4) displays in the Alignment button. Position the arrow pointer just below the tick mark (the marks on the Ruler) where you want the tab symbol to appear and then click the left mouse button. When you set a tab on the Ruler, any default tabs to the left are automatically deleted by Word. Set a center, right, decimal, or bar tab on the Ruler in a similar manner.

Before setting a tab on the Ruler, click the Alignment button at the left side of the Ruler until the appropriate tab symbol is displayed, and then set the tab. If you change the tab symbol in the Alignment button, the symbol remains until you change it again or you exit Word. If you exit and then reenter Word, the tab symbol returns to the default of left tab.

HINT

When setting tabs on the Ruler, a dotted guideline displays to help align tabs.

If you want to set a tab at a specific measurement on the Ruler, hold down the Alt key, position the arrow pointer at the desired position, and then hold down the left mouse button. This displays two measurements on the Ruler. The first measurement displays the location of the arrow pointer on the Ruler in relation to the left edge of the page. The second measurement is the distance from the location of the arrow pointer on the Ruler to the right margin. With the left mouse button held down, position the tab symbol at the desired location, and then release the mouse button and the Alt key.

HINT

Position the insertion point in any paragraph of text and tabs for the paragraph appear on the Ruler.

Inserting a Line Break

When you press the Enter key, the insertion point is moved down to the next line and a paragraph mark is inserted in the document. Paragraph formatting is stored in this paragraph mark. For example, if you make changes to tab settings, these changes are inserted in the paragraph mark. In some situations, you may want to start a new line but not a new paragraph. To do this, press Shift + Enter. Word inserts a line break symbol (visible when nonprinting characters have been turned on) and moves the insertion point to the next line.

If you change tab settings and then create columns of text using the New Line command, Shift + Enter, the tab formatting is stored in the paragraph mark at the end of the columns. If you want to make changes to the tab settings for text in the columns, position the insertion point anywhere within the columns (all of the text in the columns does not have to be selected), and then make the changes.

exercise 18

SETTING LEFT, CENTER, AND RIGHT TABS ON THE RULER

1. At a clear document screen, type the heading **WORKSHOPS** centered and bolded as shown in Figure 3.13.
2. Press Enter three times. (Be sure to return the paragraph alignment back to left and turn off bold.)
3. Set a left tab at the .5-inch mark, a center tab at the 3.5-inch mark, and a right tab at the 5.5-inch mark by completing the following steps:
   a. Click the Show/Hide ¶ button on the Standard toolbar to turn on the display of nonprinting characters.
   b. Make sure the Ruler is displayed.
   c. Make sure the left tab symbol displays in the Alignment button at the left side of the Ruler.

d. Position the arrow pointer on the .5-inch mark on the Ruler and then click the left mouse button.

e. Position the arrow pointer on the Alignment button at the left side of the Ruler and then click the left mouse button until the center tab symbol displays (see Table 3.4).

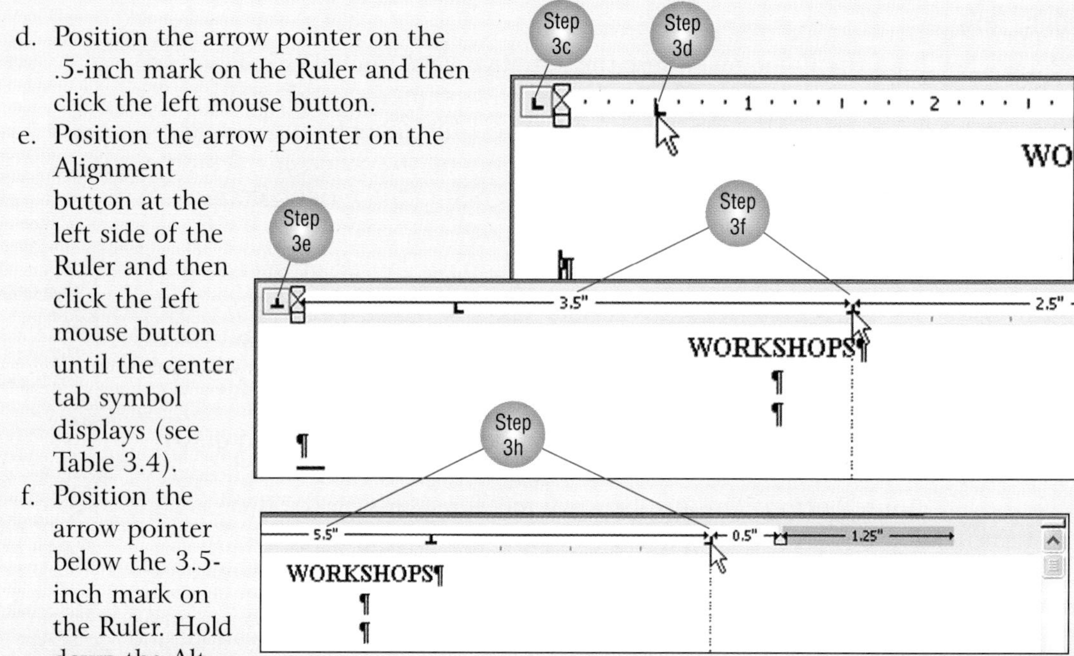

f. Position the arrow pointer below the 3.5-inch mark on the Ruler. Hold down the Alt key and then the left mouse button. Make sure the first measurement on the Ruler displays as 3.5" and then release the mouse button and the Alt key.

g. Position the arrow pointer on the Alignment button at the left side of the Ruler and then click the left mouse button until the right tab symbol displays (see Table 3.4).

h. Position the arrow pointer below the 5.5-inch mark on the Ruler. Hold down the Alt key and then the left mouse button. Make sure the first measurement on the Ruler displays as 5.5" and then release the mouse button and the Alt key.

4. Type the text in columns as shown in Figure 3.13. Press the Tab key before typing each column entry and press Shift + Enter twice after typing the text in the third column. (This moves the insertion point a double space below the text and inserts the New Line command.)
5. Save the document and name it **swc3x18**.
6. Print and then close **swc3x18**.

FIGURE 3.13 ***Exercise 18***

WORKSHOPS¶

¶

¶

Quality·Management	February·5	$150
Staff·Development	February·12	130
Streamlining·Production	March·1	115
Managing·Records	March·27	90¶

Moving Tabs

After a tab has been set on the Ruler, it can be moved to a new location. To move a single tab, position the arrow pointer on the tab symbol on the Ruler, hold down the left mouse button, drag the symbol to the new location on the Ruler, and then release the mouse button.

Deleting Tabs

To delete a tab from the Ruler, position the arrow pointer on the tab symbol you want deleted, hold down the left mouse button, drag the symbol down into the document screen, and then release the mouse button.

exercise 19

MOVING AND DELETING TABS ON THE RULER

1. Open **WordTab01**.
2. Save the document with Save As and name it **swc3x19**.
3. Move the tab settings so the columns are more balanced by completing the following steps:
   a. Select only the text in columns (do not include any blank lines above the columns of text).
   b. Position the arrow pointer on the left tab symbol at the .5-inch mark, hold down the left mouse button, drag the left tab symbol to the 1.25-inch mark on the Ruler, and then release the mouse button. ***(Hint: Use the Alt key to help you precisely position the tab symbol.)***
   c. Position the arrow pointer on the decimal tab symbol at the 3.5-inch mark, hold down the left mouse button, drag the decimal tab symbol into the document screen, and then release the mouse button. (This deletes the tab and merges the second column of text with the first column.)
   d. Click the Alignment button at the left side of the Ruler until the right tab symbol displays.
   e. Position the arrow pointer on the 4.75-inch mark on the Ruler and then click the left mouse button. ***(Hint: Use the Alt key to help you precisely position the tab symbol.)***
   f. Deselect the text.
4. Save, print, and then close **swc3x19**.

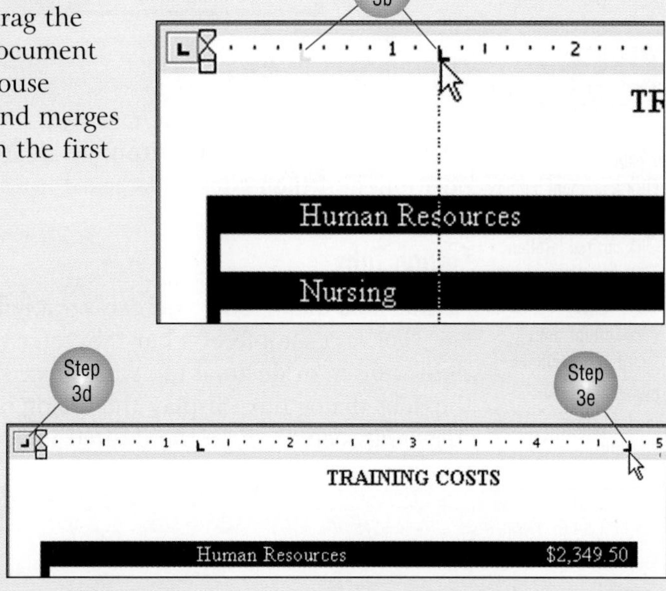

Manipulating Tabs at the Tabs Dialog Box

Use the Tabs dialog box shown in Figure 3.14 to set tabs at a specific measurement. You can also use the Tabs dialog box to set tabs with preceding leaders and clear one tab or all tabs. To display the Tabs dialog box, click Format and then Tabs.

FIGURE 3.14 ***Tabs Dialog Box***

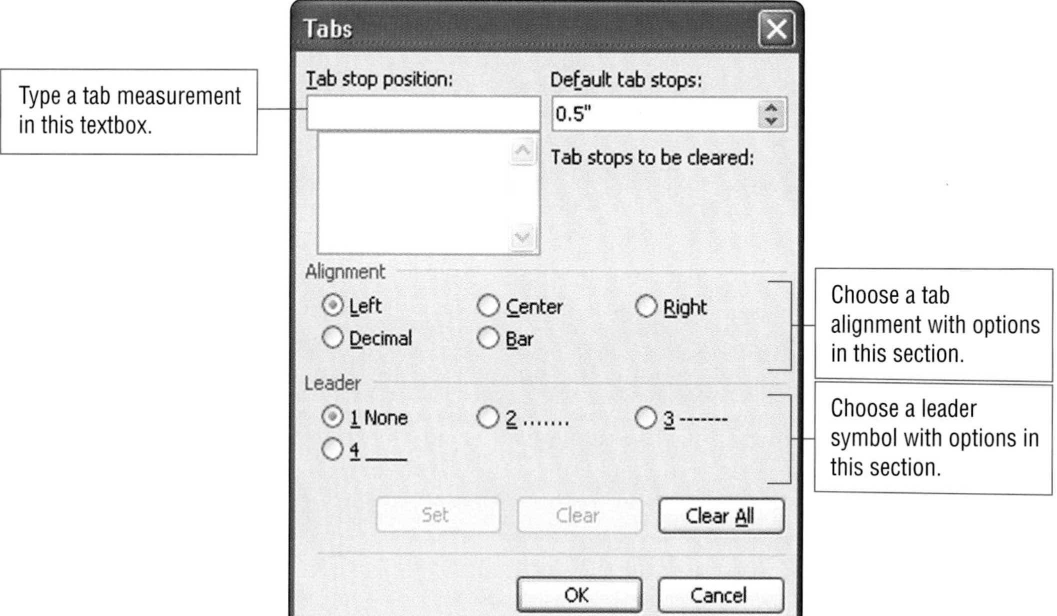

QUICK STEPS

Set Tabs
1. Click Alignment button on Ruler.
2. Click desired location on Ruler.

OR

1. Click Format, Tabs.
2. Specify tab positions, alignments, and leader options.
3. Click OK.

Clearing Tabs

At the Tabs dialog box, you can clear an individual tab or all tabs. To clear all tabs, click the Clear All button. To clear an individual tab, specify the tab position, and then click the Clear button.

Setting Tabs

At the Tabs dialog box, you can set a left, right, center, or decimal tab as well as a bar. (For an example of a bar tab, refer to Figure 3.15.) You can also set a left, right, center, or decimal tab with preceding leaders. To change the type of tab at the Tabs dialog box, display the dialog box, and then click the desired tab in the *Alignment* section. Type the desired measurement for the tab in the *Tab stop position* text box.

exercise 20

SETTING LEFT TABS AND A BAR TAB AT THE TABS DIALOG BOX

1. At a clear document screen, type the title TRAINING DATES bolded and centered as shown in Figure 3.15, press the Enter key twice, change the paragraph alignment back to left and then turn off bold.
2. Display the Tabs dialog box and then set left tabs and a bar tab by completing the following steps:
   a. Click Format and then Tabs.
   b. Make sure *Left* is selected in the *Alignment* section of the dialog box. (If not, click *Left*.)
   c. Type 1.75 in the *Tab stop position* text box. (The insertion point should automatically be positioned in the *Tab stop position* text box. If not, click in the text box.)
   d. Click the Set button.
   e. Type 3.5 in the *Tab stop position* text box and then click the Set button.
   f. Type 3 in the *Tab stop position* text box, click *Bar* in the *Alignment* section, and then click the Set button.
   g. Click OK to close the Tabs dialog box.

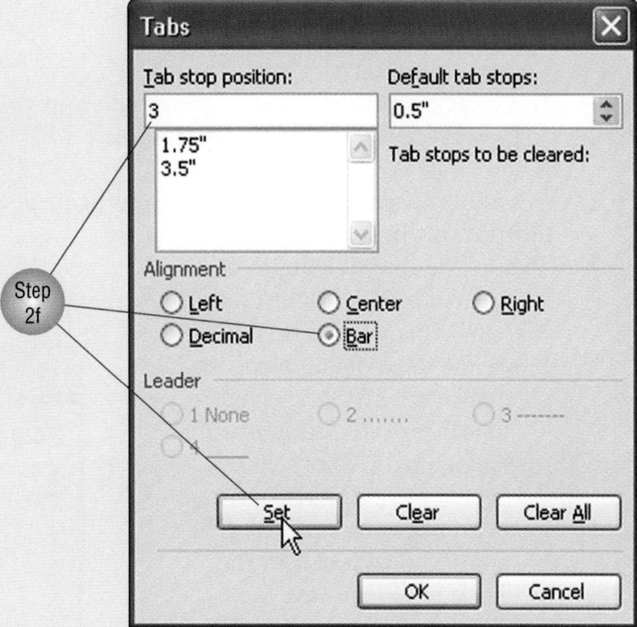

3. Type the text in columns as shown in Figure 3.15. Press the Tab key before typing each column entry. (The vertical line between columns will appear automatically. You need only to type the dates. Do not press Enter after typing the date *February 23*.)
4. Save the document and name it **swc3x20**.
5. Print and then close **swc3x20**.

FIGURE 3.15 ***Exercise 20***

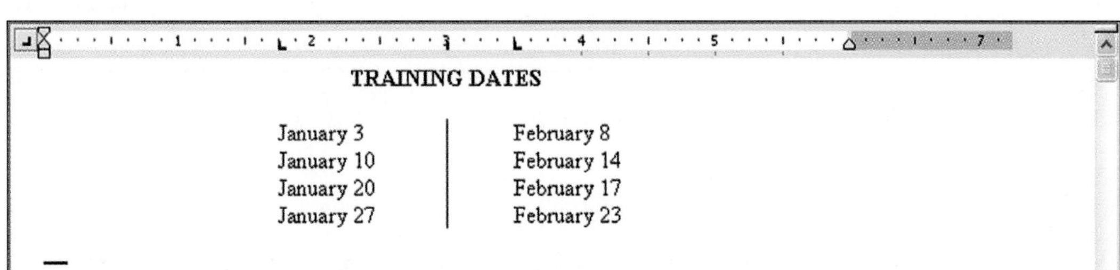

Setting Leader Tabs

The four types of tabs can also be set with leaders. Leaders are useful in a table of contents or other material where you want to direct the reader's eyes across the page. Figure 3.16 shows an example of leaders. Leaders can be periods (.), hyphens (-), or underlines (_). To add leaders to a tab, click the type of leader desired in the *Leader* section of the Tabs dialog box.

exercise 21

SETTING A LEFT TAB AND A RIGHT TAB WITH DOT LEADERS

1. At a clear document screen, change the font to 12-point Tahoma (or a similar typeface such as Univers), and then type the title **TABLE OF CONTENTS** bolded and centered as shown in Figure 3.16.
2. Press Enter three times. (Be sure to return the alignment of the paragraph back to left and turn off bold.)
3. Change the line spacing to *2*.
4. Set a left tab and a right tab with dot leaders by completing the following steps:
   a. Click Format and then Tabs.
   b. At the Tabs dialog box, make sure *Left* is selected in the *Alignment* section of the dialog box. (If not, click *Left*.)
   c. Make sure the insertion point is positioned in the *Tab stop position* text box, type 1, and then click the Set button.
   d. Type 5.5 in the *Tab stop position* text box.
   e. Click *Right* in the *Alignment* section of the dialog box.
   f. Click *2 ......* in the *Leader* section of the dialog box and then click the Set button.
   g. Click OK or press Enter.
5. Type the text in columns as shown in Figure 3.16. Press the Tab key before typing each column entry.
6. Save the document and name it **swc3x21**.
7. Print and then close **swc3x21**.

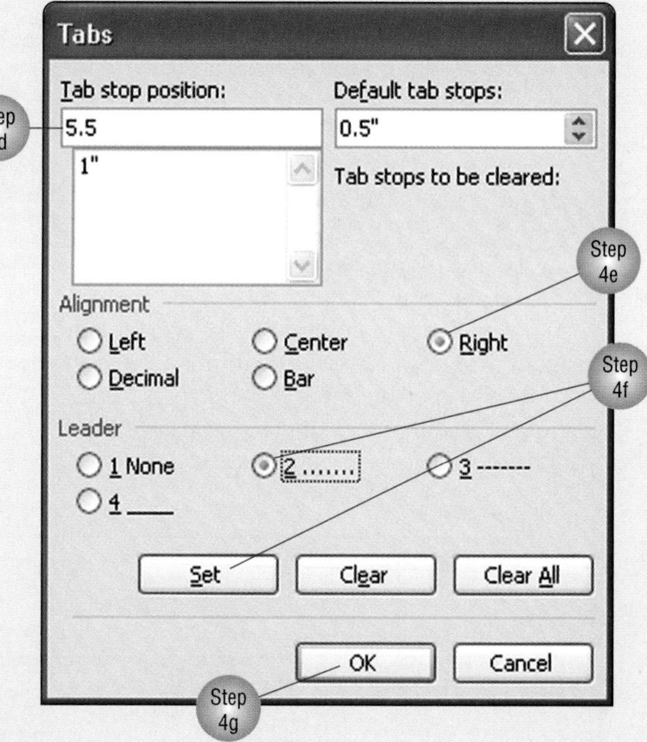

FIGURE

3.16 **Exercise 21**

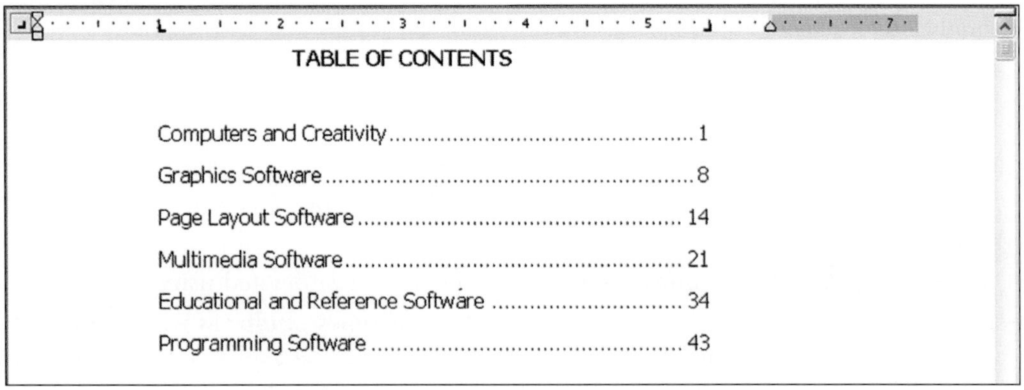

TABLE OF CONTENTS

Computers and Creativity	1
Graphics Software	8
Page Layout Software	14
Multimedia Software	21
Educational and Reference Software	34
Programming Software	43

CHAPTER summary

- To turn on or off the display of nonprinting characters such as paragraph marks, click the Show/Hide ¶ button on the Standard toolbar.
- In Word, a paragraph is any amount of text followed by a paragraph mark (a stroke of the Enter key). Word inserts into the paragraph mark any paragraph formatting that is turned on before the text is typed.
- To remove paragraph formatting from text, delete the paragraph mark or remove all paragraph formatting by pressing Ctrl + Q.
- By default, paragraphs in a Word document are aligned at the left margin and ragged at the right margin. This default alignment can be changed with buttons on the Formatting toolbar, at the Paragraph dialog box, or with shortcut commands for left, center, right, or fully aligned.
- Increase or decrease space before or after a paragraph or selected paragraphs with the *Before* and *After* options at the Paragraph dialog box.
- Indent text in paragraphs using indent buttons on the Formatting toolbar, shortcut commands, options from the Paragraph dialog box, markers on the Ruler, or with the Alignment button on the Ruler.
- Word's AutoFormat feature will automatically format numbered and bulleted lists.
- Bulleted lists with hanging indents are automatically created when a paragraph begins with *, >, or -. The type of bullet inserted depends on the type of character entered.
- Paragraphs can be numbered with the Numbering button on the Formatting toolbar and bullets can be inserted before paragraphs with the Bullets button. Numbers or bullets can also be inserted with options at the Bullets and Numbering dialog box.
- Line spacing can be changed using the Line Spacing button on the Formatting toolbar, with shortcut commands, or with options from the Paragraph dialog box.
- Repeat the last action by clicking Edit and then Repeat, by pressing Ctrl + Y, or pressing F4.
- Reveal formatting applied to text by clicking Format and then Reveal Formatting; or by clicking Help, clicking What's This, and then clicking the desired text. This displays the Reveal Formatting task pane containing information on font, paragraph, and section formatting.

- Use options from the Border button on the Formatting toolbar to insert borders around a paragraph or selected paragraphs.
- Use options at the Borders and Shading dialog box with the Borders tab selected to add a customized border to a paragraph or selected paragraphs and/or options at the Borders and Shading dialog box with the Shading tab selected to add shading or a pattern to a paragraph of text or selected paragraphs.
- By default, tabs are set every .5 inch. These settings can be changed on the Ruler or at the Tabs dialog box.
- Use the Alignment button at the left side of the Ruler to select a left, right, center, or decimal tab. When you set a tab on the Ruler, any default tabs to the left are automatically deleted.
- After a tab has been set on the Ruler, it can be moved or deleted using the mouse pointer.
- At the Tabs dialog box, you can set any of the four types of tabs as well as a bar at a specific measurement. You can also set tabs with preceding leaders and clear one tab or all tabs. Preceding leaders can be periods, hyphens, or underlines.

FEATURES summary

FEATURE	BUTTON	MENU	KEYBOARD
Display nonprinting characters	¶		Ctrl + Shift + *
Align text at left margin			Ctrl + L
Align text between margins			Ctrl + E
Align text at right margin			Ctrl + R
Align text at left and right margins			Ctrl + J
Return paragraph formatting to normal			Ctrl + Q
Paragraph dialog box		Format, Paragraph	
Bullets and Numbering dialog box		Format, Bullets and Numbering	
Change to single spacing			Ctrl + 1
Change to double spacing			Ctrl + 2
Change to 1.5-line spacing			Ctrl + 5
Repeat last action		Edit, Repeat	F4 or Ctrl + Y
Reveal Formatting task pane		Format, Reveal Formatting	Shift + F1
Borders and Shading dialog box		Format, Borders and Shading	
Display Ruler		View, Ruler	
New Line command			Shift + Enter
Tabs dialog box		Format, Tabs	

CONCEPTS check

Completion: On a blank sheet of paper, indicate the correct term, symbol, or command for each description.

1. Word inserts paragraph formatting into this mark.
2. To turn on or off the display of nonprinting characters, click this button on the Standard toolbar.
3. This is the Word default paragraph alignment.
4. You can return all paragraph formatting to normal with this keyboard command.
5. In this kind of paragraph, the first line remains at the left margin and the remaining lines are indented to the first tab setting.
6. Insert spacing before or after paragraphs with options at this dialog box.
7. Automate the creation of bulleted paragraphs with the Bullets button on this toolbar.
8. At the Paragraph dialog box, change line spacing with the *Line spacing* option or this.
9. This is the shortcut command to change line spacing to 1.5.
10. Repeat the last action by pressing F4 or with this shortcut command.
11. Click this option on the Menu bar and then click Reveal Formatting to display the Reveal Formatting task pane.
12. Click this option on the Menu bar and then click Borders and Shading to display the Borders and Shading dialog box.
13. By default, each tab is set apart from the other by this measurement.
14. This is the default tab type.
15. When setting tabs on the Ruler, choose the tab type with this button.
16. Tabs can be set on the Ruler or here.
17. List the steps you would complete to change the line spacing to 1.25.

SKILLS check

Assessment 1

1. Open **WordDocument03**.
2. Save the document with Save As and name it **swc3sc01**.
3. At the beginning of the document, type the title ECONOMIC SLOWDOWN centered and bolded. (Separate the title from the first paragraph of text by a blank line.)
4. Select the entire document and then change to a serif typeface of your choosing (other than Times New Roman).
5. Indent the first line of each of the three paragraphs of text to the .25-inch mark on the Ruler.
6. Save and then print **swc3sc01**.
7. With the document still open, make the following changes:
   a. Remove the first line indent formatting.
   b. Create a hanging indent for each of the three paragraphs of text.
   c. Change the alignment to justified for the three paragraphs of text.
   d. Change the line spacing to 1.5 for the entire document.
8. Save, print, and then close **swc3sc01**.

Assessment 2

1. Open **WordDocument05**.
2. Save the document with Save As and name it **swc3sc02**.
3. Select the entire document and then change the font to 12-point Century (or a similar serif typeface).
4. Select the title *ARE YOU PREPARING FOR RETIREMENT?* and then change the font to 14-point Century bold (or the serif typeface you chose in Step 3).
5. Select from the second paragraph (that begins *Living longer than ever,...*) to the end of the document and then add the following:
   a. Add paragraph numbering.
   b. Add 3 points of spacing before paragraphs. (To do this, select the current measurement in the *Before* text box at the Paragraph dialog box, and then type 3.)
6. Save, print, and then close **swc3sc02**.

Assessment 3

1. At a clear document screen, type the document shown in Figure 3.17.
2. After typing the text in the document, make the following changes to the document:
   a. Select the entire document and then change the font to 13-point Bookman Old Style.
   b. Select the title and then change the font to 18-point Bookman Old Style bold.
   c. Select the heading *Choices and Changes* and then change the font to 16-point Bookman Old Style bold.
3. Save the document and name it **swc3sc03**.
4. Print and then close **swc3sc03**.

FIGURE 3.17 ***Assessment 3***

GENERAL MATTERS

Choices and Changes

As long as your annuity fund certificate permits, you can choose or change any of the following:

➢ an annuity starting date;
➢ an income option;
➢ a transfer;
➢ a method of payment for death benefits;
➢ a date when the commuted value of an annuity becomes payable;
➢ an annuity partner, beneficiary, or other person named to receive payments;
➢ a cash withdrawal or other distribution; and
➢ a repurchase.

You have to make your choices or changes via a written notice satisfactory to us and received at our home offices. Transfers between accounts can currently be made by telephone. You can change the terms of a transfer, cash withdrawal, repurchase, or other cash distribution only before they are scheduled to take place.

Assessment 4

1. At a clear document screen, create the document shown in Figure 3.18 with the following specifications:
   a. Change the line spacing to double.
   b. Center, bold, and italicize text as indicated.
   c. Create hanging paragraphs as indicated.
   d. Change the paragraph alignment for all paragraphs to justified.
2. Save the document and name it **swc3sc04**.
3. Print and then close **swc3sc04**.

FIGURE 3.18 ***Assessment 4***

BIBLIOGRAPHY

Amaral, Howard G. (2004). *Economic Growth in America*, 2nd edition (pp. 103-112). Denver, CO: Goodwin Publishing Group.

Cuevas, Roxanne A. (2003). *Establishing a Stock Portfolio* (pp. 18-35). Los Angeles, CA: North Ridge, Inc.

Forsyth, Stuart M. (2004). *International Investing* (pp. 23-31). San Francisco, CA: Roosevelt & Carson Publishing.

Gudroe, Andrea G. (2005). *Global Economics*, 3rd edition (pp. 67-72). Phoenix, AZ: Desert Palm Press.

Assessment 5

1. Open **WordList04**.
2. Save the document with Save As and name it **swc3sc05**.
3. Insert numbering before each paragraph in the document (except the title and the blank line below the title).
4. Save and then print **swc3sc05**.
5. Make the following changes to the document:
   a. Delete *External fund raising*.
   b. Change *Internal fund raising* so it reads *Fund raising*.
   c. Add *Corporate* between the fourth and fifth paragraphs.
6. Save, print, and then close **swc3sc05**.

Assessment 6

1. Open **WordDocument02**.
2. Save the document with Save As and name it **swc3sc06**.
3. Select the entire document, change to a serif typeface other than Times New Roman, and then deselect the text.

4. Select the heading *QWERTY KEYBOARD* and the paragraph that follows it and then add a double-line border of your choosing and light green shading.
5. Select the heading *DVORAK KEYBOARD* and the paragraph that follows it and apply the same border and shading as in Step 4. ***(Hint: Use the Repeat command.)***
6. Save, print, and then close **swc3sc06**.

Assessment 7

1. At a clear document screen, change the font to 12-point Arial, and then type the document shown in Figure 3.19. For the text in columns, set a left tab at the 1-inch mark, the 2.5-inch mark, and the 4-inch mark on the Ruler.
2. Save the document and name it **swc3sc07**.
3. Print **swc3sc07**.
4. With the document still open, select the text in columns and then move the tab at the 1-inch mark on the Ruler to the 0.75-inch mark, the tab at the 2.5-inch mark to the 2.75-inch mark, and the tab at the 4-inch mark to the 4.5-inch mark.
5. Save, print, and then close **swc3sc07**.

FIGURE 3.19 ***Assessment 7***

SOFTWARE TRAINING SCHEDULE

Word	April 9	8:30 – 11:30 a.m.
PowerPoint	April 11	1:00 – 3:30 p.m.
Excel	May 8	8:30 – 11:30 a.m.
Access	May 10	1:00 – 3:30 p.m.

Assessment 8

1. At a clear editing window, type the document shown in Figure 3.20 with the following specifications:
   a. Change the font to 12-point Century Schoolbook (or a similar serif typeface such as Bookman Old Style or Garamond).
   b. Bold and center the title as shown.
   c. Before typing the text in columns, display the Tabs dialog box, and then set left tabs at the .5-inch mark and the 1-inch mark, and a right tab with dot leaders at the 5.5-inch mark.
2. Save the document and name it **swc3sc08**.
3. Print and then close **swc3sc08**.

FIGURE

3.20 *Assessment 8*

TABLE OF CONTENTS

Assessment 9

1. Open **swc3sc08**.
2. Save the document with Save As and name it **swc3sc09**.
3. Select the text in columns and then move the tab symbols on the Ruler as follows:
   a. Move the left tab symbol at the 1-inch mark to the 1.5-inch mark.
   b. Move the left tab at the .5-inch mark to the 1-inch mark.
   c. Move the tab at the 5.5-inch mark to the 5-inch mark.
4. Save, print, and then close **swc3sc09**.

Assessment 10

1. In some Word documents, especially documents with left and right margins wider than 1 inch, the right margin may appear quite ragged. If the paragraph alignment is changed to justified, the right margin will appear even, but there will be extra space added throughout the line. In these situations, hyphenating long words that fall at the end of the text line provides the document with a more balanced look. Use Word's Help feature to learn how to automatically hyphenate words in a document.
2. Open **WordReport01**.
3. Save the document with Save As and name it **swc3sc10**.
4. Automatically hyphenate words in the document, limiting the consecutive hyphens to 2. ***(Hint: Specify the number of consecutive hyphens at the Hyphenation dialog box.)***
5. Save, print, and then close **swc3sc10**.

CHAPTER challenge

You are the assistant to the promotions manager at the Italian Eatery, a restaurant specializing in pizza and Italian food. The promotions manager has asked you to draft a new menu that will eventually replace the existing menu. In the first section of the menu, use a leader tab format to list possible new food items and their prices. In another section of the document, indicate the prices of drinks (small, medium, and large) and then create a vertical listing (using appropriate picture bullets) showing the types of drinks available to customers. Place a border around each section. Save and then print the file.

After reviewing your draft, the promotions manager indicated that he was pleased with the borders placed around each section, but also wanted a border around the entire page. Use the Help feature to learn more about page borders. Apply an appropriate page border to the document. Save and then print the document.

The promotions manager has been informed that prices for each of the food items are to increase by 2%. He has asked you to create a spreadsheet showing the food items and their prices, as well as the prices with the 2% increase. Copy information in the first section of your draft menu to Excel and use a formula to calculate the new prices. Save and then print the Excel file.

CHAPTER 4

FORMATTING DOCUMENTS

PERFORMANCE OBJECTIVES

Upon successful completion of Chapter 4, you will be able to:

- **Change the document view**
- **Hide/show white space in Print Layout view**
- **Change document margins and page orientation**
- **Insert a hard page break and insert a section break in a document**
- **Preview a document**
- **Change the zoom, display the full screen, and view a document in Reading Layout**
- **Vertically align text in a document**
- **Use the click and type feature**
- **Format text into newspaper columns**
- **Complete a spelling check on text in a document**
- **Complete a grammar check on text in a document**
- **Add words to and delete words from the AutoCorrect dialog box**
- **Display synonyms and antonyms for specific words using the Thesaurus**

Chapter04S

WORD

Formatting can be applied to a document such as changing the document margins and inserting page breaks. In this chapter, you will learn to apply these types of formatting along with how to format text into newspaper columns, complete a spelling check on text in a document, improve the grammar of text in a document by completing a grammar check, and use the Thesaurus to find synonyms and related words for a specific word.

Preparing Multiple-Paged Documents

Word assumes that you are using standard-sized paper, which is 8.5 inches wide and 11 inches long. By default, a Word document contains 1-inch top and bottom margins and 1.25-inch left and right margins. With the default top and bottom margins of 1 inch, a total of 9 inches of text will print on a page (1 inch for the top margin, 9 inches of printed text, and then 1 inch for the bottom margin). As you create long documents, you will notice that when the insertion point nears 9.8 inches (or approximately Line 45 [this number may vary]) a page break is inserted in the document. The page break is inserted at the next line (at the 10-inch measurement). The line below the page break is the beginning of the next page.

Changing the View

Print Layout View

Normal View

The display of a page break will change depending on the view. At the Normal view, a page break displays as a row of dots. Change to the Print Layout view and a page break displays as an actual break in the page. To change to the Print Layout view, click View and then Print Layout or click the Print Layout View button at the left side of the horizontal scroll bar. (The Print Layout View button is the third button from the left side of the screen before the horizontal scroll bar.) To change back to the Normal view, click View and then Normal, or click the Normal View button at the left side of the horizontal scroll bar. (The Normal View button is the first button from the left.)

HINT

Control what displays on the screen with options at the Options dialog box with the View tab selected.

When you are working in a document containing more than one page of text, the Status bar displays the page where the insertion point is positioned and will also display the current page followed by the total number of pages in a document. For example, if the insertion point is positioned somewhere on page 3 of a 12-page document (with one section), the left side of the Status bar will display *Page 3 Sec 1 3/12*. The *3/12* indicates that the insertion point is positioned on page 3 in a document containing 12 pages.

Hiding/Showing White Space in Print Layout View

Hide White Space

Show White Space

In Print Layout view, a page displays as it will appear when printed including the white space at the top and bottom of the page representing the default margins. If Print Layout view is selected in a multiple-page document, gray space displays between pages. To save space on the screen in Print Layout view, you can remove the white space and gray space. To do this, position the mouse pointer on any gray space at the top or bottom of a page or between pages until the pointer turns into the Hide White Space button, and then click the left mouse button. To redisplay the white and gray space, position the mouse pointer on the thin gray line separating pages until the pointer turns into the Show White Space button, and then click the left mouse button.

By default, white space displays in Print Layout view. You can change this default setting at the Options dialog box with the View tab selected. Display this dialog box by clicking Tools, clicking Options, and then clicking the View tab. Remove the check mark from the *White space between pages (Print View only)* option. You must change to the Print Layout view before displaying the Options dialog box.

Changing Margins

The default margin settings are displayed in the Page Setup dialog box shown in Figure 4.1. To display the Page Setup dialog box, click File and then Page Setup or double-click a light blue area at the top of the Ruler. At the Page Setup dialog box, make sure the Margins tab is selected.

FIGURE 4.1 ***Page Setup Dialog Box with Margins Tab Selected***

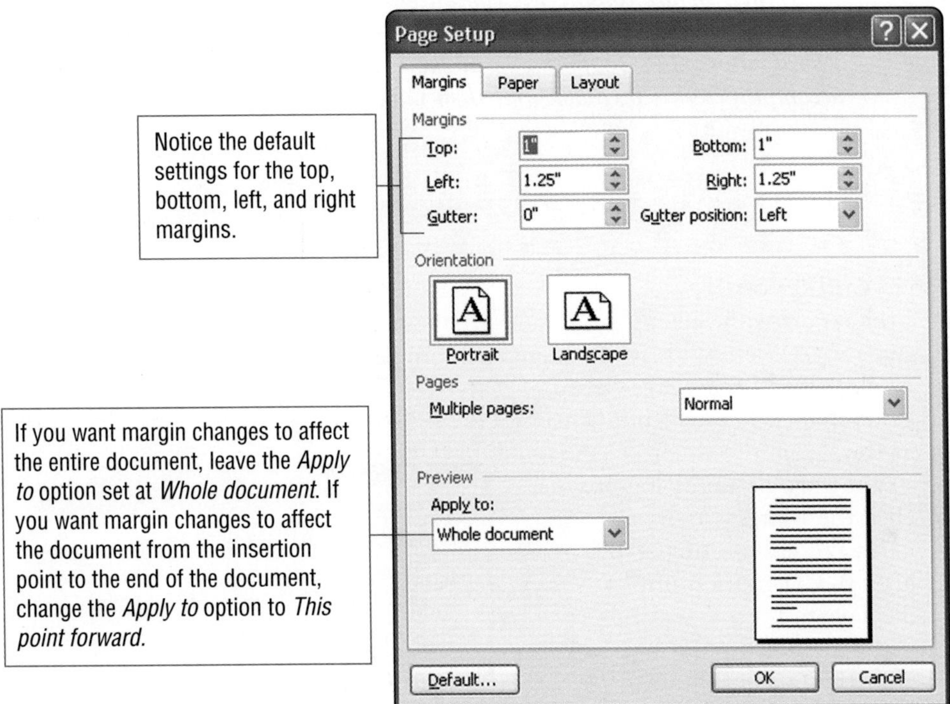

Page Setup
Margins
Paper
Layout
Margins
Top:
1"
Bottom:
1"
Left:
1.25"
Right:
1.25"
Gutter:
0"
Gutter position:
Left
Orientation
Portrait
Landscape
Pages
Multiple pages:
Normal
Preview
Apply to:
Whole document
Default...
OK
Cancel
Notice the default settings for the top, bottom, left, and right margins.
If you want margin changes to affect the entire document, leave the Apply to option set at Whole document. If you want margin changes to affect the document from the insertion point to the end of the document, change the Apply to option to This point forward.

To change margins, select the current measurement in the *Top*, *Bottom*, *Left*, or *Right* text boxes, type the new measurement for the margin, and then click OK or press Enter. As you make changes to the margin measurements at the Page Setup dialog box, the sample page in the *Preview* section illustrates the adjustments to the margins. You can also click the up- and down-pointing arrows after each margin option to increase or decrease the margin measurement.

If you want the new margins to affect the entire document, position the insertion point anywhere within the document, and then make margin changes at the Page Setup dialog box. You can also specify that margin changes affect the text in a document from the position of the insertion point to the end of the document. To do this, click the down-pointing arrow at the right of the *Apply to* option box in the Page Setup dialog box, and then click *This point forward* at the drop-down list.

HINT

Most printers contain a required margin (between one-quarter and three-eighths of an inch) because printers cannot print to the edge of the page.

Change Margins

1. Click File, Page Setup.
2. Click Margins tab.
3. Change *Top*, *Bottom*, *Left*, and *Right* options.
4. Click OK.

HINT

You can use portrait and landscape orientations in the same document. To do this, select the text you want to change, display the Page Setup dialog box, click the desired orientation, and change the *Apply to* option box to *Selected text.*

Changing Page Orientation

Word provides two orientations for pages—portrait and landscape, with portrait the default. Choose the orientation at the Page Setup dialog box with the Margins tab selected. When you switch to landscape orientation, Word automatically exchanges the top and bottom margin settings for the left and right margin setting.

Change Page Orientation

1. Click File, Page Setup.
2. Click Margins tab.
3. Click *Portrait* or *Landscape.*
4. Click OK.

(Note: Before completing computer exercises, delete the WordChapter03S folder on your disk. Next, copy to your disk the WordChapter04S subfolder from the Word2003Specialist folder on the CD that accompanies this textbook and then make WordChapter04S the active folder.)

exercise 1

CHANGING MARGINS AND VIEW

1. Open **WordReport01**.
2. Save the report with Save As and name it **swc4x01**.
3. Change the top, left, and right margins by completing the following steps:
   a. Click File and then Page Setup, or double-click a light blue area at the top of the Ruler.
   b. At the Page Setup dialog box, click the Margins tab.
   c. Click the up-pointing arrow after the *Top* option until *1.5"* displays in the *Top* text box.
   d. Click the down-pointing arrow after the *Left* option until *1"* displays in the *Left* text box.
   e. Click the down-pointing arrow after the *Right* option until *1"* displays in the *Right* text box.
   f. Click OK.

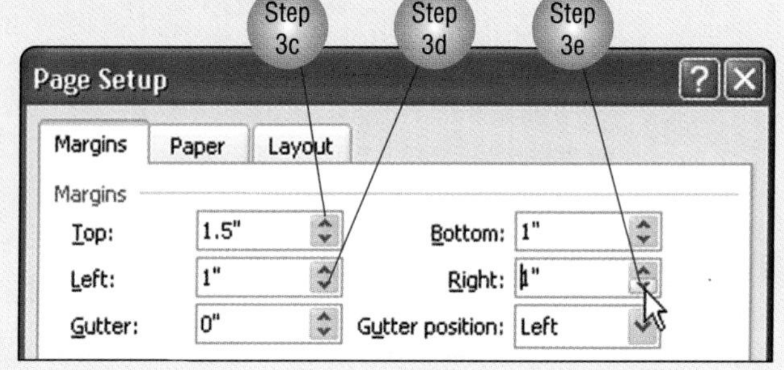

4. Make the following changes to the document:
   a. Select the title *GRAPHICS SOFTWARE* and then change the font to 18-point Arial bold.
   b. Select the heading *Early Painting and Drawing Programs* and then change the font to 14-point Arial bold.
   c. Use Format Painter to change the formatting to 14-point Arial bold for the remaining two headings, *Developments in Painting and Drawing Programs* and *Painting and Drawing Programs Today*.
5. Change the document view and hide/show white space by completing the following steps:
   a. Change to Print Layout view by clicking the Print Layout View button located at the left side of the horizontal scroll bar (third button from the left).
   b. Scroll through the document and notice how page breaks appear in the document.
   c. Display the first page in the document.

d. Position the mouse pointer on the gray space that displays above the top of the page until the pointer turns into the Hide White Space button and then click the left mouse button.
e. Scroll through the document and notice how page breaks appear without the white space.
f. Position the mouse pointer on any gray space that separates pages until the pointer turns into the Show White Space button and then click the left mouse button.
g. Change back to Normal view by clicking View and then Normal.

6. Save and then print **swc4x01**.
7. Change the page orientation by completing the following steps:
   a. Click File and then Page Setup.
   b. At the Page Setup dialog box with the Margins tab selected, click *Landscape* in the *Orientation* section.
   c. Click OK.
8. Save, print, and then close **swc4x01**.

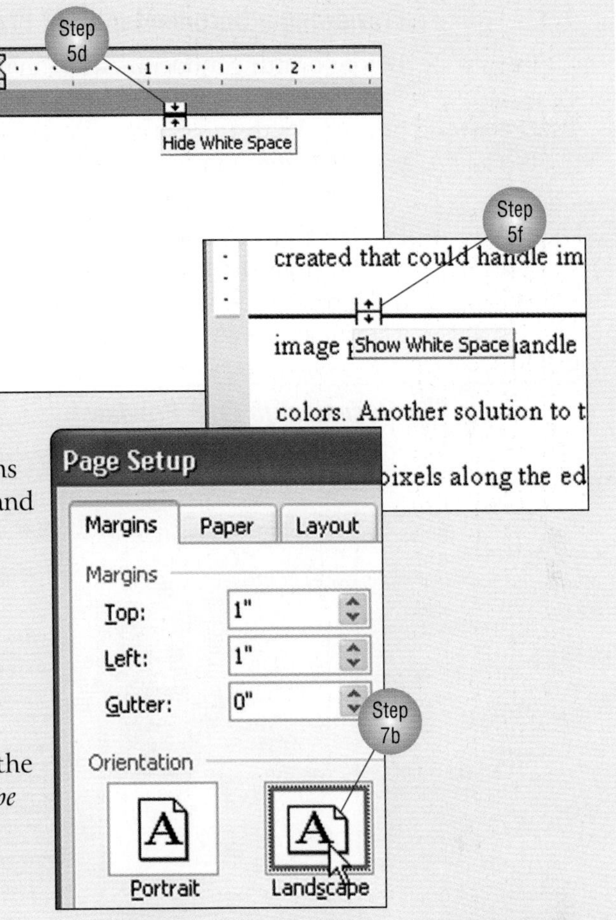

Inserting Hard Page Breaks

Insert Hard Page Break
Press Ctrl + Enter.
OR
1. Click Insert, Break.
2. Click *Page break.*
3. Click OK.

Word's default settings break each page after Line 45 (approximately 9.8 inches). Word automatically inserts page breaks in a document as you edit it. Since Word does this automatically, you may find that page breaks sometimes occur in undesirable locations. To remedy this, you can insert your own page break. A page break inserted automatically by Word is called a ***soft page break*** and a break inserted by you is called a ***hard page break***.

To insert a hard page break, position the insertion point where you want the break to occur, click Insert and then Break. At the Break dialog box, make sure *Page break* is selected, and then click OK. You can also insert a hard page break by positioning the insertion point in the document where you want the break to occur and then pressing Ctrl + Enter.

A hard page break displays in the Normal view as a line of dots with the words *Page Break* in the middle of the line. A hard page break displays in the same manner as a soft page break in the Print Layout view.

Soft page breaks automatically adjust if text is added to or deleted from a document. A hard page break does not adjust and is therefore less flexible than a soft page break. If you add or delete text from a document with a hard page break, check the break to determine whether it is still in a desirable location. To delete a hard page break, position the insertion point on the page break and then press the Delete key.

Previewing a Document in Print Preview

Print Preview

Before printing a document, it may be useful to view the document. Word's Print Preview feature displays the document on the screen as it will appear when printed. With this feature, you can view a partial page, single page, multiple pages, or zoom in on a particular area of a page.

To view a document, click File and then Print Preview or click the Print Preview button on the Standard toolbar. (The Print Preview button is the seventh button from the left on the Standard toolbar.) In Print Preview, the page where the insertion point is located displays on the screen. Figure 4.2 shows a document in Print Preview.

FIGURE 4.2 ***Document in Print Preview***

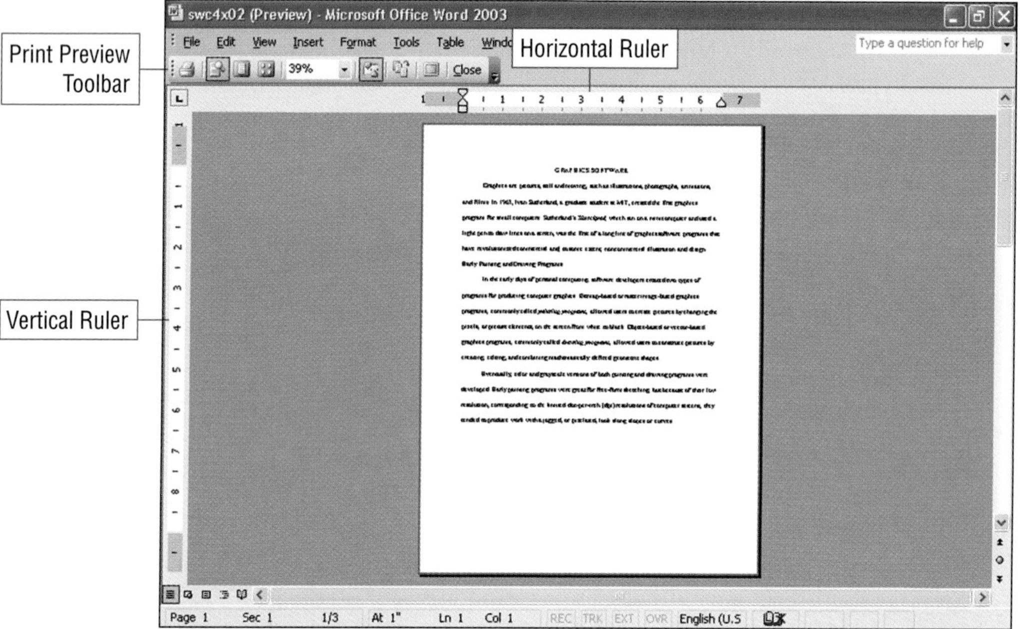

HINT

View the positioning of elements on a page in Print Preview.

The Print Preview toolbar displays along the top of the screen. With buttons from this toolbar, you can change the display of the document, send the document to the printer, and turn the display of the Ruler on or off. While in Print Preview, you can move through the document using the insertion point movement keys, the horizontal and vertical scroll bars, and/or the Page Up and Page Down keys.

exercise 2

INSERTING HARD PAGE BREAKS AND PREVIEWING A DOCUMENT

1. Open **WordReport01**.
2. Save the document with Save As and name it **swc4x02**.
3. Change the left and right margins to 1 inch.
4. Insert a hard page break by positioning the insertion point at the beginning of the heading *Developments in Painting and Drawing Programs* and then pressing Ctrl + Enter.
5. Insert a hard page break at the beginning of the remaining heading, *Painting and Drawing Programs Today*.

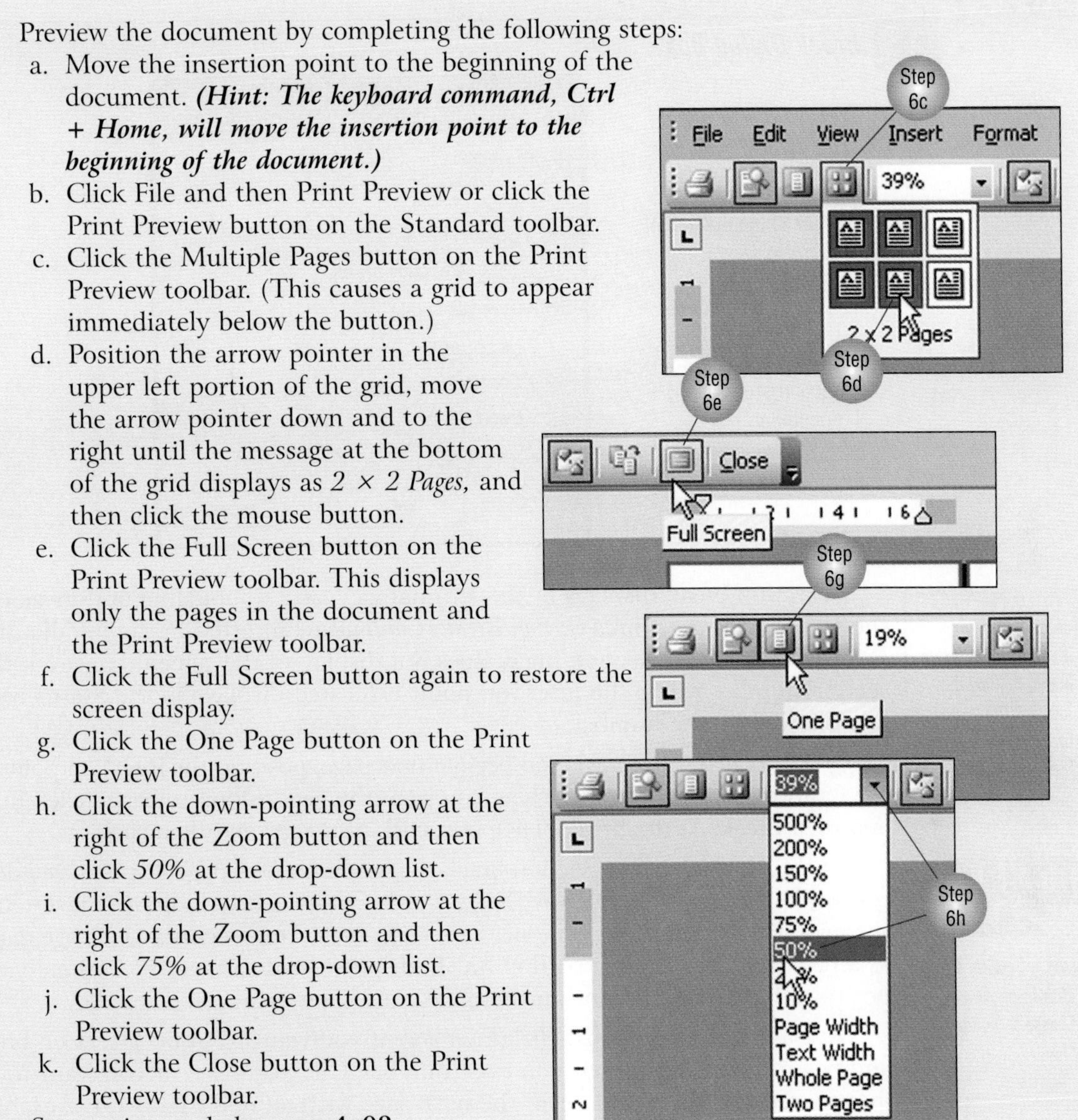

6. Preview the document by completing the following steps:
   a. Move the insertion point to the beginning of the document. ***(Hint: The keyboard command, Ctrl + Home, will move the insertion point to the beginning of the document.)***
   b. Click File and then Print Preview or click the Print Preview button on the Standard toolbar.
   c. Click the Multiple Pages button on the Print Preview toolbar. (This causes a grid to appear immediately below the button.)
   d. Position the arrow pointer in the upper left portion of the grid, move the arrow pointer down and to the right until the message at the bottom of the grid displays as *2 × 2 Pages,* and then click the mouse button.
   e. Click the Full Screen button on the Print Preview toolbar. This displays only the pages in the document and the Print Preview toolbar.
   f. Click the Full Screen button again to restore the screen display.
   g. Click the One Page button on the Print Preview toolbar.
   h. Click the down-pointing arrow at the right of the Zoom button and then click *50%* at the drop-down list.
   i. Click the down-pointing arrow at the right of the Zoom button and then click *75%* at the drop-down list.
   j. Click the One Page button on the Print Preview toolbar.
   k. Click the Close button on the Print Preview toolbar.
7. Save, print, and close **swc4x02**.

Inserting a Section Break

By default, changes made to margins in a document are applied to all text in the document. If you want margin changes to apply to specific text in a document, select the text first. Text in a document can also be divided into sections. When a document is divided into sections, each section can be formatted separately. For example, different margin settings can be applied to each section in a document.

A section can insert a page break in a document or a continuous section can be created that does not insert a page break. To insert a continuous section break in a document, position the insertion point at the location in the document where you want the new section to begin, click Insert and then click Break. At the Break dialog box shown in Figure 4.3, click *Continuous* and then click OK.

FIGURE 4.3 **Break Dialog Box**

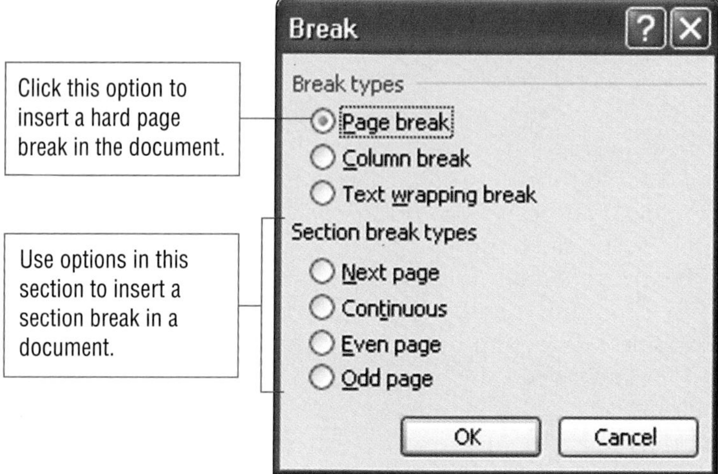

HINT

If you delete a section break, the text that followed the section break takes on the formatting of the text preceding the break.

Insert a Section Break

1. Click Insert, Break.
2. Choose section break type.
3. Click OK.

A section break displays in the Normal view as a double line of dots across the screen with the words *Section Break (Continuous)* inserted in the middle. In the Print Layout view, a section break does not display in the screen. However, the section number where the insertion point is located displays in the Status bar as *Sec* followed by the number.

To create a section break and begin a new page, position the insertion point at the location in the document where you want the new section to begin, click Insert and then Break. At the Break dialog box, click *Next page*, and then click OK.

In the Normal view, a section break that begins a new page displays as a double row of dots across the screen with the words *Section Break (Next Page)* inserted in the middle. In the Print Layout view, a section break that begins a new page displays as a new page. To delete a section break, display the document in Normal view, position the insertion point on the break, and then press the delete key.

At the Break dialog box, click *Even page* if you want to insert a section break and begin the next page with an even number. Click *Odd page* if you want to insert a section break and begin the next page with an odd number. For example, if you position the insertion point somewhere in the middle of page 4 and then insert a section break with the *Even page* option, a section break is inserted and the page below the section break is page 6.

If you change margins in a section of text, the *Apply to* option at the Page Setup dialog box will have the default setting of *This section*.

exercise 3 INSERTING SECTION BREAKS

1. Open **WordReport04**.
2. Save the document with Save As and name it **swc4x03**.
3. Bold the headings *Keyboard, Mouse, Trackball, Touch Pad and Touch Screen, Monitor,* and *Printer*.
4. Change to Print Layout view.
5. Insert a continuous section break by completing the following steps:

a. Position the insertion point at the beginning of the heading *Keyboard* (located on the first page).
   b. Click Insert and then Break.
   c. At the Break dialog box, click the *Continuous* option.
   d. Click OK.
6. Complete steps similar to those in Step 5 to insert a continuous break at the beginning of the heading *Monitor* that displays on the third page.
7. Insert a section break that begins a new page by completing the following steps:
   a. Position the insertion point at the beginning of the title *COMPUTER OUTPUT DEVICES* (located on the third page).
   b. Click Insert and then Break.
   c. At the Break dialog box, click the *Next page* option.
   d. Click OK.
8. Position the insertion point on the heading *Keyboard* and then change the left and right margins to 1.75 inches. (The margin changes affect only the text between the continuous section break and the next page section break.)
9. Position the insertion point on the heading *Monitor* and then change the left and right margins to 1.75 inches.
10. Save, print, and then close **swc4ex03**.

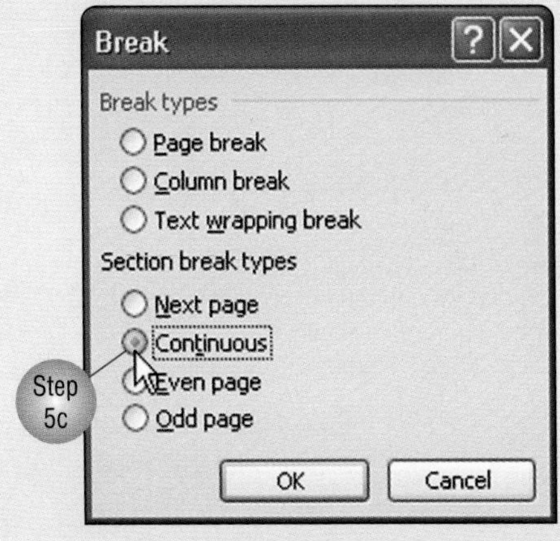

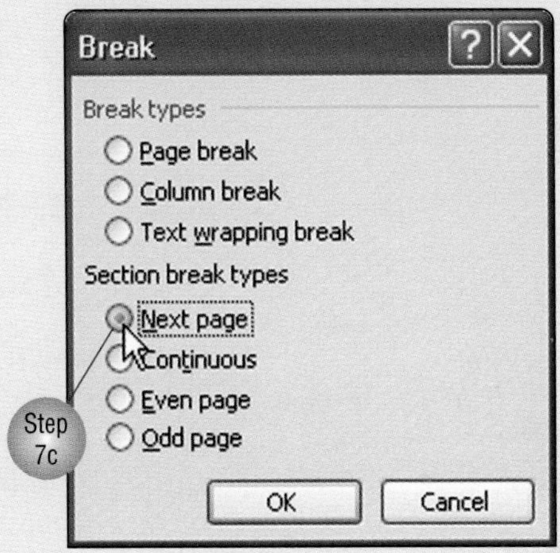

Changing the Document Zoom

You can change the display of text in the document screen with the Zoom button on the Standard toolbar or with the *Zoom* option from the View drop-down menu. Click the Zoom button and then click the desired zoom percentage, width, or page view at the drop-down menu. A Zoom change stays in effect for the document until you change to another option. The options in the Zoom drop-down menu vary depending on the view selected. For example, in Print Layout view, a number of zoom options such as *Text Width*, *Whole Page*, and *Two Pages* are available that are not available in Normal view.

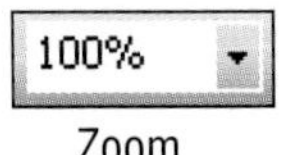

Zoom

You can change the display of text in the document screen with options from the Zoom drop-down list and also at the Zoom dialog box shown in Figure 4.4. To display the Zoom dialog box, click View and then click Zoom.

FIGURE

4.4 Zoom Dialog Box

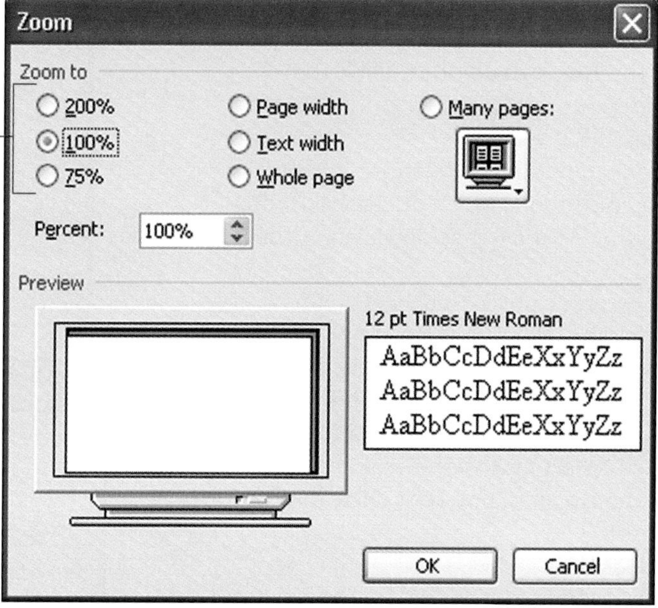

In the Normal view, the *Text Width*, *Whole page*, and *Many pages* options are dimmed and unavailable.

QUICK STEPS

Change Zoom
1. Click down-pointing arrow on Zoom button.
2. Click desired zoom option.

OR

1. Click View, Zoom.
2. Click desired zoom option.
3. Click OK.

At the Zoom dialog box you can change the display to *200%, 100%,* or *75%*. You can also change the display to *Page width*. The *Text width, Whole page,* and *Many pages* options are dimmed if the view is Normal. If the view is changed to Print Layout, the *Text width, Whole page,* and *Many pages* options are available. To specify a percentage measurement, use the *Percent* option. Changes made at the Zoom dialog box stay in effect for the document until another change is made.

Displaying the Full Screen

If you want to expand the work space on your screen, change to the Full Screen view. To do this, click View and then Full Screen. The Full Screen view hides all menus, toolbars, and other tools allowing more of your document to be visible on the screen. The Full Screen toolbar displays in Full Screen view. To restore the normal Word view, click the Close Full Screen button on the Full Screen toolbar or press the Esc key.

exercise 4 CHANGING THE DISPLAY OF TEXT USING ZOOM

1. Open **WordReport03**.
2. Change the display by completing the following steps:
   a. Click the down-pointing arrow at the right side of the Zoom button on the Standard toolbar and then click *50%* at the drop-down list.
   b. Click the down-pointing arrow at the right side of the Zoom button on the Standard toolbar and then click *Page Width* at the drop-down list.
   c. Click View and then Zoom.

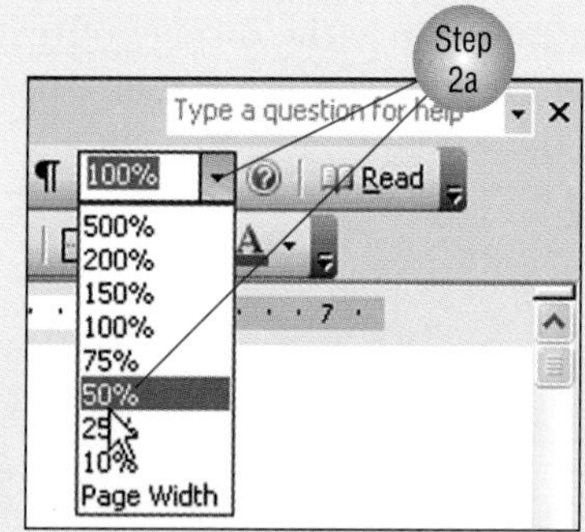

d. At the Zoom dialog box, click *200%.*
e. Click OK.
f. Click View and then Print Layout.
g. Click View and then Zoom.
h. At the Zoom dialog box, click *Whole page*.
i. Click OK.
j. Click the down-pointing arrow at the right side of the Zoom button on the Standard toolbar and then click *100%* at the drop-down list.
k. Display the full screen by clicking View and then Full Screen.
l. After viewing the document in Full Screen view, click the Close Full Screen button on the Full Screen toolbar.

3. Close **WordReport03**.

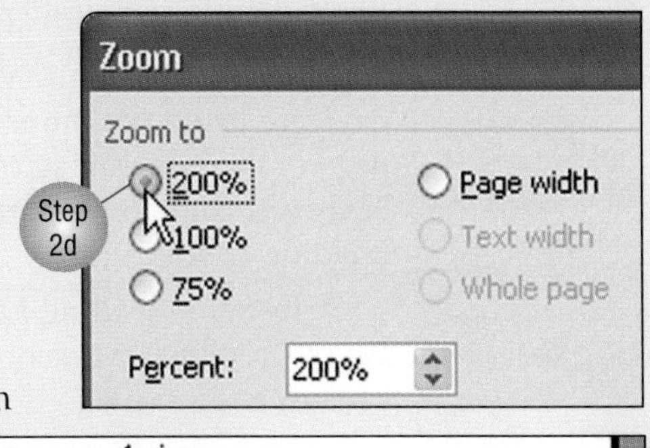

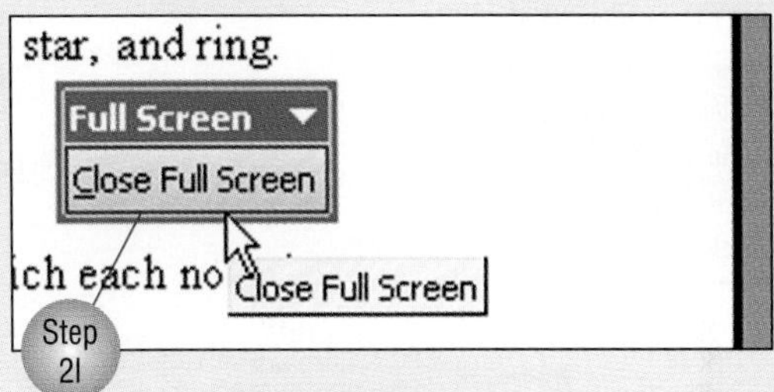

Changing to Reading Layout View

Word's Reading Layout view displays a document in a format for easy viewing and reading. To display a document in Reading Layout view, as shown in Figure 4.5, click the Read button located at the right side of the Standard toolbar, click the Reading Layout button above the Status bar, press Alt + R, or click View and then Reading Layout.

FIGURE 4.5 ***Document in Reading Layout View***

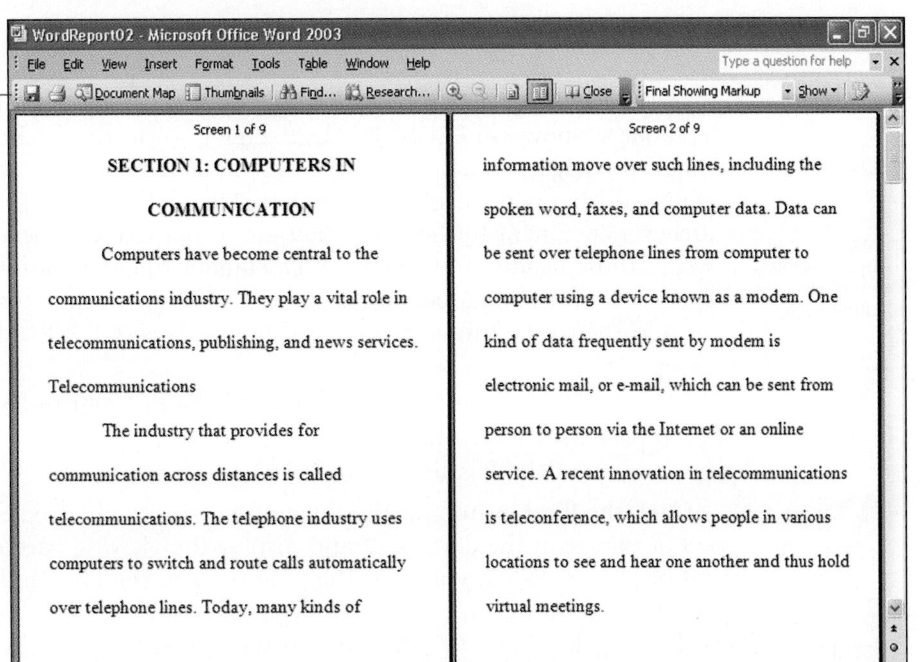

HINT

If you open a Word document that was an attachment to an e-mail, Word switches to Reading Layout. If you do not want an attached document to open in Reading Layout, remove the check mark from the *Allow starting in Reading Layout* option at the Options dialog box with the General tab selected.

Navigating in Reading Layout View

Navigate in Reading Layout view using the mouse or keys on the keyboard. To navigate using the mouse, click the down scroll arrow to display the next viewing page or click the up scroll arrow to display the previous viewing page. Use the keyboard commands shown in Table 4.1 to display various viewing pages in Reading Layout view.

Close the Reading Layout view by clicking the Close button on the Reading Layout toolbar. You can also close the view by pressing Alt + C or pressing the Esc key.

TABLE 4.1 ***Keyboard Commands in Reading Layout View***

Press this key to	***Complete this action***
Page Down key or Spacebar	Move to the next page or section
Page Up key or Backspace key	Move to the previous page or section
Right Arrow key	Move to next page
Left Arrow key	Move to previous page
Home	Move to first page in document
End	Move to last page in document
Esc	Return to previous view

In the Reading Layout view, the Reading Layout toolbar displays below the Menu bar as shown in Figure 4.5. Use some buttons on the Reading Layout toolbar to navigate in a document. Click the Document Map button and the Document Map pane displays at the left side of the screen. Document Map searches a document for headings that are formatted with heading styles and then displays those headings in the pane. Document Map will also search for and then display short lines in a document. Click a heading or line in the Document Map pane and the page containing the heading displays in the Reading Layout view area.

Document Map

Click the Thumbnails button on the Reading Layout toolbar and a thumbnail of each page displays at the left side of the screen. Click a thumbnail and that page displays in the Reading Layout view area.

Thumbnails

Click the Find button on the Reading Layout toolbar to search for a particular word or phrase in the document and display the viewing page containing the word or phrase. When you click the Find button, the Find and Replace dialog box with the Find tab selected displays. Type the word or phrase for which you are searching in the *Find what* text box and then press Enter or click the Find Next

Find

Research

button. Click the Research button on the Reading Layout toolbar and the Research task pane displays at the right side of the screen. Use the Research task pane to look up related information. Click the Start of Document button to displays the first page(s) in the document.

Customizing the Reading Layout View

Increase Text Size

Decrease Text Size

Actual Page

Allow Multiple Pages

With some of the buttons on the Reading Layout toolbar, you can customize the Reading Layout view. Click the Increase Text Size button to increase the size of text in the viewing page or click the Decrease Text Size button to reduce the size of text. Click the Actual Page button to display the page as it will appear when printed. At this view, you may not be able to read the text on the page. Click the Allow Multiple Pages button on the Reading Layout toolbar to turn off two-page view and display only one viewing page. To exit the Reading Layout view, click the Close button located at the right side of the Reading Layout toolbar.

exercise 5

VIEWING A DOCUMENT IN READING LAYOUT

1. Open **WordReport02**.
2. Click the Read button located at the right side of the Standard toolbar.
3. If two pages do not display, click the Allow Multiple Pages button on the Reading Layout toolbar.
4. Click the down scroll arrow to display the next viewing page.
5. Click the up scroll arrow to display the previous viewing page.
6. Press the End key to display the last viewing page in the document.
7. Press the Home key to display the first viewing page.
8. Click the Document Map button on the Reading Layout toolbar.
9. Click the *SECTION 2* heading in the Document Map pane. (This displays the page containing the SECTION 2 heading.)
10. Click the *SECTION 1* heading in the Document Map pane.
11. Click the Document Map button to turn off the Document Map pane.
12. Click the Thumbnails button on the Reading Layout toolbar. (This displays thumbnail miniatures of each page in the Thumbnails pane.)
13. Click the number 3 thumbnail in the Thumbnails pane.
14. Click the number 1 thumbnail in the Thumbnails pane.
15. Click the Thumbnails button to turn off the Thumbnails pane.

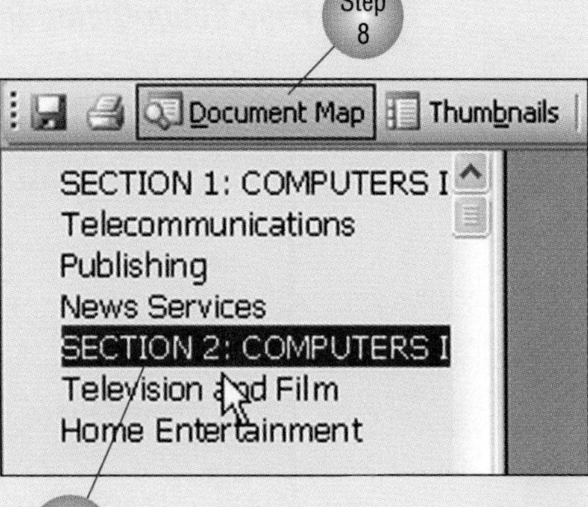

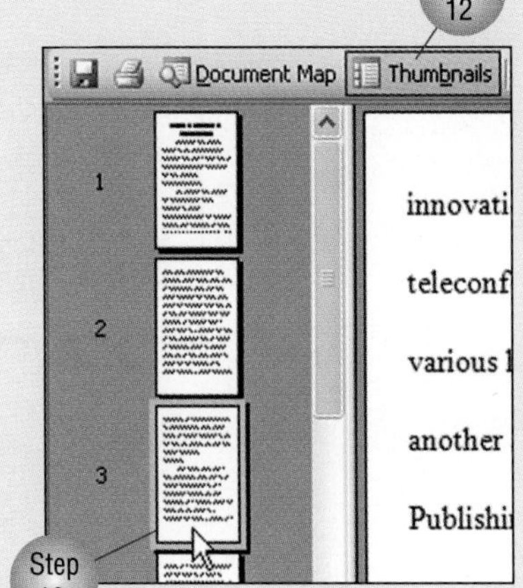

16. Click twice on the Increase Text Size button to increase the size of the text in the viewing pages.
17. Click twice on the Decrease Text Size button to decrease the size of text.
18. Click the Allow Multiple Pages button to display only one viewing page.
19. Click the Allow Multiple Pages button to display two viewing pages.
20. Click the Close button.
21. Close **WordReport02**.

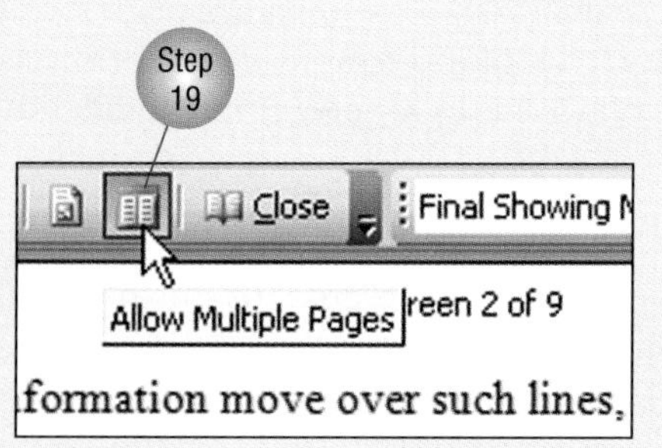

Vertically Aligning Text

Text in a Word document is aligned at the top of the page by default. This alignment can be changed with the *Vertical alignment* option at the Page Setup dialog box with the Layout tab selected as shown in Figure 4.6. Display this dialog box by clicking File and then Page Setup. At the Page Setup dialog box, click the Layout tab.

FIGURE 4.6 ***Page Setup Dialog Box***

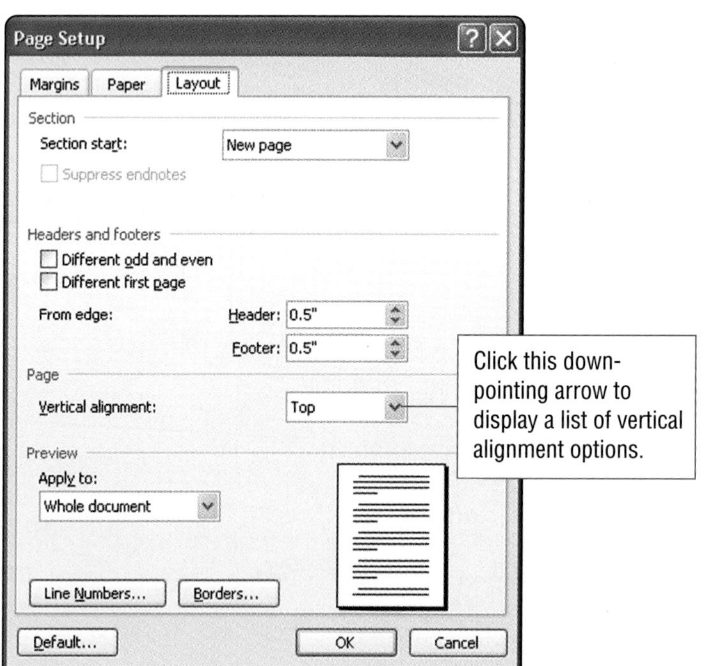

The *Vertical alignment* option from the Page Setup dialog box contains four choices—*Top*, *Center*, *Justified*, and *Bottom*. The default setting is *Top*, which aligns text at the top of the page. Choose *Center* if you want text centered vertically on the page. The *Justified* option will align text between the top and the bottom margins. The *Center* option positions text in the middle of the page vertically, while the *Justified* option adds space between paragraphs of text (not within) to fill the page from the top to bottom margins. If you center or justify text, the text does not display centered or justified on the screen in the Normal view, but it does display centered or justified in the Print Layout view. Choose the *Bottom* option to align text in the document vertically along the bottom of the page.

Vertically Align Text
1. Click File, Page Setup.
2. Click Layout tab.
3. Click *Alignment* option down-pointing arrow.
4. Click desired alignment.
5. Click OK.

exercise 6

VERTICALLY ALIGNING TEXT IN A DOCUMENT

1. Open **WordBlock01**.
2. Save the document with Save As and name it **swc4x06**.
3. Change to the Print Layout view by clicking View and then Print Layout or by clicking the Print Layout View button located at the left side of the screen before the horizontal scroll bar.
4. Select the entire document, turn on bold and change the font size to 14 points, and then deselect the text.
5. Vertically center the text in the document by completing the following steps:
   a. Click File and then Page Setup.
   b. At the Page Setup dialog box, click the Layout tab. (Skip this step if the Layout tab is already selected.)
   c. Click the down-pointing arrow at the right side of the *Vertical alignment* option box and then click *Center* at the drop-down list.
   d. Click OK to close the dialog box.
6. Display the document in Print Preview and then close Print Preview.
7. Save, print, and then close **swc4x06**.

Step 5b

Page Setup

Margins | Paper | Layout

Section
Section start: New page
Suppress endnotes

Headers and footers
Different odd and even
Different first page
From edge: Header: 0.5" Footer: 0.5"

Page
Vertical alignment: Top
Top
Center
Justified
Bottom

Preview
Apply to:

Step 5c

Using the Click and Type Feature

In Chapter 3, you learned to change paragraph alignment with buttons on the Formatting toolbar, shortcut commands, or options at the Paragraph dialog box. Another method for changing paragraph alignment is to use the ***click and type*** feature. Before using this feature, you must change to the Print Layout view.

In Print Layout view, hover the mouse pointer between the left and right margins (at approximately the 3-inch mark on the Ruler). After a few seconds, four short horizontal lines display below the I-beam pointer. These horizontal lines represent center alignment. Double-click the mouse button and the insertion point is moved to the center of the margins and the Center button on the Formatting toolbar is activated.

HINT

Turn on or off the click and type feature with the *Enable click and type* option at the Options dialog box with the Edit tab selected.

Use Click and Type
1. Change to Print Layout view.
2. Hover mouse at left margin, between left and right margins, or at right margin.
3. Double-click left mouse button.

You can change to right alignment in a similar manner. Hover the mouse pointer near the right margin and after a few seconds horizontal lines display at the left side of the I-beam pointer. These horizontal lines represent right alignment and are similar in appearance to the lines on the Align Right button on the Formatting toolbar. With the right alignment lines displayed at the left side of the I-beam pointer, double-click the left mouse button.

If the alignment lines are not displayed near the I-beam pointer and you double-click the left mouse button, a left tab is set at the position of the insertion point. If you want to change the alignment and not set a tab, be sure the alignment lines display near the I-beam pointer before double-clicking the mouse button. To change to left alignment, hover the mouse pointer near the left margin. When horizontal lines display representing left alignment, double-click the left mouse button.

exercise 7

USING CLICK AND TYPE TO ALIGN TEXT

1. At a clear document screen, change to the Print Layout view by clicking View and then Print Layout.
2. Create the centered text shown in Figure 4.7 by completing the following steps:
   a. Position the I-beam pointer between the left and right margins at about the 3-inch mark on the horizontal ruler and the 2½-inch mark on the vertical ruler.
   b. When the center alignment lines display below the I-beam pointer, double-click the left mouse button.
   c. Type the centered text shown in Figure 4.7.
3. After typing the centered text, change to right alignment by completing the following steps:
   a. Position the I-beam pointer near the right margin at approximately the 4-inch mark on the vertical ruler and the 6-inch mark on the horizontal ruler until the right alignment lines display at the left side of the I-beam pointer. (You may need to scroll down the document to display the 4-inch mark on the vertical ruler.)
   b. Double-click the left mouse button.
   c. Type the right-aligned text shown in Figure 4.7.
4. Select the centered text and then change the font to 14-point Arial bold and the line spacing to double.
5. Select the right-aligned text, change the font to 8-point Arial bold, and then deselect the text.
6. Save the document and name it **swc4x07**.
7. Print and then close **swc4x07**.

Step 2b

FIGURE 4.7 **Exercise 7**

MICROSOFT EXCEL TRAINING
Developing Financial Spreadsheets
Wednesday, October 19, 2005
Training Center
9:00 a.m. - 3:30 p.m.

Sponsored by
Cell Systems

Creating Newspaper Columns

Create Newspaper Columns
1. Click Columns button.
2. Drag to select desired number of columns.

OR

1. Click Format, Columns.
2. Specify column options.
3. Click OK.

When preparing a document containing text, readability of the document is an important point to consider. Readability refers to the ease with which a person can read and understand groups of words. The line length of text in a document can enhance or detract from the readability of text. If the line length is too long, the reader may lose his or her place on the line and have a difficult time moving to the next line. To improve the readability of some documents such as newsletters or reports, you may want to set the text in columns.

Text can be set in two different types of columns in Word. One type, called newspaper columns, is commonly used for text in newspapers, newsletters, and magazines. The other type, called side-by-side columns, is used for text that you want to keep aligned horizontally. Side-by-side columns are created using the Tables feature (covered in Chapter 7).

Newspaper columns contain text that flows up and down in the document, as shown in Figure 4.8. When the first column on the page is filled with text, the insertion point moves to the top of the next column on the same page. When the last column on the page is filled with text, the insertion point moves to the beginning of the first column on the next page.

FIGURE

4.8 Newspaper Columns

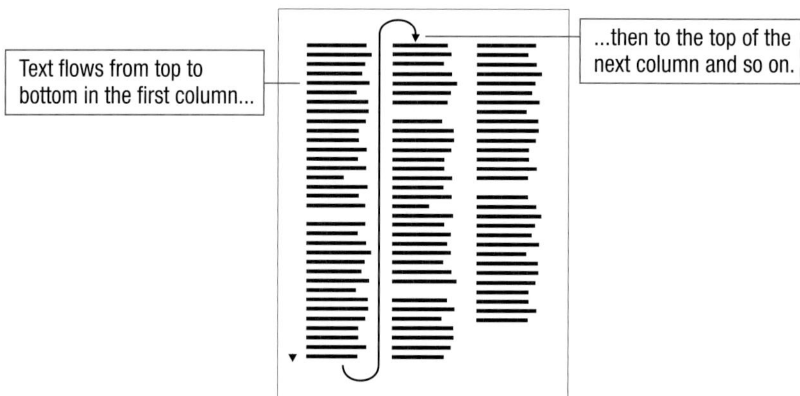
Text flows from top to bottom in the first column...
...then to the top of the next column and so on.

Columns

Create newspaper columns using the Columns button on the Standard toolbar or options from the Columns dialog box. The formatting for newspaper columns can be established before the text is typed or it can be applied to existing text. A document can include as many columns as the available space on the page. Word determines how many columns can be included on the page based on the page width, the margin widths, and the size and spacing of the columns.

Formatting Sections

Formatting text in columns affects the entire document or the section of the document in which the insert point is positioned. If you want to create different numbers or styles of columns in a document, divide the document into sections. Three methods are available for inserting a section break in a document.

One method is to use the Break dialog box (shown in Figure 4.3). Another method for inserting a section break in a document is to use the Columns dialog box and specify that text is to be formatted into columns from the location of the insertion point forward in the document. The third method is to select the text first and then apply column formatting.

Creating Newspaper Columns with the Columns Button

To create newspaper columns using the Columns button on the Standard toolbar, click the button. This causes a grid to display. Move the mouse down and to the right until the desired number of columns displays with a blue background on the Columns grid and then click the mouse button.

If a document contains a title and you want that title to span both columns, position the insertion point at the left margin at the first line of text that will begin the columns, then click Insert and then Break. At the Break dialog box (shown in Figure 4.3), click *Continuous*, and then click OK or press Enter.

In addition to the method just described, you could also format the text in a document into columns and not the title by selecting the text in the document (excluding the title), and then using the Columns button on the Standard toolbar to create the columns. A third method is explained in the next section on creating columns with options from the Columns dialog box.

In Normal view, text displays in a single column at the left side of the document screen. If you want to view columns as they will appear when printed, change to the Print Layout view.

FORMATTING TEXT INTO NEWSPAPER COLUMNS USING THE COLUMNS BUTTON

1. Open **WordReport01**.
2. Save the document with Save As and name it **swc4x08**.
3. Change to the Print Layout view.
4. Select the title and then change the font to 18-point Times New Roman bold.
5. Select the text in the document from the beginning of the first paragraph (begins with *Graphics are pictures...*) to the end of the document. With the text selected, make the following changes:

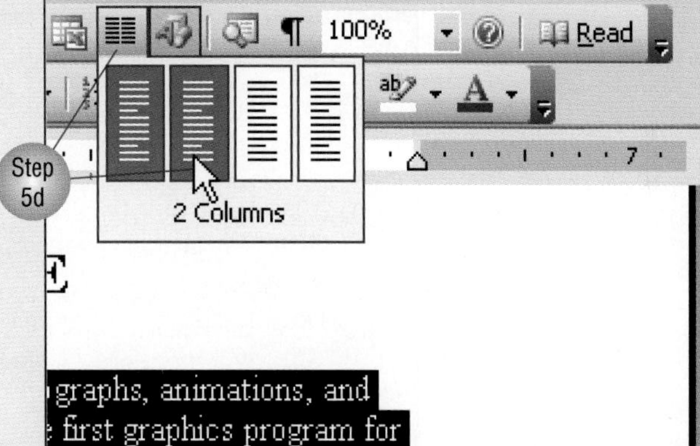

   a. Change the font to 11-point Times New Roman.
   b. Change the line spacing to single.
   c. Set a left tab on the Ruler at the .25-inch mark.
   d. Format the text into two newspaper columns by clicking the Columns button on the Standard toolbar, moving the arrow pointer down and to the right until two columns display with a dark blue background on the Columns grid (and *2 Columns* displays below the grid), and then clicking the mouse button.
   e. Deselect the text.
   f. Select and then bold each of the headings (*Early Painting and Drawing Programs*, *Developments in Painting and Drawing Programs*, and *Painting and Drawing Programs Today*).
   g. Insert 6 points of space before and after each of the three headings in the document (*Early Painting and Drawing Programs*, *Developments in Painting and Drawing Programs* and *Painting and Drawing Programs Today*). ***(Hint: Do this with the* Before *and* After *options at the Paragraph dialog box.)***

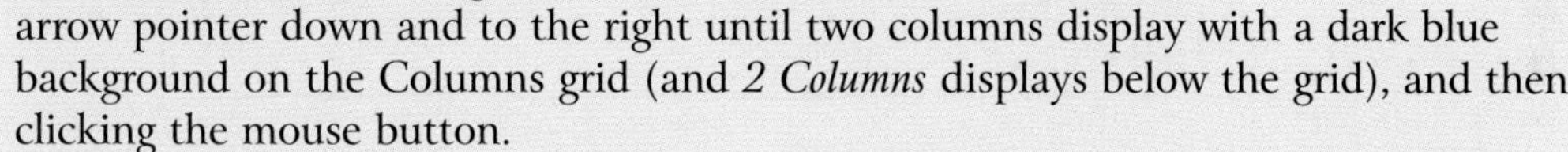

6. Save, print, and then close **swc4x08**.

Creating Newspaper Columns with the Columns Dialog Box

The Columns dialog box can be used to create newspaper columns that are equal or unequal in width. To display the Columns dialog box shown in Figure 4.9, click Format and then Columns. At the Columns dialog box, you can choose from a number of preset columns, choose your own number of columns, specify the width and spacing of specific columns, insert a line between columns, and specify where column formatting is to apply.

FIGURE 4.9 ***Columns Dialog Box***

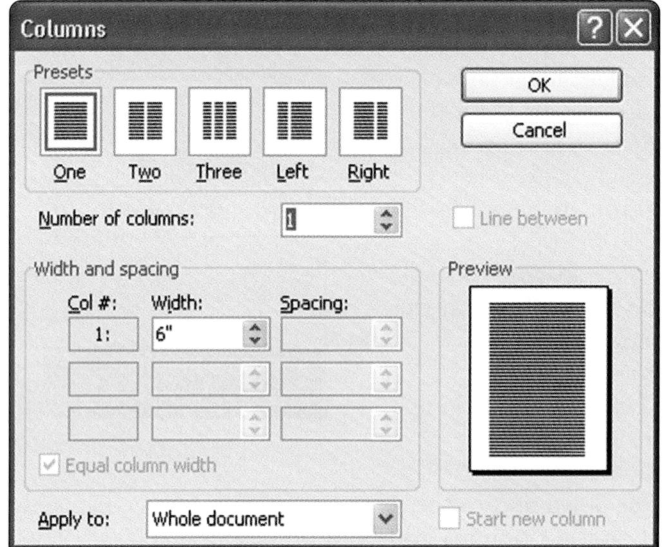

exercise 9 FORMATTING TEXT INTO UNEVEN NEWSPAPER COLUMNS WITH A LINE BETWEEN

1. Open **WordReport02**.
2. Save the document with Save As and name it **swc4x09**.
3. Delete the Section 2 portion of the document. To do this, select the text in the document from the beginning of the title *SECTION 2: COMPUTERS IN ENTERTAINMENT* (located on page 2) to the end of the document, and then press the Delete key.
4. Select the entire document and then change the font to 12-point Bookman Old Style (or a similar serif typeface).
5. Select the title *SECTION 1: COMPUTERS IN COMMUNICATION* and then change the font to 14-point Arial bold.
6. Select the heading *Telecommunications* and then change the font to 12-point Arial bold.
7. Use Format Painter to apply 12-point Arial bold to the two remaining headings (*Publishing* and *News Services*).
8. Select the text from the beginning of the first paragraph to the end of the document and then make the following changes:
   a. Change the line spacing to single.
   b. Set a left tab on the Ruler at the .25-inch mark.
9. Insert 6 points of space before and after each of the three headings (*Telecommunications*, *Publishing*, and *News Services*).

10. Format the text of the report into uneven columns with a line between by completing the following steps:
    a. Change to the Print Layout view.
    b. Position the insertion point at the left margin of the first paragraph.
    c. Click Format and then Columns.
    d. At the Columns dialog box, click the *Right* option in the *Presets* section.
    e. Click the *Line between* check box.
    f. Click the down-pointing arrow at the right side of the *Apply to* option box, and then click *This point forward* at the drop-down list.
    g. Click OK.
    h. If the heading *News Services* displays at the top of the second column, remove the 6 points of space before the heading. (If the heading moves to the bottom of the first column, position the insertion point at the beginning of the heading, and then press the Enter key. This should move the heading to the top of the second column.)
11. Save, print, and then close **swc4x09**.

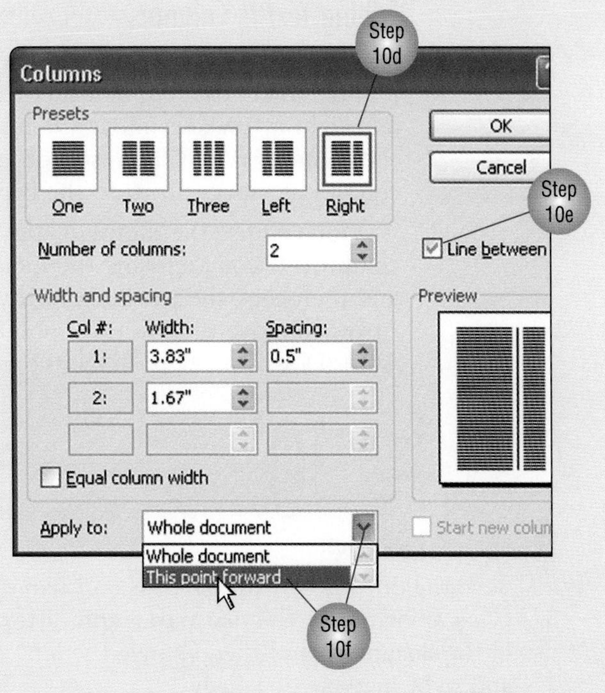

Inserting a Column and/or Page Break

When formatting text into columns, Word automatically breaks the columns to fit the page. At times, column breaks may appear in an undesirable location. For example, a heading may appear at the bottom of the column, while the text after the heading begins at the top of the next column. You can insert a column break by positioning the insertion point where you want the column to end and begin a new page by pressing Ctrl + Shift + Enter. You can also insert a column break by positioning the insertion point at the location where the new column is to begin, then clicking Insert and then Break. At the Break dialog box, click Column break, and then click OK.

HINT

Prevent Word from inserting a column break within a paragraph of text by selecting the paragraph and then clicking the *Keep lines together* option at the Paragraph dialog box with the Line and Page Breaks tab selected.

Balancing Columns on a Page

In a document containing text formatted into columns, Word automatically lines up (balances) the last line of text at the bottom of each column, except on the last page. Text in the first column of the last page may flow to the end of the page, while the text in the second column may end far short of the end of the page. Columns can be balanced by inserting a section break at the end of the text. To do this, position the insertion point at the end of the text in the last column of the section you want to balance, click Insert, and then click Break. At the Break dialog box, click *Continuous*, and then click OK.

Editing Text in Columns

To move the insertion point in a document using the mouse, position the I-beam pointer where desired, and then click the left button. On the keyboard, the left and right arrow keys move the insertion point in the direction indicated within the column. When the insertion point gets to the end of the line within the column, it moves down to the beginning of the next line within the same column.

You can use the mouse or the keyboard to move the insertion point between columns. If you are using the mouse, position the I-beam pointer where desired, and then click the left button. If you are using the keyboard, press Alt + Up Arrow to move the insertion point to the top of the previous column, or press Alt + Down Arrow to move the insertion point to the top of the next column.

exercise 10

EDITING TEXT IN NEWSPAPER COLUMNS

1. Open **swc4x08**.
2. Save the document with Save As and name it **swc4x10**.
3. Click anywhere in the first paragraph of text in the document and then change the left and right margins to 1 inch.
4. Select the entire document and then change the font to 11-point Bookman Old Style (or a similar serif typeface).
5. Change the spacing between the two columns by completing the following steps:
   a. Position the insertion point somewhere in the first paragraph.
   b. Click Format and then Columns.
   c. At the Columns dialog box, click the down-pointing arrow at the right side of the *Spacing* text box (located in the *Width and spacing* section) until *0.3"* displays.
   d. Click OK to close the dialog box.

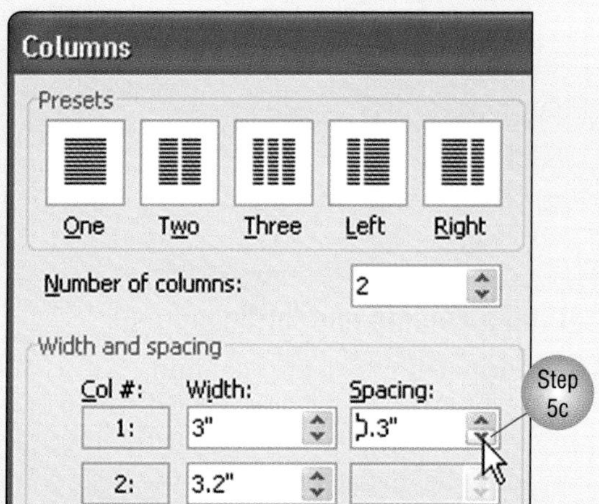

6. Select the title and then change the font to 16-point Tahoma bold.
7. Select the heading *Early Painting and Drawing Programs* and then change the font to 11-point Tahoma bold.
8. Use Format Painter to apply 11-point Tahoma bold to the two remaining headings.
9. If the heading *Developments in Painting and Drawing Programs* displays at the top of the second column, remove the 6 points of space before the heading. (If the heading moves to the bottom of the first column, position the insertion point at the beginning of the heading, and then press the Enter key. This should move the heading to the top of the second column.)
10. Balance the text on the last page by completing the following steps:
    a. Press Ctrl + End to move the insertion point to the end of the document.
    b. Click Insert and then Break.
    c. At the Break dialog box, click *Continuous*.
    d. Click OK.
11. Save, print, and then close **swc4x10**.

Removing Column Formatting

To remove column formatting using the Columns button, position the insertion point in the section containing columns, or select the text in columns. Click the Columns button on the Standard toolbar and then click the first column in the Columns grid. To remove column formatting using the Columns dialog box, position the insertion point in the section containing columns or select the text in columns, click Format, and then click Columns. At the Columns dialog box, click *One* in the *Presets* section, and then click OK or press Enter.

Checking the Spelling and Grammar of a Document

Word includes writing tools to help create a thoughtful and well-written document. Two of these tools are a spelling checker and a grammar checker. The spelling checker finds misspelled words and offers replacement words. It also finds duplicate words and irregular capitalizations. When you spell check a document, the spelling checker compares the words in your document with the words in its dictionary. If a match is found, the word is passed over. If there is no match for the word, the spelling checker will stop, select the word, and offer replacements.

The grammar checker will search a document for errors in grammar, style, punctuation, and word usage. The spelling checker and the grammar checker can help you create a well-written document but do not replace the need for proofreading. You would complete the following steps to complete a spelling and grammar check:

1. Click the Spelling and Grammar button on the Standard toolbar or click Tools and then Spelling and Grammar.
2. If a spelling error is detected, the misspelled word is selected and a Spelling and Grammar dialog box similar to the one shown in Figure 4.10 displays. The sentence containing the misspelled word is displayed in the *Not in Dictionary* text box. If a grammatical error is detected, the sentence containing the error is selected and the Spelling and Grammar dialog box similar to the one shown in Figure 4.11 displays.
3. If a misspelled word is selected, replace the word with the correct spelling, tell Word to ignore it and continue checking the document, or add the word to a custom dictionary. If a sentence containing a grammatical error is selected, the grammar checker displays the sentence in the top text box in the Spelling and Grammar dialog box. Choose to ignore or change errors found by the grammar checker.
4. When the spelling and grammar check is completed, a message displays telling you the spelling and grammar check is complete. Click OK to remove the message.

Spelling and Grammar

HINT

Complete a spelling and grammar check on a portion of a document by selecting the text first and then clicking the Spelling and Grammar button.

Check Spelling and Grammar

1. Click Spelling and Grammar button.
2. Change or ignore error.
3. Click OK.

FIGURE

4.10 ***Spelling and Grammar Dialog Box with Spelling Error Selected***

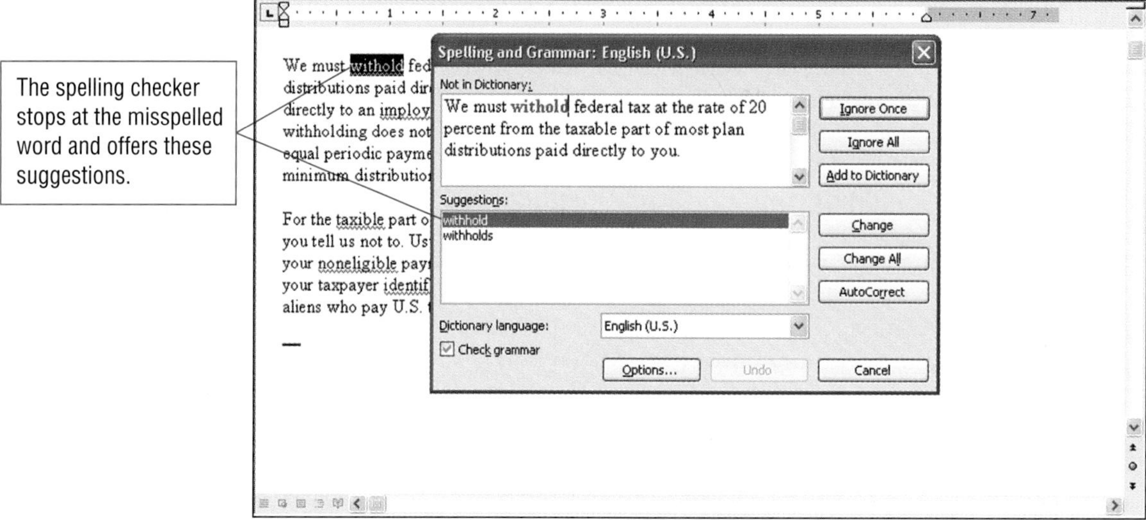

FIGURE

4.11 ***Spelling and Grammar Dialog Box with Grammar Error Selected***

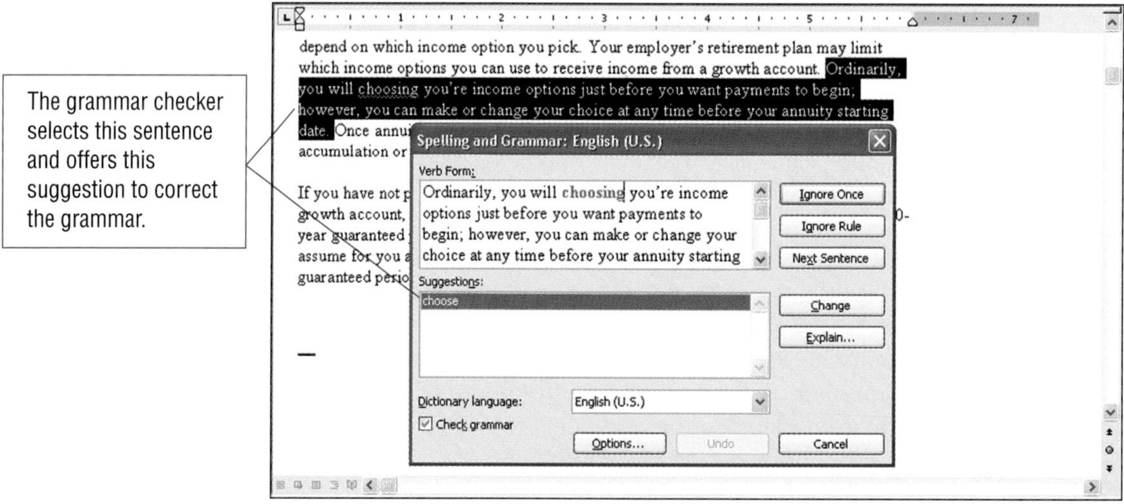

When a word is selected during a spelling and grammar check, you need to determine if the word should be corrected or if it should be ignored. Word provides buttons at the right side and bottom of the Spelling and Grammar dialog box to make decisions. The buttons will change depending on whether a misspelled word or a sentence containing a grammatical error is selected. Table 4.2 describes the buttons and the functions performed by the buttons.

TABLE 4.2 **Spelling and Grammar Checking Buttons**

Button	**Function**
Ignore Once	Click the Ignore Once button to skip the current misspelled word.
Ignore All	Click the Ignore All button to skip all occurrences of the misspelled word in the document.
Add to Dictionary	Besides the spelling checker dictionary, a custom dictionary is available. Click the Add to Dictionary button if you want to add the selected word to the custom dictionary.
Change	Replace the selected word with the word in the *Suggestions* list box by clicking the Change button. (If you want to replace the selected word with one of the other words displayed in the *Suggestions* list box, double-click the desired word.)
Change All	Click the Change All button if you want to correct the current word and the same word in other locations in the document.
AutoCorrect	Misspelled words and the correct spelling can be added to the AutoCorrect list. When the spelling checker stops at a misspelled word, make sure the proper spelling is selected in the *Suggestions* list box, and then click the AutoCorrect button.
Undo	When the Spelling and Grammar dialog box first displays, the Undo button is dimmed. Once a spelling or grammar change is made, the Undo button becomes active. Click this button if you want to reverse the most recent spelling and grammar action.

By default, the spelling and grammar are checked in a document. You can turn off the grammar checker and perform only a spelling check. To do this, click the *Check grammar* option at the Spelling and Grammar dialog box (located in the lower left corner) to remove the check mark.

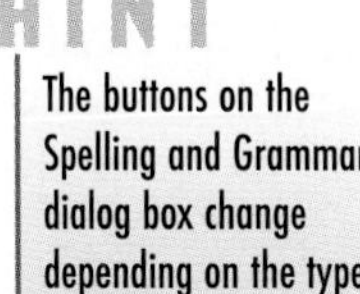

HINT

The buttons on the Spelling and Grammar dialog box change depending on the type of error selected.

exercise 11

SPELL CHECKING A DOCUMENT

1. Open **WordSpellCheck01**.
2. Save the document with Save As and name it **swc4x11**.
3. Perform a spelling check by completing the following steps:
   a. Click the Spelling and Grammar button on the Standard toolbar.

b. The spelling checker selects the word *withold*. The proper spelling is selected in the *Suggestions* list box, so click the Change All button. (Because this word is misspelled in other locations in the document, clicking the Change All button will change the other misspellings.)

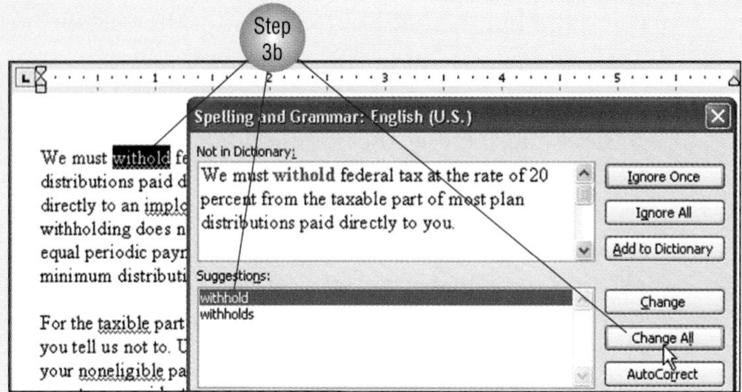

c. The spelling checker selects the word *distrabution*. The proper spelling is selected in the *Suggestions* list box, so click the Change button. (Click the Change button because the word is only misspelled once.)
d. The spelling checker selects the word *imployer*. The proper spelling is selected in the *Suggestions* list box, so click the Change button.
e. The spelling checker selects the word *fedaral*. The proper spelling is selected in the *Suggestions* list box, so click the Change All button.
f. The spelling checker selects *yaers*. The proper spelling is selected in the *Suggestions* list box, so click the Change button.
g. The spelling checker selects *taxible*. The proper spelling is selected in the *Suggestions* list box, so click the Change button.
h. If the spelling checker selects *noneligible*, click Ignore All to skip the word (it is spelled properly).
i. The spelling checker selects the word *identificatoin*. The proper spelling is selected in the *Suggestions* list box, so click the Change button.
j. At the message telling you that the spelling and grammar check is complete, click the OK button.

4. Save, print, and then close **swc4x11**.

Editing while Spell Checking

When spell checking a document, you can temporarily leave the Spelling and Grammar dialog box, make corrections in the document, and then resume spell checking. For example, suppose while spell checking you notice a sentence that you want to change. To correct the sentence, move the I-beam pointer to the location in the sentence where the change is to occur, click the left mouse button, and then make changes to the sentence. To resume spell checking, click the Resume button, which was formerly the Ignore Once button.

exercise 12

SPELL CHECKING A DOCUMENT WITH WORDS IN UPPERCASE AND WITH NUMBERS

1. Open **WordSpellCheck02**.
2. Save the document with Save As and name it **swc4x12**.
3. Check spell checking options by completing the following steps:
   a. Click Tools and then Options.
   b. At the Options dialog box, click the Spelling & Grammar tab.
   c. Make sure a check mark displays in the *Ignore words in UPPERCASE* check box. (If a check mark does not display, click in the check box before *Ignore words in UPPERCASE* to insert one.)
   d. Make sure a check mark displays in the *Ignore words with numbers* check box. (If a check mark does not display, click in the check box before *Ignore words with numbers* to insert one.)
   e. Click OK to close the dialog box.

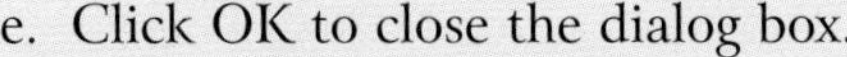

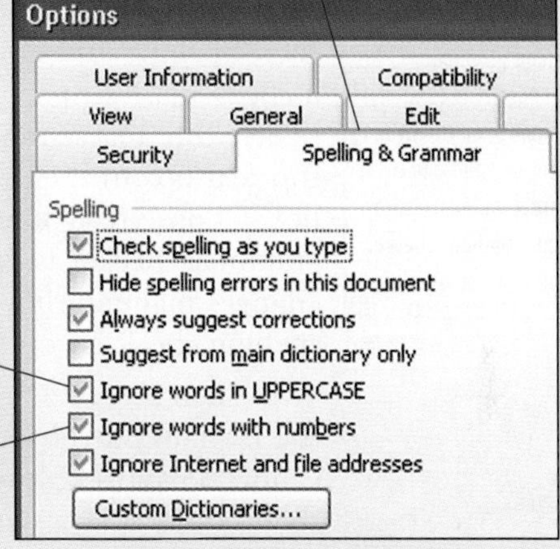

4. Perform a spelling check by completing the following steps:
   a. Click the Spelling and Grammar button on the Standard toolbar.
   b. The spelling checker selects the word *beigin*. The proper spelling is selected in the *Suggestions* list box, so click the Change button (or Change All button).
   c. The spelling checker selects the word *aney*. The proper spelling of the word is selected in the *Suggestions* list box, so click the Change button (or Change All button).
   d. The spelling checker selects *seperated*. The proper spelling is selected in the *Suggestions* list box, so click the Change button (or Change All button).
   e. The spelling checker selects *annuty*. The proper spelling is selected in the *Suggestions* list box, so click the Change button (or Change All button).
   f. The spelling checker selects *searies*. The proper spelling is selected in the *Suggestions* list box, so click the Change button (or Change All button).
   g. The spelling checker selects *gros*. The proper spelling is selected in the *Suggestions* list box, so click the Change button (or Change All button).
   h. The spelling checker selects *laess*. The proper spelling *less* is not selected in the *Suggestions* list box but it is one of the words suggested. Click *less* in the *Suggestions* list box, and then click the Change button.

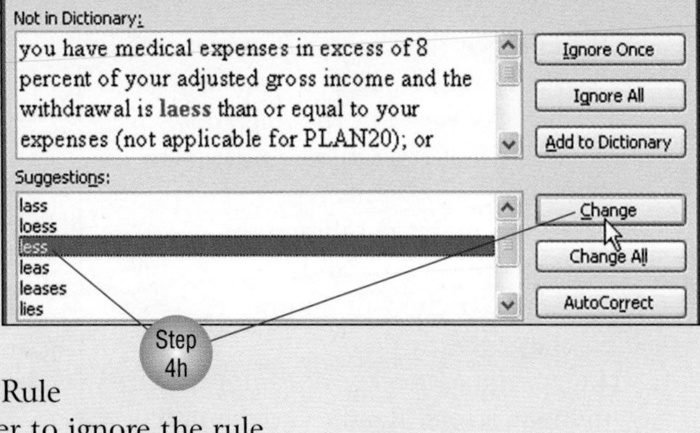

   i. The grammar checker selects *you are required to make a payment to someone besides yourself under a MIRA plan.* and displays information on commonly confused words. Click the Ignore Rule button to tell the grammar checker to ignore the rule.
   j. When the message displays telling you that the spelling and grammar check is complete, click the OK button.
5. Save, print, and then close **swc4x12**.

Checking the Grammar and Style of a Document

Word includes a grammar checking feature that you can use to search a document for grammar, style, punctuation, and word usage. Like the spelling checker, the grammar checker does not find every error in a document and may stop at correct phrases. The grammar checker can help you create a well-written document, but does not replace the need for proofreading.

HINT

Read grammar suggestions carefully. Some suggestions may not be valid and a problem identified by the grammar checker may not be a problem.

To complete a grammar check (as well as a spelling check) on a document, click the Spelling and Grammar button on the Standard toolbar or click Tools and then Spelling and Grammar. (At the Spelling and Grammar dialog box, make sure a check mark displays in the *Check grammar* check box.) The grammar checker selects the first sentence with a grammatical error and displays the sentence in the top text box in the dialog box with a suggested correction in the *Suggestions* text box. Choose to ignore or change errors found by the grammar checker. When the grammar checker is done, the open document is displayed on the screen. The changes made during the check are inserted in the document. By default, a spelling check is completed on a document during a grammar check.

When a grammar error displays in the Spelling and Grammar dialog box, click the Explain button. An explanation of the violated grammar rule displays in a yellow box next to the Office Assistant.

exercise 13

CHECKING GRAMMAR IN A DOCUMENT

1. Open **WordGrammarCheck01**.
2. Save the document with Save As and name it **swc4x13**.
3. Perform a grammar check by completing the following steps:
   a. Click the Spelling and Grammar button on the Standard toolbar.
   b. The grammar checker selects the sentence that begins *Ordinarily, you will choosing you're income options...* and displays *choose* in the *Suggestions* text box.
   c. Click the Explain button, read the information about verb forms that displays in a yellow box next to the Office Assistant, and then click the Change button.
   d. The grammar checker selects the sentence that begins *If your married, McCormack Funds may assume...* and displays *you're* in the *Suggestions* list box. Click the Change button to change *your* to *you're*.
   e. At the message telling you that the spelling and grammar check is complete, click OK.
4. The grammar checker does not find all grammar errors. Read the document and correct the errors not selected by the grammar checker.
5. Save, print, and then close **swc4x13**.

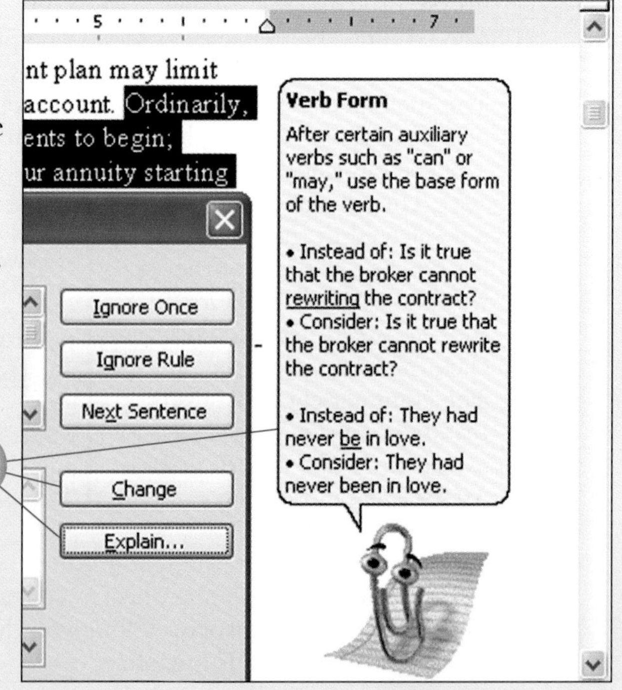
nt plan may limit
account. Ordinarily,
ents to begin;
ur annuity starting
Ignore Once
Ignore Rule
Next Sentence
Change
Explain...
Step 3c
Verb Form
After certain auxiliary verbs such as "can" or "may," use the base form of the verb.
• Instead of: Is it true that the broker cannot rewriting the contract?
• Consider: Is it true that the broker cannot rewrite the contract?
• Instead of: They had never be in love.
• Consider: They had never been in love.

Displaying Word, Paragraph, and Character Counts

With the Word Count option from the Tools menu, the number of pages, words, characters, paragraphs, and lines in a document can be displayed. To use this option, open the document for which you want the word count displayed, click Tools, and then click Word Count. This displays a Word Count dialog box similar to the one shown in Figure 4.12.

Display Word Count
Click Tools, Word Count.

FIGURE 4.12 ***Word Count Dialog Box***

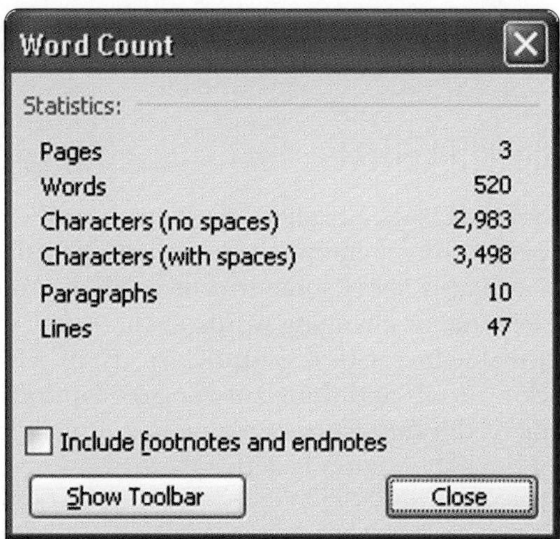

You can also display the word count in a document with the Word Count toolbar. Display this toolbar by clicking View, pointing to Toolbars, and then clicking Word Count. Another method for displaying the toolbar is to click the Show Toolbar button at the Word Count dialog box. At the Word Count toolbar, click the Recount button to display the current number of words in the document. Close the Word Count toolbar by clicking the Close button (contains an *X*) that displays in the upper right corner of the toolbar.

exercise 14 DISPLAYING WORD, PARAGRAPH, AND CHARACTER COUNTS

1. Open **WordReport01**.
2. Display a word count for the document by completing the following steps:
   a. Click Tools and then Word Count.
   b. After reading the statistics in the Word Count dialog box, click the Close button.
3. Close **WordReport01** without saving changes.
4. Open **WordReport03**.
5. Display the Word Count toolbar by clicking View, pointing to Toolbars, and then clicking Word Count.

6. Click the Recount button on the Word Count toolbar.
7. Close **WordReport03** without saving the changes.
8. Open **WordDocument05**.
9. Make sure the Word Count toolbar is displayed.
10. Click the Recount button on the Word Count toolbar.
11. Close the Word Count toolbar by clicking the Close button (contains an *X*) located in the upper right corner of the toolbar.
12. Close **WordDocument05** without saving the changes.

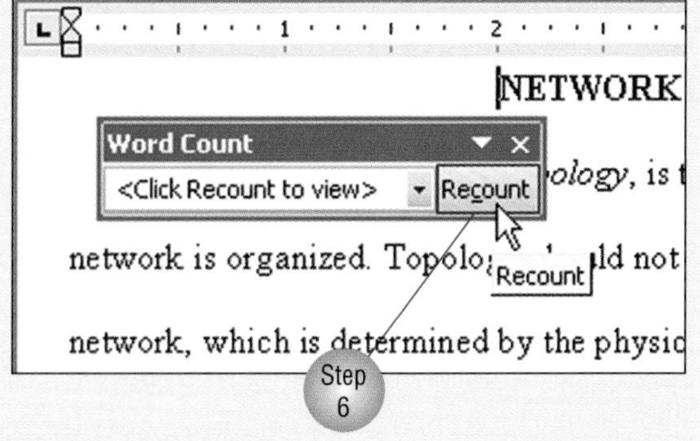

QUICK STEPS

Insert Word(s) in AutoCorrect
1. Click Tools, AutoCorrect Options.
2. Click AutoCorrect tab.
3. Type misspelled or abbreviated word.
4. Press Tab.
5. Type correctly spelled word or complete word(s).
6. Click Add button.
7. Click OK.

Customizing AutoCorrect

The AutoCorrect feature automatically detects and corrects some typographical errors, misspelled words, grammar errors, and irregular capitalizations. AutoCorrect will also insert some text or symbols. You can customize AutoCorrect by adding, deleting, or changing words at the AutoCorrect dialog box. Display the AutoCorrect dialog box with the AutoCorrect tab selected as shown in Figure 4.13, by clicking Tools and then AutoCorrect Options. Several options display at the beginning of the AutoCorrect dialog box. If a check appears in the check box before the option, the option is active.

FIGURE 4.13 ***AutoCorrect Dialog Box***

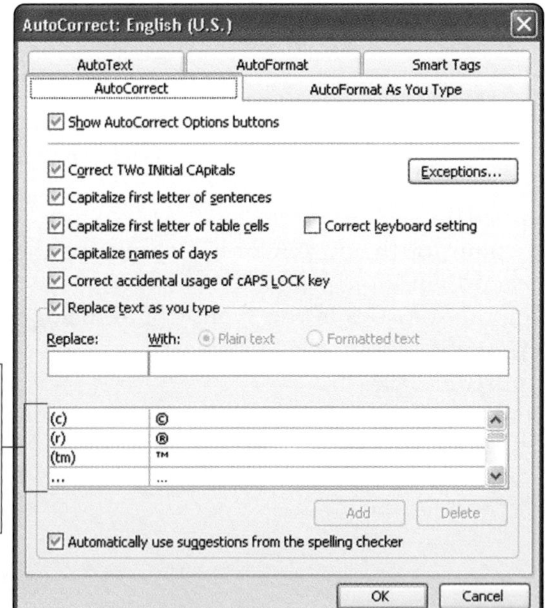

If you type the text shown in the first column of this list box and then press the spacebar, it is replaced by the text shown in the second column.

Adding a Word to AutoCorrect

Commonly misspelled words or typographical errors can be added to AutoCorrect. For example, if you consistently type *relavent* instead of *relevant*, you can add *relavent* to AutoCorrect and tell it to correct it as *relevant*. To do this, you would display the AutoCorrect dialog box, type **relavent** in the *Replace* text box, type **relevant** in the *With* text box, and then click the Add button. The next time you type *relavent* and then press the spacebar, AutoCorrect will change it to *relevant*.

HINT

Make sure the name chosen for an AutoCorrect entry is not a word you might need in a document.

Deleting a Word from AutoCorrect

A word that is contained in AutoCorrect can be deleted. To delete a word, display the AutoCorrect dialog box, click the desired word in the list box (you may need to click the down arrow to display the desired word), and then click the Delete button.

exercise 15

ADDING TEXT TO AND DELETING TEXT FROM AUTOCORRECT

1. At a clear document screen, add words to AutoCorrect by completing the following steps:
   a. Click Tools and then AutoCorrect Options.
   b. At the AutoCorrect dialog box with the AutoCorrect tab selected, make sure the insertion point is positioned in the *Replace* text box. If not, click in the *Replace* text box.
   c. Type **dtp**.
   d. Press the Tab key (this moves the insertion point to the *With* text box) and then type **desktop publishing**.
   e. Click the Add button. (This adds *dtp* and *desktop publishing* to the AutoCorrect and also selects *dtp* in the *Replace* text box.)
   f. Type **particuler** in the *Replace* text box. (When you begin typing **particuler**, *dtp* is automatically deleted.)
   g. Press the Tab key and then type **particular**.
   h. Click the Add button.
   i. With the insertion point positioned in the *Replace* text box, type **populer**.
   j. Press the Tab key and then type **popular**.
   k. Click the Add button.
   l. With the insertion point positioned in the *Replace* text box, type **tf**.
   m. Press the Tab key and then type **typeface**.
   n. Click the Add button.
   o. Click OK.

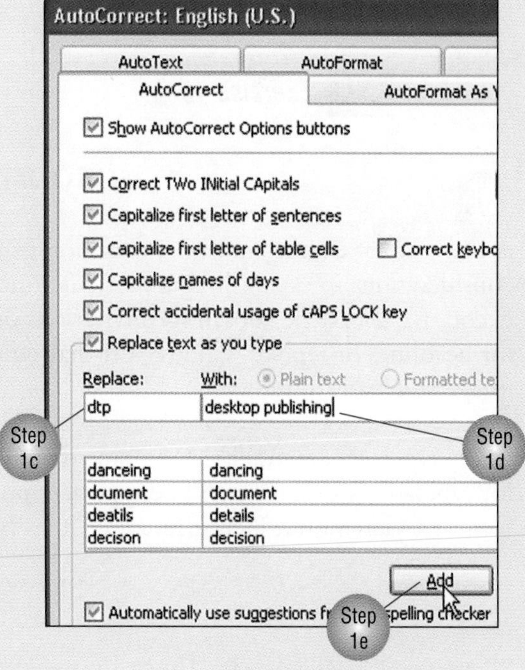

2. Type the text shown in Figure 4.14. (Type the text exactly as shown. AutoCorrect will correct words as you type.)
3. Save the document and name it **swc4x15**.
4. Print **swc4x15**.
5. Delete the words you added to AutoCorrect by completing the following steps:
    a. Click Tools and then AutoCorrect Options.
    b. At the AutoCorrect dialog box, click *dtp* in the list box. (Click the down-pointing arrow in the list box scroll bar until *dtp* is visible and then click *dtp*.)
    c. Click the Delete button.
    d. Click the *particuler* option in the list box.
    e. Click the Delete button.
    f. Click the *populer* option in the list box.
    g. Click the Delete button.
    h. Click the *tf* option in the list box.
    i. Click the Delete button.
    j. Click OK.
6. Close **swc4x15**.

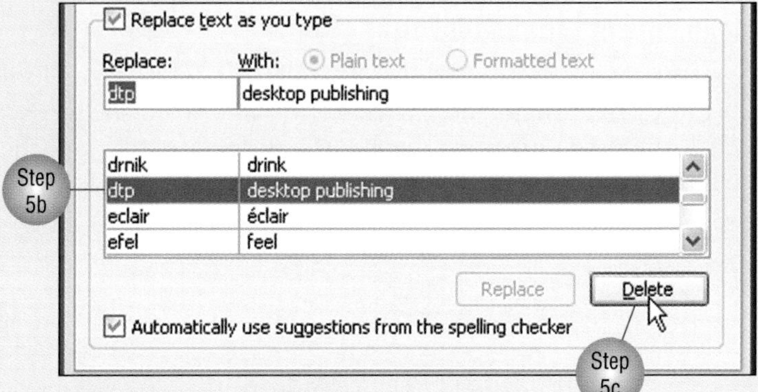

FIGURE 4.14 ***Exercise 15***

CHOOSING A TYPEFACE

A tf is a set of characters with a common general design and shape. One of teh most important considerations in establishing a particuler mood or feeling in a document is the tf. For example, a decorative tf may be chosen for invitations or menus, while a simple block-style tf may be chosen for headlines or reports. Choose a tf that reflects the contents, your audience expectations, and the image you want to project.

Many typefaces are available adn new designs are created on a regular basis. The most populer tf for typewriters is Courier. Some typefaces populer with dtp programs include Arial, Bookman, Century, Garamond, Helvetica, and Times New Roman.

Using the Thesaurus

Word offers a Thesaurus feature that can be used to find synonyms, antonyms, and related words for a particular word. Synonyms are words that have the same or nearly the same meaning. When using the Thesaurus, Word may display antonyms for some words. Antonyms are words with opposite meanings. With the Thesaurus, you can improve the clarity of business documents.

To use the Thesaurus, click Tools, point to Language, and then click Thesaurus. This displays the Research task pane. Click in the *Search for* text box located towards the top of the Research task pane, type the word for which you want to find synonyms and antonyms, and then press Enter or click the Start searching button (button containing a white arrow on a green background). This causes a list of synonyms and antonyms to display in the task pane list box. Figure 4.15 shows the Research task pane displaying synonyms and antonyms for the word *rhetoric*.

Start Searching

FIGURE 4.15 **Research Task Pane**

Type a word in this text box, press Enter, and synonyms for the word display in the list box below.

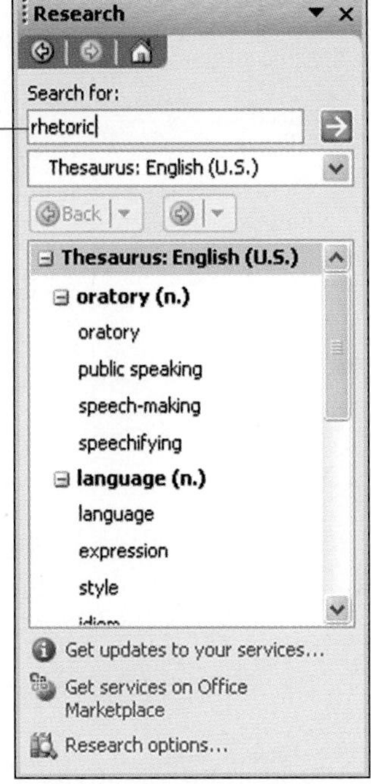

Depending on the word you are looking up, the words in the Research task pane list box may display followed by *(n.)* for *noun*, *(adj.)* for *adjective*, or *(adv.)* for *adverb*. Antonyms may display in the list of related synonyms, generally at the end of the list of related synonyms, and are followed by *(Antonym)*.

QUICK STEPS

Use Thesaurus

1. Click Tools, Language, Thesaurus.
2. Type word in *Search for* text box.
3. Press Enter.

The Thesaurus provides synonyms for the selected word as well as a list of related synonyms. For example, in the task pane list box shown in Figure 4.15, two main synonyms display for *rhetoric—oratory* and *language*—and each is preceded by a minus symbol in a square. The minus symbol indicates that the list of related synonyms is displayed. Click the minus symbol and the list of related synonyms is removed from the task pane list box and the minus symbol changes to a plus symbol. If a synonym displays preceded by a plus symbol, click this symbol to show the list of related synonyms.

As you look up synonyms and antonyms for various words, you can display the list of synonyms and antonyms for the previous word by clicking the Previous search button (contains the word *Back* and a left arrow) located above the Research task pane list box (see Figure 4.15). Click the Next search button to display the next search in the sequence. You can also click the down-pointing arrow at the right side of the Previous search or Next search buttons to display a list of words for which you have looked up synonyms and antonyms.

exercise 16

FINDING SYNONYMS USING THESAURUS

1. At a clear document screen, look up synonyms for the word *symbol* by completing the following steps:
   a. Click Tools, point to Language, and then click Thesaurus.
   b. At the Research task pane, click in the *Search for* text box, and then type **symbol**.

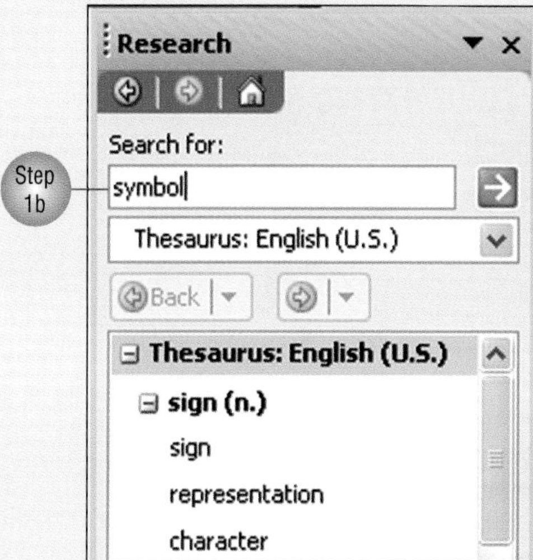

   c. Press the Enter key (or click the Start searching button located to the right of the *Search for* text box).
2. After viewing synonyms for *symbol*, look up synonyms for the word *plethora* by completing the following steps:
   a. Select the word *symbol* that displays in the *Search for* text box.
   b. Type **plethora** and then press Enter.
3. Complete steps similar to those in Step 2 to look up synonyms for the word *subtle*.
4. Close the Research task pane by clicking the Close button (contains an X) located in the upper right corner of the task pane.
5. Close the document without saving it.

If you want to look up synonyms for a word in a document, open the document, click the desired word and then click Tools, point to Language, and then click Thesaurus. To replace the selected word with one of the synonyms in the task pane list box, hover the mouse over the desired synonym until the synonym displays in a box with a down-pointing arrow at the right, and then click the down-pointing arrow. This displays a drop-down list with the options *Insert*, *Copy*, and *Look Up*. Click the *Insert* option and the synonym is inserted in the place of the selected word in the document. Click the *Copy* option to insert a copy of the synonym in the Office clipboard. To insert the copied synonym, move the insertion point to the location where you want the copied synonym, and then click the Paste button on the Standard toolbar. Click the *Look Up* option to display a list of synonyms and antonyms for the selected synonym.

Displaying Synonyms Using a Shortcut Menu

Another method for displaying synonyms for a word is to use a shortcut menu. To do this, position the mouse pointer on the word and then click the *right* mouse button. At the shortcut menu that displays, point to Synonyms, and then click the desired synonym at the side menu. Click the Thesaurus option at the bottom of the side menu to display synonyms and antonyms for the word in the Research task pane.

exercise 17

CHANGING WORDS USING THESAURUS

1. Open **WordDocument03**.
2. Save the document with Save As and name it **swc4x17**.
3. Change the word *rare* in the first paragraph to *unusual* using Thesaurus by completing the following steps:
   a. Click in the word *rare* located in the first paragraph.
   b. Click Tools, point to Language, and then click Thesaurus.
   c. At the Research task pane, hover the mouse pointer over the synonym *unusual*, click the down-pointing arrow that displays at the right of the word, and then click *Insert* at the drop-down list.

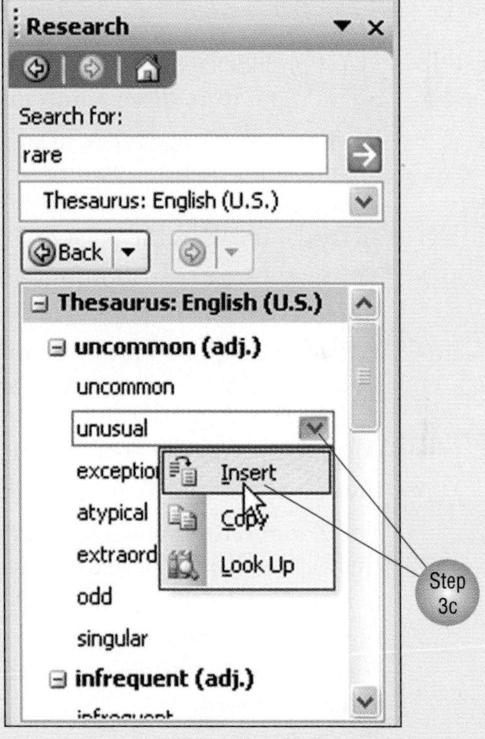

4. Follow similar steps to make the following changes using Thesaurus:
   a. Change *uneasiness* in the first paragraph to *nervousness*.
   b. Change *relatively* in the second paragraph to *comparatively*.
5. Close the Research task pane.
6. Change *phase* in the third paragraph to *stage* using a shortcut menu by completing the following steps:
   a. Position the mouse pointer on the word *phase* located in the second sentence of the third paragraph.
   b. Click the right mouse button.
   c. At the shortcut menu that displays, point to Synonyms, and then click *stage* at the side menu.

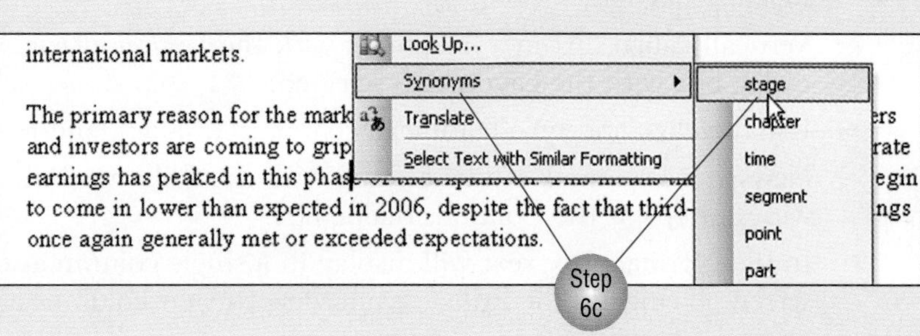

7. Save, print, and then close **swc4x17**.

CHAPTER summary

- Change to the Print Layout view by clicking View and then Print Layout or clicking the Print Layout View button at the left side of the horizontal scroll bar. Change back to the Normal view by clicking View and then Normal or clicking the Normal View button at the left side of the horizontal scroll bar.
- In Print Layout view, remove white space and gray spaces at the top and bottom of each page by positioning the mouse pointer on any gray space at the top or bottom of a page or between pages until the pointer turns into the Hide White Space button, and then click the left mouse button. Complete similar steps to redisplay white and gray spaces.
- By default, a Word document contains 1.25-inch left and right margins and 1-inch top and bottom margins. Change margins at the Page Setup dialog box with the Margins tab selected.
- Word provides two page orientations—portrait and landscape. Change the page orientation at the Page Setup dialog box with the Margins tab selected.
- Word inserts a page break at approximately 10 inches from the top of each page. With the default 1-inch top and bottom margins, this allows a total of 9 inches to be printed on a standard page. The page break displays as a row of dots in the Normal view and as an actual break in the page in Print Layout view.
- The page break that Word inserts automatically is a soft page break. A page break that you insert is a hard page break.
- With Word's Print Preview feature, you can view a partial page, single page, multiple pages, or zoom in on a particular area of a page. With buttons from the Print Preview toolbar at the top of the Print Preview screen, you can change the display of the document, send the document to the printer, and turn the display of the rulers on or off.
- Insert a section break in a document with options at the Break dialog box.
- The Zoom button changes the display of the document in Print Preview. You can also change the display of text in the document screen with the Zoom button on the Standard toolbar or with the Zoom option from the View drop-down menu.
- In Full Screen view, all menus, toolbars, and other tools are hidden, allowing more of the document to be visible on the screen. Click View, Full Screen to display the document in Full Screen view.
- The Reading Layout view displays a document in a format for easy viewing and reading. Navigate in Reading Layout view using the mouse or keys on the keyboard. Use buttons on the Reading Layout toolbar to navigate through the viewing pages and to customize Reading Layout.
- Vertically align text in a document with the *Vertical alignment* option at the Page Setup dialog box with the Layout tab selected.
- Use the click and type feature to center, right-align, and left-align text.
- Newspaper columns can be created with the Columns button on the Standard toolbar or with options at the Columns dialog box.
- In the Normal view, text will display in a single column at the left side of the document screen. Change to the Print Layout view to view columns as they will appear when printed.

- Options at the Columns dialog box let you change the spacing between columns, apply column formatting from the point of the insertion point forward, insert a line between columns, or start a new column.
- To move the insertion point in a document with columns using the mouse, position the mouse pointer where desired, and then click the left button. To move the insertion point with the keyboard, use the arrow keys.
- Column formatting can be removed with the Columns button on the Standard toolbar or at the Columns dialog box.
- Word includes a spelling and grammar checker.
- The spelling checker matches the words in your document with the words in its dictionary. If a match is not found, the word is selected and possible corrections are suggested.
- When checking the spelling and/or grammar in a document, you can temporarily leave the Spelling and Grammar dialog box, make corrections in the document, and then resume checking.
- With the grammar checker, you can search a document for correct grammar, style, punctuation, and word usage.
- Display the number of pages, words, characters, paragraphs, and lines in a document with the Word Count option from the Tools drop-down menu.
- The Word Count toolbar displays the current number of words in the document. Display this toolbar by clicking View, pointing to Toolbars, and then clicking Word Count; or by clicking the Show Toolbar button at the Word Count dialog box.
- Commonly misspelled words, typographical errors, or abbreviations can be added to or deleted from the AutoCorrect dialog box.
- The Thesaurus finds synonyms, antonyms, and related words for a particular word.

FEATURES summary

FEATURE	BUTTON	MENU	KEYBOARD
Print Layout view		View, Print Layout	
Normal view		View, Normal	
Page Setup dialog box		File, Page Setup	
Insert hard page break		Insert, Break, Page Break	Ctrl + Enter
Print Preview		File, Print Preview	Ctrl + F2
Zoom dialog box		View, Zoom	
Full Screen view		View, Full Screen	
Break dialog box		Insert, Break	
Reading Layout view		View, Reading Layout	Alt + R
Close Reading Layout		View, Normal	Alt + C or Esc

FEATURE	BUTTON	MENU	KEYBOARD
Columns dialog box		Format, Columns	
Insert column break		Insert, Break, Column break	Ctrl + Shift + Enter
Spelling and Grammar dialog box		Tools, Spelling and Grammar	F7
Word Count dialog box		Tools, Word Count	
Display Word Count toolbar		View, Toolbars, Word Count	
AutoCorrect dialog box		Tools, AutoCorrect	
Research task pane (Thesaurus)		Tools, Language, Thesaurus	Shift + F7

CONCEPTS check

Completion: On a blank sheet of paper, indicate the correct term, symbol, or command for each description.

1. Remove white and gray space in a document in Print Layout view by positioning the mouse pointer on the gray space that displays between pages until the pointer turns into this button and then clicking the left mouse button.
2. This is the default left and right margin measurement.
3. Press these keys on the keyboard to insert a hard page break.
4. This view displays the document on the screen as it will appear when printed.
5. In this view, all menus, toolbars, and other tools are hidden, allowing more of the document to be visible on the screen.
6. This view displays a document in a format for easy viewing and reading.
7. Vertically align text with the *Vertical alignment* option at the Page Setup dialog box with this tab selected.
8. The Columns button is located on this toolbar.
9. Change to this view to display columns as they will appear when printed.
10. Word provides two page orientations—portrait and this.
11. To complete a spelling and grammar check, click this button on the Standard toolbar.
12. When spell checking a document, click this button at the Spelling and Grammar dialog box to skip all occurrences of the selected word.
13. This toolbar displays the current number of words in the document.
14. This feature finds synonyms, antonyms, and related words for a particular word.
15. List the steps you would complete to add the letters *hs* and the replacement words *holograhic system* at the AutoCorrect dialog box.

SKILLS check

Assessment 1

1. Open **WordReport01**.
2. Save the document with Save As and name it **swc4sc01**.
3. Change the left and right margins to 1 inch.
4. Bold the three headings in the report—*Early Painting and Drawing Programs*, *Developments in Painting and Drawing Programs*, and *Painting and Drawing Programs Today*.
5. Select the entire document, change the line spacing to 1.5, and then deselect the text.
6. Insert a continuous section break at the beginning of the heading *Early Painting and Drawing Programs*.
7. Position the insertion point on any character in the heading *Early Painting and Drawing Programs* and then change the left and right margins to 1.5 inches.
8. Preview the document.
9. Save and then print **swc4sc01**.
10. Delete the continuous section break. ***(Hint: To do this, display the document in Normal view, position the insertion point on the section break, and then press the Delete key.)***
11. Change the page orientation to landscape.
12. Save, print, and then close **swc4sc01**.

Assessment 2

1. Open **WordReport03**.
2. Save the document with Save As and name it **swc4sc02**.
3. Change the left and right margins to 1 inch.
4. Set the title *NETWORK TOPOLOGIES* in 16-point Times New Roman bold.
5. Set the three headings in the document (*Linear Bus Networks*, *Star Networks*, and *Ring Networks*) in 14-point Times New Roman bold.
6. Select the text from the beginning of the first paragraph (begins with *A network's layout...*) to the end of the document and then make the following changes:
   a. Change the line spacing to single.
   b. Set a left tab at the .25-inch mark on the Ruler.
   c. Format the selected text into two even columns.
7. Insert 6 points of space before and after each of the three headings in the document (*Linear Bus Networks*, *Star Networks*, and *Ring Networks*).
8. Switch to Reading Layout view, navigate through the viewing pages in the document, and then turn off the Reading Layout view.
9. Display the Word Count dialog box, view the document statistics, and then close the Word Count dialog box.
10. Save, print, and then close **swc4sc02**.

Assessment 3

1. Open **swc4sc02**.
2. Save the document with Save As and name it **swc4sc03**.
3. Change the left and right margins to 1.25 inches.
4. Change the width between the columns to .3 inch and insert a line between the columns.
5. Save, print, and then close **swc4sc03**.

Assessment 4

1. Open **WordSpellCheck03**.
2. Save the document with Save As and name it **swc4sc04**.
3. Complete a spelling check on the document.
4. After completing the spell check, set the entire document in a serif typeface of your choosing (other than Times New Roman).
5. Set the title and two headings in a sans serif typeface.
6. Move the insertion point to the end of the document and then insert the current date and time.
7. Save, print, and then close **swc4sc04**.

Assessment 5

1. Open **WordGrammarCheck02**.
2. Save the document with Save As and name it **swc4sc05**.
3. Complete a grammar check on the document. You determine what to change and what to leave as written. After the grammar check is completed, proofread the document and make any necessary changes not selected by the grammar checker.
4. Set the entire document in a serif typeface of your choosing (other than Times New Roman).
5. Set the title in a larger sans serif font.
6. Double-space the paragraph in the document and change the alignment of the paragraph to justified.
7. Change the page orientation to landscape.
8. Save, print, and then close **swc4sc05**.

Assessment 6

1. At a clear document screen, add the following words to AutoCorrect:
   a. Insert *RM* in the *Replace* text box and insert *Reinburg Manufacturing* in the *With* text box.
   b. Insert *LWU* in the *Replace* text box and insert *Labor Worker's Union* in the *With* text box.
2. Type the text shown in Figure 4.16.
3. Save the document and name it **swc4sc06**.
4. Print **swc4sc06**.
5. Delete the two names you added to AutoCorrect.
6. Close **swc4sc06**.

FIGURE 4.16 ***Assessment 6***

CONTRACT NEGOTIATIONS BEGIN

Contract negotiations between RM and the LWU begin Monday, March 14, 2005. Delia Weland is the lead negotiator for RM and Avery Schaffer is lead negotiator for the LWU. For questions, comments, or concerns for RM please contact extension 4320 or extension 9392 for the LWU.

Assessment 7

1. Use the Help feature to learn how to change the writing style option from *Grammar Only* to *Grammar & Style*. ***(Hint: Make this change with the* Writing style *option at the Options dialog box with the Spelling & Grammar tab selected.)***
2. Change the writing style to *Grammar & Style* at the Options dialog box with the Spelling & Grammar tab selected.
3. Open **WordGrammarCheck02**.
4. Save the document with Save As and name it **swc4sc07**.
5. Complete a grammar check on the document. You determine what to change and what to leave as written. After the grammar check is completed, proofread the document and make any necessary changes not selected by the grammar checker.
6. Make the following changes to the document:
   a. Set the entire document in a serif typeface of your choosing (other than Times New Roman).
   b. Set the title in a larger sans serif font.
   c. Double-space the paragraph in the document and change the alignment of the paragraph to justified.
7. Display the Options dialog box with the Spelling & Grammar tab selected, change the writing style back to *Grammar Only*, and then close the dialog box.
8. Save, print, and then close **swc4sc07**.

CHAPTER challenge

Case study

You work with a financial consultant at Steven's Financial Services. You have been asked to prepare a report on managing personal budgets. The report will include a title page that is vertically and horizontally centered. You have not been given specific information for the report; however, the first page should be left blank so that text can be added later. The second page should include a monthly budget model set up in columns. Research personal budgets on the Internet and determine at least five monthly expenses that could be included. Using the columns feature, design the budget model so that in the first column the five expense areas are listed (one per row). In the second column, add a blank line (an underscore) so that percents or actual amounts for each expense can be entered later. Since this will be the only information on page two of the report, properly position and format the text for ease of reading. Save and print the file.

To add a little variety to the report, the financial consultant wants an appropriate graphic to be added to the background of the title page. Use the Help feature to learn more about watermarks. Insert a picture watermark on the title page. Save the file and print only the title page.

The financial consultant has been asked to create a PowerPoint slideshow to present the budget information at a seminar next month. Part of her presentation will consist of the personal budget model you created in the first part of the Chapter Challenge. The consultant would like you to begin creating the presentation by copying the budget model (page two of your report) onto a blank slide in PowerPoint. Add a template design to the presentation. Save the file and print the slide containing the budget model.

WORK IN Progress

Unit 1: Editing and Formatting Documents

ASSESSING proficiencies

In this unit, you have learned to create, edit, save, and print Word documents. You also learned to format characters and paragraphs and apply formatting to documents.

(Note: Before completing unit assessments, delete the WordChapter04S folder on your disk. Next, copy to your disk the WordUnit01S subfolder from the Word2003Specialist folder on the CD that accompanies this textbook and then make WordUnit01S the active folder.)

Assessment 1

1. At a clear document screen, type the text shown in Figure U1.1.
2. Save the document and name it **swu1pa01**.
3. Print and then close **swu1pa01**.

GLOSSARY

Acoustical energy: A form of energy related to signals generated by some form of sound such as a voice.

Analog signal: A continuously varying electromagnetic wave whose signal pattern changes based on the information being transmitted.

Asynchronous transmission: The transmission of data one character at a time through a method that denotes the beginning and end of each character; the devices used in sending and receiving the data are not synchronized for the transmission.

Attenuation: Decrease in the strength of a signal as it moves away from its source; the strength of the signal is generally measured in decibels, the method developed to measure the loudness of sound.

Figure U1.1 • Assessment 1

Assessment 2

1. Open **swu1pa01**.
2. Save the document with Save As and name it **swu1pa02**.
3. Make the following changes to the document:
   a. Change the top, left, and right margins to 1.5 inches.
   b. Select the paragraphs that begin with bolded words, change the paragraph alignment to justified, and then insert numbering.
   c. Select the entire document and then change the font to 12-point Century (or a similar serif typeface).
   d. Move the insertion point to the end of the document, a double-space below the text in the document, and then type the following:
      Telecommunications for Today®
      Glossary Prepared by Daria Caráquez
4. Save, print, and then close **swu1pa02**.

Assessment 3

1. Open **WordDocument09**.
2. Save the document with Save As and name it **swu1pa03**.
3. Make the following changes to the document:
   a. Bold the following text that appears at the beginning of the second through the fifth paragraphs:
      Average annual total return:
      Annual total return:
      Accumulation units:
      Accumulative rates:
   b. Select the paragraphs of text in the body of the document (all paragraphs except the title and the blank line below the title).
   c. With the paragraphs of text selected, change the paragraph alignment to justified.
   d. Select the paragraphs that begin with bolded words and then indent the text .5 inch from the left margin.
   e. Move the insertion point to the end of the document a double space below the last paragraph of text and then insert the current date as a date code.
4. Save and then print **swu1pa03**.
5. With the document still open, select the paragraphs that begin with the bolded words, and then indent the paragraphs .5 inch from the right margin (the left margin should already be indented .5 inch).
6. Save, print, and then close **swu1pa03**.

Assessment 4

1. At a clear document screen, type the text shown in Figure U1.2 with the following specifications:
   a. Bold and center the title as shown.
   b. You determine the tab settings for the text in columns.
   c. Select the entire document and then change the font to 12-point Arial.
   d. Vertically center the text on the page.

2. Save the document and name it **swu1pa04**.
3. Print and then close **swu1pa04**.

INCOME BY DIVISION

	2003	**2004**	**2005**
Public Relations	$14,375	$16,340	$16,200
Database Services	9,205	15,055	13,725
Graphic Design	18,400	21,790	19,600
Technical Support	5,780	7,325	9,600

Figure U1.2 • Assessment 4

Assessment 5

1. At a clear document screen, type the text shown in Figure U1.3 with the following specifications:
   a. Bold and center the title as shown.
   b. You determine the tab settings for the text in columns.
   c. Select the entire document and then change the font to 12-point Bookman Old Style (or a similar serif typeface).
   d. Vertically center the text on the page.
2. Save the document and name it **swu1pa05**.
3. Print and then close **swu1pa05**.

TABLE OF CONTENTS

Telecommunications Services 1

Telecommunications Facts and Figures 3

Technology in the Future 7

Electronic Mail and Messaging Systems 9

Cellular Mobile Telephone Technology 12

Local Area Networks 17

Figure U1.3 • Assessment 5

Assessment 6

1. At a clear document screen, type the text shown in Figure U1.4 with the following specifications:
   a. Change the font to 16-point Braggadocio and the color to dark blue. (If Braggadocio is not available, choose another font.)
   b. Animate the title *Telecommunications Seminar* with an animation effect of your choosing. (The animation effect will not print.)
   c. Change the line spacing to 1.5.
   d. Select the five lines of text, insert a paragraph border of your choosing, and then deselect the text.
   e. Center the text vertically on the page.
2. Save the document and name it **swu1pa06**.
3. Print and then close **swu1pa06**.

Telecommunications Seminar

Wednesday, March 16, 2005

Carson Convention Center

Room 108

8:30 a.m. - 4:30 p.m.

Figure U1.4 • Assessment 6

Assessment 7

1. Open **WordContract01**.
2. Save the document with Save As and name it **swu1pa07**.
3. Make the following changes to the document:
   a. Select the entire document and change to a serif typeface of your choosing other than Times New Roman.
   b. Select the numbered paragraphs in the *Transfers and Moving Expenses* section and change to bullets.
   c. Select the numbered paragraphs in the *Sick Leave* section and change to bullets.
   d. Change the page orientation to landscape and then change the top and bottom margins to 1 inch. (When you change the orientation to landscape, the top and bottom margins change to 1.25 inches.)
4. Save, print, and then close **swu1pa07**.

Assessment 8

1. Open **WordReport04**.
2. Save the document with Save As and name it **swu1pa08**.
3. Make the following changes to the document:

a. Select and then delete the text from the title *COMPUTER OUTPUT DEVICES* to the end of the document.
b. Select the entire document, change the line spacing to single, and then deselect the text.
c. Change the left and right margins to 1 inch.
d. Increase the amount of space after the title *COMPUTER INPUT DEVICES* to 12 points.
e. Bold each of the headings (*Keyboard*, *Mouse*, *Trackball*, and *Touch Pad and Touch Screen*) and increase the space before each heading to 9 points and the space after each heading to 6 points.
f. Format the text in the document, except the title, into two equally spaced newspaper columns with a line between.

4. Save, print, and then close **swu1pa08**.

Assessment 9

1. Open **WordSpellCheck04**.
2. Save the document with Save As and name it **swu1pa09**.
3. Make the following changes to the document:
   a. Complete a spelling check and a grammar check on the document. (You determine what to edit and what to leave as written.)
   b. Select the document and then change the font to 12-point Century (or a similar serif typeface).
   c. Set the title in 14-point Century bold.
   d. Select the paragraphs in the body of the document (excluding the title), and then indent the first line of each paragraph .5 inch and change the paragraph alignment to justified.
   e. Proofread the document. (The document contains errors that are not selected by the spelling or grammar checker.)
4. Save, print, and then close **swu1pa09**.

WRITING activity

The following activities give you the opportunity to practice your writing skills along with demonstrating an understanding of some of the important Word features you have mastered in this unit. Use correct grammar, appropriate word choices, and clear sentence constructions. Follow the steps explained below to improve your writing skills.

The Writing Process

Plan: Gather ideas, select which information to include, and choose the order in which to present the information.

Checkpoints

What is the purpose?

What information do the readers need in order to reach your intended conclusion?

Write: Following the information plan and keeping the reader in mind, draft the document using clear, direct sentences that say what you mean.

Checkpoints

What are the subpoints for each main thought?

How can you connect paragraphs so the reader moves smoothly from one idea to the next?

Revise: Improve what is written by changing, deleting, rearranging, or adding words, sentences, and paragraphs.

Checkpoints

Is the meaning clear?

Do the ideas follow a logical order?

Have you included any unnecessary information?

Have you built your sentences around strong nouns and verbs?

Edit: Check spelling, sentence construction, word use, punctuation, and capitalization.

Checkpoints

Can you spot any redundancies or clichés?

Can you reduce any phrases to an effective word (for example, change *the fact that* to *because*)?

Have you used commas only where there is a strong reason for doing so?

Did you proofread the document for errors that your spell checker cannot identify?

Publish: Prepare a final copy that could be reproduced and shared with others.

Checkpoints

Which design elements, for example, bolding and different fonts, would help highlight important ideas or sections?

Would charts or other graphics help clarify meaning?

Activity 1

Use Word's Help feature to learn about hyphenating text in a document. Learn how to hyphenate text automatically as well as manually. Create a document that contains the following:

1. Include an appropriate title that is bolded and centered.
2. Write the steps required to automatically hyphenate text in a document.
3. Write the steps required to manually hyphenate text in a document.

Save the document and name it **swu1hyphen**. Print and then close **swu1hyphen**. Open **swu1pa08** and then save it with Save As and name it **swu1act01**. Manually hyphenate text in the document. Save, print, and then close **swu1act01**.

Activity 2

Use Word's Help feature to learn about grammar and style options. Learn about grammar options and what they detect and style options and what they detect. Also, learn how to set rules for grammar and style. Once you have determined this information, create a document describing at least two grammar options and at least two style options. Also include in this document the steps required to change the writing style from grammar only to grammar and style. Save the completed document and name it **swu1act02**. Print and then close **swu1act02**.

INTERNET project

Researching Business Desktop Computer Systems

You hold a part-time job at a local newspaper, *The Daily Chronicle*, where you conduct Internet research for the staff writers. Mr. Woods, the editor, has decided to purchase nine new desktop computers for the staff. He has asked you to identify at least three different desktop PCs that can be purchased directly over the Internet, and he requests that you put your research and recommendations in writing.

Mr. Woods is looking for solid, reliable, economical, and powerful desktop computers with good warranties and service plans. He has given you a budget of $1,500 per unit.

Log on to your ISP and search the Internet for three desktop computer systems from three different manufacturers. Consider price, specifications (processor speed, amount of RAM, hard drive space, and monitor type and size), performance, warranties, and service plans when making your choice of systems. Print your research findings and include them with your report. (For helpful information on choosing a PC, read the article "Factors to Consider When Buying a PC," which is available in the Computer Concepts Resource Center at EMC/Paradigm's Web site. Go to www.emcp.com; click College Division and then click Resource Center for either *Computer Technology* or *Computers: Exploring Concepts*. Choose Student and then select the article under "Practical Tips for Computer Users.")

Using Word, write a brief report in which you summarize the capabilities and qualities of each of the three computer systems you recommend. Include a final paragraph detailing which system you suggest for purchase and why. If possible, incorporate user opinions and/or reviews about this system to support your decision. At the end of your report, include a table comparing the computer system. Format your report using the concepts and techniques you learned in Unit 1.

JOB study

Preparing Training Documentation

You are a member of the Training and Development Team of Harrison, Lawrence, & O'Mally, Inc., a legal firm specializing in immigration law. You will be conducting a full-day (9:a.m. - 4 p.m.) training session in Beginner Microsoft Word functions.

Using Unit 1 of your textbook as a guide, choose the character and paragraph formatting functions you will demonstrate in the training session. Then use those features along with other formatting functions you learned in Unit 1 to prepare attractive, professional-looking documents for the participants at the training session, including:

- an invitation to the training session to be printed in hard copy and e-mailed to training-session participants
- a schedule of the day's activities at the training session
- a "how to" manual briefly describing each function you will demonstrate and the steps to perform that function
- a questionnaire that participants will complete at the end of the training session; include five questions about the value of the training

SPECIALIST

MICROSOFT®

WORD

Unit 2: Enhancing and Customizing Documents

- Maintaining Documents
- Customizing Documents
- Creating Tables and Charts
- Enhancing Documents with Special Features

Benchmark MICROSOFT® WORD 2003

MICROSOFT OFFICE SPECIALIST SKILLS—UNIT 2

Reference No.	Skill	Pages
WW03S-1	**Creating Content**	
WW03S-1-1	Insert and edit text, symbols and special characters	
	Delete text	S166
	Cut and paste text	S166-S168
	Copy and paste text	S169-S170
	Use the Office Clipboard	S170-S172
	Use the Paste Special dialog box	S172-S173
WW03S-1-2	Insert frequently used and pre-defined text	
	Use AutoText	S201-S204
	Create, save, edit, and delete AutoText entries	S204-S207
WW03S-1-3	Navigate to specific content	
	Find and replace text	S217-S221
	Find and replace formatting	S221-S224
	Navigate in a document using Go To and Document Map	S224-S226
WW03S-1-4	Insert, position and size graphics	
	Insert, size, format, and move images	S300-S306
	Draw, size, format, and move shapes, lines, and text boxes	S307-S311
WW03S-1-5	Create and modify diagrams and charts	
	Create, size, move, format and modify charts	S281-S287
	Create and modify organizational charts and diagrams	S295-S300
WW03S-1-6	Locate, select and insert supporting information	
	Research and request information	S328-S333
	Insert research information	S329-S331
	Use Research task pane to translate text	S331-S333
WW03S-2	**Organizing Content**	
WW03S-2-1	Insert and modify tables	
	Create, edit, delete, format, size, move, and modify tables	S249-S281
	Add borders and shading to cells	S256-S258
	Insert and delete rows and columns; split and merge cells	S268-S272
	Apply autoformats to a table	S273-S274
	Convert text to table	S274-S275
WW03S-2-2	Create bulleted lists, numbered lists and outlines	
	Create an outline	S319-S322
WW03S-2-3	Insert and modify hyperlinks	
	Insert hyperlinks to Web pages	S324-S326
	Insert and modify hyperlinks to a Word document	S326-S327
WW03S-3	**Formatting Content**	
WW03S-3-1	Format text	
	Apply styles to text, lists, and tables	S312-S318
	Clear style formatting	S313-S314
WW03S-3-4	Insert and modify content in headers and footers	
	Insert, format, edit, delete, and position headers and footers	S207-S215
	Create header/footer for first page and odd/even pages	S212-S215
	Insert and format page numbering	S215-S216
WW03S-4	**Collaborating**	
WW03S-4-1	Circulate documents for review	S333-S336
WW03S-4-2	Compare and merge document versions	S238-S239
WW03S-4-3	Insert, view and edit comments	S229-S233
WW03S-4-4	Track, accept and reject proposed changes	
	Track changes	S234-S236
	Accept and/or reject changes	S236-S237
WW03S-5	**Formatting and Managing Documents**	
WW03S-5-1	Create new documents using templates	
	Create new document using a template	S226-S228
	Create new document using a wizard	S228-S229
WW03S-5-2	Review and modify document properties	S190-S191
WW03S-5-3	Organize documents using file folders	
	Create, rename, and delete folders	S158-S160
	Select documents	S159-S160
	Delete, copy, move, rename, open, and close documents	S159-S165
WW03S-5-4	Save documents in appropriate formats for different uses	
	Save a document in a different format	S165-S166
WW03S-5-5	Print documents, envelopes and labels	
	Print documents	S181-S183
	Print envelopes	S183-S186
	Print labels	S186-S189
WW03S-5-6	Preview documents and Web pages	
	Preview a document in Web Page Preview	S323-S324
WW03S-5-7	Change and organize document views and windows	
	Split and arrange windows	S175-S179
	Compare documents side by side	S180-S181

CHAPTER 5

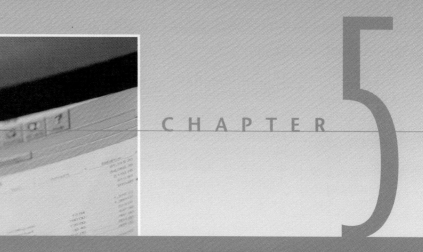

MAINTAINING DOCUMENTS

PERFORMANCE OBJECTIVES

Upon successful completion of Chapter 5, you will be able to:

- **Create and rename a folder**
- **Select, delete, copy, move, rename, and print documents**
- **Save a document in a different format**
- **Move and copy blocks of text within a document**
- **Use the Office Clipboard to collect and paste multiple items**
- **Insert one document into another**
- **Open, close, arrange, split, maximize, minimize, and restore documents**
- **Move and copy blocks of text between documents**
- **Print specific pages in a document**
- **Print multiple copies of a document**
- **Print envelopes and labels**
- **View, modify, and print document properties**

Almost every company that conducts business maintains a filing system. The system may consist of documents, folders, and cabinets; or it may be a computerized filing system where information is stored on tapes and disks. Whatever type of filing system a business uses, daily maintenance of files is important to a company's operation. In this chapter, you will learn to maintain files (documents) in Word, including such activities as creating additional folders and copying, moving, renaming, and printing documents.

Some documents may need to be heavily revised, and these revisions may include deleting, moving, or copying blocks of text. This kind of editing is generally referred to as ***cut and paste***. Cutting and pasting can be done within the same document, or text can be selected and then moved or copied to another document.

In Chapter 1, you learned to print a document with the Print button on the Standard toolbar or through the Print dialog box. By default, one copy of all pages of the currently open document is printed. In this chapter, you will learn to customize a print job with selections from the Print dialog box and print envelopes and labels.

HINT

If possible, complete all of your work in Microsoft Office on the hard drive or network drive. Use a floppy disk primarily for transporting and archiving documents.

Maintaining Documents

Many file (document) management tasks can be completed at the Open dialog box (and some can be completed at the Save As dialog box). These tasks can include copying, moving, printing, and renaming documents; opening multiple documents; and creating a new folder and renaming a folder. Perform some document maintenance tasks such as creating a folder and deleting documents using buttons on the Open dialog box toolbar shown in Figure 5.1.

FIGURE 5.1 ***Open Dialog Box Toolbar Buttons***

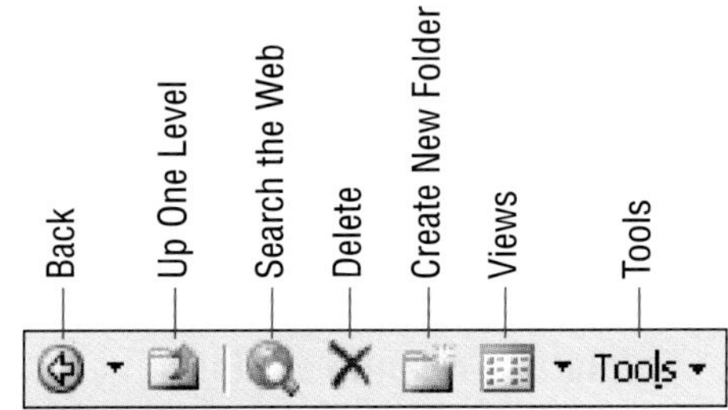

Creating a Folder

In Word, documents are grouped logically and placed in ***folders***. A folder can be created within a folder. The main folder on a disk or drive is called the ***root*** folder. Additional folders can be created as a branch of this root folder.

Create New Folder

Up One Level

At the Open dialog box (and Save As dialog box), documents display in the list box preceded by a document icon and a folder is preceded by a folder icon. Create a new folder by clicking the Create New Folder button located on the dialog box toolbar at the Open dialog box (or Save As dialog box). At the New Folder dialog box, type a name for the folder, and then click OK or press Enter. The new folder becomes the active folder.

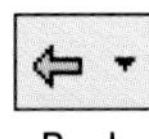

Back

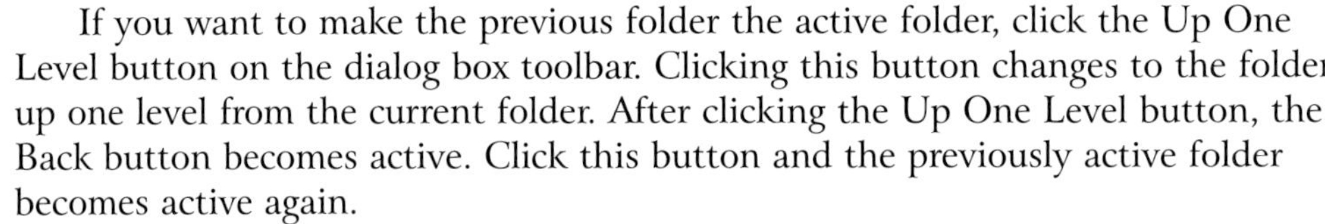

If you want to make the previous folder the active folder, click the Up One Level button on the dialog box toolbar. Clicking this button changes to the folder up one level from the current folder. After clicking the Up One Level button, the Back button becomes active. Click this button and the previously active folder becomes active again.

QUICK STEPS

Create a Folder
1. Display Open dialog box.
2. Click Create a Folder button.
3. Type folder name.
4. Press Enter.

A folder name can contain a maximum of 255 characters. Numbers, spaces, and symbols can be used in the folder name, except those symbols explained in Chapter 1 in the "Naming a Document" section.

Renaming a Folder

As you organize your files and folders, you may decide to rename a folder. Rename a folder using the Tools button on the Open dialog box toolbar or using a shortcut menu. To rename a folder using the Tools button, display the Open dialog box, click in the list box the folder you want to rename, click the Tools button on the dialog box toolbar, and then click Rename at the drop-down list. This selects the folder name and inserts a border around the name. Type the new name for the folder and then press Enter. To rename a folder using a shortcut menu, display the Open dialog box, right-click the folder name in the list box, and then click Rename at the shortcut menu. Type a new name for the folder and then press Enter.

QUICK STEPS

Rename a Folder
1. Display Open dialog box.
2. Right-click folder.
3. Type new name.
4. Press Enter.

(Note: Before completing computer exercises, delete the WordUnit01S folder on your disk. Next, copy to your disk the WordChapter05S folder from the Word2003Specialist folder on the CD that accompanies this textbook and then make WordChapter05S the active folder.)

exercise 1

CREATING A FOLDER

1. Create a folder named Correspondence on your disk by completing the following steps:
   a. Display the Open dialog box and open the WordChapter05S folder on your disk.
   b. Click the Create New Folder button (located on the dialog box toolbar).
   c. At the New Folder dialog box, type **Correspondence**.
   d. Click OK or press Enter. (The Correspondence folder is now the active folder.)
   e. Change back to the WordChapter05S folder by clicking the Up One Level button on the dialog box toolbar.
2. Rename the Correspondence folder to Documents by completing the following steps:
   a. Right-click the *Correspondence* folder name in the Open dialog box list box.
   b. Click Rename at the shortcut menu.
   c. Type **Documents** and then press Enter.
3. Click the Cancel button to close the Open dialog box.

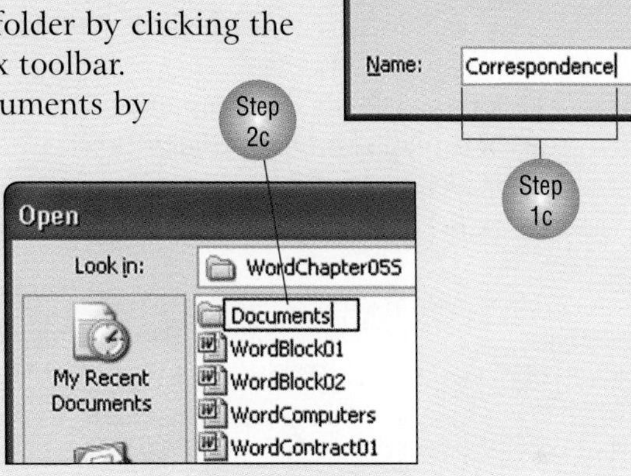

Selecting Documents

Document management tasks can be completed on one document or selected documents. For example, you can move one document to a different folder, or you can select several documents and move them at one time. Selected documents can be deleted, copied, moved, or printed. To select one document, display the Open dialog box, and then click the desired document. To select several adjacent documents (documents displayed next to each other), click the first document, hold down the Shift key, and then click the last document. You can also select documents that are not adjacent in the Open dialog box. To do this, click the first document, hold down the Ctrl key, click any other desired documents, and then release the Ctrl key.

Deleting Documents and Folders

At some point, you may want to delete certain documents from your data disk or any other disk or folder in which you may be working. If you use Word on a regular basis, you should establish a system for deleting documents. The system you choose depends on the work you are doing and the amount of folder or disk space available. To delete a document, display the Open or Save As dialog box, select the document, and then click the Delete button on the dialog box toolbar. At the dialog box asking you to confirm the deletion, click Yes.

Delete Folder/ Document
1. Display Open dialog box.
2. Click folder or document name.
3. Click Delete button.
4. Click Yes.

Tools

Delete

You can also delete a document by displaying the Open or Save As dialog box, selecting the document to be deleted, clicking the Tools button on the dialog box toolbar, and then clicking Delete at the drop-down menu. Another method for deleting a document is to display the Open or Save As dialog box, right-click the document to be deleted, and then click Delete at the shortcut menu.

A folder and all of its contents can be deleted at the Open or Save As dialog box. Delete a folder and its contents in the same manner as deleting a document or selected documents.

exercise 2

DELETING A DOCUMENT AND SELECTED DOCUMENTS

1. Open **WordDocument06** (located in the WordChapter05S folder on your disk).
2. Save the document with Save As and name it **swc5x02**.
3. Close **swc5x02**.
4. Delete **swc5x02** by completing the following steps:
   a. Display the Open dialog box with WordChapter05S the active folder.
   b. Click ***swc5x02*** to select it.
   c. Click the Delete button on the dialog box toolbar.

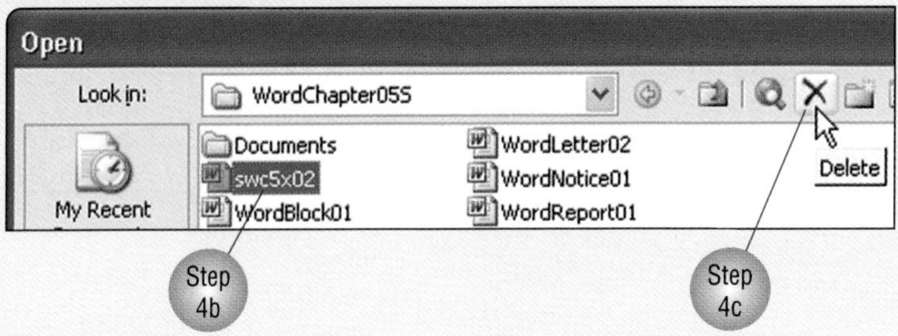

   d. At the question asking if you want to delete **swc5x02**, click Yes.
5. With the Open dialog box displayed with WordChapter05S the active folder, delete selected documents by completing the following steps:
   a. Click ***WordList01***.
   b. Hold down the Shift key and then click ***WordList03***.
   c. Position the mouse pointer on a selected document and then click the *right* mouse button.
   d. At the shortcut menu that displays, click Delete.
   e. At the question asking if you want to delete the items, click Yes.
   f. At the message telling you that **WordList01** is a read-only file and asking if you are sure you want to delete it, click the Yes to All button.
6. Close the Open dialog box.

Deleting to the Recycle Bin

Documents deleted from your data disk are deleted permanently. (Recovery programs are available, however, that will help you recover deleted text. If you accidentally delete a document or documents from a disk, do not do anything more with the disk until you can run a recovery program.) Documents deleted from the hard drive are automatically sent to the Windows Recycle Bin. If you accidentally delete a document to the Recycle Bin, it can be easily restored. To free space on the drive, empty the Recycle Bin on a periodic basis. Restoring a document from or emptying the contents of the Recycle Bin is done at the Windows desktop (not in Word).

HINT

Remember to empty the Recycle Bin on a regular basis.

To display the Recycle Bin, minimize the Word window, and then double-click the Recycle Bin icon located on the Windows desktop. At the Recycle Bin, you can restore file(s) and empty the Recycle Bin.

Copying Documents

In previous chapters, you have been opening a document from the data disk and saving it with a new name on the same disk. This process makes an exact copy of the document, leaving the original on the disk. You have been copying documents and saving the new document in the same folder as the original document. You can also copy a document into another folder and use the document's original name or give it a different name, or select documents at the Open dialog box and copy them to the same folder or into a different folder. To copy a document into another folder, open the document, display the Save As dialog box, change to the desired folder, and then click the Save button.

Copy Documents

1. Display Open dialog box.
2. Right-click document name.
3. Click Copy.
4. Navigate to desired folder.
5. Right-click blank area.
6. Click Paste.

A document can be copied to another folder without opening the document first. To do this, use the Copy and Paste options from a shortcut menu at the Open (or Save As) dialog box. A document or selected documents can be copied into the same folder. When you do this, Word names the document(s) "Copy of xxx" (where *xxx* is the current document name). You can copy one document or selected documents into the same folder.

exercise 3 — COPYING DOCUMENTS

1. Open **WordDocument02**.
2. Save the document with Save As and name it **Keyboards**. (Make sure WordChapter05S on your disk is the active folder.)
3. Save a copy of the **Keyboards** document in the Documents folder created in Exercise 1 by completing the following steps. (If your system does not contain this folder, check with your instructor to determine if another folder is available for you to use.)
   a. With **Keyboards** still open, display the Save As dialog box.
   b. At the Save As dialog box, change to the Documents folder. To do this, double-click *Documents* at the beginning of the list box (folders are listed before documents).
   c. Click the Save button located in the lower right corner of the dialog box.
4. Close **Keyboards**.
5. Display the Open dialog box and then click the Up One Level button to return to the WordChapter05S folder.
6. Copy a document to another folder by completing the following steps:

a. Position the arrow pointer on **WordDocument01**, click the *right* mouse button, and then click Copy at the shortcut menu.
b. Change to the Documents folder by double-clicking *Documents* at the beginning of the list box.
c. Position the arrow pointer in any white area (not on a document name) in the list box, click the *right* mouse button, and then click Paste at the shortcut menu.

7. Change back to the WordChapter05S folder by clicking the Up One Level button located on the dialog box toolbar.
8. Copy documents into the same folder by completing the following steps:
   a. Select **WordDocument03**, **WordDocument04**, and **WordDocument05**. (To do this, click ***WordDocument03***, hold down the Shift key, and then click ***WordDocument05***.)
   b. Position the arrow pointer on one of the selected documents, click the *right* mouse button, and then click Copy at the shortcut menu.
   c. Position the arrow pointer in any white area in the list box, click the *right* mouse button, and then click Paste at the shortcut menu. (In a few moments, Word will redisplay the Open dialog box with the following documents added: **Copy of WordDocument03**, **Copy of WordDocument04**, and **Copy of WordDocument05**.)
9. Copy several documents to the Documents folder by completing the following steps:
   a. Click once on ***WordDocument02***. (This selects the document.)
   b. Hold down the Ctrl key, click ***WordDocument04***, click ***WordDocument05***, and then release the Ctrl key.
   c. Position the arrow pointer on one of the selected documents, click the *right* mouse button, and then click Copy at the shortcut menu.
   d. Double-click the *Documents* folder.
   e. When the Documents folder displays, position the arrow pointer in any white area in the list box, click the *right* mouse button, and then click Paste at the shortcut menu.
   f. Click the Up One Level button to return to the WordChapter05S folder.
10. Close the Open dialog box by clicking the Cancel button.

Sending Documents to a Different Drive or Folder

With the Copy and Paste options from the shortcut menu at the Open or Save As dialog box, you can copy documents to another folder or drive. With the Send To option, you can quickly send a copy of a document to another drive or folder. To use this option, position the arrow pointer on the document you want copied, click the *right* mouse button, position the arrow pointer on Send To (this causes a side menu to display), and then click the desired drive or folder.

Move a Document
1. Display Open dialog box.
2. Right-click document name.
3. Click Paste.
4. Navigate to desired folder.
5. Right-click blank area.
6. Click Paste.

Cutting and Pasting a Document

Remove a document from one folder or disk and insert it in another folder or on a disk using the Cut and Paste options from the shortcut menu at the Open dialog box. To do this, display the Open dialog box, position the arrow pointer on the document to be removed (cut), click the *right* mouse button, and then click Cut at the shortcut menu. Change to the desired folder, position the arrow pointer in a white area in the list box, click the *right* mouse button, and then click Paste at the shortcut menu.

Renaming Documents

At the Open dialog box, use the Rename option from the Tools drop-down menu to give a document a different name. The Rename option changes the name of the document and keeps it in the same folder. To use Rename, display the Open dialog box, click once on the document to be renamed, and then click the Tools button on the dialog box toolbar. This causes a black border to surround the document name and the name to be selected. Type the desired name and then press Enter. You can also rename a document by right-clicking the document name at the Open dialog box and then clicking Rename at the shortcut menu. Type the desired name for the document and then press the Enter key.

Rename a Document
1. Display Open dialog box.
2. Click document name.
3. Click Tools, Rename.
4. Type new name.
5. Press Enter.

Deleting a Folder and Its Contents

As you learned earlier in this chapter, a document or selected documents can be deleted. In addition to documents, a folder (and all of its contents) can be deleted. Delete a folder in the same manner as a document is deleted.

exercise 4

CUTTING, PASTING AND RENAMING A DOCUMENT AND DELETING A FOLDER

1. Save a document into a different folder by completing the following steps:
   a. Open **WordDocument04**.
   b. Save the document with Save As and name it **EconomicOutlook**.
   c. Close **EconomicOutlook**.
2. Move **EconomicOutlook** to the Documents folder by completing the following steps:
   a. Display the Open dialog box with WordChapter05S the active folder.
   b. Position the arrow pointer on **EconomicOutlook**, click the *right* mouse button, and then click Cut at the shortcut menu.
   c. Double-click *Documents* to make it the active folder.
   d. Position the arrow pointer in the white area in the list box, click the *right* mouse button, and then click Paste at the shortcut menu.
3. Rename a document located in the Documents folder by completing the following steps:
   a. With Documents the active folder, click once on ***WordDocument05*** to select it.
   b. Click the Tools button on the dialog box toolbar.
   c. At the drop-down menu that displays, click Rename.
   d. Type **Retirement** and then press the Enter key. (Depending on your system setup, you may need to type **Retirement.doc**.)
   e. At the message asking if you are sure you want to change the name of the read-only file, click Yes.
   f. Complete steps similar to those in 3a through 3e to rename **WordDocument04** to **StockMarket** (or **StockMarket.doc**).
   g. Click the Up One Level button.

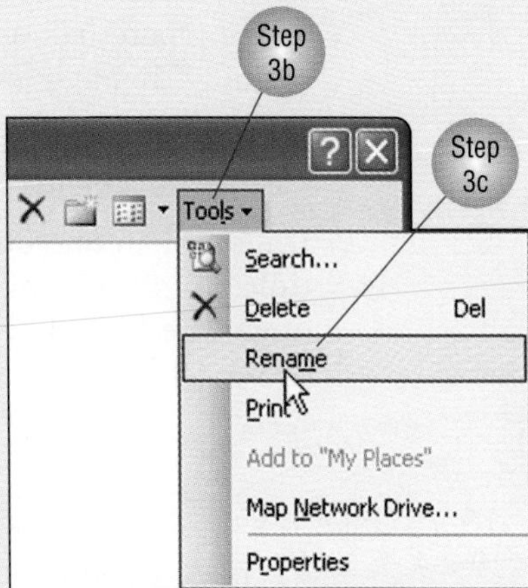

4. Delete the Documents folder and its contents by completing the following steps:
   a. With WordChapter05S the active folder, click the *Documents* folder to select it.
   b. Click the Delete button on the dialog box toolbar.
   c. At the question asking if you want to remove the folder and its contents, click Yes.
   d. At the message telling you that **WordDocument01** is a read-only file and asking if you are sure you want to delete it, click the Yes to All button.
5. Close the Open dialog box.

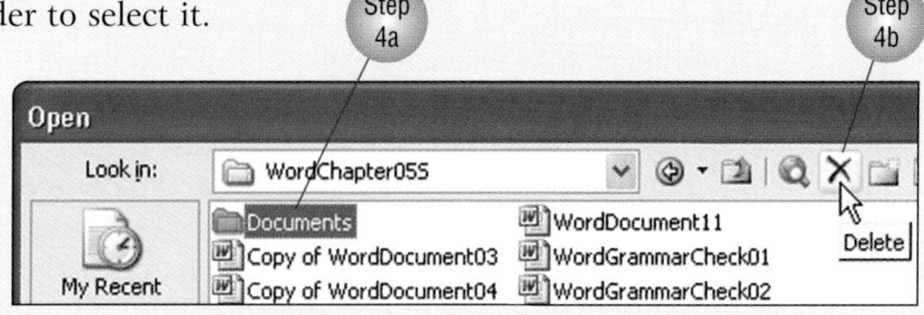

HINT You can also open a document by clicking the file name hyperlink in the *Open* section of the Getting Started task pane. This section of the task pane displays the most recently opened documents.

Opening Documents

Open a document or selected documents at the Open dialog box. To open one document, display the Open dialog box, and then double-click the document name. You can also position the arrow pointer on the desired document, click the *right* mouse button, and then click Open at the shortcut menu. To open more than one document, select the documents in the Open dialog box, and then click the Open button. You can also open multiple documents by positioning the arrow pointer on one of the selected documents, clicking the *right* mouse button, and then clicking Open at the shortcut menu.

Printing Documents

Up to this point, you have opened a document and then printed it. With the Print option from the Tools drop-down menu or the Print option from the shortcut menu at the Open dialog box, you can print a document or several documents without opening them.

Closing Documents

If more than one document is open, all open documents can be closed at the same time. To do this, hold down the Shift key, click File and then Close All. Holding down the Shift key before clicking File causes the Close option to change to Close All.

exercise 5 OPENING, CLOSING, AND PRINTING MULTIPLE DOCUMENTS

1. Open several documents by completing the following steps:
   a. Display the Open dialog box with WordChapter05S the active folder.
   b. Select ***WordDocument01***, ***WordDocument02***, ***WordDocument03***, and ***WordDocument04***.
   c. Click the Open button.

2. Close the open documents by holding down the Shift key, clicking File, and then clicking Close All.
3. Display the Open dialog box with WordChapter05S the active folder.
4. Select ***WordDocument03***, ***WordDocument04***, and ***WordDocument05***.
5. Click the Tools button on the dialog box toolbar.
6. At the drop-down menu that displays, click Print.

Saving a Document in a Different Format

A file's format is indicated by a three-letter extension after the file name.

Save Document in Different Format
1. Open document.
2. Click File, Save As.
3. Click *Save as type* option.
4. Click desired type.
5. Click Save button.

When you save a document, the document is automatically saved as a Word document. If you need to share a document with someone who is using a different Word processing program or a different version of Word, you can save the document in another format. You can also save a Word document as a Web page, in rich text format, and as plain text. To save a document with a different format, display the Save As dialog box, click the down-pointing arrow at the right side of the *Save as type* option, and then click the desired format at the drop-down list.

The Open dialog box generally displays only Word documents, which are documents containing the *.doc* extension. If you want to display all files, display the Open dialog box, click the down-pointing arrow at the right side of the *Files of type* option, and then click *All Files* at the drop-down list.

exercise 6 SAVING A DOCUMENT IN A DIFFERENT FORMAT

1. Open **WordDocument01**.
2. Change the left and right margins to 1.5 inches.
3. Save the document as plain text by completing the following steps:
   a. Click File and then Save As.
   b. At the Save As dialog box, type swc5x06 in the *File name* text box.
   c. Click the down-pointing arrow at the right side of the *Save as type* option and then click *Plain Text* at the drop-down list. (You will need to scroll down the list to display *Plain Text*.)
   d. Click the Save button.
   e. At the File Conversion dialog box, preview the document, and then click OK.
4. Close **swc5x06**.
5. Display the **swc5x06** plain text document by completing the following steps:
   a. Display the Open dialog box.

b. At the Open dialog box, click the down-pointing arrow at the right of the *Files of type* option box and then click *All Files* at the drop-down list. (This displays all files containing any extension.)

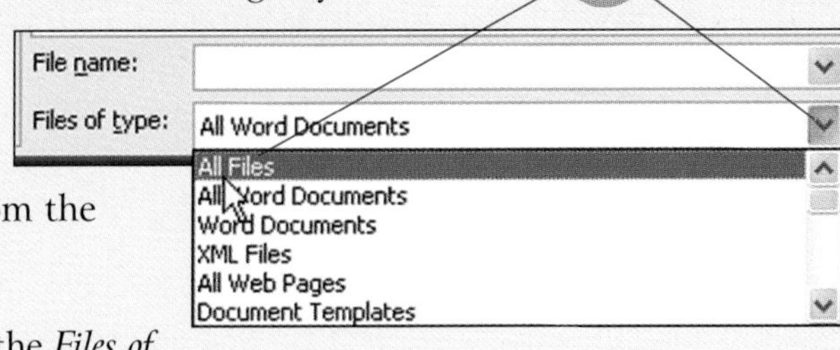

c. Double-click ***swc5x06*** in the list box. (Notice that the character and margin formatting has been removed from the document.)

d. Close **swc5x06**.

6. Display the Open dialog box, change the *Files of type* option back to *All Word Documents,* and then close the dialog box.

Working with Blocks of Text

When cutting and pasting, you work with blocks of text. A block of text is a portion of text that you have selected. (Chapter 1 covered the various methods for selecting text.) A block of text can be as small as one character or as large as an entire page or document. Once a block of text has been selected, it can be deleted, moved to a new location, or copied and pasted within a document.

Deleting a Block of Text

Word offers different methods for deleting text from a document. To delete a single character, you can use either the Delete key or the Backspace key. To delete more than a single character, select the portion of text to be deleted and then press the Delete key, click the Cut button on the Standard toolbar, or click Edit and then Cut.

HINT

The Clipboard contents are deleted when the computer is turned off. Text you want to save permanently should be saved as a separate document.

If you press Delete, the text is deleted permanently. (You can, however, restore deleted text with the Undo Clear option from the Edit menu or with the Undo or Redo buttons on the Standard toolbar.) The Cut button on the Standard toolbar and the Cut option from the Edit drop-down menu will delete the selected text and insert it in the ***Clipboard***. Word's Clipboard is a temporary area of memory. The Clipboard holds text while it is being moved or copied to a new location in the document or to a different document. Text inserted in the Clipboard stays there until other text is inserted. Delete selected text with the Delete key if you do not need it again. Use the other methods if you might want to insert deleted text in the current document or a different document. If you cut and/or copy text a second and subsequent time, the Clipboard task pane automatically displays. (You will learn more about the Clipboard task pane later in this chapter.)

Move Selected Text
1. Select text.
2. Click Cut button.
3. Move to desired location.
4. Click Paste button.

Moving a Block of Text

Word offers a variety of methods for moving text. After you have selected a block of text, move the text with buttons on the Standard toolbar or options from the Edit drop-down menu. Using buttons on the Standard toolbar, you would select the text, click the Cut button, position the insertion point where you want selected text inserted, and then click the Paste button. To move selected text with Edit menu options, select the text and then click Edit and then Cut. Position the insertion point where you want selected text inserted and then click Edit and then Paste.

In addition to the methods just described, a block of selected text can also be moved with the mouse. To do this, select the text, and then position the I-beam pointer inside the selected text until it becomes an arrow pointer. Hold down the left mouse button, drag the arrow pointer (displays with a gray box attached) to the location where you want the selected text inserted, and then release the button.

When selected text is cut from a document and inserted in the Clipboard, it stays in the Clipboard until other text is inserted in the Clipboard. For this reason, you can paste text from the Clipboard more than just once. For example, if you cut text to the Clipboard, you can paste this text in different locations within the document or other documents as many times as desired.

HINT

If you drag and then drop selected text in the wrong location, immediately click the Undo button.

Using the Paste Options Button

When you paste selected information, the Paste Options button displays in the lower right corner of the pasted information. Click this button and a drop-down list displays as shown in Figure 5.2. Use options from this drop-down list to specify how you want information pasted in the document. By default, pasted text retains the formatting of the selected text. You can choose to match the formatting of the pasted text with the formatting where the text is pasted, paste only the text without retaining formatting, or apply a style to pasted text.

FIGURE 5.2 Paste Options Button Drop-Down List

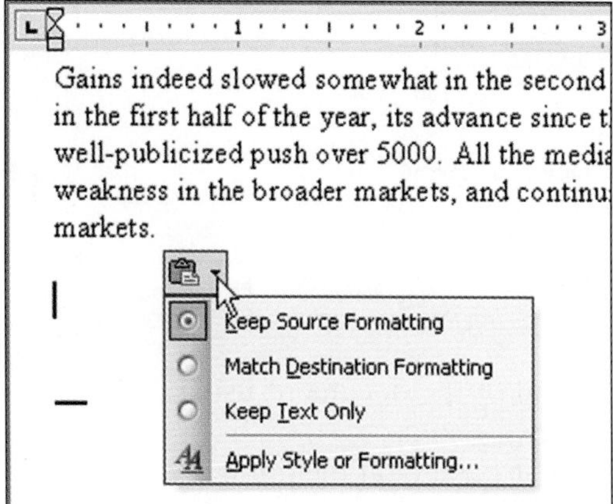

exercise 7 — MOVING SELECTED TEXT

1. Open **WordDocument03**.
2. Save the document with Save As and name it **swc5x07**.
3. Indent the third paragraph from the left and right margins by .5 inch. (Do this with the *Left* and *Right* options at the Paragraph dialog box.)
4. Move the second paragraph above the first paragraph by completing the following steps:

a. Select the second paragraph including the blank line below the paragraph.
b. Click the Cut button on the Standard toolbar.
c. Position the insertion point at the beginning of the first paragraph.
d. Click the Paste button on the Standard toolbar. (If the first and second paragraphs are not separated by a blank line, press the Enter key once.)

5. Move the third paragraph above the second paragraph without retaining the indent formatting by completing the following steps:
   a. Select the third paragraph including the blank line below the paragraph.
   b. Click Edit and then Cut. (If the Clipboard task pane displays, close it by clicking the Close button in the upper right corner of the task pane.)
   c. Position the insertion point at the beginning of the second paragraph.
   d. Click Edit and then Paste.
   e. Click the Paste Options button that displays at the end of the paragraph and then click the Keep Text Only option. (This pastes only the text and not the indent formatting.) (If the paragraphs are not separated by a blank line, press the Enter key once.)

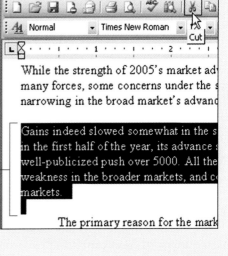

6. Move the first paragraph to the end of the document using the mouse by completing the following steps:
   a. Using the mouse, select the first paragraph including the blank line below the paragraph.
   b. Move the I-beam pointer inside the selected text until it becomes an arrow pointer.
   c. Hold down the left mouse button, drag the arrow pointer (displays with a small gray box attached) a double space below the last paragraph (make sure the insertion point, which displays as a grayed vertical bar, is positioned a double space below the last paragraph), and then release the mouse button.
   d. Deselect the text.

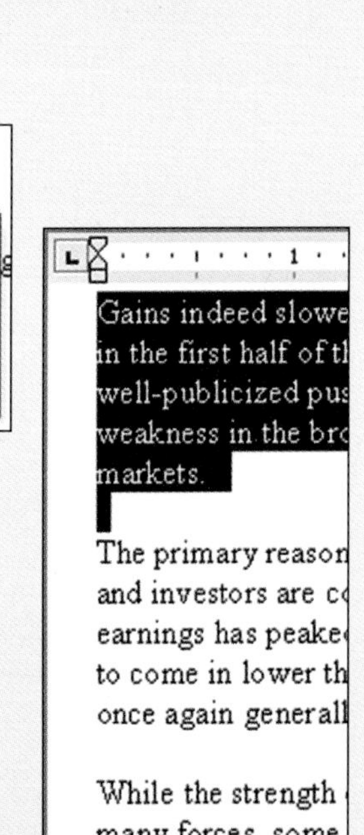

7. Save, print, and then close **swc5x07**.

Copying a Block of Text

Copy Selected Text
1. Select text.
2. Click Copy button.
3. Move to desired location.
4. Click Paste button.

Copying selected text can be useful in documents that contain repetitive portions of text. You can use this function to insert duplicate portions of text in a document instead of retyping the text. After you have selected a block of text, copy the text to a different location with the Copy and Paste buttons on the Standard toolbar, with options from the Edit drop-down menu, or using the mouse.

exercise 8

COPYING SELECTED TEXT WITH BUTTONS ON THE STANDARD TOOLBAR

1. Open **WordBlock01**.
2. Save the document with Save As and name it **swc5x08**.
3. Select the entire document and then change the font to 14-point Goudy Old Style bold (or a similar serif typeface).
4. Copy the text in the document to the end of the document by completing the following steps:
   a. Select all of the text in the document including two blank lines below the text.
   b. Click the Copy button on the Standard toolbar.
   c. Move the insertion point to the end of the document.
   d. Click the Paste button on the Standard toolbar.
5. Copy the text again at the end of the document. To do this, position the insertion point at the end of the document, and then click the Paste button on the Standard toolbar.
6. Save, print, and then close **swc5x08**.

To use the mouse to copy text, select the text, and then position the I-beam pointer inside the selected text until it becomes an arrow pointer. Hold down the left mouse button and hold down the Ctrl key. Drag the arrow pointer (displays with a small gray box and a box containing a plus symbol) to the location where you want the copied text inserted (make sure the insertion point, which displays as a grayed vertical bar, is positioned in the desired location), and then release the mouse button and then the Ctrl key.

If you select a block of text and then decide you selected the wrong text or you do not want to do anything with the block, you can deselect it. If you are using the mouse, click the left mouse button outside the selected text. If you are using the keyboard, press an arrow key to deselect text. If you selected with the Extend mode (F8), press Esc and then press an arrow key to deselect text.

exercise 9

COPYING SELECTED TEXT USING THE MOUSE

1. Open **WordBlock02**.
2. Save the document with Save As and name it **swc5x09**.
3. Copy the text in the document using the mouse by completing the following steps:
   a. Select all of the text with the mouse and include two blank lines below the text. (Consider turning on the display of nonprinting characters.)
   b. Move the I-beam pointer inside the selected text until it becomes an arrow pointer.

c. Hold down the Ctrl key and then the left mouse button. Drag the arrow pointer (displays with a small gray box and a box with a plus symbol inside) to the end of the document immediately above the end-of-document marker (make sure the insertion point, which displays as a grayed vertical bar, is positioned immediately above the end-of-document marker), release the mouse button, and then the Ctrl key.
d. Deselect the text.

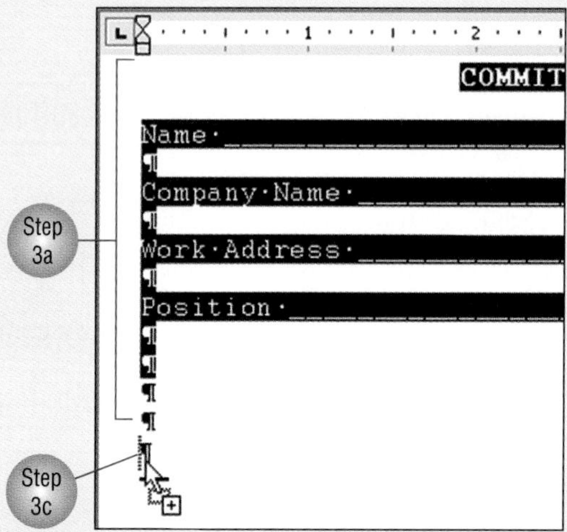

4. Select both forms using the mouse (including two blank lines below the second form) and then copy the selected forms to the end of the document.
5. Make sure all forms fit on one page. If the forms do not fit on one page, consider deleting any extra blank lines between forms.
6. Save, print, and then close **swc5x09**.

Using the Office Clipboard

Use the Office Clipboard to collect and paste multiple items. You can collect up to 24 different items and then paste them in various locations. To display the Clipboard task pane, click Edit on the Menu bar and then click Office Clipboard, or press Ctrl + C twice. You can also display the Clipboard task pane by clicking the Other Task Panes button (displays as a down-pointing arrow) located in the upper right corner of the task pane and then clicking Clipboard at the drop-down menu. The Clipboard task pane displays at the right side of the screen in a manner similar to what you see in Figure 5.3.

FIGURE 5.3 **Clipboard Task Pane**

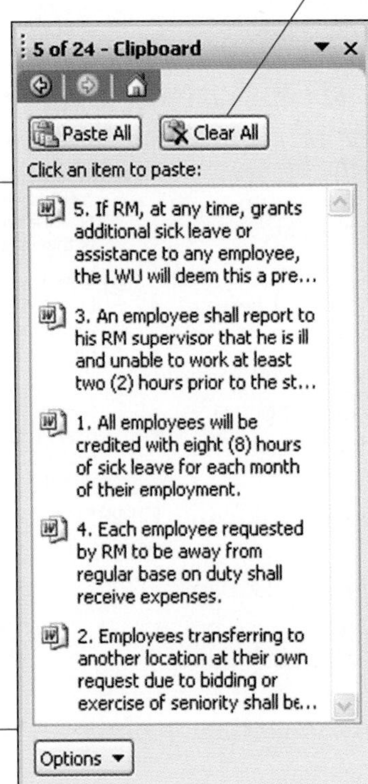

Select text or an object you want to copy and then click the Copy button on the Standard toolbar. Continue selecting text or items and clicking the Copy button. To insert an item, position the insertion point in the desired location and then click the button in the Clipboard task pane representing the item. If the copied item is text, the first 50 characters display on the Clipboard task pane. When all desired items are inserted, click the Clear All button to remove any remaining items.

HINT
You can copy items to the Clipboard from various Office applications and then paste them into any Office file.

exercise 10

COLLECTING AND PASTING PARAGRAPHS OF TEXT

1. Open **WordContract01**.
2. Turn on the display of the Clipboard task pane by clicking Edit and then Office Clipboard. (If the Clipboard task pane contains any text, click the Clear All button located towards the top of the task pane.)
3. Select paragraph 2 in the section titled *Transfers and Moving Expenses* by triple-clicking the paragraph with the mouse and then click the Copy button on the Standard toolbar. (The *2.* is not selected.)
4. Select and then copy each of the following paragraphs:

a. Paragraph 4 in the section titled *Transfers and Moving Expenses*. (The Clipboard task pane displays at the right side of the screen.)
b. Paragraph 1 in the section titled *Sick Leave*.
c. Paragraph 3 in the section titled *Sick Leave*.
d. Paragraph 5 in the section titled *Sick Leave*.

5. Paste the paragraphs by completing the following steps:
   a. Click the New Blank Document button on the Standard toolbar.
   b. Display the Clipboard task pane by pressing Ctrl + C twice.
   c. Type **CONTRACT NEGOTIATION ITEMS** centered and bolded.
   d. Press Enter twice, turn off bold, and return the paragraph alignment back to Left.
   e. Click the button in the Clipboard task pane representing paragraph 2. (When the paragraph is inserted in the document, the paragraph number changes to 1.)
   f. Click the button in the Clipboard task pane representing paragraph 4.
   g. Click the button in the Clipboard task pane representing paragraph 3.
   h. Click the button in the Clipboard task pane representing paragraph 5.
6. Click the Clear All button located toward the top of the Clipboard task pane.
7. Close the Clipboard task pane.
8. Save the document and name it **swc5x10**.
9. Print and then close **swc5x10**.
10. Close the Clipboard task pane and then close **WordContract01** without saving the changes.

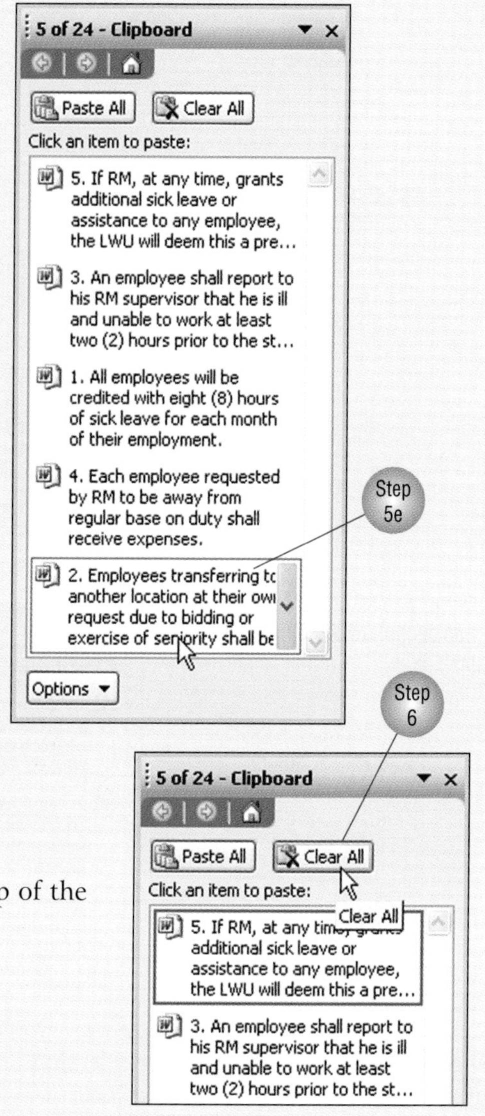

Copy and Paste Special Text/Object
1. Select text or object.
2. Click Copy button.
3. Move to desired location.
4. Click Edit, Paste Special.
5. Click desired format in *As* list box.
6. Click OK.

Pasting Text Using the Paste Special Dialog Box

Use options at the Paste Special dialog box, shown in Figure 5.4, to specify the format for pasted text. The options in the *As* list box vary depending on the cut or copied text and the source application. If you select text in a Word document, the options display in the *As* list box as shown in Figure 5.4. To use the Paste Special dialog box, cut or copy the desired text, and then paste it by clicking Edit and then Paste Special. At the Paste Special dialog box, click the desired format in the *As* list box and then click OK. For example, in Exercise 11 you will select and copy text from one document and then use the Paste Special dialog box to paste the text in a new document without the formatting.

FIGURE

5.4 Paste Special Dialog Box

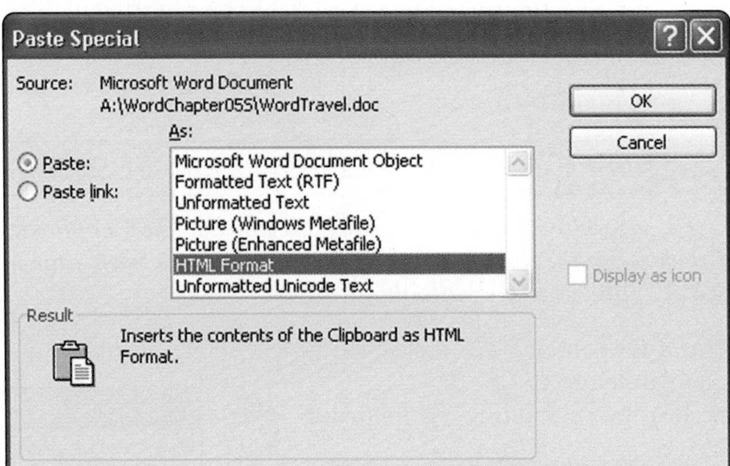

exercise 11

USING THE PASTE SPECIAL DIALOG BOX

1. Open **WordTravel**.
2. Select from the beginning of the document to just below the last bulleted item (the bullets display as earth symbols).
3. Click the Copy button on the Standard toolbar.
4. Click the New Blank Document button on the Standard toolbar.
5. Paste the text into the new blank document without formatting by completing the following steps:
   a. Click Edit and then Paste Special.
   b. At the Paste Special dialog box, click *Unformatted Text* in the *As* list box.
   c. Click OK. (The text is pasted in the document without the formatting.)
6. Make the following changes to the document:
   a. Select the first five lines of text and then click the Bold button.
   b. Delete the square and space before each of the last seven lines of text.
   c. Select the last seven lines of text and then click the Bullets button on the Formatting toolbar.
7. Save the document and name it **swc5x11**.
8. Print and then close **swc5x11**.
9. Close **WordTravel**.

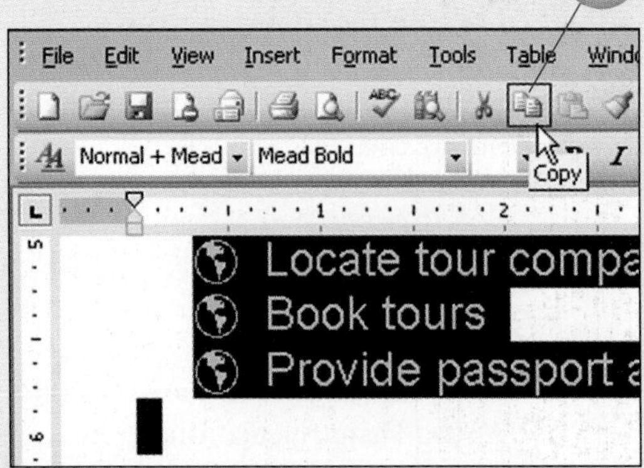

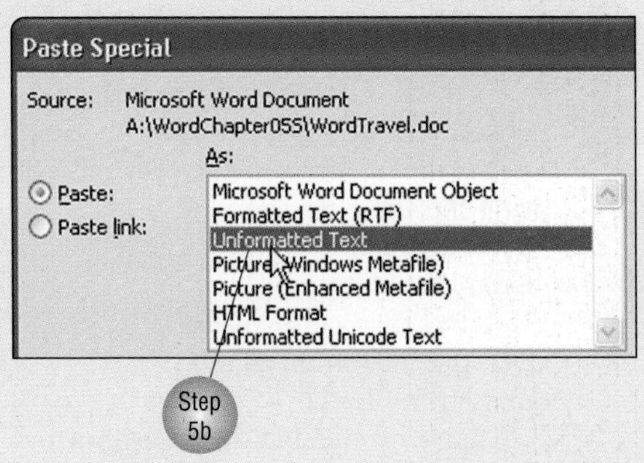

Pasting Data between Applications

Use options at the Paste Special dialog box to copy and paste data between Office applications. With the options in the *As* list box, you can specify the format for pasted data. Use the Paste Special dialog box to paste data into the destination application and retain the formatting of the originating application.

exercise 12

USING PASTE SPECIAL TO PASTE DATA BETWEEN APPLICATIONS

(Note: In Exercise 12, you will open an Excel worksheet in the Excel application, copy specific cells, and then paste the cells in a Word document. Check with your instructor to determine if the Excel application is available.)

1. Make sure Word is open and that a clear document screen displays.
2. Open Microsoft Excel.
3. Open a worksheet by completing the following steps:
   a. Click the Open button on the Excel Standard toolbar.
   b. At the Open dialog box (with WordChapter05S the active folder), double-click **Excelc5x12**.

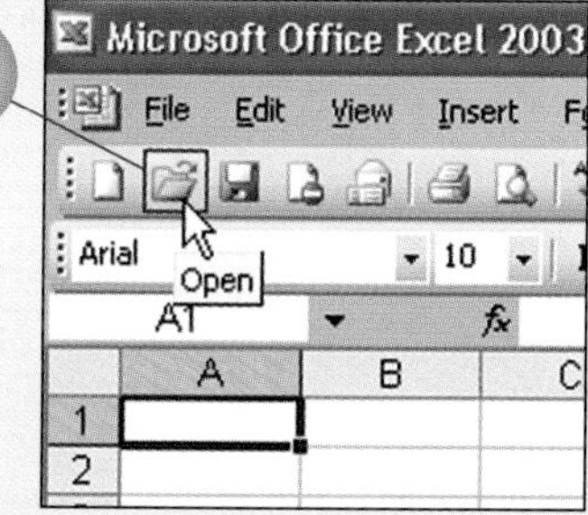

4. Select cells A1 through D5. To do this, position the mouse pointer (displays as a white plus symbol) in cell A1, hold down the left mouse button, drag down and to the right to cell D5, and then release the mouse button.
5. Click the Copy button on the Excel Standard toolbar. (A moving marquee surrounds the selected cells.)
6. Click the button on the Taskbar representing Word.
7. At the clear document screen, paste the Excel cells by completing the following steps:
   a. Click Edit and then Paste Special.
   b. At the Paste Special dialog box, click *Microsoft Excel Worksheet Object* in the *As* list box.
   c. Click OK.

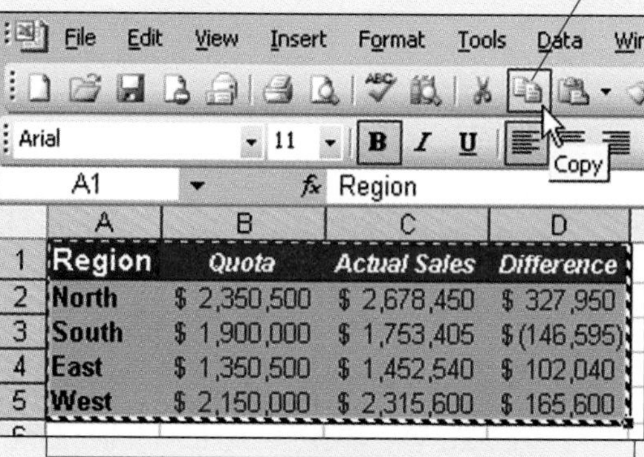

8. Press the Enter key twice and then click the Paste button on the Standard toolbar. (Notice the difference in formatting between the cells pasted using the Paste Special dialog box and the cells pasted using the Paste button.)
9. Save the document and name it **swc5x12**.
10. Print and then close **swc5x12**.
11. Click the button on the Taskbar representing Excel.
12. Exit Excel by clicking the Close button located in the upper right corner of the screen.

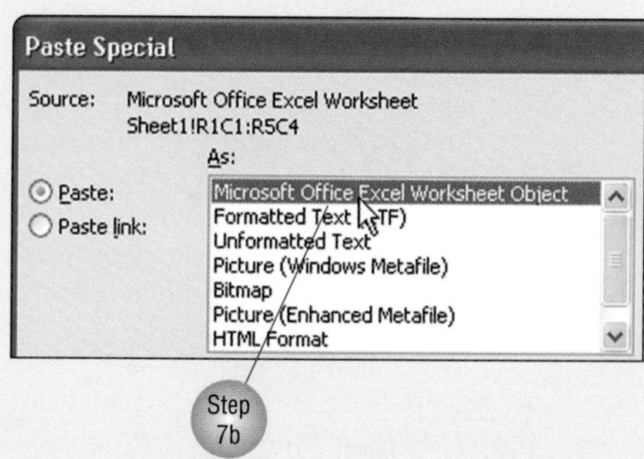

Inserting One Document into Another

Insert Document into Another
1. Open document.
2. Click Insert, File.
3. Navigate to desired folder.
4. Double-click document name.

Some documents may contain standard information—information that remains the same. For example, a legal document, such as a will, may contain text that is standard and appears in all wills. Repetitive text can be saved as a separate document and then inserted into an existing document whenever needed. Insert a separate document into an existing document by displaying the Insert File dialog box and double-clicking the desired document. To display the Insert File dialog box, click Insert and then File. The Insert File dialog box contains many of the same options as the Open and Save As dialog boxes.

exercise 13

SAVING SELECTED TEXT AND INSERTING ONE DOCUMENT INTO ANOTHER

1. Open **WordDocument04**.
2. Select the first paragraph and then save it as a separate document named **Budget** by completing the following steps:
   a. Select the first paragraph in the document.
   b. Click the Copy button on the Standard toolbar.
   c. Click the New Blank Document button on the Standard toolbar (first button on the left).
   d. At the clear document screen, click the Paste button on the Standard toolbar.
   e. Save the document and name it **Budget**.
   f. Close the **Budget** document.
3. Close **WordDocument04** without saving any changes.
4. Open **WordDocument11**.
5. Move the insertion point a double space below the first paragraph and then insert the **Budget** document by completing the following steps:
   a. Click Insert and then File.
   b. At the Insert File dialog box, double-click *Budget*. (If the second and third paragraphs are separated by a triple space, delete one of the blank lines.)
6. Save the document and name it **swc5x13**.
7. Print and then close **swc5x13**.

Working with Windows

Word operates within the Windows environment created by the Windows program. However, when working in Word, a **window** refers to the document screen. The Windows program creates an environment in which various software programs are used with menu bars, scroll bars, and icons to represent programs and files. With the Windows program, you can open several different software programs and move between them quickly. Similarly, using windows in Word, you can open several different documents and move between them quickly.

HINT
Press Ctrl + F6 to switch between open documents.

With multiple documents open, you can move the insertion point between them. You can move or copy information between documents or compare the contents of several documents. The maximum number of documents (windows) that you can have open at one time depends on the memory of your computer system and the amount of text in each document. When you open a new window, it is placed on top of the original window. Once multiple windows are open, you can resize the windows to see all or a portion of them on the screen.

When a document is open, a button displays on the Taskbar. This button represents the open document and contains a document icon, and the document name. (Depending on the length of the document name and the size of the button, not all of the name may be visible.) Another method for determining what documents are open is to click the Window option on the Menu bar. This displays a drop-down menu similar to the one shown in Figure 5.5. (The number of documents and document names displayed at the bottom of the menu will vary.)

FIGURE 5.5 ***Window Drop-Down Menu***

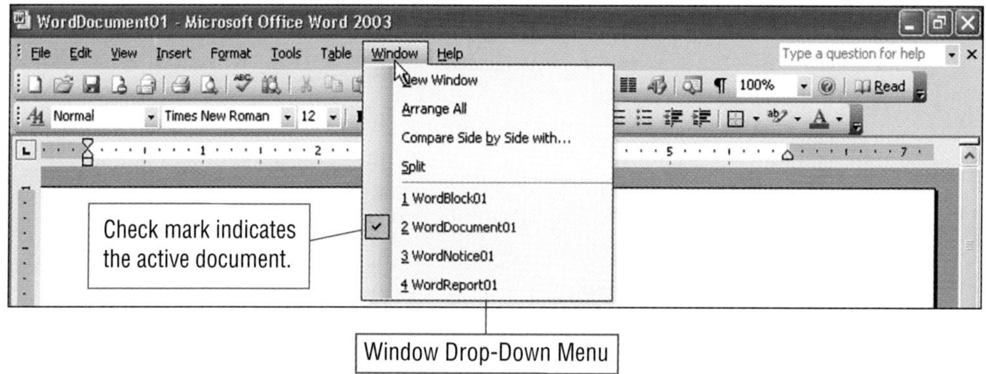

HINT

Press Ctrl + W or Ctrl + F4 to close the active document window.

The open document names are displayed at the bottom of the menu. The document name with the check mark in front of it is the ***active*** document. The active document is the document containing the insertion point. To make one of the other documents active, click the document name. If you are using the keyboard, type the number shown in front of the desired document. When you change the active document, the Window menu is removed and the new active document is displayed. ***(Note: Some virus protection software will let you open only one document at a time.)***

Arrange Windows
1. Open documents.
2. Click Windows, Arrange All.

Arranging Windows

If you have more than one document open, you can use the Arrange All option from the Window drop-down menu to view a portion of all open documents. To do this, click Window and then click Arrange All. Figure 5.6 shows a document screen with four documents open that have been arranged.

FIGURE 5.6 ***Arranged Documents***

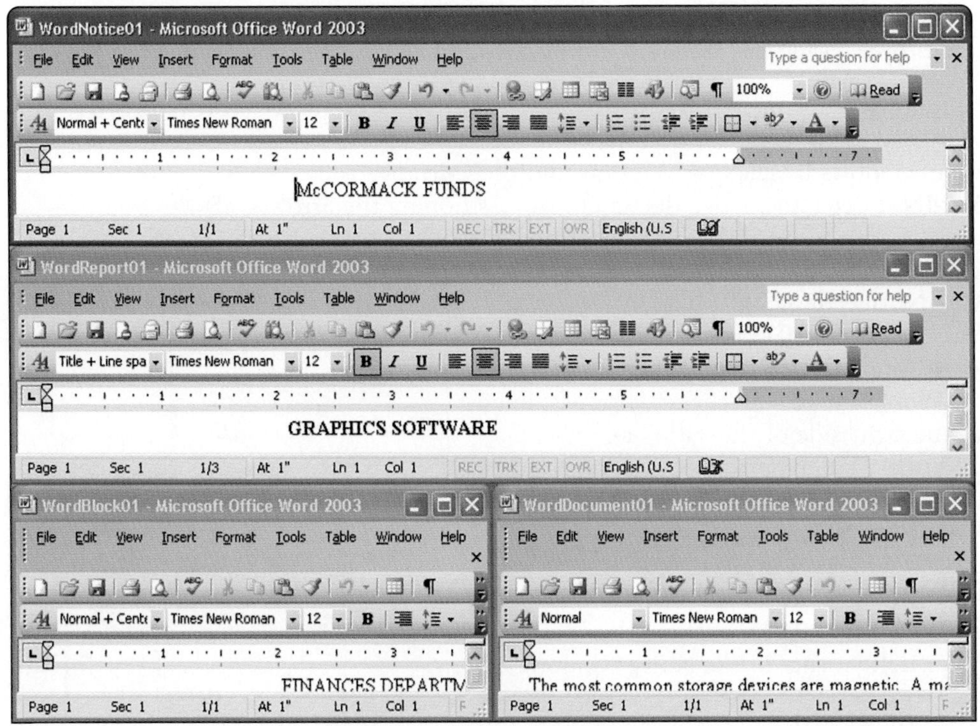

Maximizing, Restoring, and Minimizing Documents

Use the Maximize and Minimize buttons in the upper right corner of the active document window to change the size of the window. The Maximize button is the button in the upper right corner of the active document immediately to the left of the Close button. (The Close button is the button containing the *X*.) The Minimize button is located immediately to the left of the Maximize button.

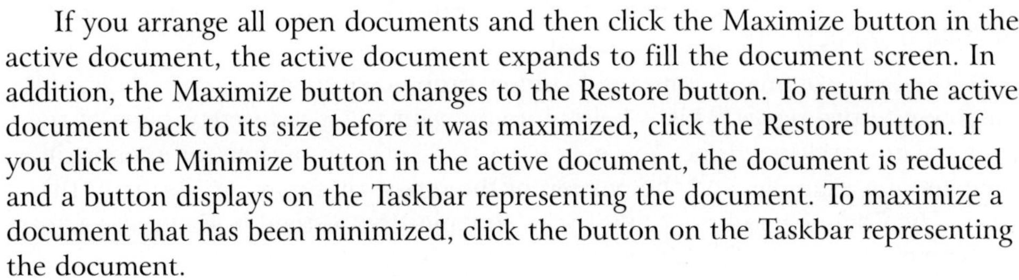

If you arrange all open documents and then click the Maximize button in the active document, the active document expands to fill the document screen. In addition, the Maximize button changes to the Restore button. To return the active document back to its size before it was maximized, click the Restore button. If you click the Minimize button in the active document, the document is reduced and a button displays on the Taskbar representing the document. To maximize a document that has been minimized, click the button on the Taskbar representing the document.

exercise 14

ARRANGING, MAXIMIZING, RESTORING, AND MINIMIZING WINDOWS

(Note: If you are using Word on a network system that contains a virus checker, you may not be able to open multiple documents at once. Continue by opening each document individually.)

1. Open the following documents: **WordBlock01**, **WordDocument01**, **WordNotice01**, and **WordReport01**.
2. Arrange the windows by clicking Window and then Arrange All.
3. Make **WordNotice01** the active document by positioning the arrow pointer on the title bar for **WordNotice01** and then clicking the left mouse button.
4. Close **WordNotice01**.
5. Make **WordDocument01** active and then close it.
6. Make **WordReport01** active and then close it.
7. Maximize **WordBlock01** by clicking the Maximize button at the right side of the Title bar. (The Maximize button is the button at the right side of the Title bar, immediately left of the Close button.)
8. Open **WordReport01**.
9. Arrange the windows.
10. Make **WordBlock01** the active window.
11. Minimize **WordBlock01** by clicking the Minimize button in the upper right corner of the active window.
12. Minimize **WordReport01**.
13. Restore **WordReport01** by clicking the button on the Taskbar representing the document.
14. Restore **WordBlock01**.
15. Make **WordReport01** the active document and then close it.
16. Maximize **WordBlock01** by clicking the Maximize button at the right side of the Title bar.
17. Close **WordBlock01**.

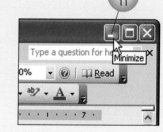

Step 7

Type a question for help

Maximize

Read

Step 11

Type a question for he

Minimize

Read

Splitting a Window

With the Split command from the Window drop-down menu you can divide a window into two ***panes***. This is helpful if you want to view different parts of the same document at one time. You may want to display an outline for a report in one pane, for example, and the portion of the report that you are editing in the other. The original window is split into two panes that extend horizontally across the screen.

Split a window with the Split option from the Window drop-down menu or with the Split bar. To split the current document window using the Split option, click Window and then Split. This causes a wide gray line to display in the middle of the screen and the mouse pointer to display as a double-headed arrow pointing up and down with a small double line between. Move this double-headed arrow pointer up or down, if desired, by dragging the mouse or by pressing the Up and/or Down Arrow keys on the keyboard. When the double-headed arrow is positioned at the desired location in the document, click the left mouse button or press the Enter key.

HINT

You can move text or graphics by selecting the desired object and then dragging and dropping it across the split bar.

You can also split the window with the split bar. The split bar is the small gray horizontal bar above the up scroll arrow on the vertical scroll bar. To split the window with the split bar, position the arrow pointer on the split bar until it turns into a short double line with an up- and down-pointing arrow. Hold down the left mouse button, drag the double-headed arrow into the document screen to the location where you want the window split, and then release the mouse button.

Split Window
1. Open document.
2. Click Window, Split.
OR
Drag split bar.

When a window is split, the insertion point is positioned in the bottom pane. To move the insertion point to the other pane with the mouse, position the I-beam pointer in the other pane, and then click the left mouse button. If you are using the keyboard, press F6 to move to the next pane. (You can also press Shift + F6, which is the Previous Pane command.)

To remove the split line from the document, click Window and then Remove Split. You can also double-click the split bar or drag the split bar to the top or bottom of the screen.

exercise 15

MOVING SELECTED TEXT BETWEEN SPLIT WINDOWS

1. Open **WordReport02**.
2. Save the document with Save As and name it **swc5x15**.
3. Click Window and then Split.
4. With the split line displayed in the middle of the document screen, click the left mouse button.
5. With the insertion point positioned in the bottom pane, move the *SECTION 1: COMPUTERS IN COMMUNICATION* section below the *SECTION 2: COMMUNICATIONS IN ENTERTAINMENT* section by completing the following steps:
   a. Select the *SECTION 1: COMPUTERS IN COMMUNICATION* section from the title to right above *SECTION 2: COMPUTERS IN ENTERTAINMENT*.
   b. Click the Cut button on the Standard toolbar.
   c. Position the arrow pointer at the end of the document in the top window pane and then click the left mouse button.
   d. Click the Paste button on the Standard toolbar.
   e. Change the number in the two titles to *SECTION 1: COMPUTERS IN ENTERTAINMENT* and *SECTION 2: COMPUTERS IN COMMUNICATION*.
6. Insert a section break that begins a new page above *SECTION 2: COMPUTERS IN COMMUNICATION* by completing the following steps:
   a. Position the arrow pointer immediately left of the *S* in *SECTION 2: COMPUTERS IN COMMUNICATION* in the bottom window pane and then click the left mouse button.
   b. Click Insert and then Break.
   c. At the Break dialog box, click *Next page*.
   d. Click OK.
7. Remove the split from the window by clicking Window and then Remove Split.
8. Check page breaks in the document and, if necessary, make corrections to the page breaks.
9. Save, print, and then close **swc5x15**.

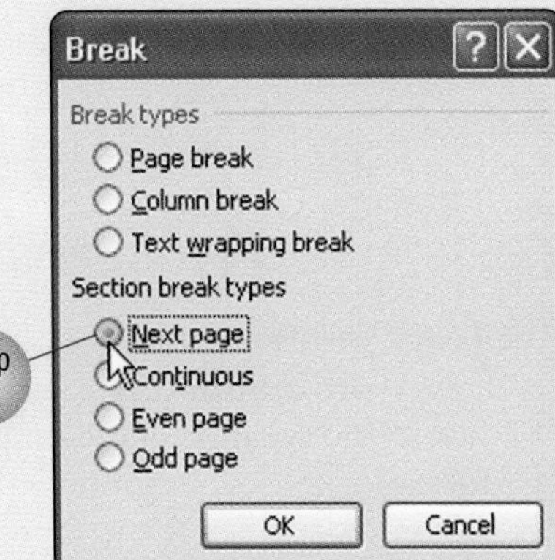

Comparing Documents Side by Side

Compare Side by Side
1. Open two documents.
2. Click Window, Compare Side by Side with *(Document name)*.

If you want to compare the contents of two documents, open both documents, click Window, and then click Compare Side by Side with *(Document Name)*. Both documents are arranged in the screen side by side and the Compare Side by Side toolbar displays as shown in Figure 5.7. By default, the Synchronous Scrolling button on the toolbar is active. With this button active, scrolling in one document causes the same scrolling to occur in the other document. This feature is useful in situations where you want to compare text, formatting, or other features between documents. If you want to scroll in one document and not the other, click the Synchronous Scrolling button to turn it off.

FIGURE 5.7 ***Comparing Documents Side by Side***

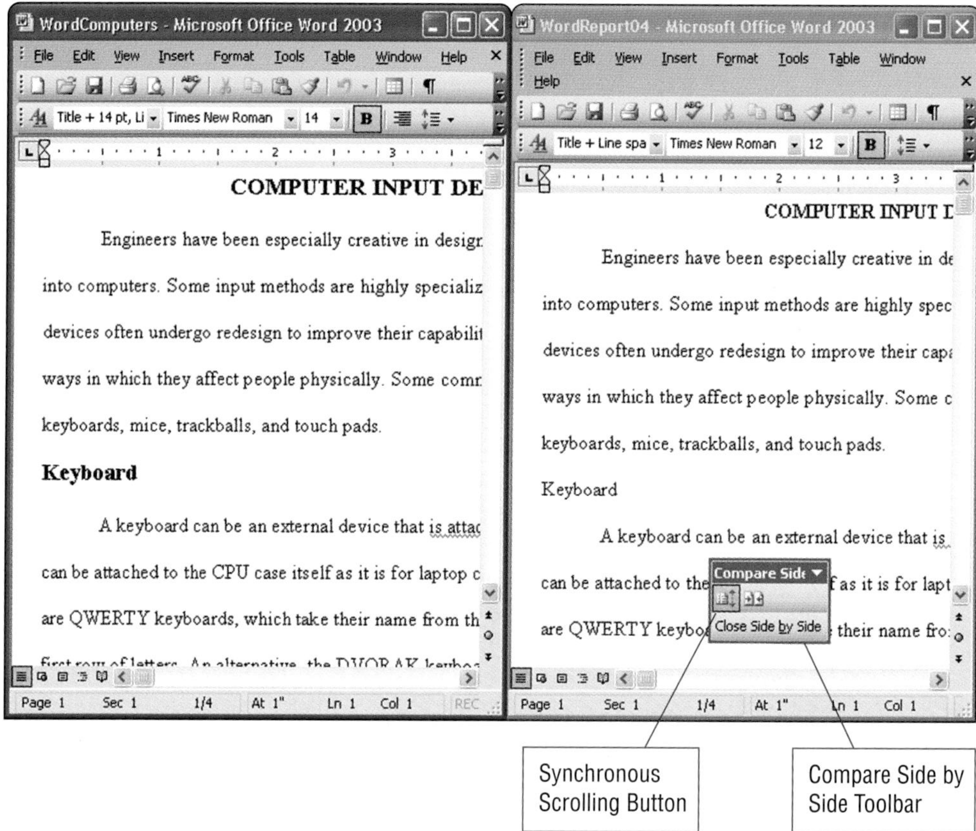

exercise 16 COMPARING DOCUMENTS SIDE BY SIDE

1. Open **WordReport04**.
2. Open **WordComputers**.
3. Click Window and then Compare Side by Side with WordReport04.
4. Make sure the Synchronous Scrolling button is active on the Compare Side by Side toolbar.

5. Scroll through both documents simultaneously. Notice the difference between the two documents. (The only difference is that the titles and headings in **WordComputers** are set in a different size and type style than the title and headings in **WordReport04**.) Select and then format each title and heading in the **WordReport04** document so they are set in the same size and style as the titles and headings in **WordComputers**.
6. Save the **WordReport04** document with Save As and name it **swc5x16**.
7. Print and then close **swc5x16**.
8. Close **WordComputers**.

Cutting and Pasting Text between Windows

With several documents open, you can easily move, copy, and/or paste text from one document to another. To move, copy, and/or paste text between documents, use the cutting and pasting options you learned earlier in this chapter together with the information about windows.

exercise 17

COPYING SELECTED TEXT FROM ONE OPEN DOCUMENT TO ANOTHER

1. Open **WordDocument03**.
2. Save the document with Save As and name it **swc5x17**.
3. With **swc5x17** still open, open **WordDocument04**.
4. With **WordDocument04** the active document, copy the first two paragraphs in the document and paste them into **swc5x17** by completing the following steps:
   a. Select the first two paragraphs in **WordDocument04**.
   b. Click the Copy button on the Standard toolbar.
   c. Deselect the text.
   d. Make **swc5x17** the active document.
   e. Position the insertion point a double space below the last paragraph and then click the Paste button on the Standard toolbar.
5. Make **WordDocument04** the active document and then close it. (This displays **swc5x17**.)
6. With **swc5x17** displayed, make the following changes to the document:
   a. Type the title **ECONOMIC OUTLOOK** at the beginning of the document, centered and in bold.
   b. Select the entire document and then change the font to 12-point Garamond (or a similar serif typeface).
7. Save, print, and then close **swc5x17**.

Printing Documents

In Chapter 1, you learned to print the document displayed in the document screen at the Print dialog box. By default, one copy of all pages of the currently open document prints. With options at the Print dialog box, you can specify the number of copies to print and also specific pages for printing. To display the Print dialog box shown in Figure 5.8, click File and then Print.

HINT
Save a document before printing it.

FIGURE 5.8 ***Print Dialog Box***

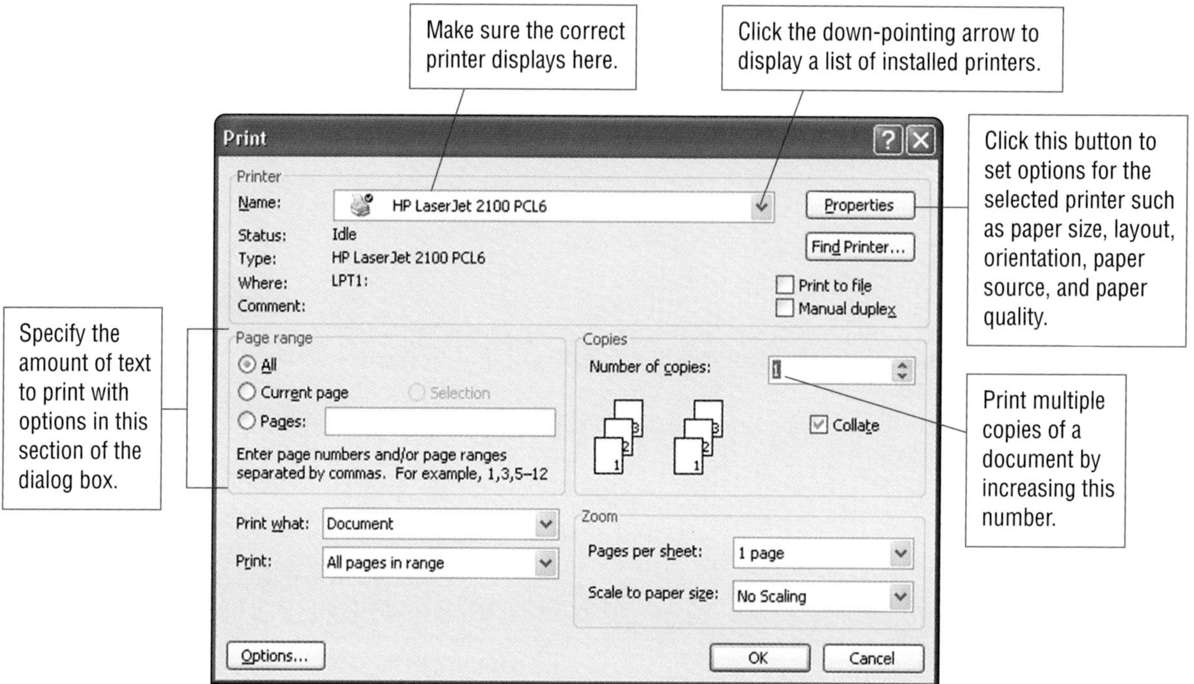
Make sure the correct printer displays here.
Click the down-pointing arrow to display a list of installed printers.
Click this button to set options for the selected printer such as paper size, layout, orientation, paper source, and paper quality.
Specify the amount of text to print with options in this section of the dialog box.
Print multiple copies of a document by increasing this number.
Print
Printer
Name:
HP LaserJet 2100 PCL6
Properties
Status: Idle
Type: HP LaserJet 2100 PCL6
Where: LPT1:
Comment:
Find Printer...
Print to file
Manual duplex
Page range
All
Current page
Selection
Pages:
Enter page numbers and/or page ranges separated by commas. For example, 1,3,5–12
Copies
Number of copies:
Collate
Print what: Document
Print: All pages in range
Zoom
Pages per sheet: 1 page
Scale to paper size: No Scaling
Options...
OK
Cancel

Printing Specific Text or Pages

The *Page range* section of the Print dialog box contains settings you can use to specify the amount of text you want printed. At the default setting of *All*, all pages of the current document are printed. Choose the *Current page* option to print the page where the insertion point is located. If you want to select and then print a portion of the document, choose the *Selection* option at the Print dialog box. This prints only the text that has been selected in the current document. (This option is dimmed unless text is selected in the document.)

With the *Pages* option, you can identify a specific page, multiple pages, and/or a range of pages. If you want specific multiple pages printed, use a comma (,) to indicate *and* and use a hyphen (-) to indicate *through*. For example, to print pages 2 and 5, you would type 2,5 in the *Pages* text box. To print pages 6 through 10, you would type 6-10.

Printing Multiple Copies

If you want to print more than one copy of a document, use the *Number of copies* option from the Print dialog box. If you print several copies of a document containing multiple pages, Word prints the pages in the document collated. For example, if you print two copies of a three-page document, pages 1, 2, and 3 are printed, and then the pages are printed a second time. Printing pages collated is helpful but takes more printing time. To speed up the printing time, you can tell Word *not* to print the pages collated. To do this, remove the check mark from the *Collate* option at the Print dialog box. With the check mark removed, Word will print all copies of the first page, and then all copies of the second page, and so on.

exercise 18 PRINTING MULTIPLE COPIES OF SPECIFIC PAGES

1. Open **WordReport04**.
2. Print two copies of pages 1 and 3 of the report (not collated) by completing the following steps:
   a. Display the Print dialog box by clicking File and then Print.
   b. Type 2 in the *Number of copies* text box.
   c. Click in the *Pages* text box and then type 1,3.
   d. Click the *Collate* option to remove the check mark.
   e. Click OK or press Enter.

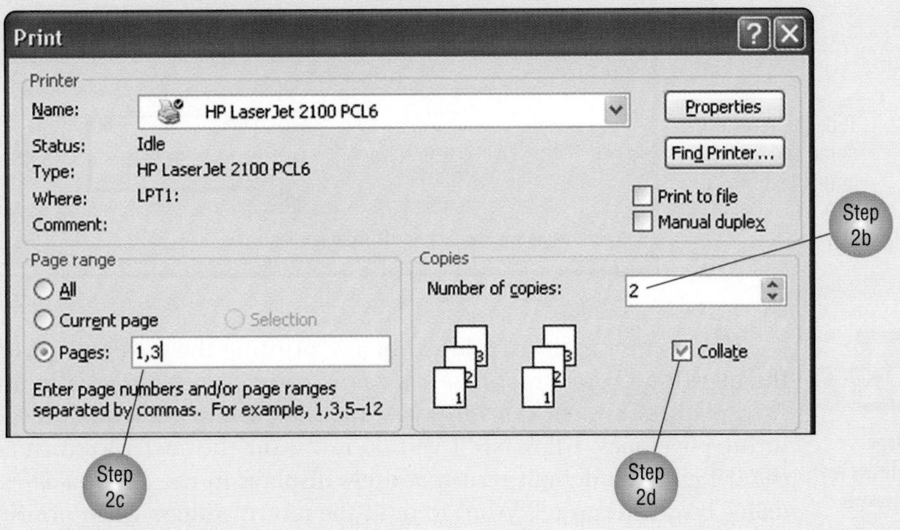

3. Close **WordReport04**.

Printing Envelopes

Word automates the creation of envelopes with options at the Envelopes and Labels dialog box with the Envelopes tab selected as shown in Figure 5.9. Display this dialog box by clicking Tools, pointing to Letters and Mailings, and then clicking Envelopes and Labels. At the dialog box, type the delivery address in the *Delivery address* text box and the return address in the *Return address* text box.

At the Envelopes and Labels dialog box, you can send the envelope directly to the printer by clicking the Print button or insert the envelope in the current document by clicking the Add to Document button.

FIGURE

5.9 Envelopes and Labels Dialog Box with Envelopes Tab Selected

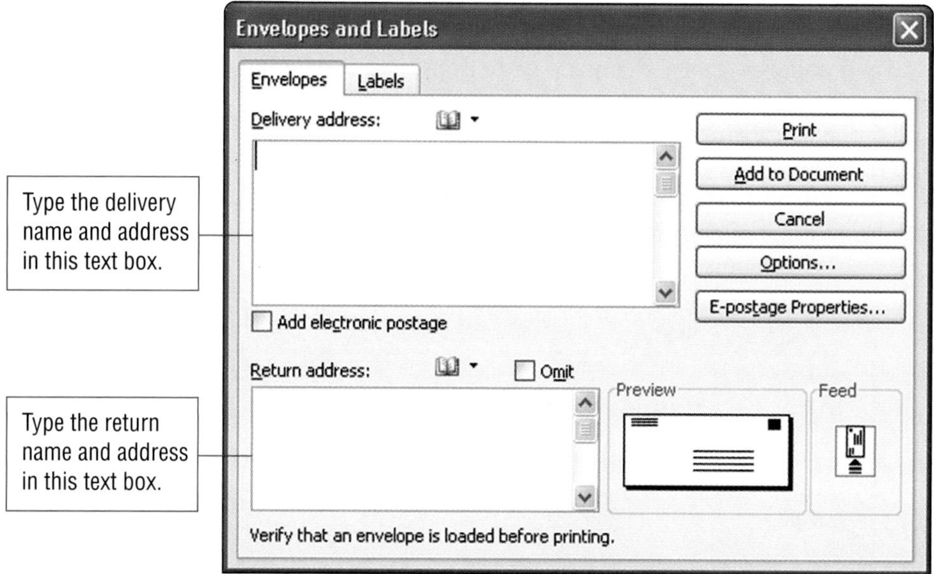

QUICK STEPS

Create Envelope
1. Click Tools, Letters and Mailings, Envelopes and Labels.
2. Click Envelopes tab.
3. Type delivery address.
4. Click in *Return address* text box.
5. Type return address.
6. Click Add to Document button or Print button.

If you enter a return address before printing the envelope, Word will display the question *Do you want to save the new return address as the default return address?* At this question, click Yes if you want the current return address available for future envelopes. Click No if you do not want the current return address used as the default. If a default return address displays in the *Return address* section of the dialog box, you can tell Word to omit the return address when printing the envelope by clicking the *Omit* check box to remove the check mark.

The Envelopes and Labels dialog box contains a *Preview* sample box and a *Feed* sample box. The *Preview* sample box shows how the envelope will appear when printed and the *Feed* sample box shows how the envelope will be inserted into the printer.

When addressing envelopes, consider following general guidelines issued by the United States Postal Service (USPS). The USPS guidelines suggest using all capital letters with no commas or periods for return and delivery addresses. Figure 5.10 shows envelope addresses following the USPS guidelines. Use abbreviations for street suffixes (such as *ST* for *STREET* and *AVE* for *Avenue*). For a complete list of address abbreviations, visit the USPS Web site at www.emcp.net/usps and then search for *Official USPS Abbreviations*.

exercise 19

PRINTING AN ENVELOPE

1. At a clear document screen, create an envelope that prints the delivery address and return address shown in Figure 5.10 by completing the following steps:
   a. Click Tools, point to Letters and Mailings, and then click Envelopes and Labels.
   b. At the Envelopes and Labels dialog box with the Envelopes tab selected, type the delivery address shown in Figure 5.10 (the one containing the name *GREGORY WATANABE*). (Press the Enter key to end each line in the name and address.)

c. Click in the *Return address* text box. (If any text displays in the *Return address* text box, select and then delete it.)
d. Type the return address shown in Figure 5.10 (the one containing the name *WENDY STEINBERG*). (Press the Enter key to end each line in the name and address.)
e. Click the Add to Document button.
f. At the message *Do you want to save the new return address as the default return address?*, click No.

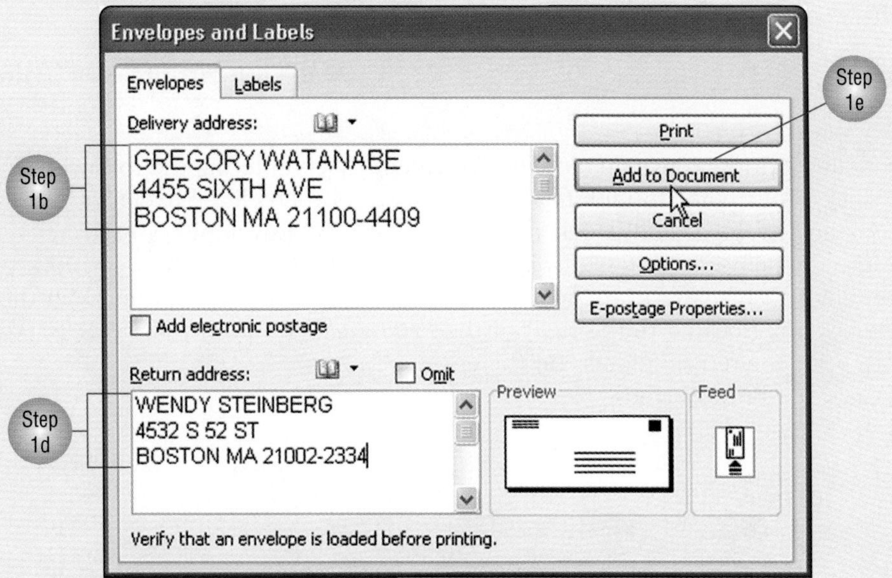

2. Save the document and name it **swc5x19**.
3. Print and then close **swc5x19**. ***(Note: Manual feed of the envelope may be required. Please check with your instructor.)***

FIGURE 5.10 ***Exercise 19***

WENDY STEINBERG
4532 S 52 ST
BOSTON MA 21002-2334

GREGORY WATANABE
4455 SIXTH AVE
BOSTON MA 21100-4409

If you open the Envelopes and Labels dialog box in a document containing a name and address, the name and address are automatically inserted in the *Delivery address* section of the dialog box. To do this, open a document containing a name and address, and then display the Envelopes and Labels dialog box. The name and address are inserted in the *Delivery address* section as they appear in the letter and may not conform to the USPS guidelines. The USPS guidelines for addressing envelopes are only suggestions, not requirements.

exercise 20

CREATING AN ENVELOPE IN AN EXISTING DOCUMENT

1. Open **WordLetter02**.
2. Create and print an envelope for the document by completing the following steps:
   a. Click Tools, point to Letters and Mailings, and then click Envelopes and Labels.
   b. At the Envelopes and Labels dialog box (with the Envelopes tab selected), make sure the delivery address displays properly in the *Delivery address* section.
   c. If any text displays in the *Return address* section, insert a check mark in the *Omit* check box (located to the right of the *Return address* option). (This tells Word not to print the return address on the envelope.)
   d. Click the Print button.

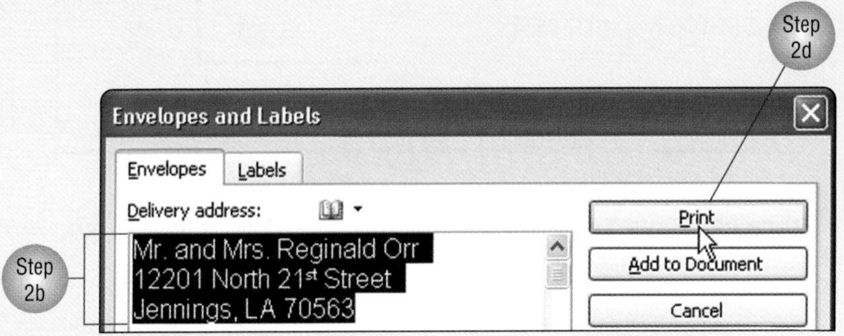

3. Close **WordLetter02** without saving the changes.

Printing Labels

Use Word's labels feature to print text on mailing labels, file labels, disk labels, or other types of labels. Word includes a variety of predefined labels that can be purchased at an office supply store. To create a sheet of mailing labels with the same name and address using the default options, display the Envelopes and Labels dialog box with the Labels tab selected as shown in Figure 5.11. Type the desired address in the *Address* text box and then click the New Document button to insert the mailing label in a new document, or click the Print button to send the mailing label directly to the printer.

FIGURE

5.11 ***Envelopes and Labels Dialog Box with Labels Tab Selected***

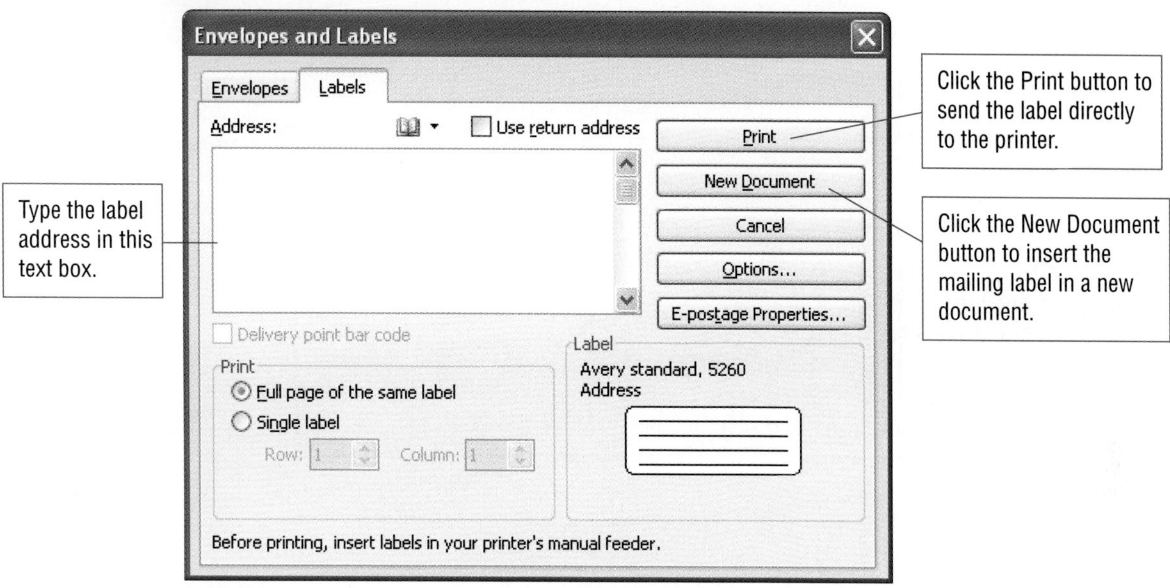

If you open the Envelopes and Labels dialog box (with the Labels tab selected) in a document containing a name and address, the name and address are automatically inserted in the *Address* section of the dialog box. To enter different names in each of the mailing labels, start at a clear document screen, display the Envelopes and Labels dialog box with the Labels tab selected, and then click the New Document button. The Envelopes and Labels dialog box is removed from the screen and the document screen displays with label forms. The insertion point is positioned in the first label form. Type the name and address in this label and then press the Tab key to move the insertion point to the next label. Pressing Shift + Tab will move the insertion point to the preceding label.

Create Labels

1. Click Tools, Letters and Mailings, Envelopes and Labels.
2. Click Labels tab.
3. Type delivery address(es).
4. Click New Document button or Print button.

Changing Label Options

Click the Options button at the Envelopes and Labels dialog box with the Labels tab selected and the Label Options dialog box displays as shown in Figure 5.12. At the Label Options dialog box, choose the type of printer, the desired label product, and the product number. This dialog box also displays information about the selected label such as type, height, width, and paper size. When you select a label, Word automatically determines label margins. If, however, you want to customize these default settings, click the Details button at the Label Options dialog box.

FIGURE 5.12 ***Label Options Dialog Box***

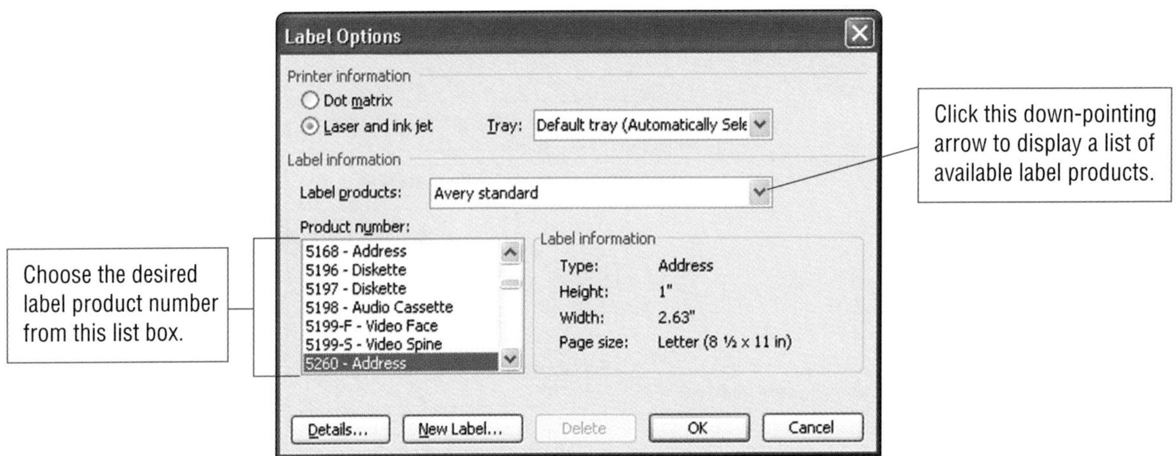

exercise 21 CREATING MAILING LABELS

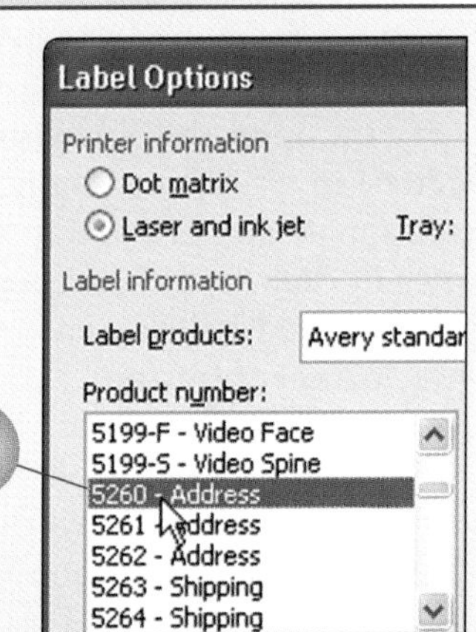

1. Open **WordLetter02**.
2. Create mailing labels with the delivery address by completing the following steps:
   a. Click Tools, point to Letters and Mailings, and then click Envelopes and Labels.
   b. At the Envelopes and Labels dialog box, click the Labels tab.
   c. Click the Options button.
   d. At the Label Options dialog box, make sure *Avery Standard* displays in the *Label Products* option box.
   e. Scroll through the *Product number* list box until *5260 – Address* is visible and then click *5260 – Address*.
   f. Click OK or press Enter.
   g. Make sure the delivery address displays properly in the *Address* text box.
   h. Click the New Document button.

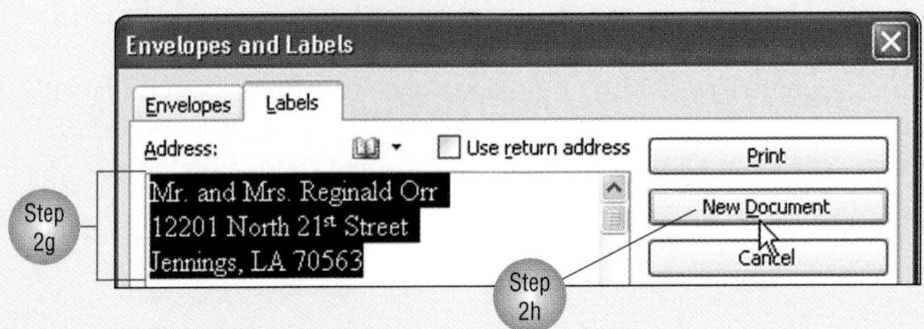

3. Save the mailing label document and name it **swc5x21**.
4. Print and then close **swc5x21**.
5. Close **WordLetter02**.

exercise 22

CREATING CUSTOMIZED MAILING LABELS

1. At a clear document screen, create mailing labels by completing the following steps:
   a. Click Tools, point to Letters and Mailings, and then click Envelopes and Labels.
   b. Make sure the Labels tab is selected. (If not, click Labels.)
   c. Click the Options button.
   d. At the Label Options dialog box, make sure *Avery standard* displays in the *Label products* text box.
   e. Click the down-pointing arrow at the right side of the *Product number* list box until *5662 - Address* is visible, and then click *5662 - Address*.
   f. Click OK or press Enter.
   g. At the Envelopes and Labels dialog box, click the New Document button.
   h. At the document screen, type the first name and address shown in Figure 5.13 in the first label.
   i. Press the Tab key twice to move the insertion point to the next label and then type the second name and address shown in Figure 5.13.
   j. Press the Tab key once (this moves the insertion point to the label below the label containing the name *DAVID LOWRY*).
   k. Type the third name and address shown in Figure 5.13. Continue in this manner until all names and addresses have been typed.
2. Save the document and name it **swc5x22**.
3. Print and then close **swc5x22**.
4. At the clear document screen, close the document screen without saving changes.

FIGURE 5.13 **Exercise 22**

DAVID LOWRY 12033 S 152 ST HOUSTON TX 77340	MARCELLA SANTOS 394 APPLE BLOSSOM FRIENDSWOOD TX 77533
AL AND DONNA SASAKI 1392 PIONEER DR BAYTOWN TX 77903	JACKIE RHYNER 29039 107 AVE E HOUSTON TX 77302

Viewing, Modifying, and Printing Document Properties

Word provides specific details about a document at the Properties dialog box. Figure 5.14 displays the Properties dialog box for WordContract01. Display the Properties dialog box by clicking File and then Properties. You can also display the Open (or Save As) dialog box, select the desired document, click the Tools button and then click Properties. Another method for displaying the Properties dialog box is to display the Open (or Save As) dialog box, right-click the desired document, and then click Properties at the shortcut menu.

FIGURE 5.14 ***WordContract01 Properties Dialog Box***

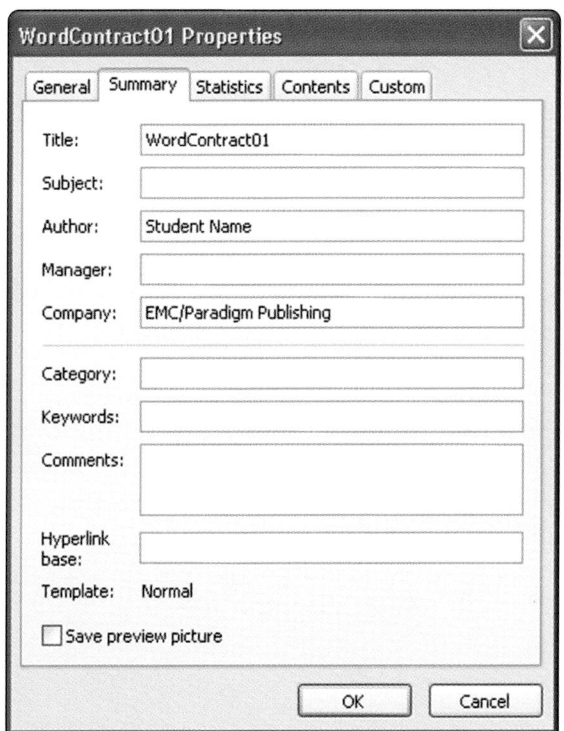

Display/Modify Document Properties
1. Open document.
2. Click File, Properties.
3. Type desired information in specific text boxes.
4. Click OK.

HINT

You can search for documents based on document properties.

The Properties dialog box with the Summary tab selected contains fields such as title, subject, author, company, category, keywords, and comments. Some of these fields may contain information while others are blank. You can type specific information in each of these fields to describe the document. To move the insertion point to the next field, press the Tab key. To move the insertion point to the previous field, press Shift + Tab.

Other tabs can be selected at the Properties dialog box to view additional information about the document. If you click the General tab, information about the document type, size, and location displays. Click the Statistics tab to view information such as the number of pages, paragraphs, lines, words, characters, and bytes included in the document. You can view the document without bringing it to the document screen by clicking the Contents tab. This displays a portion of the document in a viewing window. Click the Custom tab if you want to customize the properties of a document.

You can use the *Print what* option at the Print dialog box to print document properties. To do this, click File and then Print. At the Print dialog box, click the down-pointing arrow at the right side of the *Print what* option and then click *Document properties* at the drop-down list. Click OK to close the Print dialog box.

exercise 23

VIEWING AND MODIFYING INFORMATION AT THE PROPERTIES DIALOG BOX

1. Open **WordReport03**.
2. Save the document with Save As and name it **swc5x23**.
3. Click File and then click Properties.
4. At the swc5x23 Properties dialog box, make sure the Summary tab is selected, and then type the following text in the specified text box:

Subject	=	**Network Topologies**
Category	=	**Networks**
Keywords	=	**network, topologies, linear, star, ring**
Comments	=	**This report contains information on common network topologies including linear bus, star, and ring.**

5. Click OK to close the swc5x23 Properties dialog box.
6. Print the document properties by completing the following steps:
   a. Click File and then Print.
   b. At the Print dialog box, click the down-pointing arrow at the right side of the *Print what* option and then click *Document properties*.
   c. Click OK.
7. Save and then close **swc5x23**.

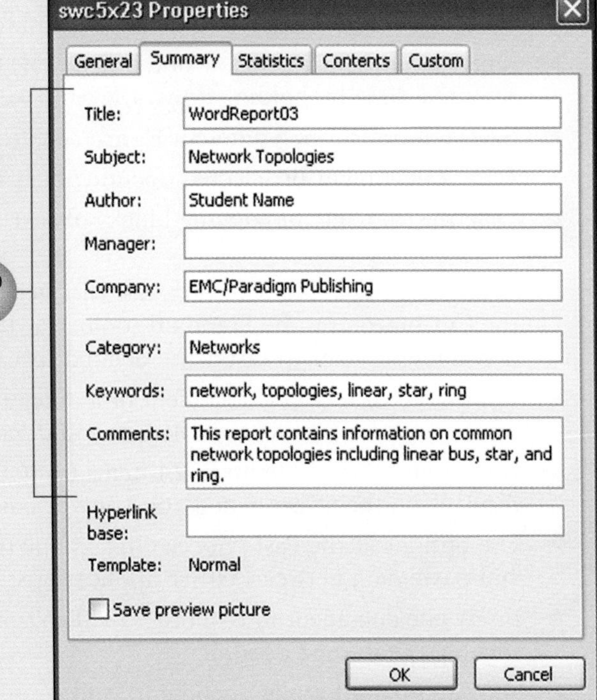

CHAPTER summary

- Group Word documents logically into folders. Create a new folder at the Open or Save As dialog box.
- You can select one or several documents at the Open dialog box. Copy, move, rename, delete, print, or open a document or selected documents.
- Make a copy of a document by opening the document and then saving it with a different name. You can also make a copy of a document with the Copy option from the Open dialog box shortcut menu. Copy a document or selected documents to the same folder or to a different folder. Word adds *Copy of* before a document name copied to the same folder.
- Use the Cut and Paste options from the Open dialog box shortcut menu to move a document from one folder to another.
- Use the Rename option from the Open dialog box Tools drop-down menu or the shortcut menu to give a document a different name.
- Delete documents and/or folders with the Delete button on the Open or Save As dialog box toolbar or the Delete option from the shortcut menu. Documents deleted from the hard drive are sent to the Windows Recycle Bin. Documents can be emptied or recovered from the Recycle Bin at the Windows desktop.
- Open several documents at one time at the Open dialog box. Close all open documents at the same time by holding down the Shift key, then clicking File and then Close All.
- Save a document in a different format with the *Save as type* option at the Save As dialog box.
- Print a document or selected documents at the Open dialog box.
- Deleting, moving, or copying blocks of text within a document is generally referred to as cutting and pasting.
- When deleting a block of text, use the Delete key if you do not need that text again; use the Cut button on the Standard toolbar or the Cut option from the Edit drop-down menu if you might want to insert the deleted text in the current or a different document.
- Copy selected text in a document or a different document using the Copy and Paste buttons on the Standard toolbar or the Copy and Paste options from the Edit drop-down menu.
- Collect and then paste up to 24 items using the Office Clipboard. The Clipboard task pane displays on the screen when you copy or cut two different items consecutively.
- Use options at the Paste Special dialog box to specify the format for pasted text or to copy and paste data between Office applications.
- Insert one document into another by displaying the Insert File dialog box and then double-clicking the desired document.
- You can open multiple documents and copy or move text between documents.
- Each open document fills the entire editing window. Move among the open documents by clicking the button on the Taskbar representing the desired document, or by clicking Window and then clicking the desired document name. The active document is the document containing the insertion point.
- Use the Arrange All option from the Window drop-down menu to view a portion of all open documents.
- Use the Minimize, Maximize, and Restore buttons in the upper right corner of the window to reduce or increase the size of the active window.

- With the Split command from the Window drop-down menu, you can divide a window into two panes. This enables you to view different parts of the same document at one time.
- Compare the contents of two documents by opening both documents, clicking Window, and then clicking Compare Side by Side with *(Document Name)*.
- The options available at the Print dialog box can help to customize a print job.
- The *Page range* section of the Print dialog box contains settings you can use to specify the amount of text you want printed. With the *Pages* option, you can identify a specific page for printing, multiple pages, and/or a range of pages.
- If you want to print more than one copy of a document, use the *Number of copies* option from the Print dialog box.
- Create and print an envelope with options at the Envelopes and Labels dialog box.
- Use Word's labels feature to print text on mailing labels, file labels, disk labels, or other types of labels.
- Word provides specific details about a document at the Properties dialog box. The Properties dialog box contains several tabs with each tab providing different information about the document.

FEATURES summary

FEATURE	BUTTON	MENU	KEYBOARD
Open dialog box		File, Open	Ctrl + O
Close all open documents		Hold down Shift key, click File, Close All	
Delete selected text		Edit, Cut	Ctrl + X
Copy selected text		Edit, Copy	Ctrl + C
Paste text		Edit, Paste	Ctrl + V
Clipboard task pane		Edit, Office Clipboard	Ctrl + C twice
Paste Special dialog box		Edit, Paste Special	
Insert File dialog box		Insert, File	
Arrange all open documents		Window, Arrange All	
Minimize document			
Restore document			
Maximize document			
Split a window		Window, Split	
Remove split from window		Window, Remove Split	

FEATURE	BUTTON	MENU	KEYBOARD
Move insertion point to other window			F6 or Shift + F6
Compare documents side by side		Window, Compare Side by Side with *(document name)*	
Print dialog box		File, Print	Ctrl + P
Envelopes and Labels dialog box		Tools, Letters and Mailings, Envelopes and Labels	
Properties dialog box		File, Properties	

CONCEPTS check

Completion: On a blank sheet of paper, indicate the correct term, command, or number for each description.

1. Create a new folder with this button at the Open or Save As dialog box.
2. Click this button at the Open or Save As dialog box to change to the folder that is up one level from the current folder.
3. To display the Open dialog box shortcut menu, display the Open dialog box, position the arrow pointer on a document, and then click this mouse button.
4. To select documents at the Open dialog box that are not adjacent using the mouse, hold down this key while clicking the desired documents.
5. To close all open documents at once, hold down this key, click File, and then click Close All.
6. When a document is deleted from the hard drive, the document is sent to this bin.
7. This choice from the Window drop-down menu causes each open document to appear in a separate window with no windows overlapping.
8. To remove a split line from a document, click Remove Split from this drop-down menu.
9. If more than one document is open, this word describes the document where the insertion point is located.
10. Compare the contents of two documents by opening both documents, clicking Window, and then clicking this.
11. Use options at this dialog box to specify the format for pasted text or data.
12. Click this button if you want a document to fill the editing window.
13. To print pages 1 through 4 in a document, type this in the *Pages* text box at the Print dialog box.
14. Display the Envelopes and Labels dialog box by clicking Tools, pointing to this option, and then clicking Envelopes and Labels.
15. The Properties dialog box with this tab selected contains fields such as title, subject, author, company, category, keywords, and comments.
16. List the steps you would complete to open several consecutive documents at one time.
17. List the steps you would complete to print pages 2 through 8 and page 12 of the open document.

SKILLS check

Assessment 1

1. Display the Open dialog box with WordChapter05S the active folder and then create a new folder named CheckingTools.
2. Copy (be sure to copy and not cut) all documents that begin with *WordSpellCheck* and *WordGrammarCheck* into the CheckingTools folder.
3. With the CheckingTools folder as the active folder, rename the following documents:
   a. Rename **WordSpellCheck01** to **Plans**. (Depending on your system setup, you may need to rename it **Plans.doc**.)
   b. Rename **WordSpellCheck02** to **Total Return**. (Depending on your system setup, you may need to rename it **Total Return.doc**.)
4. Make WordChapter05S the active folder and then close the Open dialog box.

Assessment 2

1. Display the Open dialog box with WordChapter05S the active folder and then delete the CheckingTools folder and all documents contained within it.
2. Delete the following documents:
   Copy of WordDocument03
   Copy of WordDocument04
   Copy of WordDocument05
3. Close the Open dialog box.

Assessment 3

1. Open **WordReport01**.
2. Save the document with Save As and name it **swc5sc03**.
3. Make the following changes to the report:
   a. Select the entire document and then change to a serif typeface other than Times New Roman (you determine the typeface) and change the line spacing to single.
   b. Select and then delete the last sentence in the document.
   c. Move the entire section titled *Painting and Drawing Programs Today* above the section titled *Developments in Painting and Drawing Programs*.
   d. Set the title and three headings in a larger, bold, sans serif typeface.
   e. Change the left and right margins to 1 inch.
4. Display the Properties dialog box with the Summary tab selected and then add the following information to the specified field:

Subject	=	Graphics Software
Category	=	Painting and Drawing Programs
Keywords	=	graphics, software, drawing, painting
Comments	=	This report contains information on graphics software including early drawing and painting programs, the development of graphics software, and current uses.

5. Print the document properties.
6. Save, print, and then close **swc5sc03**.

Assessment 4

1. At a clear document screen, create the document shown in Figure 5.15. Double-space between lines and triple-space after the last line in the document.
2. Make the following changes to the document:
   a. Change the font for the entire document to 14-point Copperplate Gothic Bold. (If this font is not available, choose Bookman Old Style.)
   b. Select and then copy the text a triple space below the original text.
   c. Paste the text two more times. (The document should contain a total of four forms when you are done and they should fit on one page.)
3. Save the document and name it **swc5sc04**.
4. Print and then close **swc5sc04**.

FIGURE 5.15 ***Assessment 4***

NEWS FLASH!!

LIFETIME ANNUITY FUNDS WORKSHOP TODAY!

Friday, October 21, 2005

North Bay Conference Hall

Assessment 5

1. Make sure Word is open and that a clear document screen displays.
2. Open Microsoft Excel.
3. Open the worksheet named **Excelc5sc05**.
4. Select cells A1 through C5 and then click the Copy button on the Excel Standard toolbar.
5. Click the button on the Taskbar representing Word.
6. At the clear document screen, paste the Excel cells using the Paste Special dialog box.
7. Press the Enter key twice and then paste the Excel cells by clicking the Paste button on the Standard toolbar.
8. Save the document and name it **swc5sc05**.
9. Print and then close **swc5sc05**.
10. Click the button on the Taskbar representing Excel.
11. Exit Excel.

Assessment 6

1. Open **WordBlock01**, **WordNotice01**, and **WordSpellCheck01**.
2. Make **WordSpellCheck01** the active document.
3. Make **WordBlock01** the active document.
4. Arrange all of the windows.
5. Make **WordSpellCheck01** the active document and then minimize it.
6. Minimize the remaining documents.
7. Restore **WordBlock01** by clicking the button on the Taskbar representing the document.

8. Restore **WordNotice01**.
9. Restore **WordSpellCheck01**.
10. Close **WordSpellCheck01**.
11. Close **WordNotice01**.
12. Maximize **WordBlock01**.
13. Close **WordBlock01**.

Assessment 7

1. Open **WordDocument03** and **WordDocument04**.
2. Make **WordDocument03** the active document and then save it with Save As and name it **swc5sc07**.
3. Make the following changes to the open documents:
   a. Select and then delete the last paragraph of text in **swc5sc07**.
   b. Copy the first two paragraphs in **WordDocument04** and then paste them at the end of **swc5sc07**.
   c. Check the spacing of paragraphs in **swc5sc07** and make sure there is a blank line between each paragraph.
4. Make sure **swc5sc07** is the active document and then make the following changes:
   a. Type the title ECONOMIC GROWTH IN THE 1990s at the beginning of the document, making it bold and centered.
   b. Set the entire document in a serif typeface (other than Times New Roman).
5. Save, print, and then close **swc5sc07**.
6. Close **WordDocument04**.

Assessment 8

1. Open **WordDocument01**.
2. Print two copies of the document, displaying the Print dialog box only once.
3. Close **WordDocument01**.

Assessment 9

1. At a clear document screen, create an envelope with the text shown in Figure 5.16.
2. Save the envelope document and name it **swc5sc09**.
3. Print and then close **swc5sc09**.

FIGURE 5.16 ***Assessment 9***

DR ROSEANNE HOLT
21330 CEDAR DR
LOGAN UT 84598

GENE MIETZNER
4559 CORRIN AVE
SMITHFIELD UT 84521

Assessment 10

1. Create mailing labels with the names and addresses shown in Figure 5.17. Use the Avery standard, 5660 – Address label.
2. Save the document and name it **swc5sc10**.
3. Print and then close **swc5sc10**.
4. At the clear document screen, close the document screen without saving changes.

FIGURE 5.17 ***Assessment 10***

SUSAN LUTOVSKY 1402 MELLINGER DR FAIRHOPE OH 43209	LEONARD KRUEGER 13290 N 120TH CANTON OH 43291	JIM AND PAT KIEL 413 JACKSON ST AVONDALE OH 43887
VINCE KILEY 14005 288TH S CANTON OH 43287	IRENE HAGEN 12930 147TH AVE E CANTON OH 43296	HELGA GUNDSTROM PO BOX 3112 AVONDALE OH 43887

Assessment 11

1. Use Word's Help feature to learn how to create a POSTNET bar code and a FIM-A code for an envelope.
2. At a clear document screen, create an envelope that contains the addresses shown in Figure 5.18. Add a POSTNET bar code and a FIM-A code to the envelope.
3. Save the envelope document and name it **swc5sc11**.
4. Print and then close **swc5sc11**.

FIGURE 5.18 ***Assessment 11***

CANDACE BRYNER
2604 LINDEN BLVD
MONTGOMERY AL 36334

CHAD FRAZIER
610 VALLEY AVE
MONTGOMERY AL 36336

CHAPTER challenge

You have been asked by your professor to create diskette labels that will be placed on the disks submitted for your homework. Create a full sheet of diskette labels that include your first and last names and the name of this course. Also, select a picture from ClipArt and position it so that it appears on each of the labels. Save and then print the labels.

You have been asked by your professor to locate information about eServices and especially about electronic postage. Use the Help feature and the Internet to learn about eServices and how electronic postage can be added to envelopes and labels. Summarize your findings in a memo to your professor. Save and then print the memo.

Use Microsoft Paint to create a simple graphic that can be placed on the same diskette labels that were created in the first part of the Chapter Challenge. Remove the existing picture from the labels. Copy the newly created graphic to all of the diskette labels. Save and then print the labels.

CUSTOMIZING DOCUMENTS

PERFORMANCE OBJECTIVES

Upon successful completion of Chapter 6, you will be able to:

- **Add text to a document with the AutoText feature**
- **Save, insert, edit, and delete an AutoText entry**
- **Create, format, edit, and delete a header or footer**
- **Create a different header or footer on the first page of a document**
- **Create a header or footer for odd pages and another for even pages**
- **Insert page numbering in a document**
- **Find and replace text and formatting**
- **Navigate using Go To and Document Map**
- **Create a document using a Word template and a wizard**
- **Create, view, delete, and print comments**
- **Compare and merge documents**

In this chapter you will learn to use the AutoText feature to simplify inserting commonly used words, names, or phrases in a document, and you will learn a variety of features to customize a Word document. For example, you will learn how to create and customize headers and footers, insert page numbering, find and replace text, use templates and wizards to create custom documents, insert comments in a document, and compare an original document with a revised document.

Using AutoText

Use the AutoText feature to quickly insert text that you use on a frequent basis. Word comes with built-in AutoText entries you can insert a document or you can create your own AutoText entry. Insert an AutoText entry in a document with the Insert, AutoText side menu, the All Entries button on the AutoText toolbar, or with options at the AutoCorrect dialog box with the AutoText tab selected. Create your own AutoText entry by selecting the desired text and then displaying the Create AutoText dialog box.

HINT

Insert an AutoText entry in a document by double-clicking the entry at the AutoCorrect dialog box with the AutoText tab selected.

Inserting a Built-in AutoText Entry

Word contains a number of built-in AutoText entries you can insert in a document. These built-in AutoText entries can be inserted in a document with the Insert, AutoText side menu or by selecting an entry at the AutoCorrect dialog box with the AutoText tab selected. To insert an AutoText entry with the side menu, position the insertion point at the desired location in the document, click Insert, point to AutoText, point to the desired category name, and then click the desired entry. Figure 6.1 displays the side menu categories.

FIGURE 6.1 ***AutoText Entry Side Menu Categories***

Insert Built-In AutoText
Click Insert, point to AutoText, point to category, click desired entry.
OR
Click All Entries button on AutoText toolbar, point to category, click desired entry.

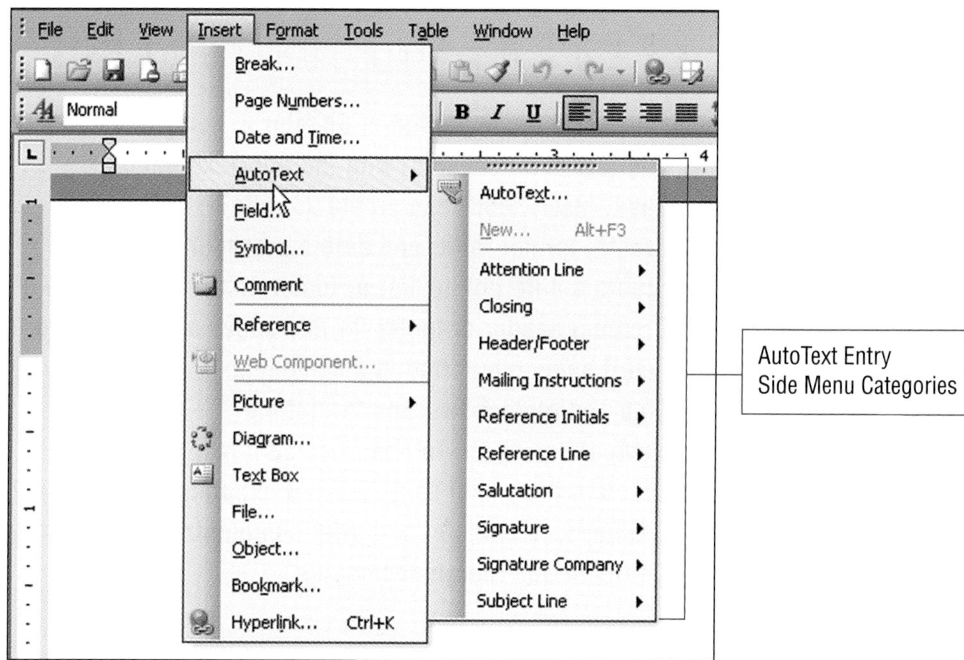

You can also display built-in AutoText entries with a button on the AutoText toolbar. To display this toolbar, click View, point to Toolbars, and then click AutoText. Click the All Entries button on the AutoText toolbar and a drop-down menu displays with AutoText categories as shown in Figure 6.2.

FIGURE

6.2 All Entries Drop-Down Menu Categories

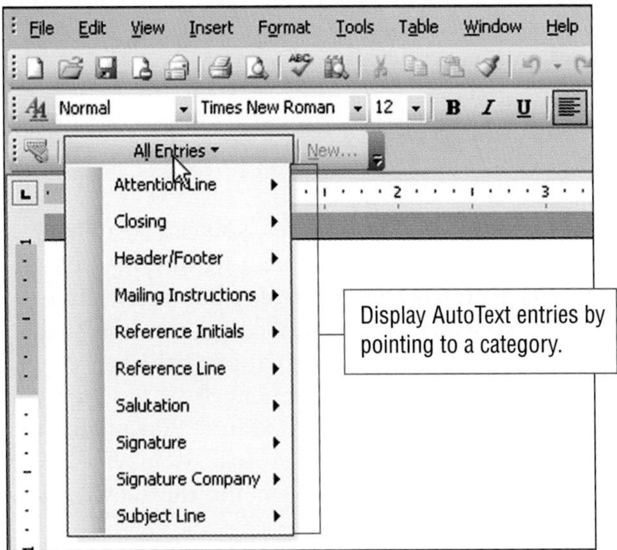

exercise 1

CREATING A LETTER AND INSERTING BUILT-IN AUTOTEXT ENTRIES

1. At a clear document screen, press the Enter key six times.
2. Insert the current date. (Insert the date with the month spelled out and day and year in figures, such as *February 23, 2005*).
3. Press the Enter key five times.
4. Insert a salutation by clicking Insert, pointing to AutoText, pointing to Salutation, and then clicking Ladies and Gentlemen:.
5. Press the Enter key twice.
6. Insert the file named **WordLetter04** located in the WordChapter06S folder. (Click Insert and then File to insert the document into the current document.)
7. Display the AutoText toolbar by clicking View, pointing to Toolbars, and then clicking AutoText.
8. With the insertion point positioned a double space below the inserted text, insert a complimentary close by clicking the All Entries button on the AutoText toolbar, pointing to Closing, and then clicking Sincerely yours,.

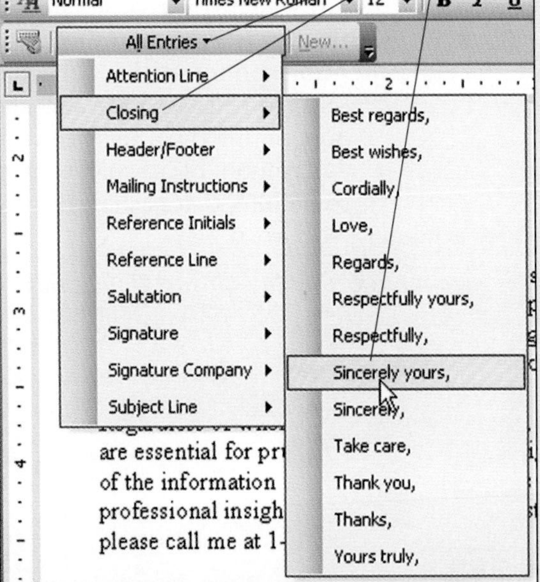

9. Press the Enter key four times.
10. Insert the current user name by clicking the All Entries button on the AutoText toolbar, pointing to Signature, and then clicking the user name that displays at the side menu.
11. Press the Enter key twice and then type your initials. ***(Note: The typist's initials are generally typed in lowercase letters. Word's AutoCorrect feature, by default,***

automatically changes the first letter to an uppercase. For this reason, uppercase letters are used for the initials. If you want to type initials in lowercase letters, consider turning off the* Capitalize first letter of sentences *option at the AutoCorrect dialog box. To display the AutoCorrect dialog box, click Tools and then AutoCorrect Options.)

12. Save the document and name it **swc6x01**.
13. Print and then close **swc6x01**.

Creating an AutoText Entry

Along with built-in AutoText entries, you can create your own entries. The AutoText feature is similar to the AutoCorrect feature you learned about in a previous chapter. With AutoCorrect, the text is automatically inserted in a document when the spacebar is pressed. For example, if you assigned the letters *HC* to *Hartland Corporation*, when you type and then press the spacebar, *Hartland Corporation* is automatically inserted in the document. If you use text on a less frequent basis and do not want it automatically inserted in the document when you press the spacebar, use Word's AutoText feature. An AutoText entry is inserted in the document with an option from the AutoText side menu, the shortcut key, F3, or by pressing the Enter key.

QUICK STEPS

Create an AutoText Entry

1. Type text.
2. Select text.
3. Click Insert, point to AutoText, click New.
4. Type entry.
5. Click OK.

Saving an AutoText Entry

The AutoText feature is useful for items such as addresses, company logos, lists, standard text, letter closing, or any other text that you use on a frequent basis. To save an AutoText entry, type the desired text, applying any necessary formatting. Select the text, click Insert, point to AutoText, and then click New. At the Create AutoText dialog box shown in Figure 6.3, type a short name for the text, and then click OK.

When you save selected text as an AutoText entry, the formatting applied to the text is also saved. If you are saving a paragraph or paragraphs of text that have paragraph formatting applied, make sure you include the paragraph mark with the selected text. To make sure the paragraph mark is included, turn on the display of nonprinting characters before selecting the text. An AutoText entry name can contain a maximum of 32 characters and can include spaces. Try to name the AutoText something that is short but also gives you an idea of the contents of the entry.

FIGURE 6.3 ***Create AutoText Dialog Box***

Insert an AutoText Entry

1. Type AutoText name.
2. Press Enter or F3.

Inserting an AutoText Entry

Insert an AutoText entry in a document by typing the name of the AutoText and then pressing the Enter key or the shortcut key, F3. An AutoText entry name must be at least four characters in length to display the AutoText with the Enter key.

Use the shortcut key, F3, on an AutoText entry name of any length. To insert an AutoText entry with the Enter key, type the name given (at least four characters) to the AutoText entry (the full entry displays in a yellow box above the insertion point), and then press the Enter key. To insert an AutoText entry with the shortcut key, type the name given the AutoText entry, and then press F3.

HINT

Make sure a check mark displays in the *Show AutoComplete suggestions* option at the AutoCorrect dialog box with the AutoText tab selected.

Editing/Deleting an AutoText Entry

Edit an AutoText entry by inserting the entry in a document, making any necessary changes, and then saving it again with the same AutoText entry name. When a message displays asking if you want to redefine the AutoText entry, click Yes.

Delete an AutoText entry at the AutoCorrect dialog box with the AutoText tab selected. Display this dialog box by clicking Insert, pointing to AutoText, and then clicking AutoText. At the AutoCorrect dialog box, click the entry to be deleted in the list box, and then click the Delete button.

exercise 2

CREATING AND DELETING AUTOTEXT ENTRIES

1. At a clear document screen, create an AutoText entry for Individual Retirement Pension Fund, by completing the following steps:
   a. Type **Individual Retirement Pension Fund**.
   b. Select *Individual Retirement Pension Fund*. (Be sure you do not include the paragraph symbol when selecting text. You may want to turn on the display of nonprinting characters.)
   c. Click Insert, point to AutoText, and then click New.
   d. At the Create AutoText dialog box, type **irpf**.
   e. Click OK.
   f. Deselect the text.
   g. Close the document without saving it.

2. At a clear document screen, create an AutoText entry for the letter complimentary closing shown in Figure 6.4 by completing the following steps:
   a. Type the text as shown in Figure 6.4. (Insert your initials where you see the *XX*.)
   b. Select the text.
   c. Click Insert, point to AutoText, and then click New.
   d. At the Create AutoText dialog box, type **cc**.
   e. Click OK.
   f. Deselect the text.
   g. Close the document without saving it.
3. At a clear document screen, create the letter shown in Figure 6.5 with the following specifications:
   a. While typing the letter, insert the *irpf* AutoText by typing **irpf** (this displays *Individual Retirement Pension Fund* in a yellow box above the insertion point), and then pressing the Enter key.
   b. Insert the *cc* AutoText entry at the end of the letter by typing **cc** and then pressing F3.
4. When the letter is completed, save it and name it **swc6x02**.
5. Print and then close **swc6x02**.

6. At a clear document screen, delete the *irpf* AutoText entry by completing the following steps:
   a. Click Insert, point to AutoText, and then click AutoText.
   b. At the AutoCorrect dialog box with the AutoText tab selected, click *irpf* in the list box below the *Enter AutoText entries here* text box.
   c. Click the Delete button.

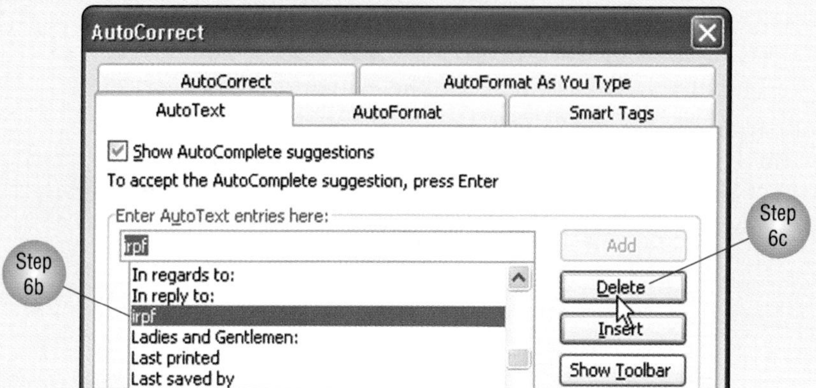

   d. Complete steps similar to those in 6b and 6c to delete the *cc* entry.
   e. Click OK to close the dialog box.

FIGURE 6.4 **Exercise 2**

Sincerely,

Chris Warren
Director of Financial Services

XX:

FIGURE 6.5 ***Exercise 2***

November 7, 2005

Dear Investors:

Stradford Funds is offering the new irpf for investors. This new fund offers an excellent opportunity for self-employed individuals as well as those who want to supplement their existing retirement fund. The irpf will be available to investors beginning January 1.

If you would like more information on the irpf, please give me a call at 1-888-555-3455. I can send you a brochure explaining the fund along with a fact sheet prepared by Stradford Funds. The irpf is an exciting opportunity and I would like to schedule a private consultation with you to determine if it fits with your investment needs.

cc

Creating a Header or Footer

HINT

Consider inserting a header or footer in any document longer than one page in length.

Text that appears at the top of every page is called a **header** and text that appears at the bottom of every page is referred to as a **footer**. Headers and footers are common in manuscripts, textbooks, reports, and other publications. Create a header or footer with the Header and Footer option from the View drop-down menu. Click View and then Header and Footer and Word automatically changes to the Print Layout view, dims the text in the document, inserts a pane where the header or footer is entered, and inserts the Header and Footer toolbar. Figure 6.6 shows a document with a header pane and the Header and Footer toolbar displayed, and Table 6.1 identifies the buttons on the Header and Footer toolbar.

Create a Header
1. Click View, Header and Footer.
2. Type header text.

Create a Footer
1. Click View, Header and Footer.
2. Click Switch Between Header and Footer button.
3. Type footer text.

FIGURE

6.6 Header Pane and Header and Footer Toolbar

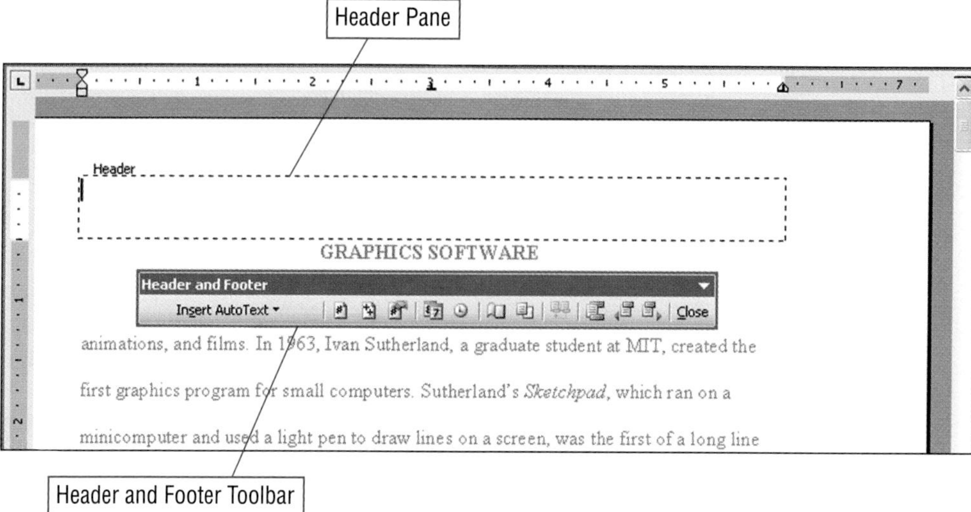

TABLE

6.1 Header and Footer Toolbar Buttons

Click this button	*Named*	*To do this*
Insert AutoText ▾	Insert AutoText	Insert AutoText into header/footer.
	Insert Page Number	Insert page number in header/footer.
	Insert Number of Pages	Prints the total number of pages in the active document.
	Format Page Number	Format the page numbers in the current section.
	Insert Date	Insert date in header/footer.
	Insert Time	Insert time in header/footer.
	Page Setup	Display Page Setup dialog box.
	Show/Hide Document Text	Turn on/off the display of document text.
	Save as Previous	Link/unlink header/footer to or from previous section.
	Switch Between Header and Footer	Switch between the header pane and the footer pane.

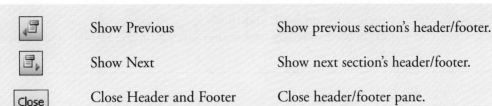

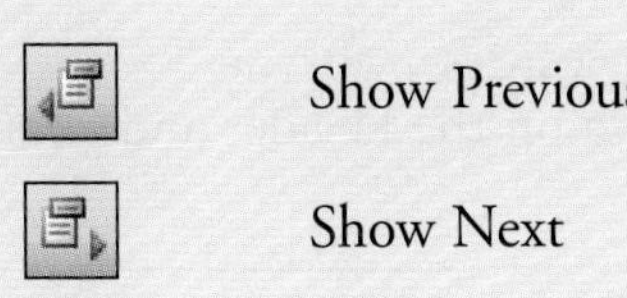	Show Previous	Show previous section's header/footer.
	Show Next	Show next section's header/footer.
	Close Header and Footer	Close header/footer pane.

Switch Between Header and Footer

By default, the insertion point is positioned in the header pane. Type the header text in the header pane. If you are creating a footer, click the Switch Between Header and Footer button on the Header and Footer toolbar. This displays a footer pane where footer text is typed.

Format header and footer text in the same manner as text in the document. For example, the font of header or footer text can be changed; character formatting such as bolding, italicizing, and underlining can be added; margins can be changed; and much more.

HINT

For reference purposes in a document, consider inserting a footer that contains the document name and path.

After typing the header or footer text, click the Close Header and Footer button on the Header and Footer toolbar. Closing the header or footer pane returns you to the previous view. If the Normal view was selected before a header was created, you are returned to the Normal view. If the Print Layout view was selected before a header was created, you are returned to that view. In the Normal view, a header or footer does not display on the screen. A header or footer will display dimmed in the Print Layout view. If you want to view how a header and/or footer will print, click the Print Preview button on the Standard toolbar. By default, a header and/or footer prints on every page in the document. Later in this chapter you will learn how to create headers/footers for specific sections of a document.

Show/Hide Document Text

When creating a header or footer, the main document text displays but is dimmed. This dimmed text can be hidden while creating a header or footer by clicking the Show/Hide Document Text button on the Header and Footer toolbar. To redisplay the dimmed document text, click the button again.

exercise 3 CREATING A HEADER AND A FOOTER

1. Open **WordReport01**.
2. Save the document with Save As and name it **swc6x03**.
3. Create the header *Graphics Software* and a footer that inserts the file name and path by completing the following steps:
   a. Click View and then Header and Footer.

b. At the header pane, turn on bold, and then type **Graphics Software**.
c. Click the Switch Between Header and Footer button on the Header and Footer toolbar. (This displays the footer pane.)

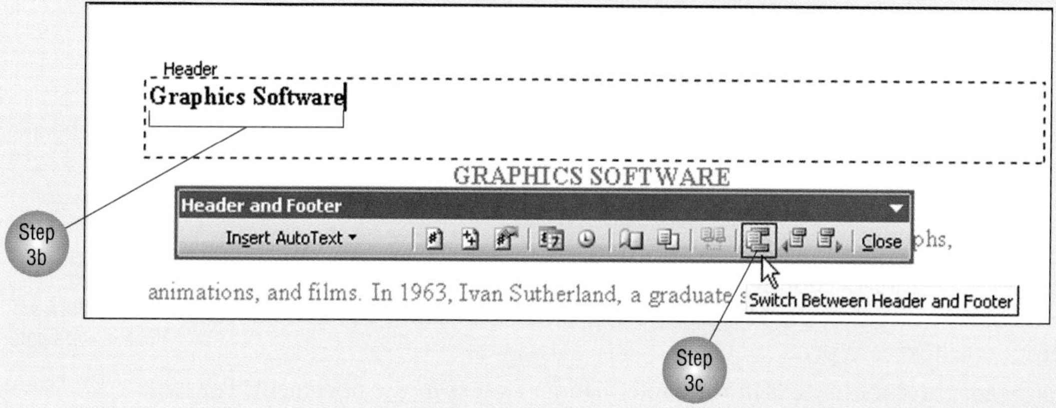

d. At the footer pane, click the Insert AutoText button on the Header and Footer toolbar and then click *Filename and path* at the drop-down list.
e. Click the Close button on the Header and Footer toolbar.

4. Display Print Preview to see how the header and footer will appear on each page when printed. (Press the Page Down key to view the second and then third page of the report.) After previewing the document, close Print Preview.
5. Save, print, and then close **swc6x03**.

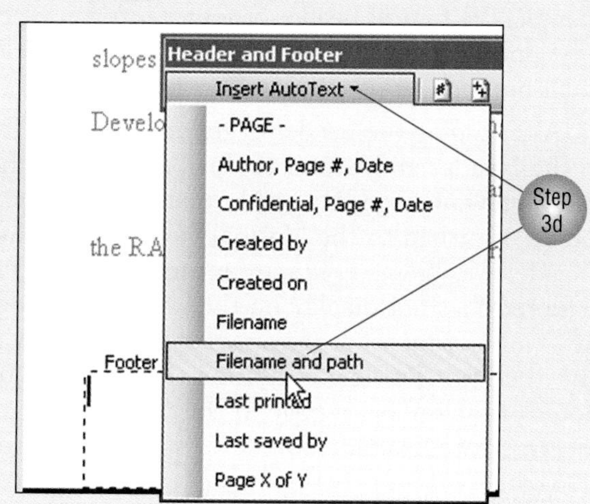

Formatting a Header or Footer

Double-click a header or footer in the Print Layout view to open the header or footer pane for editing.

Header or footer text does not take on the character formatting of the document. For example, if you change the font for the document text, header or footer text remains at the default font. However, margin changes made to the document text do affect header or footer text. If you want header or footer text character formatting to be the same as the document text, you must format header or footer text in the header or footer pane in the normal manner.

A header or footer contains three tab settings. (These settings are designed to work with the default left and right margins of 1.25 inches. If changes are made to the margins, these settings may not operate as described.) If you want text aligned at the left margin, make sure the insertion point is positioned at the left side of the header or footer pane, and then type the text. To center text in the header or footer pane, press the Tab key. This moves the insertion point to a preset tab. From the left margin, pressing the Tab key twice will move the insertion point to the right margin of the header or footer pane. Text typed at this tab will be right-aligned.

Editing a Header or Footer

Edit a header or footer by changing to the Print Layout view and then double-clicking the dimmed header or footer you want to edit. Edit the header or footer and then double-click the dimmed document text to make the document active.

Another method for editing a header or footer is to click View and then Header and Footer. Edit the header and then click the Close button on the Header and Footer toolbar. If you want to edit a footer, click the Switch Between Header and Footer button to display the footer. If the document contains more than one header or footer, click the Show Next button or Show Previous button to display the desired header/footer.

Show Next

Show Previous

exercise 4 CREATING, FORMATTING, AND EDITING A FOOTER

1. Open **WordReport01**.
2. Save the document with Save As and name it **swc6x04**.
3. Change the top margin to 1.5 inches.
4. Select the entire document, change the font to 12-point Century and then deselect the text. (If Century is not available, choose another serif typeface such as Bookman Old Style or Garamond.)
5. Create a footer by completing the following steps:
   a. Click View and then Header and Footer.
   b. Click the Switch Between Header and Footer button on the Header and Footer toolbar. (This displays the footer pane.)
   c. Change the font to 12-point Century bold (or the serif typeface you chose in Step 4).
   d. Type Painting and Drawing Programs.
   e. Press the Tab key twice.
   f. Type Page and then press the spacebar once.
   g. Click the Insert Page Number button on the Header and Footer toolbar.
   h. Select the page number and then change the font to 12-point Century bold (or the serif typeface you chose in Step 4).
   i. Click the Close button on the Header and Footer toolbar.

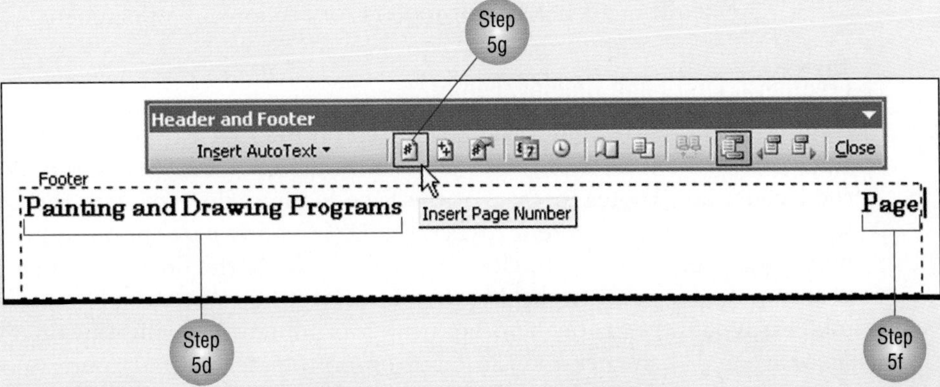

6. View the document in Print Preview and then close Print Preview.
7. Save and then print **swc6x04**.
8. Change the left and right margins to 1 inch.
9. Edit the footer by completing the following steps:
   a. Click View and then Header and Footer.

b. Click the Switch Between Header and Footer button on the Header and Footer toolbar.
c. Delete *Painting and Drawing Programs* from the footer pane. (Leave *Page #*, which is located toward the right margin.)
d. Type **Graphics Software** at the left margin in the footer pane.
e. Move the right tab on the Ruler from the 6-inch mark to the 6.5-inch mark.
f. Click the Close button on the Header and Footer toolbar.

10. Save, print, and then close **swc6x04**.

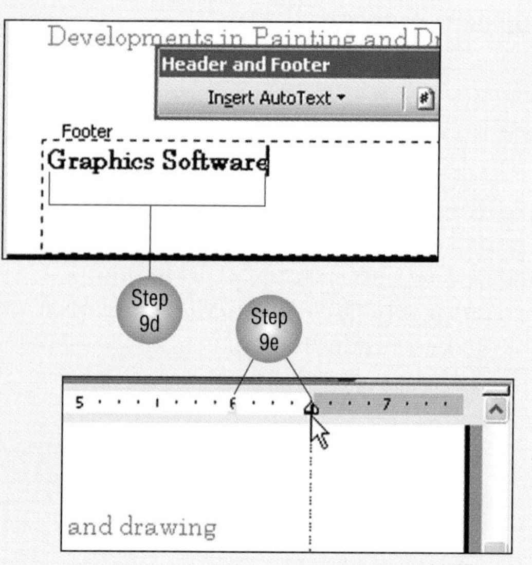

Deleting a Header or Footer

Delete a header or footer from a document by deleting it from the header or footer pane. Display the pane containing the header or footer to be deleted, select the header or footer text, and then press the Delete key.

Creating Different Headers/Footers in a Document

By default, Word will insert a header or footer on every page in the document. You can create different headers or footers within one document. For example, you can do the following:

- create a unique header or footer on the first page;
- omit a header or footer on the first page;
- create different headers or footers for odd and even pages; or
- create different headers or footers for sections in a document.

Creating a First Page Header/Footer

Page Setup

A different header or footer can be created on the first page of a document. To do this, display the header or footer pane and then click the Page Setup button on the Header and Footer toolbar. At the Page Setup dialog box with the Layout tab selected as shown in Figure 6.7, click the *Different first page* option to insert a check mark, and then click OK to close the dialog box. At the document, open another header or footer pane by clicking the Show Next button on the Header and Footer toolbar. Type the text for the other header or footer that will print on all but the first page and then click the Close button on the Header and Footer toolbar.

FIGURE

6.7 **Page Setup Dialog Box with Layout Tab Selected**

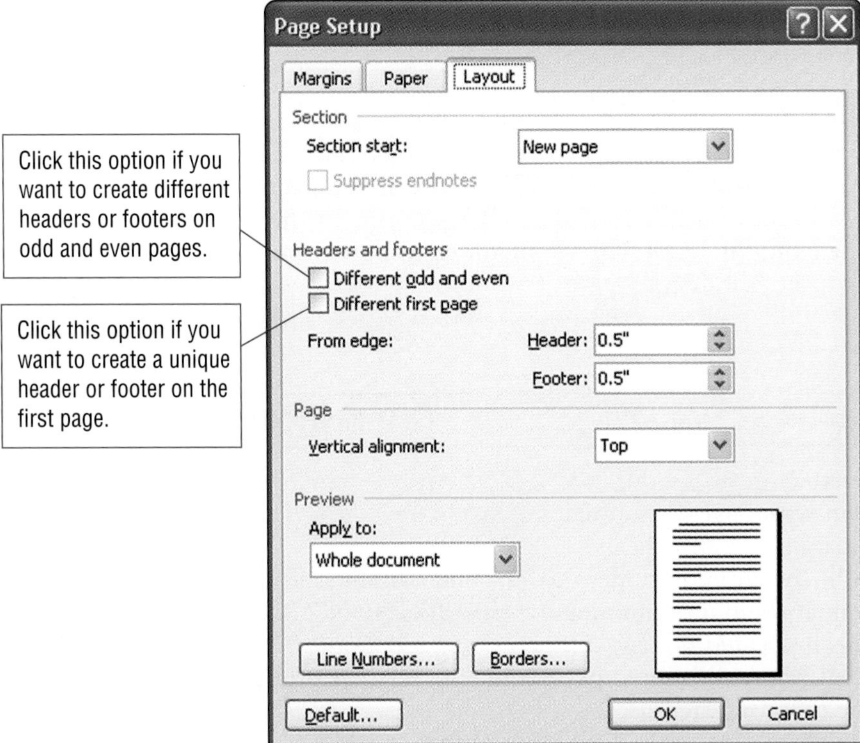

exercise 5

CREATING A HEADER THAT PRINTS ON ALL PAGES EXCEPT THE FIRST PAGE

1. Open **WordReport02**.
2. Save the document with Save As and name it **swc6x05**.
3. Create a header that prints at the right margin on all pages except the first page by completing the following steps:
   a. Position the insertion point anywhere in the first page.
   b. Click View and then Header and Footer.
   c. Click the Page Setup button on the Header and Footer toolbar.
   d. At the Page Setup dialog box, click the Layout tab.
   e. Click *Different first page*. (This inserts a check mark in the check box.)
   f. Click OK or press Enter.
   g. With the First Page Header pane displayed, click the Show Next button on the Header and Footer toolbar. (This opens another header pane.)

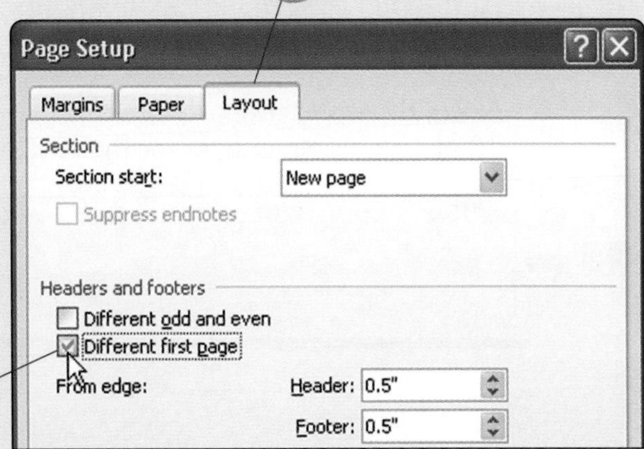

h. Press the Tab key twice, turn on bold, and then type **Computer Technology**.
i. Click the Close button on the Header and Footer toolbar.

4. Save, print, and then close **swc6x05**.

Creating a Header/Footer for Odd/Even Pages

Printing one header or footer on even pages and another header or footer on odd pages may be useful. You may want to do this in a document that will be bound after printing. Use the *Different odd and even* option at the Page Setup dialog box with the Layout tab selected to create different headers and/or footers for odd and even pages.

exercise 6 — CREATING A FOOTER FOR ODD AND EVEN PAGES

1. Open **WordReport02**.
2. Save the document with Save As and name it **swc6x06**.
3. Change the top margin to 1.5 inches.
4. Change the font for the entire document to 12-point Garamond (or a similar typeface).
5. Insert a page break at the line containing the title SECTION 2: COMPUTERS IN ENTERTAINMENT (located on page 2).
6. Create a footer that prints on all odd pages and another that prints on all even pages by completing the following steps:
   a. Move the insertion point to the beginning of the document and then click View and then Header and Footer.
   b. Click the Switch Between Header and Footer button.
   c. Click the Page Setup button.
   d. At the Page Setup dialog box, click the Layout tab.
   e. Click *Different odd and even*. (Make sure the *Different first page* option does not contain a check mark.)
   f. Click OK or press Enter.
   g. At the Odd Page Footer pane, press the Tab key twice and then type **Communication and Entertainment**.
   h. Select the footer text *Communication and Entertainment* and then change the font to 12-point Garamond bold (or the serif typeface you chose in Step 4).

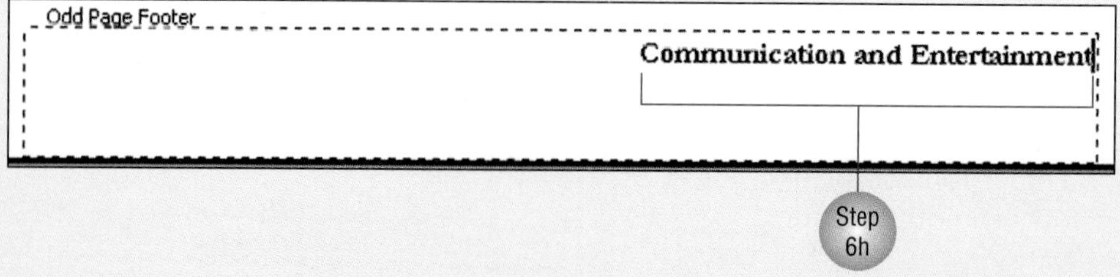

i. Click the Show Next button on the Header and Footer toolbar.
j. At the Even Page Footer pane, type **Computers**.
k. Select the footer text *Computers* and then change the font to 12-point Garamond bold (or the serif typeface you chose in Step 4).
l. Click the Close button on the Header and Footer toolbar.

7. Save, print, and then close **swc6x06**.

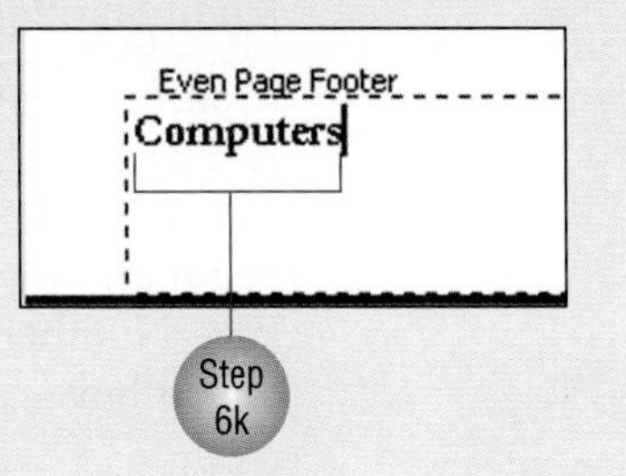

Inserting Page Numbering in a Document

Word, by default, does not print page numbers on a page. For documents such as memos and letters, this is appropriate. For longer documents, however, page numbers may be needed. Page numbers can be added to documents with options from the Page Numbers dialog box or in a header or footer. Earlier in this chapter, you learned about the Insert Page Number button on the Header and Footer toolbar. Clicking this button inserts page numbering in a header or footer.

In addition to a header or footer, page numbering can be added to a document with options from the Page Numbers dialog box shown in Figure 6.8. To display this dialog box, click Insert and then Page Numbers. With options at the Page Numbers dialog box you can specify the position and alignment of page numbers and whether or not you want the page number to appear on the first page.

Insert Page Numbering
1. Click Insert, Page Numbers.
2. Specify position and alignment.
3. Click OK.

FIGURE 6.8 ***Page Numbers Dialog Box***

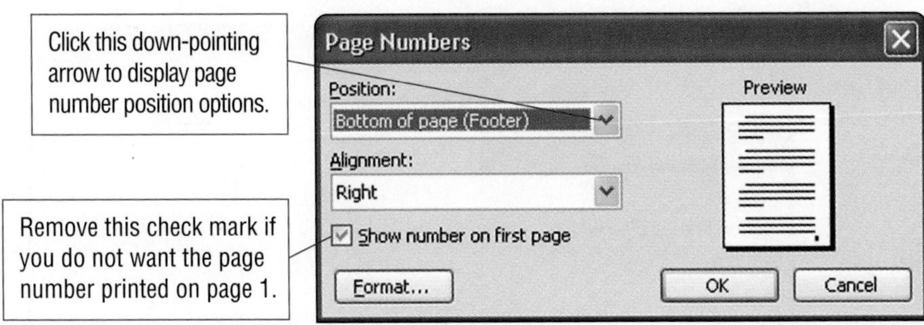

Deleting Page Numbering

Delete page numbering in a document in the same manner as deleting a header or footer. To delete page numbering, click View and then Header and Footer. Display the header or footer pane containing the page numbering, select the page numbering, and then press the Delete key. Click the Close button on the Header and Footer toolbar.

Modifying Page Numbering Format

Modify page numbering with options at the Page Number Format dialog box shown in Figure 6.9. With options at this dialog box, you can change the numbering format, add chapter numbering, and specify where you want page numbering to begin and in what sections you want page numbering to appear. To display the Page Number Format dialog box, click the Format button at the Page Numbers dialog box.

FIGURE 6.9 ***Page Number Format Dialog Box***

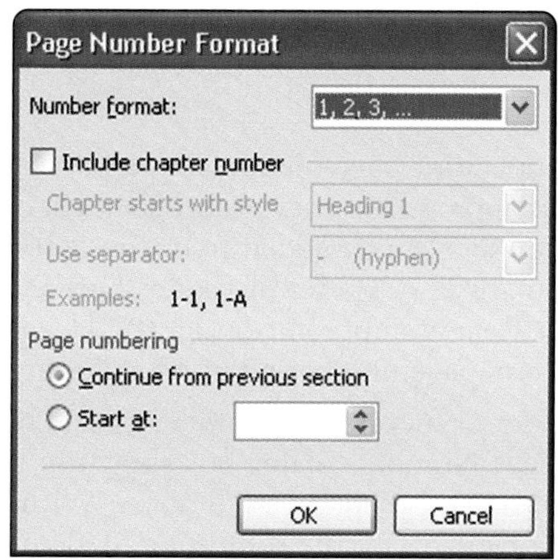

exercise 7

INSERTING AND MODIFYING PAGE NUMBERS

1. Open **WordComputers**.
2. Save the document with Save As and name it **swc6x07**.
3. Insert and modify page numbers by completing the following steps:
   a. Click Insert and then Page Numbers.
   b. At the Page Numbers dialog box, click the down-pointing arrow at the right of the *Alignment* option, and then click *Outside*.
   c. Click the Format button.
   d. At the Page Number Format dialog box, click the down-pointing arrow at the right of the *Number format* option box and then click *i, ii, iii, ...* at the drop-down list.
   e. Click *Start at* and then type 3.
   f. Click OK or press Enter to close the Page Number Format dialog box.
   g. Click OK or press Enter to close the Page Numbers dialog box.
4. Save, print, and then close **swc6x07**.

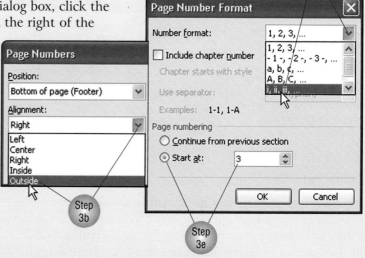

Finding and Replacing Text

With Word's Find feature you can search for specific characters or formatting. With the Find and Replace feature, you can search for specific characters or formatting and replace with other characters or formatting. Using the Find feature, or the Find and Replace feature, you can:

- Search for overly used words or phrases in a document.
- Use abbreviations for common phrases when entering text and then replace the abbreviations with the actual text.
- Set up standard documents with generic names and replace them with other names to make personalized documents.
- Find and replace formatting.

HINT

Press Ctrl + F to display the Find and Replace dialog box with the Find tab selected.

Finding Text

To find specific text or formatting in a document, click Edit and then Find. This displays the Find and Replace dialog box with the Find tab selected as shown in Figure 6.10. Enter the characters for which you are searching in the *Find what* text box. You can enter up to 256 characters in this text box. Click the Find Next button and Word searches for and selects the first occurrence of the text in the document. Make corrections to the text if needed and then search for the next occurrence by clicking the Find Next button again. Click the Cancel button to close the Find and Replace dialog box.

Find Text
1. Click Edit, Find.
2. Type find text.
3. Click Find Next button.

FIGURE 6.10 **Find and Replace Dialog Box with Find Tab Selected**

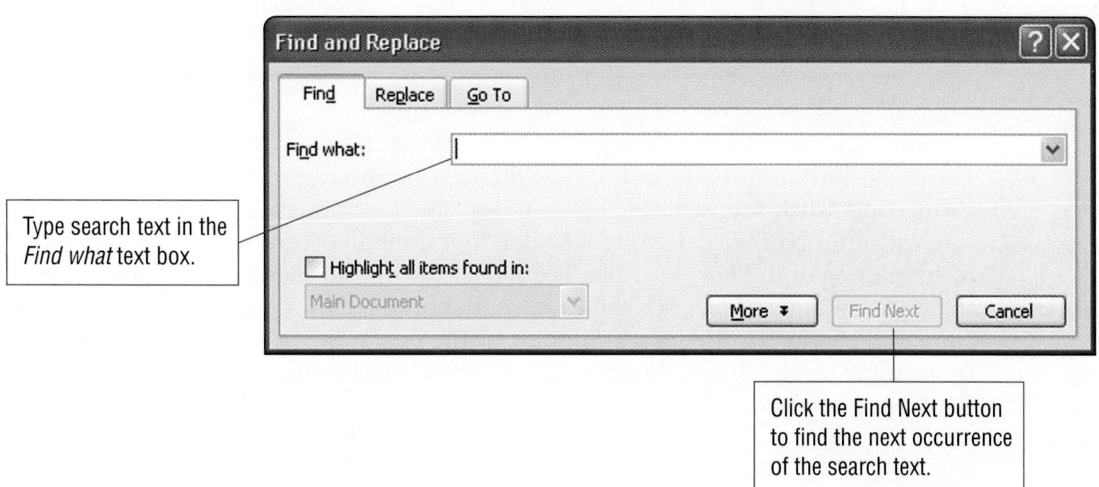

The next time you open the Find and Replace dialog box, you can display a list of text for which you have searched by clicking the down-pointing arrow at the right of the *Find what* text box. For example, if you searched for *type size* and then performed another search for *type style,* the third time you open the Find and Replace dialog box, clicking the down-pointing arrow after the *Find what* text box will display a drop-down list with *type style* and *type size*. Click text from this drop-down list if you want to perform a search on that text.

HINT
Press Ctrl + H to display the Find and Replace dialog box with the Replace tab selected.

QUICK STEPS

Find and Replace Text
1. Click Edit, Replace.
2. Type find text.
3. Press Tab key.
4. Type replace text.
5. Click Replace or Replace All.

Finding and Replacing Text

To find and replace text, click Edit and then Replace. This displays the Find and Replace dialog box with the Replace tab selected as shown in Figure 6.11. Enter the characters and/or formatting for which you are searching in the *Find what* text box. Press the Tab key to move the insertion point to the *Replace with* text box and then type the replacement text or insert the replacement formatting. You can also move the insertion point to the *Replace with* text box by clicking inside the text box.

FIGURE 6.11 ***Find and Replace Dialog Box with the Replace Tab Selected***

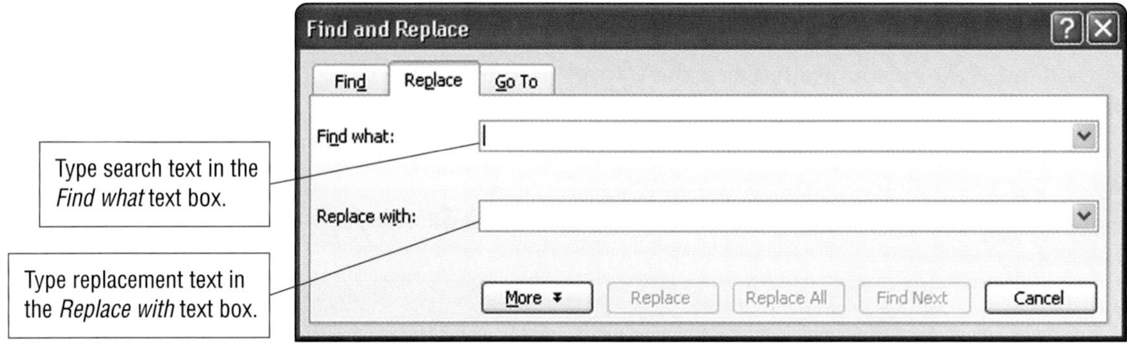

HINT
If the Find and Replace dialog box is in the way of specific text, drag the dialog box to a different location.

The Find and Replace dialog box contains several command buttons. Click the Find Next button to tell Word to find the next occurrence of the characters and/or formatting. Click the Replace button to replace the characters or formatting and find the next occurrence. If you know that you want all occurrences of the characters or formatting in the *Find what* text box replaced with the characters or formatting in the *Replace with* text box, click the Replace All button. This replaces every occurrence from the location of the insertion point to the beginning or end of the document (depending on the search direction). Click the Cancel button to close the Find and Replace dialog box.

exercise 8 FINDING AND REPLACING TEXT

1. Open **WordLegal01**.
2. Save the document with Save As and name it **swc6x08**.
3. Find all occurrences of *NAME1* and replace with *SUSAN R. LOWE* by completing the following steps:
   a. With the insertion point positioned at the beginning of the document, click Edit and then Replace.

b. At the Find and Replace dialog box with the Replace tab selected, type NAME1 in the *Find what* text box.
c. Press the Tab key to move the insertion point to the *Replace with* text box.
d. Type SUSAN R. LOWE.
e. Click the Replace All button.

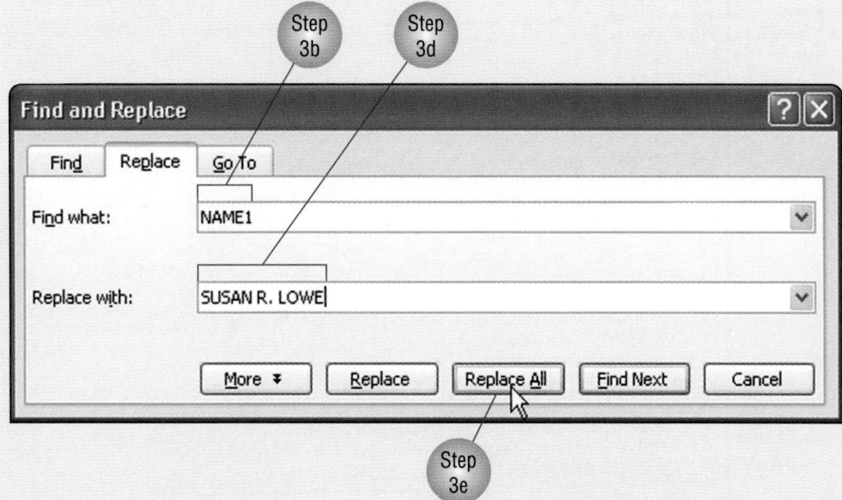

f. At the message *Word has completed its search of the document and has made 5 replacements*, click OK. (Do not close the Find and Replace dialog box.)

4. With the Find and Replace dialog box still open, complete steps similar to those in Steps 3b through 3f to find all occurrences of *NAME2* and replace with *MARY A. LANGE.*
5. With the Find and Replace dialog box still open, complete steps similar to those in Steps 3b through 3f to find the one occurrence of *NUMBER* and replace with *C-3546*.
6. Close the Find and Replace dialog box.
7. Save, print, and then close **swc6x08**.

Choosing Find Check Box Options

The Find and Replace dialog box contains a variety of check boxes with options you can choose for completing a search. To display these options, click the More button located at the bottom of the dialog box. This causes the Find and Replace dialog box to expand as shown in Figure 6.12. Each option and what will occur if it is selected is described in Table 6.2. To remove the display of options toward the bottom of the Find and Replace dialog box, click the Less button. (The Less button was previously the More button.)

HINT

If you make a mistake when replacing text, close the Find and Replace dialog box, and then click the Undo button on the Standard toolbar.

FIGURE

6.12 ***Expanded Find and Replace Dialog Box***

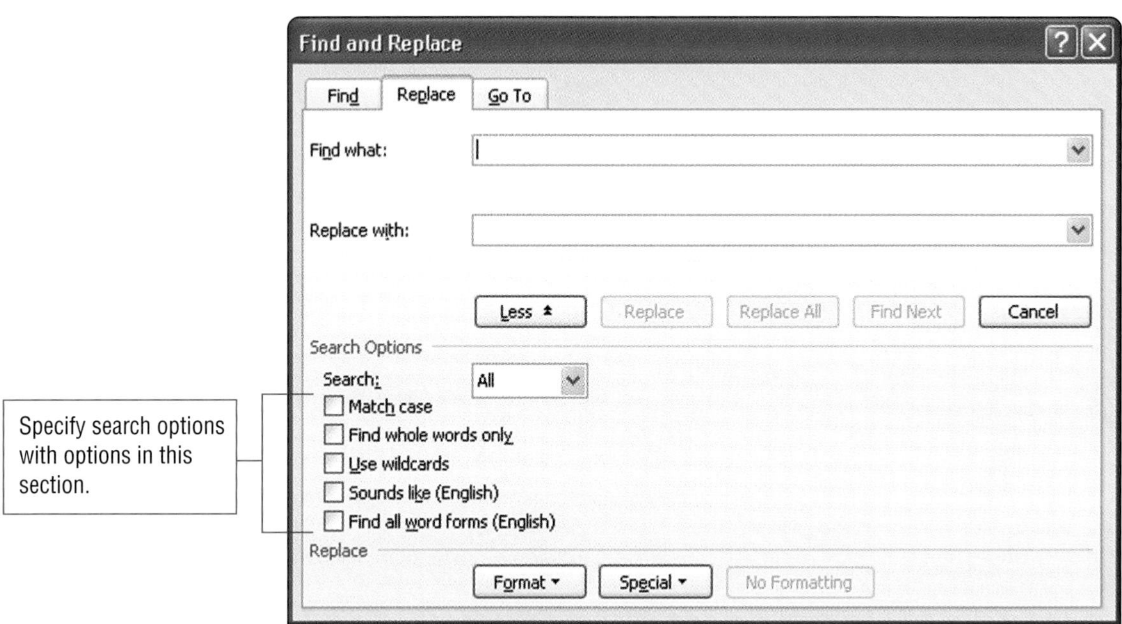

TABLE

6.2 ***Options at the Expanded Find and Replace Dialog Box***

Choose this option	***To***
Match case	Exactly match the case of the search text. For example, if you search for *Book* and select the *Match case* option, Word will stop at *Book* but not *book* or *BOOK*.
Find whole words only	Find a whole word, not a part of a word. For example, if you search for *her* and did not select *Find whole words only*, Word would stop at t*her*e, *her*e, *her*s, and so on.
Use wildcards	Search for wildcards, special characters, or special search operators.
Sounds like	Match words that sound alike but are spelled differently such as *know* and *no*.
Find all word forms	Find all forms of the word entered in the *Find what* text box. For example, if you enter *hold*, Word will stop at *held* and *holding*.

FINDING AND REPLACING WORD FORMS

1. Open **WordDocument06**.
2. Save the document with Save As and name it **swc6x09**.
3. Find all forms of the word *produce* and replace it with forms of *create* by completing the following steps:
   a. Make sure the insertion point is positioned at the beginning of the document.
   b. Click Edit and then Replace.
   c. At the Find and Replace dialog box with the Replace tab selected, type **produce** in the *Find what* text box.
   d. Press the Tab key and then type **create** in the *Replace with* text box.
   e. Click the More button.
   f. Click the *Find all word forms* option. (This inserts a check mark in the check box.)
   g. Click the Replace All button.
   h. At the message *Replace All is not recommended with Find All Word Forms. Continue with Replace All?*, click OK.
   i. At the message *Word has completed its search of the document and has made 7 replacements*, click OK.
   j. Click the *Find all word forms* option to remove the check mark.
   k. Click the Less button.
   l. Click the Close button to close the Find and Replace dialog box.
4. Save, print, and then close **swc6x09**.

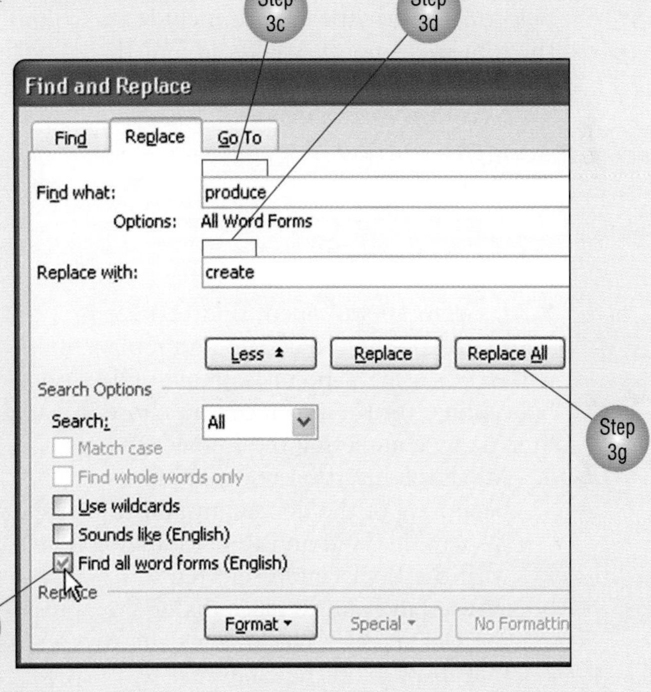

Finding and Replacing Formatting

With options at the Find and Replace dialog box with the Replace tab selected, you can search for specific formatting or characters containing specific formatting and replace it with other characters or formatting. For example, you can search for the text *Desktop Publishing* set in 14-point Arial and replace it with the text *Desktop Publishing* set in 18-point Times New Roman.

FINDING AND REPLACING FONTS

1. Open **WordSurvey01**.
2. Save the document with Save As and name it **swc6x10**.
3. Change the top and bottom margins to 0.75 inch and the left and right margins to 1 inch.
4. Change the font for the entire document to 12-point Bookman Old Style (or a similar serif typeface such as Century or Garamond).
5. Select the title, *TEACHER DEVELOPMENT TOPICS*, and the subtitle, *Activities within Your Classroom*, and then change the font to 16-point Arial bold and the color to dark red.
6. Select *Directions:* (be sure to include the colon) in the first paragraph and then change the font to 14-point Arial bold and the color to dark red. Use Format Painter to change the font to 14-point Arial bold and the color to dark red for the following:
   Classroom Presentations:
   Expertise in Your Discipline:
   Information Technology:
   Thinking Skills:
   Active Listening:
7. Save and then print **swc6x10**.
8. With **swc6x10** still open, find text set in 16-point Arial bold dark red and replace it with text set in 14-point Bookman Old Style bold indigo (or the typeface you chose in Step 4) by completing the following steps:
   a. Move the insertion point to the beginning of the document and then display the Find and Replace dialog box with the Replace tab selected.
   b. At the Find and Replace dialog box, press the Delete key. (This deletes any text that displays in the *Find what* text box.)
   c. Click the More button. (If a check mark displays in the *Find all word forms* check box, click the option to remove the check mark.)
   d. With the insertion point positioned in the *Find what* text box, click the Format button located at the bottom of the dialog box and then click Font at the drop-down list.

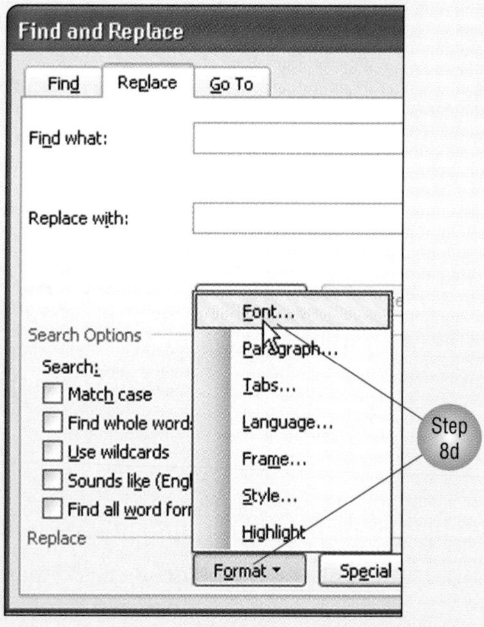

e. At the Find Font dialog box, change the font to *Arial*, the font style to *Bold*, the size to *16*, and the font color to Dark Red.
f. Click OK or press Enter to close the Find Font dialog box.
g. At the Find and Replace dialog box, click inside the *Replace with* text box. (Delete any text that displays.)
h. Click the Format button located at the bottom of the dialog box and then click Font at the drop-down list.
i. At the Replace Font dialog box, change the font to *Bookman Old Style* (or the typeface you chose in Step 4), the font style to *Bold*, the size to *14*, and the font color to Indigo.
j. Click OK or press Enter to close the Replace Font dialog box.
k. At the Find and Replace dialog box, click the Replace All button.
l. At the message telling you that the search of the document is complete and two replacements were made, click OK.

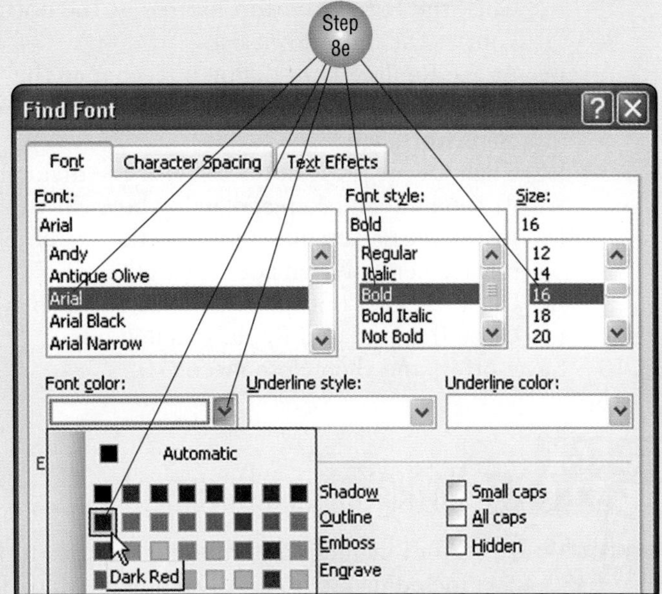

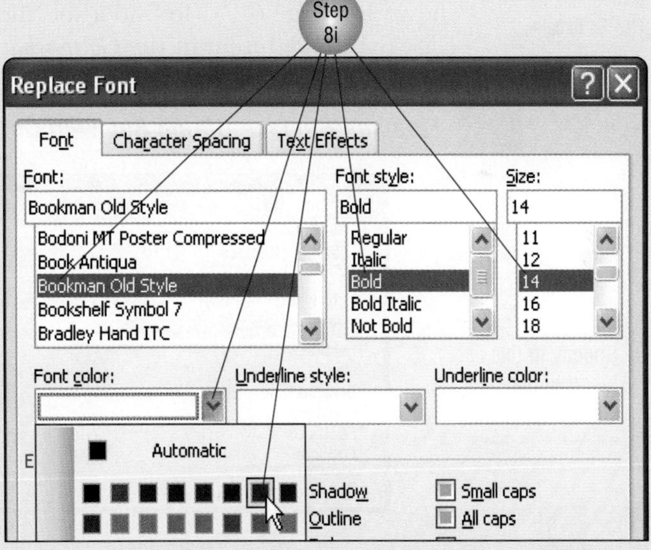

9. With the Find and Replace dialog box still open, find all text set in 14-point Arial bold dark red and replace it with text set in 12-point Bookman Old Style bold indigo by completing the following steps:
   a. Click inside the *Find what* text box at the Find and Replace dialog box.
   b. Click the No Formatting button located at the bottom of the dialog box.
   c. With the insertion point still positioned in the *Find what* text box, click the Format button located at the bottom of the dialog box and then click Font at the drop-down list.
   d. At the Find Font dialog box, change the font to *Arial*, the font style to *Bold*, the size to *14*, and the font color to Dark Red.
   e. Click OK or press Enter to close the Find Font dialog box.
   f. At the Find and Replace dialog box, click inside the *Replace with* text box.
   g. Click the No Formatting button located at the bottom of the dialog box.

h. Click the Format button located at the bottom of the dialog box and then click Font at the drop-down list.
i. At the Replace Font dialog box, change the font to *Bookman Old Style* (or the typeface you chose in Step 4), the font style to *Bold*, the size to *12*, and the font color to Indigo.
j. Click OK or press Enter to close the dialog box.
k. At the Find and Replace dialog box, click the Replace All button.
l. At the message telling you that the search of the document is complete and six replacements were made, click OK.
m. Click the Less button to turn off the display of the additional options.
n. Close the Find and Replace dialog box.

10. Save, print, and then close **swc6x10**.

QUICK STEPS

Navigate with Go To
1. Click Edit, Go To.
2. Specify item and number.
3. Click Go To button.

Navigating in a Document

Word includes a number of features to help you navigate easily in a document including Go To and Document Map. To use the Go To feature to navigate in a document, display the Find and Replace dialog box with the Go To tab selected as shown in Figure 6.13. To find a specific item in a document such as a page or line, click the desired item in the *Go to what* list box, and then click the Go To button.

FIGURE 6.13 ***Find and Replace Dialog Box with Go To Tab Selected***

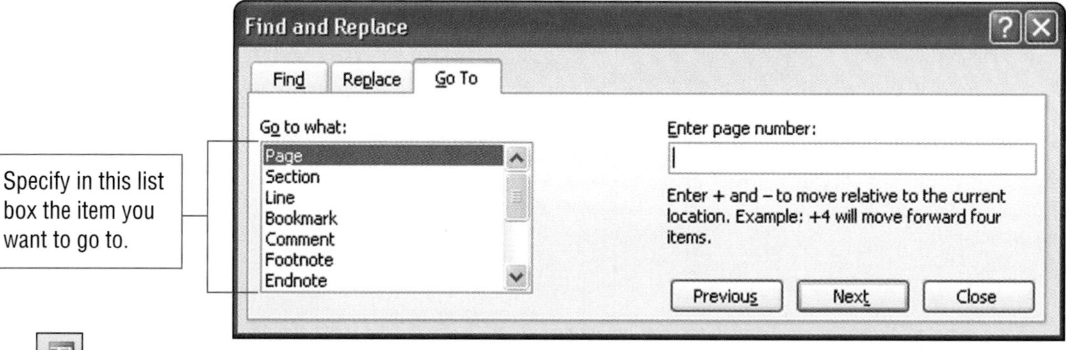

Document Map

HINT
You can display the Document Map pane by clicking View and then Document Map.

To navigate using the Document Map feature, click the Document Map button on the Standard toolbar. This displays the Document Map pane at the left side of the document as shown in Figure 6.14. The Document Map pane displays any headings formatted with styles or text that looks like headings, such as short lines set in a larger type size. Navigate to a specific location in the document by clicking the heading in the Document Map pane.

Navigate with Document Map
1. Click Document Map button.
2. Click desired heading.

FIGURE 6.14 **Document Map Pane**

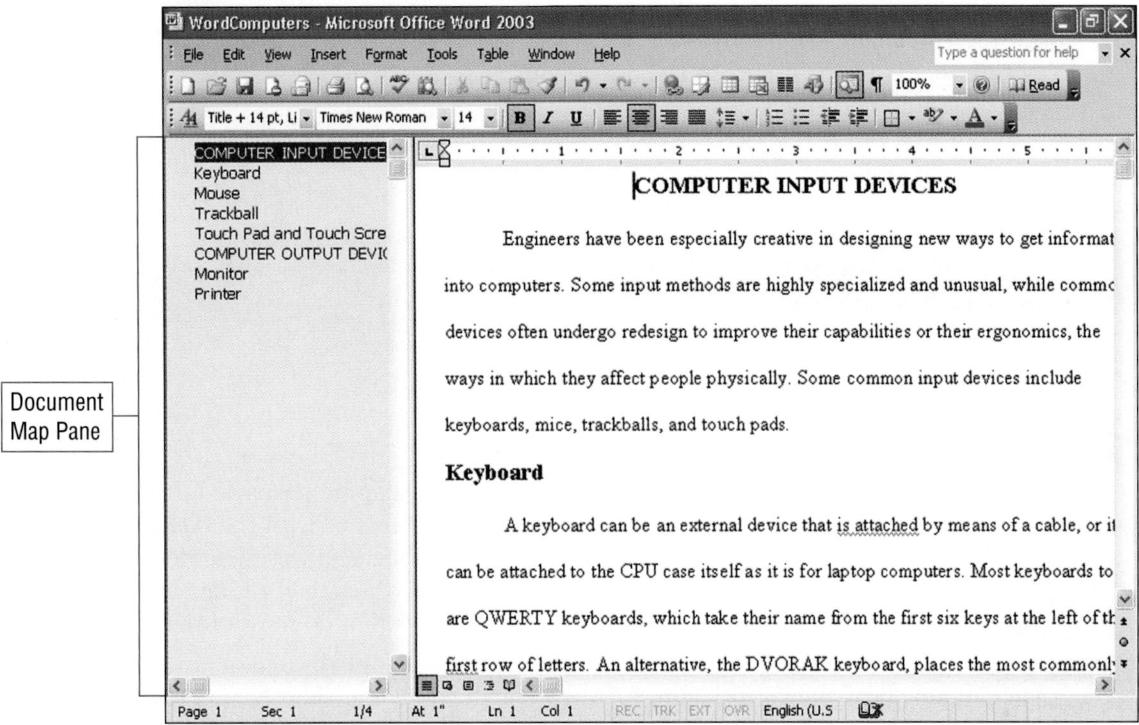

exercise 11

NAVIGATING IN A DOCUMENT USING GO TO AND DOCUMENT MAP

1. Open **WordComputers**.
2. Position the insertion point at the beginning of the document and then move the insertion point to specific locations in the document by completing the following steps:
   a. Click Edit and then Go To.
   b. At the Find and Replace dialog box with the Go To tab selected, click *Line* in the *Go to what* list box.
   c. Click in the *Enter line number* text box and then type 10.
   d. Click the Go To button. (This moves the insertion point to line 10 on the first page of the document—check the Status bar.)

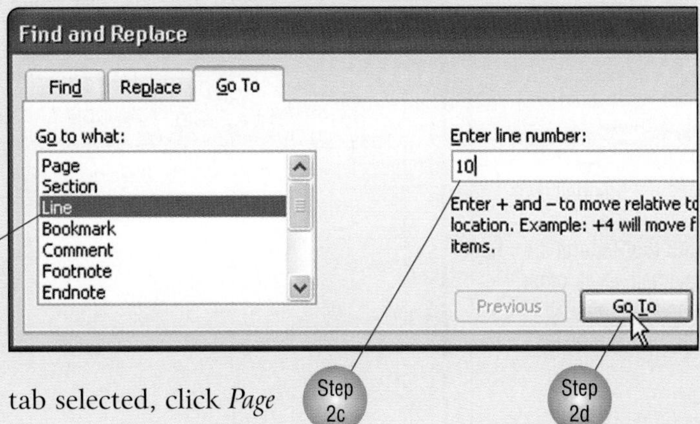

   e. At the Find and Replace dialog box with the Go To tab selected, click *Page* in the *Go to what* list box.

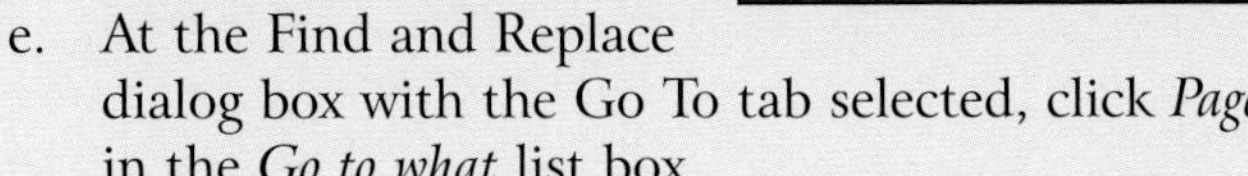

   f. Click in the *Enter page number* text box and then type 2.

g. Click the Go To button. (This moves the insertion point to the beginning of page 2.)
h. Click the Close button to close the Find and Replace dialog box.

3. Click the Document Map button on the Standard toolbar.
4. Navigate to specific locations in the document by completing the following steps:
   a. Click the *COMPUTER OUTPUT DEVICES* title.
   b. Click the *Printer* heading.
   c. Click the *COMPUTER INPUT DEVICES* title.
   d. Click the Document Map button on the Standard toolbar to turn off the display of the Document Map pane.
5. Close **WordComputers**.

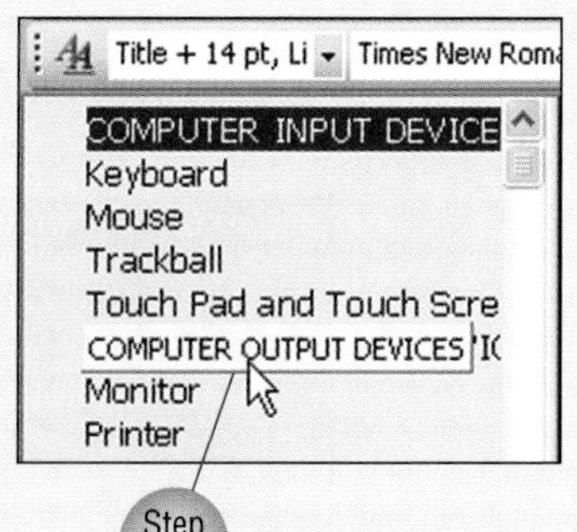

HINT

Use Word wizards and templates to create a variety of professionally designed documents.

Using Templates and Wizards

Word includes a number of ***template*** documents that are formatted for specific uses. Each Word document is based on a template document with the ***Normal*** template the default. With Word templates, you can easily create a variety of documents such as letters, memos, and awards, with specialized formatting. Along with templates, Word also includes ***wizards***. Wizards are templates that do most of the work for you.

QUICK STEPS

Create Document using Template/Wizard

1. Click File, New.
2. Click On my computer... hyperlink.
3. Click desired tab.
4. Double-click desired template or wizard.

Templates and wizards are available at the Templates dialog box. Display this dialog box, shown in Figure 6.15, by clicking File and then New. This displays the New Document task pane at the right side of the screen. At this task pane, click the On my computer hyperlink located in the *Templates* section. The Templates dialog box contains several tabs for displaying a variety of templates and wizards. Click the various tabs located at the top of the dialog box to display the available templates and wizards.

FIGURE 6.15 ***Templates Dialog Box***

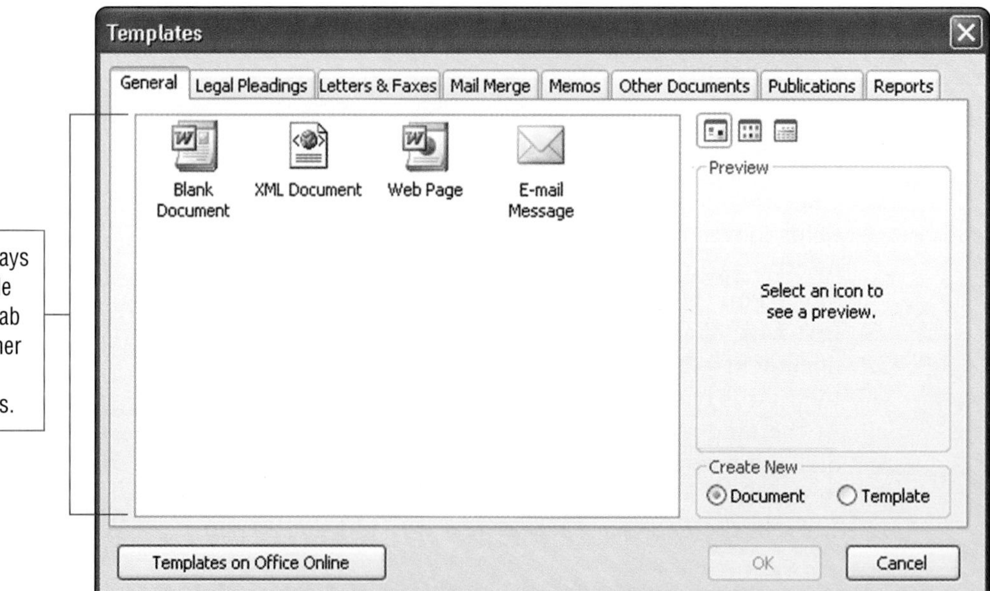

This list box displays templates available with the General tab selected. Click other tabs to display different templates.

Creating a Document Using a Template

To create a document based on a different template, double-click the desired template. If you click just once on the desired template, a sample template displays in the Preview box at the right side of the dialog box. When you double-click a template, a template document opens with formatting already applied. You enter specific information in the template document and then save it in the normal manner.

exercise 12

CREATING A CONTEMPORARY MEMO WITH A MEMO TEMPLATE

1. Click File and then New. (This displays the New Document task pane.)
2. Click the On my computer hyperlink located in the *Templates* section of the task pane.
3. At the Templates dialog box, click the Memos tab.
4. Double-click the *Contemporary Memo* icon.
5. At the Contemporary Memo template document, complete the following steps to type the text in the memo:
   a. Position the I-beam pointer on the word *here* in the bracketed text *[Click **here** and type name]* after *To:*, click the left mouse button, and then type **Sylvia Monroe, Vice President**.
   b. Position the I-beam pointer on the word *here* in the bracketed text *[Click **here** and type name]* after *CC:*, click the left mouse button, and then type **Jacob Sharify, President**.
   c. Position the I-beam pointer on the word *here* in the bracketed text *[Click **here** and type name]* after *From:*, click the left mouse button, and then type **Jamie Rodriquez, Design Department Manager**.
   d. Position the I-beam pointer on the word *here* in the bracketed text *[Click **here** and type subject]* after *Re:*, click the left mouse button, and then type **Color Scanners**.
   e. Select the text in the memo from *How To Use This Memo Template* to the end of the document and then type the text shown in Figure 6.16.
6. Save the memo and name it **swc6x12**.
7. Print and then close **swc6x12**. (This memo template will print with several graphics including horizontal and vertical lines as well as lightened images.)

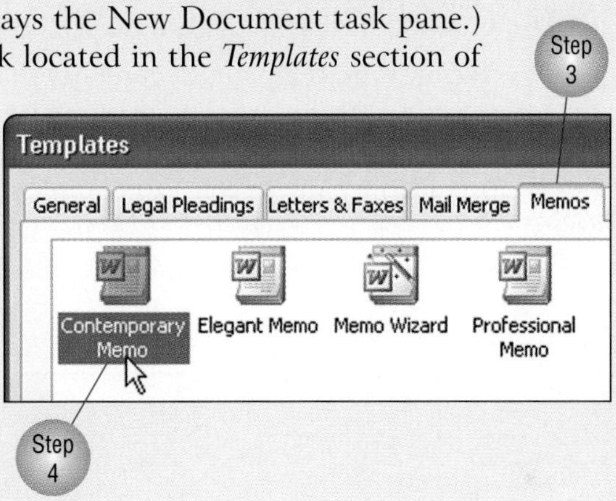

Step 3

Templates

General | Legal Pleadings | Letters & Faxes | Mail Merge | Memos

Contemporary Memo | Elegant Memo | Memo Wizard | Professional Memo

Step 4

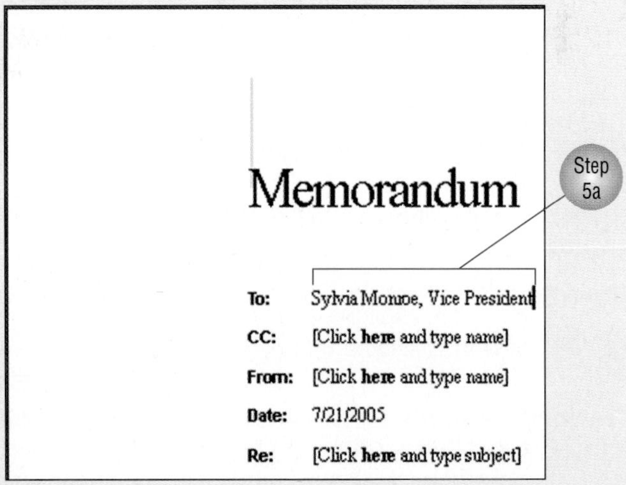

Memorandum

Step 5a

To: Sylvia Monroe, Vice President
CC: [Click **here** and type name]
From: [Click **here** and type name]
Date: 7/21/2005
Re: [Click **here** and type subject]

FIGURE 6.16 **Exercise 12**

The amount of company material produced by the Graphics Department has increased 200 percent in the past six months. To meet the demands of the increased volume, I am requesting two new color scanners. These scanners are needed to scan photographs, pictures, and other images. The total price of the two scanners is approximately $425. I will complete a product request form and forward it to you immediately.

HINT

You can download additional templates and wizards from the Microsoft Office Online Templates Home Web page.

Creating a Document Using a Wizard

Wizards are template documents that do most of the work for you. When you select a Wizard template document, Word asks you questions and provides choices about what type of formatting you want applied to the document. Follow the steps provided by the Wizard to complete the document.

exercise 13 CREATING A LETTER USING A WIZARD

1. Click File and then New to display the New Document task pane.
2. Click the On my computer hyperlink located in the *Templates* section of the task pane.
3. At the Templates dialog box, click the Letters & Faxes tab.
4. Double-click the *Letter Wizard* icon.
5. At the message that displays, make sure the *Send one letter* option is selected, and then click OK.

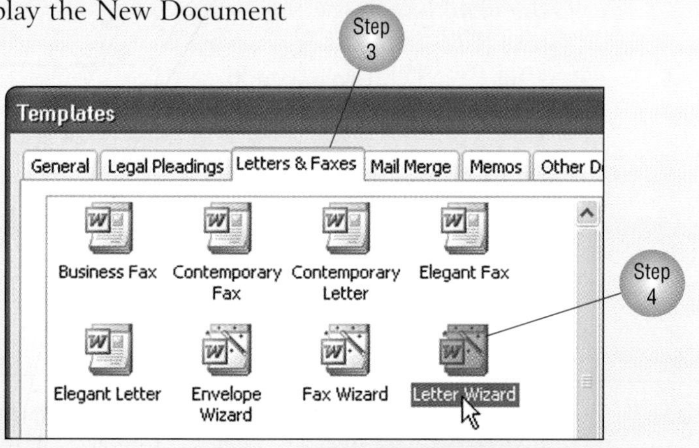

6. At the Letter Wizard – Step 1 of 4 dialog box, complete the following steps:
   a. Click the down-pointing arrow at the right side of the *Choose a page design* option, and then click *Contemporary Letter* at the drop-down list.
   b. Click the Next button.
7. At the Letter Wizard – Step 2 of 4 dialog box, complete the following steps:
   a. Type **Mr. Gregory Todd** in the *Recipient's name* text box.
   b. Press the Tab key. (This moves the insertion point to the *Delivery address* text box.)

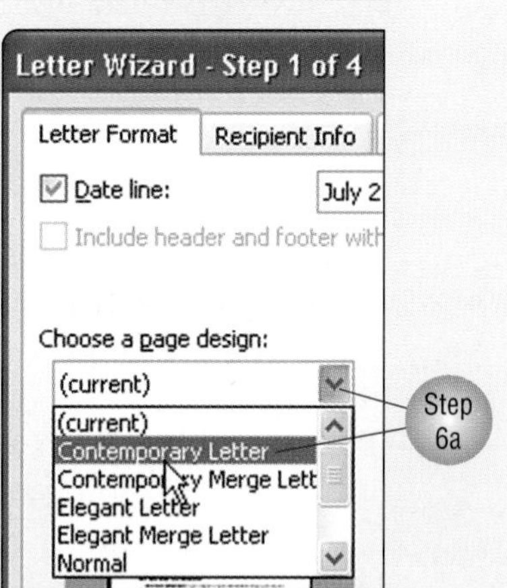

c. Type **12001 North 32nd Avenue**.
d. Press Enter.
e. Type **New York, NY 10225**.
f. Click the *Business* option located toward the bottom of the dialog box.
g. Click the Next button.

8. At the Letter Wizard – Step 3 of 4 dialog box, click the Next button.
9. At the Letter Wizard – Step 4 of 4 dialog box, complete the following steps:
   a. Select the text that currently displays in the *Sender's name* text box, and then type **Louis Hamilton**.
   b. Click in the *Job title* text box and then type **Investment Manager**.
   c. Click in the *Writer/typist initials* text box and then type your initials.
   d. Click the Finish button.
10. At the letter, insert a file for the body of the letter by completing the following steps:
    a. Select the text *Type your letter here. To add, remove, or change letter elements, double-click ✉. Or, on the Tools menu, point to Letters and Mailings, and then click Letter Wizard.* and then press the Delete key.
    b. Click Insert and then File.
    c. At the Insert File dialog box, make sure WordChapter06S is the active folder, and then double-click **WordLetter01**.
11. Move down the name and inside address by positioning the insertion point at the beginning of the name *Mr. Gregory Todd* and then pressing the Enter key twice.
12. Save the letter and name it **swc6x13**.
13. Print and then close **swc6x13**.

Sharing Documents

Some employees in a company may be part of a ***workgroup***, which is a networked collection of computers sharing files, printers, and other resources. In a workgroup, you generally make your documents available to your colleagues. With the Windows operating system and Office applications, you can share and distribute your documents quickly and easily to members of your workgroup from your desktop computer.

If you are part of a workgroup, several options are available for distributing documents to colleagues. You can make the document available on the shared network drive for anyone in your workgroup to open and edit; members in your workgroup can open and edit copies of a document; or you can route a document to specific members in your workgroup.

Creating Comments

If you want to make comments in a document, or if a reviewer wants to make comments in a document written by someone else, insert a comment. Insert a comment in a Comment balloon or in the Reviewing pane. More than one user can insert comments in a document. Word distinguishes comments from users by color. Comments from the first user are inserted in a pink balloon or with a pink shading in the Reviewing pane. Blue is used for comments from the second user.

HINT

Use comments to add notes, suggestions, or explanations, or add a comment to communicate with other members in your workgroup.

To create a comment, select the text or item on which you want to comment or position the insertion point at the end of the text, click Insert, and then click Comment. You can also click the Insert Comment button on the Reviewing toolbar.

Insert Comment

HINT
If your computer has a sound card and a microphone, you can record voice comments.

If you are in Print Layout view, a Comment balloon displays in the right margin and the Reviewing toolbar displays below the Formatting toolbar as shown in Figure 6.17. (The location of your Reviewing toolbar may vary from what you see in Figure 6.17.) Type the desired comment in the Comment balloon.

FIGURE 6.17 Comment Balloon and Reviewing Toolbar

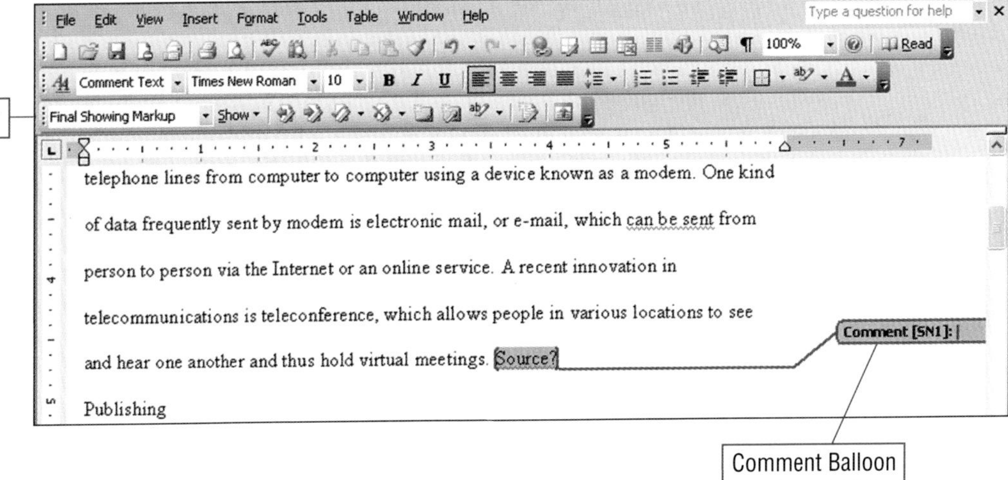

Reviewing Pane

If you are in Normal view, the Reviewing pane, shown in Figure 6.18, automatically opens and the Reviewing toolbar displays below the Formatting toolbar. Type the desired comment in the Reviewing pane. Close the Reviewing pane by clicking the Reviewing Pane button on the Reviewing toolbar.

FIGURE 6.18 Reviewing Pane

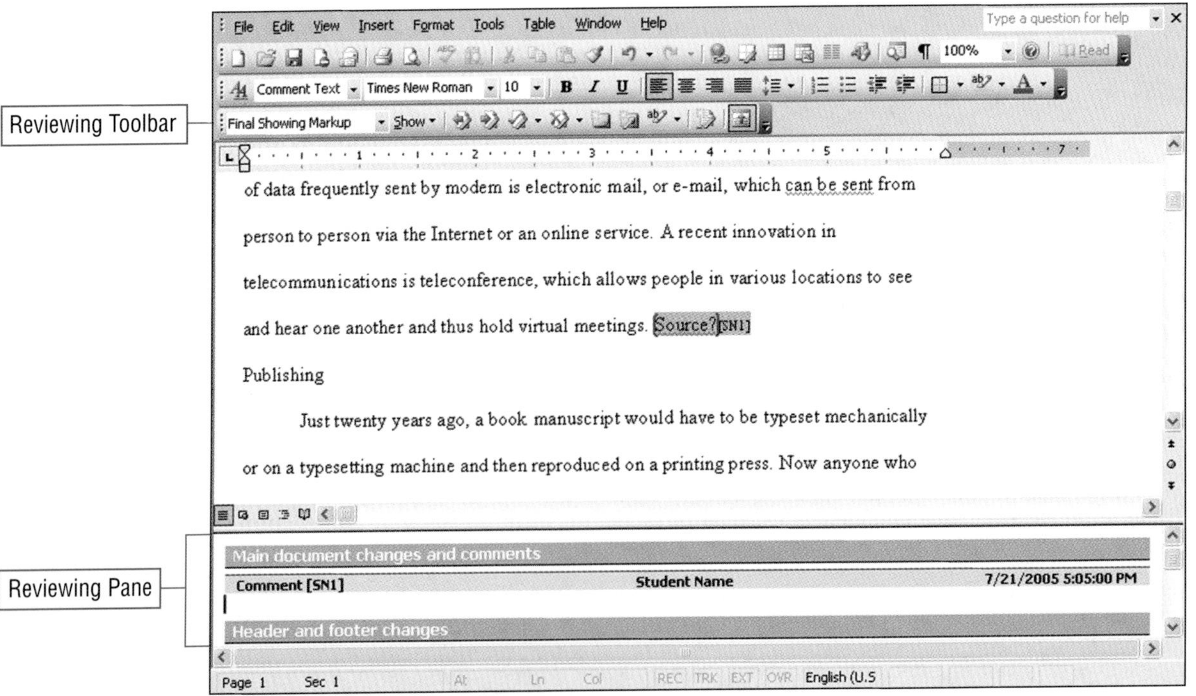

To edit a comment in Print Layout view, click in the Comment balloon, make the desired changes, and then click outside the balloon. To edit a comment in the Normal view, first turn on the display of the Reviewing Pane. To do this, display the Reviewing toolbar and then click the Reviewing Pane button on the Reviewing toolbar. Click in the comment text in the Reviewing pane, make the desired changes, and then click in the document.

Insert a Comment
1. Select text.
2. Click Insert, Comment or click Insert Comment button.
3. Type comment.

Print a document containing comments with the comments or print just the comments and not the document. To print a document and comments, display the Print dialog box, click the down-pointing arrow at the right side of the *Print what* option, and then click *Document showing markup* at the drop-down list. To print only comments, display the Print dialog box, click the down-pointing arrow at the right side of the *Print what* option, and then click *List of markup* at the drop-down list. This prints the contents of the Reviewing pane including comments as well as any tracked changes or changes to headers, footers, text boxes, footnotes, or endnotes.

Delete a comment by clicking the Next button on the Reviewing toolbar (this moves the insertion point to the next comment in the document) and then clicking the down-pointing arrow at the right side of the Reject Change/Delete Comment button. At the drop-down list that displays, click Reject Change/Delete Comment to delete the current comment, or click Reject All Comments to delete all comments in the document. In Print Layout view, you can also delete a comment by right-clicking the Comment balloon and then clicking Delete Comment at the pop-up list. This deletes the Comment balloon as well as the comment text in the Reviewing pane.

Next

Reject Change/
Delete Comment

exercise 14 CREATING COMMENTS IN A DOCUMENT

1. Open **WordReport02**.
2. Save the document with Save As and name it **swc6x14**.
3. Make sure that the document displays in Normal view.
4. Create a comment by completing the following steps:
   a. Position the insertion point at the end of the first paragraph of text in the *Telecommuniations* section.
   b. Press the spacebar once and then type **Source?**.
   c. Select *Source?*.
   d. Click Insert and then Comment. (This inserts the Reviewing pane at the bottom of the screen and also displays the Reviewing toolbar below the Formatting toolbar.)
   e. Type **Please add the source for the information in this paragraph.** in the Reviewing pane.
   f. Click in the document.

telecommunications is teleconference, which allows people in various locations to see and hear one another and thus hold virtual meetings. Source?[SN1]

Main document changes and comments

Comment [SN1] Student Name

Please add the source for the information in this paragraph.

Header and footer changes

Step 4e

5. Create another comment by completing the following steps:
   a. Move the insertion point to the end of the only paragraph of text in the *Publishing* section.
   b. Press the spacebar once, type **Images and/or pictures.**, and then select *Images and/or pictures.*
   c. Click the Insert Comment button on the Reviewing toolbar.
   d. Type **Include several images and/or pictures of publishing equipment.** in the Reviewing pane.
   e. Click in the document.

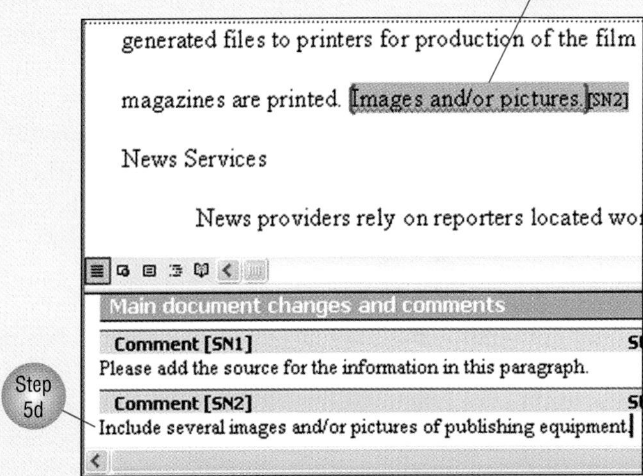

6. Click the Reviewing Pane button on the Reviewing toolbar to turn off the display of the Reviewing pane.
7. Change to the Print Layout view.
8. Create another comment by completing the following steps:
   a. Move the insertion point to the end of the first paragraph in the *Television and Film* section.
   b. Press the spacebar once, type **Web sites?**, and then select *Web sites?*.
   c. Click the Insert Comment button on the Reviewing toolbar.
   d. Type **Include hyperlinks related to Web sites.** in the Comment balloon.
   e. Click in the document.

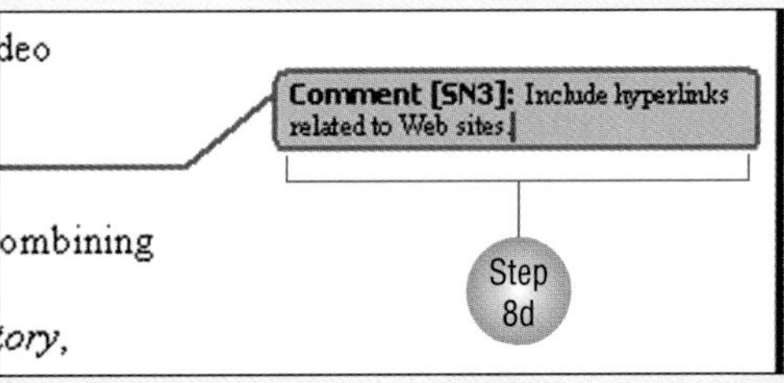

9. Edit the first comment by completing the following steps:
   a. Scroll up the document until the first Comment balloon is visible and then click in the text located inside the balloon.
   b. Move the insertion point immediately left of the period at the end of the sentence and then type **and include any pertinent Web sites**.
   c. Click in the document, outside any Comment balloons.

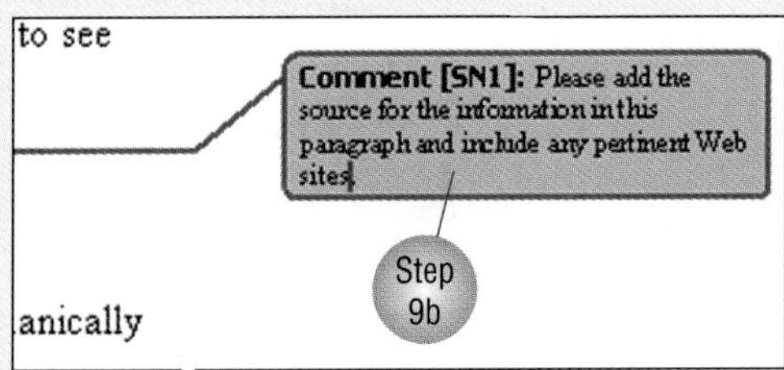

10. Save the document again with the same name (**swc6x14**).

11. Print the document and the comments by displaying the Print dialog box, clicking the down-pointing arrow at the right side of the *Print what* option, and then clicking *Document showing markup* at the drop-down list.
12. Print just the information in the Reviewing pane by displaying the Print dialog box, clicking the down-pointing arrow at the right side of the *Print what* option, and then clicking *List of markup* at the drop-down list.
13. Delete a comment by completing the following steps:
    a. Move the insertion point to the beginning of the document.
    b. Click the Next button on the Reviewing toolbar.

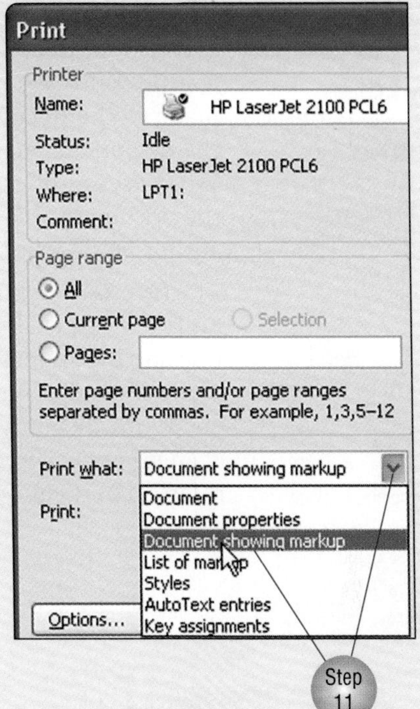

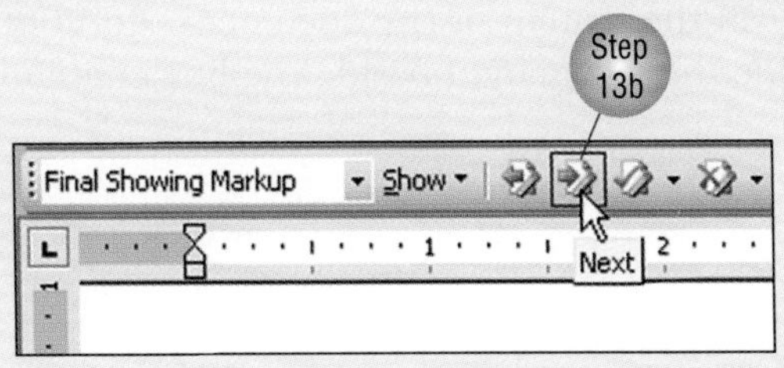

    c. Click the Next button again. (This moves the insertion point to the second comment.)
    d. Click the down-pointing arrow at the right side of the Reject Change/Delete Comment button.
    e. At the drop-down list, click Reject Change/Delete Comment.
    f. Select and then delete *Images and/or pictures*. (This text is located at the end of the only paragraph in the *Publishing* section.)

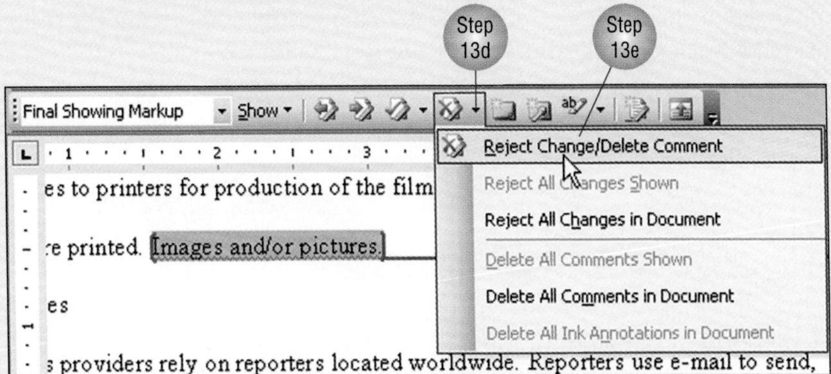

14. Turn off the display of the Reviewing toolbar.
15. Print only the comments.
16. Save and then close **swc6x14**.

Track Changes
1. Display Reviewing toolbar.
2. Click Track Changes button.
3. Make corrections or deletions.

Track Changes

HINT

Customize tracking formatting with options at the Options dialog box with the Track Changes tab selected.

Tracking Changes to a Document

If you want to edit a document and keep track of the changes, turn on the tracking feature. With the tracking feature on, each deletion, insertion, or formatting change made to the document is tracked. For example, deleted text is not removed from the document but instead displays with a line through it and in a different color. Word uses a different color (up to eight) for each person in making changes to the document. In this way, the person looking at the document can identify which author made what change.

Turn on tracking by clicking Tools and then Track Changes, pressing Ctrl + Shift + E, or clicking the Track Changes button on the Reviewing toolbar. Turn off tracking by completing the same steps. When tracking is on, the letters *TRK* display in black on the Status bar (located toward the bottom of the screen). With tracking on, Word displays some changes (such as insertion) in the text line and other changes appear in balloons in the margin of the document. Additionally, Word inserts a vertical line outside the left margin beside the line containing a change.

exercise 15 TRACKING CHANGES TO A DOCUMENT

1. Open **WordContract01**.
2. Save the document with Save As and name it **swc6x15**.
3. Change to the Print Layout view.
4. Turn on the display of the Reviewing toolbar by clicking View, pointing to Toolbars, and then clicking Reviewing.
5. Make changes to the contract and track the changes by completing the following steps:
   a. Click the Track Changes button on the Reviewing toolbar.

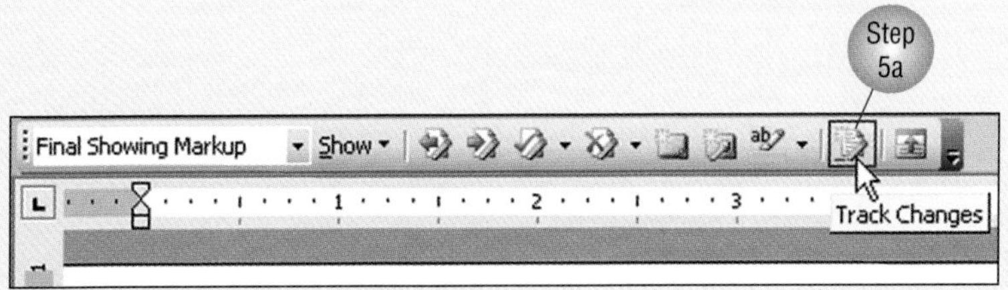

   b. Delete *4,000* in paragraph number 3 in the *Transfers and Moving Expenses* section (the deleted text is inserted in a balloon at the right side of the screen).
   c. Type 6,000. (The text you type displays in the document underlined and in red.)

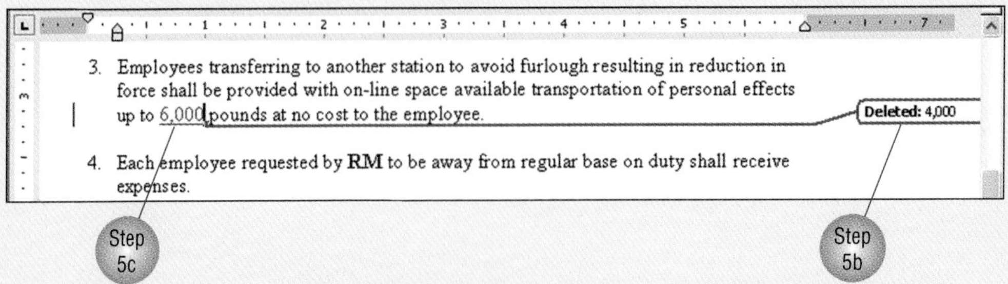

d. Delete *two (2)* in paragraph number 3 in the *Sick Leave* section and then type three (3).

Step 5d

3. An employee shall ~~report to~~ his **RM** supervisor that he is ill and unable to work at least three (3) hours prior to the start of his shift if at all possible.

Deleted: two (2)

4. The employee and the **LWU** recognize their obligations to prevent absence for other reasons than illness and injury, or other abuses of the sick leave provisions, and pledge their wholehearted cooperation to **RM** to prevent abuse.

e. Click in the document (outside the balloon).
f. Turn off tracking by clicking the Track Changes button on the Reviewing toolbar.

6. Save, print, and then close **swc6x15**.

Display information on tracking changes by positioning the mouse pointer on a change. After approximately one second, a box displays above the change containing the author's name, date, time, and the type of change (for example, whether it was a deletion or insertion). You can also display information on tracking changes by displaying the Reviewing pane. To do this, click the Reviewing Pane button on the Reviewing toolbar or click the Show button and then click Reviewing Pane at the drop-down menu. Each change is listed separately in the Reviewing pane. Use the arrow keys at the right side of the Reviewing pane to scroll through the pane and view each change. To remove the Reviewing pane, click the Reviewing Pane button on the Reviewing toolbar.

If changes are made to the document by another person with different User Information, the changes display in a different color. In the next exercise, you will pretend to be another author, change User Information, and then make changes to the contract. Change user information at the Options dialog box with the User Information tab selected.

exercise 16

TRACKING CHANGES TO A DOCUMENT MADE BY ANOTHER AUTHOR

(Note: Check with your instructor before completing this exercise to determine if you can change User Information.)

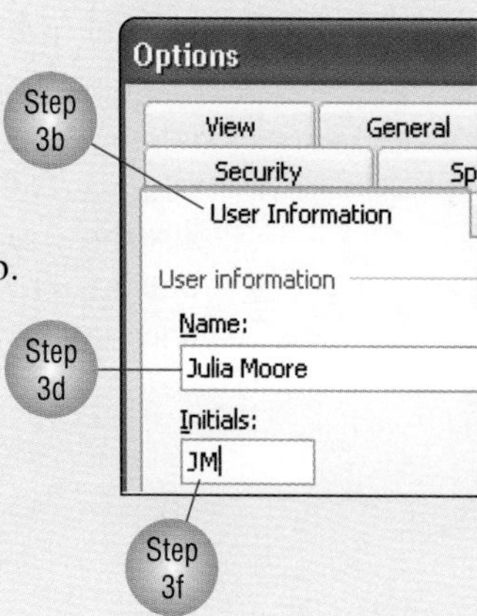

1. Open **swc6x15**.
2. Save the document with Save As and name it **swc6x16**.
3. Change user information by completing the following steps:
   a. Click Tools and then Options.
   b. At the Options dialog box, click the User Information tab.
   c. At the Options dialog box with the User Information tab selected, make a note of the current name, initials, and mailing address. (You will reenter this information later in this exercise.)
   d. Type **Julia Moore** in the *Name* text box.
   e. Press the Tab key. (This moves the insertion point to the *Initials* text box.)
   f. Type JM.
   g. Click OK to close the Options dialog box.

4. Make additional changes to the contract and track the changes by completing the following steps:
   a. Make sure the Reviewing toolbar is displayed.
   b. Turn on tracking by clicking the Track Changes button on the Reviewing toolbar.
   c. Add the text **up to $5,000** to the end of the sentence in paragraph number 4 in the *Transfers and Moving Expenses* section. (Notice that the change displays in a different color.)

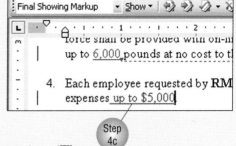

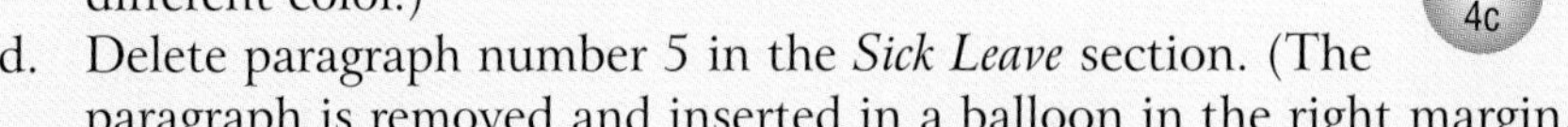

   d. Delete paragraph number 5 in the *Sick Leave* section. (The paragraph is removed and inserted in a balloon in the right margin.)
5. Turn off tracking by clicking the Track Changes button on the Reviewing toolbar.
6. View the changes in the Reviewing pane by completing the following steps:
   a. Click the Reviewing Pane button on the Reviewing toolbar.
   b. Use the arrows at the right side of the Reviewing pane to scroll through the pane and review the changes. (Notice the changes made in the first exercise are in a different color than the changes made in this exercise.)
   c. Click the Reviewing Pane button to turn off the display of the Reviewing pane.
7. Change the User Information back to the information that displayed before you typed *Julia Moore* and the initials *JM* by completing the following steps:
   a. Click Tools and then Options.
   b. At the Options dialog box, make sure the User Information tab is selected.
   c. At the Options dialog box with the User Information tab selected, type the original name in the *Name* text box.
   d. Press the Tab key and then type the original initials in the *Initials* text box.
   e. Click OK to close the dialog box.
8. Print the document showing markup.
9. Save and then close **swc6x16**.

Previous

Next

Accept Change

In a longer document containing several changes, use buttons on the Reviewing toolbar to move the insertion point to a change in the document. Click the Previous button on the Reviewing toolbar to move to the previous change in the document or click the Next button to move to the next change in the document.

Changes made to a document can be accepted or rejected. Click the Accept Change button on the Reviewing toolbar to accept the change or click the Reject Change/Delete Comment button to specify changes you want to reject. You can also position the mouse pointer over the change and then click the *right* mouse button. This causes a shortcut menu to display with options for accepting or rejecting the change.

exercise 17

ACCEPTING/REJECTING CHANGES IN A DOCUMENT

1. Open **swc6x16**.
2. Save the document with Save As and name it **swc6x17**.
3. Accept the change from *4,000* to *6,000* by completing the following steps:
   a. Make sure the Reviewing toolbar is displayed. (If not, right-click on the Standard toolbar and then click Reviewing.)
   b. Click the Next button on the Reviewing toolbar.
   c. With *4,000* selected in the Deleted balloon, click the Accept Change button on the Reviewing toolbar.

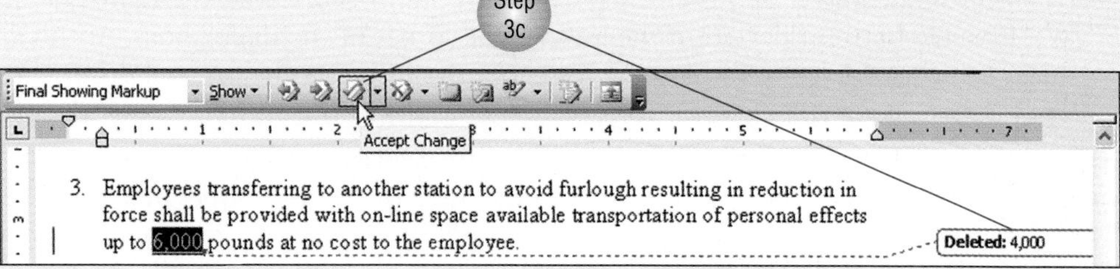

4. Accept *6,000* by completing steps similar to those in Step 3.
5. Click the Next button on the Reviewing toolbar and then accept the change adding *up to $5,000* to the end of the sentence in paragraph number 4 in the *Transfers and Moving Expenses* section.
6. Reject the change from *two (2)* to *three (3)* by completing the following steps:
   a. Click the Next button on the Reviewing toolbar.
   b. Position the mouse pointer over *two (2)* in the Deleted balloon. (This text is selected.)
   c. Click the *right* mouse button.
   d. At the shortcut menu that displays, click Reject Deletion.
   e. Click the Next button on the Reviewing toolbar.
   f. Reject the change inserting *three (3)* by clicking the Reject Change/Delete Comment button on the Reviewing toolbar.

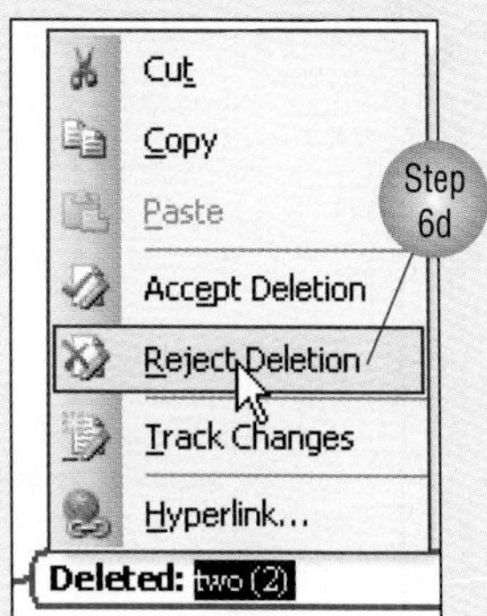

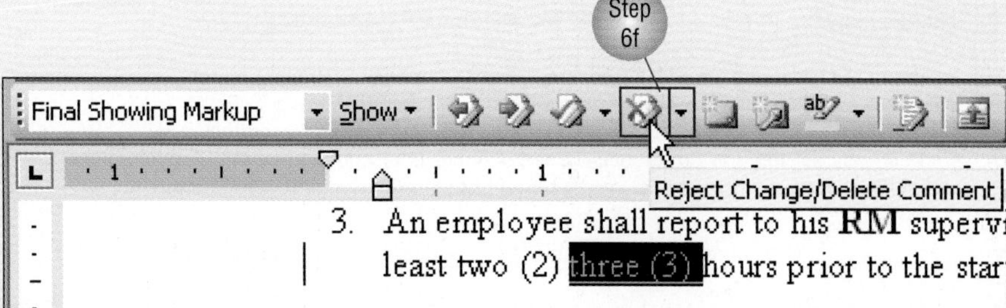

7. Reject the change deleting paragraph number 5 in the *Sick Leave* section.
8. Deselect the text.
9. Turn off the display of the Reviewing toolbar.
10. Save, print, and then close **swc6x17**.

QUICK STEPS

Compare and Merge Documents

1. Open document.
2. Click Tools, Compare and Merge Documents.
3. Click document name to compare.
4. Click down-pointing arrow at Merge button.
5. Specify merge location.

HINT

If multiple reviewers edit copies of the same document, you can merge all of the changes into a single document.

Comparing and Merging Documents

Use Word's Compare and Merge feature to compare two documents and display the differences between the documents as tracked changes. This might be useful in a setting where multiple individuals will make changes to separate copies of the original document. Merge all of the changes made by each individual using the Compare and Merge feature. When you compare and merge documents, you can choose to display the results in the original document, in the currently open document, or in a new document.

To compare and merge documents, open the desired document, click Tools, and then click Compare and Merge Documents. At the Compare and Merge Documents dialog box, click once on the document you want to compare with the currently open document, and then click the down-pointing arrow at the right side of the Merge button (located in the lower right corner of the dialog box). At the drop-down list, click Merge to display the results of the merge in the original document, click *Merge into current document* to display the results in the currently open document, or click *Merge into new document* to display the results in a new document.

Results of the compare and merge are shown in the document as tracked changes. In Print Layout view, the results display in the document as well as in balloons in the right margin. Figure 6.19 displays the results of the compare and merge you will complete in Exercise 18.

FIGURE 6.19 ***Results of Compare and Merge***

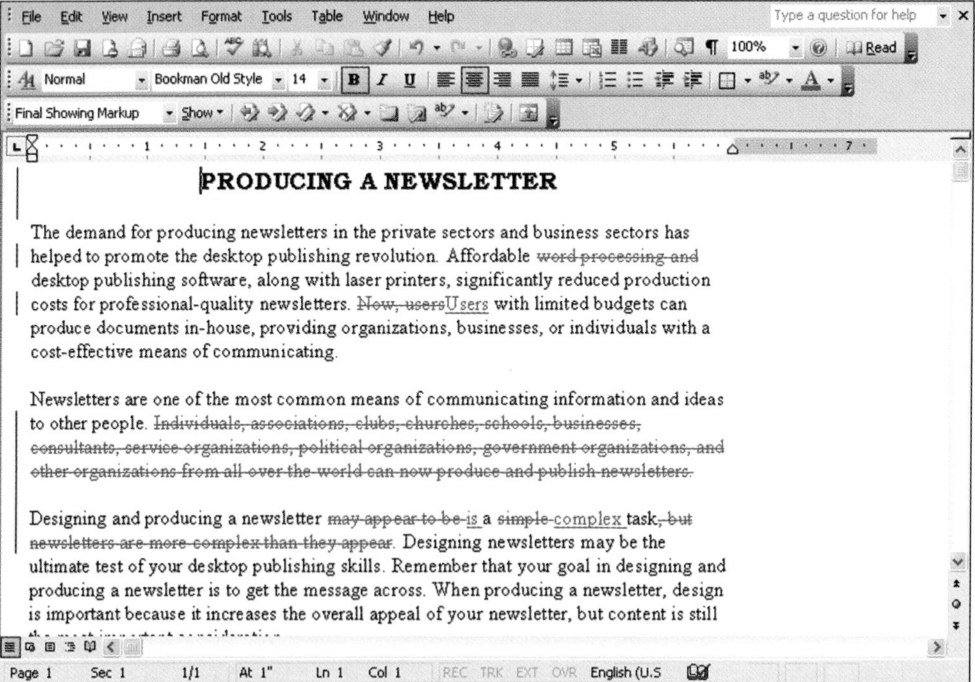

After viewing the results, you can choose to accept or reject individual changes. To accept all of the changes, click the down-pointing arrow at the right side of the Accept Change button on the Reviewing toolbar, and then click Accept All Changes in Document at the drop-down list. To reject all of the changes, click the down-pointing arrow at the right side of the Reject Change/Delete Comment button on the Reviewing toolbar, and then click Reject All Changes in Document at the drop-down list.

exercise 18

COMPARING AND MERGING DOCUMENTS

1. Open **WordEditedDoc06**.
2. Compare it with **WordDocument06** by completing the following steps:
   a. Click Tools and then Compare and Merge Documents.
   b. At the Compare and Merge Documents dialog box, make sure that the WordChapter06S folder on your disk is the active folder and then click once on ***WordDocument06***.
   c. Click the down-pointing arrow at the right side of the Merge button (located in the lower right corner of the dialog box).
   d. Click *Merge into new document* at the drop-down list.

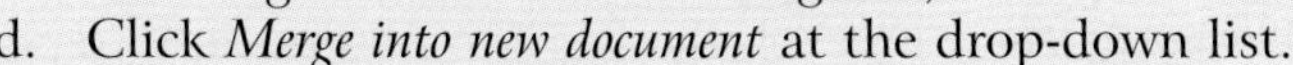

3. Change to the Print Layout view. (Notice the results of the compare and merge.)
4. Print the document with the marked changes by completing the following steps:
   a. Click File and then Print.
   b. At the Print dialog box, make sure the *Print what* option is set at *Document showing markup*, and then click OK.
5. Accept all of the changes by completing the following steps:
   a. Display the Reviewing toolbar.
   b. Click the down-pointing arrow at the right side of the Accept Change button.
   c. Click *Accept All Changes in Document* at the drop-down list.
6. Save the document and name it **swc6x18**.
7. Print and then close **swc6x18**.
8. Close **WordEditedDoc06**.

CHAPTER summary

- Use the AutoText feature to insert text you use on a frequent basis. Word comes with built-in AutoText entries that you can insert in a document with the Insert, AutoText side menu, the All Entries button on the AutoText toolbar, or options at the AutoCorrect dialog box with the AutoText tab selected.
- You can create your own AutoText entry and then insert it in a document with the Enter key, the shortcut key, F3, or with options at the AutoCorrect dialog box with the AutoText tab selected.

- Text that appears at the top of every page is called a header; text that appears at the bottom of every page is called a footer. Click View and then Header and Footer to display the Header and Footer toolbar and a header pane.
- Click the Switch Between Header and Footer button on the Header and Footer toolbar to display a footer pane.
- A header or footer does not display in the Normal view but will display dimmed in the Print Layout view. To see how the header or footer will print, display Print Preview.
- Insert page numbering in a document with options from the Page Numbers dialog box or in a header or footer. Modify page numbers at the Page Number Format dialog box.
- Use the find feature to search for specific characters or formatting. Use the find and replace feature to search for specific characters or formatting and replace with other characters or formatting.
- At the Find and Replace dialog box, click the Find Next button to find the next occurrence of the characters and/or formatting. Click the Replace button to replace the characters or formatting and find the next occurrence; or, click the Replace All button to replace all occurrences of the characters or formatting.
- Click the More button at the Find and Replace dialog box to display additional options for completing a search such as *Match case*, *Find whole words only*, *Use wildcards*, *Sounds like*, and *Find all word forms*.
- You can search a document for some character and paragraph formatting such as bold characters, specific fonts, indents, and spacing and replace with other text and/or formatting.
- Navigate through a document with options at the Find and Replace dialog box with the Go To tab selected or with the Document Map feature.
- Use Word templates and wizards to create a variety of documents such as letters, memos, and awards. Templates and wizards provided by Word are available at the Templates dialog box.
- If you want to make comments in a document you are creating, or if a reviewer wants to make comments in a document written by someone else, insert a comment. Insert a comment by clicking Insert and then Comment or by clicking the Insert Comment button on the Reviewing toolbar.
- In Print Layout view you insert a comment in a Comment balloon and in Normal view you insert a comment in the Reviewing pane.
- Edit a comment in Print Layout view by clicking in the Comment balloon, and edit a comment in Normal view by clicking in the comment text in the Reviewing pane.
- Print a document containing comments with the comments or choose to print just the comments and not the document.
- Use the Reject Change/Delete Comment button on the Reviewing toolbar to delete a comment. Another method for deleting a comment is to right-click the Comment balloon and then click Delete Comment at the shortcut list.
- Use the tracking feature when more than one person is reviewing a document and making editing changes. Turn on tracking by clicking Tools and then Track Changes, pressing Ctrl + Shift + E, or clicking the Track Changes button on the Reviewing toolbar.
- When tracking is on, Word displays some changes in the text line and other changes appear in balloons at the right margin. Control how changes display in the document with options from the Display for Review button on the Reviewing toolbar.

- Display information on tracking changes such as author's name, date, time, and type of change by positioning the mouse pointer on a change. After approximately one second, a box displays with the information. You can also display information on tracking changes by displaying the Reviewing pane. Display this pane by clicking the Reviewing Pane button on the Reviewing toolbar.
- If changes are made to a document by another person with different user information, the changes display in a different color. Change user information at the Options dialog box with the User Information tab selected.
- Move to the next change in a document by clicking the Next button on the Reviewing toolbar or click the Previous button to move to the previous change. Changes made to a document can be accepted or rejected.
- Use the Compare and Merge feature to compare two documents and display the differences between the documents as tracked changes.
- When comparing and merging documents, you can choose to display the results in the original document, in the currently open document, or in a new document.

FEATURES summary

FEATURE	BUTTON	MENU	KEYBOARD
Create AutoText dialog box		Insert, AutoText, New	
Display header pane		View, Header and Footer	
Find and Replace dialog box with Find tab selected		Edit, Find	Ctrl + F
Find and Replace dialog box with Replace tab selected		Edit, Replace	Ctrl + H
Find and Replace dialog box with Go To tab selected		Edit, Go To	Ctrl + G
Page Numbers dialog box		Insert, Page Numbers	
Insert comment		Insert, Comment	
Turn on tracking		Tools, Track Changes	Ctrl + Shift + E
Options dialog box		Tools, Options	
Compare and Merge dialog box		Tools, Compare and Merge Documents	

CONCEPTS check

Completion: On a blank sheet of paper, indicate the correct term, command, or number for each description.

1. If an AutoText entry name is less than four characters in length, type the AutoText entry name and then press this key on the keyboard to insert the full text.
2. After clicking View and then Header and Footer, the insertion point is automatically positioned here.
3. To create a footer, click this button on the Header and Footer toolbar.
4. Create footers on odd and/or even pages at this dialog box.
5. Page numbers can be inserted in a header or footer or with options at this dialog box.
6. Change the beginning page number with this option at the Page Number Format dialog box.
7. If you want to replace every occurrence of what you are searching for in a document, click this button at the Find and Replace dialog box.
8. Click this button at the Find and Replace dialog box if you do not want to replace an occurrence with the replace text.
9. Click this option at the Find and Replace dialog box if you are searching for a word and all of its forms.
10. Choose a template or wizard at this dialog box.
11. One method for creating a comment is to click the New Comment button on this toolbar.
12. In Print Layout view, clicking Insert and then Comment causes this to display in the right margin.
13. In Normal view, clicking Insert and then Comment causes this to open.
14. Use this feature to compare two documents and display the differences between the documents as tracked changes.
15. List the steps you would complete to create the footer *Computers and Technology* that prints bolded and centered on each page of the document.
16. List the steps you would complete to insert page numbering in a document that prints at the bottom right side on each page and begins with page number 5.
17. List the steps you would complete to find all occurrences of the word *remove* and all of its word forms and replace it with *delete* and all of its word forms.

SKILLS check

Assessment 1

1. Create an AutoText entry for *Stradford Annuity Mutual Funds* and use the initials *samf*.
2. Type the document shown in Figure 6.20 using the AutoText entry you created.
3. Save the document and name it **swc6sc01**.
4. Move the insertion point to the end of the document, press the Enter key, and then insert the built-in AutoText entry *Filename and path*. (To do this, click Insert, point to AutoText, point to Header/Footer, and then click Filename and path.)
5. Print and then close **swc6sc01**.
6. At a clear document screen, delete the *samf* AutoText entry.

FIGURE

6.20 ***Assessment 1***

STRADFORD ANNUITY ASSOCIATION

The samf complement your traditional retirement savings by putting your after-tax dollars to work. The samf offer some very important advantages that can make your retirement dreams a reality including:

- No-loads
- Exceptionally low operating costs
- A low $250 initial investment
- Easy access to your money
- No marketing or distribution fees

The samf are backed by the investment expertise that has made Stradford Annuity Association one of the most respected companies in the financial industry.

Assessment 2

1. Open **WordReport03**.
2. Save the document with Save As and name it **swc6sc02**.
3. Change the top margin to 1.5 inches.
4. Select the entire document, change the font to 12-point Bookman Old Style (or a similar serif typeface), and then deselect the text.
5. Select the title *NETWORK TOPOLOGIES* and then change the font to 18-point Tahoma bold.
6. Select the heading *Linear Bus Networks* and then change the font to 14-point Tahoma bold.
7. Use the Format Painter to change the font to 14-point Tahoma bold for the remaining two headings *Star Networks* and *Ring Networks*.
8. Create the footer *Network Topologies* that is set in 12-point Tahoma bold and prints at the center of the footer pane.
9. Save, print, and then close **swc6sc02**.

Assessment 3

1. Open **swc6sc02**.
2. Save the document with Save As and name it **swc6sc03**.
3. Delete the footer in the document.
4. Create the footer *Page #* (where the correct page number is inserted at the #) that is set in 12-point Tahoma bold and prints at the right margin on all odd pages.
5. Create the footer *Types of Networks* that is set in 12-point Tahoma bold and prints at the left margin on all even pages.
6. Save, print, and then close **swc6sc03**.

Assessment 4

1. Open **WordContract01**.
2. Save the document with Save As and name it **swc6sc04**.
3. Find all occurrences of *REINBERG MANUFACTURING* and replace with *QUALITY SYSTEMS*.
4. Find all occurrences of *RM* and replace with *QS*.
5. Find all occurrences of *LABOR WORKER'S UNION* and replace with *INDUSTRIAL WORKER'S UNION*.
6. Find all occurrences of *LWU* and replace with *IWU*.
7. Save, print, and then close **swc6sc04**.

Assessment 5

1. Open **WordMortgage**.
2. Save the document with Save As and name it **swc6sc05**.
3. Insert the title *MORTGAGE CONTRACT* centered at the beginning of the document. Separate the title from the first paragraph of text in the document by a blank line.
4. Select the title and then change the font to 18-point Tahoma bold.
5. Select the heading *Delinquency:* (be sure to include the colon [:]) and then change the font to 14-point Tahoma bold.
6. Use Format Painter to change the font for the remaining headings in the document to 14-point Tahoma bold.
7. Save and then print **swc6sc05**.
8. With the document still open, make the following changes:
   a. Search for 18-point Tahoma bold formatting and replace with 16-point Arial bold formatting.
   b. Search for 14-point Tahoma bold formatting and replace with 13-point Arial bold formatting.
9. Save, print, and then close **swc6sc05**.

Assessment 6

1. Use the Contemporary Fax template (displays when the Letters & Faxes tab is selected at the Templates dialog box) to create a fax cover sheet. Select the text in brackets, delete it, and then type the information as shown below:

   Click anywhere in the text *[Click here and type address]* located in the upper right corner of the fax page and then type the following:

   4509 Jackson Avenue
   St. Paul, MN 55230

   Type the following text in the specified location:

To:	**Rene LeJeune**
Fax:	**(412) 555-8122**
From:	**Claire Monroe**
Re:	**Order Number 3420**
Pages:	**1**
CC:	**Mark Frazier**

   Select the text in the body of the fax, delete it, and then type the following:

   This fax is to confirm your order number 3420. All items on that order are in stock and will be shipped within three business days. This order will be shipped by two-day express delivery. If you need overnight delivery, please call (304) 555-9855.

2. Save the completed fax cover sheet and name it **swc6sc06**.
3. Print and then close **swc6sc06**.

Assessment 7

1. Open **WordReport01**.
2. Save the document with Save As and name it **swc6sc07**.
3. Select the entire document and then change the font to 13-point Garamond (or a similar serif typeface).
4. Set the title and the headings in 14-point Arial bold.
5. Select the text in the body of the report (everything except the title) and then make the following change:
   a. Change the line spacing to single.
   b. Change the spacing before and after paragraphs to 6 points.
6. Create a comment at the end of the first paragraph in the report. To do this, type the word **History**, select it, and then create the comment with the following text: *Include additional historical facts about graphics programs.*
7. Create a comment at the end of the last paragraph in the *Early Painting and Drawing Programs* section of the report. To do this, type the word **Define**, select it, and then create the comment with the following text: *Provide further information on resolution.*
8. Create a comment at the end of the first paragraph in the *Developments in Painting and Drawing Programs* section of the report. To do this, type the word **Examples**, select it, and then create the comment with the following text: *Include examples of pixelization and antialiasing.*
9. Save the document again with the same name (**swc6sc07**).
10. Print the document with the comments.
11. Close **swc6sc07**.

Assessment 8

1. Open **WordEditedDoc02**.
2. Merge and compare **WordEditedDoc02** with **WordDocument02**. Save the results in a new document.
3. At the new document, change to the Print Layout view, and then print the document with the marked changes.
4. Accept all of the changes in the document.
5. Save the document and name it **swc6sc08**.
6. Print and then close **swc6sc08**.
7. Close **WordEditedDoc02**.

Assessment 9

1. Open **WordMortgage**.
2. Save the document with Save As and name it **swc6sc09**.
3. Turn on tracking and then make the following changes to the document:
   a. Change *ten (10)* in the *Delinquency* paragraph to *fifteen (15)*.
   b. Delete the words *charge computed as if Buyers had prepaid in full* that display at the end of the *Demand for Full Payment* paragraph.
   c. Insert the words *and safe* between *good* and *condition* in the second sentence in the *Use of the Collateral* paragraph.
   d. Turn off tracking.
4. Save, print, and then close **swc6sc09**.

Assessment 10

1. Open **swc6sc09**.
2. Save the document with Save As and name it **swc6sc10**.
3. Display the Options dialog box with the User Information tab selected and then complete the following steps:.
   a. Make a note of the current name, initials, and mailing address. (You will reenter this information later in this assessment.)
   b. Type **Lewis Granger** in the *Name* text box.
   c. Type **LG** in the *Initials* text box.
   d. Close the Options dialog box.
4. Turn on tracking and then make the following change to the document:
   a. Insert the word *all* between *pay* and *reasonable* in the last sentence in the *Delinquency* paragraph.
   b. Delete the words *at the time of the default or any time after default,* in the first sentence in the *Demand for Full Payment* paragraph.
   c. Insert the words *unless agreed upon by Sellers* between *contract* and the period that ends the last sentence in the *Use of the Collateral* paragraph.
   d. Turn off tracking.
5. Display the Options dialog box with the User Information tab selected, change back to the information that displayed before you typed *Lewis Granger* and the initials *LG*, and then close the dialog box.
6. Save, print, and then close **swc6sc10**.

Assessment 11

1. Open **swc6sc10**.
2. Save the document with Save As and name it **swc6sc11**.
3. With the insertion point positioned at the beginning of the document, accept the following changes in the document:
   a. Accept the change from *ten (10)* to *fifteen (15)* in the *Delinquency* paragraph.
   b. Accept the change inserting the word *all* between *pay* and *reasonable* in the last sentence in the *Delinquency* paragraph.
   c. Accept the change deleting the words *charge computed as if Buyers had prepaid in full* that display at the end of the *Demand for Full Payment* paragraph.
   d. Accept the change inserting the words *unless agreed upon by Sellers* between *Contract* and the period that ends the last sentence in the *Use of the Collateral* paragraph.
4. Move the insertion point to the beginning of the document and then reject the following changes in the document:
   a. Reject the change deleting the words *at the time of the default or any time after default,* in the first sentence in the *Demand for Full Payment* paragraph.
   b. Reject the change inserting the words *and safe* between *good* and *condition* in the second sentence in the *Use of the Collateral* paragraph.
5. Save, print, and then close **swc6sc11**.

Assessment 12

1. Use the Help files to learn about creating a calendar using a wizard.
2. Use the Calendar Wizard to create a calendar for the next month.
3. Save the calendar document and name it **swc6sc12**.
4. Print and then close **swc6sc12**.

CHAPTER challenge

You are the office manager for a medium-sized lumber company. You have been with the company for a year. Without any training and little guidance, you learned many of the tasks delegated to and required of you. You see a need for a training and procedures manual so that other newly hired people do not have to struggle as you did. You decide to use the Manual wizard provided in the Templates dialog box. You will want to make a few minor changes to the template. First, insert the current date in the left corner of the footer and position the page number in the right corner, adding the word *Page* prior to the number. Second, replace all occurrences of the Garamond font with the Rockwell font. Save the manual as **Company Manual**.

As you continue to review and make changes to the company manual, you decide that you would like to format the manual's index differently. Learn how to format indexes by using the Help feature and then apply a different format to the existing index. Save the manual again. Print the index page only.

To make the manual more distinctive, you decide to insert a company logo at the beginning of each chapter. Create a simple logo in the Paint program. Copy and paste the logo into the header of the first chapter of the manual. The logo will be used frequently as more chapters are added. Create an AutoText entry for the logo, using the word *logo* as the AutoText entry name. Save the manual again.

Optional: Switch disks with another student in class. Make at least two corrections with the tracking feature and provide at least two suggestions using the comment feature. Print only those pages on which the revisions or comments were made.

7

CREATING TABLES AND CHARTS

PERFORMANCE OBJECTIVES

Upon successful completion of Chapter 7, you will be able to:

- **Create, edit, and format a table**
- **Delete a table**
- **Apply formatting with an AutoFormat**
- **Create and format a table using buttons on the Tables and Borders toolbar**
- **Create and modify charts**

Some Word data can be organized in a table, which is a combination of columns and rows. With the Tables feature, you can insert data in columns and rows. This data can consist of text, values, and formulas. In this chapter you will learn how to create and format a table and insert and format data in the table. You will also learn how to convert data in a table to a chart, which presents data in a more visual manner.

Creating a Table

Use the Tables feature to create boxes of information called ***cells***. A cell is the intersection between a row and a column. A cell can contain text, characters, numbers, data, graphics, or formulas. Create a table with the Insert Table button on the Standard toolbar or the Table option from the Menu bar. To create a table with the Insert Table button, position the mouse pointer on the Insert Table button on the Standard toolbar, hold down the left mouse button, drag down and to the right until the correct number of rows and columns displays, and then release the mouse button.

Insert Table

You can also create a table with options at the Insert Table dialog box shown in Figure 7.1. Click Table, point to Insert, and then click Table to display the Insert Table dialog box. Enter the desired number of columns and rows and then click OK to close the dialog box. A table is inserted in the document at the location of the insertion point.

FIGURE

7.1 Insert Table Dialog Box

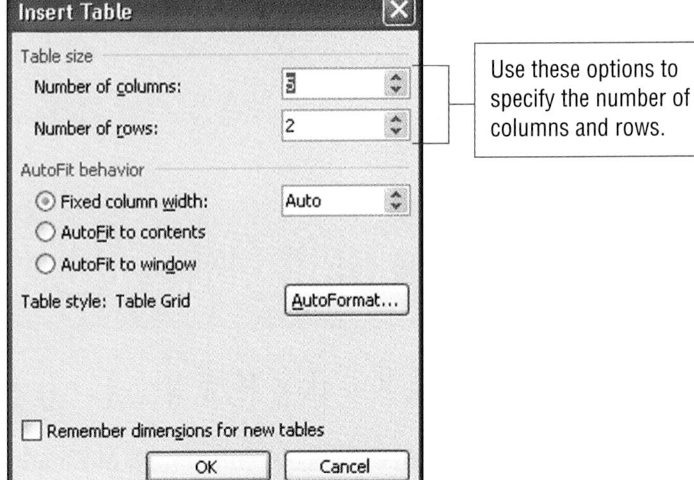

QUICK STEPS

Create a Table

1. Position mouse pointer on Insert Table button.
2. Hold down left mouse button.
3. Drag to create desired number of columns and rows.
4. Release mouse button.

OR

1. Click Table, Insert, Table.
2. Specify number of columns and rows.
3. Click OK.

Figure 7.2 shows an example of a table with four columns and three rows. Various parts of the table are identified in Figure 7.2 such as the gridlines, move table column marker, end-of-cell marker, end-of-row marker, and the resize handle. In a table, nonprinting characters identify the end of a cell and the end of a row. To view these characters, click the Show/Hide ¶ button on the Standard toolbar. The end-of-cell marker displays inside each cell and the end-of-row marker displays at the end of a row of cells. These markers are identified in Figure 7.2.

FIGURE

7.2 Table Features

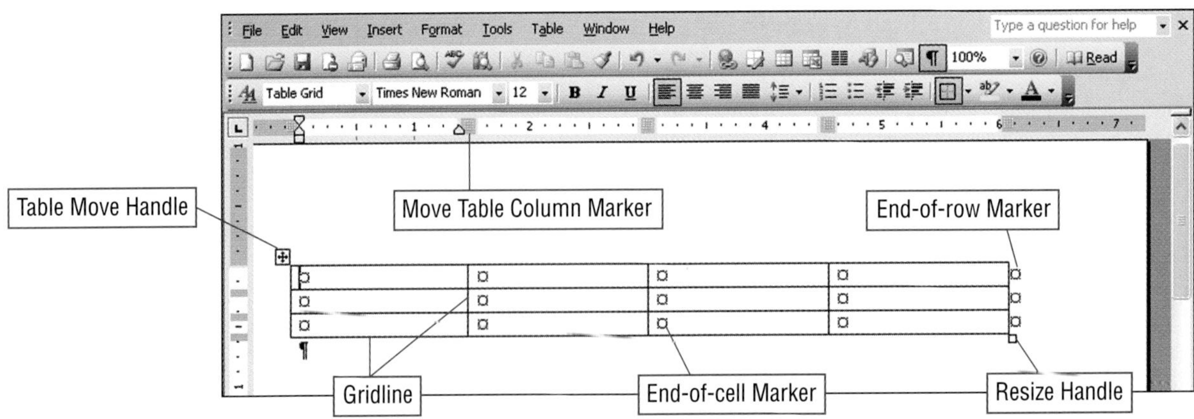

HINT

You can create a table within a table, creating a ***nested*** table.

When you create a table, the insertion point is located in the cell in the upper left corner of the table. Cells in a table contain a cell designation. Columns in a table are lettered from left to right, beginning with *A*. Rows in a table are numbered from top to bottom beginning with *1*. The cell in the upper left corner of the table is cell A1. The cell to the right of A1 is B1, the cell to the right of B1 is C1, and so on.

If the Ruler is displayed at the top of the document screen, move table column markers display on the Ruler. These markers represent the end of a column and are useful in changing the width of columns. Figure 7.2 identifies a move table column marker.

Entering Text in Cells

With the insertion point positioned in a cell, type or edit text. Move the insertion point to other cells with the mouse by clicking in the desired cell. If you are using the keyboard, press the Tab key to move the insertion point to the next cell or press Shift + Tab to move the insertion point to the previous cell.

If the text you type does not fit on one line, it wraps to the next line within the same cell. Or, if you press Enter within a cell, the insertion point is moved to the next line within the same cell. The cell vertically lengthens to accommodate the text, and all cells in that row also lengthen. Pressing the Tab key in a table causes the insertion point to move to the next cell in the table. If you want to move the insertion point to a tab stop within a cell, press Ctrl + Tab. If the insertion point is located in the last cell of the table and you press the Tab key, Word adds another row to the table. Insert a page break within a table by pressing Ctrl + Enter. The page break is inserted between rows, not within.

HINT

Pressing the Tab key in a table moves the insertion point to the next cell. Pressing Ctrl + Tab moves the insertion point to the next tab within a cell.

Moving the Insertion Point within a Table

To move the insertion point to a different cell within the table using the mouse, click in the desired cell. To move the insertion point to different cells within the table using the keyboard, refer to the information shown in Table 7.1.

TABLE 7.1 ***Insertion Point Movement within a Table Using the Keyboard***

To move the insertion point	*Press these keys*
To next cell	Tab
To preceding cell	Shift + Tab
Forward one character	Right Arrow key
Backward one character	Left Arrow key
To previous row	Up Arrow key
To next row	Down Arrow key
To first cell in the row	Alt + Home
To last cell in the row	Alt + End
To top cell in the column	Alt + Page Up
To bottom cell in the column	Alt + Page Down

exercise 1

CREATING A TABLE WITH THE INSERT TABLE BUTTON

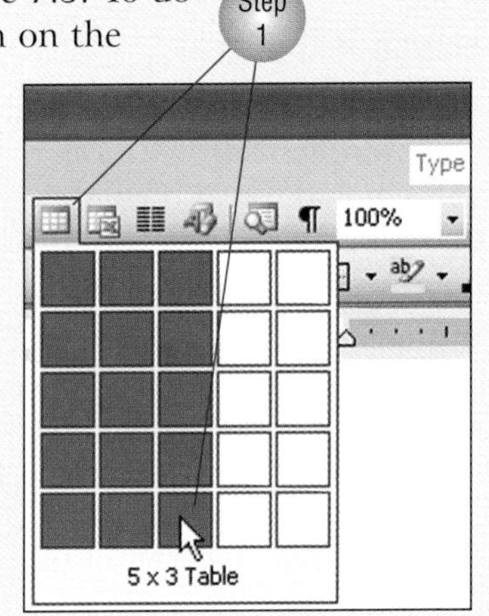

1. At a clear document screen, create the table shown in Figure 7.3. To do this, position the insertion point on the Insert Table button on the Standard toolbar, hold down the left mouse button, drag down and to the right until the number below the grid displays as 5 × 3, and then release the mouse button.
2. Type the text in the cells as indicated in Figure 7.3. Press the Tab key to move to the next cell or press Shift + Tab to move to the preceding cell. (If you accidentally press the Enter key within a cell, immediately press the Backspace key. Do not press Tab after typing the text in the last cell. If you do, another row is inserted in the table. If this happens, immediately click the Undo button on the Standard toolbar.)

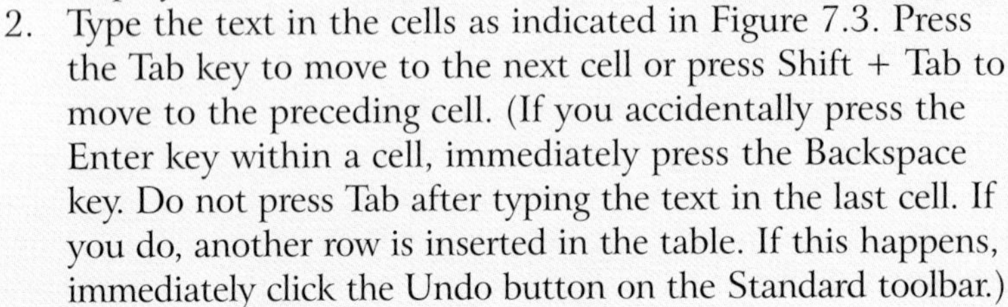

3. Save the table and name it **swc7x01**.

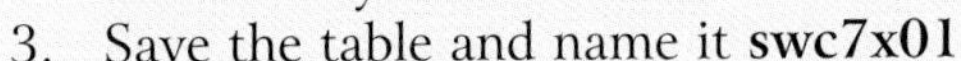

4. Print and then close **swc7x01**.

FIGURE 7.3 ***Exercise 1***

Maggie Rivera	First Trust Bank	(203) 555-3440
Regina Stahl	United Fidelity	(301) 555-1221
Stanley White Cloud	Key One Savings	(360) 555-8966
Les Cromwell	Madison Trust	(602) 555-4900
Cecilia Nordyke	American Financial Trust	(509) 555-3995

exercise 2

CREATING A TABLE AT THE INSERT TABLE DIALOG BOX

1. At a clear document screen, change the paragraph alignment to center, turn on bold, and then type the title **OPTIONAL PLAN PREMIUM RATES** shown in Figure 7.4.
2. Press the Enter key twice, turn off bold, and then change the paragraph alignment to left.
3. Click Table, point to Insert, and then click Table.
4. At the Insert Table dialog box, type 3 in the *Number of columns* text box. (The insertion point is automatically positioned in this text box.)
5. Press the Tab key (this moves the insertion point to the *Number of rows* text box) and then type 5.
6. Click OK or press Enter.

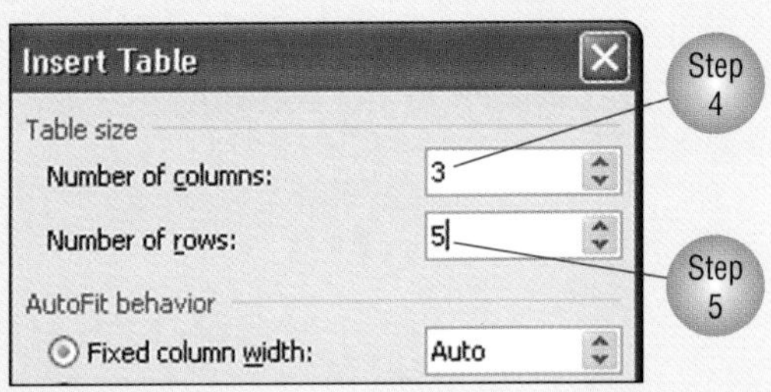

7. Type the text in the cells as indicated in Figure 7.4. Press the Tab key to move to the next cell or press Shift + Tab to move to the preceding cell. To indent the text in cells B2 through B5 and cells C2 through C5, press Ctrl + Tab to move the insertion to a tab within cells, and then type the text.
8. Save the table and name it **swc7x02**.
9. Print and then close **swc7x02**.

FIGURE 7.4 ***Exercise 2***

OPTIONAL PLAN PREMIUM RATES

Waiting Period	Plan 2005 Employees	Basic Plan Employees
60 days	0.79%	0.67%
90 days	0.59%	0.49%
120 days	0.35%	0.30%
180 days	0.26%	0.23%

Selecting Cells

You can format a table in special ways. For example, you can change the alignment of text in cells or rows or you can add character formatting. To identify the cells that are to be affected by the formatting, select the specific cells.

Selecting in a Table with the Mouse

Use the mouse pointer to select a cell, row, column, or an entire table. Table 7.2 describes methods for selecting a table with the mouse. The left edge of each cell, between the left column border and the end-of-cell marker (in an empty cell) or first character in the cell (in a cell containing text), is called the **cell selection bar**. When you position the mouse pointer in the cell selection bar, it turns into an arrow pointing up and to the right (instead of up and to the left). Each row in a table contains a **row selection bar**, which is the space just to the left of the left edge of the table. When you position the mouse pointer in the row selection bar, the mouse pointer turns into an arrow pointing up and to the right.

HINT

You can move text to a different cell by selecting only the text and then dragging the selected text to a different cell.

TABLE

7.2 Selecting in a Table with the Mouse

To select this	Do this
A cell	Position the mouse pointer in the cell selection bar at the left edge of the cell until it turns into an arrow pointing up and to the right and then click the left mouse button.
A row	Position the mouse pointer in the row selection bar at the left edge of the table until it turns into an arrow pointing up and to the right and then click the left mouse button.
A column	Position the mouse pointer on the uppermost horizontal gridline of the table in the appropriate column until it turns into a short, down-pointing arrow and then click the left mouse button.
Adjacent cells	Position the mouse pointer in the first cell to be selected, hold down the left mouse button, drag the mouse pointer to the last cell to be selected, and then release the mouse button.
All cells in a table	Click the table move handle; or position the mouse pointer in any cell in the table, hold down the Alt key, and then double-click the left mouse button. You can also position the mouse pointer in the row selection bar for the first row at the left edge of the table until it turns into an arrow pointing up and to the right, hold down the left mouse button, drag down to select all rows in the table, and then release the left mouse button.
Text within a cell	Position the mouse pointer at the beginning of the text and then hold down the left mouse button as you drag the mouse across the text. (When a cell is selected, the entire cell is changed to black. When text within cells is selected, only those lines containing text are selected.)

exercise 3

SELECTING AND FORMATTING CELLS IN A TABLE

1. Open **swc7x01**.
2. Save the document with Save As and name it **swc7x03**.
3. Select and then bold the text in the cells in the first column using the mouse by completing the following steps:
   a. Position the mouse pointer on the uppermost horizontal gridline of the first column in the table until it turns into a short, down-pointing arrow.
   b. Click the left mouse button.
   c. Click the Bold button on the Standard toolbar.
   d. Deselect the column.
4. Select and then italicize the text in the cells in the third column by completing steps similar to those in Step 3.
5. Save, print, and then close **swc7x03**.

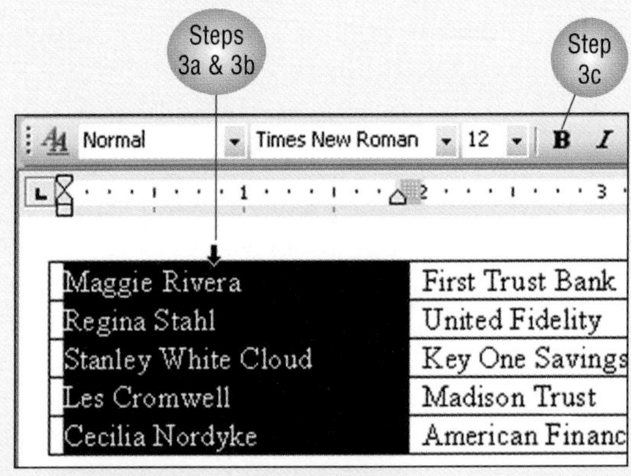

Selecting in a Table with the Keyboard

In addition to the mouse, you can also use the keyboard to select specific cells within a table. Table 7.3 displays the commands for selecting specific amounts of a table.

TABLE 7.3 ***Selecting in a Table with the Keyboard***

To select	*Press*
The next cell's contents	Tab
The preceding cell's contents	Shift + Tab
The entire table	Alt + 5 (on numeric keypad with Num Lock off)
Adjacent cells	Hold down Shift key, then press an arrow key repeatedly
A column	Position insertion point in top cell of column, hold down Shift key, then press Down Arrow key until column is selected

If you want to select only text within cells, rather than the entire cell, press F8 to turn on the Extend mode, and then move the insertion point with an arrow key. When a cell is selected, the entire cell is changed to black. When text within a cell is selected, only those lines containing text are selected.

Selecting Cells with the Table Drop-Down Menu

You can select a row or column of cells or all cells in a table with options from the Table drop-down menu. For example, to select a row of cells in a table, position the insertion point in any cell in the row, click Table, point to Select, and then click Row.

To select cells in a column, position the insertion point in any cell in the column, click Table, point to Select, and then click Column. To select all cells in the table, position the insertion point in any cell in the table, click Table, point to Select, and then click Table.

exercise 4 SELECTING AND FORMATTING CELLS USING THE KEYBOARD AND TABLE DROP-DOWN MENU

1. Open **swc7x02**.
2. Save the document with Save As and name it **swc7x04**.
3. Select and then bold the text in the cells in the first column using the keyboard by completing the following steps:
   a. Position the insertion point in the first cell of the first column (cell A1).
   b. Hold down the Shift key and then press the Down Arrow key four times. (This should select all cells in the first column.)
   c. Press Ctrl + B.

4. Select and then italicize the text in the cells in the second column using the Table drop-down menu by completing the following steps:
   a. Position the insertion point in any cell in the second column.
   b. Click Table, point to Select, and then click Column.
   c. Click the Italic button on the Standard toolbar.

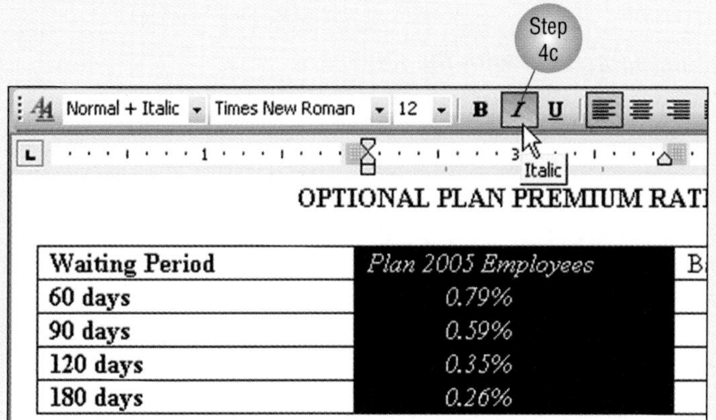

5. Select and then italicize the text in the cells in the third column by completing steps similar to those in Step 4.
6. Save, print, and then close **swc7x04**.

Deleting a Table or Table Contents

You can delete all text in cells within a table, leaving the table gridlines, or you can delete all text and the gridlines. To delete table contents, leaving the gridlines, select the table or specific cells within the table, and then press the Delete key. You can also click Edit, point to Clear, and then click Contents. The text in each selected cell is deleted leaving the gridlines. To delete the entire table, including cell contents and gridlines, click Table, point to Delete, and then click Table.

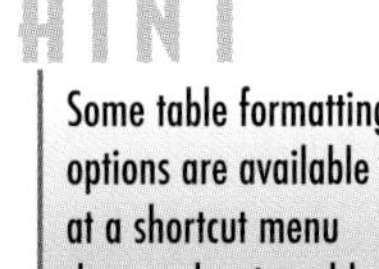

HINT Some table formatting options are available at a shortcut menu that can be viewed by right-clicking a table.

Formatting a Table

A table created with Word's Tables feature can be formatted in a variety of ways. For example, borders and shading can be added to cells; rows and columns can be inserted or deleted; cells can be split or merged; and the alignment of the table can be changed.

Adding Borders and Shading

The gridlines creating a table can be customized with border options. Borders can be added to a selected cell(s) or an entire table with options at the Borders and Shading dialog box shown in Figure 7.5. To display this dialog box, click Format and then Borders and Shading.

FIGURE

7.5 Borders and Shading Dialog Box with Borders Tab Selected

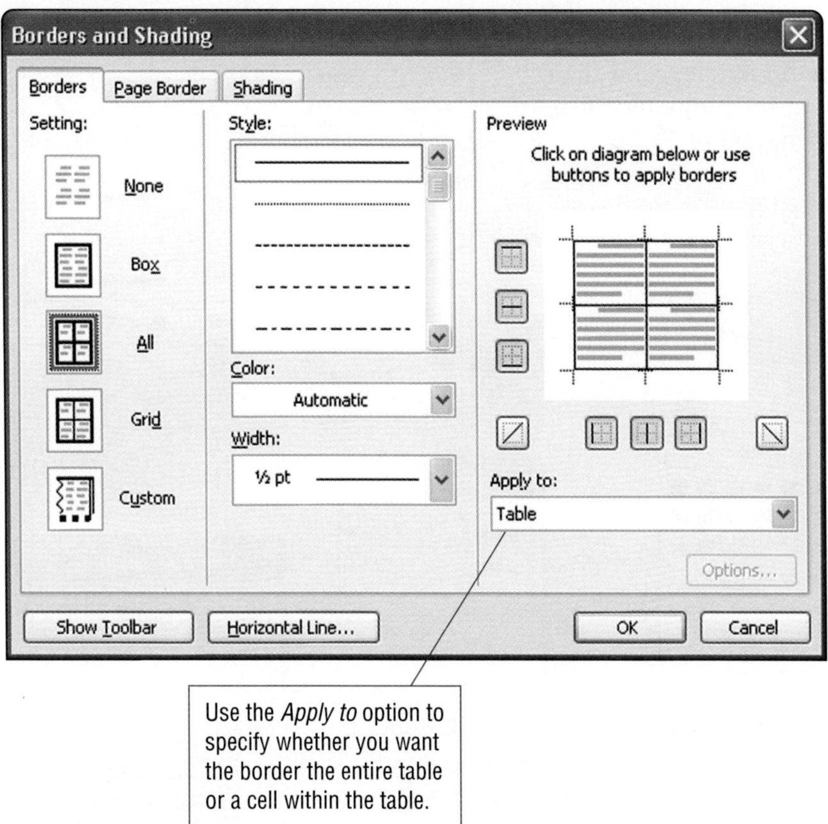

Use the *Apply to* option to specify whether you want the border the entire table or a cell within the table.

If you want a border option to apply to a specific cell, select the cell first and then display the Borders and Shading dialog box. The *Apply to* option at the Borders and Shading dialog box will display with *Cell* in the option box. If the insertion point is positioned in a table (with no cell selected) or if the entire table is selected, changes made at the Borders and Shading dialog box will affect the entire table and the *Apply to* option will display with *Table*.

To add visual appeal to a table, shading can be added to cells. Shading can be added to cells or selected cells with options at the Borders and Shading dialog box with the Shading tab selected. With options at this dialog box you can add a fill and apply a pattern to cells.

HINT

If you make a mistake while formatting a table, immediately click the Undo button on the Standard toolbar.

exercise 5

CREATING A TABLE WITH BORDER LINES AROUND AND BETWEEN CELLS

1. Open **swc7x02**.
2. Save the document with Save As and name it **swc7x05**.
3. Add thick blue lines around the table and add light turquoise shading by completing the following steps:
   a. Position the insertion point in any cell in the table. (Make sure no text or cell is selected.)

b. Click Format and then Borders and Shading.
c. At the Borders and Shading dialog box with the Borders tab selected, click the down-pointing arrow at the right side of the *Width* option box, and then click *4 ½ pt* at the drop-down list.
d. Click the down-pointing arrow at the right side of the *Color* option and then click Blue (sixth option from the left in the second row) at the color palette.

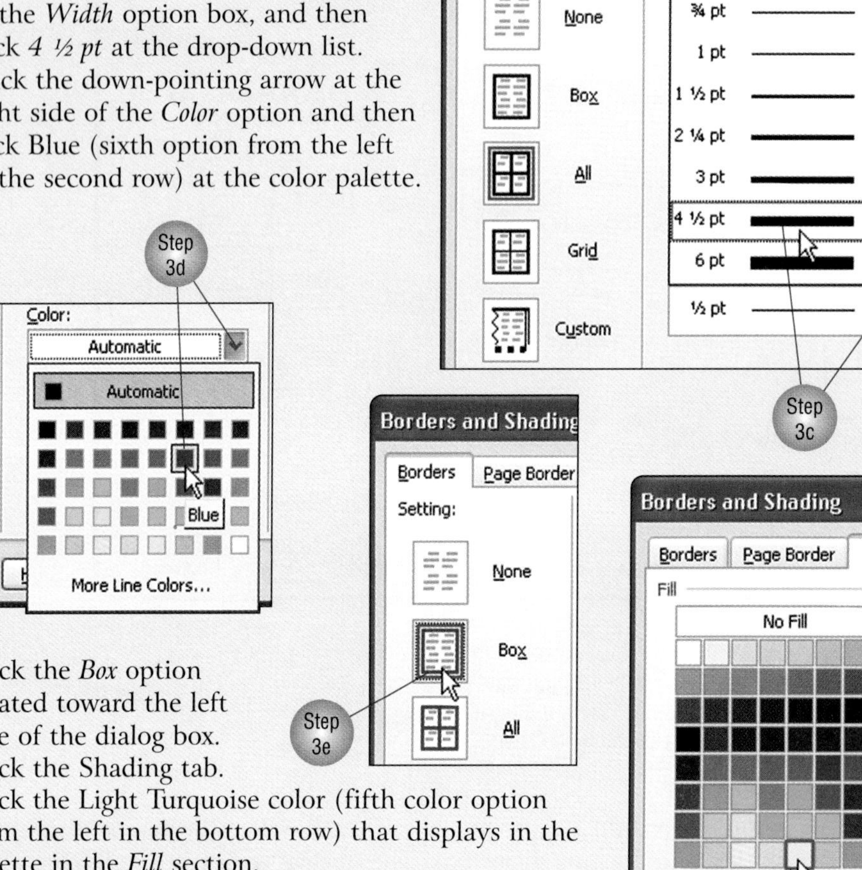

e. Click the *Box* option located toward the left side of the dialog box.
f. Click the Shading tab.
g. Click the Light Turquoise color (fifth color option from the left in the bottom row) that displays in the palette in the *Fill* section.
h. Click OK.

4. Save, print, and then close **swc7x05**.

Changing Column Width

HINT

Change column widths by dragging column markers on the Ruler.

When you create a table, the columns are the same width. The width of the columns depends on the number of columns as well as the document margins. In some tables, you may want to change the width of certain columns to accommodate more or less text. You can change the width of columns using the mouse on the Ruler, in a table, or with options from the Table Properties dialog box.

To change column width using the Ruler, position the mouse pointer on a move table column marker until it turns into a left and right arrow, and then drag the marker to the desired position. Hold down the Alt key while dragging a table column marker and measurements display on the horizontal ruler.

exercise 6

CREATING A TABLE AND THEN CHANGING COLUMN WIDTH WITH THE RULER

1. At a clear document screen, create a table with 3 columns and 7 rows (7 × 3) as shown in Figure 7.6.
2. Change the width of the second column using the mouse by completing the following steps:
   a. Make sure the Ruler is displayed.
   b. Position the mouse pointer on the move table column marker on the 4-inch mark on the Ruler until it turns into an arrow pointing left and right.
   c. Hold down the Shift key and then the left mouse button.
   d. Drag the marker to the 3.25-inch mark, release the Shift key and then release the mouse button.

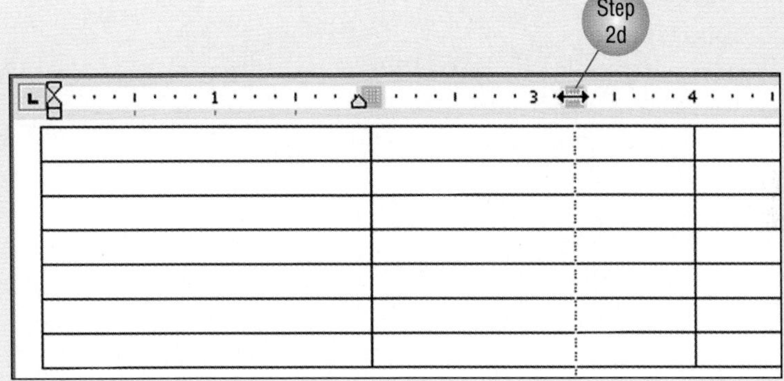

3. Change the width of the third column using the mouse by completing the following steps:
   a. Position the mouse pointer on the move table column marker on the 6-inch mark on the Ruler until it turns into an arrow pointing left and right.
   b. Hold down the Shift key and then the left mouse button.
   c. Drag the marker to the 4.75-inch mark, release the Shift key and then release the mouse button.

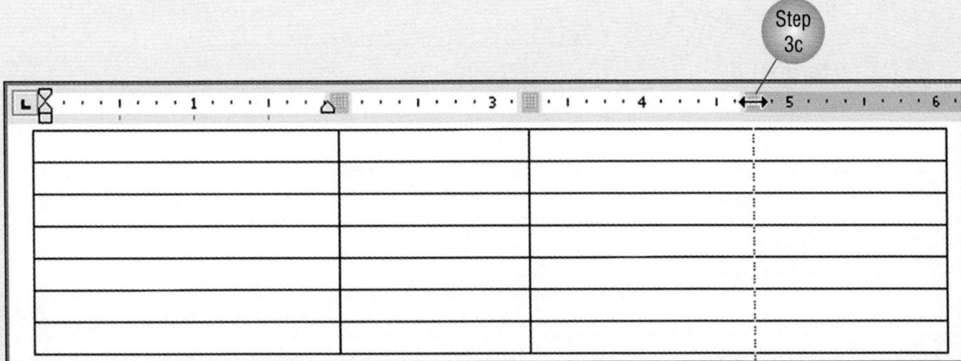

4. Type the text in the cells, bolding and centering the text as shown in Figure 7.6.
5. Add a thick/thin double-line border around the table by completing the following steps:
   a. With the insertion point positioned in any cell in the table, click Format and then Borders and Shading.
   b. At the Borders and Shading dialog box, make sure the Borders tab is selected.

c. Scroll down the *Style* list box until the first thick/thin double-line option displays and then click the double-line option.

d. Click the *Grid* option that displays at the left side of the dialog box.

e. Click OK to close the dialog box.

6. Add 10% fill to cells A1, B1, and C1 by completing the following steps:

a. Select cells A1, B1, and C1.

b. Click Format and then Borders and Shading.

c. At the Borders and Shading dialog box, click the Shading tab.

d. At the Borders and Shading dialog box with the Shading tab selected, click the down-pointing arrow at the right side of the *Style* option, and then click *10%* at the drop-down list.

e. Click OK to close the Borders and Shading dialog box.

f. Deselect the cells.

7. Save the document and name it **swc7x06**.

8. Print and then close **swc7x06**.

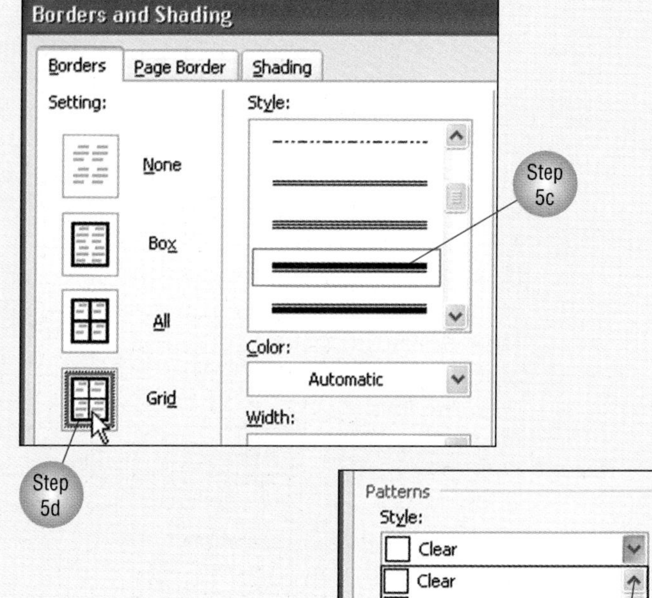

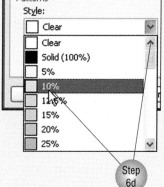

FIGURE 7.6 ***Exercise 6***

Name	Employee #	Department
Kevin Gerome	222-104-6608	Human Resources
Louella Arellano	433-196-9817	Human Resources
Gale Meschke	533-119-6780	Financial Planning
Paul Tjerne	114-457-3221	Sales
William Whitlock	652-671-9910	Sales
Madeline Zevenbergen	552-900-6221	Support Services

Change column width using gridlines by positioning the arrow pointer on the gridline separating columns until the insertion point turns into a left- and right-pointing arrow with a vertical line between, and then drag the gridline to the desired position. If you want to see the column measurements on the Ruler as you drag a gridline, hold down the Alt key.

If you know the exact measurement for columns in a table, you can change column widths at the Table Properties dialog box with the Column tab selected as shown in Figure 7.7. To display this dialog box, click Table and then Table Properties. At the Table Properties dialog box, click the Column tab. To change the column width, select the current measurement in the *Preferred width* text box, and then type the desired measurement. You can also click the up- or down-pointing arrow to increase or decrease the current measurement.

FIGURE 7.7 **Table Properties Dialog Box with Column Tab Selected**

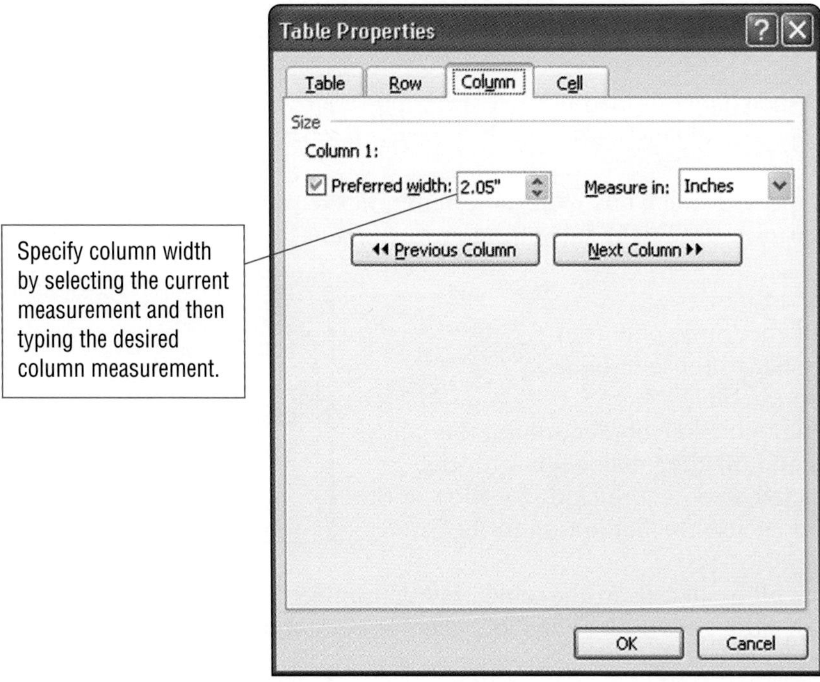

In a table containing text or other features, you can adjust the width of one column to accommodate the longest line of text in the column. To do this, position the mouse pointer on the right column gridline until it turns into a left- and right-pointing arrow with a vertical double line, and then double-click the left mouse button. To automatically size more than one column, select the columns first, and then double-click on a gridline.

exercise 7

CHANGING COLUMN WIDTH IN A TABLE

1. Open **swc7x02**.
2. Save the document with Save As and name it **swc7x07**.
3. Select and then delete the title *OPTIONAL PLAN PREMIUM RATES*.
4. Change the width of the first column by completing the following steps:
   a. Click in the top cell in the first column.
   b. Position the mouse pointer on the gridline separating the first and second columns until it turns into a left- and right-pointing arrow with a vertical double line between.
   c. Hold down the Alt key and then the left mouse button, drag the gridline to the left until the first measurement on the horizontal ruler displays as *1.25"*, then release the Alt key and then the mouse button.

Step 4c

1.25" 2.55"

Waiting Period	Plan 2005 Empl
60 days	0.79%
90 days	0.59%
120 days	0.35%
180 days	0.26%

5. Change the width of the second column by completing the following steps:
   a. Click in the top cell in the middle column.
   b. Click Table and then Table Properties.
   c. At the Table Properties dialog box, click the Column tab.
   d. At the Table Properties dialog box with the Column tab selected, click the down-pointing arrow at the right side of the *Preferred width* text box until *1.7"* displays.
   e. Click OK or press Enter.

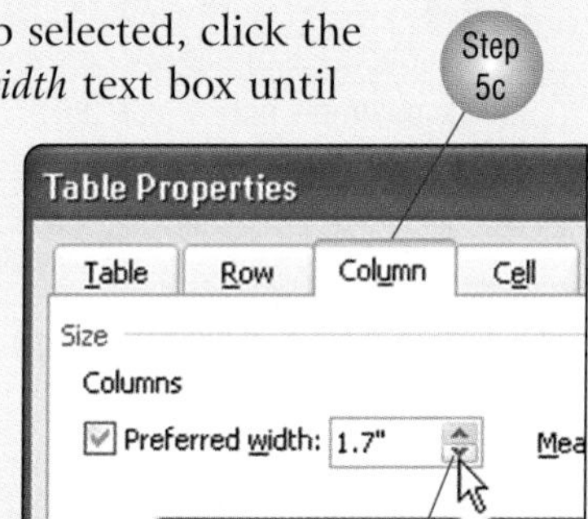

6. Change the width of the third column to 1.7" by completing steps similar to those in Step 5.
7. Add the following to the table:
   a. Add a thick/thin double-line border around the table. (At the Borders and Shading dialog box with the Borders tab selected, choose a thick/thin option in the *Style* list box and choose the *Box* option in the *Setting* section.)
   b. Add a light color fill to all cells in the table (you determine the color).
8. Save, print, and then close **swc7x07**. (The table will not be centered between the margins.)

Changing Column Width with AutoFit

Use the AutoFit option from the Table drop-down menu to make the column widths in a table automatically fit the contents. To do this, position the insertion point in any cell in the table, click Table, point to AutoFit, and then click AutoFit to Contents at the side menu.

Changing Table Size with the Resize Handle

In Print Layout with the insertion point positioned inside a table, the resize handle displays in the lower right corner of the table. Drag this resize handle to increase and/or decrease the size and proportion of the table.

exercise 8 — CHANGING COLUMN WIDTHS USING AUTOFIT AND RESIZING THE TABLE

1. Open **swc7x01**.
2. Save the document with Save As and name it **swc7x08**.
3. Change the width of the columns to fit the contents by completing the following steps:
   a. Make sure the insertion point is positioned in a cell within the table.
   b. Click Table, point to AutoFit, and then click AutoFit to Contents at the side menu.
4. Make the following changes to the table:
   a. Change the border line around the table from a single line to a line of your choosing (other than single). (At the Borders and Shading dialog box with the Borders tab selected, choose the *Grid* option in the *Setting* section.)
   b. Add shading of your choosing to the table.
5. Save and then print **swc7x08**.
6. With **swc7x08** still open, increase the size of the table by completing the following steps:
   a. Change to the Print Layout view.
   b. Position the mouse pointer on the resize handle located in the lower right corner of the table.
   c. Hold down the left mouse button, drag down and to the right until the width and height of the table increase approximately .5 inch, and then release the mouse button.

Maggie Rivera	First Trust Bank	(203) 555-3440
Regina Stahl	United Fidelity	(301) 555-1221
Stanley White Cloud	Key One Savings	(360) 555-8966
Les Cromwell	Madison Trust	(602) 555-4900
Cecilia Nordyke	American Financial Trust	(509) 555-3995

Step 6c

7. Save, print, and then close **swc7x08**.

Changing Row Height

Change row height in a table in much the same manner as changing column width. For example, you can change row height with an adjust table row marker on the vertical ruler, by dragging a gridline, or with options at the Table Properties dialog box.

Changing Cell Alignment

By default, text in cells aligns at the left side of the cell. Like normal text, this alignment can be changed to centered, right, or justified. To change the alignment of text in cells, select the cells, and then click the desired alignment button on the Formatting toolbar. You can also change the alignment of text in selected cells with the *Alignment* option at the Paragraph dialog box with the Indents and Spacing tab selected or with a shortcut command.

The methods just described change the horizontal alignment of text in cells. You can also change the vertical alignment of text in cells at the Table Properties dialog box with the Cell tab selected as shown in Figure 7.8. The default vertical alignment of text in a cell is *Top*. This can be changed to *Center* or *Bottom*.

FIGURE 7.8 *Table Properties Dialog Box with Cell Tab Selected*

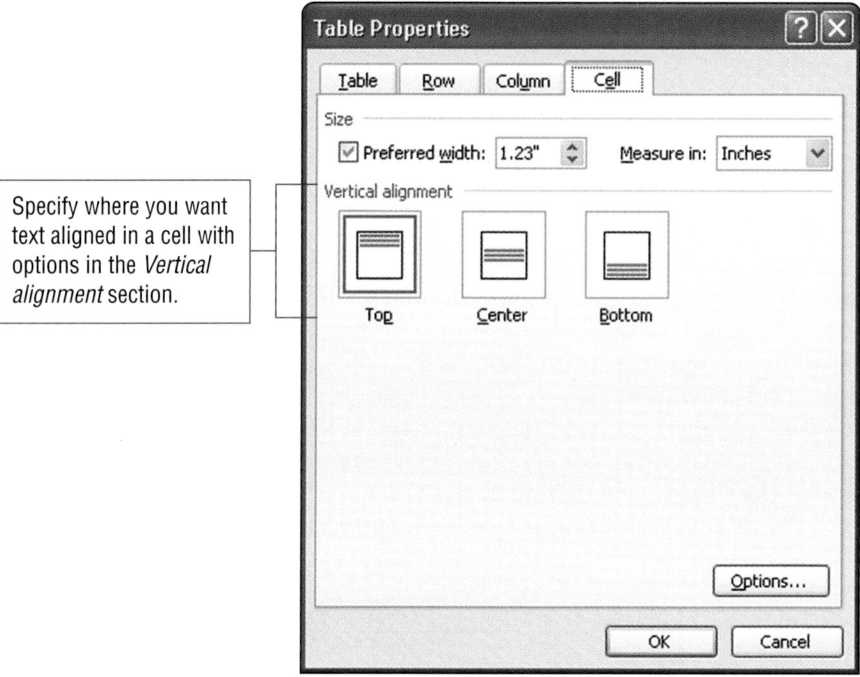

Aligning a Table

By default, a table aligns at the left margin. Change this alignment with options at the Table Properties dialog box with the Table tab selected as shown in Figure 7.9. To change the alignment, click the desired alignment option in the *Alignment* section of the dialog box.

FIGURE 7.9 *Table Properties Dialog Box with Table Tab Selected*

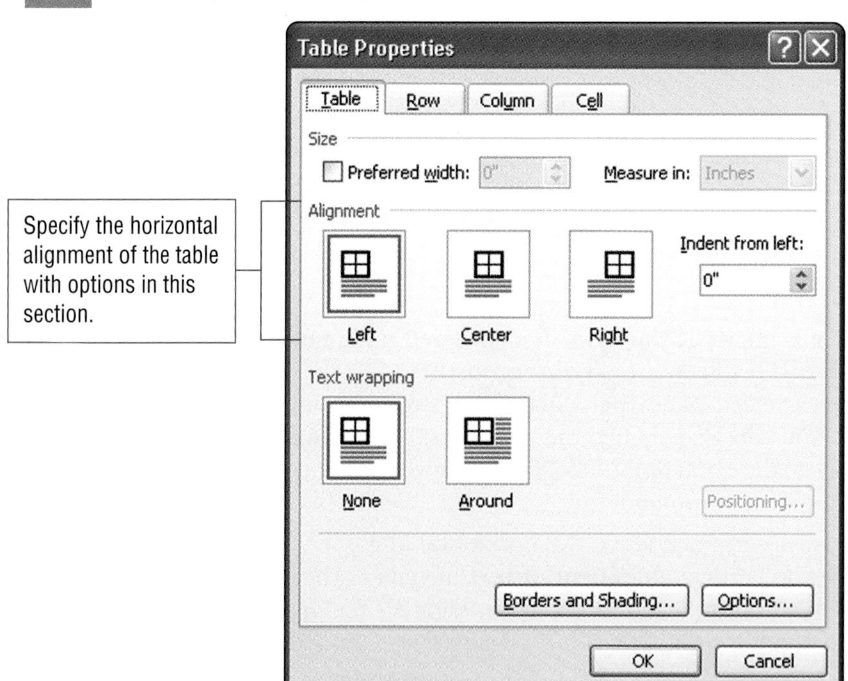

exercise 9

CHANGING ROW HEIGHT, CELL ALIGNMENT, AND TABLE ALIGNMENT

1. Open **WordTable01**.
2. Save the document with Save As and name it **swc7x09**.
3. Increase the height of the first row in the table by completing the following steps:
   a. Change to the Print Layout view.
   b. Position the mouse pointer on the first adjust table row marker on the vertical ruler.
   c. Hold down the left mouse button and hold down the Alt key.
   d. Drag the adjust table row marker down until the first row measurement on the vertical ruler displays as *1"*, then release the mouse button and then the Alt key.

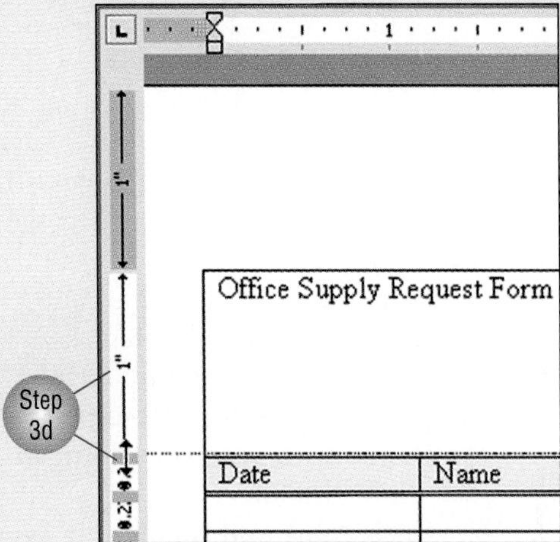

4. Increase the height of second row by completing the following steps:
   a. Position the arrow pointer on the gridline that displays at the bottom of the second row until the arrow pointer turns into an up- and down-pointing arrow with a vertical double line between.
   b. Hold down the left mouse button and then hold down the Alt key.
   c. Drag the gridline down until the second row measurement on the vertical ruler displays as *0.58"*, then release the mouse button and then the Alt key.

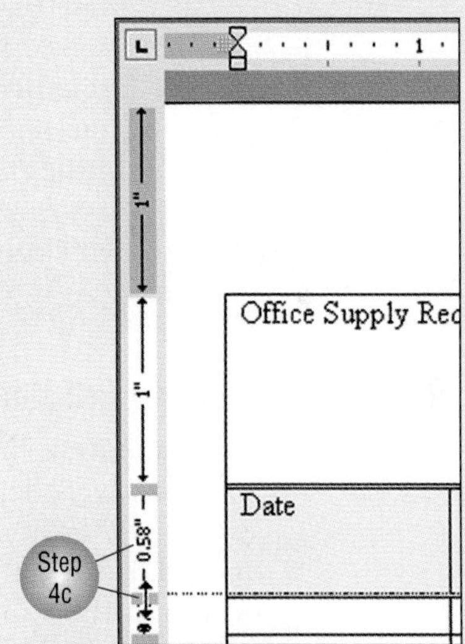

5. Increase the height of rows 3 through 11 (the remaining rows) by completing the following steps:
   a. Select rows 3 through 11.
   b. Click Table and then Table Properties.
   c. At the Table Properties dialog box, click the Row tab.
   d. At the Table Properties dialog box with the Row tab selected, click the *Specify height* option.
   e. Click the up-pointing arrow at the right side of the *Specify height* option until *0.5"* displays in the *Specify height* text box.
   f. Click OK to close the dialog box.

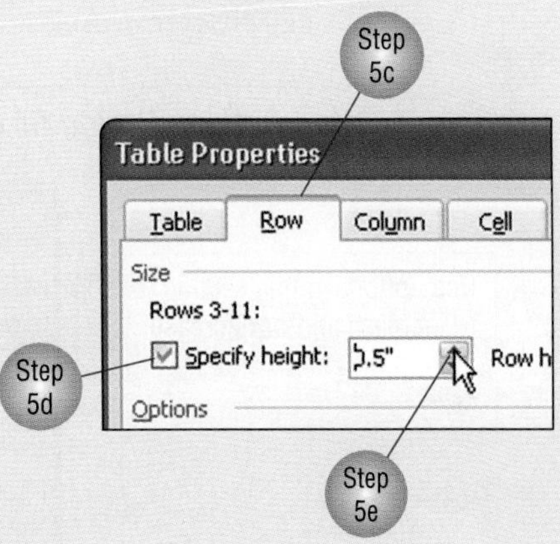

6. Change the vertical and horizontal alignment of text in rows 1 and 2 by completing the following steps:
   a. Select rows 1 and 2.
   b. Click Table and then Table Properties.

c. At the Table Properties dialog box, click the Cell tab.
d. At the Table Properties dialog box with the Cell tab selected, click the *Center* option in the *Vertical alignment* section of the dialog box.
e. Click OK to close the dialog box.
f. With rows 1 and 2 still selected, click the Center button on the Formatting toolbar.
7. Select only row 1 and then change the font to 24-point Arial bold.
8. Select only row 2 and then change the font to 14-point Arial bold.
9. Center the table horizontally by completing the following steps:
   a. Position the insertion point in any cell in the table.
   b. Click Table and then Table Properties.
   c. At the Table Properties dialog box, click the Table tab.
   d. At the Table Properties dialog box with the Table tab selected, click the *Center* option in the *Alignment* section.
   e. Click OK or press Enter.
10. Save, print, and then close **swc7x09**.

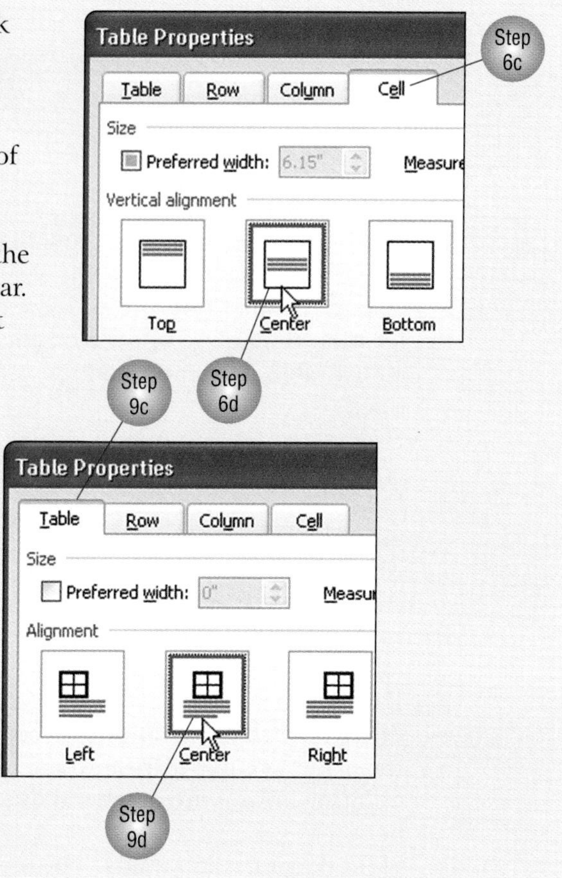

Changing Cell Margin Measurements

By default, cells in a table contain specific margin settings. Top and bottom margins in a cell have a default measurement of *0"* and left and right margins have a default setting of *0.08"*. Change these default settings with options at the Table Options dialog box shown in Figure 7.10. Display this dialog box by clicking the Options button at the Table Properties dialog box with the Table tab selected. Use the options in the Default cell margins section to change the top, bottom, left, and/or right cell margin measurements.

FIGURE 7.10 ***Table Options Dialog Box***

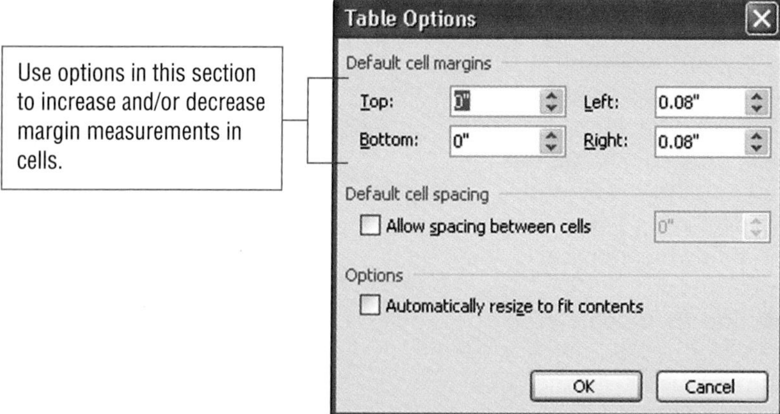

Changes to cell margins will affect all cells in a table. If you want to change the cell margin measurements for one cell or for selected cells, position the insertion point in the cell or select the desired cells, display the Table Properties dialog box with the Cell tab selected, and then click the Options button. This displays the Cell Options dialog box shown in Figure 7.11.

FIGURE 7.11 ***Cell Options Dialog Box***

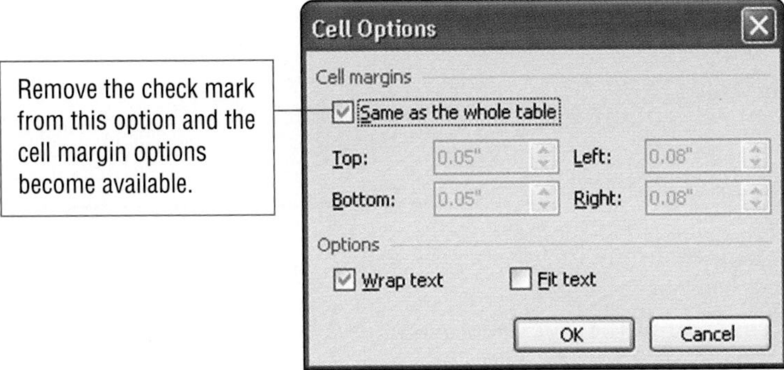

Before setting the new cell margin measurements, remove the check mark from the *Same as the whole table* option. With the check mark removed from this option, the cell margin options become available. Specify the new cell margin measurements and then click OK to close the dialog box.

exercise 10

CHANGING CELL MARGIN MEASUREMENTS

1. Open **WordTable10**.
2. Save the document with Save As and name it **swc7x10**.
3. Change the top and bottom margins for all cells in the table by completing the following steps:
   a. Position the insertion point in any cell in the table, click Table, and then click Table Properties.
   b. At the Table Properties dialog box, click the Table tab. (Skip this step if the Table tab is already selected.)
   c. Click the Options button.
   d. At the Table Options dialog box, change the *Top* and *Bottom* measurements to *0.05"*.
   e. Click OK to close the Table Options dialog box.
   f. Click OK to close the Table Properties dialog box.
4. Save and then print **swc7x10**.

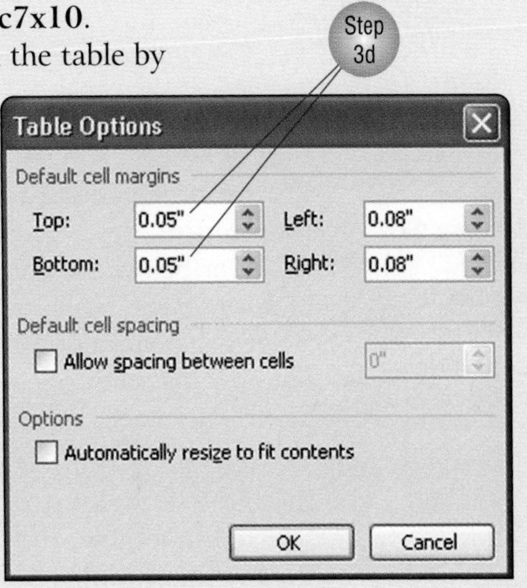

5. Change the top and bottom cell margin measurements for the first row of cells by completing the following steps:
   a. Select the first row of cells (the cells containing *Salesperson*; *Sales, First Half*; and *Sales, Second Half*).
   b. Click Table and then Table Properties.
   c. At the Table Properties dialog box, click the Cell tab.
   d. Click the Options button.
   e. At the Cell Options dialog box, remove the check mark from the *Same as the whole table* option.
   f. Change the *Top* and *Bottom* measurements to *0.1″*.
   g. Click OK to close the Cell Options dialog box.
   h. Click OK to close the Table Properties dialog box.

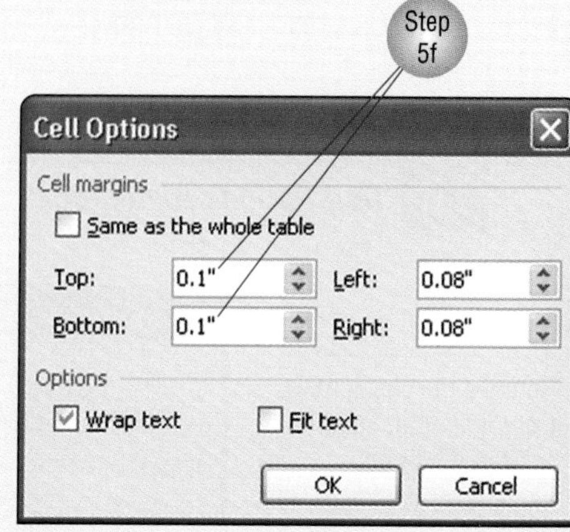

6. Change the left cell margin measurement for specific cells by completing the following steps:
   a. Select only the cells containing the salespersons' names (this includes the cells containing *Bushing, Tyler*; *Catalano, Gina*; *Hebert, Rene*; *Lipinski, Steve*; and *Raymond, Jeanette*).
   b. Display the Table Properties dialog box with the Cell tab selected.
   c. Click the Options button.
   d. At the Cell Options dialog box, remove the check mark from the *Same as the whole table* option.
   e. Change the *Left* measurement to *0.3″*.
   f. Click OK to close the Cell Options dialog box.
   g. Click OK to close the Table Properties dialog box.

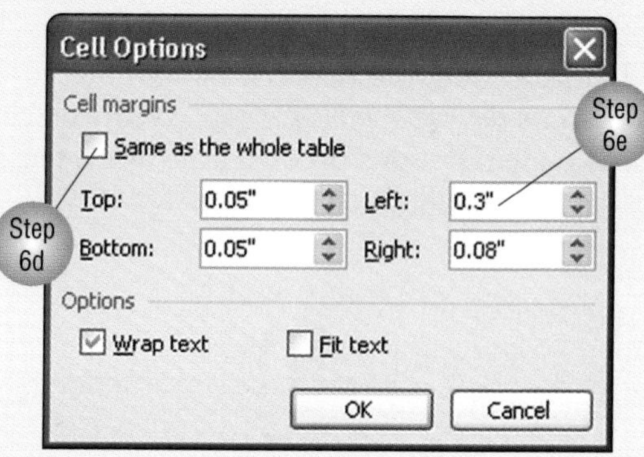

7. Save, print, and then close **swc7x10**.

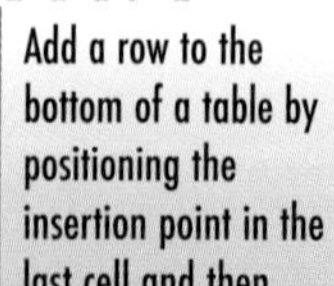

Inserting Rows

Rows can be added (inserted) to an existing table. Several methods are available for inserting rows. You can use options from the Insert side menu to insert rows above or below the current row. To do this, position the insertion point in a cell in a row, click Table, point to Insert, and then click either Rows Above or Rows Below (depending on where you want the row inserted). If you want more than one row inserted, select the desired number of rows, click Table, point to Insert, and then choose Rows Above or Rows Below.

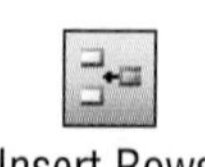
Insert Rows

You can also insert rows by selecting a row or several rows and then clicking the Insert Rows button on the Standard toolbar. When a row or several rows are selected in a table, the Insert Table button becomes the Insert Rows button on the Standard toolbar.

Another method for inserting a row or several rows is to select a row (or rows) in a table, position the mouse pointer inside the table, click the *right* mouse button, and then click Insert Rows. Also, you can insert a row at the end of the table by positioning the insertion point in the last cell in the table and then pressing the Tab key.

Inserting Columns

Insert columns in a table in much the same way as rows. To insert a column, position the insertion in a cell within the table, click Table, point to Insert, and then click Columns to the Left or Columns to the Right. If you want to insert more than one column, select the desired number of columns first.

Insert Columns

Another method for inserting a column (or columns) is to select the column and then click the Insert Columns button on the Standard toolbar. When a column or columns are selected, the Insert Table button on the Standard toolbar becomes the Insert Columns button.

You can also insert a column or group of columns by selecting the column(s), clicking the *right* mouse button, and then clicking Insert Columns at the shortcut menu. Word inserts a column or columns to the left of the selected column or columns. If you want to add a column to the right side of the table, select all of the end-of-row markers, and then click the Insert Columns button on the Standard toolbar.

exercise 11

INSERTING ROWS AND A COLUMN IN A TABLE

1. Open **WordTable11**.
2. Save the document with Save As and name it **swc7x11**.
3. Add two rows to the table by completing the following steps:
   a. Select the fourth and fifth rows in the table.
   b. Click Table, point to Insert, and then click Rows Above.

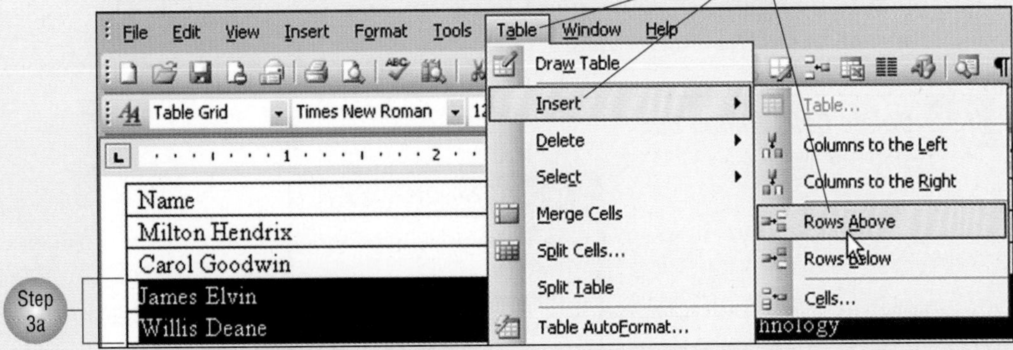

   c. Deselect the rows.
   d. Position the insertion point in cell A4 (below *Carol Goodwin*) and then type **Steven Harrison**.
   e. Type the following text in the specified cells:

B4	=	**Financial Planning**
A5	=	**Howard Kline**
B5	=	**Human Resources**

4. Add a column to the right side of the table and change the alignment to center by completing the following steps:
   a. Click in the cell containing the title *Department*.
   b. Click Table, point to Insert, and then click Columns to the Right. (This inserts a column at the right side of the table and also selects the column.)
   c. Click the Center button on the Formatting toolbar.
   d. Deselect the column.
5. Type the following text in the specified cells:
   C1 = Extension
   C2 = 2331
   C3 = 1035
   C4 = 2098
   C5 = 1564
   C6 = 2109
   C7 = 1822
   C8 = 2311
   C9 = 3442
6. Make the following changes to the table:
   a. Use the AutoFit feature to make the columns in the table automatically fit the contents.
   b. Center the text in cells A1 and B1.
   c. Bold the text in cells A1, B1, and C1.
   d. Center the table horizontally.
7. Save, print, and then close **swc7x11**.

Deleting Cells, Rows, or Columns

Delete a column, row, or cell with options from the Delete side menu. For example, to delete a column, position the insertion point in any cell within the column, click Table, point to Delete, and then click Columns. To delete a row, click Table, point to Delete, and then click Rows. To delete a specific cell, position the insertion point in the cell, click Table, point to Delete, and then click Cells. This displays the Delete Cells dialog box shown in Figure 7.12.

FIGURE 7.12 ***Delete Cells Dialog Box***

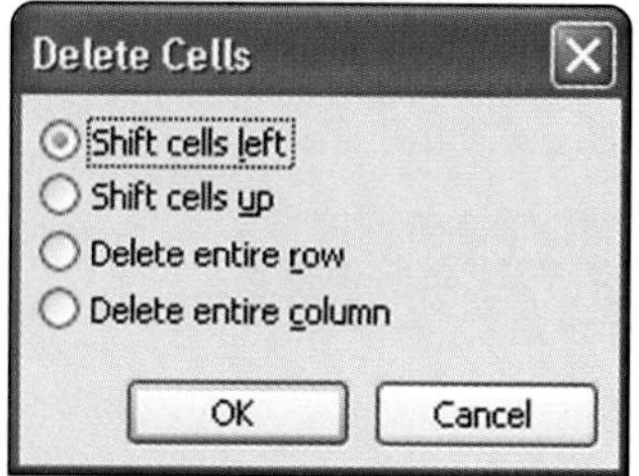

At the Delete Cells dialog box, the *Shift cells left* option is selected by default. At this option, cells will shift left after the cell (or selected cells) is deleted. Click the *Shift cells up* option if you want cells moved up after the cell (or selected cells) is deleted. Click *Delete entire row* to delete the row where the insertion point is positioned or click *Delete entire column* to delete the column where the insertion point is positioned.

The Delete Cells dialog box can also be displayed by positioning the mouse pointer in the table, clicking the *right* mouse button, and then clicking Delete Cells at the shortcut menu.

Deleting Cell Content

If you want to delete just the contents of cells and not a row or column, select the desired cells and then press the Delete key. You can also select the cells, click Edit on the Menu bar, point to Clear, and then click Contents.

Merging and Splitting Cells

Merge cells with the Merge Cells option from the Table drop-down menu. To do this, select the cells to be merged, click Table and then click Merge Cells. Split a cell or a row or column of cells with options at the Split Cells dialog box shown in Figure 7.13. To display this dialog box, position the insertion point in the cell to be split, click Table and then Split Cells. At the Split Cells dialog box, make sure the desired number of columns displays in the *Number of columns* text box, and then click OK or press Enter. To split an entire column or row of cells, select the column or row first, click Table and then click Split Cells.

FIGURE 7.13 **Split Cells Dialog Box**

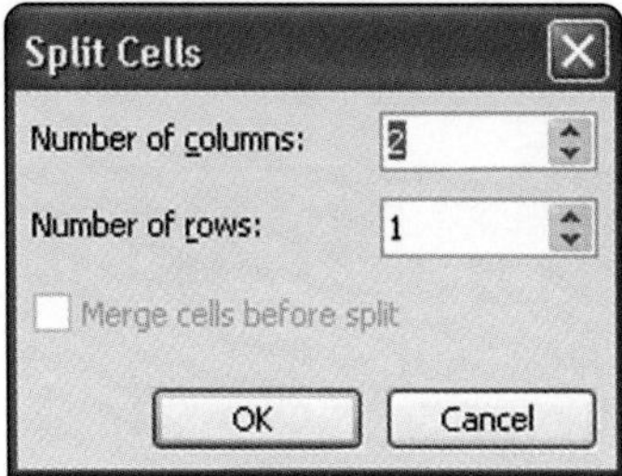

exercise 12 DELETING ROWS, COLUMNS, AND CELL CONTENT; MERGING AND SPLITTING CELLS

1. Open **swc7x06**.
2. Save the document with Save As and name it **swc7x12**.
3. Delete the row containing information on *William Whitlock* by positioning the insertion point in the cell containing *William Whitlock*, clicking Table, pointing to Delete, and then clicking Rows.
4. Delete the second column by positioning the insertion point in the cell containing the title *Employee #*, clicking Table, pointing to Delete, and then clicking Columns.
5. Insert a row at the beginning of the table, merge cells in the row, and insert text by completing the following steps:
   a. Position the insertion point in the cell containing the title *Name*.
   b. Click Table, point to Insert, and then click Rows Above.

c. With the cells selected in the new row, click Table and then click Merge Cells.
d. Type McCORMACK FUNDS CORPORATION.

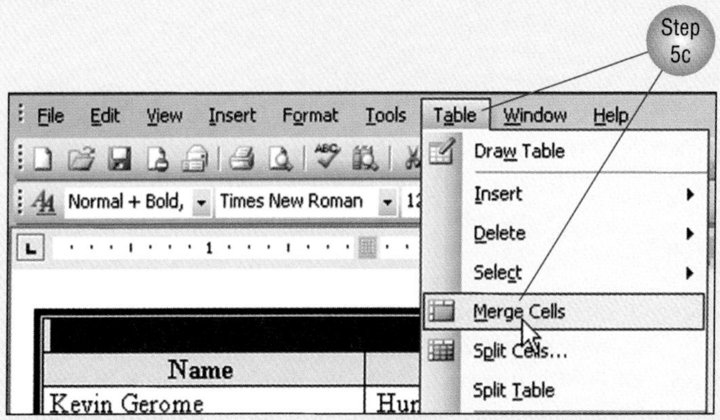

6. Save and then print **swc7x12**.
7. Delete the content of cells by completing the following steps:
   a. Select cells beginning with the cell containing the name *Kevin Gerome* and ending with the cell containing the text *Support Services* (this includes all cells except the top two rows).
   b. Press the Delete key. (This deletes the cell contents but not the cells.)
8. Split cells by completing the following steps:
   a. Select the cells below the *Name* cell (five cells).
   b. Click Table and then Split Cells.

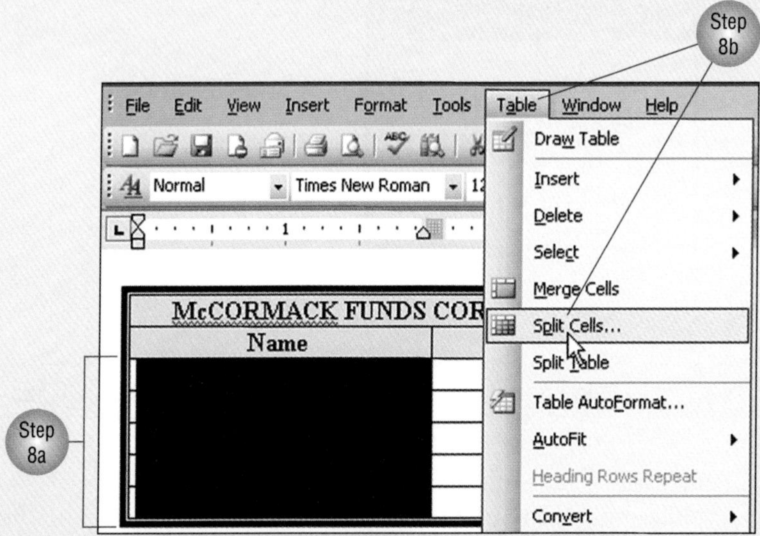

   c. At the Split Cells dialog box, make sure *2* displays in the *Number of columns* text box, and then click OK.
   d. Deselect the cells.
9. Save, print, and then close **swc7x12**.

Formatting with AutoFormat

Formatting a table such as adding borders or shading, aligning text in cells, changing fonts, and so on, can take some time. Word has provided predesigned table styles that can quickly format your table for you. Table styles are contained in the Table AutoFormat dialog box shown in Figure 7.14. To display this dialog box, position the insertion point in any cell in a table, click Table and then Table AutoFormat. Click the desired style in the *Table styles* list box (notice the table in the *Preview* section) and then click the Apply button (located toward the bottom of the dialog box).

HINT

Save a document containing a table before applying an autoformat.

FIGURE 7.14 ***Table AutoFormat Dialog Box***

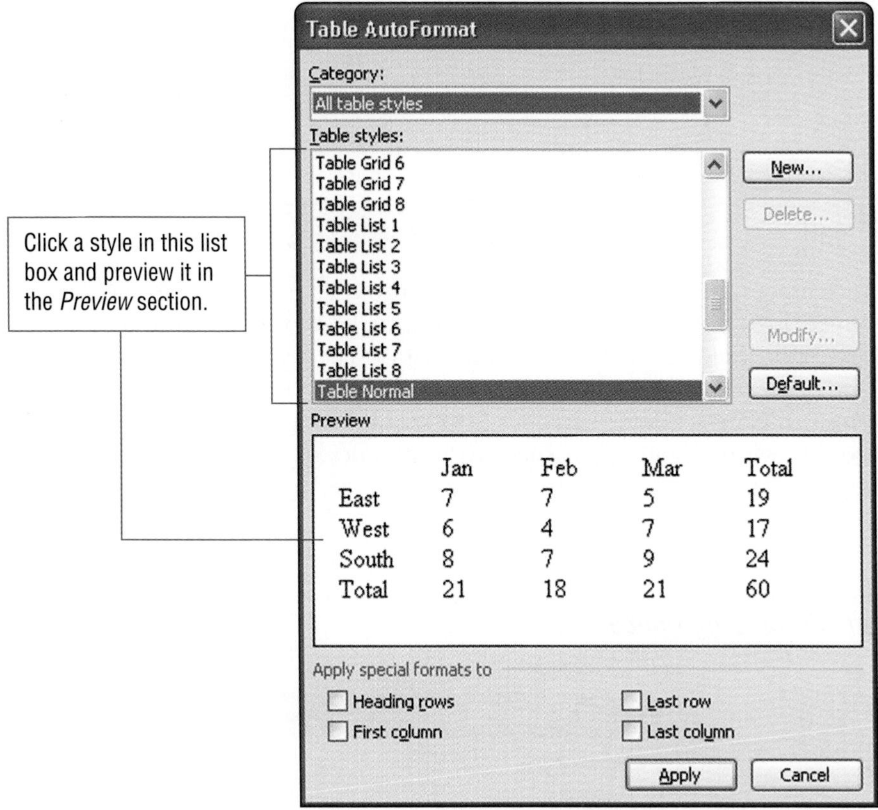

QUICK STEPS

Apply Autoformatting to Table

1. Select table.
2. Click Table, Table AutoFormat.
3. Click desired autoformat.
4. Click OK.

exercise 13 FORMATTING A TABLE USING THE TABLE AUTOFORMAT DIALOG BOX

1. Open **swc7x01**.
2. Save the document with Save As and name it **swc7x13**.
3. Make sure the insertion point is positioned in cell A1 and then insert a row above the current row.
4. With the new row selected, click the Bold button on the Formatting toolbar and then the Center button.
5. Type the following text in the specified cells (the text will be bold and centered):

A1 = Name
B1 = Company
C1 = Telephone Number

6. Automatically format the table by completing the following steps:
   a. Position the insertion point in any cell in the table.
   b. Click Table and then Table AutoFormat.
   c. At the Table AutoFormat dialog box, click *Table List 7* in the *Table styles* list box.
   d. Click the Apply button or press Enter.
7. Use the AutoFit feature to make the columns in the table automatically fit the contents.
8. Center the table horizontally.
9. Save, print, and then close **swc7x13**.

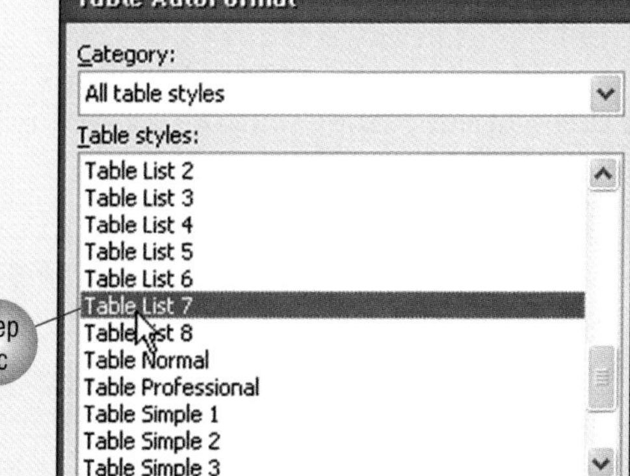

Converting Text to a Table

QUICK STEPS

Convert Text to Table
1. Select text.
2. Click Table, Convert, Text to Table.
3. Specify number of columns, rows, and AutoFit behavior.
4. Click OK.

You can create a table and then enter data in the cells or you create the data and then convert it to a table. To convert text to a table, type the text and separate it with a separator character such as a comma or tab. The separator character identifies where you want text divided into columns. To convert text, select the text, click Table, point to Convert, and then click Text to Table. At the Convert Text to Table dialog box shown in Figure 7.15, specify the number of columns and rows, the AutoFit behavior, and the separator character.

FIGURE 7.15 ***Convert Text to Table Dialog Box***

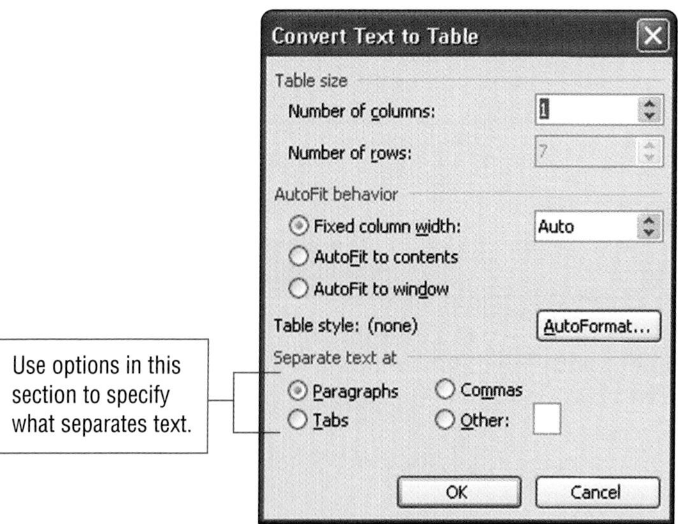

exercise 14 — CONVERTING TEXT TO A TABLE

1. Open **WordList03**.
2. Save the document with Save As and name it **swc7x14**.
3. Convert the text to a table by completing the following steps:
   a. Select the text.
   b. Click Table, point to Convert, and then click Text to Table.
   c. At the Convert Text to Table dialog box, make the following changes:
      1) Type 2 in the *Number of columns* text box.
      2) Click the *AutoFit to contents* option in the *AutoFit behavior* section.
      3) Click the *Commas* option in the *Separate text at* section.
      4) Click OK.

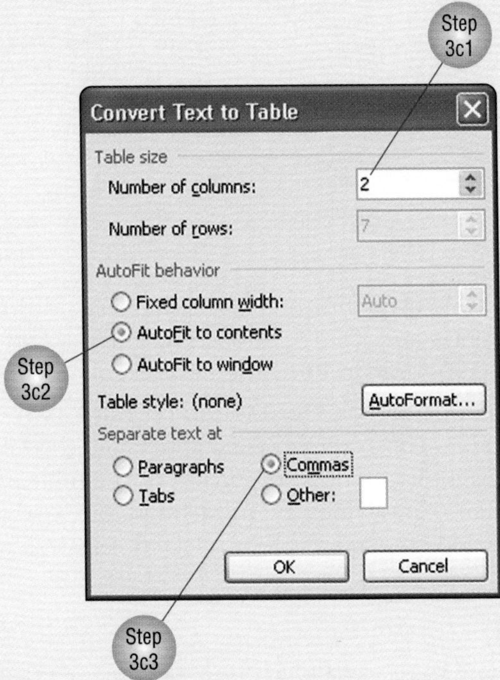

4. Select and merge the cells in the top row (the row containing the title *CEDAR RIVER SERVICES*) and then change the alignment to Center.
5. Apply the *Table Colorful 3* autoformat to the table.
6. Save, print, and then close **swc7x14**.

Creating a Table Using the Tables and Borders Toolbar

Word includes a Tables and Borders toolbar with options you can use to create a more free-form table. With buttons on the Tables and Borders toolbar shown in Figure 7.16, you can draw a table with specific borders as well as add shading and fill. To display this toolbar, click the Tables and Borders button on the Standard toolbar.

Tables and Borders

FIGURE 7.16 *Tables and Borders Toolbar*

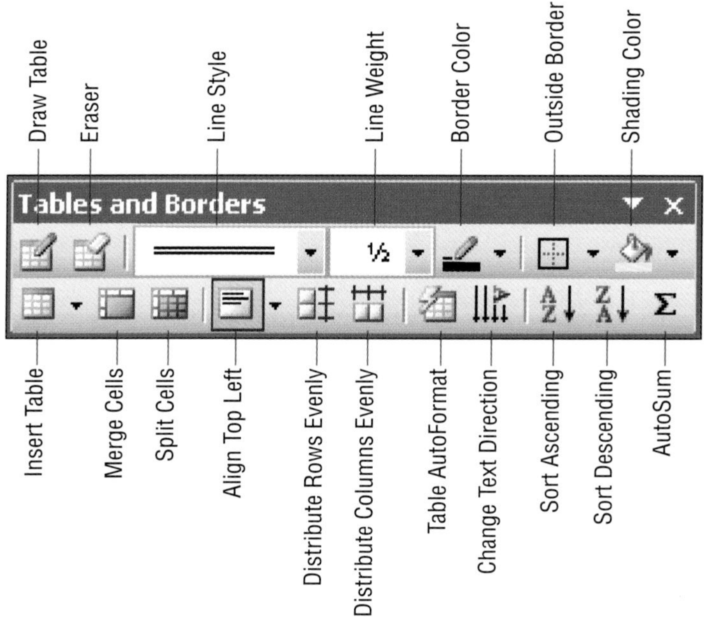

HINT
Use buttons on the Tables and Borders toolbar to create a more free-form table.

HINT
Hold down the Shift key and the Draw Table tool turns into the Eraser tool.

To create a table using buttons on the Tables and Borders toolbar, turn on the display of the Tables and Borders toolbar. Using the mouse (the mouse pointer displays as a pencil), drag to draw the desired columns and rows.

Many of the buttons on the Tables and Borders toolbar can be used to customize the table. For example, you can change the line style with Line Style options and then draw the desired portion of the table. Or, you can change the line style and then redraw lines in an existing table. Use options from the Shading Color button to add color to a cell or selected cells in a table.

exercise 15 DRAWING A TABLE USING THE TABLES AND BORDERS TOOLBAR

1. At a clear document screen, type the title centered and bolded as shown in Figure 7.17. (Press the Enter key once, turn off bold, return paragraph alignment to left, and then press the Enter key two more times.)
2. Turn on the display of the Tables and Borders toolbar by clicking the Tables and Borders button on the Standard toolbar.
3. Make sure the line style is single. To do this, click the down-pointing arrow at the right side of the Line Style button and then click the first single-line option.
4. Position the mouse pointer (displays as a pencil) in the editing window and draw the table, row, and column lines as shown in Figure 7.17. (To draw the lines, position the pencil in the desired location, hold down the left mouse button, draw the line, and then release the button. If you want to erase a line, hold down the Shift key and then drag across the line. Release the Shift key and then continue drawing the table.)
5. When the table is drawn, click the Draw Table button on the Tables and Borders toolbar button to deactivate it.

6. Change the vertical alignment of text in cells by completing the following steps:
   a. Select all cells in the table.
   b. Click the down-pointing arrow at the right side of the Align Top Left button located on the Tables and Borders toolbar.
   c. At the palette of alignment choices, click the Align Center Left option (first option from the left in the second row).

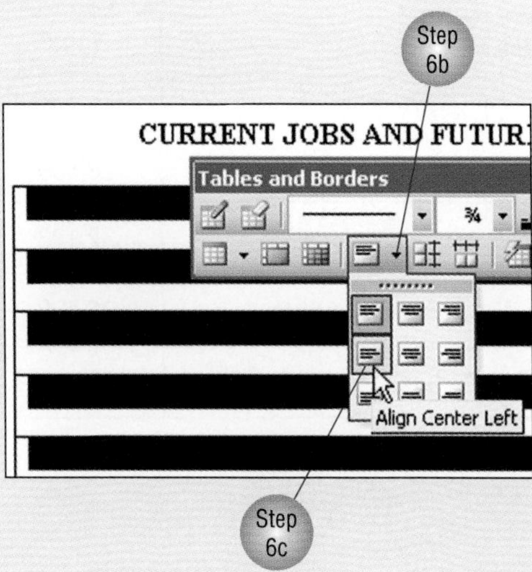

7. With all cells in the table still selected, click the Distribute Rows Evenly button on the Tables and Borders toolbar.

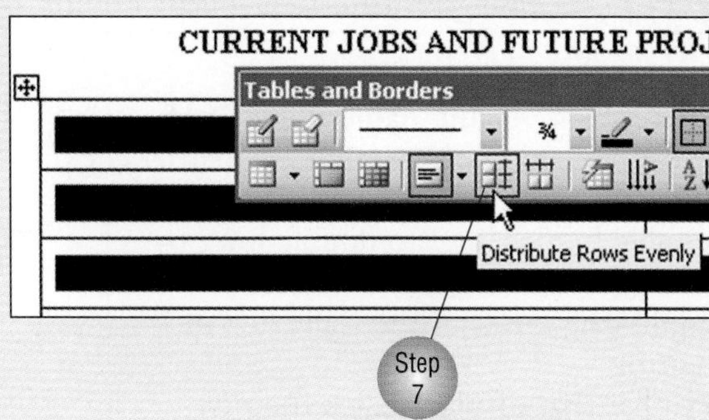

8. Select all cells in the second and third columns and then click the Center button on the Formatting toolbar (not the Tables and Borders toolbar).
9. Click in the first cell.
10. Type the text in the cells as shown in Figure 7.17. (If text wraps in a cell, widen the column.)
11. Turn off the display of the Tables and Borders toolbar by clicking the Tables and Borders button on the Standard toolbar.
12. Save the document and name it **swc7x15**.
13. Print and then close **swc7x15**.

FIGURE

7.17 *Exercise 15*

CURRENT JOBS AND FUTURE PROJECTIONS

Occupation	1998	2010
Agriculture, Forestry, Fishery	18,342	15,423
Executive, Managerial, Administrative	26,459	28,109
Marketing, Sales	32,188	33,009
Operators, Fabricators, Laborers	35,429	32,677
Professional, Technical	51,239	55,438

exercise 16

CUSTOMIZING A TABLE WITH THE TABLES AND BORDERS TOOLBAR

1. Open **swc7x15**.
2. Save the document with Save As and name it **swc7x16**.
3. Turn on the display of the Tables and Borders toolbar by clicking the Tables and Borders button on the Standard toolbar.
4. Change the outside table border lines to double lines by completing the following steps:
   a. Click the down-pointing arrow at the right side of the Line Style button.
   b. At the drop-down list that displays, click the first double-line style.
   c. Position the pencil pointer in the upper left corner of the table, hold down the left mouse button, drag the pencil down the left side of the table until it reaches the bottom, and then release the mouse button. (This changes the single line to a double line.)
   d. Change the bottom border of the table to a double line by dragging the pencil across the bottom border. (Be sure to hold down the left mouse button as you drag.)
   e. Change the right border of the table to a double line by dragging the pencil along the right border.
   f. Change the top border of the table to a double line by dragging the pencil along the top border.
5. Click the Draw Table button to deselect it.

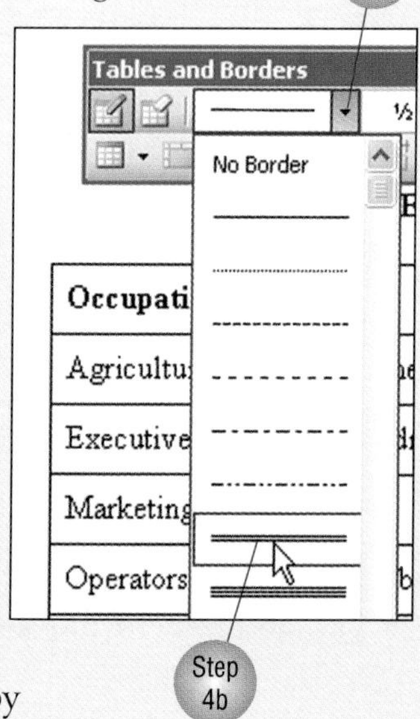

6. Add gray shading to cells by completing the following steps:
   a. Select cells A2 through C6.
   b. Click the down-pointing arrow at the right side of the Shading Color button on the Tables and Borders toolbar.
   c. At the palette of color choices that displays, click the Gray-25% color (this is the second option from the *right* in the top row).

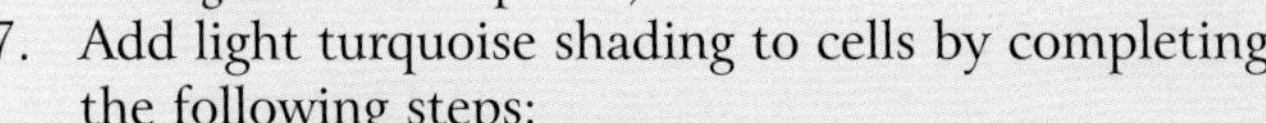

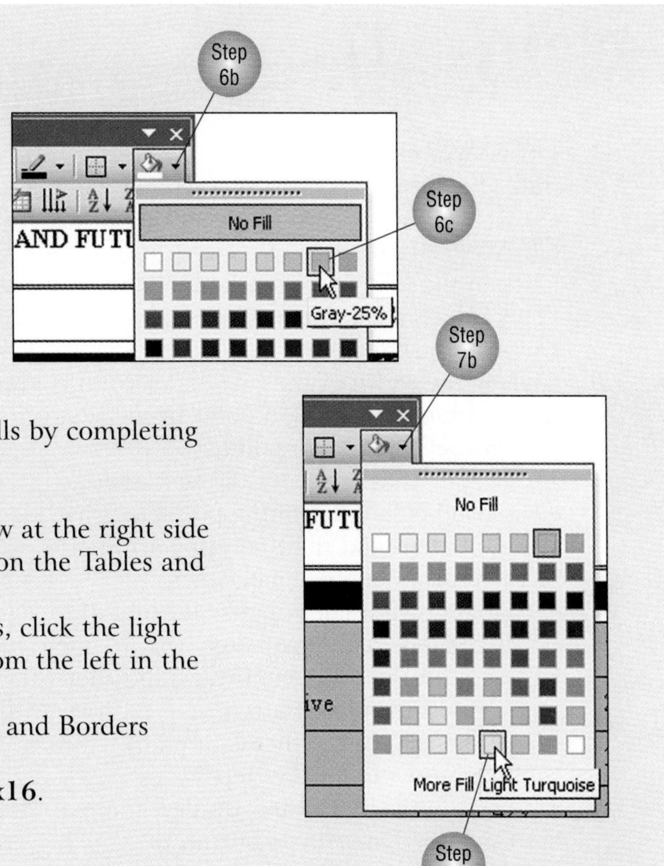

7. Add light turquoise shading to cells by completing the following steps:
   a. Select cells A1, B1, and C1.
   b. Click the down-pointing arrow at the right side of the Shading Color button on the Tables and Borders toolbar.
   c. At the palette of color choices, click the light turquoise color (fifth color from the left in the bottom row).
8. Turn off the display of the Tables and Borders toolbar.
9. Save, print, and then close **swc7x16**.

Moving a Table

Position the mouse pointer in a table drawn with options from the Tables and Borders toolbar and a table move handle displays in the upper left corner. Use this handle to move the table in the document. Position the mouse pointer on the table move handle until the pointer turns into a four-headed arrow, hold down the left mouse button, drag the table to the desired position, and then release the mouse button.

To move a table, changing the document view can be helpful. With options from the Zoom button on the Standard toolbar, you can change the display percentage and also select options such as *Page Width*, *Text Width*, *Whole Page*, and *Two Pages*. The options available from the Zoom button depend on the view selected. To move a table, consider changing to the Print Layout view and then changing the Zoom to *Whole Page*. To change the zoom, click the down-pointing arrow at the right side of the Zoom button and then click *Whole Page* at the drop-down list.

exercise 17 — INSERTING A COLUMN, CHANGING TEXT DIRECTION, AND MOVING THE TABLE

1. Open **swc7x15**.
2. Save the document with Save As and name it **swc7x17**.
3. Customize the table so it appears as shown in Figure 7.18. To begin, delete the title *CURRENT JOBS AND FUTURE PROJECTIONS*.
4. Click in the first cell, click Table, point to Insert, and then click Columns to the Left. (This inserts a column at the left side of the table.)
5. Deselect the column.
6. Change the width of the first and second columns by completing the following steps:
   a. Position the insertion point in the first cell (cell A1).
   b. Position the mouse pointer on the gridline that separates the first and second column until the pointer turns into a left- and right-pointing arrow with a vertical double line between.
   c. Hold down the left mouse button, drag to the left to approximately the .75-inch mark on the horizontal ruler, and then release the mouse button.

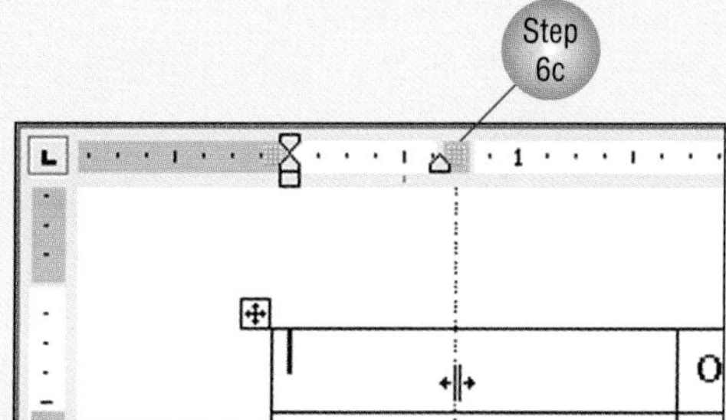

7. Merge the cells in the first column by completing the following steps:
   a. Display the Tables and Borders toolbar.
   b. Click the Draw Table button to deactivate it.
   c. Select the first column.
   d. Click the Merge Cells button on the Tables and Borders toolbar.
8. Type the text in the first cell as shown in Figure 7.18 by completing the following steps:
   a. Make sure the insertion point is positioned in the first cell.
   b. Change the text direction by clicking twice on the Change Text Direction button on the Tables and Borders toolbar.
   c. Click the Center button on the Formatting toolbar.
   d. Change the font to 24-point Times New Roman bold.
   e. Type **Future Jobs**.

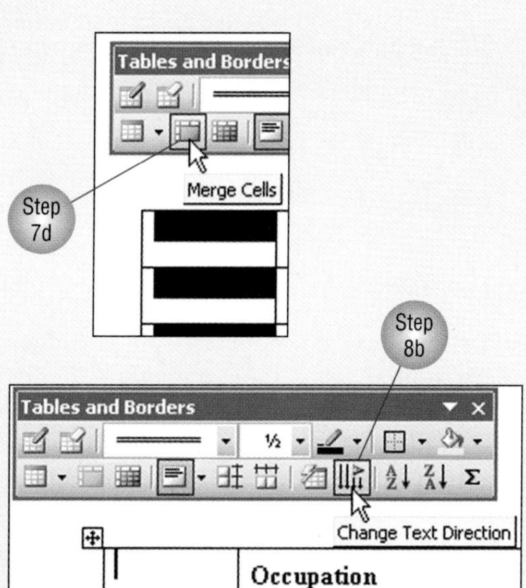

9. Turn off the display of the Tables and Borders toolbar.
10. Center the table horizontally.
11. Move the table to the middle of the page by completing the following steps:
    a. Click the down-pointing arrow at the right side of the Zoom button on the Standard toolbar and then click *Whole Page* at the drop-down list.
    b. Position the mouse pointer in the table until the table move handle displays in the upper left corner of the table.

c. Position the mouse pointer on the table move handle until the pointer turns into a four-headed arrow.
d. Hold down the left mouse button, drag the outline of the table to the middle of the page, and then release the mouse button.
e. Click the down-pointing arrow at the right side of the Zoom button on the Standard toolbar and then click *100%* at the drop-down list.

12. Save, print, and then close **swc7x17**.

FIGURE 7.18 ***Exercise 17***

Future Jobs	Occupation	1998	2010
	Agriculture, Forestry, Fishery	18,342	15,423
	Executive, Managerial, Administrative	26,459	28,109
	Marketing, Sales	32,188	33,009
	Operators, Fabricators, Laborers	35,429	32,677
	Professional, Technical	51,239	55,438

Creating a Chart with Data in a Word Table

While data established in a Word table does an adequate job of representing data, you can create a chart from data in a table to provide a more visual presentation of the data. A chart is sometimes referred to as a **graph** and is a picture of numeric data. Create a chart with data in a table or data in a spreadsheet created in other programs such as Microsoft Excel. Create charts with the Microsoft Graph Chart application. With Microsoft Graph Chart, you can create a variety of charts including bar and column charts, pie charts, area charts, and much more.

Create a Chart
1. Select table.
2. Click Insert, Picture, Chart.

Create a chart in Word by entering data in a datasheet provided by Microsoft Graph Chart, or create a chart from data in a table. In this section, you will learn how to create a chart using data from a Word table. To create a chart in Word using data in a table, select the table and then click Insert, point to Picture and then click Chart. A datasheet is inserted in the document above the table and the chart created by Microsoft Graph Chart is inserted below the table. Click outside the chart to close Microsoft Graph Chart and remove the datasheet.

exercise 18 CREATING A CHART WITH DATA IN A TABLE

1. Open **WordTable04**.
2. Save the document with Save As and name it **swc7x18**.
3. Create the chart shown in Figure 7.19. To begin, position the insertion point in any cell in the table and then select the table by clicking Table, pointing to Select, and then clicking Table.
4. Click Insert, point to Picture, and then click Chart.
5. When the datasheet and chart display, click outside the chart and the datasheet. (This closes Graph and removes the datasheet.)
6. Delete the table in the document by positioning the insertion point in any cell in the table, clicking Table, pointing to Delete, and then clicking Table.
7. Save, print, and then close **swc7x018**.

FIGURE 7.19 ***Exercise 18***

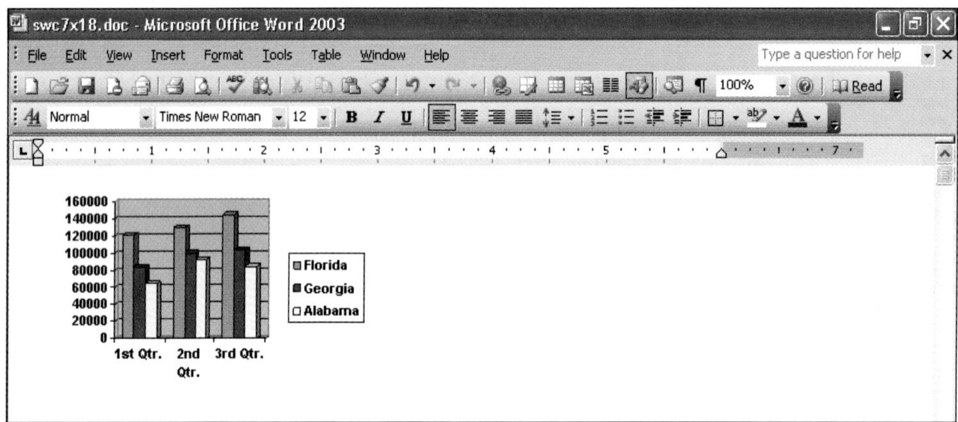

In a chart, the data in the first row is used for the ***x-axis***. The x-axis is the horizontal axis that runs along the bottom of the chart. The left side of the chart displays the values and is referred to as the ***z-axis***. The z-axis is generally marked like a ruler and is broken into units by marks called ***ticks***. Next to each tick mark is the amount of the value at that particular point on the axis. The values in the chart created in Exercise 18 are broken into tick marks by twenty thousands beginning with zero and continuing to 160,000. The values for the z-axis will vary depending on the data in the table.

Drawing

HINT

Precisely size a chart with measurements at the Format Object dialog box. Display this dialog box by selecting the chart, clicking Format, and then clicking Object.

Sizing and Moving a Chart

Increase the size of a chart by selecting the chart and then dragging a sizing handle. To move a chart, change the black sizing handles to white sizing handles and then drag the chart to the desired location. To change to white sizing handles, change text wrapping for the chart. Do this with the Draw button on the Drawing toolbar. Display the Drawing toolbar by clicking the Drawing button on the Standard toolbar. To change the text wrapping, click the Draw button on the Drawing toolbar, point to Text Wrapping, and then click the desired wrapping option at the side menu.

exercise 19

SIZING AND MOVING A CHART

1. Open **swc7x18**.
2. Save the document with Save As and name it **swc7x19**.
3. Change to the Print Layout view.
4. Change the Zoom to Whole Page. To do this, click the down-pointing arrow at the right of the Zoom button on the Standard toolbar, and then click *Whole Page* at the drop-down menu.
5. Click in the chart to select it. (Black sizing handles display around the chart.)
6. Drag the middle sizing handle at the right side of the chart to the right to approximately the 5-inch mark on the horizontal ruler.

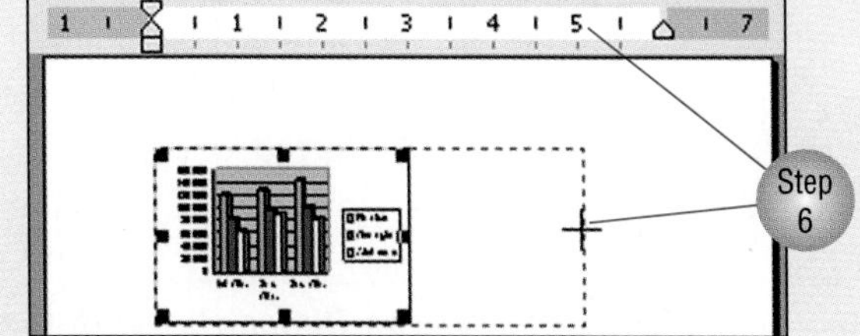

7. Drag the middle sizing handle at the bottom of the chart down to approximately the 4-inch mark on the vertical ruler.

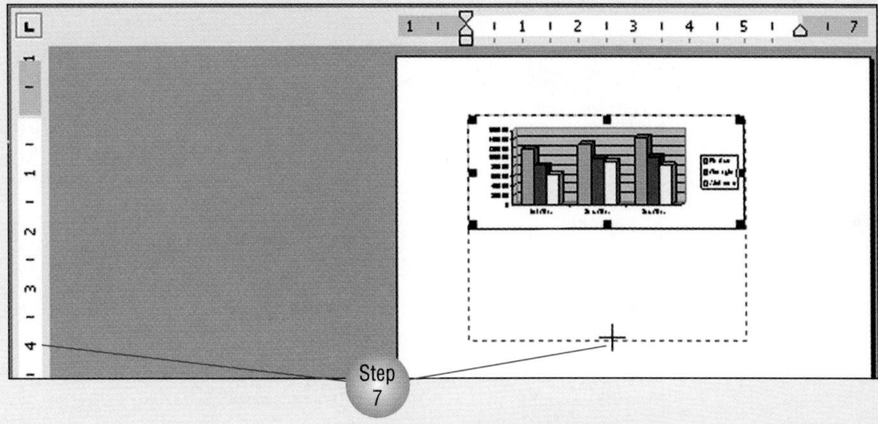

8. Change the text wrapping for the chart by completing the following steps:
   a. Display the Drawing toolbar by clicking the Drawing button on the Standard toolbar. (Skip this step if the Drawing toolbar is already displayed.)
   b. Make sure the chart is selected.
   c. Click the Draw button on the Drawing toolbar, point to Text Wrapping, and then click Through at the side menu.

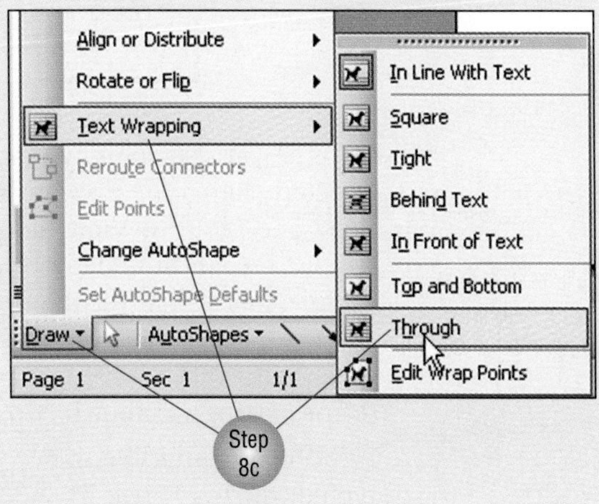

9. Position the arrow pointer (displays with a four-headed arrow attached) inside the chart, hold down the left mouse button, drag the outline of the chart to the middle of the page, and then release the mouse button.
10. Click outside the chart to deselect it.
11. Change the Zoom back to 100%. To do this, click the down-pointing arrow at the right of the Zoom button, and then click *100%* at the drop-down menu.
12. Save, print, and then close **swc7x19**.

Changing the Chart Type

Chart Type

The default chart type created by Graph is a Column chart. Change this default chart type with the Chart Type button on the Graph Standard toolbar. (The chart must be displayed in Microsoft Graph Chart for the Graph Standard toolbar to display. To display Microsoft Graph Chart for an existing chart, double-click the chart.) To change the chart type, click the down-pointing arrow at the right side of the button, and then click the desired chart type at the drop-down list. The drop-down list contains a visual representation of chart types. Click the chart that represents the desired chart type. (If the Chart Type button is not visible on the Graph Standard toolbar, click the Toolbar Options button.)

You can also select a chart type at the Chart Type dialog box with the Standard Types tab selected, as shown in Figure 7.20. To display this dialog box, click Chart and then Chart Type.

FIGURE 7.20 **Chart Type Dialog Box with Standard Types Tab Selected**

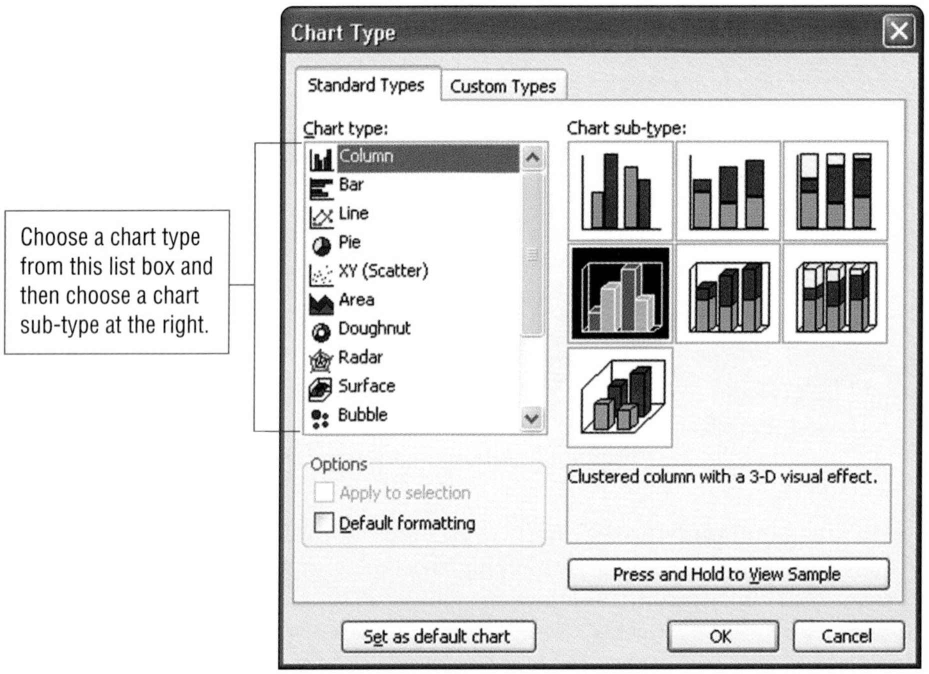

The various chart types display in the *Chart type* list box. A description of the selected chart type displays in the lower right corner of the dialog box (above the Press and Hold to View Sample button). Click a different chart type in the *Chart type* list box and the description changes. When you click a different chart type, the sample charts that display in the *Chart sub-type* list box change. Graph provides chart sub-types that contain different combinations of enhancements for each chart type. With these sub-types, you can choose a chart with different enhancements or formatting without having to customize the chart yourself.

HINT

Up to 14 chart types are available in Microsoft Graph Chart.

If you would like to see a sample of a particular chart, click the desired chart type in the *Chart type* list box and then click the desired sub-type chart in the *Chart sub-type* list box. Position the arrow pointer on the Press and Hold to View Sample button and hold down the left mouse button. This causes a sample chart to display in the selected chart type and sub-type chosen.

The default chart type is a Column chart. Change this default by clicking the desired chart type in the *Chart type* list box and then clicking the *Set as default chart* button that displays toward the bottom of the dialog box.

exercise 20

CHANGING THE CHART TYPE

1. Open **swc7x19**.
2. Save the document with Save As and name it **swc7x20**.
3. Change the chart type to Line by completing the following steps:
   a. Change the Zoom to Whole Page.
   b. Position the arrow pointer in the chart and then double-click the left mouse button.
   c. Close the datasheet. (To do this, click the View Datasheet button on the Graph Standard toolbar; or, click the Close button that displays in the upper right corner of the datasheet.)
   d. Click Chart on the Menu bar and then click Chart Type.
   e. At the Chart Type dialog box, click *Line* in the *Chart type* list box.
   f. Change the chart sub-type by clicking the first chart in the second row in the *Chart sub-type* list box. (Skip this step if the sub-type is already selected.)
   g. View a sample of how this sub-type chart will display by positioning the arrow pointer on the Press and Hold to View Sample button and then holding down the left mouse button. After viewing a sample of the selected Line chart, release the mouse button.
   h. Click OK to close the Chart Type dialog box.
   i. Click outside the chart to close Graph and deselect the chart.
   j. Change the Zoom to 100%.
4. Save, print, and then close **swc7x20**.

Changing the Data Series

When a chart is created, Graph uses the data in the first row (except the first cell) to create the x-axis (the information along the bottom of the chart) and uses the data in the first column (except the first cell) to create the legend. When a chart is created, the By Row button on the Graph Standard toolbar is active by default. This indicates that Graph uses the data in the first row (except the first cell) to create the x-axis for the chart. This can be changed by clicking the By Column button on the Graph Standard toolbar. Click the By Column button and the data in the first column (except the first cell) is used to create the x-axis. The active button on the Graph Standard toolbar displays with a light gray background. If the By Row or By Column button is not visible, click the Toolbar Options button on the Graph Standard toolbar.

By Row

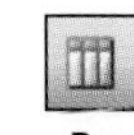
By Column

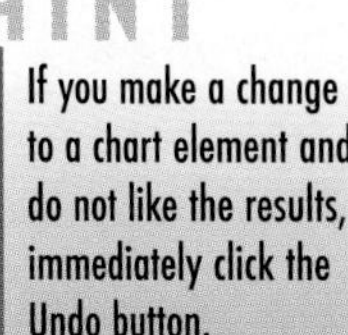

HINT
If you make a change to a chart element and do not like the results, immediately click the Undo button.

Adding Chart Elements

HINT

Format chart elements by double-clicking the element while in Microsoft Graph Chart.

Microsoft Graph Chart automatically inserts certain chart elements, including a chart legend and labels for the axes. You can add other chart elements, such as a chart title and data labels. Add these elements to a chart with options at the Chart Options dialog box shown in Figure 7.21. To display this dialog box, click Chart and then Chart Options. You can also display this dialog box by positioning the arrow pointer in a white portion of the chart (outside any chart elements), clicking the *right* mouse button, and then clicking Chart Options at the shortcut menu that displays. To add a chart element, click the desired tab at the Chart Options dialog box, and then choose the desired chart element.

FIGURE 7.21 ***Chart Options Dialog Box with Titles Tab Selected***

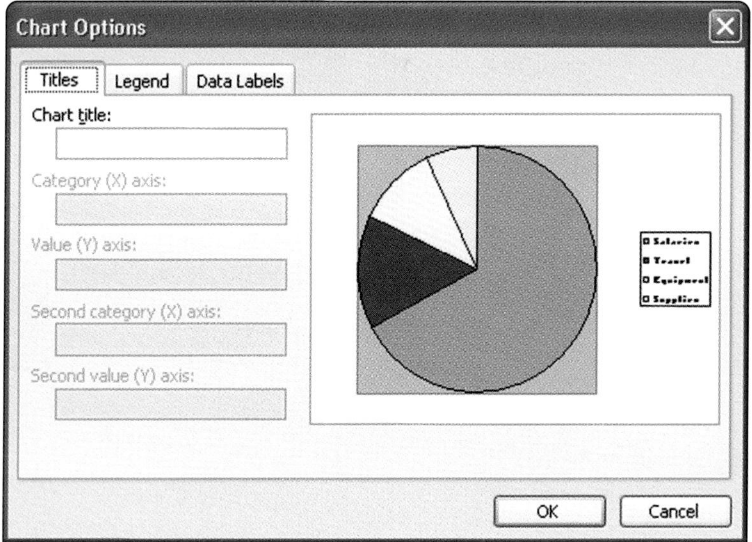

exercise 21

CREATING A PIE CHART AND ADDING CHART ELEMENTS

1. Open **WordTable05**.
2. Save the document with Save As and name it **swc7x21**.
3. Select the table.
4. Click Insert, point to Picture, and then click Chart.
5. When the datasheet and chart display, close the datasheet.
6. Change to a Pie chart by completing the following steps:
   a. Click the down-pointing arrow at the right side of the Chart Type button. (If the Chart Type button is not visible, click the Toolbar Options button on the Graph Standard toolbar.)
   b. At the drop-down palette of chart type options, click the first pie chart option in the fifth row.

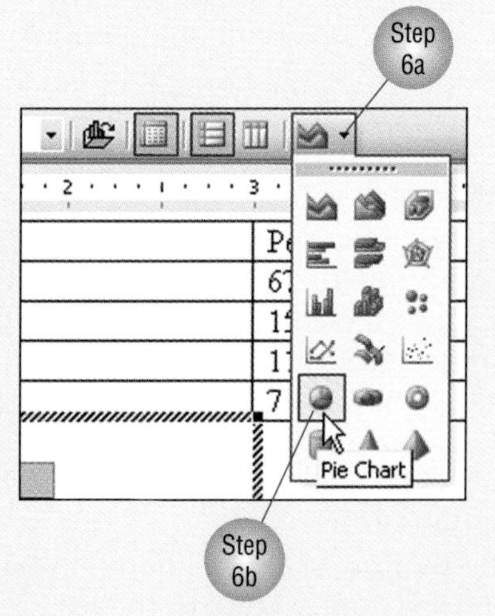

7. Click the By Column button on the Graph Standard toolbar. (If the By Column button is not visible, click the Toolbar Options button on the Graph Standard toolbar.)
8. Add a title and data labels to the Pie chart and move the legend by completing the following steps:
   a. Click Chart on the Menu bar and then click Chart Options.
   b. At the Chart Options dialog box, click the Titles tab. (Skip this step if the Titles tab is already selected.)
   c. At the Chart Options dialog box with the Titles tab selected, click inside the *Chart title* text box, and then type DEPARTMENT EXPENSES BY PERCENTAGE.

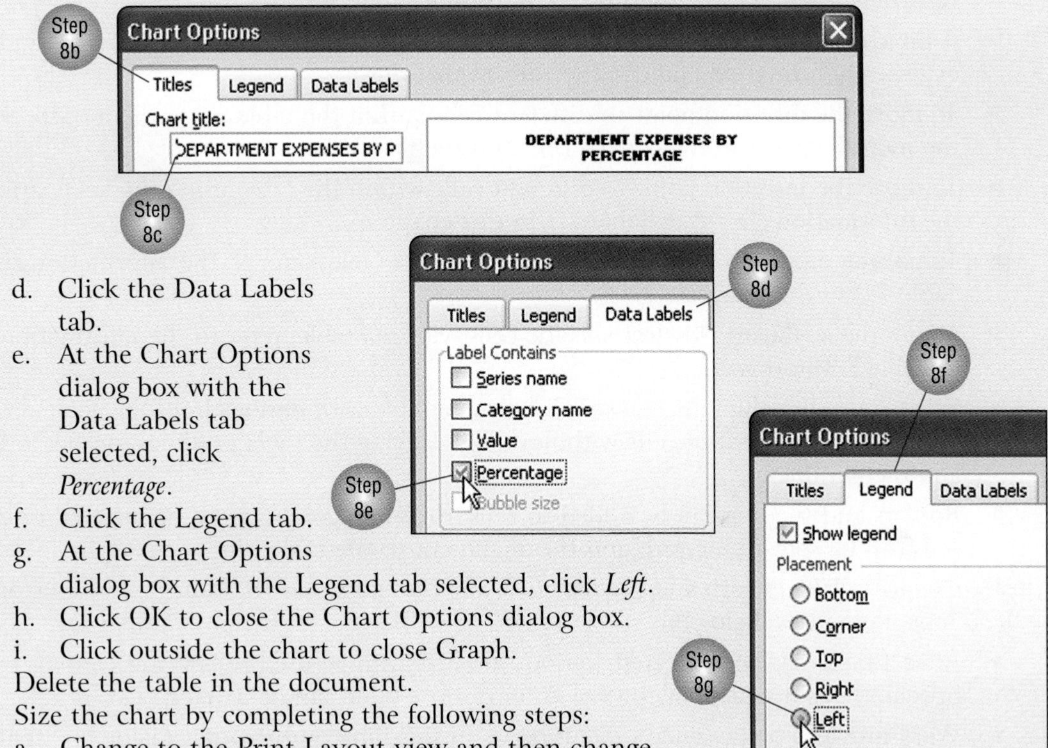

   d. Click the Data Labels tab.
   e. At the Chart Options dialog box with the Data Labels tab selected, click *Percentage*.
   f. Click the Legend tab.
   g. At the Chart Options dialog box with the Legend tab selected, click *Left*.
   h. Click OK to close the Chart Options dialog box.
   i. Click outside the chart to close Graph.
9. Delete the table in the document.
10. Size the chart by completing the following steps:
    a. Change to the Print Layout view and then change the Zoom to Whole Page.
    b. Click in the chart to select it.
    c. Drag the middle sizing handle at the right side of the chart to approximately the 5-inch mark on the horizontal ruler.
    d. Drag the middle sizing handle at the bottom of the chart to approximately the 4-inch mark on the vertical ruler.
11. With the chart selected, move the chart by completing the following steps:
    a. Change the text wrapping by clicking the Draw button on the Drawing toolbar, pointing to Text Wrapping, and then clicking Through.
    b. With the chart selected, position the arrow pointer (displays with a four-headed arrow attached) inside the chart, hold down the left mouse button, drag the outline of the chart to the middle of the page, and then release the mouse button.
    c. Click outside the chart to deselect it.
12. Change the Zoom back to 100%.
13. Save, print, and then close **swc7x21**.

CHAPTER summary

- Use the Tables feature to create columns and rows of information. A table can be created with the Insert Table button on the Standard toolbar or at the Insert Table dialog box.
- A cell is the intersection between a row and a column. The lines that form the cells of the table are called gridlines. Columns in a table are lettered from left to right beginning with *A*. Rows are numbered from top to bottom beginning with *1*.
- A table can contain text, characters, numbers, data, graphics, or formulas. It can be extensively formatted and can include calculations.
- To move the insertion point to different cells within the table using the mouse, position the mouse pointer in the desired cell, and then click the left button.
- To move the insertion point to different cells within the table using the keyboard, refer to the information shown in Table 7.1 in this chapter.
- To use the mouse to select specific cells within a table, refer to the information shown in Table 7.2 in this chapter.
- To use the keyboard to select specific cells within a table, refer to the information shown in Table 7.3 in this chapter.
- Select a row or column of cells or all cells in a table with options from the Table drop-down menu. Delete all text in cells within a table, leaving the table gridlines, or delete all text and the gridlines.
- Borders and shading can be added to cells; rows and columns can be inserted or deleted; cells can be split or merged; and the alignment of the table can be changed.
- Change column width and row height using the mouse on the Ruler, in a table, or at the Table Properties dialog box.
- After a table has been created, various methods can be used to add rows and/or columns. Specific cells in a table or rows or columns in a table can be deleted.
- Word provides predesigned table formats in the Table AutoFormat dialog box that can quickly format a table.
- Use buttons on the Tables and Borders toolbar to create and customize a table. Click the Tables and Borders button on the Standard toolbar to turn on the display of the Tables and Borders toolbar.
- Create a chart from data in a table to provide a more visual presentation of the data. Create charts with the Microsoft Graph Chart application.
- To create a chart, select the table, click Insert, point to Picture, and then click Chart.
- Click outside a chart to close Microsoft Graph Chart and remove the datasheet.
- Data in the first row of a table is used for the x-axis in the chart. The left side of a chart is generally referred to as the z-axis.
- Increase the size of a chart by selecting the chart and then dragging a sizing handle.
- To move a chart, change the black sizing to white sizing handles, and then drag the chart to the desired position. Change to white sizing handles by changing text wrapping for the chart.
- The default chart type created by Graph is a Column chart. Change this chart type with options at the Chart Type dialog box.

- Microsoft Graph Chart uses the first row of data (except the first cell) to create the x-axis and uses the data in the first column (except the first cell) to create the legend. You can reverse this by clicking the By Column button on the Graph Standard toolbar.
- Add elements to a chart and customize the elements with options at the Chart Options dialog box.

FEATURES summary

FEATURE	BUTTON	MENU	KEYBOARD
Insert Table dialog box		Table, Insert, Table	
Move insertion point to next cell			Tab
Move insertion point to previous cell			Shift + Tab
Insert page break within table		Insert, Break, Page Break, OK	Ctrl + Enter
Select row, column, or all cells		Table, Select, Table, then Column, Row, or Cell	
Delete table		Table, Delete, Table	
Table Properties dialog box		Table, Table Properties	
Table AutoFormat dialog box		Table, Table AutoFormat	
Tables and Borders toolbar		View, Toolbars, Tables and Borders	
Create a chart		Select table, click Insert, Picture, Chart	
Chart Type dialog box		Chart, Chart Type	
Chart Options dialog box		Chart, Chart Options	

CONCEPTS check

Completion: On a blank sheet of paper, indicate the correct term, command, or number for each description.

1. Use this button on the Standard toolbar to create a table.
2. This is another name for the lines that form the cells of the table.
3. Use this keyboard command to move the insertion point to the previous cell.
4. Use this keyboard command to insert a tab within a cell.
5. To add shading to a cell or selected cells, display this dialog box.
6. Text in cells aligns at this side of the cell by default.

7. To merge cells A1 and B1, select A1 and B1, click Table, and then click this at the drop-down menu.
8. To divide one cell into two columns, click this at the Table drop-down menu.
9. Choose predesigned table formats at this dialog box.
10. Click this button on the Tables and Borders toolbar to add, modify, or remove fill color from selected objects.
11. Click this button on the Tables and Borders toolbar to change the border-line style.
12. Create charts from data in a table using this application.
13. The left side of a chart is generally referred to as this axis.
14. Increase the size of a chart by selecting the chart and then dragging one of these.
15. This is the default chart type created by Graph.
16. Select a chart type at the Chart Type dialog box with this tab selected.

SKILLS check

Assessment 1

1. At a clear document screen, create the table shown in Figure 7.22 with the following specifications:
   a. Press the Enter key once and then create a table with 2 columns and 9 rows (9 × 2).
   b. Change the width of the first column to 4.5 inches and the width of the second column to 1.5 inches.
   c. Change the alignment of cells in the second column to right.
   d. Select the entire table and then change the font to 12-point Arial.
   e. Merge cells in the first row (cells A1 and B1).
   f. Type the text in the cells as indicated. Bold and center the text in the first cell. Before typing the text in the first cell, press the Enter key once. After typing the text in the cell centered and bolded, press the Enter key once.
2. Save the document and name it **swc7sc01**.
3. Print and then close **swc7sc01**.

FIGURE 7.22 ***Assessment 1***

PROPERTY Replacement Cost	
Business Personal Property Including Stock & Equipment	$1,367,400
Blanket Earnings & Expenses	4,883,432
Total Valuable Papers	73,000
Transit Domestic & Foreign	41,000
Excess Legal Liability	550,000
Accounts Receivable	40,000
Computer Coverage	35,000
Fire Department Service Charge	15,000

Assessment 2

1. Open **WordTable02**.
2. Save the document with Save As and name it **swc7sc02**.
3. Make the following changes to the table:
   a. Select cells B2 through C6 and then change the alignment to right.
   b. Select the first row, center and bold the text, and then deselect the text.
   c. Use the AutoFit feature to make the columns in the table automatically fit the contents.
   d. Apply the Table Contemporary table style at the Table AutoFormat dialog box.
   e. Center the table horizontally.
4. Save, print, and then close **swc7sc02**.

Assessment 3

1. Open **WordTable03**.
2. Save the document with Save As and name it **swc7sc03**.
3. Customize the table in the document so it displays as shown in Figure 7.23.
4. Save, print, and then close **swc7sc03**.

FIGURE 7.23 *Assessment 3*

Jobs in Demand	Position	Weekly Income	Yearly Openings
	Accountants/Auditors	$675	821
	Financial Managers	$645	357
	Loan Officers	$695	278
	Registered Nurses	$752	1,450
	Teachers, Elementary	$680	1,008
	Teachers, Secondary	$750	1,326

Assessment 4

1. Open **WordTable06**.
2. Save the document with Save As and name it **swc7sc04**.
3. Select the table and then create a chart with the default settings.
4. After creating the chart, delete the table.
5. Make the following changes to the chart:
   a. Display the chart in Graph and then add the title *PRODUCT GROSS SALES*.

b. Click outside the chart to close Graph.
c. Make sure the view is Print Layout and then change the Zoom to Whole Page.
d. Select the chart and then change the text wrapping to Through.
e. With the chart still selected, increase the width and height of the chart approximately 2 inches, move the chart to the middle of the page, and then deselect the chart.
f. Change the Zoom to 100%.

6. Save, print, and then close **swc7sc04**.

Assessment 5

1. Open **WordTable07**.
2. Save the document with Save As and name it **swc7sc05**.
3. Select the table and then create a chart with the default settings.
4. After creating the chart, delete the table.
5. Make the following changes to the chart:
   a. Change the chart type to Pie.
   b. Click the By Column button on the Graph Standard toolbar.
   c. Add the title *Investment Assets* to the chart.
   d. Add percentage data labels to the pie.
6. Click outside the chart to close Graph.
7. Select the chart and then change the text wrapping to Through.
8. With the chart still selected, increase the width and height of the chart approximately 2 inches, move the chart to the middle of the page, and then deselect the chart.
9. Save, print, and then close **swc7sc05**.

Assessment 6

1. In this chapter, you learned how to convert text to a table. Use Word's Help feature to learn how to convert a table to text and print the information.
2. After reading the information on converting a table to text, open **swc7sc01** and then convert the table to text. (You determine with what to separate the text.)
3. Save the converted table and name it **swc7sc06**.
4. Print and then close **swc7sc06**.

CHAPTER challenge

You have recently been hired as an accounting clerk for a landscaping business, Beyond Bushes, which has two small offices in your city. Each of the offices has its own accounting clerk; you will be working in the east side office. The accounting clerk prior to you kept track of monthly sales using Word, and the manager would prefer that you continue using that application. Open the file called **Monthly Sales**. After reviewing the information, you decide that a table would be a better way of maintaining and displaying the data. Convert this data to a table and modify its appearance so that it is easy to read and understand. Apply an AutoFormat style to the table. Save the file as **Beyond Bushes Monthly Sales** and then print it.

The manager mentioned that she would like to know the average sales per month for each item as well as the total sales for each month. As you learned in this chapter, Word tables consist of cells that can contain text, characters, numbers, data, graphics, or formulas. Use the Help feature to learn about performing calculations in a table. Using the table created in the first part of the Chapter Challenge, add a column to the right of the *August* column and insert a formula to calculate the average of each of the items. Add a row to the bottom of the table and insert a formula to calculate the total sales for each of the months. Add appropriate titles for the new column and row. Save the file again and then print it.

The manager would like to compare sales with the west side office. She has obtained the data from their accounting clerk and has given you the disk to analyze. Since you know that charts are a good way of comparing data, you decide to create a bar chart with the data from the west side office and a bar chart with the data from the east side office. The data from your office should not be difficult to graph since you know how to create charts from data in a table; however, when you open the file from the west side office, you discover that the file was created using Excel. Fortunately, you know how to import Excel data into a Word table. Create a bar chart, using the data from the Excel file called **Monthly Sales West Side**. Properly format the chart, save the file, and then print the chart.

CHAPTER 8

ENHANCING DOCUMENTS WITH SPECIAL FEATURES

PERFORMANCE OBJECTIVES

Upon successful completion of Chapter 8, you will be able to:

- **Create and modify diagrams and organizational charts**
- **Insert and format images in a document**
- **Draw and customize shapes, lines, and text boxes**
- **Apply styles to text in a document**
- **Display and format a document in Outline view**
- **Assign headings in an outline and collapse and expand an outline**
- **Save a document as a Web page and format and preview a Web page**
- **Insert hyperlinks to Web pages and Word documents**
- **Search for and request specific information from online sources**
- **Use the translation feature to translate words from English to other languages**
- **Send a document as an e-mail and route a document**

WORD Chapter08S

Microsoft Word contains a variety of features that help you enhance the visual appeal of a document. In this chapter, you will learn how to create and modify diagrams and organizational charts; insert and format images; and draw and customize shapes, lines, and text boxes. You will also learn how to save a Word document as a Web page, preview the page, insert hyperlinks to Web pages and Word documents, and send and route an e-mail. With options at the Research task pane you will learn how to search for and request specific information from online sources and translate words from English to other languages.

Insert Diagram or Organization Chart

Creating Diagrams and Organizational Charts

Use the Diagram Gallery to create organizational charts or other types of diagrams. Display the Diagram Gallery dialog box, shown in Figure 8.1, by clicking the Insert Diagram or Organization Chart button on the Drawing toolbar or by clicking Insert and then Diagram.

FIGURE

8.1 **Diagram Gallery Dialog Box**

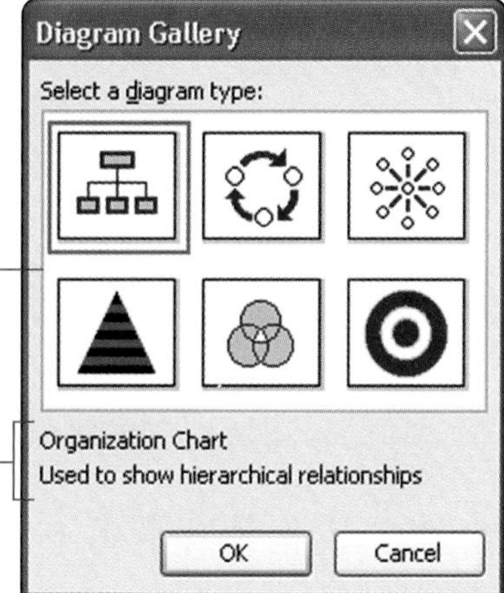

Click a diagram in this list box and the type of diagram displays below the list box along with a description of the diagram.

HINT

Use an organizational chart to visually illustrate hierarchical data.

QUICK STEPS

Create a Diagram/Chart

1. Click Insert Diagram or Organization Chart button.
2. Click desired option.
3. Click OK.

HINT

Use a diagram to illustrate a concept and enhance the visual appeal of a document.

At the Diagram Gallery dialog box, click the desired option in the *Select a diagram type* list box and then click OK. If you click an organizational chart option, chart boxes appear in the drawing canvas and the Organization Chart toolbar displays. Use buttons on this toolbar to create additional boxes in the chart, specify the layout of the chart, expand or scale the chart, select specific elements in the chart, apply an autoformat to the chart, or specify a text wrapping option.

If you click a diagram option at the Diagram Gallery dialog box, the diagram is inserted in the drawing canvas and the Diagram toolbar displays. Use buttons on this toolbar to insert additional shapes; move shapes backward or forward or reverse the diagram; expand, scale, or fit the contents of the diagram; apply an autoformat to the diagram; or change the type of diagram (choices include Cycle, Radial, Pyramid, Venn, and Target).

exercise 1

CREATING AND CUSTOMIZING AN ORGANIZATIONAL CHART

1. At a clear document screen, create the organizational chart shown in Figure 8.2. To begin, display the Drawing toolbar by clicking the Drawing button on the Standard toolbar. (Skip this step if the Drawing toolbar is already displayed.)
2. Click the Insert Diagram or Organization Chart button on the Drawing toolbar.
3. At the Diagram Gallery dialog box, click the first option from the left in the top row in the *Select a diagram type* list box, and then click OK. (This inserts an organizational chart in the drawing canvas in the document.)

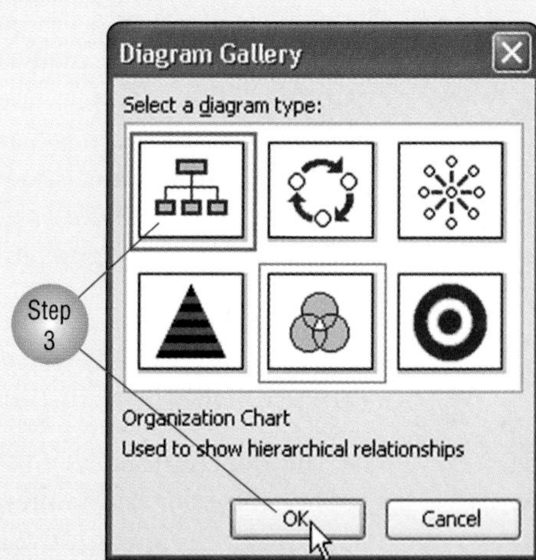

4. With the top box selected (round circles containing *X*'s display around the top box), add the assistant box by completing the following steps:
   a. Click the down-pointing arrow at the right side of the Insert Shape button on the Organization Chart toolbar.
   b. At the drop-down list that displays, click Assistant.
5. Remove the third organizational chart box at the right side of the chart by completing the following steps:
   a. Position the mouse pointer on one of the edges of the third box at the right side of the organizational chart until the pointer turns into a four-headed arrow and then click the left mouse button. (This selects the box and displays round circles containing *X*'s around the box.)

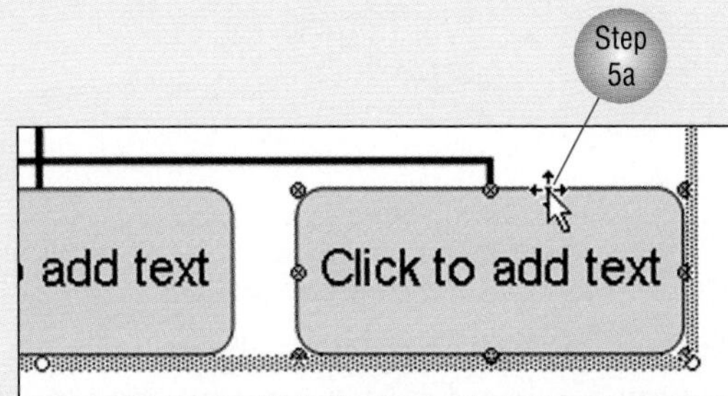

   b. Press the Delete key.
6. Apply an autoformat to the chart by completing the following steps:
   a. Click the Autoformat button on the Organization Chart toolbar.

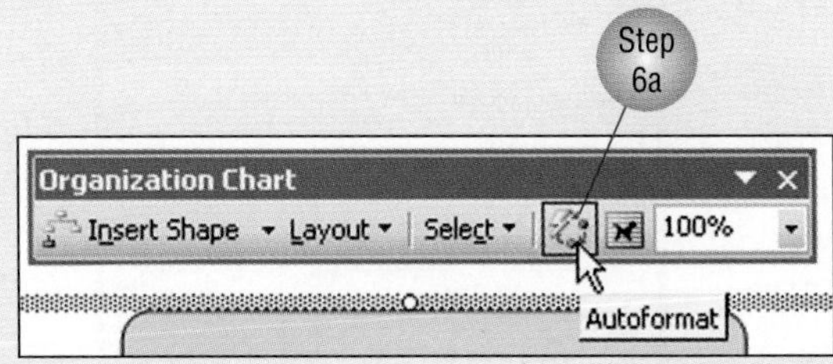

   b. At the Organization Chart Style Gallery dialog box, click *Primary Colors* in the *Select a Diagram Style* list box.
   c. Click OK.
7. Create the text in the top box as shown in Figure 8.2 by completing the following steps:
   a. Click inside the top box.
   b. Type **Liam Kilgallon** and then press Enter.
   c. Type **Manager**.
8. Complete steps similar to those in Step 7 to insert the text in the three remaining boxes.
9. Set the text in each box in 18-point Arial bold.
10. Save the organizational chart document and name it **swc8x01**.
11. Print and then close **swc8x01**.

FIGURE

8.2 ***Exercise 1***

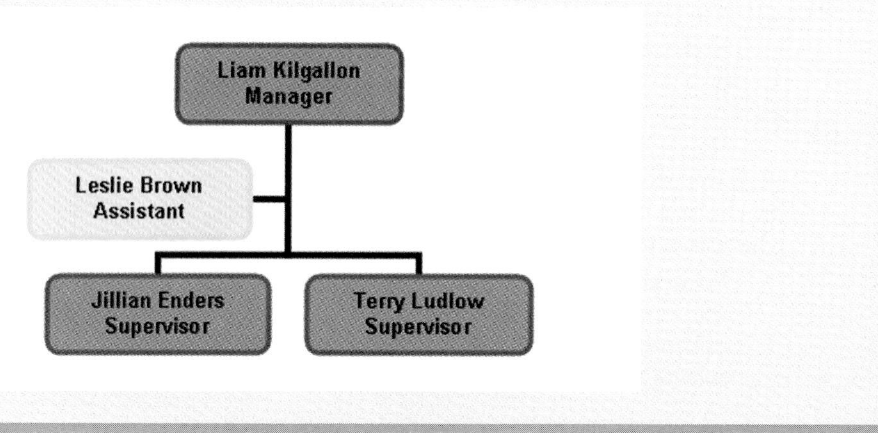

exercise 2

CREATING AND CUSTOMIZING A DIAGRAM

1. At a clear document screen, create the diagram shown in Figure 8.3. To begin, click the Insert Diagram or Organization Chart button on the Drawing toolbar.
2. At the Diagram Gallery dialog box, click the last option from the left in the bottom row in the *Select a diagram type* list box, and then click OK. (This inserts a Target diagram in the drawing canvas in the document.)
3. Click the Insert Shape button on the Diagram toolbar. (This inserts an additional circle in the Target diagram. The diagram should now contain four circles.)
4. Expand the diagram to better fill the drawing canvas by clicking the Layout button on the Diagram toolbar and then clicking Expand Diagram at the drop-down list.
5. Apply an autoformat to the diagram by completing the following steps:
   a. Click the AutoFormat button on the Diagram toolbar.
   b. At the Diagram Style Gallery dialog box, click *3-D Color* in the *Select a Diagram Style* list box.
   c. Click OK.

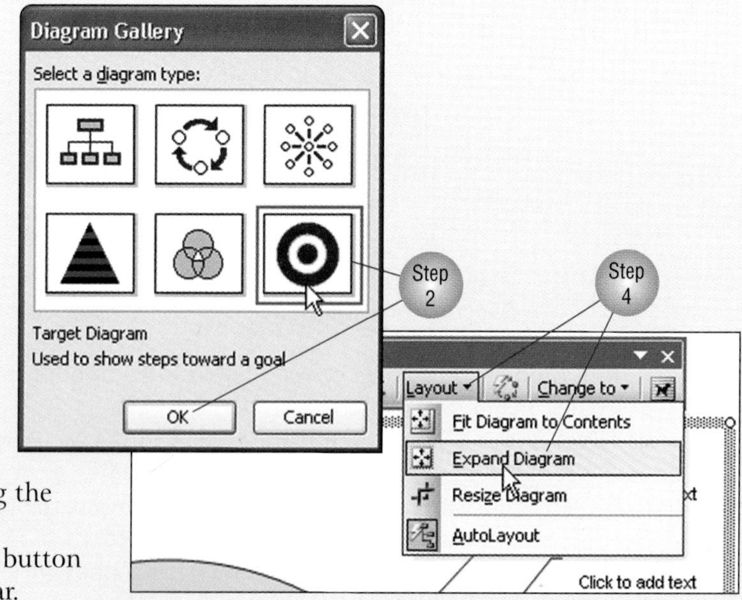

6. Click *Click to add text* that displays at the top of the drawing canvas and then type **Goal**.

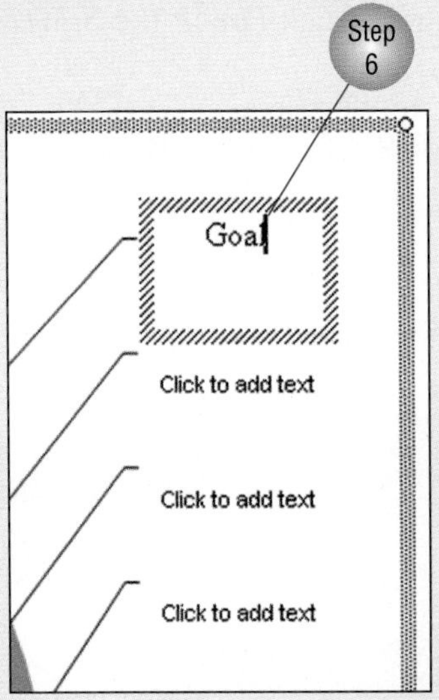

7. Click the second *Click to add text* and then type **Step 3**.
8. Click the third *Click to add text* and then type **Step 2**.
9. Click the fourth *Click to add text* and then type **Step 1**.
10. Click outside the diagram to deselect it.
11. Save the diagram document and name it **swc8x02**.
12. Print **swc8x02**.
13. With the document still open, change to a Radial diagram by completing the following steps:
    a. Click the diagram to select it.
    b. Click the Change to button on the Diagram toolbar.
    c. Click Radial at the drop-down list.

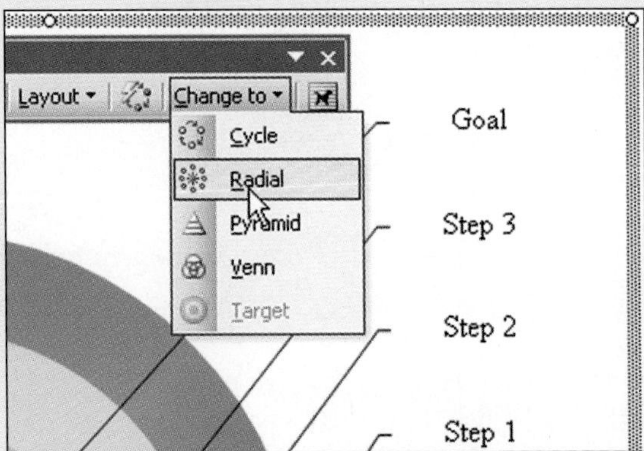

    d. Click at the beginning of the text *Step 3* in the top circle and then press Enter twice.
    e. Press Enter twice before the text *Goal*, *Step 1*, and *Step 2* in each of the remaining circles.

14. Apply a different autoformat by completing the following steps:
    a. Click the AutoFormat button on the Diagram toolbar.
    b. At the Diagram Style Gallery, click *Fire* in the *Select a Diagram Style* list box.
    c. Click OK.
15. Click outside the diagram to deselect it.
16. Save, print, and then close **swc8x02**.

FIGURE 8.3 ***Exercise 2***

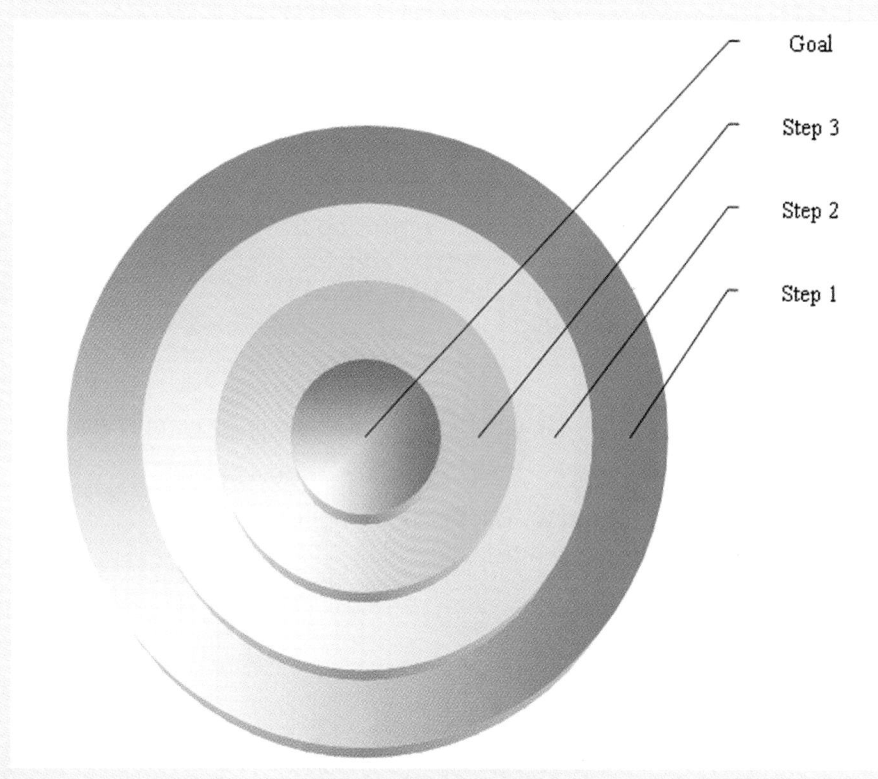

Inserting Images in a Document

Microsoft Office includes a gallery of media images that can be inserted in a document such as clip art, photographs, and movie images, as well as sound clips. To insert an image in a Word document, click Insert, point to Picture, and then click Clip Art. This displays the Clip Art task pane at the right side of the screen as shown in Figure 8.4.

FIGURE 8.4 **Clip Art Task Pane**

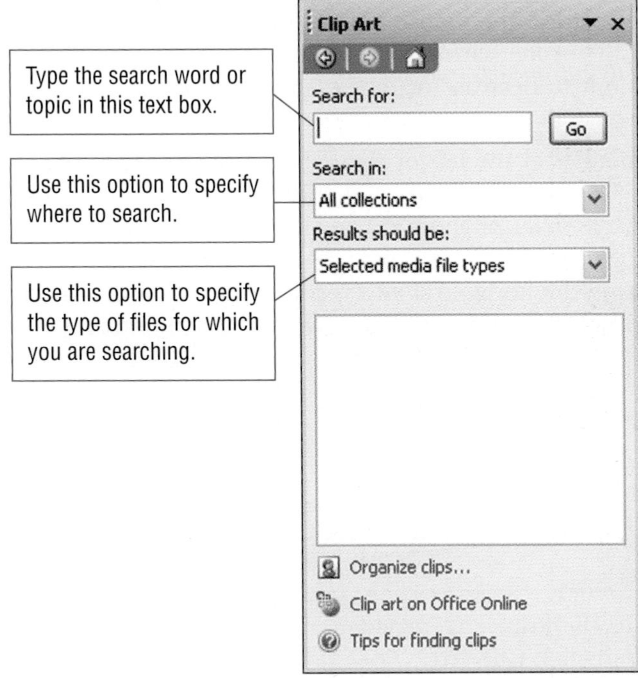
Type the search word or topic in this text box.
Use this option to specify where to search.
Use this option to specify the type of files for which you are searching.
Clip Art
Search for:
Go
Search in:
All collections
Results should be:
Selected media file types
Organize clips...
Clip art on Office Online
Tips for finding clips

Another method for displaying the Clip Art task pane is to click the Insert Clip Art button on the Drawing toolbar. To display the Drawing toolbar, click the Drawing button on the Standard toolbar. You can also display the toolbar by right-clicking on any currently displayed toolbar and then clicking Drawing at the pop-up list; or by clicking View, pointing to Toolbars, and then clicking Drawing.

Insert Clip Art

Drawing

To view all picture, sound, and motion files, make sure no text displays in the *Search for* text box at the Clip Art task pane, and then click the Go button. When the desired image is visible, click the image to insert it in the document.

Narrowing a Search

By default (unless it has been customized), the Clip Art task pane looks for all media images and sound clips found in all locations. You can narrow the search to specific locations and to specific images. The *Search in* option at the Clip Art task pane has a default setting of *All collections*. This can be changed to *My Collections*, *Office Collections*, and *Web Collections*. The *Results should be* option has a default setting of *Selected media file types*. Click the down-pointing arrow at the right side of this option to display media types. To search for a specific media type, remove the check mark before all options at the drop-down list but the desired type. For example, if you are searching only for photograph images, remove the check mark before Clip Art, Movies, and Sound.

HINT

You can drag a clip art image from the Clip Art task pane to your document.

QUICK STEPS

Insert Clip Art Image
1. Click Insert Clip Art button.
2. Type search word or topic.
3. Press Enter.
4. Click desired image.

If you are searching for specific images, click in the *Search for* text box, type the desired word, and then click the Go button. For example, if you want to find images related to computers, click in the *Search for* text box, type **computer**, and then click the Go button. Clip art images related to *computer* display in the viewing area of the task pane. If you are connected to the Internet, Word will search for images at the Microsoft Design Gallery Live Web site matching the topic.

HINT

Resize a selected object proportionally by holding down the Shift key and then dragging a corner sizing handle.

HINT

Resize a selected object horizontally, vertically, or diagonally from the center outward by holding down the Ctrl key and then dragging a sizing handle.

Sizing an Image

Once an image is inserted in a document, it can be sized using the sizing handles that display around a selected image. To change the size of an image, click in the image to select it, and then position the mouse pointer on a sizing handle until the pointer turns into a double-headed arrow. Hold down the left mouse button, drag the sizing handle in or out to decrease or increase the size of the image, and then release the mouse button.

Use the middle sizing handles at the left or right side of the image to make the image wider or thinner. Use the middle sizing handles at the top or bottom of the image to make the image taller or shorter. Use the sizing handles at the corners of the image to change both the width and height at the same time. When sizing an image, consider using the horizontal and vertical rulers that display in the Print Layout view. To deselect an image, click anywhere in the document outside the image.

exercise 3

VIEWING, INSERTING, AND SIZING AN IMAGE

1. At a clear document screen, change to the Print Layout view.
2. Click Insert, point to Picture, and then click Clip Art.
3. At the Clip Art task pane, click in the *Search for* text box.
4. Type **buildings** and then click the Go button.
5. View the building images. If necessary, scroll down the viewing window to display all of the images.
6. Click the down-pointing arrow at the right side of the *Results should be* option box and make sure only Clip Art contains a check mark. Click outside the drop-down list to remove it.
7. Select the word *buildings* in the *Search for* text box, type **computer**, and then click the Go button.
8. Click the computer image shown in the figure. (If this computer clip art image is not available, click another image that interests you.)
9. Click the computer image in the document screen. (This displays sizing handles around the image.)
10. Position the mouse pointer on the bottom right sizing handle until it turns into a diagonally pointing two-headed arrow.

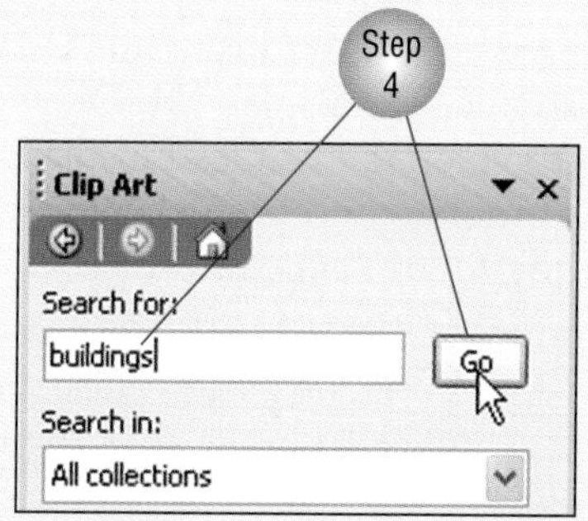

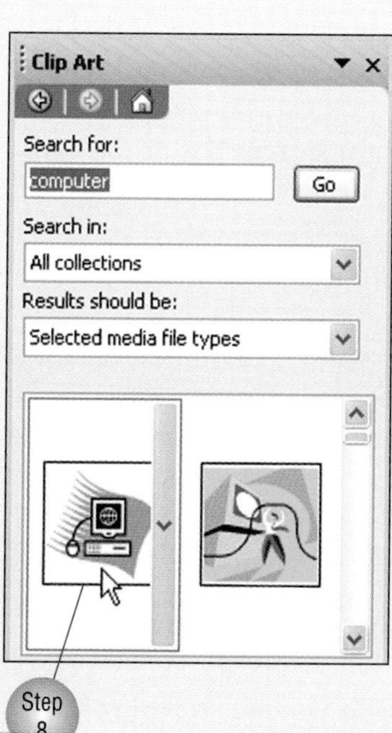

11. Hold down the left mouse button, drag down and to the right until the width and height increase by approximately 1 inch, and then release the mouse button.
12. Deselect the image.
13. Close the Clip Art task pane by clicking the Close button (contains an *X*) located in the upper right corner of the task pane.
14. Save the document and name it **swc8x03**.
15. Print and then close **swc8x03**.

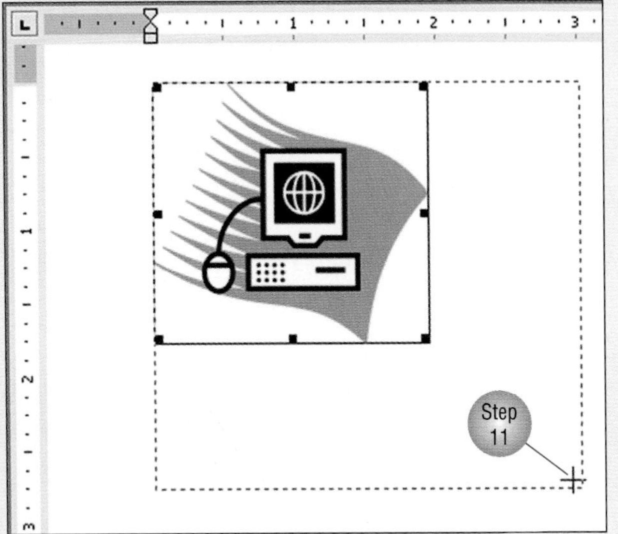

Formatting Images with Buttons on the Picture Toolbar

You can format images in a variety of ways. Formatting might include adding fill color and border lines, increasing or decreasing the brightness or contrast, choosing a wrapping style, and cropping the image. Format an image with buttons on the Picture toolbar or options at the Format Picture dialog box. Display the Picture toolbar by clicking an image or by right-clicking an image and then clicking Show Picture Toolbar at the shortcut menu. Figure 8.5 identifies the buttons on the Picture toolbar.

FIGURE 8.5 ***Picture Toolbar Buttons***

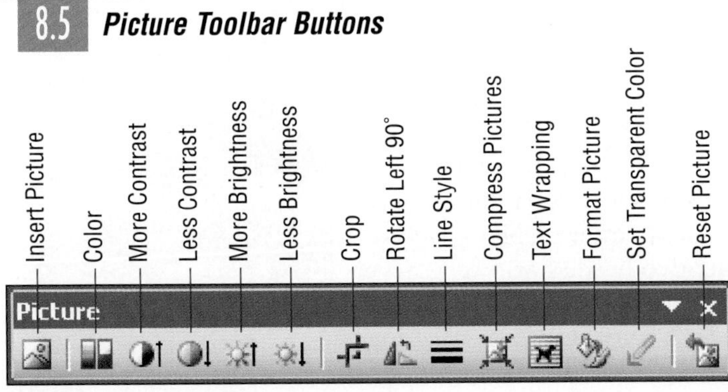

Moving an Image

Text Wrapping

To move an image in a document you must first choose a text wrapping option. To do this, select the image, click the Text Wrapping button on the Picture toolbar, and then click a wrapping option. This changes the sizing handles that display around the selected image from squares to white circles and also inserts a green rotation handle. To move the image, position the mouse pointer inside the image until the pointer turns into a four-headed arrow. Hold down the left mouse button, drag the image to the desired position, and then release the mouse button. Rotate the image by positioning the mouse pointer on the green, round rotation handle until the pointer displays as a circular arrow. Hold down the left mouse button, drag in the desired direction, and then release the mouse button.

HINT
Move an image up, down, left, or right in small increments by clicking the Draw button, pointing to Nudge, and then clicking the desired direction option.

exercise 4

INSERTING, MOVING, SIZING, AND CUSTOMIZING AN IMAGE IN A DOCUMENT

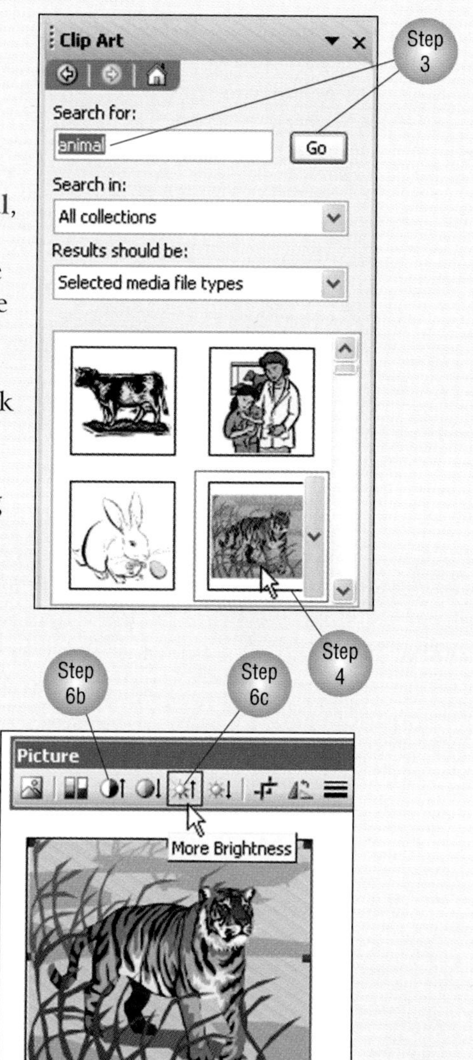

1. At a clear document screen, change to the Print Layout view.
2. Click the Insert Clip Art button on the Drawing toolbar.
3. Search for clip art images related animals. To do this, click in the *Search for* text box in the Clip Art task pane (or select any existing text), type **animal**, and then click the Go button.
4. Click once on the image of the tiger. (If this image is not available, click another animal clip art image of your choosing.)
5. Close the Clip Art task pane by clicking the Close button located in the upper right corner of the task pane.
6. Customize the image of the animal using buttons on the Picture toolbar by completing the following steps:
   a. Click the image to select it (sizing handles display around the image). (Make sure the Picture toolbar displays. If it does not, click View, point to Toolbars, and then click Picture.)
   b. Click six times on the More Contrast button on the Picture toolbar. (This increases the contrast of the colors used in the image.)
   c. Click twice on the More Brightness button on the Picture toolbar.
7. Change the size of the image by completing the following steps:
   a. Position the mouse pointer on the sizing handle that displays in the lower right corner of the image until the pointer displays as a diagonally pointing two-headed arrow.
   b. Hold down the left mouse button, drag down and to the right until the size of the image measures approximately 4 inches in width and 3.25 inches in height, and then release the mouse button. (Use the horizontal and vertical rulers to help you approximate the size.)
8. Move the image by completing the following steps:
   a. With the image still selected, click the Text Wrapping button on the Picture toolbar, and then click Through at the drop-down list. (This changes the sizing handles to white circles.)
   b. Position the mouse pointer inside the image (displays as a four-headed arrow).

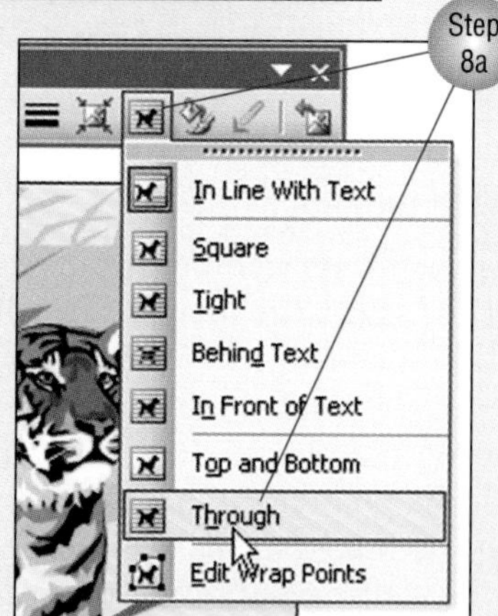

c. Hold down the left mouse button, drag the outline of the image to the right until the left edge of the image is positioned at approximately the 1-inch mark on the horizontal ruler, and then release the mouse button.

9. Add a border line to the image by clicking the Line Style button on the Picture toolbar and then clicking the first *3 pt* option that displays at the drop-down list.

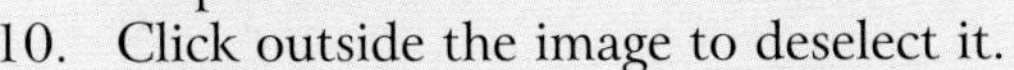

10. Click outside the image to deselect it.
11. Save the document and name it **swc8x04**.
12. Print and then close **swc8x04**.

Formatting Images at the Format Picture Dialog Box

The options on the Picture toolbar are also available at the Format Picture dialog box along with some additional options. To display the Format Picture dialog box, select an image, and then click the Format Picture button on the Picture toolbar.

Format Picture

The Format Picture dialog box displays with a variety of tabs. Click the Colors and Lines tab and options are available for choosing fill color; line color, style, and weight; and arrows. Click the Size tab and display options for specifying the height, width, and rotation degree of the image. Options at the Format Picture dialog box with the Layout tab selected include wrapping style and horizontal alignment. Click the Picture tab to display options for cropping the image and changing the color.

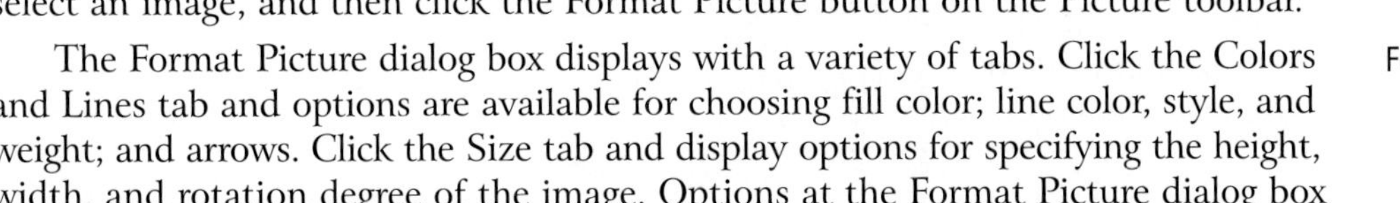

exercise 5

FORMATTING AN IMAGE AT THE FORMAT PICTURE DIALOG BOX

1. Open **WordDocument08**.
2. Save the document with Save As and name it **swc8x05**.
3. Select the entire document and then change the font to 13-point Garamond. (If this typeface is not available, choose a similar serif typeface such as Century.)
4. Deselect the text and then move the insertion point to the beginning of the document.
5. Insert an image of a computer in the document as shown in Figure 8.6 by completing the following steps:
   a. Change to the Print Layout view.
   b. Click Insert, point to Picture, and then click Clip Art.
   c. At the Clip Art task pane, click in the *Search for* text box (or select any existing text), type **computer**, and then press Enter.
   d. Click once on the computer image shown in Figure 8.6. (You may need to scroll down the list of images. If this image is not available, choose another computer image.)
   e. Close the Clip Art task pane.

f. Click once on the image to select it.

g. Change the wrapping style by clicking the Text Wrapping button on the Picture toolbar and then clicking Through at the drop-down list. (This changes the sizing handles to white circles.)

h. With the image still selected, click the Format Picture button on the Picture toolbar.

i. At the Format Picture dialog box, click the Colors and Lines tab.

j. Click the down-pointing arrow at the right side of the *Color* option box in the *Line* section and then click the Black color option (first option in the top row).

k. Click the up-pointing arrow at the right side of the *Weight* text box until *1 pt* displays in the text box.

l. Click the Size tab located at the top of the dialog box.

m. Select the current measurement in the *Height* text box and then type 1.5.

n. Click the Layout tab.

o. Click the *Left* option in the *Horizontal alignment* section of the dialog box.

p. Click OK to close the Format Picture dialog box.

6. At the document screen, click outside the image to deselect it. (Make sure the computer image displays at the left margin next to the first paragraph of text. If the image appears to be out of alignment, select the image, and then drag it to a more desirable location.)

7. Save, print, and then close **swc8x05**.

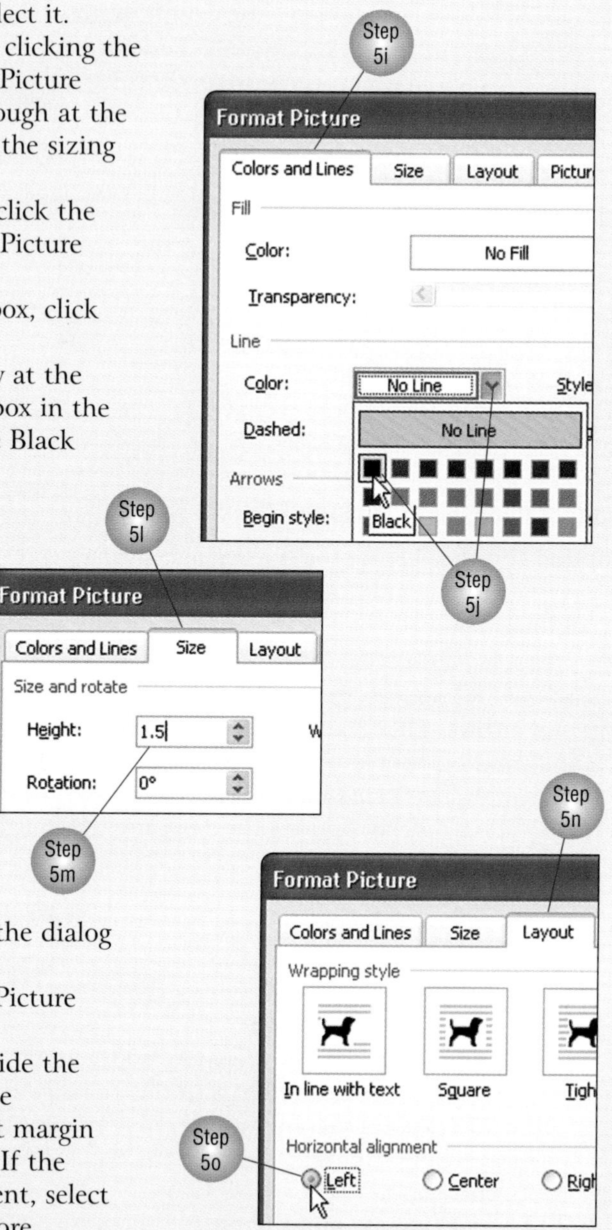

FIGURE

8.6 Exercise 5

Word, one of the best-selling word processing programs for microcomputers, includes a wide variety of desktop publishing features. The scope and capabilities of these features have expanded with each new Word version. Some of the desktop publishing features include a wide variety of fonts and special symbols, drawing, charting, text design capabilities, graphic manipulation, templates, and much more.

Design can be learned by studying design and by experimentation. Collect and study designs that are attractive and visually interesting. Analyze what makes the design and layout unique and try using the same principles or variations in your publications. Take advantage of the special design and layout features that Word for Windows has to offer. Take the time to design. Layout and design is a lengthy process of revising, refining, and making adjustments. Start with small variations from the default formats to create designs that are attractive and visually interesting.

Drawing Shapes, Lines, and Text Boxes

With buttons on the Drawing toolbar, you can draw a variety of shapes such as circles, squares, rectangles, ovals, straight lines, free-form lines, lines with arrowheads, and much more. You can also draw text boxes and autoshapes. To display the Drawing toolbar, shown in Figure 8.7, click the Drawing button on the Standard toolbar. When you click a button on the Drawing toolbar, Word switches to the Print Layout view and inserts a drawing canvas. You can draw objects inside the drawing canvas or delete the canvas and draw directly in the document. Using the drawing canvas, you can create objects with an absolute position and also protect objects from being split by a page break.

QUICK STEPS

Draw a Shape

1. Click desired shape button on Drawing toolbar.
2. Drag in drawing canvas or document screen to create shape.

FIGURE

8.7 Drawing Toolbar

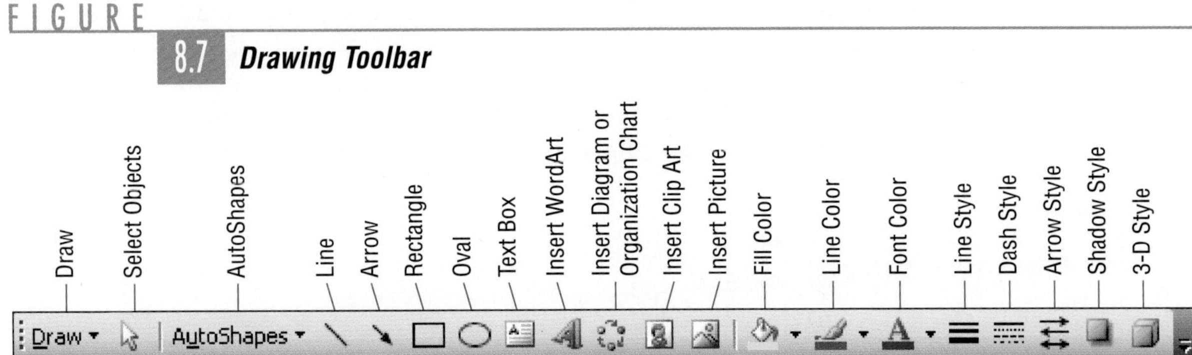

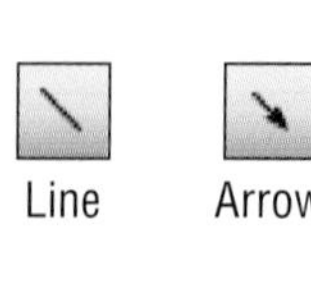

With some of the buttons on the Drawing toolbar, you can draw a shape. If you draw a shape with the Line button or the Arrow button, the shape you draw is considered a **line drawing**. If you draw a shape with the Rectangle or Oval button, the shape you draw is considered an **enclosed object**. If you want to draw the same shape more than once, double-click the shape button on the Drawing toolbar. After drawing the shapes, click the button again to deactivate it.

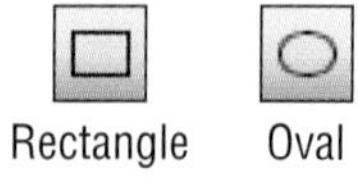

Use the Rectangle button on the Drawing toolbar to draw a square or rectangle in a document. If you want to draw a square, hold down the Shift key while drawing the shape. The Shift key keeps all sides of the drawn object equal. Use the Oval button to draw a circle or an oval object. To draw a circle, hold down the Shift key while drawing the object.

exercise 6

DRAWING A CIRCLE AND SQUARE

1. At a clear document screen, draw a circle and a square by completing the following steps:
   a. Display the Drawing toolbar by clicking the Drawing button on the Standard toolbar. (Skip this step if the Drawing toolbar is already displayed.)
   b. Click the Oval button on the Drawing toolbar. (This inserts a drawing canvas on the document screen.)
   c. Position the crosshairs in the drawing canvas toward the left side.
   d. Hold down the Shift key and the left mouse button, drag the mouse down and to the right until the outline image displays as approximately a 2-inch circle, release the mouse button, and then the Shift key.
   e. Click the Rectangle button on the Drawing toolbar.
   f. Position the crosshairs in the drawing canvas toward the right side.
   g. Hold down the Shift key and the left mouse button, drag the mouse down and to the right until the outline image displays as approximately a 2-inch square, release the mouse button, and then the Shift key.
2. Save the document and name it **swc8x06**.
3. Print and then close **swc8x06**.

With the Line button, you can draw a line in the drawing canvas. To do this, click the Line button on the Drawing toolbar. Position the crosshairs where you want to begin the line, hold down the left mouse button, drag the line to the location where you want the line to end, and then release the mouse button.

You can add as many lines as desired on the document screen by repeating the steps above. For example, you can draw a triangle by drawing three lines. If you want to draw more than one line, double-click the Line button. This makes the button active. After drawing all of the necessary lines, click the Line button again to deactivate it.

exercise 7

CREATING A LINE WITH THE ARROW BUTTON

1. At a clear document screen, create the document shown in Figure 8.8. To begin make sure the Drawing toolbar is displayed.
2. Change the font to 24-point Copperplate Gothic Bold (or a similar decorative typeface).
3. Click the Center button on the Formatting toolbar.
4. Type **Mainline Manufacturing**. (The Copperplate Gothic Bold typeface uses small caps for lowercase letters.)
5. Press the Enter key.
6. Click the Arrow button on the Drawing toolbar.
7. Delete the drawing canvas by pressing the Delete key. (You will be drawing the arrow in the document, rather than the drawing canvas.)
8. Hold down the Shift key and then draw the line in the document as shown in Figure 8.8. (The line will display with an arrow on one end. This will be changed in the next step.)
9. With the line still selected (a white sizing handle displays at each end), click the Arrow Style button on the Drawing toolbar.
10. At the pop-up list that displays, click the second option from the bottom of the list (Arrow Style 10).
11. Click outside the line to deselect it and display the arrow style.
12. Save the completed document and name it **swc8x07**.
13. Print and then close **swc8x07**.

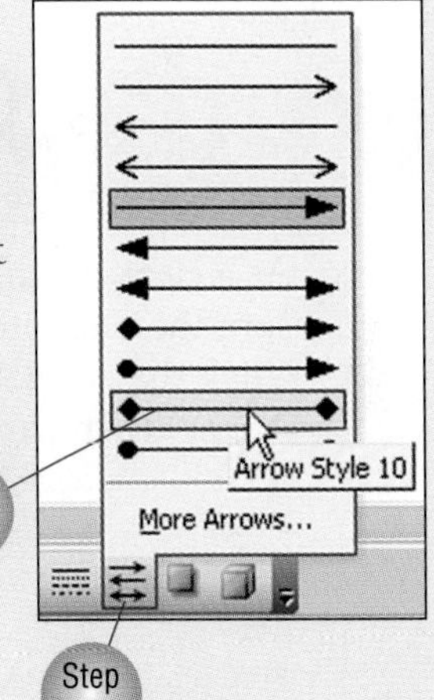

FIGURE 8.8 *Exercise 7*

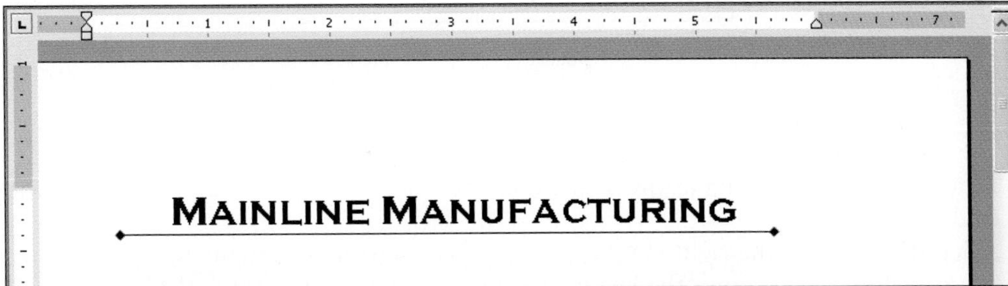

Use the Text Box button on the Drawing toolbar to create a box and then insert text inside the box. Text inside a box can be formatted in the normal manner. For example, you can change the font, alignment, or indent of the text. To create a text box, click the Text Box button, position the crosshairs in the drawing canvas or on the document screen where you want the text to appear, hold down the left mouse button, drag to create the box, and then release the mouse button. This inserts a text box in the document in which you can type text. If the text you type fills more than the first line in the box, the text wraps to the next line. (The box, however, will not increase in size. If you need more room in the text box, select the box, and then use the sizing handles to make it bigger.)

Text Box

QUICK STEPS

Draw a Text Box
1. Click Text Box button on Drawing toolbar.
2. Drag in drawing canvas or document screen to create shape.

Draw an AutoShape
1. Click Draw button.
2. Point to shape category.
3. Click desired autoshape.
4. Drag in drawing canvas or document screen to create shape.

Draw a variety of shapes with options from the AutoShapes button. Click the AutoShapes button and a pop-up menu displays. Point to the desired menu option and a side menu displays. This side menu offers autoshape choices for the selected option. For example, if you point to the Basic Shapes option, a number of shapes display at the right side of the pop-up menu such as a circle, square, triangle, box, stop sign, and so on. Click the desired shape and the mouse pointer turns into crosshairs. Position the crosshairs in the drawing canvas or on the document screen, hold down the left mouse button, drag to create the shape, and then release the button.

exercise 8

CREATING A TEXT BOX AND AUTOSHAPE

1. At a clear document screen, create the document shown in Figure 8.9. To begin, make sure the Drawing toolbar is displayed.
2. Click the AutoShapes button, point to Block Arrows, and then click Striped Right Arrow (first arrow in the fifth row from the top).

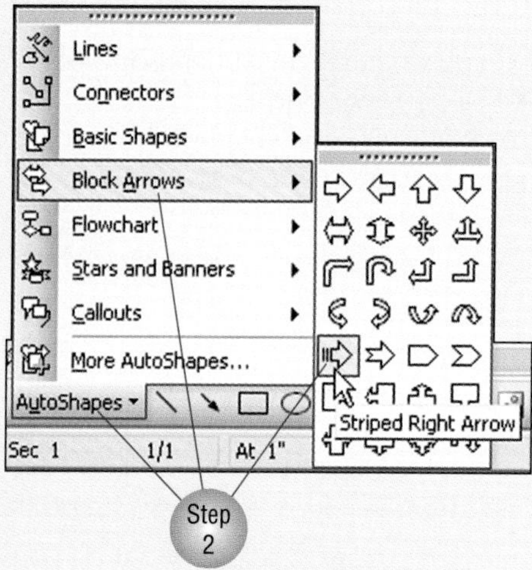

3. Press the Delete key to delete the drawing canvas.
4. Draw the down-pointing arrow in the document that is approximately 5 inches wide and 4 inches tall.
5. Click the arrow at the right side of the Fill Color button and then click the Yellow option (third option from the left in the fourth row from the top).

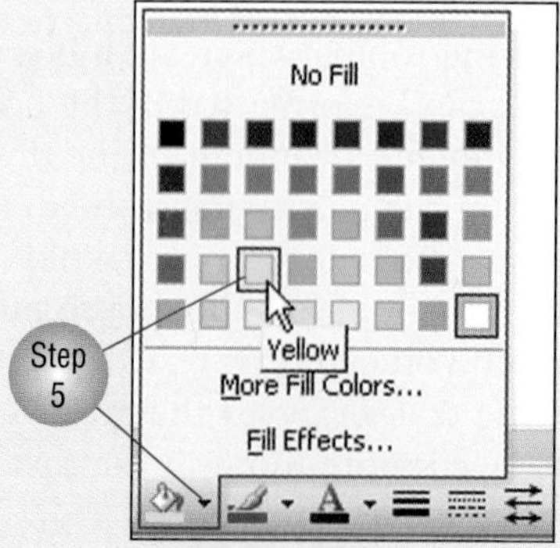

6. Click the Text Box button on the Drawing toolbar.
7. Using the mouse, draw a text box inside the arrow that is approximately 2 inches wide and 1 inch high.
8. With the insertion point positioned inside the text box, change the font size to 24 points, turn on bold, change the alignment to center, and then type the text shown in Figure 8.9.
9. Remove the line around the text box by clicking the down-pointing arrow at the right side of the Line Color button on the Drawing toolbar and then clicking No Line at the color palette.
10. Add yellow fill to the text box by clicking the Fill Color button. (The default color for the Fill Color button should be yellow.)
11. Click outside the text box to deselect it.
12. Save the completed document and name it **swc8x08**.
13. Print and then close **swc8x08**.

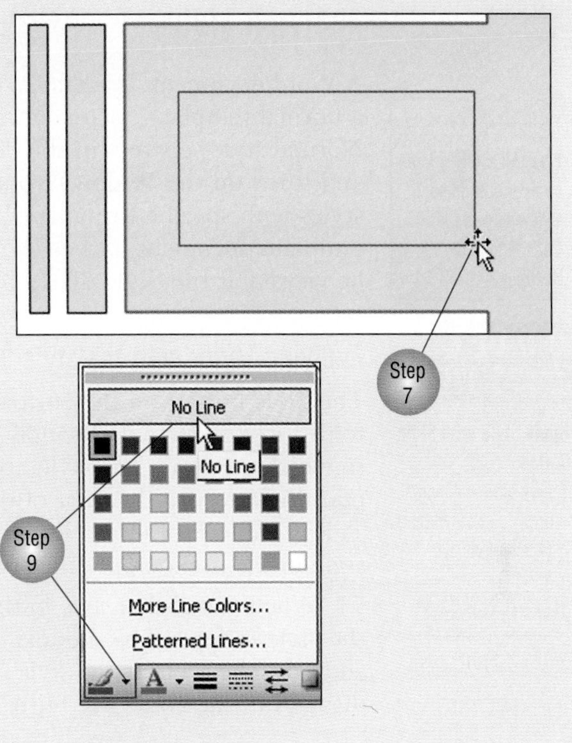

FIGURE 8.9 ***Exercise 8***

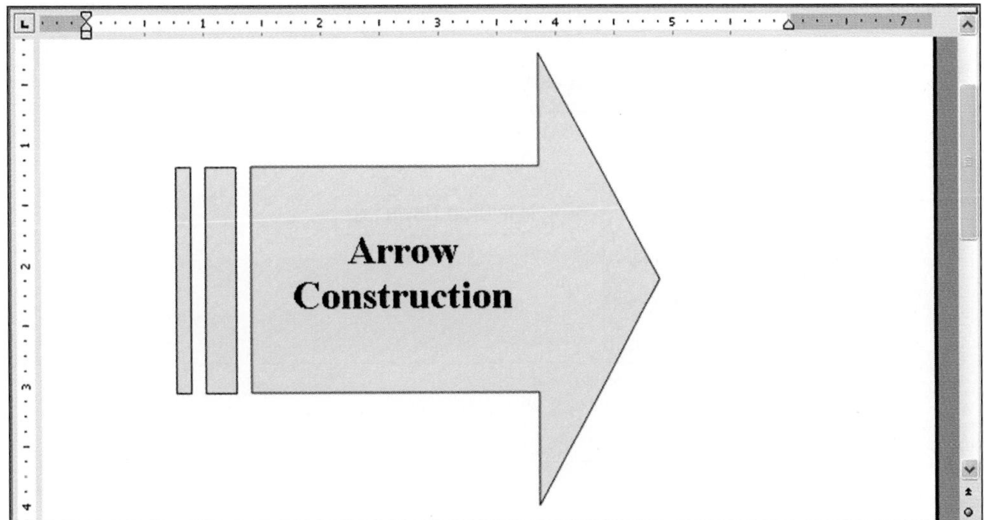

Normal

Style

HINT

Press Alt + Ctrl + 1 to apply the Heading 1 style and press Alt + Ctrl + 2 to apply the Heading 2 style.

Applying Styles

A Word document, by default, is based on the Normal template document. Within a normal template document, a Normal style is applied to text by default. This Normal style sets text in the default font, uses left alignment and single spacing, and turns on the Widow/Orphan control. In addition to this Normal style, other styles with specific formatting are available in a document based on the Normal template document. Other Word templates contain additional styles, which can be viewed at the Style dialog box.

QUICK STEPS

Apply Style with Style Button

1. Click down-pointing arrow on Style button.
2. Click desired style.

Times New Roman

Font

12

Font Size

Applying Styles with the Style Button

The Style button on the Formatting toolbar offers one method for applying a style to text in a document. To apply a style, position the insertion point in the paragraph to which you want the style applied, or select the text, and then click the down-pointing arrow to the right of the Style button (the second button from the left). This causes a drop-down list to display as shown in Figure 8.10. Click the desired style in the list to apply the style to the text in the document.

When you click a style in the drop-down list, the list is removed from the screen, the style is applied to the text, and the style name displays in the Style button. In addition, the font for the style displays in the Font button and the size for the style displays in the Font Size button.

FIGURE 8.10 ***Style Drop-Down List***

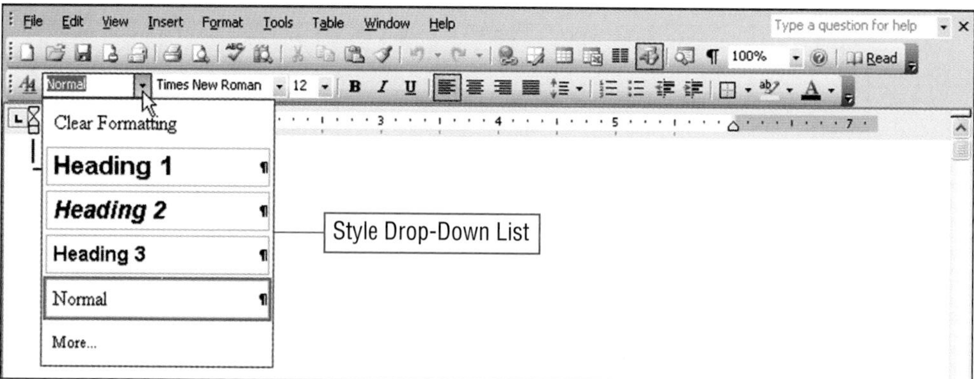

HINT

Applying a ready-to-use style ensures a consistent visual appearance of document elements.

Clearing Formatting

Clear all formatting applied to text, such as styles, bullets, numbering, alignment, font, and other character and paragraph formatting by selecting the text, clicking the down-pointing arrow at the right side of the Style button on the Formatting toolbar, and then clicking *Clear Formatting*. You can also clear formatting by selecting text, clicking Edit, pointing to Clear, and then clicking Format or by applying the Normal style.

HINT
Press Ctrl + Shift + N to apply the Normal style.

exercise 9 APPLYING PREDESIGNED STYLES AND CLEARING FORMATTING

1. Open **WordReport02**.
2. Save the document with Save As and name it **swc8x09**.
3. Select the entire document, change the line spacing to single, and then deselect the document.
4. Apply the Heading 1 style to the title by completing the following steps:
   a. Position the insertion point on any character in the title *SECTION 1: COMPUTERS IN COMMUNICATION*.
   b. Click the down-pointing arrow at the right side of the Style button on the Formatting toolbar.
   c. At the drop-down list that displays, click *Heading 1*.
5. Apply the Heading 2 style to the first heading by completing the following steps:
   a. Position the insertion point on any character in the heading *Telecommunications*.
   b. Click the down-pointing arrow at the right side of the Style button on the Formatting toolbar.
   c. At the drop-down list that displays, click *Heading 2*.
6. Complete steps similar to those in Steps 4 or 5 to apply the specified style to the following text:

Publishing	=	Heading 2
News Services	=	Heading 2
SECTION 2: COMPUTERS IN ENTERTAINMENT	=	Heading 1
Television and Film	=	Heading 2
Home Entertainment	=	Heading 2

7. Save and then print **swc8x09**.
8. Clear formatting by completing the following steps:
   a. Position the insertion point on any character in the title *SECTION 1: COMPUTERS IN COMMUNICATION*.
   b. Click the down-pointing arrow at the right side of the Style button on the Formatting toolbar and then click *Clear Formatting* at the drop-down list.
   c. Position the insertion point on any character in the title *SECTION 2: COMPUTERS IN ENTERTAINMENT*.
   d. Click the down-pointing arrow at the right side of the Style button on the Formatting toolbar and then click *Clear Formatting* at the drop-down list.

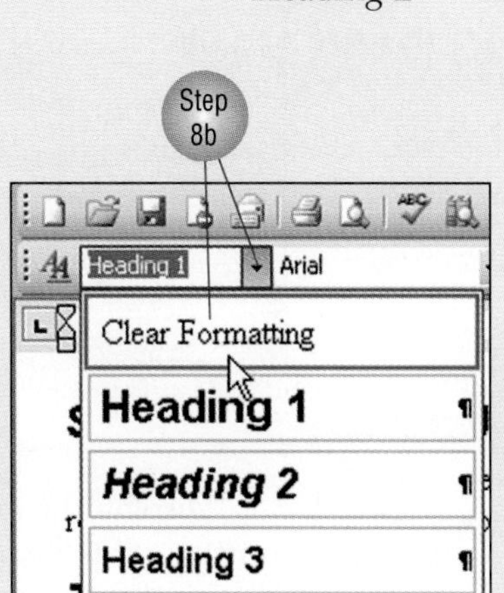

9. Apply the following formatting to the title *SECTION 1: COMPUTERS IN COMMUNICATION*:
   a. Change the font size to 14, turn on bold, and change the alignment to center.
   b. Insert 6 points of spacing after the title. ***(Hint: Do this at the Paragraph dialog box with the Indents and Spacing tab selected.)***
10. Apply the following formatting to the title *SECTION 2: COMPUTERS IN ENTERTAINMENT*:
    a. Change the font size to 14, turn on bold, and change the alignment to center.
    b. Insert 6 points of spacing before and 6 points of spacing after the title.
11. Save, print, and then close **swc8x09**.

Applying Styles with Options at the Styles and Formatting Task Pane

Styles and Formatting

Click the Styles and Formatting button on the Formatting toolbar (first button from the left) and the Styles and Formatting task pane displays as shown in Figure 8.11. By default, *Available formatting* is selected in the *Show* option box (located at the bottom of the task pane). This includes three built-in heading styles, any direct formatting you applied, and any styles you have created. Change what styles display by choosing a different option at the drop-down list.

FIGURE 8.11 ***Styles and Formatting Task Pane***

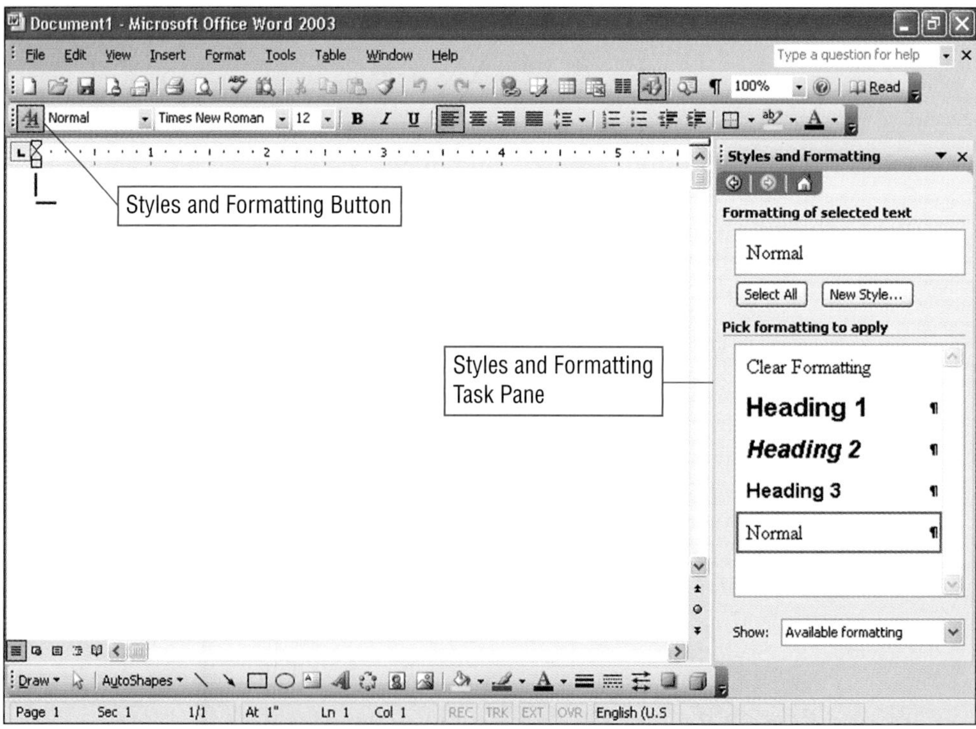

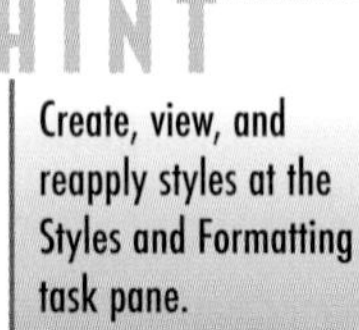

HINT

Create, view, and reapply styles at the Styles and Formatting task pane.

Display the entire list of styles provided by Word by choosing the *All styles* option. This displays additional styles in the *Pick formatting to apply* list box. Paragraph styles are followed by the ¶ symbol and character styles are followed by the **a** symbol. To apply a paragraph style at the Styles and Formatting task pane, position the insertion point anywhere in the paragraph and then click the desired style in the *Pick formatting to apply* list box. To apply a character style, select the text, and then click the desired style.

The Styles and Formatting task pane with *All styles* selected contains different types of styles you can apply to text. The *Pick formatting to apply* list box contains styles you can apply to body text, headings, lists, tables, and much more.

Apply Style at Styles and Formatting Task Pane

1. Click Styles and Formatting button on Formatting toolbar.
2. Click desired style in *Pick formatting to apply* list box.

exercise 10

APPLYING A LIST STYLE

1. Open **WordList01**.
2. Save the document with Save As and name it **swc8x10**.
3. Apply a list bullet style and a list number style to text in the document by completing the following steps:
   a. Click the Styles and Formatting button on the Formatting toolbar. (This displays the Styles and Formatting task pane.)
   b. Click the down-pointing arrow to the right of the *Show* option box (located towards the bottom of the Styles and Formatting task pane) and then click *All styles* at the drop-down list.
   c. Select the list of text in the document (from *Investment Practices of the Account* through *Expense Deductions*).
   d. Scroll through the list of styles in the *Pick formatting to apply* list box until List Bullet 4 is visible and then click *List Bullet 4*.
   e. Deselect the text.
   f. Save and then print **swc8x10**.
   g. Select the list of text in the document (from *Investment Practices of the Account* through *Expense Deductions*).
   h. Apply the List Number 4 style (located in the *Pick formatting to apply* list box in the Styles and Formatting task pane).
   i. Deselect the text.
4. Close the Styles and Formatting task pane.
5. Save, print, and then close **swc8x10**.

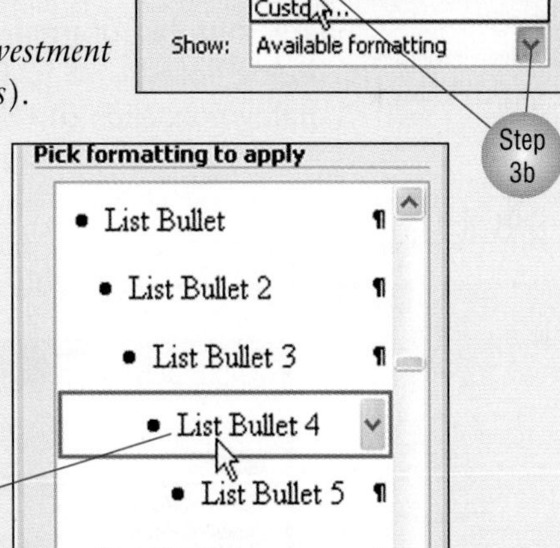

APPLYING A TABLE STYLE

1. Open **WordTab01**.
2. Save the document with Save As and name it **swc8x11**.
3. Apply a table style to the document by completing the following steps:
   a. Click the Styles and Formatting button to display the Styles and Formatting task pane.

b. Click the down-pointing arrow to the right of the *Show* option box (located towards the bottom of the Styles and Formatting task pane) and then click *All styles* at the drop-down list.
c. Press Ctrl + A to select the entire document.
d. Scroll through the list of styles in the *Pick formatting to apply* list box until Table Colorful 2 is visible and then click *Table Colorful 2*.
e. Autofit the contents of the table. (To do this, click Table, point to AutoFit and then click AutoFit to Contents.)
f. Using the mouse, drag the right border of the table to the right approximately .5 inch.

4. Close the Styles and Formatting task pane.
5. Save, print, and then close **swc8x11**.

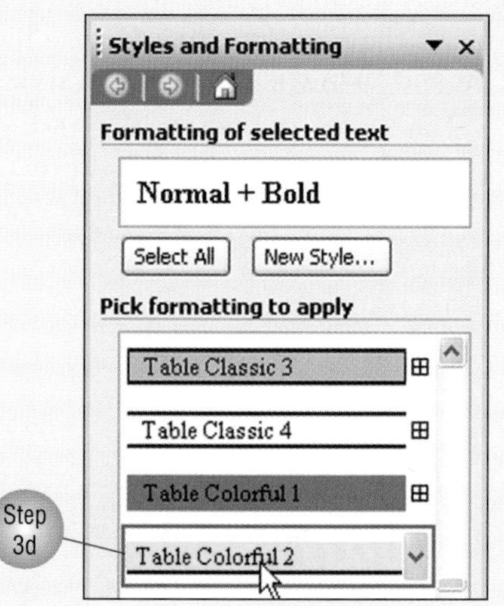

QUICK STEPS

Format Text with Style Gallery

1. Click Format, Theme.
2. Click Style Gallery button.
3. Click desired template in Template list box.
4. Click OK.

Formatting Text with the Style Gallery

As you learned in an earlier chapter, each document is based on a template, with the Normal template document the default. Word also provides predesigned styles with other template documents. You can use the Style Gallery dialog box to apply styles from other templates to the current document. This provides you with a large number of predesigned styles for formatting text. To display the Style Gallery dialog box shown in Figure 8.12, click Format and then Theme. At the Theme dialog box, click the Style Gallery button (located at the bottom of the dialog box).

FIGURE 8.12 ***Style Gallery Dialog Box***

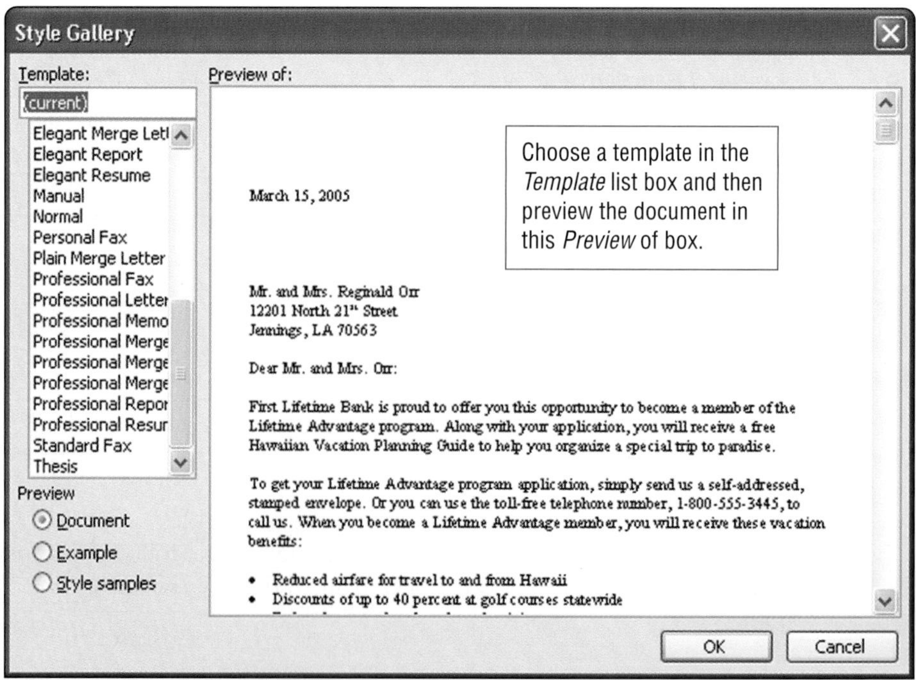

At the Style Gallery dialog box, the template documents are displayed in the *Template* list box. The open document is displayed in the *Preview of* section of the dialog box. With this section, you can choose templates from the *Template* list box and see how the formatting is applied to the open document.

At the bottom of the Style Gallery dialog box, the *Document* option is selected in the *Preview* section. If you click *Example,* Word will insert a sample document in the *Preview of* section that displays the formatting applied to the document. Click *Style samples* and styles will display in the *Preview of* section of the dialog box rather than the document or sample document.

exercise 12

FORMATTING A LETTER WITH STYLES FROM A LETTER TEMPLATE

1. Open **WordLetter02**.
2. Save the document with Save As and name it **swc8x12**.
3. Format the letter at the Style Gallery by completing the following steps:
   a. Click Format and then Theme.
   b. At the Theme dialog box, click the Style Gallery button (located at the bottom of the dialog box).
   c. At the Style Gallery dialog box, click *Elegant Letter* in the *Template* list box. (You may need to scroll up the list.)
   d. Click OK.

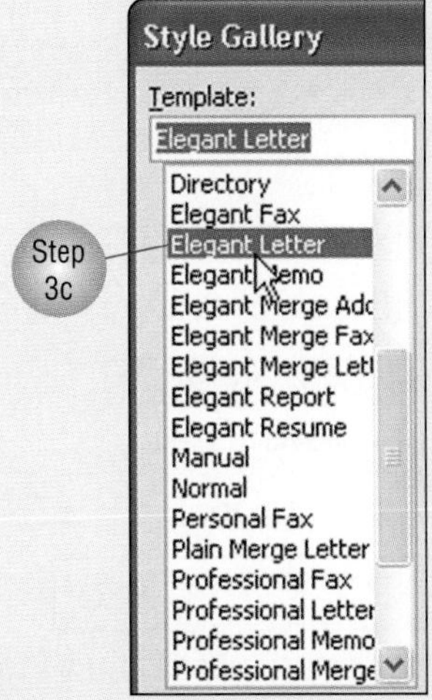

4. Save, print, and then close **swc8x12**.

When you select a template at the Style Gallery, the template styles are available at the Style button on the Formatting toolbar and at the Styles and Formatting task pane. Paragraph styles are followed by the ¶ symbol and character styles are followed by the **a** symbol. Use the template styles to format specific text in a document.

exercise 13

APPLYING SPECIFIC STYLES TO A REPORT

1. Open **WordReport01**.
2. Save the document with Save As and name it **swc8x13**.
3. Select a template at the Style Gallery by completing the following steps:
   a. Click Format and then Theme.
   b. At the Theme dialog box, click the Style Gallery button.
   c. At the Style Gallery dialog box, click *Elegant Report* in the *Template* list box.
   d. Click OK.

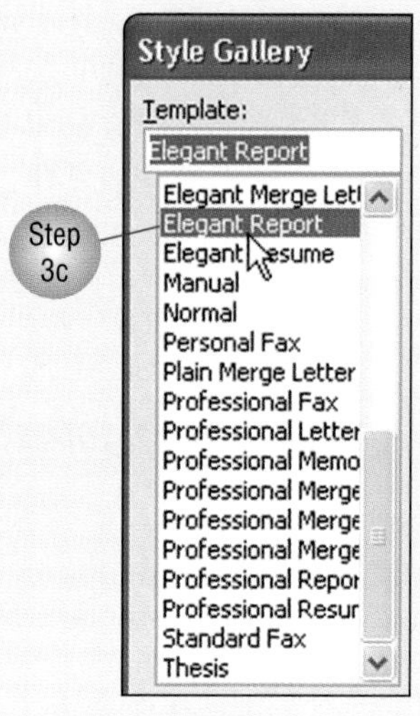

4. Click the Styles and Formatting button on the Formatting toolbar to turn on the display of the Styles and Formatting task pane.
5. Apply the Body Text style by completing the following steps:
   a. Select text from the beginning of the first paragraph of text (the paragraph that begins *Graphics are pictures, still and moving, such as…*) to the end of the document.
   b. Click the *Body Text* paragraph style in the *Pick formatting to apply* list box.

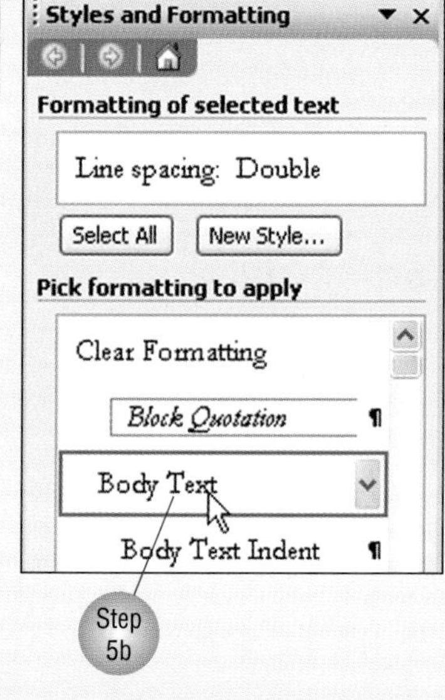

6. Click anywhere in the title *GRAPHICS SOFTWARE* and then click the *CHAPTER LABEL* paragraph style in the *Pick formatting to apply* list box.

7. Select the heading *Early Painting and Drawing Programs* and then click the *EMPHASIS* character style in the *Pick formatting to apply* list box.

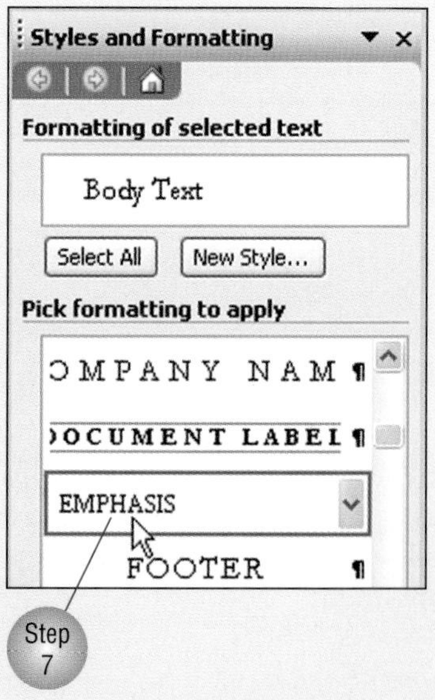

8. Select each of the remaining headings individually (*Developments in Painting and Drawing Programs* and *Painting and Drawing Programs Today*) and apply the EMPHASIS character style.
9. Close the Styles and Formatting task pane.
10. Save, print, and then close **swc8x13**.

Creating an Outline

Word's outlining feature will format headings within a document as well as let you view formatted headings and body text in a document. With the outlining feature you can quickly see an overview of a document by collapsing parts of a document so that only the headings show. With headings collapsed, you can perform such editing functions as moving or deleting sections of a document.

To create an outline, you identify particular headings and subheadings within a document as certain heading levels. The Outline view is used to assign particular heading levels to text. You can also enter text and edit text while working in Outline view. To change to Outline view, click the Outline View button at the left side of the horizontal scroll bar or click View and then Outline. Figure 8.13 shows the WordReport01 document as it will appear in Exercise 14 with heading formatting applied in Outline view.

Outline View

FIGURE 8.13 **Document in Outline View**

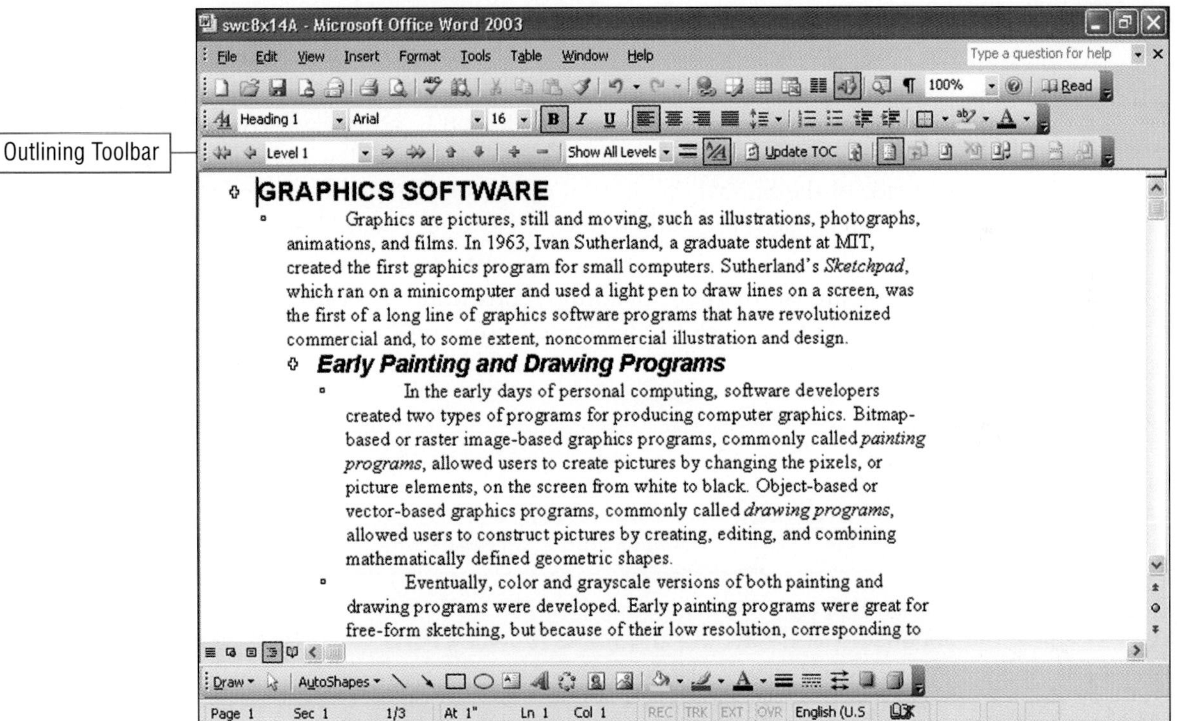

In Figure 8.13, the title *GRAPHICS SOFTWARE* is identified as a first-level heading, the heading *Early Painting and Drawing Programs* is identified as a second-level heading, and the paragraphs following are normal text. When a document contains headings and text formatted in the Outline view, each paragraph is identified as a particular heading level or as normal text. Paragraphs are identified by **outline symbols** that appear in the selection bar at the left side of the screen. Use the outline symbols to select text in the document. To do this, position the arrow pointer on the outline symbol next to text you want to select until it turns into a four-headed arrow, and then click the left mouse button.

HINT

Create an outline in Word and then use the outline as a basis for preparing a PowerPoint presentation.

Assign Headings in Outline

1. Open document.
2. Click Outline View button.
3. Click heading.
4. Click Promote or Demote button.

Promote to Heading 1 Demote

Collapse an outline before moving text.

Show Level

Collapse Expand

Assigning Headings

In Outline view, the Outlining toolbar displays below the Formatting toolbar. Use buttons on this toolbar to promote and demote headings, expand or collapse the outline, or show specific headings in an outline. To change a paragraph that is identified as normal text to a first-level heading, position the insertion point on any character in the text (or select the text), and then click the Promote to Heading 1 button on the Outlining toolbar. This applies the Heading 1 style to the paragraph. To change a paragraph to a second-level heading, position the insertion point anywhere within the text, and then click the Demote button. This applies the Heading 2 style to the text.

Collapsing and Expanding Outline Headings

One of the major benefits of working in the Outline view is the ability to see a condensed outline of your document without all of the text in between headings or subheadings. Word lets you collapse a heading level in an outline. This causes any text or subsequent lower heading levels to disappear temporarily. When heading levels are collapsed, viewing the outline of a document is much easier. For example, when an outline is collapsed, you can see an overview of the entire document and move easily to different locations in the document. You can also move headings and their subordinate headings to new locations in the outline.

To collapse an outline, click the down-pointing arrow at the right side of the Show Level button, and then click the desired heading level. For example, if a document contains three heading levels, clicking the down-pointing arrow at the right side of the Show Level button on the Outlining toolbar and then clicking *Show Level 2* will collapse the outline so only Heading 1 and Heading 2 text displays.

To collapse all of the text beneath a particular heading (including the text following any subsequent headings), position the insertion point within the heading, and then click the Collapse button on the Outlining toolbar. To make the text appear again, click the Expand button on the Outlining toolbar.

exercise 14

FORMATTING A DOCUMENT WITH BUTTONS ON THE OUTLINING TOOLBAR

1. Open **WordReport01**.
2. Save the document with Save As and name it **swc8x14A**.
3. Change to the Outline view by clicking the Outline View button at the left side of the horizontal scroll bar.
4. Promote and demote heading levels by completing the following steps:
   a. Position the insertion point anywhere in the title *GRAPHICS SOFTWARE* and then click the Promote button on the Outlining toolbar. (*Heading 1* will display in the Style button on the Formatting toolbar.)

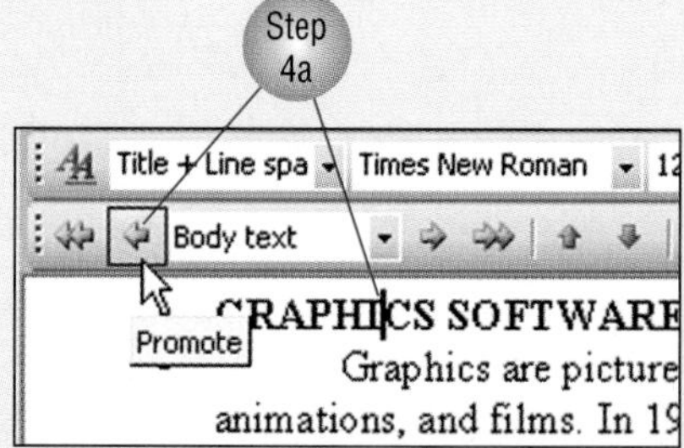

b. Position the insertion point anywhere in the heading *Early Painting and Drawing Programs* and then click the Demote button on the Outlining toolbar. (*Heading 2* will display in the Style button on the Formatting toolbar.)

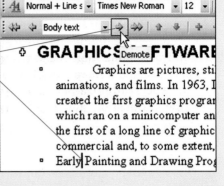

c. Position the insertion point anywhere in the heading *Developments in Painting and Drawing Programs* and then click the Promote button on the Outlining toolbar. (*Heading 2* will display in the Style button on the Formatting toolbar.)

d. Position the insertion point anywhere in the heading *Painting and Drawing Programs Today* and then click the Promote button on the Outlining toolbar. (*Heading 2* will display in the Style button on the Formatting toolbar.)

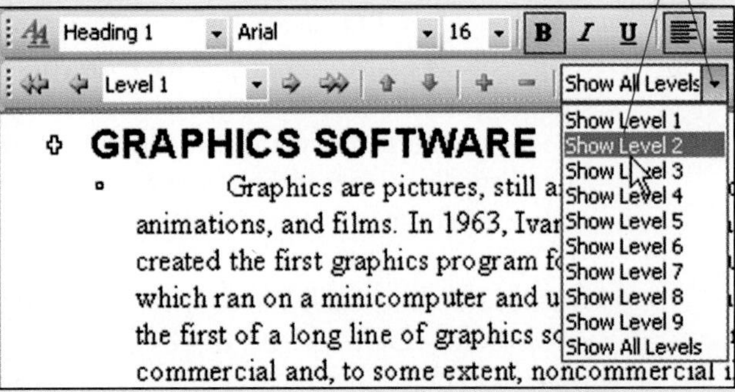

5. Save and then print **swc8x14A**.
6. Press Ctrl + Home to move the insertion point to the beginning of the document.
7. Click the down-pointing arrow at the right side of the Show Level button on the Outlining toolbar and then click *Show Level 2* at the drop-down list.
8. With the outline collapsed, position the mouse pointer on the plus symbol immediately left of the *Painting and Drawing Programs Today* heading until the pointer turns into a four-headed arrow, and then click the left mouse button. (This selects the heading.)

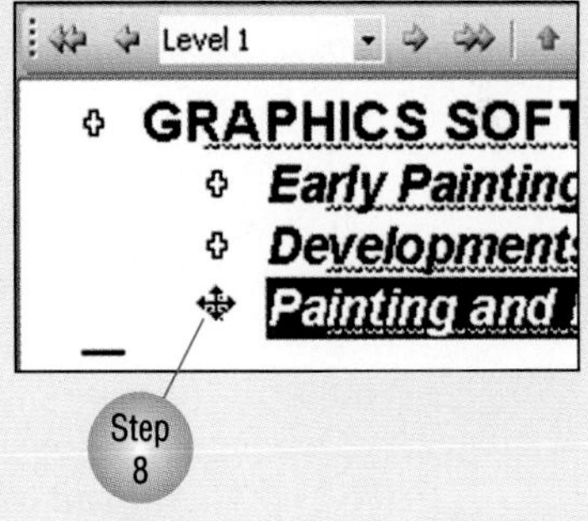

9. Press the Delete key. (This deletes the heading and all text below the heading.)
10. Save the document with Save As and name it **swc8x14B**.
11. Print and then close **swc8x14B**. (This will print the collapsed outline, not the entire document.)

Organizing an Outline

Collapsing and expanding headings within an outline is only part of the versatility offered by Word's outline feature. It also offers you the ability to rearrange an entire document by reorganizing an outline. You can rearrange whole sections of a document by moving the headings at the beginning of those sections. Text collapsed beneath the headings is moved at the same time. For example, to move a second-level heading below other second-level headings, you would collapse the outline, select the second-level heading to be moved, and then click the Move Down button on the Outlining toolbar until the second-level heading is in the desired position.

Move Down

If headings are collapsed, you only need to select the heading and move it to the desired location. Any subsequent hidden text is moved automatically. You can also move headings in a document by positioning the arrow pointer on the plus symbol before the desired heading until it turns into a four-headed arrow, holding down the mouse button, dragging the heading to the desired location, and then releasing the mouse button. As you drag the mouse, a gray horizontal line displays in the document with an arrow attached. Use this horizontal line to help you move the heading to the desired location.

exercise 15

MOVING HEADINGS IN A DOCUMENT

1. Open **swc8x14A**.
2. Save the document with Save As and name it **swc8x15**.
3. In Outline view, make sure the insertion point is positioned at the beginning of the document, click the down-pointing arrow at the right side of the Show Level button, and then click *Show Level 2* at the drop-down list.
4. Move *Painting and Drawing Programs Today* above *Developments in Painting and Drawing Programs* by completing the following steps:
   a. Position the insertion point anywhere in the heading *Painting and Drawing Programs Today*.
   b. Click once on the Move Up button on the Outlining toolbar.
5. Move the heading *Early Painting and Drawing Programs* below *Developments in Painting and Drawing Programs* by completing the following steps:
   a. Position the arrow pointer on the plus symbol immediately left of the heading *Early Painting and Drawing Programs* until it turns into a four-headed arrow.
   b. Hold down the left mouse button, drag the mouse down until the gray horizontal line with the arrow attached is positioned below *Developments in Painting and Drawing Programs*, and then release the mouse button.
   c. Deselect the text.
6. Save and then print **swc8x15**.
7. Click the down-pointing arrow at the right side of the Show Level button and then click *Show All Levels* at the drop-down list.
8. Close **swc8x15**.

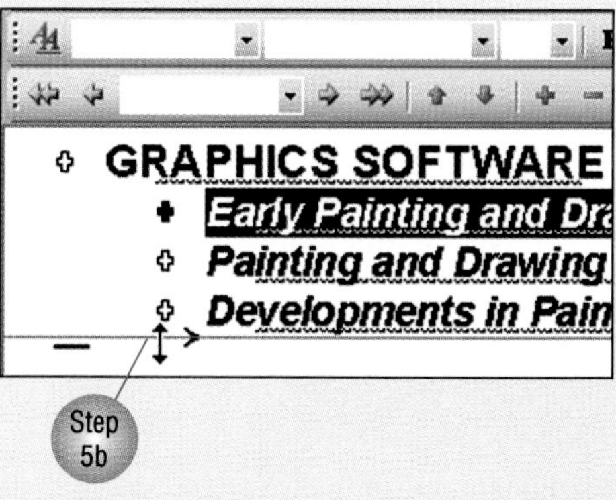

Save Document as Web Page
1. Click Save, Save as Web Page.
2. Type name in *File name* text box.
3. Click Save.

Creating a Web Page

Many businesses and corporations as well as some individuals have Web sites on the Internet. These Web sites generally consist of a number of Web pages probably created using a language called Hypertext Markup Language (HTML). Web browsers use this language to read hypertext documents. In the past, a person needed knowledge of HTML to design a Web page. Now you can create a Web page in Word and save the document as a Web page.

To save a Word document as a Web page, click File, and then click Save as Web Page. At the Save As dialog box, type a name for the Web page document, and then press Enter or click the Save button. (Word automatically changes the *Save as type* option to *Single File Web Page*.)

When saving a document as a Web page, click the Change Title button at the Save As dialog box and the Set Page Title dialog box displays. At this dialog box, type a name for the Web page that you want to display in the title bar of the Web browser and then click OK.

Changing to the Web Layout View

When you save a document as a Web page, Word automatically changes to the Web Layout view. The Web Layout view displays a page as it will appear when published to the Web or an intranet. You can also change to the Web Layout view by clicking the Web Layout View button located at the left side of the horizontal scroll bar or by clicking View and then Web Layout.

Web Layout View

Previewing a Document in Web Page Preview

When creating a Web page, you may want to preview it in your default Web browser. To do this, click File, and then click Web Page Preview. This displays the currently open document in the default Web browser and displays formatting supported by the browser.

exercise 16

CREATING AND PREVIEWING A WEB PAGE

1. Open **BeltwayHomePage**.
2. Insert, move, and size the clip art image shown in Figure 8.14 by completing the following specifications:
   a. Search for clip art images related to *Travel* and then insert the image shown in Figure 8.14. (If this clip art image is not available, choose a similar image.)
   b. Change the wrapping style to Square.
   c. Size and move the image so it is positioned as shown in Figure 8.14.
3. Save the document as a Web page by completing the following steps:
   a. Click File and then Save as Web Page.
   b. At the Save As dialog box, click the Change Title button.
   c. At the Set Page Title dialog box, type Travel with Beltway! and then click OK.

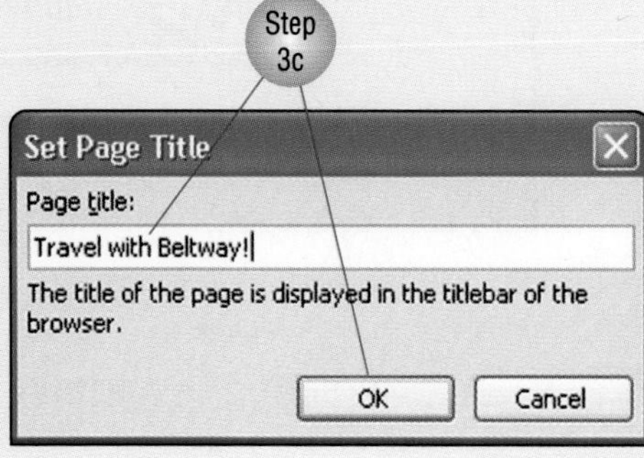

d. At the Save As dialog box, select the current name that displays in the *File name* text box and then type BeltwayWebPage.
e. Click the Save button.

Step 3d

Page title: Travel with Beltway!
Change Title...
File name: BeltwayWebPage
Save
Save as type: Single File Web Page
Cancel

Step 3e

f. If a message displays telling you that some features are not supported by Microsoft Internet Explorer, click the Continue button.

4. Preview the document in Web Page Preview by completing the following steps:
   a. Click File and then click Web Page Preview.
   b. After viewing the document in the Web browser, click File and then Close.
5. Save the document again with the same name (**BeltwayWebPage**).
6. Print and then close **BeltwayWebPage**.

FIGURE 8.14 ***Exercise 16***

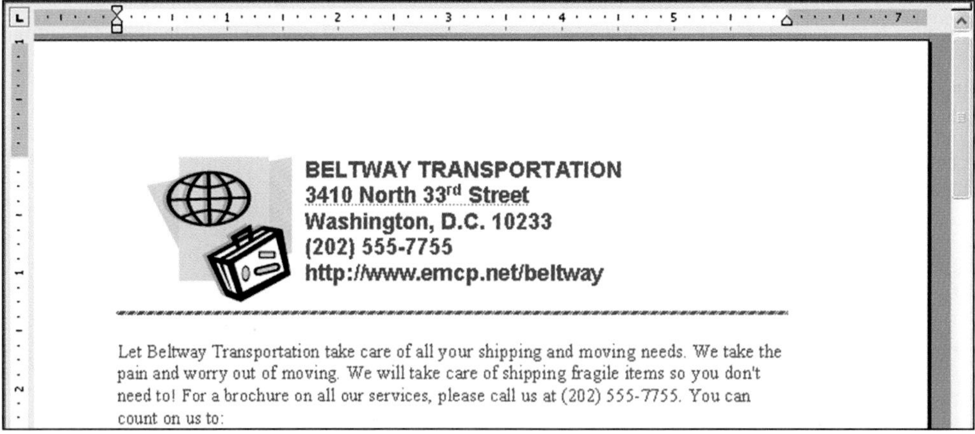

BELTWAY TRANSPORTATION
3410 North 33rd Street
Washington, D.C. 10233
(202) 555-7755
http://www.emcp.net/beltway
Let Beltway Transportation take care of all your shipping and moving needs. We take the pain and worry out of moving. We will take care of shipping fragile items so you don't need to! For a brochure on all our services, please call us at (202) 555-7755. You can count on us to:

Creating Hyperlinks

Insert Hyperlink

Web pages use hyperlinks to display other pages or Web sites. You can create your own hyperlink in your Web page. To do this, select the text you want specified as the hyperlink, and then click the Insert Hyperlink button on the Standard toolbar. At the Insert Hyperlink dialog box shown in Figure 8.15, type the Web site address in the *Address* text box, and then click OK.

FIGURE

8.15 ***Insert Hyperlink Dialog Box***

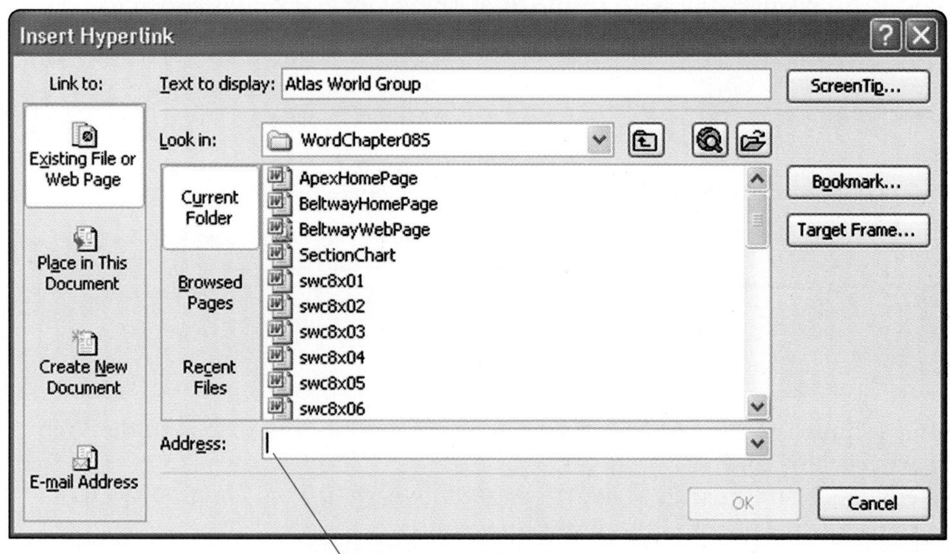

Insert Hyperlink
1. Select text.
2. Click Insert Hyperlink button.
3. Type Web address of document name.
4. Click OK.

Another method for creating a hyperlink is to type the Web site address in a Word document. When you type the complete Web site address, Word automatically converts the address to a hyperlink and changes the color of the Web site address. To link to the specified Web page, position the mouse pointer on the hyperlink text, hold down the Ctrl key, and then click the left mouse button.

exercise 17

CREATING HYPERLINKS

1. Open **BeltwayWebPage**.
2. Create a hyperlink so that clicking Atlas World Group displays the Atlas World Group Web page by completing the following steps:
   a. Select the text *Atlas World Group* that displays toward the end of the document (after a bullet).
   b. Click the Insert Hyperlink button on the Standard toolbar.

c. At the Insert Hyperlink dialog box, type www.atlasworldgroup.com in the *Address* text box. (When you begin typing the Web site address, *http://* is automatically inserted in the *Address* text box.)
d. Click OK. (This changes the color of the *Atlas World Group* text and also adds underlining to the text.)

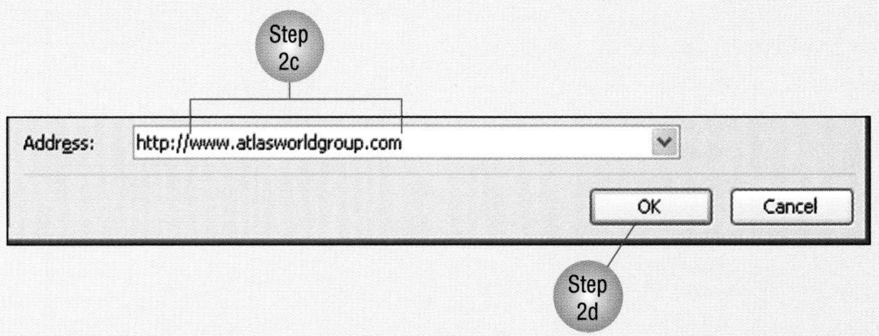

3. Complete steps similar to those in Step 2 to create a hyperlink from *Bekins* to the Web site address www.bekins.com.
4. Complete steps similar to those in Step 2 to create a hyperlink from *United Van Lines* to the Web site address www.unitedvanlines.com.
5. Click the Save button on the Standard toolbar to save the Web page with the hyperlinks added.
6. Jump to the hyperlink sites by completing the following steps:
   a. Hold down the Ctrl key, position the mouse pointer on the Atlas World Group hyperlink that displays toward the end of the document, click the left mouse button, and then release the Ctrl key.
   b. When the Atlas World Group Web page displays, scroll through the page, and then click on a hyperlink that interests you.
   c. After looking at this next page, click File and then Close.
   d. At the Beltway Web page document, hold down the Ctrl key, and then click the Bekins hyperlink.
   e. After viewing the Bekins home page, click File and then Close.
   f. At the Beltway Web page document, hold down the Ctrl key, and then click the United Van Lines hyperlink.
   g. After viewing the United Van Lines home page, click File and then Close.
7. Close the **BeltwayWebPage** document.

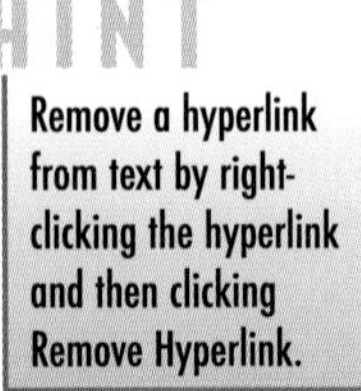

HINT

Remove a hyperlink from text by right-clicking the hyperlink and then clicking Remove Hyperlink.

You can modify or change hyperlink text or the hyperlink destination. To do this, right-click the hyperlink, and then click Edit Hyperlink. At the Edit Hyperlink dialog box, make any desired changes, and then close the dialog box. The Edit Hyperlink dialog box contains the same options as the Insert Hyperlink dialog box.

Insert Exercise 17, you created a hyperlink from a Word document to a Web site on the Internet. You can also create a hyperlink in a Word document to another Word document.

exercise 18

CREATING AND MODIFYING A HYPERLINK TO A WORD WORKSHEET

1. Open **WordDocument12**.
2. Save the document with Save As and name it **swc8x18**.
3. Create a hyperlink that will display the **SectionChart** document by completing the following steps:
   a. Press Ctrl + End to move the insertion point to the end of the document.
   b. Type Section Chart.
   c. Select *Section Chart*.
   d. Click the Insert Hyperlink button on the Standard toolbar.
   e. At the Insert Hyperlink dialog box, make sure WordChapter08S is the active folder (displays in the *Look in* option box).
   f. Double-click *SectionChart* in the WordChapter08S folder on your disk. (This closes the Insert Hyperlink dialog box and displays the *Section Chart* text as a hyperlink in the document.)

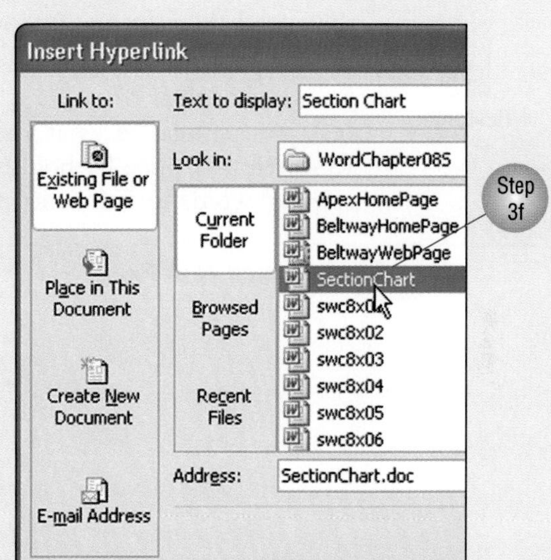

4. Display the **SectionChart** document by positioning the mouse pointer on the hyperlink text Section Chart, holding down the Ctrl key, clicking the left mouse button, and then releasing the Ctrl key.
5. Close the **SectionChart** document.
6. Modify the hyperlink text by completing the following steps:
   a. Position the mouse pointer on the Section Chart hyperlink, click the *right* mouse button, and then click Edit Hyperlink.
   b. At the Edit Hyperlink dialog box, select the text *Section Chart* in the *Text to display* text box and then type 2004 Fund Section Breakdown.
   c. Click OK.

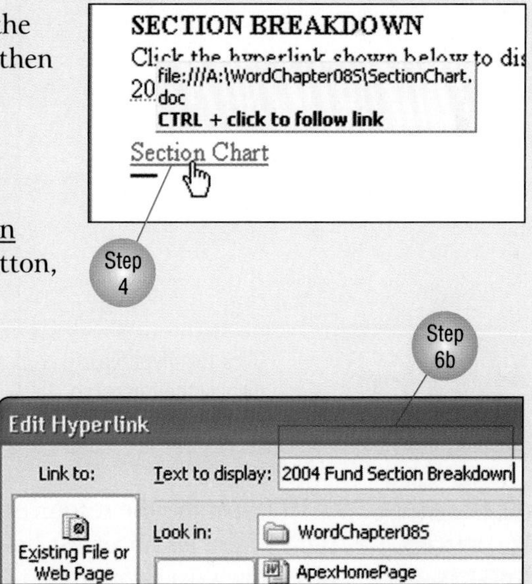

7. At the memo document, position the mouse pointer over the 2004 Fund Section Breakdown hyperlink, hold down the Ctrl key, click the left mouse button, and then release the Ctrl key.
8. Close the **SectionChart** document.
9. Save, print, and then close **swc8x18**.

Researching and Requesting Information

In Chapter 4, you used the Research task pane to search for synonyms for a specific word. You can also use options at this task pane to search for and request specific information from online sources and to translate words from and to a variety of languages. The online resources available to you depend on the locale to which your system is set, authorization information indicating that you are allowed to download the information, and your Internet service provider.

Research

Display the Research task pane by clicking the Research button on the Standard toolbar or clicking Tools and then Research. This displays the Research task pane similar to what you see in Figure 8.16. You can also display the Research task pane by holding down the Alt key and clicking a specific word or selected words in a document.

FIGURE 8.16 **Research Task Pane**

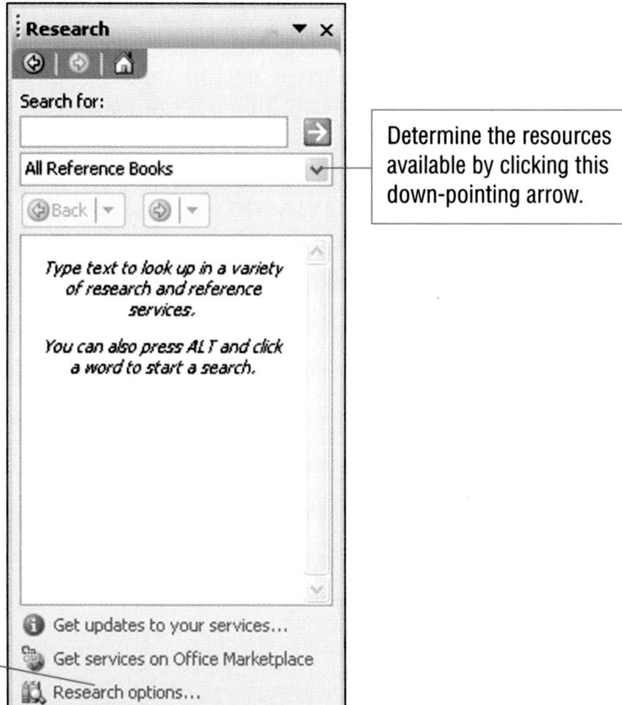

Request Information from Online Sources
1. Click Research button.
2. Type word or topic.
3. Specify resources.
4. Click Start searching button.

Determine the resources available by clicking the down-pointing arrow at the right of the resources list box (the list box located below the *Search for* text box). The drop-down list contains lists of reference books, research sites, business and financial sites, and other services. If you want to use a specific reference in your search, click the desired reference at the drop-down list, type the desired word or topic in the *Search for* text box, and then press Enter. Items matching your word or topic display in the task pane list box. Depending on the item, the list box may contain hyperlinks you can click to access additional information on the Internet.

HINT

Click the Parental Control button at the Research Options dialog box to turn on content filtering that blocks offensive results.

You can control the available research options by clicking the Research options hyperlink located at the bottom of the Research task pane. This displays the Research Options dialog box shown in Figure 8.17. At this dialog box, insert a check mark before those items you want available and remove the check mark from those items you do not want available.

FIGURE

8.17 ***Research Options Dialog Box***

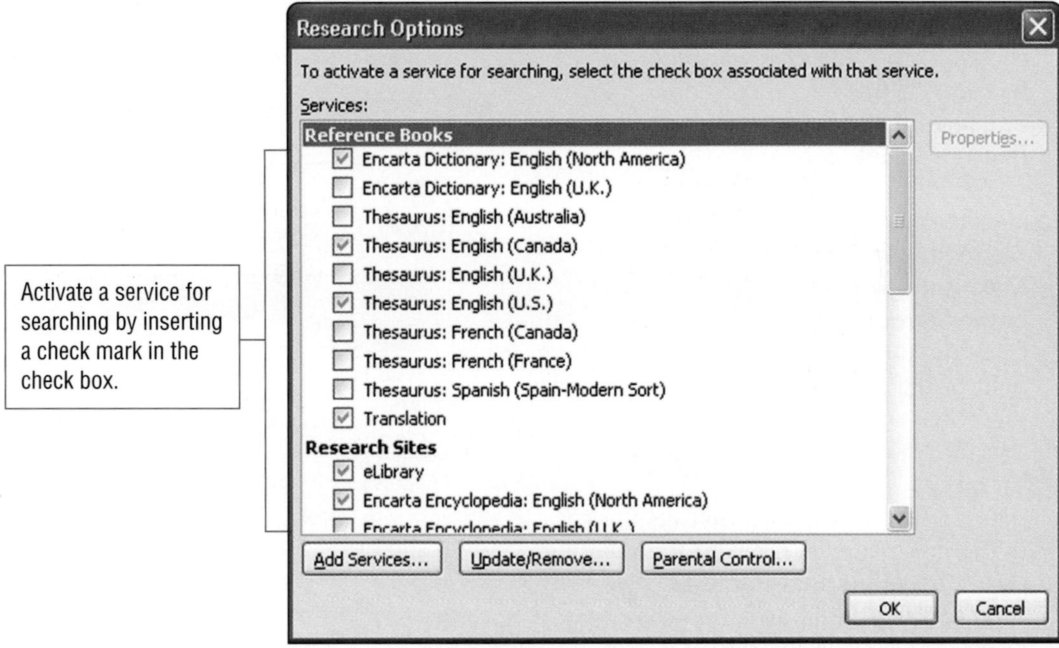

Inserting Research Information

You can insert into your document some of the information that displays in the Research task pane and other information you can copy and paste into your document. If you look up stock prices, an *Insert Price* button is available for inserting the stock table in your document. If information displays in your browser, select the desired information, click Edit on the Browser's menu bar and then click Copy at the drop-down menu. Make your document active, click Edit, and then click Paste or click the Paste button.

exercise 19

RESEARCHING AND REQUESTING INFORMATION

(Note: Your computer must be connected to the Internet to complete this exercise.)

1. At a clear document screen, display the Research task pane by clicking the Research button on the Standard toolbar.
2. Search for information on artificial intelligence in a dictionary by completing the following steps:
    a. Click in the *Search for* text box or select any text that displays in the text box and then type **artificial intelligence**.

b. Click the down-pointing arrow to the right of the resources list box (the down-pointing arrow immediately below the Start searching button).
c. At the drop-down list of resources, click *Encarta Dictionary: English (North America)*. If this reference is not available, click any other dictionary that is available to you.

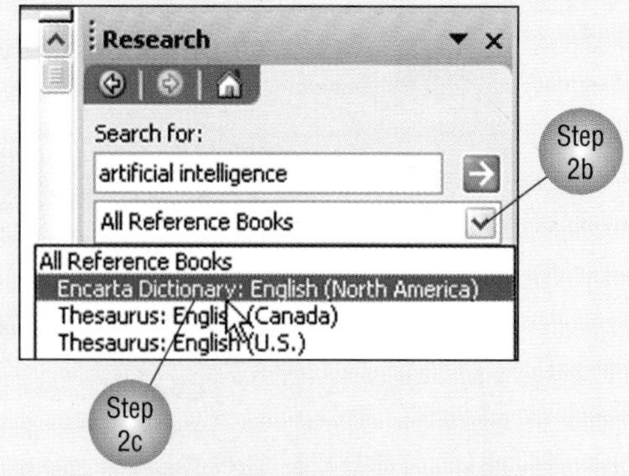

3. Search for information on artificial intelligence in an encyclopedia by completing the following steps:
   a. Make sure *artificial intelligence* displays in the *Search for* text box.
   b. Click the down-pointing arrow at the right of the resources list box and then click an encyclopedia listed in the *All Research Sites* section of the list box.
   c. Look at the information that displays in the task pane list box and then click a hyperlink that interests you.
   d. After reading the information that displays in your Web browser, close the browser window.

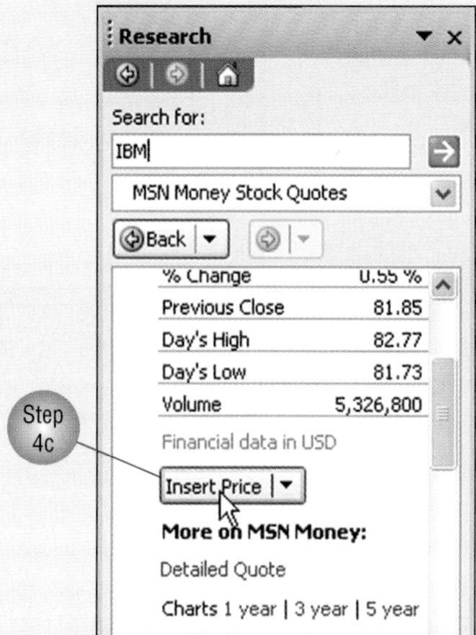

4. Search for stock information and then insert the information in your document by completing the following steps:
   a. Select the text *artificial intelligence* in the *Search for* text box and then type **IBM**.
   b. Click the down-pointing arrow at the right of the resources list box and then click *MSN Money Stock Quotes*.
   c. Scroll down the Research task pane until the Insert Price button is visible and then click the button.
   d. Press the Enter key twice.
   e. Select *IBM* in the *Search for* text box, type **MSFT** and then press Enter.
   f. Click the Insert Price button.
   g. Press the Enter key twice.

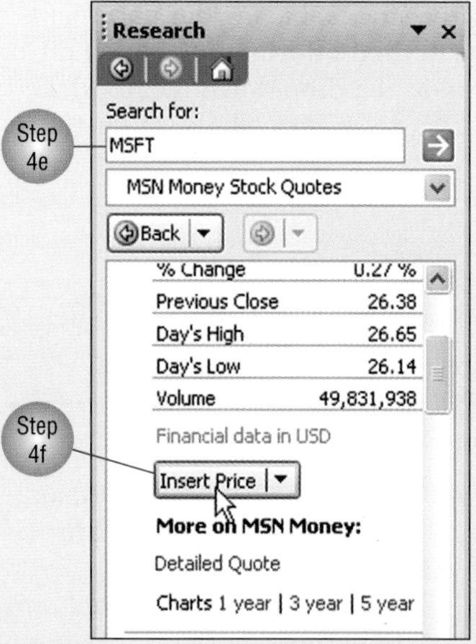

5. Search for a company profile and insert the profile in your document by completing the following steps:
   a. Click the down-pointing arrow at the right of the resources list box and then click *Gale Company Profiles*.

b. Click the View Complete Profile hyperlink that displays below the first Microsoft company profile. (This displays the company profile information in your Web browser.)
c. Select the company profile information that displays in the Web browser window.
d. Click Edit and then Copy.
e. Click the button on the Taskbar representing your Word document.
f. Position the insertion point a double space below the Microsoft stock price.
g. Click Edit and then Paste.
h. Close the Research task pane.
i. Save the document and name it **swc8x19**.
j. Print and then close **swc8x19**.
k. Click the button on the Taskbar representing your browser and then close the browser.

6. Open **WordReport01**.
7. Search for information on specific words by completing the following steps:
   a. Position the mouse pointer on the word *minicomputer* that displays in the third sentence of the first paragraph, hold down the Alt key, and then click the left mouse button.
   b. Click the down-pointing arrow to the right of the references list box and then click *All Reference Books* at the drop-down list. (This displays the Research task pane with information and resources available on minicomputers.)
   c. If the task pane contains any hyperlinks, click a hyperlink that interests you, read the information in your Web browser, and then close the browser.
   d. Select the words *graphics software programs* that display in the third sentence of the first paragraph of the document.
   e. Position the mouse pointer on the selected text, hold down the Alt key, and then click the left mouse button.
   f. If the task pane contains any hyperlinks, click a hyperlink that interests you, read the information in your Web browser, and then close the browser.
   g. Close the Research task pane.
8. Close **WordReport01**.

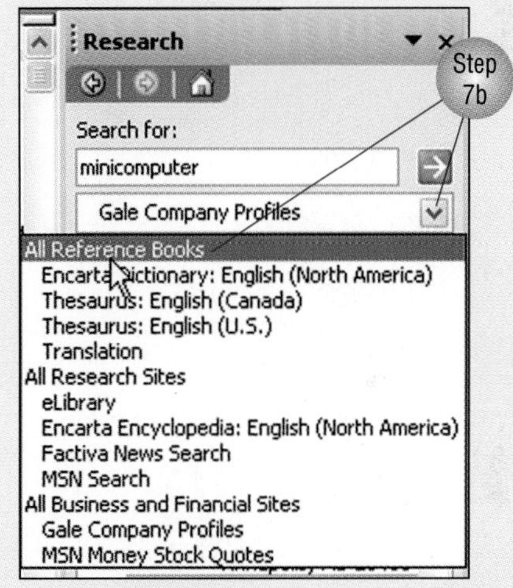

Translating Text

Translate Text
1. Click Research button.
2. Type word in *Search for* text box.
3. Click down-pointing arrow at right of resource list box.
4. Click desired language.

The Research task pane includes a translator for translating words from one language into another. This feature must be installed before it can be used. To translate a word, type the word in the *Search for* text box. Click the down-pointing arrow at the right of the resources list box and then click *Translation*. In the translation list box, specify the languages you are translating to and from. For example, to translate *family* from English to Spanish, type **family** in the *Search for* text box. Click the down-pointing arrow at the right of the resources list box and then click *Translation*. Click the down-pointing arrow at the right of the *To* list box in the *Translation* section and then click *Spanish (Spain-Modern Sort)* at the drop-down list. The translation displays in the task pane as shown in Figure 8.18.

FIGURE 8.18 **Research Task Pane with Translation**

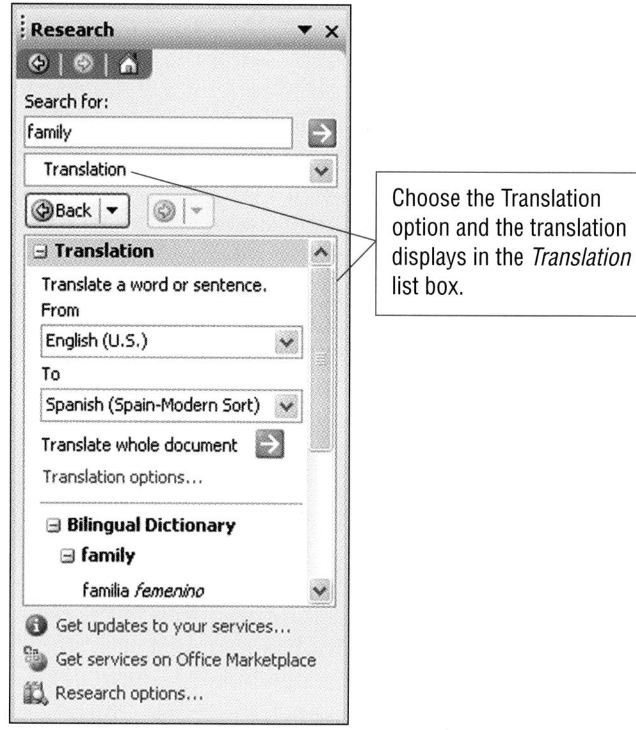

exercise 20

TRANSLATING WORDS

1. At a clear document screen, use the translation feature to translate *keyboard* from English to Spanish and English to French by completing the following steps:
   a. Click the Research button on the Standard toolbar.
   b. Click in the *Search for* text box and then type **keyboard**.
   c. Click the down-pointing arrow at the right of the resource list box and then click *Translation* at the drop-down list.
   d. Make sure that *English (U.S.)* displays in the *From* option box. (If it does not, click the down-pointing arrow at the right of the *From* option and then click *English (U.S.)* at the drop-down list.)
   e. Click the down-pointing arrow to the right of the *To* option and then click *Spanish (Spain-Modern Sort)* at the drop-down list.

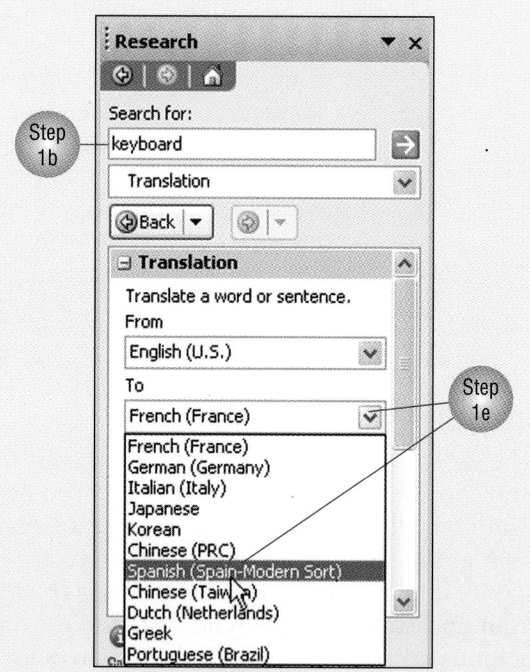

f. Click the down-pointing arrow to the right of the *To* option and then click *French (France)* at the drop-down list.

2. Use the translation feature to translate *mouse* from English to French.
3. Use the translation feature to translate *monitor* from English to Spanish.
4. Use the translation feature to translate *printer* from English to another language of your choosing (other than Spanish or French).
5. Close the Research task pane.
6. Close the document without saving it.

Sending and Routing Documents

In a corporate or business setting, you may work on a project with others in a group. In a situation where a number of people are working on individual documents that will be combined into a larger document, sending and routing documents can be very helpful. In Word, you can send a document to a project member in an Outlook e-mail message or route a document to several project members, one after the other.

To complete exercises in this section, you will need to have Outlook available on your system. System configurations can be quite varied. You may find that your screen does not exactly match what you see in figures in this section. Steps in exercises may need to be modified to accommodate your system. Before completing exercises in this section, please check with your instructor for any modifications or changes to information and exercises.

Sending a Document in an E-Mail

You can send a document in an e-mail to others for review, as an attachment to the e-mail, or as the body of the e-mail message. To send a document as an e-mail message for review, click File, point to Send To, and then click Mail Recipient (for Review). To send a document as an e-mail attachment, click File, point to Send To, and then click Mail Recipient (as Attachment). (To send a document as an e-mail attachment, you must be using Microsoft Outlook, Microsoft Outlook Express, Microsoft Exchange, or an e-mail program compatible with the Messaging Application Programming Interface (MAPI).) To send a document as the body of an e-mail message, click the E-mail button on the Standard toolbar or click File, point to Send to, and then click Mail Recipient. (You must be using Outlook 2003 to complete this procedure.)

Send Document as E-Mail
1. Click E-mail button.
2. Fill in recipient information.
3. Click Send a Copy button.

To send a document as the body of an e-mail message, click the E-mail button on the Standard toolbar and the e-mail header displays below the Formatting toolbar, as shown in Figure 8.19. When the e-mail header displays, Outlook is automatically opened. Depending on how Outlook has been configured, you may need to enter your user name and password to connect to the e-mail server.

FIGURE

8.19 E-Mail Header

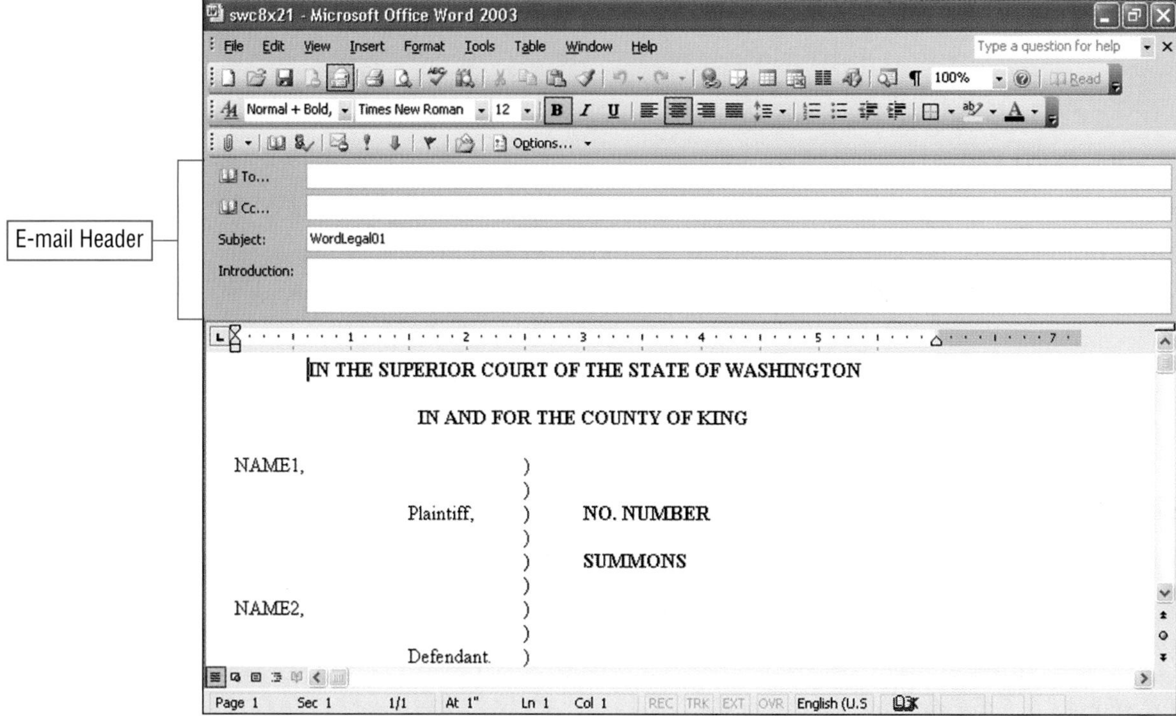

At the e-mail header, fill in the recipient information and then click the Send a Copy button. Word sends a copy of the document to the recipient and closes the e-mail header. The original document remains open for editing. When the document is saved, the e-mail information is saved with the document.

In the *To* text box in the e-mail header, type the e-mail address of the person to receive the document. If the e-mail name and address have been established in an address folder, click the book icon that displays immediately before *To* and the Select Names dialog box displays. At this dialog box, select the name to receive the document in the list box and then click the *To* button. This inserts the name in the *Message Recipients* list box. Click OK to close the dialog box.

In the exercises in this chapter, you will send the e-mail to your instructor. If your system is networked and your computer is not part of an intranet system, skip the step instructing you to click the Send a Copy button.

exercise 21

CREATING AND PRINTING AN OUTLOOK E-MAIL MESSAGE

(Note: Before completing this exercise, check to see if you can send e-mail messages. If you cannot, consider completing all of the steps in the exercise except Step 3d.)

1. Open **WordLegal01**.
2. Save the document with Save As and name it **swc8x21**.
3. Create the **swc8x21** document as an Outlook e-mail by completing the following steps:
   a. Click the E-mail button on the Standard toolbar. If necessary, type your user name and password to log on to the mail server.
   b. At the e-mail header, type your instructor's name in the *To* text box. (Depending on how the system is configured, you may need to type your instructor's e-mail address.)
   c. Click the Importance: High button.
   d. Click the Send a Copy button.
   e. If necessary, click the E-mail button on the Standard toolbar to turn off the display of the e-mail header.
4. Save and then close **swc8x21**.

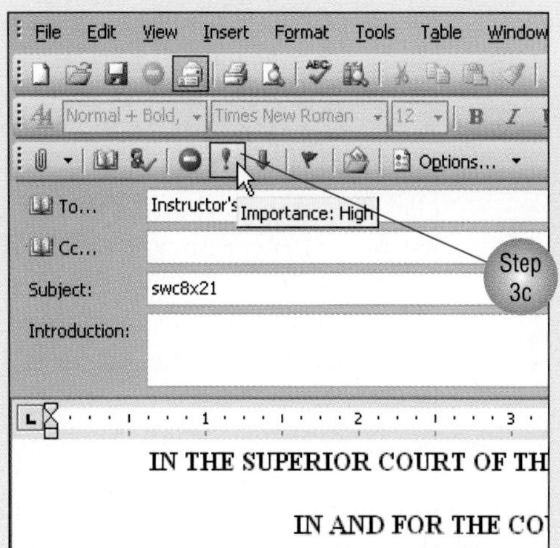

Routing a Document

Routing a document differs from sending a document in that the first recipient receives the document, makes comments or changes, and then it is sent to the next person on the list. In this way, one document is edited by several people rather than several people editing versions of the same document. To route a document, open the document, click File, point to Send To, and then click Routing Recipient. Click Yes, if a Microsoft Outlook message box displays warning you that a program is trying to access e-mail addresses you have stored in Outlook. This displays the Routing Slip dialog box. At the Routing Slip dialog box, click the Address button and the Address Book dialog box displays.

Route Document
1. Click File, Send To, Routing Recipient.
2. Click Address button.
3. Double-click desired names.
4. Click OK.
5. Click Route button.

At the Address Book dialog box, double-click the name of each recipient in the order they are to receive the document. Double-clicking a name inserts the name in the *To* list box that displays at the bottom of the dialog box. When all names are displayed in the *To* list box, click OK. At the Routing Slip dialog box, make sure the names are displayed in the proper order. (If not, click one of the Move buttons to move the names into the proper order.) Type a message in the *Message* text box. Make sure *One after another* is selected in the *Route to recipients* section, and then click the Route button that displays at the top right side of the dialog box.

ROUTING A DOCUMENT

1. Open **swc8x21**.
2. Route the document by completing the following steps:
   a. Click File, point to Send To, and then click Routing Recipient. (Click Yes if a Microsoft Outlook message box displays warning you that a program is trying to access e-mail addresses you have stored in Outlook.)
   b. At the Routing Slip dialog box, click the Address button.
   c. At the Address Book dialog box, double-click any names that display in the *Name* list box. (If necessary, check with your instructor for the list of recipients to whom you should route this document.)
   d. Click OK to close the Address Book dialog box.
   e. At the Routing Slip dialog box, click the Route button to route the document to the first recipient. (Click Yes if a Microsoft Outlook message box displays warning you that a program is trying to automatically send e-mail on your behalf. Depending on your system configuration, you may not be able to send this e-mail. If that is the case, click the Cancel button instead of the Route button.)
3. Close **swc8x21**.

Routing Slip

From: Unknown

To:

Move

Address...

Remove

Subject:

Step 2b

CHAPTER summary

- Create organizational charts and other types of diagrams with options at the Diagram Gallery dialog box.
- If you choose an organizational chart option at the Diagram Gallery dialog box, the Organization Chart toolbar displays. Use buttons on this toolbar to customize the organizational chart. If you choose a diagram, the Diagram toolbar displays with options for customizing the diagram.
- You can insert clip art images, photographs, movie images, and/or sound clips in a document. Do this with options at the Clip Art task pane.
- Search for specific images and/or pictures by typing the specific topic in the *Search for* text box and then clicking the Go button.
- You can narrow the search for images to specific locations with the *Search in* and the *Results should be* options at the Clip Art task pane.
- Size an image using the sizing handles that display around a selected image.

- To move an image, choose a text wrapping style (this changes the black sizing handles to white sizing handles), and then drag the image to the desired position.
- Customize images with buttons on the Picture toolbar. This toolbar generally displays when an image is selected. You can also customize images with options at the Format Picture dialog box.
- With buttons on the Drawing toolbar, you can draw a variety of objects such as shapes, autoshapes, lines, and text boxes. When you click a button on the Drawing toolbar to draw an object, Word changes to the Print Layout and inserts a drawing canvas in the screen. Draw objects in this canvas or delete the canvas and draw directly in the document.
- Customize objects with buttons on the Drawing toolbar.
- A Word document is based on the Normal template document and the Normal style is applied to text by default. Other styles are available in a document based on the Normal template document as well as other Word templates.
- Use options from the Style button on the Formatting toolbar to apply a style to a paragraph of text or selected text.
- You can also apply styles to text in a document with options in the Styles and Formatting task pane. Display this task pane by clicking the Styles and Formatting button on the Formatting toolbar.
- Display the entire list of styles provided by Word by clicking the down-pointing arrow to the right of the *Show* option box (in the Styles and Formatting task pane) and then clicking *All styles* at the drop-down list.
- Paragraph styles arc followed by the ¶ symbol and character styles are followed by the **a** symbol.
- Clear formatting applied to text by applying the Clear Formatting style or by clicking Edit, pointing to Clear, and then clicking Format.
- Use the Style Gallery dialog box to apply styles from other templates to text in the current document.
- Use the Outline view to format headings in a document and assign particular heading levels to text.
- Headings and text formatted in the Outline view are identified by outline symbols that display at the left side of the screen.
- The Outlining toolbar displays below the Formatting toolbar in Outline view. Use buttons on this toolbar to promote and demote headings, move headings up or down, expand or collapse the outline, or show specific headings in an outline.
- You can save a Word document as a Web page. When you save a document as a Web page, Word automatically changes to the Web Layout view. This view displays the page as it will appear when published to the Web or an intranet.
- Preview a Web page document by clicking File and then Web Page Preview.
- You can insert a hyperlink that connects to a Web site address or insert a hyperlink that connects to another Word document.
- Edit a hyperlink by right-clicking the hyperlink and then clicking Edit Hyperlink at the shortcut menu. At the Edit Hyperlink dialog box, make the desired changes, and then close the dialog box.
- Use options at the Research task pane to search for and request specific information from online sources and to translate words from a variety of languages.
- Send a document in an Outlook e-mail for others to review, as an attachment to an e-mail, or as the body of the e-mail message.

- Click the E-mail button on the Standard toolbar to display the E-mail header. The E-mail header contains buttons you can use to customize the e-mail message.
- When a document is routed, one document is edited by several people rather than several people editing versions of the same document.

FEATURES summary

FEATURE	BUTTON	MENU	KEYBOARD
Diagram Gallery dialog box		Insert, Diagram	
Clip Art task pane		Insert, Picture, Clip Art	
Format Picture dialog box			
Drawing toolbar		View, Toolbars, Drawing	
Styles and Formatting task pane		Format, Styles and Formatting	
Styles Gallery dialog box		Format, Theme, Style Gallery button	
Outline view		View, Outline	
Save as Web page		File, Save as Web Page	
Web Layout view		View, Web Layout	
Insert Hyperlink dialog box		Insert, Hyperlink	Ctrl + K
Research task pane		Tools, Research	Alt + click
E-mail header		File, Send To, Mail Recipient	
Routing Slip dialog box		File, Send To, Routing Recipient	

CONCEPTS check

Completion: On a blank sheet of paper, indicate the correct term, command, or number for each description.

1. Click the Insert Diagram or Organization Chart button on this toolbar to display the Diagram Gallery dialog box.
2. If you click an organizational chart option at the Diagram Gallery dialog box, this toolbar displays.
3. Click this button on the Drawing toolbar to display the Clip Art task pane.

4. Display the Format Picture dialog box by clicking this button on the Picture toolbar.
5. Options at the Format Picture dialog box with this tab selected include wrapping style and horizontal alignment.
6. A Word document, by default, is based on this template document.
7. Display the Styles and Formatting task pane by clicking the Styles and Formatting button on this toolbar.
8. Use options from this dialog box to apply styles from other templates.
9. Use this view to format headings in a document and assign particular heading levels to text.
10. Click this button on the Outlining toolbar to move the selected heading up one level.
11. To collapse an outline, click the down arrow at the right side of this button on the Outlining toolbar, and then click the desired heading level.
12. This view displays a page as it will appear when published to the Web or an intranet.
13. To preview a Web page document in your default Web browser, click File and then this.
14. Use options at this task pane to search for and request specific information from online sources.
15. Click this button on the Standard toolbar to display the E-mail header.
16. Click File, point to Send To, and then click Routing Recipient and this dialog box displays.

SKILLS check

Assessment 1

1. At a clear document screen, type the title bolded and centered as shown in Figure 8.20. Set the title in 18-point Arial bold.
2. Press the Enter key twice and then create the organizational chart with the following specifications:
   a. Choose the first option in the top row at the Diagram Gallery dialog box.
   b. Delete the third box at the right side of the chart.
   c. Add a subordinate box below the box at the left by clicking the Insert Shape button on the Organization Chart toolbar and then clicking Subordinate at the drop-down list.
   d. Add a subordinate box below the box at the right. (You should now have the same boxes as those shown in Figure 8.20.)
   e. Apply the Thick Outline autoformat to the chart.
   f. Click in the top box and then type **Director**. (Make sure the text is centered. If not, click the Center button on the Formatting toolbar.)
   g. Type the text centered in the remaining boxes as shown in Figure 8.20.
   h. Select the text *Director* in the top box and then change the font to 24-point Arial bold in green. (Make these changes at the Font dialog box.)
   i. Select *Trainer* in one of the boxes and then press F4. (Pressing F4 repeats the last command, which was applying the font formatting.)
   j. Apply the font formatting to the remaining text in the other boxes.
3. Save the document and name it **swc8sc01**.
4. Print and then close **swc8sc01**.

FIGURE 8.20 ***Assessment 1***

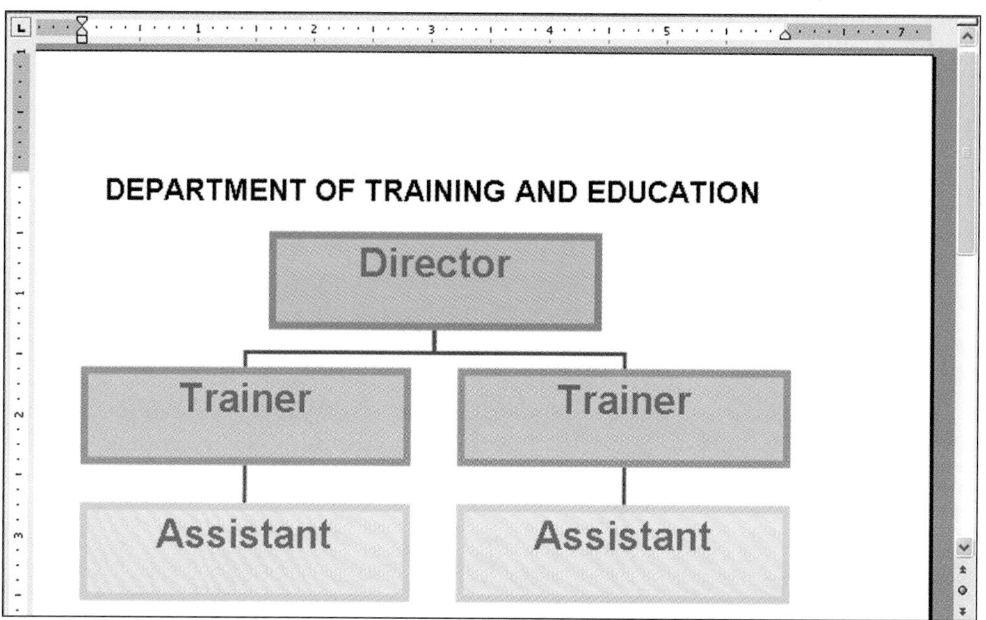

Assessment 2

1. At a clear document screen, create the diagram shown in Figure 8.21 with the following specifications:
   a. Choose the last option from the left in the top row at the Diagram Gallery dialog box (Radial Diagram).
   b. Apply the Primary Colors autoformat to the diagram.
   c. Click in the top box, press the Enter key twice, and then type **Fabrication**. Insert text in the other circles following the same steps. (Press the Enter key only once for the two bottom circles.)
   d. Select the text *Fabrication* in the top circle and then change the font to 10-point Arial bold.
   e. Change the font for the text in the remaining circles to 10-point Arial bold. ***(Hint: Use the Repeat command, F4.)***
2. Save the document and name it **swc8sc02**.
3. Print and then close **swc8sc02**.

FIGURE 8.21 **Assessment 2**

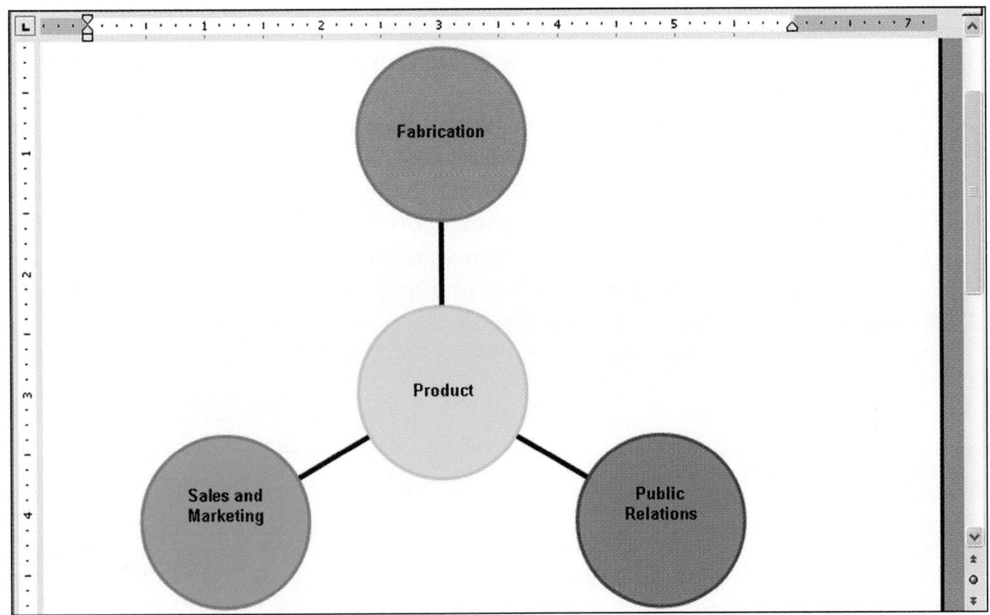

Assessment 3

1. At a clear document screen, display the Clip Art task pane.
2. Search for clip art images related to *people*.
3. Insert into the document a clip art image of your choosing related to people.
4. Close the Clip Art task pane.
5. Increase the size of the clip art image until it is approximately double the original size.
6. Change the text wrapping to Through for the image.
7. Change to the Print Layout view.
8. Change the Zoom to Whole Page.
9. Move the image so it is centered horizontally and vertically on the page.
10. Insert a double-line border of your choosing around the image.
11. Change the Zoom back to 100%.
12. Save the document and name it **swc8sc03**.
13. Print and then close **swc8sc03**.

Assessment 4

1. At a clear document screen, create a letterhead document that contains the following information:

   CONTINENTAL TRAVEL
   1005 Century Plaza
   St. Louis, MO 63045
   (612) 555-4040
   www.emcp.net/ctravel
2. Set the above text in a decorative typeface and type size of your choosing.
3. Insert a clip art image related to travel and position it in an appealing location toward the top of the page (near the text and/or balanced with the text).
4. Save the document and name it **swc8sc04**.
5. Print and then close **swc8sc04**.

Assessment 5

1. At a clear document screen, create the object shown in Figure 8.22 with the following specifications:
    a. Use the Heart autoshape (located in the Basic Shapes side menu).
    b. Draw a heart that is approximately 5 inches wide and 4 inches tall.
    c. Fill the heart with red fill.
    d. Draw a text box inside the heart shape and then type the text center aligned shown in Figure 8.22. Set the text *St. Valentine's Day Sale* in 18-point Lucida Calligraphy bold (or a similar decorative typeface), set the text *Monday, February 14* in 16-point Lucida Calligraphy bold, and set the text *9:00 a.m. – 10:30 p.m.* in 14-point Lucida Calligraphy bold. Change the font color to white for all of the text.
    e. Remove the line around the text box and add red fill to the text box.
2. Save the document and name it **swc8sc05**.
3. Print and then close **swc8sc05**.

FIGURE 8.22 ***Assessment 5***

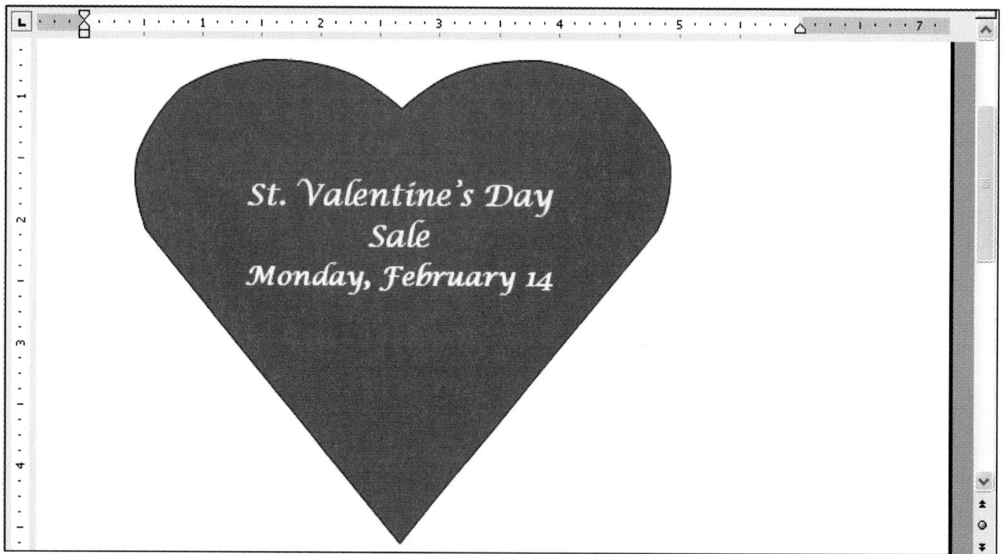

Assessment 6

1. Open **WordContract01**.
2. Save the document with Save As and name it **swc8sc06**.
3. Format the document at the Style Gallery with the Contemporary Report template.
4. Save, print, and then close **swc8sc06**.

Assessment 7

1. Open **WordLetter03**.
2. Save the document with Save As and name it **swc8sc07**.
3. Display the Style Gallery, select the Contemporary Letter template, and then close the Style Gallery.

4. Turn on the display of the Styles and Formatting task pane.
5. Make sure the insertion point is positioned at the beginning of the document and then type **Langley, Koch & Townsend**.
6. Apply the Company Name paragraph style to the text *Langley, Koch & Townsend* that you just typed and then click the Center button on the Formatting toolbar.
7. Select the text *Re: Callahan v. Rosario* and then apply the EMPHASIS character style.
8. Save, print, and then close **swc8sc07**.

Assessment 8

1. Open **WordReport04**.
2. Save the document with Save As and name it **swc8sc08**.
3. Change to the Outline view and then promote or demote the following titles and headings:

COMPUTER INPUT DEVICES	=	Heading 1
Keyboard	=	Heading 2
Mouse	=	Heading 2
Trackball	=	Heading 2
Touch Pad and Touch Screen	=	Heading 2
COMPUTER OUTPUT DEVICES	=	Heading 1
Monitor	=	Heading 2
Printer	=	Heading 2

4. Collapse the outline so only the two heading levels display.
5. Move the *COMPUTER INPUT DEVICES* title and the headings below it after the *COMPUTER OUTPUT DEVICES* title and the headings below it.
6. Move the heading *Trackball* below the heading *Touch Pad and Touch Screen*.
7. Save, print, and then close **swc8sc08**.

Assessment 9

1. Open the **ApexHomePage** document.
2. Save the document as a Web page with the name **ApexWebPage** and change the title to *Low-cost Computer Software*.
3. Make the following formatting changes to the document:
   a. Insert a clip art image related to computers.
   b. Move and size the image. (You determine the location of the image in the document.)
   c. Consider changing the font, font color, and alignment of the text.
   d. Preview the document in the default Web browser. After viewing the document, close the Web browser.
4. Create the following hyperlinks:
   a. Select *Apple Computer* and then create a hyperlink to www.apple.com.
   b. Select *Blizzard Entertainment* and then create a hyperlink to www.blizzard.com.
   c. Select *Microsoft Corporation* and then create a hyperlink to www.microsoft.com.
5. If you are connected to the Internet, click each hyperlink you created to view the company Web page.
6. Save, print, and then close **ApexWebPage**.

CHAPTER challenge

As president of the Student Government Association at your campus, you have decided that showing and explaining the structure of your campus would be very helpful for new members. Create an organizational chart to be used as a tool for explaining the structure of your college. The organizational chart should begin with college president or chancellor at the top and proceed down through your professor. Apply an AutoFormat to the organizational chart and save the chart.

After creating the organizational chart, you decide that it might be beneficial to have the option of quickly accessing the college's Web page from within the file. Insert a title at the top of the organizational chart. Use the Help feature to learn about changing the default for following or opening hyperlinks. Create a hyperlink so that by clicking (not by pressing the CTRL key while clicking the hyperlink) the title, your college's Web page displays. Save the organizational chart again and then print it.

You will be conducting an orientation for the new members of the Student Government Association. Part of the orientation will include a short PowerPoint presentation describing the history of the association and aspects of campus life. You will include the organizational chart that you created in the first two parts of the Chapter Challenge. Begin the PowerPoint presentation by creating a title slide. On slide 2, insert the organizational chart as an object. Save the PowerPoint presentation. Print the two slides so that they appear on only one page.

Workplace Ready

Enhancing and Customizing Documents

ASSESSING proficiencies

In this unit, you have learned to manage files, print envelopes and labels, create and edit headers and footers, find and replace text, create documents using templates and wizards, prepare outlines, create and edit tables, and enhance documents with special features such as charts, diagrams, images, and styles.

Assessment 1

1. At a clear document screen, type the title **KEY LIFE HEALTH PLAN** bolded and centered.
2. Press Enter twice and then type the subtitle **Plan Information** bolded and centered.
3. Press Enter three times, turn off bold, and return the paragraph alignment to left.
4. Save the document and name it **swu2pa01**.
5. With **swu2pa01** still open, open the document named **KeyLifeHealthPlan**. (This document is located on your disk.)
6. With **KeyLifeHealthPlan** the active document, select the second heading *HOW THE PLAN WORKS* and the three paragraphs of text below this heading, and then copy and paste it at the end of the **swu2pa01** document.
7. Make **KeyLifeHealthPlan** the active document. Select the first heading *PLAN HIGHLIGHTS* and the six paragraphs of text below this heading and then copy and paste the selected text at the end of the **swu2pa01** document.
8. Make **KeyLifeHealthPlan** the active document. Select the fourth heading *PROVIDER NETWORK* and the two paragraphs of text below this heading and then copy and paste it to the end of the **swu2pa01**.
9. Make **KeyLifeHealthPlan** the active document. Select the third heading *QUALITY ASSESSMENT* and the six paragraphs of text below this heading (two paragraphs and four bulleted paragraphs) and then copy and paste it at the end of the **swu2pa01** document.
10. Close **KeyLifeHealthPlan**. (If you are asked if you want to save the changes, click No.)
11. Make the following changes to **swu2pa01**:
    a. Change the top margin to 1.5 inches and the left and right margins to 1 inch.
    b. Set the entire document in 12-point Century (or a similar serif typeface).
    c. Set the title and subtitle in 16-point Arial bold.

d. Set the following headings in 14-point Arial bold: ***(Hint: Use Format Painter.)***
   HOW THE PLAN WORKS
   PLAN HIGHLIGHTS
   PROVIDER NETWORK
   QUALITY ASSESSMENT
e. Check the spacing in the document. A double space should display above and below headings (except between the subtitle and the first heading—that should be a triple space) and between paragraphs. If spacing above and below contain any extra blank lines, delete them.
f. Insert a footer in the document that prints *Key Life Health Plan* set in 12-point Century bold (or a similar serif typeface) at the left margin and prints the page number in bold at the right margin. ***(Hint: Drag the right tab alignment marker to the 6.5-inch mark on the Ruler. This moves the page number to the right margin.)***

12. Save, print, and then close **swu2pa01**.

Assessment 2

1. Open **swu2pa01**.
2. Save the document with Save As and name it **swu2pa02**.
3. Delete the footer.
4. Select the entire document and then change line spacing to 1.2. (To do this, display the Paragraph dialog box, type **1.2** in the *At* text box, and then close the dialog box. This should increase the size of the document to three pages. If your document is not three pages in length, consider increasing the line spacing to *1.3*.)
5. Create the header *Key Life Health Plan* that is set in 12-point Century bold and prints at the right margin on every page except the first page. ***(Hint: Drag the right tab alignment marker to the 6.5-inch mark on the Ruler. This moves the header text to the right margin.)***
6. Save, print, and then close **swu2pa02**.

Assessment 3

1. At a clear document screen, create an envelope with the text shown in Figure U2.1.
2. Save the envelope document and name it **swu2pa03**.
3. Print and then close **swu2pa03**.

Mrs. Eileen Hebert
15205 East 42nd Street
Lake Charles, LA 71098

Mr. Earl Robicheaux
1436 North Sheldon Street
Jennings, LA 70542

FIGURE U2.1 • Assessment 3

Assessment 4

1. Create mailing labels with the name and address for Mrs. Eileen Hebert shown in Figure U2.1 using the Avery standard, 5660 – Address label.
2. Save the document and name it **swu2pa04**.
3. Print and then close **swu2pa04**.

Assessment 5

1. Open **WordReport04**.
2. Save the document with Save As and name it **swu2pa05**.
3. Apply the following styles to the specified titles and headings:

COMPUTER INPUT DEVICES	=	Heading 1
Keyboard	=	Heading 2
Mouse	=	Heading 2
Trackball	=	Heading 2
Touch Pad and Touch Screen	=	Heading 2
COMPUTER OUTPUT DEVICES	=	Heading 1
Monitor	=	Heading 2
Printer	=	Heading 2

4. Change the top margin to 1.5 inches.
5. Insert a page break at the beginning of *COMPUTER OUTPUT DEVICES*.
6. Create the footer *Computer Input and Output Devices* that is bolded and prints at the right margin on all odd pages.
7. Create a footer that inserts the file name and path at the left margin on all even pages.
8. Save, print, and then close **swu2pa05**.

Assessment 6

1. Open the document named **WordEditedDoc04**.
2. Merge and compare **WordEditedDoc04** with the document named **WordDocument04**. Save the results in a new document.
3. At the new document, change to the Print Layout view, and then print the document with the marked changes.
4. Accept all of the changes in the document.
5. Save the document and name it **swu2pa06**.
6. Print and then close **swu2pa06**.
7. Close **WordEditedDoc04**.

Assessment 7

1. At a clear document screen, create the table shown in Figure U2.2. Include the lines and shading as shown in the figure.
2. Save the document and name it **swu2pa07**.
3. Print and then close **swu2pa07**.

REINBERG MANUFACTURING		
Technology Development Committee Members		
Name	Department	Extension

FIGURE U2.2 • Assessment 7

Assessment 8

1. At a clear document screen, create a table using the information shown in Figure U2.3 with the following specifications:
   a. Include the title *STRATEGIC INCOME FUND* in the table.
   b. Autofit the contents of the table.
   c. Apply an autoformat of your choosing to the table.
   d. Horizontally and vertically center the table on the page.
2. Save the document and name it **swu2pa08**.
3. Print and then close **swu2pa08**.

STRATEGIC INCOME FUND

Expense	**Class A**	**Class B**
Expenses after 1 year	$156.25	$168.30
Expenses after 3 years	198.30	201.40
Expenses after 5 years	295.55	310.90
Expenses after 10 years	398.50	420.75

FIGURE U2.3 • Assessment 8

Assessment 9

1. At a clear document screen, create the organizational boxes shown in Figure U2.4 with the following specifications:
   a. Choose the first option in the top row at the Diagram Gallery dialog box.
   b. Insert the box below the Vice President Marketing box by clicking the Vice President Marketing box, clicking the down-pointing arrow at the right side of the Insert Shape button, and then clicking Assistant.
   c. Complete steps similar to those in Step 1b to insert the box below the Vice President Production box.
   d. Apply the Beveled Gradient autoformat.

e. Press the Enter key once before typing the text in each box.
f. Set the text inside the boxes in 10-point Arial bold.

2. Save the document and name it **swu2pa09**.
3. Print and then close **swu2pa09**.

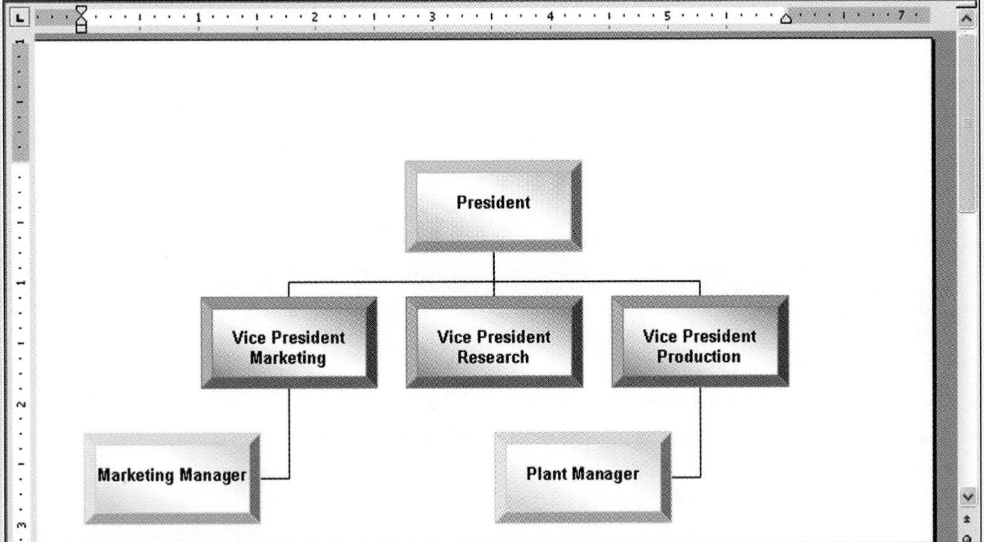

FIGURE U2.4 • Assessment 9

Assessment 10

1. At a clear document screen, create the document shown in Figure U2.5 by completing the following steps:
   a. Change the font to 18-point Arial bold.
   b. Change the paragraph alignment to center.
   c. Type the text shown in Figure U2.5.
   d. Insert the clip art image shown in the figure. (Search for this image by typing **buildings** in the *Search for* text box in the Clip Art task pane. If this clip art image is not available, choose a similar image.)
   e. Change the wrapping style of the clip art image to Square.
   f. Format the clip art image so that the height is 2.3 inches (leave the width measurement that is automatically inserted).
   g. Drag the clip art image to the position shown in Figure U2.5.
2. Save the document and name it **swu2pa10**.
3. Print and then close **swu2pa10**.

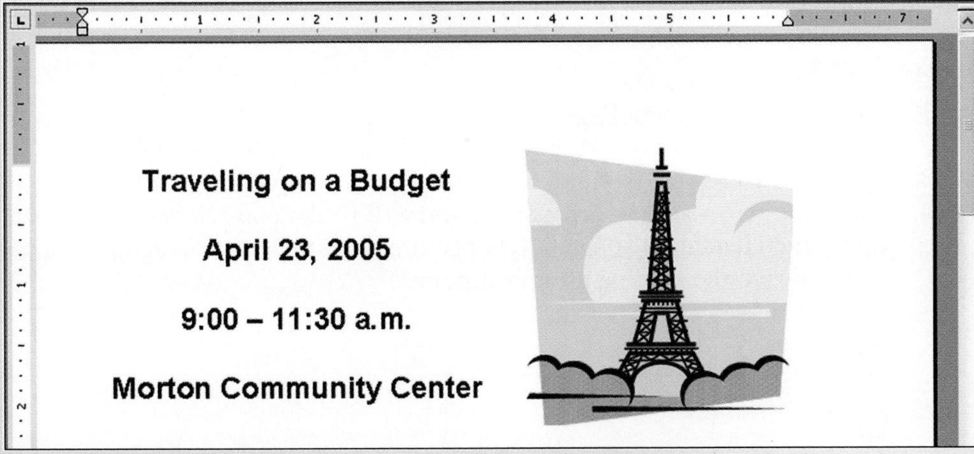

FIGURE U2.5 • Assessment 10

Assessment 11

1. Open **WordDocument08**.
2. Save the document with Save As and name it **swu2pa11**.
3. Insert the title *DESKTOP PUBLISHING* centered and bolded so that it displays at the beginning of the document a double space above the first paragraph of text.
4. Insert a clip art image with the following specifications:
   a. Insert a clip art image related to computers. (Choose an appropriate image related to the text in the document.)
   b. Change the text wrapping for the image to Tight.
   c. Move the image so it is located at the left margin of the first paragraph. Increase and/or decrease the size of the image so it is the same approximate height as the lines of text in the first paragraph.
5. Save, print, and then close **swu2pa11**.

Assessment 12

1. Open **WordTable08**.
2. Save the document with Save As and name it **swu2pa12**.
3. Create a Column chart with the table with the following elements:
   a. Add the title *REVENUE SOURCES* to the chart.
   b. Delete the table.
   c. Increase the size of the chart. (You determine the size. Make sure the chart fits within the margins.)
   d. Move the chart to the middle of the page.
4. Save, print, and then close **swu2pa12**.

Assessment 13

1. Open **WordTable09**.
2. Save the document with Save As and name it **swu2pa13**.
3. Create a Pie chart with the table with the following elements:
   a. Change the chart type to Pie.
   b. Make sure the data is displayed properly in the Pie chart. ***(Hint: You may need to click the By Column button on the Graph Standard toolbar.)***
   c. Add the title *EXPENDITURES* to the chart.
   d. Add percentage data labels to the pieces of the pie in the chart.
   e. Delete the table.
   f. Increase the size of the chart. (You determine the size. Make sure the chart fits within the margins.)
   g. Move the chart to the middle of the page.
4. Save, print, and then close **swu2pa13**.

Assessment 14

1. Open **GoldburgHomePage**.
2. Save the document as a Web page and name it **GoldburgWebPage**.
3. Apply the Heading 1 style to the name *DEVIN M. GOLDBURG*.
4. Select the street address; city, state, and ZIP Code; and telephone number. Apply the Heading 2 style and change the spacing before paragraphs to 3 points (leave the spacing after at 3 points).

5. Apply the Heading 3 style to the following headings:
   Career Objective
   Education
   Work Experience
   Hobbies and Interests
   Relocation
6. Preview the document in Web Page Preview. After viewing the document in the default browser, close the browser.
7. Save, print, and then close **Goldburg Web Page**.

WRITING activities

Activity 1

Use Word's Help feature to learn how to insert a page border in a document. Create a document that explains the steps required to insert a page border. Save the completed document and name it **swu2PageBorder**. Print and then close **swu2PageBorder**. Open **WordNotice02**. Save the document with Save As and name it **swu2act01**. Insert a page border of your choosing in the document. Save, print, and then close **swu2act01**.

Activity 2

Use Word's Help feature to learn about watermarks. Learn how to create text watermarks and picture watermarks. Once you have determined this information, create a document describing the steps required to create a text watermark and the steps required to create a picture watermark. Save the completed document and name it **swu2Watermarks**. Print and then close **swu2Watermarks**. Open **swu2act01** and then save the document with Save As and name it **swu2act02**. Insert a watermark in the document using the image named *pc* that is located in the ClipArt subfolder on the CD that accompanies this textbook. ***(Hint: At the Insert Picture dialog box, navigate to the ClipArt subfolder folder on the CD that accompanies this textbook.)*** Save, print, and then close **swu2act02**.

INTERNET project

Creating a Web Page

Osborne Medical Equipment Corporation sells medical equipment to hospitals and universities throughout the United States and Europe. As an incentive to increase sales in your division, the director of sales has authorized a sales contest with a grand prize of a one-week paid vacation to Cancun, Mexico.

To promote interest in the contest, the sales director has asked you to create a Web page that will be published on your company's intranet. You will use Microsoft Word to create the Web page. The content of the Web page is all about Cancun, Mexico—location, weather, health and safety issues, currency, language, culture and history, activities, tours, shopping, dining, and nightlife.

Conduct a search to gather information about Cancun, Mexico. Plan the layout of the information on your Web page. Include text, graphics, photographs, and a chart created in Microsoft Graph. Also include active hyperlinks to several of the pages you visited on the Web. Utilize other elements such as styles and images to enhance the page. Print a copy of the final product.

JOB study

Developing Recycling Program Communications

The Chief Operating Officer of Harrington Engineering has just approved your draft of the company's new recycling policy (see the file named RecyclingPolicy located in the WordUnit02S folder) with a note that you need to add some statistics on national average costs of recycling, which you can locate on the Internet. You will copyedit the draft and prepare a final copy of the policy along with a memorandum to all employees describing the new guidelines. To support the company's energy resources conservation effort, the policy will be published on the company's Web site and sent via e-mail to all employees; however, hard copies of the new policy will be sent to the Somerset Recycling Program president and to directors of Somerset Chamber of Commerce.

Using the concepts and techniques you learned in this unit, prepare the following documents:

- Recycling policy manual, including a cover page, appropriate headers and footers, and page numbers. Add at least one graphic and one diagram where appropriate. Format the document using Word's Styles feature.
- Memorandum from Susan Gerhardt, Chief Operating Officer of Harrington Engineering to all employees introducing the new recycling program. Copy the "Procedure" section of the recycling policy manual into the memorandum where appropriate. Include a table listing five employees who will act as Recycling Coordinators at Harrington Engineering (make up the names). Add columns for the employees' department names and their telephone extension.
- Letter to the President of the Somerset Recycling Program, William Elizondo, enclosing a copy of the recycling policy manual. Add a notation indicating copies with enclosures to all members of the Somerset Chamber of Commerce.
- Mailing labels (see Figure U2.6).

William Elizondo, President
Somerset Recycling Program
700 West Brighton Road
Somerset, NJ 55123

Paul Schwartz
Somerset Chamber of Commerce
45 Wallace Road
Somerset, NJ 55123

Ashley Crighton
Somerset Chamber of Commerce
45 Wallace Road
Somerset, NJ 55123

Carol Davis
Somerset Chamber of Commerce
45 Wallace Road
Somerset, NJ 55123

Robert Knight
Somerset Chamber of Commerce
45 Wallace Road
Somerset, NJ 55123

FIGURE U2.6 • Mailing Labels

INDEX

SPECIALIST

MICROSOFT® EXCEL

Tracking and analyzing numerical data is a large component of the daily activity in today's workplace. Microsoft Excel 2003 is a popular choice among individuals and companies for organizing, analyzing, and presenting numerical information.

Organizing Information

Numbers are the foundation of every business transaction. Think about all of the various numbers that a person needs to organize for a typical purchase: account numbers, stock numbers, quantities, sale price, cost price, taxes, total due, amount received—just to name a few. Now consider a different scenario in which you want to track the egg production of a chicken farm. You might want to factor in the volume of feed, the number of eggs produced each day by each hen, the total production by day, by week, by month, and so on. These are just two examples of the type of information for which you could find a use for Excel.

Spreadsheet software organizes data in columns and rows—an electronic version of an accountant's ledger—only with a lot more power and versatility. In Microsoft Excel, information is organized by creating column and row headings called

SPECIALIST

Making EXCEL Work for YOU!

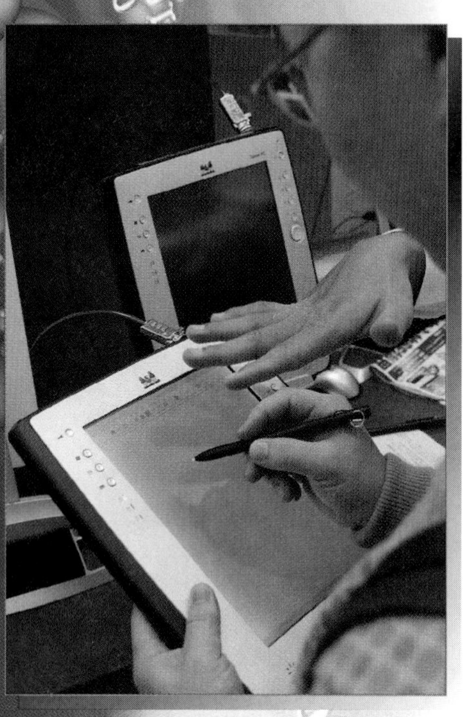

labels. Numbers, called ***values,*** are entered below and beside the headings and then formulas are created to perform calculations. The completed document is referred to as a ***worksheet.***

The potential uses for an application like Excel are only limited by your imagination—any type of document that can be set up in the column/row format is a candidate for an Excel worksheet.

Not sure how to set up the information you want to track? Go to Office Online and browse the templates at the Microsoft Web site. Several templates are available that already contain labels and formulas, so all you have to do is fill in the data. You can preview a template before downloading it to make sure it will meet your needs. The templates site is continually updated, so keep checking for new additions.

Oak Springs Animal Clinic

INVOICE RECORDS: Small Animals

Invoice #	Owner's Name	Pet Name	Classification	Service Rendered	Vet	Amount	Paid
55017	Heckman, Ellen	Carl	Dog	Office Call/Examination	Frobose	$ 20.00	Yes
55017	Heckman, Ellen	Carl	Dog	Rabies Shot	Frobose	$ 20.00	Yes
55018	Wegman, Marcy	Raven	Dog	Call/Examination	Martin	$ 20.00	Yes
55018	Wegman, Marcy	Raven	Dog		Martin	$ 20.00	Yes
55019	Wegman, Marcy	Homer	Cat			$ 20.00	Yes
55019	Wegman, Marcy	Homer	Cat				Yes
55019	Wegman, Marcy						
55020	Fox, Alan						
55020							

Personal Budget

Balance Sheet
The Waterfront Bistro
May 26, 2005

	2004	2005
	15,000.00	17,500.00
	27,000.00	29,847.00
	55,250.00	57,843.00
	12,675.00	11,349.00
	$ 109,925.00	$ 116,539.00

Assets
Current Assets:
Total Assets

EQUIPMENT USAGE REPORT												
Hours	Jan	Feb	Mar	Apr	May	Jun	Jul	Aug	Sep	Oct	Nov	Dec
Total Hours Available	2,300	2,430	2,530	2,400	2,440	2,240	2,520	2,520	2,390	2,540	2,310	2,210
Avoidable Delays	19	12	16	20	14	15	9	8	12	7	12	5
Unavoidable Delays	9	8	6	12	9	10	10	13	8	9	5	7
Repairs	5	7	12	9	10	6	7	8	10	13	9	8
Servicing	6	13	7	6	4	5	8	3	12	6	11	12
Unassigned	128	95	85	135	95	75	145	120	124	112	95	120
In Use	2,040	2,105	2,320	2,180	2,050	1,995	2,320	2,250	2,190	1,945	2,005	1,830

Analyzing Information

The true power of Excel lies in its ability to analyze information at the click of a mouse. Once a worksheet has been created you can play the *what-if* game. For example, suppose you have used Excel to set up a personal budget. You can use its calculating and projecting features to answer questions: What if I receive an increase in wages? What if I spend less on groceries? What if I put more money down on the house I want to buy? Whenever you change a value in a worksheet, Excel automatically recalculates other values that are

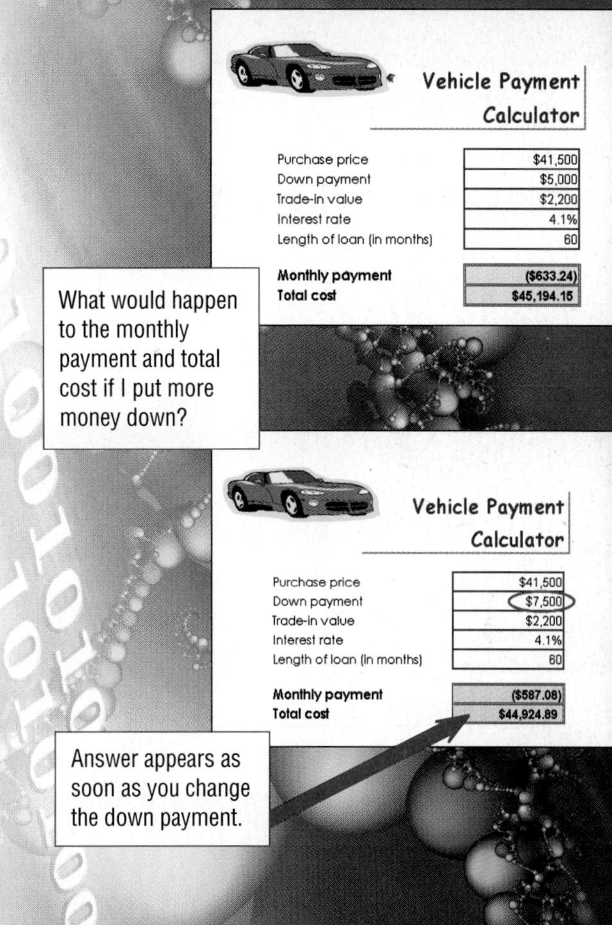

dependent on the number you changed. In an instant you have your answer.

Excel includes several predefined formulas, called ***functions*** that make the task of constructing complex worksheets easier to manage. So math is not your favorite subject? Not a problem with Excel's Insert Function dialog box, which helps you build a formula by prompting you with explanations for each parameter.

Use the Sort and Filter features in Excel to help you analyze the data in various arrangements. With the click of a button on the toolbar you can rearrange the order of the worksheet to sort in ascending or descending order by a single column or by multiple columns. Use the Filter by Selection or Filter by Form commands to reduce the data you are viewing by temporarily hiding rows that do not meet your criteria. For

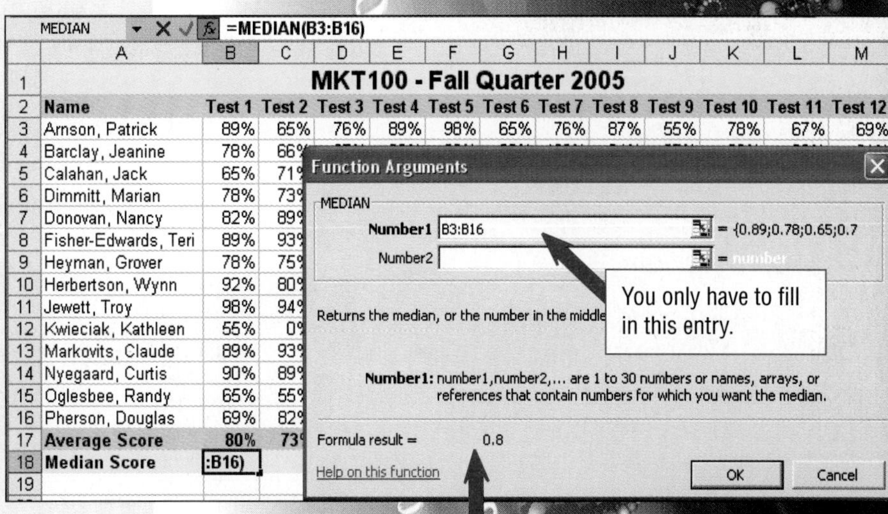

The dialog box provides assistance with building complex formulae by providing explanations of each requirement. As you fill in the dialog box, Excel creates the corresponding formula including all required syntax.

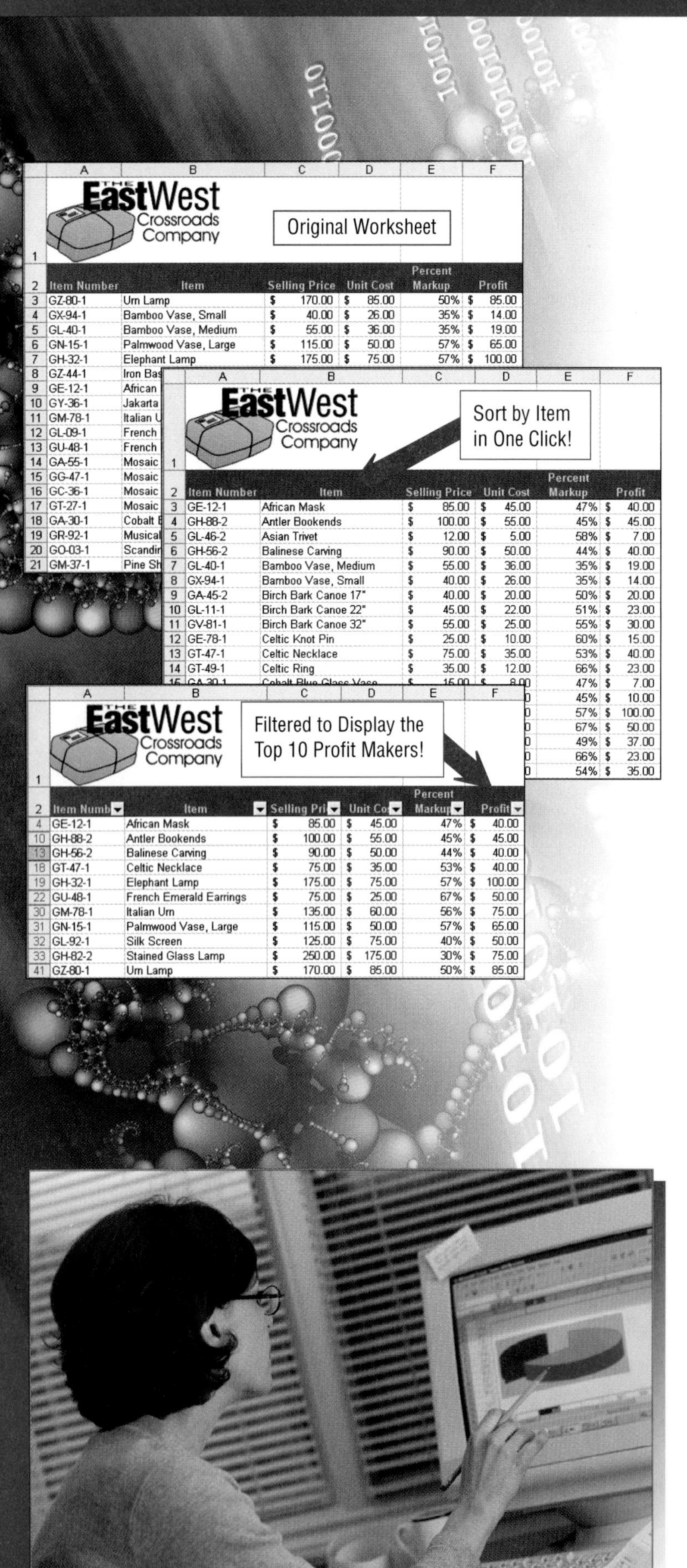

example, in a workplace scenario, you might want to view only the top ten sales amounts to identify the star performers in your organization.

Presenting Information

With information already structured in columns and rows, the task of interpreting the results is already simplified. Add some color and other rich text enhancements to draw the reader's attention to important titles, totals, or other results and you have just made the process even easier! Add clip art, photographs, or other media to a worksheet using the ClipArt task pane.

It is said that a picture is worth a thousand words. Why not use Excel's charting capabilities to turn those numbers into a chart—a pictorial representation that enables a reader to more easily distinguish the impact of the differences between columns of numbers? Excel can render both two-dimensional and three-dimensional charts in several chart types, a sampling of which are: column, bar, line, pie, area, radar, doughnut, and scatter.

Knowing how to use Excel is a prerequisite for many jobs in our information-driven economy. Creating worksheets in Microsoft Excel 2003 is as simple as one, two, three:

1. Set up the column and row headings.
2. Enter the data.
3. Create the formulas.

Within a short period of time, you will *excel* at creating, editing, and formatting worksheets!

SPECIALIST

MICROSOFT®

EXCEL

UNIT 1: Preparing and Formatting a Worksheet

- Preparing an Excel Worksheet
- Formatting an Excel Worksheet
- Inserting Formulas in a Worksheet
- Enhancing a Worksheet

BENCHMARK MICROSOFT® EXCEL 2003

MICROSOFT OFFICE SPECIALIST SKILLS—UNIT 1

Reference No.	Skill	Pages
XL03S-1	**Creating Data and Content**	
XL03S-1-1	Enter and Edit Cell Contents	
	Enter data (text and symbols) in a cell	S10-S20
	Automatically enter data (AutoComplete, AutoCorrect, AutoFill)	S17-S20
	Edit data in a cell	S15-S17
	Enter and edit numbers in cells	S42-S47
	Clear data in cells	S54-S55
XL03S-2	**Analyzing Data**	
XL03S-2-1	Filter lists using AutoFilter	S127-S129
XL03S-2-2	Sort lists	S122-S126
XL03S-2-3	Insert and modify formulas	
	Use AutoSum button to insert formula	S69-S71
	Write formulas with mathematical operators and edit formulas	S71-S76
	Insert formulas with the Insert Function button and edit formulas	S76-S89
	Use absolute and mixed cell references in formulas	S89-S91
XL03S-3	**Formatting Data and Content**	
XL03S-3-1	Apply and modify cell formats	
	Format cells with AutoFormat	S23-S25
	Apply formatting with buttons on the Formatting toolbar	S35-S37
	Format data in cells	S42-S51
	Apply borders and shading to cells	S55-S61
XL03S-3-3	Modify row and column formats	
	Change column width and row heights	S37-S42
	Insert rows and columns	S51-S54
	Align, indent, and rotate data in cells	S47-S49
	Hide and unhide columns and rows	S111-S113
XL03S-5	**Managing Workbooks**	
XL03S-5-2	Insert, delete, and move cells	
	Insert and delete cells, rows, and columns	S51-S55
XL03S-5-5	Preview data in other views	
	Preview a worksheet	S33-S34
	Display worksheet in Page Break view	S106-S108
XL03S-5-7	Setup pages for printing	
	Print specific area of a worksheet	S113-S114
	Change worksheet orientation	S98-S101
	Insert headers and footers in a worksheet	S99-S103
	Change worksheet margins	S103-S105
	Center a worksheet horizontally and vertically	S105-S106
	Print column and row titles on multiple pages	S108-S110
	Print gridlines and row and column headings	S110-S111
XL03S-5-8	Print data	
	Print a workbook	S12
	Set up, customize, and print worksheets and selected data	S97-S116

CHAPTER 1

PREPARING AN EXCEL WORKSHEET

PERFORMANCE OBJECTIVES

Upon successful completion of Chapter 1, you will be able to:

- **Identify the various elements of an Excel worksheet**
- **Create, save, and print a worksheet**
- **Enter data in a worksheet**
- **Edit data in a worksheet**
- **Apply an AutoFormat to cells in a worksheet**
- **Use the Help feature**

Many companies use a spreadsheet for numerical and financial data and to analyze and evaluate information. An Excel spreadsheet can be used for such activities as creating financial statements, preparing budgets, managing inventory, and analyzing cash flow. In addition, numbers and values can be easily manipulated to create "what if" situations. For example, using a spreadsheet, a person in a company can ask questions such as "What if the value in this category is decreased? How would that change affect the department budget?" Questions like these can be easily answered in an Excel spreadsheet. Change the value in a category and Excel will recalculate formulas for the other values. In this way, a spreadsheet can be used not only for creating financial statements or budgets, but also as a planning tool.

Creating a Worksheet

start

Open Excel by clicking the Start button at the left side of the Taskbar, pointing to All Programs, pointing to Microsoft Office, and then clicking Microsoft Office Excel 2003. (Depending on your operating system, these steps may vary.) When Excel is open, you are presented with a blank worksheet like the one shown in Figure 1.1. The elements of a blank Excel worksheet are described in Table 1.1.

On your screen, the Standard and Formatting toolbars may display side by side with only a portion of the buttons visible. If this is the case, move the Formatting toolbar below the Standard toolbar by completing the following steps:

1. Click Tools and then Customize.
2. At the Customize dialog box, click the Options tab.
3. Click the *Show Standard and Formatting toolbars on two rows* option to insert a check mark in the check box.
4. Click the Close button to close the dialog box.

The display of the Standard and Formatting toolbars (as well as other toolbars) can be turned on or off. To do this, position the mouse pointer anywhere on a toolbar, and then click the *right* mouse button. At the drop-down menu that displays, click the toolbar name you want turned on or off. You can also turn on or off the display of a toolbar by clicking View on the Menu bar, pointing to Toolbars, and then clicking the toolbar name.

FIGURE 1.1 ***Blank Excel Worksheet***

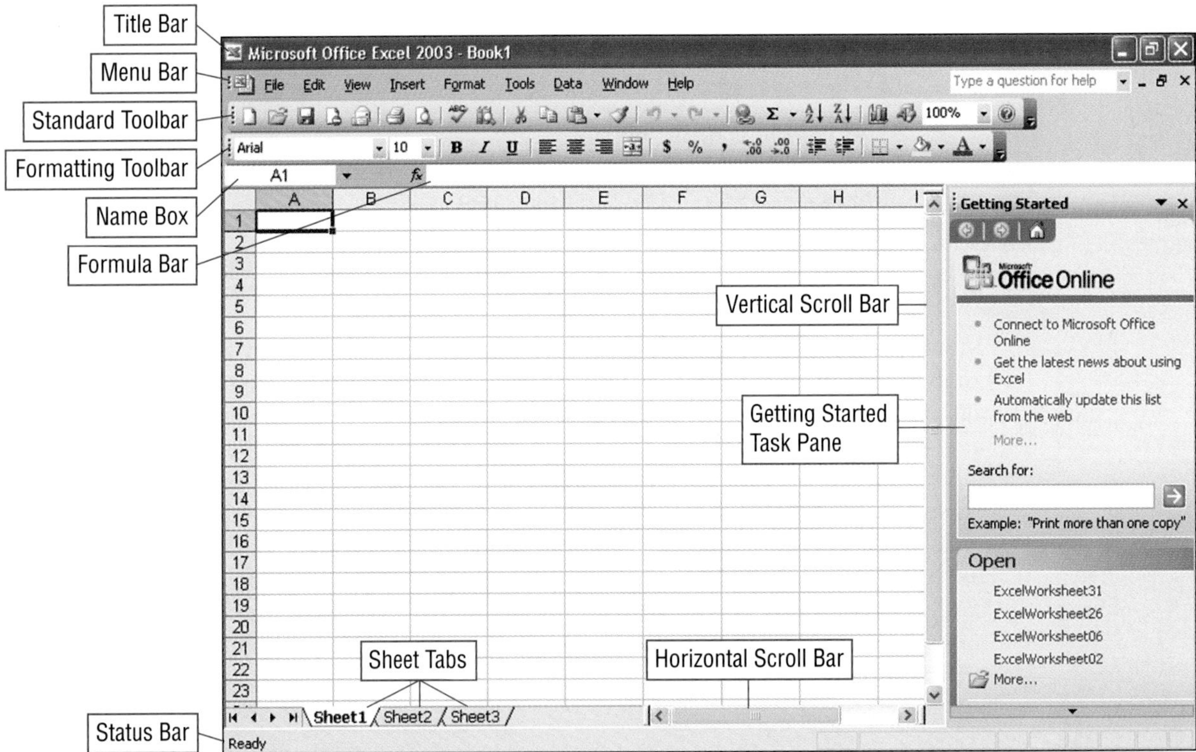

TABLE 1.1 ***Elements of an Excel Worksheet***

Title bar	The Title bar displays the name of the program along with the name of a workbook. The buttons at the far right side of the Title bar can be used to minimize, restore, or close Excel.
Menu bar	Excel commands are grouped into related functions and placed on the Menu bar. For example, options for formatting cells, rows, or columns are grouped in the Format option on the Menu bar.
Standard toolbar	Icons for the most common commands in Excel are placed on the Standard toolbar.
Formatting toolbar	Options that are used to format elements of a worksheet are placed on buttons on the Formatting toolbar.
Name box	The cell address, also called the cell reference, displays in the Name box and includes the column letter and row number.
Formula bar	The Formula bar provides information about the active cell. Formulas can be entered and edited in the Formula bar.
Scroll bars	A vertical scroll bar displays toward the right side of the worksheet (immediately left of the task pane) and a horizontal scroll bar displays at the bottom of the worksheet. These scroll bars are used to navigate within a worksheet.
Task pane	The task pane presents features to help the user easily identify and use more of the program. The name of the task pane and the features contained in the task pane change depending on the actions being performed by the user.
Sheet tabs	Sheet tabs identify the current worksheet. The tab for the active worksheet displays with a white background while the inactive worksheets display with a gray background (the background color may vary depending on the Windows color scheme).
Status bar	The Status bar is located below the horizontal scroll bar and displays information about the worksheet and the currently active cell.
Worksheet area	The worksheet area is a collection of cells where information such as labels, values, or formulas is entered. (A cell is an intersection between a row and a column.)

A document created in Excel is referred to as a ***workbook***. An Excel workbook consists of individual worksheets (or ***sheets***) like the sheets of paper in a notebook. Notice the tabs located toward the bottom of the Excel window that are named *Sheet1*, *Sheet2*, and so on. The area containing the gridlines in the Excel window is called the ***worksheet area***. Figure 1.2 identifies the elements of the worksheet area. Create a worksheet in the worksheet area that will be saved as part of a workbook. Columns in a worksheet are labeled with letters of the alphabet and rows are numbered.

FIGURE 1.2 ***Elements of a Worksheet Area***

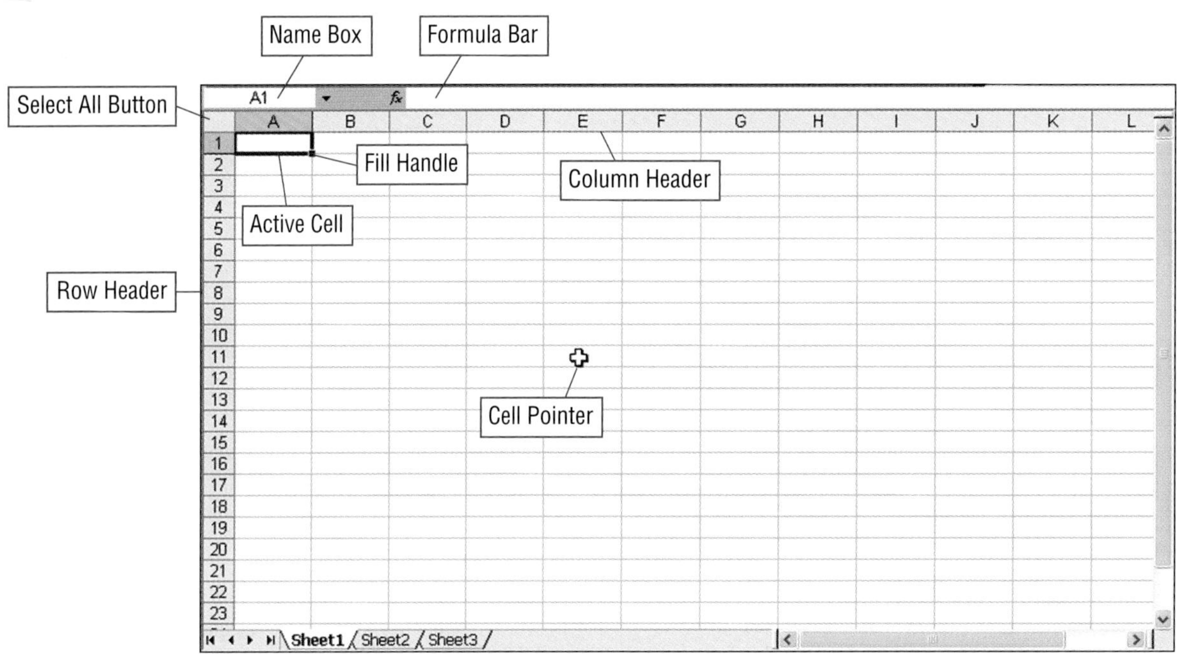

HINT

To make a cell active, position the cell pointer in the cell and then click the left mouse button.

The gray horizontal and vertical lines that define the cells in the worksheet area are called ***gridlines***. When the insertion point (which displays as a thick white plus sign) is positioned in a cell, the ***cell address***, also called the ***cell reference***, displays at the left side of the Formula bar in what is called the ***Name box***. The cell reference includes the column letter and row number. For example, if the insertion point is positioned in the first cell of the worksheet, the cell reference *A1* displays in the Name box located at the left side of the Formula bar. In a worksheet, the cell containing the insertion point is considered the ***active cell*** and a thick black border surrounds the active cell.

Entering Data in a Cell

Enter data such as a heading, number, or value in a cell. To enter data in a cell, make the desired cell active, and then type the data. To move the insertion point to the next cell in the worksheet, press the Tab key. Other commands for moving the insertion point within a worksheet are displayed in Table 1.2.

TABLE

1.2 Commands for Moving Insertion Point in a Worksheet

To move the insertion point here	***Press***
Down to the next cell	Enter
Up to the next cell	Shift + Enter
Next cell	Tab
Previous cell	Shift + Tab
Cell at beginning of row	Home
Next cell in the direction of the arrow	Up, Down, Left, or Right Arrow key
Last cell in worksheet	Ctrl + End
First cell in worksheet	Ctrl + Home
Cell in next window (approximately 16-24 rows)	Page Down
Cell in previous window (approximately 16-24 rows)	Page Up
Cell in window to right (approximately 8-11 columns)	Alt + Page Down
Cell in window to left (approximately 8-11 columns)	Alt + Page Up

Another method for moving the insertion point to a specific cell is to use the Go To feature. To use this feature, click Edit and then Go To. At the Go To dialog box, type the cell reference in the *Reference* text box, and then click OK.

HINT

Ctrl + G is the keyboard command to display the Go To dialog box.

When you are ready to type data into the active cell, check the Status bar. The word *Ready* should display at the left side. As data is being typed in the cell, the word *Ready* changes to *Enter*. Data being typed in a cell displays in the cell as well as in the Formula bar. If the data being typed is longer than the cell can accommodate, the data overlaps the next cell to the right (it does not become a part of the next cell—it simply overlaps it). You will learn how to change column widths to accommodate data later in this chapter.

If the data you enter in a cell consists of text and the text does not fit into the cell, it overlaps the next cell. If, however, you enter a number in a cell, specify it as a number (rather than text) and the number is too long to fit in the cell, Excel changes the display of the number to number symbols *(###)*. This is because Excel does not want you to be misled by a number when you see only a portion of it in the cell.

In addition to moving the insertion point with the keyboard, you can also move it using the mouse. To make a specific cell active with the mouse, position the mouse pointer, which displays as a white plus sign (called the ***cell pointer***), on the desired cell, and then click the left mouse button. The cell pointer displays as a white plus sign when positioned in a cell in the worksheet and displays as an arrow pointer when positioned on other elements of the Excel window such as toolbars or scroll bars.

Scroll through a worksheet using the horizontal and/or vertical scroll bars. Scrolling shifts the display of cells in the worksheet area, but does not change the active cell. Scroll through a worksheet until the desired cell is visible and then click the desired cell.

Save

Save a Workbook
1. Click Save button.
2. Type workbook name.
3. Press Enter.

Saving a Workbook

Save an Excel workbook, which may consist of a worksheet or several worksheets, by clicking the Save button on the Standard toolbar, clicking File and then Save, or by pressing Ctrl + S. At the Save As dialog box, type a name for the workbook in the *File name* text box, and then press Enter or click Save. A workbook file name can contain up to 255 characters, including drive letter and any folder names, and can include spaces. Some symbols cannot be used in a file name, such as:

forward slash (/)	question mark (?)
backslash (\)	quotation mark (")
greater than sign (>)	colon (:)
less than sign (<)	semicolon (;)
asterisk (*)	pipe symbol (|)

To save an Excel workbook in the ExcelChapter01S folder on your disk, display the Save As dialog box and then click the down-pointing arrow at the right side of the *Save in* option box. Click *3½ Floppy (A:)* that displays in the drop-down list and then double-click *ExcelChapter01S* in the list box. Note that you cannot give a workbook the same name in first uppercase and then lowercase letters.

Open

Open a Workbook
1. Click Open button.
2. Display desired folder.
3. Double-click workbook name.

Opening a Workbook

Open an Excel workbook by displaying the Open dialog box and then double-clicking the desired workbook name. Display the Open dialog box by clicking the Open button on the Standard toolbar or by clicking File and then Open, or by pressing Ctrl + O.

Print

Print a Workbook
Click Print button.
OR
1. Click File, Print.
2. Click OK.

Printing a Workbook

Click the Print button on the Standard toolbar to print the active worksheet. You can also print a worksheet by clicking File and then Print, or by pressing Ctrl + P. At the Print dialog box that displays, click the OK button.

Closing a Workbook and Exiting Excel

Close

Excel

To close an Excel workbook, click the Close button that displays at the right side of the Menu bar (the second Close button from the top) or click File and then Close. To exit Excel, click the Close button that displays at the right side of the Title bar (the first Close button from the top) or click File and then Exit. You can also exit Excel by double-clicking the *Excel* icon that displays at the left side of the Menu bar.

Close a Workbook
Click Close button.
OR
Click File, Close.

Expanding Drop-Down Menus

Microsoft Excel personalizes menus and toolbars as you work. When you click an option on the Menu bar, only the most popular options display (considered first-rank options). A drop-down menu that displays first-rank options is referred to as an ***adaptive menu***. To expand a drop-down menu and display the full set of options (first-rank options as well as second-rank options), click the down-pointing arrows that display at the bottom of the drop-down menu. A drop-down menu will also expand if you click an option on the Menu bar and then pause on the menu for a few seconds. Second-rank options on the expanded drop-down menu display in a light gray color. If you choose a second-rank option, it is promoted and becomes a first-rank option the next time the drop-down menu is displayed.

If you want all menu options displayed when you click an option, you would complete the following steps:

1. Click Tools, expand the drop-down menu by clicking the down-pointing arrows that display at the bottom of the menu, and then click Customize.
2. At the Customize dialog box, click the Options tab.
3. At the Customize dialog box with the Options tab selected, click in the *Always show full menus* check box to insert a check mark.
4. Click the Close button to close the dialog box.

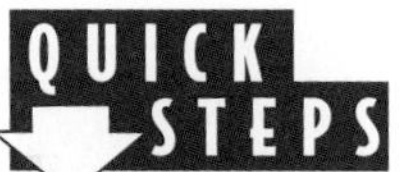

Display Full Drop-Down Menus
1. Click Tools, Customize.
2. Click Options tab.
3. Click *Always show full menus* option.
4. Click Close button.

In this textbook, you will not be instructed to expand the drop-down menu. If you do not see a specified option, click the down-pointing arrows that display at the bottom of the menu to expand it. Or, consider following the steps above to show full menus.

Completing Computer Exercises

At the end of sections within chapters and at the end of chapters, you will be completing hands-on exercises at the computer. These exercises will provide you with the opportunity to practice the presented functions and commands. The skill assessment exercises at the end of each chapter include general directions. If you do not remember how to perform a particular function, refer to the text in the chapter.

Copying Data Workbooks

In several exercises in each chapter, you will be opening workbooks provided with this textbook. Before beginning each chapter, copy the chapter folder from the CD that accompanies this textbook to a floppy disk (or other folder). For this chapter, copy to your disk or directory the ExcelChapter01S subfolder from the Excel2003Specialist folder on the CD that accompanies this textbook. Steps on how to copy a folder from the CD to your floppy disk are printed on the inside of the back cover of this textbook.

Changing the Default Folder

At the end of this and the remaining chapters in the textbook, you will be saving workbooks. More than likely, you will want to save workbooks onto a disk. You will also be opening workbooks that have been saved on your disk. To save workbooks in and open workbooks from the chapter folder on your disk, you will need to specify the drive where your disk is located as the default folder. Once you specify the chapter folder on your disk, Excel uses this as the default folder until you exit the Excel program. The next time you open Excel, you will again need to specify the drive where your disk is located.

Change the default folder at the Open dialog box or the Save As dialog box. To change the folder to the ExcelChapter01S folder on the disk in drive A at the Open dialog box, you would complete the following steps:

1. Click the Open button on the Standard toolbar (the second button from the left), or click File and then Open.
2. At the Open dialog box, click the down-pointing arrow at the right side of the *Look in* option box.
3. From the drop-down list that displays, click *3½ Floppy (A:)*.
4. Double-click *ExcelChapter01S* that displays in the list box.
5. Click the Cancel button in the lower right corner of the dialog box.

Change Default Folder
1. Click Tools, Options.
2. Click General tab.
3. Type desired folder in *Default file location* text box.
4. Click OK.

If you want to change the default folder permanently, make the change at the Options dialog box with the General tab selected, as shown in Figure 1.3. To permanently change the default folder to drive A, you would complete these steps:

1. Click Tools and then Options.
2. At the Options dialog box, click the General tab.
3. Select the text that displays in the *Default file location* text box and then type A:\.
4. Click the OK button.

FIGURE 1.3 ***Options Dialog Box with General Tab Selected***

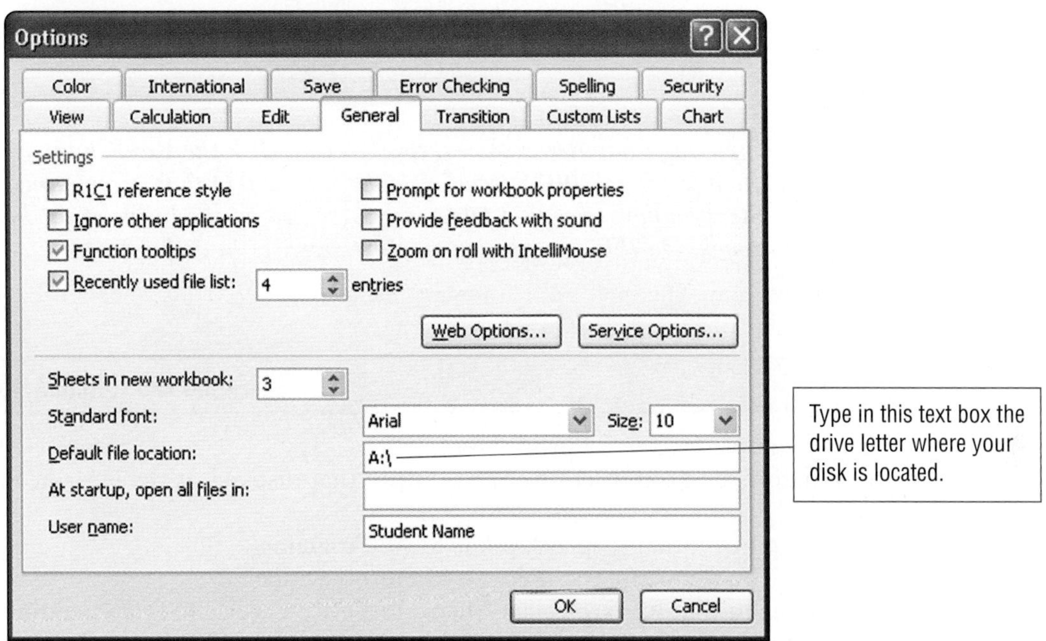

Editing Data in a Cell

Edit data being typed in a cell by pressing the Backspace key to delete the character left of the insertion point or pressing the Delete key to delete the character to the right of the insertion point. To change the data in a cell, click the cell once to make it active, and then type the new data. When a cell containing data is active, anything typed will take the place of the existing data. If you want to edit only a portion of the data in a cell, double-click the cell. This makes the cell active, moves the insertion point inside the cell, and displays the word *Edit* at the left side of the Status bar. Move the insertion point using the arrow keys or the mouse and then make the needed corrections. If you are using the keyboard, you can press the Home key to move the insertion point to the first character in the cell or Formula bar, or press the End key to move the insertion point to the last character.

When you are done editing the data in the cell, be sure to change out of the Edit mode. To do this, make another cell active. You can do this by pressing Enter, Tab, or Shift + Tab. You can also change out of the Edit mode and return to the Ready mode by clicking another cell or clicking the Enter button on the Formula bar.

If the active cell does not contain data, the Formula bar displays only the cell reference (by column letter and row number). As data is being typed in a cell, the two buttons shown in Figure 1.4 display on the Formula bar to the right of the Name box. Click the Cancel button to delete the current cell entry. You can also delete the cell entry by pressing the Esc key. Click the Enter button to indicate that you are done typing or editing the cell entry. When you click the Enter button on the Formula bar, the word *Enter* (or *Edit*) located at the left side of the Status bar changes to *Ready*.

Cancel

Enter

FIGURE

1.4 Buttons on the Formula Bar

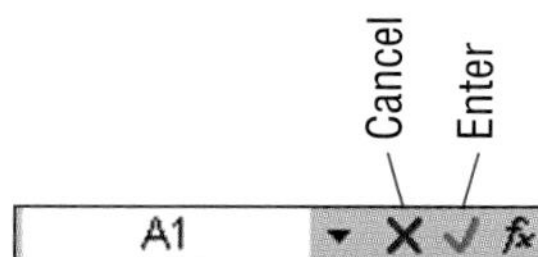

(Before completing computer exercises, copy to your disk the ExcelChapter01S subfolder from the Excel2003Specialist folder on the CD that accompanies this textbook. Steps on how to copy a folder are presented on the inside of the back cover of this textbook. Do this every time you start exercises in a chapter.)

exercise 1

CREATING AND EDITING A WORKSHEET

1. Open Excel by completing the following steps:
   a. At the Windows desktop, click the Start button that displays at the left side of the Taskbar.
   b. At the pop-up menu that displays, point to All Programs.
   c. At the side menu that displays, point to Microsoft Office.
   d. At the side menu that displays, click Microsoft Office Excel 2003. (Depending on your operating system, these steps may vary.)
2. At the Excel worksheet that displays, create the worksheet shown in Figure 1.5 by completing the following steps:
   a. With cell A1 the active cell (displays with a thick black border), type **Name**.
   b. Press the Tab key. (This makes cell B1 the active cell.)
   c. Type **Hours** and then press the Tab key. (This makes cell C1 the active cell.)
   d. Type **Rate** and then press Enter to move the insertion point to cell A2.
   e. With A2 the active cell, type the name **Avery**.
   f. Continue typing the data shown in Figure 1.5. Type the dollar signs as shown in the figure. Use the Tab key to move to the next cell in the row, press Shift + Tab to move to the previous cell in the row, or press the Enter key to move down a row to the cell at the left margin. (For other commands for moving the insertion point, refer to Table 1.2.)
3. After typing the data shown in the cells in Figure 1.5, save the worksheet by completing the following steps:
   a. Click the Save button on the Standard toolbar.
   b. At the Save As dialog box, click the down-pointing arrow to the right of the *Save in* option.
   c. From the drop-down list that displays, click *3½ Floppy (A:)* (this may vary depending on your system).
   d. Double-click the *ExcelChapter01S* folder that displays in the list box.
   e. Select the text in the *File name* text box and then type **sec1x01**.
   f. Press Enter or click the Save button.

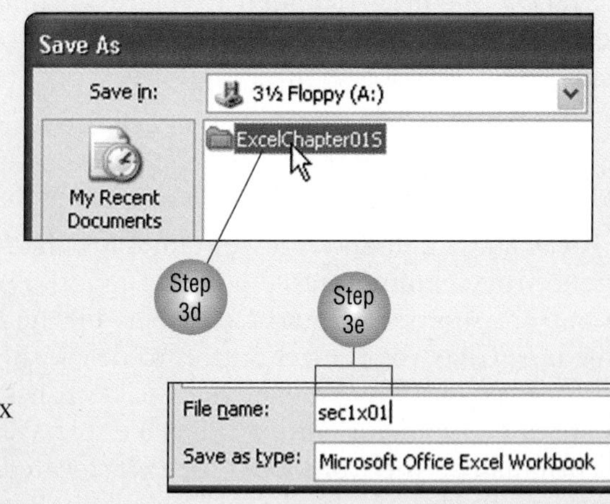

4. Print **sec1x01** by clicking the Print button on the Standard toolbar. (The gridlines will not print.)
5. With the worksheet still open, make the following edits:
   a. Double-click cell A6 (contains *Mikulich*).
   b. Move the insertion point immediately left of the *k* and then type c. (This changes the spelling to *Mickulich*.)
   c. Click once in cell A3 (contains *Connors*) and then type **Bryant**. (Clicking only once allows you to type over the existing data.)
   d. Click once in cell B4 (contains *24*), type **30**, and then press Enter.
   e. Edit cell C7 by completing the following steps:
      1) Click Edit and then Go To.
      2) At the Go To dialog box, type **C7** in the *Reference* text box, and then click OK.
      3) Type **$14.25** (over *$10.00*).
   f. Click once in any other cell.
6. Click the Save button on the Standard toolbar to save the worksheet again.
7. Click the Print button on the Standard toolbar to print the worksheet again.
8. Close the worksheet by clicking File on the Menu bar and then clicking Close at the drop-down menu.

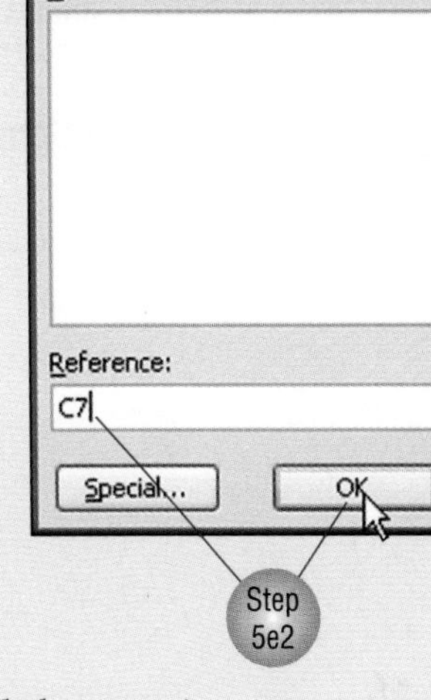

FIGURE 1.5 ***Exercise 1***

	A	B	C	D
1	Name	Hours	Rate	
2	Avery	45	$19.50	
3	Connors	35	$18.75	
4	Estrada	24	$15.00	
5	Juergens	24	$17.50	
6	Mikulich	20	$15.25	
7	Talbot	15	$10.00	
8				

Using Automatic Entering Features

Excel contains several features that help you enter data into cells quickly and efficiently. These features include ***AutoComplete***, which automatically inserts data in a cell that begins the same as a previous entry; ***AutoCorrect***, which automatically corrects many common typographical errors; and ***AutoFill***, which will automatically insert words, numbers, or formulas in a series.

The AutoComplete feature will automatically insert data in a cell that begins the same as a previous entry. If the data inserted by AutoComplete is the data you want in the cell, press Enter. If it is not the desired data, simply continue typing the correct data. This feature can be very useful in a worksheet that contains repetitive data entries. For example, consider a worksheet that repeats the word *Payroll*. The second and subsequent times this word is to be inserted in a cell, simply typing the letter *P* will cause AutoComplete to insert the entire word.

The AutoCorrect feature automatically corrects many common typing errors. To see what symbols and words are in the AutoCorrect feature, click Tools and then AutoCorrect Options. This displays the AutoCorrect dialog box with the AutoCorrect tab selected as shown in Figure 1.6 with a list box containing the replacement data.

FIGURE 1.6 ***AutoCorrect Dialog Box with AutoCorrect Tab Selected***

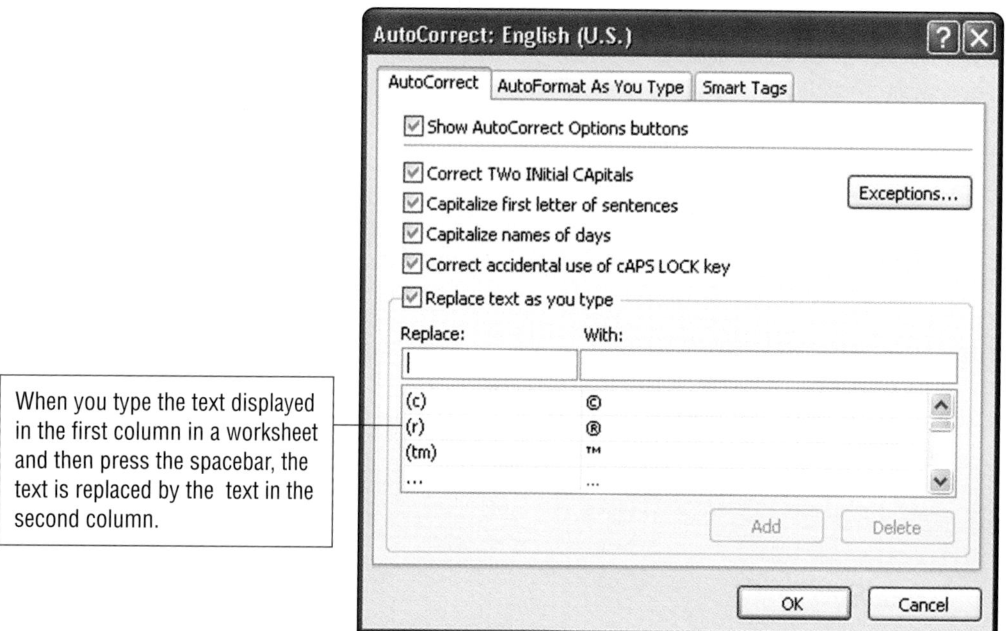

At the AutoCorrect dialog box, type the text shown in the first column in the list box and the text in the second column is inserted in the cell. Along with symbols, the AutoCorrect dialog box contains commonly misspelled words and common typographical errors. The AutoCorrect feature is a helpful tool when entering text in cells.

exercise 2

INSERTING DATA IN CELLS WITH AUTOCOMPLETE

1. Create the worksheet shown in Figure 1.7. To begin, display a clear worksheet window. (If a blank screen displays, click the New button on the Standard toolbar [first button from the left].)
2. Type the text in cell A1 and insert the ® symbol by typing **(r)**. AutoCorrect will change (r) to ® when you press the Enter key.
3. Type the remaining text in the cells. AutoCorrect will correct the spelling of *Benifits*. When you type the W in *West* in cell B5, the AutoComplete feature will insert *West*. Accept this by pressing the Tab key. (Pressing the Tab key accepts *West* and also makes the next cell in the row active.) Use the AutoComplete feature to enter *West* in B6 and B8 and *North* in cell B7. Use AutoComplete to enter the second and subsequent occurrences of *No* and *Yes*.
4. Save the worksheet and name it **sec1x02**.
5. Print **sec1x02**.
6. Close **sec1x02**.

FIGURE

1.7 ***Exercise 2***

	A	B	C	D
1	Team Net®			
2	Employee	Location	Benefits	
3	Abbot	West	No	
4	Blalock	North	No	
5	Calhoun	West	Yes	
6	Davis	West	Yes	
7	Hogan	North	Yes	
8	Mikelson	West	No	
9				

When a cell is active, a thick black border surrounds it and a small black square displays in the bottom right side of the border. This black square is called the AutoFill ***fill handle*** (see Figure 1.2). With the fill handle, you can quickly fill a range of cells with the same data or with consecutive data. For example, suppose you need to insert the year 2005 in consecutive cells. To do this quickly, type 2005 in the first cell, position the mouse pointer on the fill handle, hold down the left mouse button, drag across the cells where you want the year inserted, and then release the mouse button.

You can also use the fill handle to insert a series in consecutive cells. For example, suppose you are creating a worksheet with data for all of the months in the year. Type January in the first cell, position the mouse pointer on the fill handle, hold down the left mouse button, drag down or across to 11 more cells, and then release the mouse button. Excel automatically inserts the other 11 months in the year in the proper order. When using the fill handle, the cells must be adjacent. Table 1.3 identifies the sequence inserted in cells by Excel when specific data is entered.

TABLE

1.3 ***AutoFill Fill Handle Series***

Enter this data *(Commas represent data in separate cells.)*	***And the fill handle will insert this sequence in adjacent cells***
January	February, March, April, and so on…
Jan	Feb, Mar, Apr, and so on…
Jan 04, Jan 05	Jan-04, Jan-05, Jan-06, Jan-07, and so on…
Monday	Tuesday, Wednesday, Thursday, and so on…
Product 1	Product 2, Product 3, Product 4, and so on…
Qtr 1	Qtr 2, Qtr 3, Qtr 4
2, 4	6, 8, 10, and so on…

HINT

If you do not want a series to increment, hold down the Ctrl key while dragging the fill handle.

Auto Fill Options

Certain sequences, such as *2, 4* and *Jan 04, Jan 05,* require that both cells be selected before using the fill handle. If only the cell containing *2* is active, the fill handle will insert *2*s in the selected cells. The list in Table 1.3 is only a sampling of what the fill handle can do. You may find a variety of other sequences that can be inserted in a worksheet using the fill handle.

An Auto Fill Options button displays when you fill cells with the fill handle. Click this button and a list of options displays for filling the cells. By default, data and formatting are filled in each cell. You can choose to fill only the formatting in the cells or fill only the data without the formatting.

Turning On/Off and Maneuvering in the Task Pane

When you first open Microsoft Excel, the Getting Started task pane displays at the right side of the screen. With options in the Getting Started task pane, you can open a specific worksheet, create a new worksheet, or search for specific information about Office. Depending on the actions you are performing, the task pane may be removed from the screen. For example, if you click the New button on the Standard toolbar, a clear worksheet window displays and the task pane is removed. You can control whether the display of the task pane is on or off by clicking View and then Task Pane. You can also close the task pane by clicking the Close button (contains an *X*) located in the upper right corner of the task pane.

As you learn more features in Excel, the options in the task pane as well as the task pane name may change. Maneuver within various task panes with buttons on the task pane toolbar. Click the Back button (contains a left arrow) on the toolbar to display the previous task pane or click the Forward button (contains a right arrow) to display the next task pane. Click the Home button to return to the Getting Started task pane. You can also maneuver within various task panes by clicking the Other Task Panes button (contains the name of the task pane and a down arrow) and then clicking the desired task pane at the drop-down list.

The task pane can be docked and undocked. By default, the task pane is docked at the right side of the screen. Undock (move) the task pane by positioning the mouse pointer to the right of the task pane toolbar, holding down the left mouse button (mouse pointer turns into a four-headed arrow), and then dragging the task pane to the desired location. If you undock the task pane, you can dock it back at the right side of the screen by double-clicking to the right of the task pane toolbar.

exercise 3

INSERTING DATA IN CELLS WITH THE FILL HANDLE

1. Create the worksheet shown in Figure 1.8. To begin, display a clear worksheet window. (If a blank screen displays, click the New button on the Standard toolbar [first button from the left].)
2. Type **January** in cell B1.

3. Position the mouse pointer on the fill handle for cell B1, hold down the left mouse button, drag across to cell G1, and then release the mouse button.

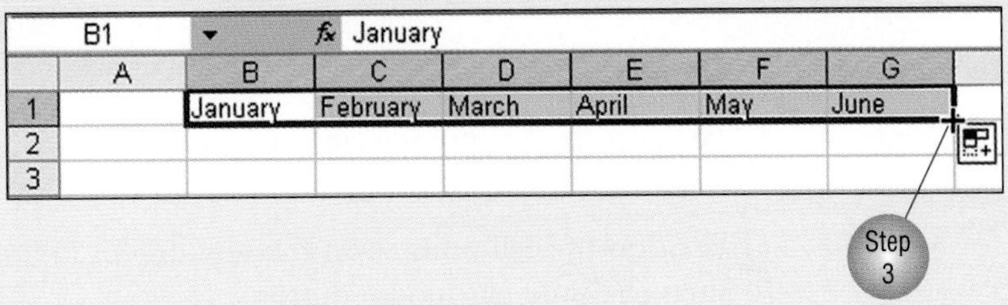

	A	B	C	D	E	F	G
1		January	February	March	April	May	June
2							
3							

Step 3

4. Type the years (2002, 2003, and so on) in cells A2 through A5.
5. Make cell B2 active and then type **100**.
6. Drag the fill handle for cell B2 to cell E2. (This inserts *100* in cells C2, D2, and E2.)

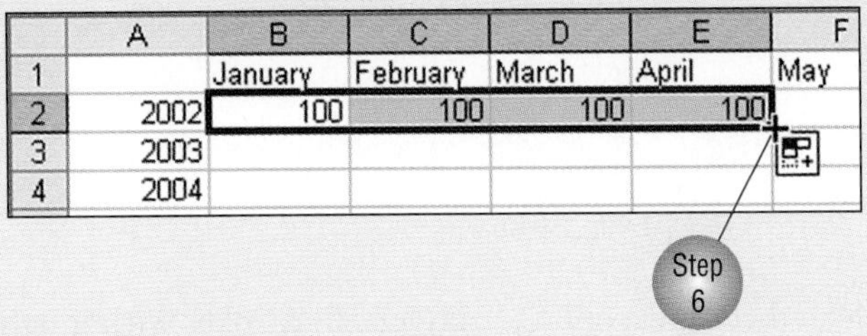

	A	B	C	D	E	F
1		January	February	March	April	May
2	2002	100	100	100	100	
3	2003					
4	2004					

Step 6

7. Type the text in the remaining cells as shown in Figure 1.8. Use the fill handle to fill adjacent cells.
8. Save the worksheet and name it **sec1x03**.
9. Print and then close **sec1x03**.

FIGURE 1.8 ***Exercise 3***

	A	B	C	D	E	F	G	H
1		January	February	March	April	May	June	
2	2002	100	100	100	100	125	125	
3	2003	150	150	150	150	175	175	
4	2004	200	200	200	150	150	150	
5	2005	250	250	250	250	250	250	
6								

Selecting Cells

Cells within a worksheet can be formatted in a variety of ways. For example, the alignment of data in cells or rows can be changed or character formatting can be added. To identify the cells that are to be affected by the formatting, select the specific cells.

Selecting Cells Using the Mouse

Select specific cells in a worksheet using the mouse or select columns or rows. Methods for selecting cells using the mouse display in Table 1.4.

TABLE 1.4 *Selecting with the Mouse*

To select this	*Do this*
Column	Position the cell pointer on the column header (a letter) and then click the left mouse button.
Row	Position the cell pointer on the row header (a number) and then click the left mouse button.
Adjacent cells	Drag with mouse to select specific cells.
Nonadjacent cells	Hold down the Ctrl key while clicking column header, row header, or specific cells.
All cells in worksheet	Click Select All button (refer to Figure 1.2).

HINT

Select nonadjacent columns or rows by holding down the Ctrl key while selecting cells.

Selected cells, except the active cell, display with a light blue background (this may vary) rather than a white background. The active cell is the first cell in the selection block and displays in the normal manner (white background with black data). Selected cells remain selected until you click a cell with the mouse or press an arrow key on the keyboard.

HINT

The first cell in a range displays with a white background and is the active cell.

Selecting Cells Using the Keyboard

The keyboard can be used to select specific cells within a worksheet. Table 1.5 displays the commands for selecting specific cells.

TABLE 1.5 *Selecting Cells Using the Keyboard*

To select	*Press*
Cells in direction of arrow key	Shift + arrow key
To beginning of row	Shift + Home
To beginning of worksheet	Shift + Ctrl + Home
To last cell in worksheet containing data	Shift + Ctrl + End
An entire column	Ctrl + spacebar
An entire row	Shift + spacebar
An entire worksheet	Ctrl + A or Ctrl + Shift + spacebar

Selecting Data within Cells

The selection commands presented select the entire cell. You can also select specific characters within a cell. To do this with the mouse, position the cell pointer in the desired cell, and then double-click the left mouse button. Drag with the I-beam pointer through the data you want selected. If you are using the keyboard, hold down the Shift key, and then press the arrow key that moves the insertion point in the desired direction. Data the insertion point passes through will be selected. You can also press F8 to turn on the Extend mode, move the insertion point in the desired direction to select the data, and then press F8 to turn off the Extend mode. When the Extend mode is on, the letters *EXT* display towards the right side of the Status bar.

Formatting with AutoFormat

Format with AutoFormat
1. Select cells.
2. Click Format, AutoFormat.
3. Double-click desired autoformat.

An Excel worksheet contains default formatting. For example, letters and words are aligned at the left of a cell, numbers are aligned at the right, and data is set in a 10-point sans serif typeface (usually Arial). Excel contains the AutoFormat feature you can use to apply a variety of predesigned formats to cells in a worksheet. Choose formatting at the AutoFormat dialog box shown in Figure 1.9. Display this dialog box by clicking Format and then AutoFormat.

FIGURE 1.9 ***AutoFormat Dialog Box***

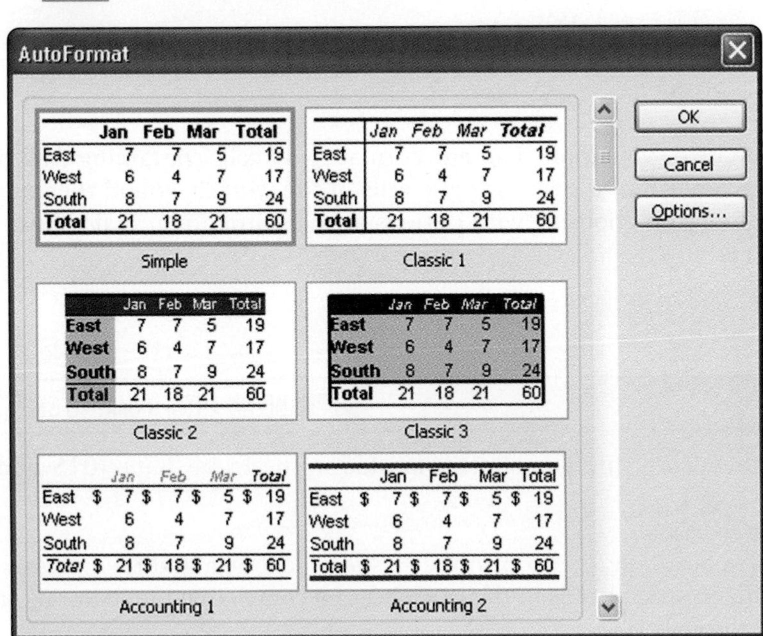

To automatically format a worksheet, select the cells that make up the worksheet, click Format, and then click AutoFormat. (Do not click the Select All button—this selects the entire worksheet, even the empty cells. If you apply an autoformat to all cells, it may lock up your computer.) At the AutoFormat dialog box, double-click the desired worksheet format.

exercise 4

FORMATTING A WORKSHEET WITH AUTOFORMAT

1. Open **ExcelWorksheet01**. (This worksheet is located in the ExcelChapter01S folder on your disk.)
2. Click File and then Save As. At the Save As dialog box, type **sec1x04** in the *File name* text box, and then press Enter.
3. Apply autoformatting to the worksheet by completing the following steps:
   a. Select cells A1 through D10.
   b. Click Format and then AutoFormat.
   c. At the AutoFormat dialog box, click the down scroll arrow on the vertical scroll bar until the *Colorful 1* sample worksheet displays.
   d. Double-click *Colorful 1*.

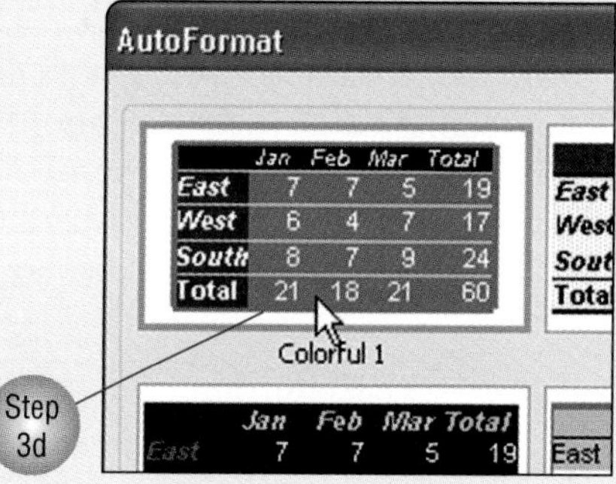

   e. At the worksheet, click in cell A1. (This deselects the cells.)
4. Save, print, and then close **sec1x04**.

In Exercise 4, you applied an autoformat to all cells containing data in the worksheet. You can also select specific cells in the worksheet and then apply an autoformat of your choosing with options at the AutoFormat dialog box.

exercise 5

APPLYING AN AUTOFORMAT TO SELECTED CELLS

1. Open **ExcelWorksheet26**. (This worksheet is located in the ExcelChapter01S folder on your disk.)
2. Click File and then Save As.
3. At the Save As dialog box, type **sec1x05** in the *File name* text box, and then press Enter.
4. Apply autoformatting to specific cells in the worksheet by completing the following steps:
   a. Select cells A2 through H16.
   b. Click Format and then AutoFormat.

c. At the AutoFormat dialog box, click the down scroll arrow on the vertical scroll bar until the *List 1* sample worksheet displays.

d. Double-click *List 1*.

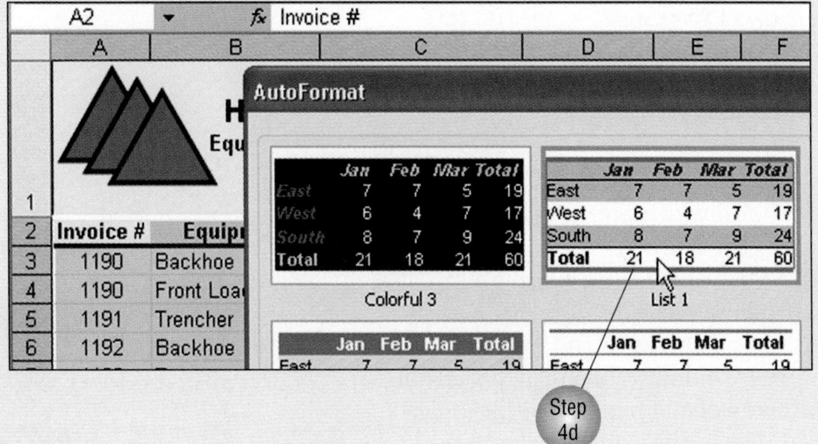

e. At the worksheet, click in cell A1. (This deselects the cells.)

5. Save, print, and then close **sec1x05**.

Using Help

Excel's Help feature is an on-screen reference manual containing information about all Excel features and commands. Excel's Help feature is similar to the Windows Help and the Help features in Word, PowerPoint, and Access. Get help using the Ask a Question text box on the Menu bar or with options at the Excel Help task pane.

Ask a Question

Getting Help Using the Ask a Question Text Box

Click the text inside the Ask a Question text box located at the right side of the Menu bar (this removes the text), type a help question, and then press Enter. A list of topics matching key words in your question displays in the Search Results task pane.

QUICK STEPS

Use Ask a Question Text Box

1. Click in Ask a Question text box.
2. Type help question.
3. Press Enter.

exercise 6

GETTING HELP USING THE ASK A QUESTION TEXT BOX

1. At a clear Excel worksheet, click the text inside the Ask a Question text box located at the right side of the Menu bar.
2. Type **How do I change column width?**.
3. Press the Enter key.
4. At the Search Results task pane, click the Change column width and row height hyperlink in the list box.
5. When the Microsoft Office Excel Help window displays, click the Show All hyperlink that displays in the upper right corner of the window. (This displays all the information available related to the topic.)
6. Read the information contained in the window, and then click the Close button (contains an *X*) located in the upper right corner of the Microsoft Office Excel Help window.
7. Close the Search Results task pane.

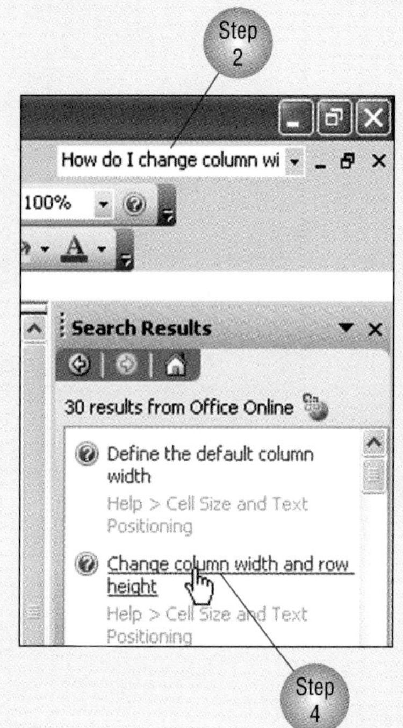

Getting Help from the Excel Help Task Pane

Microsoft Office Excel Help

Use Help Feature
1. Click Microsoft Office Excel Help button.
2. Type help question.
3. Press Enter.

You can type a question in the Ask a Question text box or type a question or topic in the Excel Help task pane. Display this task pane by clicking the Microsoft Office Excel Help button on the Standard toolbar or by clicking Help on the Menu bar and then clicking Microsoft Office Excel Help at the drop-down menu.

In the Excel Help task pane, type a topic, feature, or question in the *Search* text box and then press Enter or click the Start searching button (key containing white arrow on green background). Topics related to the topic, feature, or question display in the Search Results task pane. Click a topic in the results list box and information about that topic displays in the Microsoft Office Excel Help window. If the window contains a Show All hyperlink in the upper right corner, click this hyperlink and the information expands to show all help information related to the topic. When you click the Show All hyperlink, it becomes the Hide All hyperlink.

(Note: If the Office Assistant displays when you click the Microsoft Office Excel Help button, turn off the display of the Office Assistant. To do this, click the Options button in the yellow box above the Office Assistant. At the Office Assistant dialog box, click the Use the Office Assistant *option to remove the check mark from the check box, and then click OK.)*

exercise 7

GETTING HELP

1. At a clear document screen, display information on entering data in a worksheet. To begin, click the Microsoft Office Excel Help button on the Standard toolbar. (This displays the Excel Help task pane.)
2. Type **How do I enter data in a cell?** in the *Search* text box and then press Enter.
3. Click the Enter data in worksheet cells hyperlink in the results list box. (This displays the Microsoft Office Excel Help window.)
4. Click the Show All hyperlink that displays in the upper right corner of the window.
5. Read the information about entering data in cells. (You will need to scroll down the window to display all of the information.)
6. Click the Close button to close the Microsoft Office Excel Help window.
7. Close the Search Results task pane.

CHAPTER summary

- Use an Excel spreadsheet to create financial statements, prepare budgets, manage inventory, and analyze cash flow. Numbers and values can be easily manipulated in an Excel spreadsheet to answer "what if" questions.
- A document created in Excel is called a workbook. A workbook consists of individual worksheets. The intersections of columns and rows in a worksheet are referred to as cells.
- An Excel window contains the following elements: Title bar, Menu bar, Standard toolbar, Formatting toolbar, Formula bar, worksheet area, task pane, scroll bars, sheet tabs, and Status bar.
- The gray horizontal and vertical lines that define cells in the worksheet area are called gridlines.
- When the insertion point is positioned in a cell, the cell reference displays in the Name box located at the left side of the Formula bar. The cell reference includes the column letter and row number.
- To enter data in a cell, make the cell active, and then type the data. To move the insertion point to the next cell, press the Tab key. To move the insertion point to the previous cell, press Shift + Tab. For other insertion point movement commands, refer to Table 1.2.

- Data being entered in a cell displays in the cell as well as in the Formula bar.
- If data entered in a cell consists of text (letters) and the text does not fit into the cell, it overlaps the cell to the right. However, if the data being entered are numbers and do not fit in the cell, the numbers are changed to number symbols (###).
- To replace data in a cell, click the cell once, and then type the new data. To edit data within a cell, double-click the cell, and then make necessary changes.
- The AutoComplete feature will automatically insert a previous entry if the character or characters being typed in a cell match a previous entry.
- The AutoCorrect feature corrects many common typographical errors.
- Use the AutoFill fill handle to fill a range of cells with the same or consecutive data.
- The task pane presents features to help the user easily identify and use more of the program.
- Select all cells in a column by clicking the column header. Select all cells in a row by clicking the row header. Select all cells in a worksheet by clicking the Select All button located immediately to the left of the column headers.
- To select cells with the mouse, refer to Table 1.4; to select cells using the keyboard, refer to Table 1.5.
- Apply automatic formatting to selected cells in a worksheet with autoformats available at the AutoFormat dialog box.
- Get help by typing a question in the Ask a Question text box located at the right side of the Menu bar.
- Display the Excel Help task pane by clicking the Microsoft Office Excel Help button on the Standard toolbar or by clicking Help and then Microsoft Office Excel Help.

FEATURES summary

FEATURE	BUTTON	MENU	KEYBOARD
Save As dialog box		File, Save As	Ctrl + S
Open dialog box		File, Open	Ctrl + O
Print worksheet			
Print dialog box		File, Print	Ctrl + P
Close worksheet		File, Close	
AutoFormat dialog box		Format, AutoFormat	
Excel Help task pane		Help, Microsoft Office Excel Help	F1

CONCEPTS check

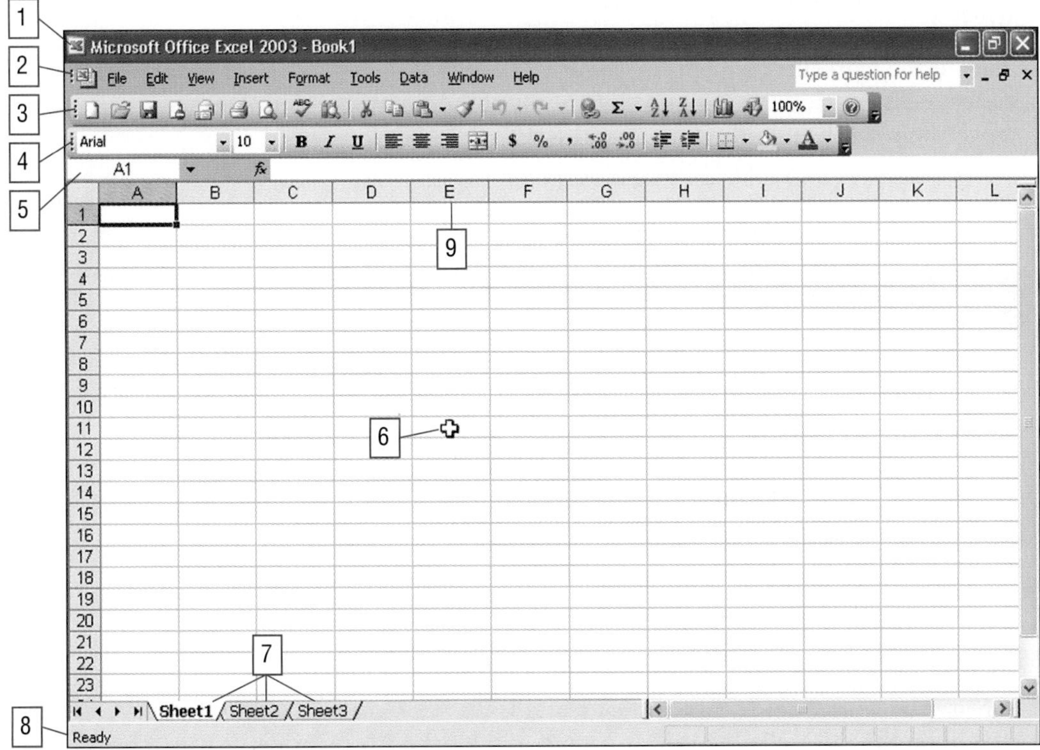

Identifying: Look at the Excel screen shown above. This screen contains numbers with lines pointing to specific items. On a blank sheet of paper, write the name of the item that corresponds with the number in the Excel screen.

Completion: On a blank sheet of paper, indicate the correct term, symbol, or command for each description.

1. Press this key on the keyboard to move the insertion point to the next cell.
2. Press these keys on the keyboard to move the insertion point to the previous cell.
3. Columns in a worksheet are labeled with this.
4. Rows in a worksheet are labeled with this.
5. Click this button in the worksheet area to select all cells in the table.
6. The gray horizontal and vertical lines that define the cells in a worksheet area are referred to as this.
7. If a number entered in a cell is too long to fit inside the cell, the number is changed to this.
8. Data being typed in a cell displays in the cell as well as here.
9. This is the name of the small black square that displays in the bottom right corner of the active cell.
10. To select nonadjacent columns using the mouse, hold down this key on the keyboard while clicking the column headers.
11. Automatically apply formatting to selected cells in a worksheet with formats available at this dialog box.

SKILLS check

Assessment 1

1. Create the worksheet shown in Figure 1.10.
2. Select cells A1 through C5 and then apply the *Accounting 1* AutoFormat.
3. Save the worksheet and name it **sec1sc01**.
4. Print and then close **sec1sc01**.

FIGURE 1.10 ***Assessment 1***

	A	B	C	D
1	Expense	Original	Current	
2	Labor	97000	98500	
3	Material	129000	153000	
4	Permits	1200	1350	
5	Tax	1950	2145	
6				

Assessment 2

1. Create the worksheet shown in Figure 1.11. To create the © symbol in cell A1, type (c). Type the misspelled words as shown and let the AutoCorrect feature correct the spelling. Use the AutoComplete feature to insert the second occurrence of *Category, Available,* and *Balance.*
2. Select cells A1 through B7 and then apply the *Classic 2* AutoFormat.
3. Save the worksheet and name it **sec1sc02**.
4. Print and then close **sec1sc02**.

FIGURE 1.11 ***Assessment 2***

	A	B	C
1	Premiere Plan©		
2	Plan A	Catagory	
3		Availalbe	
4		Balence	
5	Plan B	Category	
6		Available	
7		Balance	
8			

Assessment 3

1. Create the worksheet shown in Figure 1.12. Type **Monday** in cell B2 and then use the fill handle to fill in the remaining days of the week. Use the fill handle to enter other repetitive data.
2. Select cells A1 through F4 and then apply an autoformat of your choosing.
3. Save the worksheet and name it **sec1sc03**.
4. Print and then close **sec1sc03**.

FIGURE 1.12 ***Assessment 3***

	A	B	C	D	E	F	G
1	CAPITAL INVESTMENTS						
2		Monday	Tuesday	Wednesday	Thursday	Friday	
3	Budget	350	350	350	350	350	
4	Actual	310	425	290	375	400	
5							

Assessment 4

1. Use the Help feature to learn more about how to scroll within an Excel worksheet.
2. Read and then print the information provided by Help.
3. Create a worksheet containing the information. Set this up as a worksheet with two columns (cells will contain only text—not numbers). Create a title for the worksheet.
4. Apply an autoformat to the cells in the table.
5. Save the completed worksheet and name it **sec1sc04**.
6. Print and then close **sec1sc04**.

CHAPTER challenge

You have been hired to manage a small business, Barry's Better Built Barns, which specializes in selling and building yard barns. Barry has asked you to prepare a sample budget based on last year's data. His operating income last year was $500,000. His expenses included: Salaries, $75,000; Building Materials, $122,000; Paint, $15,000; and Miscellaneous, $17,000. Create a worksheet showing this information. Apply an autoformat to the cells in the worksheet. Save the workbook.

Barry would like to know what his net income was for last year. This can be calculated by subtracting the total expenses from gross income. Use the Help feature to learn how to create simple formulas. Using the worksheet created in the first part of the Chapter Challenge, insert a formula that adds the total expenses and identify that amount appropriately. Also, insert a formula that subtracts total expenses from the net income. Again, identify the amount appropriately. Save and print the workbook.

In Word, create a short memo to Barry that includes the information from the worksheet created in the first part of the Chapter Challenge. Copy the information into the memo. Explain how the net income was calculated. Also, provide an explanation of your recommendations for the upcoming year's budget based on last year's information. Save the memo and print it.

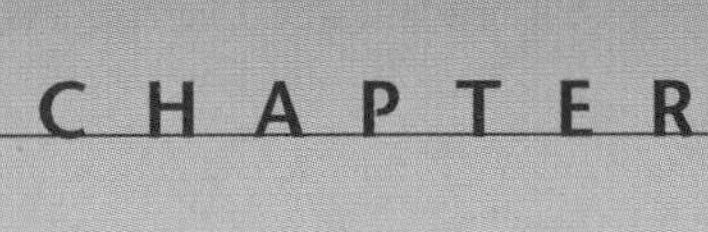

FORMATTING AN EXCEL WORKSHEET

PERFORMANCE OBJECTIVES

Upon successful completion of Chapter 2, you will be able to:

- **Preview a worksheet**
- **Apply formatting to data in cells**
- **Change column widths**
- **Change row heights**
- **Format numbers in a worksheet**
- **Insert rows and columns in a worksheet**
- **Delete cells, rows, and columns in a worksheet**
- **Clear data in cells**
- **Add borders, shading, and patterns to cells in a worksheet**
- **Repeat the last action**
- **Automate formatting with Format Painter**

The appearance of a worksheet on the screen and how it looks when printed is called the ***format***. In the previous chapter, you learned how to apply formatting automatically with choices at the AutoFormat dialog box. You can also apply specific formatting to cells in a worksheet. For example, you can change column width and row height; apply character formatting such as bold, italics, and underlining; specify number formatting; insert and delete rows and columns; and apply borders, shading, and patterns to cells.

QUICK STEPS

Preview a Worksheet
Click Print Preview button in Print dialog box.
OR
Click Print Preview button on Standard toolbar.
OR
Click File, Print Preview.

Print Preview

Previewing a Worksheet

Before printing a worksheet, consider previewing it to see how it will appear when printed. To preview a worksheet, click the Preview button in the Print dialog box; click the Print Preview button on the Standard toolbar; or click File and then Print Preview. This causes the worksheet to display on the screen as it will appear when printed. Figure 2.1 displays the worksheet named ExcelWorksheet01 in Print Preview. Note that the gridlines in the worksheet will not print.

FIGURE

2.1 **Worksheet in Print Preview**

Print Preview Toolbar

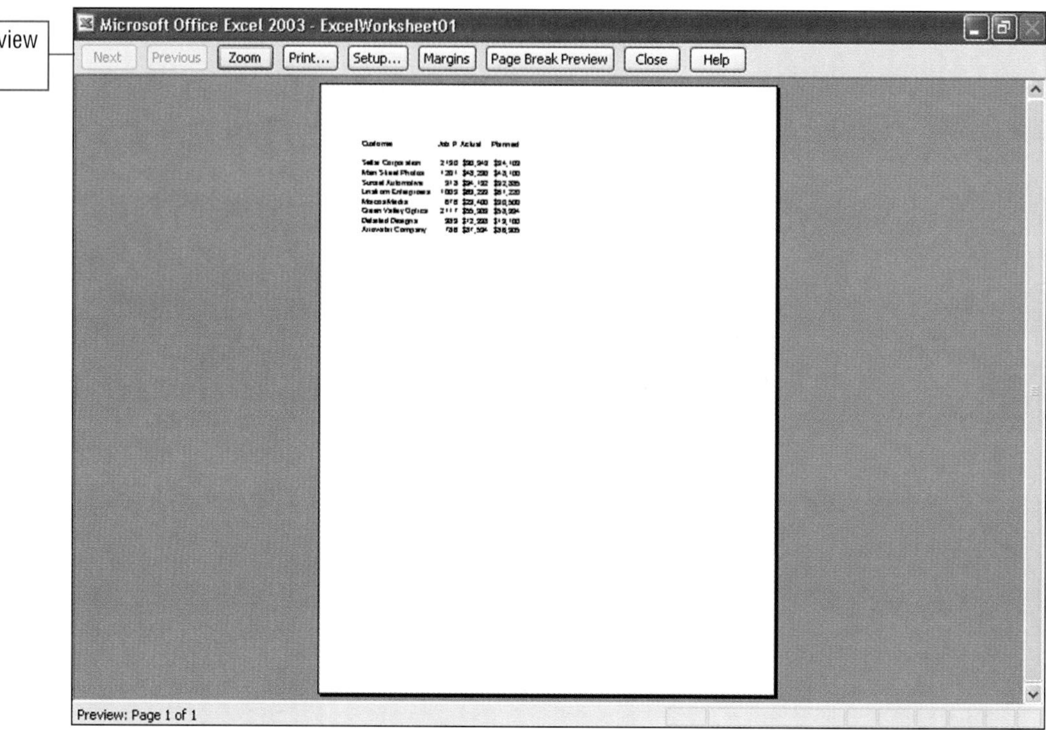

HINT

In Print Preview with the Margins button active, change worksheet margins by dragging margin borders.

To zoom in on the worksheet and make the display bigger, click the Zoom button on the Print Preview toolbar. This toolbar displays at the top of the screen immediately below the Title bar. Click the Print button on the Print Preview toolbar to send the worksheet to the printer. Click the Setup button and the Page Setup dialog box displays where you can specify the orientation of the page and the paper size. Clicking the Margins button causes margin boundary lines to display on the worksheet. Clicking this button again removes the margin boundary lines. After viewing the worksheet, click the Close button to remove Print Preview and return to the worksheet.

Changing the Zoom Setting

HINT

Click the *Selection* option at the Zoom drop-down list and the selected area fills the window.

100%

Zoom

In Print Preview, you can zoom in on the worksheet and make the display bigger. You can also change the size of the display at the worksheet (not in Print Preview) with the options on the Zoom button. To change the percentage of display, click the down arrow at the right side of the Zoom button on the Standard toolbar and then click the desired percentage at the drop-down list. You can also click the Zoom button to select the current percentage measurement, type a new percentage, and then press Enter.

Applying Formatting with Buttons on the Formatting Toolbar

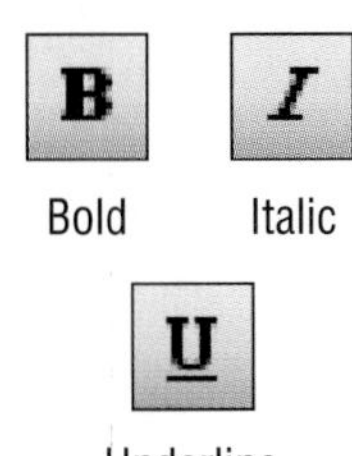

A variety of formatting can be applied to cells in a worksheet using buttons on the Formatting toolbar. With buttons on the Formatting toolbar shown in Figure 2.2, you can change the font and font size and bold, italicize, and underline data in cells. To apply bold to a cell or selected cells, click the Bold button on the Formatting toolbar; click the Italic button to apply italics; and click the Underline button to apply underlining formatting.

FIGURE 2.2 **Formatting Toolbar**

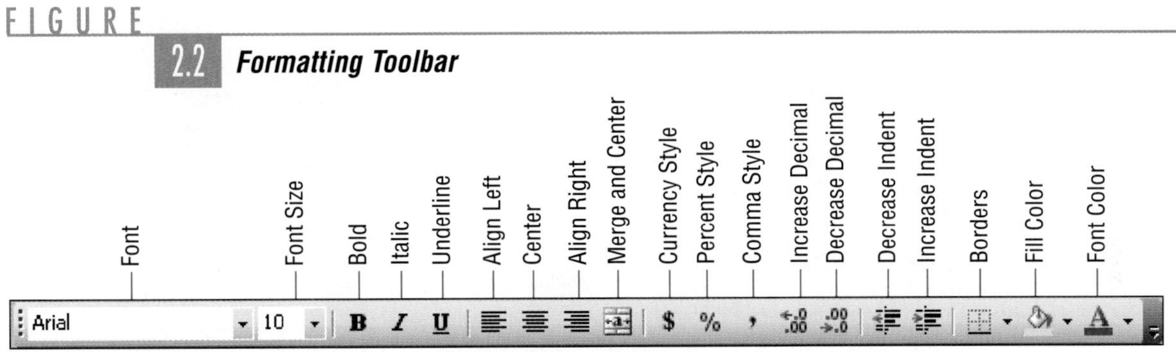

With other buttons on the Formatting toolbar, you can change the alignment of text within cells, increase or decrease the number of digits after a decimal point, increase or decrease indents, change the cell border, add fill color to a cell, and change text color.

(Note: Before completing computer exercises, delete the ExcelChapter01S folder on your disk. Next, copy the ExcelChapter02S subfolder from the Excel2003Specialist folder on the CD that accompanies this textbook to your disk and then make ExcelChapter02S the active folder.)

exercise 1

FORMATTING AND PREVIEWING A WORKSHEET

1. Open **ExcelWorksheet01**.
2. Save the worksheet with Save As and name it **sec2x01**.
3. Select and then bold and italicize the first row by completing the following steps:
   a. Position the cell pointer on the row 1 header (this is the number 1 that displays at the left side of the screen, immediately left of *Customer*) and then click the left mouse button.
   b. Click the Bold button and then click the Italic button on the Formatting toolbar.

Step 3b

Arial 10 B I U

A1 fx Customer

Step 3a

	A	B	C
1	Customer	Job #	Actual
2			
3	Sellar Corporation	2130	$30,349
4	Main Street Photos	1201	$48,290
5	Sunset Automotive	318	$34,192

4. Select and then bold the data in cells A3 through A10 by completing the following steps:

   a. Position the cell pointer in cell A3, hold down the left mouse button, drag the cell pointer to cell A10, and then release the mouse button.
   b. Click the Bold button on the Formatting toolbar.

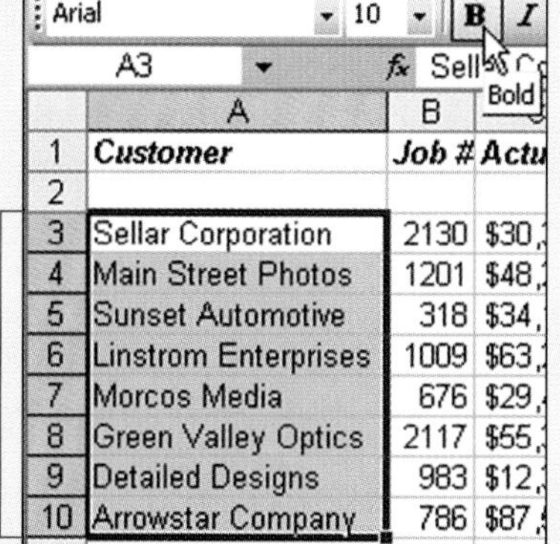

5. Select and then italicize the data in cells B3 through D10 by completing the following steps:
   a. Position the cell pointer in cell B3, hold down the left mouse button, drag the cell pointer to cell D10, and then release the mouse button.
   b. Click the Italic button on the Formatting toolbar.
6. Click in cell A1. (This deselects the cells.)
7. Preview the worksheet by completing the following steps:
   a. Click the Print Preview button on the Standard toolbar.
   b. At the print preview screen, click the Zoom button. (This increases the display of the worksheet cells.)
   c. After viewing the worksheet, click the Close button.
8. Change the zoom display by completing the following steps:
   a. Click the down-pointing arrow at the right side of the Zoom button on the Standard toolbar and then click *200%* at the drop-down list.
   b. After viewing the worksheet at 200% display, click the Zoom button (this selects *200%*), type 150, and then press Enter. (This changes the zoom percentage to 150%.)
   c. Change the zoom back to 100% by clicking the down-pointing arrow at the right side of the Zoom button and then clicking *100%* at the drop-down list.
9. Save, print, and then close **sec2x01**. (The gridlines will not print.)

exercise 2

CHANGING THE FONT AND FONT COLOR FOR DATA IN A WORKSHEET

1. Open **ExcelWorksheet01**.
2. Save the worksheet with Save As and name it **sec2x02**.
3. Select the entire worksheet and then change the font and font color by completing the following steps:
   a. Click the Select All button. (This is the gray button that displays immediately left of column header A and immediately above row header 1.)
   b. Click the down-pointing arrow at the right side of the Font button on the Formatting toolbar.
   c. At the drop-down list that displays, scroll down the list and then click *Garamond*. (If Garamond is not available, choose another serif typeface such as Century.)
   d. Click the down-pointing arrow at the right side of the Font Size button on the Formatting toolbar and then click *11* at the drop-down list.

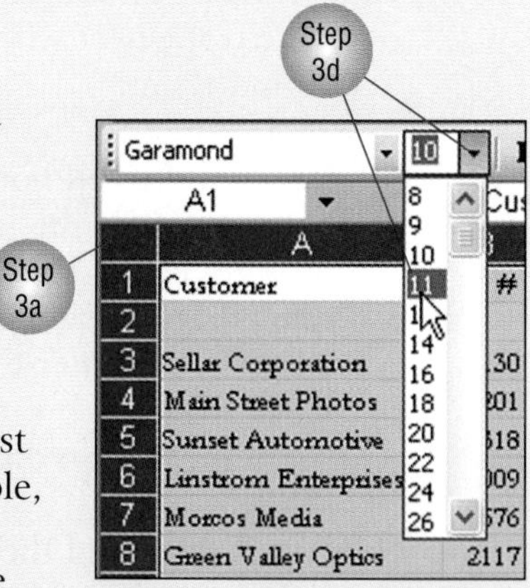

e. Click the down-pointing arrow at the right side of the Font Color button (this is the last button on the Formatting toolbar). At the palette of color choices, click the Blue color that is the sixth color from the left in the second row.

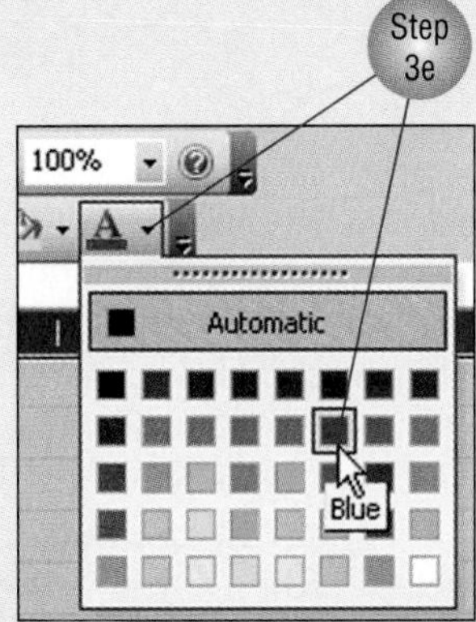

4. Click once in cell A6 and then change *Linstrom Enterprises* to *Jefferson, Inc.*
5. Double-click in cell A7 and then change *Morcos Media* to *Morcos Corp.* (Include the period after *Corp.*)
6. Click once in cell C6 and then change *$63,293* to *$59,578*.
7. Click once in any other cell.
8. Preview the worksheet by completing the following steps:

	A	B	C	D
1	Customer	Job #	Actual	Planned
2				
3	Sellar Corporation	2130	$30,349	$34,109
4	Main Street Photos	1201	$48,290	$48,100
5	Sunset Automotive	318	$34,192	$32,885
6	Jefferson, Inc.	1009	$59,578	$61,220
7	Morcos Corp.	676	$29,400	$30,500
8	Green Valley Optics	2117	$55,309	$58,394
9	Detailed Designs	983	$12,398	$13,100
10	Arrowstar Company	786	$87,534	$86,905

Step 4

Step 5

   a. Click the Print Preview button on the Standard toolbar.
   b. At the print preview screen, increase the size of the display by clicking the Zoom button. (Skip this step if the size is already increased.)
   c. After viewing the worksheet, click the Close button.
9. Save, print, and then close **sec2x02**. (The gridlines will not print. If you are not printing on a color printer, the data will print in black rather than blue.)

Changing Column Width

Columns in a worksheet are the same width by default. In some worksheets you may want to change column widths to accommodate more or less data. Changes to column widths can be made using the mouse on column boundaries or at a dialog box.

QUICK STEPS

Change Column Width
Drag column boundary line.
OR
Double-click column boundary.
OR
1. Click Format, Column, Width.
2. Type desired number.
3. Click OK.

Changing Column Width Using Column Boundaries

The mouse can be used to change the width of a column or selected columns. For example, to change the width of column B, you would position the mouse pointer on the black boundary line between columns B and C in the column header until the mouse pointer turns into a double-headed arrow pointing left and right and then drag the boundary to the right to increase the size or to the left to decrease the size. The width of selected columns that are adjacent can be changed at the same time. To do this, select the columns and then drag one of the column boundaries within the selected columns. As the boundary is being dragged, the column width changes for all selected columns.

As a column boundary is being dragged, the column width displays in a yellow box above the mouse pointer. The column width number that displays represents the average number of characters in the standard font that can fit in a cell.

exercise 3

CHANGING COLUMN WIDTH USING A COLUMN BOUNDARY

1. At a blank Excel worksheet, create the worksheet shown in Figure 2.3. To begin, change the width of column A by completing the following steps:
   a. Position the mouse pointer on the column boundary in the column header between columns A and B until it turns into a double-headed arrow pointing left and right.
   b. Hold down the left mouse button, drag the column boundary to the right until *Width: 17.00 (124 pixels)* displays in the yellow box, and then release the mouse button.
2. Change the width of columns B, C, and D by completing the following steps:
   a. Select columns B, C, and D. To do this, position the cell pointer on the letter *B* in the column header, hold down the left mouse button, drag the cell pointer to the letter *D* in the column header, and then release the mouse button.
   b. Position the cell pointer on the column boundary between columns B and C until it turns into a double-headed arrow pointing left and right.
   c. Hold down the left mouse button, drag the column boundary to the right until *Width: 13.00 (96 pixels)* displays in the yellow box, and then release the mouse button.
3. Type the data in the cells as shown in Figure 2.3. Type the dollar signs and decimal points as shown. (Consider using the fill handle for the months. To do this, type **October** in cell B1, position the mouse pointer on the fill handle, hold down the left mouse button, drag to cell D1, and then release the mouse button.)

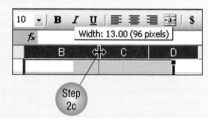

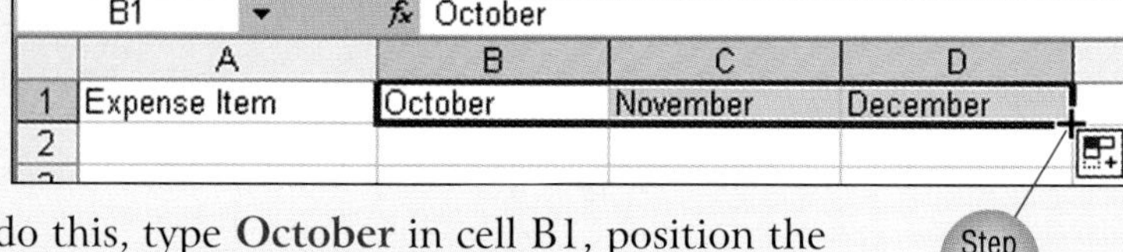

4. After typing the data in the cells, make the following formatting changes:
   a. Select the entire worksheet and then change the font to 12-point Tahoma (or a similar typeface).
   b. Select row 1 and then apply bold and italic formatting.
5. Click in cell A1. (This deselects the cells.)
6. Save the worksheet and name it **sec2x03**.
7. Preview the worksheet.
8. Print and then close **sec2x03**.

FIGURE 2.3 ***Exercise 3***

	A	B	C	D	E
1	Expense Item	October	November	December	
2	Salaries	$25,450.50	$26,090.65	$26,445.00	
3	Lease	$5,650.00	$5,650.00	$5,650.00	
4	Insurance	$5,209.65	$5,335.55	$5,621.45	
5	Utilities	$2,100.50	$2,249.75	$2,441.35	
6	Maintenance	$1,430.00	$1,119.67	$1,450.50	
7					

A column width in an existing worksheet can be adjusted to fit the longest entry in the column. To automatically adjust a column width to the longest entry, position the cell pointer on the column boundary at the right side of the column and then double-click the left mouse button.

exercise 4

CHANGING COLUMN WIDTH AUTOMATICALLY IN AN EXISTING WORKSHEET

1. Open **ExcelWorksheet01**.
2. Save the worksheet with Save As and name it **sec2x04**.
3. Select the entire worksheet and then change the font to 14-point Times New Roman.
4. Adjust the width of the first column to accommodate the longest entry in the column by completing the following steps:
   a. Position the cell pointer on the column boundary between columns A and B until it turns into a double-headed arrow pointing left and right.
   b. Double-click the left mouse button.
5. Select row 1 and then click the Bold button on the Formatting toolbar.
6. Click in cell A1. (This deselects the cells.)
7. Save, preview, print, and then close **sec2x04**.

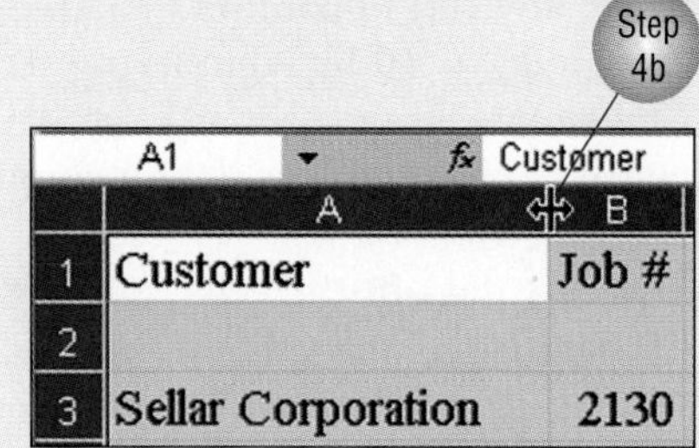

Changing Column Width at the Column Width Dialog Box

At the Column Width dialog box shown in Figure 2.4, you can specify a column width number. The column width number represents the average number of characters in the standard font that will fit in a cell. Increase the column width number to make the column wider or decrease the column width number to make the column narrower.

To display the Column Width dialog box, click Format, point to Column, and then click Width. At the Column Width dialog box, type the number representing the average number of characters in the standard font that you want to fit in the column, and then press Enter or click OK.

FIGURE 2.4 ***Column Width Dialog Box***

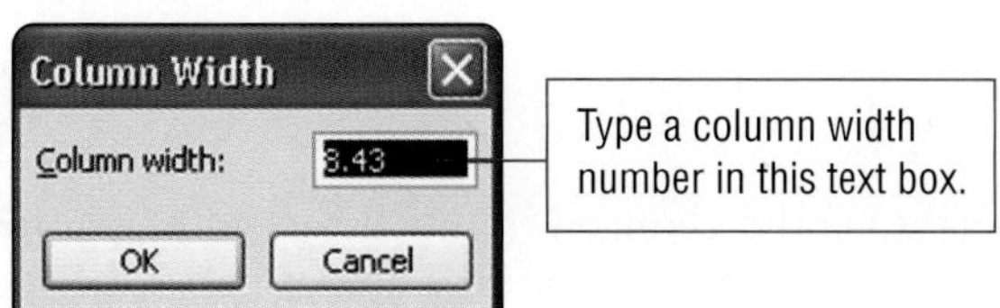

exercise 5

CHANGING COLUMN WIDTH AT THE COLUMN WIDTH DIALOG BOX

1. At a blank Excel worksheet, create the worksheet shown in Figure 2.5. To begin, change the width of column A by completing the following steps:
   a. Make sure any cell in column A is active.
   b. Click Format, point to Column, and then click Width.
   c. At the Column Width dialog box, type **10** in the *Column width* text box.
   d. Click OK to close the dialog box.
2. Make any cell in column B active and then change the width of column B to *5* by completing steps similar to those in Step 1.
3. Make any cell in column C active and then change the width of column C to *10* by completing steps similar to those in Step 1.
4. Make any cell in column D active and then change the width of column D to *10* by completing steps similar to those in Step 1.
5. Type the data in the cells as shown in Figure 2.5. Use the fill handle to insert the months.
6. After typing the data in the cells, make the following formatting changes:
   a. Select the entire worksheet and then change the font to 12-point Garamond (or a similar serif typeface).
   b. Select row 1 and then apply bold formatting.
7. Click in cell A1.
8. Save the worksheet and name it **sec2x05**.
9. Preview, print, and then close **sec2x05**.

FIGURE 2.5 ***Exercise 5***

	A	B	C	D	E
1	Month	Emp	Actual	Budget	
2	January	320	$3,121.50	$3,005.60	
3	February	197	$3,450.78	$3,500.20	
4	March	763	$2,109.45	$2,229.67	
5	April	804	$4,312.50	$4,110.30	
6	May	334	$5,110.40	$4,995.00	
7	June	105	$1,894.35	$1,995.15	
8					

Change Row Height
Drag row boundary line.
OR
1. Click Format, Row, Height.
2. Type desired number.
3. Click OK.

Changing Row Height

Row height can be changed in much the same manner as column width. For example, you can change the row height using the mouse on a row boundary, or at the Row Height dialog box.

Changing Row Height Using Row Boundaries

Change row height using a row boundary in the same manner as you learned to change column width. To do this, position the cell pointer on the boundary between rows in the row header until it turns into a double-headed arrow pointing up and down, hold down the left mouse button, drag up or down until the row is the desired height, and then release the mouse button.

The height of selected rows that are adjacent can be changed at the same time. (The height of nonadjacent rows will not all change at the same time.) To do this, select the rows, and then drag one of the row boundaries within the selected rows. As the boundary is being dragged, the row height changes for all selected rows.

As a row boundary is being dragged, the row height displays in a yellow box above the mouse pointer. The row height number that displays represents a point measurement. A vertical inch contains approximately 72 points. Increase the point size to increase the row height; decrease the point size to decrease the row height.

exercise 6

CHANGING ROW HEIGHT USING A ROW BOUNDARY

1. Open **ExcelWorksheet05**.
2. Save the worksheet with Save As and name it **sec2x06**.
3. Change the font size of *January* to 14 by completing the following steps:
   a. Make cell A1 the active cell.
   b. Click the down-pointing arrow at the right of the Font Size button on the Formatting toolbar.
   c. From the drop-down list that displays, click *14*.
4. Change the height of row 1 by completing the following steps:
   a. Position the cell pointer in the row header on the row boundary between rows 1 and 2 until it turns into a double-headed arrow pointing up and down.
   b. Hold down the left mouse button, drag the row boundary down until *Height: 27.00 (36 pixels)* displays in the yellow box, and then release the mouse button.

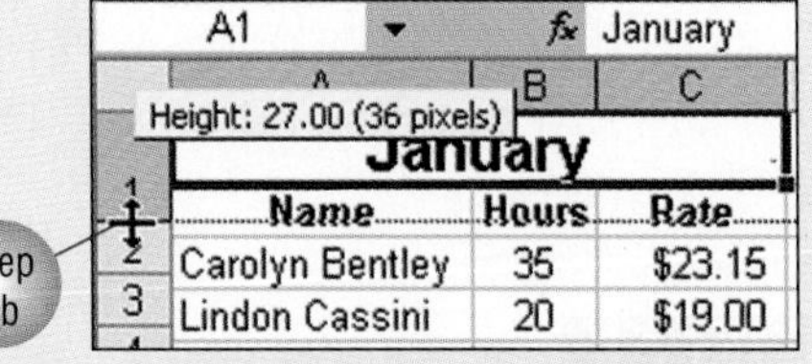

5. Change the height of rows 2 through 8 by completing the following steps:
   a. Select rows 2 through 8. To do this, position the cell pointer on the number 2 in the row header, hold down the left mouse button, drag the cell pointer to the number 8 in the row header, and then release the mouse button.
   b. Position the cell pointer on the row boundary between rows 2 and 3 until it turns into a double-headed arrow pointing up and down.
   c. Hold down the left mouse button, drag the row boundary down until *Height: 21.00 (28 pixels)* displays in the yellow box, and then release the mouse button.

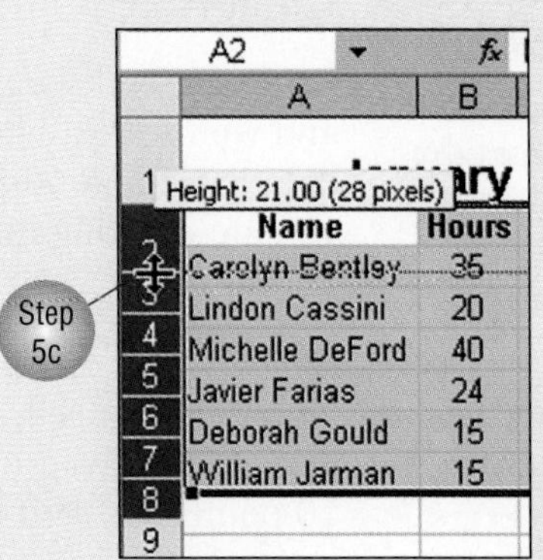

6. Click in cell A1.
7. Save, preview, print, and then close **sec2x06**.

Changing Row Height at the Row Height Dialog Box

At the Row Height dialog box shown in Figure 2.6, you can specify a row height number. To display the Row Height dialog box, click Format, point to Row, and then click Height.

FIGURE 2.6 ***Row Height Dialog Box***

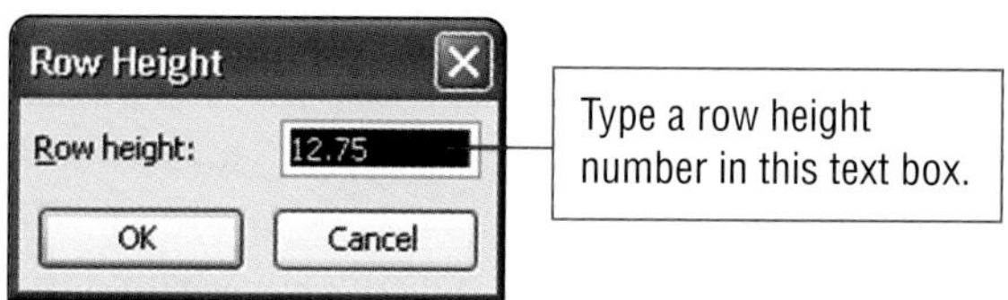

exercise 7

CHANGING ROW HEIGHT AT THE ROW HEIGHT DIALOG BOX

1. Open **ExcelWorksheet07**.
2. Save the worksheet with Save As and name it **sec2x07**.
3. Change the font size of *REAL PHOTOGRAPHY* to 14 points.
4. Change the height of row 1 by completing the following steps:
   a. With cell A1 active, click Format, point to Row, and then click Height.
   b. At the Row Height dialog box, type **30** in the *Row height* text box, and then click OK.
5. Change the height of rows 2 through 10 by completing the following steps:
   a. Select rows 2 through 10.
   b. Click Format, point to Row, and then click Height.
   c. At the Row Height dialog box, type **20** in the *Row height* text box, and then press Enter or click OK.
6. Click in cell A1.
7. Save, preview, print, and then close **sec2x07**.

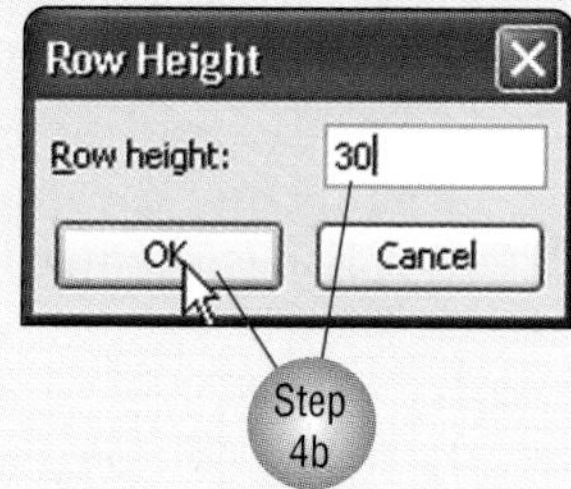

QUICK STEPS

Format Data in Cells
Click button on toolbar representing desired formatting.
OR
1. Click Format, Cells.
2. Click desired tab.
3. Use options in dialog box to apply desired formatting.
4. Click OK.

Formatting Data in Cells

An Excel worksheet contains default formatting. For example, by default, letters and words are aligned at the left of a cell, numbers are aligned at the right, and data is set in a 10-point sans serif typeface such as Arial. Depending on the data you are entering in cells, you may want to change some of these default settings.

Formatting Numbers

Numbers in a cell, by default, are aligned at the right and decimals and commas are not displayed unless they are typed in the cell. Also, numbers display in a 10-point sans serif typeface such as Arial. Depending on the type of numbers used in a worksheet, you may want to change these default settings. You can format numbers using a format symbol, or change number formatting with buttons on the Formatting toolbar or with options at the Format Cells dialog box.

Format symbols you can use to format numbers include a percent sign (%), a comma (,), and a dollar sign ($). For example, if you type the number *$45.50* in a cell, Excel automatically applies Currency formatting to the number. If you type *45%*, Excel automatically applies the Percent formatting to the number.

Five buttons on the Formatting toolbar can be used to format numbers in cells. The five buttons are shown and described in Table 2.1.

TABLE 2.1 ***Number Formatting Buttons on Formatting Toolbar***

Click this button	***Named***	***To do this***
$	Currency Style	Add a dollar sign, any necessary commas, and a decimal point followed by two decimal digits, if none are typed; right-align number in cell
%	Percent Style	Multiply cell value by 100 and display result with a percent symbol; right-align number in cell
,	Comma Style	Add any necessary commas and a decimal point followed by two decimal digits, if none are typed; right-align number in cell
←.0 .00	Increase Decimal	Increase number of decimal places displayed after decimal point in selected cells
.00 →.0	Decrease Decimal	Decrease number of decimal places displayed after decimal point in selected cells

Specify the formatting for numbers in cells in a worksheet before typing the numbers, or format existing numbers in a worksheet. The Increase Decimal and Decrease Decimal buttons on the Formatting toolbar will change decimal places for existing numbers only.

Increase Decimal

Decrease Decimal

exercise 8

FORMATTING NUMBERS WITH BUTTONS ON THE FORMATTING TOOLBAR

1. Open **ExcelWorksheet08**.
2. Save the worksheet with Save As and name it **sec2x08**.
3. Change the width of column A to 13.00.
4. Select columns B, C, and D, and then change the column width to 10.00.
5. Change the width of column E to 8.00.
6. Make the following number formatting changes:
   a. Select cells B3 through D12.
   b. Click the Currency Style button on the Formatting toolbar.
   c. Click twice the Decrease Decimal button on the Formatting toolbar. (The numbers in the selected cells should not contain any decimal places.)

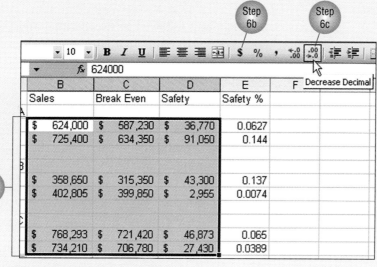

Step 6b

Step 6c

Decrease Decimal

Step 6a

B	C	D	E	F
Sales	Break Even	Safety	Safety %	
$ 624,000	$ 587,230	$ 36,770	0.0627	
$ 725,400	$ 634,350	$ 91,050	0.144	
$ 358,650	$ 315,350	$ 43,300	0.137	
$ 402,805	$ 399,850	$ 2,955	0.0074	
$ 768,293	$ 721,420	$ 46,873	0.065	
$ 734,210	$ 706,780	$ 27,430	0.0389	

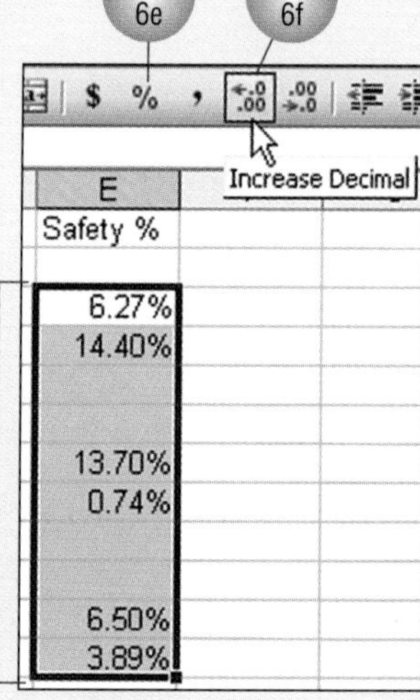

   d. Select cells E3 through E12.
   e. Click the Percent Style button on the Formatting toolbar.
   f. Click twice the Increase Decimal button on the Formatting toolbar. (There should now be two decimal places in the percent numbers in the selected cells.)

Step 6d

7. Select and then bold column A.
8. Select cells B1 through E1 and then click the Bold button.
9. Click in cell A1.
10. Save, print, and then close **sec2x08**.

HINT

Another method for displaying the Format Cells dialog box is to right-click a cell and then click Format Cells at the shortcut menu.

Numbers in cells can also be formatted with options at the Format Cells dialog box with the Number tab selected as shown in Figure 2.7. Display this dialog box by clicking Format and then Cells.

FIGURE

2.7 Format Cells Dialog Box with Number Tab Selected

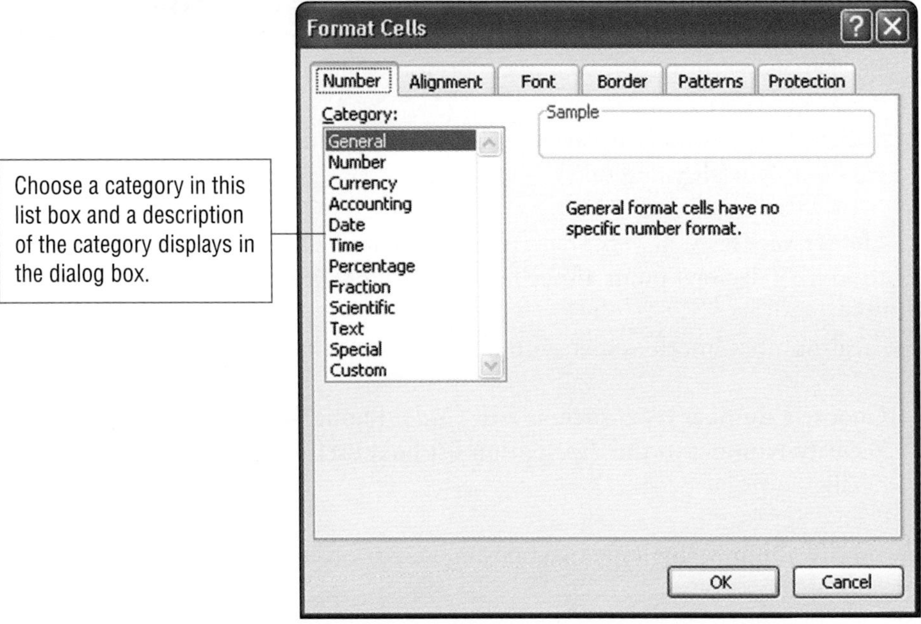

The left side of the dialog box displays number categories. The default category is *General*. At this setting no specific formatting is applied to numbers except right-aligning numbers in cells. The other number categories are described in Table 2.2.

TABLE

2.2 Number Categories at the Format Cells Dialog Box

Click this category	To apply this number formatting
Number	Specify number of decimal places and whether or not a thousand separator should be used; choose the display of negative numbers; right-align numbers in cell
Currency	Apply general monetary values; dollar sign is added as well as commas and decimal points, if needed; right-align numbers in cell
Accounting	Line up the currency symbol and decimal points in a column; add dollar sign and two digits after a decimal point; right-align numbers in cell
Date	Display date as date value; specify the type of formatting desired by clicking an option in the *Type* list box; right-align date in cell
Time	Display time as time value; specify the type of formatting desired by clicking an option in the *Type* list box; right-align time in cell

Continued on next page

Click this category	To apply this number formatting
Percentage	Multiply cell value by 100 and display result with a percent symbol; add decimal point followed by two digits by default; number of digits can be changed with the *Decimal places* option; right-align number in cell
Fraction	Specify how fraction displays in cell by clicking an option in the *Type* list box; right-align fraction in cell
Scientific	Use for very large or very small numbers. Use the letter *E* to tell Excel to move a decimal point a specified number of positions
Text	Treat number in cell as text; number is displayed in cell exactly as typed
Special	Choose a number type, such as ZIP Code, Phone Number, or Social Security Number in the *Type* option list box; useful for tracking list and database values
Custom	Specify a numbering type by choosing an option in the *Type* list box

exercise 9

FORMATTING NUMBERS AT THE FORMAT CELLS DIALOG BOX

1. Open **ExcelWorksheet02**.
2. Save the worksheet with Save As and name it **sec2x09**.
3. Change the number formatting by completing the following steps:
   a. Select cells B2 through D8.
   b. Click Format and then Cells.
   c. At the Format Cells dialog box with the Number tab selected, click *Currency* in the *Category* list box.
   d. Click the down-pointing arrow at the right of the *Decimal places* option until *0* displays in the *Decimal places* text box.
   e. Click OK to close the dialog box.

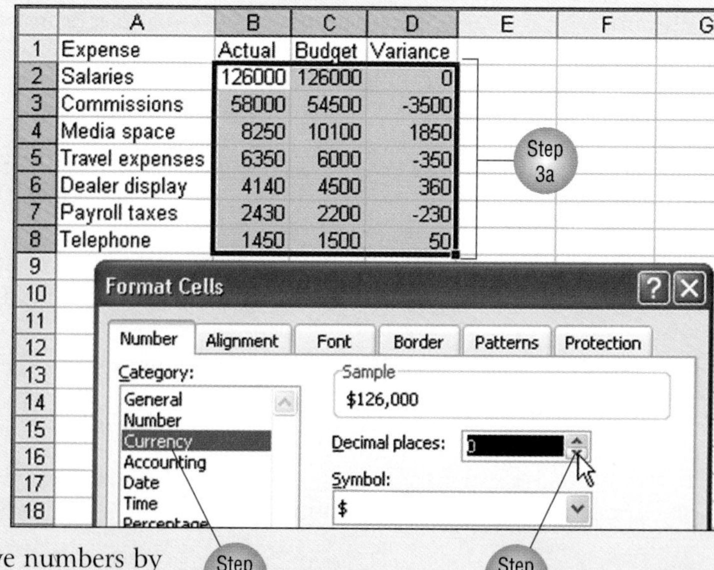

4. Select and then bold and italicize row 1.
5. Save and then print **sec2x09**.
6. With **sec2x09** still open, change the display of negative numbers by completing the following steps:

a. Select cells D2 through D8.
b. Click Format and then Cells.
c. At the Format Cells dialog box, click the fourth option displayed in the Negative numbers list box (displays as *($1,234)*).
d. Click OK to close the dialog box.
e. Click in cell A1.

7. Save, print, and then close **sec2x09**.

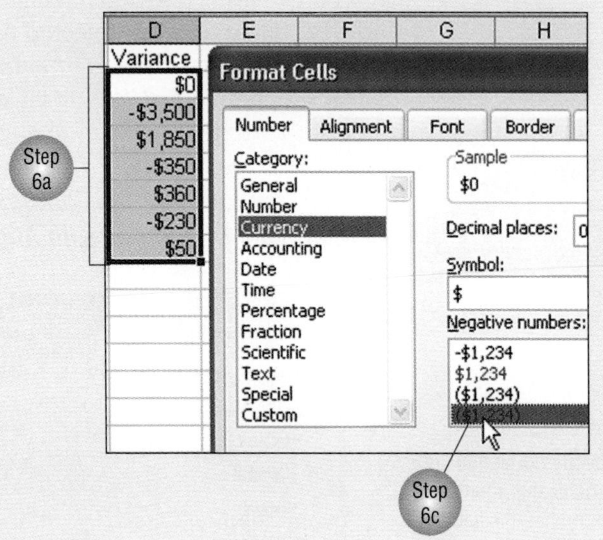

Aligning, Indenting, and Rotating Data in Cells

The alignment of data in cells depends on the type of data entered. For example, words or text combined with numbers entered in a cell are aligned at the left edge of the cell while numbers are aligned at the right. Alignment of data can be controlled with buttons on the Formatting toolbar or options at the Format Cells dialog box with the Alignment tab selected.

Four buttons on the Formatting toolbar, shown in Figure 2.8, can be used to control the alignment of data in a cell or selected cells. Click the Align Left button to align data at the left side of a cell, click the Center button to align data between the left and right side of a cell, and click Align Right to align data at the right side of a cell. Click the Merge and Center button to merge selected cells and center data within the merged cells. If you have merged cells and want to split them again, select the cells and then click the Merge and Center button.

Indent text within a cell or selected cells by clicking the Increase Indent button or the Decrease Indent button on the Formatting toolbar. These buttons are identified in Figure 2.8. The Increase Indent button will move text within the cell or selected cells to the right while the Decrease Indent button will move text to the left.

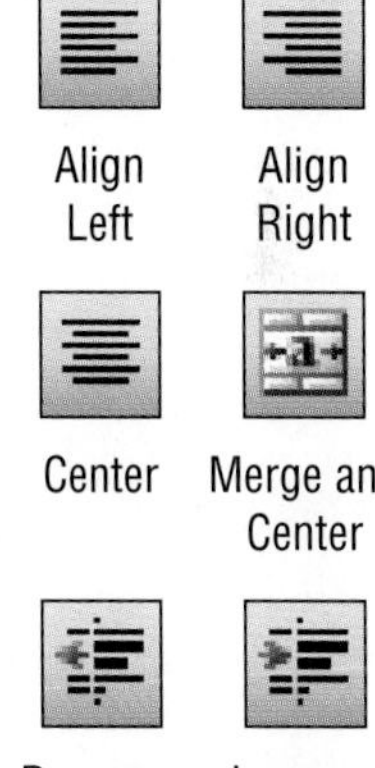

FIGURE 2.8 ***Alignment and Indent Buttons on the Formatting Toolbar***

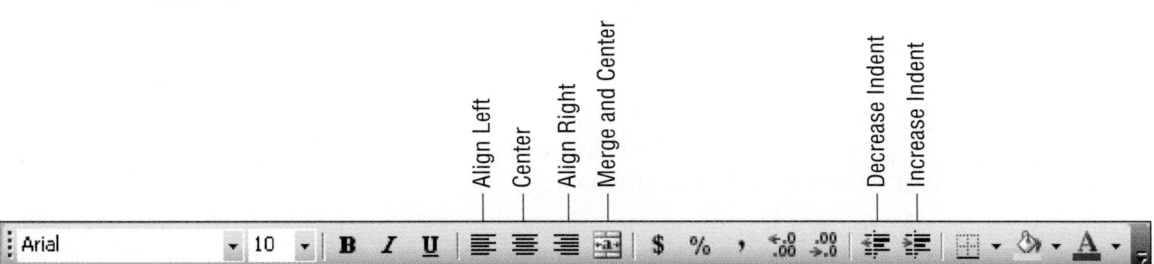

You can also control data aligning and indenting at the Format Cells dialog box with the Alignment tab selected as shown in Figure 2.9. Click the down-pointing arrow at the right of the *Horizontal* option box and a list of alignment options displays including *Left (Indent), Center, Right, Fill, Justify,* and *Center Across Selection*. Choose the desired horizontal alignment from this list.

FIGURE 2.9 **Format Cells Dialog Box with Alignment Tab Selected**

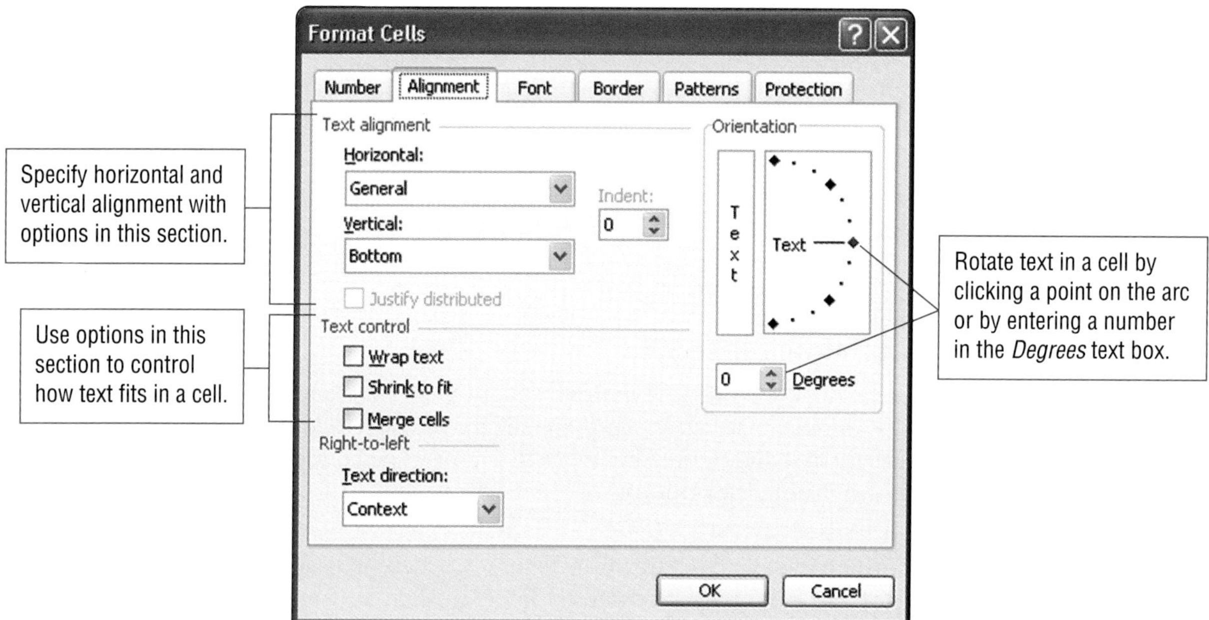

By default, data in a cell is aligned at the bottom of the cell. Change this alignment to top, center, or justify with choices from the *Vertical* drop-down list. To display this list, click the down-pointing arrow at the right side of the *Vertical* option. Use the *Indent* text box to indent cell contents from the left side of the cell. Each increment entered in the *Indent* text box is equivalent to the width of one character.

In the *Orientation* section, you can choose to rotate data. A portion of the *Orientation* section shows points on an arc. Click a point on the arc to rotate the text along that point. You can also type a rotation degree in the *Degrees* text box. Type a positive number to rotate selected text from the lower left to the upper right of the cell. Type a negative number to rotate selected text from the upper left to the lower right of the cell.

As you learned earlier, if data typed in a cell is longer than the cell, it overlaps the next cell to the right. If you want data to remain in a cell and wrap to the next line within the same cell, click the *Wrap text* option in the *Text control* section of the dialog box. Click the *Shrink to fit* option to reduce the size of the text font so all selected data fits within the column. Use the *Merge cells* option to combine two or more selected cells into a single cell.

If you want to enter data on more than one line within a cell, enter the data on the first line and then press Alt + Enter. Pressing Alt + Enter moves the insertion point to the next line within the same cell.

ALIGNING AND ROTATING DATA IN CELLS

1. Open **ExcelWorksheet01**.
2. Save the worksheet with Save As and name it **sec2x10**.
3. Select the entire worksheet and then change the font to 12-point Tahoma (or a similar sans serif typeface).
4. Automatically increase the width of column A by positioning the cell pointer on the boundary between columns A and B and then double-clicking the left mouse button.
5. Select row 1, click the Bold button, and then click the Center button on the Formatting toolbar.
6. Select cells B3 through B10 and then click the Center button on the Formatting toolbar.
7. Change the orientation of data in cells by completing the following steps:
   a. Select cells B1 through D1.
   b. Click Format and then Cells.
   c. At the Format Cells dialog box, click the Alignment tab.
   d. Select *0* in the *Degrees* text box and then type 45.
   e. Click OK to close the dialog box.

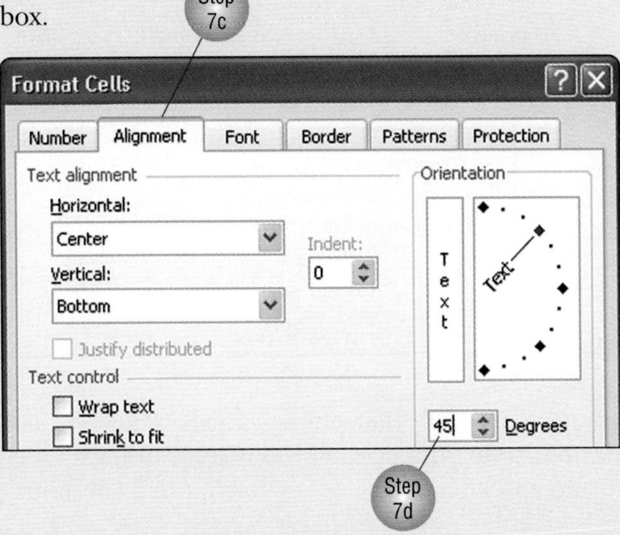

8. Merge and center data in a cell by completing the following steps:
   a. Select cells A12 through D12.
   b. Click the Merge and Center button on the Formatting toolbar.
   c. Double-click in the newly merged cell.
   d. Turn on bold, type **YEARLY JOB REPORT**, and then press Enter.

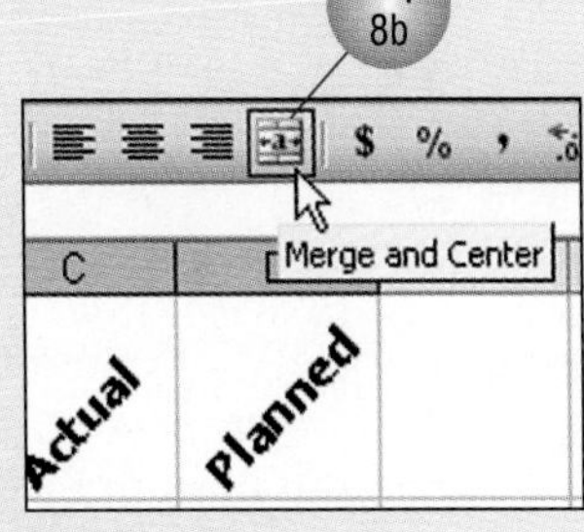

9. Enter text on a separate line in cell A1 by completing the following steps:
   a. Double-click cell A1.
   b. Move the insertion point to the end of *Customer*.
   c. Press Alt + Enter.
   d. Type **Products Dept.**
10. Save, print, and then close **sec2x10**.

HINT

Use the Format Painter button on the Standard toolbar to copy formatting from one range of cells to another.

Changing the Font at the Format Cells Dialog Box

As you learned earlier in this chapter, the font for data can be changed with the Font button on the Formatting toolbar and the font size can be changed with the Font Size button. The font for data in selected cells can also be changed at the Format Cells dialog box with the Font tab selected as shown in Figure 2.10.

FIGURE 2.10 ***Format Cells Dialog Box with Font Tab Selected***

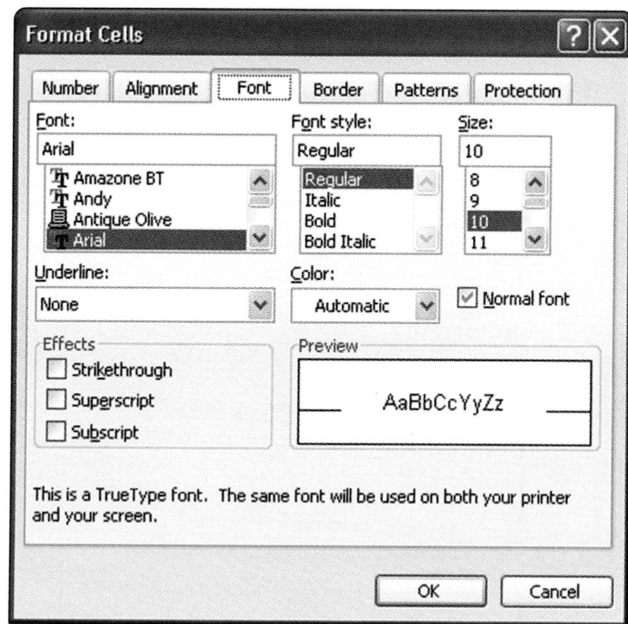

At the Format Cells dialog box with the Font tab selected, you can change the font, font style, font size, and font color. You can also change the underlining method and add effects such as superscript and subscript.

exercise 11

CHANGING THE FONT AND FONT COLOR OF DATA IN CELLS

1. Open **ExcelWorksheet02**.
2. Save the worksheet with Save As and name it **sec2x11**.
3. Change the font and font color by completing the following steps:
   a. Select the entire worksheet.
   b. Click Format and then Cells.
   c. At the Format Cells dialog box, click the Font tab.

d. At the Format Cells dialog box with the Font tab selected, click *Garamond* in the *Font* list box (you will need to scroll down the list to make this font visible).
e. Click *12* in the *Size* list box (you will need to scroll down the list to make this size visible).
f. Click the down-pointing arrow at the right of the *Color* option box (contains the word *Automatic*).
g. At the palette of color choices that displays, click the Blue color.
h. Click OK to close the dialog box.

4. Change the font color for the cells in row 1 by completing the following steps:
   a. Select row 1.
   b. Click Format and then Cells.
   c. At the Format Cells dialog box, make sure the Font tab is selected.
   d. Click the down-pointing arrow at the right side of the *Color* option box.
   e. At the palette of color choices, click a red color (you choose the red).
   f. Click OK to close the dialog box.
5. Select cells B2 through D8 and then change the number formatting to *Currency* with zero decimal places.
6. Select cells A2 through A8 and then click twice on the Increase Indent button on the Formatting toolbar. (This indents the text from the left side of the cells.)
7. Automatically adjust the width of columns A, B, C, and D.
8. Save, print, and then close **sec2x11**.

Inserting/Deleting Cells, Rows, and Columns

HINT

At the Insert dialog box, specify the direction in which cells should move.

New data may need to be included in an existing worksheet. For example, a row or several rows of new data may need to be inserted into a worksheet; or, data may need to be removed from a worksheet.

Inserting Rows

Insert Row
Click Insert, Rows.
OR
1. Click Insert, Cells.
2. Click Entire row.
3. Click OK.

After a worksheet has been created, rows can be added (inserted) to the worksheet. Insert a row with options from the Insert drop-down menu or with options at the Insert dialog box. By default, a row is inserted above the row containing the active cell. To insert a row in a worksheet, make a cell active in the row below where the row is to be inserted, click Insert and then click Rows. If you want to insert more than one row, select the number of rows in the worksheet that you want inserted, click Insert and then click Rows.

You can also insert a row by making a cell active in the row below where the row is to be inserted, clicking Insert, and then clicking Cells. This causes the Insert dialog box to display as shown in Figure 2.11. At the Insert dialog box, click *Entire row*. This inserts an entire row above the active cell.

FIGURE 2.11 ***Insert Dialog Box***

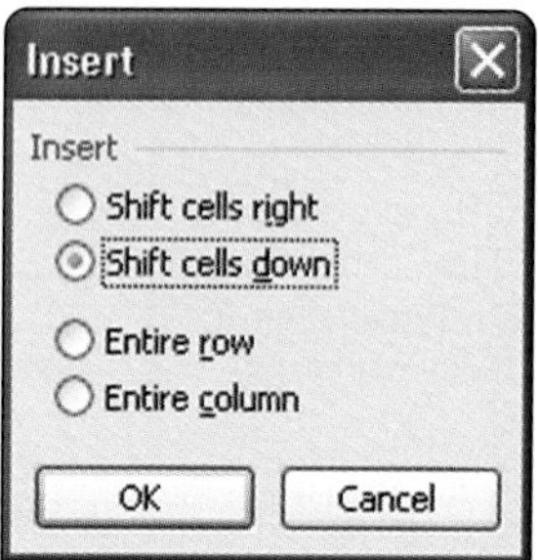

exercise 12 INSERTING ROWS IN A WORKSHEET

1. Open **ExcelWorksheet01**.
2. Save the worksheet with Save As and name it **sec2x12**.
3. Add two rows and enter data in the new cells by completing the following steps:
   a. Select rows 7 and 8 in the worksheet.
   b. Click Insert and then Rows.
   c. Type the following data in the specified cells (you do not need to type the dollar sign or the comma in cells containing money amounts):

A7	=	**Summit Clinic**
B7	=	**570**
C7	=	**33056**
D7	=	**32500**
A8	=	**Franklin Center**
B8	=	**690**
C8	=	**19745**
D8	=	**19250**

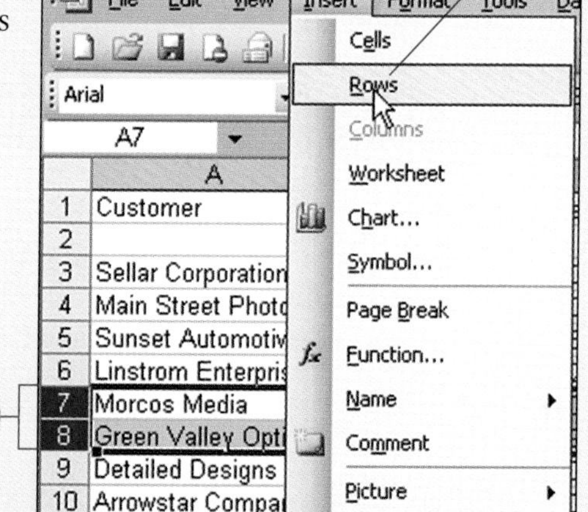

4. Select cells A1 through D12 and then apply an autoformat of your choosing. (Make sure the numbers display properly.)
5. Save, print, and then close **sec2x12**.

QUICK STEPS

Insert Column
Click Insert, Column.
OR
1. Click Insert, Cells.
2. Click Entire column.
3. Click OK.

Inserting Columns

Insert columns in a worksheet in much the same way as rows. Insert a column with options from the Insert drop-down menu or with options at the Insert dialog box. By default, a column is inserted immediately to the left of the column containing the active cell. To insert a column in a worksheet, make a cell active in the column immediately to the right of where the new column is to be inserted, click Insert

and then click Columns. If you want to insert more than one column, select the number of columns in the worksheet that you want inserted, click Insert and then click Columns.

You can also insert a column by making a cell active in the column immediately to the right of where the new column is to be inserted, clicking Insert, and then clicking Cells. This causes the Insert dialog box to display. At the Insert dialog box, click *Entire column*. This inserts an entire column immediately to the left of the active cell.

exercise 13

INSERTING A COLUMN IN A WORKSHEET

1. Open **ExcelWorksheet03**.
2. Save the worksheet with Save As and name it **sec2x13**.
3. Add a column to the worksheet and enter data in the new cells by completing the following steps:
   a. Click in any cell in column D.
   b. Click Insert and then Columns.
   c. Type the following data in the specified cells:

D2	=	**Next Year**
D3	=	0.55
D4	=	0.4
D5	=	1.12
D6	=	1.85
D7	=	0.22
D8	=	0.055

C	D	E
Planned	Next Year	Prior Year
0.6	0.55	0.57
0.39	0.4	0.41
1.15	1.12	1.2
1.9	1.85	1.87
0.2	0.22	0.28
0.06	0.055	0.06

Step 3c

4. Select cells B3 through E8 and then click the Percent Style button on the Formatting toolbar.
5. Select cells A1 through E8 and then apply an autoformat of your choosing.
6. Save, print, and then close **sec2x13**.

Deleting Cells, Rows, or Columns

Specific cells in a worksheet or rows or columns in a worksheet can be deleted. To delete a specific cell, make the cell active, and then press the Delete key. You can also select the cells to be deleted and then press the Delete key. If you use the Delete key to delete cell(s), only the cell text is deleted. The empty cell(s) remains in the worksheet.

If you want to delete the cell(s) as well as the cell text, make the specific cell active or select cells, click Edit, and then click Delete. At the Delete dialog box shown in Figure 2.12, choose what you want deleted, and then click OK.

FIGURE 2.12 ***Delete Dialog Box***

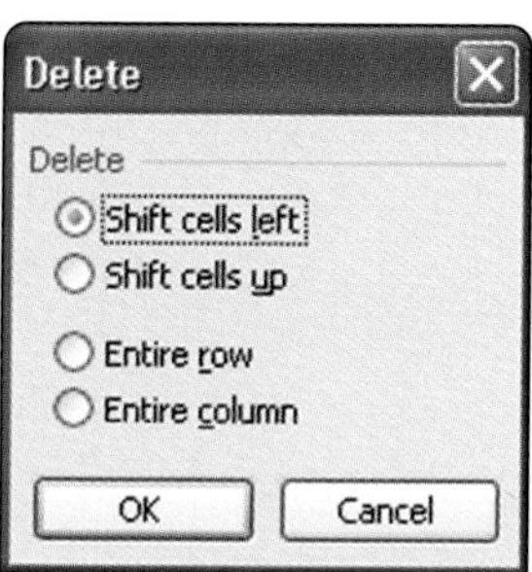

The Delete dialog box can also be displayed by positioning the cell pointer in the worksheet, clicking the *right* mouse button, and then clicking *Delete* on the shortcut menu. To delete several rows of cells, select the rows, click Edit, and then click Delete. To delete several columns of cells, select the columns, click Edit, and then click Delete.

HINT

One method for clearing the contents of a cell is to right-click the cell and then click Clear Contents at the shortcut menu.

Clearing Data in Cells

With the Clear option from the Edit drop-down menu, the contents of selected cells can be cleared. This is useful in a situation where the cells are to remain but the contents need to be changed. To clear cell contents, select the cells, click Edit, point to Clear, and then click All. This deletes the cell contents and the cell formatting. Click Formats to remove formatting from selected cells while leaving the data. Click Contents to remove the contents of the cell, leaving any formatting. You can also click the Delete key to clear the contents of the selected cells.

Clear Data in Cells
1. Select cells.
2. Click Edit, Clear, All.

exercise 14 DELETING COLUMNS AND DELETING AND CLEARING ROWS IN A WORKSHEET

1. Open **ExcelWorksheet02**.
2. Save the worksheet with Save As and name it **sec2x14**.
3. Delete column D in the worksheet by completing the following steps:
   a. Click in any cell in column D.
   b. Click Edit and then Delete.
   c. At the Delete dialog box, click *Entire column*.
   d. Click OK or press Enter.
4. Delete row 5 by completing the following steps:
   a. Select row 5.
   b. Click Edit and then Delete.
5. Clear row contents by completing the following steps:
   a. Select rows 5 and 6.
   b. Click Edit, point to Clear, and then click Contents.

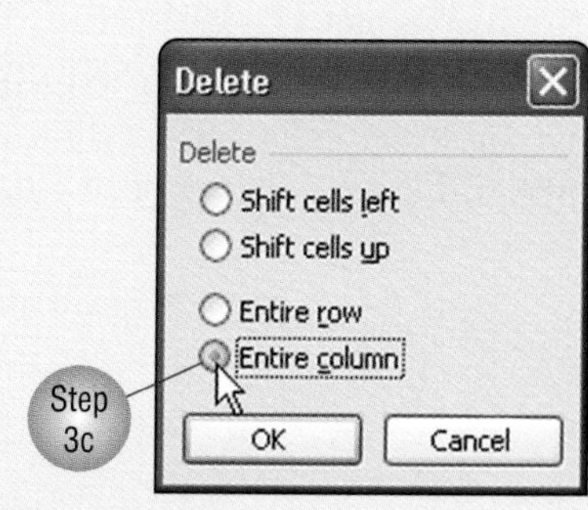

6. Type the following data in the specified cells:

A5	=	**Lodging**
B5	=	**4535**
C5	=	**5100**
A6	=	**Entertainment**
B6	=	**3210**
C6	=	**3000**

Step 6

	A	B	C
1	Expense	Actual	Budget
2	Salaries	126000	126000
3	Commissions	58000	54500
4	Media space	8250	10100
5	Lodging	4535	5100
6	Entertainment	3210	3000
7	Telephone	1450	1500

7. Select cells A1 through C7 and then apply the Accounting 1 autoformat.
8. Clear cell formatting and then apply different formatting by completing the following steps:
   a. Select cells A1 through C1.
   b. Click Edit, point to Clear, and then click Formats.
   c. With cells A1 through C1 still selected, click the Bold button on the Formatting toolbar and then click the Center button.
9. Save, print, and then close **sec2x14**.

Adding Borders and Shading to Cells

The gridlines that display in a worksheet do not print. Borders that will print can be added to cells, however. Add borders with options from the Borders button on the Formatting toolbar or with options from the Format Cells dialog box with the Border tab selected.

To add a border to a cell or selected cells, make the desired cell active or select the desired cells, and then click the Borders button on the Formatting toolbar. By default, a single-line border is added to the bottom of the active cell or the selected cells. To change the style of border, click the down-pointing arrow at the right of the Borders button. This causes a palette of border style choices to display. Click the choice that represents the type of border desired for the cell or selected cells. Clicking the desired border style removes the palette and also applies that border style to the active cell or the selected cells.

Click the down arrow at the right side of the Borders button, click the Draw Borders option, and the Borders toolbar displays. Use buttons on this toolbar to draw, customize, and erase border lines. If you click the Erase button on the Borders toolbar and the mouse pointer turns into an eraser. Use this pointer to erase borders from cells.

QUICK STEPS

Add Border to Cells
1. Select cells.
2. Click Borders button.

OR

1. Select cells.
2. Click Format, Cells.
3. Click Border tab.
4. Use options in dialog box to apply desired border.
5. Click OK.

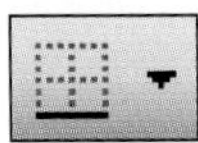

Borders

exercise 15

ADDING BORDERS TO CELLS USING THE BORDERS BUTTON

1. Open **ExcelWorksheet01**.
2. Save the worksheet with Save As and name it **sec2x15**.
3. Select row 1 and then turn on bold and change the alignment to center.
4. Select cells B3 through B10 and then change the alignment to center.

5. Add a border to all cells in the worksheet (that contain data) by completing the following steps:
   a. Click the down-pointing arrow at the right side of the Borders button on the Formatting toolbar and then click the Draw Borders option. (The mouse pointer turns into a pencil and the Borders toolbar displays in the worksheet area.)
   b. Click the down-pointing arrow at the right side of the Line Style button on the Borders toolbar and then click the double-line option.
   c. Using the mouse pointer (pencil), draw a double-line border around the outside of the cells containing data.

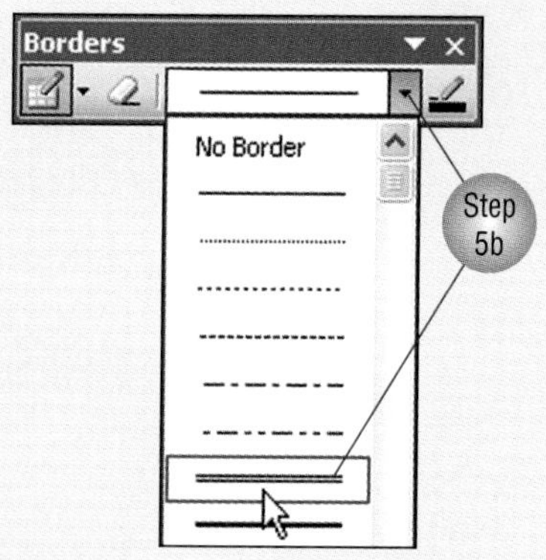

	A	B	C	D
1	**Customer**	**Job #**	**Actual**	**Planned**
2				
3	Sellar Corporation	2130	$30,349	$34,109
4	Main Street Photos	1201	$48,290	$48,100
5	Sunset Automotive	318	$34,192	$32,885
6	Linstrom Enterprises	1009	$63,293	$61,220
7	Morcos Media	676	$29,400	$30,500
8	Green Valley Optics	2117	$55,309	$58,394
9	Detailed Designs	983	$12,398	$13,100
10	Arrowstar Company	786	$87,534	$86,905

Step 5c

   d. Change back to a single line by clicking the down-pointing arrow at the right side of the Line Style button on the Borders toolbar, and then clicking the top single-line option.
   e. Turn off the display of the Borders toolbar by clicking the Close button (contains an *X*) located in the upper right corner of the toolbar.
6. Add a single-line border to specific cells by completing the following steps:
   a. Select cells A1 through D1.
   b. Click the down-pointing arrow at the right of the Borders button on the Formatting toolbar.
   c. At the palette of border style choices that displays, click the Thick Bottom Border option (second option from the left in the middle row).

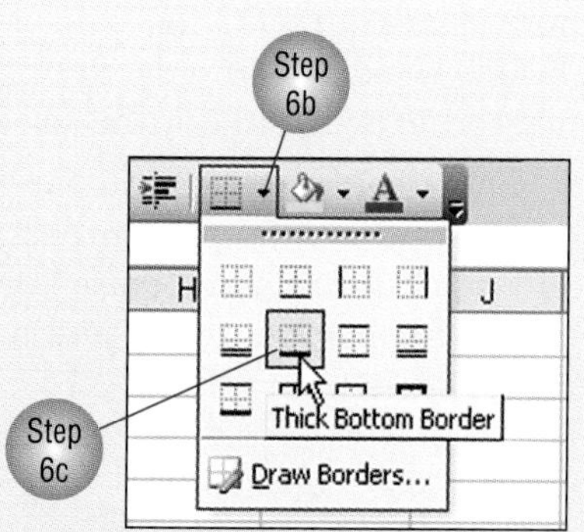

7. Click in cell A1.
8. Save, print, and then close **sec2x15**.

You can also add borders to the active cell or selected cells with options at the Format Cells dialog box with the Border tab selected as shown in Figure 2.13. With options in the *Presets* section, you can remove borders with the *None* option, add only outside borders with the *Outline* option, or click the *Inside* option to add borders to the inside of selected cells. In the *Border* section of the dialog box, specify the side of the cell or selected cells to which you want to apply a border. Choose the style of line desired for the border with the options that display in the *Style* list box. Add color to border lines with choices from the color palette that displays when you click the down arrow located at the right side of the *Color* option box (contains the word *Automatic*).

FIGURE 2.13 **Format Cells Dialog Box with Border Tab Selected**

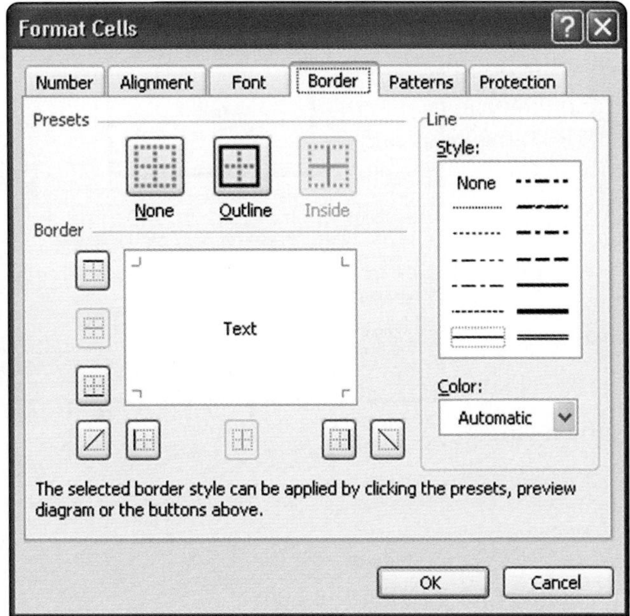

exercise 16 ADDING BORDERS TO CELLS AT THE FORMAT CELLS DIALOG BOX

1. Open **ExcelWorksheet02**.
2. Save the worksheet with Save As and name it **sec2x16**.
3. Select the entire worksheet, display the Format Cells dialog box with the Font tab selected, change the font to 12-point Century (or a similar serif typeface), the color to green (you determine the green), and then close the dialog box.
4. Select row 1 and then turn on bold and change the alignment to center.
5. Select cells B2 through D8, display the Format Cells dialog box with the Number tab selected, change the *Category* option to *Currency* with zero decimal places, and then close the dialog box.
6. Automatically adjust the width of columns A, B, C, and D.
7. Add a green outline border to the worksheet by completing the following steps:
   a. Select cells A1 through D8 (all cells containing data).
   b. Click Format and then Cells.

c. At the Format Cells dialog box, click the Border tab.
d. Click the sixth option from the top in the second column in the *Style* list box.
e. Click the down-pointing arrow located at the right side of the *Color* option box (contains the word *Automatic*).
f. At the palette of color choices, click the same green color that you chose for the font.
g. Click the *Outline* option in the *Presets* section of the dialog box.
h. Click OK to close the dialog box.

8. Click in cell A1.
9. Save, print, and then close **sec2x16**.

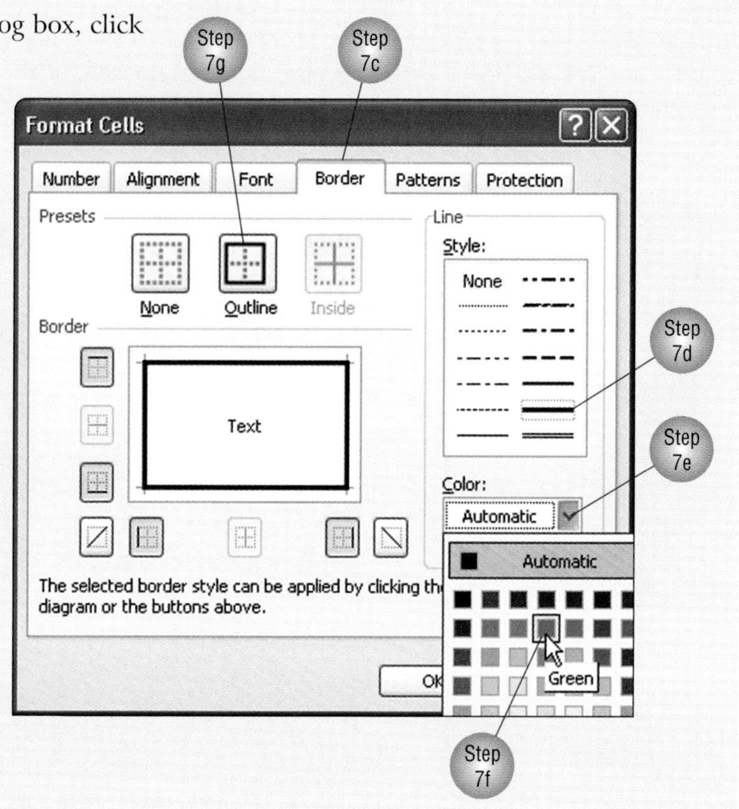

HINT

Apply shading and patterns to cells at the Format Cells dialog box with the Patterns tab selected.

Fill Color

QUICK STEPS

Add Shading to Cells

1. Select cells.
2. Click down-pointing arrow at right of Fill Color button.
3. Click desired color.

OR

1. Select cells.
2. Click Format, Cells.
3. Click Patterns tab.
4. Use options in dialog box to apply desired border.

Adding Shading and a Pattern to Cells

To enhance the visual display of cells and data within cells, consider adding shading and/or a pattern to cells. Add color shading to cells in a worksheet by clicking the Fill Color button on the Formatting toolbar. You can also add color shading and/or a pattern to cells in a worksheet with options at the Format Cells dialog box with the Patterns tab selected.

To add color shading using the Fill Color button on the Formatting toolbar, make the desired cell active or select the desired cells, and then click the Fill Color button. By default, the color yellow is added to the cell or selected cells. To add a shading of a different color, click the down-pointing arrow at the right of the Fill Color button, and then click the desired color at the palette that displays.

Add color shading as well as a pattern to the active cell or selected cells with options at the Format Cells dialog box with the Patterns tab selected as shown in Figure 2.14. Choose a color shading for a cell or selected cells by clicking a color choice in the *Color* section. To add a pattern to a cell or selected cells, click the down-pointing arrow at the right of the *Pattern* option box, and then click the desired pattern. When you click a pattern, that pattern displays in the Sample box in the dialog box. The Sample box also displays any chosen color shading.

FIGURE

2.14 *Format Cells Dialog Box with Patterns Tab Selected*

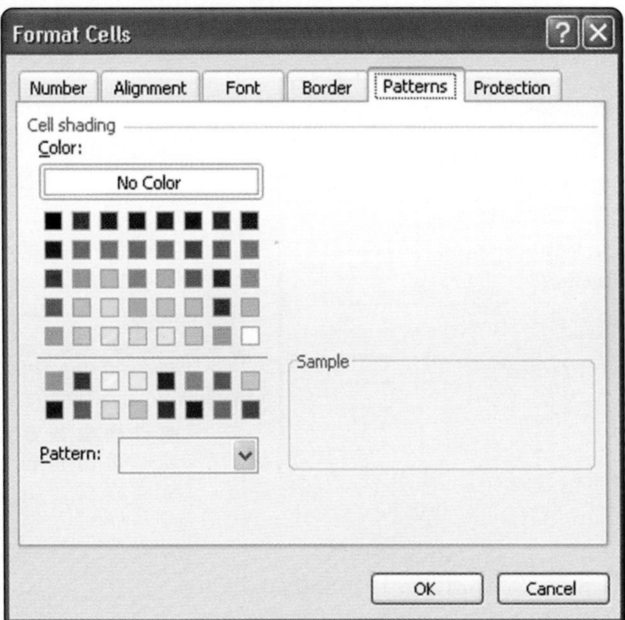

Repeating the Last Action

If you want to apply other types of formatting, such as number, border, or shading formatting to other cells in a worksheet, use the Repeat command by pressing F4 or Ctrl + Y. The Repeat command repeats the last action performed. You can also repeat formatting by clicking Edit and then Repeat. The Repeat option will change depending on the most recent function performed. For example, if you apply shading formatting to a selected cell, click Edit and Repeat Format Cells displays in the drop-down menu.

Repeat Last Action
1. Apply formatting.
2. Press F4; Ctrl + Y; or Edit, Repeat.

exercise 17

ADDING SHADING AND A PATTERN TO CELLS

1. Open **ExcelWorksheet08**.
2. Save the worksheet with Save As and name it **sec2x17**.
3. Select cells B3 through D12 and then click the Currency Style button on the Formatting toolbar.
4. Select cells E3 through E12, click the Percent Style button, and then click twice on the Increase Decimal button on the Formatting toolbar.
5. Apply a double-line border around cells by completing the following steps:
   a. Select cells A1 through E12.
   b. Click Format and then Cells.
   c. At the Format Cells dialog box, click the Border tab.

d. Click the double-line option in the *Style* list box.
e. Click the Outline button in the *Presets* section.
f. Click OK to close the dialog box.

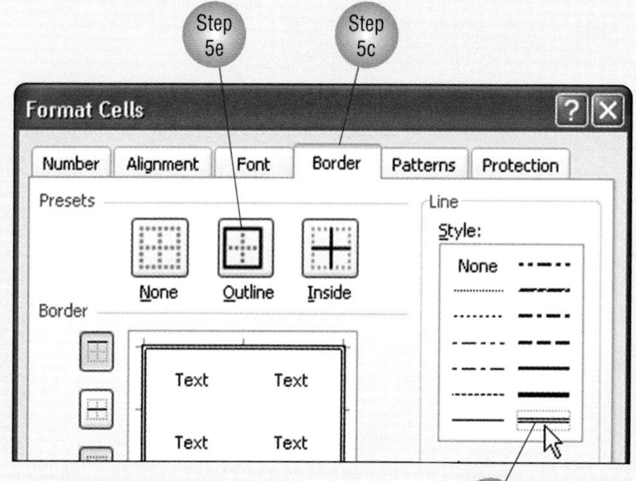

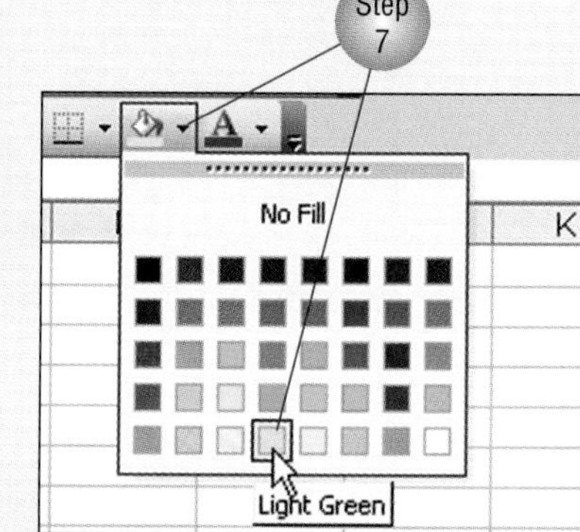

6. Select cells B1 through E1 and then turn on bold and change the alignment to center.
7. With cells B1 through E1 selected, apply shading by clicking the down-pointing arrow at the right of the Fill Color button and then clicking the Light Green color.
8. Repeat the shading by selecting cells A2 through A12 and then pressing F4 or Ctrl + Y.
9. Apply shading to specific cells by completing the following steps:
   a. Select cells B3 through E4.
   b. Click Format and then Cells.
   c. At the Format Cells dialog box, click the Patterns tab.
   d. Click the Light Yellow color in the *Color* section.
   e. Click OK.

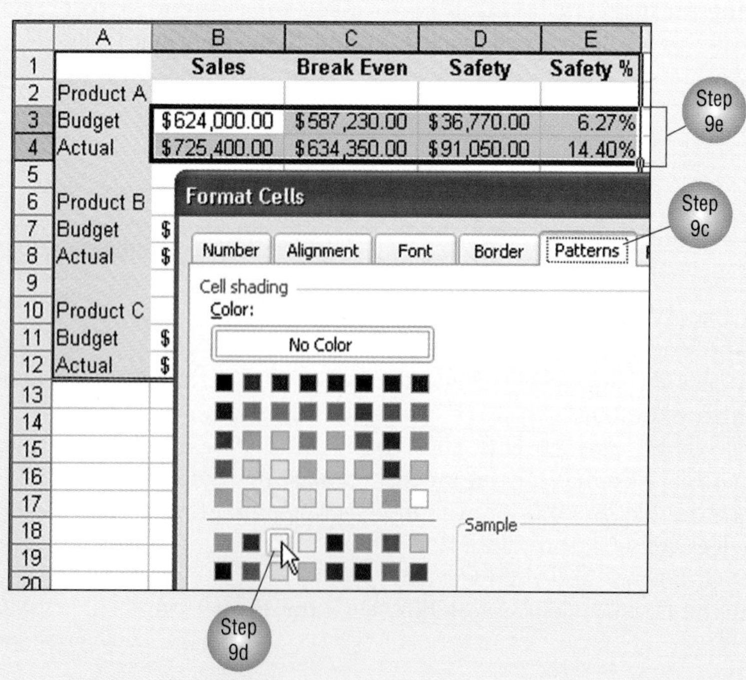

10. Use the Repeat command, F4 or Ctrl + Y, to apply the same light yellow shading to cells B7 through E8 and also to cells B11 through E12.
11. Apply a pattern to cells by completing the following steps:
    a. Select cells B2 through E2 (these are empty cells).
    b. Click Format and then Cells.
    c. At the Format Cells dialog box with the Patterns tab selected, click the down-pointing arrow at the right side of the *Pattern* option box, and then click the Thin Diagonal Stripe option (fourth option from the left in the bottom row).
    d. Click OK.
12. Use the Repeat command, F4 or Ctrl + Y, to apply the same pattern to cells B5 through E6 and also to cells B9 through E10.
13. Click in cell A1.
14. Save, print, and then close **sec2x17**.

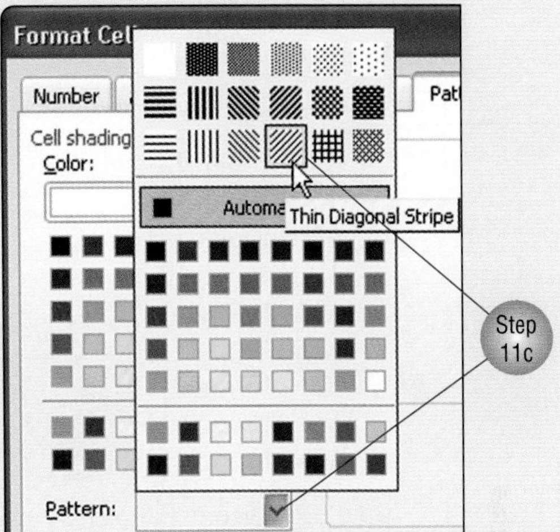

Formatting with Format Painter

The Standard toolbar contains a button that can be used to copy formatting to different locations in the worksheet. This button is called the Format Painter and displays on the Standard toolbar as a paintbrush. To use the Format Painter button, make a cell or selected cells active that contain the desired formatting, click the Format Painter button, and then click the cell or selected cells to which you want the formatting applied.

Format Painter

Format with Format Painter
1. Apply formatting.
2. Double-click Format Painter button.
3. Select cells.
4. Click Format Painter button.

When you click the Format Painter button, the mouse pointer displays with a paintbrush attached. If you want to apply formatting a single time, click the Format Painter brush once. If, however, you want to apply the character formatting in more than one location in the worksheet, double-click the Format Painter button. If you have double-clicked the Format Painter button, turn off the feature by clicking the Format Painter button once.

exercise 18

FORMATTING WITH FORMAT PAINTER

1. Open **ExcelWorksheet06**.
2. Save the worksheet with Save As and name it **sec2x18**.
3. Select and then delete columns K through M.
4. Use Format Painter to "paint" formatting to cells by completing the following steps:
    a. Select cells B1 through B20 and then apply pale blue shading to the cells.
    b. Make a cell active that contains a percentage number in column B.
    c. Double-click the Format Painter button on the Standard toolbar.

d. Select the following cells in each column:

   D1 through D20
   F1 through F20
   H1 through H20
   J1 through J20

e. Select the following cells in each row:

   A3 through J3
   A5 through J5
   A7 through J7
   A9 through J9
   A11 through J11
   A13 through J13
   A15 through J15
   A17 through J17
   A19 through J19

f. Turn off Format Painter by clicking the Format Painter button on the Standard toolbar.

g. Select row 1 and then click twice on the Bold button on the Formatting toolbar. (The Format Painter removed the bold formatting from the cells you formatted with pale blue shading. Selecting the row and then clicking the Bold button the first time removes bold from all headings. Clicking the Bold button the second time inserts bold formatting for the headings.)

5. Save, print, and then close **sec2x18**.

CHAPTER summary

- Preview a worksheet by clicking the Preview button in the Print dialog box; clicking the Print Preview button on the Standard toolbar; or clicking File and then Print Preview.
- Change the size of the worksheet display with options on the Zoom button on the Standard toolbar.
- Apply character formatting to selected cells with buttons on the Formatting toolbar such as Font, Font Size, Bold, Italic, Underline, and Font Color.
- Change column width using the mouse on column boundaries or with options at the Column Width dialog box.
- To automatically adjust a column to accommodate the longest entry in the column, double-click the column header boundary on the right.
- Change row height using the mouse on row boundaries or with options at the Row Height dialog box.

- Format numbers in cells with the Currency Style, Percent Style, Comma Style, Increase Decimal, and Decrease Decimal buttons on the Formatting toolbar.
- Numbers in cells can also be formatted at the Format Cells dialog box with the Number tab selected.
- Change alignment of data within cells with these buttons on the Formatting toolbar: Align Left, Center, Align Right, and Merge and Center.
- You can also change the alignment of data within cells at the Format Cells dialog box with the Alignment tab selected.
- Indent text in a cell or selected cells by clicking the Increase Indent button on the Formatting toolbar. Decrease the indent of text in a cell or selected cells by clicking the Decrease Indent button.
- Change font type, font size, font style, and font color for data in a cell or selected cells with options at the Format Cells dialog box with the Font tab selected.
- Insert a row in a worksheet by clicking Insert and then Rows. To insert more than one row, select the number of rows you want inserted, click Insert, and then click Rows. A row can also be inserted at the Insert dialog box.
- Insert a column in a worksheet by clicking Insert and then Columns. To insert more than one column, select the number of columns you want inserted, click Insert, and then click Columns. A column can also be inserted at the Insert dialog box.
- Delete a specific cell by clicking Edit and then Delete. This displays the Delete dialog box where you can specify if you want to delete just the cell or an entire row or column.
- Remove contents of a cell with the Clear option from the Edit drop-down menu or by pressing the Delete key.
- Add borders to a cell or selected cells with the Borders button on the Formatting toolbar or options at the Format Cells dialog box with the Border tab selected.
- Click the down-pointing arrow at the right side of the Borders button, click the Draw Borders option, and the Borders toolbar displays. Use buttons on this toolbar to draw borders.
- Add color shading to a cell or selected cells with the Fill Color button on the Formatting toolbar. Shading as well as a pattern can be added to a cell or selected cells with options at the Format Cells dialog box with the Patterns tab selected.
- Press F4 or Ctrl + Y to repeat the last action performed. You can also click Edit and then Repeat.
- Use the Format Painter button on the Standard toolbar to copy formatting to different locations in a worksheet.

FEATURES summary

FEATURE	BUTTON	MENU	KEYBOARD
Print Preview		File, Print Preview	
Zoom	100%	View, Zoom	
Column Width dialog box		Format, Column, Width	
Row Height dialog box		Format, Row, Height	
Format Cells dialog box		Format, Cells	Ctrl + 1
Insert dialog box		Insert, Cells	
Delete dialog box		Edit, Delete	
Repeat last action		Edit, Repeat	F4 or Ctrl + Y
Format Painter			

CONCEPTS check

Completion: On a blank sheet of paper, indicate the correct term, symbol, or command for each description.

1. To preview a worksheet, click this button on the Standard toolbar.
2. This toolbar contains buttons for applying character formatting to data within selected cells.
3. To automatically adjust a column width to accommodate the longest entry in the cell, do this with the mouse on the column header boundary.
4. As a column boundary is being dragged, the column width displays in this.
5. Click this button on the Formatting toolbar to multiply the value of numbers in selected cells by 100 and display the result followed by a percent symbol.
6. Click this button on the Formatting toolbar to add a dollar sign, any necessary commas, and a decimal point followed by two decimal digits to numbers in selected cells.
7. Click this button on the Formatting toolbar to merge selected cells and center any data within the cells.
8. Rotate data in cells with options at the Format Cells dialog box with this tab selected.
9. By default, a row is inserted in this direction from the row containing the active cell.

10. By default, a column is inserted in this direction from the column containing the active cell.
11. Add color shading to selected cells in a worksheet with options at the Format Cells dialog box with this tab selected.
12. Press this key to repeat the last action.
13. Use this button on the Standard toolbar to copy formatting to different locations in a worksheet.

SKILLS check

Assessment 1

1. Create the worksheet shown in Figure 2.15 with the following specifications:
   a. Select the entire worksheet and then change the font to 12-point Garamond (or a similar typeface).
   b. Change the width of column A to 14.00 and the width of columns B and C to 9.00.
   c. Type the text in the cells as shown in Figure 2.15. (Bold and center the data in row 1 as shown in the figure.)
   d. After typing the data, select cells B2 through C6, and then change the number formatting to *Currency* with zero decimal places.
2. Save the worksheet and name it **sec2sc01**.
3. Print and then close **sec2sc01**.

FIGURE 2.15 ***Assessment 1***

	A	B	C	D
1	**Expense**	**Original**	**Current**	
2	Labor	97000	98500	
3	Material	129000	153000	
4	Subcontracts	20450	21600	
5	Permits	1200	1350	
6	Tax	1950	2145	
7				

Assessment 2

1. Open **ExcelWorksheet03**.
2. Save the worksheet with Save As and name it **sec2sc02**.
3. Select the entire worksheet and then change the font to 11-point Tahoma (or a similar sans serif typeface).
4. Select row 1 and then turn on bold.
5. Select row 2 and then turn on bold and italics and change the alignment to center.
6. Select cells A1 through D1 and then click the Merge and Center button on the Formatting toolbar.

7. Select cells B3 through D8 and then click the Percent Style button on the Formatting toolbar.
8. Select rows 1 through 8 and then change the row height to 18.00.
9. Automatically adjust the widths of columns A through D.
10. Save, print, and then close **sec2sc02**.

Assessment 3

1. Open **sec2sc01**.
2. Save the worksheet with Save As and name it **sec2sc03**.
3. Change the font for the entire worksheet to 14-point Arial and change the font color to Violet.
4. Change the font color to Dark Blue for the cells in row 1.
5. Automatically adjust the widths of columns A, B, and C.
6. Add a single-line outside border to cells A1 through C6.
7. Save, print, and then close **sec2sc03**.

Assessment 4

1. Open **sec2sc02**.
2. Save the worksheet with Save As and name it **sec2sc04**.
3. Change the font for the entire worksheet to 12-point Garamond (or a similar serif typeface) and the font color to Violet.
4. Select row 2, turn off bold and italics, and then change the font color to Dark Blue.
5. Select row 1 and then change the font color to Dark Blue.
6. Select cells A1 through D8 and then add an outside border with a line style of your choosing.
7. Save, print, and then close **sec2sc04**.

Assessment 5

1. Open **sec2sc01**.
2. Save the worksheet with Save As and name it **sec2sc05**.
3. Select rows 5 and 6, insert two new rows, and then insert the following data in the new specified cells:

   A5 = **Insurance**
   B5 = **2000**
   C5 = **1300**
   A6 = **Management**
   B6 = **20000**
   C6 = **14500**

4. Insert a new column between columns B and C and then insert the following data in the specified cells:

   C1 = **Budgeted**
   C2 = **95000**
   C3 = **130000**
   C4 = **22000**
   C5 = **2000**
   C6 = **18000**
   C7 = **1500**
   C8 = **2000**

5. Automatically adjust the widths of columns A, B, C, and D.
6. Select cells A1 through D8 and then add a border around the cells (you choose the border-line style).
7. With the cells still selected, add light yellow shading to the selected cells.
8. Select cells A1 through D1 and then add a pattern of your choosing to the cells.
9. Save, print, and then close **sec2sc05**.

Assessment 6

1. Create an Excel worksheet with the information shown in Figure 2.16. You determine the following:
   a. Font
   b. Width of columns
   c. Number formatting
2. Add the following enhancements to the worksheet:
   a. Add a border to all cells in the worksheet containing data.
   b. Add a color shading to all cells in the worksheet containing data.
   c. Add a pattern to column headings (the cells containing *Project, Projected*, and *Actual*).
3. Save the completed worksheet and name it **sec2sc06**.
4. Print and then save **sec2sc06**.

FIGURE 2.16 **Assessment 6**

CAPITAL PROJECT SUMMARY		
Project	Projected	Actual
Rail siding installation	$43,300	$41,200
Cement slabs	$12,000	$13,980
Silos	$28,420	$29,600
Conveying system	$56,700	$58,200
Modulators	$8,210	$8,100
Winder	$6,400	$7,100

Assessment 7

1. Use the Help feature to learn how to shrink the font size to show all data in a cell. ***(Hint: To do this, display the Excel Help task pane, type*** Change formatting of text ***in the Search for text box and then press Enter. When the results display, click the Change formatting of text hyperlink. In the Microsoft Office Excel Help window, click the Shrink the font size to show all data in a cell hyperlink.)***
2. Open **ExcelWorksheet03**.
3. Save the worksheet with Save As and name it **sec2sc07**.
4. Select cells A1 through D8 and then change the font size to 12.
5. Select cells A1 through D2 and then shrink the font size to show all data in the selected cells.
6. Save, print, and then close **sec2sc07**.

CHAPTER challenge

You work with a fitness trainer at Exercise for Life Athletic Club. The fitness trainer has asked you to monitor members' activities as they use the club. You decide to create a weekly workout log for the members. Information will be compiled from a daily log sheet that members complete each time they work out. The weekly log will consist of the member's name, number of workouts per week, facilities used (i.e., pool, tennis courts, etc.), and additional fees (if any). Add at least five members (use information about yourself as one of the members) to this weekly log. Save the worksheet and print it.

To enhance the appearance of the log, you would like to format the worksheet with an appropriate background. Use the Help feature to learn how to format worksheets with a background. Choose an appropriate background for the workout log and add it to the worksheet. Save the worksheet.

After several weeks of maintaining this workout log in Excel, you decide that the information could be more easily maintained if it were stored in Access. Create a database in Access called **ExerciseforLife** and import the Excel worksheet as an Access table. Save the database and print the newly imported table.

CHAPTER 3

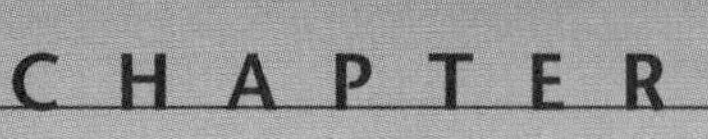

INSERTING FORMULAS IN A WORKSHEET

PERFORMANCE OBJECTIVES

Upon successful completion of Chapter 3, you will be able to:

- **Insert a formula in a cell using the AutoSum button**
- **Write formulas with mathematical operators**
- **Type a formula in the Formula bar**
- **Copy a formula**
- **Use the Insert Function feature to insert a formula in a cell**
- **Write formulas with the AVERAGE, MAX, MIN, COUNT, PMT, FV, DATE, NOW, and IF functions**
- **Create an absolute and mixed cell reference**

Chapter03S

EXCEL

Excel is a powerful decision-making tool containing data that can be manipulated to answer "what if" situations. Insert a formula in a worksheet and then manipulate the data to make projections, answer specific questions, and use as a planning tool. For example, the manager of a department might use an Excel worksheet to prepare a department budget and then determine the impact on the budget of hiring a new employee or increasing the volume of production.

Insert a formula in a worksheet to perform calculations on values. A formula contains a mathematical operator, value, cell reference, cell range, and a function. Formulas can be written that add, subtract, multiply, and/or divide values. Formulas can also be written that calculate averages, percentages, minimum and maximum values, and much more. Excel includes an AutoSum button on the Standard toolbar that inserts a formula to calculate the total of a range of cells. Insert Function is an Excel feature that offers a variety of functions to create a formula.

Using the AutoSum Button

To perform a calculation in a worksheet, make active the cell in which you want to insert the formula (this cell should be empty). Type the formula in the cell and the formula displays in the cell as well as in the Formula bar. When the formula is completed and you exit the cell, the result of the formula displays in the active cell while the actual formula displays in the Formula bar.

Enter

You can also enter a formula in the Formula bar located below the Formatting toolbar. To do this, click in the Formula bar text box, type the desired formula, and then press Enter or click the Enter button (contains a green check mark) on the Formula bar.

HINT

Use the AutoSum button to automatically add numbers in a range of cells.

One of the advantages of using formulas in a worksheet is that cell entries can be changed and the formula will automatically recalculate the values and insert the result in the cell containing the formula. This is what makes an Excel worksheet a decision-making tool.

In addition to typing a formula in a cell, you can also use the AutoSum button on the Standard toolbar. The AutoSum button adds numbers automatically with the SUM function. When you click the AutoSum button, Excel looks for a range of cells containing numbers above the active cell. If no cell above contains numbers, then Excel looks to the left of the active cell. Excel suggests the range of cells to be added. If the suggested range is not correct, drag through the desired range with the mouse, and then press Enter. You can also just double-click the AutoSum button and this will insert the SUM function with the range Excel chooses.

QUICK STEPS

Write Formula Using AutoSum Button

Click AutoSum button on Standard toolbar.

OR

1. Click down-pointing arrow at right of AutoSum button.
2. Click desired function.

(Note: Before completing computer exercises, delete the ExcelChapter02S folder on your disk. Next, copy the ExcelChapter03S subfolder from the Excel2003Specialist folder on the CD that accompanies this textbook to your disk and then make ExcelChapter03S the active folder.)

exercise 1

ADDING VALUES WITH THE AUTOSUM BUTTON

1. Open **ExcelWorksheet02**.
2. Save the worksheet with Save As and name it **sec3x01**.
3. Calculate the sum of cells by completing the following steps:
   a. Make B9 the active cell.
   b. Click the AutoSum button on the Standard toolbar.
   c. Excel inserts the formula *=SUM(B2:B8)* in cell B9. This is the correct range of cells, so press Enter.
   d. Make C9 the active cell.
   e. Click the AutoSum button on the Standard toolbar.
   f. Excel inserts the formula *=SUM(C2:C8)* in cell C9. This is the correct range of cells, so press Enter.
   g. Make D9 the active cell.
   h. Double-click the AutoSum button on the Standard toolbar. (This inserts the formula *=SUM(D2:D8)* in cell D9 and inserts the sum *-1820*.)
4. Select cells A1 through D9 and then apply the Accounting 1 autoformat.

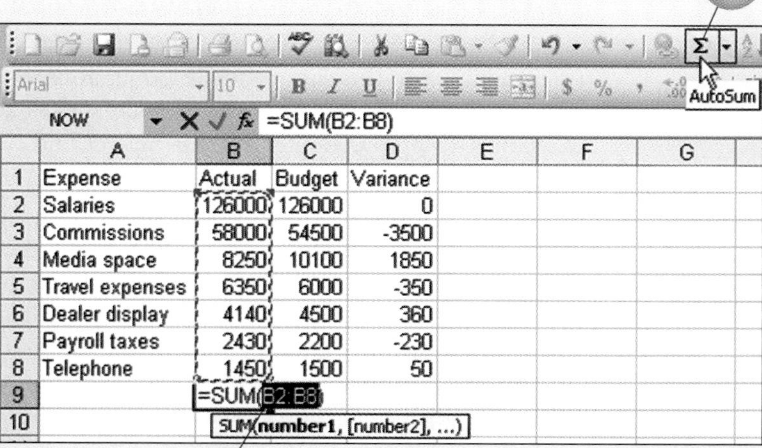

5. Save and then print **sec3x01**.
6. With the worksheet still open, make the following changes to cell entries:

   B4: Change *8,250.00* to *9550*
   D4: Change *1,850.00* to *550*
   B7: Change *2,430.00* to *2050*
   D7: Change *(230.00)* to *150*

7. Save, print, and then close **sec3x01**.

Writing Formulas with Mathematical Operators

The AutoSum button on the Standard toolbar essentially creates the formula for you. You can also write your own formulas using mathematical operators. Commonly used mathematical formulas and their functions are described in Table 3.1.

When writing your own formula, begin the formula with the equals (=) sign. For example, to divide the contents of cell B2 by the contents of cell C2 and insert the result in cell D2, you would make D2 the active cell, and then type **=B2/C2**.

HINT
After typing a formula in a cell, press the Enter key, the Tab key, Shift + Tab, or click the Enter button on the Formula bar.

TABLE 3.1 ***Mathematical Operators***

Function	***Operator***
Addition	+
Subtraction	-
Multiplication	*
Division	/
Percent	%
Exponentiation	^

If a formula contains two or more operators, Excel uses the same order of operations used in algebra. From left to right in a formula, this order, called the ***order of operations***, is: negations (negative number—a number preceded by -) first, then percents (%), then exponentiations (^), followed by multiplications (*), divisions (/), additions (+), and finally subtractions (-). If you want to change the order of operations, use parentheses around the part of the formula you want calculated first.

Copying a Formula with Relative Cell References

In many worksheets, the same basic formula is used repetitively. In a situation where a formula is copied to other locations in a worksheet, use a ***relative cell reference***. Copy a formula containing relative cell references and the cell references change. For example, if you enter the formula *=SUM(A2:C2)* in cell D2 and then

HINT
Display formulas in a worksheet rather than the calculated values by pressing Ctrl + ` (accent grave).

QUICK STEPS

Copy Relative Formula
1. Insert formula in cell.
2. Select cell containing formula and all cells you want to contain formula.
3. Click Edit, Fill, then click desired direction.

OR

1. Insert formula in cell.
2. Make active the cell containing formula.
3. Using fill handle, drag through cells you want to contain formula.

copy it relatively to cell D3, the formula in cell D3 displays as *=SUM(A3:C3)*. (Additional information on cell references is discussed later in this chapter in the "Using an Absolute Cell Reference in a Formula" section.)

To copy a formula relatively in a worksheet, use the Fill option from the Edit drop-down menu. To do this, select the cell containing the formula as well as the cells to which you want the formula copied, and then click Edit. At the Edit drop-down menu, point to Fill. This causes a side menu to display. The choices active in this side menu vary depending on the selected cells. For example, if you select cells down a column, options such as Down and Up will be active. If cells in a row are selected, options such as Right and Left will be active. Click the desired direction and the formula is copied relatively to the selected cells.

exercise 2

FINDING VARIANCES BY INSERTING AND COPYING A FORMULA

1. Open **ExcelWorksheet01**.
2. Save the worksheet with Save As and name it **sec3x02**.
3. Change the width of column A to 19.00.
4. Make cell E1 active and then type **Variance**.
5. Insert a formula by completing the following steps:
   a. Make E3 the active cell.
   b. Type the formula =D3-C3.
   c. Press Enter.
6. Copy the formula to cells E4 through E10 by completing the following steps:
   a. Select cells E3 through E10.
   b. Click Edit, point to Fill, and then click Down.

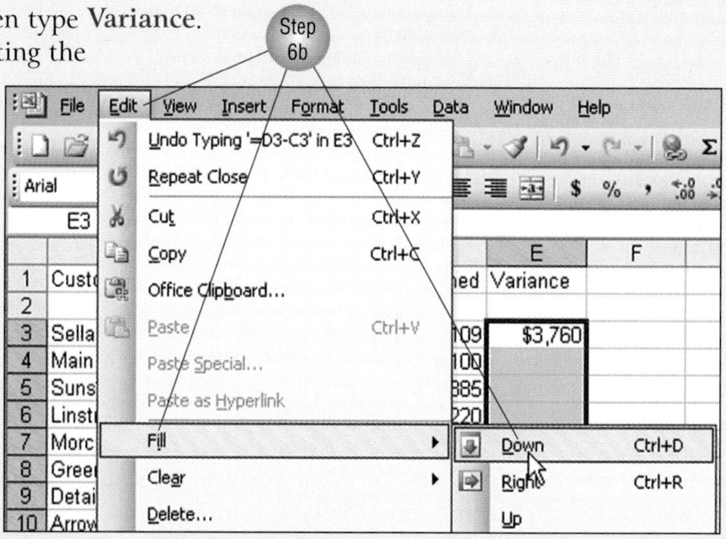

7. Select cells A1 through E10 and then apply the Colorful 1 autoformat.
8. Select cells B3 through B10 and then change the alignment to right.
9. Save and then print **sec3x02**.
10. With the worksheet still open, make the following changes to cell contents:

    C4: Change *$48,290* to *46425*
    D6: Change *$61,220* to *60000*
    C8: Change *$55,309* to *57415*
    C9: Change *$12,398* to *14115*

11. Save, print, and then close **sec3x02**.

Copying Formulas with the Fill Handle

Use the fill handle to copy a formula up, down, left, or right within a worksheet. To use the fill handle, insert the desired data in the cell (text, value, formula, and so on). With the cell active, position the mouse pointer (white plus sign) on the fill handle until the mouse pointer turns into a thin black cross. Hold down the left mouse button, drag and select the desired cells, and then release the mouse button. If you are dragging a cell containing a formula, a relative version of the formula is copied to the selected cells.

HINT

Use the fill handle to copy a relative version of a formula.

exercise 3

CALCULATING SALARY BY INSERTING AND COPYING A FORMULA USING THE FILL HANDLE

1. Open **ExcelWorksheet05**.
2. Save the worksheet with Save As and name it **sec3x03**.
3. Make cell D2 active, turn on bold, change the alignment to center, and then type Salary.
4. Insert a formula by completing the following steps:
   a. Make D3 the active cell.
   b. Click in the Formula bar and then type =C3*B3.
   c. Click the Enter button on the Formula bar.
5. Copy the formula to cells D4 through D8 by completing the following steps:
   a. Make sure cell D3 is the active cell.
   b. Position the mouse pointer (white plus sign) on the fill handle that displays at the lower right corner of cell D3 until the pointer turns into a thin black cross.
   c. Hold down the left mouse button, drag down to cell D8, and then release the mouse button.
6. Save and then print **sec3x03**.
7. With the worksheet still open, make the following changes to cell contents:

   B4: Change *20* to *28*
   C5: Change *$18.75* to *19.10*
   B7: Change *15* to *24*

8. Save, print, and then close **sec3x03**.

Step 4c | Step 4b

NOW ▾ X ✓ fx =C3*B3

	A	B	C	D
1	January			
2	Name	Hours	Rate	Salary
3	Carolyn Bentley	35	$23.15	=C3*B3
4	Lindon Cassini	20	$19.00	

C	D
Rate	Salary
$23.15	$810.25
$19.00	$380.00
$18.75	$750.00
$16.45	$394.80
$11.50	$172.50
$11.50	$172.50

Step 5c

Writing a Formula by Pointing

In Exercises 2 and 3, you wrote formulas using cell references such as *=D3-C3*. Another method for writing a formula is to "point" to the specific cells that are to be part of the formula. Creating a formula by pointing is more accurate than typing the cell reference since a mistake can happen when entering the cell reference.

To write a formula by pointing, click the cell that will contain the formula, type the equals sign to begin the formula, and then click the cell you want to reference in the formula. This inserts a moving border around the cell and also changes the mode from Enter to Point. (The word *Point* displays at the left side of the Status bar.) Type the desired mathematical operator and then click the next cell reference.

Write Formula by Pointing
1. Click cell that will contain formula.
2. Type equals sign.
3. Click cell you want to reference in formula.
4. Type desired mathematical operator.
5. Click next cell reference.

Continue in this manner until all cell references are specified and then press the Enter key. This ends the formula and inserts the result of the calculation of the formula in the active cell. When writing a formula by pointing, you can also select a range of cells you want included in a formula.

exercise 4 WRITING A FORMULA BY POINTING THAT CALCULATES PERCENTAGE OF ACTUAL BUDGET

1. Open **ExcelWorksheet02**.
2. Save the worksheet with Save As and name it **sec3x04**.
3. Delete column D.
4. Make cell D1 active and then type **% of Actual**.
5. Enter a formula by pointing that calculates the percentage of actual budget by completing the following steps:
   a. Make cell D2 active.
   b. Type the equals sign.
   c. Click cell C2. (This inserts a moving border around the cell and the mode changes from Enter to Point.)
   d. Type the forward slash symbol (/).
   e. Click cell B2.
   f. Make sure the formula looks like this *=C2/B2* and then press Enter.
6. Make cell D2 active and then click the Percent Style button on the Formatting toolbar.
7. With cell D2 still active, position the mouse pointer on the fill handle, drag down to cell D8, and then release the mouse button.
8. Select cells B2 through C8 and then click the Currency Style button on the Formatting toolbar.
9. Automatically increase the width of column D to accommodate the column heading.
10. Select cells A1 through D8 and then apply the Classic 2 AutoFormat.
11. Save, print, and then close **sec3x04**.

	A	B	C	D
1	Expense	Actual	Budget	% of Actual
2	Salaries	126000	126000	=C2/B2
3	Commissions	58000	54500	
4	Media space	8250	10100	
5	Travel expenses	6350	6000	
6	Dealer display	4140	4500	
7	Payroll taxes	2430	2200	
8	Telephone	1450	1500	

Steps 5a–5e

C	D
Budget	% of Actual
126000	100%
54500	94%
10100	122%
6000	94%
4500	109%
2200	91%
1500	103%

Step 7

Using the Trace Error Button

Trace Error

As you are working in a worksheet, you may occasionally notice a button pop up near the active cell. The general term for this button is ***smart tag***. The display of the smart tag button varies depending on the action performed. In Exercise 5, you will insert a formula that will cause a smart tag button, named the Trace Error button, to appear. When the Trace Error button appears, a small dark green triangle also displays in the upper left corner of the cell. Click the Trace Error button and a drop-down list displays with options for updating the formula to include specific cells, getting help on the error, ignoring the error, editing the error in the Formula bar, and completing an error check. In Exercise 5, two of the formulas you insert return the desired results. You will click the Trace Error button, read information on what Excel perceives as the error, and then tell Excel to ignore the error.

exercise 5

WRITING A FORMULA BY POINTING THAT CALCULATES PERCENTAGE OF DOWN TIME

1. Open **ExcelWorksheet09**.
2. Save the worksheet with Save As and name it **sec3x05**.
3. Make cell A11 active, type **Percentage of**, press Alt + Enter, and then type **Down Time**.
4. Enter a formula by pointing that computes the percentage of equipment down time by completing the following steps:
   a. Make cell B11 active.
   b. Type the equals sign followed by the left parenthesis (=().
   c. Click cell B3. (This inserts a moving border around the cell and the mode changes from Enter to Point.)
   d. Type the minus symbol (-).
   e. Click cell B9.
   f. Type the right parenthesis followed by the forward slash ()/).
   g. Click cell B3.
   h. Make sure the formula looks like this *=(B3-B9)/B3* and then press Enter.
5. Make cell B11 active and then click the Percent Style button on the Formatting toolbar.
6. With cell B11 still active, position the mouse pointer on the fill handle, drag across to cell M11, and then release the mouse button.
7. Enter a formula by dragging through a range of cells by completing the following steps:
   a. Click in cell A13, type **Hours Available**, press Alt + Enter, and then type **Jan - June**.
   b. Click in cell B13 and then click the AutoSum button on the Standard toolbar.
   c. Select cells B3 through G3.
   d. Click the Enter button on the Formula bar. (This inserts *14,340* in cell B13.)
8. Click in cell A14, type **Hours Available**, press Alt + Enter, and then type **July - Dec**.
9. Click in cell B14 and then complete steps similar to those in Steps 7b through 7d to create a formula that totals hours available from July through December (cells H3 through M3). (This inserts *14,490* in cell B14.)
10. Click in cell B13 and notice the Trace Error button that displays. Complete the following steps to read about the error and then tell Excel to ignore the error:

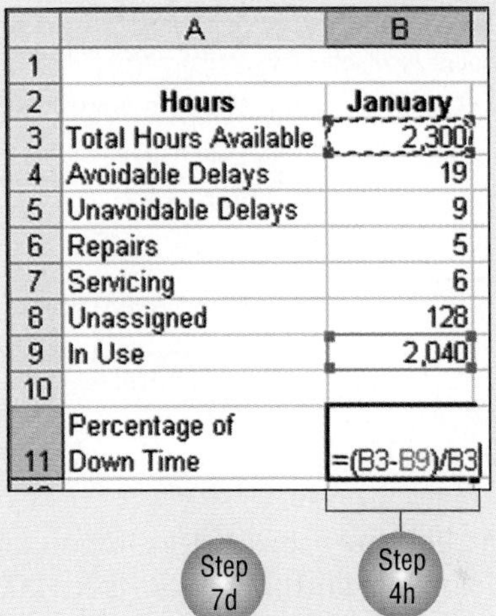

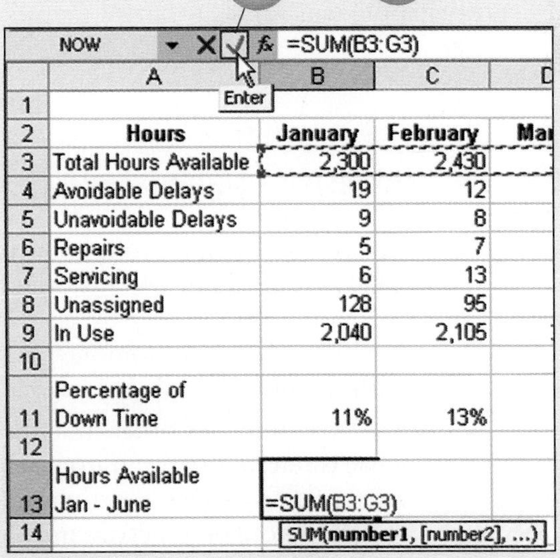

a. Click the Trace Error button.
b. At the drop-down menu that displays, click the *Help on this error* option.
c. Read the information on *Formula Omits Cells in Region* that displays in the Microsoft Excel Help window and then close the window.
d. Click the Trace Error button again and then click *Ignore Error* at the drop-down menu.

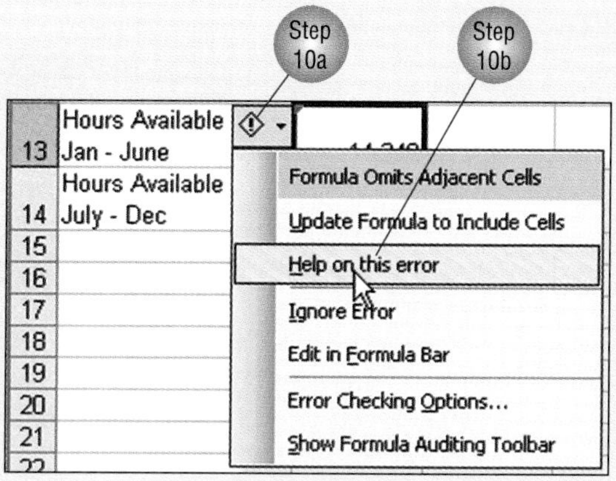

Step 10a
Step 10b
Hours Available
13 Jan - June
Hours Available
14 July - Dec
Formula Omits Adjacent Cells
Update Formula to Include Cells
Help on this error
Ignore Error
Edit in Formula Bar
Error Checking Options...
Show Formula Auditing Toolbar

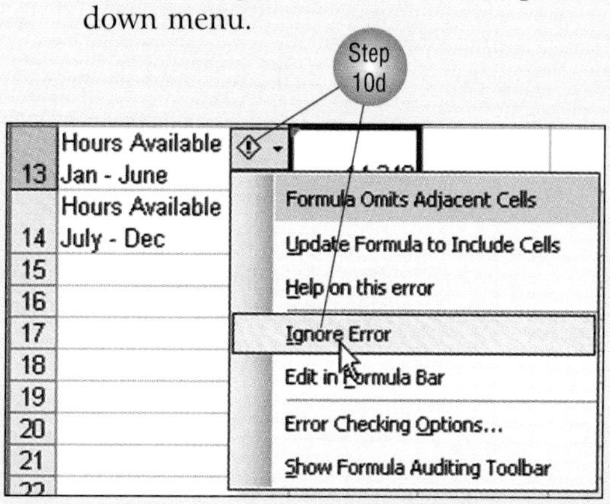

Step 10d
Hours Available
13 Jan - June
Hours Available
14 July - Dec
Formula Omits Adjacent Cells
Update Formula to Include Cells
Help on this error
Ignore Error
Edit in Formula Bar
Error Checking Options...
Show Formula Auditing Toolbar

11. Remove the dark green triangle from cell B14 by completing the following steps:
    a. Click in cell B14.
    b. Click the Trace Error button and then click *Ignore Error* at the drop-down menu.
12. Save, print, and then close **sec3x05**. (The worksheet will print on two pages. In the next chapter, you will learn about features that control how worksheets are printed.)

Inserting a Formula with the Insert Function Button

In Exercise 1, the AutoSum button inserted a formula that began with *=SUM*. This part of the formula is called a ***function***, which is a built-in formula. Using a function takes less keystrokes when creating a formula. For example, the *=SUM* function saved you from having to type each cell to be included in the formula with the plus (+) symbol between cell entries.

Excel provides other functions for writing formulas. A function operates on what is referred to as an ***argument***. An argument may consist of a constant, a cell reference, or another function (referred to as a nested function). In Exercise 1, when you made cell B10 active and then clicked the AutoSum button, the formula *=SUM(B3:B9)* was inserted in the cell. The cell range *(B3:B9)* is an example of a cell reference argument. An argument may also contain a ***constant***. A constant is a value entered directly into the formula. For example, if you enter the formula *=SUM(B3:B9,100)*, the cell range *B3:B9* is a cell reference argument and *100* is a constant. In this formula, 100 is always added to the sum of the cells. If a function is included in an argument within a function, it is called a ***nested function***. (You will learn about nested functions later in this chapter.)

When a value calculated by the formula is inserted in a cell, this process is referred to as ***returning the result***. The term ***returning*** refers to the process of calculating the formula and the term ***result*** refers to inserting the value in the cell.

You can type a function in a cell in a worksheet or you can use the Insert Function button on the Formula bar to help you write the formula. When you click the Insert Function button, or click Insert and then Function, the Insert Function dialog box displays as shown in Figure 3.1.

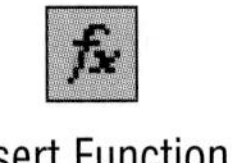

Insert Function

FIGURE 3.1 ***Insert Function Dialog Box***

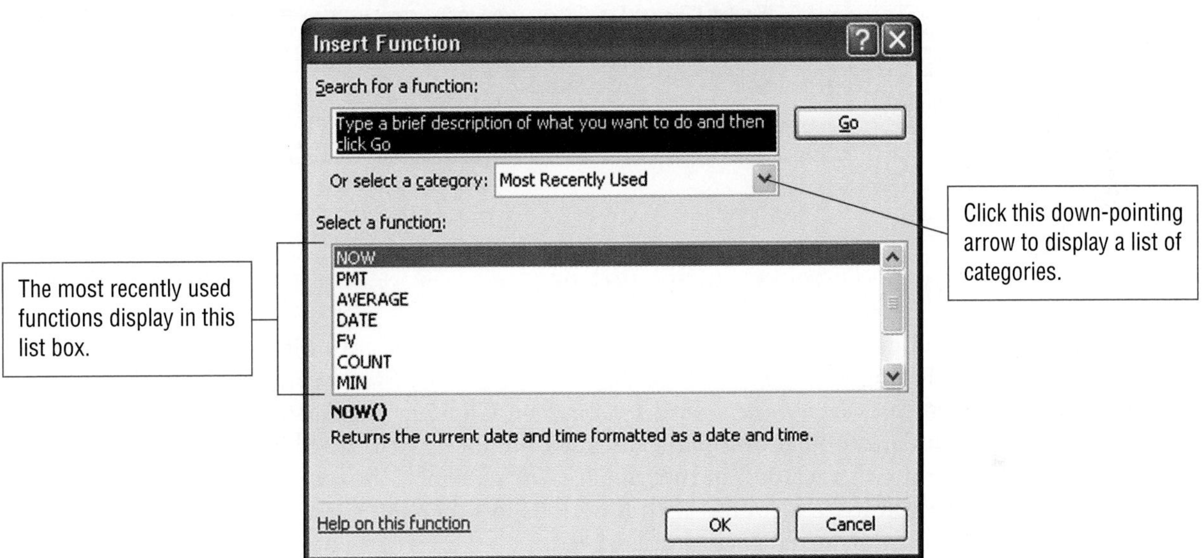

At the Insert Function dialog box, the most recently used functions display in the *Select a function* list box. You can choose a function category by clicking the down arrow at the right side of the *Or select a category* list box, and then clicking the desired category at the drop-down list. Use the *Search for a function* option to locate a specific function.

With the desired function category selected, choose a function in the *Select a function* list box and then click OK. This displays a Function Arguments palette like the one shown in Figure 3.2. At this palette, enter in the *Number1* text box the range of cells you want included in the formula, enter any constants that are to be included as part of the formula, or enter another function. After entering a range of cells, a constant, or another function, click the OK button. More than one argument can be included in a function. If the function you are creating contains more than one argument, press the Tab key to move the insertion point to the *Number2* text box, and then enter the second argument.

HINT

You can also display the Insert Function dialog box by clicking the down-pointing arrow at the right side of the AutoSum button and then clicking More Functions.

HINT

If you need to display a specific cell or cells behind the formula palette, move the palette by clicking and dragging it.

FIGURE 3.2 *Example Function Arguments Palette*

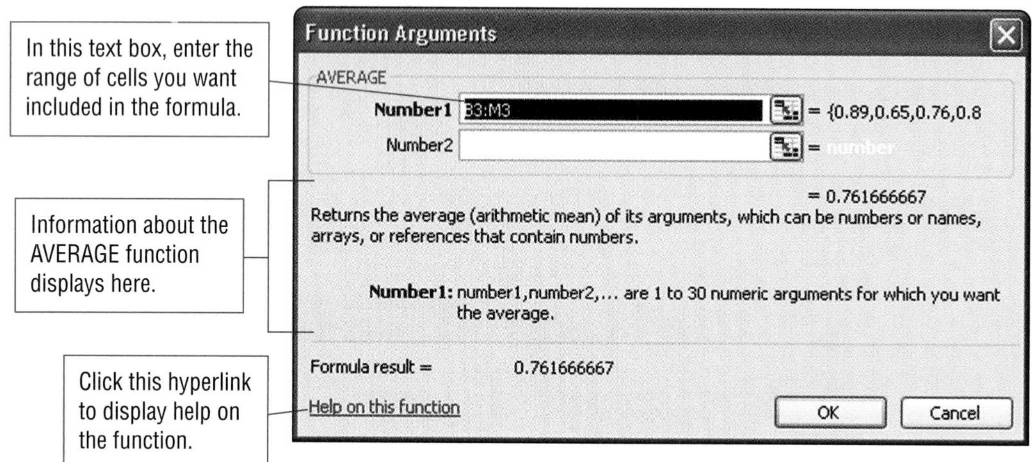

Writing Formulas with Functions

HINT
Click the down-pointing arrow at the right side of the AutoSum button and common functions display in a drop-down list.

Excel includes over 200 functions that are divided into nine different categories including *Financial*, *Date & Time*, *Math & Trig*, *Statistical*, *Lookup & Reference*, *Database*, *Text*, *Logical*, and *Information*. Clicking the AutoSum button on the Standard toolbar automatically adds numbers with the SUM function. The SUM function is included in the *Math & Trig* category. In some sections in this chapter, you will write formulas with functions in other categories including *Statistical*, *Financial*, *Date & Time*, and *Logical*.

Writing Formulas with Statistical Functions

In this section, you will learn to write formulas with the statistical functions AVERAGE, MAX, MIN, and COUNT. The AVERAGE function returns the average (arithmetic mean) of the arguments. The MAX function returns the largest value in a set of values and the MIN function returns the smallest number in a set of values. Use the COUNT function to count the number of cells that contain numbers within the list of arguments.

Finding Averages

A common function in a formula is the AVERAGE function. With this function, a range of cells is added together and then divided by the number of cell entries. In Exercise 6 you will use the AVERAGE function, which will add all test scores for a student and then divide that number by the total number of tests. You will use the Insert Function feature to simplify the creation of the formula containing an AVERAGE function.

One of the advantages to using formulas in a worksheet is the ability to easily manipulate data to answer certain questions. In Exercise 6 you will learn the impact of retaking certain tests on the final average score.

exercise 6

AVERAGING TEST SCORES IN A WORKSHEET

1. Open **ExcelWorksheet06**.
2. Save the worksheet with Save As and name it **sec3x06**.
3. Make cell N1 the active cell, turn on bold, and then type Average.
4. Use the Insert Function feature to find the average of test scores by completing the following steps:
   a. Make N3 the active cell.
   b. Click the Insert Function button on the Formula bar.
   c. At the Insert Function dialog box, click the down-pointing arrow at the right side of the *Or select a category* options box, and then click *Statistical* at the drop-down list.
   d. Click *AVERAGE* in the *Select a function* list box.

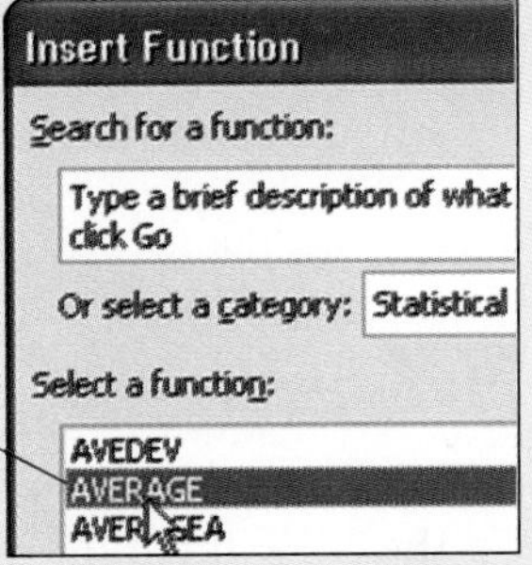

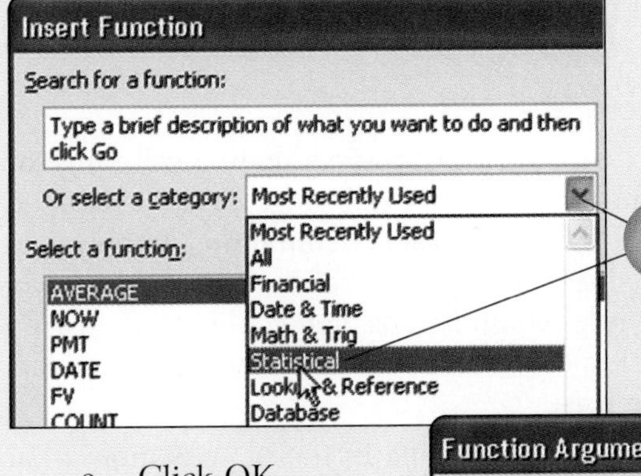

   e. Click OK.
   f. At the Function Arguments palette, make sure *B3:M3* displays in the *Number1* text box. (If not, type **B3:M3** in the *Number1* text box.)
   g. Click OK.
5. Copy the formula by completing the following steps:
   a. Make cell N3 active.
   b. Position the mouse pointer on the fill handle until the pointer turns into a thin black cross.
   c. Hold down the left mouse button, drag down to cell N20, and then release the mouse button.

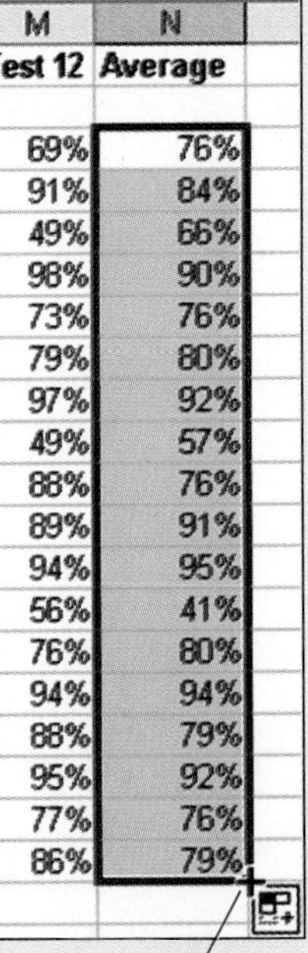

6. Save and then print **sec3x06**. (The worksheet will print on two pages.)
7. After viewing the averages of test scores, you notice that a couple of people have a low average. You decide to see what happens to the average score if students make up tests where they scored the lowest. You decide that a student can make up to a 70% on a retake of the test. Make the following changes to test scores to see how the changes will affect the test average.

   L5: Change *45%* to *70%*
   M5: Change *49%* to *70%*

C10: Change *45%* to *70%*
M10: Change *49%* to *70%*
C14: Change *0%* to *70%*
I14: Change *0%* to *70%*
J14: Change *0%* to *70%*

8. Save, print, and then close **sec3x06**. (Compare the test averages for Jack Calahan, Stephanie Flanery, and Kathleen Kwieciak to see what the effect of retaking the tests has on their final test averages.)

When a formula such as the AVERAGE formula you inserted in a cell in Exercise 6 calculates cell entries, it ignores certain cell entries. The AVERAGE function will ignore text in cells and blank cells (not zeros). For example, in the worksheet containing test scores, a couple of cells contained a *0%* entry. This entry was included in the averaging of the test scores. If you did not want that particular test to be included in the average, enter text in the cell such as *N/A* (for *not applicable*) or leave the cell blank.

Finding Maximum and Minimum Values

The MAX function in a formula returns the maximum value in a cell range and the MIN function returns the minimum value in a cell range. As an example, you could use the MAX and MIN functions in a worksheet containing employee hours to determine which employee worked the most number of hours and which worked the least. In a worksheet containing sales commissions, you could use the MAX and MIN functions to determine the salesperson who earned the most commission dollars and the one who earned the least.

Insert a MAX and MIN function into a formula in the same manner as an AVERAGE function. In Exercise 7, you will use the Insert Function feature to insert MAX and MIN functions in cells to determine the highest test score average and the lowest test score average.

exercise 7

FINDING MAXIMUM AND MINIMUM VALUES IN A WORKSHEET

1. Open **sec3x06**.
2. Save the worksheet with Save As and name it **sec3x07**.
3. Type the following in the specified cells:

   A22: Turn on bold and then type **Highest Test Average**.
   A23: Turn on bold and then type **Lowest Test Average**.
   A24: Turn on bold and then type **Average of All Tests**.

4. Automatically adjust the width of column A.
5. Insert a formula to identify the highest test score average by completing the following steps:
   a. Make cell B22 active.
   b. Click the Insert Function button on the Formula bar.

c. At the Insert Function dialog box, make sure *Statistical* is selected in the *Or select a category* option box. (If not, click the down-pointing arrow at the right side of the *Or select a category* option box and then click *Statistical* at the drop-down list.)
d. Click *MAX* in the *Select a function* list box. (You will need to scroll down the list to display *MAX*.)
e. Click OK.
f. At the Function Arguments palette, type N3:N20 in the *Number1* text box.
g. Click OK.

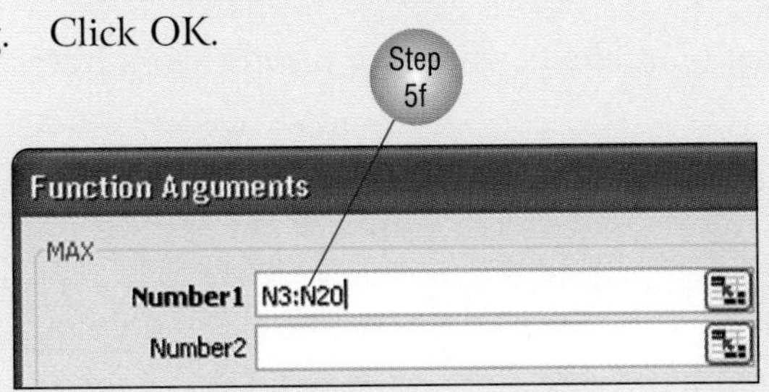

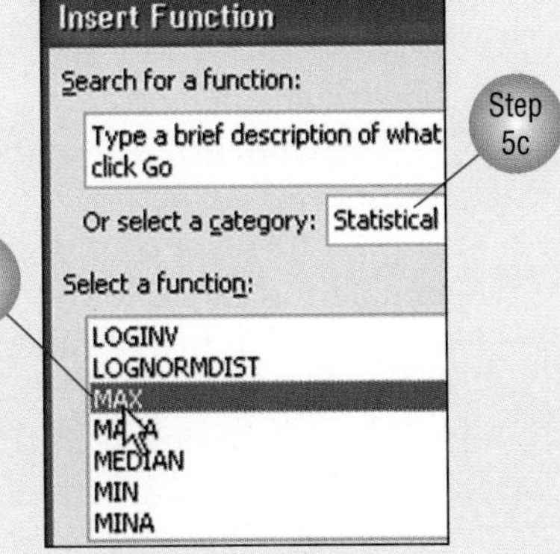

6. Insert a formula to identify the lowest test score average by completing the following steps:
   a. Make cell B23 active.
   b. Click the Insert Function button on the Formula bar.
   c. At the Insert Function dialog box, make sure *Statistical* is selected in the *Or select a category* option box, and then click *MIN* in the *Select a function* list box. (You will need to scroll down the list to display *MIN*.)
   d. Click OK.
   e. At the Function Arguments palette, type N3:N20 in the *Number1* text box, and then click OK.
7. Insert a formula to determine the average of all test scores by completing the following steps:
   a. Make cell B24 active.
   b. Click the Insert Function button on the Formula bar.
   c. At the Insert Function dialog box, make sure *Statistical* is selected in the *Or select a category* option box and then click *AVERAGE* in the *Select a function* list box.
   d. Click OK.
   e. At the Function Arguments palette, type N3:N20 in the *Number1* text box, and then click OK.
8. Save and then print **sec3x07**. (The worksheet will print on two pages.)
9. Change the *70%* values (which were previously *0%*) in cells C14, I14, and J14 to *N/A*. (This will cause the average of test scores for Kathy Kwieciak to increase and will change the minimum number and average of all test scores.)
10. Save, print, and then close **sec3x07**.

Counting Numbers in a Range

Use the COUNT function to count the numeric values in a range. For example, in a range of cells containing cells with text and cells with numbers, you can count how many cells in the range contain numbers. In Exercise 8, you will use the COUNT function to specify the number of students taking the midterm test and the number taking the final test. In this worksheet, a cell is left blank if a student did not take a test. If a value such as *0%* was entered into the cell, the COUNT function would count this as a cell with a number.

exercise 8

COUNTING THE NUMBER OF STUDENTS TAKING TESTS

1. Open **ExcelWorksheet19**.
2. Save the worksheet and name it **sec3x08**.
3. Make cell A22 active.
4. Type **Number of students**, press Alt + Enter, and then type **completing the midterm**.
5. Make cell B22 active.
6. Insert a formula counting the number of students who have taken the midterm test by completing the following steps:
   a. Click the Insert Function button on the Formula bar.
   b. At the Insert Function dialog box, make sure *Statistical* is selected in the *Or select a category* option box. (If not, click the down-pointing arrow at the right side of the *Or select a category* option box and then click *Statistical* at the drop-down list.)
   c. Scroll down the list of functions in the *Select a function* list box until COUNT is visible and then double-click *COUNT*.
   d. At the Function Arguments palette, type **B3:B20** in the *Value1* text box.
   e. Click OK.

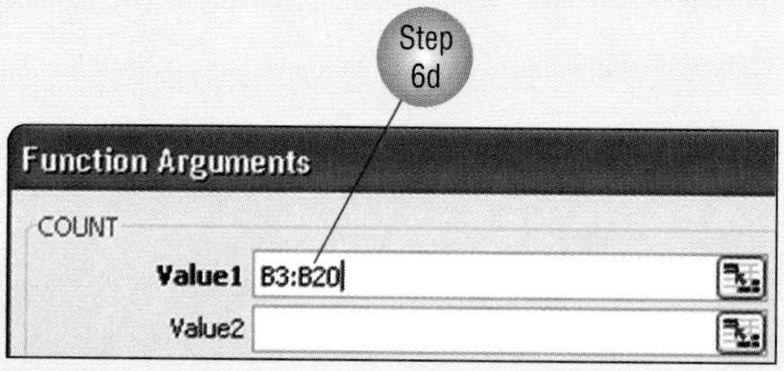

Step 6d

Function Arguments

COUNT

Value1 B3:B20

Value2

7. Count the number of students who have taken the final test by completing the following steps:
   a. Make cell A23 active.
   b. Type **Number of students**, press Alt + Enter, and then type **completing the final**.
   c. Make cell B23 active.

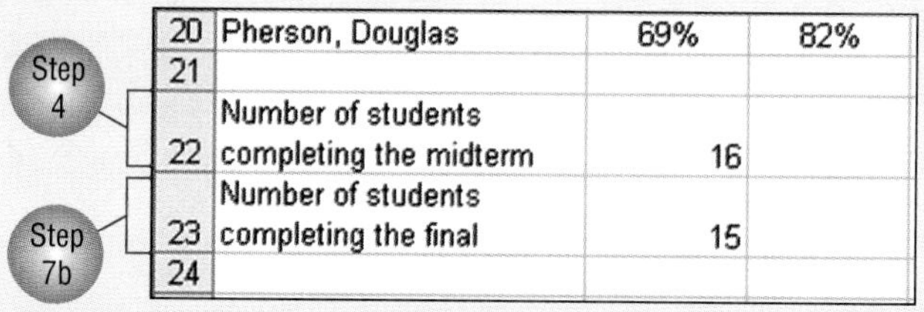

Step 4

Step 7b

20	Pherson, Douglas	69%	82%
21			
22	Number of students completing the midterm	16	
23	Number of students completing the final	15	
24			

8. Insert a formula counting the number of students who have taken the final test by completing the following steps:
   a. Click the Insert Function button on the Formula bar.
   b. At the Insert Function dialog box, make sure *Statistical* is selected in the *Or select a category* option box.
   c. Scroll down the list of functions in the *Select a function* list box until COUNT is visible and then double-click *COUNT*.
   d. At the Function Arguments palette, type **C3:C20** in the *Value1* text box, and then click OK.
9. Save and then print **sec3x08**.
10. Add test scores by completing the following steps:
    a. Make cell B14 active and then type **68**.
    b. Make cell C14 active and then type **70**.
    c. Make cell C19 active and then type **55**.
    d. Press Enter.
11. Save, print, and then close **sec3x08**.

Writing Formulas with Financial Functions

In this section, you will learn to write formulas with the financial functions PMT and FV. The PMT function calculates the payment for a loan based on constant payments and a constant interest rate. Use the FV function to return the future value of an investment based on periodic, constant payments and a constant interest rate.

Finding the Periodic Payments for a Loan

The PMT function finds the periodic payment for a loan based on constant payments and a constant interest rate. The PMT function contains the arguments Nper, Pv, Fv, and Type. The Nper argument is the number of payments that will be made to an investment or loan, Pv is the current value of amounts to be received or paid in the future, Fv is the value of a loan or investment at the end of all periods, and Type determines whether calculations will be based on payments made in arrears (at the end of each period) or in advance (at the beginning of each period).

CALCULATING PAYMENTS

1. Open **ExcelWorksheet20**.
2. Save the worksheet with Save As and name it **sec3x09**.
3. The owner of Real Photography is interested in purchasing a new developer and needs to determine monthly payments on three different models. Insert a formula that calculates monthly payments and then copy that formula by completing the following steps:
   a. Make cell E7 active.
   b. Click the Insert Function button on the Formula bar.
   c. At the Insert Function dialog box, click the down-pointing arrow at the right side of the *Or select a category* option box and then click *Financial* at the drop-down list.
   d. Scroll down the *Select a function* option box until *PMT* is visible and then double-click *PMT*.
   e. At the Function Arguments palette, type C7/12 in the *Rate* text box. (This tells Excel to divide the interest rate by 12 months.)
   f. Press the Tab key. (This moves the insertion point to the *Nper* text box.)
   g. Type D7. (This is the total number of months in the payment period.)
   h. Press the Tab key. (This moves the insertion point to the *Pv* text box.)
   i. Type -B7. (Excel displays the result of the PMT function as a negative number since the loan represents a negative cash flow to the borrower. Insert a minus sign before *B7* to show the monthly payment as a positive number rather than a negative number.)
   j. Click OK. (This closes the palette and inserts the monthly payment of *$316.98* in cell E7.)

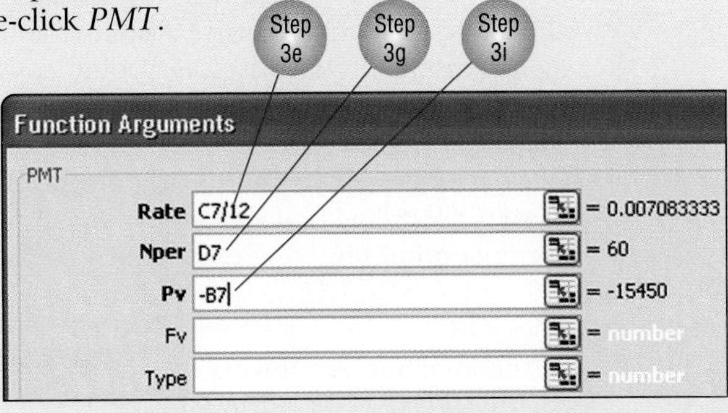

k. Copy the formula in cell E7 down to cells E8 and E9.

4. Insert a formula in cell F7 that calculates the total amount of the payments by completing the following steps:
   a. Make cell F7 active.
   b. Type **=E7*D7** and then press Enter.
   c. Make cell F7 active and then copy the formula down to cells F8 and F9.
5. Insert a formula in cell G7 that calculates the total amount of interest paid by completing the following steps:
   a. Make cell G7 active.
   b. Type **=F7-B7** and then press Enter.
   c. Make cell G7 active and then copy the formula down to cells G8 and G9.
6. Save, print, and then close **sec3x09**.

Monthly Payments	Total Payments	Total Interest
$316.98	$ 19,018.82	$ 3,568.82
$615.39	$ 36,923.60	$ 6,928.60
$711.92	$ 42,715.42	$ 8,015.42

Step 5c

Finding the Future Value of a Series of Payments

The FV function calculates the future value of a series of equal payments or an annuity. Use this function to determine information such as how much money can be earned in an investment account with a specific interest rate and over a specific period of time.

exercise 10 FINDING THE FUTURE VALUE OF AN INVESTMENT

1. Open **ExcelWorksheet21**.
2. Save the worksheet with Save As and name it **sec3x10**.
3. The owner of Real Photography has decided to save money to purchase a new developer and wants to compute how much money can be earned by investing the money in an investment account that returns 9% annual interest. The owner determines that $1,200 per month can be invested in the account for three years. Determine the future value of the investment account by completing the following steps:
   a. Make cell B6 active.
   b. Click the Insert Function button on the Formula bar.
   c. At the Insert Function dialog box, make sure *Financial* displays in the *Or select a category* option box.
   d. Click *FV* in the *Select a function* list box.
   e. Click OK.
   f. At the Function Arguments palette, type **B3/12** in the *Rate* text box.
   g. Press the Tab key.
   h. Type **B4** in the *Nper* text box.
   i. Press the Tab key.
   j. Type **B5** in the *Pmt* text box.
   k. Click OK. (This closes the palette and also inserts the future value of *$49,383.26* in cell B6.)

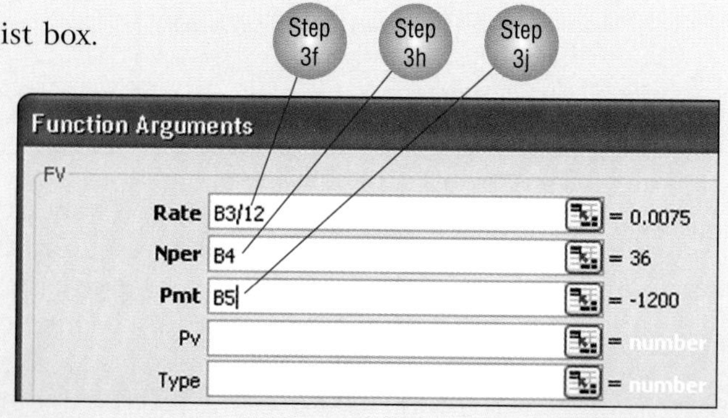

4. Save and then print **sec3x10**.
5. The owner decides to determine the future return after two years. To do this, change the amount in cell B4 from *36* to *24* and then press Enter. (This recalculates the future investment amount in cell B6.)
6. Save, print, and then close **sec3x10**.

	A	B
1	REAL PHOTOGRAPHY	
2	Future Value of Investment	
3	Rate	9%
4	Number of Months	24
5	Monthly Payment	$ (1,200.00)
6	Future Value	$31,426.16

Step 5

Writing Formulas with Date and Time Functions

In this section, you will learn to write formulas with the date and time functions NOW and DATE. The NOW function returns the serial number of the current date and time. The DATE function returns the serial number that represents a particular date. Excel can make calculations using dates because the dates are represented as serial numbers. To calculate a date's serial number, Excel counts the days since the beginning of the twentieth century. The date serial number for January 1, 1900, is 1. The date serial number for January 1, 2000, is 36,526.

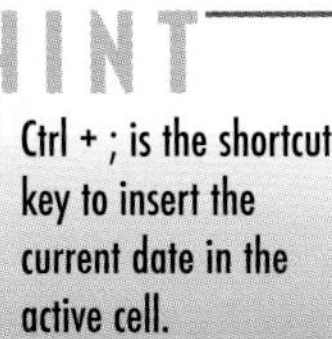

HINT
Ctrl + ; is the shortcut key to insert the current date in the active cell.

exercise 11

USING THE DATE AND NOW FUNCTIONS

1. Open **ExcelWorksheet23**.
2. Save the worksheet with Save As and name it **sec3x11**.
3. This worksheet establishes overdue dates for accounts. Enter a formula in cell D5 that returns the serial number for the date March 21, 2005, by completing the following steps:
   a. Make cell D5 active.
   b. Click the Insert Function button on the Formula bar.
   c. At the Insert Function dialog box, click the down-pointing arrow at the right side of the *Or select a category* option box and then click *Date & Time* at the drop-down list.
   d. Double-click *DATE* in the *Select a function* list box.
   e. At the Function Arguments palette, type **2005** in the *Year* text box.
   f. Press the Tab key and then type **03** in the *Month* text box.
   g. Press the Tab key and then type **21** in the *Day* text box.
   h. Click OK.

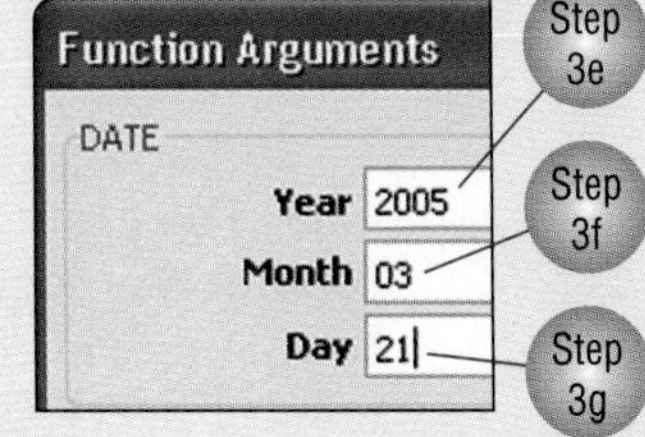

4. Complete steps similar to those in Step 3 to enter the following dates as serial numbers in the specified cells:

D6	=	March 27, 2005
D7	=	April 2, 2005
D8	=	April 10, 2005

5. Enter a formula in cell F5 that inserts the due date (the purchase date plus the number of days in the Terms column) by completing the following steps:
   a. Make cell F5 active.

b. Type =D5+E5 and then press Enter.
c. Make cell F5 active and then copy the formula down to cells F6, F7, and F8.

Purchase Date	Terms	Due Date
3/21/2005	30	4/20/2005
3/27/2005	15	4/11/2005
4/2/2005	15	4/17/2005
4/10/2005	30	5/10/2005

Step 5c

6. Make cell A10 active and then type your name.
7. Insert the current date and time as a serial number by completing the following steps:
   a. Make cell A11 active.
   b. Click the Insert Function button on the Formula bar.
   c. At the Insert Function dialog box, make sure *Date & Time* displays in the *Or select a category* option box.
   d. Scroll down the *Select a function* list box until *NOW* is visible and then double-click *NOW*.
   e. At the Function Arguments palette telling you that the function takes no argument, click OK.
   f. With cell A11 still active, click the Align Left button on the Formatting toolbar.
8. Save, print, and then close **sec3x11**.

Writing a Formula with the IF Logical Function

The IF function is considered a ***conditional function***. With the IF function you can perform conditional tests on values and formulas. A question that can be answered with true or false is considered a ***logical test***. The IF function makes a logical test and then performs a particular action if the answer is true and another action if the answer is false.

For example, an IF function can be used to write a formula that calculates a salesperson's bonus as 10% if the quota of $100,000 is met or exceeded, and zero if the quota is less than $100,000. That formula would look like this: *=IF(quota=>100000,quota*0.1,0)*. The formula contains three parts—the condition or logical test *IF(quota=>100000)*, action taken if the condition or logical test is true *(quota*0.1)*, and the action taken if the condition or logical test is false *(0)*. Commas separate the condition and the actions. In the bonus formula, if the quota is equal to or greater than $100,000, then the quota is multiplied by 10%. If the quota is less than $100,000, then the bonus is zero.

In Exercise 12, you will write a formula with cell references rather than cell data. The formula in Exercise 12 is *=IF(C2>B2,C2*0.15,0)*. In this formula the condition or logical test is whether or not the number in cell C2 is greater than the number in cell B2. If the condition is true and the number is greater, then the number in cell C2 is multiplied by 0.15 (providing a 15% bonus). If the condition is false and the number in cell C2 is less than the number in cell B2, then nothing happens (no bonus). Notice how commas are used to separate the logical test from the actions.

Editing a Formula

Enter

Edit a formula by making active the cell containing the formula and then editing the formula in the cell or in the Formula bar text box. After editing the formula, press Enter or click the Enter button on the Formula bar and Excel will recalculate the result of the formula.

exercise 12

WRITING A FORMULA WITH AN IF FUNCTION AND EDITING THE FORMULA

1. Open **ExcelWorksheet10**.
2. Save the worksheet with Save As and name it **sec3x12**.
3. Write a formula with the IF function by completing the following steps. (The formula will determine if the quota has been met and, if it has, will insert the bonus [15% of the actual sales]. If the quota has not been met, the formula will insert a zero.)
   a. Make cell D2 active.
   b. Type **=IF(C2>B2,C2*0.15,0)** and then press Enter.
   c. Make cell D2 active and then use the fill handle to copy the formula to cells D3 through D7.
   d. With cells D2 through D7 selected, click the Currency Style button on the Formatting toolbar. 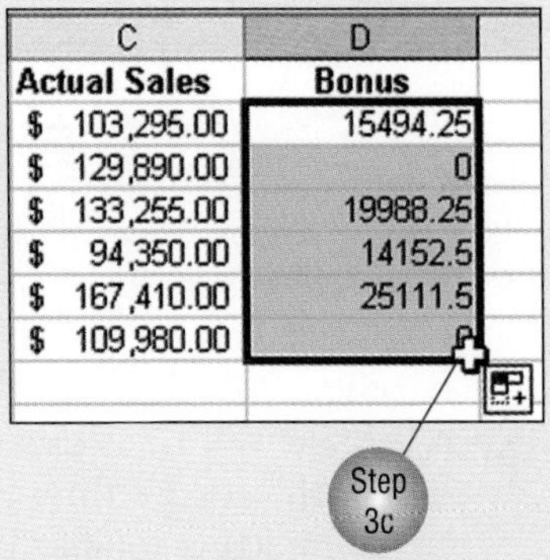
4. Print the worksheet.
5. Revise the formula so it will insert a 25% bonus if the quota has been met by completing the following steps:
   a. Make cell D2 active.
   b. Click in the Formula bar, edit the formula so it displays as *=IF(C2>B2,C2*0.25,0)*, and then click the Enter button on the Formula bar. 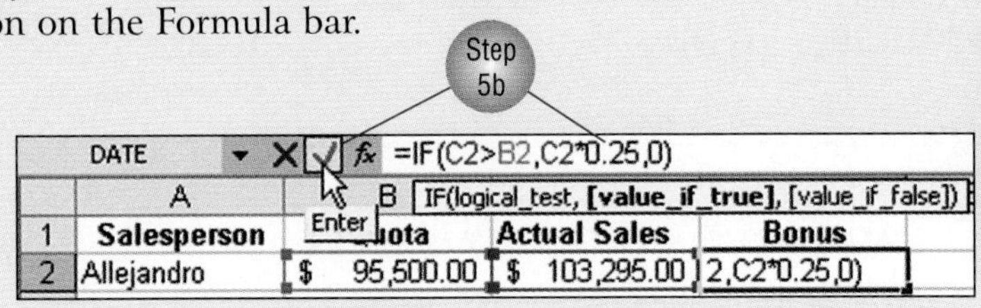 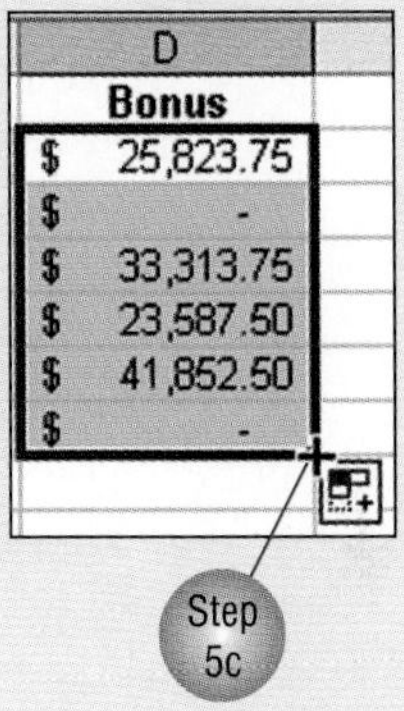
   c. Copy the formula down to cells D3 through D7.
6. Save, print, and then close **sec3x12**.

Writing a Nested IF Condition

In Exercise 12, the IF function had only two possible actions—the actual sales times 15% or a zero. In a formula where more than two actions are required, use nested IF functions. For example, in Exercise 13, you will write a formula with IF conditions that has four possible actions—a letter grade of A, B, C, or D. When writing nested IF conditions, insert symbols such as commas, quotation marks, and parentheses in the proper locations. If you want an IF condition to insert text, insert quotation marks before and after the text. The formula you will be writing in Exercise 13 is shown below.

=IF(E2>89,"A",IF(E2>79,"B",IF(E2>69,"C",IF(E2>59,"D"))))

This formula begins with the condition *=IF(E2>89,"A",*. If the number in cell E2 is greater than 89, then the condition is met and the grade of A is returned. The formula continues with a nested condition, *IF(E2>79,"B",*. If the number in cell E2 does not meet the first condition (greater than 89), then Excel looks to the next condition—is the number in cell E2 greater than 79? If it is, then the grade of B is inserted in cell E2. The formula continues with another nested condition,

HINT

If you enter a complicated formula in a worksheet, consider protecting the worksheet. To do this, click Tools, point to Protection, and then click Protect Sheet. At the Protect Sheet dialog box, enter a password, and then click OK.

IF(E2>69,"C",. If the number in cell E2 does not match the first condition, Excel looks to the second condition, and if that condition is not met, then Excel looks to the third condition. If the number in cell E2 is greater than 69, then the grade of C is inserted in cell E2. The final nested condition is *IF(E2>59,"D"*. If the first three conditions are not met but this one is, then the grade of D is inserted in cell E2. The four parentheses at the end of the formula end each condition in the formula.

exercise 13

WRITING A FORMULA WITH NESTED IF CONDITIONS

1. Open **ExcelWorksheet11**.
2. Save the worksheet with Save As and name it **sec3x13**.
3. Insert a formula to average the scores by completing the following steps:
   a. Make cell E2 active.
   b. Type =AVERAGE(B2:D2) and then press Enter.
   c. Make cell E2 active and then copy the formula down to cells E3 through E6.
   d. With cells E2 through E6 still selected, click the Decrease Decimal button on the Formatting toolbar five times.
4. Insert a formula with nested IF conditions by completing the following steps:
   a. Make cell F2 active.
   b. Type =IF(E2>89,"A",IF(E2>79,"B",IF(E2>69,"C",IF(E2>59,"D")))) and then press Enter.

E	F	G	H	I	J
Average	Grade				
78	=IF(E2>89,"A",IF(E2>79,"B",IF(E2>69,"C",IF(E2>59,"D"))))				
90					
88					
98					
67					

Step 4b

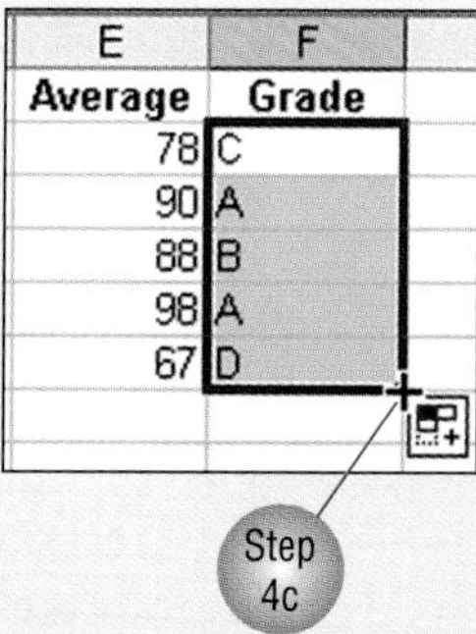

E	F
Average	Grade
78	C
90	A
88	B
98	A
67	D

Step 4c

   c. Make cell F2 active and then use the fill handle to copy the formula down to cells F3 through F6.
   d. With cells F2 through F6 still selected, click the Center button on the Formatting toolbar.
5. Save, print, and then close **sec3x13**.

As you typed the formula with nested IF conditions in Step 4b of Exercise 13, did you notice that the parentheses were different colors? Each color represents a condition. The four right parentheses at the end of the formula ended each of the conditions and each matched in color a left parenthesis. If an average in column E in sec3x13 is less than 59, the nested formula inserts *FALSE* in the cell. If you want the formula to insert a letter grade, such as *F*, instead of *FALSE*, include another nested IF condition in the formula. A maximum of seven IF functions can be nested in a formula.

Using Absolute and Mixed Cell References in Formulas

A reference identifies a cell or a range of cells in a worksheet and can be relative, absolute, or mixed. Relative cell references refer to cells relative to a position in a formula. Absolute references refer to cells in a specific location. When a formula is copied, a relative cell reference adjusts while an absolute cell reference remains constant. A mixed cell reference does both—either the column remains absolute and the row is relative or the column is relative and the row is absolute. Distinguish between relative, absolute, and mixed cell references using the dollar sign ($). Type a dollar sign before the column and/or row cell reference in a formula to specify that the column or row is an absolute cell reference.

Using an Absolute Cell Reference in a Formula

In this chapter you have learned to copy a relative formula. For example, if the formula =*SUM(A2:C2)* in cell D2 is copied relatively to cell D3, the formula changes to =*SUM(A3:C3)*. In some situations, you may want a formula to contain an absolute cell reference, which always refers to a cell in a specific location. In Exercise 14, you will add a column for projected job earnings and then perform "what if" situations using a formula with an absolute cell reference.

To identify an absolute cell reference, insert a $ symbol before the row and also the column. For example, the absolute cell reference C12 would be typed as *$C$12* in a formula.

exercise 14

INSERTING AND COPYING A FORMULA WITH AN ABSOLUTE CELL REFERENCE

1. Open **ExcelWorksheet01**.
2. Save the worksheet with Save As and name it **sec3x14**.
3. Delete columns B and D by completing the following steps:
   a. Click the column B header (the letter *B* at the top of the column).
   b. Hold down the Ctrl key and then click the column D header. (This selects column B and column D.)
   c. Click Edit and then Delete.
4. Type **Projected** in cell C1.
5. Center and bold the text in cells A1 through C1.
6. Determine the effect on actual job earnings with a 20% increase by completing the following steps:
   a. Type **% Increase/Decrease** in cell A12.
   b. Type **1.2** in cell B12 and then press Enter. (This number will be used in a formula to determine a 20% increase.)
   c. Make cell B12 active and then change the number formatting to General. (To do this, click Format and then Cells. At the Format Cells dialog box, click the Number tab, click *General* in the *Category* list box, and then click OK.)
   d. Make cell C3 active, type the formula **=B3*$B$12**, and then press Enter.
   e. Make cell C3 active and then use the fill handle to copy the formula to cells C4 through C10.

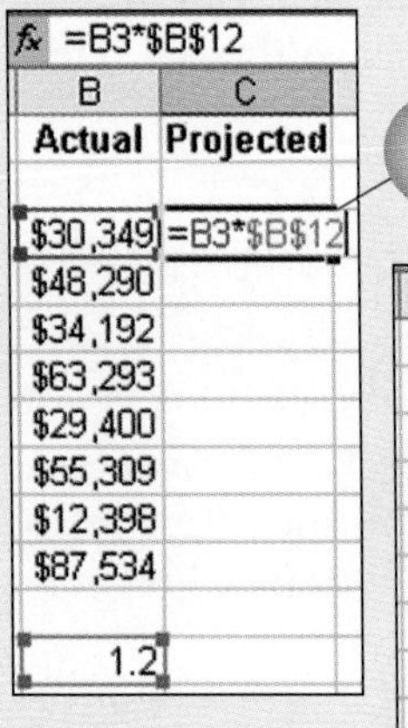

Step 6d

B	C
Actual	Projected
$30,349	36418.8
$48,290	57948
$34,192	41030.4
$63,293	75951.6
$29,400	35280
$55,309	66370.8
$12,398	14877.6
$87,534	105040.8
1.2	

Step 6e

f. Select cells B3 through C10 and then click the Currency Style button on the Formatting toolbar.
g. With cells B3 through C10 still selected, click twice on the Decrease Decimal button on the Formatting toolbar.

7. Save and then print the worksheet.
8. With the worksheet still open, determine the effect on actual job earnings with a 10% decrease by completing the following steps:
   a. Make cell B12 active.
   b. Type **0.9** and then press Enter.
9. Save and then print **sec3x14**.
10. Determine the effects on actual job earnings with a 10% increase. (To do this, type **1.1** in cell B12.)
11. Save, print, and then close **sec3x14**.

B	C
Actual	Projected
$ 30,349	$ 27,314
$ 48,290	$ 43,461
$ 34,192	$ 30,773
$ 63,293	$ 56,964
$ 29,400	$ 26,460
$ 55,309	$ 49,778
$ 12,398	$ 11,158
$ 87,534	$ 78,781
0.9	

Step 8b

Using a Mixed Cell Reference in a Formula

The formula you created in Step 6d in Exercise 14 contained a relative cell reference (B3) and an absolute cell reference ($B$12). A formula can also contain a mixed cell reference. In a mixed cell reference either the column remains absolute and the row is relative or the column is relative and the row is absolute. In Exercise 15, you will create the formula *=$A3*B$2*. In the first cell reference in the formula, *$A3*, the column is absolute and the row is relative. In the second cell reference, *B$2*, the column is relative and the row is absolute. The formula containing the mixed cell references allows you to fill in the column and row data using only one formula.

Identify an absolute or mixed cell reference by typing a dollar sign before the column and/or row reference or press the F4 function key to cycle through the various cell references. For example, type **=A3** in a cell, press F4, and the cell reference changes to *=$A$3*. Press F4 again and the cell reference changes to *=A$3*. The next time you press F4, the cell reference changes to *=$A3*. Press it again to change the cell reference back to *=A3*.

exercise 15

DETERMINING SIMPLE INTEREST USING A FORMULA WITH MIXED CELL REFERENCES

1. Open **ExcelWorksheet12**.
2. Save the worksheet with Save As and name it **sec3x15**.
3. Make cell B3 the active cell and then insert a formula containing mixed cell references by completing the following steps:
   a. Type **=A3** and then press the F4 function key three times. (This changes the cell reference to *$A3*.)
   b. Type ***B2** and then press the F4 function key twice. (This changes the cell reference to *B$2*.)
   c. Make sure the formula displays as *=$A3*B$2* and then press Enter.

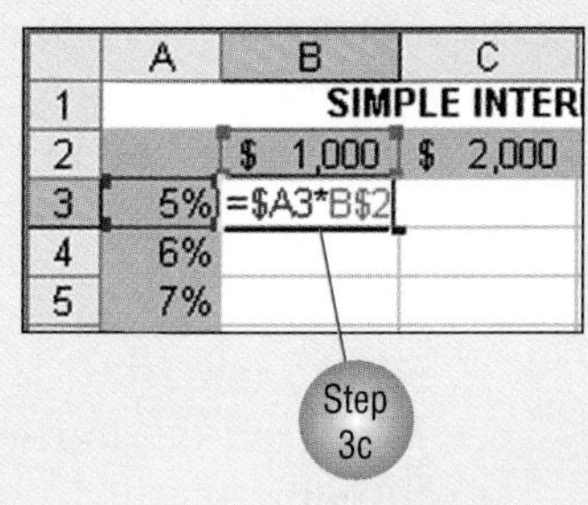

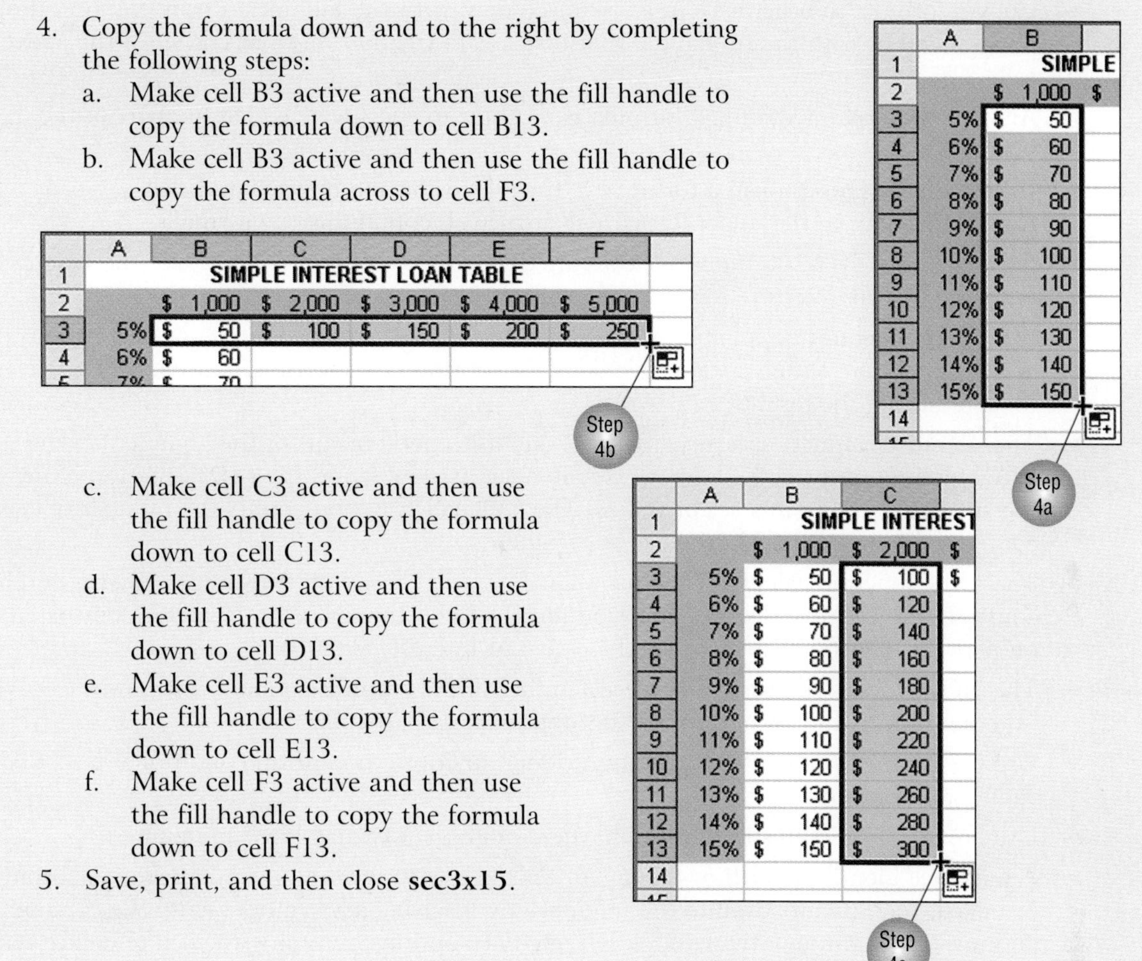

4. Copy the formula down and to the right by completing the following steps:
   a. Make cell B3 active and then use the fill handle to copy the formula down to cell B13.
   b. Make cell B3 active and then use the fill handle to copy the formula across to cell F3.
   c. Make cell C3 active and then use the fill handle to copy the formula down to cell C13.
   d. Make cell D3 active and then use the fill handle to copy the formula down to cell D13.
   e. Make cell E3 active and then use the fill handle to copy the formula down to cell E13.
   f. Make cell F3 active and then use the fill handle to copy the formula down to cell F13.
5. Save, print, and then close **sec3x15**.

You only had to type one formula in Exercise 15 to create the data in the simple interest table. The mixed cell references allowed you to copy the formula down columns and across rows.

CHAPTER summary

- Type a formula in a cell and the formula displays in the cell as well as in the Formula bar. If cell entries are changed, a formula will automatically recalculate the values and insert the result in the cell.
- Use the AutoSum button on the Standard toolbar to automatically add numbers in rows or columns.
- Create your own formula with commonly used operators such as addition (+), subtraction (-), multiplication (*), division (/), percent (%), and exponentiation (^). When writing a formula, begin with the equals (=) sign.

- Copy a formula to other cells in a row or column with the Fill option from the Edit drop-down menu or with the fill handle that displays in the bottom right corner of the active cell.
- Another method for writing a formula is to point to specific cells that are part of the formula.
- If Excel detects an error in a formula, a Trace Error button appears and a dark green triangle displays in the upper left corner of the cell containing the formula.
- Excel includes over 200 functions that are divided into nine categories. Use the Insert Function feature to create formulas using built-in functions.
- A function operates on an argument, which may consist of a cell reference, a constant, or another function. When a value calculated by a formula is inserted in a cell, this is referred to as returning the result.
- The AVERAGE function returns the average (arithmetic mean) of the arguments. The MAX function returns the largest value in a set of values, and the MIN function returns the smallest number in a set of values. The COUNT function counts the number of cells containing numbers within the list of arguments.
- The PMT function calculates the payment for a loan based on constant payments and a constant interest rate. The FV function returns the future value of an investment based on periodic, constant payments and a constant interest rate.
- The NOW function returns the serial number of the current date and time and the DATE function returns the serial number that represents a particular date.
- Use the IF function, considered a conditional function, to perform conditional tests on values and formulas.
- Use nested IF functions in a formula where more than two actions are required.
- A reference identifies a cell or a range of cells in a worksheet and can be relative, absolute, or mixed. Identify an absolute cell reference by inserting a $ symbol before the column and row. Cycle through the various cell reference options by typing the cell reference and then pressing F4.

FEATURES summary

FEATURE	BUTTON	MENU	KEYBOARD
AutoSum function	Σ ▾	Insert, Function, SUM	
Insert Function dialog box	fx	Insert, Function	
Cycle through cell reference options			F4

CONCEPTS check

Completion: On a blank sheet of paper, indicate the correct term, symbol, or command for each description.

1. When typing a formula, begin the formula with this sign.
2. Click this button on the Standard toolbar to automatically add numbers in cells.
3. This is the operator for division that is used when writing a formula.
4. This is the operator for multiplication that is used when writing a formula.
5. This is the name of the small black box located at the bottom right corner of a cell that can be used to copy a formula to adjacent cells.
6. A function operates on this, which may consist of a constant, a cell reference, or another function.
7. This function returns the largest value in a set of values.
8. This function finds the periodic payment for a loan based on constant payments and a constant interest rate.
9. This function returns the serial number of the current date and time.
10. This function is considered a conditional function.
11. To identify an absolute cell reference, type this symbol before the column and row.
12. Suppose that cell B2 contains the budgeted amount and cell C2 contains the actual amount. Write the formula (including the IF conditions) that would insert the word *under* if the actual amount was less than the budgeted amount and insert the word *over* if the actual amount was greater than the budgeted amount.

SKILLS check

Assessment 1

1. Create a worksheet with the information shown in Figure 3.3 with the following specifications:
   a. Type the data shown in Figure 3.3 with the appropriate formatting.
   b. Insert the formula to calculate the difference (actual amount minus the budget amount) and then copy the formula down to the other cells.
   c. Use AutoSum to insert the total amounts.
   d. Format the numbers in cells as currency with zero decimal places.
2. Save the worksheet and name it **sec3sc01**.
3. Print and then close **sec3sc01**.

FIGURE 3.3 *Assessment 1*

SUMMARY OF PERFORMANCE

	Actual	Budget	Difference
Northeast division	2,505,250	2,250,000	
Southeast division	1,895,200	1,550,000	
Northwest division	2,330,540	2,200,000	
Southwest division	1,850,340	1,950,500	
Total			

Assessment 2

1. Open **ExcelWorksheet13**.
2. Save the worksheet with Save As and name it **sec3sc02**.
3. Make the following changes to the worksheet:
   a. Determine the average monthly sales using the AVERAGE function.
   b. Format the numbers in cell B3 through H8 as currency with zero decimal places.
   c. Automatically adjust columns B through H.
4. Save, print, and then close **sec3sc02**.

Assessment 3

1. Open **sec3sc02**.
2. Save the worksheet with Save As and name it **sec3sc03**.
3. Make the following changes to the worksheet:
   a. Total each monthly column. (Create an appropriate title for the row and resize column widths, if necessary.)
   b. Use the MAX function to determine the highest monthly total (for cells B3 through G8). (You determine where you want this maximum monthly total to appear in the worksheet. Be sure to include a cell title.)
   c. Use the MIN function to determine the lowest monthly total (for cells B3 through G8). (You determine where you want this minimum monthly total to appear in the worksheet. Be sure to include a cell title.)
4. Save, print, and then close **sec3sc03**.

Assessment 4

1. Open **ExcelWorksheet24**.
2. Save the worksheet with Save As and name it **sec3sc04**.
3. The manager of Clearline Manufacturing is interested in refinancing a loan for either $125,000 or $300,000 and wants to determine the monthly payments, total payments, and total interest paid. Insert a formula with the following specifications:
   a. Make cell E5 active.
   b. Use the Insert Function button on the Formula bar to insert a formula using the PMT function. At the formula palette, enter the following:

Rate	=	C5/12
Nper	=	D5
Pv	=	-B5

   c. Copy the formula in cell E5 down to cells E6 through E8.
4. Insert a formula in cell F5 that multiplies the amount in E5 by the amount in D5.
5. Copy the formula in cell F5 down to cells F6 through F8.
6. Insert a formula in cell G5 that subtracts the amount in B5 from the amount in F5. (The formula is ***=F5-B5***.)
7. Copy the formula in cell G5 down to cells G6 through G8.
8. Save, print, and then close **sec3sc04**.

Assessment 5

1. Open **ExcelWorksheet21**.
2. Save the worksheet with Save As and name it **sec3sc05**.
3. Make the following changes to the worksheet:
   a. Change the percentage in cell B3 from *9%* to *10%*.
   b. Change the number in cell B4 from *36* to *60*.
   c. Change the amount in cell B5 from *($1,200)* to *-500*.
   d. Use the FV function to insert a formula that calculates the future value of the investment. ***(Hint: For help with the formula, refer to Exercise 10.)***
4. Save, print, and then close **sec3sc05**.

Assessment 6

1. Open **ExcelWorksheet14**.
2. Save the worksheet with Save As and name it **sec3sc06**.
3. Make the following changes to the worksheet:
   a. Insert a formula using an absolute reference to determine the projected quotas at 10% of the current quotas.
   b. Save and then print **sec3sc06**.
   c. Determine the projected quotas at 15% of the current quota by changing cell A14 to *15% Increase* and cell B14 to *1.15*.
   d. Save and then print **sec3sc06**.
   e. Determine the projected quotas at 20% of the current quota.
4. Save, print, and then close **sec3sc06**.

Assessment 7

1. Learn about specific options in the Options dialog box by completing the following steps:
   a. Open a blank workbook and then display the Options dialog box by clicking Tools and then Options.
   b. At the Options dialog box, click the View tab.
   c. Read information about the options in the *Window options* section of the dialog box. (To do this, click the Help button [displays with a question mark] that displays in the upper right corner of the dialog box. At the Microsoft Office Excel Help window, click the View hyperlink. Scroll down the window and read information about the options in the Window options section.)
   d. Close the blank workbook.
2. After reading information about the options in the Window options section, complete the following steps:

a. Open **sec3sc04**.
b. Save the worksheet with Save As and name it **sec3sc07**.
c. Display the formulas in the worksheet (rather than the results) using information you learned from the Options dialog box.

3. Save, print, and then close **sec3sc07**.

CHAPTER challenge

You are a loan officer for Loans R Us. You work in the department that specializes in home loans. To quickly determine monthly payments for potential customers, create a worksheet that displays the following labels: Price of Home, Down Payment, Loan Amount, Interest Rate, Term of Loan, and Monthly Payment. Use a formula to calculate the loan amount. Use the PMT function to determine the Monthly Payment. Insert amounts of your choosing for the other parts. In addition to calculating the monthly payment, customers whose down payment is less than 10% of the price of the home will be required to purchase private mortgage insurance. In another area of the worksheet, use the IF function to determine if the customer would have to purchase insurance. If the customer's down payment is less than 10%, display "purchase insurance" in the cell. If customer's down payment is 10% or greater, "no insurance necessary" should appear in the cell. Use cell references whenever possible. Format the worksheet so that it is easy to read and understand. Save the file and print it.

When a customer is required to purchase private mortgage insurance, you would like to provide information to the customer quickly concerning this insurance. Use the Help feature to learn about creating hyperlinks in Excel. Locate a helpful Web site that specializes in private mortgage insurance. Create a hyperlink in the worksheet that will jump to the Web site. Save the file again.

Once a loan has been approved and finalized, a letter will be sent to the customer explaining the details of the loan. Use a letter template in Word to create a letter that will be sent to a customer. Copy and link the information in the worksheet created in the first part of the Chapter Challenge to the customer letter. Save the letter and print it.

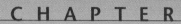

CHAPTER 4

ENHANCING A WORKSHEET

PERFORMANCE OBJECTIVES

Upon successful completion of Chapter 4, you will be able to:

- **Create headers and footers**
- **Change worksheet margins**
- **Center a worksheet horizontally and vertically on the page**
- **Insert a page break in a worksheet**
- **Print gridlines and row and column headings**
- **Hide and unhide a worksheet, column, or row**
- **Set and clear a print area**
- **Specify more than one print area in Page Break Preview**
- **Change the print quality**
- **Complete a spelling check on a worksheet**
- **Find and replace data and cell formatting in a worksheet**
- **Sort data in cells in ascending and descending order**
- **Filter a list using AutoFilter**
- **Plan and create a worksheet**

Excel contains features you can use to enhance and control the formatting of a worksheet. In this chapter, you will learn how to create headers and footers, change worksheet margins, print column and row titles, print gridlines, and center a worksheet horizontally and vertically on the page. You will also learn how to complete a spell check on text in a worksheet, find and replace specific data and formatting in a worksheet, sort and filter data, and plan and create a worksheet.

Formatting a Worksheet Page

Worksheets, by default, are printed in portrait orientation with default top and bottom margins of 1 inch and left and right margins of .75 inch. These settings can be changed with options at the Page Setup dialog box. The Page Setup dialog box contains several tabs for controlling the appearance of the worksheet page.

Controlling the Page Layout

The Page Setup dialog box with the Page tab selected as shown in Figure 4.1 provides options for controlling the layout of the worksheet on the page. To display this dialog box, click File and then Page Setup. You can also display the Page Setup dialog box while in Print Preview by clicking the Setup button. At the Page Setup dialog box, make sure the Page tab is selected.

FIGURE 4.1 **Page Setup Dialog Box with Page Tab Selected**

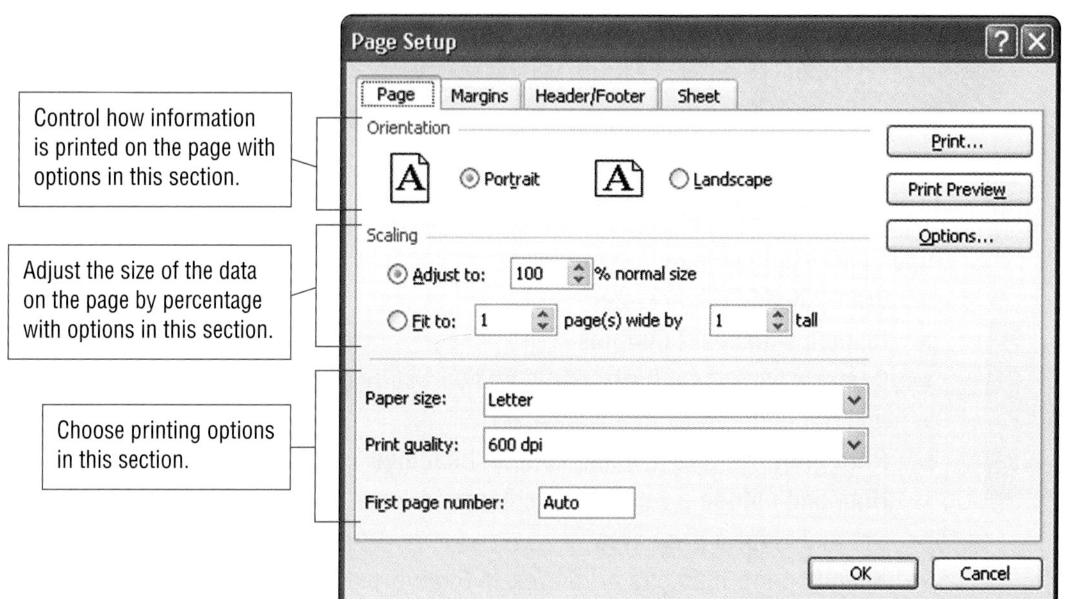

Control how information is printed on the page with choices in the *Orientation* section of the Page Setup dialog box. The two choices in the *Orientation* section are represented by sample pages. A sample page that is taller than it is wide shows how the default orientation (*Portrait*) prints data on the page. The other choice, *Landscape*, will rotate the data and print it on a page that is wider than it is tall. The landscape orientation might be useful in a worksheet that contains more columns than rows.

With options in the *Scaling* section of the Page Setup dialog box, you can adjust the size of the data in the worksheet by percentage. You can also specify on how many pages you want the data to fit. For example, if a worksheet contains too many columns to print on one page, choosing *Fit to* and leaving *1* as the number of pages will cause the display percentage to be decreased until the columns all fit on one page.

By default, an Excel worksheet is printed on standard paper, which is 8.5 inches wide and 11 inches long. Change this paper size with options from the Paper size drop-down list. Paper size choices will vary depending on the selected printer. To view the list of paper sizes, click the down-pointing arrow at the right of the *Paper size* option box.

Depending on the printer you are using, you may or may not have choices for setting the print quality. The data that displays in the *Print quality* option box will vary depending on the selected printer. To view a list of print quality choices, click the down-pointing arrow at the right side of the *Print quality* option box. Choose a higher dpi (dots per inch) number to improve the quality of the print.

The worksheets you have printed so far have not been numbered. If you turn on page numbering (discussed in the "Inserting Headers/Footers" section), the first worksheet page is numbered 1 and any additional pages are incrementally numbered. With the *First page number* option, you can specify a different beginning page number. To do this, select *Auto* in the *First page number* text box, and then type the new starting number.

Inserting Headers/Footers

Use options at the Page Setup dialog box with the Header/Footer tab selected as shown in Figure 4.2 to insert text that will print at the top and/or bottom of each page of the worksheet. Click the down-pointing arrow after the *Header* option box and a drop-down list displays with options for inserting the user's name, workbook name, current date, and page number. The same list will display if you click the down-pointing arrow at the right of the *Footer* option box.

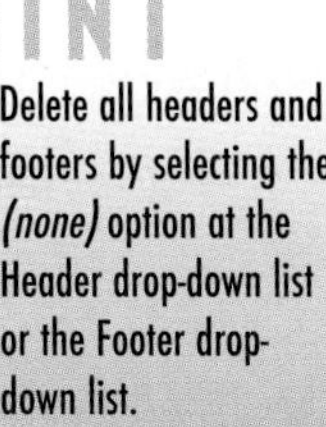

Delete all headers and footers by selecting the *(none)* option at the Header drop-down list or the Footer drop-down list.

FIGURE 4.2 **Page Setup Dialog Box with Header/Footer Tab Selected**

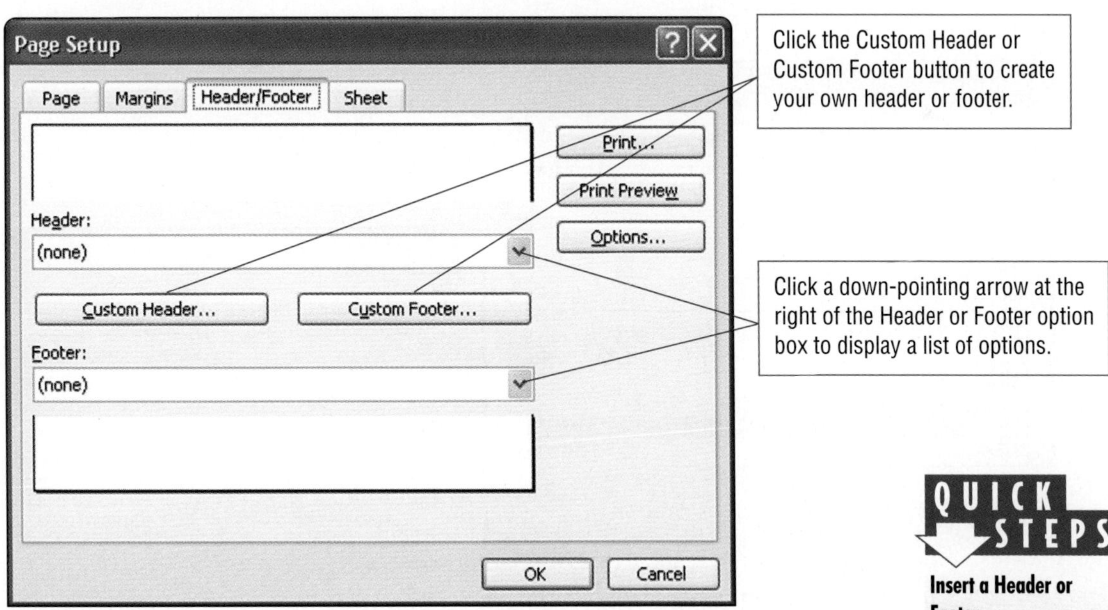

QUICK STEPS

Insert a Header or Footer

1. Click File, Page Setup.
2. Click Header/Footer tab.
3. Use options to insert desired header or footer.
4. Click OK.

(Note: Before completing computer exercises, delete the ExcelChapter03S folder on your disk. Next, copy the ExcelChapter04S subfolder from the Excel2003Specialist folder on the CD that accompanies this textbook to your disk and then make ExcelChapter04S the active folder.)

exercise 1

CHANGING PAGE ORIENTATION AND INSERTING PAGE NUMBERING

1. Open **ExcelWorksheet06**.
2. Save the worksheet with Save As and name it **sec4x01**.
3. Change the orientation of the worksheet and insert a header and footer by completing the following steps:
   a. Click File and then Page Setup.
   b. At the Page Setup dialog box, click the Page tab.
   c. Click the *Landscape* option.
   d. Click twice on the up-pointing arrow at the right side of the *Adjust to* text box. (This inserts *110* in the text box.)
   e. Click the Header/Footer tab.
   f. At the Page Setup dialog box with the Header/Footer tab selected, click the down-pointing arrow at the right of the *Header* option box, and then click ***sec4x01*** in the drop-down list box. (If ***sec4x01*** is not visible in the list box, scroll down the list box.)

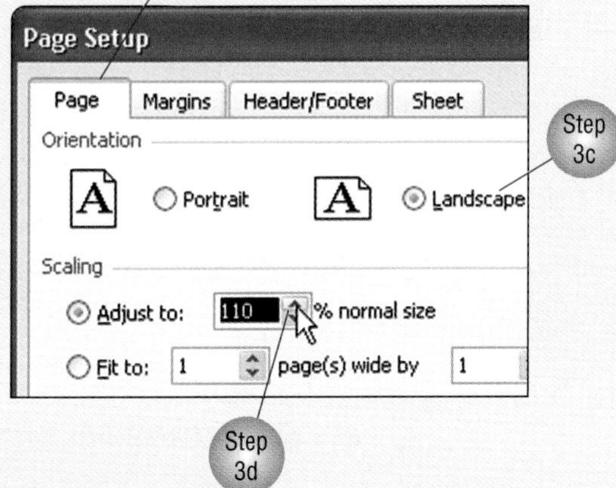

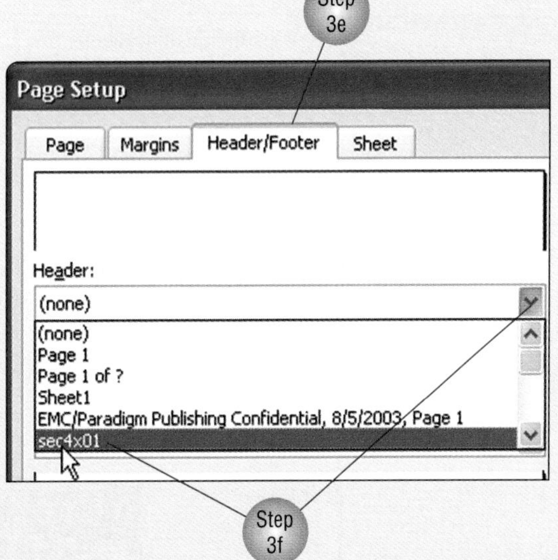

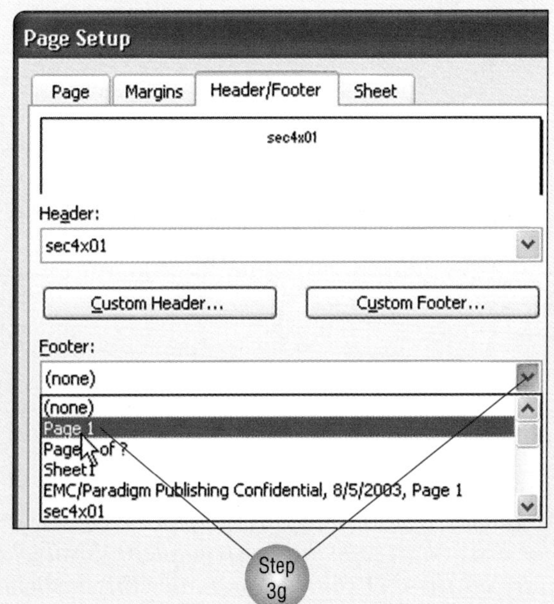

   g. Click the down-pointing arrow at the right of the *Footer* option box and then click *Page 1* at the drop-down list box. (If *Page 1* is not visible in the list box, scroll down the list box.)
   h. Click OK to close the Page Setup dialog box.
4. Save and then preview **sec4x01**.
5. Print **sec4x01**. (Before printing this worksheet, check with your instructor to determine if your printer can print in landscape orientation.)

6. With **sec4x01** still open, change the page orientation, scale the size of the worksheet so it fits on one page, and change the beginning page number to 3 by completing the following steps:
   a. Click File and then Page Setup.
   b. At the Page Setup dialog box, click the Page tab.
   c. Click the *Portrait* option.
   d. Click the *Fit to* option.
   e. Select *Auto* that displays in the *First page number* text box and then type 3.
   f. Click OK to close the dialog box.
7. Save, preview, print, and then close **sec4x01**.

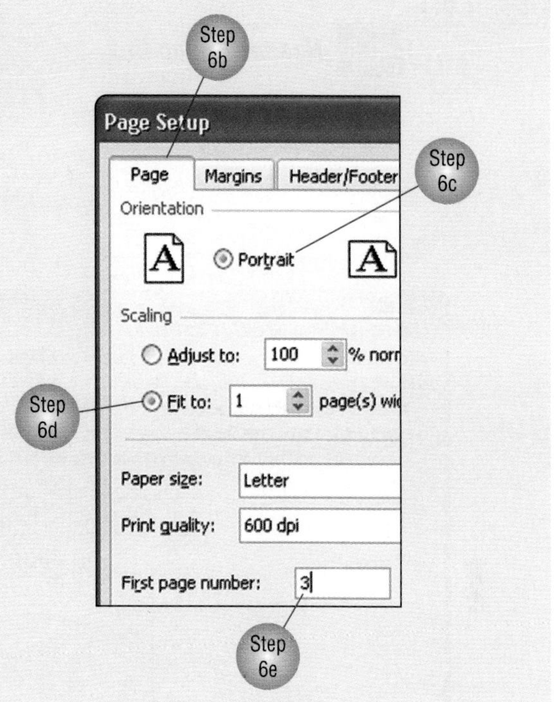

Creating Custom Headers/Footers

If you want to create a custom header, click the Custom Header button at the Page Setup dialog box with the Header/Footer tab selected. This displays the Header dialog box shown in Figure 4.3. Create a custom footer by clicking the Custom Footer button. This displays the Footer dialog box containing the same options as the Header dialog box. The Header dialog box and Footer dialog box contain a toolbar with buttons for customizing header/footer text; inserting text such as a page number, date, time, and path and file name; and inserting a picture. Buttons on this toolbar are identified in Figure 4.3.

To insert text in a custom header or footer, click in the desired section text box (such as *Left section*, *Center section*, or *Right section*) and then click the button on the toolbar that inserts the desired text or type the desired text. For example, to insert the workbook file name and path at the top center of the page, click in the *Center section* text box, and then click the Path & File button on the toolbar.

QUICK STEPS

Insert a Custom Header
1. Click File, Page Setup.
2. Click Header/Footer tab.
3. Click Custom Header button.
4. Type or insert desired data.
5. Click OK.
6. Click OK.

Insert a Custom Footer
1. Click File, Page Setup.
2. Click Header/Footer tab.
3. Click Custom Footer button.
4. Type or insert desired data.
5. Click OK.
6. Click OK.

FIGURE 4.3 **Header Dialog Box**

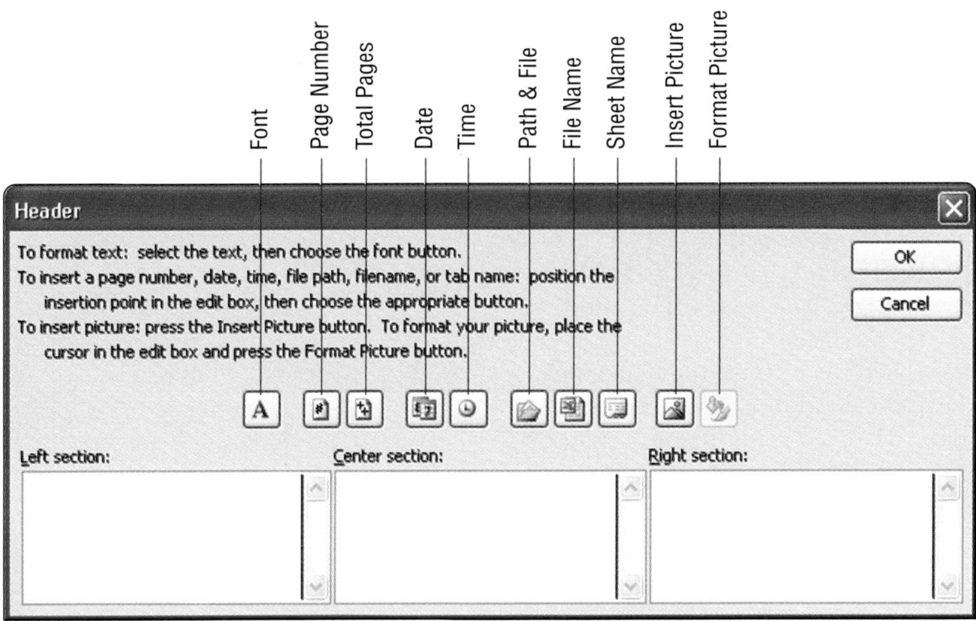

exercise 2 CREATING A HEADER AND FOOTER

1. Open **ExcelWorksheet06**.
2. Save the worksheet with Save As and name it **sec4x02**.
3. Delete row 2.
4. Insert the text *Average* in cell N1.
5. Insert a formula in cell N2 that averages the percentages in cells B2 through M2.
6. Copy the formula in cell N2 relatively to cells N3 through N19.
7. Insert a header and footer in the worksheet by completing the following steps:
   a. Click File and then Page Setup.
   b. At the Page Setup dialog box, click the Header/Footer tab.
   c. At the Page Setup dialog box with the Header/Footer tab selected, click the Custom Header button.
   d. At the Header dialog box, click in the text box below *Right section*, and then type your name.
   e. Click OK to close the Header dialog box.
   f. At the Page Setup dialog box, click the Custom Footer button.
   g. At the Footer dialog box, click in the text box below *Center section*, and then click the File Name button on the toolbar.

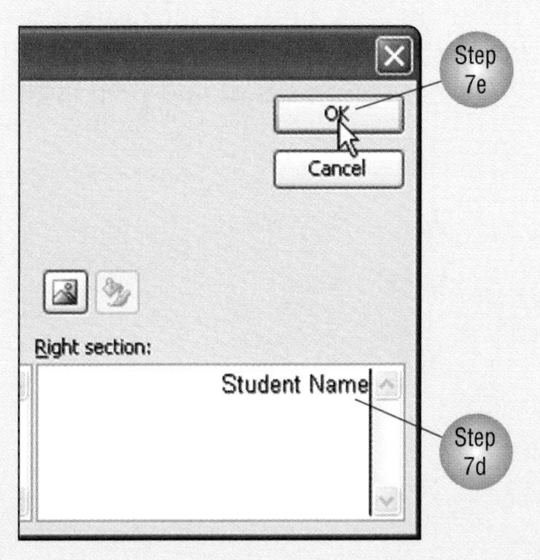

h. Click OK to close the Footer dialog box.
i. Click OK to close the Page Setup dialog box.

8. Save, preview, print, and then close **sec4x02**.

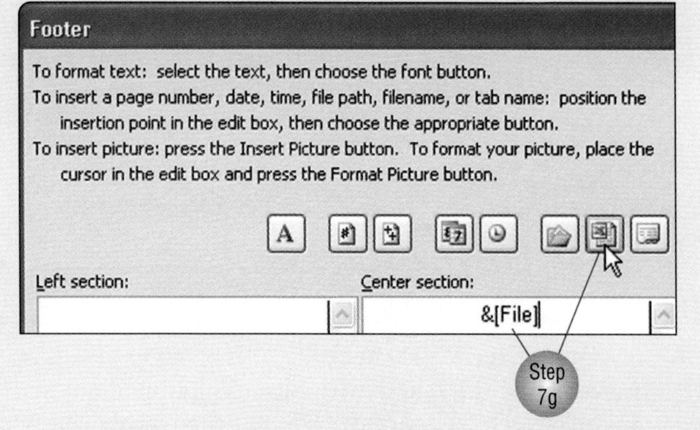

Changing Worksheet Margins

Excel uses 1-inch top and bottom margins for a worksheet and 0.75-inch left and right margins. You can change these default margins at the Page Setup dialog box with the Margins tab selected as shown in Figure 4.4.

Change Worksheet Margins

1. Click File, Page Setup.
2. Click Margins tab.
3. Change the top, left, right, and/or bottom measurements.
4. Click OK.

FIGURE 4.4 ***Page Setup Dialog Box with Margins Tab Selected***

Changes made to margin measurements are reflected in the sample worksheet page.

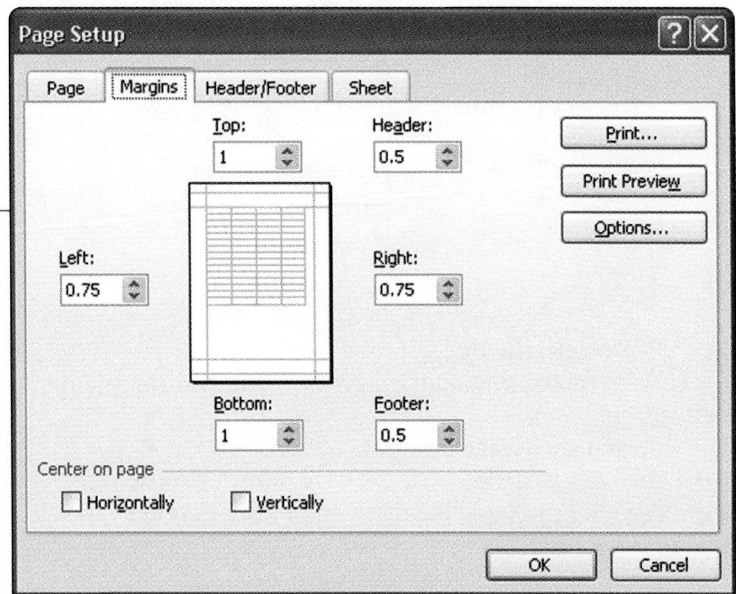

A worksheet page showing the cells and margins displays in the dialog box. As you increase or decrease the Top, Bottom, Left, or Right margin measurements, the sample worksheet page reflects the change. You can also increase or decrease the measurement from the top of the page to the header with the *Header* option or the measurement from the footer to the bottom of the page with the *Footer* option.

exercise 3 CHANGING WORKSHEET MARGINS

1. Open **ExcelWorksheet02**.
2. Save the worksheet with Save As and name it **sec4x03**.
3. Select cells A1 through D8 and then apply the Accounting 2 autoformat.
4. Change the orientation of the worksheet and change the worksheet margins by completing the following steps:
   a. Click File and then Page Setup.
   b. At the Page Setup dialog box, click the Page tab.
   c. Click the *Landscape* option.
   d. Click the Margins tab.
   e. At the Page Setup dialog box with the Margins tab selected, click the up-pointing arrow at the right of the *Top* text box until *3.5* displays.
   f. Click the up-pointing arrow at the right of the *Left* text box until *3.5* displays.

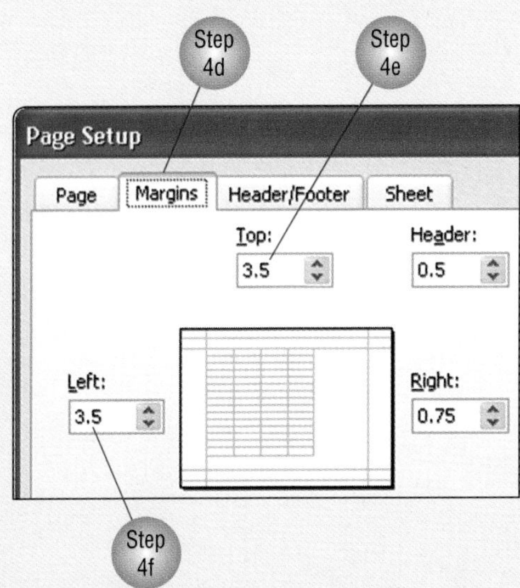

   g. Click OK to close the dialog box.
5. Create a custom footer that contains your name and the file name by completing the following steps:
   a. Click File and then Page Setup.
   b. At the Page Setup dialog box, click the Header/Footer tab.
   c. At the Page Setup dialog box with the Header/Footer tab selected, click the Custom Footer button.

d. At the Footer dialog box, click in the text box below *Left section*, and then type your name.
e. Click in the text box below *Right section* and then click the File Name button on the toolbar.
f. Click OK to close the Footer dialog box.

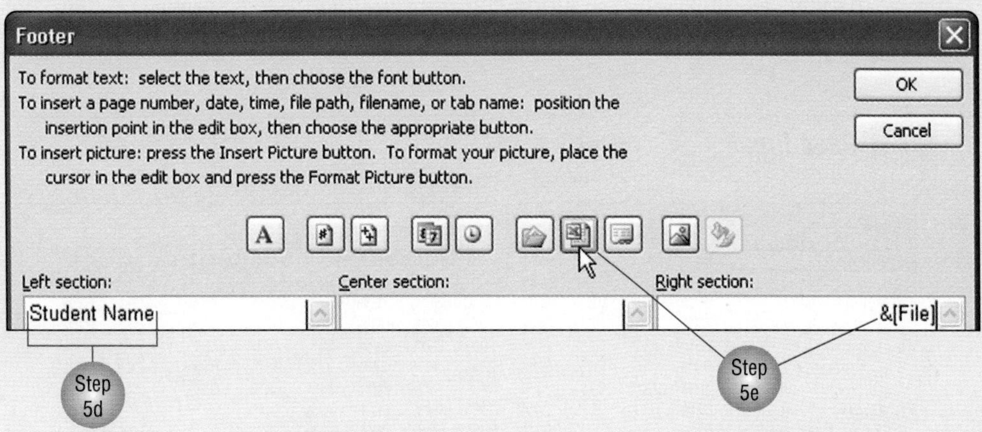

g. Click OK to close the Page Setup dialog box.
6. Save, preview, print, and then close **sec4x03**.

Centering a Worksheet Horizontally and/or Vertically

By default, worksheets print in the upper left corner of the page. You can center a worksheet on the page by changing the margins; however, an easier method for centering a worksheet is to use the *Horizontally* and/or *Vertically* options that display at the bottom of the Page Setup dialog box with the Margins tab selected. If you choose one or both of these options, the worksheet page in the *Preview* section displays how the worksheet will print on the page.

Center Worksheet Horizontally/Vertically
1. Click File, Page Setup.
2. Click Margins tab.
3. Click *Horizontally* option and/or click *Vertically* option.
4. Click OK.

exercise 4 — HORIZONTALLY AND VERTICALLY CENTERING A WORKSHEET

1. Open **ExcelWorksheet03**.
2. Save the worksheet with Save As and name it **sec4x04**.
3. Select cells B3 through D8 and then click the Percent Style button on the Formatting toolbar.
4. Select cells A1 through D8 and then apply the Colorful 2 autoformat.
5. Horizontally and vertically center the worksheet by completing the following steps:
   a. Click File and then Page Setup.
   b. At the Page Setup dialog box, click the Margins tab.
   c. Click the *Horizontally* option. (This inserts a check mark.)
   d. Click the *Vertically* option. (This inserts a check mark.)
   e. Click OK to close the dialog box.
6. Save, preview, print, and then close **sec4x04**.

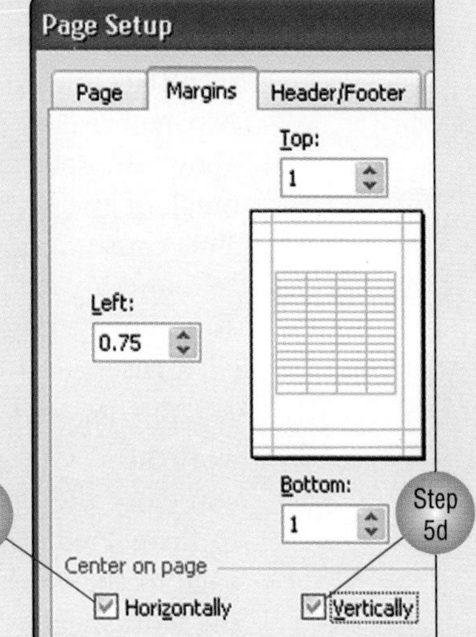

Insert Page Break
1. Select column or row.
2. Click Insert, Page Break.

Inserting and Removing Page Breaks

The default left and right margins of .75 inch allow a total of 7 inches of cells across the page (8.5 inches minus 1.5 inches equals 7 inches). If a worksheet contains more than 7 inches of cells across the page, a page break is inserted in the worksheet and the remaining columns are moved to the next page. A page break displays as a broken line along cell borders. Figure 4.5 shows the page break in ExcelWorksheet06. (The location of your page break may vary.)

FIGURE 4.5 ***Page Break***

A1 | Name

	A	B	C	D	E	F	G	H	I	J	K	L	M	N
1	**Name**	**Test 1**	**Test 2**	**Test 3**	**Test 4**	**Test 5**	**Test 6**	**Test 7**	**Test 8**	**Test 9**	**Test 10**	**Test 11**	**Test 12**	
2														
3	Arnson, Patrick	89%	65%	76%	89%	98%	65%	76%	87%	55%	78%	67%	69%	
4	Barclay, Jeanine	78%	66%	87%	90%	92%	82%	100%	84%	67%	86%	82%	91%	
5	Calahan, Jack	65%	71%	64%	66%	70%	81%	64%	59%	76%	76%	45%	49%	
6	Cumpston, Kurt	89%	91%	90%	93%	86%	80%	84%	93%	95%	81%	96%	98%	
7	Dimmitt, Marian	78%	73%	81%	82%	67%	69%	82%	72%	85%	83%	71%	73%	
8	Donovan, Nancy	82%	89%	79%	74%	80%	82%	86%	72%	74%	82%	76%	79%	
9	Fisher-Edwards, Teri	89%	93%	100%	91%	86%	90%	88%	86%	100%	98%	90%	97%	
10	Flanery, Stephanie	58%	45%	63%	51%	60%	59%	63%	52%	66%	67%	53%	49%	
11	Heyman, Grover	78%	75%	87%	88%	64%	76%	70%	67%	55%	87%	82%	88%	
12	Herbertson, Wynn	92%	80%	93%	90%	86%	84%	95%	100%	98%	88%	95%	89%	
13	Jewett, Troy	98%	94%	99%	89%	100%	93%	100%	95%	96%	91%	87%	94%	
14	Kwieciak, Kathleen	55%	0%	42%	65%	72%	40%	65%	0%	0%	48%	52%	56%	
15	Leibrand, Maxine	78%	69%	83%	87%	84%	69%	80%	82%	88%	79%	83%	76%	
16	Markovits, Claude	89%	93%	84%	100%	95%	92%	95%	100%	89%	94%	98%	94%	
17	Moonstar, Siana	73%	87%	67%	83%	90%	84%	73%	81%	75%	65%	84%	88%	
18	Nyegaard, Curtis	90%	89%	84%	85%	93%	85%	100%	94%	98%	93%	100%	95%	
19	Oglesbee, Randy	65%	55%	73%	90%	87%	67%	85%	77%	85%	73%	78%	77%	
20	Pherson, Douglas	69%	82%	87%	74%	70%	82%	84%	85%	66%	77%	91%	86%	
21														
22														
23														

Sheet1 / Sheet2 / Sheet3

Page Break

A page break also displays horizontally in a worksheet. By default, a worksheet can contain approximately 9 inches of cells vertically down the page. This is because the paper size is set by default at 11 inches. With the default top and bottom margins of 1 inch, this allows 9 inches of cells to print on one page.

Excel automatically inserts a page break in a worksheet. You can insert your own if you would like more control over what cells print on a page. To insert your own page break, select the column or row, click Insert, and then click Page Break. A page break is inserted immediately left of the selected column or immediately above the selected row. If you want to insert both a horizontal and vertical page break at the same time, make a cell active, click Insert, and then click Page Break. This causes a horizontal page break to be inserted immediately above the active cell, and a vertical page break to be inserted at the left side of the active column. To remove a page break, select the column or row or make the desired cell active, click Insert and then click Remove Page Break.

The page break automatically inserted by Excel may not be visible initially in a worksheet. One way to display the page break is to preview the worksheet. When you close the Print Preview screen, the page break will display in the worksheet. In Print Preview, click the Next button on the Preview bar to display the next page in the worksheet. Click the Previous button to display the previous page in the worksheet.

Excel provides a Page Break view that will display worksheet pages and page breaks. To display this view, click View and then Page Break Preview. This causes the worksheet to display similarly to the worksheet shown in Figure 4.6. The word *Page* along with the page number is displayed in gray behind the cells in the worksheet. A blue line displays indicating the page break. You can move the page break by positioning the arrow pointer on the blue line, holding down the left mouse button, dragging the line to the desired location, and then releasing the mouse button. To return to the Normal view, click View and then Normal.

HINT

You can edit a worksheet in Page Break Preview.

FIGURE

4.6 *Worksheet in Page Break Preview*

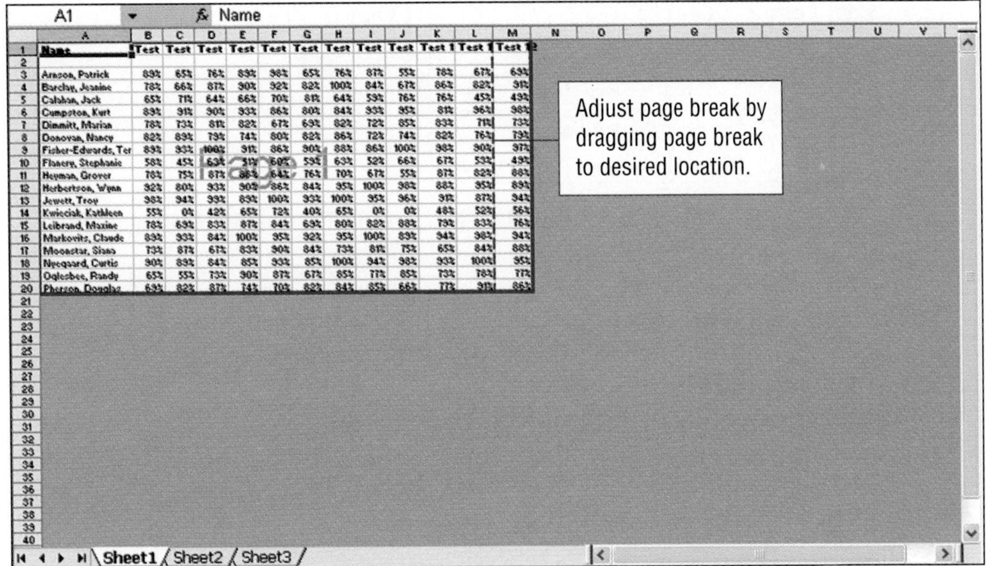
A1
Name
Adjust page break by dragging page break to desired location.
Sheet1
Sheet2
Sheet3

exercise 5

INSERTING A PAGE BREAK IN A WORKSHEET

1. Open **ExcelWorksheet06**.
2. Save the worksheet with Save As and name it **sec4x05**.
3. View the default page break inserted automatically by Excel by completing the following steps:
   a. Click the Print Preview button on the Standard toolbar.
   b. After previewing the worksheet, click the Close button.
   c. At the worksheet, click the right scroll arrow at the right side of the horizontal scroll bar until columns L and M are visible. The default page break should display between columns L and M. (The default page break displays as a dashed line. The location of the page break may vary slightly.)
4. Select the entire worksheet and then change the font to 12-point Century (or a similar serif typeface such as Garamond).
5. If necessary, automatically adjust the width of column A.
6. Select columns B through M and then drag one of the selected column boundaries to the right until the column width displays as *9.00* in the yellow box.

7. Insert a page break between columns F and G by completing the following steps:
   a. Select column G.
   b. Click Insert and then Page Break.
   c. Click once in any cell in column F.

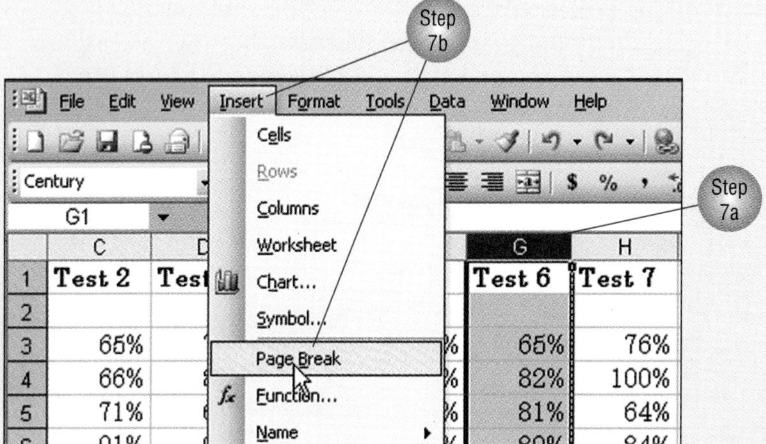

8. View the worksheet in Page Break Preview by completing the following steps:
   a. Click View and then Page Break Preview.
   b. View the pages and page breaks in the worksheet.
   c. Click View and then Normal to return to the Normal view.
9. Horizontally and vertically center the worksheet by completing the following steps:
   a. Click File and then Page Setup.
   b. At the Page Setup dialog box, click the Margins tab.
   c. Click the *Horizontally* option. (This inserts a check mark.)
   d. Click the *Vertically* option. (This inserts a check mark.)
   e. Click OK to close the dialog box.
10. Save, preview, print, and then close **sec4x05**.

Print Column and Row Titles
1. Click File, Page Setup.
2. Click Sheet tab.
3. Type row range in *Rows to repeat at top* option.
4. Type column range in *Columns to repeat at left* option.
5. Click OK.

Printing Column and Row Titles on Multiple Pages

Columns and rows in a worksheet are usually titled. For example, in ExcelWorksheet06, column titles include *Name, Test 1, Test 2, Test 3,* and so on. Row titles include the names of the people who have taken the tests. If a worksheet prints on more than one page, having column and/or row titles printing on each page can be useful. For example, when you printed sec4x05, the names of the people did not print on the second page. This makes matching test scores with names difficult.

You can print column and/or row titles on each page of a worksheet. To do this, click File and then Page Setup. At the Page Setup dialog box, click the Sheet tab. This displays the dialog box as shown in Figure 4.7.

FIGURE

4.7 Page Setup Dialog Box with Sheet Tab Selected

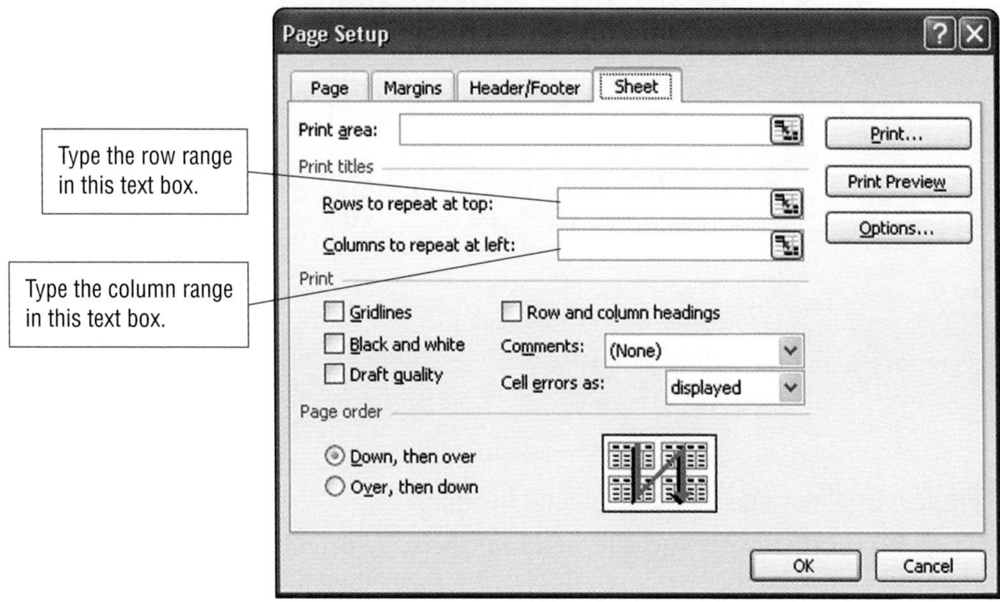

At the Page Setup dialog box with the Sheet tab selected, specify the range of row cells you want to print on every page in the *Rows to repeat at top* text box. Type a cell range using a colon. For example, if you want cells A1 through J1 to print on every page, you would type **A1:J1** in the *Rows to repeat at top* text box. Type the range of column cells you want to print on every page in the *Columns to repeat at left* text box.

exercise 6

PRINTING COLUMN TITLES ON EACH PAGE OF A WORKSHEET

1. Open **ExcelWorksheet06**.
2. Save the worksheet with Save As and name it **sec4x06**.
3. Select the entire worksheet and then change the font to 12-point Garamond (or a similar serif typeface).
4. If necessary, automatically adjust the width of column A.
5. Select columns B through M and then drag one of the selected column boundaries to the right until the column width displays as *8.00* in the yellow box above the mouse pointer. (This will change the width of columns B through M to *8.00*.)
6. Select row 1 and then change the alignment to center.
7. Specify that you want column titles to print on each page by completing the following steps:
    a. Click File and then Page Setup.
    b. At the Page Setup dialog box, click the Sheet tab.
    c. At the Page Setup dialog box with the Sheet tab selected, click in the *Columns to repeat at left* text box.

d. Type A1:A20.
e. Click OK to close the dialog box.

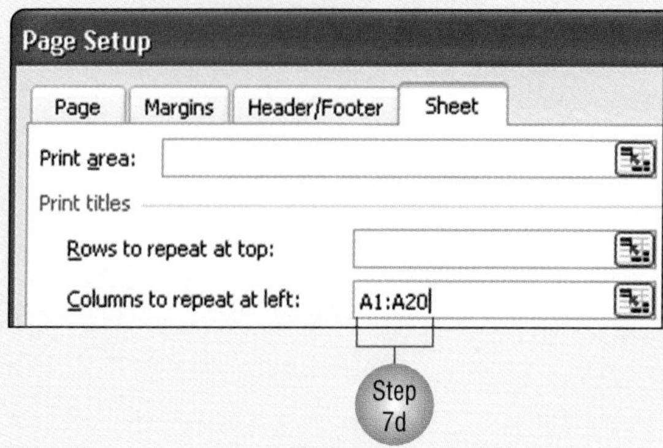

8. Save, preview, print, and then close **sec4x06**.

Printing Gridlines and Row and Column Headings

QUICK STEPS

Print Gridlines
1. Click File, Page Setup.
2. Click Sheet tab.
3. Click *Gridlines* option.
4. Click OK.

The gridlines that create the cells in a worksheet, by default, do not print. If you would like these gridlines to print, display the Page Setup dialog box with the Sheet tab selected, and then click *Gridlines* in the *Print* section. This inserts a check mark in the check box. At the Page Setup dialog box with the Sheet tab selected, you can also click *Row and column headings* and the row numbers and column letters will print with the worksheet.

If you are printing with a color printer, you can print the worksheet in black and white. To do this, display the Page Setup dialog box with the Sheet tab selected, and then click *Black and white*. This option is located in the *Print* section of the dialog box.

exercise 7

PRINTING GRIDLINES AND ROW AND COLUMN HEADINGS

1. Open **ExcelWorksheet05**.
2. Save the worksheet with Save As and name it **sec4x07**.
3. Insert the text *Total* in cell D2.
4. Merge and center cells A1 through D1. (You must click the Merge and Center button twice.)
5. Make cell D3 active and then insert a formula that multiplies the contents of cell C3 with B3.
6. Copy the formula in cell D3 relatively to cells D4 through D8.

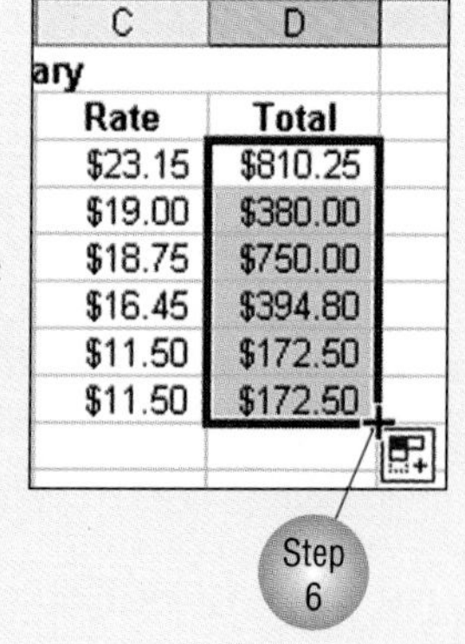

7. Specify that the gridlines and row and column headings are to print by completing the following steps:
   a. Click File and then Page Setup.
   b. At the Page Setup dialog box, click the Sheet tab.

c. At the Page Setup dialog box with the Sheet tab selected, click the *Gridlines* check box in the *Print* section to insert a check mark.

d. Click the *Row and column headings* check box in the *Print* section to insert a check mark.

8. With the Page Setup dialog box still displayed, click the Margins tab.
9. At the Page Setup dialog box with the Margins tab selected, click the *Horizontally* option, click the *Vertically* option, and then click OK to close the dialog box.
10. Save, preview, print, and then close **sec4x07**.

Hiding and Unhiding Columns/Rows

If a worksheet contains columns and/or rows of sensitive data or data that you are not using or do not want to view, consider hiding the columns and/or rows. To hide columns in a worksheet, select the columns to be hidden, click Format, point to Column, and then click Hide. To hide selected rows, click Format, point to Row, and then click Hide. To make a hidden column visible, select the column to the left and the column to the right of the hidden column, click Format, point to Column, and then click Unhide. To make a hidden row visible, select the row above and the row below the hidden row, click Format, point to Row, and then click Unhide.

Hide Columns
1. Select columns.
2. Click Format, Column, Hide.

If the first row or column is hidden, use the Go To feature to make the row or column visible. To do this, click Edit and then Go To. At the Go To dialog box, type A1 in the *Reference* text box, and then click OK. At the worksheet, click Format, point to either Column or Row, and then click Unhide.

You can also unhide columns or rows using the mouse. If a column or row is hidden, the gray boundary line in the column or row header displays as a slightly thicker gray line. To unhide a column, position the mouse pointer on the slightly thicker gray line that displays in the column header until the mouse pointer changes to left- and right-pointing arrows with a double line between. (Make sure the mouse pointer displays with two lines between the arrows. If a single line displays, you will simply change the size of the visible column.) Hold down the left mouse button, drag to the right until the column displays at the desired width, and then release the mouse button. Unhide a row in a similar manner. Position the mouse pointer on the slightly thicker gray line in the row header until the mouse pointer changes to up- and down-pointing arrows with a double line between. Drag down to display the row and then release the mouse button. If two or more adjacent columns or rows are hidden, you will need to unhide each column or row separately.

Hide Rows
1. Select rows.
2. Click Format, Row, Hide.

exercise 8

HIDING/UNHIDING COLUMNS AND ROWS

1. Open **ExcelWorksheet26**.
2. Save the worksheet with Save As and name it **sec4x08**.
3. Hide the rows containing rental information on the forklift by completing the following steps:
   a. Click cell A9 to make it the active cell.
   b. Click Format, point to Row, and then click Hide.
   c. Click cell A16 to make it the active cell.
   d. Click Format, point to Row, and then click Hide.

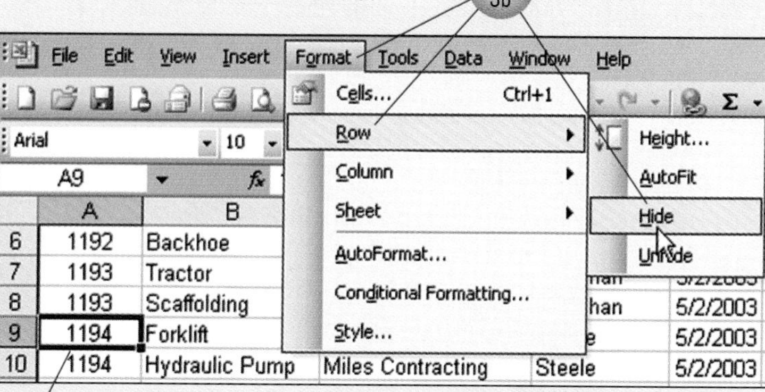

4. Hide the column containing the names of the service representatives by completing the following steps:
   a. Click cell D3 to make it the active cell.
   b. Click Format, point to Column, and then click Hide.

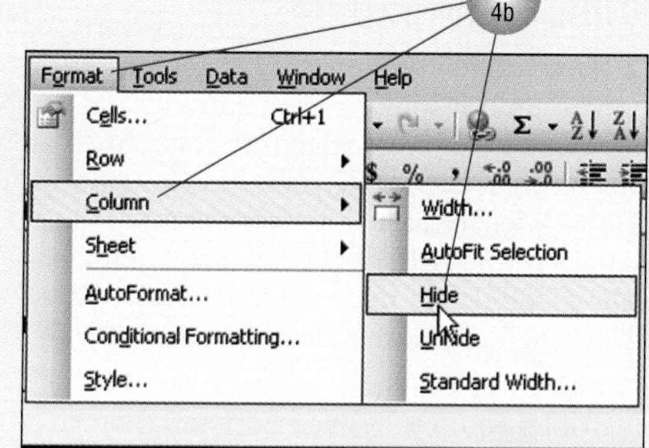

5. Create a custom footer that prints your name at the left margin and the file name at the right margin. ***(Hint: For assistance, refer to Exercise 3, Step 5.)***
6. Save and then print **sec4x08**.
7. Unhide row 9 by completing the following steps:
   a. Select rows 8 and 10.
   b. Click Format, point to Row, and then click Unhide.
8. Unhide row 16 by completing the following steps:

a. Position the mouse pointer on the thicker gray line that displays between rows 15 and 17 in the header row until the pointer turns into arrows pointing up and down with a double line between.
b. Hold down the left mouse button, drag down until *Height: 12.75 (17 pixels)* displays in the yellow box above the mouse pointer, and then release the mouse button.

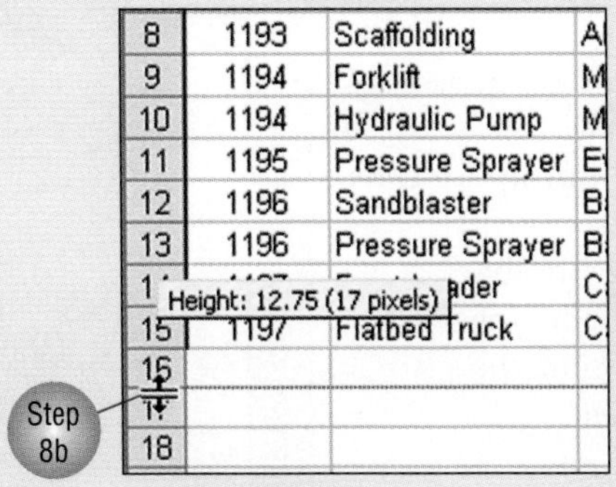

8	1193	Scaffolding	A
9	1194	Forklift	M
10	1194	Hydraulic Pump	M
11	1195	Pressure Sprayer	E
12	1196	Sandblaster	B
13	1196	Pressure Sprayer	B
1	Height: 12.75 (17 pixels)	ader	C
15	1197	Flatbed Truck	C
16			
17			
18			

Step 8b

9. Save, print, and then close **sec4x08**.

Printing a Specific Area of a Worksheet

Use the Print Area feature to select and print specific areas in a worksheet. To use this feature, select the cells you want to print, click File, point to Print Area, and then click Set Print Area. This inserts a border around the selected cells. Click the Print button on the Standard toolbar and the cells within the border are printed.

You can specify more than one print area in a worksheet in Page Break Preview. To do this, display the worksheet in Page Break Preview. Select the first group of cells, click File, point to Print Area, and then click Set Print Area. Select the next group of cells, right-click in the selected cells, and then click Add to Print Area at the shortcut menu. Clear a print area by clicking File, pointing to Print Area, and then clicking Clear Print Area.

Each area specified as a print area will print on a separate page. If you want nonadjacent print areas to print on the same page, consider hiding columns and/or rows in the worksheet to bring the areas together.

Changing Print Quality

Most printers have more than one level of print quality. The print quality choices vary with printers and may include options such as *High*, *Medium*, *Low*, and *Draft*. Print quality choices are available at the Page Setup dialog box with the Page tab selected. At this dialog box, click the down-pointing arrow at the right side of the *Print quality* option, and then click the desired print quality at the drop-down list.

exercise 9

CUSTOMIZING A PRINTING JOB

1. Open **ExcelWorksheet06**.
2. Specify a print area by completing the following steps:
   a. Select cells A1 through B20.
   b. Click File, point to Print Area, and then click Set Print Area.
   c. With the border surrounding the cells A1 through B20, click the Print button on the Standard toolbar.
   d. Clear the print area by clicking File, pointing to Print Area, and then clicking Clear Print Area.

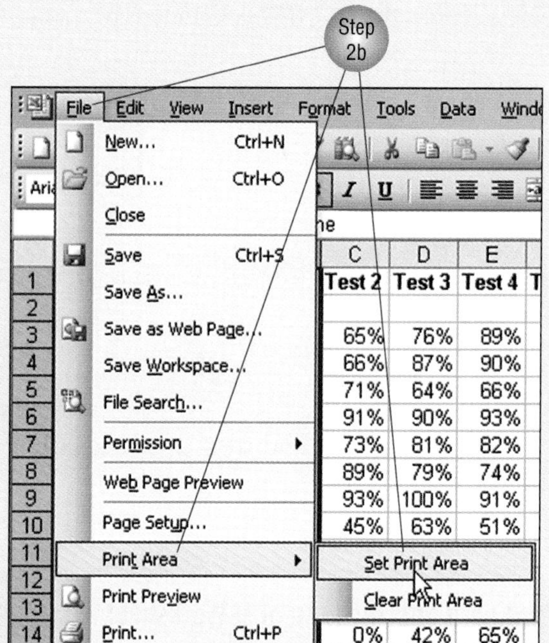

3. Suppose you want to print all of the student names and just the percentages for Test 6 and you want the information to print on one page. To do this, hide columns B through F and select the print area by completing the following steps:
   a. Select columns B through F.
   b. Click Format, point to Column, and then click Hide.
   c. Select cells A1 through G20. (Columns A and G are now adjacent.)
   d. Click File, point to Print Area, and then click Set Print Area.

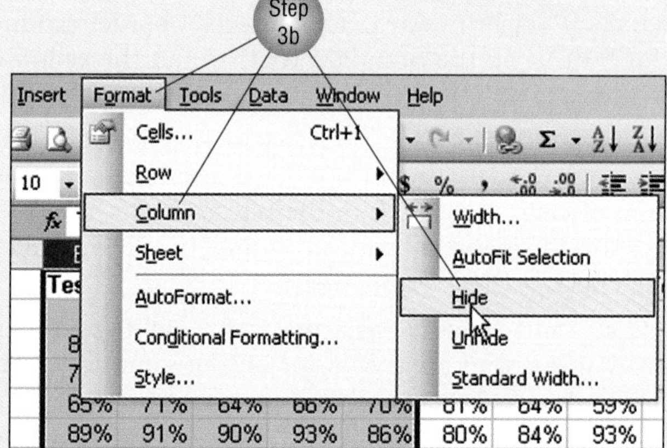

4. Change the print quality and print the specified print area by completing the following steps:
   a. Click File and then Page Setup.
   b. At the Page Setup dialog box, click the Page tab.
   c. At the Page Setup dialog box with the Page tab selected, click the down-pointing arrow at the right side of the *Print quality* option, and then click *Draft* (or a similar quality or lower *dpi*) at the drop-down list.
   d. Click the Print button.
   e. At the Print dialog box, click OK.
5. Clear the print area by making sure cells A1 through G20 are selected, clicking File, pointing to Print Area, and then clicking Clear Print Area.
6. With cells A1 through G20 selected, make the hidden columns visible by clicking Format, pointing to Column, and then clicking Unhide.
7. Close **ExcelWorksheet06** without saving the changes.

Customizing Print Jobs

The Print dialog box provides options for customizing a print job. Display the Print dialog box shown in Figure 4.8 by clicking File and then Print. Use options at the Print dialog box to print a specific range of cells, selected cells, or multiple copies of a workbook.

FIGURE 4.8 ***Print Dialog Box***

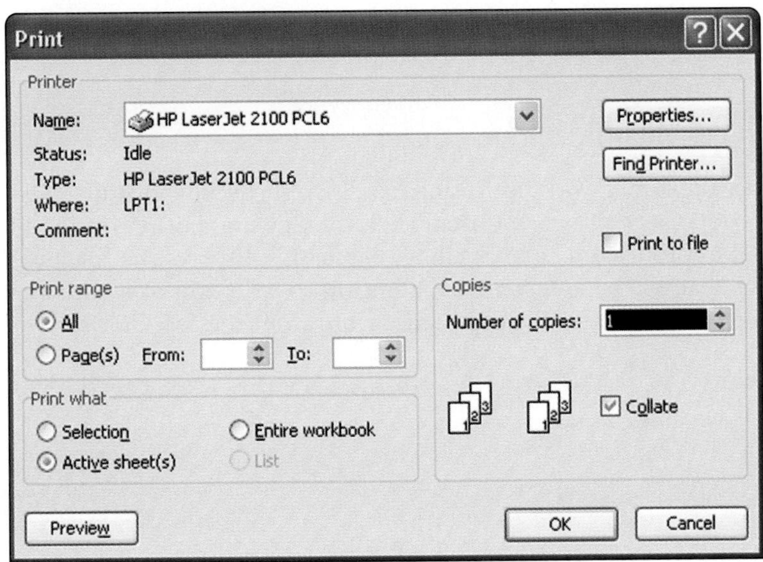

At the Print dialog box, the currently selected printer name displays in the *Name* option box. If other printers are installed, click the down-pointing arrow at the right side of the *Name* option box to display a list of printers.

The *Active sheet(s)* option in the *Print what* section is selected by default. At this setting, the currently active worksheet will print. If you want to print an entire workbook that contains several worksheets, click *Entire workbook* in the *Print what* section. Click the *Selection* option in the *Print what* section to print the currently selected cells.

If you want more than one copy of a worksheet or workbook printed, change to the desired number of copies with the *Number of copies* option in the *Copies* section. If you want the copies collated, make sure the *Collate* check box in the *Copies* section contains a check mark.

A worksheet within a workbook can contain more than one page. If you want to print specific pages of a worksheet within a workbook, click *Page(s)* in the *Print range* section, and then specify the desired page numbers in the *From* and *To* text boxes.

If you want to preview the worksheet before printing, click the Preview button that displays at the bottom left corner of the dialog box. This displays the worksheet as it will appear on the printed page. After viewing the worksheet, click the Close button that displays toward the top of the Preview screen.

exercise 10

PRINTING SPECIFIC CELLS IN A WORKSHEET

1. Open **ExcelWorksheet24**.
2. Print selected cells by completing the following steps:
   a. Select cells A4 through D8.
   b. Click File and then Print.
   c. At the Print dialog box, click *Selection* in the *Print what* section.
   d. Click OK.
3. Close **ExcelWorksheet24**.

Spelling

Complete a Spelling Check
1. Click Spelling button on Standard toolbar.
2. Replace or ignore selected word.

Completing a Spelling Check

To spell check text in a worksheet using Excel's spell checking feature, make the first cell in the worksheet active, and then click the Spelling button on the Standard toolbar or click Tools and then Spelling. Figure 4.9 displays the Spelling dialog box. At this dialog box, you can click a button to tell Excel to ignore a word or you can replace a misspelled word with a word from the *Suggestions* list box.

FIGURE 4.9 ***Excel Spelling Dialog Box***

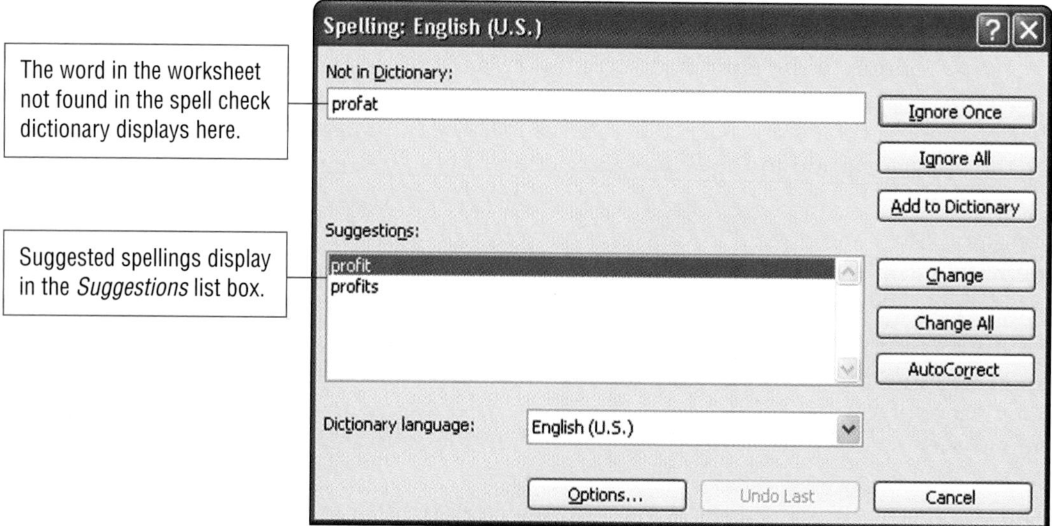

Using Undo and Redo

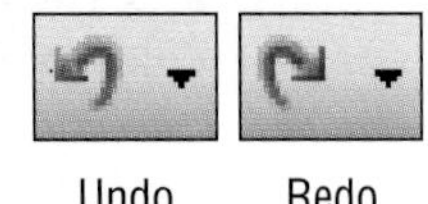

Excel includes an Undo button on the Standard toolbar that will reverse certain commands or delete the last data typed in a cell. For example, if you apply an autoformat to selected cells in a worksheet and then decide you want the autoformatting removed, click the Undo button on the Standard toolbar. If you decide you want the autoformatting back again, click the Redo button on the Standard toolbar.

In addition to the Undo and Redo buttons on the Standard toolbar, you can use options from the Edit drop-down menu to undo or repeat actions. The first two options at the Edit drop-down menu will vary depending on the last action completed. For example, if you just clicked the Currency Style button on the Formatting toolbar and then displayed the Edit drop-down menu, the first option displays as Undo Style and the second option displays as Repeat Style. If you decide you do not want the currency style applied, click Edit and then Undo Style. You can also just click the Undo button on the Standard toolbar.

HINT
Ctrl + Z is the keyboard command to Undo a command.

exercise 11

SPELL CHECKING AND FORMATTING A WORKSHEET

1. Open **ExcelWorksheet04**.
2. Save the worksheet with Save As and name it **sec4x11**.
3. Complete a spelling check on the worksheet by completing the following steps:
   a. Make sure cell A1 is the active cell.
   b. Click the Spelling button on the Standard toolbar.
   c. Click the Change button as needed to correct misspelled words in the worksheet.
   d. At the message telling you the spelling check is completed, click OK.

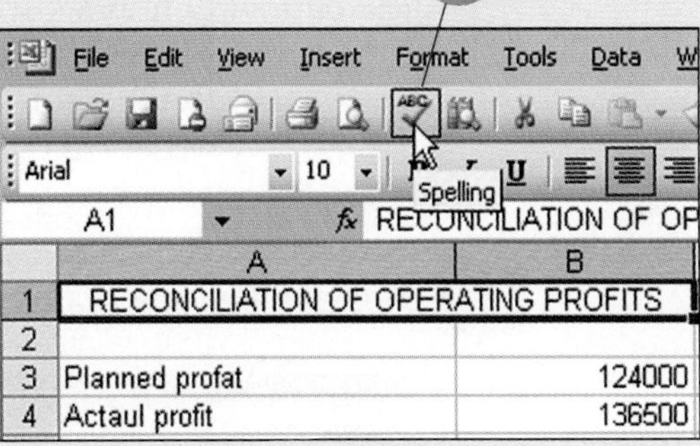

4. Select the entire worksheet and then change the font to 11-point Univers (or a similar sans serif typeface such as Tahoma).
5. Select cells A1 through B12 and then apply the Accounting 4 autoformat.
6. Select cells B3 through B12 and then click the Currency Style button on the Formatting toolbar.
7. With cells B3 through B12 still selected, click twice the Decrease Decimal button on the Formatting toolbar.
8. Make cell B4 active and then add a single-line border at the bottom of the cell. (To do this, click the down-pointing arrow at the right side of the Borders button on the Formatting toolbar and then click the Bottom Border option.)
9. Make cell B5 active and then add a double-line border at the bottom of the cell. (To do this, click the down-pointing arrow at the right side of the Borders button on the Formatting toolbar and then click the Bottom Double Border option.)
10. Make cell B10 active and then add a single-line border at the bottom of the cell.
11. Make cell B12 active and then add a double-line border at the bottom of the cell.
12. Select row 1 and then turn on bold.

13. Select cells A1 through B12 and then add a pale blue color shading.
14. After looking at the worksheet with the pale blue color shading, you decide you want to remove it. To do this, click the Undo button on the Standard toolbar.
15. Save, print, and then close **sec4x11**.

Finding and Replacing Data in a Worksheet

Find Data
1. Click Edit, Find.
2. Type data in *Find what* text box.
3. Click Find Next button.

Excel provides a Find feature you can use to look for specific data and either replace it with nothing or replace it with other data. This feature is particularly helpful in a large worksheet with data you want to find quickly. Excel also includes a find and replace feature. Use this to look for specific data in a worksheet and replace with other data.

To find specific data in a worksheet, click Edit and then Find. This displays the Find and Replace dialog box with the Find tab selected as shown in Figure 4.10. Type the data you want to find in the *Find what* text box and then click the Find Next button. Continue clicking the Find Next button to move to the next occurrence of the data. Ctrl + F is the keyboard command to display the Find and Replace dialog box with the Find tab selected.

FIGURE 4.10 ***Find and Replace Dialog Box with Find Tab Selected***

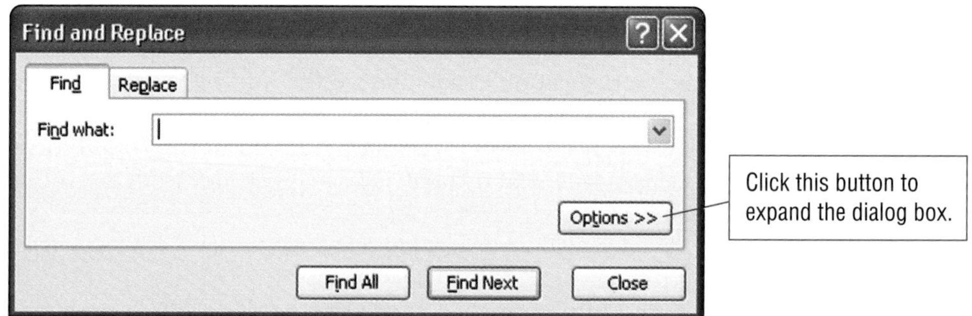

QUICK STEPS

Find and Replace Data
1. Click Edit, Replace.
2. Type data in *Find what* text box.
3. Type data in *Replace with* text box.
4. Click Replace button or Replace All button.

To find specific data in a worksheet and replace it with other data, click Edit and then Replace. This displays the Find and Replace dialog box with the Replace tab selected as shown in Figure 4.11. Enter the data for which you are looking in the *Find what* text box. Press the Tab key or click in the *Replace with* text box and then enter the data that is to replace the data in the *Find what* text box. Ctrl + H is the keyboard command to display the Find and Replace dialog box with the Replace tab selected.

FIGURE 4.11 ***Find and Replace Dialog Box with Replace Tab Selected***

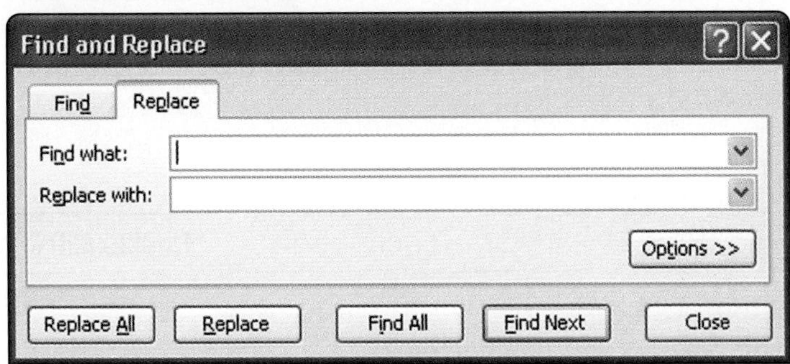

Click the Find Next button to tell Excel to find the next occurrence of the data. Click the Replace button to replace the data and find the next occurrence. If you know that you want all occurrences of the data in the *Find what* text box replaced with the data in the *Replace with* text box, click the Replace All button. Click the Close button to close the Replace dialog box.

Display additional find and replace options by clicking the Options button. This expands the dialog box as shown in Figure 4.12. By default, Excel will look for any data that contains the same characters as the data in the *Find what* text box, without concern for the characters before or after the entered data. For example, in Exercise 12, you will be looking for test scores of 0%. If you do not specify to Excel that you want to find cells that contain only *0%,* Excel will stop at any cell containing *0%.* In this example, Excel would stop at a cell containing *90%* or a cell containing *100%.* To specify that the only data that should be contained in the cell is what is entered in the *Find what* text box, click the Options button to expand the dialog box, and then insert a check mark in the *Match entire cell contents* check box.

HINT

If the Find and Replace dialog box obstructs your view of the worksheet, move the box by clicking and dragging the Title bar.

FIGURE 4.12 ***Expanded Find and Replace Dialog Box***

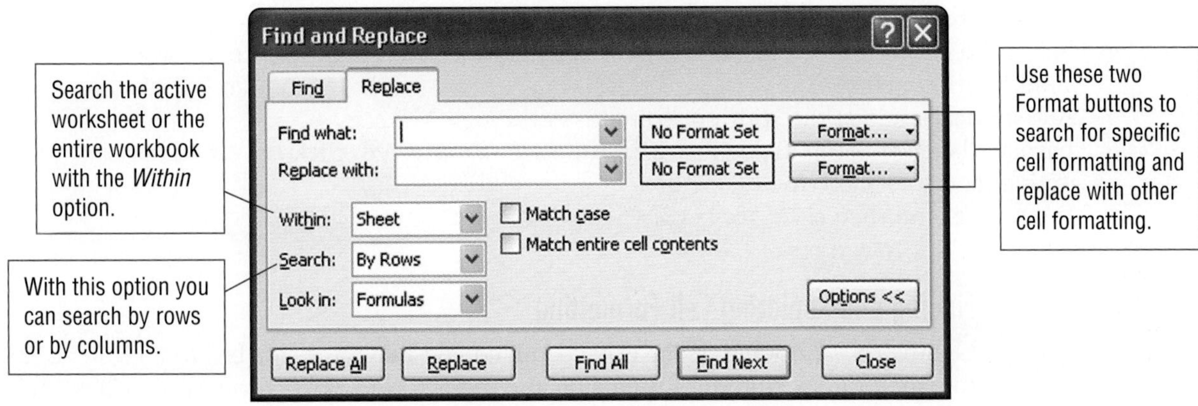

If the *Match case* option is active (contains a check mark), Excel will look for only that data that exactly matches the case of the data entered in the *Find what* text box. Remove the check mark from this check box if you do not want Excel to find exact case matches. Excel will search in the current worksheet. If you want Excel to search an entire workbook, change the *Within* option to *Workbook*. Excel, by default, searches by rows in a worksheet. This can be changed to *By Columns* with the *Search* option.

exercise 12

FINDING AND REPLACING DATA

1. Open **ExcelWorksheet06**.
2. Save the worksheet with Save As and name it **sec4x12**.
3. Find all occurrences of *0%* in the worksheet and replace with *70%* by completing the following steps:
   a. Click Edit and then Replace.
   b. At the Find and Replace dialog box with the Replace tab selected, type 0% in the *Find what* text box.
   c. Press the Tab key (this moves the insertion point to the *Replace with* text box).
   d. Type 70%.
   e. Click the Options button to display additional options. (If additional options already display, skip this step.)
   f. Click the *Match entire cell contents* option to insert a check mark in the check box.
   g. Click the Replace All button.
   h. At the message telling you that Excel has completed the search and has made three replacements, click OK.
   i. Click the Options button to decrease the size of the Find and Replace dialog box and then close the dialog box.

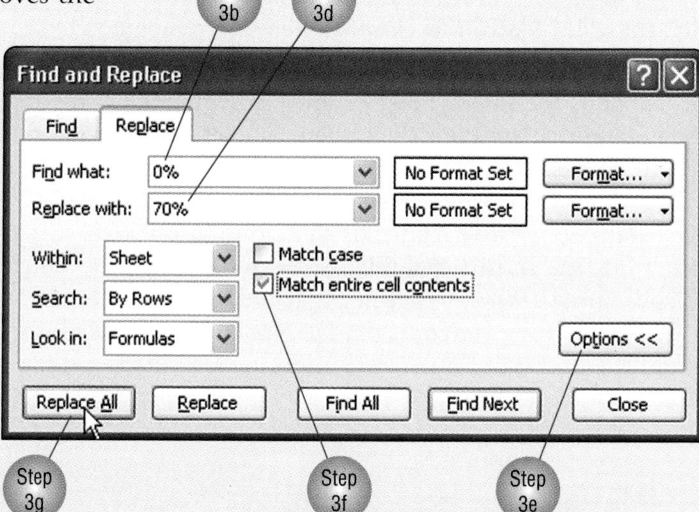

4. Select the entire worksheet and then change the font to 10-point Century (or a similar serif typeface).
5. Automatically adjust the width of columns A through M.
6. Display the Page Setup dialog box with the Page tab selected, click the *Landscape* option, and then close the dialog box.
7. Print, save, and then close **sec4x12**.

Finding and Replacing Cell Formatting

Use the *Format* options at the expanded Find and Replace dialog box (see Figure 4.12) to search for specific cell formatting and replace with other formatting. Click the down-pointing arrow at the right side of the Format button and a drop-down menu displays. Click the *Format* option and the Find Format dialog box displays with the Number, Alignment, Font, Border, Patterns, and Protection tabs. Specify formatting at this dialog box. Click the *Choose Format From Cell* option and the mouse pointer displays with a pointer tool attached. Click in the cell containing the desired formatting and the formatting displays in the Preview box to the left of the Format button. Click the *Clear Find Format* option and any formatting in the Preview box is removed.

exercise 13

FINDING AND REPLACING CELL FORMATTING

1. Open **ExcelWorksheet28**.
2. Save the worksheet with Save As and name it **sec4x13**.
3. Search for orange shading and replace it with light purple shading by completing the following steps:
   a. Click Edit and then Replace.
   b. At the Find and Replace dialog box with the Replace tab selected, make sure the dialog box is expanded. (If not, click the Options button.)
   c. Select and then delete any text that displays in the *Find what* text box.
   d. Select and then delete any text that displays in the *Replace with* text box.
   e. Make sure the boxes immediately preceding the two Format buttons display with the text *No Format Set*. (If not, click the down-pointing arrow at the right of the Format button, and then click the *Clear Find Format* option at the drop-down list. Do this for each Format button.)
   f. Click the down-pointing arrow at the right side of the top Format button (the one at the far right side of the *Find what* text box) and then click Format at the drop-down menu.
   g. At the Find Format dialog box, click the Patterns tab.
   h. Click the Light Orange color (as shown below on the left).
   i. Click OK to close the dialog box.
   j. Click the down-pointing arrow at the right side of the second Format button (the one at the far right side of the *Replace with* text box and then click Format at the drop-down menu.
   k. At the Replace Format dialog box with the Patterns tab selected, click the Light Purple color (as shown at the far right).
   l. Click OK to close the dialog box.
   m. At the Find and Replace dialog box, click the Replace All button.
   n. At the message telling you that Excel has completed the search and made replacements, click OK.

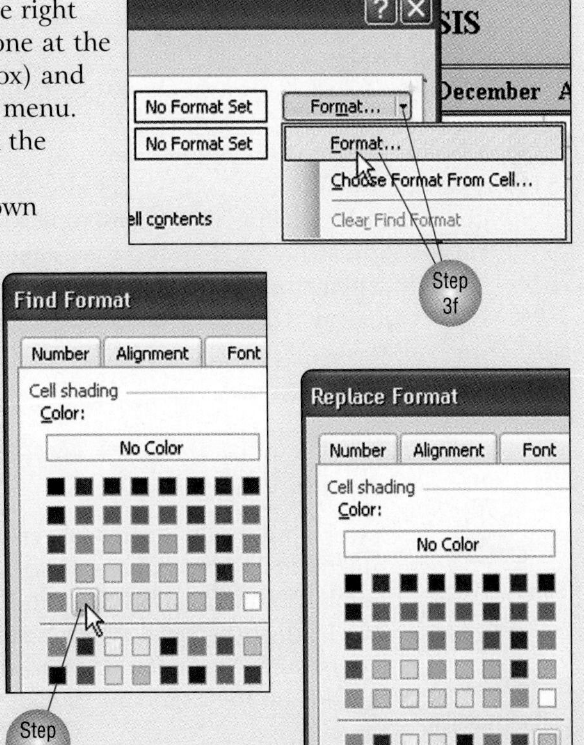

4. Complete steps similar to those in Steps 3f through 3n to search for light yellow shading and replace it with light green shading.

5. Search for 11-point Times New Roman formatting and replace with 10-point Arial formatting by completing the following steps:
   a. Clear formatting from the top Format button by clicking the down-pointing arrow and then clicking the *Clear Find Format* option at the drop-down menu.
   b. Clear formatting from the bottom Format button by clicking the down-pointing arrow and then clicking *Clear Replace Format.*
   c. Click the down-pointing arrow at the right side of the top Format button and then click Format at the drop-down menu.
   d. At the Find Format dialog box, click the Font tab.
   e. Click *Times New Roman* in the *Font* list box (you will need to scroll down the list to display this typeface).
   f. Click *11* in the *Size* text box.
   g. Click OK to close the dialog box.
   h. Click the down-pointing arrow at the right side of the second Format button and then click Format at the drop-down menu.
   i. At the Find Format dialog box with the Font tab selected, click *Arial* in the *Font* list box.
   j. Click *10* in the *Size* list box.
   k. Click OK to close the dialog box.
   l. At the Find and Replace dialog box, click the Replace All button.
   m. At the message telling you that Excel has completed the search and made replacements, click OK.

6. At the Find and Replace dialog box, remove formatting from both Format buttons.
7. Click the Close button to close the Find and Replace dialog box.
8. Click in cell H3 and then insert a formula that finds the average of cells B3 through G3.
9. Copy the formula in cell H3 down to cells H4 through H8.
10. Copying the formula removed the double-line border at the bottom of cell H8. Replace the border by clicking the down-pointing arrow at the right side of the Borders button on the Formatting toolbar and then clicking the Bottom Double Border option at the drop-down palette.
11. Save, print, and then close **sec4x13**.

Sorting Data

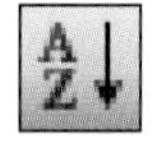

Sort Ascending

Sort Descending

Excel is primarily a spreadsheet program, but it also includes some basic database functions. With a database program, you can alphabetize information or arrange numbers numerically. Data can be sorted by columns in a worksheet. By default, Excel will sort special symbols such as *, /, @, and # first, numbers second, and letters third. Sort data in a worksheet using the Sort Ascending or Sort Descending buttons on the Standard toolbar or at the Sort dialog box.

Sorting Data Using Buttons on the Standard Toolbar

To sort data in a worksheet using the buttons on the Standard toolbar, open the worksheet, select the cells containing data you want to sort, and then click the Sort Ascending button (sorts text A through Z; sorts numbers lowest to highest) or the Sort Descending button (sorts text Z through A; sorts numbers highest to lowest). If you select more than one column in a worksheet, Excel will sort the data in the first selected column.

exercise 14 — SORTING DATA USING THE SORT ASCENDING AND SORT DESCENDING BUTTONS

1. Open **ExcelWorksheet03**.
2. Save the worksheet with Save As and name it **sec4x14**.
3. Merge and center the data in cell A1 across cells A1 through D1.
4. Bold the data in cell A1.
5. Bold the data in cells B2 through D2.
6. Automatically adjust the width of columns A through D.
7. Select cells B3 through D8 and then click the Percent Style button on the Formatting toolbar.
8. Sort the data in the first column alphabetically in ascending order by completing the following steps:
   a. Select cells A3 through D8.
   b. Click the Sort Ascending button on the Standard toolbar.

Step 8b

Sort Ascending

A3 Stockholder's equity ratio

	A	B	C	D	E	F	G
1	ANALYSIS OF FINANCIAL CONDITION						
2		Actual	Planned	Prior Year			
3	Stockholder's equity ratio	62%	60%	57%			
4	Bond holder's equity ratio	45%	39%	41%			
5	Liability liquidity ratio	122%	115%	120%			
6	Fixed obligation security ratio	196%	190%	187%			
7	Fixed interest ratio	23%	20%	28%			
8	Earnings ratio	7%	6%	6%			

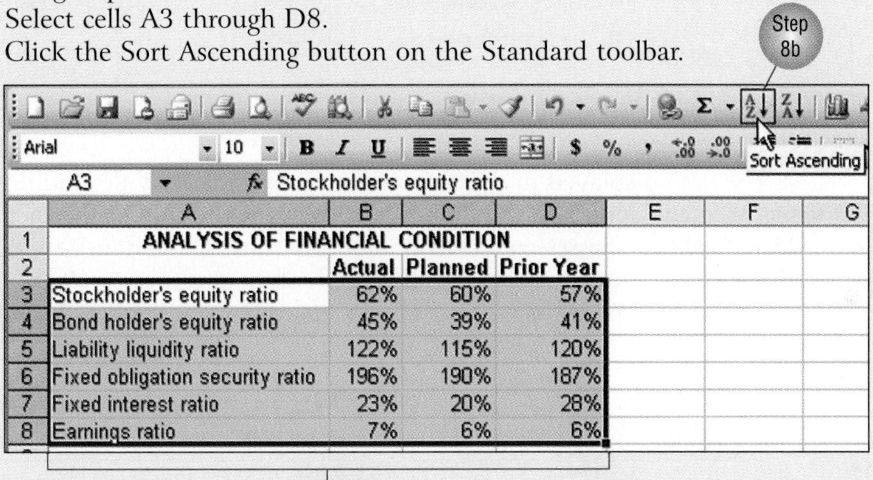

Step 8a

9. Save and print **sec4x14**.
10. Sort the data in the first column alphabetically in descending order by completing steps similar to those in Step 8, except click the Sort Descending button on the Standard toolbar.
11. Save, print, and then close **sec4x14**.

Sorting Data at the Sort Dialog Box

If you want to sort data in a column other than the first selected column, use the Sort dialog box. If you select just one column in a worksheet and then click the Sort Ascending or Sort Descending button on the Standard toolbar, only the data in that column is sorted. If this data is related to data to the left or right of the data in the column, that relationship is broken. For example, if you sort cells B3 through B8 in sec4x13, the percentages for *Bondholder's equity ratio* are now *23%, 39%,* and *41%*, when they should be *45%, 39%,* and *41%*.

QUICK STEPS

Sort Data
1. Select cells.
2. Click Sort Ascending button or Sort Descending button.

OR

1. Select cells.
2. Click Data, Sort.
3. Specify options at Sort dialog box.
4. Click OK.

HINT

If you are not satisfied with the results of a sort, immediately click the Undo button.

Use the Sort dialog box to sort data and maintain the relationship of all cells. To sort using the Sort dialog box, select the cells you want sorted, click Data, and then click Sort. This displays the Sort dialog box shown in Figure 4.13.

FIGURE

4.13 Sort Dialog Box

The data displayed in the *Sort by* option box will vary depending on what you have selected. Generally, the data that displays is the title of the first column of selected cells. If the selected cells do not have a title, the data may display as *Column A*. Use this option to specify what column you want sorted. Using the Sort dialog box to sort data in a column maintains the relationship of the data.

exercise 15

SORTING DATA USING THE SORT DIALOG BOX

1. Open **sec4x14**.
2. Save the worksheet with Save As and name it **sec4x15**.
3. Sort the percentages in cells B3 through B8 in ascending order and maintain the relationship to the other data by completing the following steps:
   a. Select cells A3 through D8.
   b. Click Data and then Sort.
   c. At the Sort dialog box, click the down-pointing arrow at the right of the *Sort by* option box, and then click *Actual* from the drop-down list.
   d. Make sure *Ascending* is selected in the *Sort by* section of the dialog box. If not, click *Ascending*.
   e. Click OK to close the dialog box.
4. Save and then print **sec4x15**.
5. Sort the percentages in cells B3 through B8 in *descending* order and maintain the relationship of the data by completing steps similar to those in Step 3.
6. Save, print, and then close **sec4x15**.

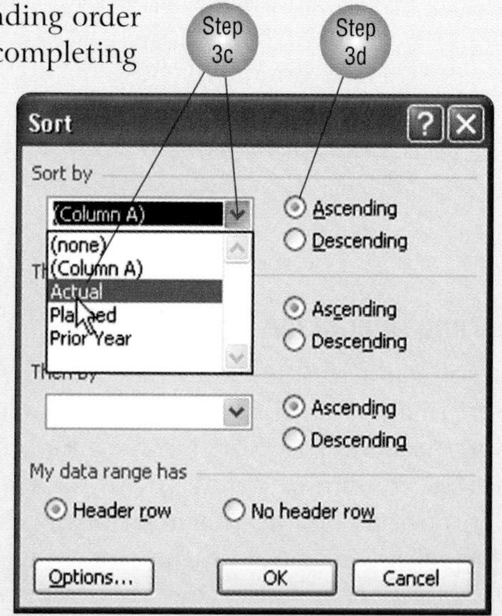

Sorting More than One Column

When sorting data in cells, you can sort in more than one column. For example, in Exercise 16, you will be sorting the average test scores in ascending order and then sorting the names of the students alphabetically. In this sort, the test averages are sorted first and then students with the same average are sorted alphabetically within that average. For example, the worksheet contains several average scores of 76%. Students within that average are sorted alphabetically—not all students.

To sort in more than one column, select all columns in the worksheet that need to remain relative, and then display the Sort dialog box. At the Sort dialog box, specify the first column you want sorted in the *Sort by* option box, and then specify the second column in the first *Then by* text box. In Excel, you can sort in up to three columns. If you want to sort the data in a third column, you would specify that in the second *Then by* option box.

exercise 16

SORTING DATA IN TWO COLUMNS

1. Open **ExcelWorksheet06**.
2. Save the worksheet with Save As and name it **sec4x16**.
3. Select and then delete row 2.
4. Sort the Test 1 percentages in cells B2 through B19 in ascending order and then sort alphabetically by the names in the first column by completing the following steps:
   a. Select cells A2 through M19.
   b. Click Data and then Sort.
   c. At the Sort dialog box, click the down-pointing arrow at the right side of the *Sort by* option box, and then click *Test 1* from the drop-down list.
   d. Make sure *Ascending* is selected in the *Sort by* section of the dialog box. If not, click *Ascending*.
   e. Click the down-pointing arrow at the right of the first *Then by* option box and then click *Name* in the drop-down list.
   f. Make sure *Ascending* is selected in the first *Then by* section.
   g. Click OK to close the dialog box.

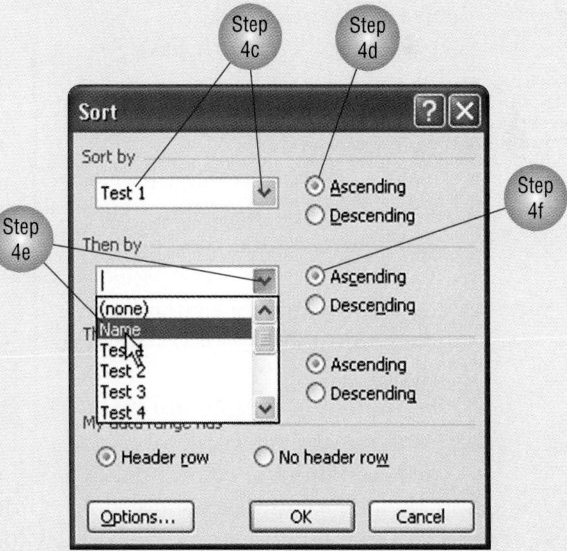

5. Display the Page Setup dialog box with the Page tab selected, click the *Landscape* option, and then close the dialog box.
6. Print the worksheet. (Notice how the names of the students with the same Test 1 percentages are alphabetized.)
7. Save and then close **sec4x16**.

Creating a List

QUICK STEPS

Create a List
1. Click Data, List, Create List.
2. Click OK at Create List dialog box.

A list in an Excel worksheet is a series of rows that contain related data such as a specific customer name, invoice number, product, and so forth. Each column in a list must be labeled and contain specific information. For example, in Exercise 17 you will identify cells in a worksheet as a list that contains specific columns of information including a column for invoice numbers, a column for equipment, another for client, and so on.

To identify a list in a worksheet, click Data on the Menu bar, point to List, and then click Create List. This displays the Create List dialog box and also inserts a moving border around all cells in the worksheet. If you want all selected cells included in the list, click the OK button. If your worksheet contains cells that you do not want included in the list (such as cells containing headings or titles), first select the cells you want included in the list and then click Data, point to List, and then click Create List. At the Create List dialog box, click OK. When you select specific cells, you must make sure that the first row is the row containing column labels.

When you click OK at the Create List dialog box, the dialog box is removed from the screen and a button containing a down arrow is inserted at the right side of each column label cell. Click this down arrow and a drop-down list displays with options for sorting and filtering records in the list.

exercise 17

CREATING AND SORTING A LIST

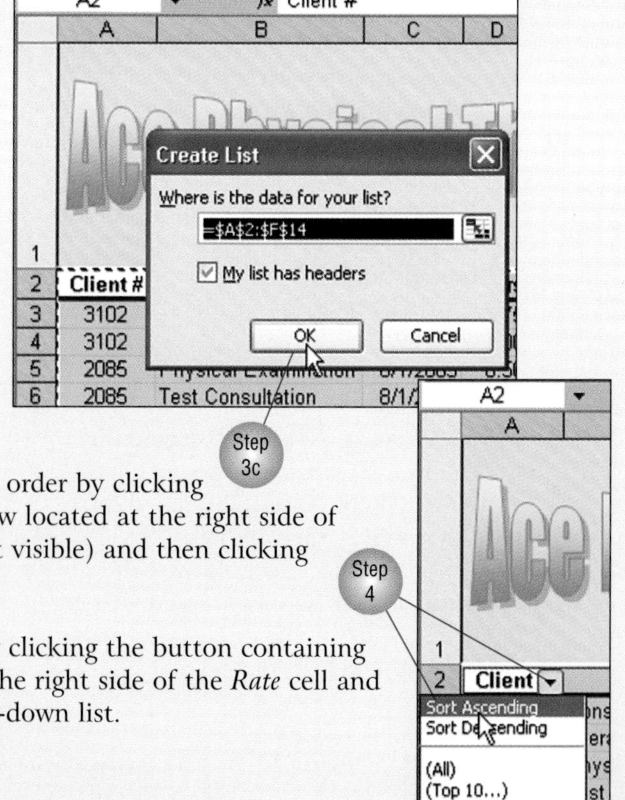

1. Open **ExcelWorksheet27**.
2. Save the worksheet with Save As and name it **sec4x17**.
3. Create a list by completing the following steps:
   a. Select cells A2 through F14.
   b. Click Data on the Menu bar, point to List, and then click Create List.
   c. At the Create List dialog box, click OK. (This removes the dialog box and inserts a button containing a down-pointing arrow at the right side of each cell containing a column label.)
4. Sort the client numbers in ascending order by clicking the button containing the down arrow located at the right side of the *Client #* cell (the # symbol is not visible) and then clicking *Sort Ascending* at the drop-down list.
5. Save and then print **sec4x17**.
6. Sort the rates in descending order by clicking the button containing the down-pointing arrow located at the right side of the *Rate* cell and then click *Sort Descending* at the drop-down list.
7. Save, print, and then close **sec4x17**.

Filtering a List

You can place a restriction, called a ***filter***, on data in a worksheet to isolate temporarily a specific list. You can apply only one filter to a worksheet at a time. You can filter data in a worksheet by first creating a list or by using the AutoFilter feature. To use the AutoFilter feature, click in a cell containing data you want to filter, click Data, point to Filter, and then click AutoFilter. This causes a down arrow to appear in each column label in the worksheet as shown in Figure 4.14. Unlike creating a list, the AutoFilter feature automatically searches for column labels—you do not need to first select the cells.

To filter a list, click the down-pointing arrow in the heading you want to filter. This causes a drop-down list to display with options to filter all records in the list, display the top 10 records, create a custom filter, or select an entry that appears in one or more of the cells in the list.

Filter a List

1. Click Data, Filter, AutoFilter.
2. Click down-pointing arrow of heading to filter.
3. Click desired option at drop-down list.

FIGURE **4.14** ***Using AutoFilter***

Activate the AutoFilter feature and down-pointing triangles display in column heading.

	A	B	C	D	E	F	G	H
1	Hilltop Equipment Rental							
2	Invoice	Equipment	Client	Service Re	Date	Hour	Ra	Tota
3	1190	Backhoe	Lakeside Trucking	Monahan	5/1/2003	8	$75	$ 600
4	1190	Front Loader	Lakeside Trucking	Monahan	5/1/2003	8	$65	$ 520
5	1191	Trencher	Martin Plumbing	Steele	5/1/2003	4	$45	$ 180
6	1192	Backhoe	Country Electrical	Leuke	5/1/2003	16	$75	$1,200
7	1193	Tractor	Able Construction	Monahan	5/2/2003	5	$55	$ 275
8	1193	Scaffolding	Able Construction	Monahan	5/2/2003	5	$25	$ 125
9	1194	Forklift	Miles Contracting	Steele	5/2/2003	10	$70	$ 700
10	1194	Hydraulic Pump	Miles					
11	1195	Pressure Sprayer	Ever					
12	1196	Sandblaster	Barri					
13	1196	Pressure Sprayer	Barri					
14	1197	Front Loader	Casc					
15	1197	Flatbed Truck	Casc					
16	1198	Forklift	Allie					

Click the down-pointing triangle in the Service Rep column, click *Monahan* at the drop-down list, and only those rows containing *Monahan* display.

	A	B	C	D	E	F	G	H
1	Hilltop Equipment Rental							
2	Invoice	Equipment	Client	Service Re	Date	Hour	Ra	Tota
3	1190	Backhoe	Lakeside Trucking	Monahan	5/1/2003	8	$75	$ 600
4	1190	Front Loader	Lakeside Trucking	Monahan	5/1/2003	8	$65	$ 520
7	1193	Tractor	Able Construction	Monahan	5/2/2003	5	$55	$ 275
8	1193	Scaffolding	Able Construction	Monahan	5/2/2003	5	$25	$ 125
16	1198	Forklift	Allied Builders	Monahan	5/3/2003	6	$70	$ 420
17								

The Top 10 option displays in a list that contains values rather than text. Click *(Top 10...)* and the Top 10 AutoFilter dialog box displays as shown in Figure 4.15. With options at this dialog box, you can choose to show the top values, the bottom values, and the number you want filtered.

FIGURE

4.15 *Top 10 AutoFilter Dialog Box*

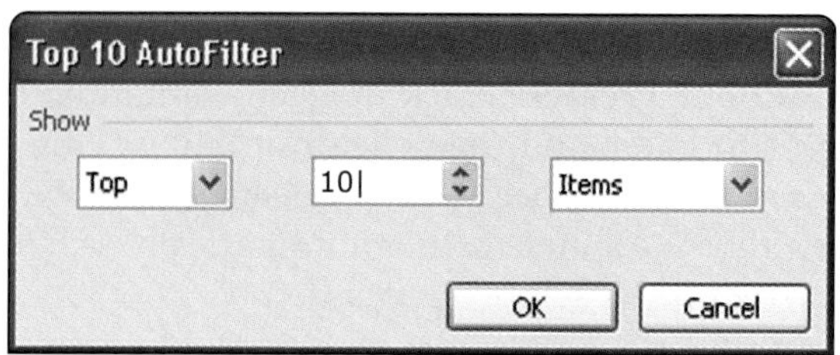

When you filter a list, the down-pointing arrow in the column heading turns blue as well as the row number for the selected rows. This color indicates that rows in the worksheet have been filtered. To deactivate AutoFilter, click Data, point to Filter, and then click AutoFilter.

exercise 18

FILTERING LISTS USING AUTOFILTER

1. Open **ExcelWorksheet26**.
2. Save the worksheet with Save As and name it **sec4x18**.
3. Apply the AutoFilter by clicking Data, pointing to Filter, and then clicking AutoFilter. (This causes down-pointing arrows to appear in heading cells.)
4. Filter and then print a list of rows containing companies renting a forklift by completing the following steps:
   a. Click the down-pointing arrow at the right side of the *Equipment* heading.
   b. Click *Forklift* at the drop-down list.
   c. Print the list by clicking the Print button on the Standard toolbar.
   d. Redisplay all cells containing data by clicking the down-pointing arrow at the right side of the *Equipment* heading and then clicking *(All)* at the drop-down list.
5. Filter and then print a list of rows containing equipment rented by the service representative Monahan by completing the following steps:
   a. Click the down-pointing arrow at the right side of the *Service Rep* heading.
   b. Click *Monahan* at the drop-down list.
   c. Click the Print button.
   d. Redisplay all cells containing data by clicking the down-pointing arrow at the right side of the *Service Rep* heading and then clicking *(All)* at the drop-down list.

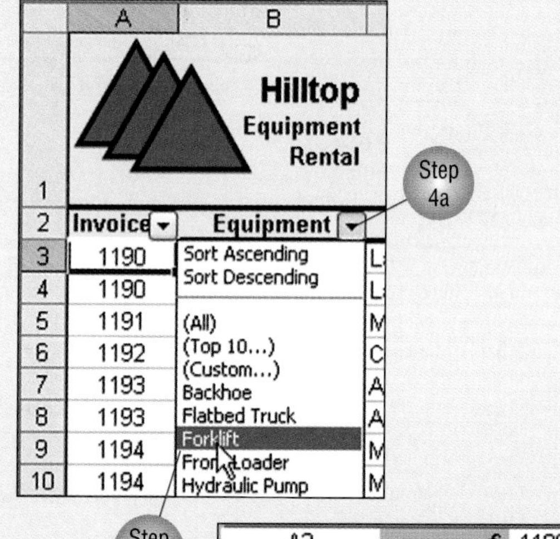

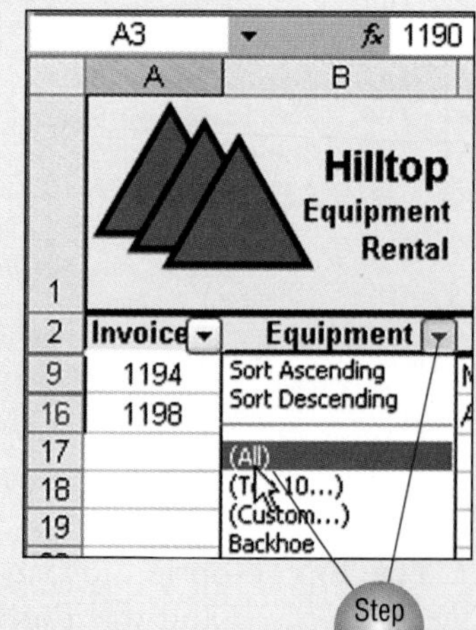

6. Filter and then print a list of rows containing only the client *Cascade Enterprises* by completing steps similar to those in Steps 4 or 5. (Make sure you return the list to *(All)*.)
7. Display the top 3 highest totals by completing the following steps:
   a. Click the down-pointing arrow at the right side of the *Total* heading and then click *(Top 10...)* at the drop-down list.
   b. At the Top 10 AutoFilter dialog box, select *10* in the middle text box and then type 3.
   c. Click OK.
   d. Click the Print button to print the list.
   e. Click the down-pointing arrow at the right side of the *Total* heading and then click *(All)* at the drop-down list.

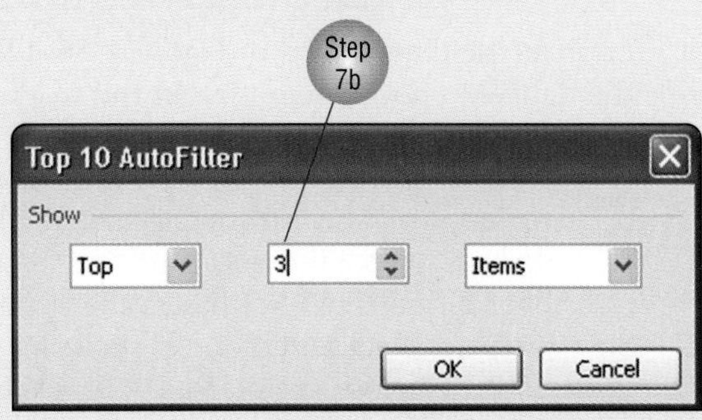

8. Deactivate AutoFilter by clicking Data, pointing to Filter, and then clicking AutoFilter.
9. Save, print, and then close **sec4x18**.

Planning a Worksheet

The worksheets you have worked with so far basically have already been planned. If you need to plan a worksheet yourself, some steps you can follow are listed below. These are basic steps—you may think of additional steps or additional information to help you plan a worksheet.

- **Step 1: Identify the purpose of the worksheet.** The more definite you are about your purpose, the easier organizing your data into an effective worksheet will be. Consider things such as the purpose of the worksheet, the intended audience, the desired output or results, and the data required.
- **Step 2: Design the worksheet.** To do this, you need to determine how the data is to be organized, the titles of columns and rows, and how to emphasize important information. Designing the worksheet also includes determining any calculations that need to be performed.
- **Step 3: Create a sketch of the worksheet.** A diagram or sketch can help create a logical and well-ordered worksheet. With a sketch, you can experiment with alternative column and row configurations and titles and headings. When creating a sketch, start with the heading or title of the worksheet, which should provide a quick overview of what the data represents in the worksheet. Determine appropriate column and row titles that clearly identify the data.
- **Step 4: Enter the data in the worksheet.** Type the data in the worksheet, including the worksheet title, column titles, row titles, and data within cells. Enter any required formulas into the worksheet and then format the worksheet to make it appealing and easy to read.
- **Step 5: Test the worksheet data.** After preparing the worksheet and inserting any necessary formulas, check the data to be sure that the calculations are performed correctly. Consider verifying the formula results by completing the formula on a calculator.

exercise 19

PLANNING AND CREATING A WORKSHEET

1. Look at the data shown in Figure 4.16. (The first paragraph is simply a description of the data—do not include this in the worksheet.) After reviewing the data, complete the following steps:
   a. Create a sketch of how you think the worksheet should be organized.
   b. Create a worksheet from the sketch. (Be sure to include the necessary formula to calculate the total costs.)
   c. Apply formatting to enhance the appearance of the worksheet.
2. Save the worksheet and name it **sec4x19**.
3. Print and then close **sec4x19**.

FIGURE 4.16 ***Exercise 19***

The following data itemizes budgeted direct labor hours and dollars by department for planning purposes. This data is prepared quarterly and sent to the plant manager and production manager.

DIRECT LABOR BUDGET

	Labor Rate	Total Hours	Total Costs
April			
Assembly	12.75	723	
Electronics	16.32	580	
Machining	27.34	442	
May			
Assembly	12.75	702	
Electronics	16.32	615	
Machining	27.34	428	
June			
Assembly	12.75	694	
Electronics	16.32	643	
Machining	27.34	389	

CHAPTER summary

- By default, a worksheet prints on the page in portrait orientation. This can be changed to landscape orientation at the Page Setup dialog box with the Page tab selected.
- Adjust the percentage size of data in a worksheet with options in the *Scaling* section of the Page Setup dialog box with the Page tab selected.
- Change the paper size with the *Paper size* option at the Page Setup dialog box with the Page tab selected.
- Create a header and/or footer for worksheet pages with options at the Page Setup dialog box with the Header/Footer tab selected.
- Create a custom header at the Header dialog box and create a custom footer at the Footer dialog box.
- Excel uses 1-inch top and bottom margins and .75-inch left and right margins for a worksheet. Change these default margins at the Page Setup dialog box with the Margins tab selected.
- Center a worksheet horizontally and/or vertically on a page with options at the Page Setup dialog box with the Margins tab selected.
- Insert a page break in a worksheet with Insert and then Page Break.
- Print column and row titles on every page of a multiple-page worksheet with options at the Page Setup dialog box with the Sheet tab selected.
- Print gridlines, column letters, and row numbers with options at the Page Setup dialog box with the Sheet tab selected.
- You can hide and unhide columns or rows in a worksheet.
- Use the Print Area feature to select and print specific areas in a worksheet. Specify more than one print area in Page Break Preview.
- Change the print quality for most printers with options at the Properties dialog box. Print quality choices are available at the Page Setup dialog box with the Page tab selected.
- Use options at the Print dialog box to print a specific range of cells, selected cells, or multiple copies of a workbook.
- Complete a spelling check on a worksheet by clicking the Spelling button on the Standard toolbar or clicking Tools and then Spelling.
- Click the Undo button to reverse certain commands or delete the last data typed in a cell. Click the Redo button to repeat the last command or action, if possible.
- Find data with options at the Find and Replace dialog box with the Find tab selected, and find and replace data in a worksheet with options at the Find and Replace dialog box with the Replace tab selected.
- Use options at the expanded Find and Replace dialog box to search for specific cell formatting and replace with other formatting.
- Sort the first column of selected cells with the Sort Ascending or Sort Descending buttons on the Standard toolbar.
- Use the Sort dialog box to sort in a column other than the first column, to maintain the relationship of the data, or to sort in more than one column.

- A list in an Excel worksheet is a series of rows that contain related data. Once you identify a list in a worksheet, you can sort and filter the information in the list.
- Use the AutoFilter feature to isolate temporarily a specific list. With the AutoFilter, you can filter all records in the list, display the top 10 records, create a custom filter, or select an entry that appears in one or more of the cells in the list.
- Plan a worksheet by completing these basic steps: identify the purpose of the worksheet, design the worksheet, create a sketch of the worksheet, enter the data in the worksheet, and test the worksheet data.

FEATURES summary

FEATURE	BUTTON	MENU	KEYBOARD
Page Setup dialog box		File, Page Setup	
Header dialog box		File, Page Setup, Header/Footer tab, Custom Header	
Footer dialog box		File, Page Setup, Header/Footer tab, Custom Footer	
Insert page break		Insert, Page Break	
Hide columns		Format, Column, Hide	
Hide rows		Format, Row, Hide	
Unhide columns		Format, Column, Unhide	
Unhide rows		Format, Row, Unhide	
Set a print area		File, Print Area, Set Print Area	
Clear a print area		File, Print Area, Clear Print Area	
Print dialog box		File, Print	Ctrl + P
Spelling dialog box		Tools, Spelling	F7
Undo command		Edit, Undo	Ctrl + Z

FEATURE	BUTTON	MENU	KEYBOARD
Redo command		Edit, Redo	Ctrl + Y
Find and Replace dialog box		Edit, Find or Edit, Replace	Ctrl + F or Ctrl + H
Sort column in ascending order			
Sort column in descending order			
Sort dialog box		Data, Sort	
Create a list		Data, List, Create List	Ctrl + L
Activate/Deactivate AutoFilter		Data, Filter, AutoFilter	

CONCEPTS check

Completion: On a blank sheet of paper, indicate the correct term, symbol, or command for each description.

1. By default, a worksheet prints in this orientation on a page.
2. Change the page orientation at the Page Setup dialog box with this tab selected.
3. This is the default paper size.
4. Display the Header dialog box by clicking this button at the Page Setup dialog box with the Header/Footer tab selected.
5. This is the worksheet default top and bottom margin measurement.
6. This is the worksheet default left and right margin measurement.
7. A worksheet can be horizontally and/or vertically centered with options at the Page Setup dialog box with this tab selected.
8. Click this to insert a page break in a worksheet.
9. Print gridlines with an option at the Page Setup dialog box with this tab selected.
10. To make a hidden column visible, select these columns, click Format, point to Column, and then click Unhide.
11. Use this feature to print specific areas in a worksheet.
12. To complete a spelling check on a worksheet, click this button on the Standard toolbar.
13. To display the Sort dialog box, click Sort from this drop-down menu.
14. Use this feature to isolate temporarily a specific list of rows in a worksheet containing related data.
15. List the steps you would complete to print column titles in a multiple-page worksheet.
16. List the steps you would complete to find all occurrences of *January* in a worksheet and replace with *July*.

SKILLS check

Assessment 1

1. Open **ExcelWorksheet28**.
2. Save the worksheet with Save As and name it **sec4sc01**.
3. Make the following changes to the worksheet:
   a. Insert a formula in cell H3 that averages the amounts in cells B3 through G3.
   b. Copy the formula in cell H3 down to cells H4 through H8.
   c. Copying the formula removed the double-line border at the bottom of cell H8. Use the Borders button to insert a double-line border at the bottom of cell H8.
   d. Change the orientation of the worksheet to landscape.
   e. Change the top margin to 3 inches and the left margin to 1.5 inches.
4. Save, print, and then close **sec4sc01**.

Assessment 2

1. Open **ExcelWorksheet06**.
2. Save the worksheet with Save As and name it **sec4sc02**.
3. Make the following changes to the worksheet:
   a. Select the worksheet and then change the font to 11-point Garamond (or a similar serif typeface).
   b. Automatically adjust columns A through M.
   c. Delete row 2.
   d. Create a footer that prints *Page x* (where *x* represents the correct page number) at the bottom center of the page.
   e. Create a custom header that prints your name at the left margin and the text *Excel Test Scores* at the right margin.
4. Save the worksheet again with the same name (**sec4sc02**).
5. Print the worksheet so the column titles (names) print on both pages.
6. Close **sec4sc02**.

Assessment 3

1. Open **ExcelWorksheet13**.
2. Save the worksheet with Save As and name it **sec4sc03**.
3. Make the following changes to the worksheet:
   a. Delete column H.
   b. Type Total in cell A9.
   c. Make cell B9 active and then use the AutoSum button to sum the amounts in B3 through B8.
   d. Copy the formula in cell B9 to cells C9 through G9.
4. Print the worksheet including gridlines and the row and column headings.
5. Save and then close **sec4sc03**.

Assessment 4

1. Open **ExcelWorksheet26**.
2. Save the worksheet with Save As and name it **sec4sc04**.
3. Make the following changes to the worksheet:
   a. Find all occurrences of cells containing *75* and replace with *90*.

   b. Find all occurrences of cells containing *20* and replace with *25*.
   c. Find all occurrences of *Barrier Concrete* and replace with *Lee Sand and Gravel*.
4. Save the worksheet again with the same name (**sec4sc04**).
5. Print the worksheet horizontally and vertically centered on the page.
6. Close **sec4sc04**.

Assessment 5

1. Open **ExcelWorksheet06**.
2. Print student names and scores for Test 12 on one page by completing the following steps:
   a. Hide columns B through L.
   b. Specify A1 through M20 as a print area.
   c. Print the print area. (Make sure the cells print on one page.)
   d. Clear the print area.
   e. Make columns B through L visible.
3. Close **ExcelWorksheet06** without saving the changes.

Assessment 6

1. Open **ExcelWorksheet23**.
2. Save the worksheet with Save As and name it **sec4sc06**.
3. Search for 11-point Arial formatting and replace with 12-point Garamond formatting (or another serif typeface such as Century or Times New Roman).
4. Search for 10-point Arial formatting and replace with 11-point Garamond formatting (or the typeface you chose in Step 3) with a light yellow background color.
5. Save, print, and then close **sec4sc06**. (This worksheet will contain blank cells in columns D and F.

Assessment 7

1. Open **ExcelWorksheet27**.
2. Save the worksheet with Save As and name it **sec4sc07**.
3. Select cells A3 through F14 and then click the Sort Ascending button on the Standard toolbar.
4. Print the worksheet horizontally and vertically centered on the page.
5. With the worksheet still open, select cells A3 through F14, and then sort the text in column B (Treatment) in ascending order (do this at the Sort dialog box).
6. Print the worksheet horizontally and vertically centered on the page.
7. With the worksheet still open, select cells A3 through F14, and then sort by the *Client #* in ascending order and then by *Treatment* in ascending order. (This is one sort.)
8. Save the worksheet again with the same name (**sec4sc07**).
9. Print the worksheet horizontally and vertically centered on the page.
10. Close **sec4sc07**.

Assessment 8

1. Open **ExcelWorksheet27**.
2. Save the worksheet with Save As and name it **sec4sc08**.
3. Filter and then print a list of rows containing only the treatment *Physical Therapy*. (After printing, return the list to *(All)*.)
4. Filter and then print a list of rows containing only the client number *2085*. (After printing, return the list to *(All)*.)

5. Filter and then print a list of rows containing the top 2 highest rates.
6. After printing, return the list to *(All)*. ***(Hint: Excel will display the three highest rates because there is a tie.)***
7. Save, print, and then close **sec4sa08**.

Assessment 9

1. Using the Ask a Question text box on the Menu bar, ask the question *What is Excel's default sorting order?*
2. Display information on default sort orders. After reading and printing the information presented, create a worksheet containing a summary of the information. Create the worksheet with the following features:
    a. Create a title for the worksheet.
    b. Set the data in cells in a serif typeface and change the data color.
    c. Add borders to the cells (you determine the border style).
    d. Add a color shading to cells (you determine the color—make it complementary to the data color).
    e. Create a custom footer that prints your name at the left margin and the file name at the right margin.
3. Save the completed worksheet and name it **sec4sc09**.
4. Print and then close **sec4sc09**.

CHAPTER challenge

You have been hired by See It Again video store. The store manager would like you to create and maintain a list of the store's videos and DVDs using Excel. The list should include the name of the movie, type of movie (comedy, horror, drama, etc.), rating, checkout date, return date, and any other fields you feel would be appropriate. Add at least 10 movies and their associated information to the list. Sort the list by movie names. Save and print the file.

A customer has entered the store and wants a list of the comedy and drama movies. Use the Help feature to learn about creating a custom filter that filters more than one criterion. Then use the custom filter to filter the comedy and drama movies. Print the results.

Business continues to grow for See It Again. You have spoken with the manager about maintaining the list of information in Access, since it is a more powerful database application, and Excel is limited in the database features it can use. Many of the individuals who maintain the current list are more familiar with Excel, so the transition from using Excel to Access will be gradual. Therefore, the information will be maintained in both Excel and Access. Create a database in Access called **SeeItAgain** and link the Excel list as a table. By linking the information, changes made in one application will take effect in the other application. Save the database and print the table.

WORK IN Progress

Preparing and Formatting a Worksheet

ASSESSING proficiency

In this unit, you have learned to create, save, print, edit, and format Excel worksheets; create and insert formulas; and enhance worksheets with features such as headers and footers, page numbering, sorting, and filtering.

(Note: Before completing computer exercises, delete the ExcelChapter04S folder on your disk. Next, copy the ExcelUnit01S subfolder from the Excel2003Specialist folder on the CD that accompanies this textbook to your disk and then make ExcelUnit01S the active folder.)

Assessment 1

1. Create the Excel worksheet shown in Figure U1.1. Format the cells as you see them in the figure. (Include a formula in cell D3 that subtracts the Quota sales from the Actual sales and then copy the formula down to cells D4 through D9.) *(Hint: The formula should look like this:* =C3-B3.*)*
2. Print the worksheet with gridlines and centered horizontally and vertically on the page.
3. Save the completed worksheet and name it **seu1pa01**.
4. Close **seu1pa01**.

	A	B	C	D	E
1	SALES QUOTA REPORT				
2	**Salesperson**	**Quota**	**Actual**	**Over/(Under)**	
3	Chavis	$55,000	$63,450		
4	Hampton	$85,000	$74,000		
5	Martindale	$48,000	$51,250		
6	Enriquez	$93,000	$86,300		
7	Gorham	$45,000	$45,000		
8	Kline	$75,000	$78,560		
9	McGuinness	$65,000	$71,450		
10					

FIGURE U1.1 • Assessment 1

Assessment 2

1. Open **seu1pa01**.
2. Save the worksheet with Save As and name it **seu1pa02**.
3. Make the following changes to the worksheet:

a. Add a row above row 7.
b. Type the following data in the specified cells:

A7	=	**Dillinger**
B7	=	**95000**
C7	=	**89650**

c. Make cell E2 the active cell and then type **% of Quota**.
d. Insert a formula in cell E3 that divides the actual amount by the quota. Copy this formula down to the other cells. (The result will be a decimal point. Select the decimal numbers that are a result of the formula and then click the Percent Style button on the Formatting toolbar.)
e. Select cells A1 through E10 and then apply an autoformat of your choosing.

4. Save, print, and then close **seu1pa02**.

Assessment 3

1. Open **seu1pa01**.
2. Save the worksheet with Save As and name it **seu1pa03**.
3. Make the following changes to the worksheet:
   a. Type **Quota Met** in cell E2.
   b. Select cells A1 through E1 and then merge and center the cells. (To do this, click the Merge and Center button twice.)
   c. Increase the height of row 1 to 30.00.
   d. Increase the height of row 2 to 24.00.
   e. Vertically center the text in cell A1. ***(Hint: To do this, make cell A1 active, click Format, and then click Cells. At the Format Cells dialog box, click the Alignment tab. Click the down-pointing triangle at the right of the* Vertical *option and then click* Center *at the drop-down list.)***
   f. Vertically center the text in cells A2 through E2.
   g. Change the width of column A to 16.00 and the width of columns B, C, D, and E to 14.00.
   h. Set the text in cell A1 in 14-point Arial bold.
   i. Set the text in cells A2 through E2 in 12-point Arial bold.
   j. Insert a formula in cell E3 that inserts the word *YES* if the quota is met and inserts *NO* if the quota is not met. ***(Hint: Use the IF function to write the formula, which should look like this:* =IF(D3>=0,"YES",IF(D3<0,"NO")).*)***
   k. Copy the formula in cell E3 down to cells E4 through E9.
   l. Center align the text in cells E3 through E9.
   m. Select cells A1 through E9 and then apply an outline border to the selected cells.
   n. Select cells A2 through E2 and then apply to the cells a top and bottom border and light gray shading.
   o. Select cells A4 through E4 and then apply light yellow shading.
   p. Apply the light yellow shading to cells A6 through E6 and cells A8 through E8.
4. Hide column D and then print the worksheet.
5. Redisplay column D.
6. Create the custom footer that prints your name at the left margin and *Annual Report* at the right margin.
7. Save and then close **seu1pa03**.

Assessment 4

1. Open **ExcelWorksheet30**.
2. Save the worksheet with Save As and name it **seu1pa04**.
3. The owner of Hilltop Equipment Rental is interested in purchasing a new tractor and needs to determine monthly payments on three different models. Insert a formula with the following specifications:
   a. Make cell E4 active.
   b. Use the Insert Function button on the Formula bar to insert a formula using the PMT function. At the formula palette, enter the following:

      Rate = C4/12
      Nper = D4
      Pv = -B4

   c. Copy the formula in cell E4 down to cells E5 and E6.
4. Insert a formula in cell F4 that multiplies the amount in E4 by the amount in D4.
5. Copy the formula in cell F4 down to cells F5 and F6.
6. Insert a formula in cell G4 that subtracts the amount in B4 from the amount in F4. ***(Hint: The formula is =F4-B4.)***
7. Copy the formula in cell G4 down to cells G5 and G6.
8. Save, print, and then close **seu1pa04**.

Assessment 5

1. Open **ExcelWorksheet29**.
2. Save the worksheet with Save As and name it **seu1pa05**.
3. Using the DATE function, enter a formula in each of the specified cells that returns the serial number for the specified date:

   C5 = **February 7, 2005**
   C6 = **February 9, 2005**
   C7 = **March 4, 2005**
   C8 = **March 4, 2005**

4. Enter a formula in cell E5 that inserts the due date (date of service plus the number of days in the Terms column).
5. Copy the formula in cell E5 down to cells E6 through E8.
6. Make cell A10 active and then type your name.
7. Make cell A11 active and then use the NOW function to insert the current date and time as a serial number.
8. Save, print, and then close **seu1pa05**.

Assessment 6

1. Open **seu1pa02**.
2. Save the worksheet with Save As and name it **seu1pa06**.
3. Sort the names of the salespersons alphabetically in ascending order.
4. Save the worksheet again with the same name (**seu1pa06**).
5. Print **seu1pa06**.
6. Sort the quota amounts in column B in descending order.
7. Save the worksheet again with the same name (**seu1pa06**).
8. Print **seu1pa06**.
9. Close **seu1pa06**.

Assessment 7

1. Open **ExcelWorksheet06**.
2. Save the worksheet with Save As and name it **seu1pa07**.
3. Make the following changes to the worksheet:
   a. Delete row 2.
   b. Insert a formula to average test scores for each student.
   c. Sort the data in the worksheet by the average test scores in ascending order.
   d. Select all cells in the worksheet and then change the font to 11-point Tahoma (or a similar sans serif typeface).
   e. Automatically adjust the widths of columns A through N.
   f. Add shading (you determine the color) to the first row.
   g. Create a footer that prints *Page x* (where *x* represents the correct page number) at the bottom center of each page.
   h. Create a custom header that prints your name at the left margin and *Student Test Scores* at the right margin.
4. Print the worksheet so the column titles (names) print on both pages.
5. Save and then close **seu1pa07**.

Assessment 8

1. Open **ExcelWorksheet31**.
2. Save the worksheet with Save As and name it **seu1pa08**.
3. Insert a formula in cell G5 that multiplies the amount in E5 by the percentage in F5 and then adds that total to the amount in E5. ***(Hint: The formula should look like this:* =(E5*F5)+E5.*)***
4. Copy the formula in cell G5 down to cells G6 through G14.
5. Print **seu1pa08**.
6. Make the following changes to the worksheet:
   a. Find all occurrences of cells containing *11-279* and replace with *10-005*.
   b. Find all occurrences of cells containing *8.5%* and replace with *9.0%*.
   c. Search for 10-point Arial formatting and replace with 11-point Times New Roman formatting.
7. Filter and then print a list of rows containing only the client number *04-325*. (After printing, return the list to *(All)*.)
8. Filter and then print a list of rows containing only the service *Development*. (After printing, return the list to *(All)*.)
9. Filter and then print a list of rows containing the top 3 highest amounts. (After printing, return the list to *(All)*.)
10. Save and then close **seu1pa08**.

WRITING activities

The following activities give you the opportunity to practice your writing skills along with demonstrating an understanding of some of the important Excel features you have mastered in this unit. Use correct grammar, appropriate word choices, and clear sentence constructions.

Activity 1

Plan and prepare a worksheet with the information shown in Figure U1.2. Apply formatting of your choosing to the worksheet either with an autoformat or with formatting at the Format Cells dialog box. Save the completed worksheet and name it **seu1act01**. Print and then close **seu1act01**.

Prepare a weekly summary of orders taken that itemizes the product coming into the company and the average order size.

The products and average order size include:

Black and gold wall clock—$2,450 worth of orders, average order size of $125
Traveling alarm clock—$1,358 worth of orders, average order size of $195
Water-proof watch—$890 worth of orders, average order size of $90
Dashboard clock—$2,135 worth of orders, average order size of $230
Pyramid clock—$3,050 worth of orders, average order size of $375
Gold chain watch—$755 worth of orders, average order size of $80

In the worksheet, total the amount ordered, and also calculate the average weekly order size. Sort the data in the worksheet by the order amount in descending order.

FIGURE U1.2 • Activity 1

Activity 2

Assets within a company, such as equipment, can be depreciated over time. Several methods are available for determining the amount of depreciation such as the straight-line depreciation method, fixed-declining balance method, and the double-declining method. Use Excel's Help feature to learn about two depreciation methods—straight-line and double-declining depreciation. After reading about the two methods, create an Excel worksheet with the following information:

- An appropriate title
- A heading for straight-line depreciation
- The straight-line depreciation function
- The name and a description for each straight-line depreciation function argument category
- A heading for double-declining depreciation
- The double-declining depreciation function
- The name and a description for each double-declining depreciation function argument category

Apply formatting of your choosing to the worksheet. Save the completed worksheet and name it **seu1act02**. Print the worksheet horizontally and vertically centered on the page. Close **seu1act02**.

Open **ExcelWorksheet32**. Save the worksheet with Save As and name it **seu1slnact**. Insert the function to determine straight-line depreciation in cell E3. Copy the formula down to cells E4 through E10. Apply formatting of your choosing to the worksheet. Print the worksheet horizontally and vertically centered on the page. Save and then close **seu1slnact**.

INTERNET project

Make sure you are connected to the Internet. Use a search engine of your choosing to look for information on traveling to a specific country that interests you. Find sites that provide cost information for airlines, hotels, meals, entertainment, and car rentals. Create a travel planning worksheet for the country that includes the following:

- appropriate title
- appropriate headings
- airline costs
- hotel costs (off-season and in-season rates if available)
- estimated meal costs
- entertainment costs
- car rental costs

Save the completed worksheet and name it **seu1intact**. Print and then close **seu1intact**.

JOB study

You are the owner of a small lawn mowing business. You need to prepare a budget with separate sections for income and expenses for April through November. Your worksheet will include these monthly expenses:

- **Gasoline** (5-gallon container)—Each gallon will mow 8 yards. Create an absolute reference to figure the gas price. Use the current gas price in your area.
- **Mower** (a new push mower with a bag attachment)—Select a model advertised in your local paper or go online to find the cost. Figure depreciation on the mower by taking the purchase price plus your local tax on the mower purchase price and dividing by 8 months.
- **Blade sharpening**—$15 each month.

Figure your income based on the following parameters:

- You will mow at least 15 yards per week.
- You will provide services based on the following rates:

  mowing - $25 per yard
  bagging grass - $10 extra per yard
  trimming and edging - $10 per yard

Sort the expenses in ascending order and then sort the income in ascending order. Create totals using formulas and functions. Determine the minimum, maximum, and average for each month's income and expenses sections. Apply formats where necessary (header/footers, centering, shading, numeric formats, bolding, and so on). Save your worksheet as **LawnBusiness** and print one copy.

SPECIALIST

MICROSOFT®

EXCEL

Unit 2: Maintaining and Enhancing Workbooks

- Moving Data within and between Workbooks
- Maintaining Workbooks
- Creating a Chart in Excel
- Enhancing the Display of Workbooks

BENCHMARK MICROSOFT® EXCEL 2003

MICROSOFT OFFICE SPECIALIST SKILLS—UNIT 2

Reference No.	Skill	Pages
XL03S-1	**Creating Data and Content**	
XL03S-1-3	Locate, select, and insert supporting information	
	Research and request information	S249-S252
	Insert research information	S250-S252
XL03S-2	**Analyzing Data**	
XL03S-2-4	Use statistical, date and time, financial, and logical functions	
	Name a range and use a range in a formula	S158-S159
XL03S-2-5	Create, modify, and position diagrams and charts based on worksheet data	
	Create and customize diagrams	S257-S259
	Create, preview, print, delete, move, size, format, and customize charts	S213-S235
XL03S-3	**Formatting Data and Content**	
XL03S-3-2	Apply and modify cell styles	S194-S200
XL03S-3-4	Format worksheets	
	Customize worksheet tabs	S151-S153
	Hide and unhide a worksheet in a workbook	S153-S155
	Add a background image to a worksheet	S245-S247
XL03S-4	**Collaborating**	
XL03S-4-1	Insert, view, and edit comments	S200-S204
XL03S-5	**Managing Workbooks**	
XL03S-5-1	Create new workbooks from templates	S204-S207
XL03S-5-2	Insert, delete, and move cells	
	Move, copy, and paste cells	S145-S149
	Move, copy, and paste data using Paste Special	S164-S170
XL03S-5-3	Create and modify hyperlinks	S244-S248
XL03S-5-4	Organize Worksheets	
	Delete, copy, cut, paste, and rename worksheets	S181-S187
	Copy a worksheet to another workbook	S187-S188
	Move a worksheet to another workbook	S189-S191
XL03S-5-5	Preview data in other views	
	Preview a workbook in Web Page Preview	S243-S247
XL03S-5-6	Customize window layout	
	Split a worksheet into windows and freeze and unfreeze panes	S161-S163
	Arrange workbooks	S162-S163
	Hide and unhide workbooks	S163-S164
	Size and move workbooks	S155-S158
XL03S-5-8	Print data	
	Print a workbook containing multiple worksheets	S150-S151
XL03S-5-9	Organize workbooks using file folders	
	Create a folder	S180-S181
	Delete and rename a folder	S181-182
XL03S-5-10	Save data in appropriate formats for different uses	
	Save workbooks un a variety of formats	S191-S194
	Save a workbook as a Web page	S241-S247

CHAPTER 5

MOVING DATA WITHIN AND BETWEEN WORKBOOKS

PERFORMANCE OBJECTIVES

Upon successful completion of Chapter 5, you will be able to:

- **Move, copy, and paste cells within a worksheet**
- **Create a workbook with multiple worksheets**
- **Split a worksheet into windows and freeze panes**
- **Name a range of cells and use a range in a formula**
- **Open and close workbooks**
- **Arrange, size, and move workbooks**
- **Copy and paste data between workbooks**
- **Link data between worksheets**
- **Link worksheets with a 3-D reference**
- **Copy and paste a worksheet between programs**

Moving and pasting or copying and pasting selected cells in different locations in a worksheet is useful for rearranging data in a worksheet or for saving time. Up to this point, the workbooks you have been working in have consisted of only one worksheet. In this chapter, you will learn to create a workbook with several worksheets and complete tasks such as copying and pasting data within and between worksheets. You will also work with multiple workbooks and complete tasks such as arranging, sizing, and moving workbooks, and opening and closing multiple workbooks.

Excel uses styles to automate formatting in a large workbook containing multiple worksheets. A style is a predefined set of formatting attributes. In this chapter, you will learn to define, apply, modify, remove, delete, and copy styles.

Moving, Copying, and Pasting Cells

Situations may arise where you need to move cells to a different location within a worksheet or you may need to copy repetitive data in a worksheet. You can perform these actions by selecting cells and then using the Move, Copy, and/or Paste buttons on the Standard toolbar. You can also perform these actions with the mouse or with options from the Edit drop-down menu.

Moving Selected Cells

Cut

Paste

You can move selected cells and cell contents in a worksheet and between worksheets. Move selected cells with the Cut and Paste buttons on the Standard toolbar, by dragging with the mouse, or with options on the Edit drop-down menu.

Move and Paste Cells
1. Select cells.
2. Click Cut button.
3. Click desired cell.
4. Click Paste button.

Ctrl + X is the keyboard command to cut selected data. Ctrl + V is the keyboard command to paste data.

To move selected cells with buttons on the Standard toolbar, select the cells, and then click the Cut button. This causes a moving dashed line border to display around the selected cells. Click the cell where you want the first selected cell inserted and then click the Paste button on the Standard toolbar. If you change your mind and do not want to move the selected cells, press the Esc key to remove the moving dashed line border or double-click in any cell.

To move selected cells with the mouse, select the cells, and then position the mouse pointer on any border of the selected cells until it turns into an arrow pointer. Hold down the left mouse button, drag the outline of the selected cells to the desired location, and then release the mouse button.

Selected cells can also be moved by selecting the cells, clicking Edit, and then clicking Cut. This causes a moving dashed line to display around the selected cells. Click the cell where you want the first selected cell inserted, click Edit, and then click Paste.

exercise 1

MOVING SELECTED CELLS IN A WORKSHEET

1. Open **ExcelWorksheet02**.
2. Save the worksheet with Save As and name it **sec5x01**.
3. Move cells in column D to column E by completing the following steps:
   a. Select cells D1 through D8.
   b. Click the Cut button on the Standard toolbar.
   c. Click cell E1 to make it active.
   d. Click the Paste button on the Standard toolbar.
4. Move cells in column B to column D by completing the following steps:
   a. Select cells B1 through B8.
   b. Position the mouse pointer on any boundary of the selected cells until it turns into an arrow pointer with a four-headed arrow attached.
   c. Hold down the left mouse button, drag the outline of the selected cells to column D, and then release the mouse button. (After the cells are moved, they should occupy cells D1 through D8.)

	A	B	C	D	E
1	Expense	Actual	Budget		Variance
2	Salaries	126000	126000		D1:D8 0
3	Commissions	58000	54500		-3500
4	Media space	8250	10100		1850
5	Travel expenses	6350	6000		-350
6	Dealer display	4140	4500		360
7	Payroll taxes	2430	2200		-230
8	Telephone	1450	1500		50

Step 4a　Step 4c

5. Delete column B.
6. Select cells A1 through D8 and then apply the Accounting 2 autoformat.
7. Select row 1 and then turn on Bold and change the alignment to center.
8. Save, print, and then close **sec5x01**.

Copying Selected Cells

Copy

Copying selected cells can be useful in worksheets that contain repetitive data. To copy cells, select the cells, and then click the Copy button on the Standard toolbar. Click the cell where you want the first selected cell copied and then click the Paste button on the Standard toolbar.

HINT

Ctrl + C is the keyboard command to copy selected data.

Selected cells can also be copied using the mouse and the Ctrl key. To do this, select the cells to be copied, and then position the mouse pointer on any border around the selected cells until it turns into an arrow pointer. Hold down the Ctrl key and the left mouse button, drag the outline of the selected cells to the desired location, release the left mouse button, and then release the Ctrl key.

Copy and Paste Cells
1. Select cells.
2. Click Copy button.
3. Click desired cell.
4. Click Paste button.

You can also use the Copy and Paste options from the Edit drop-down menu to copy selected cells in a worksheet. To do this, select the cells, click Edit, and then click Copy. Click the cell where you want the first selected cell copied, click Edit, and then click Paste.

exercise 2

COPYING SELECTED CELLS IN A WORKSHEET

1. Open **ExcelWorksheet05**.
2. Save the worksheet with Save As and name it **sec5x02**.
3. Type Total in cell D2.
4. Make cell D3 active and then insert a formula that multiplies the contents of cell C3 with the contents of cell B3.
5. Copy the formula in cell D3 down to cells D4 through D8.
6. Select cells A1 through D1.
7. Click the Merge and Center button on the Formatting toolbar. (This splits the cells.)
8. Click the Merge and Center button again. (This merges cells A1 through D1.)
9. Copy and paste cells by completing the following steps:
   a. Select cells A1 through D8.
   b. Position the mouse pointer on any boundary of the selected cells until it turns into an arrow pointer with a four-headed arrow attached.
   c. Hold down the Ctrl key and then the left mouse button.
   d. Drag the outline of the selected cells so the top left corner of the outline is positioned at the top of cell A10.
   e. Release the left mouse button and then the Ctrl key.

	A	B	C	D
1	January			
2	Name	Hours	Rate	Total
3	Carolyn Bentley	35	$23.15	$810.25
4	Lindon Cassini	20	$19.00	$380.00
5	Michelle DeFord	40	$18.75	$750.00
6	Javier Farias	24	$16.45	$394.80
7	Deborah Gould	15	$11.50	$172.50
8	William Jarman	15	$11.50	$172.50
9				
10				
11				
12				
13				
14				
15				
16				
17				
18				
19				

Step 9d

A10:D17

10. Change the contents of the following cells to the specified data:

    A10: From *January* to *February*
    B12: From *35* to *40*
    B14: From *40* to *32*
    B16: From *15* to *30*

11. Select cells A1 through D8 and then apply the Colorful 2 autoformat.
12. Select cells A10 through D17 and then apply the Colorful 2 autoformat.
13. Save, print, and then close **sec5x02**.

QUICK STEPS

Copy and Paste Multiple Items

1. Click Edit, Office Clipboard.
2. Select desired cells.
3. Click Copy button.
4. Continue selecting desired cells and then clicking the Copy button.
5. Make active the desired cell.
6. Click item in Clipboard task pane that you want inserted in the worksheet.
7. Continue pasting desired items from the Clipboard task pane.

Using the Office Clipboard

Use the Office Clipboard feature to collect and paste multiple items. You can collect up to 24 different items and then paste them in various locations. To use the Office Clipboard feature, display the Clipboard task pane, by clicking Edit on the Menu bar and then clicking Office Clipboard, or by pressing Ctrl + C twice. You can also display the Clipboard task pane by clicking the Other Task Panes button (displays with a down-pointing arrow at the right side) located at the top of the task pane and then clicking Clipboard at the drop-down menu. The Clipboard task pane displays at the right side of the screen in a manner similar to what you see in Figure 5.1.

The Clipboard task pane holds up to 24 items. After that number, items are discarded beginning with the oldest item.

FIGURE 5.1 ***Clipboard Task Pane***

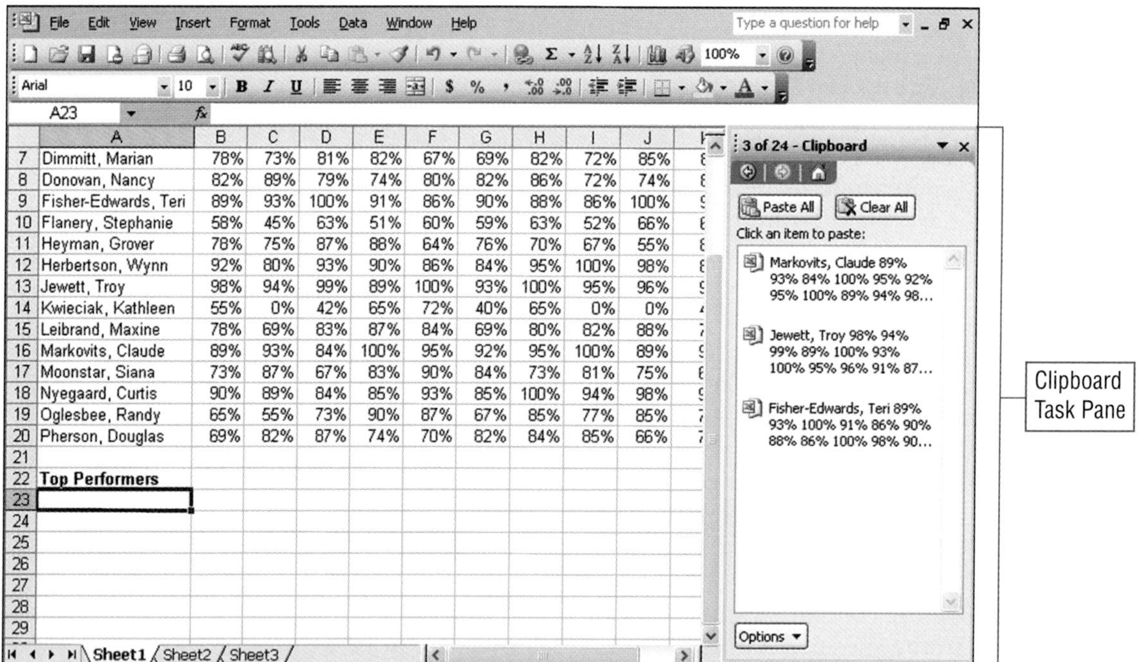

	A	B	C	D	E	F	G	H	I	J
7	Dimmitt, Marian	78%	73%	81%	82%	67%	69%	82%	72%	85%
8	Donovan, Nancy	82%	89%	79%	74%	80%	82%	86%	72%	74%
9	Fisher-Edwards, Teri	89%	93%	100%	91%	86%	90%	88%	86%	100%
10	Flanery, Stephanie	58%	45%	63%	51%	60%	59%	63%	52%	66%
11	Heyman, Grover	78%	75%	87%	88%	64%	76%	70%	67%	55%
12	Herbertson, Wynn	92%	80%	93%	90%	86%	84%	95%	100%	98%
13	Jewett, Troy	98%	94%	99%	89%	100%	93%	100%	95%	96%
14	Kwieciak, Kathleen	55%	0%	42%	65%	72%	40%	65%	0%	0%
15	Leibrand, Maxine	78%	69%	83%	87%	84%	69%	80%	82%	88%
16	Markovits, Claude	89%	93%	84%	100%	95%	92%	95%	100%	89%
17	Moonstar, Siana	73%	87%	67%	83%	90%	84%	73%	81%	75%
18	Nyegaard, Curtis	90%	89%	84%	85%	93%	85%	100%	94%	98%
19	Oglesbee, Randy	65%	55%	73%	90%	87%	67%	85%	77%	85%
20	Pherson, Douglas	69%	82%	87%	74%	70%	82%	84%	85%	66%
21										
22	Top Performers									

HINT Click the Paste All button in the Clipboard task pane to paste all items at once.

Select data or an object you want to copy and then click the Copy button on the Standard toolbar. Continue selecting text or items and clicking the Copy button. To insert an item, position the insertion point in the desired location and then click that item in the Clipboard task pane. If the copied item is text, the first 50 characters display. When all desired items are inserted, click the Clear All button to remove any remaining items.

exercise 3

COLLECTING AND PASTING CELLS

1. Open **ExcelWorksheet06**.
2. Save the worksheet with Save As and name it **sec5x03**.
3. Make cell A22 the active cell, turn on bold, and then type **Top Performers**.
4. Display the Clipboard task pane by clicking Edit and then Office Clipboard.
5. Collect several rows of cells and then paste them by completing the following steps:
    a. Click the row header for row 9 (this selects the entire row).
    b. Click the Copy button on the Standard toolbar.
    c. Click the row header for row 13 and then click the Copy button on the Standard toolbar.
    d. Click the row header for row 16 and then click the Copy button on the Standard toolbar.

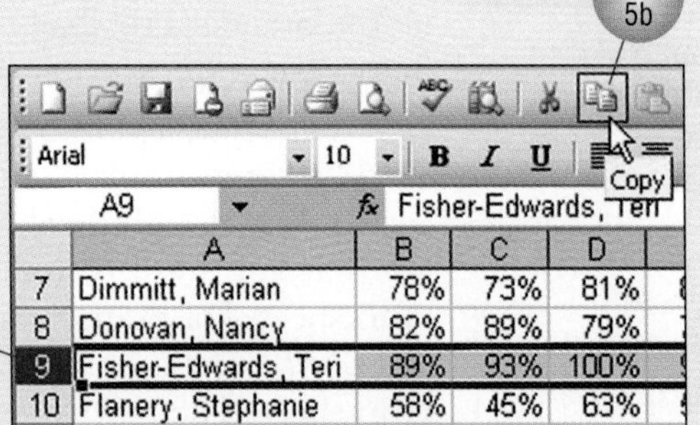

6. Paste the copied cells by completing the following steps:
    a. Make cell A23 active.
    b. Click the item in the Clipboard task pane representing row 13 (the row for Jewett).
    c. Make cell A24 active.
    d. Click the item in the Clipboard task pane representing row 16 (the row for Markovits).
    e. Make cell A25 active.
    f. Click the item in the Clipboard task pane representing row 9 (the row for Fisher-Edwards).

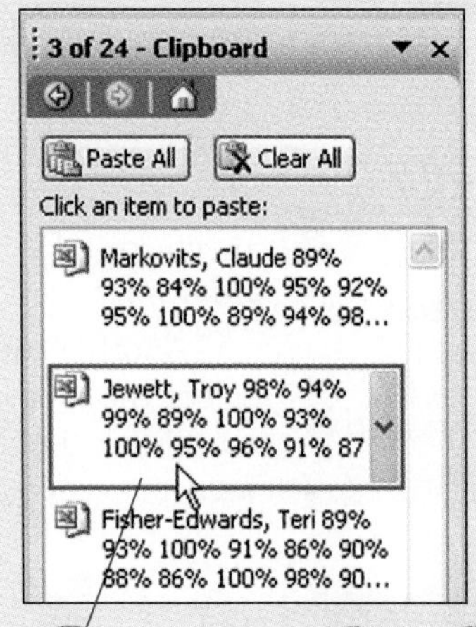

7. Click the Clear All button located toward the top of the Clipboard task pane.
8. Close the Clipboard task pane by clicking the Close button (contains an *X*) located in the upper right corner of the task pane.
9. Create a custom footer that prints your name at the left margin and the file name at the right margin.
10. Print the worksheet in landscape orientation.
11. Save the worksheet.
12. Close **sec5x03**.

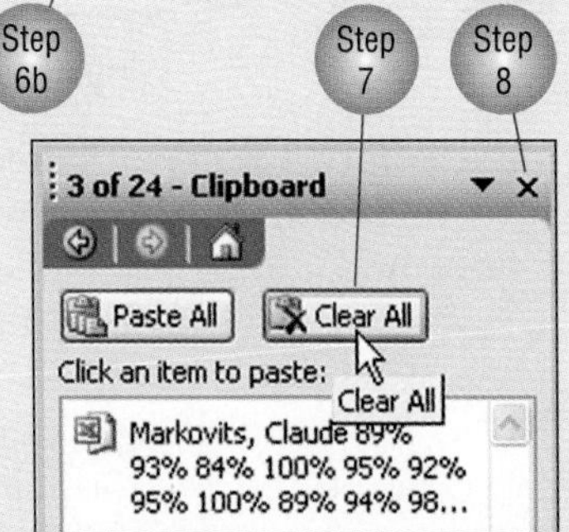

Creating a Workbook with Multiple Worksheets

Up to this point, each workbook you have created has contained one worksheet. A workbook can contain several worksheets. You can create a variety of worksheets within a workbook for related data. For example, a workbook may contain a worksheet for the expenses for each salesperson in a company and another worksheet for the monthly payroll for each department within the company. Another example is recording sales statistics for each quarter in individual worksheets within a workbook.

HINT

By default, a workbook contains three worksheets. You can change this number with the *Sheets in new workbook* option at the Options dialog box with the General tab selected.

The copy and paste features can be useful in creating more than one worksheet within a workbook. These features are helpful if some data within each worksheet is consistent. For example, you can create a worksheet containing information on a product and then copy this information to another worksheet where you would change data in specific cells.

QUICK STEPS

Insert Worksheet
1. Click worksheet tab that you want to follow the new worksheet.
2. Click Insert, Worksheet.

To copy selected cells to a new worksheet, select the cells, click the Copy button on the Standard toolbar, click the worksheet tab (displayed immediately above the Status bar) representing the desired worksheet, and then click the Paste button.

By default, a workbook contains three worksheets named *Sheet1*, *Sheet2*, and *Sheet3*. (Later in this chapter, you will learn how to change these default names.) You can insert additional worksheets in a workbook. To do this, click the worksheet tab that you want to follow the new worksheet, click Insert, and then click Worksheet. For example, if you want to insert a new worksheet between *Sheet1* and *Sheet2*, click the *Sheet2* tab to make it active, click Insert, and then click Worksheet. The new worksheet, by default, is named *Sheet4*.

HINT

Print specific worksheets in a workbook by selecting the desired worksheet tabs.

Printing a Workbook Containing Multiple Worksheets

In Exercise 4, you will create a workbook that contains four worksheets. When printing this workbook, by default, Excel will print the worksheet currently displayed. If you want to print all worksheets in a workbook, display the Print dialog box by clicking File and then Print. At the Print dialog box, click *Entire workbook* in the *Print what* section, and then click OK.

Print all Worksheets in a Workbook
1. Click File, Print.
2. Click *Entire workbook*.
3. Click OK.

Another method for printing specific worksheets within a workbook is to select the tabs of the worksheets you want to print. To do this, open the desired workbook, hold down the Ctrl key, and then click the desired tabs. If the tabs are adjacent, you can use the Shift key.

exercise 4 — COPYING CELLS TO DIFFERENT WORKSHEETS

1. Open **ExcelWorksheet34**.
2. Save the worksheet with Save As and name it **sec5x04**.
3. Add a fourth worksheet by clicking Insert and then Worksheet. (This adds a *Sheet4* tab before the *Sheet1* tab.)
4. Click *Sheet1* to make worksheet 1 active and then make the following changes to the worksheet:
   a. Insert the formula =B3-C3 in cell D3 to subtract the amount in C3 from the amount in B3.
   b. Copy the formula in cell D3 down to cells D4 through D9.

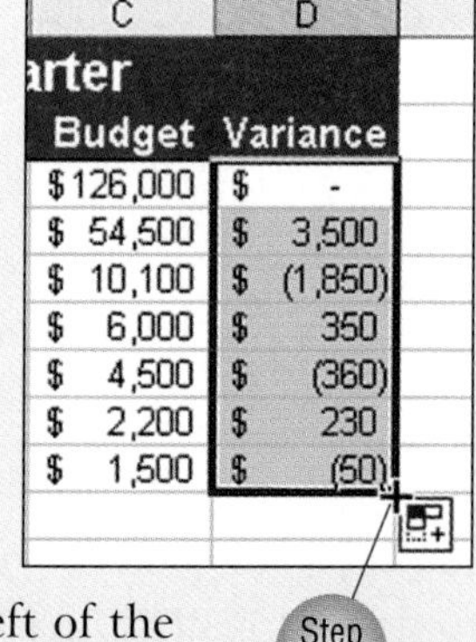

C
D
arter
Budget
Variance
$126,000
$ -
$ 54,500
$ 3,500
$ 10,100
$ (1,850)
$ 6,000
$ 350
$ 4,500
$ (360)
$ 2,200
$ 230
$ 1,500
$ (50)
Step 4b

5. Copy cells and paste them into worksheets 2, 3, and 4 by completing the following steps:
   a. Click the Select All button that displays immediately to the left of the column A header and immediately above the row 1 header.
   b. Click the Copy button on the Standard toolbar.
   c. Click the *Sheet2* tab that displays immediately above the Status bar.
   d. At worksheet 2, make sure cell A1 is the active cell, and then click the Paste button.

23
Sheet4 / Sheet1 / Sheet2 / Sheet3
Select destination and press ENTER or choose Paste
Step 5c

e. Click the *Sheet3* tab that displays immediately above the Status bar.
f. At worksheet 3, make sure cell A1 is the active cell, and then click the Paste button.
g. Click the *Sheet4* tab.
h. At worksheet 4, make sure cell A1 is the active cell, and then click the Paste button.

6. Click the *Sheet2* tab and then make the following changes to cell entries in worksheet 2:

   A1: From *First Quarter* to *Second Quarter*
   B4: From *58,000* to *60,500*
   C4: From *54,500* to *58,500*
   B8: From *2,430* to *2,510*
   C8: From *2,200* to *2,350*

7. Click the *Sheet3* tab and then make the following changes to cell entries in worksheet 3:

   A1: From *First Quarter* to *Third Quarter*
   B4: From *58,000* to *60,200*
   C4: From *54,500* to *60,500*
   B8: From *2,430* to *2,500*
   C8: From *2,200* to *2,550*

8. Click the *Sheet4* tab and then make the following changes to cell entries in worksheet 4:

   A1: From *First Quarter* to *Fourth Quarter*
   B4: From *58,000* to *61,000*
   C4: From *54,500* to *60,500*
   B8: From *2,430* to *2,550*
   C8: From *2,200* to *2,500*

9. Save the workbook again with the same name (**sec5x04**).
10. Print all of the worksheets in the workbook by completing the following steps:
    a. Make sure no cells are selected (just an active cell).
    b. Click File and then Print.
    c. At the Print dialog box, click *Entire workbook* in the *Print what* section.
    d. Click OK. (Each worksheet will print on a separate piece of paper.)
11. Close **sec5x04**.

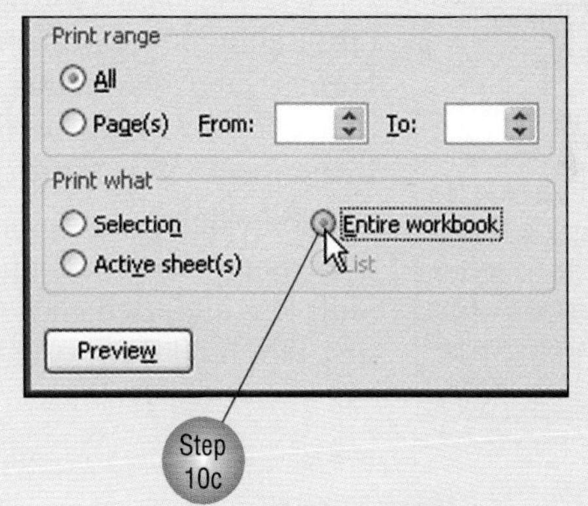

Managing Worksheets

Right-click a sheet tab and a shortcut menu displays as shown in Figure 5.2 with the options Insert, Delete, Rename, Move or Copy, Select All Sheets, Tab Color, and View Code. Use these options to manage worksheets in a workbook. For example, remove a worksheet by clicking the Delete option. Move or copy a worksheet by clicking the Move or Copy option. Clicking this option causes a Move or Copy dialog box to display where you specify what sheet you want to move or copy the selected sheet. By default, Excel names worksheets in a workbook *Sheet1, Sheet2, Sheet3,* and so on. To rename a worksheet, click the Rename option (this selects the default sheet name), and then type the desired name.

HINT
Use the tab scroll buttons, located to the left of the sheet tabs, to bring into view any worksheet tabs not currently visible.

FIGURE 5.2 **Sheet Tab Shortcut Menu**

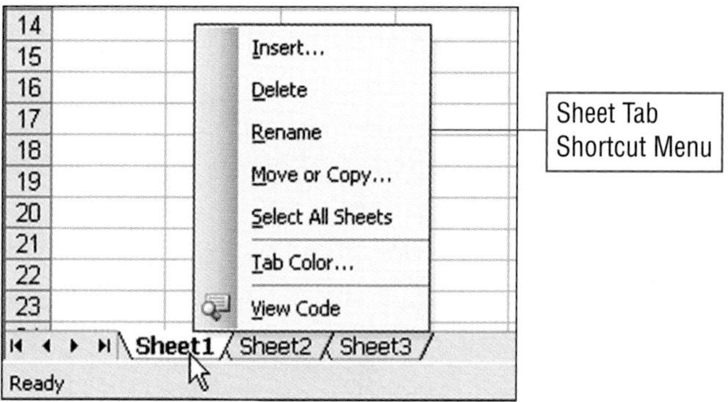

Move or Copy a Worksheet
1. Right-click sheet tab.
2. Click Move or Copy.
3. At Move or Copy dialog box, click desired worksheet name in *Before sheet* list box.
4. Click OK.

OR

Drag worksheet tab to the desired position (hold down Ctrl key while dragging to copy).

Recolor Sheet Tab
1. Right-click sheet tab.
2. Click Tab Color.
3. Click desired color.
4. Click OK.

HINT

Copy a worksheet in a workbook by holding down the Ctrl key and then dragging a tab from one location to another.

In addition to the shortcut menu options, you can use the mouse to move or copy worksheets. To move a worksheet, position the mouse pointer on the worksheet tab, hold down the left mouse button (a page icon displays next to the mouse pointer), drag the page icon to the desired position, and then release the mouse button. For example, to move *Sheet2* tab after *Sheet3* tab you would position the mouse pointer on the *Sheet2* tab, hold down the left mouse button, drag the page icon so it is positioned after the *Sheet3* tab, and then release the mouse button. To copy a worksheet, hold down the Ctrl key while dragging the sheet tab.

Use the Tab Color option at the shortcut menu to apply a color to a worksheet tab. Right-click a worksheet tab, click Tab Color at the shortcut menu, and the Format Tab Color dialog box displays. At this dialog box, click the desired color and then click OK. Only a strip of color displays at the bottom of the active sheet tab. If the sheet tab is not the active tab, the entire tab displays with the selected color.

You can manage more than one worksheet at a time by first selecting the worksheets. To select adjacent worksheet tabs, click the first tab, hold down the Shift key, and then click the last tab. To select nonadjacent worksheet tabs, click the first tab, hold down the Ctrl key, and then click any other tabs you want selected.

exercise 5

SELECTING, DELETING, RENAMING, AND CHANGING THE COLOR OF WORKSHEET TABS

1. Open **sec5x04**.
2. Save the workbook with Save As and name it **sec5x05**.
3. Delete worksheets 3 and 4 by completing the following steps:
   a. Click the left mouse button on *Sheet3* that displays at the bottom of the workbook window.
   b. Hold down the Ctrl key, click *Sheet4*, and then release the Ctrl key.
   c. Position the arrow pointer on the *Sheet4* tab and then click the *right* mouse button.

d. At the shortcut menu that displays, click Delete.
e. At the message telling you that the selected sheets will be permanently deleted, click the Delete button.

4. Rename worksheets 1 and 2 by completing the following steps:
   a. Right-click the *Sheet1* tab and then click Rename.
   b. Type **First Quarter** and then press Enter.
   c. Right-click the *Sheet2* tab and then click Rename.
   d. Type **Second Quarter** and then press Enter.
5. Move the *Second Quarter* sheet tab by completing the following steps:
   a. Right-click the *Second Quarter* sheet tab and then click Move or Copy at the shortcut menu.
   b. At the Move or Copy dialog box, make sure *First Quarter* is selected in the *Before sheet* list box, and then click OK.
6. Change the color of the *First Quarter* sheet tab by completing the following steps:
   a. Right-click the *First Quarter* sheet tab.
   b. Click Tab Color at the shortcut menu.
   c. At the Format Tab Color dialog box, click a blue color of your choosing, and then click OK.
7. Follow steps similar to those in Step 6 to change the *Second Quarter* sheet tab to a red color of your choosing.
8. Save and then print the entire workbook (two worksheets).
9. Close **sec5x05**.

Hiding a Worksheet in a Workbook

In a workbook containing multiple worksheets, you can hide a worksheet that may contain sensitive data or data you do not want to display or print with the workbook. To hide a worksheet in a workbook, click Format, point to Sheet, and then click Hide. To make a hidden worksheet visible, click Format, point to Sheet, and then click Unhide. At the Unhide dialog box shown in Figure 5.3, double-click the name of the hidden worksheet you want to display.

HINT
If the Hide command is unavailable, the workbook is protected from change.

FIGURE 5.3 ***Unhide Dialog Box***

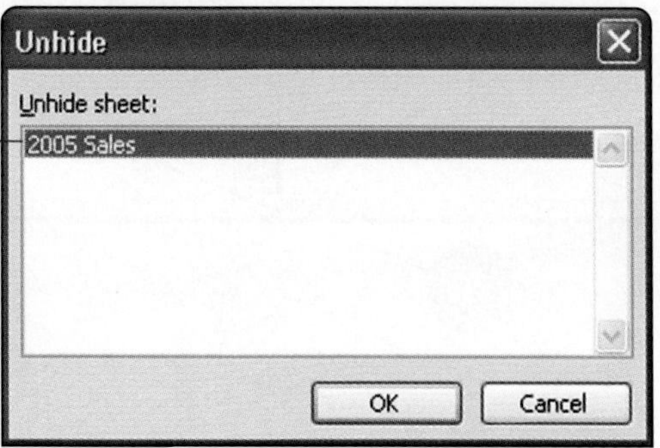

The names of hidden worksheets display in this list box.

Hide a Worksheet
Click Format, Sheet, Hide.

Unhide a Worksheet
Click Format, Sheet, Unhide.

Formatting Multiple Worksheets

When you apply formatting to a worksheet, such as changing margins, orientation, or inserting a header or footer, and so on, the formatting is applied only to the active worksheet. If you want formatting to apply to multiple worksheets in a workbook, select the tabs of the desired worksheets and then apply the formatting. For example, if a workbook contains three worksheets and you want to apply formatting to the first and second worksheets only, select the tabs for the first and second worksheets and then apply the formatting.

exercise 6

HIDING A WORKSHEET AND FORMATTING MULTIPLE WORKSHEETS

1. Open **ExcelWorksheet41**.
2. Save the workbook with Save As and name it **sec5x06**. (This workbook contains three worksheets.)
3. Make the following changes to the worksheet tabs:
   a. Rename *Sheet1* to *2003 Sales*.
   b. Rename *Sheet2* to *2004 Sales*.
   c. Rename *Sheet3* to *2005 Sales*.
4. Hide the *2005 Sales* worksheet by completing the following steps:
   a. Click the *2005 Sales* worksheet tab.
   b. Click Format, point to Sheet, and then click Hide.
5. Change the margins and insert a custom footer to multiple worksheets by completing the following steps:
   a. Click the *2003 Sales* tab.
   b. Hold down the Shift key and then click the *2004 Sales* tab. (This selects both tabs.)
   c. Click File and then Page Setup.
   d. At the Page Setup dialog box, click the Margins tab.
   e. At the Page Setup dialog box with the Margins tab selected, change the *Top* margin measurement to *2* and the *Left* margin measurement to *2.25*.
   f. Click the Header/Footer tab.
   g. At the Page Setup dialog box with the Header/Footer tab selected, click the Custom Footer button.
   h. At the Footer dialog box, type your name in the *Left section* text box, insert the page number in the *Center section* text box, and insert the file name in the *Right section* text box.
   i. Click OK to close the Footer dialog box.

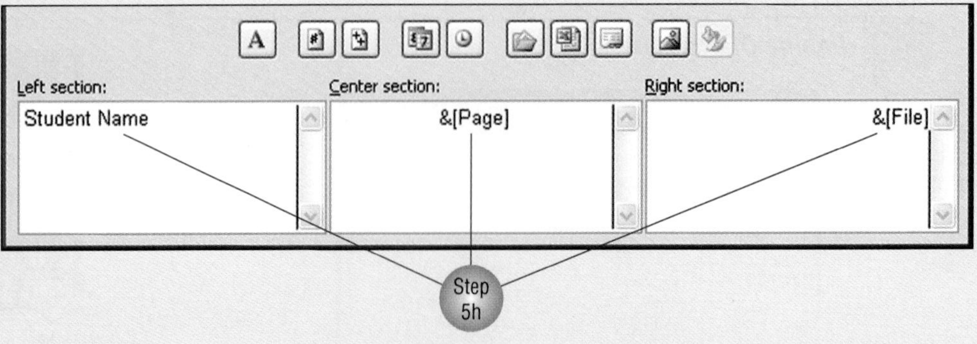

j. Click OK to close the Page Setup dialog box.
6. Print the entire workbook (except the hidden worksheet) by displaying the Print dialog box, clicking *Entire workbook* in the *Print what* section, and then clicking OK.
7. Unhide the *2005 Sales* worksheet by completing the following steps:
   a. Click Format, point to Sheet, and then click Unhide.
   b. At the Unhide dialog box, make sure *2005 Sales* is selected in the *Unhide sheet* list box, and then click OK.
8. Save and then close **sec5x06**.

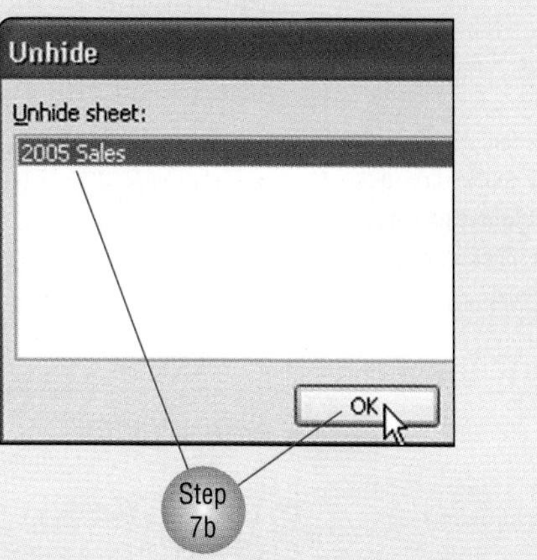

Splitting a Worksheet into Windows and Freezing and Unfreezing Panes

In some worksheets, not all cells display at one time in the worksheet area (such as ExcelWorksheet06). When working in worksheets with more cells than can display at one time, you may find splitting the worksheet window into panes helpful. Split the worksheet window into panes with the Split option from the Window drop-down menu or use the split bars that display at the top of the vertical scroll bar and at the right side of the horizontal scroll bar. Figure 5.4 identifies these split bars.

Split a Worksheet
Click Window, Split.
OR
Drag horizontal and/or vertical split bars.

FIGURE 5.4 ***Split Bars***

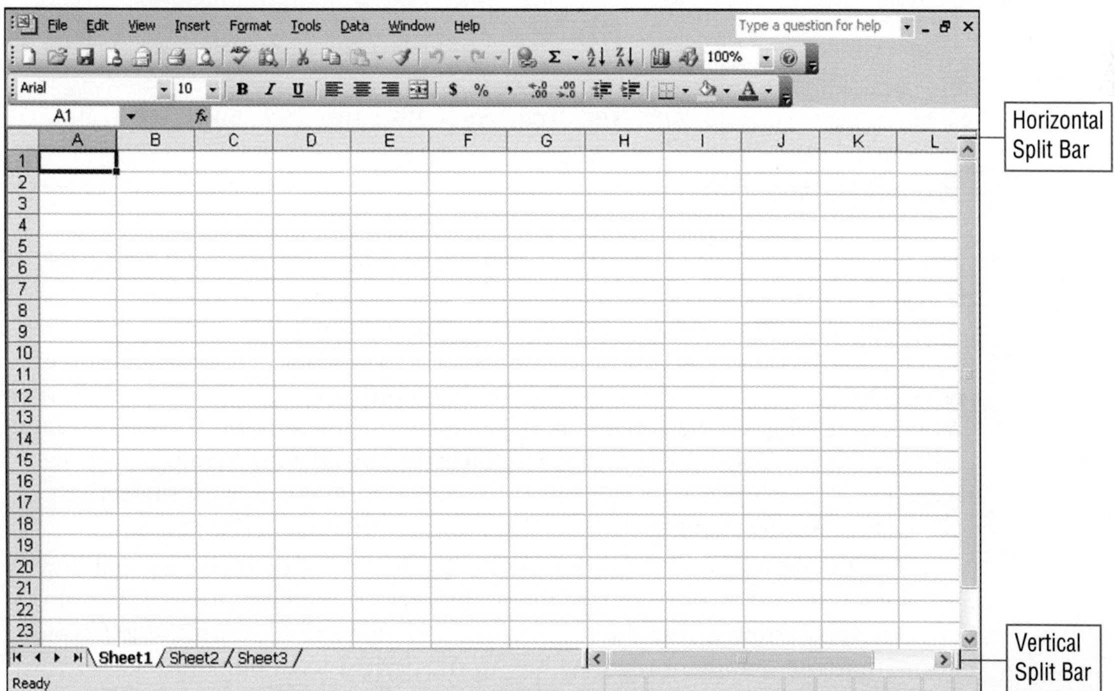

To split a window with the split bar located at the top of the vertical scroll bar, position the mouse pointer on the split bar until it turns into a double-headed arrow with a short double line in the middle. Hold down the left mouse button, drag down the thick gray line that displays until the pane is the desired size, and then release the mouse button. Split the window vertically with the split bar at the right side of the horizontal scroll bar.

HINT

Restore a split window by double-clicking anywhere on the split bar that divides the panes.

To split a worksheet window with the Window drop-down menu, click Window and then Split. This causes the worksheet to split into four window panes as shown in Figure 5.5. The windows are split by thick gray lines (with a three-dimensional look). To remove a split from a worksheet window, click Window, Remove Split; or, drag the split bars to the upper left corner of the worksheet.

FIGURE 5.5 ***Split Window***

	A	B	C	D	E	F	G	H	I	J	K	L
1	**Name**	**Test 1**	**Test 2**	**Test 3**	**Test 4**	**Test 5**	**Test 6**	**Test 7**	**Test 8**	**Test 9**	**Test 10**	**Test 11**
2												
3	Arnson, Patrick	89%	65%	76%	89%	98%	65%	76%	87%	55%	78%	67%
4	Barclay, Jeanine	78%	66%	87%	90%	92%	82%	100%	84%	67%	86%	82%
5	Calahan, Jack	65%	71%	64%	66%	70%	81%	64%	59%	76%	76%	45%
6	Cumpston, Kurt	89%	91%	90%	93%	86%	80%	84%	93%	95%	81%	96%
7	Dimmitt, Marian	78%	73%	81%	82%	67%	69%	82%	72%	85%	83%	71%
8	Donovan, Nancy	82%	89%	79%	74%	80%	82%	86%	72%	74%	82%	76%
9	Fisher-Edwards, Teri	89%	93%	100%	91%	86%	90%	88%	86%	100%	98%	90%
10	Flanery, Stephanie	58%	45%	63%	51%	60%	59%	63%	52%	66%	67%	53%
11	Heyman, Grover	78%	75%	87%	88%	64%	76%	70%	67%	55%	87%	82%
12	Herbertson, Wynn	92%	80%	93%	90%	86%	84%	95%	100%	98%	88%	95%
13	Jewett, Troy	98%	94%	99%	89%	100%	93%	100%	95%	96%	91%	87%
14	Kwieciak, Kathleen	55%	0%	42%	65%	72%	40%	65%	0%	0%	48%	52%
15	Leibrand, Maxine	78%	69%	83%	87%	84%	69%	80%	82%	88%	79%	83%
16	Markovits, Claude	89%	93%	84%	100%	95%	92%	95%	100%	89%	94%	98%
17	Moonstar, Siana	73%	87%	67%	83%	90%	84%	73%	81%	75%	65%	84%
18	Nyegaard, Curtis	90%	89%	84%	85%	93%	85%	100%	94%	98%	93%	100%
19	Oglesbee, Randy	65%	55%	73%	90%	87%	67%	85%	77%	85%	73%	78%
20	Pherson, Douglas	69%	82%	87%	74%	70%	82%	84%	85%	66%	77%	91%

A window pane will display the active cell. As the insertion point is moved through the pane, another active cell with a blue background may display. This additional active cell displays when the insertion point passes over one of the gray lines that creates the pane. As you move through a worksheet, you may see both active cells—one with a normal background and one with a blue background. If you make a change to the active cell, the change is made in both. If you want only one active cell to display, freeze the window panes by clicking Window and then Freeze Panes. With panes frozen, only the display of the pane with the active cell will change. To unfreeze panes, click Window and then Unfreeze Panes.

Using the mouse, you can move the thick gray lines that divide the window into panes. To do this, position the mouse pointer on the line until it turns into a double-headed arrow with a double line in the middle. Hold down the left mouse button, drag the outline of the gray line to the desired location, and then release the mouse button. If you want to move both the horizontal and vertical lines at the same time, position the mouse pointer on the intersection of the thick gray lines until it turns into a four-headed arrow. Hold down the left mouse button, drag the thick gray lines in the desired direction, and then release the mouse button.

By splitting a worksheet into windows, you can maintain the display of column headings while editing or typing text in cells. You can do the same for row headings. You will be doing this with a worksheet in Exercise 7.

exercise 7

SPLITTING WINDOWS AND EDITING CELLS

1. Open **ExcelWorksheet06**.
2. Save the worksheet with Save As and name it **sec5x07**.
3. Select the entire worksheet and then change the font size to 11 points.
4. Automatically adjust the width of the columns.
5. Make cell A1 active and then split the window by clicking Window and then Split. (This causes the window to split into four panes.)
6. Drag both the horizontal and vertical gray lines by completing the following steps:
   a. Position the mouse pointer on the intersection between the horizontal and vertical lines until it turns into a four-headed black arrow.
   b. Hold down the left mouse button, drag up and to the left until the horizontal gray line is immediately below the first row and the vertical gray line is immediately to the right of the first column, and then release the mouse button. 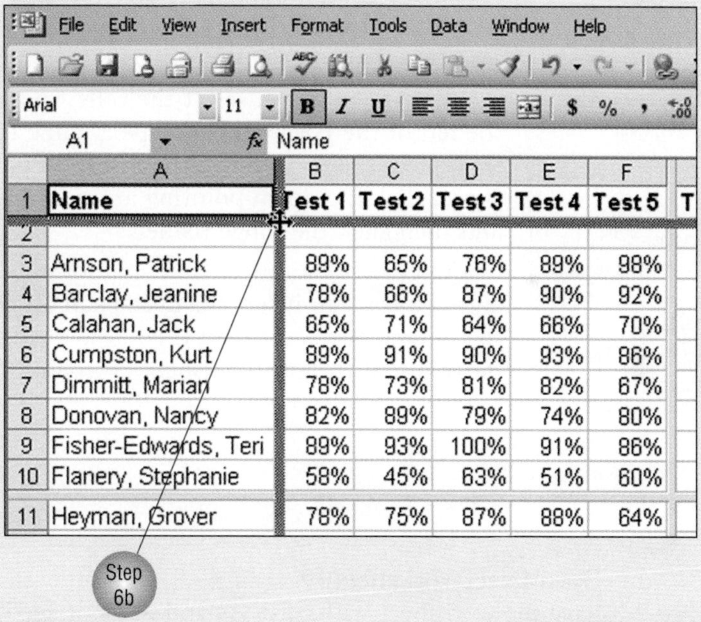
7. Freeze the window panes by clicking Window and then Freeze Panes.
8. Add two rows by completing the following steps:
   a. Select rows 18 and 19.
   b. Click Insert and then Rows.
9. Type the following text in the specified cells:

A18	=	Nauer, Sheryl	A19	=	Nunez, James
B18	=	75	B19	=	98
C18	=	83	C19	=	96
D18	=	85	D19	=	100
E18	=	78	E19	=	90
F18	=	82	F19	=	95
G18	=	80	G19	=	93
H18	=	79	H19	=	88
I18	=	82	I19	=	91
J18	=	92	J19	=	89
K18	=	90	K19	=	100
L18	=	86	L19	=	96
M18	=	84	M19	=	98

10. Edit the text in the following cells:

    D3: Change *76%* to *92%*
    K6: Change *81%* to *74%*
    E8: Change *74%* to *90%*
    M12: Change *89%* to *95%*
    C14: Change *0%* to *70%* ***(Note: Be sure to press Enter to change from the Enter mode to the Ready mode.)***

11. Unfreeze the window panes by clicking Window and then Unfreeze Panes.
12. Remove the panes by clicking Window and then Remove Split.
13. Save the worksheet and then print it in landscape orientation.
14. Close **sec5x07**.

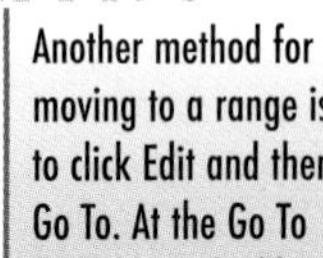

Name a Range
1. Select cells.
2. Click in Name Box button.
3. Type range name.
4. Press Enter.

HINT

Another method for moving to a range is to click Edit and then Go To. At the Go To dialog box, double-click the range name.

Working with Ranges

A selected group of cells is referred to as a ***range***. A range of cells can be formatted, moved, copied, or deleted. You can also name a range of cells and then move the insertion point to the range or use a named range as part of a formula.

To name a range, select the cells, and then click in the Name Box button to the left of the Formula bar. Type a name for the range (do not use a space) and then press Enter. To move the insertion point to a specific range and select the range, click the down-pointing arrow at the right side of the Name Box button and then click the range name.

You can use a range name in a formula. For example, if a range is named *Profit* and you want to insert the average of all cells in the *Profit* range, you would make the desired cell active and then type =AVERAGE(Profit). You can use a named range in the current worksheet or in another worksheet within the workbook.

exercise 8

NAMING A RANGE AND USING A RANGE IN A FORMULA

1. Open **ExcelWorksheet09**.
2. Save the worksheet with Save As and name it **sec5x08**.
3. Click the *Sheet2* tab and then type the following text in the specified cell:

A1	=	EQUIPMENT USAGE REPORT
A2	=	Yearly Hours
A3	=	Avoidable Delays
A4	=	Unavoidable Delays
A5	=	Total Delay Hours
A6	=	(leave blank)
A7	=	Repairs
A8	=	Servicing
A9	=	Total Repair/Servicing Hours

4. Make the following formatting changes to the worksheet:
    a. Automatically adjust the width of column A.
    b. Center and bold the text in cells A1 and A2.

5. Select a range of cells in worksheet 1, name the range, and use it in a formula in worksheet 2 by completing the following steps:
   a. Make worksheet 1 active by clicking the *Sheet1* tab.
   b. Select cells B4 through M4.
   c. Click in the Name Box button to the left of the Formula bar.
   d. Type **adhours** (for Avoidable Delays Hours) and then press Enter.
   e. Click the *Sheet2* tab to make worksheet 2 active.
   f. Make cell B3 active.
   g. Type the equation **=SUM(adhours)** and then press Enter.

Step 5d

adhours | fx 19

	A	B	C
1			
2	Hours	January	February
3	Total Hours Available	2,300	2,430
4	Avoidable Delays	19	12
5	Unavoidable Delays	9	8

DATE | fx =SUM(adhours)

	A	B	C
1	EQUIPMENT USAGE REPORT		
2	Yearly Hours		
3	Avoidable Delays	=SUM(adhours)	
4	Unavoidable Delays		
5	Total Delay Hours		
6			
7	Repairs		
8	Servicing		
9	Total Repair/Servicing Hours		

Step 5g

6. Make worksheet 1 active and then complete the following steps:
   a. Select cells B5 through M5 and then name the range *udhours*.
   b. Make worksheet 2 active, make cell B4 active, and then type the equation **=SUM(udhours)**.
   c. Make worksheet 1 active.
   d. Select cells B6 through M6 and then name the range *rhours*.
   e. Make worksheet 2 active, make cell B7 active, and then type the equation **=SUM(rhours)**.
   f. Make worksheet 1 active.
   g. Select cells B7 through M7 and then name the range *shours*.
   h. Make worksheet 2 active, make cell B8 active, and then type the equation **=SUM(shours)**.
7. With worksheet 2 still active, make the following changes:
   a. Make cell B5 active.
   b. Click the AutoSum button on the Standard toolbar and then press Enter.
   c. Make cell B9 active.
   d. Double-click the AutoSum button on the Standard toolbar.
8. Save the workbook and then print worksheet 2.
9. Make worksheet 1 active and then move to the range *adhours* by clicking the down-pointing arrow at the right side of the Name Box button and then clicking *adhours* at the drop-down list.
10. Close **sec5x08**.

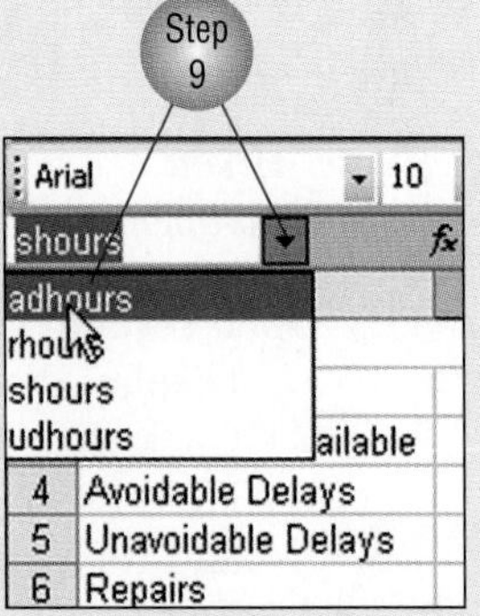

Working with Windows

You can open multiple workbooks in Excel and arrange the open workbooks in the Excel window. With multiple workbooks open, you can cut and paste or copy and paste cell entries from one workbook to another using the same techniques discussed earlier in this chapter with the exception that you activate the destination workbook before executing the Paste command.

Opening Multiple Workbooks

With multiple workbooks open, you can move or copy information between workbooks or compare the contents of several workbooks. The maximum number of workbooks that you can have open at one time depends on the memory of your computer system and the amount of information in each workbook. When you open a new workbook, it is placed on top of the original workbook. Once multiple workbooks are opened, you can resize the workbooks to see all or a portion of them on the screen.

Open multiple workbooks at one time at the Open dialog box. If workbooks are adjacent, display the Open dialog box, click the first workbook name to be opened, hold down the Shift key, and then click the last workbook name to be opened. If the workbooks are nonadjacent, click the first workbook name to be opened, and then hold down the Ctrl key while clicking the remaining desired workbook names. Release the Shift key or the Ctrl key and then click the Open button.

To see what workbooks are currently open, click Window on the Menu bar. The names of the open workbooks display at the bottom of the drop-down menu. The workbook name with the check mark in front of it is the *active* workbook. The active workbook is the workbook containing the active cell. To make one of the other workbooks active, click the desired workbook.

Closing Multiple Workbooks

Close all open workbooks at one time by holding down the Shift key, clicking File on the Menu bar, and then clicking Close All. The Close option becomes the Close All option when the Shift key is down.

exercise 9 OPENING AND CLOSING MULTIPLE WORKBOOKS

(Note: If you are using Excel on a network system that contains a virus checker, you may not be able to open multiple workbooks at one time.)

1. Open several workbooks at the same time by completing the following steps:
   a. Display the Open dialog box.
   b. Click the workbook named **ExcelWorksheet02**.
   c. Hold down the Ctrl key, click ***ExcelWorksheet04***, and then click ***ExcelWorksheet06***.
   d. Release the Ctrl key and then click the Open button in the dialog box.
2. Make **ExcelWorksheet06** the active workbook by clicking Window and then clicking 3 at the drop-down menu.
3. Make **ExcelWorksheet02** the active workbook by clicking Window and then clicking 2 at the drop-down menu.
4. Close all open workbooks by completing the following steps:
   a. Hold down the Shift key.
   b. Click File on the Menu bar.
   c. Click Close All.
   d. Release the Shift key.

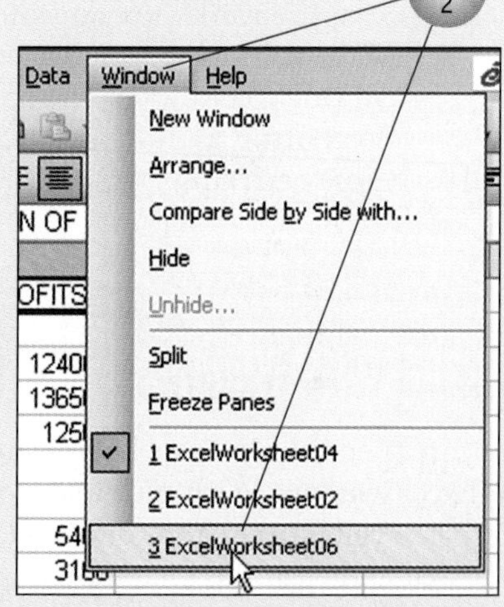

Arranging Workbooks

If you have more than one workbook open, you can arrange the workbooks at the Arrange Windows dialog box shown in Figure 5.6. To display this dialog box, open several workbooks, click Window, and then click Arrange. At the Arrange Windows dialog box, click *Tiled* to display a portion of each open workbook. Figure 5.7 displays four tiled workbooks.

Arrange Workbooks

1. Click Window, Arrange.
2. At Arrange Windows dialog box, click desired arrangement.
3. Click OK.

FIGURE 5.6 ***Arrange Windows Dialog Box***

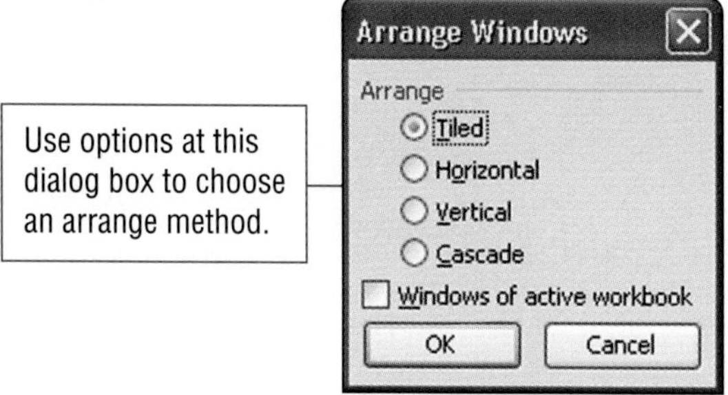

FIGURE 5.7 ***Tiled Workbooks***

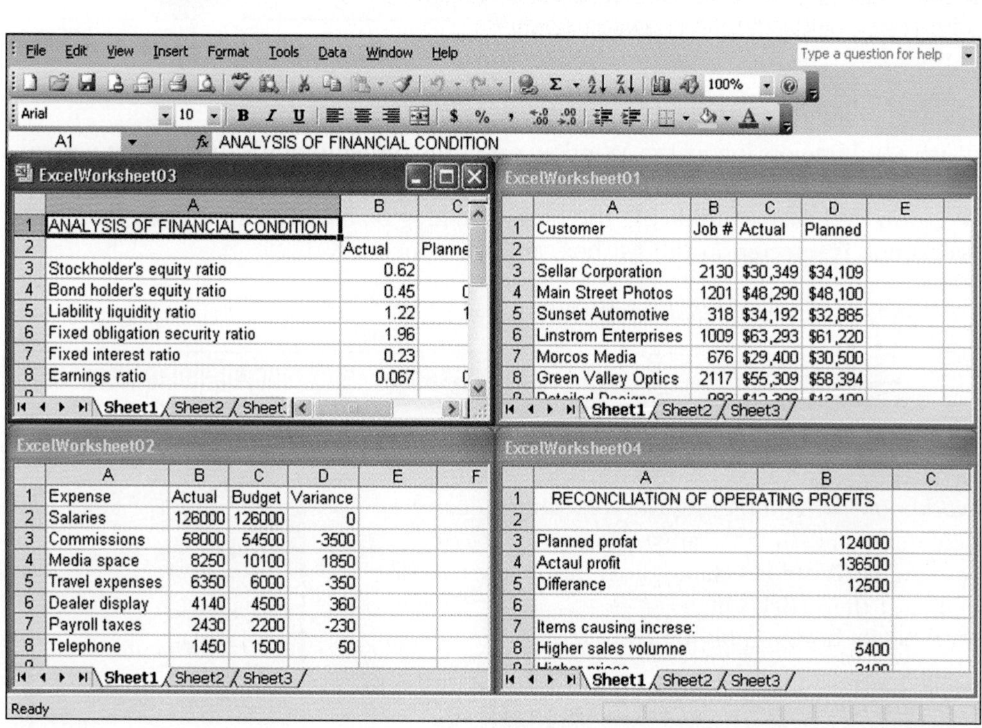

Choose the *Horizontal* option at the Arrange Windows dialog box and the open workbooks display across the screen. The *Vertical* option displays the open workbooks up and down the window. The last option, *Cascade*, displays the Title bar of each open workbook. Figure 5.8 shows four cascaded workbooks.

FIGURE 5.8 ***Cascaded Workbooks***

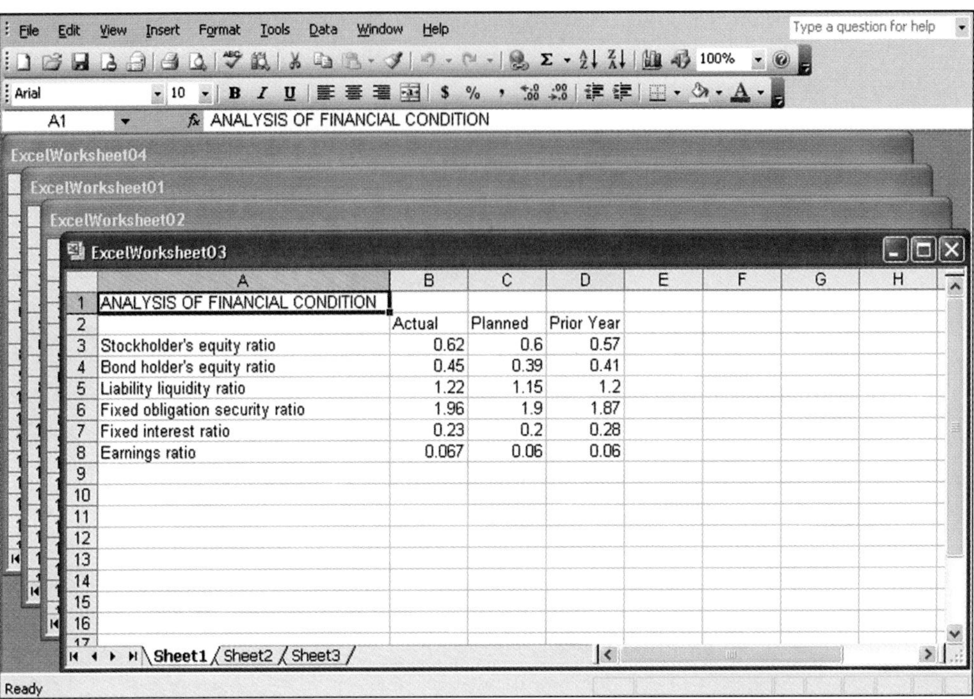

Hiding/Unhiding Workbooks

With the Hide option at the Window drop-down menu, you can hide the active workbook. If a workbook has been hidden, redisplay the workbook by clicking Window and then Unhide. At the Unhide dialog box, make sure the desired workbook is selected in the list box, and then click OK.

exercise 10 ARRANGING AND HIDING/UNHIDING WORKBOOKS

1. Open the following workbooks: **ExcelWorksheet01**, **ExcelWorksheet02**, **ExcelWorksheet03**, and **ExcelWorksheet04**.
2. Tile the workbooks by completing the following steps:
   a. Click Window and then Arrange.
   b. At the Arrange Windows dialog box, make sure *Tiled* is selected, and then click OK.

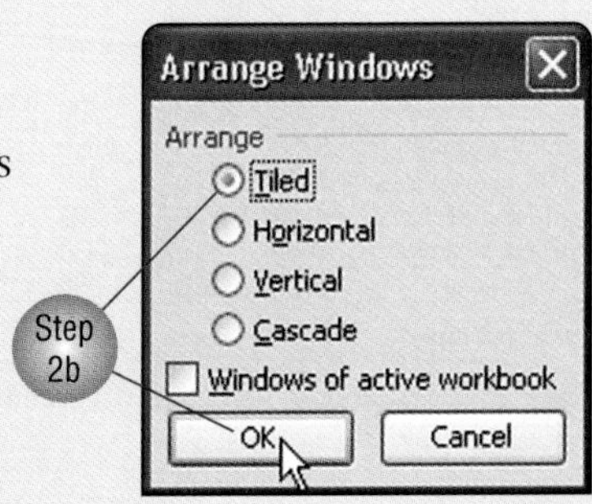

3. Tile the workbooks horizontally by completing the following steps:
   a. Click Window and then Arrange.
   b. At the Arrange Windows dialog box, click *Horizontal*.
   c. Click OK.
4. Cascade the workbooks by completing the following steps:
   a. Click Window and then Arrange.
   b. At the Arrange Windows dialog box, click *Cascade*.

c. Click OK.

5. Hide and unhide workbooks by completing the following steps:
   a. Click the ExcelWorksheet01 title bar to make it the active workbook.
   b. Click Window and then Hide.
   c. Click the ExcelWorksheet04 title bar to make it the active workbook.
   d. Click Window and then Hide.
   e. Click Window and then Unhide.
   f. At the Unhide dialog box, click ***ExcelWorksheet01*** in the list box, and then click OK.
   g. Click Window and then Unhide.
   h. At the Unhide dialog box, make sure **ExcelWorksheet04** is selected in the list box, and then click OK.

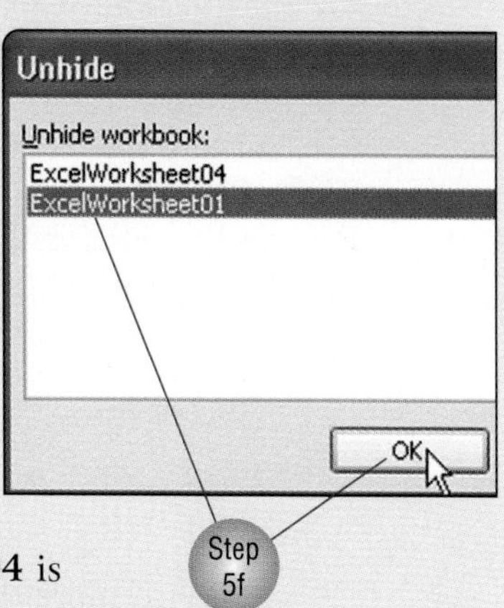

6. Close all of the open workbooks by holding down the Shift key, clicking File, and then clicking Close All. (If a message displays asking you to save the worksheet, click No.)

Sizing and Moving Workbooks

The Maximize and Minimize buttons in the upper right corner of the active workbook window can be used to change the size of the window. The Maximize button is the button in the upper right corner of the active workbook immediately to the left of the Close button. (The Close button is the button containing the *X*.) The Minimize button is located immediately to the left of the Maximize button.

Maximize

Minimize

Close

Restore

If you arrange all open workbooks and then click the Maximize button in the active workbook, the active workbook expands to fill the screen. In addition, the Maximize button changes to the Restore button. To return the active workbook back to its size before it was maximized, click the Restore button.

Clicking the Minimize button causes the active workbook to be reduced and positioned as a button on the Taskbar. In addition, the Minimize button changes to the Restore button. To maximize a workbook that has been reduced, click the button on the Taskbar representing the workbook.

exercise 11

MINIMIZING, MAXIMIZING, AND RESTORING WORKBOOKS

1. Open **ExcelWorksheet01**.
2. Maximize **ExcelWorksheet01** by clicking the Maximize button at the right side of the workbook Title bar. (The Maximize button is the button at the right side of the Title bar, immediately to the left of the Close button.)
3. Open **ExcelWorksheet03** and **ExcelWorksheet05**.
4. Make the following changes to the open workbooks:
   a. Tile the workbooks.
   b. Make **ExcelWorksheet01** the active workbook (Title bar displays with a blue background [the background color may vary depending on how Windows is customized]).

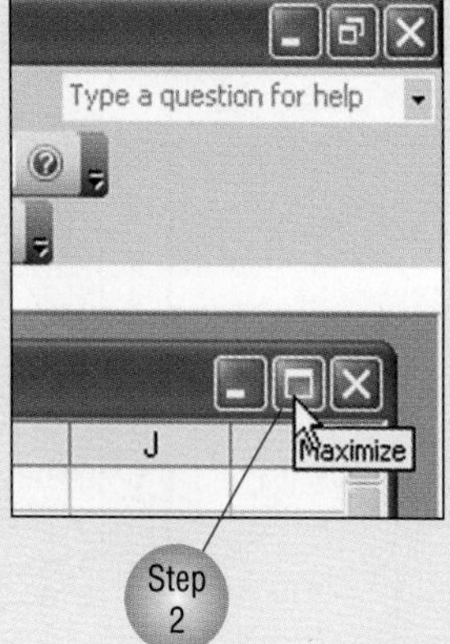

c. Minimize **ExcelWorksheet01** by clicking the Minimize button that displays at the right side of the Title bar.
d. Make **ExcelWorksheet03** the active workbook and then minimize it.
e. Minimize **ExcelWorksheet05**.
5. Close all workbooks by holding down the Shift key, clicking File, and then clicking Close All.

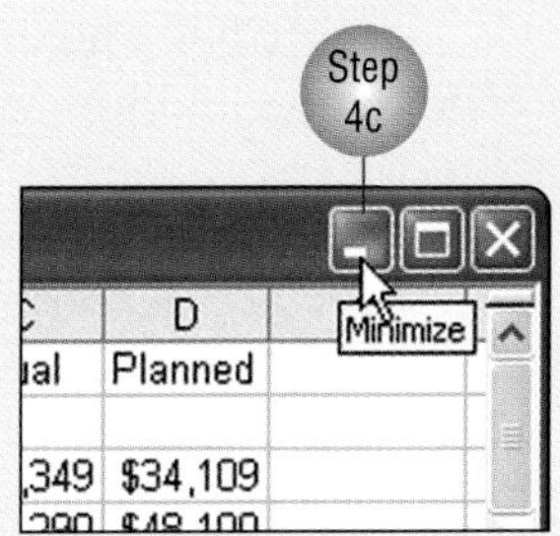

Moving, Copying, and Pasting Data

With more than one workbook open, you can move, copy, and/or paste data from one workbook to another. To move, copy, and/or paste data between workbooks, use the cutting and pasting options you learned earlier in this chapter, together with the information about windows in this chapter.

exercise 12

COPYING SELECTED CELLS FROM ONE OPEN WORKSHEET TO ANOTHER

1. Open **ExcelWorksheet35**.
2. If you just completed Exercise 11, click the Maximize button so the worksheet fills the entire worksheet window.
3. Save the worksheet and name it **sec5x12**.
4. With **sec5x12** still open, open **ExcelWorksheet01**.
5. Select and then copy text from **ExcelWorksheet01** to **sec5x12** by completing the following steps:
   a. With **ExcelWorksheet01** the active workbook, select cells A5 through D10.
   b. Click the Copy button on the Standard toolbar.
   c. Click Window and then click *2 sec5x12*.

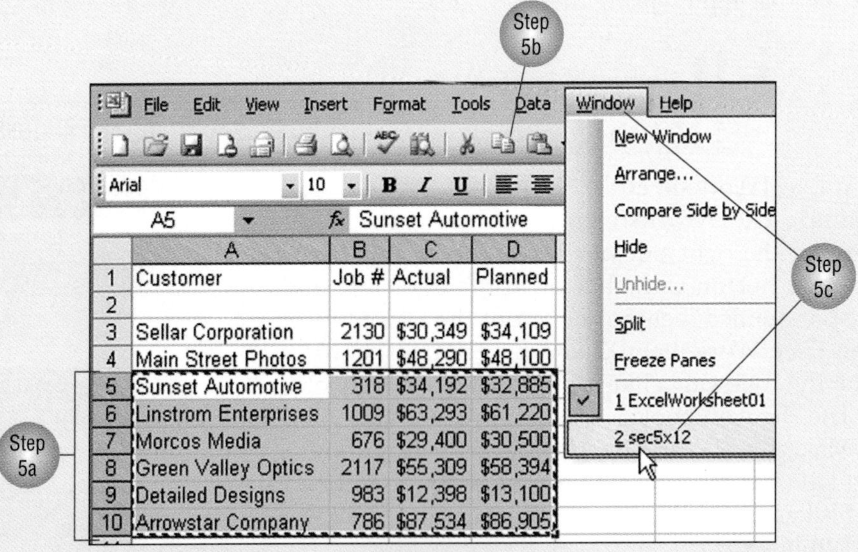

d. Make cell A7 the active cell and then click the Paste button on the Standard toolbar.

6. Select cells A1 through D12 in **sec5x11** and then apply the Colorful 1 autoformat.
7. Print **sec5x12** horizontally and vertically centered on the page.
8. Save the worksheet again with the same name (**sec5x12**).
9. Close **sec5x12**.
10. Close **ExcelWorksheet01**.

Step 5d

Arial 10 B I U Paste

A7

	A	B	C	D
1	FEBRUARY			
2	Customer	Job #	Actual	Planned
3	Real Photography	129	$42,350	$41,000
4	Jenkins Corporation	3310	$88,450	$90,000
5	Bridgway Electronics	1023	$19,340	$17,500
6	Moss Bay Productions	894	$68,340	$65,000
7				

Linking Data between Worksheets

In workbooks containing multiple worksheets or between related workbooks, you may want to create a link between worksheets or workbooks with data in cells. When data is linked, a change made in a linked cell is automatically made to the other cells in the link. Links can be made with individual cells or with a range of cells.

Linking cells between worksheets creates what is called a ***dynamic link***. Dynamic links are useful in worksheets or workbooks that need to maintain consistency and control over critical data. The worksheet that contains the original data is called the ***source*** worksheet and the worksheet relying on the source worksheet for the data in the link is called the ***dependent*** worksheet.

To create a link, make active the cell containing the data to be linked (or select the cells), and then click the Copy button on the Standard toolbar. Make active the worksheet where you want to paste the cell or cells, click Edit, and then click Paste Special. This displays the Paste Special dialog box as shown in Figure 5.9.

QUICK STEPS

Link Data between Worksheets

1. Select cells.
2. Click Copy button.
3. Click desired worksheet tab.
4. Click in desired cell.
5. Click Edit, Paste Special.
6. Click Paste Link button.

FIGURE 5.9 ***Paste Special Dialog Box***

HINT

To open the source of a link, open the dependent workbook, click Edit, and then click Links. Click the workbook name in the Source box and then click the Open Source button.

At the Paste Special dialog box, specify what in the cell you want to copy and what operators you want to include, and then click the Paste Link button. When a change is made to the cell or cells in the source worksheet, the change is automatically made to the linked cell or cells in the dependent worksheet.

exercise 13

LINKING CELLS BETWEEN WORKSHEETS

1. Open **ExcelWorksheet34**.
2. Save the worksheet with Save As and name it **sec5x13**.
3. Make the following changes to the worksheet:
   a. Change the text in cell A1 from *First Quarter* to *FIRST HALF, 2004*.
   b. Insert the formula **=B3-C3** in cell D3.
   c. Copy the formula in cell D3 down to cells D4 through D9.
4. Copy data in the worksheet to *Sheet2* by completing the following steps:
   a. Select cells A1 through D9.
   b. Click the Copy button on the Standard toolbar.
   c. Click the *Sheet2* tab.
   d. With cell A1 the active cell, click the Paste button on the Standard toolbar.
   e. Automatically adjust the widths of the cells.
   f. Select cells C3 through C9 and then delete the cell data.
5. Link cells C3 through C9 from *Sheet1* to *Sheet2* by completing the following steps:
   a. Click the *Sheet1* tab.
   b. Select cells C3 through C9.
   c. Click the Copy button on the Standard toolbar.
   d. Click the *Sheet2* tab.
   e. Make cell C3 active.
   f. Click Edit and then Paste Special.
   g. At the Paste Special dialog box, make sure *All* is selected in the *Paste* section of the dialog box, and then click the Paste Link button.

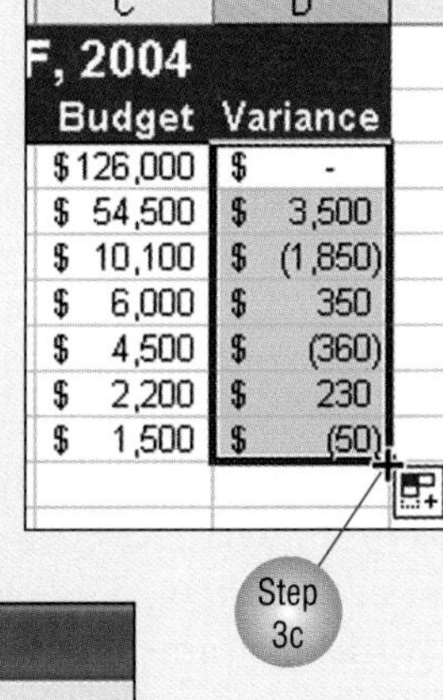

C
D
F, 2004
Budget
Variance
$126,000
$ -
$ 54,500
$ 3,500
$ 10,100
$ (1,850)
$ 6,000
$ 350
$ 4,500
$ (360)
$ 2,200
$ 230
$ 1,500
$ (50)
Step 3c

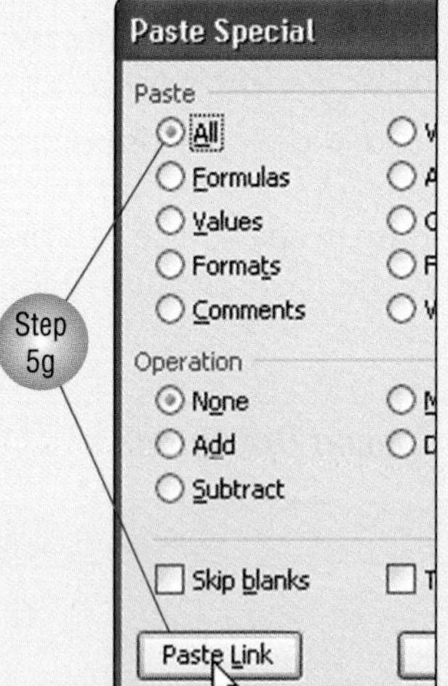

6. With *Sheet2* still the active worksheet, make the following changes to the specified cells:

   A1: Change *FIRST HALF, 2004* to *SECOND HALF, 2004*
   B3: Change *$126,000* to *123,500*
   B4: Change *$58,000* to *53,000*
   B6: Change *$6,350* to *6,125*

7. Make *Sheet1* the active worksheet and then make the following changes to some of the linked cells:

   C3: Change *$126,000* to *128,000*
   C4: Change *$54,500* to *56,000*
   C8: Change *$2,200* to *2,400*

	A	B	C	D
1	SECOND HALF, 2004			
2	Expense	Actual	Budget	Variance
3	Salaries	$123,500	$126,000	$ (2,500)
4	Commissions	$ 53,000	$ 54,500	$ (1,500)
5	Media space	$ 8,250	$ 10,100	$ (1,850)
6	Travel expenses	$ 6,125	$ 6,000	$ 125
7	Dealer display	$ 4,140	$ 4,500	$ (360)
8	Payroll taxes	$ 2,430	$ 2,200	$ 230
9	Telephone	$ 1,450	$ 1,500	$ (50)

Step 6

8. Click the *Sheet2* tab and notice that the values in cells C3, C4, and C8 automatically changed (because they are linked to *Sheet1*).
9. Save the worksheet with the same name (**sec5x13**).
10. Print both worksheets in the workbook.
11. Close **sec5x13**.

Linking Worksheets with a 3-D Reference

In multiple worksheet workbooks, you can use a 3-D reference to analyze data in the same cell or range of cells. A 3-D reference includes the cell or range of cells, preceded by a range of worksheet names. For example, you can add all of the values contained in cells in B2 through B5 in worksheets 1 and 2 in a workbook using a 3-D reference. To do this, you would complete these basic steps:

1. Make active the cell where you want to enter the function.
2. Type =SUM(and then click the *Sheet1* tab.
3. Hold down the Shift key and then click the *Sheet2* tab.
4. Select cells B2 through B5 in the worksheet.
5. Type) (this is the closing parenthesis that ends the formula) and then press Enter.

exercise 14 — LINKING WORKSHEETS WITH A 3-D REFERENCE

1. Open **ExcelWorksheet33**.
2. Save the workbook with Save As and name it **sec5x14**.
3. Make sure *Sales 2002* is the active worksheet.
4. Select columns B, C, and D and change the width to 14.00.
5. Make the following changes to the *Sales 2002* worksheet:
   a. Make cell B10 active.
   b. Click the Center button and then the Bold button on the Formatting toolbar.

c. Type **January Sales** and then press Alt + Enter.
d. Type **2002-2004** and then press Enter.

6. Link the *Sales 2002*, *Sales 2003*, and *Sales 2004* worksheets with a 3-D reference by completing the following steps:
   a. With cell B11 active, type =SUM(.
   b. Hold down the Shift key, click the *Sales 2004* sheet tab, and then release the Shift key. (This selects all three sheet tabs.)
   c. Select cells B3 through B8.
   d. Type) and then press Enter.
   e. Make cell B11 active.
   f. Click the Currency Style button on the Formatting toolbar and then click twice on the Decrease Decimal button.

DATE =SUM('Sales 2002:Sales 2004'!B3:B8

	A	B	C	D
1	FIRST-QUARTER SALES - 2002			
2	Customer	January	February	March
3	Lakeside Trucking	$ 84,231	$ 73,455	$ 97,549
4	Gresham Machines	$ 33,199	$ 40,390	$ 50,112
5	Real Photography	$ 30,891	$ 35,489	$ 36,400
6	Genesis Productions	$ 72,190	$ 75,390	$ 83,219
7	Landower Company	$ 22,188	$ 14,228	$ 38,766
8	Jewell Enterprises	$ 19,764	$ 50,801	$ 32,188
9				
10		January Sales 2002-2004		
11		=SUM('Sales 2002:Sales 2004'!B3:B8		
12		SUM(number1, [number2], ...)		

7. Complete steps similar to those in Step 5 to add *February Sales 2002-2004* (on two lines) in cell C10 and complete steps similar to those in Step 6 to insert the formula with the 3-D reference in cell C11.
8. Complete steps similar to those in Step 5 to add *March Sales 2002-2004* (on two lines) in cell D10 and complete steps similar to those in Step 6 to insert the formula with the 3-D reference in cell D11.
9. Save the workbook again with the same name (**sec5x14**).
10. Print the *Sales 2002* worksheet of the workbook.
11. Close **sec5x14**.

Copying and Pasting a Worksheet between Programs

Microsoft Office is a suite that allows integration, which is the combining of data from two or more programs into one file. Integration can occur by copying and pasting data between programs. The program containing the data to be copied is called the ***source*** program and the program where the data is pasted is called the ***destination*** program. For example, you can create a worksheet in Excel and then copy it to a Word document. The steps to copy and paste between programs are basically the same as copying and pasting within the same program.

When copying data between worksheets or from one program to another, you can copy and paste, copy and link, or copy and embed the data. Consider the following when choosing a method for copying data:

- Copy data in the source program and paste it in the destination program when the data will not need to be edited.
- Copy data in the source program and then link it in the destination program when the data is updated regularly in the source program and you want the update reflected in the destination program.

- Copy data in the source program and then embed it in the destination program when the data will be edited in the destination program (with the tools of the source program).

Earlier in this chapter, you copied and pasted cells within and between worksheets and you also copied and linked cells between worksheets. You can also copy and link data between programs. Copy and embed data using options at the Paste Special dialog box. In Exercise 15, you will copy cells in a worksheet and then embed the cells in a Word document. With the worksheet embedded in a Word document, double-click the worksheet and Excel tools display in the document for editing the worksheet.

exercise 15

COPYING AND PASTING A WORKSHEET INTO A WORD DOCUMENT

1. Open the Word program and then open **WordLetter02**.
2. Save the document and name it **seWordc5x15**.
3. With **seWordc5x15** still open, make Excel the active program.
4. Open **ExcelWorksheet03**.
5. Save the worksheet with Save As and name it **sec5x15**.
6. Make the following changes to the worksheet:
   a. Select cells B3 through D8 and then click the Percent Style button on the Formatting toolbar.
   b. Select cells A1 through D8 and then apply the Classic 2 autoformat.
7. Save the worksheet again with the same name (**sec5x15**).
8. Copy the worksheet to the letter in **seWordc5x15** by completing the following steps:
   a. Select cells A1 through D8.
   b. Click the Copy button on the Standard toolbar.
   c. Click the button on the Taskbar representing the Word document **seWordc5x15**.
   d. Position the insertion point a double space below the first paragraph of text in the body of the letter.
   e. Click Edit and then Paste Special.
   f. At the Paste Special dialog box, click *Microsoft Office Excel Worksheet Object* in the *As* list box, and then click OK.

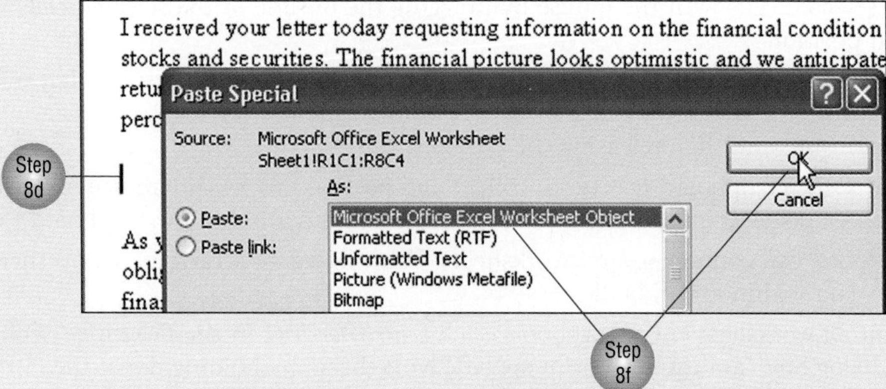

9. Edit a few of the cells in the worksheet by completing the following steps:
   a. Double-click anywhere in the worksheet. (This displays the Excel toolbar for editing.)
   b. Click in each of the following cells and make the change indicated:

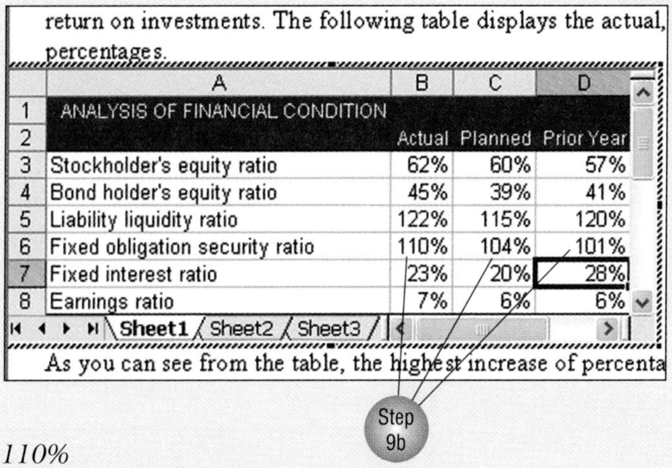

      B6: Change *196%* to *110%*
      C6: Change *190%* to *104%*
      D6: Change *187%* to *101%*

   c. Click outside the worksheet to remove the Excel tools (and deselect the worksheet).
10. Save, print, and then close **seWordc5x15**.
11. Exit Word.
12. With Excel the active program, close **sec5x15**.

return on investments. The following table displays the actual, percentages.

	A	B	C	D
1	ANALYSIS OF FINANCIAL CONDITION			
2		Actual	Planned	Prior Year
3	Stockholder's equity ratio	62%	60%	57%
4	Bond holder's equity ratio	45%	39%	41%
5	Liability liquidity ratio	122%	115%	120%
6	Fixed obligation security ratio	110%	104%	101%
7	Fixed interest ratio	23%	20%	28%
8	Earnings ratio	7%	6%	6%

Sheet1 / Sheet2 / Sheet3

As you can see from the table, the highest increase of percenta

Step 9b

CHAPTER summary

- Move selected cells and cell contents in and between worksheets using the Cut, Copy, and Paste buttons on the Standard toolbar; dragging with the mouse; or with options from the Edit drop-down menu.
- Move selected cells with the mouse by dragging the outline of the selected cells to the desired position.
- Copy selected cells with the mouse by holding down the Ctrl key and the left mouse button, dragging the outline of the selected cells to the desired location, releasing the left mouse button, and then releasing the Ctrl key.
- Use the Office Clipboard feature to collect and paste up to 24 different items within and between worksheets and workbooks. To use this feature, display the Clipboard task pane.
- A workbook can contain several worksheets. You can create a variety of worksheets for related data within a workbook.
- To print all worksheets in a workbook, click *Entire workbook* in the *Print what* section of the Print dialog box. You can also print specific worksheets by holding down the Ctrl key and then clicking the tabs of the worksheets you want printed.
- Perform maintenance activities, such as deleting and renaming, on worksheets within a workbook by clicking the right mouse button on a sheet tab, and then clicking the desired option at the shortcut menu.

- You can use the mouse to move or copy worksheets. To move a worksheet, drag the worksheet tab with the mouse. To copy a worksheet, hold down the Ctrl key, and then drag the worksheet tab with the mouse.
- Use the Tab Color option at the worksheet shortcut menu to apply a color to a worksheet tab.
- Manage more than one worksheet at a time by first selecting the worksheets. Use the mouse together with the Shift key to select adjacent worksheet tabs and use the mouse together with the Ctrl key to select nonadjacent worksheet tabs.
- Hide a worksheet by clicking Format, pointing to Sheet, and then clicking Hide. To unhide a worksheet, click Format, point to Sheet, and then click Unhide. At the Unhide dialog box, double-click the name of the worksheet you want to unhide.
- If you want formatting to apply to multiple worksheets in a workbook, select the tabs of the desired worksheets and then apply the formatting.
- Split the worksheet window into panes with the Split option from the Window drop-down menu or with the split bars on the horizontal and vertical scroll bars.
- Remove the split window by clicking Window and then Remove Split; or drag the split bars.
- Freeze window panes by clicking Window and then Freeze Panes. When panes are frozen, only the display of the pane with the active cell changes. Unfreeze window panes by clicking Window and then Unfreeze Panes.
- A selected group of cells is referred to as a range. A range can be named and used in a formula. Name a range by typing the name in the Name Box button located to the left of the Formula bar.
- To open multiple workbooks that are adjacent, display the Open dialog box, click the first workbook, hold down the Shift key, click the last workbook, and then click the Open button. If workbooks are nonadjacent, click the first workbook, hold down the Ctrl key, click the desired workbooks, and then click the Open button.
- Click Window on the Menu bar to see a list of open workbooks.
- Close all open workbooks at one time by holding down the Shift key, clicking File and then clicking Close All.
- Arrange multiple workbooks in a window with options at the Arrange Windows dialog box.
- Click the Maximize button located at the right side of the Title bar of the active workbook to make the workbook fill the entire window area. Click the Minimize button to shrink the active workbook to a button on the Taskbar. Click the Restore button to return the workbook to its previous size.
- You can move, copy, and/or paste data between workbooks.
- Copy and then link data if you make changes in the source worksheet and you want the changes reflected in the destination worksheet. The worksheet containing the original data is called the source worksheet and the worksheet relying on the source worksheet for data in the link is called the dependent worksheet.
- Copy and link data using the Paste Special dialog box.
- You can copy data from a document in one program (called the source program) and paste the data into a file in another program (called the destination program).
- Use a 3-D reference to analyze data in the same cell or range of cells.
- You can copy and then paste, link, or embed data between programs in the Office suite. Integrating is the combining of data from two or more programs in the Office suite.

FEATURES summary

FEATURE	BUTTON	MENU	KEYBOARD
Cut selected cells		Edit, Cut	Ctrl + X
Paste selected cells		Edit, Paste	Ctrl + V
Copy selected cells		Edit, Copy	Ctrl + C
Clipboard task pane		Edit, Office Clipboard	Ctrl + C, Ctrl + C
Hide worksheet		Format, Sheet, Hide	
Unhide dialog box		Format, Sheet, Unhide	
Split window into panes		Window, Split	
Freeze window panes		Window, Freeze Panes	
Unfreeze window panes		Window, Unfreeze Panes	
Arrange Windows dialog box		Window, Arrange	
Paste Special dialog box		Edit, Paste Special	

CONCEPTS check

Completion: On a blank sheet of paper, indicate the correct term, symbol, or command for each description.

1. To copy selected cells with the mouse, hold down this key while dragging the outline of the selected cells to the desired location.
2. Press Ctrl + C twice and this task pane displays.
3. Click this option at the Print dialog box to print all worksheets in the workbook.
4. Use this option at the worksheet shortcut menu to apply a color to a worksheet tab.
5. To hide a worksheet, click Format, point to this, and then click Hide.
6. To split a window using a split bar, position the mouse pointer on the split bar until the mouse pointer turns into this.
7. Clicking Window and then Split causes the active worksheet to be split into this number of windows.

8. To see what workbooks are currently open, click this option on the Menu bar.
9. To close all open workbooks at the same time, hold down this key while clicking File and then Close All.
10. Arrange all open workbooks with options from this dialog box.
11. Click this button to shrink the active workbook to a button on the Taskbar.
12. Click this button to return the workbook back to its original size.
13. Click this button to make the active workbook fill the entire window area.
14. When copying and pasting data between programs, the program containing the original data is called this.
15. List the steps you would complete to open all of the following workbooks at one time: ExcelWorksheet02, ExcelWorksheet03, and ExcelWorksheet05.
16. List the steps you would complete to copy a range of cells from one workbook to another.

SKILLS check

Assessment 1

1. Open **ExcelWorksheet34**.
2. Save the worksheet with Save As and name it **sec5sc01**.
3. Make the following changes to the worksheet:
   a. Insert a column between columns C and D. (The new column will be column D.)
   b. Move the content of cells B2 through B9 to D2 through D9.
   c. Delete the blank column B.
   d. Insert a formula in cell D3 that subtracts the Actual amount from the Budget amount.
   e. Copy the formula in cell D3 down to cells D4 through D9.
4. Save, print, and then close **sec5sc01**.

Assessment 2

1. Open **ExcelWorksheet05**.
2. Save the worksheet with Save As and name it **sec5sc02**.
3. Make the following changes:
   a. Copy cells A1 through C8 to *Sheet2*.
   b. With *Sheet2* active, make the following changes:

      A1: Change *January* to *February*
      B3: Change *35* to *40*
      B6: Change *24* to *20*
      B7: Change *15* to *20*
      C4: Change *$19.00* to *20.15*
      C6: Change *$16.45* to *17.45*

   c. Automatically adjust the width of column A.
   d. Copy cells A1 through C8 to *Sheet3*.
   e. With *Sheet3* active, make the following changes:

      A1: Change *February* to *March*
      B4: Change *20* to *35*
      B8: Change *15* to *20*

f. Automatically adjust the width of column A.
4. Rename *Sheet1* to *Jan. Payroll*, *Sheet2* to *Feb. Payroll*, and *Sheet3* to *Mar. Payroll*.
5. Change the color of the *Jan. Payroll* sheet tab to green, the color of the *Feb. Payroll* tab to yellow, and the color of the *Mar. Payroll* tab to red.
6. Save the worksheets again and then print all worksheets in the **sec5sc02** workbook.
7. Close **sec5sc02**.

Assessment 3

1. Open **ExcelWorksheet09**.
2. Save the worksheet with Save As and name it **sec5sc03**.
3. Make the following changes to the worksheet:
   a. Split the window.
   b. Drag the intersection of the horizontal and vertical gray lines so that the horizontal gray line is immediately below row 9 and the vertical gray line is immediately to the right of column A.
   c. Freeze the window panes.
   d. Insert a new row 8 and then type the following in the specified cells:

      A8 = **Loaned Out**
      B8 = **10**
      C8 = **0**
      D8 = **5**
      E8 = **0**
      F8 = **11**
      G8 = **3**
      H8 = **16**
      I8 = **0**
      J8 = **0**
      K8 = **5**
      L8 = **0**
      M8 = **0**

   e. Remove the split.
   f. Select rows 1 through 10 and then change the row height to 18.00.
4. Print the worksheet in landscape orientation (it will print on two pages) so the row titles print on each page.
5. Save and then close **sec5sc03**.

Assessment 4

1. Open **ExcelWorksheet01**.
2. Save the worksheet with Save As and name it **sec5sc04**.
3. Make the following changes to the worksheet:
   a. Type **Difference** in cell E1.
   b. Insert the formula *=D3-C3* in cell E3 and then copy it down to E4 through E10.
   c. Select cells E3 through E10 and then name the range *Difference*.
   d. Type **Max Difference** in cell A13.
   e. Insert the formula *=MAX(Difference)* in cell B13.
   f. Type **Min Difference** in cell A14.
   g. Insert the formula *=MIN(Difference)* in cell B14.
   h. Type **Ave Difference** in cell A15.
   i. Insert the formula *=AVERAGE(Difference)* in cell B15.

j. Select cells B13 through B15 and then click the Currency Style button on the Formatting toolbar.
k. With cells B13 through B15 selected, click twice the Decrease Decimal button.
l. Automatically adjust the width of column B.
m. Bold and center the text in cells A1 through E1.
4. Save and then print **sec5sc04**.
5. Make the following changes to the worksheet:
   a. Change *63,293* in cell C6 to *55,500*.
   b. Change *12,398* in cell C9 to *13,450*.
   c. Create a custom header that prints *Customer Jobs* centered at the top of the page.
6. Save, print, and then close **sec5sc04**.

Assessment 5

1. Create the worksheet shown in Figure 5.10 (change the width of column A to 21.00).
2. Save the worksheet and name it **sec5sc05**.
3. With **sec5sc05** still open, open **ExcelWorksheet09**.
4. Select and copy the following cells from **ExcelWorksheet09** to **sec5sc05**:
   a. Copy cells A3 through G3 in **ExcelWorksheet09** and paste them into **sec5sc05** beginning with cell A12.
   b. Copy cells A9 through G9 in **ExcelWorksheet09** and paste them into **sec5sc05** beginning with cell A13.
5. With **sec5sc05** the active worksheet, apply an autoformat of your choosing to cells A1 through G13.
6. Print **sec5sc05** in landscape orientation and centered horizontally and vertically on the page.
7. Save and then close **sec5sc05**.
8. Close **ExcelWorksheet09** without saving the changes.

FIGURE 5.10 **Assessment 5**

	A	B	C	D	E	F	G	H
1				EQUIPMENT USAGE REPORT				
2		January	February	March	April	May	June	
3	Machine #12							
4	Total Hours Available	2,300	2,430	2,530	2,400	2,440	2,240	
5	In Use	2,040	2,105	2,320	2,180	2,050	1,995	
6								
7	Machine #25							
8	Total Hours Available	2,100	2,240	2,450	2,105	2,390	1,950	
9	In Use	1,800	1,935	2,110	1,750	2,215	1,645	
10								
11	Machine #30							
12								

Assessment 6

1. Open **ExcelWorksheet33**.
2. Save the workbook with Save As and name it **sec5sc06**.
3. Change the color of the *Sales 2002* tab to light purple, the color of the *Sales 2003* tab to light blue, and the color of the *Sales 2004* tab to light green.
4. Make the following changes to the workbook:
   a. Make sure the *Sales 2002* worksheet is the active worksheet.

b. Select columns B, C, and D and then change the width to 15.00.
c. Insert the heading *Average January Sales 2002-2004* (on multiple lines) in cell B10.
d. Insert a formula in cell B11 with a 3-D reference that averages the total in cells B3 through B8 in the *Sales 2002*, *Sales 2003*, and *Sales 2004* worksheets.
e. Make cell B11 active and then change to the Currency Style with zero decimal places.
f. Insert the heading *Average February Sales 2002-2004* (on multiple lines) in cell C10.
g. Insert a formula in cell C11 with a 3-D reference that averages the total in cells C3 through C8 in the *Sales 2002*, *Sales 2003*, and *Sales 2004* worksheets.
h. Make cell C11 active and then change to the Currency Style with zero decimal places.
i. Insert the heading *Average March Sales 2002-2004* (on multiple lines) in cell D10.
j. Insert a formula in cell D11 with a 3-D reference that averages the total in cells D3 through D8 in the *Sales 2002*, *Sales 2003*, and *Sales 2004* worksheets.
k. Make cell D11 active and then change to the Currency Style with zero decimal places.

5. Save the workbook and then print only the *Sales 2002* worksheet.
6. Close **sec5sc06**.

Assessment 7

1. Use Excel's Help feature to learn about linking data between programs.
2. After locating and reading the information on linking, open the Word program and then open **WordLetter02**.
3. Save the document and name it **seWordc5sc07**.
4. Make Excel the active program and then open **ExcelWorksheet03**.
5. Save the worksheet with Save As and name it **sec5sc07**.
6. Make the following changes to the worksheet:
   a. Select cells B3 through D8 and then click the Percent Style button on the Formatting toolbar.
   b. Select cells A1 through D8 and then apply the Colorful 2 autoformat.
7. Save and then print the worksheet.
8. Copy the worksheet and link it to **seWordc5sc07** (between the two paragraphs in the body of the letter).
9. Save and then print **seWordc5sc07**.
10. Click the button on the Taskbar representing the Excel worksheet **sec5sc07** and then make the following changes to data in cells:
    a. Change the title in cell A1 from *ANALYSIS OF FINANCIAL CONDITION* to *FINANCIAL ANALYSIS*.
    b. Change the content of cell B3 from *62%* to *80%*.
    c. Change the content of cell B4 from *45%* to *70%*.
11. Save, print, and then close **sec5sc07**.
12. Make active the Word document **seWordc5sc07** and then close the document.
13. Open **seWordc5sc07** and update the links.
14. Save, print, and then close **seWordc5sc07**.
15. Exit Word.

CHAPTER challenge

You are the sales manager for Campton's Camera Company and have been asked by the regional sales manager to report to him the first quarter sales for the last three years. You decide to provide him with a detailed summary. Create an Excel workbook containing three worksheets (one for each of the three years). In each of the worksheets show first quarter sales for the following camera models: Models A, B, and C. In a fourth worksheet, called *Totals*, link the three worksheets using a 3-D reference. The *Totals* sheet should show the total monthly sales for each of the camera models. Name each of the sheet tabs appropriately. Attractively format all of the worksheets. Save the workbook.

Although naming sheet tabs is very useful in keeping a workbook organized and understandable, you feel that using tab color would be helpful as your regional sales manager interprets the information in the workbook. Use the Help feature to learn about tab color, then apply tab colors to the various sheet tabs in the workbook created in the first part of the Chapter Challenge. Save the workbook again.

The regional sales manager was so impressed with your work that he has asked you to present the information to the Board of Directors. Create a PowerPoint presentation that includes the information created in the first part of the Chapter Challenge. Begin the presentation with a title slide and then include the information from each of the worksheets on a separate slide. The information from the *Totals* sheet should be linked to the presentation. Save the presentation.

CHAPTER 6

MAINTAINING WORKBOOKS

PERFORMANCE OBJECTIVES

Upon successful completion of Chapter 6, you will be able to:

- **Create and rename a folder**
- **Delete workbooks and folders**
- **Copy and move workbooks within and between folders**
- **Copy, move, and rename worksheets within a workbook**
- **Save a workbook in a variety of formats**
- **Search for specific workbooks**
- **Maintain consistent formatting with styles**
- **Use comments for review and response**
- **Create financial forms using templates**

Once you have been working with Excel for a period of time you will have accumulated several workbook files. Workbooks should be organized into folders to facilitate fast retrieval of information. Occasionally you should perform file maintenance activities such as copying, moving, renaming, and deleting workbooks to ensure the workbook list in your various folders is manageable.

Maintaining Workbooks

Many workbook management tasks can be completed at the Open and Save As dialog boxes. These tasks can include copying, moving, printing, and renaming workbooks; opening multiple workbooks; and creating and renaming a new folder. Some file maintenance tasks such as creating a folder and deleting files are performed by using buttons on the Open dialog box or Save As dialog box toolbar. Figure 6.1 displays the Open dialog box toolbar buttons.

FIGURE 6.1 **Open Dialog Box Toolbar Buttons**

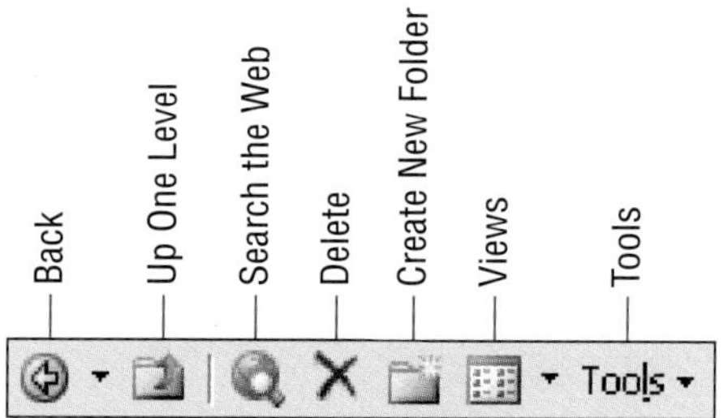

Create a Folder
1. Click File, Open.
2. Click Create New Folder button.
3. Type folder name.
4. Press Enter.

Change the default folder with the *Default file location* option at the Options dialog box with the General tab selected.

New Folder

Creating a Folder

In Excel, workbooks should be grouped logically and stored in folders. For example, all of the workbooks related to one department could be stored in one folder with the department name being the folder name. A folder can be created within a folder (called a ***subfolder***). If you create workbooks for a department by individual, each individual could have a subfolder name within the department folder. The main folder on a disk or drive is called the root folder. Additional folders are created as a branch of this root folder.

At the Open or Save As dialog boxes, workbook file names display in the list box preceded by a workbook icon and a folder name is preceded by a folder icon. Create a new folder by clicking the Create New Folder button located on the dialog box toolbar at the Open dialog box or Save As dialog box. At the New Folder dialog box shown in Figure 6.2, type a name for the folder in the *Name* text box, and then click OK or press Enter. The new folder becomes the active folder.

FIGURE 6.2 **New Folder Dialog Box**

Up One Level

Back

If you want to make the previous folder the active folder, click the Up One Level button on the dialog box toolbar. Clicking this button changes to the folder that is up one level from the current folder. After clicking the Up One Level button, the Back button becomes active. Click this button and the previously active folder becomes active again.

A folder name can contain a maximum of 255 characters. Numbers, spaces, and symbols can be used in the folder name, except those symbols explained in Chapter 1 in the "Saving a Workbook" section.

Renaming a Folder

Rename a Folder
1. Click File, Open.
2. Right-click folder name.
3. Click Rename.
4. Type new name.
5. Press Enter.

As you organize your files and folders, you may decide to rename a folder. Rename a folder using the Tools button on the Open dialog box toolbar or using a shortcut menu. To rename a folder using the Tools button, display the Open dialog box, click in the list box the folder you want to rename, click the Tools button on the dialog box toolbar, and then click Rename at the drop-down menu. This selects the folder name and inserts a border around the name. Type the new name for the folder and then press Enter. To rename a folder using a shortcut menu, display the Open dialog box, right-click the folder name in the list box, and then click Rename at the shortcut menu. Type a new name for the folder and then press Enter.

HINT

Display all files in a folder by changing the *Files of type* option at the Open dialog box to *All Files.*

exercise 1

CREATING AND RENAMING A FOLDER

1. Create a folder named *Payroll* on your disk. To begin, display the Open dialog box.
2. Double-click the *ExcelChapter06S* folder name to make it the active folder.
3. Click the Create New Folder button (located on the dialog box toolbar).
4. At the New Folder dialog box, type **Payroll**.
5. Click OK or press Enter. (The Payroll folder is now the active folder.)
6. Change back to the ExcelChapter06S folder by clicking the Up One Level button on the dialog box toolbar.
7. Rename the Payroll folder to *Finance* by completing the following steps:
   a. Right-click the *Payroll* folder name in the Open dialog box list box.
   b. Click Rename at the shortcut menu.
   c. Type **Finance** and then press Enter.
8. Click the Cancel button to close the Open dialog box.

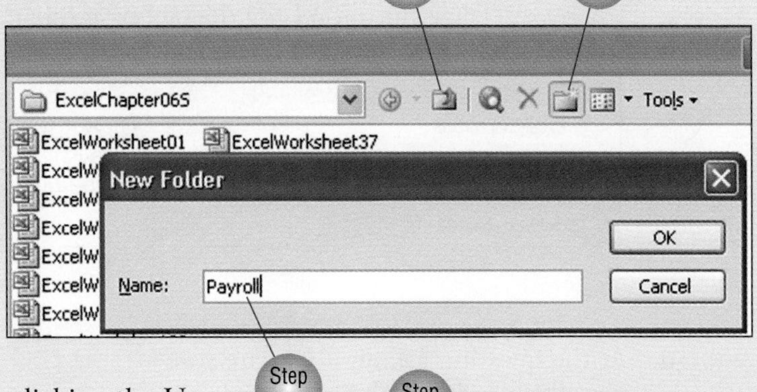

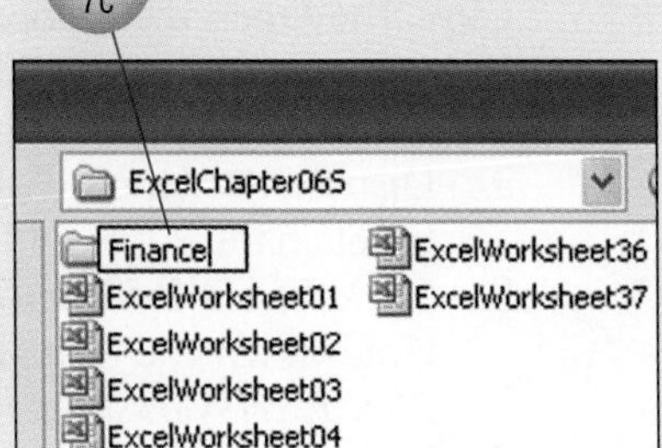

Deleting Workbooks and Folders

At some point, you may want to delete certain workbooks from your data disk or any other disk or folder in which you may be working. If you use Excel on a regular basis, you should establish a periodic system for deleting workbooks that are no longer used. The system you choose depends on the work you are doing and the amount of folder or disk space available. To delete a workbook, display the Open or Save As dialog box, select the workbook, and then click the Delete button on the dialog box toolbar. At the dialog box asking you to confirm the deletion, click Yes.

Delete

Tools

Delete Workbook/ Folder
1. Click File, Open.
2. Click workbook or folder name.
3. Click Delete button.
4. Click Yes.

You can also delete a workbook by displaying the Open dialog box, selecting the workbook to be deleted, clicking the Tools button on the dialog box toolbar, and then clicking Delete at the drop-down menu. Another method for deleting a workbook is to display the Open dialog box, right-click the workbook to be deleted, and then click Delete at the shortcut menu. Delete a folder and all of its contents in the same manner as deleting a workbook or selected workbooks.

exercise 2

DELETING A WORKBOOK AND SELECTED WORKBOOKS

1. Open **ExcelWorksheet05**.
2. Save the worksheet with Save As and name it **sec6x02**.
3. Close **sec6x02**.
4. Delete **sec6x02** by completing the following steps:
   a. Display the Open dialog box with the ExcelChapter06S folder active.
   b. Click ***sec6x02*** to select it.
   c. Click the Delete button on the dialog box toolbar.

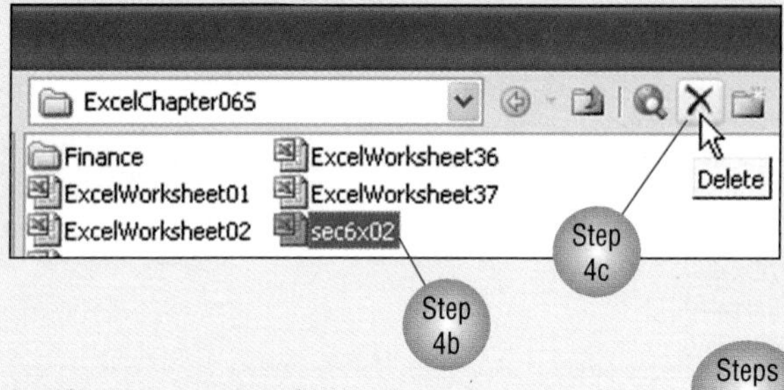

   d. At the question asking if you are sure you want to delete the item, click Yes.
5. Close the Open dialog box.
6. Delete selected workbooks by completing the following steps:
   a. Display the Open dialog box with the ExcelChapter06S folder active.
   b. Click ***ExcelWorksheet02***.
   c. Hold down the Shift key and then click ***ExcelWorksheet04***.
   d. Position the mouse pointer on one of the selected workbooks and then click the right mouse button.
   e. At the shortcut menu that displays, click Delete.
   f. At the question asking if you are sure you want to delete the items, click Yes.
   g. At the message telling you that **ExcelWorksheet02** is a read-only file and asking if you want to delete it, click the Yes to All button.
7. Close the Open dialog box.

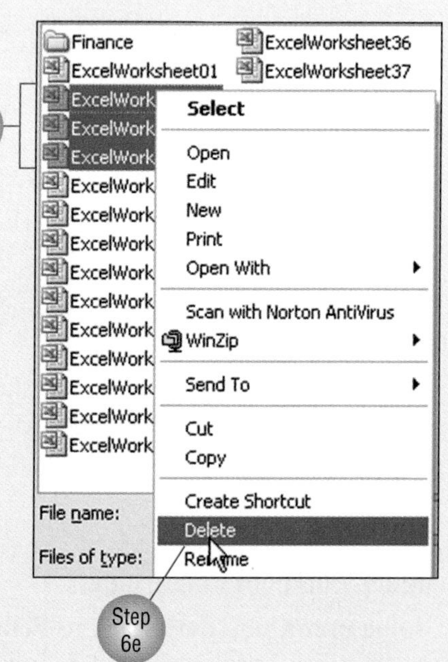

Deleting to the Recycle Bin

Workbooks deleted from your data disk are deleted permanently. (Recovery programs are available, however, that will help you recover deleted text. If you accidentally delete one or more workbooks from a disk, do not do anything more with the disk until you can run a recovery program.) Workbooks deleted from the hard drive are automatically sent to the Windows Recycle Bin. If you accidentally delete a workbook to the Recycle Bin, it can be easily restored. To free space on the drive, empty the Recycle Bin on a periodic basis. Restoring a workbook from or emptying the contents of the Recycle Bin is done at the Windows desktop (not in Excel).

To display the Recycle Bin, minimize the Excel window, and then double-click the *Recycle Bin* icon located on the Windows desktop. At the Recycle Bin, you can restore file(s) and empty the Recycle Bin.

Copying Workbooks

In previous chapters, you opened a workbook from the data disk and saved it with a new name on the same disk. This process makes an exact copy of the workbook, leaving the original on the disk. You copied workbooks and saved the new workbook in the same folder as the original. You can also copy a workbook into another folder and use the workbook's original name or give it a different name, or select workbooks at the Open dialog box and copy them to the same folder or into a different folder. To copy a workbook into another folder, open the workbook, display the Save As dialog box, change to the desired folder, and then click the Save button.

The Open and Save As dialog boxes contain an Up One Level button (located on the dialog box toolbar). Use this button if you want to change to the folder that is up one level from the current folder.

Copy a Workbook
1. Click File, Open.
2. Right-click workbook name.
3. Click Copy.
4. Navigate to desired folder.
5. Right-click white area in list box.
6. Click Paste.

exercise 3

SAVING A COPY OF AN OPEN WORKBOOK

1. Open **ExcelWorksheet10**.
2. Save the workbook with Save As and name it **Quota&Bonus**. (Make sure ExcelChapter06S is the active folder.)
3. Save a copy of the Quota&Bonus workbook in the Finance folder created in Exercise 1 by completing the following steps. (If you did not complete Exercise 1, check with your instructor before continuing.)
   a. With **Quota&Bonus** still open, display the Save As dialog box.
   b. At the Save As dialog box, change to the Finance folder. To do this, double-click *Finance* at the beginning of the list box (folders are listed before workbooks).
   c. Click the Save button located in the lower right corner of the dialog box.
4. Close **Quota&Bonus**.
5. Change back to the ExcelChapter06S folder by completing the following steps:
   a. Display the Open dialog box.
   b. Click the Up One Level button located on the dialog box toolbar.
   c. Close the Open dialog box.

A workbook can be copied to another folder without opening the workbook first. To do this, use the Copy and Paste options from a shortcut menu at the Open (or Save As) dialog box.

exercise 4

COPYING A WORKBOOK AT THE OPEN DIALOG BOX

1. Copy **ExcelWorksheet07** to the Finance folder. To begin, display the Open dialog box with the ExcelChapter06S folder active.
2. Position the arrow pointer on ***ExcelWorksheet07***, click the right mouse button, and then click Copy at the shortcut menu.
3. Change to the Finance folder by double-clicking *Finance* at the beginning of the list box.
4. Position the arrow pointer in any white area (not on a workbook name) in the list box, click the right mouse button, and then click Paste at the shortcut menu.
5. Change back to the ExcelChapter06S folder by clicking the Up One Level button located on the dialog box toolbar.
6. Close the Open dialog box.

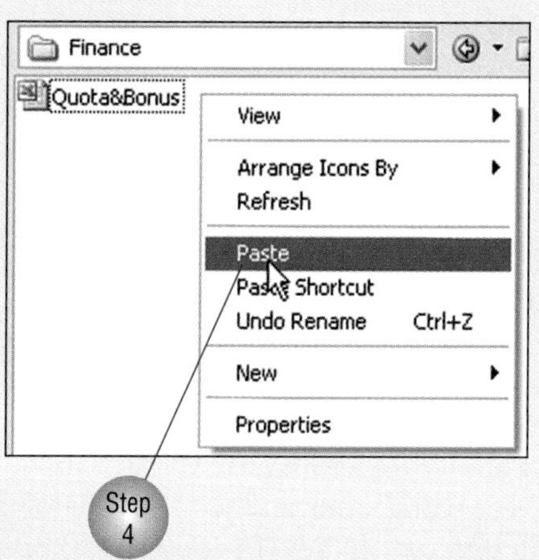

A workbook or selected workbooks can be copied into the same folder. When you do this, Excel names the duplicated workbook(s) "Copy of xxx" (where *xxx* is the current workbook name). You can copy one workbook or selected workbooks into the same folder.

exercise 5

COPYING SELECTED WORKBOOKS INTO THE SAME FOLDER

1. Copy workbooks into the same folder. To begin, display the Open dialog box with ExcelChapter06S the active folder.
2. Select ***ExcelWorksheet01***, ***ExcelWorksheet07***, and ***ExcelWorksheet09***. (To do this, hold down the Ctrl key while clicking each workbook name.)
3. Position the arrow pointer on one of the selected workbooks, click the right mouse button, and then click Copy at the shortcut menu.
4. Position the arrow pointer in any white area in the list box, click the right mouse button, and then click Paste at the shortcut menu. (In a few seconds, Excel will redisplay the Open dialog box with the following workbooks added: Copy of ExcelWorksheet01, Copy of ExcelWorksheet07, and Copy of ExcelWorksheet09.)
5. Close the Open dialog box.

exercise 6

COPYING SELECTED WORKBOOKS INTO A DIFFERENT FOLDER

1. Copy selected workbooks to the Finance folder. To begin, display the Open dialog box with ExcelChapter06S the active folder.
2. Select ***ExcelWorksheet06, ExcelWorksheet08,*** and ***ExcelWorksheet10***.
3. Position the arrow pointer on one of the selected workbooks, click the right mouse button, and then click Copy at the shortcut menu.
4. Double-click the *Finance* folder.
5. Position the arrow pointer in any white area in the list box, click the right mouse button, and then click Paste at the shortcut menu.
6. Click the Up One Level button to change back to the ExcelChapter06S folder.
7. Close the Open dialog box.

Sending Workbooks to a Different Drive or Folder

Copy workbooks to another folder or drive with the Copy and Paste options from the shortcut menu at the Open or Save As dialog box. With the Send To option, you can quickly send a copy of a workbook to another drive or folder. To use this option, position the arrow pointer on the workbook you want copied, click the right mouse button, point to Send To (this causes a side menu to display), and then click the desired drive or folder.

Move a Workbook
1. Click File, Open.
2. Right-click workbook name.
3. Click Cut.
4. Navigate to desired folder.
5. Right-click white area in list box.
6. Click Paste.

Cutting and Pasting a Workbook

You can remove a workbook from one folder or disk and insert it in another folder or on another disk using the Cut and Paste options from the shortcut menu at the Open dialog box. To do this, display the Open dialog box, position the arrow pointer on the workbook to be removed (cut), click the right mouse button, and then click Cut at the shortcut menu. Change to the desired folder or drive, position the arrow pointer in a white area in the list box, click the right mouse button, and then click Paste at the shortcut menu.

exercise 7

CUTTING AND PASTING A WORKBOOK

1. Move a workbook to a different folder. To begin, display the Open dialog box with the ExcelChapter06S folder active.
2. Position the arrow pointer on ***ExcelWorksheet05,*** click the right mouse button, and then click Cut at the shortcut menu.
3. Double-click *Finance* to make it the active folder.
4. Position the arrow pointer in the white area in the list box, click the right mouse button, and then click Paste at the shortcut menu.
5. At the Confirm File Move dialog box asking if you are sure you want to move the file, click Yes. (This dialog box usually does not appear when you cut and paste. Since the files you copied from your student CD-ROM are read-only files, this warning message appears.)
6. Click the Up One Level button to make the ExcelChapter06S folder the active folder.
7. Close the Open dialog box.

Renaming Workbooks

Rename a Workbook
1. Click File, Open.
2. Right-click workbook name.
3. Click Rename.
4. Type new name.
5. Press Enter.

At the Open dialog box, use the Rename option from the Tools drop-down menu or the shortcut menu to give a workbook a different name. The Rename option changes the name of the workbook and keeps it in the same folder. To use Rename, display the Open dialog box, click once on the workbook to be renamed, click the Tools button on the dialog box toolbar, and then click Rename. This causes a thin black border to surround the workbook name and the name to be selected. Type the new name and then press Enter.

You can also rename a workbook by right-clicking the workbook name at the Open dialog box and then clicking Rename at the shortcut menu. Type the new name for the workbook and then press the Enter key.

exercise 8

RENAMING A WORKBOOK

1. Rename a workbook located in the Finance folder. To begin, display the Open dialog box with ExcelChapter06S the active folder.
2. Double-click *Finance* to make it the active folder.
3. Click once on ***ExcelWorksheet07*** to select it.
4. Click the Tools button on the dialog box toolbar.
5. At the drop-down menu that displays, click Rename.
6. Type **Equipment** and then press the Enter key.
7. At the message asking if you are sure you want to change the name of the read-only file, click Yes.
8. Complete steps similar to those in Steps 3 through 6 to rename **ExcelWorksheet06** to *TestScores*.
9. Click the Up One Level button.
10. Close the Open dialog box.

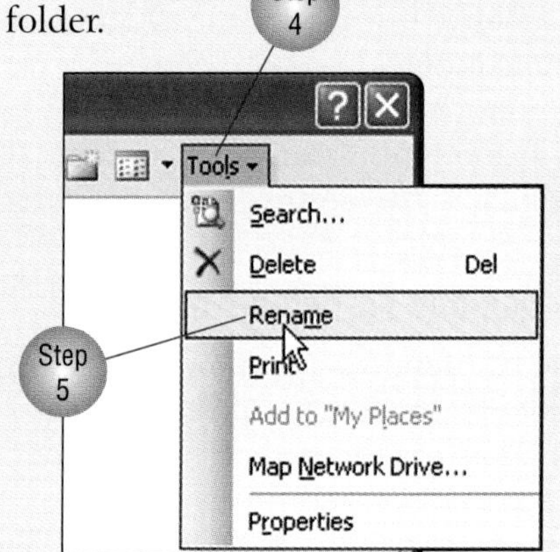

Deleting a Folder and Its Contents

As you learned earlier in this chapter, a workbook or selected workbooks can be deleted. In addition to workbooks, a folder (and all of its contents) can be deleted. Delete a folder in the same manner as a workbook is deleted.

exercise 9

DELETING A FOLDER AND ITS CONTENTS

1. Delete the Finance folder and its contents. To begin, display the Open dialog box with the ExcelChapter06S folder active.
2. Right-click on the *Finance* folder.
3. Click Delete at the shortcut menu.
4. At the Confirm Folder Delete dialog box, click Yes.
5. At the Confirm File Delete dialog box, click the Yes to All button.
6. Close the Open dialog box.

Printing Workbooks

Up to this point, you have opened a workbook and then printed it. With the Print option from the Tools drop-down menu or the Print option from the shortcut menu at the Open dialog box, you can print a workbook or several workbooks without opening them.

exercise 10

PRINTING WORKBOOKS

1. Display the Open dialog box with the ExcelChapter06S folder active.
2. Select ***ExcelWorksheet01*** and ***ExcelWorksheet08***.
3. Click the Tools button on the dialog box toolbar.
4. At the drop-down menu that displays, click Print.

Managing Worksheets

Individual worksheets within a workbook can be moved or copied within the same workbook or to another existing workbook. Exercise caution when moving sheets since calculations or charts based on data on a worksheet might become inaccurate if you move the worksheet.

Copying a Worksheet to Another Workbook

To copy a worksheet to another existing workbook, open both the source and the destination workbooks. Activate the sheet you want to copy in the source workbook, click Edit, and then click Move or Copy Sheet, or right-click the sheet tab located at the bottom of the screen just above the Status bar and then click Move or Copy at the shortcut menu. At the Move or Copy dialog box shown in Figure 6.3, select the destination workbook name from the *To book* drop-down list, select the worksheet that you want the copied worksheet placed before in the *Before sheet* list box, click the *Create a copy* check box, and then click OK.

HINT

Make a duplicate of a worksheet in the same workbook by holding the Ctrl key and then dragging the worksheet tab to the desired position.

FIGURE 6.3 ***Move or Copy Dialog Box***

Insert a check mark in this check box if you want to copy the worksheet.

exercise 11 COPYING A WORKSHEET TO ANOTHER WORKBOOK

1. Open **ExcelWorksheet26** and **Copy of ExcelWorksheet09**.
2. Copy the Equipment Usage Report worksheet from the workbook named Copy of ExcelWorksheet09 to the ExcelWorksheet26 workbook by completing the following steps:
   a. Make sure **Copy of ExcelWorksheet09** is the active workbook.
   b. Right-click the *Sheet1* tab located at the bottom left of the screen just above the Status bar, and then click Move or Copy at the shortcut menu.

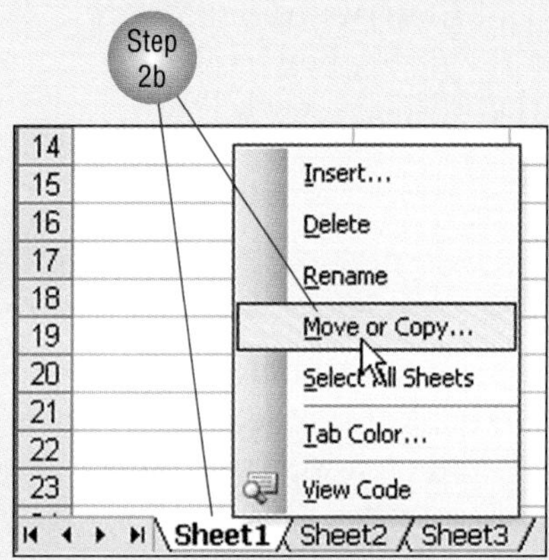

   c. Click the down-pointing arrow next to the *To book* option box and then click *ExcelWorksheet26.xls* at the drop-down list.
   d. Click *Sheet2* in the *Before sheet* list box.
   e. Click the *Create a copy* check box to insert a check mark.
   f. Click OK. (Excel switches to the workbook **ExcelWorksheet26** and inserts the copied sheet with the sheet name *Sheet1 (2)*.)
3. Save **ExcelWorksheet26** with Save As and name it **sec6x11**.
4. Print the entire **sec6x11** workbook. ***(Hint: Do this with the*** **Entire workbook** ***option at the Print dialog box.)***
5. Close **sec6x11**.
6. Close **Copy of ExcelWorksheet09**.

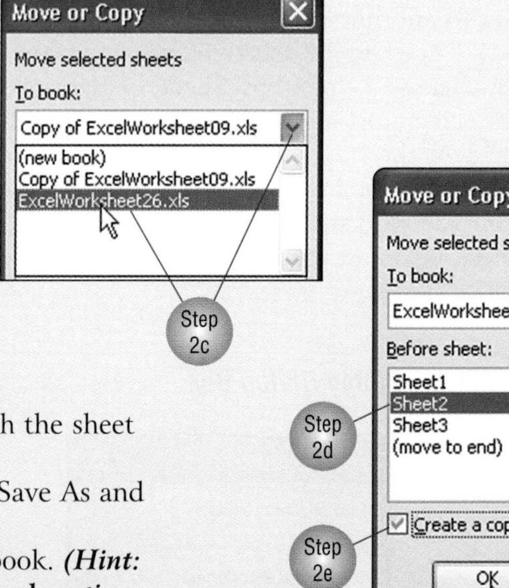

Moving a Worksheet to Another Workbook

To move a worksheet to another existing workbook, open both the source and the destination workbooks. Make active the sheet you want to move in the source workbook, click Edit, and then Move or Copy Sheet, or right-click the sheet tab located at the bottom of the screen just above the Status bar and click Move or Copy at the shortcut menu. At the Move or Copy dialog box shown in Figure 6.3, select the destination workbook name from the *To book* drop-down list, select the worksheet that you want the worksheet placed before in the *Before sheet* list box, and then click OK.

HINT

To reposition a worksheet tab, drag the tab to the desired position.

Be careful when moving a worksheet to another workbook file. If formulas exist in the workbook that depend on the contents of the cells in the worksheet that is moved, they will no longer calculate properly.

exercise 12

MOVING A WORKSHEET TO ANOTHER WORKBOOK

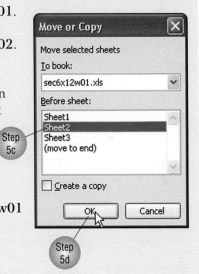

1. Open **ExcelWorksheet01**.
2. Save the workbook with Save As and name it **sec6x12w01**.
3. Open **ExcelWorksheet10**.
4. Save the workbook with Save As and name it **sec6x12w02**.
5. Move *Sheet1* from **sec6x12w02** to **sec6x12w01** by completing the following steps:
   a. With **sec6x12w02** the active workbook, click Edit on the Menu bar, and then click Move or Copy Sheet at the drop-down menu.
   b. Click the down-pointing arrow next to the *To book* option box and then click ***sec6x12w01.xls*** at the drop-down list.
   c. Click *Sheet2* in the *Before sheet* list box.
   d. Click OK. (Excel switches to the workbook **sec6x12w01** and inserts the moved sheet with the sheet name *Sheet1 (2)*.)
6. Save the worksheet with the same name (**sec6x12w01**).
7. Print the entire **sec6x12w01** workbook.
8. Close **sec6x12w01**.
9. Close **sec6x12w02** without saving changes.

Searching for Specific Workbooks

Use options at the Basic File Search task pane shown in Figure 6.4 to search for specific workbooks. To display this task pane, click File and then File Search. (If the Advanced File Search task pane displays, scroll down to the end of the task pane and then click the Basic File Search hyperlink.) At the Basic File Search task pane, click in the *Search text* box and then enter one or more words specific to the workbooks for which you are searching. The word or words can be contained in the workbook name, the text of the workbook, keywords assigned to the workbook, or in the workbook properties. After entering the search word or words, click the Go button and workbooks matching the search criteria display in the Search Results task pane.

FIGURE 6.4 **Basic File Search Task Pane**

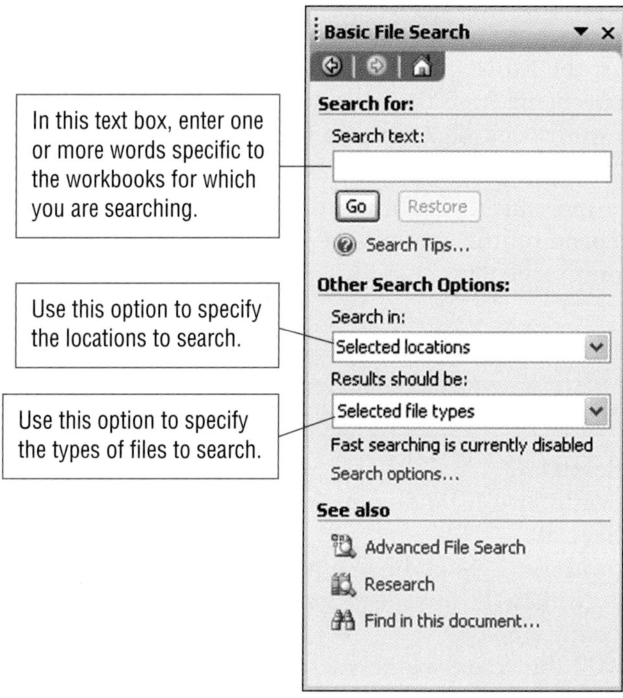

HINT

Click the Advanced File Search hyperlink to display the Advanced File Search task pane containing options for setting limits and conditions on the search.

Specify the locations to search with the *Search in* option. Click the down-pointing arrow at the right side of the *Search in* option box. This displays a drop-down list containing folders and network places. Click the plus symbol preceding a folder name to expand the display to include any subfolders. Insert a check mark in the check boxes next to any folders you want searched. Click a check box once and a check mark is inserted in the box and only that folder is searched. Click a check box a second time to specify that you want the folder and all subfolders searched. When you click the check box a second time, the check box changes to a cascading check box (check boxes overlapping). Click a check box a third time and the folder is deselected but all subfolders remain selected. Click a check box a fourth time and all subfolders are deselected.

Specify the types of files to search with the *Results should be* option. Click the down-pointing arrow at the right side of the *Results should be* option box and then, at the drop-down list that displays, insert a check mark in the check boxes before the types of files you want searched. For example, if you want only Excel files displayed, insert a check mark in the *Excel Files* check box.

exercise 13

FINDING WORKBOOKS CONTAINING SPECIFIC TEXT

1. At a blank Excel worksheet, click File and then File Search. (If the Advanced File Search task pane displays, scroll down to the end of the task pane and then click the Basic File Search hyperlink.)
2. Search for all Excel workbooks on your disk in drive A that contain the company name *Real Photography* by completing the following steps:
   a. Click in the *Search text* box. (If text displays in the text box, select the text and then delete it.)
   b. Type **Real Photography** in the *Search text* box.
   c. Click the down-pointing arrow at the right side of the *Search in* option box.
   d. Click the plus sign that precedes *My Computer*.
   e. Click twice in the *3½ Floppy (A:)* check box to insert a check mark (and cascade the check box). (Make sure that it is the only check box containing a check mark.)
   f. Click in the task pane outside the *Search in* list box to remove the list.
   g. Click the down-pointing arrow at the right side of the *Results should be* option box.
   h. At the drop-down list, click in the *Excel Files* check box to insert a check mark. (Make sure that it is the only check box containing a check mark.)
   i. Click in the task pane outside the *Results should be* list box to remove the list.
   j. Click the Go button. (In a few moments, the Search Results task pane will display with workbook names containing *Real Photography*.)
   k. When the list of workbooks displays in the Search Results task pane, double-click ***ExcelWorksheet07*** in the task pane. (This opens the **ExcelWorksheet07** workbook.)
   l. Close **ExcelWorksheet07**.
3. Close the Search Results task pane.

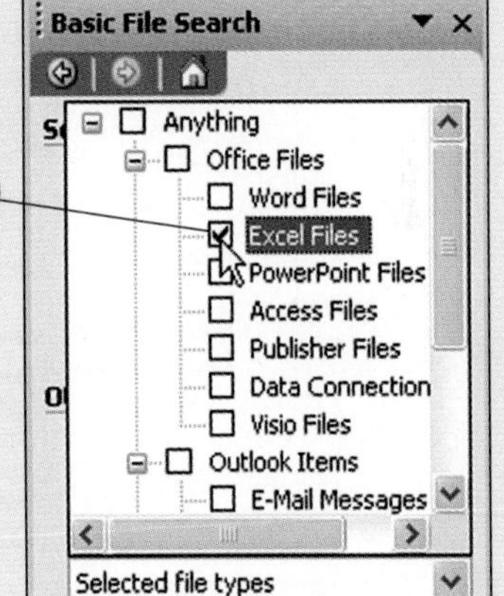

Saving Workbooks in a Variety of Formats

In some situations, you may want to share Excel data with other users who may open the data in an application other than Excel. Excel offers a variety of file formats for saving Excel data allowing for transportability of the data. For example, you can save data in an Excel worksheet as text and then open that text file in Word or save Excel data in XML (Extensible Markup Language), which is a method for putting data in a text file that follows specific standard guidelines that can be read by a variety of applications.

HINT

Formatting rules for XML data are generally organized into style sheets, which format the data appropriately.

Save Workbook in Different Format
1. Click File, Save As.
2. Type name for workbook.
3. Click down-pointing arrow at right of *Save as type* option box.
4. Click desired type in drop-down list.
5. Click Save button.

To save an Excel workbook in a different format, open the workbook, and then display the Save As dialog box. At the Save As dialog box, click the down-pointing arrow at the right side of the *Save as type* option, and then click the desired format at the drop-down list. In Exercise 14, you will save an Excel worksheet as a text file with tab delimiters, as a text file with comma delimiters, and as an XML spreadsheet. You will then open each of the three files in Microsoft Word.

exercise 14

SAVING A WORKSHEET IN A VARIETY OF FORMATS

1. Open **ExcelWorksheet19**.
2. Save the worksheet with Save As and name it **sec6x14**.
3. Save the worksheet in the Text (Tab delimited) format by completing the following steps:
   a. Click File and then Save As.
   b. At the Save As dialog box, type **sec6x14tab** in the *File name* text box.
   c. Click the down-pointing arrow at the right side of the *Save as type* list box, and then click *Text (Tab delimited)* at the drop-down list.
   d. Click the Save button.

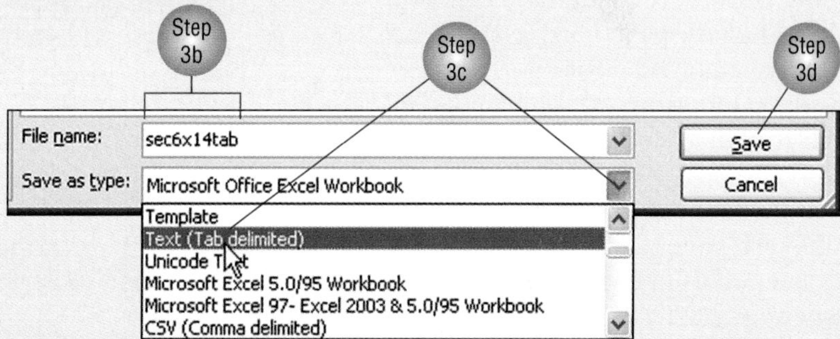

   e. At the message telling you that the selected file type does not support workbooks that contain multiple worksheets, click OK.
   f. At the message telling you that the file may contain features that are not compatible with Text (Tab delimited) and asking if you want to keep the workbook in the format, click Yes.
   g. Close the workbook. (At the message asking if you want to save the changes, click Yes. At the message telling you that the file type does not support workbooks containing multiple worksheets, click OK. At the message asking if you want to keep the workbook in the format, click Yes.)
4. Open **sec6x14** and then save it in the CSV (Comma delimited) format by completing the following steps:
   a. Click File and then Save As.

b. At the Save As dialog box, type **sec6x14comma** in the *File name* text box.
c. Click the down-pointing arrow at the right side of the *Save as type* list box, and then click *CSV (Comma delimited)* at the drop-down list.
d. Click the Save button.

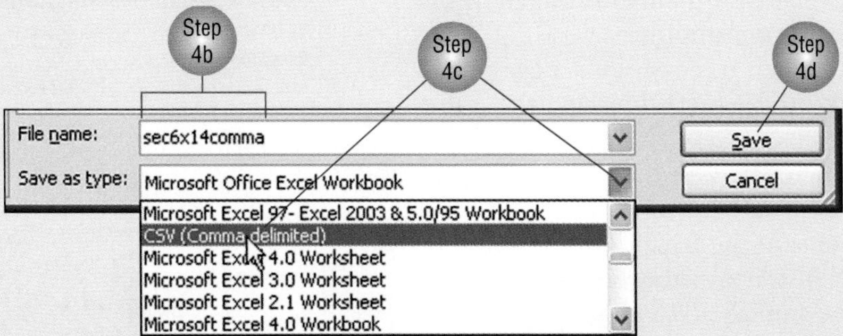

e. At the message telling you that the selected file type does not support workbooks that contain multiple worksheets, click OK.
f. At the message telling you that the file may contain features that are not compatible with CSV (Comma delimited) and asking if you want to keep the workbook in the format, click Yes.
g. Close the workbook. (At the message asking if you want to save the changes, click Yes. At the message telling you that the file type does not support workbooks containing multiple worksheets, click OK. At the message asking if you want to keep the workbook in the format, click Yes.)

5. Open **sec6x14** and then save it in the XML format by completing the following steps:
   a. Click File and then Save As.
   b. At the Save As dialog box, type **sec6x14xml** in the *File name* text box.
   c. Click the down-pointing arrow at the right side of the *Save as type* list box, and then click *XML Spreadsheet* at the drop-down list.
   d. Click the Save button.
   e. Close the workbook.
6. Open and then print **sec6x14tab** in Microsoft Word by completing the following steps:
   a. Open Microsoft Word.
   b. Click the Open button on the Standard toolbar.
   c. At the Open dialog box, navigate to the ExcelChapter06S folder on your disk.
   d. Click the down-pointing arrow at the right side of the *Files of type* list box and then click *All Files* at the drop-down list.
   e. Double-click ***sec6x14tab*** in the list box.
   f. With the file open, click the Print button on the Standard toolbar.
   g. Click File and then Close to close the **sec6x14tab** file.

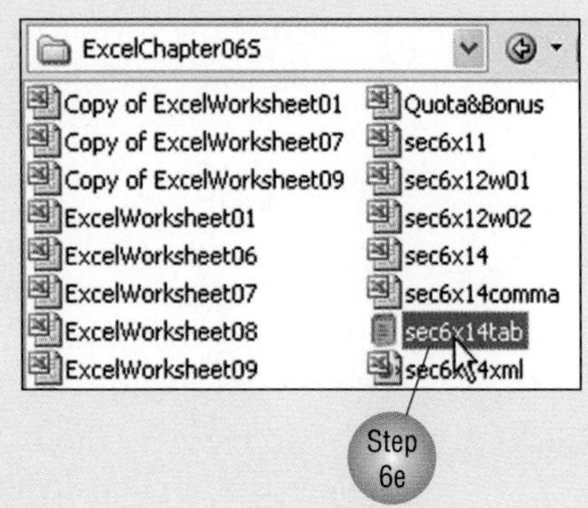

7. Open and then print **sec6x14comma** by completing the following steps:
   a. In Microsoft Word, click the Open button on the Standard toolbar.
   b. Make sure the ExcelChapter06S folder on your disk in the active folder.
   c. Make sure the *Files of type* option is set at *All Files*.

d. Double-click ***sec6x14comma*** in the list box.
e. With the file open, click the Print button on the Standard toolbar.
f. Click File and then Close to close the **sec6x14comma** file.

8. Open and then print the first page of the **sec6x14xml** file by completing the following steps:
   a. In Microsoft Word, click the Open button on the Standard toolbar.
   b. Make sure the ExcelChapter06S folder on your disk is the active folder.
   c. Make sure the *Files of type* option is set at *All Files*.
   d. Double-click ***sec6x14xml*** in the list box.
   e. With the file open, print only the first page by completing the following steps:
      1) Click File and then Print.
      2) At the Print dialog box, click in the *Pages* text box, and then type 1.
      3) Click OK.
   f. Click File and then Close to close the **sec6x14xml** file.
   g. Close Microsoft Word.

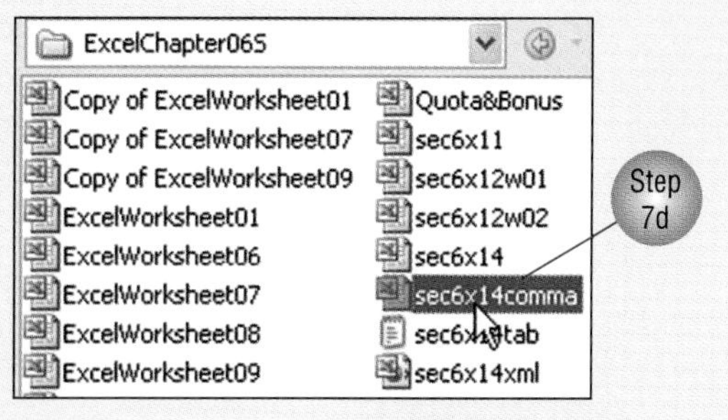

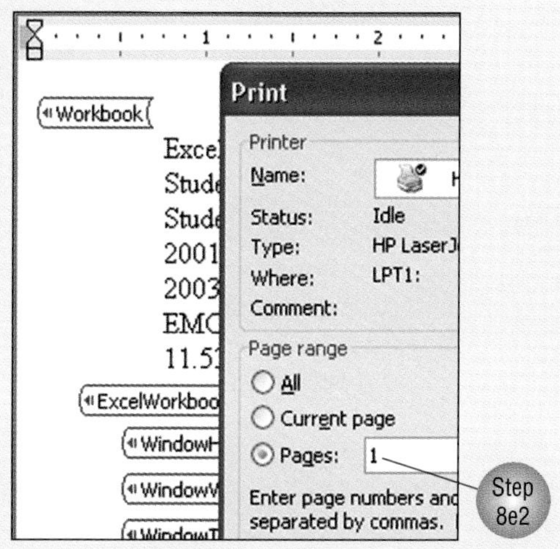

Formatting with Styles

To automate the formatting of cells in a workbook, consider defining and applying a style. A style, which is a predefined set of formatting attributes such as font, font size, alignment, borders, shading, and so forth, is particularly useful in large workbooks with data requiring a considerable amount of formatting.

Using a style to apply formatting has several advantages. A style helps to ensure consistent formatting from one worksheet to another. Once you define all attributes for a particular style, you do not have to define them again. If you need to change the formatting, change the style, and all cells formatted with that style automatically reflect the change.

Defining a Style

Excel contains some common number styles you can apply with buttons on the Formatting toolbar. For example, clicking the Currency Style button on the Formatting toolbar applies currency formatting to the cell or selected cells. The Percent Style and Comma Style buttons also apply styles to cells.

Two basic methods are available for defining your own style. You can define a style with formats already applied to a cell or you can display the Style dialog box, click the Modify button, and then choose formatting options at the Format Cells dialog box. Styles you create are only available in the workbook in which they are created. To define a style with existing formatting, you would complete these steps:

1. Select the cell or cells containing the desired formatting.
2. Click Format and then Style.
3. At the Style dialog box, shown in Figure 6.5, type a name for the new style in the *Style name* text box.
4. Click OK to close the dialog box.

Define a Style with Existing Formatting
1. Select cell containing formatting.
2. Click Format, Style.
3. Type a name for the style.
4. Click OK.

FIGURE 6.5 ***Style Dialog Box***

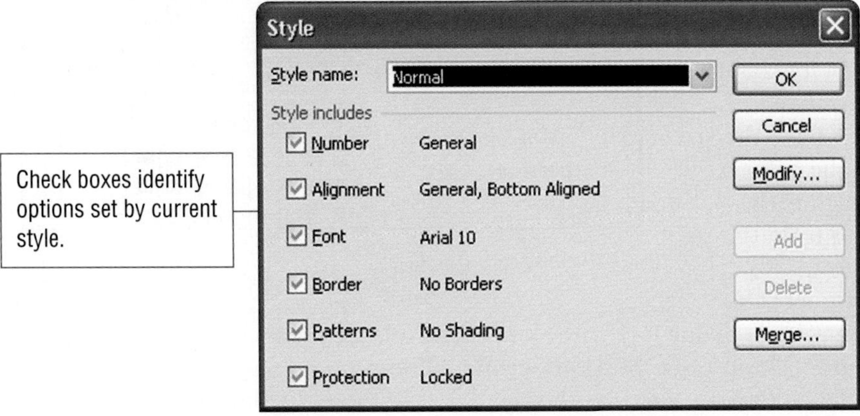

To define a new style without first applying the formatting, you would complete the following steps:

1. Click Format and then Style.
2. At the Style dialog box, type a name for the new style in the *Style name* text box.
3. Click the Modify button.
4. At the Format Cells dialog box, select the formats you want included in the style.
5. Click OK to close the Format Cells dialog box.
6. At the Style dialog box, remove the check mark from any formats that you do not want included in the style.
7. Click OK to define and apply the style to the selected cell. To define the style without applying it to the selected cell, click the Add button, and then click the Close button.

QUICK STEPS

Define a Style
1. Click Format, Style.
2. Type a name for the style.
3. Click Modify button.
4. Choose desired formatting at the Format Cells dialog box.
5. Click OK.

Applying a Style

To apply a style, select the cells you want to format, and then display the Style dialog box. At the Style dialog box, click the down-pointing arrow at the right side of the *Style name* text box, and then click the desired style name. Click OK to close the dialog box and apply the style.

Apply a Style
1. Select cells.
2. Click Format, Style.
3. Click down-pointing arrow at right of *Style name* text box.
4. Click desired style at drop-down list.
5. Click OK.

exercise 15

DEFINING AND APPLYING STYLES

1. Open **ExcelWorksheet36**.
2. Save the worksheet with Save As and name it **sec6x15**.
3. Format a cell and then define a style with the formatting by completing the following steps:
   a. Make sure cell A1 is active.
   b. Change the font and apply a bottom border by completing the following steps:
      1) Click Format and then Cells.
      2) At the Format Cells dialog box, click the Font tab.
      3) At the Font tab, change the font to *Tahoma*, the font style to *Bold*, the size to *12*, and the color to *Indigo*. (Indigo is the second color from the right in the top row.)

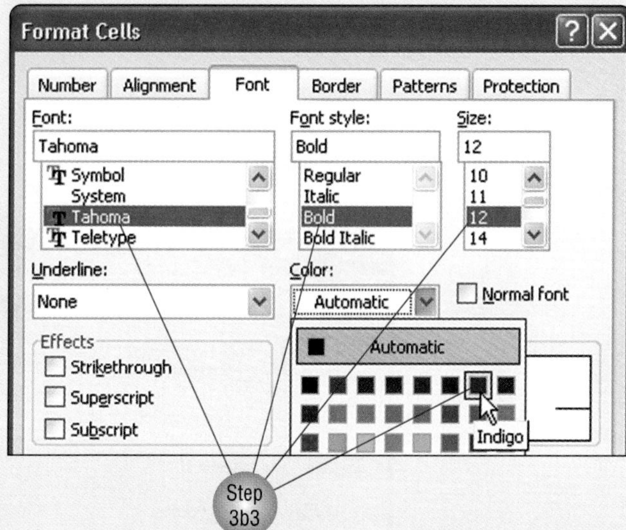

      4) Click the Border tab.
      5) At the Format Cells dialog box with the Border tab selected, click the sixth *Line Style* option from the top in the second column.
      6) Click the down-pointing arrow at the right side of the *Color* option and then click the Violet color at the color palette (seventh color from the left in the third row from the top).
      7) Click the bottom border of the preview cell in the dialog box.

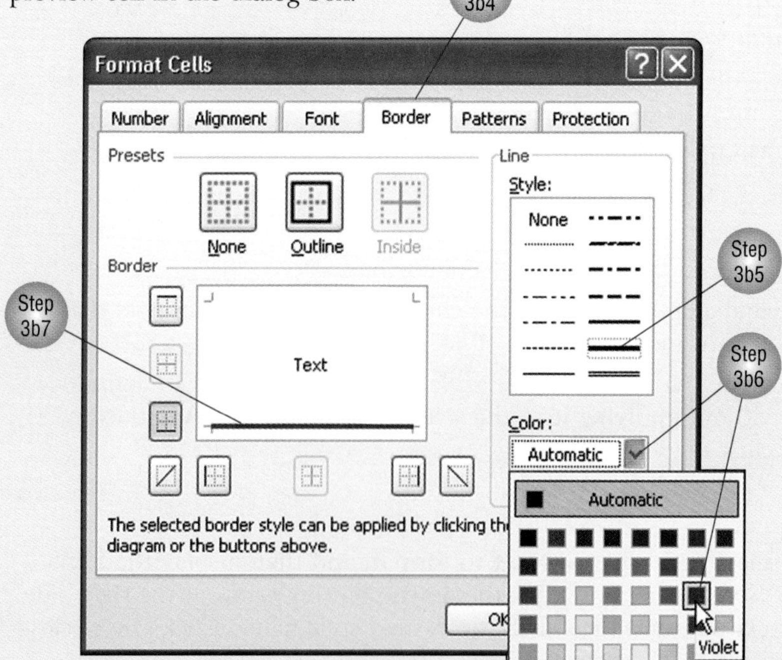

8) Click OK to close the Format Cells dialog box.

c. With cell A1 still the active cell, define a style named Title with the formatting you just applied by completing the following steps:
   1) Click Format and then Style.
   2) At the Style dialog box, type **Title** in the *Style name* text box.
   3) Click the Add button.
   4) Click the Close button.

4. Apply the Title style to cell A1 by completing the following steps:
   a. Make sure cell A1 is the active cell. (Even though cell A1 is already formatted, the style has not been applied to it. Later, you will modify the style and the style must be applied to the cell for the change to affect it.)
   b. Click Format and then Style.
   c. At the Style dialog box, click the down-pointing arrow at the right side of the *Style name* text box, and then click *Title* at the drop-down list.
   d. Click OK to close the Style dialog box.

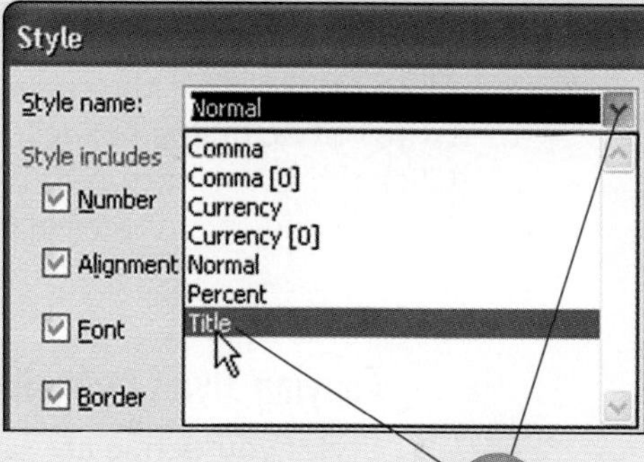

5. Apply the Title style to other cells by completing the following steps:
   a. Select cells A2 through D2.
   b. Click Format and then Style.
   c. At the Style dialog box, click the down-pointing arrow at the right side of the *Style name* text box, and then click *Title* at the drop-down list.
   d. Click OK to close the Style dialog box.
6. Define a new style named Font without first applying the formatting by completing the following steps:
   a. Click in any empty cell.
   b. Click Format and then Style.
   c. At the Style dialog box, type **Font** in the *Style name* text box.
   d. Click the Modify button.
   e. At the Format Cells dialog box, click the Font tab.
   f. At the Format Cells dialog box with the Font tab selected, change the font to *Tahoma*, the size to *12*, and the color to *Indigo*.
   g. Click the Patterns tab.
   h. At the Format Cells dialog box with the Patterns tab selected, click a light blue color of your choosing in the color palette.
   i. Click OK to close the Format Cells dialog box.
   j. At the Style dialog box, click the Add button.
   k. Click the Close button. (Do not click the OK button.)
7. Apply the Font style by completing the following steps:

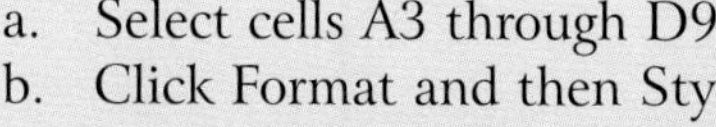

   a. Select cells A3 through D9.
   b. Click Format and then Style.
   c. At the Style dialog box, click the down-pointing arrow at the right side of the *Style name* text box, and then click *Font* at the drop-down list.
   d. Click OK to close the Style dialog box.

8. Make the following changes to the worksheet:
   a. Select cells B3 through D9.
   b. Click the Currency Style button on the Formatting toolbar.
   c. Click twice on the Decrease Decimal button on the Formatting toolbar.
   d. Automatically adjust columns A through D.
9. Save and then print **sec6x15**.
10. With **sec6x15** still open, modify the Title style by completing the following steps:
    a. Click in any empty cell.
    b. Display the Style dialog box.
    c. Click the down-pointing arrow at the right side of the *Style name* text box and then click *Title* at the drop-down list.
    d. Click the Modify button.
    e. At the Format Cells dialog box, click the Alignment tab.
    f. At the Format Cells dialog box with the Alignment tab selected, click the down-pointing arrow to the right of the *Vertical* option box, and then click *Center* at the drop-down list.
    g. Click OK to close the Format Cells dialog box.
    h. At the Style dialog box, click the Add button.
    i. Click the Close button to close the Style dialog box.
11. Save, print, and then close **sec6x15**.

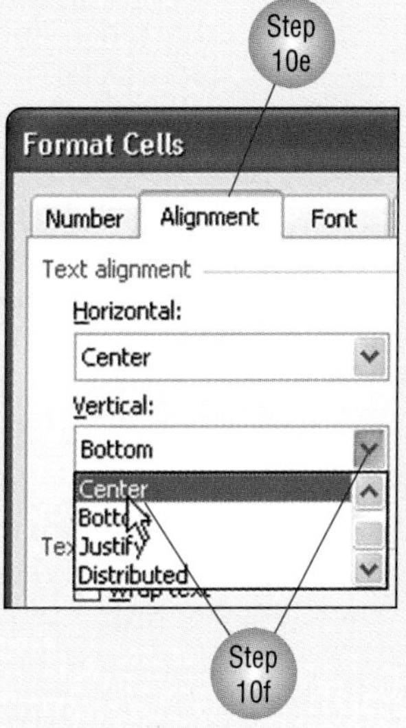

Copying Styles to Another Workbook

HINT
The Undo command will not reverse the effects of the Merge Style dialog box.

Styles you define are saved with the workbook in which they are created. You can, however, copy styles from one workbook to another. To do this, you would complete the following steps:

1. Open the workbook containing the styles you want to copy.
2. Open the workbook into which you want to copy the styles.
3. Display the Style dialog box.
4. At the Style dialog box, click the Merge button.
5. At the Merge Styles dialog box shown in Figure 6.6, double-click the name of the workbook that contains the styles you want to copy.
6. Click OK to close the Style dialog box.

FIGURE 6.6 **Merge Styles Dialog Box**

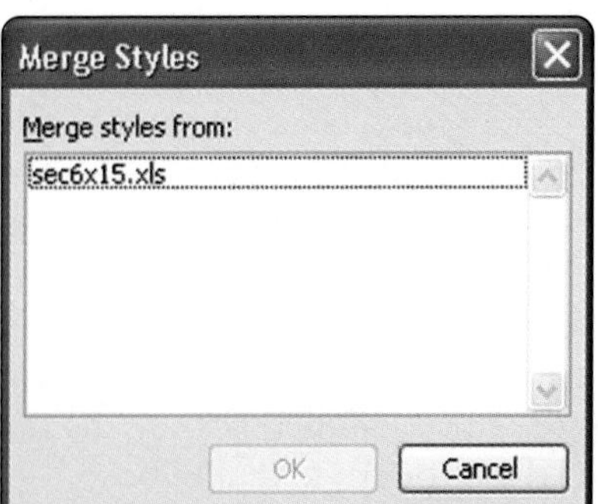

Removing a Style

If you apply a style to text and then decide you do not want the formatting applied, remove the style. To do this, select the cells formatted with the style you want to remove and then display the Style dialog box. At the Style dialog box, click the down-pointing arrow at the right side of the *Style name* text box, and then click *Normal* at the drop-down list.

Deleting a Style

Delete a style at the Style dialog box. To do this, display the Style dialog box, click the down-pointing arrow at the right side of the *Style name* text box. At the drop-down list that displays, click the style you want deleted, and then click the Delete button.

exercise 16 — COPYING AND REMOVING STYLES

1. Open **sec6x15**.
2. Open **ExcelWorksheet13**.
3. Save the workbook with Save As and name it **sec6x16**.
4. Delete column H.
5. Copy the styles in **sec6x15** into **sec6x16** by completing the following steps:
   a. Display the Style dialog box.
   b. At the Style dialog box, click the Merge button.
   c. At the Merge Styles dialog box, double-click ***sec6x15.xls*** in the *Merge styles from* list box.
   d. Click OK to close the Style dialog box.

6. Modify the Font style by completing the following steps:
   a. Click in any empty cell.
   b. Display the Style dialog box.
   c. At the Style dialog box, click the down-pointing arrow at the right side of the *Style name* text box, and then click *Font*.
   d. Click the Modify button.
   e. At the Format Cells dialog box, click the Font tab.
   f. Change the font to *Arial* and the size to *10*.
   g. Click OK to close the Format Cells dialog box.
   h. At the Style dialog box, click the Add button.
   i. Click the Close button to close the Style dialog box.
7. Apply the following styles:
   a. Select cells A1 through G2 and then apply the Title style.
   b. Select cells A3 through G8 and then apply the Font style.
8. Remove the Font style from cells B3 through B8 by completing the following steps:
   a. Select cells B3 through B8.
   b. Display the Style dialog box.
   c. At the Style dialog box, click the down-pointing arrow at the right side of the *Style name* text box, and then click *Normal*.

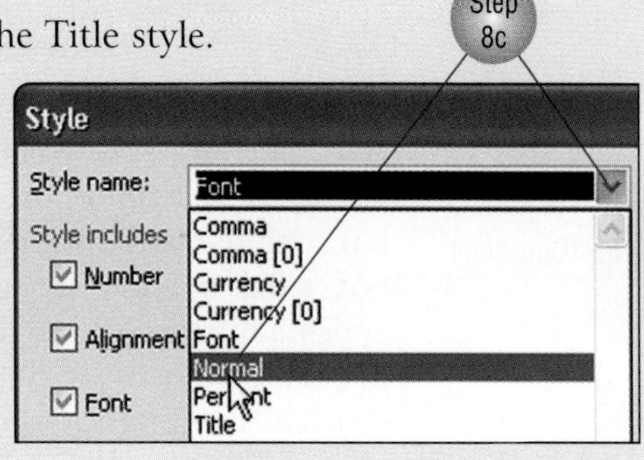

d. Click OK to close the dialog box.
9. Select cells D3 through D8 and then press F4. (This repeats the last action, which was changing the style to *Normal*.)
10. Select cells F3 through F8 and then press F4.
11. Make the following changes to the workbook:
    a. Change the width of columns B through G to 11.00.
    b. Select cells B3 through G8, click the Currency button on the Formatting toolbar, and then click twice on the Decrease Decimal button.
12. Save, print, and then close **sec6x16**.
13. Close **sec6x15**.

Inserting Comments

Insert a Comment
1. Click Insert, Comment.
2. Type comment.

OR

1. Display Reviewing toolbar.
2. Click New Comment button.
3. Type comment.

If you want to make comments in a worksheet, or if a reviewer wants to make comments in a worksheet prepared by someone else, insert a comment. A comment is useful for providing specific instructions, identifying critical information, or for multiple individuals reviewing the same worksheet to insert comments. Some employees in a company may be part of a ***workgroup***, which is a networked collection of computers sharing files, printers, and other resources. In a workgroup, you may collaborate with coworkers on a specific workbook. Comments provide a method for reviewing the workbook and responding to others in the workgroup.

Insert a comment by clicking Insert and then Comment or by clicking the New Comment button on the Reviewing toolbar. The Reviewing toolbar contains buttons for inserting and managing comments. Display this toolbar, shown in Figure 6.7, by clicking View, pointing to Toolbars, and then clicking Reviewing.

FIGURE 6.7 ***Reviewing Toolbar Buttons***

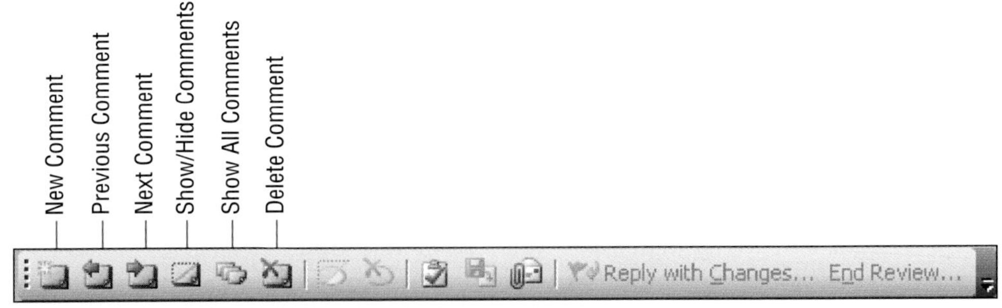

Inserting a Comment

New Comment

Insert a comment by clicking Insert and then Comment or by clicking the New Comment button on the Reviewing toolbar. This displays a yellow pop-up comment box with the user's name. Type the desired information or comment in this comment box. Click outside the comment box and the box is removed. A small, red triangle appears in the upper right corner of a cell containing a comment. You can also insert a comment by right-clicking a cell and then clicking Insert Comment at the shortcut menu.

Displaying a Comment

Show All Comments

Show/ Hide Comments

Next Comment

Previous Comment

Hover the mouse over a cell containing a comment and the comment box displays. Turn on the display of all comments by clicking the Show All Comments button on the Reviewing toolbar. Turn on the display of an individual comment by making the cell active and then clicking the Show/Hide Comments button on the Reviewing toolbar. Hide the display of an individual comment by making the cell active and then clicking the Hide Comment button on the Reviewing toolbar. (The Show/Hide Comments button becomes the Hide Comment button if the comment in the active cell is visible.) Move to comments in a worksheet by clicking the Next Comment or Previous Comment buttons on the Reviewing toolbar.

HINT
You can also display all comments by clicking View and then Comments.

Printing a Comment

By default, comments do not print. If you want comments to print, display the Page Setup dialog box with the Sheet tab selected and then click the down-pointing arrow at the right side of the *Comments* option box. At the drop-down menu that displays, choose *At end of sheet* to print comments on the page after cell contents, or choose the *As displayed on sheet* option to print the comments in the comment box in the worksheet.

INSERTING, DISPLAYING, AND PRINTING COMMENTS

1. Open **ExcelWorksheet26**.
2. Save the worksheet with Save As and name it **sec6x17**.
3. Turn on the display of the Reviewing toolbar by clicking View, pointing to Toolbars, and then clicking Reviewing. (Skip this step if the Reviewing toolbar is already displayed.)
4. Insert a comment by completing the following steps:
   a. Click cell F3 to make it active.
   b. Click the New Comment button on the Reviewing toolbar.
   c. In the comment box, type **Bill Lakeside Trucking for only 7 hours for the backhoe and front loader on May 1.**
   d. Click outside the comment box.

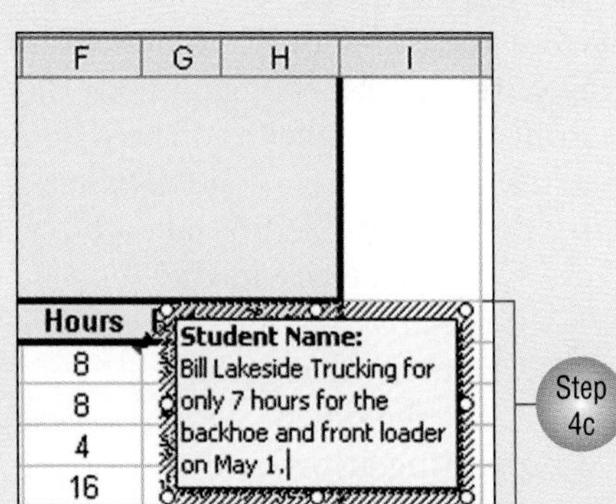

5. Insert another comment by completing the following steps:
   a. Click cell C6 to make it active.
   b. Click the New Comment button on the Reviewing toolbar.
   c. In the comment box, type **I think Country Electrical has changed their name to Northwest Electrical.**
   d. Click outside the comment box.

Client	Service Rep	Date
Lakeside Trucking	Monahan	5/1/2003
Lakeside Trucking	Monahan	5/1/2003
Martin Plumbing		
Country Electrical		
Able Construction		
Able Construction		
Miles Contracting		

Student Name:
I think Country Electrical has changed their name to Northwest Electrical.

Step 5c

6. Assume that more than one person is reviewing and commenting on this worksheet. Change the user name and then insert additional comments by completing the following steps:
   a. Click Tools and then Options.
   b. At the Options dialog box, click the General tab.
   c. Select the current name in the *User name* text box (remember the name you are selecting) and then type **Jean Coen**.
   d. Click OK to close the dialog box.
   e. Click cell D11 to make it active.
   f. Click the New Comment button on the Reviewing toolbar.
   g. In the comment box, type **This rental should be credited to *Monahan* instead of *Leuke*.**
   h. Click outside the comment box.
   i. Click cell G11 to make it active.
   j. Click the New Comment button on the Reviewing toolbar.
   k. In the comment box, type **The hourly rental for the pressure sprayer is $25.**
   l. Click outside the comment box.
   m. Complete steps similar to those in Steps 6a through 6d to return the user name back to the original name (the name that displayed before you changed it to *Jean Coen*).

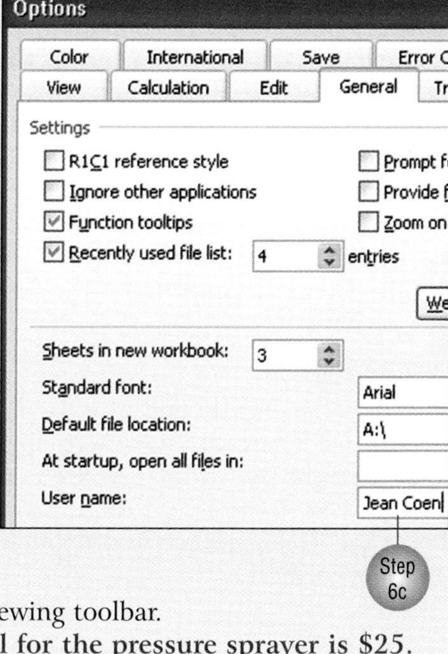

7. Click the Show All Comments button to turn on the display of all comments.
8. Save the worksheet again with the same name (**sec6x17**).
9. Print the worksheet and the comments by completing the following steps:
   a. Click File and then Page Setup.
   b. At the Page Setup dialog box, click the Page tab.
   c. Click *Landscape* in the *Orientation* section.
   d. Click the Sheet tab.
   e. Click the down-pointing arrow at the right side of the *Comments* option and then click *As displayed on sheet*.
   f. Click the Print button that displays toward the upper right corner of the dialog box.
   g. At the Print dialog box, click OK.

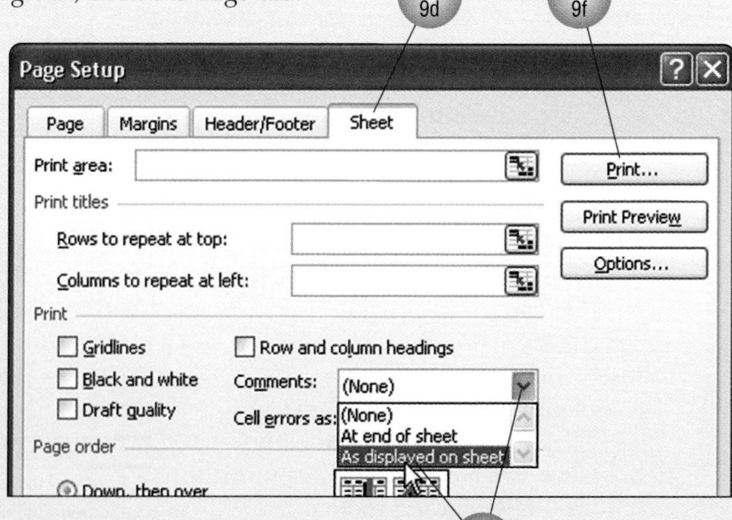

10. Click the Hide All Comments button (previously the Show All Comments button) to turn off the display of comments.
11. Save and then close **sec6x17**.

Editing a Comment

Edit Comment

To edit a comment, click the cell containing the comment, and then click the Edit Comment button on the Reviewing toolbar. (The New Comment button changes to the Edit Comment button when the active cell contains a comment.) You can also edit a comment by right-clicking the cell containing the comment and then clicking Edit Comment at the shortcut menu.

Deleting a Comment

Delete Comment

Cell comments exist in addition to data in a cell. Deleting data in a cell does not delete the comment. To delete a comment, click the cell containing the comment, and then click the Delete Comment button on the Reviewing toolbar. You can also delete a comment by clicking Edit, pointing to Clear, and then clicking Comments.

exercise 18

EDITING, DELETING, AND RESPONDING TO COMMENTS

1. Open **sec6x17**.
2. Save the worksheet with Save As and name it **sec6x18**.
3. Make sure the Reviewing toolbar is displayed.
4. Display comments by completing the following steps:
   a. Click cell A3 to make it the active cell.
   b. Click the Next Comment button on the Reviewing toolbar.
   c. Read the comment and then click the Next Comment button.
   d. Continue clicking the Next Comment button until a message displays telling you that Microsoft Excel has reached the end of the workbook and asking if you want to continue reviewing from the beginning of the workbook. At this message, click the Cancel button.
   e. Click outside the comment box.
5. Edit a comment by completing the following steps:
   a. Click cell D11 to make it active.
   b. Click the Edit Comment button.
   c. Edit the comment so it displays as **This rental should be credited to *Steele* instead of *Leuke*.**
6. Delete a comment by completing the following steps:
   a. Click cell C6 to make it active.
   b. Click the Delete Comment button on the Reviewing toolbar.
7. Respond to the comments by making the following changes:
   a. Change the contents of F3 from *8* to *7*.
   b. Change the contents of F4 from *8* to *7*.
   c. Change the contents of D11 from *Leuke* to *Steele*.
   d. Change the contents of G11 from *$20* to *$25*.

Step 4b
Next Comment
A3 1190
Hilltop Equipment Rental
Step 4a

	Invoice #	Equipment
2	Invoice #	Equipment
3	1190	Backhoe
4	1190	Front Loader
5	1191	Trencher

Date	Hours	Rate	Total
5/1/2003	8	$75	$ 600
5/1/2003	8	$65	$ 520
5/1/2003	4	$45	$ 180
5/1/2003	16	$75	$1,200
5/2/2003	5	$55	$ 275
5/2/2003	5	$25	$ 125
5/2/2003	10	$70	$ 700
			$ 200
			$ 160
			$ 120
			$ 160
			$ 650
5/3/2003	10	$55	$ 550

Jean Coen:
This rental should be credited to *Steele* instead of *Leuke*.

Step 5c

8. Save the worksheet again with the same name (**sec6x18**).
9. Print the worksheet and the comments by completing the following steps:
   a. Click File and then Page Setup.
   b. At the Page Setup dialog box, click the Sheet tab.
   c. Click the down-pointing arrow at the right side of the *Comments* option and then click *At end of sheet*.
   d. Click the Print button that displays toward the upper right corner of the dialog box.
   e. At the Print dialog box, click OK. (The worksheet will print on one page and the comments will print on a second page.)
10. Close **sec6x18**.

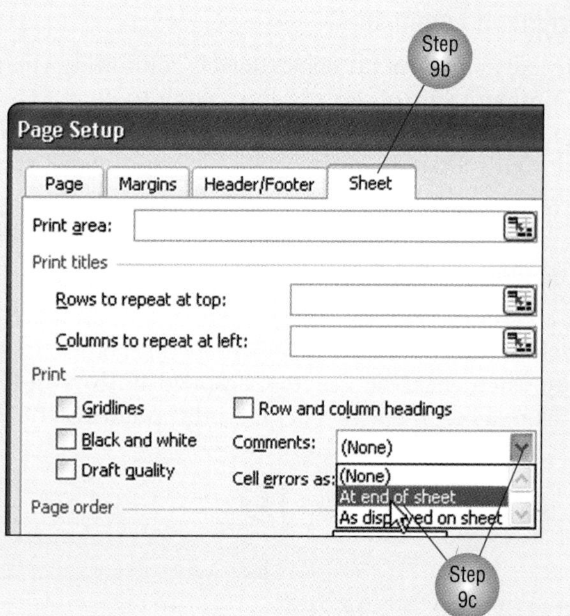

Using Excel Templates

HINT

If it fits your needs, consider using an Excel template worksheet form.

Excel has included a number of *template* worksheet forms formatted for specific uses. For example, Excel has provided template forms for a balance sheet, expense statement, loan amortization, sales invoice, and timecard. To view the templates available with Excel, click File and then New to display the New Workbook task pane. At the task pane, click the On my computer hyperlink. At the Templates dialog box, click the Spreadsheet Solutions tab and the template forms display as shown in Figure 6.8.

FIGURE 6.8 ***Templates Dialog Box with Spreadsheet Solutions Tab Selected***

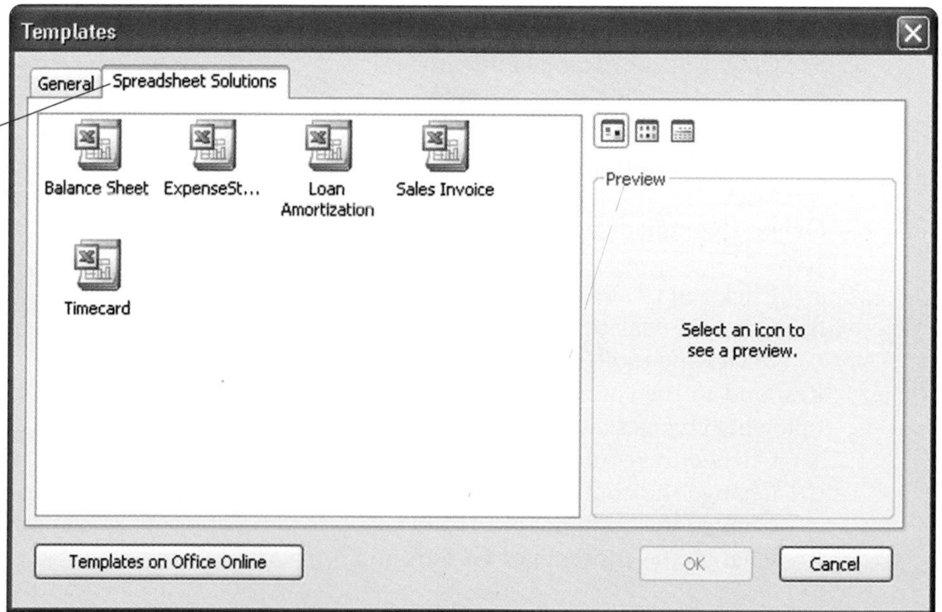

Entering Data in a Template

Templates contain unique areas where information is entered at the keyboard. For example, in the Sales Invoice template shown in Figure 6.9, you enter information such as the customer name, address, and telephone number, and also the quantity, description, and unit price of products. To enter information in the appropriate location, position the mouse pointer (white plus sign) in the location where you want to type data, and then click the left mouse button. After typing the data, click the next location. You can also move the insertion point to another cell using the commands learned in Chapter 1. For example, press the Tab key to make the next cell active, press Shift + Tab to make the previous cell active.

Use an Excel Template
1. Click File, New.
2. Click On my computer hyperlink.
3. Click Spreadsheet Solutions tab.
4. Double-click desired template.

FIGURE 6.9 **Sales Invoice Template**

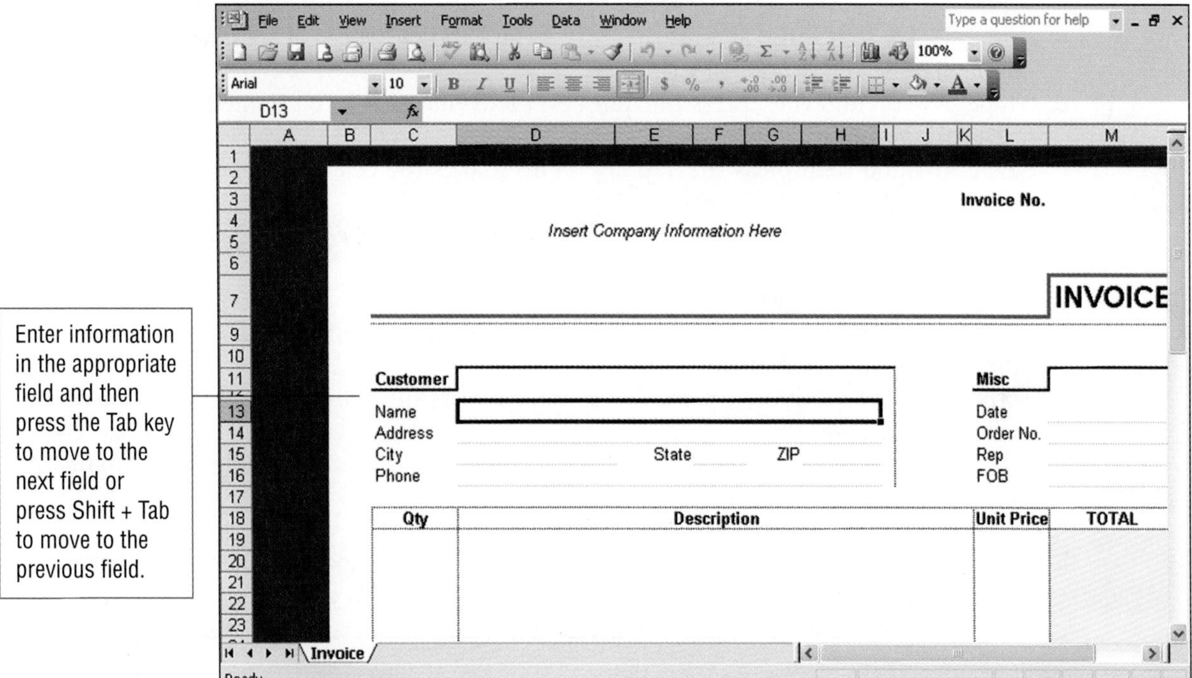

exercise 19

PREPARING A SALES INVOICE USING A TEMPLATE

1. Click File and then New.
2. At the New Workbook task pane, click the On my computer hyperlink.
3. At the Templates dialog box, click the Spreadsheet Solutions tab.

4. At the Templates dialog box with the Spreadsheet Solutions tab selected, double-click *Sales Invoice*.
5. Depending on your system, Microsoft may display a message box telling you that the workbook you are opening contains macros. Check with your instructor to make sure your system is secure and, if it is, click Enable Macros.

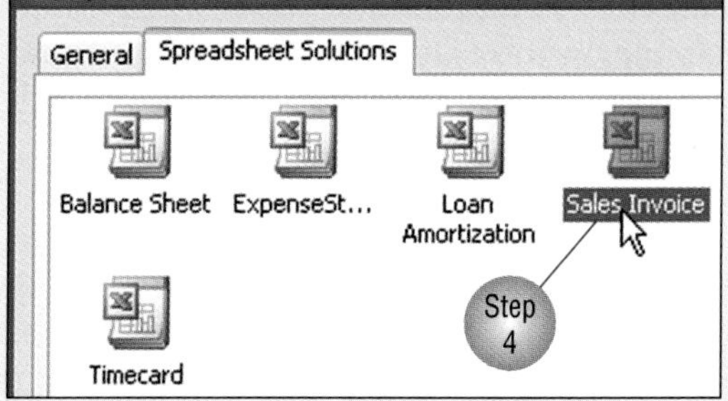

6. Type data in the invoice by completing the following steps:
   a. Type **IN-FLOW SYSTEMS** in the cell immediately to the right of *Name*. (This cell is automatically active when the sales invoice displays.)
   b. Press the Enter key. (This makes the cell immediately to the right of *Address* active.)
   c. Type **320 Milander Way** and then press the Tab key twice. (This makes the cell immediately to the right of *City* active.)
   d. Type **Boston** and then press the Tab key. (This makes the cell immediately to the right of *State* active.)
   e. Type **MA** and then press the Tab key. (This makes the cell immediately to the right of *ZIP* active.)
   f. Type **02188** and then press the Tab key twice. (This makes the cell immediately to the right of *Phone* active.)
   g. Type **(617) 555-3900**.
   h. Position the mouse pointer (white plus sign) to the right of *Order No.* and then click the left mouse button.
   i. Type **2388-348** and then press Enter. (This makes the cell immediately to the right of *Rep* active.)
   j. Type **Jenkins** and then press Enter. (This makes the cell immediately to the right of *FOB* active.)
   k. Type **Boston** and then press the Tab key.
   l. Type the following data immediately *below* the specified heading (use the mouse, the Tab key, and/or the Enter key to make the desired cell active):

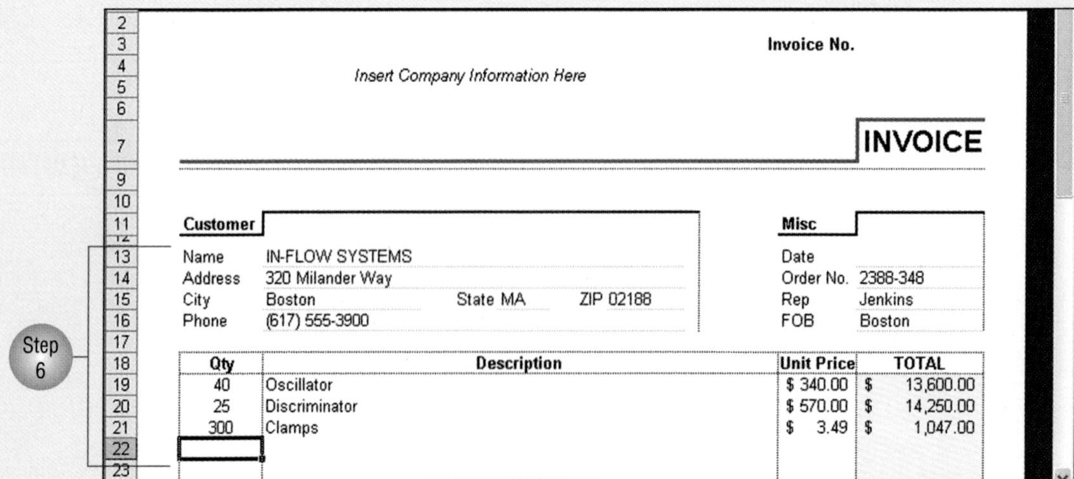

Qty.	=	40
Description	=	Oscillator
Unit Price	=	340
Qty.	=	25
Description	=	Discriminator
Unit Price	=	570
Qty.	=	300
Description	=	Clamps
Unit Price	=	3.49

7. Save the completed invoice and name it **sec6x19**.
8. Print and then close **sec6x19**.

CHAPTER summary

- Perform file management tasks such as copying, moving, printing, and renaming workbooks and creating a new folder and renaming a folder at the Open or Save As dialog boxes.
- Create a new folder by clicking the Create New Folder button located on the dialog box toolbar at the Open dialog box or Save As dialog box. A folder name can contain a maximum of 255 characters.
- To delete a workbook use the Delete button on the Open or Save As dialog box toolbar, the Delete option at the Tools button drop-down menu or with a shortcut menu option.
- Workbooks deleted from your data disk are deleted permanently. Workbooks and/or folders deleted from the hard drive are automatically sent to the Windows Recycle Bin where they can be restored or permanently deleted.
- Create a copy of an existing workbook by opening the workbook and then using the Save As command to assign the workbook a different file name.
- Use the Copy and Paste options from the shortcut menu at the Open (or Save As) dialog box to copy a workbook from one folder to another folder or drive.
- When you copy a workbook into the same folder from which it originates, Excel names the duplicated workbook "Copy of xxx" (where *xxx* is the original workbook name).
- Use the Send To option from the shortcut menu to send a copy of a workbook to another drive or folder.
- Remove a workbook from a folder or disk and insert it in another folder or disk using the Cut and Paste options from the shortcut menu.
- Use the Rename option from the Tools drop-down menu or the shortcut menu to give a workbook a different name.
- To move or copy a worksheet to another existing workbook, open both the source and the destination workbooks and then open the Move or Copy Sheet dialog box.
- Change the name of worksheets to help identify the data contained in them.
- Save a workbook in a different format with the *Save as type* option at the Save As dialog box. Click the down-pointing arrow at the right of the *Save as type* option and a drop-down list displays with the available formats.

- Use options at the Basic File Search task pane to search for specific workbooks. Display this task pane by clicking File and then File Search.
- Automate the formatting of cells in a workbook by defining and then applying styles. A style is a predefined set of formatting attributes.
- A style helps to ensure consistent formatting from one worksheet to another. All formatting attributes for a particular style are defined only once. Modify a style and all cells to which the style is applied automatically reflect the change.
- Define a style with formats already applied to a cell or display the Style dialog box, click the Modify button, and then choose formatting options at the Format Cells dialog box.
- Define, apply, modify, remove, and delete styles at the Style dialog box.
- Styles are saved in the workbook in which they are created. Styles can be copied, however, to another workbook. Do this with the Merge button at the Style dialog box.
- Insert comments in a worksheet to provide specific instructions, identify critical information, and review a workbook and respond to others in a workgroup about the workbook.
- Insert, display, edit, and delete comments using buttons on the Reviewing toolbar.
- By default, comments do not print. To print comments, display the Page Setup dialog box with the Sheet tab selected, and then choose the printing location with the *Comments* option.
- Excel provides preformatted templates for creating forms such as a balance sheet, expense statement, loan amortization, sales invoice, and timecard.
- Templates contain unique areas where information is entered at the keyboard. These areas vary depending on the template.

FEATURES summary

FEATURE	BUTTON	MENU	KEYBOARD
Open dialog box		File, Open	Ctrl + O
Save As dialog box		File, Save As	Ctrl + S
Print dialog box		File, Print	Ctrl + P
Move or Copy Sheet dialog box		Edit, Move or Copy Sheet	
Basic File Search task pane		File, File Search	
Style dialog box		Format, Style	
Merge Styles dialog box		Format, Style, Merge	
Reviewing toolbar		View, Toolbars, Reviewing	
Templates dialog box		File, New, On my computer	

CONCEPTS check

Completion: On a blank sheet of paper, indicate the correct term, symbol, or command for each description.

1. File management tasks such as copying, moving, or deleting workbooks can be performed at the Open dialog box or this dialog box.
2. Click this button on the Open dialog box toolbar to display the folder that is up a level from the current folder.
3. Workbooks and/or folders deleted from the hard drive can be restored by opening this feature in Windows.
4. Click the down-pointing arrow at the right side of this option at the Save As dialog box to display a list of available workbook formats.
5. Search for specific workbooks with options at this task pane.
6. Click this button at the Style dialog box to display the Format Cells dialog box.
7. In a cell containing a comment, this displays in the upper right corner of the cell.
8. Print comments by choosing the desired printing location with the *Comments* option at the Page Setup dialog box with this tab selected.
9. Click this button on the Reviewing toolbar to display all comments in the worksheet.
10. Click this hyperlink in the New Workbook task pane to display the Templates dialog box.

SKILLS check

Assessment 1

1. Display the Open dialog box with ExcelChapter06S the active folder.
2. Create a new folder named *Sales* in the ExcelChapter06S folder.
3. Copy **ExcelWorksheet01** and **ExcelWorksheet10** to the Sales folder.
4. Rename **ExcelWorksheet01** to **SalesByJob** in the Sales folder. (At the message asking if you are sure you want to rename the read-only file, click Yes.)
5. Rename **ExcelWorksheet10** to **SalesbySalesperson** in the Sales folder. (At the message asking if you are sure you want to rename the read-only file, click Yes.)
6. Change the active folder back to ExcelChapter06S.
7. Close the Open dialog box.

Assessment 2

1. Display the Open dialog box.
2. Delete all of the workbooks in the ExcelChapter06S folder that begin with *Copy of*.
3. Move **ExcelWorksheet07** and **ExcelWorksheet29** to the *Sales* folder.
4. Change the active folder back to ExcelChapter06S.
5. Close the Open dialog box.

Assessment 3

1. Display the Open dialog box and make Sales the active folder.
2. Open **ExcelWorksheet07** and **ExcelWorksheet29**.
3. Make **ExcelWorksheet07** the active workbook and then copy *Sheet1* from **ExcelWorksheet07** and position it before Sheet2 in **ExcelWorksheet29**.
4. With **ExcelWorksheet29** the active workbook, rename *Sheet1* to *Accounts*.
5. With **ExcelWorksheet29** the active workbook, rename *Sheet1 (2)* to *Depreciation*.
6. Save **ExcelWorksheet29** with Save As and name it **sec6sc03**.
7. Print the entire workbook and then close **sec6sc03**.
8. Close **ExcelWorksheet07**.

Assessment 4

1. Use the Basic File Search task pane to search for all workbooks on your disk containing the word *Equipment*.
2. Search for all workbooks on your disk containing the words *Lakeside Trucking*.

Assessment 5

1. At a clear worksheet, define a style named *Heading* that contains the following formatting:
   a. 14-point Times New Roman bold in Blue-Gray color
   b. Horizontal alignment of Center
   c. Double-line top and bottom border in Dark Red color
   d. Light purple shading
2. Define a style named *Column01* that contains the following formatting:
   a. 12-point Times New Roman in Blue-Gray color
   b. Light purple shading
3. Define a style named *Column02* that contains 12-point Times New Roman in Blue-Gray color.
4. Save the worksheet and name it **sec6style01**.
5. With **sec6style01** open, open **ExcelWorksheet09**.
6. Save the worksheet with Save As and name it **sec6sc05**.
7. Copy the styles from **sec6style01** into **sec6sc05**. ***(Hint: Do this through the Style dialog box.)***
8. Select cells A1 through M1 and then click the Merge and Center button on the Formatting toolbar.
9. Apply the following styles:
   a. Select cells A1 through M2 and then apply the Heading style.
   b. Select cells A3 through A9 and then apply the Column01 style.
   c. Select cells B3 through G9 and then apply the Column02 style.
   d. Select cells H3 through M9 and then apply the Column01 style.
10. Automatically adjust the widths of columns A through M.
11. Save the worksheet again and then print **sec6sc05** on one page in landscape orientation. (Make sure you choose the *Fit to* option at the Page Setup dialog box.)
12. With **sec6sc05** still open, modify the following styles:
   a. Modify the Heading style so it changes the font color to Plum (instead of Blue-Gray) and inserts a solid, thick top and bottom border in Plum (instead of a double-line top and bottom border in Dark Red).
   b. Modify the Column02 style so it adds a font style of Bold Italic (leave all of the other formatting attributes).
13. Automatically adjust the widths of columns A through M.

14. Save the worksheet again and then print **sec6sc05** on one page and in landscape orientation.
15. Close **sec6sc05**.
16. Close **sec6style01**.

Assessment 6

1. Open **ExcelWorksheet37**.
2. Save the worksheet with Save As and name it **sec6sc06**.
3. Insert the following comments in the specified cells:

B7	=	**Should we include Sun Valley, Idaho, as a destination?**
B12	=	**Please include the current exchange rate.**
G8	=	**What other airlines fly into Aspen, Colorado?**

4. Save **sec6sc06**.
5. Turn on the display of all comments.
6. Print the worksheet in landscape orientation with the comments as displayed on the worksheet.
7. Turn off the display of all comments.
8. Delete the comment in cell B12.
9. Print the worksheet again with the comments printed at the end of the worksheet. (The comments will print on a separate page from the worksheet.)
10. Save and then close **sec6sc06**.

Assessment 7

1. In this chapter, you learned about the styles feature, which automates formatting in a workbook. Another formatting feature is Conditional Formatting. Use Excel's Help feature to learn about Conditional Formatting.
2. Open **ExcelWorksheet06**.
3. Save the worksheet with Save As and name it **sec6sc07**.
4. Select cells B3 through M20 and then use Conditional Formatting to display all percentages between 95% and 100% in red and with a red border.
5. Save, print in landscape orientation, and then close **sec6sc07**.

CHAPTER challenge

You have recently opened a new business called Sit and Soak Spas. You decide to create a financial form based on Excel's Timecard template. Use the Timecard template to create an Excel workbook called Employee Time Card. Save the workbook in a new folder named Financial Forms. Since each of the employees will complete the time card on the computer, you decide providing additional information might be helpful. Insert comments in at least three different areas that would benefit the employees when they are completing the time card. Also, create and apply a new style (containing formats of your choice) to the bolded headings. Do not apply the style to the main title of the form, "TIMECARD". Save the workbook again.

Although Excel has several templates from which to choose, you may have a need for a variety of other templates. Use the Help feature to learn how to obtain additional templates. Access the World Wide Web and locate a template (not already located on your computer) that would be helpful in your new business. Download the template to your computer. Complete the template with information of your own and save it as an Excel workbook in the folder Financial Forms.

To give customers more exposure to your new business and to help them in the decision-making process of buying a spa, you decide to make the template downloaded in the second part of the Chapter Challenge available on the Web. If the template is not appropriate, choose another one or use the Loan Amortization template located under the Spreadsheets Solutions tab. Save the template as a Web page in the Financial Forms folder.

CHAPTER 7

CREATING A CHART IN EXCEL

PERFORMANCE OBJECTIVES

Upon successful completion of Chapter 7, you will be able to:

- **Create a chart with data in an Excel worksheet**
- **Create a chart in a separate worksheet**
- **Print a selected chart and print a worksheet containing a chart**
- **Size, move, and delete a chart**
- **Change the type of chart**
- **Choose a custom chart type**
- **Change data in a chart**
- **Add, delete, and customize elements in a chart**

In the previous Excel chapters, you learned to create data in worksheets. While a worksheet does an adequate job of representing data, you can present some data more visually by charting the data. A chart is sometimes referred to as a ***graph*** and is a picture of numeric data. In this chapter, you will learn to create and customize charts in Excel.

Creating a Chart

Chart Wizard

QUICK STEPS

Create a Chart
1. Select cells.
2. Click Chart Wizard button.
3. Complete the four steps of the wizard.

In Excel, create a chart by selecting cells containing the data you want to chart, and then clicking the Chart Wizard button on the Standard toolbar. Four steps are involved in creating a chart with the Chart Wizard. Suppose you wanted to create a chart with the worksheet shown in Figure 7.1. To create the chart with the Chart Wizard, you would complete the following steps:

1. Select the cells containing data (in the worksheet in Figure 7.1, this would be cells A1 through C4).
2. Click the Chart Wizard button on the Standard toolbar.
3. At the Chart Wizard - Step 1 of 4 - Chart Type dialog box shown in Figure 7.2, choose the desired chart type and chart sub-type, and then click the Next button.

HINT

Press F11 to create a chart using the Chart Wizard with all default settings.

4. At the Chart Wizard - Step 2 of 4 - Chart Source Data dialog box shown in Figure 7.3, make sure the data range displays correctly (for the chart in Figure 7.1, the range will display as *=Sheet1!$A$1:$C$4*), and then click the Next button.
5. At the Chart Wizard - Step 3 of 4 - Chart Options dialog box shown in Figure 7.4, make any changes to the chart, and then click the Next button.
6. At the Chart Wizard - Step 4 of 4 - Chart Location dialog box shown in Figure 7.5, specify where you want the chart inserted, and then click the Finish button.

If the chart was created with all of the default settings at the Chart Wizard dialog boxes, the chart would display below the cells containing data as shown in Figure 7.6.

FIGURE 7.1 ***Excel Worksheet***

	A	B	C	D
1	**Salesperson**	**June**	**July**	
2	Chaney	$34,239	$39,224	
3	Ferraro	$23,240	$28,985	
4	Jimenez	$56,892	$58,450	
5				

FIGURE 7.2 ***Chart Wizard - Step 1 of 4 - Chart Type Dialog Box***

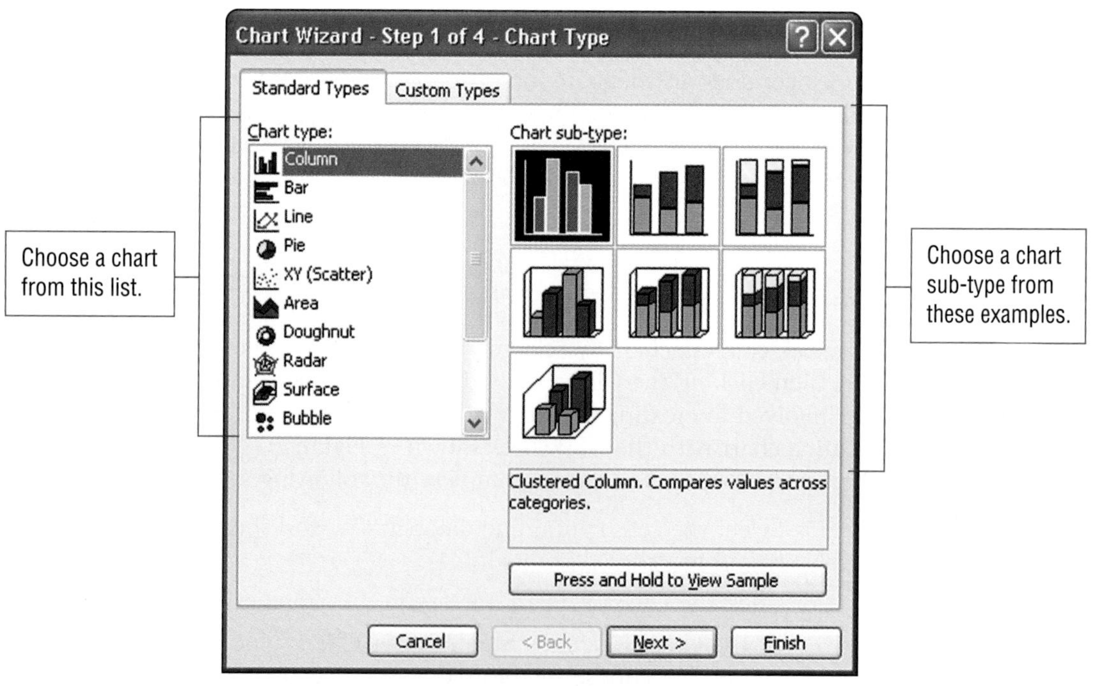

FIGURE 7.3 ***Chart Wizard - Step 2 of 4 - Chart Source Data Dialog Box***

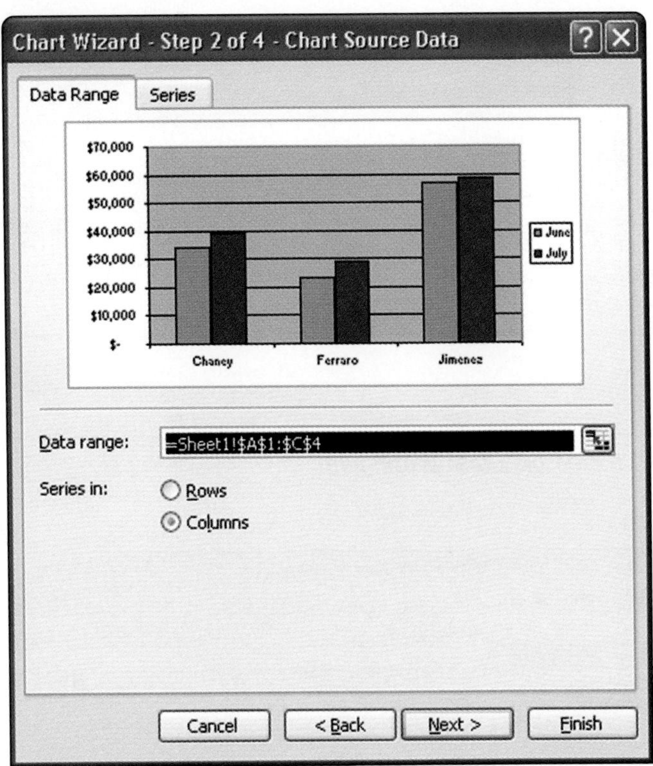

FIGURE 7.4 ***Chart Wizard - Step 3 of 4 - Chart Options Dialog Box***

Add and/or format chart elements with options from this dialog box with various tabs selected.

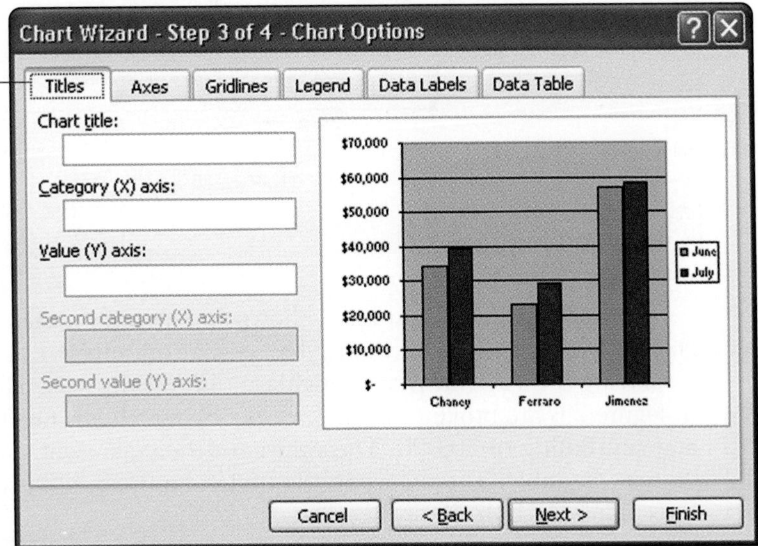

FIGURE

7.5 Chart Wizard - Step 4 of 4 - Chart Location Dialog Box

To insert a chart in the active window, leave this at the default setting of *As object in*. Choose the *As new sheet* option to create the chart in a separate sheet.

Chart Wizard - Step 4 of 4 - Chart Location

Place chart:

As new sheet: Chart1

As object in: Sheet1

Cancel | < Back | Next > | Finish

FIGURE

7.6 Chart Based on Excel Worksheet

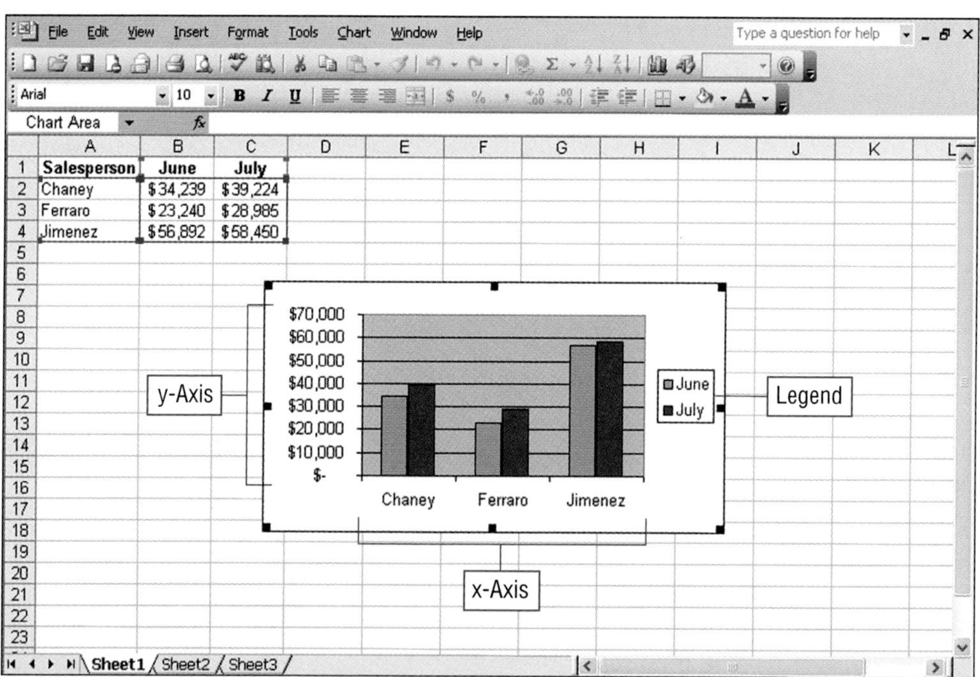

HINT

Preview the chart at Step 1 of the Chart Wizard by positioning the arrow pointer on the Press and Hold to View Sample button and then holding down the left mouse button.

In the chart created in Excel shown in Figure 7.6, the left vertical side of the chart is referred to as the y-axis. The y-axis contains tick marks with amounts displaying the value at that particular point on the axis. The values in the chart in Figure 7.6 are broken into tick marks by ten thousands beginning with zero and continuing to 70,000. The values for the y-axis will vary depending on the data in the table. The names in the first column are used for the x-axis, which runs along the bottom of the chart.

exercise 1

CREATING A CHART IN EXCEL WITH DATA IN A WORKSHEET

1. Open **ExcelWorksheet15**.
2. Save the worksheet with Save As and name it **sec7x01**.
3. Create a chart using the Chart Wizard by completing the following steps:
   a. Select cells A1 through E5.
   b. Click the Chart Wizard button on the Standard toolbar.

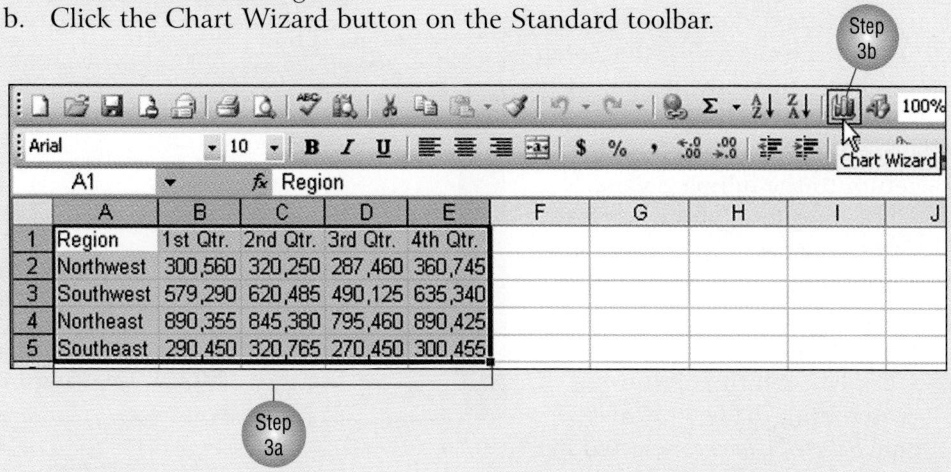

Step 3b
100%
Arial
10
Chart Wizard
A1
Region
	A	B	C	D	E
1	Region	1st Qtr.	2nd Qtr.	3rd Qtr.	4th Qtr.
2	Northwest	300,560	320,250	287,460	360,745
3	Southwest	579,290	620,485	490,125	635,340
4	Northeast	890,355	845,380	795,460	890,425
5	Southeast	290,450	320,765	270,450	300,455
Step 3a

   c. At the Chart Wizard - Step 1 of 4 - Chart Type dialog box, click the Next button.
   d. At the Chart Wizard - Step 2 of 4 - Chart Source Data dialog box, make sure the data range displays as *=Sheet1!$A$1:$E$5* and then click the Next button.
   e. At the Chart Wizard - Step 3 of 4 - Chart Options dialog box, click the Next button.
   f. At the Chart Wizard - Step 4 of 4 - Chart Location dialog box, make sure the *As object in* option is selected and that *Sheet1* displays in the text box, and then click the Finish button.
   g. Click outside the chart to deselect the chart.
4. Print **sec7x01** in landscape orientation.
5. Save and then close **sec7x01**.

Printing Only the Chart

In a worksheet containing data in cells as well as a chart, you can print only the chart. To do this, click the chart to select it and then display the Print dialog box. At the Print dialog box, *Selected Chart* will automatically be selected in the *Print what* section. Click OK to print only the selected chart.

Previewing a Chart

Preview a chart by clicking the Print Preview button on the Standard toolbar or by clicking File and then Print Preview. This displays the worksheet containing the chart in Print Preview. After previewing the chart, click the Close button, or print the worksheet by clicking the Print button on the Print Preview toolbar and then clicking OK at the Print dialog box.

exercise 2

PREVIEWING AND THEN PRINTING ONLY THE CHART IN EXCEL

1. Open **sec7x01**.
2. Preview the chart by completing the following steps:
   a. Click the Print Preview button on the Standard toolbar.
   b. In Print Preview, click the Zoom button to make the display of the worksheet bigger.
   c. Click the Zoom button again to return to the full-page view.
   d. Click the Close button to close Print Preview.
3. Print only the chart by completing the following steps:
   a. Click the chart to select it.
   b. Click File and then Print.
   c. At the Print dialog box, make sure *Selected Chart* is selected in the *Print what* section of the dialog box and then click OK.
4. Close **sec7x01**.

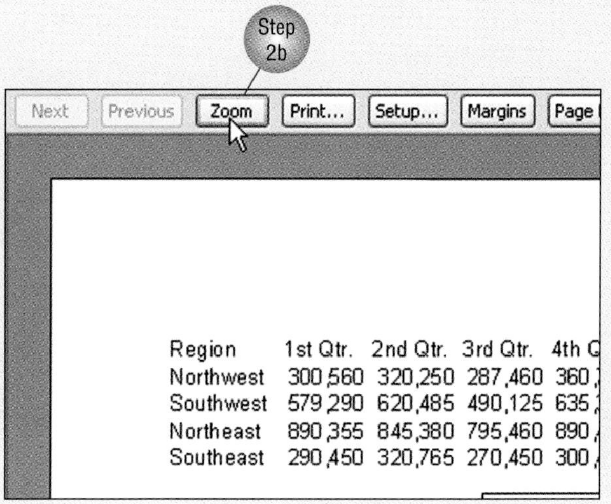

Creating a Chart in a Separate Worksheet

The chart you created in Excel in Exercise 1 was inserted in the same worksheet as the cells containing data. You should not delete the data (displaying only the chart) because the data in the chart will also be deleted. If you want to create a chart in a worksheet by itself, click the *As new sheet* option at the Chart Wizard - Step 4 of 4 - Chart Location dialog box. When the chart is completed, it displays in a separate sheet and fills most of the page. The sheet containing the chart is labeled *Chart1*. This sheet label displays on a tab located toward the bottom of the screen. The worksheet containing the data is located in *Sheet 1*. You can move between the chart and the worksheet by clicking the desired tab.

exercise 3

CREATING A CHART IN A SEPARATE EXCEL WORKSHEET

1. Open **ExcelWorksheet15**.
2. Save the worksheet with Save As and name it **sec7x03**.
3. Create a chart as a separate sheet using the Chart Wizard by completing the following steps:
   a. Select cells A1 through E5.
   b. Click the Chart Wizard button on the Standard toolbar.
   c. At the Chart Wizard - Step 1 of 4 - Chart Type dialog box, click the Next button.

d. At the Chart Wizard - Step 2 of 4 - Chart Source Data dialog box, make sure the data range displays as *=Sheet1!$A$1:$E$5*, and then click the Next button.
e. At the Chart Wizard - Step 3 of 4 - Chart Options dialog box, click the Next button.

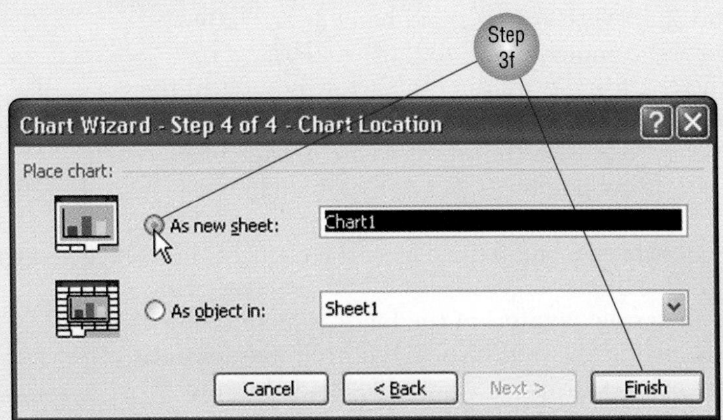

f. At the Chart Wizard - Step 4 of 4 - Chart Location dialog box, click *As new sheet*, and then click the Finish button.

4. Save the workbook (two sheets) again and then print only the sheet containing the chart. (To do this, make sure the sheet containing the chart displays, and then click the Print button on the Standard toolbar.)
5. Close **sec7x03**.

Deleting a Chart

Delete a chart created in Excel by clicking once in the chart to select it and then pressing the Delete key. If a chart created in a new worksheet is deleted, the chart is deleted but the worksheet is not. To delete the chart as well as the worksheet, position the mouse pointer on the *Chart1* tab, click the *right* mouse button, and then click Delete at the shortcut menu. At the message box telling you that selected sheets will be permanently deleted, click OK.

Sizing and Moving a Chart

You can change the size of a chart created in Excel in the same worksheet as the data containing cells. To do this, click the chart once to select it (this inserts black square sizing handles around the chart), and then drag the sizing handles in the desired direction.

A chart created with data in a worksheet can be moved by selecting the chart and then dragging it with the mouse. To move a chart, click once inside the chart to select it. Position the arrow pointer inside the chart, hold down the left mouse button, drag the outline of the chart to the desired location, and then release the button.

exercise 4

SIZING A CHART

1. Open **sec7x01**.
2. Save the worksheet with Save As and name it **sec7x04**.
3. Size the chart by completing the following steps:
   a. Select the chart by positioning the arrow pointer in the white portion of the chart just inside the chart border until a yellow box with the words *Chart Area* displays next to the arrow pointer (takes approximately one second) and then clicking the left mouse button. (Do not click on a chart element. This selects the element, not the entire chart.)
   b. Position the arrow pointer on the black, square sizing handle located in the middle of the bottom border until the arrow pointer turns into a double-headed arrow pointing up and down.
   c. Hold down the left mouse button, drag the outline of the bottom border of the chart down approximately five rows, and then release the mouse button.
   d. Position the arrow pointer on the black square sizing handle located in the middle of the right border until the arrow pointer turns into a double-headed arrow pointing left and right.
   e. Hold down the left mouse button, drag the outline of the border to the right approximately two columns, and then release the mouse button.
   f. Deselect the chart. (To do this, click in an empty cell somewhere in the worksheet.)
4. Change the page orientation to landscape and then print **sec7x04**.
5. Save the worksheet again with the same name (**sec7x04**).
6. Close **sec7x04**.

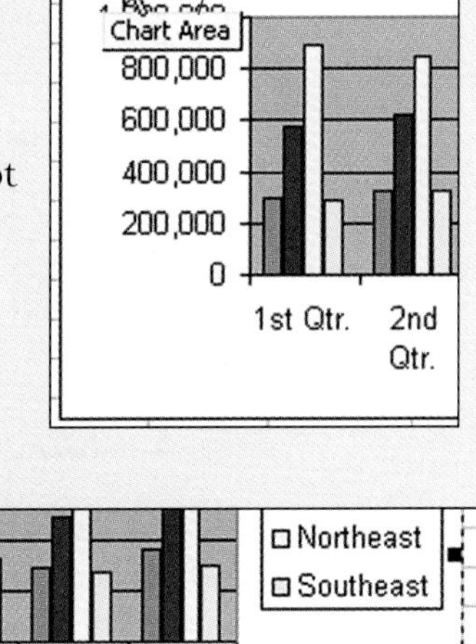

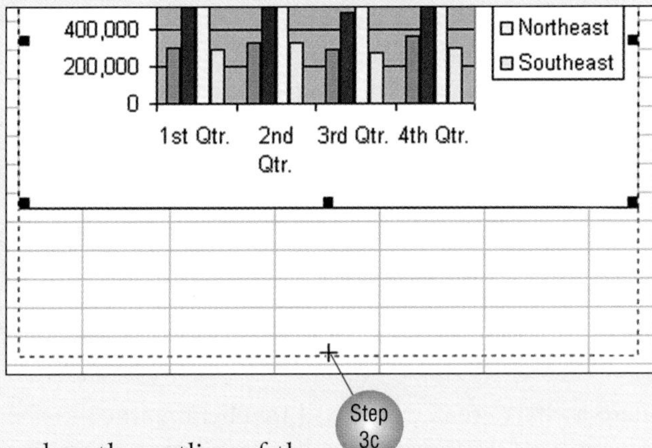

Changing the Chart Type

QUICK STEPS

Change Chart Type
1. Make the chart active.
2. Click Chart, Chart Type.
3. Click the desired type.
4. Click OK.

In Exercises 1 and 3, you created a column chart, which is the default. The Chart Wizard offers 14 basic chart types along with built-in autoformats you can apply to save time to get the desired look for the chart. Table 7.1 shows an illustration and explanation of the 14 chart types.

TABLE

7.1 **Chart Types**

Icon	Chart Type	Description
	Area	An Area chart emphasizes the magnitude of change, rather than time and the rate of change. It also shows the relationship of parts to a whole by displaying the sum of the plotted values.
	Bar	A Bar chart shows individual figures at a specific time, or shows variations between components but not in relationship to the whole.
	Bubble	A Bubble chart compares sets of three values in a manner similar to a scatter chart, with the third value displayed as the size of the bubble marker.
	Column	A Column chart compares separate (noncontinuous) items as they vary over time.
	Cone	A Cone chart displays columns with a conical shape.
	Cylinder	A Cylinder chart displays columns with a cylindrical shape.
	Doughnut	A Doughnut chart shows the relationship of parts of the whole.
	Line	A Line chart shows trends and change over time at even intervals. It emphasizes the rate of change over time rather than the magnitude of change.
	Pie	A Pie chart shows proportions and relationships of parts to the whole.
	Pyramid	A Pyramid chart displays columns with a pyramid shape.
	Radar	A Radar chart emphasizes differences and amounts of change over time and variations and trends. Each category has its own value axis radiating from the center point. Lines connect all values in the same series.
	Stock	A Stock chart shows four values for a stock—open, high, low, and close.
	Surface	A Surface chart shows trends in values across two dimensions in a continuous curve.
	XY (Scatter)	A Scatter chart either shows the relationships among numeric values in several data series or plots the interception points between *x* and *y* values. It shows uneven intervals of data and is commonly used in scientific data.

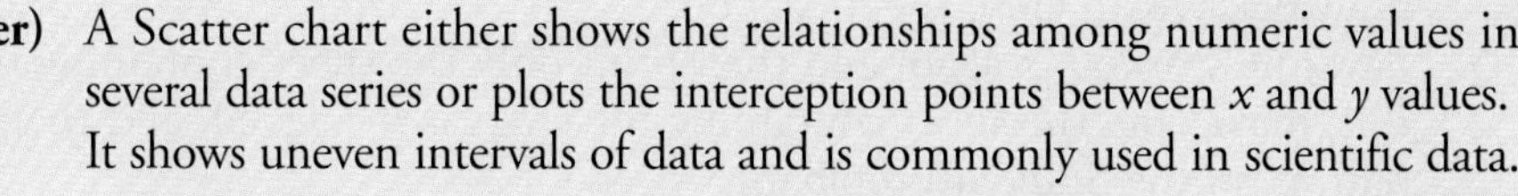

You can choose a chart type in Step 1 of the Chart Wizard steps or change the chart type for an existing chart. When creating a chart with the Chart Wizard, choose the desired chart type and sub-type at the first Chart Wizard dialog box. To change the chart type for an existing chart, make sure the chart is active, click Chart, and then click Chart Type. This displays the Chart Type dialog box. Choose the desired chart type and chart sub-type at this dialog box and then click the OK button.

You can also change the chart type in an existing chart with a shortcut menu. To do this, position the arrow pointer in a white portion of the chart (inside the chart but outside any chart element), and then click the *right* mouse button. At the shortcut menu that displays, click Chart Type. This displays the Chart Type dialog box that contains the same options as the Chart Wizard - Step 1 of 4 - Chart Type dialog box.

exercise 5 CHANGING CHART TYPE IN EXCEL

1. Open **sec7x03**.
2. Save the workbook with Save As and name it **sec7x05**.
3. Make sure the chart is displayed. If not, click the *Chart1* tab located at the bottom of the worksheet window.
4. Change the chart type to a Line chart by completing the following steps:
   a. Click Chart and then Chart Type.
   b. At the Chart Type dialog box, click *Line* in the *Chart type* list box.
   c. Change the chart sub-type by clicking the first chart in the second row in the *Chart sub-type* list box.

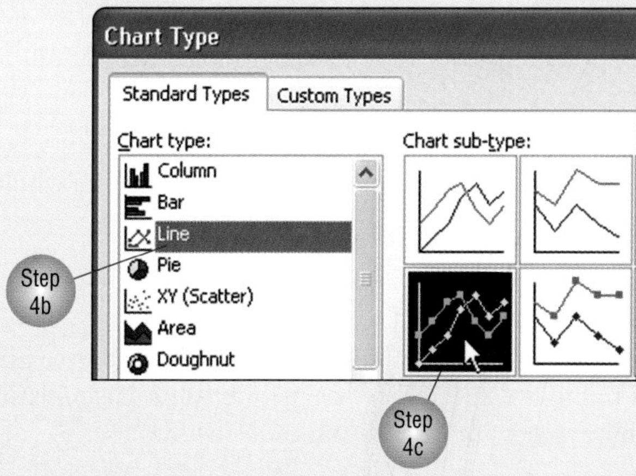

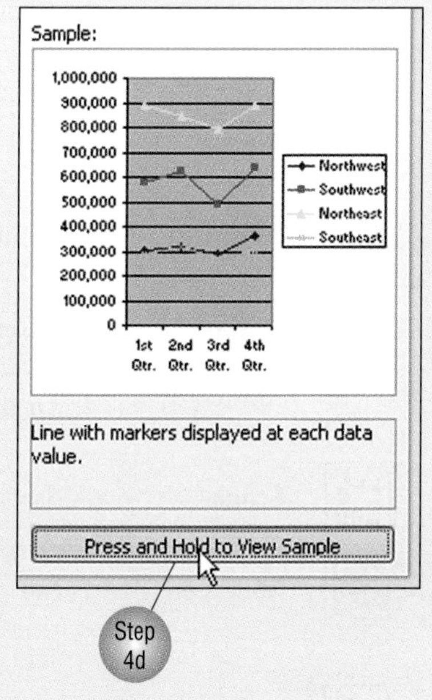

   d. View a sample of how this sub-type chart will display by positioning the arrow pointer on the Press and Hold to View Sample button and then holding down the left mouse button. After viewing a sample of the selected Line chart, release the mouse button.
   e. Click OK to close the dialog box.
5. Save the workbook again and then print only the sheet containing the chart. (To do this, make sure the sheet containing the chart is displayed, and then click the Print button on the Standard toolbar.)

6. With **sec7x05** still open, change the chart type to *Bar* by completing the following steps:
   a. Click Chart and then Chart Type.
   b. At the Chart Type dialog box, click *Bar* in the *Chart type* list box.
   c. Change the chart sub-type by clicking the first chart in the second row in the *Chart sub-type* list box.

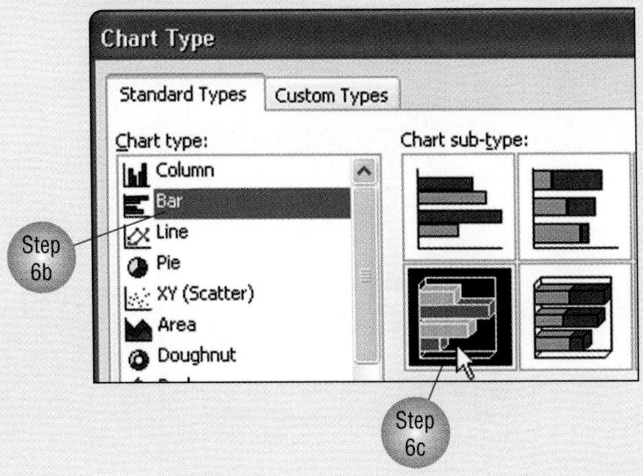

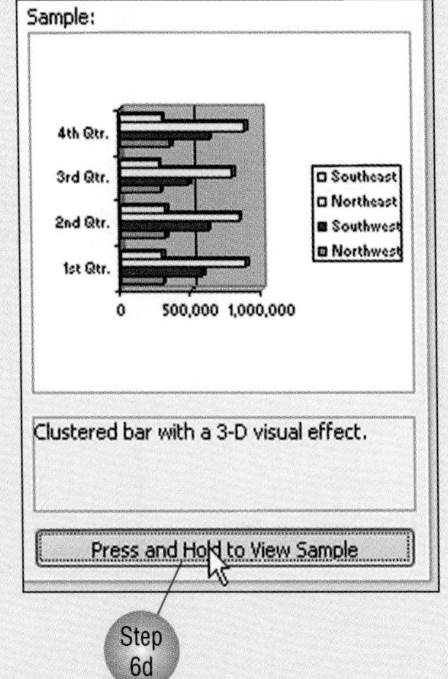

   d. View a sample of how this sub-type chart will display by positioning the arrow pointer on the Press and Hold to View Sample button and then holding down the left mouse button. After viewing a sample of the selected Bar chart, release the mouse button.
   e. Click OK to close the dialog box.
7. Save the workbook again and then print only the sheet containing the chart. (To do this, make sure the sheet containing the chart displays, and then click the Print button on the Standard toolbar.)
8. Close **sec7x05**.

Choosing a Custom Chart Type

The chart feature offers a variety of preformatted custom charts. A custom chart can be chosen in Step 1 of the Chart Wizard steps or a custom chart type can be chosen for an existing chart. To choose a custom chart type while creating a chart, click the Custom Types tab at the Chart Wizard - Step 1 of 4 - Chart Type dialog box.

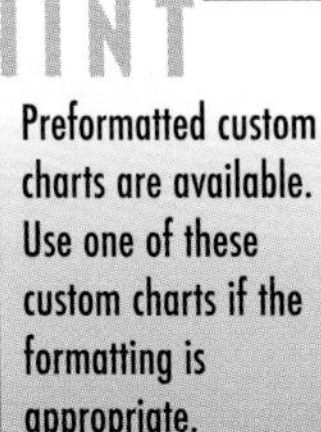

HINT
Preformatted custom charts are available. Use one of these custom charts if the formatting is appropriate.

You can also choose a custom chart for an existing chart. To do this, click Chart and then Chart Type. At the Chart Type dialog box, click the Custom Types tab. This displays the Chart Type dialog box as shown in Figure 7.7. You can also display the Chart Type dialog box by positioning the arrow pointer in the chart, clicking the *right* mouse button, and then clicking Chart Type at the shortcut menu. At the Chart Type dialog box with the Custom Types tab selected, click the desired custom chart type in the *Chart type* list box.

FIGURE

7.7 Chart Type Dialog Box with Custom Types Tab Selected

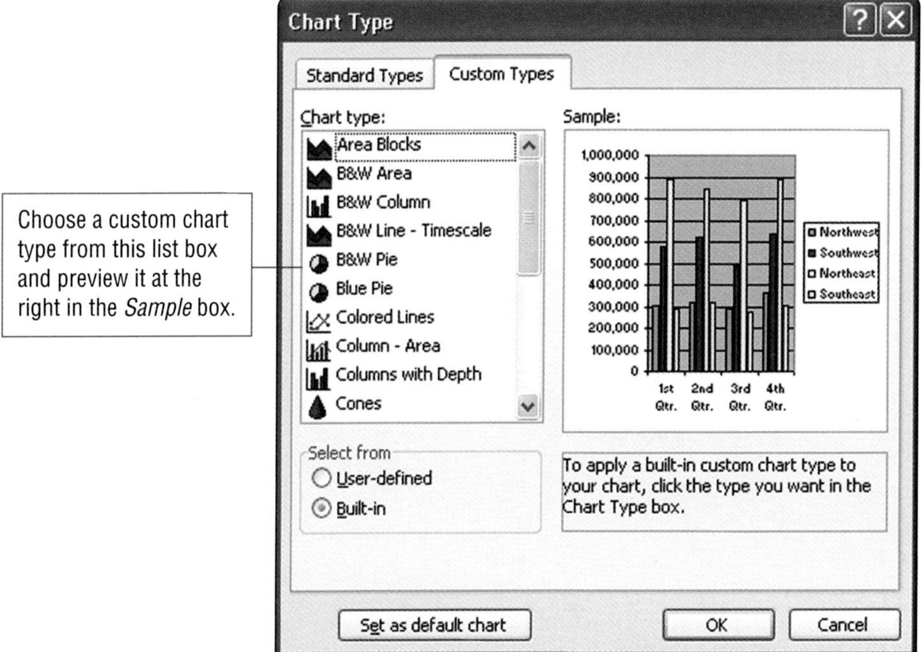

exercise 6

CHOOSING A CUSTOM CHART TYPE

1. Open **sec7x03**.
2. Save the workbook with Save As and name it **sec7x06**.
3. Choose a custom chart type by completing the following steps:
   a. Click Chart and then Chart Type.
   b. At the Chart Type dialog box, click the Custom Types tab.
   c. At the Chart Type dialog box with the Custom Types tab selected, click *Columns with Depth* in the *Chart type* list box.
   d. Click OK to close the Chart Type dialog box.
4. Save the workbook again and then print only the sheet containing the chart.
5. Close **sec7x06**.

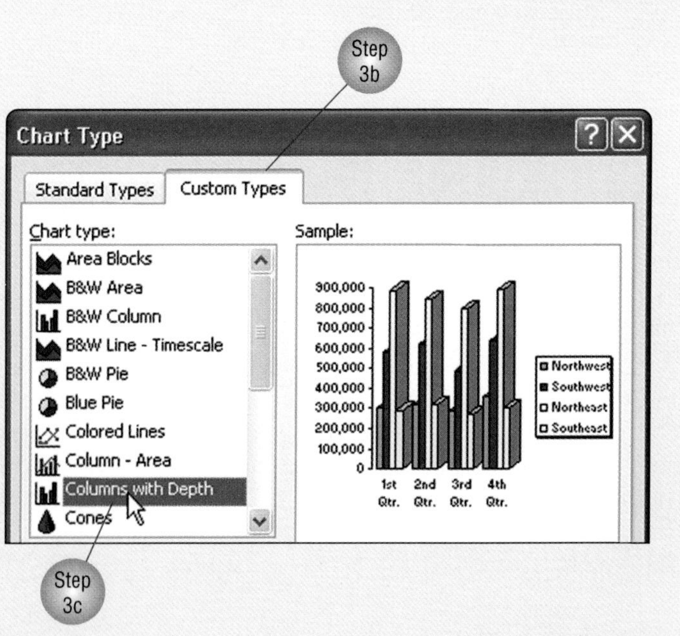

Changing Data in Cells

The Excel chart feature uses data in cells to create a chart. This data can be changed and the chart will reflect the changes. When a change is made to data in a worksheet, the change is also made to any chart created with the cells in the worksheet. The change is reflected in a chart whether it is located in the same worksheet as the changed cells or in a new sheet.

HINT

The chart is linked to the selected cells. If data is changed in a selected cell, the chart is automatically updated.

exercise 7

CHANGING NUMBERS IN AN EXCEL WORKSHEET

1. Open **sec7x03**.
2. Save the workbook with Save As and name it **sec7x07**.
3. Make sure the worksheet containing the cells (not the chart) is active. If not, click the *Sheet1* tab located at the bottom of the worksheet window.
4. Make the following changes to the specified cells:

   C2: Change *320,250* to *295,785*
   D3: Change *490,125* to *550,350*
   C5: Change *320,765* to *298,460*
   E5: Change *300,455* to *275,490*

5. Display the worksheet containing the chart *(Chart1)*.
6. Save the workbook again and then print only the sheet containing the chart.
7. Close **sec7x07**.

Changing the Data Series

When a chart is created, the Chart Wizard uses the data in the first column (except the first cell) to create the x-axis (the information along the bottom of the chart) and uses the data in the first row (except the first cell) to create the legend. For example, in the chart in Figure 7.6, the names (Chaney, Ferraro, and Jimenez) were used for the x-axis (along the bottom of the chart) and the months (June and July) were used for the legend.

When a chart is created, the option *Columns* is selected by default at the Chart Wizard - Step 2 of 4 - Chart Source Data dialog box. Change this to *Rows* and the data in the first row (except the first cell) will be used to create the x-axis and the data in the first column will be used to create the legend.

Change the data series in an existing chart by making the chart active, clicking Chart, and then clicking Source Data. This displays the Source Data dialog box shown in Figure 7.8. Another method for displaying the Source Data dialog box is to position the arrow pointer in a white portion of the chart (inside the chart but outside any chart element) and then click the *right* mouse button. At the shortcut menu that displays, click Source Data. The Source Data dialog box contains the same options as the Chart Wizard - Step 2 of 4 - Chart Source Data dialog box.

HINT

A data series is information represented on the chart by bars, lines, columns, pie slices, and so on.

QUICK STEPS

Change Chart Data Series

1. Make the chart active.
2. Click Chart, Source Data.
3. Click the desired tab and options.
4. Click OK.

FIGURE 7.8 ***Source Data Dialog Box***

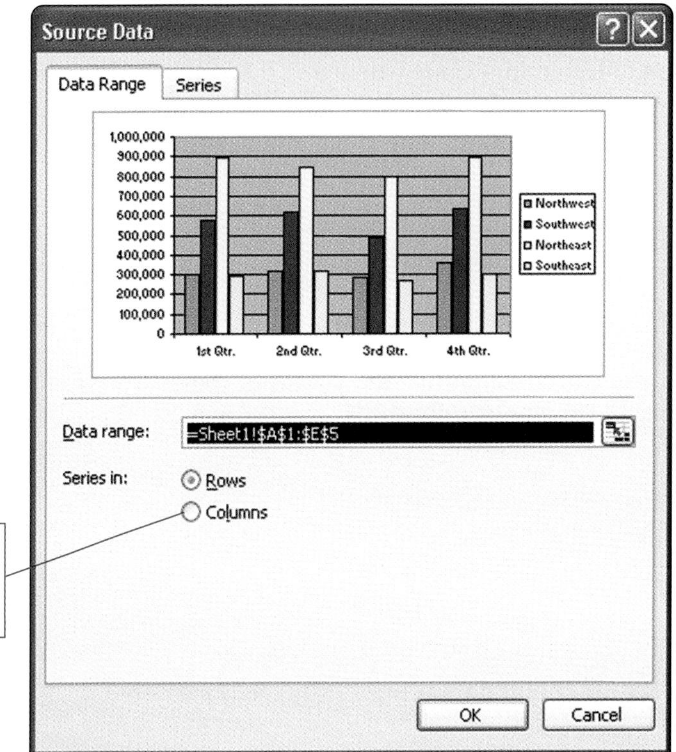

Choose the *Columns* option to reverse the x-axis and the legend.

exercise 8

CHANGING DATA SERIES IN AN EXCEL CHART

1. Open **sec7x01**.
2. Save the workbook with Save As and name it **sec7x08**.
3. Change the data series by completing the following steps:
   a. Position the arrow pointer in a white portion of the chart (inside the chart but outside any chart element) and then click the *right* mouse button.
   b. At the shortcut menu that displays, click Source Data.
   c. At the Source Data dialog box, click the *Columns* option.
   d. Click OK to close the Source Data dialog box.
   e. Click outside the chart to deselect it.
4. Save, print in landscape orientation, and then close **sec7x08**.

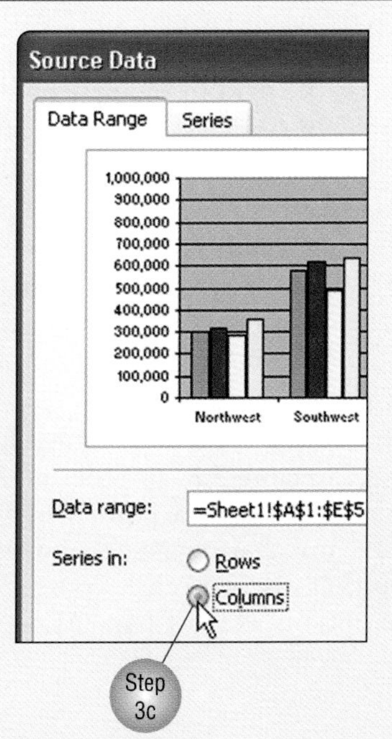

exercise 9

CREATING A PIE CHART IN EXCEL USING CHART WIZARD

1. Open **ExcelWorksheet16**.
2. Save the worksheet with Save As and name it **sec7x09**.
3. Create a pie chart by completing the following steps:
   a. Select cells A4 through B10.
   b. Click the Chart Wizard button on the Standard toolbar.
   c. At the Chart Wizard - Step 1 of 4 - Chart Type dialog box, click *Pie* in the *Chart type* list box, and then click the Next button.
   d. At the Chart Wizard - Step 2 of 4 - Chart Source Data dialog box, make sure the data range displays as *=Sheet1!$A$4:$B$10*. Click the *Rows* option to see what happens to the pie when the data series is changed, click *Columns* to return the data series back, and then click the Next button.
   e. At the Chart Wizard - Step 3 of 4 - Chart Options dialog box, click the Data Labels tab.
   f. At the dialog box with the Data Labels tab selected, click *Percentage*.
   g. Click the Next button.
   h. At the Chart Wizard - Step 4 of 4 - Chart Location dialog box, click *As new sheet* and then click the Finish button.
4. Save the workbook again and then print only the sheet containing the chart.
5. Close **sec7x09**.

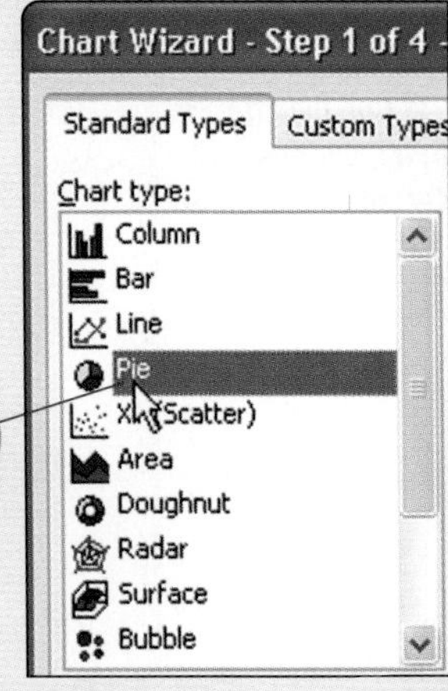

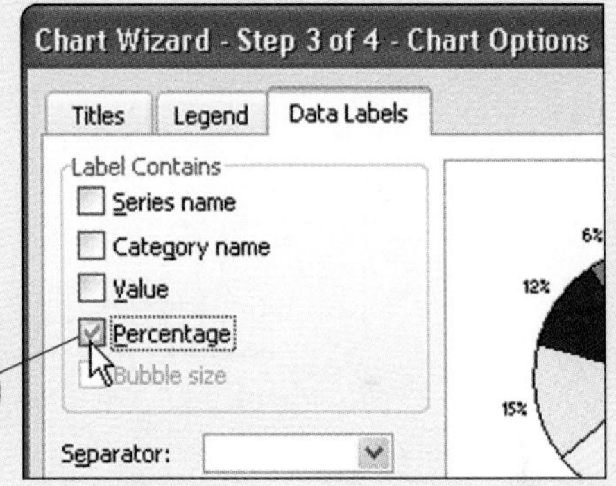

Adding Chart Elements

Certain chart elements are automatically inserted in a chart created by the Chart Wizard including a chart legend and labels for the x-axis and y-axis. Add other chart elements such as a chart title and data labels at the Chart Wizard - Step 3 of 4 - Chart Options dialog box. Add chart elements to an existing chart by making the chart active, clicking Chart, and then clicking Chart Options. This displays the Chart Options dialog box shown in Figure 7.9. Another method for displaying this dialog box is to position the arrow pointer in a white portion of the chart (inside the chart but outside any chart element), click the *right* mouse button, and then click Chart Options. The Chart Options dialog box contains the same options as the Chart Wizard - Step 3 of 4 - Chart Options dialog box.

HINT

The legend identifies which data series is represented by which data marker.

Add a Chart Element

1. Make the chart active.
2. Click Chart, Chart Options.
3. Click the desired tab and options.
4. Click OK.

FIGURE

7.9 Chart Options Dialog Box with Titles Tab Selected

Customize a chart with options at this dialog box with the various tabs selected.

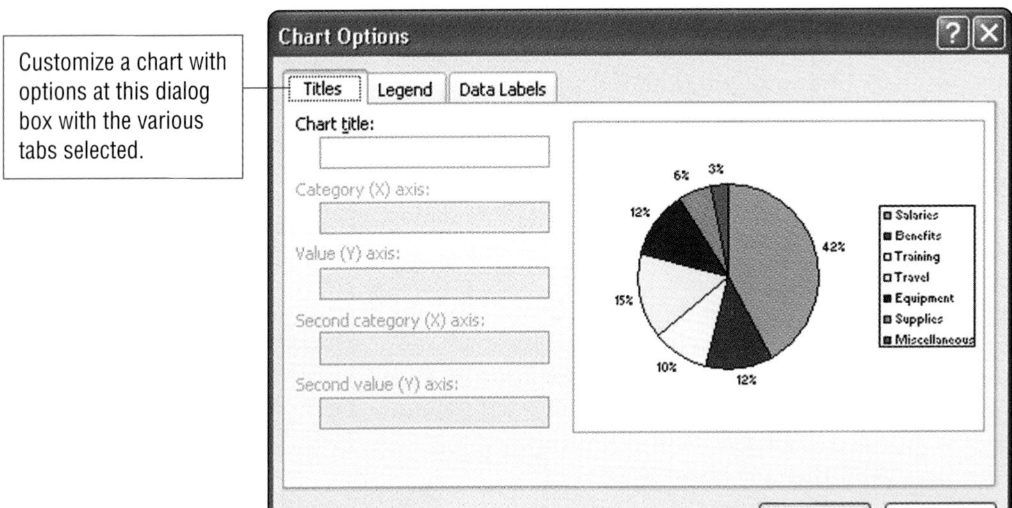

exercise 10

ADDING A TITLE TO A CHART AND CHANGING THE LEGEND LOCATION

1. Open **sec7x09**.
2. Save the workbook with Save As and name it **sec7x10**.
3. Add a title and data labels to the chart and change the location of the chart legend by completing the following steps:
   a. Make sure the sheet *(Chart1)* containing the pie chart displays.
   b. Click Chart and then Chart Options.
   c. At the Chart Options dialog box, click the Titles tab. (Skip this step if the Titles tab is already selected.)
   d. Click inside the *Chart title* text box and then type DEPARTMENT EXPENSES BY PERCENTAGE.

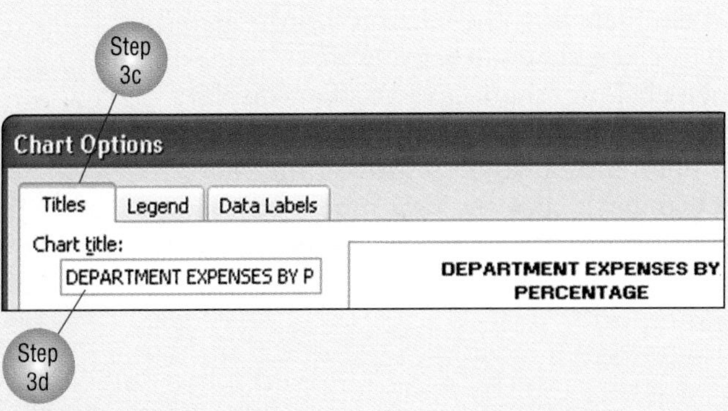

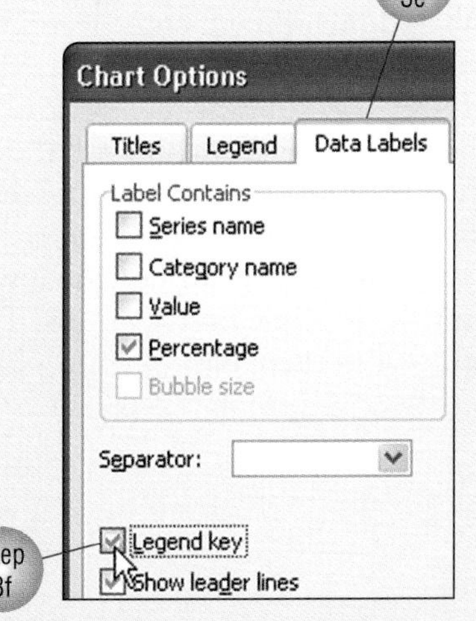

   e. Click the Data Labels tab.
   f. Click the *Legend key* option to insert a check mark.

g. Click the Legend tab.
h. At the Chart Options dialog box with the Legend tab selected, click *Left*.
i. Click the OK button to close the dialog box.

4. Save the workbook again and then print only the sheet containing the pie chart.
5. Close **sec7x10**.

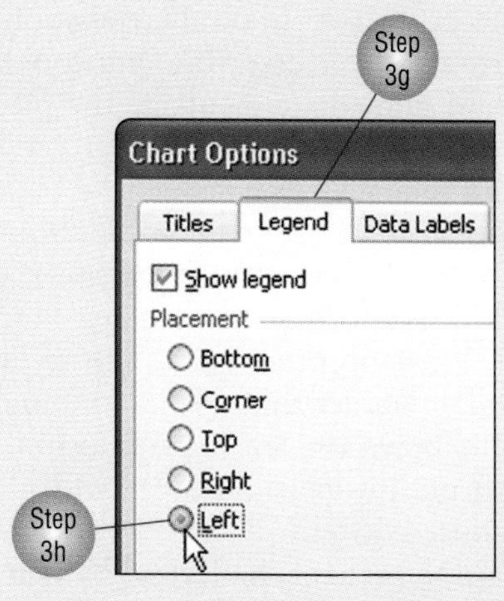

Moving/Sizing Chart Elements

When additional elements are added to a chart, the chart can become quite full and elements may overlap. If elements in a chart overlap, an element can be selected and then moved. To select an element, position the arrow pointer on a portion of the element, and then click the left mouse button. This causes sizing handles to display around the element. Position the mouse pointer toward the edge of the selected element until it turns into an arrow pointer, hold down the left mouse button, drag the element to the desired location, and then release the mouse button. To change the size of an element, drag the sizing handles in the desired direction.

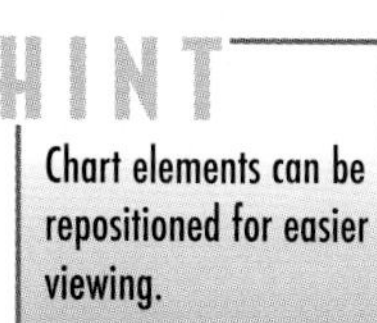

HINT
Chart elements can be repositioned for easier viewing.

Deleting/Removing Chart Elements

Chart elements can be selected by clicking the desired element. Once an element is selected, it can be moved and it can also be deleted. To delete a selected element, press the Delete key. If you delete a chart element in a chart and then decide you want it redisplayed in the chart, immediately click the Undo button on the Standard toolbar.

exercise 11

MOVING/SIZING/ADDING CHART ELEMENTS

1. Open **sec7x10**.
2. Save the workbook with Save As and name it **sec7x11**.
3. Move the legend to the right side of the chart by completing the following steps:
   a. Click the legend to select it.
   b. With the arrow pointer positioned in the legend, hold down the left mouse button, drag the outline of the legend to the right side of the chart, and then release the mouse button.
4. Move the pie to the left by completing the following steps:

a. Select the pie. To do this, position the arrow pointer in a white portion of the chart immediately outside the pie (a yellow box displays with *Plot Area* inside) and then click the left mouse button. (This should insert a square border around the pie. If not, try selecting the pie again.)

b. With the pie selected (square border around the pie), position the arrow pointer inside the square border that displays around the pie (not inside the pie), hold down the left mouse button, drag the outline of the pie to the left until it looks balanced with the legend, and then release the mouse button.

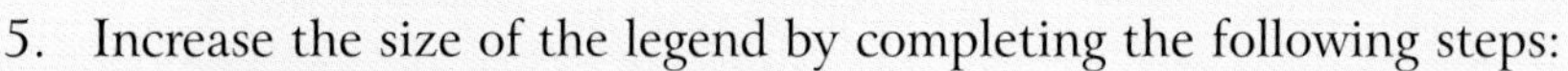

5. Increase the size of the legend by completing the following steps:
   a. Click the legend to select it.
   b. Use the sizing handles that display around the legend to increase the size. (You determine the direction to drag the sizing handles and the final size of the legend. Make sure the pie and legend are balanced.)

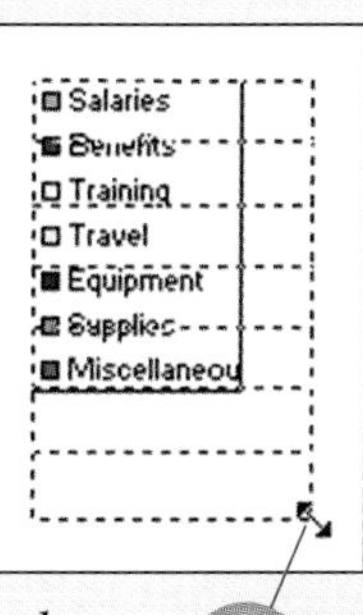

6. Save the workbook again and then print only the sheet containing the pie chart.
7. With **sec7x11** still open, delete the legend by completing the following steps:
   a. Click the legend to select it.
   b. Press the Delete key.
8. Change the data labels by completing the following steps:
   a. Position the arrow pointer in a white portion of the chart (outside any chart element) and then click the *right* mouse button.
   b. At the shortcut menu that displays, click Chart Options.
   c. At the Chart Options dialog box, click the Data Labels tab.
   d. At the Chart Options dialog box with the Data Labels tab selected, click the *Category name* option to insert a check mark. (Make sure the *Percentage* option still contains a check mark.)
   e. Click OK to close the Chart Options dialog box.

9. Move the pie by completing the following steps:
   a. Make sure the pie is selected. (If the pie is not selected, select it by positioning the arrow pointer in a white portion of the chart outside but immediately left or right at the top or bottom of the pie [a yellow box displays with *Plot Area* inside] and then clicking the left mouse button.)
   b. With the pie selected (square border around the pie), position the arrow pointer inside the square border that displays around the pie (not inside the pie), hold down the left mouse button, drag the outline of the pie until it looks centered between the left and right sides of the chart, and then release the mouse button.
10. Save the workbook again and then print only the sheet containing the pie chart.
11. Close **sec7x11**.

Adding Gridlines

Gridlines can be added to a chart for the category, series, and value. Depending on the chart, some but not all of these options may be available. To add gridlines, display the Chart Options dialog box and then click the Gridlines tab. This displays the Chart Options dialog box with the Gridlines tab selected as shown in Figure 7.10. At this dialog box, insert a check mark in those options for which you want gridlines.

FIGURE 7.10 **Chart Options Dialog Box with Gridlines Tab Selected**

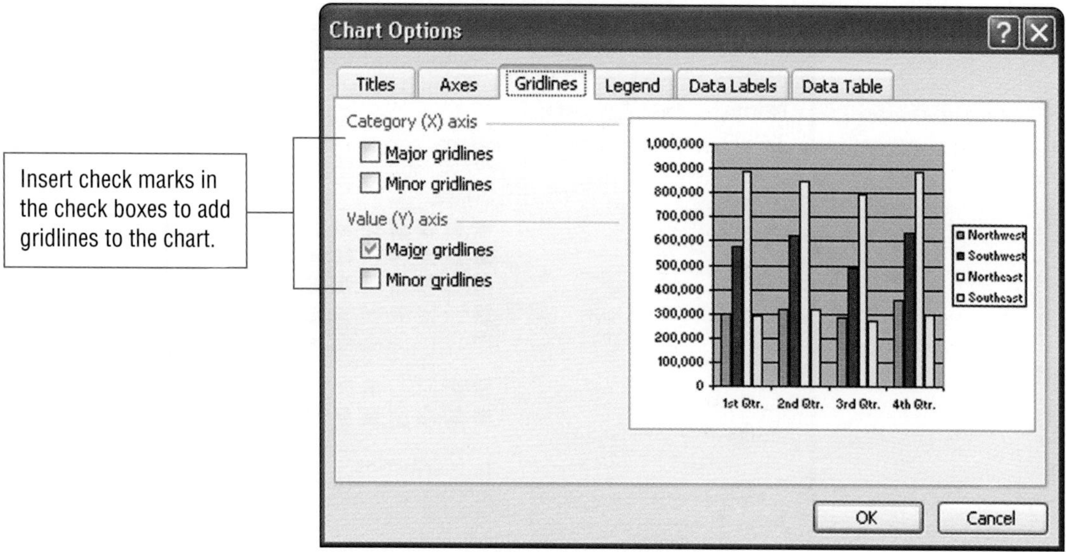

exercise 12

ADDING GRIDLINES TO A CHART

1. Open **sec7x03**.
2. Save the workbook with Save As and name it **sec7x12**.
3. Add gridlines to the chart by completing the following steps:
   a. Make sure the sheet containing the chart is displayed. (If not, click the *Chart1* tab located toward the bottom of the screen.)
   b. Click Chart and then Chart Options.
   c. At the Chart Options dialog box, click the Gridlines tab.
   d. At the Chart Options dialog box with the Gridlines tab selected, insert a check mark in the two options in the *Category (X) axis* section and also the two options in the *Value (Y) axis* section.
   e. Click OK to close the Chart Options dialog box.
4. Save the workbook again and then print only the sheet containing the chart.
5. Close **sec7x12**.

Step 3c

Chart Options
Titles Axes Gridlines
Category (X) axis
Major gridlines
Minor gridlines
Value (Y) axis
Major gridlines
Minor gridlines

Step 3d

Formatting Chart Elements

A variety of formatting options is available for a chart or chart elements. Formatting can include adding a pattern, changing background and foreground colors of the selected element or chart, changing the font, and changing the alignment or placement. To customize a chart, double-click in the chart area (outside any chart element). This displays the Format Chart Area dialog box with the Patterns tab selected as shown in Figure 7.11. You can also display this dialog box by clicking once in the chart area, clicking Format, and then clicking Selected Chart Area.

FIGURE 7.11 ***Format Chart Area Dialog Box with Patterns Tab Selected***

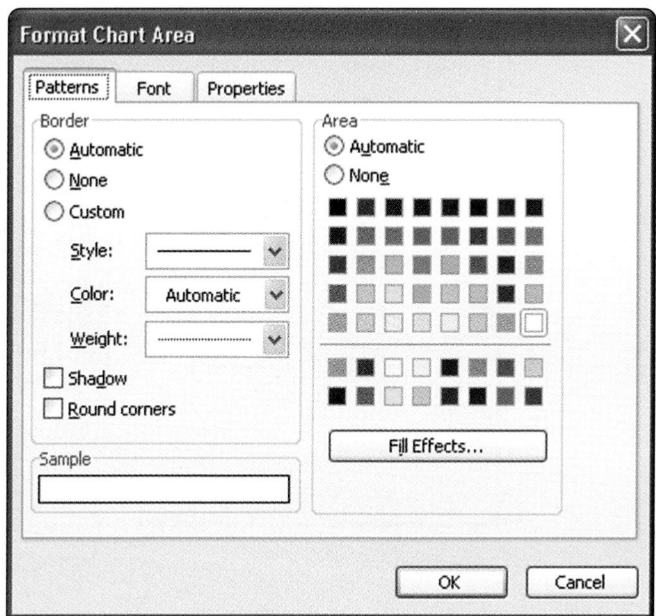

Customize the chart area by adding a pattern and/or fill color and background at the Format Chart Area dialog box with the Patterns tab selected. Click the Font tab and options for changing the typeface, type style, and type size display.

The font and pattern of chart elements can also be customized along with additional formatting for specific elements. For example, if you double-click a chart title, the Format Chart Title dialog box displays. (You can also display this dialog box by clicking once on the title, clicking Format, and then clicking Selected Chart Title.) This dialog box contains three tabs—Patterns, Font, and Alignment. Clicking the Patterns or the Font tab displays the same options as those available at the Format Chart Area dialog box. Click the Alignment tab and options for changing the text alignment (horizontal or vertical) display along with options for the title orientation.

Double-click a chart legend and the Format Legend dialog box displays with three tabs—Patterns, Font, and Placement. (You can also display this dialog box by clicking once on the legend, clicking Format, and then clicking Selected Legend.) Clicking the Patterns or the Font tab displays the same options as those available at the Format Chart Area dialog box. Click the Placement tab to display options for specifying the location of the legend in relation to the chart.

Each chart element contains a formatting dialog box. To display this dialog box, double-click the desired chart element. For example, double-click text in either the x-axis or the y-axis and the Format Axis dialog box displays.

exercise 13

CUSTOMIZING ELEMENTS IN AN EXCEL CHART

1. Open **ExcelWorksheet25**.
2. Save the worksheet with Save As and name it **sec7x13**.
3. Create a Column chart with the data in the worksheet by completing the following steps:
   a. Select cells A4 through C7.
   b. Click the Chart Wizard button on the Standard toolbar.
   c. At the Chart Wizard - Step 1 of 4 - Chart Type dialog box, click the Next button.
   d. At the Chart Wizard - Step 2 of 4 - Chart Source Data dialog box, make sure the data range displays as *=Sheet1!$A$4:$C$7* and then click the Next button.
   e. At the Chart Wizard - Step 3 of 4 - Chart Options dialog box, make the following changes:
      1) Click the Titles tab.
      2) Click inside the *Chart title* text box and then type **NORTHWEST REGION**.
      3) Click the Next button.
   f. At the Chart Wizard - Step 4 of 4 - Chart Location dialog box, click the *As new sheet* option, and then click the Finish button.

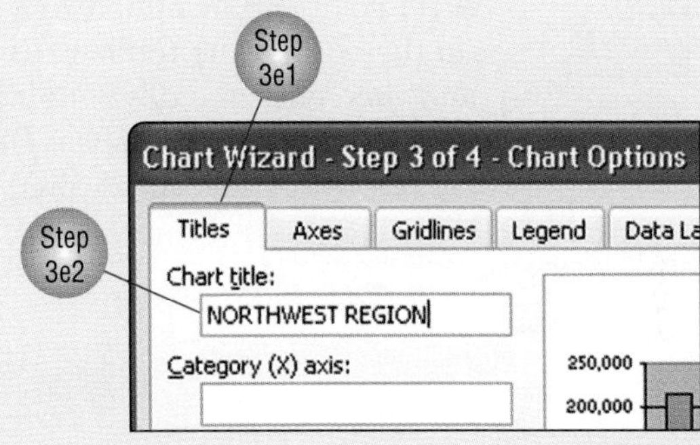

4. Change the font for the title and legend and add a border and shading by completing the following steps:
   a. Double-click the title *NORTHWEST REGION*.
   b. At the Format Chart Title dialog box, click the Font tab, and then change the font to 24-point Century bold (or a similar serif typeface).
   c. Click the Patterns tab.
   d. Click the white circle before *Custom* in the *Border* section of the dialog box.
   e. Click the down-pointing arrow to the right of the *Weight* text box. From the drop-down list that displays, click the third option.
   f. Click the check box before the *Shadow* option.
   g. Add the Light Green color by clicking the fourth color from the left in the fifth row.
   h. Click OK to close the Format Chart Title dialog box.

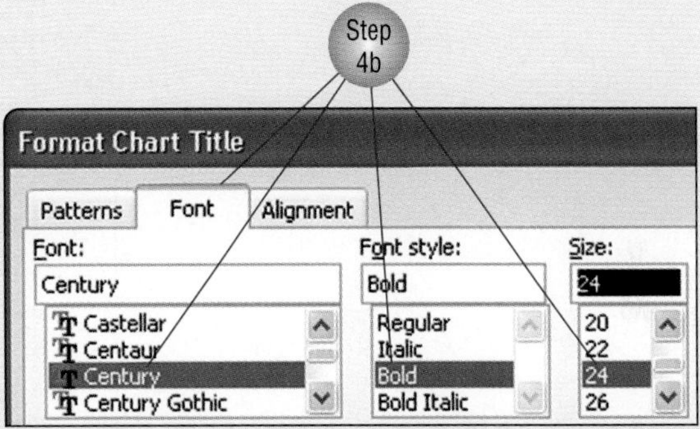

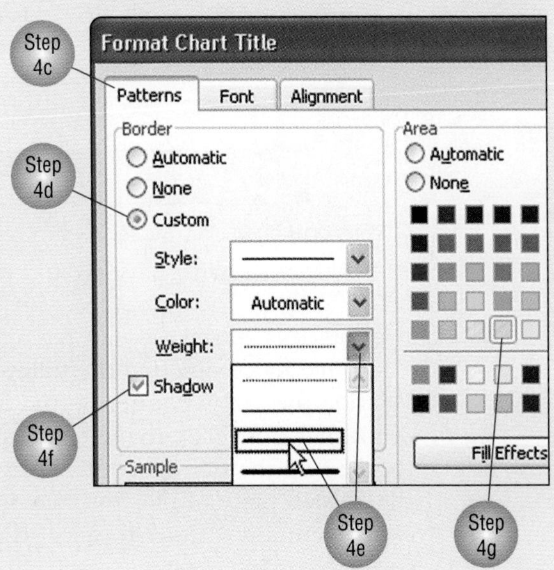

5. Format the legend with the same options as the title (complete steps similar to those in Step 4, except change the font to 10-point Century bold instead of 24-point).
6. With the legend still selected, increase the width by dragging the left middle sizing handle to the left so the legend slightly overlaps the chart. (Make sure *# of Computers* is completely visible in the legend.)
7. Save the workbook again and then print only the sheet containing the chart.
8. Close **sec7x13**.

Changing Element Colors

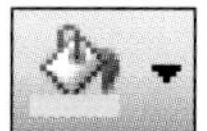

Fill Color

A fill color can be added to a chart or a chart element with the Fill Color button on the Formatting toolbar. To add a fill color, select the chart or the chart element, and then click the down-pointing arrow at the right side of the Fill Color button on the Formatting toolbar. This displays a palette of color choices as shown in Figure 7.12. Click the desired color on the palette.

FIGURE 7.12 ***Fill Color Button Palette***

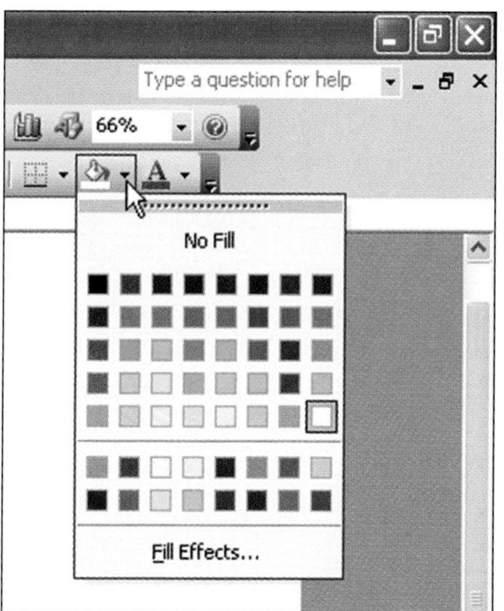

exercise 14 CHANGING ELEMENT COLORS IN A CHART

1. Open **sec7x09**.
2. Save the workbook with Save As and name it **sec7x14**.
3. Change the color of the piece of pie representing *Salaries* to red by completing the following steps:
   a. Position the arrow pointer on the *Salaries* piece of pie and then click the left mouse button. (Make sure the sizing handles surround only the *Salaries* piece of pie. You may need to experiment a few times to select the piece correctly.)

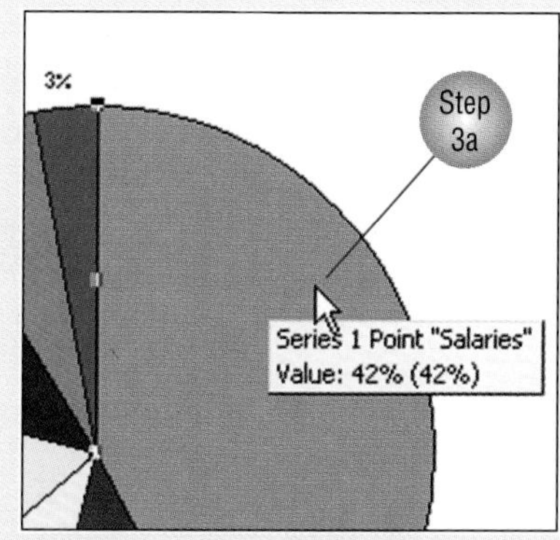

b. Click the down-pointing arrow at the right of the Fill Color button on the Formatting toolbar.
   c. At the color palette, click the Red color (first color in the third row).
4. Change the color of the *Miscellaneous* piece of pie to green by completing steps similar to those in Step 3. (You determine the shade of green.)
5. Change the color of the *Supplies* piece of pie to yellow by completing steps similar to those in Step 3. (You determine the shade of yellow.)
6. Change the color of the *Equipment* piece of pie to blue by completing steps similar to those in Step 3. (You determine the shade of blue.)
7. Change the color of the *Travel* piece of pie to violet by completing steps similar to those in Step 3.
8. Change the color of the *Training* piece of pie to light turquoise by completing steps similar to those in Step 3.
9. Change the color of the *Benefits* piece of pie to a color you have not used on the other pieces of pie by completing steps similar to those in Step 3.
10. Add a background color to the chart by completing the following steps:
    a. Select the entire chart. (To do this, position the arrow pointer inside the chart window but outside the chart, and then click the left mouse button.)
    b. Click the down-pointing arrow at the right of the Fill Color button on the Formatting toolbar.
    c. From the color palette that displays, click a light blue color of your choosing.
11. Save the workbook again and then print only the sheet containing the pie chart.
12. Close **sec7x14**.

CHAPTER summary

- Create a chart with data in an Excel worksheet. A chart is a visual presentation of data.
- Create a chart by selecting the cells containing the data to be charted and then clicking the Chart Wizard button on the Standard toolbar. Complete the four steps in the Chart Wizard.
- Insert a chart in the same worksheet as the cells containing data or in a separate sheet. If a chart is created in a separate sheet, the sheet is named *Chart1*.
- The left vertical side of a chart is referred to as the y-axis, and the bottom of the chart is referred to as the x-axis.
- In a worksheet containing cells of data as well as a chart, the chart can be printed (rather than all data in the worksheet) by selecting the chart first and then displaying the Print dialog box.
- To delete a chart in a worksheet, click the chart to select it, and then press the Delete key. To delete a chart created in a separate sheet, position the mouse pointer on the chart tab, click the right mouse button, and then click Delete.

- Change the size of a chart in an Excel worksheet by clicking the chart and then dragging the sizing handles in the desired direction. To move a chart, select the chart, position the arrow pointer inside the chart, hold down the left mouse button, drag the outline of the chart to the desired location, and then release the mouse button.
- Fourteen basic chart types are available and include Area, Bar, Bubble, Column, Cone, Cylinder, Doughnut, Line, Pie, Pyramid, Radar, Stock, Surface, and XY (scatter).
- The default chart type is a Column chart. Change this default type at the first Chart Wizard dialog box or at the Chart Type dialog box.
- A variety of custom charts are available at the Chart Type dialog box with the Custom Types tab selected.
- Change data in a cell used to create a chart and the data in the chart reflects the change.
- Add chart elements to a chart at the Step 3 Chart Wizard dialog box or at the Chart Options dialog box.
- Move a chart element by selecting the element and then dragging the element to the desired location.
- Size a chart element by selecting the chart element and then dragging a sizing handle to the desired size.
- Delete a chart element by selecting the element and then pressing the Delete key.
- Customize the formatting of a chart element by double-clicking the element. This causes a formatting dialog box to display. The options at the dialog box will vary depending on the chart element.
- Add fill color to a chart or a chart element by selecting the chart or element and then clicking the Fill Color button on the Formatting toolbar. Click the desired color at the palette of color choices that displays.

FEATURES summary

FEATURE	BUTTON	MENU	KEYBOARD
Create default chart			F11
Begin Chart Wizard		Insert, Chart	
Chart Type dialog box		Chart, Chart Type	
Chart Source Data dialog box		Chart, Source Data	
Chart Options dialog box		Chart, Chart Options	
Format Chart Area dialog box		Format, Selected Chart Area	Ctrl + 1

CONCEPTS check

Completion: On a blank sheet of paper, indicate the correct term, symbol, or command for each description.

1. Create a chart by selecting the cells containing data and then clicking this button on the Standard toolbar.
2. To create a chart as a separate worksheet, click this option at the Chart Wizard - Step 4 of 4 - Chart Location dialog box.
3. Change the size of a selected chart by dragging these.
4. This axis is located at the bottom of the chart.
5. Double-click a legend in a chart and this dialog box displays.
6. Choose a custom chart type at the Chart Type dialog box with this tab selected.
7. Double-click in a chart area and this dialog box displays.
8. Add fill color to a chart element by selecting the element and then clicking this button on the Formatting toolbar.
9. List the steps you would complete to create a default chart in Excel with cells A1 through D8 and insert the chart in a separate worksheet.

SKILLS check

Assessment 1

1. Open **ExcelWorksheet01**.
2. Save the worksheet with Save As and name it **sec7sc01**.
3. Make the following changes to the worksheet:
   a. Delete column B.
   b. Delete row 2.
4. Select cells A1 through C9 and then create a chart in a separate sheet with the following specifications:
   a. At Step 1 of the Chart Wizard, do not make any changes.
   b. At Step 2, make sure the proper cell range displays.
   c. At Step 3, add the title *COMPANY SALES*.
   d. At Step 4, specify that the chart is to be created as a new sheet.
   e. After the chart is created, change the font size of the title to 24 points.
5. Save the workbook again and then print only the sheet containing the chart.
6. Close **sec7sc01**.

Assessment 2

1. Open **ExcelWorksheet22**.
2. Save the worksheet with Save As and name it **sec7sc02**.
3. Select cells A1 through E3 and then create a chart in a new worksheet with the following specifications:
   a. At Step 1 of the Chart Wizard, choose the Line chart type.
   b. At Step 2, make sure the proper cell range displays.

c. At Step 3, add the title *COMPANY SALES*.
d. At Step 4, specify that the chart is to be created as a new sheet.

4. After creating the chart, make the following customizations:
   a. Add a light background color to the entire chart.
   b. Add a complementary light background color to the legend.
   c. Change the legend font to a serif typeface (you determine the typeface).
   d. Change the font for the title *COMPANY SALES* to the same serif typeface you chose for the legend and increase the font size.
   e. If some of the text in the legend is not visible, select the legend and then increase the size of the legend.
5. Save the workbook again and then print only the sheet containing the chart.
6. Close **sec7sc02**.

Assessment 3

1. Open **ExcelWorksheet03**.
2. Save the worksheet with Save As and name it **sec7sc03**.
3. Make the following changes to the worksheet:
   a. Delete column D.
   b. Select cells B3 through C8 and then click the Percent Style button on the Standard toolbar.
4. Select cells A2 through C8 and then create a chart in a new sheet with the default settings in Chart Wizard, except add the chart title *ANALYSIS OF FINANCIAL CONDITION*.
5. Make the following changes to the chart:
   a. Change the color of the bars in the chart (you determine the colors).
   b. Change the font of the title and add a border (you determine the font and border style).
   c. Change the background shading of the chart to light turquoise.
   d. Add the following gridlines: *Major gridlines* in *Category (X) axis* and *Minor gridlines* in *Value (Y) axis*.
6. Save the workbook again and then print only the sheet containing the chart.
7. Close **sec7sc03**.

Assessment 4

1. At a clear worksheet window, create a worksheet with the following data:

Fund Allocations

Fund	Percentage
Annuities	23%
Stocks	42%
Bonds	15%
Money Market	20%

2. Create a pie chart as a separate worksheet with the data with the following specifications:
   a. Create a title for the pie chart.
   b. Add data labels to the chart.
   c. Add any other enhancements that will improve the visual presentation of the data.
3. Save the workbook and name it **sec7sc04**.
4. Print only the sheet containing the chart.
5. Close **sec7sc04**.

Assessment 5

1. Open **sec7sc04**.
2. Save the workbook with Save As and name it **sec7sc05**.
3. Choose a custom chart type at the Chart Type dialog box with the Custom Types tab selected. (Choose a custom pie chart.)
4. Save the workbook again and then print only the sheet containing the chart.
5. Close **sec7sc05**.

Assessment 6

1. Open **ExcelWorksheet18**.
2. Save the workbook with Save As and name it **sec7sc06**.
3. Look at the data in the worksheet and then create a chart to represent the data. Add a title to the chart and add any other enhancements to improve the visual display of the chart.
4. Save the workbook again and then print the chart.
5. Close **sec7sc06**.

Assessment 7

1. Use Excel's Help feature to learn more about an XY (scatter) chart.
2. After reading the information presented by Help, create a worksheet with the data shown in Figure 7.13. Create a scatter chart from the data in a separate sheet and create an appropriate title for the chart. (Excel will change the date *July 1* to *1-Jul* and change the other dates in the same manner. The XY scatter chart will display time in five-day intervals.)
3. Save the completed workbook and name it **sec7sc07**.
4. Print both sheets of the workbook (the sheet containing the data in cells and the sheet containing the chart).
5. Close **sec7sc07**.

FIGURE 7.13 **Assessment 7**

HIGHLAND PARK ATTENDANCE

Week	Projected	Actual
July 1	35,000	42,678
July 8	33,000	41,065
July 15	30,000	34,742
July 22	28,000	29,781
July 29	28,000	26,208

CHAPTER challenge

You work with the manager in a recreational department store named Stephan's Sporting Goods. The manager would like you to compare the sales for the last six months for each of the three departments in the store. (You determine the three departments.) Since you know that charts are the best way to compare and interpret data, you decide to create a column chart based on the sales data from the last six months. Format the chart appropriately and include a legend (if necessary) and appropriate titles. Save the workbook as **StephansSportingGoods**.

Formatting and customizing worksheets and charts so that others can interpret the information easily is very critical. One of the ways to customize a chart is to use pictures in the data series. Use the Help feature to learn how to use a picture in a chart. Using the chart created in the first part of the Chapter Challenge, locate and use appropriate pictures for each of the columns. (Apply the Stack format to the pictures). Save the workbook again.

The manager will be sharing this information with the department managers in a PowerPoint presentation. Help him get started by linking the chart used in the second part of the Chapter Challenge to a PowerPoint presentation. Save the presentation as **StephansSportingGoods**.

CHAPTER 8

ENHANCING THE DISPLAY OF WORKBOOKS

PERFORMANCE OBJECTIVES

Upon successful completion of Chapter 8, you will be able to:

- **Save a workbook as a Web page**
- **Preview a Web page using Web Page Preview**
- **Create and modify a hyperlink**
- **Search for and request specific information from online sources**
- **Add a background image to a worksheet**
- **Insert, size, move, and format a clip art image**
- **Insert and customize a diagram**
- **Create, size, move, and customize WordArt**
- **Draw and customize shapes, lines, and autoshapes using buttons on the Drawing toolbar**

Chapter08S

EXCEL

You can save an Excel workbook as a Web page and then view it in Web Page Preview and in a Web browser. You can also insert hyperlinks in a workbook that connect to a Web site or to another workbook and use options at the Research task pane to search for and request information from online sources. Microsoft Excel contains a variety of features that help you enhance the visual appeal of a workbook. Some methods for adding visual appeal that you will learn in this chapter include inserting and modifying images, inserting and customizing a diagram, creating and customizing WordArt text, and drawing and aligning shapes.

Creating and Viewing a Web Page

You can save an Excel workbook as a Web page. The Web page can be viewed in the default Web browser software, and hyperlinks can be inserted in the Web page to jump to other workbooks or sites on the Internet with additional information pertaining to the workbook content. In an organization, an Excel workbook can be saved as a Web page and posted on the company intranet as a timely method of distributing the workbook to the company employees.

HINT

Web pages are documents containing special formatting codes written in HTML (Hypertext Markup Language).

QUICK STEPS

Save Workbook as a Web Page

1. Click File, Save as Web Page.
2. Type name in *File name* text box.
3. Click Save button.

Saving a Workbook as a Web Page

If you want to make a workbook available on the Internet, save the workbook as a Web page. You can save a workbook as a Web page as a folder with an HTML file and all supporting files or you can save a workbook as a Web page as a single file with all supporting files. *HTML* is an acronym for Hypertext Markup Language, which is the programming language used to code pages to display graphically on the World Wide Web. HTML is a collection of instructions that include *tags* applied to text and graphics to instruct the Web browser software how to properly display the page. If you save your workbook as a Web page, the file is saved as an HTML file with the *.htm* file extension. If you save a workbook as a single file, the file is saved as a MHTML file with the *.mht* file extension. (The *m* refers to *MIME*, which is a list of standards for conveying multimedia objects via the Internet and identifies all of the workbook elements in the single file.)

When you save a workbook as a Web page, you can choose to save the workbook as interactive or noninteractive. If you save the workbook as an interactive Web page, users are able to interact with the workbook in a variety of ways, such as applying formatting, manipulating data, changing formulas, and switching between worksheets. If you save the workbook as noninteractive, users cannot change or interact with the data in the Web browser.

Save a workbook as a Web page by opening the workbook, clicking File, and then clicking Save as Web Page. At the Save As dialog box shown in Figure 8.1, specify which part of the workbook you want published, whether the worksheet is to be interactive or not, and if you want to add an HTML title to the Web page. Click the Publish button and the Publish as Web Page dialog box appears as shown in figure 8.2. This dialog box contains advanced options for publishing a Web page.

By default, a Web page is saved as a static page (cannot be modified). You can save a workbook as an interactive Web page (can be modified) by inserting a check mark in the *Add interactivity* check box at the Save As dialog box.

FIGURE 8.1 ***Save As Dialog Box***

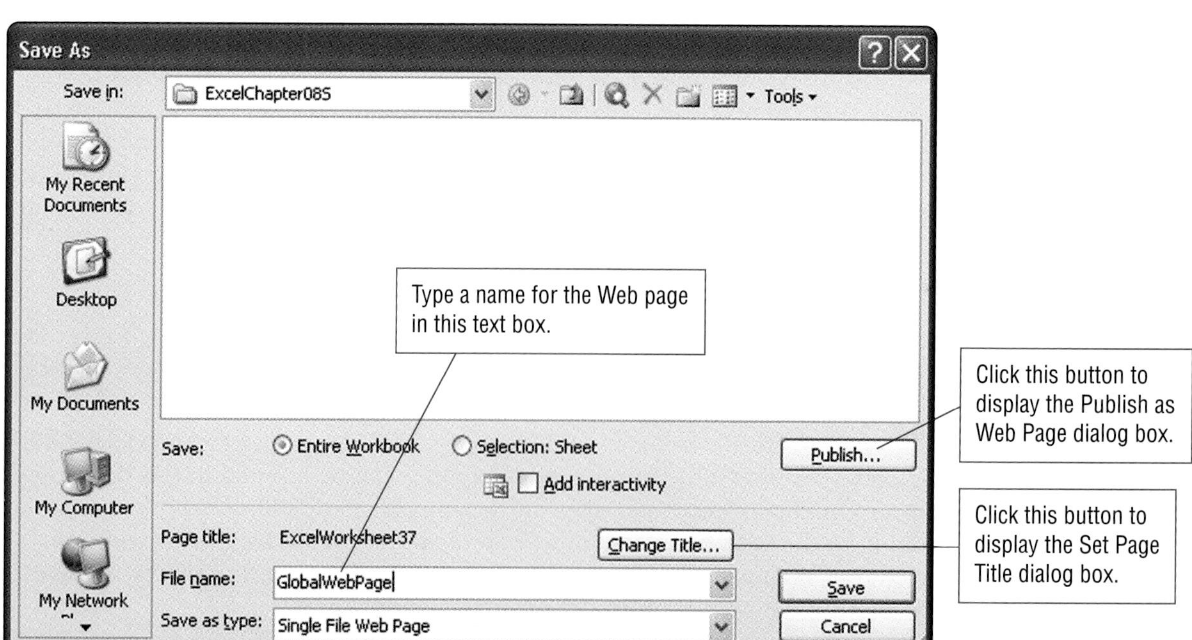

FIGURE

8.2 ***Publish as Web Page Dialog Box***

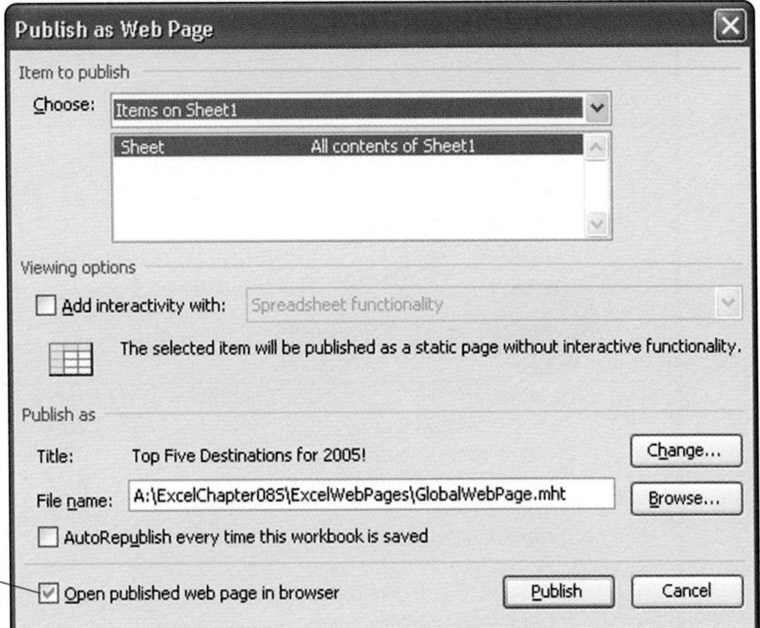

Insert a check mark in this check box if you want the worksheet to automatically display in the default Web browser.

Previewing a Workbook in Web Page Preview

When creating a Web page, you may want to preview it in your default Web browser. Depending on the browser you are using, some of the formatting in a workbook may not display in the browser. To preview a workbook in your default Web browser, click File and then click Web Page Preview. This displays the currently open worksheet in the default Web browser and displays formatting supported by the browser. Close the Web browser window when you are finished previewing the page to return to Microsoft Excel. Figure 8.3 displays the GlobalWebPage file in Web Page Preview.

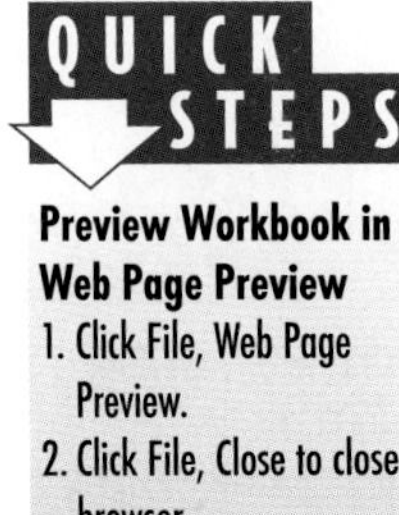

Preview Workbook in Web Page Preview

1. Click File, Web Page Preview.
2. Click File, Close to close browser.

FIGURE 8.3 ***GlobalWebPage in Web Page Preview***

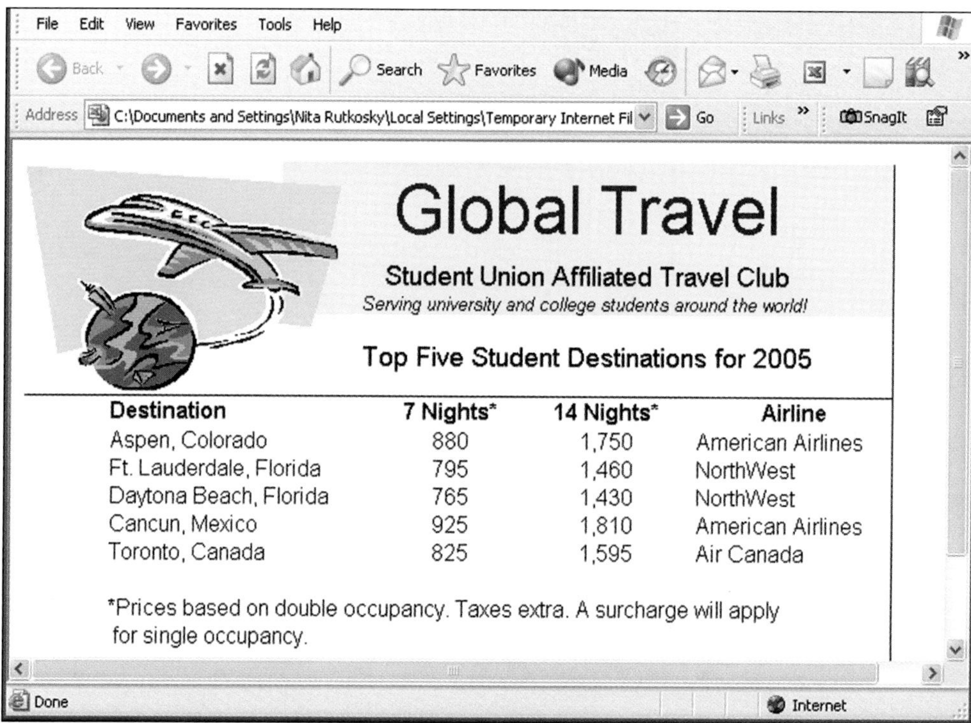

Creating Hyperlinks

Create a Hyperlink
1. Click desired cell.
2. Click Insert Hyperlink button on Standard toolbar.
3. Type Web address or file name.
4. Click OK.

Insert Hyperlink

A hyperlink is text or an object that you click to go to a different file, an HTML page on the Internet, or an HTML page on an intranet. Create a hyperlink in an Excel worksheet by typing the address of an existing Web page such as www.emcp.com. By default, the automatic formatting of hyperlinks is turned on and the Web address is formatted as a hyperlink (text is underlined and the color changes to blue). (You can turn off the automatic formatting of hyperlinks. To do this, display the AutoCorrect dialog box by clicking Tools and then AutoCorrect Options. At the AutoCorrect dialog box, click the AutoFormat As You Type tab, and then remove the check mark from the *Internet and network paths with hyperlinks* check box.)

You can also create a customized hyperlink by clicking the desired cell in a workbook and then clicking the Insert Hyperlink button on the Standard toolbar. At the Insert Hyperlink dialog box shown in Figure 8.4, type the file name or Web site address in the *Address* text box, and then click OK. You can also use the *Look in* option to browse to the desired folder and file and then double-click the file name. To link to the specified file or Web page, position the mouse pointer on the hyperlink, and then click the left mouse button.

FIGURE 8.4 ***Insert Hyperlink Dialog Box***

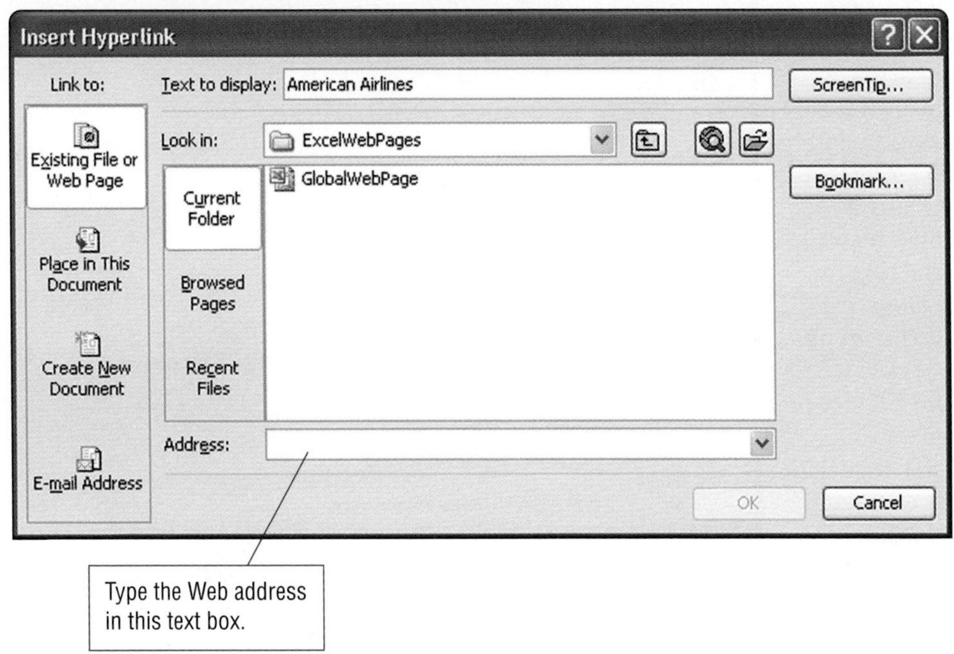

Adding a Background Image to a Worksheet

Add a Background Image to Worksheet
1. Click Format, Sheet, Background.
2. Navigate to desired folder.
3. Double-click desired image.

Add visual interest to a worksheet by adding a background image. To insert a background image in a workbook, click Format, point to Sheet, and then click Background. This displays the Sheet Background dialog box with the contents of the My Pictures folder. (This default may vary.) Navigate to the folder containing the image you want to insert in the worksheet and then double-click the desired image.

A background image inserted in a worksheet does not print and is not retained in individual worksheets saved as Web pages. If you want to retain the worksheet background image, publish the entire workbook as a Web page.

exercise 1

SAVING A WORKBOOK AS A WEB PAGE, PREVIEWING THE WEB PAGE, AND CREATING HYPERLINKS

1. Create a folder named *ExcelWebPages* within the ExcelChapter08S folder on your disk.
2. Open **ExcelWorksheet37**.
3. Save the workbook with Save As and name it **sec8x01**.
4. Save the worksheet as a single Web page in the ExcelWebPages folder by completing the following steps:
   a. Click File and then Save as Web Page.
   b. At the Save As dialog box, double-click *ExcelWebPages* in the list box.

c. Make sure the *Save as type* option is set at *Single File Web Page*. (If it is not, click the down-pointing arrow at the right of the *Save as type* option and then click *Single File Web Page* at the drop-down menu.)

d. Select the text in the *File name* text box and then type **GlobalWebPage**.

e. Click the Change Title button.

f. At the Set Page Title dialog box, type **Top Five Destinations for 2005!** in the *Page title* text box, and then click OK.

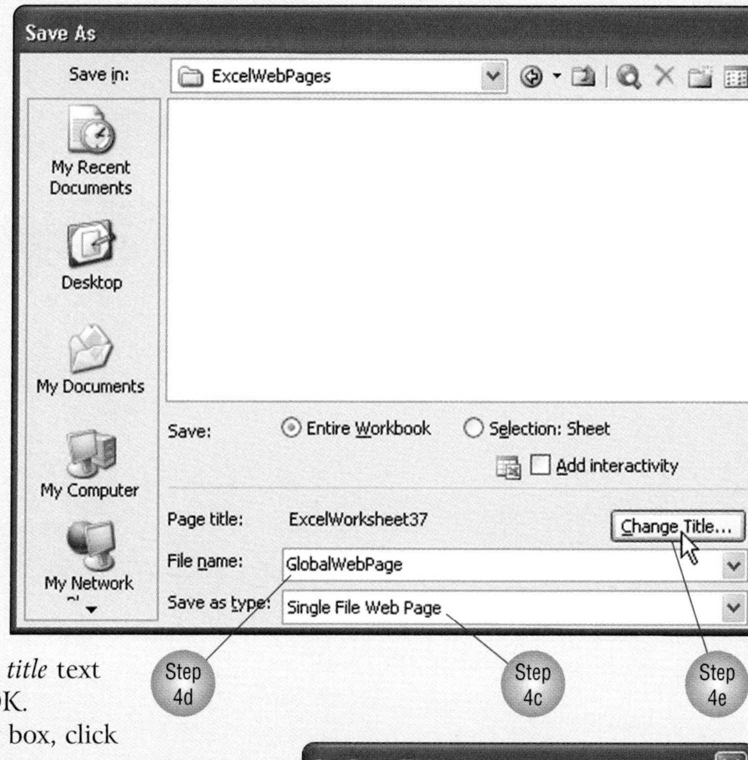

g. At the Save As dialog box, click the Publish button.

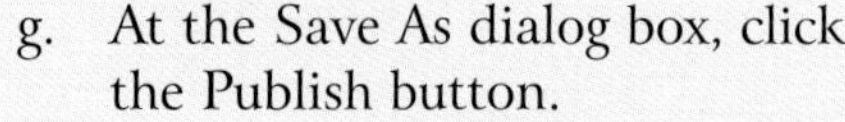

h. At the Publish as Web Page dialog box, click the *Open published web page in browser* option to insert a check mark.

i. Click the Publish button. (This automatically displays the worksheet in your default Web browser.)

Set Page Title
Page title:
Top Five Destinations for 2005!
The title of the page is displayed in the title bar of the browser.
OK
Cancel
Step 4f

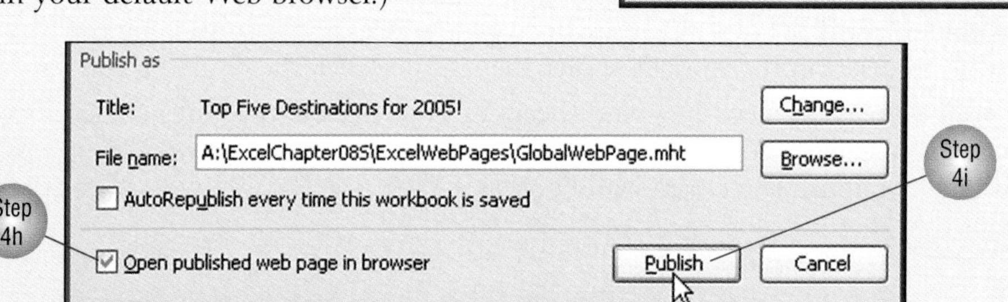

j. After viewing your Web page, close the Web page browser.

k. Save and then close **sec8x01**.

5. Preview the workbook in Web Page Preview by completing the following steps:
   a. Display the Open dialog box and then open the **GlobalWebPage** file.
   b. Click File and then click Web Page Preview.
   c. If the viewing area in the browser is limited, click the Maximize button located in the upper right corner of the browser window.
   d. After viewing the worksheet in the Web browser, click File and then Close.
6. Create a hyperlink so that clicking *American Airlines* displays the American Airlines Web page by completing the following steps:
   a. Click cell G10 (this is the cell containing *American Airlines*).
   b. Click the Insert Hyperlink button on the Standard toolbar.

c. At the Insert Hyperlink dialog box, type **www.aa.com** in the *Address* text box. (The *http://* is automatically inserted in the address.)
d. Click OK. (This changes the color of the *American Airlines* text and also adds underlining to the text.)
e. Repeat Steps 6b through 6d in cell G13.

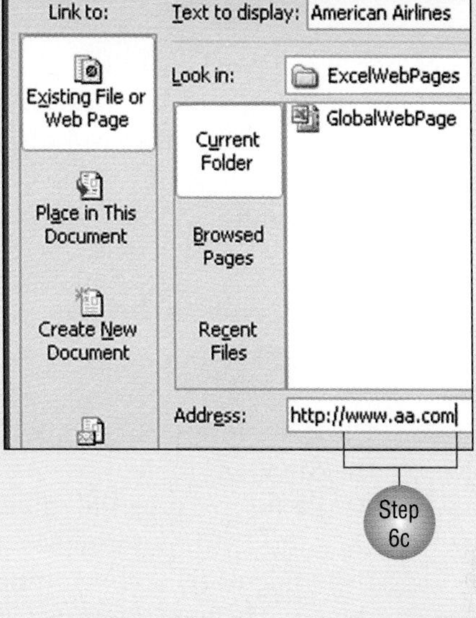

7. Complete steps similar to those in Step 6 to create a hyperlink from *Northwest Airlines* to the URL www.nwa.com in cells G11 and G12.
8. Complete steps similar to those in Step 6 to create a hyperlink from *Air Canada* to the URL www.aircanada.ca in cell G14.
9. Click the Save button on the Standard toolbar to save the Web page with the hyperlinks added.
10. Jump to the hyperlinked sites by completing the following steps:
    a. Make sure you are connected to the Internet.
    b. Click one of the American Airlines hyperlinks.
    c. When the American Airlines Web page displays, scroll through the page, and then click a hyperlink that interests you.
    d. After looking at this next page, click File and then Close.
    e. At the **GlobalWebPage** workbook, click the Air Canada hyperlink.
    f. At the Air Canada Web page, click the hyperlink to see their site displayed in English.
    g. After viewing the Air Canada page, click File and then Close.
    h. At the **GlobalWebPage** workbook, click one of the Northwest hyperlinks.
    i. At the Northwest Airlines Web page, click a link that interests you.
    j. After viewing the Northwest Airlines page, click File and then Close.
11. Save and then print **GlobalWebPage**.
12. Add a background image to the worksheet by completing the following steps:
    a. With **GlobalWebPage** open, click Format, point to Sheet, and then click Background.
    b. At the Sheet Background dialog box, navigate to the Background folder on the CD that accompanies this text. (The Background folder is located in the Excel2003Specialist folder.)
    c. Double-click the ***Beach*** file that displays in the list box.
    d. View the worksheet in Web Page Preview by clicking File and then Web Page Preview.
    e. After viewing the worksheet in the Web browser, click File and then Close.
13. Close **GlobalWebPage** without saving the changes.

In Exercise 1, you created hyperlinks from an Excel workbook to sites on the Web. You can also insert hyperlinks in a workbook that link to other Excel workbooks or files in other programs in the Office suite. In Exercise 2, you will create a hyperlink that, when clicked, displays another Excel workbook.

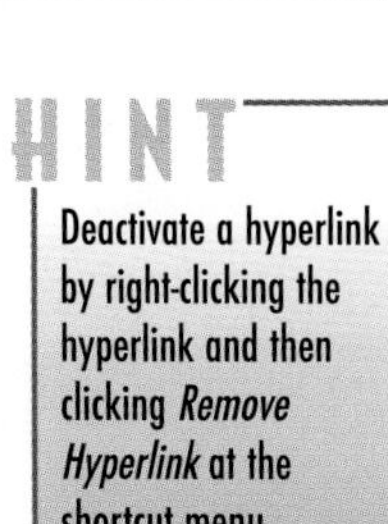

HINT
Deactivate a hyperlink by right-clicking the hyperlink and then clicking *Remove Hyperlink* at the shortcut menu.

You can modify or change hyperlink text or the hyperlink destination. To do this, right-click the hyperlink, and then click Edit Hyperlink. At the Edit Hyperlink dialog box, make any desired changes, and then close the dialog box. The Edit Hyperlink dialog box contains the same options as the Insert Hyperlink dialog box.

exercise 2

CREATING AND MODIFYING A HYPERLINK TO AN EXCEL WORKSHEET

1. Open **ExcelWorksheet33**.
2. Save the workbook with Save As and name it **sec8x02**.
3. Create a hyperlink that will display **ExcelWorksheet28** by completing the following steps:
   a. Make cell A10 active.
   b. Type **Semiannual Sales** and then press Enter.
   c. Click cell A10 to make it the active cell.
   d. Click the Insert Hyperlink button on the Standard toolbar.
   e. At the Insert Hyperlink dialog box, click the down-pointing arrow at the right side of the *Look in* option and then navigate to the ExcelChapter08S folder on your disk.
   f. Double-click ***ExcelWorksheet28*** in the ExcelChapter08S folder on your disk. (This closes the Insert Hyperlink dialog box and displays the *Semiannual Sales* text as a hyperlink in the workbook.)

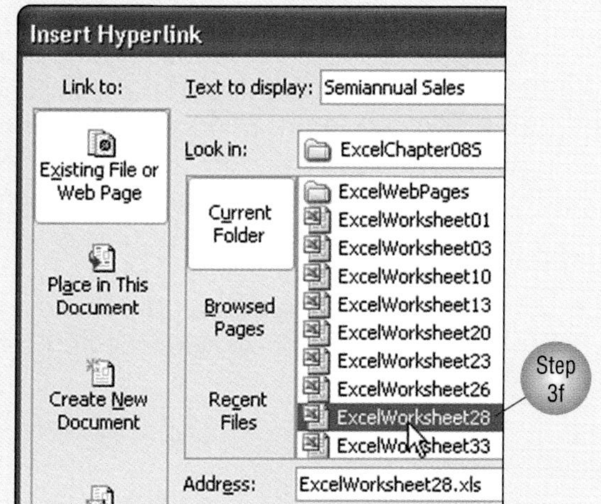

	A	B	C
1	FIRST-QUARTER SALES - 2002		
2	Customer	January	February
3	Lakeside Trucking	$84,231	$ 73,455
4	Gresham Machines	$33,199	$ 40,390
5	Real Photography	$30,891	$ 35,489
6	Genesis Productions	$72,190	$ 75,390
7	Landower Company	$22,188	$ 14,228
8	Jewell Enterprises	$19,764	$ 50,801
9			
10	Semiannual Sales		
11			
12			
13			

file:///A:\ExcelChapter08S\ExcelWorksheet28.xls - Click once to follow. Click and hold to select this cell.

Step 4

4. Display **ExcelWorksheet28** by clicking the Semiannual Sales hyperlink.
5. Close **ExcelWorksheet28**.
6. Print **sec8x02**.
7. Modify the hyperlink text in **sec8x02** by completing the following steps:
   a. Position the mouse pointer on the Semiannual Sales hyperlink, click the *right* mouse button, and then click Edit Hyperlink.
   b. At the Edit Hyperlink dialog box, select the text *Semiannual Sales* in the *Text to display* text box and then type **Customer Sales Analysis**.
   c. Click OK.
8. Click the Customer Sales Analysis hyperlink.
9. Close **ExcelWorksheet28**.
10. Save, print, and then close **sec8x02**.

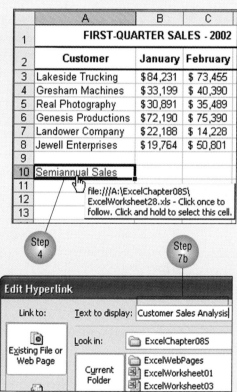

Step 7b

Edit Hyperlink
Link to:
Text to display: Customer Sales Analysis
Existing File or Web Page
Look in: ExcelChapter08S
Current Folder
ExcelWebPages
ExcelWorksheet01
ExcelWorksheet03

Researching and Requesting Information

QUICK STEPS

Research and Request Information

1. Click Research button on Standard toolbar.
2. Type desired word or topic in the *Search for* text box.
3. Click the down-pointing arrow at right of resources list box and then click desired resource.

Use options at the Research task pane to search for and request specific information from online sources and to translate words from and to a variety of languages. The online resources available to you depend on the locale to which your system is set, authorization information indicating that you are allowed to download the information, and your Internet service provider.

Display the Research task pane by clicking the Research button on the Standard toolbar or clicking Tools and then Research. This displays the Research pane similar to what you see in Figure 8.5. You can also display the Research task pane by holding down the Alt key and clicking a specific word or selected words in a document.

FIGURE 8.5 **Research Task Pane**

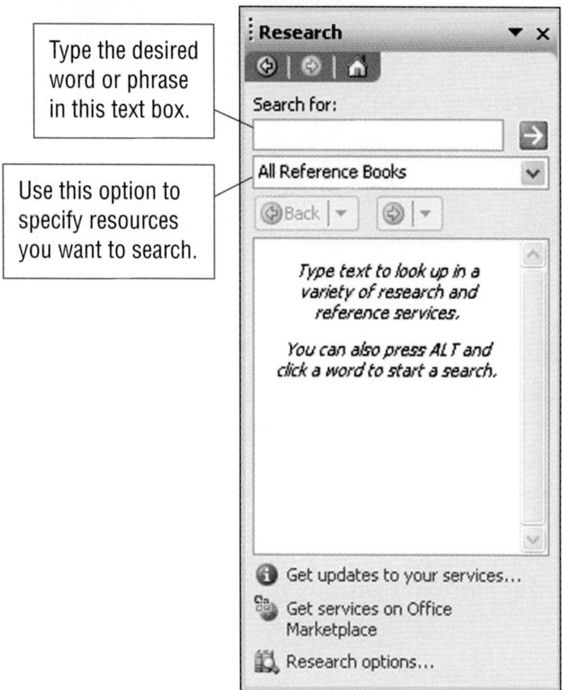

Determine the resources available by clicking the down-pointing arrow at the right of the resources list box (the list box located below the *Search for* text box). The drop-down list contains lists of reference books, research sites, business and financial sites, and other services. If you want to use a specific reference in your search click the desired reference at the drop-down list, type the desired word or topic in the *Search for* text box, and then press Enter. Items matching your word or topic display in the task pane list box. Depending on the item, the list box may contain hyperlinks you can click to access additional information on the Internet.

You can control the available research options by clicking the Research options hyperlink located at the bottom of the Research task pane. This displays the Research Options dialog box shown in Figure 8.6. At this dialog box, insert a check mark before those items you want available and remove the check mark from those items you do not want available.

FIGURE

8.6 Research Options Dialog Box

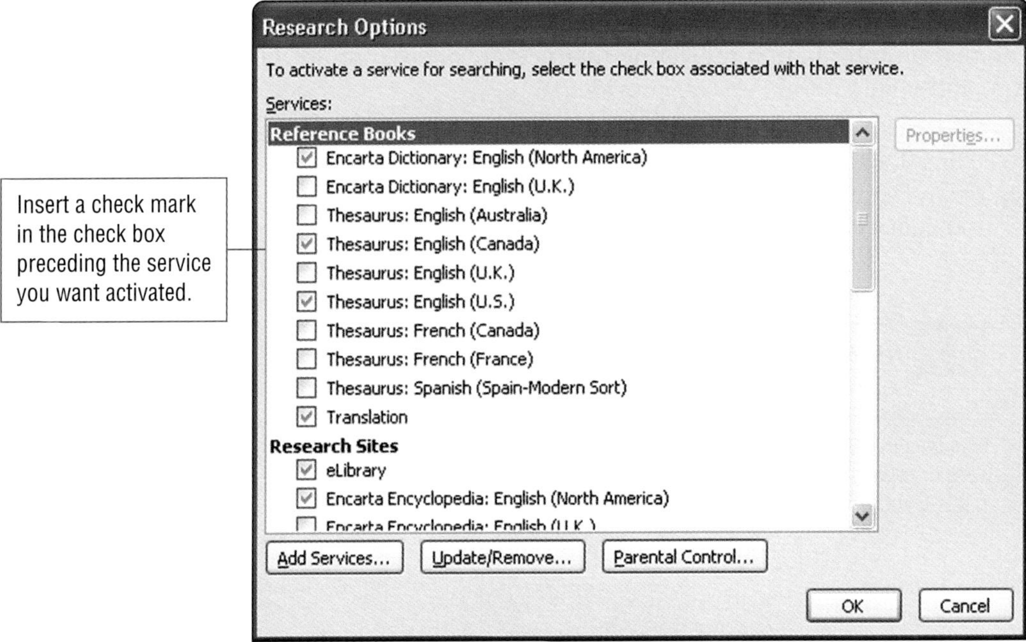

Inserting Research Information

You can insert into your worksheet some of the information that displays in the Research task pane and other information you can copy and paste into your worksheet. If you look up stock prices, an *Insert Stock Price* option is available for inserting the stock information in your worksheet. If information displays in your browser, select the desired information, click Edit on the Browser's menu bar and then click Copy at the drop-down menu. Make your worksheet active, click Edit, and then click Paste or click the Paste button.

exercise 3

RESEARCHING AND REQUESTING INFORMATION

(Note: Your computer must be connected to the Internet to complete this exercise.)

1. At a clear document screen, display the Research task pane by clicking the Research button on the Standard toolbar.
2. Search for information in a dictionary on Venn diagrams (one of the diagrams you can create with the Diagram feature) by completing the following steps:

a. Click in the *Search for* text box or select any text that displays in the text box and then type **Venn**.
b. Click the down-pointing arrow to the right of the resources list box (the down-pointing arrow immediately below the Start searching button).
c. At the drop-down list of resources, click *Encarta Dictionary: English (North America)*. If this reference is not available, click any other dictionary that is available to you.

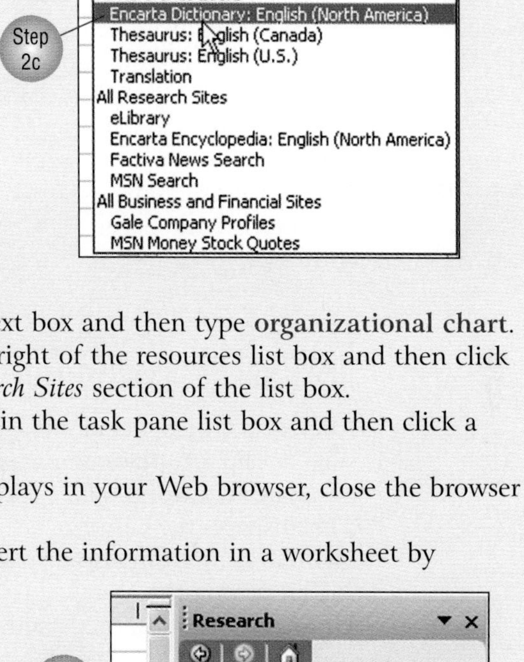

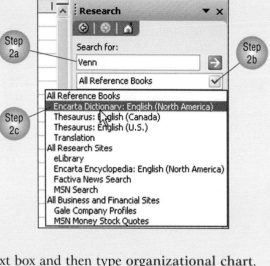

3. Search for information on organizational charts in an encyclopedia by completing the following steps:
   a. Select the text *Venn* in the *Search for* text box and then type **organizational chart**.
   b. Click the down-pointing arrow at the right of the resources list box and then click an encyclopedia listed in the *All Research Sites* section of the list box.
   c. Look at the information that displays in the task pane list box and then click a hyperlink that interests you.
   d. After reading the information that displays in your Web browser, close the browser window.
4. Search for stock information and then insert the information in a worksheet by completing the following steps:
   a. Open **ExcelWorksheet44**.
   b. Save the worksheet with Save As and name it **sec8x03**.
   c. Make sure cell B4 is the active cell.
   d. Select the text *organizational chart* in the *Search for* text box and then type **IBM**.
   e. Click the down-pointing arrow at the right of the resources list box and then click *MSN Money Stock Quotes*.
   f. Scroll down the Research task pane and then click the Insert Price button.
   g. Make cell B5 active.
   h. Select *IBM* in the *Search for* text box, type **MSFT**, and then press Enter. (This will display the stock information for Microsoft.)
   i. Scroll down the Research task pane and then click the Insert Price button.
   j. Make cell B6 active.
   k. Select *Microsoft* in the *Search for* text box, type **Dell**, and then press Enter.
   l. Scroll down the Research task pane and then click the Insert Price button.

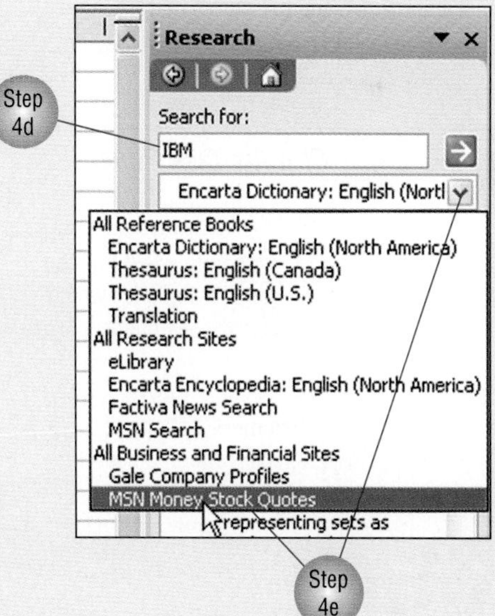

5. Save, print, and then close **sec8x03**.
6. Open a blank worksheet.
7. Insert Microsoft stock information in the worksheet by completing the following steps:
   a. Make sure cell A1 is the active cell and that the Research task pane is displayed.
   b. Make sure *MSN Money Stock Quotes* displays in the resources list box.

c. Select *Dell* that displays in the *Search for* text box, type **MSFT**, and then press Enter.
d. Scroll down the Research task pane until the Insert Price button is visible.
e. Click the down-pointing arrow at the right side of the Insert Price button.
f. Click *Insert Refreshable Stock Data* in the drop-down list. (This inserts stock data into the worksheet.) (If this option does not display, go to the Internet Resource Center for this book at www.emcp.com and click Text Updates.)

8. Save the worksheet and name it **sec8Stocks**.
9. Print the worksheet in landscape orientation and scale it to fit on one page.
10. Close **sec8Stocks**.

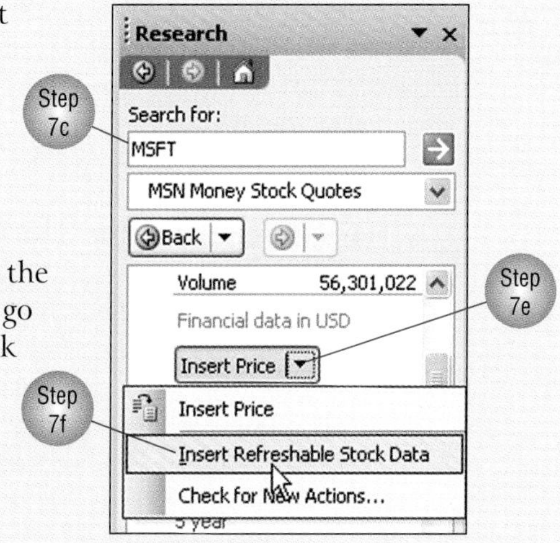

Inserting Images in a Workbook

Insert Clip Art

Drawing

Microsoft Office includes a gallery of media images you can insert in a workbook such as clip art, photographs, and movie images, as well as sound clips. To insert an image in a workbook, click Insert, point to Picture, and then click Clip Art. This displays the Clip Art task pane at the right side of the screen as shown in Figure 8.7. You can also display the Clip Art task pane by clicking the Insert Clip Art button on the Drawing toolbar. (Display the Drawing toolbar by clicking the Drawing button on the Standard toolbar.)

FIGURE 8.7 ***Clip Art Task Pane***

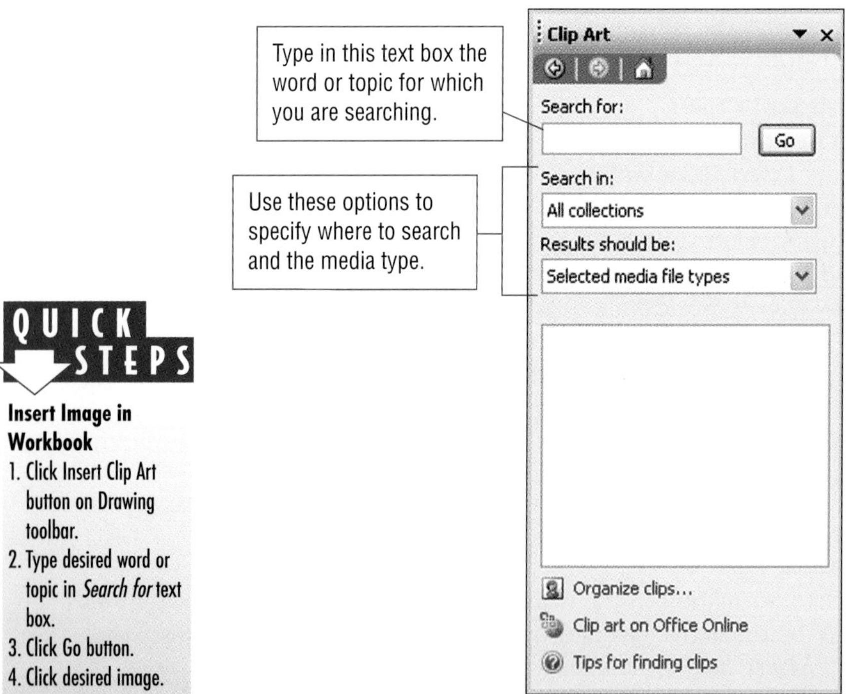

QUICK STEPS

Insert Image in Workbook

1. Click Insert Clip Art button on Drawing toolbar.
2. Type desired word or topic in *Search for* text box.
3. Click Go button.
4. Click desired image.

To view all picture, sound, and motion files, make sure no text displays in the *Search for* text box at the Clip Art task pane, and then click the Go button. Display the desired image and then click the image to insert it in the worksheet.

Narrowing a Search

By default (unless it has been customized), the Clip Art task pane looks for all media images and sound clips found in all locations. You can narrow the search to specific locations and to specific images. The *Search in* option at the Clip Art task pane has a default setting of *All collections*. You can change this to *My Collections*, *Office Collections*, and *Web Collections*. The *Results should be* option has a default setting of *All media file types*. Click the down-pointing arrow at the right side of this option to display media types. To search for a specific media type, remove the check mark before all options at the drop-down list but the desired type. For example, if you are searching only for clip art images, remove the check mark before *Photographs*, *Movies*, and *Sound*.

If you are searching for specific images, click in the *Search for* text box, type the desired word, and then click the Go button. For example, if you want to find images related to computers, click in the *Search for* text box, type **computer**, and then click the Go button. Clip art images related to *computer* display in the viewing area of the task pane.

Sizing an Image

Size an image in a workbook using the sizing handles that display around a selected image. To change the size of an image, click in the image to select it, and then position the mouse pointer on a sizing handle until the pointer turns into a double-headed arrow. Hold down the left mouse button, drag the sizing handle in or out to decrease or increase the size of the image, and then release the mouse button.

Use the middle sizing handles at the left or right side of the image to make the image wider or thinner. Use the middle sizing handles at the top or bottom of the image to make the image taller or shorter. Use the sizing handles at the corners of the image to change both the width and height at the same time. When sizing an image, consider using the horizontal and vertical rulers that display in the Print Layout view. To deselect an image, click anywhere in the workbook outside the image.

HINT

Drag one of the corner sizing handles to maintain the original proportions of the image.

Moving and Deleting an Image

To move an image, select the image, and then position the mouse pointer inside the image until the pointer turns into a four-headed arrow. Hold down the left mouse button, drag the image to the desired position, and then release the mouse button. Rotate an image by positioning the mouse pointer on the green, round rotation handle until the pointer displays as a circular arrow. Hold down the left mouse button, drag in the desired direction, and then release the mouse button. Delete a clip art image by selecting the image and then pressing the Delete key.

HINT

You can use arrow keys on the keyboard to move a selected object.

exercise 4

INSERTING AND SIZING A CLIP ART IMAGE IN A WORKSHEET

1. Open **ExcelWorksheet03**.
2. Save the worksheet with Save As and name it **sec8x04**.
3. Select the first four rows of the worksheet, click Insert and then click Rows. (This inserts four new rows at the beginning of the worksheet.)
4. Click in cell A2, type **MYLAN COMPUTERS**, and then press Enter.
5. Select cells A1 through D12 and then apply the Accounting 1 autoformat.
6. Select cells B7 through D12 and then click the Percent Style button on the Formatting toolbar.
7. Insert an image in the worksheet by completing the following steps:
   a. Make cell C1 active.
   b. Click Insert, point to Picture, and then click Clip Art.
   c. At the Clip Art task pane, click in the *Search for* text box.
   d. Type **computer** and then click the Go button.
   e. Click the computer image shown in the figure at the right. (If this computer clip art image is not available, click another image that interests you.)
   f. Close the Clip Art task pane.
   g. With the computer image selected (white sizing handles display around the image), position the mouse pointer on the bottom right sizing handle until it turns into a diagonally pointing two-headed arrow.
   h. Hold down the left mouse button, drag into the image to decrease the size until the image is approximately the size shown at the right, and then release the mouse button.

Step 7d

Clip Art
Search for:
computer
Go
Search in:
All collections
Results should be:
Selected media file types

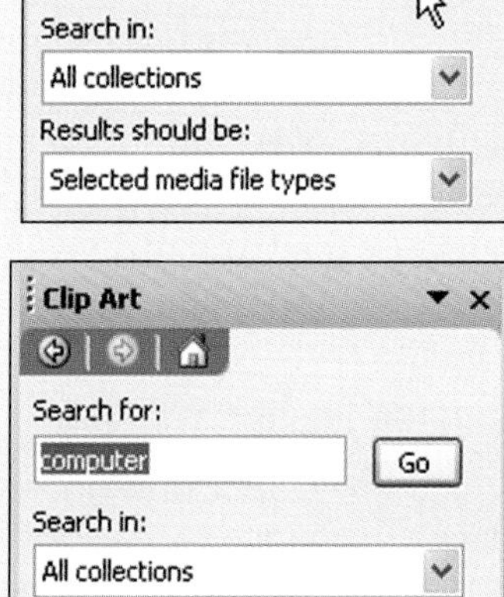

Step 7e

	A	B	C	D
1				
2	MYLAN COMPUTERS			
3				
4				
5	ANALYSIS OF FINANCIAL CONDITION			
6		Actual	Planned	Prior Year
7	Stockholder's equity ratio	62%	60%	57%

Step 7h

   i. If necessary, move the image so it is positioned as shown at the right.
   j. Click outside the image to deselect it.
8. Print the worksheet horizontally and vertically centered on the page.
9. Save and then close **sec8x04**.

Formatting Images with Buttons on the Picture Toolbar

You can format images in a variety of ways. Formatting might include adding fill color and border lines, increasing or decreasing the brightness or contrast, choosing a wrapping style, and cropping the image. Format an image with buttons on the Picture toolbar or options at the Format Picture dialog box. Display the Picture toolbar by clicking an image or by right-clicking an image and then clicking Show Picture Toolbar at the shortcut menu. Table 8.1 identifies the buttons on the Picture toolbar.

TABLE 8.1 ***Picture Toolbar Buttons***

Button	Name	Function
	Insert Picture From File	Displays the Insert Picture dialog box with a list of subfolders containing additional images.
	Color	Displays a drop-down list with options for controlling how the image displays. Options include *Automatic*, *Grayscale*, *Black & White*, and *Washout*.
	More Contrast	Increases contrast of the image.
	Less Contrast	Decreases contrast of the image.
	More Brightness	Increases brightness of the image.
	Less Brightness	Decreases brightness of the image.
	Crop	Crops image so only a specific portion of the image is visible.
	Rotate Left 90°	Rotates the image 90 degrees to the left.
	Line Style	Inserts a border around the image and specifies the border line style.
	Compress Pictures	Reduces resolution or discards extra information to save room on the hard drive or to reduce download time.

Continued on next page

	Format Picture	Displays Format Picture dialog box with options for formatting the image. Tabs in the dialog box include Colors and Lines, Size, Position, Wrapping, and Picture.
	Set Transparent Color	This button is not active. (When an image contains a transparent area, the background color or texture of the page shows through the image. Set transparent color in Microsoft Photo Editor.)
	Reset Picture	Resets image to its original size, position, and color.

exercise 5

INSERTING, MOVING, AND CUSTOMIZING AN IMAGE IN A WORKBOOK

1. Open **ExcelWorksheet13**.
2. Save the worksheet with Save As and name it **sec8x05**.
3. Delete column H.
4. Insert a row at the beginning of the worksheet.
5. Change the height of the new row to 99.00.
6. Select cells A1 through G1 and then click the Merge and Center button on the Formatting toolbar.
7. With cell A1 the active cell, make the following changes:
   a. Display the Format Cells dialog box. (To do this, click Format and then Cells.)
   b. At the Format Cells dialog box, click the Alignment tab.
   c. At the Format Cells dialog box with the Alignment tab selected, change the *Horizontal* option to *Right (Indent)* and the *Vertical* option to *Center*.
   d. Click the Font tab.
   e. At the Format Cells dialog box with the Font tab selected, change the font to 32-point Arial bold.
   f. Click OK to close the dialog box.
8. Type **Global Transport**.
9. Click outside cell A1 and then click cell A1 again.
10. Display the Clip Art task pane by clicking Insert, pointing to Picture, and then clicking Clip Art.
11. Select the text in the *Search for* text box and then type **maps**.
12. Click the Go button.
13. Click the image shown at the right. (If this image is not available, choose another image related to maps.)
14. Close the Clip Art task pane.

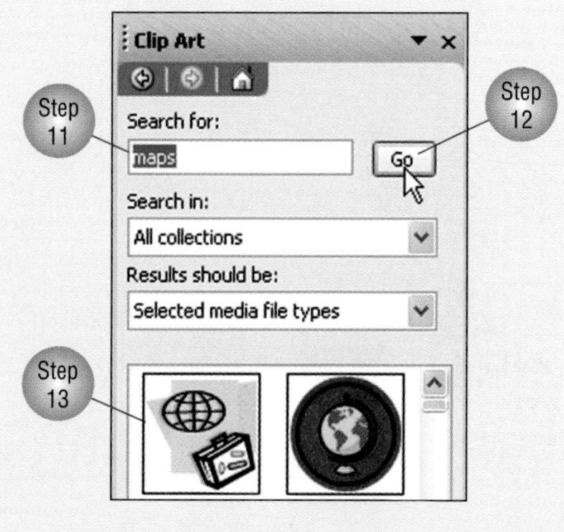

15. Change the size of the image by completing the following steps:
    a. With the clip art image selected, click the Format Picture button on the Picture toolbar. (If the Picture toolbar is not visible, click View, point to Toolbars, and then click Picture.)
    b. At the Format Picture dialog box, click the Size tab.
    c. Select the current measurement in the *Height* text box (in the *Size and rotate* section) and then type 1.5.
    d. Click OK to close the dialog box.
16. Click twice on the More Contrast button on the Picture toolbar.
17. Print the worksheet centered horizontally and vertically on the page.
18. Save and then close **sec8x05**.

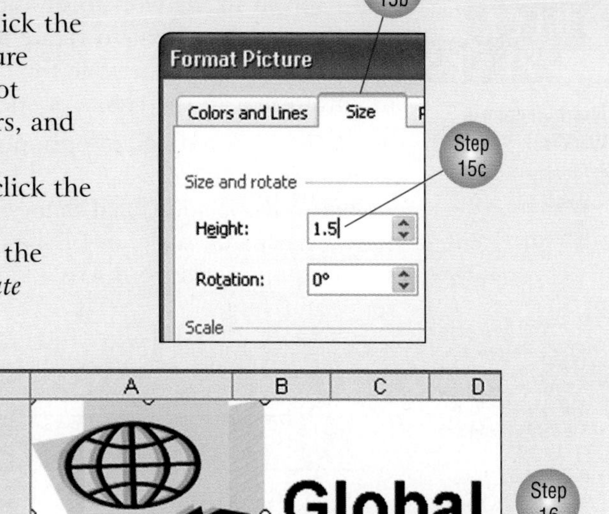

Creating Diagrams and Organizational Charts

Use the Diagram Gallery to create organizational charts or other types of diagrams. Display the Diagram Gallery dialog box, shown in Figure 8.8, by clicking the Insert Diagram or Organization Chart button on the Drawing toolbar or by clicking Insert and then Diagram.

FIGURE 8.8 **Diagram Gallery Dialog Box**

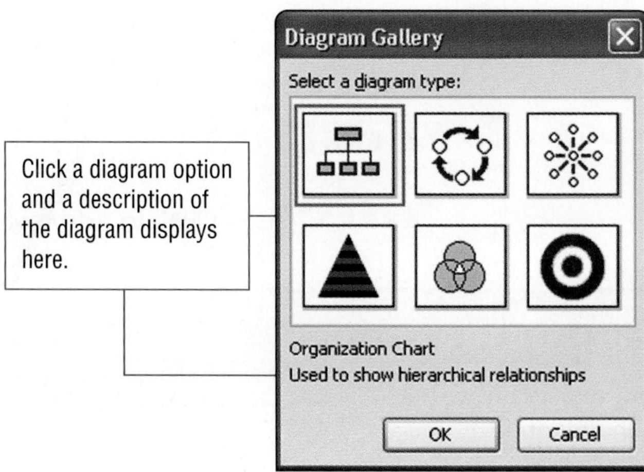

At the Diagram Gallery dialog box, click the desired option in the *Select a diagram type* list box and then click OK. If you click an organizational chart option, chart boxes appear in the worksheet and the Organization Chart toolbar displays. Use buttons on this toolbar to create additional boxes in the chart, specify the layout of the chart, expand or scale the chart, select specific elements in the chart, apply an autoformat to the chart, or specify a text wrapping option.

Insert Diagram in Workbook

1. Click Insert, Diagram.
2. Double-click desired diagram.

If you click a diagram option at the Diagram Gallery dialog box, the diagram is inserted in the worksheet and the Diagram toolbar displays. Use buttons on this toolbar to insert additional shapes; move shapes backward or forward or reverse the diagram; expand, scale, or fit the contents of the diagram; apply an autoformat to the diagram; or change the type of diagram (choices include Cycle, Radial, Pyramid, Venn, and Target).

exercise 6 CREATING AND CUSTOMIZING A DIAGRAM

1. Open **ExcelWorksheet43**.
2. Save the worksheet with Save As and name it **sec8x06**.
3. Insert a Pyramid diagram in cell A1 and modify the diagram by completing the following steps:
   a. Click Insert and then Diagram.
   b. At the Diagram Gallery, double-click the Pyramid diagram (first diagram from the left in the second row).
   c. Click the AutoFormat button on the Diagram toolbar.
   d. At the Diagram Style Gallery, double-click the *Square Shadows* option in the *Select a Diagram Style* list box.
   e. Scroll down the screen until the bottom right sizing handle (small, white circle) displays.
   f. Using the bottom right sizing handle, decrease the size of the Pyramid diagram so it is approximately two columns wide and eight rows high (the approximate size shown in Figure 8.9).
   g. Click the text *Click to add text* that displays towards the bottom of the pyramid and then press the spacebar once. (This removes the text and replaces it with a space, which does not show in the pyramid.)

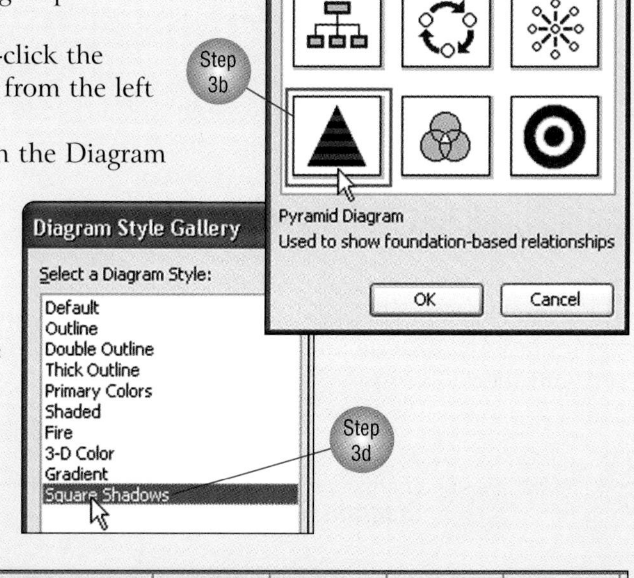

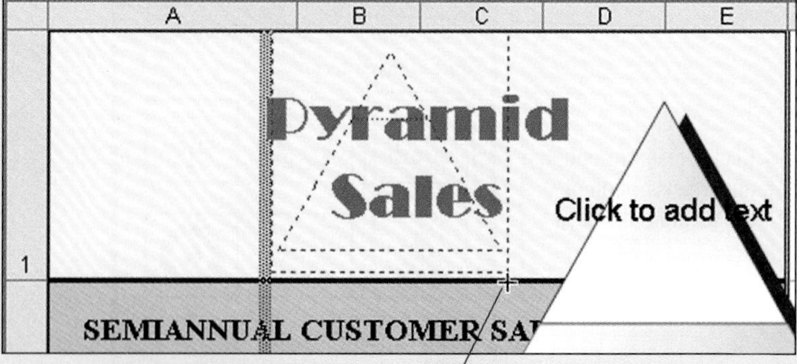

h. Click the text *Click to add text* that displays towards the middle of the pyramid and then press the spacebar.
i. Click the text *Click to add text* that displays towards the top of the pyramid and then press the spacebar.
j. Drag the Pyramid diagram so it displays at the left side of cell A1 as shown in Figure 8.9.
k. Copy the pyramid (hold down the Ctrl key while dragging the pyramid) to the right side of cell A1 as shown in Figure 8.9.

4. Save and then print **sec8x06**.

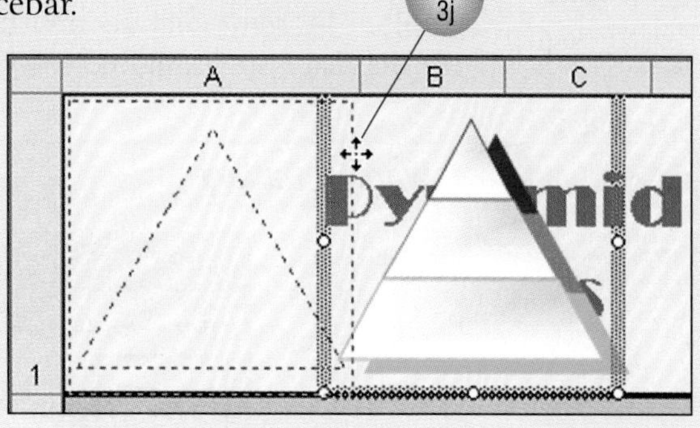

FIGURE 8.9 ***Exercise 6***

Pyramid Sales

	A	B	C	D	E
2	**SEMIANNUAL CUSTOMER SALES ANALYSIS**				
3	**Customer**	**October**	**November**	**December**	**Average**
4	**Lakeside Trucking**	$ 84,231	$ 73,455	$ 97,549	$ 85,078
5	**Gresham Machines**	$ 33,199	$ 40,390	$ 50,112	$ 41,234
6	**Real Photography**	$ 30,891	$ 35,489	$ 36,400	$ 34,260
7	**Genesis Productions**	$ 72,190	$ 75,390	$ 83,219	$ 76,933
8	**Landower Company**	$ 22,188	$ 14,228	$ 38,766	$ 25,061
9	**Jewell Enterprises**	$ 19,764	$ 50,801	$ 32,188	$ 34,251

Creating WordArt

With the WordArt application, you can distort or modify text to conform to a variety of shapes. This is useful for creating company logos and headings. With WordArt, you can change the font, style, and alignment of text. You can also use different fill patterns and colors, customize border lines, and add shadow and three-dimensional effects.

To insert WordArt in an Excel workbook click Insert, point to Picture, and then click WordArt. This displays the WordArt Gallery shown in Figure 8.10. You

QUICK STEPS

Create WordArt

1. Click Insert WordArt button on Drawing toolbar.
2. Double-click desired option at WordArt Gallery.
3. Type desired text at Edit WordArt Text box.
4. Click OK.

can also display the WordArt Gallery by clicking the Insert WordArt button on the WordArt toolbar or the Drawing toolbar. Display the WordArt or Drawing toolbar by right-clicking a visible toolbar, and then clicking Drawing or WordArt at the drop-down menu.

FIGURE 8.10 **WordArt Gallery**

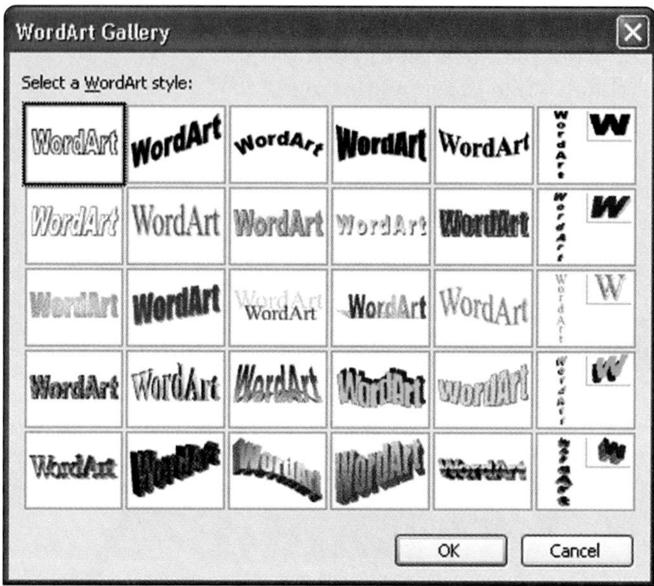

Entering Text

Double-click a WordArt choice at the WordArt Gallery and the Edit WordArt Text dialog box displays as shown in Figure 8.11. At the Edit WordArt Text dialog box, type the WordArt text and then click the OK button. At the Edit WordArt Text dialog box, you can change the font and/or size of text and also apply bold or italic formatting.

FIGURE 8.11 **Edit WordArt Text Dialog Box**

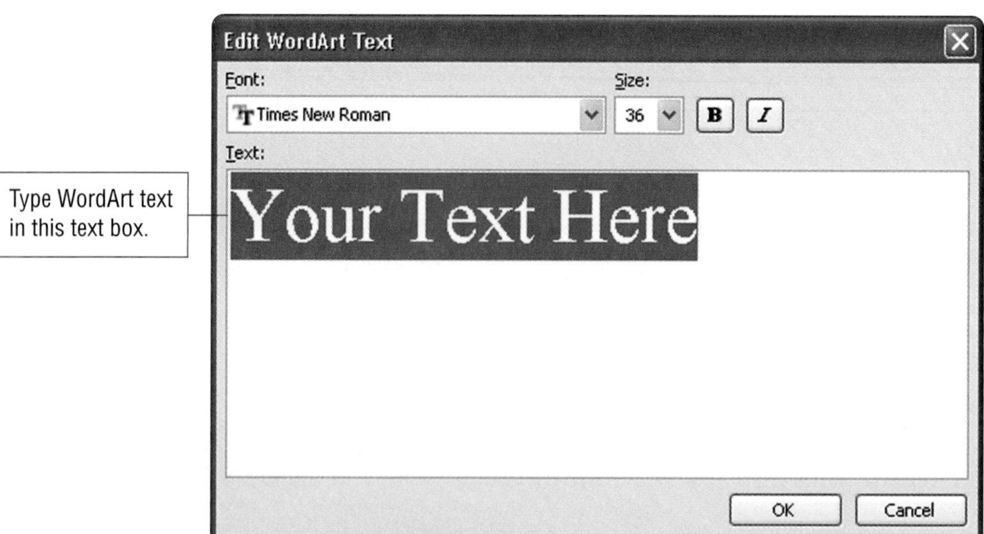

Sizing and Moving WordArt

WordArt text is inserted in the workbook with the formatting selected at the WordArt Gallery. The WordArt text is surrounded by white sizing handles and the WordArt toolbar displays near the text. Use the white sizing handles to change the height and width of the WordArt text. Use the yellow diamond located at the bottom of the WordArt text to change the slant of the WordArt text. To do this, position the arrow pointer on the yellow diamond, hold down the left mouse button, drag to the left or right, and then release the mouse button.

HINT
Use the small, green circle that displays when an object, such as WordArt, is selected to rotate the object.

To move WordArt text, position the arrow pointer on any letter of the WordArt text until the arrow pointer displays with a four-headed arrow attached. Hold down the left mouse button, drag the outline of the WordArt text box to the desired position, and then release the mouse button.

exercise 7

INSERTING WORDART IN A WORKSHEET

1. Open **ExcelWorksheet01**.
2. Save the worksheet with Save As and name it **sec8x07**.
3. Select cells A1 through D10 and then apply the Classic 3 autoformat.
4. Insert the WordArt as shown in Figure 8.12 by completing the following steps:
   a. Make cell E1 the active cell.
   b. Click Insert, point to Picture, and then click WordArt.
   c. At the WordArt Gallery, double-click the second option from the left in the second row.
   d. At the Edit WordArt Text dialog box, type **Cambridge** in the *Text* box and then press Enter.
   e. Type **Construction**.
   f. Click the down-pointing arrow at the right side of the *Font* text box and then click *Tahoma*.
   g. Click the OK button to close the Edit WordArt Text dialog box.

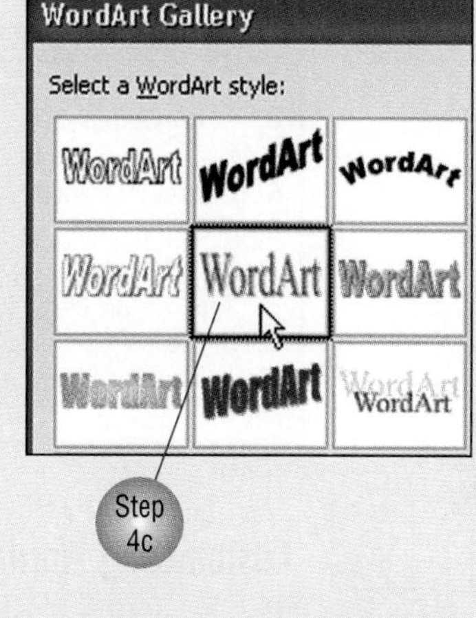

5. Change the location of the WordArt text by completing the following steps:
   a. Position the arrow pointer on any letter in the WordArt text until the arrow pointer displays with a four-headed arrow attached.
   b. Hold down the left mouse button, drag the outline of the WordArt text box so the upper left corner of the outline is located in cell E1, and then release the mouse button.

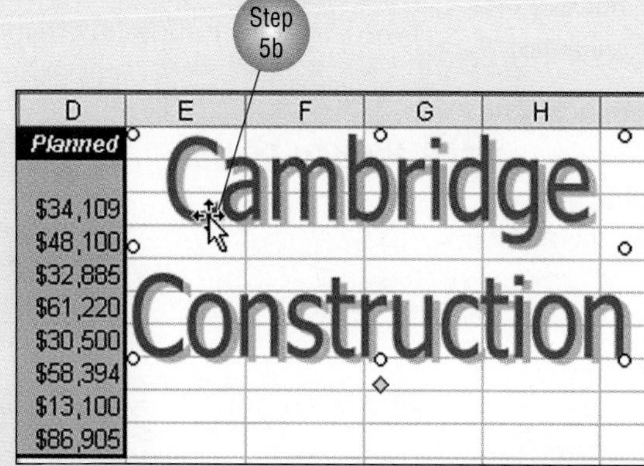

6. Change the size of the WordArt text by completing the following steps:
   a. Position the arrow pointer on the middle white sizing handle located at the bottom of the WordArt text.

b. Hold down the left mouse button, drag down until the outline of the WordArt box is positioned at the bottom of row 10, and then release the mouse button.
7. Click outside the WordArt text to deselect it.
8. Print **sec8x07** in landscape orientation and horizontally and vertically centered on the page.
9. Save the worksheet again with the same name (**sec8x07**).
10. Close **sec8x07**.

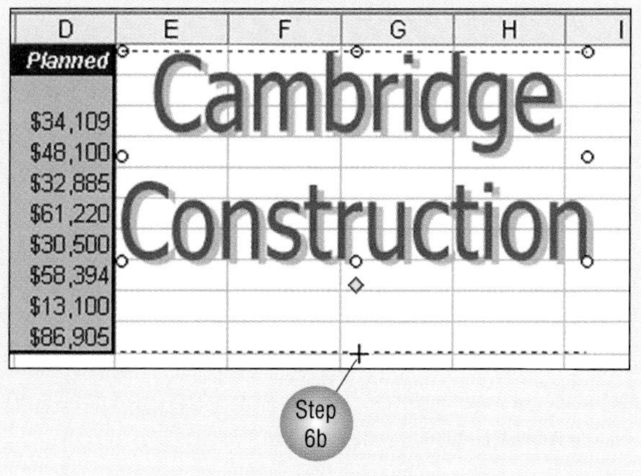

FIGURE 8.12 ***Exercise 7***

	A	B	C	D	E	F	G	H	I
1	*Customer*	*Job #*	*Actual*	*Planned*					
2									
3	Sellar Corporation	2130	$30,349	$34,109					
4	Main Street Photos	1201	$48,290	$48,100					
5	Sunset Automotive	318	$34,192	$32,885					
6	Linstrom Enterprises	1009	$63,293	$61,220					
7	Morcos Media	676	$29,400	$30,500					
8	Green Valley Optics	2117	$55,309	$58,394					
9	Detailed Designs	983	$12,398	$13,100					
10	Arrowstar Company	786	$87,534	$86,905					
11									

Cambridge Construction

WordArt Gallery

Format WordArt

Edit Text

Customizing WordArt

The WordArt toolbar, shown in Figure 8.13, contains buttons for customizing the WordArt text. Click the Insert WordArt button and the WordArt Gallery shown in Figure 8.8 displays. You can also display this gallery by clicking the WordArt Gallery button on the WordArt toolbar. Click the Edit Text button and the Edit WordArt Text dialog box displays.

FIGURE 8.13 ***WordArt Toolbar***

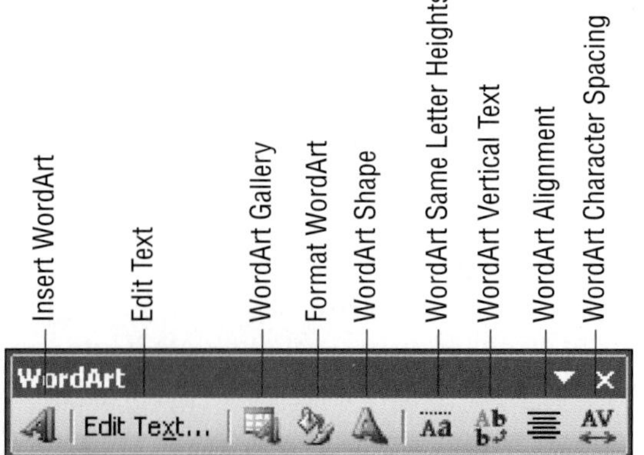

Customizing WordArt with Options at the Format WordArt Dialog Box

Customize WordArt text at the Format WordArt dialog box shown in Figure 8.14. To display this dialog box, click the Format WordArt button on the WordArt toolbar.

FIGURE 8.14 **Format WordArt Dialog Box with the Colors and Lines Tab Selected**

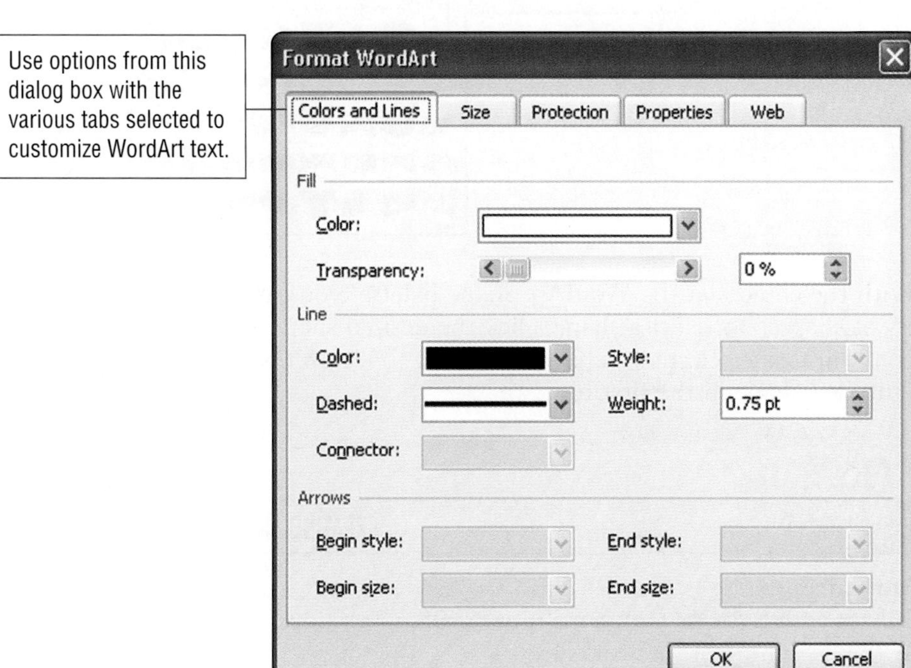

Change the color of the WordArt text and the line creating the text at the Format WordArt dialog box with the Colors and Lines tab selected. Click the Size tab and the dialog box displays with options for changing the size and rotation of the WordArt text as well as the scale of the text. At the Format WordArt dialog box with the Protection tab selected, you can specify if you want the WordArt text locked. You can only lock the WordArt text if the worksheet is protected. (Protect a worksheet with options at the Protect Sheet dialog box. Display this dialog box by clicking Tools, pointing to Protection, and then clicking Protect Sheet.)

Use options at the Format WordArt dialog box with the Properties tab selected to specify the positioning of the WordArt text. Choices include moving and sizing WordArt text with cells, moving but not sizing with cells, and not sizing or moving with cells. If you are going to post your worksheet on the Web, click the last tab, Web, and specify what text you want displayed while your WordArt text is being loaded.

Changing Shapes

The WordArt Gallery contains a variety of predesigned WordArt options. Formatting is already applied to these gallery choices. You can, however, customize the gallery choices with buttons on the WordArt toolbar. Use options from the WordArt

WordArt Shape

Shape button to customize the shape of WordArt text. Click the WordArt Shape button on the WordArt toolbar and a palette of shape choices displays as shown in Figure 8.15.

FIGURE 8.15 ***WordArt Shape Palette***

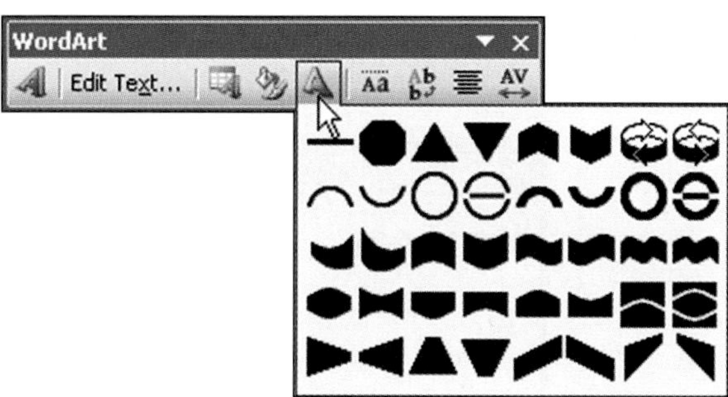

With the choices at the WordArt Shape palette, you can conform text to a variety of shapes. To select a shape, click the desired shape, and the WordArt text will conform to the selected shape. If you want to return text to the default shape, click the first shape in the first row.

exercise 8 CREATING AND SHAPING WORDART TEXT

1. Open **ExcelWorksheet28**.
2. Save the worksheet with Save As and name it **sec8x08**.
3. Insert a row at the beginning of the worksheet.
4. Change the height of row 1 (the new row) to 90.00.
5. Select cells A1 through H1 and then click the Merge and Center button.
6. Insert a formula in cell H4 that averages the amounts in B4 through G4.
7. Copy the formula in cell H4 down to cells H5 through H9.
8. Insert a double-line border at the bottom of cell H9. (The border is removed when you copy the formula.)
9. Insert WordArt in row 1, as shown in Figure 8.16, by completing the following steps:
   a. Click Insert, point to Picture, and then click WordArt.
   b. In the *Select a WordArt style* section, double-click the first option from the left in the top row.
   c. At the Edit WordArt Text dialog box, type **Cascade Manufacturing**.
   d. Click the OK button.
   e. Change the shape of the WordArt text by clicking the WordArt Shape button on the WordArt toolbar and then clicking the first option from the left in the fourth row (Inflate).

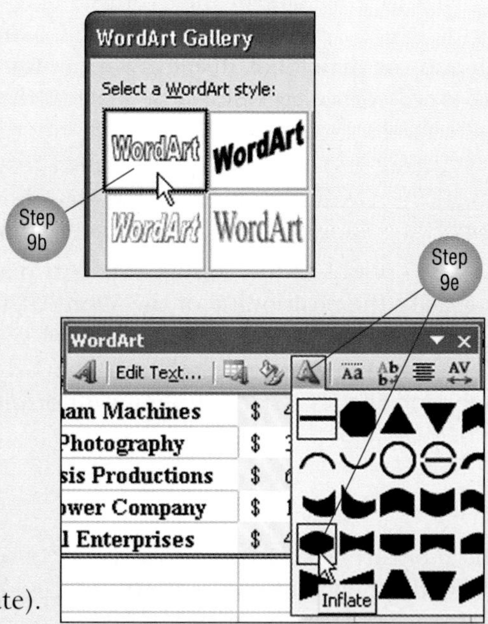

10. Change the size and color of the WordArt text by completing the following steps:
    a. Click the Format WordArt button on the WordArt toolbar.
    b. At the Format WordArt dialog box, click the Size tab.
    c. Select the current measurement in the *Height* text box and then type 1.4.
    d. Select the current measurement in the *Width* text box and then type 6.8.
    e. Click the Colors and Lines tab.
    f. At the Format WordArt dialog box with the Colors and Lines tab selected, click the down-pointing arrow at the right side of the *Color* option (in the *Fill* section) and then click the Tan color (second color from the left in the fifth row).
    g. Click OK to close the dialog box.
11. Drag the WordArt text so it is positioned in row 1 as shown in Figure 8.16.
12. Print the worksheet in landscape orientation, horizontally and vertically centered on the page.
13. Save the worksheet again with the same name (**sec8x08**).
14. Close **sec8x08**.

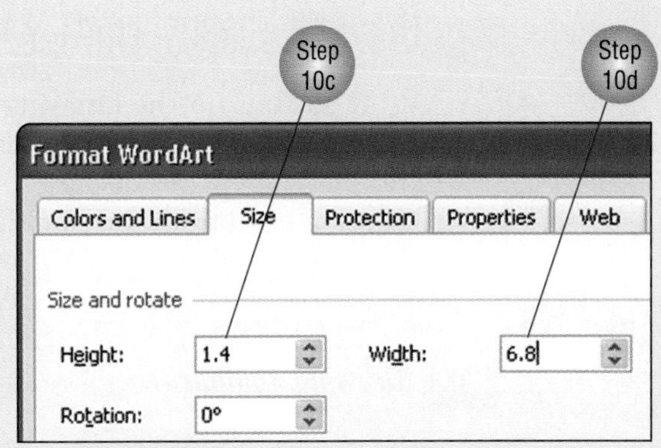

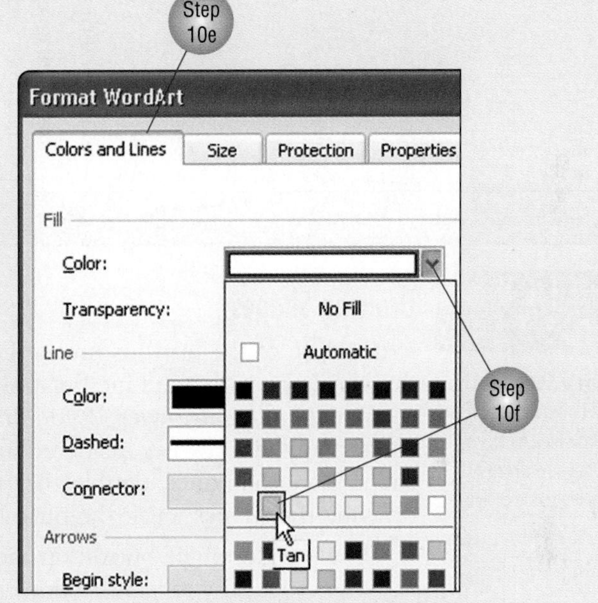

FIGURE 8.16 **Exercise 8**

	A	B	C	D	E	F	G	H	I
1	Cascade Manufacturing								
2	SEMIANNUAL CUSTOMER SALES ANALYSIS								
3	Customer	July	August	September	October	November	December	Average	
4	Lakeside Trucking	$ 89,450	$ 75,340	$ 98,224	$ 84,231	$ 73,455	$ 97,549	$ 86,375	
5	Gresham Machines	$ 45,210	$ 28,340	$ 53,400	$ 33,199	$ 40,390	$ 50,112	$ 41,775	
6	Real Photography	$ 30,219	$ 28,590	$ 34,264	$ 30,891	$ 35,489	$ 36,400	$ 32,642	
7	Genesis Productions	$ 65,290	$ 51,390	$ 79,334	$ 72,190	$ 75,390	$ 83,219	$ 71,136	
8	Landower Company	$ 12,168	$ 19,355	$ 45,209	$ 22,188	$ 14,228	$ 38,766	$ 25,319	
9	Jewell Enterprises	$ 44,329	$ 21,809	$ 33,490	$ 19,764	$ 50,801	$ 32,188	$ 33,730	
10									

Drawing Shapes, Lines, and Autoshapes

Drawing

With buttons on the Drawing toolbar, you can draw a variety of shapes such as circles, squares, rectangles, ovals, straight lines, free-form lines, lines with arrowheads, and much more. To display the Drawing toolbar, shown in Figure 8.17, click the Drawing button on the Standard toolbar.

FIGURE 8.17 ***Drawing Toolbar***

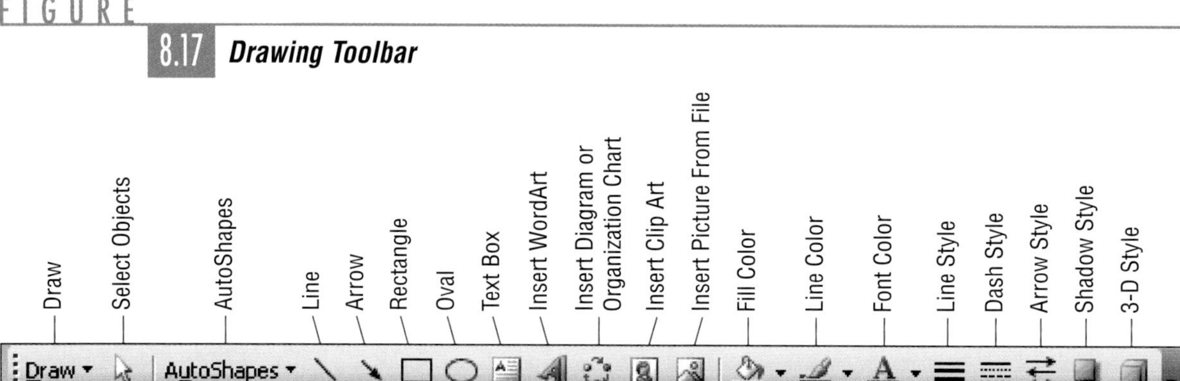

QUICK STEPS

Draw a Shape or Line

1. Click desired button on Drawing toolbar.
2. Drag in worksheet to create shape or line.

Line

Arrow

Rectangle

Oval

Drawing Shapes

With some of the buttons on the Drawing toolbar, you can draw a shape. If you draw a shape with the Line button or the Arrow button, the shape you draw is considered a ***line drawing***. If you draw a shape with the Rectangle or Oval button, the shape you draw is considered an ***enclosed object***. If you want to draw the same shape more than once, double-click the shape button on the Drawing toolbar. After drawing the shapes, click the button again to deactivate it.

Use the Rectangle button on the Drawing toolbar to draw a square or rectangle in a workbook. If you want to draw a square, hold down the Shift key while drawing the shape. The Shift key keeps all sides of the drawn object equal. Use the Oval button to draw a circle or an oval object. To draw a circle, hold down the Shift key while drawing the object.

Adding Fill Color

Fill Color

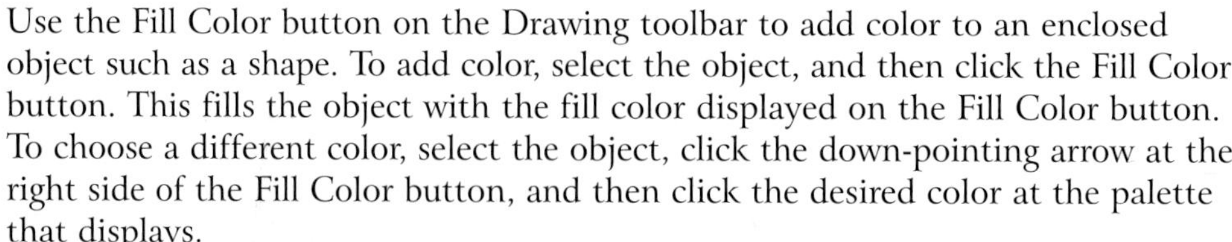

Use the Fill Color button on the Drawing toolbar to add color to an enclosed object such as a shape. To add color, select the object, and then click the Fill Color button. This fills the object with the fill color displayed on the Fill Color button. To choose a different color, select the object, click the down-pointing arrow at the right side of the Fill Color button, and then click the desired color at the palette that displays.

Changing Line Color

Line Color

Change the color of the line around a shape or a line drawn with the Arrow button with the Line Color button on the Drawing toolbar. To change the color, click the object, and then click the Line Color button. The line color of the selected object changes to the color displayed on the button. To change to a different color, click the down-pointing arrow at the right side of the button, and then click the desired color at the color palette.

Aligning Objects

Distribute and align objects with the Draw button on the Drawing toolbar. To align and distribute objects, select the objects, click the Draw button on the Drawing toolbar, and then point to Align or Distribute. Choose the desired alignment and distribution option from the side menu that displays.

To identify the objects you want to align and/or distribute, click the Select Objects button on the Drawing toolbar and then draw a border around the objects. Another method for selecting objects is to click the first object, hold down the Shift key, and then click any other objects you want aligned.

HINT

If objects overlap, click the Draw button, point to Order, and then use options from the side menu to specify how objects should overlap.

Draw

Select Objects

DRAWING, CUSTOMIZING, AND COPYING CIRCLES

1. Open **ExcelWorksheet38**.
2. Save the worksheet with Save As and name it **sec8x09**.
3. Click the Drawing button on the Standard toolbar to turn on the display of the Drawing toolbar. (The Drawing toolbar displays toward the bottom of the screen, above the Status bar.)
4. Draw a circle in cell A1 and then format the circle by completing the following steps:
   a. With cell A1 the active cell, click the Oval button on the Drawing toolbar.
   b. Hold down the Shift key and then use the mouse to draw a circle the approximate size of the circle shown in Figure 8.18. After drawing the circle, release the mouse button.

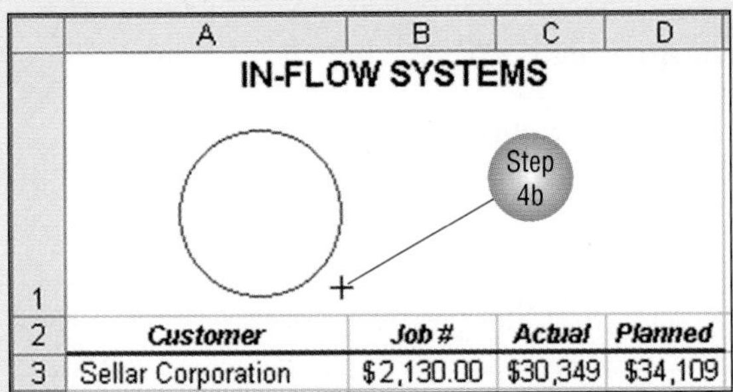

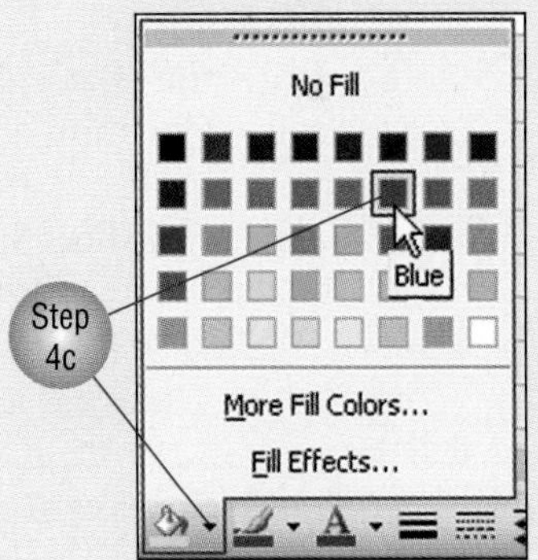

   c. With the circle selected (small, white circles [sizing handles] display around the circle), click the down-pointing arrow at the right side of the Fill Color button on the Drawing toolbar, and then click the Blue color (sixth color from the left in the second row).
   d. Click the down-pointing arrow at the right side of the Line Color button and then click the Black color (first color from the left in the top row).
   e. Click the Line Style button and then click *2¼ pt* at the palette that displays.

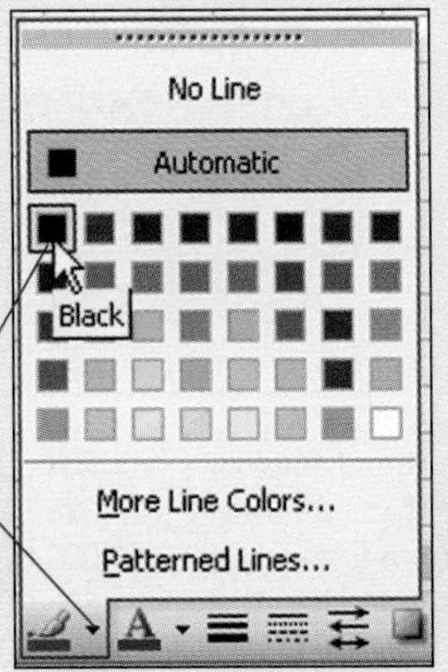

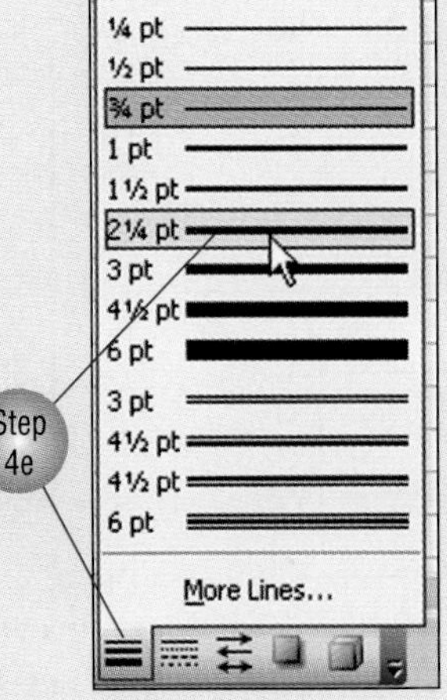

5. With the circle selected, copy the circle three times by completing the following steps:
   a. Position the mouse pointer on the circle and hold down the Ctrl key.
   b. Hold down the left mouse button, drag to the right (refer to Figure 8.18), and then release the mouse button.
   c. With the Ctrl key down, drag the second circle to the right (refer to Figure 8.18), and then release the mouse button.
   d. With the Ctrl key down, drag the third circle to the right (refer to Figure 8.18), and then release the mouse button.

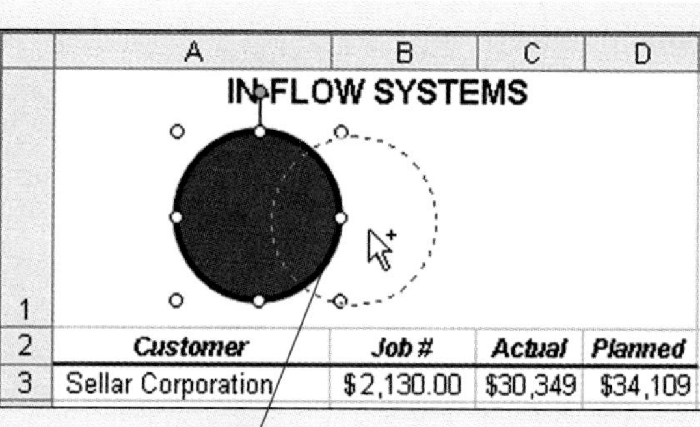

6. Align and distribute the four circles by completing the following steps:
   a. Click the Select Objects button on the Drawing toolbar.
   b. Using the mouse, draw a box around the four circles. (When you release the mouse button, white sizing handles display around each of the circles.)
   c. Click the Draw button on the Drawing toolbar, point to Align or Distribute, and then click Distribute Horizontally.
   d. With the circles still selected, click the Draw button, point to Align or Distribute, and then click Align Bottom.
   e. With the circles still selected, drag the circles so they are positioned in cell A1 as shown in Figure 8.18.

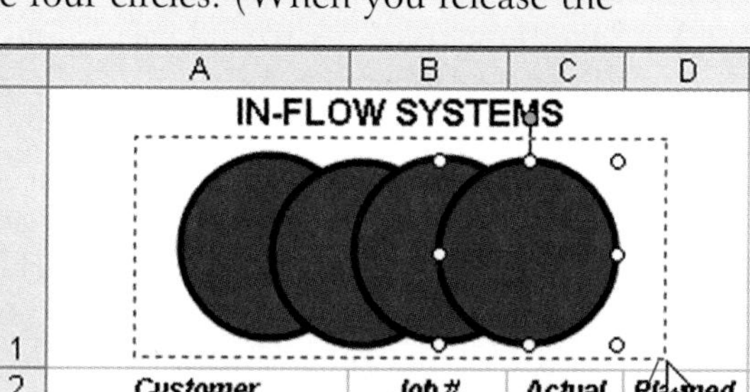

7. Print the worksheet horizontally and vertically centered on the page.
8. Save the worksheet with the same name (**sec8x09**).
9. Close **sec8x09**.

FIGURE **8.18** ***Exercise 9***

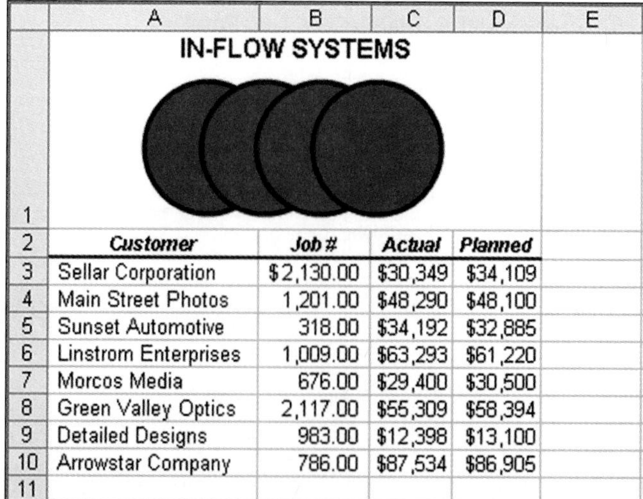

	A	B	C	D	E
1	IN-FLOW SYSTEMS				
2	*Customer*	*Job #*	*Actual*	*Planned*	
3	Sellar Corporation	$2,130.00	$30,349	$34,109	
4	Main Street Photos	1,201.00	$48,290	$48,100	
5	Sunset Automotive	318.00	$34,192	$32,885	
6	Linstrom Enterprises	1,009.00	$63,293	$61,220	
7	Morcos Media	676.00	$29,400	$30,500	
8	Green Valley Optics	2,117.00	$55,309	$58,394	
9	Detailed Designs	983.00	$12,398	$13,100	
10	Arrowstar Company	786.00	$87,534	$86,905	
11					

Drawing Lines

To draw a line in a worksheet, click the Line button on the Drawing toolbar. Position the crosshairs where you want to begin the line, hold down the left mouse button, drag the line to the location where you want the line to end, and then release the mouse button. Customize a line by changing the line color, line style, or by applying an arrow style.

exercise 10 — DRAWING AND CUSTOMIZING LINES

1. Open **ExcelWorksheet10**.
2. Save the worksheet with Save As and name it **sec8x10**.
3. Delete column D (contains the heading *Bonus*).
4. Click in cell E1, turn on bold, type **Top Sales**, and then press Enter.
5. Click in cell A8.
6. Draw and customize two lines as shown in Figure 8.19 by completing the following steps:
   a. Click the Arrow button on the Drawing toolbar.
   b. Position the crosshairs at the left side of the text *Top Sales* (located in cell E1).
   c. Hold down the left mouse button, drag down and to the left until the crosshairs are positioned near the contents of cell C4 (refer to Figure 8.20), and then release the mouse button.
   d. With the line selected, click the down-pointing arrow at the right side of the Line Color button, and then click the Red color (first color from the left in the third row).
   e. Click the Arrow button on the Drawing toolbar and then draw another arrow as shown in Figure 8.19.
   f. With the second arrow selected, click the Line Color button. (This changes the line to red since that was the last color selected.)
7. Save, print, and then close **sec8x10**.

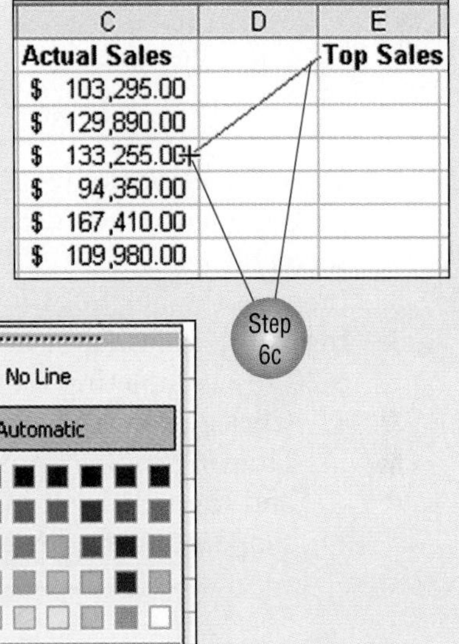

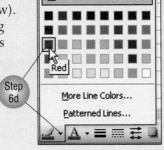

FIGURE 8.19 ***Exercise 10***

	A	B	C	D	E	F
1	**Salesperson**	**Quota**	**Actual Sales**		**Top Sales**	
2	Allejandro	$ 95,500.00	$ 103,295.00			
3	Crispin	$ 137,000.00	$ 129,890.00			
4	Frankel	$ 124,000.00	$ 133,255.00			
5	Hiesmann	$ 85,500.00	$ 94,350.00			
6	Jarvis	$ 159,000.00	$ 167,410.00			
7	Littleman	$ 110,500.00	$ 109,980.00			
8						

Creating Autoshapes

AutoShapes

Draw a variety of shapes with options from the AutoShapes button. Click the AutoShapes button, point to the desired menu option, and then click the desired shape. When you choose an autoshape, the mouse pointer turns into crosshairs. Position the crosshairs in the workbook, hold down the left mouse button, drag to create the shape, and then release the button.

Draw an Autoshape
1. Click AutoShapes button on Drawing toolbar.
2. Point to desired menu option.
3. Click desired shape.
4. Drag in worksheet to create autoshape.

Flipping and Rotating an Object

A selected object, such as a shape or line, can be rotated and flipped horizontally or vertically. To rotate or flip an object, select the object, click the Draw button on the Drawing toolbar, point to Rotate or Flip, and then click the desired rotation or flip option at the side menu that displays.

Choose an autoshape and then click in the worksheet and Excel will insert a standard-sized autoshape object. Display the AutoShapes toolbar by clicking Insert, pointing to Picture, and then clicking AutoShapes.

exercise 11

DRAWING AND ROTATING AN AUTOSHAPE

1. Open **ExcelWorksheet23**.
2. Save the worksheet with Save As and name it **sec8x11**.
3. Increase the height of row 2 to 60.00.
4. Insert the autoshapes in cell B2 (refer to Figure 8.20) by completing the following steps:
   a. Click the AutoShapes button on the Drawing toolbar, point to Block Arrows, and then click Striped Right Arrow (first shape from the left in the fifth row).

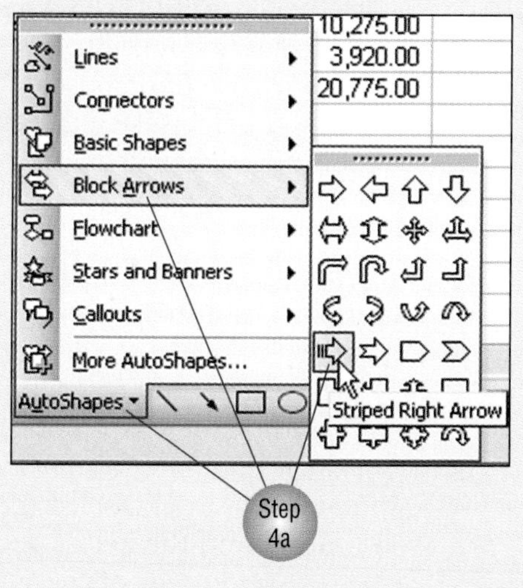

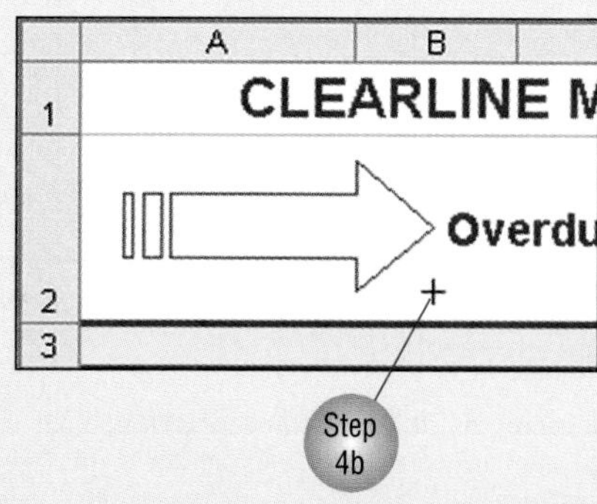

   b. Position the crosshairs at the left side of the text *Overdue Accounts*, hold down the Shift key, and then draw an arrow approximately the size of the arrow in Figure 8.20.
   c. With the arrow selected, click the down-pointing arrow at the right side of the Fill Color button, and then click the Light Turquoise color (fifth color from the left in the bottom row).

d. With the arrow selected, hold down the Ctrl key, drag the arrow to the right of the text *Overdue Accounts*, then release the mouse button and then the Ctrl key.

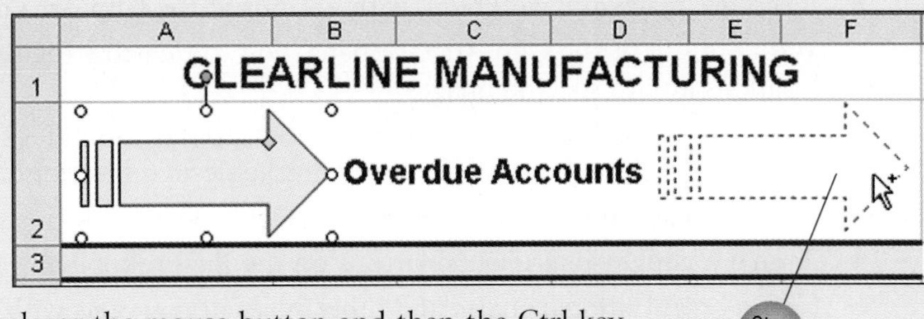

e. Flip the arrow by clicking the Draw button, pointing to Rotate or Flip, and then clicking Flip Horizontal.

5. Save, print, and then close **sec8x11**.

FIGURE 8.20 ***Exercise 11***

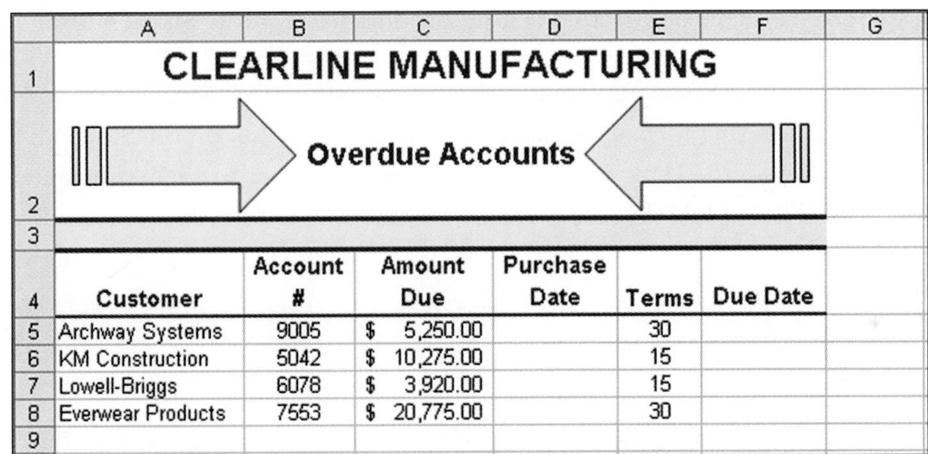

	A	B	C	D	E	F	G
1	CLEARLINE MANUFACTURING						
2	Overdue Accounts						
3							
4	Customer	Account #	Amount Due	Purchase Date	Terms	Due Date	
5	Archway Systems	9005	$ 5,250.00		30		
6	KM Construction	5042	$ 10,275.00		15		
7	Lowell-Briggs	6078	$ 3,920.00		15		
8	Everwear Products	7553	$ 20,775.00		30		
9							

CHAPTER summary

- Save a workbook as a Web page by opening the workbook, clicking File, and then clicking Save as Web Page. Type the name of the Web page in the Save As dialog box and then click Save.
- To preview a workbook in your default Web browser, click File and then click Web Page Preview.
- To create a hyperlink in a workbook, select the text to which you want to attach the hyperlink, click the Insert Hyperlink button on the Standard toolbar, and then type the file name or Web site URL in the *Address* text box.
- To modify or edit a hyperlink, right-click the hyperlink and then click Edit Hyperlink at the shortcut menu.
- Add visual interest to a worksheet that is viewed in a Web browser by adding a background image. A background image inserted in a worksheet does not print.
- Use options at the Research task pane to search for and request specific information from online sources and to translate words from and to a variety of languages.

- Insert an image in a workbook with options at the Clip Art task pane.
- With options at the Clip Art task pane, you can narrow the search for images to specific locations and to specific images.
- Size an image using the sizing handles that display around a selected image and move a selected image by dragging the image to the desired location using the mouse.
- Delete a selected image by pressing the Delete key.
- Format a clip art image with buttons on the Picture toolbar.
- Create organizational charts and other types of diagrams with options at the Diagram Gallery dialog box.
- Use WordArt to create, distort, modify, and/or conform text to a variety of shapes. The WordArt Gallery contains a variety of predesigned WordArt.
- Size WordArt using the sizing handles that display around selected WordArt text and move selected WordArt by dragging it to the desired location using the mouse.
- Customize WordArt text with buttons on the WordArt toolbar and/or with options at the Format WordArt dialog box.
- Customize the shape of WordArt text by clicking the WordArt Shape button on the WordArt toolbar and then clicking the desired shape at the palette that displays.
- Use buttons on the Drawing toolbar to draw and customize shapes, lines, and autoshapes.
- Display the Drawing toolbar by clicking the Drawing button on the Standard toolbar.
- Use options from the Draw button on the Drawing toolbar to align, distribute, rotate and/or flip selected objects.

FEATURES summary

FEATURE	BUTTON	MENU	KEYBOARD
Save as Web page		File, Save as Web Page	
Web Page Preview		File, Web Page Preview	
Insert Hyperlink dialog box		Insert, Hyperlink	Ctrl + K
Sheet Background dialog box		Format, Sheet, Background	
Research task pane		Tools, Research	Alt + click
Clip Art task pane		Insert, Picture, Clip Art	
Diagram Gallery dialog box		Insert, Diagram	
WordArt Gallery		Insert, Picture, WordArt	
Format WordArt dialog box		Format, WordArt	Ctrl + 1
Drawing toolbar		View, Toolbars, Drawing	

CONCEPTS check

Completion: On a blank sheet of paper, indicate the correct term, symbol, or command for each description.

1. If you want to view a workbook in a Web browser, save the workbook as this.
2. This term refers to text or an object you click to go to a different file or HTML page on the Internet.
3. Use options at this task pane to search for and request specific information from online sources.
4. Insert an image in a workbook with options at this task pane.
5. Select a clip art image in a workbook and these display around the image.
6. Use buttons on this toolbar to format a selected image.
7. Click the Insert Diagram or Organization Chart button on this toolbar to display the Diagram Gallery dialog box.
8. Use this application to distort or modify text to conform to a variety of shapes.
9. Click this button on the WordArt toolbar to display a palette of shape options.
10. Customize WordArt text with options at this dialog box.
11. To draw a circle, click the Oval button on the Drawing toolbar, hold down this key, and then use the mouse to draw the circle.
12. Distribute and align objects with this button on the Drawing toolbar.
13. Draw a variety of shapes with options from this button on the Drawing toolbar.
14. Write the steps you would complete to insert a clip art image in a workbook related to summer.

SKILLS check

Assessment 1

1. Display the Open dialog box with ExcelChapter08S the active folder.
2. Open **ExcelWorksheet39**.
3. Save the workbook as a Single File Web Page in the ExcelWebPages folder (you created this folder in Exercise 1) on your disk, name it **BooksGaloreWebPage**, and then change the title to *Books Galore*.
4. Preview the Web page in the default browser.
5. Close the browser application window.
6. Print **BooksGaloreWebPage** in landscape orientation.
7. Close **BooksGaloreWebPage**.

Assessment 2

1. Open **BooksGaloreWebPage**.
2. Select E12 and hyperlink it to www.microsoft.com.
3. Select E13 and hyperlink it to www.symantec.com.
4. Select E14 and hyperlink it to www.nasa.gov.
5. Select E15 and hyperlink it to www.cnn.com.
6. Make sure you are connected to the Internet and then click the hyperlink to NASA.
7. Jump to a link from the NASA Web page that interests you.

8. Print the page you viewed from NASA and then close the browser application window.
9. Jump to each of the remaining links in the Web page. At each Web page, jump to a link that interests you, print the page, and then close the browser application window.
10. Close **BooksGaloreWebPage**.

Assessment 3

1. Open **ExcelWorksheet44**.
2. Save the worksheet with Save As and name it **sec8sc03**.
3. Display the Research task pane.
4. Insert current stock prices for the following companies in the specified cells:

B4	=	UPS (for United Parcel Service, Inc.)
B5	=	AAPL (for Apple Computer, Inc.)
B6	=	DIS (for Walt Disney Company)

5. Save, print, and then close **sec8sc03**.

Assessment 4

1. Open **ExcelWorksheet20**.
2. Save the worksheet with Save As and name it **sec8sc04**.
3. Increase the height of row 1 to 75.00.
4. Insert the clip art image shown in Figure 8.21 (search for this clip art by typing **camera** in the *Search for* text box). If this clip art image is not available, choose another image related to *camera* or *photography*.
5. Size and move the clip art image so it is positioned as shown in Figure 8.21.
6. Insert a formula in cell E7 using the PMT function that calculates monthly payments. ***(Hint: Refer to Chapter 3, Exercise 9.)***
7. Copy the formula in cell E7 down to cells E8 and E9.
8. Insert a formula in cell F7 that calculates the total amount of the payments. ***(Hint: Refer to Chapter 3, Exercise 9.)***
9. Copy the formula in cell F7 down to cells F8 and F9.
10. Insert a formula in cell G7 that calculates to the total amount of interest paid. ***(Hint: Refer to Chapter 3, Exercise 9.)***
11. Copy the formula in cell G7 down to cells G8 and G9.
12. Print the worksheet in landscape orientation.
13. Save and then close **sec8sc04**.

FIGURE 8.21 ***Assessment 4***

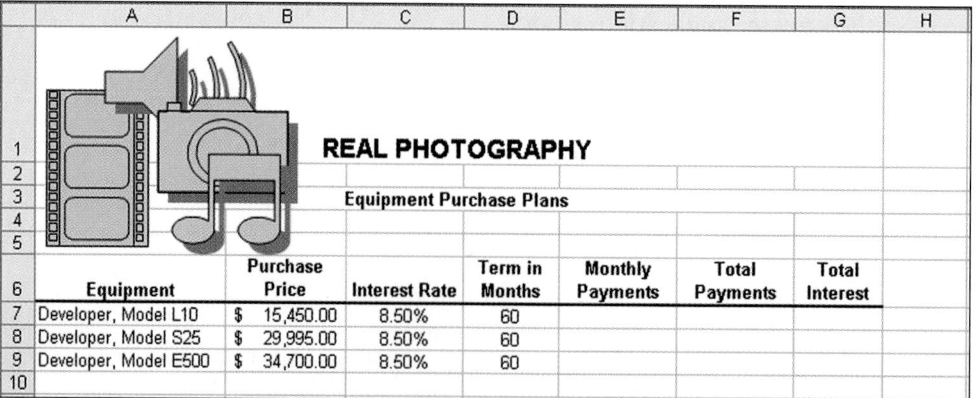

	A	B	C	D	E	F	G	H
1			REAL PHOTOGRAPHY					
2								
3			Equipment Purchase Plans					
4								
5								
6	Equipment	Purchase Price	Interest Rate	Term in Months	Monthly Payments	Total Payments	Total Interest	
7	Developer, Model L10	$ 15,450.00	8.50%	60				
8	Developer, Model S25	$ 29,995.00	8.50%	60				
9	Developer, Model E500	$ 34,700.00	8.50%	60				
10								

Assessment 5

1. Open **ExcelWorksheet34**.
2. Save the worksheet with Save As and name it **sec8sc05**.
3. Insert a new row at the beginning of the worksheet.
4. Select cells A1 through D1 and then click the Merge and Center button.
5. Increase the height of row 1 to 90.00.
6. Insert a formula in cell D4 that subtracts the Actual amount from the Budget amount.
7. Copy the formula in cell D4 down to cells D5 through D10.
8. Insert the text *EZ Sports* as WordArt in cell A1. You determine the formatting and shape of the WordArt. Move and size the WordArt so it fits in cell A1.
9. Save, print, and then close **sec8sc05**.

Assessment 6

1. Open **ExcelWorksheet33**.
2. Save the worksheet with Save As and name it **sec8sc06**.
3. Make sure *Sales 2002* is the active tab. (This workbook contains three worksheets.)
4. Insert a new row at the beginning of the worksheet.
5. Select cells A1 through D1 and then click the Merge and Center button.
6. Increase the height of row 1 to 75.00.
7. In cell A1, type **Mountain**, press Alt + Enter, and then type **Systems**.
8. Select *Mountain Systems* and then change the font to 18-point Arial bold.
9. Change the horizontal alignment to *Left (Indent)* and the vertical alignment to *Center*.
10. Click outside cell A1.
11. Use the Isosceles Triangle shape (to find it click AutoShapes, point to Basic Shapes, and then click Isosceles Triangle) to draw a triangle as shown in Figure 8.22.
12. Copy the triangle three times, add fill to the triangles, and position the triangles as shown in Figure 8.22.
13. Print only the *Sales 2002* worksheet.
14. Save and then close **sec8sc06**.

FIGURE 8.22 ***Assessment 6***

	A	B	C	D	E
1	**Mountain Systems**				
2	**FIRST-QUARTER SALES - 2002**				
3	**Customer**	**January**	**February**	**March**	
4	Lakeside Trucking	$84,231	$ 73,455	$97,549	
5	Gresham Machines	$33,199	$ 40,390	$50,112	
6	Real Photography	$30,891	$ 35,489	$36,400	
7	Genesis Productions	$72,190	$ 75,390	$83,219	
8	Landower Company	$22,188	$ 14,228	$38,766	
9	Jewell Enterprises	$19,764	$ 50,801	$32,188	
10					

Assessment 7

1. The Drawing toolbar contains buttons for applying shadow effects and 3-D effects to shapes. Use the Help feature to learn how to apply a shadow style to a shape and then apply shadow formatting by following these basic steps:
   a. Open **sec8x11**.
   b. Save the worksheet with Save As and name it **sec8sc07A**.
   c. Select the left arrow autoshape and apply a shadow style of your choosing.
   d. Select the right arrow autoshape and apply a shadow style of your choosing. (Choose a shadow style that complements the shadow style you applied to the left arrow.)
   e. Save, print, and then close **sec8sc07A**.
2. Use the Help feature to learn how to apply a 3-D effect to a shape and then apply 3-D formatting by following these basic steps:
   a. Open **ExcelWorksheet26**.
   b. Save the worksheet with Save As and name it **sec8sc07B**.
   c. Select all of the triangle shapes in cell A1 and then apply the 3-D Style 7 formatting.
   d. Save, print, and then close **sec8sc07B**.

CHAPTER challenge

Allen's Auto Sales has hired you to maintain the inventory of vehicles on its lot. Ultimately, this information will be placed on the Web. To begin the task, create a worksheet that contains at least five different types (brand name) of vehicles. Also include the price of the vehicle, destination charges, rebate (if applicable), and final price (use a formula to calculate). Format the worksheet appropriately, using at least three different formatting tools learned in this chapter. Since the worksheet will ultimately be placed on the Web to be used by potential customers, save the workbook as a Web Page. To provide further information for the customer, include two hyperlinks in the Web page. One hyperlink should be to a recommended financial institution Web site, where customers can learn more about financing their vehicle. The second hyperlink should be to a Web site that provides additional information about buying a new or used car. Save the file again.

After you show the workbook (created in the first part of the Chapter Challenge) to the owner, he suggests sorting the list in a different order. Use the Help feature to learn how to perform single and multiple sorts. After reading about ways to sort, provide the owner with various types of sorts. First, sort the list in descending order by final price. Print the workbook. Then sort the list in ascending order by type of vehicle and then by price (ascending order.) Save the workbook again.

After working at Allen's Auto Sales for six months, you decide that maintaining the inventory of vehicles could be managed better in a database application. Use Microsoft Access to create a database named **Cars**. Using the workbook created in the first part of the Chapter Challenge, import the section of the worksheet that includes the vehicle type, price, destination charges, rebate, and final price as a table into the **Cars** database. Add one more record to the table. Save the table.

WORKPLACE Ready

Maintaining and Enhancing Workbooks

ASSESSING proficiency

In this unit, you have learned to create, save, print, edit, and format Excel In this unit, you have learned how to work with multiple windows; move, copy, link and paste data between workbooks and applications; create and customize charts with data in a worksheet; save a workbook as a Web page; insert hyperlinks; and insert and customize clip art images, diagrams, WordArt, and drawn objects.

Assessment 1

1. Open **ExcelWorksheet19**.
2. Save the worksheet with Save As and name it **seu2pa01**.
3. Make the following changes to the worksheet:
   a. Type **Ave.** in cell D2.
   b. Apply the same top and bottom border to cell D2 that is applied to cells A2 through C2.
   c. Merge and center cells A1 through D1.
   d. Delete row 14 (the row for Kwieciak, Kathleen).
   e. Insert a formula in cell D3 that averages the percentages in cells B3 and C3.
   f. Copy the formula in cell D3 down to cells D4 through D19.
   g. Make cell A21 active, turn on bold, and then type **Highest Averages**.
   h. Display the Clipboard task pane. (Make sure the Clipboard task pane is empty.)
   i. Select and then copy each of the following rows (individually): row 6, 9, 13, 15, and 17.
   j. Make cell A22 active and then paste row 13 (the row for Jewett, Troy).
   k. Make cell A23 active and then paste row 6 (the row for Cumpston, Kurt).
   l. Make cell A24 active and then paste row 9 (the row for Fisher-Edwards, Teri).
   m. Make cell A25 active and then paste row 15 (the row for Markovits, Claude).
   n. Make cell A26 active and then paste row 17 (the row for Nyegaard, Curtis).
   o. Click the Clear All button in the Clipboard task pane and then close the task pane.
4. Save, print, and then close **seu2pa01**.

Assessment 2

1. Open **ExcelWorksheet17**.
2. Save the worksheet with Save As and name it **seu2pa02**.
3. Select cells A1 through C11 and then copy the cells to *Sheet2*.
4. With *Sheet2* displayed, make the following changes:
   a. Automatically adjust the width of columns A, B, and C.
   b. Delete the contents of cell B2.
   c. Change the contents of the following cells:

      A6: Change *January* to *July*
      A7: Change *February* to *August*
      A8: Change *March* to *September*
      A9: Change *April* to *October*
      A10: Change *May* to *November*
      A11: Change *June* to *December*
      B6: Change *8.30%* to *8.10%*
      B8: Change *9.30%* to *8.70%*

5. Make *Sheet1* active and then copy cell B2 and paste link it to cell B2 in *Sheet2*.
6. Make *Sheet1* active and then determine the effect on projected monthly earnings if the projected yearly income is increased by 10% by changing the number in cell B2 to *$1,480,380*.
7. Save the workbook (two worksheets) again and then print both worksheets of the workbook so they are horizontally and vertically centered on each page.
8. Determine the effect on projected monthly earnings if the projected yearly income is increased by 20% by changing the number in cell B2 to *$1,614,960*.
9. Save the workbook again and then print both worksheets of the workbook so they are horizontally and vertically centered on each page.
10. Save and then close **seu2pa02**.

Assessment 3

1. Open **ExcelWorksheet41**.
2. Save the workbook with Save As and name it **seu2pa03**.
3. Make the following changes to the workbook:
   a. Insert the heading *Average Sales 2003-2005* (on multiple lines) in cell A13.
   b. Insert a formula in cell B13 with a 3-D reference that averages the total in cells B4 through B11 in *Sheet1*, *Sheet2*, and *Sheet3*.
   c. Make cell B13 active and then change to the Currency Style with zero decimal places.
   d. Insert a formula in cell C13 with a 3-D reference that averages the total in cells C4 through C11 in *Sheet1*, *Sheet2*, and *Sheet3*.
   e. Make cell C13 active and then change to the Currency Style with zero decimal places.
4. Rename *Sheet1* to *2003 Sales*, rename *Sheet2* to *2004 Sales*, and rename *Sheet3* to *2005 Sales*.
5. Save the workbook and then print the entire workbook.
6. Close **seu2pa03**.

Assessment 4

1. Open Excel and then type the following information in a worksheet (The text *Country* and *Total Sales* should be set in bold.):

Country	**Total Sales**
Denmark	$85,345
Finland	$71,450
Norway	$135,230
Sweden	$118,895

2. Using the data just entered in the worksheet, create a column chart as a separate sheet.
3. Save the workbook (worksheet plus chart sheet) and name it **seu2pa04**.
4. Print only the sheet containing the chart.
5. Change the column chart to a line chart of your choosing.
6. Print only the sheet containing the chart.
7. Save and then close **seu2pa04**.

Assessment 5

1. Open **ExcelWorksheet42**.
2. Save the worksheet with Save As and name it **seu2pa05**.
3. Create a pie chart as a separate sheet with the data in cells A3 through B10. You determine the type of pie. Include an appropriate title for the chart and include percentage labels.
4. Print only the sheet containing the chart.
5. Save and then close **seu2pa05**.

Assessment 6

1. Create a new folder named *TravelWebPages* in the ExcelUnit02S folder on your disk.
2. Open **ExcelWorksheet40**.
3. Save the worksheet as a Single File Web Page in the TravelWebPages folder with the following specifications:
   a. Name the Web page **TravelAdvantageWebPage**.
   b. Change the title to *Winter Getaway Destinations!*
4. Preview the Web page in the default browser.
5. Make sure you are connected to the Internet and then search for sites that might be of interest to tourists for each of the cities in the TravelAdvantageWebPage. Write down the URL for the best Web page you find for each city.
6. Create a hyperlink in TravelAdvantageWebPage for each city to jump to the URL you wrote down in Step 5.
7. Test the hyperlinks to make sure you entered the URLs correctly by clicking each hyperlink and then closing the Web browser.
8. Save, print, and then close **TravelAdvantageWebPage**.

Assessment 7

1. Open **ExcelWorksheet14**.
2. Save the worksheet with Save As and name it **seu2pa07**.
3. Make the following changes to the worksheet:
   a. Insert a formula in cell C3 using an absolute reference to determine the projected quotas at 10% of the current quotas.

b. Copy the formula in cell C3 down to cells C4 through C12.
c. Increase the height of row 1 (you determine the height) and then insert a clip art image in row 1 related to *money*. You determine the size and position of the clip art image.

4. Save, print, and then close **seu2pa07**.

Assessment 8

1. Open **ExcelWorksheet33**.
2. Save the worksheet with Save As and name it **seu2pa08**.
3. Make the following changes to the worksheet:
   a. Insert a new row at the beginning of the worksheet.
   b. Select and then merge cells A1 through D1.
   c. Increase the height of row 1 to approximately 100.00.
   d. Insert the text **Custom Interiors** as WordArt in cell A1. You determine the formatting and shape of the WordArt. Move and size the WordArt so it fits in cell A1.
   e. Insert the following comments in the specified cells:

      D4 = **Increase amount to $100,000.**
      A5 = **Change the name to Gresham Technology.**
      A9 = **Decrease amounts for this company by 5%.**

4. Turn on the display of all comments.
5. Print the worksheet with the comments as displayed on the worksheet.
6. Turn off the display of all comments.
7. Delete the comment in A5.
8. Print the worksheet again with the comments printed at the end of the worksheet. (The comments will print on a separate page from the worksheet.)
9. Save and then close **seu2pa08**.

Assessment 9

1. Open **ExcelWorksheet03**.
2. Save the worksheet with Save As and name it **seu2pa09**.
3. Make the following changes to the worksheet so it displays as shown in figure U2.1:
   a. Insert a new row at the beginning of the worksheet.
   b. Select and then merge cells A1 through D1.
   c. Select cells A2 through D9 and then apply the List 2 autoformat.
   d. Select cells B4 through D9 and then click the Percent Style button.
   e. Increase the height of row 1 to the approximate size shown in figure U2.1.
   f. Insert the text **SOLAR ENTERPRISES** in cell A1 centered horizontally and vertically and set the text in 18-point Arial bold.
   g. Insert and fill the shapes using the AutoShapes button on the Drawing toolbar. (To find the Sun shape, click Draw, point to Basic Shapes, and then click Sun.)
4. Save, print, and then close **seu2pa09**.

	A	B	C	D	E
1	SOLAR ENTERPRISES				
2	ANALYSIS OF FINANCIAL CONDITION				
3		Actual	Planned	Prior Year	
4	Stockholder's equity ratio	62%	60%	57%	
5	Bond holder's equity ratio	45%	39%	41%	
6	Liability liquidity ratio	122%	115%	120%	
7	Fixed obligation security ratio	196%	190%	187%	
8	Fixed interest ratio	23%	20%	28%	
9	Earnings ratio	7%	6%	6%	
10					

FIGURE U2.1 • Assessment 9

WRITING activities

The following activities give you the opportunity to practice your writing skills along with demonstrating an understanding of some of the important Excel features you have mastered in this unit. Use correct grammar, appropriate word choices, and clear sentence constructions.

Activity 1

Suppose that you are the accounting assistant in the financial department of McCormack Funds and you have been asked to prepare a yearly proposed department budget. The total amount for the department is $1,450,000. You are given the percentages for the proposed budget items, which are: Salaries, 45%; Benefits, 12%; Training, 14%; Administrative Costs, 10%; Equipment, 11%; and Supplies, 8%. Create a worksheet with this information that shows the projected yearly budget, the budget items in the department, the percentage of the budget, and the amount for each item. After the worksheet is completed, save it and name it **seu2act01**. Print and then close **seu2act01**.

Activity 2

Prepare a worksheet in Excel for Carefree Travels that includes the following information (the text *Scandinavian Tours, Country* and *Tours Booked* should be set in bold):

Scandinavian Tours

Country	Tours Booked
Norway	52
Sweden	62
Finland	29
Denmark	38

Use the information in the worksheet to create a bar chart as a separate worksheet. Save the workbook (worksheet and chart) and name it **seu2act02**. Print only the sheet containing the chart and then close **seu2act02**.

Activity 3

Prepare a worksheet for Carefree Travels that advertises a snow skiing trip. Include the following information in the announcement:

- At the beginning of the worksheet, create a company logo that includes the company name *Carefree Travels* and a clip art image related to travel.
- Include the heading *Whistler Ski Vacation Package* in the worksheet.
- Include the following below the heading:
  - Round-trip air transportation: $395
  - Hotel accommodations for seven nights: $1,550
  - Four all-day ski passes: $425
  - Compact rental car with unlimited mileage: $250
  - Total price of the ski package: (calculate the total price)
- Include the following information somewhere in the worksheet:
  - Book your vacation today at special discount prices
  - Two-for-one discount at many of the local ski resorts

Save the completed worksheet and name it **seu2act03**. Print and then close **seu2act03**.

INTERNET project

Make sure you are connected to the Internet. Using a search engine of your choosing, locate two companies on the Internet that sell new books. At the first new book company site, locate three books on Microsoft Excel. Record the title, author, and price for each book. At the second new book company site, locate the same three books and record the prices. Create an Excel worksheet that includes the following information:

- Name of each new book company
- Title and author of the three books
- Prices for each book from the two book company sites

Create a hyperlink for each book company to the URL on the Internet. Save the completed worksheet and name it **seu2intact**. Print and then close **seu2intact**.

JOB study

Create an invoice form in Excel for the customers of your lawn business from the Unit 1 Job Study. Using the drawing tools, design a logo that will go at the top left corner. Use borders and shading to separate various sections. You can use the Invoice template found within Excel as a sample. Save your template file as **LawnTemplate**. Print one copy. Be sure to copy your template file to the Microsoft template files folder found on your computer's hard drive. Print out a picture of the directory containing your new **LawnTemplate** file and the other Excel templates.

Open the file *LawnBusiness* you created in the Unit 1 Job Study and create three different chart types for the expenses section and three different chart types for the income section. You determine the options for each chart. Print each chart on a separate worksheet tab. Rename the worksheet tabs accordingly. You will incorporate these six charts into a presentation about your expansion project for the following year that you will give to a potential lender. Save your file as **LawnCharts**.

INDEX

SPECIALIST

MICROSOFT® ACCESS

Each of us interacts with a database more often than we realize. Did you use a bank machine to get some cash today? Did you search the library's catalog for a book that you need? Did you browse an online retail catalog or flip through the pages of a printed catalog? If you did any of these activities, you were accessing and/or updating a database. Any time you look for something by accessing an organized file system you are probably using a database. Microsoft Access is the database management system included with Microsoft Office.

Organizing Information

Information in a database is organized into a collection of *tables* that can be related to each other for purposes of exchanging data. Each table is broken down into a series of columns (called *fields*) and rows (called *records*). If you are

SPECIALIST

Making ACCESS Work for YOU!

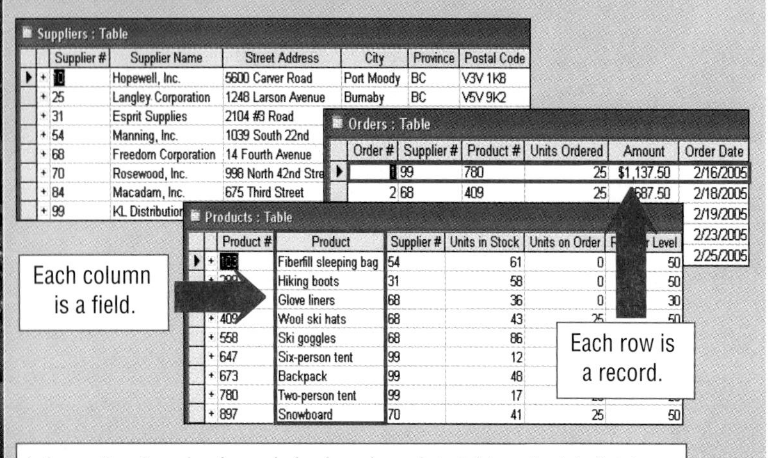
Each column is a field.
Each row is a record.

Information for a business is broken down into tables of related data. In this example, Supplier information is in a separate table from Product information and Order information.

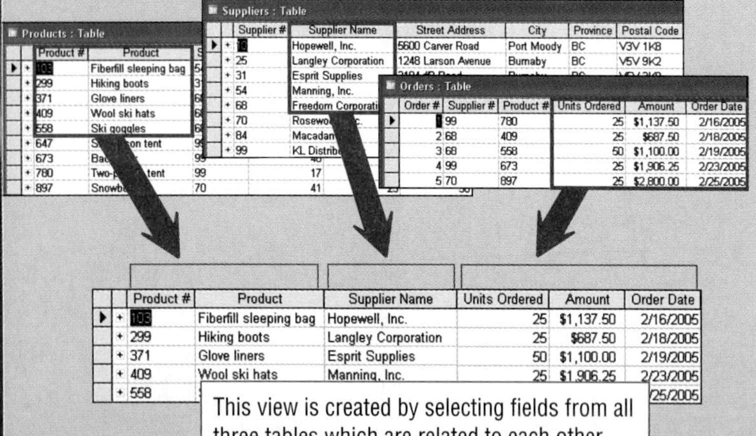
This view is created by selecting fields from all three tables which are related to each other.

familiar with a spreadsheet program such as Excel, you will be comfortable viewing a datasheet in Access. Much thought is put into the design of a database and its tables since all of the data a business collects in a database must be organized into logical groups.

Defining a *relationship* between two tables enables data from more than one table to be shared or exchanged for viewing, updating, or reporting purposes. Access allows for three kinds of relationships that can be created: one-to-one, one-to-many, and many-to-many.

Records within tables can be sorted and filtered numerous ways to allow the data to be reorganized to suit many needs. Sorting by one column and by multiple columns is accomplished with just a few mouse clicks. Temporarily hide records that don't meet your criteria by filtering the table. Edit, view and/or print as required and then redisplay the remaining records.

Forms allow those using a database to interact with the table by viewing and updating only one record at a time. Large tables clutter the screen, overwhelming the user

City	Supplier Name	Street Address	Province	Postal Code
Burnaby	Esprit Supplies	2104 #3 Road	BC	V5V 3K9
Burnaby	Langley Corporation	1248 Larson Avenue	BC	V5V 9K2
Port Moody	Hopewe			V3V 1K8
Port Moody	KL Dist			V3V 3K8
Vancouver	Freedor			V2V 5K4
Vancouver	Macada			V2V 6K3
Vancouver	Manning, Inc.	1039 South 22nd	BC	V2V 5K9
Vancouver	Rosewood, Inc.	998 North 42nd Street	BC	V2V 8K1

Sorted by City and then by Supplier name

Supplier #	Supplier Name	Street Address	City	Province	Postal Code
10	Hopewell, Inc.	5600 Carver Road	Port Moody		
25	Langley Corporation	1248 Larson Avenue	Burnaby	BC	V5V 9K2
31	Esprit Supplies		Burnaby	BC	V5V 3K9
54	Manning, Inc.		Vancouver	BC	V2V 5K9
68	Freedom Corporation	14 Fourth Avenue	Vancouver	BC	V2V 5K4
70	Rosewood, Inc.	998 North 42nd Street	Vancouver	BC	V2V 8K1
84	Macadam, Inc.	675 Third Street	Vancouver	BC	V2V 6K3
99	KL Distributions	402 Yukon Drive	Port Mood		

Original Table

Supplier Name	Street Address	City	Province	Postal Code
Freedom Corporation	14 Fourth Avenue	Vancouver	BC	V2V 5K4
Macadam, Inc.	675 Third Street	Vancouver	BC	V2V 6K3
Mann				
Rose				

Filtered to show only those suppliers in Vancouver and then sorted by Supplier Name

with data and requiring scrolling to view all of the fields. Creating a form solves this problem by presenting the table data in a more user-friendly interface. Additional explanatory text can be added to forms, providing information about using the form or following business practices.

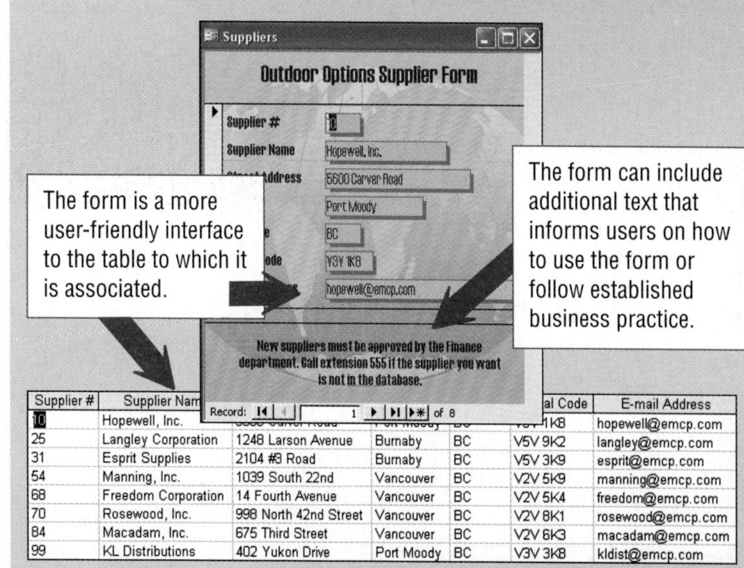

Suppliers
Outdoor Options Supplier Form
Supplier #
Supplier Name
Hopewell, Inc.
5600 Carver Road
Port Moody
BC
V3V 1K8
hopewell@emcp.com
New suppliers must be approved by the Finance department. Call extension 555 if the supplier you want is not in the database.
Record: 1 of 8
The form is a more user-friendly interface to the table to which it is associated.
The form can include additional text that informs users on how to use the form or follow established business practice.

Supplier #	Supplier Nam...				...al Code	E-mail Address
10	Hopewell, Inc.				...1K8	hopewell@emcp.com
25	Langley Corporation	1248 Larson Avenue	Burnaby	BC	V5V 9K2	langley@emcp.com
31	Esprit Supplies	2104 #3 Road	Burnaby	BC	V5V 3K9	esprit@emcp.com
54	Manning, Inc.	1039 South 22nd	Vancouver	BC	V2V 5K9	manning@emcp.com
68	Freedom Corporation	14 Fourth Avenue	Vancouver	BC	V2V 5K4	freedom@emcp.com
70	Rosewood, Inc.	998 North 42nd Street	Vancouver	BC	V2V 8K1	rosewood@emcp.com
84	Macadam, Inc.	675 Third Street	Vancouver	BC	V2V 6K3	macadam@emcp.com
99	KL Distributions	402 Yukon Drive	Port Moody	BC	V3V 3K8	kldist@emcp.com

Analyzing Information

Databases store a wealth of data that can be extracted in various ways. A *query* is one method for extracting information from tables. A basic query might simply list fields from several tables in one datasheet. This method is shown on the facing page, where individual fields from three tables are selected for viewing in one datasheet. In more complex queries, data can be selected for viewing based on meeting a single criterion or multiple criteria, and calculations can be performed on fields.

For more sophisticated analysis, tables can be grouped and then filtered on more than one field. Open a table or query and then switch to PivotTable View or PivotChart View. Access has simplified the task of creating pivot tables and pivot charts by incorporating a drag and drop technique in the view.

Interact with the pivot table or pivot chart by clicking one of the filter arrows, selecting or deselecting the items you want to view, and then click OK. The data in the view is instantly updated to reflect the new settings.

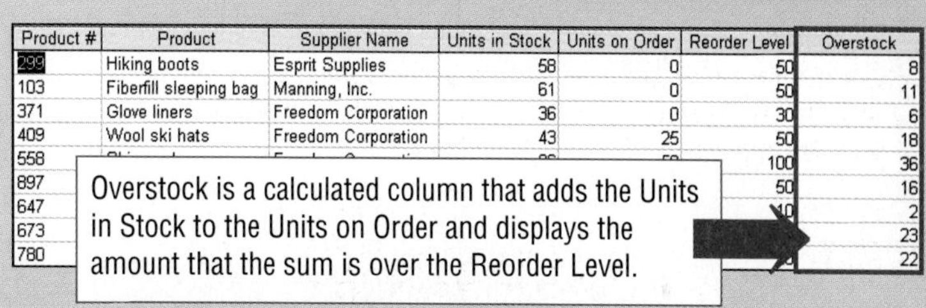

Overstock is a calculated column that adds the Units in Stock to the Units on Order and displays the amount that the sum is over the Reorder Level.

Product #	Product	Supplier Name	Units in Stock	Units on Order	Reorder Level	Overstock
299	Hiking boots	Esprit Supplies	58	0	50	8
103	Fiberfill sleeping bag	Manning, Inc.	61	0	50	11
371	Glove liners	Freedom Corporation	36	0	30	6
409	Wool ski hats	Freedom Corporation	43	25	50	18
558					100	36
897					50	16
647						2
673						23
780						22

In this query only records with a value above zero in Units on Order to the supplier named Freedom Corporation are displayed.

Product #	Product	Supplier Name	Units in Stock	Units on Order
409	Wool ski hats	Freedom Corporation	43	25
558	Ski goggles	Freedom Corporation	86	50

Product #	Product	Supplier Name	Units Ordered	Amount	Order Date
780	Two-person tent	KL Distributions	25	$1,137.50	2/16/2005
409	Wool ski hats	Freedom Corporation	25	$687.50	2/18/20...
558	Ski goggles	Freedom Corporation	50	$1,100.00	...2005
673	Backpack	KL Distributions	25	$1,9...	2/23/2005
897	Snowboard	Rosewood, Inc.	3...	...,800.00	2/25/2005

Transform data in a table for analysis in a pivot table (left) or pivot chart (right).

Order Date By Month: All

Supplier Name	Backpack Amount	Ski goggles Amount	Snowboard Amount	Two-person tent Amount	Wool ski hats Amount	Grand Total Total Amount
Freedom Corporation		$1,100.00 $1,100.00			$687.50 $687.50	$1,787.50
KL Distributions	$1,906.25 $1,906.25			$1,137.50 $1,137.50		$3,043.75
Rosewood, Inc.			$2,800.00 $2,800.00			$2,800.00
Grand Total	$1,906.25	$1,100.00	$2,800.00	$1,137.50	$687.50	$7,631.25

Presenting Information

Having critical business information stored electronically and the ability to easily extract specific data from the database is a valuable asset to a business. However, there are still times when a printed report is a necessity. Reports in Access are used to create professional-looking, high-quality output. Reports can be grouped and sorted and can include calculations. Access includes the Report Wizard, which can be used to create a report such as the one shown at left by choosing the table or query for the source data, specifying a group or sort order, and choosing from predefined styles and layouts. Once the report is generated, you can easily modify its design by moving, resizing, adding, or deleting objects, changing the layout or sort order, adding a calculation, drawing lines, and so on.

In today's global workplaces, the Web is often the environment of choice for conducting business. Putting Access information on the Web is as easy as creating an object called a *data access page*. Data in tables can be linked to a data access page for easier viewing and updating by those not familiar with a database. Access includes the Page Wizard, which is similar to the Report Wizard and can be used to generate a Web page.

A business cannot survive without a well designed database that is easy to update and maintain. Microsoft Access is a database management system that is easy to learn and use. In just a few pages, you will be exploring the world of databases and learning how to access the technology that drives business success.

Product #	Product	Supplier Name	Units in Stock	Units on Order	Reorder Level	Overstock
299	Hiking boots	Esprit Supplies	58	0	50	8
103	Fiberfill sleeping bag	Manning, Inc.	61	0	50	11
371	Glove liners	Freedom Corporation	36	0	30	6
409	Wool ski hats	Freedom Corporation	43	25	50	18
558	Ski goggles	Freedom Corporation	86	50	100	36
897	Snowboard	Rosewood, Inc.	41	25	50	16
647	Six-person tent	KL Distributions	12	0	10	2
673	Backpack	KL Distributions	48	25	50	23
780	Two-person tent	KL Distributions	17	25	20	22

Create a report to produce high-quality output.

Overstock Report by Supplier Name

Supplier Name	Product	Product #	Units in Stock	Units on Order	Reorder Level	Overstock
Esprit Supplies						
	Hiking boots	299	58	0	50	8
			Total Overstock by Supplier Name:			8
Freedom Corporation						
	Glove liners	371	36	0	30	6
	Ski goggles	558	86	50	100	36
	Wool ski hats	409	43	25	50	18
			Total Overstock by Supplier Name:			60
KL Distributions						
	Backpack	673	48	25	50	23
	Six-person tent	647	12	0	10	2
	Two-person tent	780	17	25	20	22
			Total Overstock by Supplier Name:			47

Information in Access tables can be put on the Web by creating a data access page.

Order Entry Web Page

Supplier # 68
Order #: 2
Product #: 409
Units 25
Amount: $687.50
Order Date: 2/18/2005

SPECIALIST

MICROSOFT®

ACCESS

Unit 1: Creating Database Tables, Queries, and Filters

- Maintaining Databases
- Customizing Databases
- Creating Queries, Forms, and Reports
- Enhancing Databases with Special Features

MICROSOFT ACCESS 2003

MICROSOFT OFFICE ACCESS 2003 SPECIALIST SKILLS – UNIT 1

Reference No.	Skill	Pages
AC03S-1	**Structuring Databases**	
AC03S-1-1	Create Access databases	S7-S20
AC03S-1-2	Create and modify tables	
	Create a table in design view	S8-S17
	Create a table using the Table Wizard	S67-S76
	Modify a table	S22-S27
AC03S-1-3	Define and create field types	
	Define, assign, and create field types	S8-S17
	Create Lookup field	S27-S32
AC03S-1-4	Modify field properties	
	Create input masks	S26-S32
	Change field data type	S9-S17
AC03S-1-5	Create and modify one-to-many relationships	
	Create a one-to-many relationship between tables	S41-S57
	Edit a one-to-many relationship	S57-S60
AC03S-1-6	**Enforce referential integrity**	**S49-S52**
AC03S-1-7	Create and modify queries	
	Create queries using the Simple Query Wizard	S93-S108
	Create queries with Aggregate Functions	S108-S112
	Create a Crosstab query	S113-S115
	Create a Find Duplicates query	S115-S119
	Create an Unmatched query	S119-S120
AC03S-2	**Entering Data**	
AC03S-2-1	Enter, edit and delete records	
	Enter data in a table	S17-S20
	Add and delete records	S24-S25
AC03S-2-2	Find and move among records	
	Find records with specific data and replace with other data	S77-S80
	Find duplicate records using the Find Duplicates query	S115-S119
AC03S-3	**Organizing Data**	
AC03S-3-1	Create and modify calculated fields and aggregate functions	S105-S112
AC03S-3-4	Format datasheets	S20-S23
AC03S-3-5	Sort records	
	Sort records in a table	S33-S34
	Sort fields in a query	S100-S101
AC03S-3-6	Filter records	
	Filter by selection	S120-S121
	Filter by form	S122-S124
AC03S-4	**Managing Databases**	
AC03S-4-3	Print database objects and data	
	Print a database table	S20-S23
	Print database relationships	S50-S54
AC03S-4-5	Back up a database	S81-S83
AC03S-4-6	Compact and repair databases	S81-S83

CHAPTER 1

CREATING A DATABASE TABLE

PERFORMANCE OBJECTIVES

Upon successful completion of Chapter 1, you will be able to:

- **Design a database table**
- **Determine fields and assign data types in a database table**
- **Enter data in a database table**
- **Open, save, print, and close a database table**
- **Add and delete records in a database table**
- **Modify a database table by adding, deleting, or moving fields**
- **Use the Input Mask Wizard and the Lookup Wizard**

Managing information in a company is an integral part of operating a business. Information can come in a variety of forms, such as data on customers, including names, addresses, and telephone numbers; product data; purchasing and buying data; information on services performed for customers or clients; and much more. Most companies today manage data using a database management system software program. Microsoft Office Professional includes a database management system software program called *Access*. With Access, you can organize, store, maintain, retrieve, sort, and print all types of business data.

As an example of how Access might be used to manage data in an office, suppose a bookstore decides to send a mailer to all customers who have purchased a certain type of book in the past month (such as autobiographies). The bookstore uses Access and maintains data on customers, such as names, addresses, types of books purchased, and types of books ordered. With this data in Access, the manager of the bookstore can easily select those customers who have purchased or ordered autobiographies in the past month and send a mailer announcing a visit by an author who has just completed writing an autobiography. The bookstore could also use the information to determine what types of books have been ordered by customers in the past few months and use this information to determine what inventory to purchase.

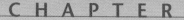

Use the information in a database to perform a wide variety of functions. This chapter contains just a few ideas. With a properly designed and maintained database management system, a company can operate smoothly with logical, organized, and useful information. The Access program displays in the Start pop-up menu preceded by a picture of a key, and a key is displayed in the Taskbar when Access is open. The key symbolizes the importance of managing and maintaining data to a company's survival and success.

Organizing Data in a Database Table

HINT
Organize data in tables to minimize or eliminate duplication.

Data is not very useful to a company if it is not organized in a logical manner. Organizing data in a manageable and logical manner allows the data to be found and used for a variety of purposes.

Determining Fields

Microsoft Access is a database management system software program that allows you to design, create, input, maintain, manipulate, sort, and print data. Access is considered a relational database in which you organize data in related tables. In this chapter, you will be creating one table as part of a database file. In a later chapter, you will create a related table within the same database file.

HINT
A database table contains fields that describe a person, customer, client, object, place, idea, or event.

The first step in creating a table is to determine the fields. A field is one piece of information about a person, a place, or an item. For example, one field could be a customer's name, another field could be a customer's address, and another a customer number. All fields for one unit, such as a customer, are considered a record. For example, in Exercise 1, a record is all the information pertaining to one employee of Premium Health Services. A collection of records becomes a database table.

When designing a database table, determine fields for information to be included on the basis of how you plan to use the data. When organizing fields, be sure to consider not only current needs for the data but also any future needs. For example, a company may need to keep track of customer names, addresses, and telephone numbers for current mailing lists. In the future, the company may want to promote a new product to customers who purchase a specific type of product. For this situation, a field that identifies product type must be included in the database. When organizing fields, consider all potential needs for the data but also try to keep the fields logical and manageable.

After deciding what data you want included in a database table, you need to determine field names. Consider the following guidelines when naming fields in a database table:

- Each field must contain a unique name.
- The name must describe the contents of the field.
- A field name can contain up to 64 characters.
- A field name can contain letters, numbers, spaces, and symbols except the period (.), comma (,), exclamation point (!), square brackets ([]), and grave accent (`).
- A field name cannot begin with a space.

In Exercise 1, you will create a database table containing information on employees of a medical corporation. The fields in this table and the names you will give to each field are shown in Figure 1.1.

FIGURE 1.1 ***Field Information and Names for Exercise 1***

Employee Information	Field Name
ID number	*Emp #*
Last name	*Last Name*
First name	*First Name*
Middle initial	*Middle Initial*
Street address	*Street Address*
City	*City*
State	*State*
ZIP Code	*ZIP Code*
Date of hire	*Hire Date*
Department code	*Dept Code*

Assigning a Data Type to Fields

Assign a data type for each field that determines the values that can be entered for the field.

Part of the process of designing a database table includes specifying or assigning a data type to each field. The data type specifies the type of data you can enter in a field. Assigning a data type to fields helps maintain and manage the data and helps identify for anyone entering information into the field what type of data is expected. The data types that are available in Access along with a description of each and the field size are shown in Table 1.1.

TABLE 1.1 ***Data Types***

Assign this data type	***To this type of field***
Text	Assign to a field where text will be entered, such as names, addresses, and numbers that do not require calculations, such as telephone numbers, dates, Social Security numbers, and ZIP Codes. A maximum number of 255 characters can be stored in a text data field; 50 characters is the default.
Memo	Assign to a field where more than 255 characters are needed. Up to 64,000 characters can be stored in a memo data field.
Number	Assign to a field where positive and/or negative numbers are to be entered for mathematical calculations, except calculations that involve money or require a high degree of accuracy. A maximum of 15 digits can be stored in a number data field.

Continued on next page

Currency	Assign to a field where you do not want calculations rounded off during a calculation. A maximum of 15 digits can be stored in a currency data field.
Date/Time	Assign to a field where a date and/or time will be entered. Eight characters is the default.
AutoNumber	Create a field that automatically enters a number when a record is added. Three types of numbers can be generated—sequential numbers that change by one, random numbers, and replication ID numbers. A maximum of nine digits can be stored in an *AutoNumber* data field.
Yes/No	Assign to a field where data is to be limited to Yes or No, True or False, or On or Off.
OLE Object	Assign to an object such as an Excel spreadsheet or Word document linked to or embedded in an Access table. Up to 1 gigabyte of characters can be stored in the field.
Hyperlink	Assign to text or a combination of text and numbers stored as text and used as a hyperlink address. A hyperlink address can contain up to three parts and each part can contain up to 2,048 characters.
Lookup Wizard	Click this option to start the Lookup Wizard, which creates a *Lookup* field. When the wizard is completed, Access sets the data type based on the values selected during the wizard steps.

When designing a database table, determine the data type that is to be assigned to a field. The fields in Exercise 1 will be assigned the data types and field sizes shown in Figure 1.2.

FIGURE 1.2 ***Data Types for Exercise 1***

Field Name	**Data Type**
Emp #	Text (Field Size = 5)
Last Name	Text (Field Size = 30)
First Name	Text (Field Size = 30)
Middle Initial	Text (Field Size = 2)
Street Address	Text (Field Size = 30)
City	Text (Field Size = 20)
State	Text (Field Size = 2)
ZIP Code	Text (Field Size = 5)
Dept Code	Text (Field Size = 2)
Hire Date	Date/Time

Data entered for some fields in Exercise 1, such as *ZIP Code,* will be numbers. These numbers, however, are not values and will not be used in calculations. This is why they are assigned the data type of Text (rather than Number or Currency).

During the process of creating the database table, field sizes are assigned. By default, a field is assigned the default number as described in Table 1.1. You can, however, specify a maximum field size. For example, a Text data type sets the field size at 50 characters by default. For a field in Exercise 1 such as the *ZIP Code,* a specific maximum number can be assigned, such as 5 (if you are only using the five-number ZIP Code). When assigning a field size, consider the data that will be entered in the field, and then shorten or lengthen the maximum number to accommodate any possible entries. For the *First Name* field or the *Last Name* field, for example, shortening the number to 30 would be appropriate, ensuring that all names would fit in the field. The two-letter state abbreviation will be used in the *State* field, so the number of characters is changed to 2.

Creating a Database Table

Once the fields, field names, and data types have been determined, you are ready to create the database table. To create a database table, you would follow these general steps:

1. Open Access. To do this, click the Start button on the Taskbar, point to *All Programs*, point to *Microsoft Office*, and then click *Microsoft Office Access 2003*. (These steps may vary.)
2. At the blank Access screen, click the New button located at the left side of the Database toolbar.
3. At the New File task pane, click the Blank database hyperlink. (The New File task pane displays at the right side of the window as shown in Figure 1.3.)
4. At the File New Database dialog box shown in Figure 1.4, change to the drive where your disk is located, type a name for the database in the *File name* text box, and then press Enter or click the Create button.
5. At the Database window shown in Figure 1.5, double-click *Create table in Design view* in the list box.
6. At the Table1 : Table window shown in Figure 1.6, type the first field name in the *Field Name* text box, and then press Tab. (This moves the insertion point to the *Data Type* text box and inserts the word *Text*.)
7. With the insertion point positioned in the *Data Type* text box and the word *Text* inserted in the box, press Tab to move the insertion point to *Description* or change the data type and then press Tab.
8. With the insertion point positioned in the *Description* text box, type a description of the field, and then press Tab.
9. Continue typing field names, assigning a data type to each field, and typing a description of all fields.
10. When all fields have been typed, click File and then Save, or click the Save button on the Table Design toolbar.
11. At the Save As dialog box shown in Figure 1.7, type a name for the table in the *Table Name* text box, and then press Enter or click OK.
12. A message displays telling you that no primary key is defined and asking if you want to create one. At this message, click No. (You will learn more about primary keys in Chapter 2.)
13. Click File and then Close to close the database table.

Create a Database Table
1. Click New button.
2. Click Blank database hyperlink.
3. Type file name.
4. Press Enter or click Create button.
5. Double-click *Create table in Design view.*
6. Type field names, specify types, and include descriptions.
7. Click Save button.
8. Type name for table.
9. Press Enter or click OK.

Provide full descriptions of fields in a database file if other users will be maintaining the database.

Save

FIGURE 1.3 *Microsoft Access Screen*

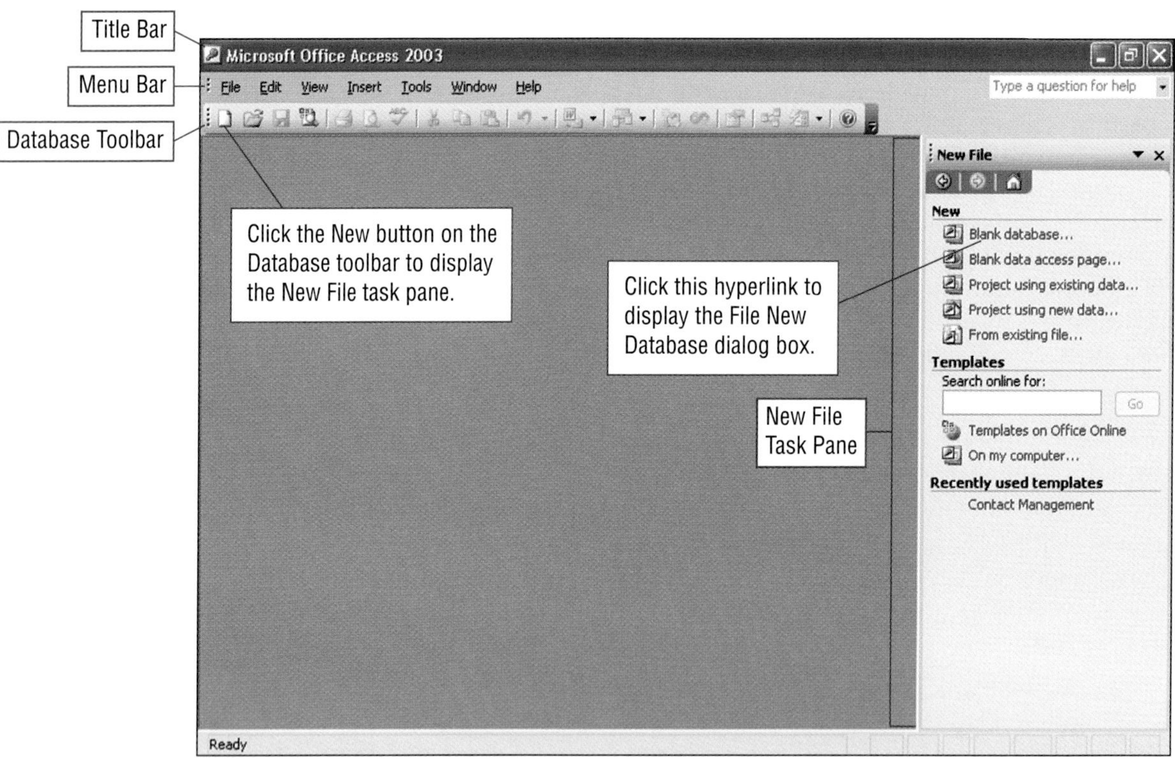

FIGURE 1.4 *File New Database Dialog Box*

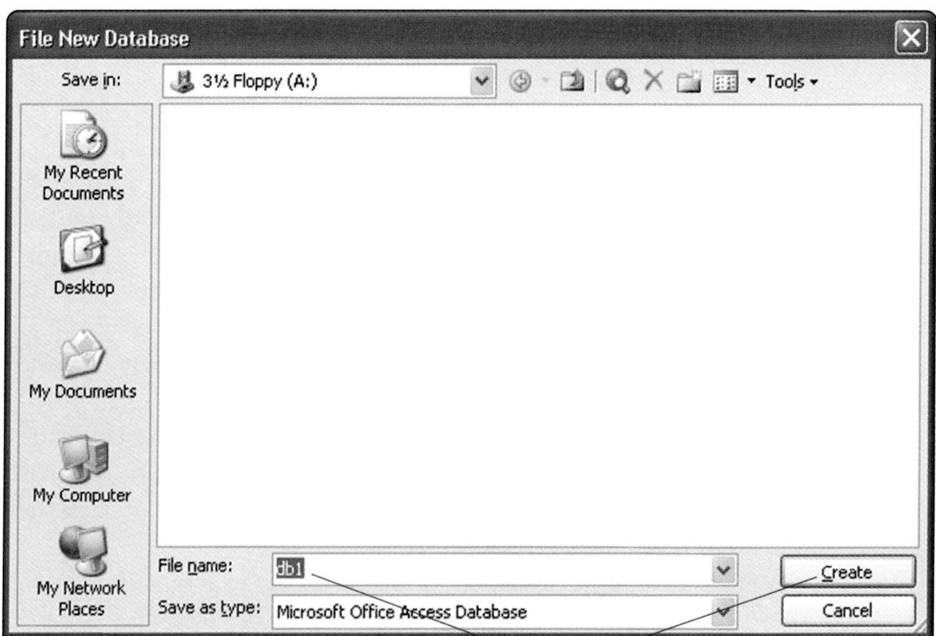

FIGURE

1.5 *Database Window*

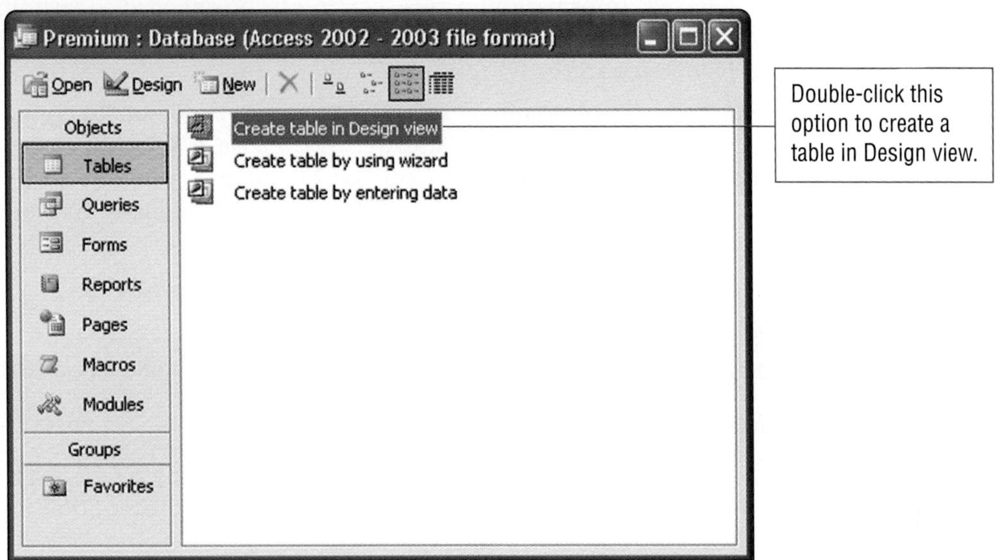

FIGURE

1.6 *Table1 : Table Window*

At this window, assign field names and data types; also provide a description.

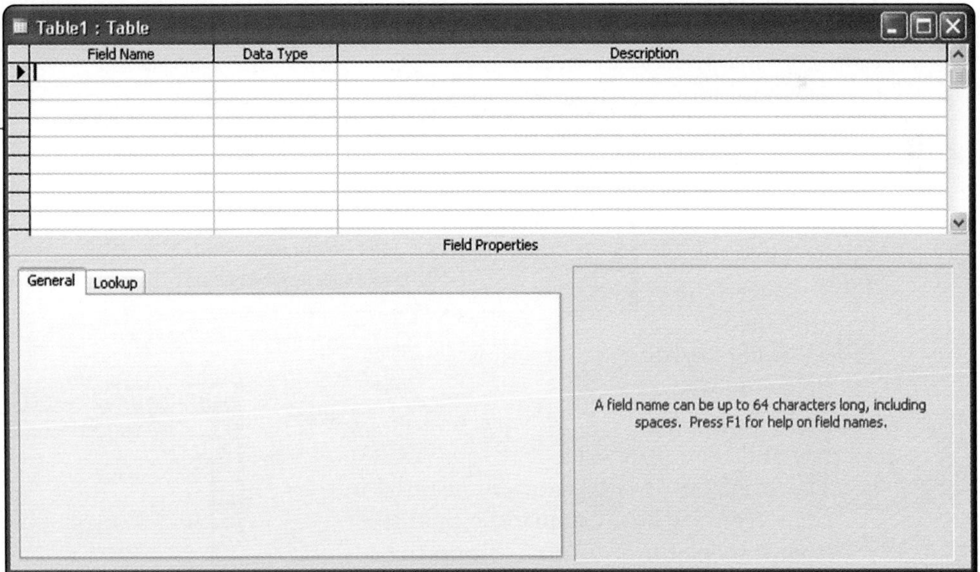

FIGURE

1.7 *Save As Dialog Box*

Type a name for the table in this text box.

Save As
Table Name:
Table1
OK
Cancel

At the Table window shown in Figure 1.6, field names are entered, data types are assigned, and descriptions are typed. When assigning a data type, Access displays information in the bottom portion of the window in a section with the General tab selected. Information in this section can be changed to customize a data type for a field. For example, you can specify that only a maximum of two characters can be entered in the *Middle Initial* field.

A database file can contain more than one table. Tables containing related data are saved in the same database. In Exercise 1, you will create a table named Employees that is part of the database file named Premium. In Exercise 2, you will create another table as part of the Premium database that includes payroll information.

exercise 1 — CREATING AN EMPLOYEE DATABASE TABLE

(Note: Insert a blank formatted disk before beginning Exercise 1.)

1. Open Access by clicking Start button on the Taskbar, pointing to *All Programs*, pointing to *Microsoft Office*, and then clicking *Microsoft Office Access 2003*.
2. At the blank Access screen, click the New button (first button from the left) on the Database toolbar.
3. At the New File task pane, click the Blank database hyperlink located in the *New* section.

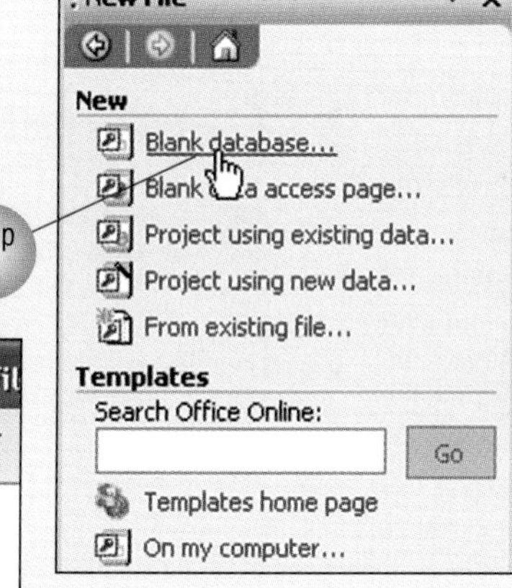

4. At the File New Database dialog box (see Figure 1.4), change to the drive where your disk is located, type **Premium** in the *File name* text box, and then press Enter or click the Create button.
5. At the Premium : Database window, double-click *Create table in Design view* in the list box.
6. At the Table1 : Table window, type the fields shown in Figure 1.8 by completing the following steps:
   a. Type **Emp #** in the *Field Name* text box and then press Tab.
   b. The word *Text* is automatically inserted in the *Data Type* text box. Change the field size from the default of 50 to 5. To do this, select *50* that displays after *Field Size* in the *Field Properties* section of the window and then type 5.

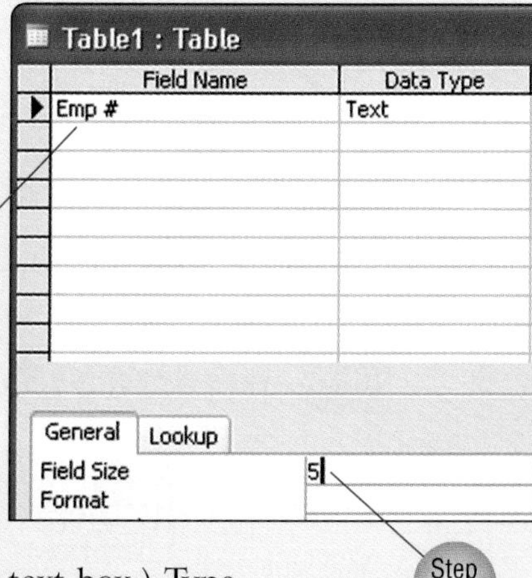

   c. Position the I-beam pointer in the *Description* text box (for the *Emp #* field), and then click the left mouse button. (You can also press F6 to switch to the top of the window, and then press Tab to move the insertion point to the *Description* text box.) Type **Employee number** in the *Description* text box and then press Tab.

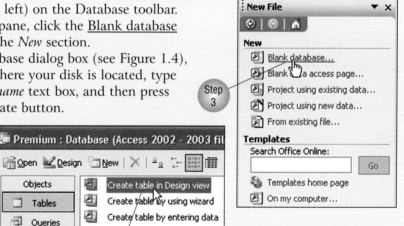

d. Type **Last Name** in the *Field Name* text box and then press Tab.
e. Change the field size to 30 and then click in the *Description* text box for the *Last Name* field (or press F6 and then press Tab). Type **Employee last name** and then press Tab.
f. Type **First Name** in the *Field Name* text box and then press Tab.
g. Change the field size to 30 and then click in the *Description* text box for the *First Name* field (or press F6 and then press Tab). Type **Employee first name** and then press Tab.
h. Continue typing the field names, data types, and descriptions as shown in Figure 1.8. Refer to Figure 1.2 for the text field sizes. To change the Data Type for the *Hire Date* field, click the down-pointing arrow after *Text* and then click *Date/Time* in the drop-down list.

7. When all of the fields are entered, save the database table by completing the following steps:
   a. Click the Save button on the Table Design toolbar.
   b. At the Save As dialog box, type **Employees** in the text box, and then press Enter or click OK.
   c. At the message telling you that no primary key is defined and asking if you want to create one, click No. (You will learn more about primary keys in Chapter 2.)
8. Close the Employees table by clicking File and then Close or clicking the Close button located in the upper right corner of the window.
9. Close the **Premium** database file by clicking File and then Close or clicking the Close button located at the right side of the Title bar.

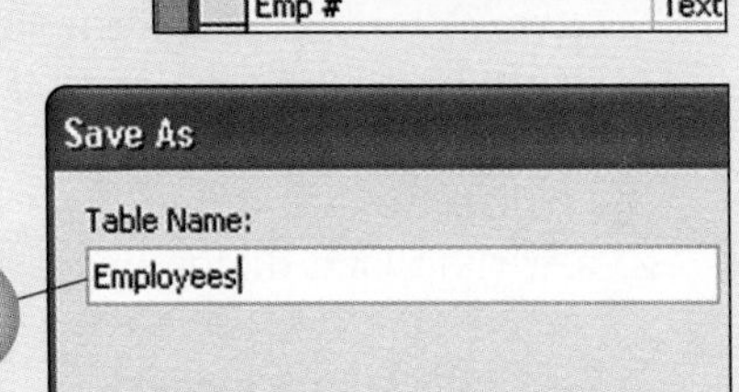

FIGURE 1.8 ***Exercise 1***

Table1 : Table

Field Name	Data Type	Description
Emp #	Text	Employee number
Last Name	Text	Employee last name
First Name	Text	Employee first name
Middle Initial	Text	Employee middle initial
Street Address	Text	Employee street address
City	Text	Employee city
State	Text	Employee state
Zip Code	Text	Employee Zip code
Dept Code	Text	Department code
Hire Date	Date/Time	Date of hire

HINT
The active database is saved automatically on a periodic basis and also when the database is closed.

HINT
If you are working with a database file saved on a floppy disk, never remove the disk while the database file is open. If you do, Access will have problems when trying to automatically save the database.

In Exercise 1, you saved the table containing the fields with the name Employees and then closed the Premium database file. Access automatically saves an open (or active) database on a periodic basis and also when the database is closed. If you are working with a database that is saved on a disk, never remove the disk while the database is open because Access saves the database periodically. If the disk is not in the drive when Access tries to save it, problems will be encountered and you run the risk of damaging the database. Exit (close) Access by clicking the Close button located in the upper right corner of the Access Title bar (contains an *X*) or by clicking File and then Exit.

The Employees table contains a *Dept Code* field. This field will contain a two-letter code identifying the department within the company. In Exercise 2, you will create a table named Departments containing only two fields—the department code and the department name. Establishing a department code decreases the amount of data entered in the Employees table. For example, in an employee record, you type a two-letter code identifying the employee department rather than typing the entire department name. Imagine the time this saves when entering hundreds of employee records. This is an example of the power of a relational database.

(Note: If a Security warning message box appears when opening a database stating that unsafe expressions are not blocked, click Yes to confirm that you want to open the file. This message may or may not appear depending on the security level setting on the computer you are using. If the message appears, expect that it will reappear each time you open a database file.)

exercise 2

CREATING A DEPARTMENT TABLE

1. At the blank Access screen, click the Open button on the Database toolbar. (The Database toolbar displays directly below the Menu bar.)
2. At the Open dialog box, make sure the drive is active where your disk is located and then double-click ***Premium*** in the list box.

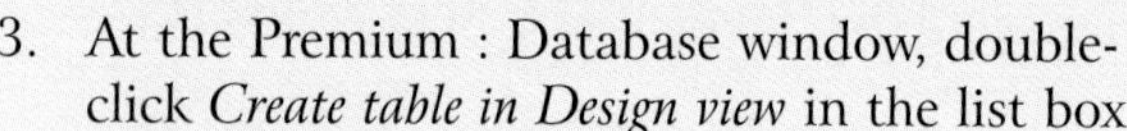

3. At the Premium : Database window, double-click *Create table in Design view* in the list box.

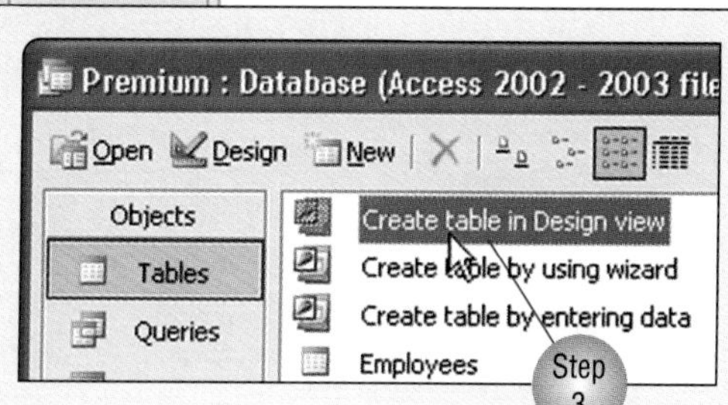

4. At the Table1 : Table window, type the fields shown in Figure 1.9 by completing the following steps:
   a. Type **Dept Code** in the *Field Name* text box and then press Tab.
   b. Change the field size to 2, and then click in the *Description* text box for the *Dept Code* field.
   c. Type **Department code** in the *Description* text box and then press the Tab key.
   d. Type **Department** in the *Field Name* text box and then press Tab.
   e. Change the field size to 30, and then click in the *Description* text box for the *Department* field.
   f. Type **Department name** in the *Description* text box.
5. When all of the fields are entered, save the database table by completing the following steps:
   a. Click the Save button on the Table Design toolbar.
   b. At the Save As dialog box, type **Departments** in the text box, and then press Enter or click OK.

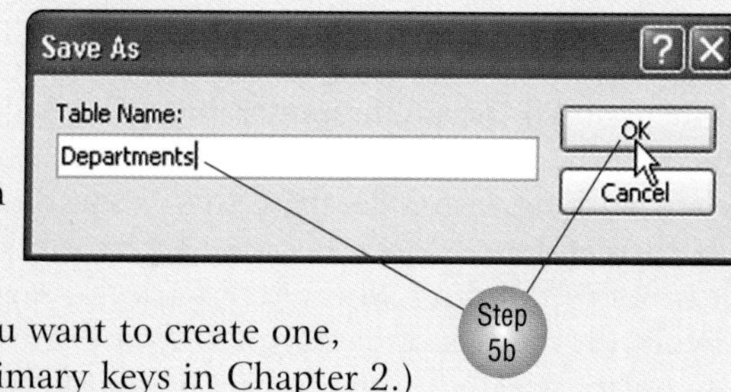

   c. At the message telling you that no primary key is defined and asking if you want to create one, click No. (You will learn more about primary keys in Chapter 2.)
6. Close the Departments table by clicking File and then Close or clicking the Close button located in the upper right corner of the window.
7. Close the **Premium** database file by clicking File and then Close or clicking the Close button located at the right side of the Title bar.

FIGURE 1.9 ***Exercise 2***

Table1 : Table

Field Name	Data Type	Description
Dept Code	Text	Department code
Department	Text	Department name

Entering Data in a Table

After a database table has been designed with the necessary fields and has been created in Access, the next step is to input the data. One method for entering data into a database table is to change to the Datasheet view. A table datasheet displays the contents of a table in rows and columns in the same manner as a Word table or Excel worksheet. Each row in a datasheet represents one record. In the Employees table of the Premium database, one record will contain the information for one employee.

Opening a Database File

To open a database file, click the Open button on the Database toolbar or click File and then Open. At the Open dialog box, double-click the desired database file name in the Open dialog box list box.

Open

Opening a Table

Open a database file and a database window displays similar to the one shown in Figure 1.10. Open a specific table in the database file by double-clicking the table name in the list box.

HINT
Only one database file can be open at a time.

FIGURE 1.10 ***Premium : Database Window***

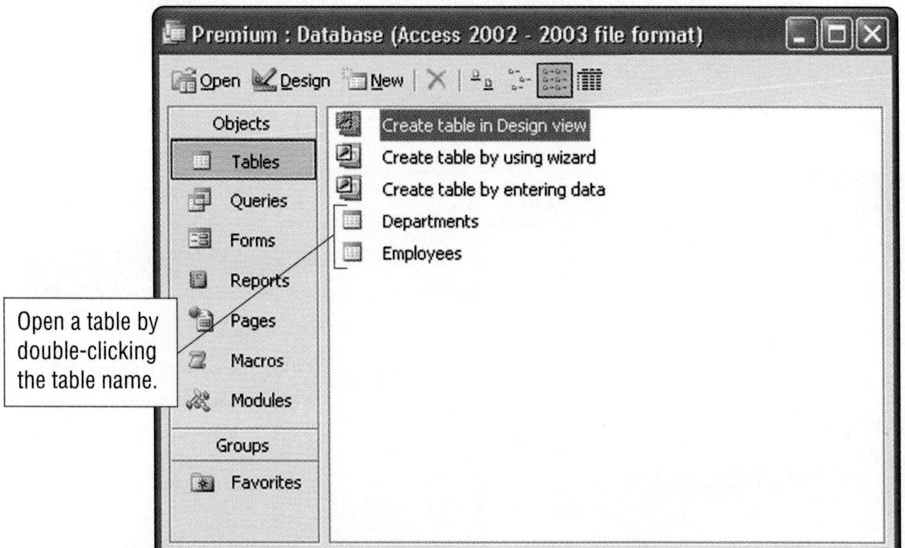

Entering Data in a Database Table

Open a database table and the table displays in the Datasheet view. This is the view needed for entering data in the table. Type data for each field in the table, pressing Tab to move the insertion point from field to field. For example, the Employees database table in the Premium database file will display as shown in Figure 1.11. (Data has been entered in this database table.)

FIGURE 1.11 ***Employees Table in Premium Database***

Microsoft Office Access 2003

File Edit View Insert Format Records Tools Window Help — Type a question for help

Employees : Table

	Emp #	Last Name	First Name	Middle Initial	Street Address	City	State	Zip Cc
✎	21043	Brown	Leland	C.	112 Kansas Ave	Missoula	MT	84311
	19034	Guenther	Julia	A.	215 Bridge Wes	Lolo	MT	86308
	27845	Oaklee	Thomas	E.	2310 Keating Ri	Missola	MT	84325
	08921	Avery	Michael	W.	23155 Neadham	Florence	MT	85901
	30091	Latora	Gina	M.	13221 138th Str	Missoula	MT	84302
*								

Enter Data in a Table
1. Click Open button.
2. Double-click database file name.
3. Double-click database table name.
4. Make sure table displays in Datasheet view.
5. Type data in fields.
6. Click Save button.

When you type data for the first field in the record, another row of cells is automatically inserted below the first row. Type the data for the first record, pressing Tab to move from field to field. The description you typed for each field when creating the database table displays at the left side of the Access Status bar. This description reminds you what data is expected in the field.

If you assigned the Yes/No data type to a field, a square displays in the field. This square can be left empty or a check mark can be inserted. If the field is asking a yes/no question, an empty box signifies "No" and a box with a check mark signifies "Yes." If the field is asking for a true/false answer, an empty box signifies "False" and a box with a check mark signifies "True." This field can also have an on/off response. An empty box signifies "Off" and a box with a check mark signifies "On." To insert a check mark in the box, tab to the field, and then press the spacebar.

When all records have been entered in the table, save the table again by clicking the Save button on the Table Datasheet toolbar. (The Table Datasheet toolbar displays directly below the Menu bar.)

exercise 3

ENTERING DATA IN THE EMPLOYEES AND THE DEPARTMENTS TABLES

1. At the blank Access screen, click the Open button on the Database toolbar.
2. At the Open dialog box, make sure the drive is active where your disk is located, and then double-click ***Premium*** in the list box.
3. At the Premium : Database window, double-click *Employees* in the list box.

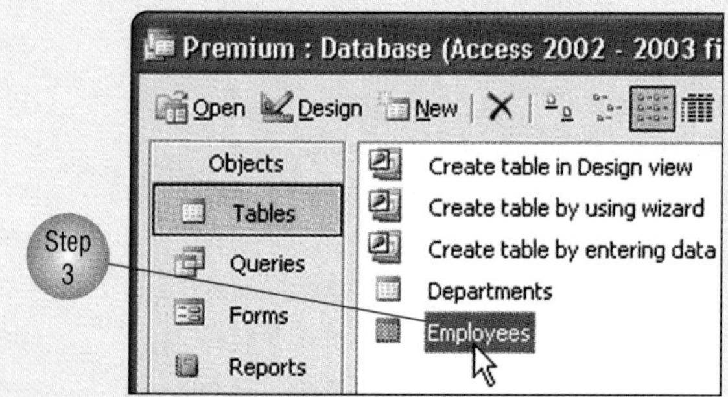

4. At the Employees : Table window, type the following data for five records in the specified fields. (Press Tab to move the insertion point to the next field or press Shift + Tab to move the insertion point to the previous field.) When typing data, not all of the data may be visible. You will adjust column widths in a later exercise.

Emp # = 21043
Last Name = Brown
First Name = Leland
Middle Initial = C.
Street Address = 112 Kansas Avenue
City = Missoula
State = MT
ZIP Code = 84311
Dept Code = PA
Hire Date = 11/5/1999

Emp # = 19034
Last Name = Guenther
First Name = Julia
Middle Initial = A.
Street Address = 215 Bridge West
City = Lolo
State = MT
ZIP Code = 86308
Dept Code = MS
Hire Date = 2/15/1994

Emp # = 27845
Last Name = Oaklee
First Name = Thomas
Middle Initial = E.
Street Address = 2310 Keating Road
City = Missoula
State = MT
ZIP Code = 84325
Dept Code = HR
Hire Date = 6/8/2000

Emp # = 08921
Last Name = Avery
First Name = Michael
Middle Initial = W.
Street Address = 23155 Neadham Avenue
City = Florence
State = MT
ZIP Code = 85901
Dept Code = PA
Hire Date = 11/5/1999

Emp # = 30091
Last Name = Latora

First Name	=	Gina
Middle Initial	=	M.
Street Address	=	13221 138th Street
City	=	Missoula
State	=	MT
ZIP Code	=	84302
Dept Code	=	HR
Hire Date	=	9/16/2004

5. After typing the data, save the database table by clicking the Save button on the Table Datasheet toolbar.
6. Close the Employees table by clicking File and then Close or by clicking the Close button in the upper right corner of the window.
7. At the Premium : Database window, double-click *Departments* in the list box.
8. At the Departments : Table window, type the following data for four departments in the specified fields (press Tab to move the insertion point to the next field or press Shift + Tab to move the insertion point to the previous field):

Dept Code	=	IS
Department Name	=	Information Services
Dept Code	=	HR
Department Name	=	Human Resources
Dept Code	=	MS
Department Name	=	Medical Services
Dept Code	=	PA
Department Name	=	Patient Accounts

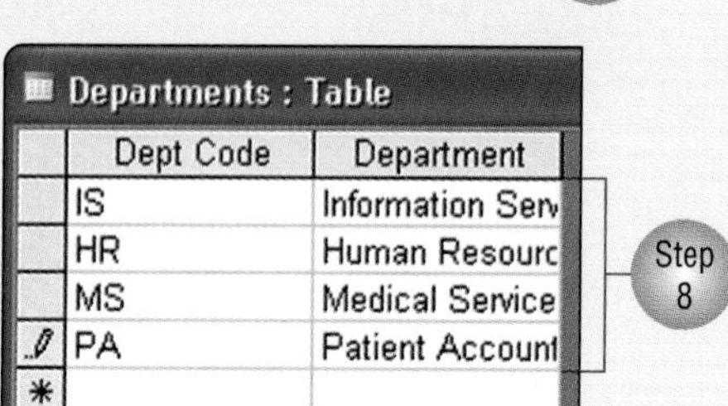

9. After typing the data, save the database table by clicking the Save button on the Table Datasheet toolbar.
10. Close the Departments table by clicking File and then Close or by clicking the Close button in the upper right corner of the window.
11. Close the **Premium** database file by clicking File and then Close or by clicking the Close button at the right side of the Title bar.

Printing a Database Table

Print

QUICK STEPS

Print a Table

1. Open database file.
2. Open database table.
3. Click Print button.

Various methods are available for printing data in a database table. One method for printing is to open the database table and then click the Print button on the Table Datasheet toolbar. This sends the information directly to the printer without any formatting changes. In some fields created in the Employees database table, this means that you would not be able to see all printed text in a field if all of the text did not fit in the field. For example, when typing the data in Exercise 3, did you notice that the Street Address data was longer than the field column could accommodate? You can change the database table layout to ensure that all data is visible. You will first print the Employees and Departments tables with the default settings, learn about changing the layout, and then print the tables again.

exercise 4 PRINTING THE EMPLOYEES AND DEPARTMENTS TABLES WITH THE DEFAULT SETTINGS

1. At the blank Access screen, open the **Premium** database file.
2. Open the Employees table.
3. Click the Print button on the Table Datasheet toolbar.
4. Close the Employees table.
5. Open the Departments table.
6. Click the Print button on the Table Datasheet toolbar.
7. Close the Departments table.
8. Close the **Premium** database file.

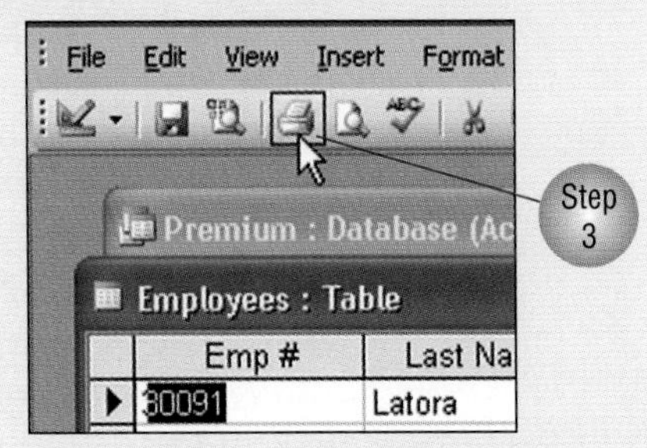

Look at the printing of the Employees table and notice how the order of records displays differently in the printing (and in the table) than the order in which the records were typed. Access automatically sorted the records by the ZIP Code in ascending order. Access automatically sorted the records in the Departments table alphabetically by department name. You will learn more about sorting later in this chapter.

Changing Page Setup

The Employees table printed on two pages in the Portrait orientation with default margins. The page orientation and page margins can be changed with options at the Page Setup dialog box with either the Margins or the Page tab selected. To display the Page Setup dialog box shown in Figure 1.12, you would open the Employees or Departments database table, click File, and then click Page Setup.

Display Page Setup Dialog Box
1. Open database file.
2. Open database table.
3. Click File, Page Setup.

FIGURE 1.12 ***Page Setup Dialog Box with Margins Tab Selected***

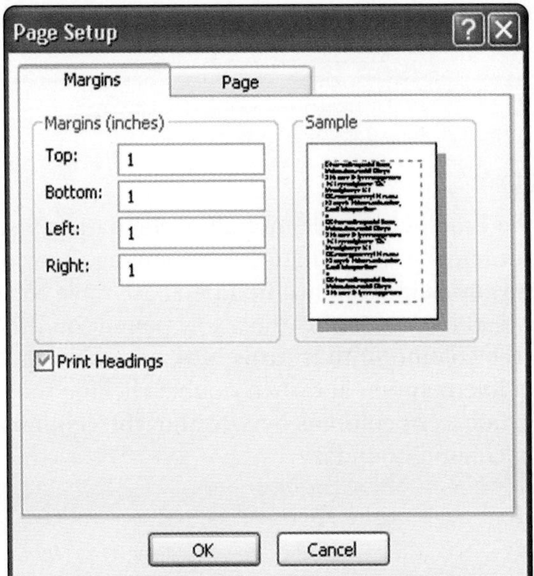

At the Page Setup dialog box with the Margins tab selected, notice that the default margins are 1 inch. Change these defaults by typing a different number in the desired margin text box. By default, the table name prints at the top center of the page. For example, when you printed the Employees table, *Employees* printed at the top of the page along with the current date (printed at the right side of the page). *Page 1* also printed at the bottom of the page. If you do not want the name of the table and the date as well as the page number printed, remove the check mark from the *Print Headings* option at the Page Setup dialog box with the Margins tab selected.

HINT

A table can be printed in landscape orientation.

Change the table orientation at the Page Setup dialog box with the Page tab selected as shown in Figure 1.13. To change to landscape orientation, click *Landscape*. You can also change the paper size with options in the *Paper* section of the dialog box and specify the printer with options in the *Printer for (table name)* section of the dialog box.

FIGURE 1.13 **Page Setup Dialog Box with Page Tab Selected**

HINT

Automatically adjust column widths in an Access database table in the same manner as adjusting column widths in an Excel worksheet.

Changing Field Width

In the printing of the Employees table, not all of the data is visible in the *Street Address* field. You can remedy this situation by changing the width of the fields. Automatically adjust one field (column) in a database table to accommodate the longest entry in the field by positioning the arrow pointer on the column boundary at the right side of the column until it turns into a double-headed arrow pointing left and right with a line between and then double-clicking the left mouse button. Automatically adjust adjacent columns by selecting the columns first and then double-clicking on a column boundary.

QUICK STEPS

Changing Field Width

1. Open database table in Datasheet view.
2. Drag column boundary to desired position.

exercise 5

CHANGING PAGE SETUP AND THEN PRINTING THE EMPLOYEES TABLE

1. Open the **Premium** database file and then open the Employees database table.
2. Change the page margins and orientation by completing the following steps:
   a. Click File and then Page Setup.
   b. At the Page Setup dialog box, click the Page tab.
   c. At the Page Setup dialog box with the Page tab selected, click *Landscape* in the *Orientation* section.

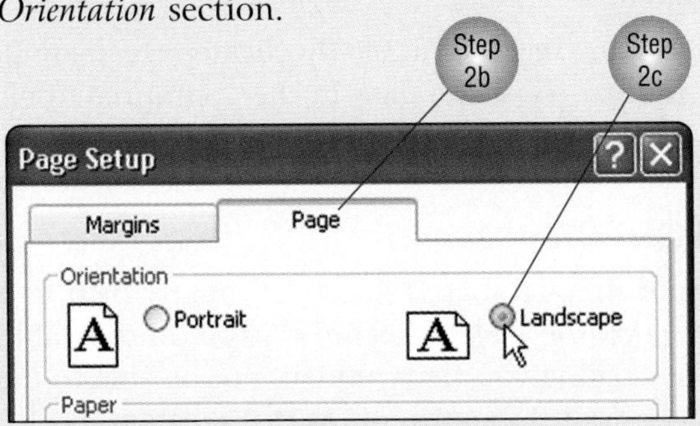

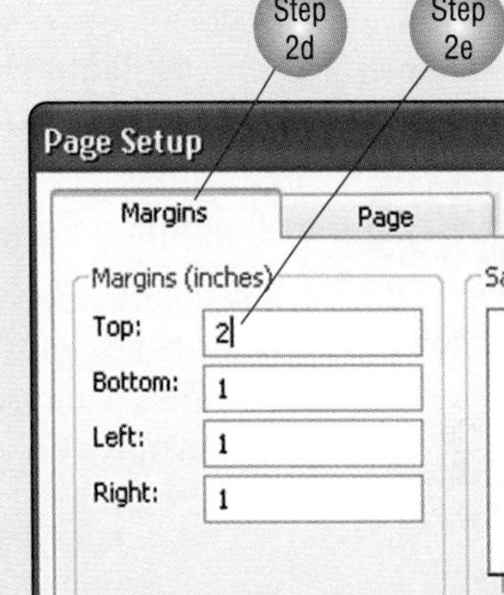

   d. Click the Margins tab.
   e. At the Page Setup dialog box with the Margins tab selected, select *1* in the *Top* text box, and then type 2.
   f. Click OK to close the dialog box.
3. Automatically adjust all columns in the table to accommodate the longest entry by completing the following steps:
   a. Position the arrow pointer on the *Emp #* field name (the arrow pointer turns into a down-pointing black arrow).
   b. Hold down the left mouse button, drag the arrow pointer to the *Hire Date* field name, and then release the mouse button. (This selects all data in the table.)
   c. Position the arrow pointer on one of the column boundaries until it turns into a double-headed arrow pointing left and right with a line between, and then double-click the left mouse button. (If a column boundary is not visible, click the left scroll arrow at the left side of the horizontal scroll bar until a column boundary is visible.)

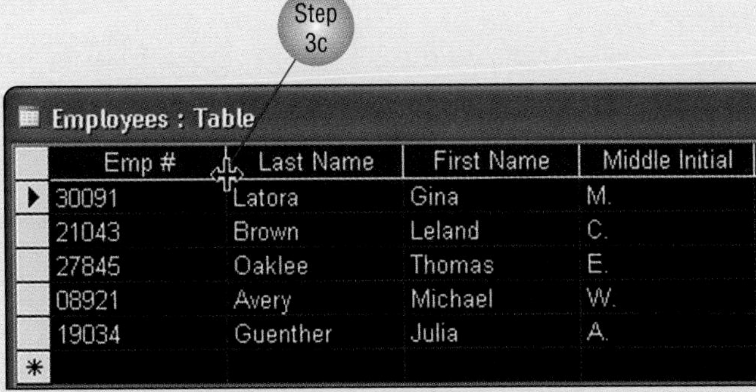

   d. Deselect the data by clicking in any field in the table.
4. Save the database table again by clicking the Save button on the Table Datasheet toolbar.
5. Send the table to the printer by clicking the Print button on the Table Datasheet toolbar.
6. Close the Employees database table and then close the **Premium** database file.

New Record

Delete Record

Maintaining a Database Table

Once a database table is created, more than likely it will require maintenance. For example, newly hired employees will need to be added to the Employees table. A system may be established for deleting an employee record when an employee leaves the company. The type of maintenance required on a database table is related to the type of data stored in the table.

Add a Record to a Table
1. Open database table in Datasheet view.
2. Click New Record button.

Adding a Record to a Table

Add a new record to an existing database table by clicking the New Record button on the Table Datasheet toolbar. Type the data in the appropriate fields and then save the table again.

Delete a Record from a Table
1. Open database table in Datasheet view.
2. Click Delete Record button.

Deleting a Record in a Table

To delete an existing record in a database table, click in any field in the row you want to delete, and then click the Delete Record button on the Table Datasheet toolbar. A message displays telling you that you will not be able to undo the delete operation and asking if you want to continue. At this message, click Yes.

exercise 6

ADDING AND DELETING RECORDS IN THE EMPLOYEES TABLE

1. Open the **Premium** database file and then open the Employees database table.
2. Add two new records to the table by completing the following steps:
   a. Click the New Record button on the Table Datasheet toolbar.
   b. Type the following data in the specified fields:

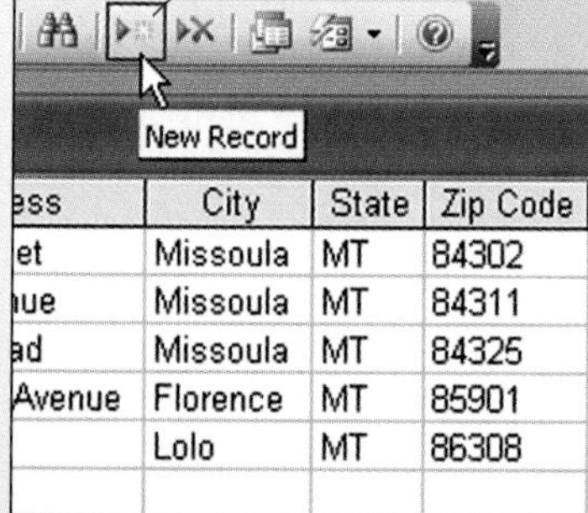

Emp #	=	30020
Last Name	=	Pang
First Name	=	Brian
Middle Initial	=	R.
Street Address	=	15512 Country Drive
City	=	Lolo
State	=	MT
ZIP Code	=	86308
Dept Code	=	IS
Hire Date	=	8/15/2005

   c. Click the New Record button on the Table Datasheet toolbar (or, just press the Tab key).
   d. Type the following data in the specified fields:

Emp #	=	30023
Last Name	=	Zajac
First Name	=	Elizabeth
Middle Initial	=	A.
Street Address	=	423 Corrin Avenue
City	=	Missoula

State	=	MT
ZIP Code	=	84325
Dept Code	=	HR
Hire Date	=	8/15/2005

3. Delete a record in the table by completing the following steps:
   a. Click anywhere in the last name *Guenther*.
   b. Click the Delete Record button on the Table Datasheet toolbar.
   c. At the message telling you that you will not be able to undo the delete operation and asking if you want to continue, click Yes.
4. Click the Save button on the Table Datasheet toolbar to save the Employees table.
5. Print the Employees database table in landscape orientation. (You will need to change to the *Landscape* orientation at the Page Setup dialog box with the Page tab selected.)
6. Close the Employees table and then close the **Premium** database file.

Modifying a Table

Maintaining a database table involves adding and/or deleting records as needed. It can also involve adding, moving, changing, or deleting fields in the database table. These types of changes modify the structure of the database table and are done in the Design view. To display a database table in the Design view, open the database table, and then click the down-pointing arrow at the right side of the View button (first button from the left). When you click the down-pointing arrow, a drop-down list displays with two viewing choices—Design View and Datasheet View. Click Design View to change the display of the database table. In the Design view, *Field Name*, *Data Type*, and *Description* display at the top of the window and *Field Properties* displays toward the bottom of the window. In the Design view, you can add fields, remove fields, and change the order of fields.

View

In addition to clicking the down-pointing arrow at the right side of the View button, you can also just click the button. If the current view is the Datasheet view, clicking the button will change to the Design view. If the Design view is the current view, clicking the button will change to the Datasheet view.

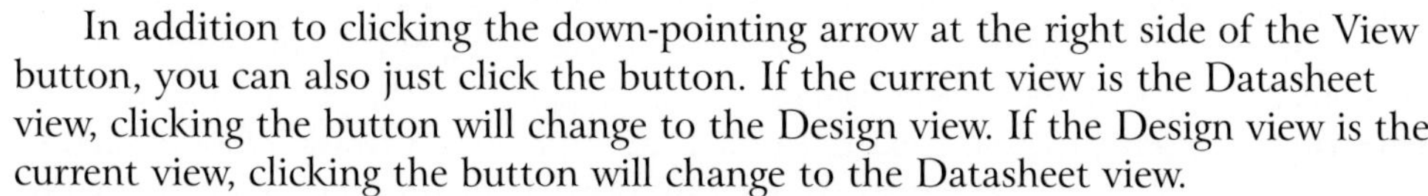

Adding a Field

Situations change within a company, and a database table must be flexible to accommodate changes that occur with new situations. Adding a field is a change that may need to be made to an existing database table. For example, more information may be required to manage the data or an additional field may be needed for accounting purposes. Whatever the reason, being able to add a new field to an existing database table is a necessity.

Add a Field to a Table
1. Open database table in Design view.
2. Click in row that will follow the new field.
3. Click Insert Rows button.

Add a row for a new field to an existing database table with a button on the Table Design toolbar, an option from the Insert drop-down menu, or a shortcut menu. To add a row for a new field, position the insertion point on any text in the row that will be immediately *below* the new field, and then click the Insert Rows button on the Table Design toolbar; click Insert and then Rows; or position the insertion point on any text in the row that will be immediately *below* the new field, click the *right* mouse button, and then click the left mouse button on Insert Rows. If you insert a row for a new field and then change your mind, immediately click the Undo button on the Table Design toolbar.

Insert Rows

Undo

Delete a Field from a Table

1. Open database table in Design view.
2. Click in row to be deleted.
3. Click Delete Rows button.

Delete Rows

Deleting a Field

Delete a field in a database table and all data entered in that field is also deleted. When a field is deleted it cannot be undone with the Undo button. Delete a field only if you are sure you really want it and the data associated with it completely removed from the database table.

To delete a field, open the database table, and then change to the Design view. Position the insertion point in any text in the row containing the field you want deleted, and then click the Delete Rows button on the Table Design toolbar, or click Edit and then Delete Rows. At the message asking if you want to permanently delete the field and all of the data in the field, click Yes.

Use Input Mask

1. Open database table in Design view.
2. Type text in *Field Name* column.
3. Press Tab key.
4. Click Save button.
5. Click in Input Mask text box.
6. Click button containing three black dots.
7. At first Input Mask Wizard dialog box, click desired option.
8. Press Next.
9. At second Input Mask Wizard dialog box, make any desired changes.
10. Click Next.
11. At third Input Mask Wizard dialog box, make any desired changes.
12. Click Next.
13. Click Finish.

Using the Input Mask Wizard

For some fields, you may want to control the data entered in the field. For example, in a *ZIP Code* field, you may want the nine-digit ZIP Code entered (rather than the five-digit ZIP Code); or you may want the three-digit area code included in a telephone number. Use the *Input Mask* field property to set a pattern for how data is entered in a field. An input mask ensures that data in records conforms to a standard format. Access includes an Input Mask Wizard that guides you through creating an input mask.

Use the Input Mask Wizard when assigning a data type to a field. After specifying the *Field Size* in the *Field Properties* section of the Table window, click the *Input Mask* text box. Run the Input Mask Wizard by clicking the button containing the three black dots that appears to the right of the *Input Mask* text box. This displays the first Input Mask Wizard dialog box as shown in Figure 1.14. In the *Input Mask* list box, choose which input mask you want your data to look like, and then click the Next button. At the second Input Mask Wizard dialog box as shown in Figure 1.15, specify the appearance of the input mask and the desired placeholder character, and then click the Next button. At the third Input Mask Wizard dialog, specify whether you want the data stored with or without the symbol in the mask, and then click the Next button. At the fourth dialog box, click the Finish button.

FIGURE 1.14 ***First Input Mask Wizard Dialog Box***

Input Mask Wizard

Which input mask matches how you want data to look?

To see how a selected mask works, use the Try It box.

To change the Input Mask list, click the Edit List button.

Input Mask:	Data Look:
Phone Number	(206) 555-1212
Social Security Number	531-86-7180
Zip Code	98052-6399
Extension	63215
Password	*******

Try It:

Edit List | Cancel | < Back | Next > | Finish

Choose the desired input mask from this list box.

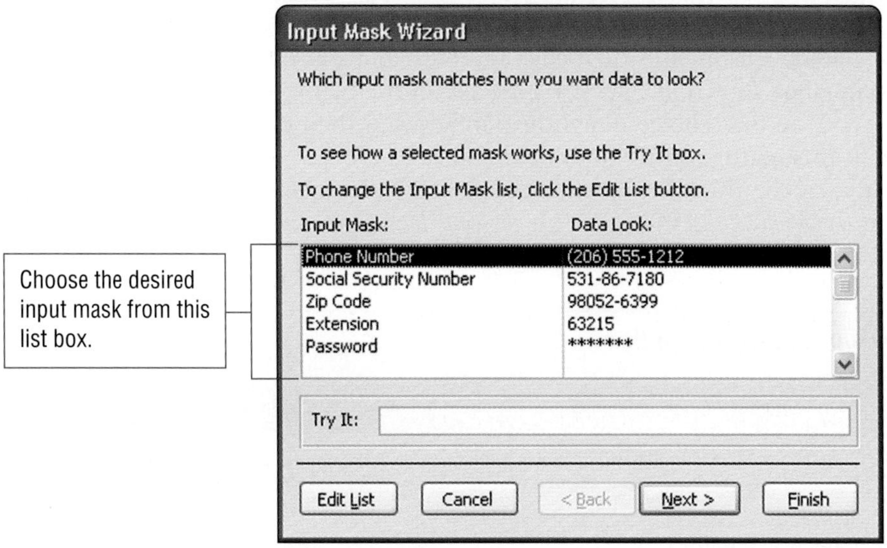

FIGURE 1.15 ***Second Input Mask Wizard Dialog Box***

Input Mask Wizard

Do you want to change the input mask?

Input Mask Name: Phone Number

Input Mask: !(999) 000-0000

What placeholder character do you want the field to display?

Placeholders are replaced as you enter data into the field.

Placeholder character: _

Try It:

Cancel | < Back | Next > | Finish

Use this option to specify the placeholder character.

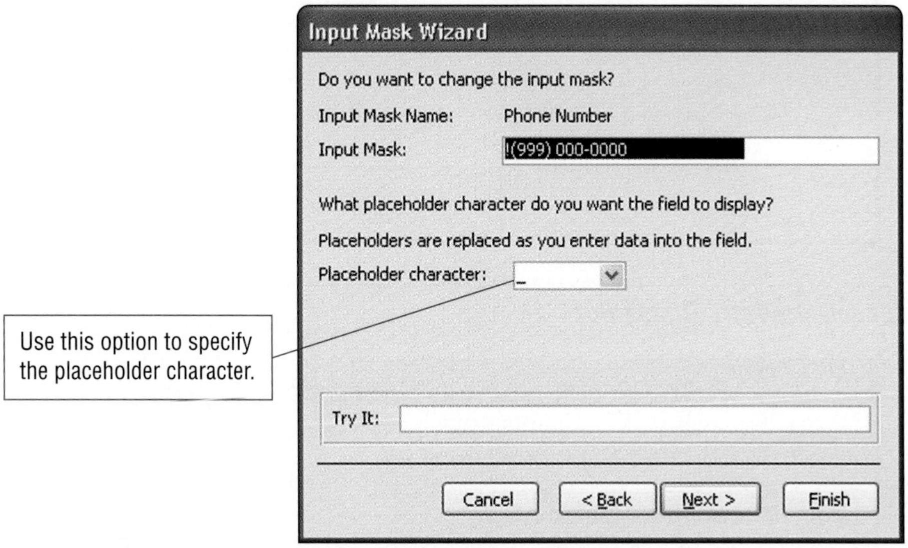

Using the Lookup Wizard

Like the Input Mask Wizard, you can use the Lookup Wizard to control the data entered in a field. Use the Lookup Wizard to confine the data entered into a field to a specific list of items. For example, in Exercise 7 you will use the Lookup Wizard to restrict the new *Employee Category* field to one of three choices—*Salaried*, *Hourly*, and *Temporary*. When the user clicks in the field in the datasheet, a down-pointing arrow displays. The user clicks this down-pointing arrow to display a drop-down list of available entries and then clicks the desired item.

QUICK STEPS

Use Lookup Wizard

1. Open table in Design view.
2. Type text in *Field Name* column.
3. Press Tab key.
4. Click down-pointing arrow.
5. Click *Lookup Wizard.*
6. At first Lookup Wizard dialog box, make desired changes.
7. Click Next.
8. At second Lookup Wizard dialog box, click in blank text box.
9. Type desired text.
10. Press Tab key.
11. Continue typing text and pressing Tab until all desired text is entered.
12. Click Next.
13. Click Finish.

Use the Lookup Wizard when assigning a data type to a field. Click in the *Data Type* text box and then click the down-pointing arrow that displays at the right side of the box. At the drop-down menu that displays, click *Lookup Wizard*. This displays the first Lookup Wizard dialog box as shown in Figure 1.16. At this dialog box, indicate that you want to enter the field choices by clicking the *I will type in the values that I want.* option, and then click the Next button. At the second Lookup Wizard dialog box shown in Figure 1.17, click in the blank text box below *Col1* and then type the first choice. Press the Tab key and then type the second choice. Continue in this manner until all desired choices are entered and then click the Next button. At the third Lookup Wizard dialog box, make sure the proper name displays in the *What label would you like for your lookup column?* text box, and then click the Finish button.

FIGURE 1.16 **First Lookup Wizard Dialog Box**

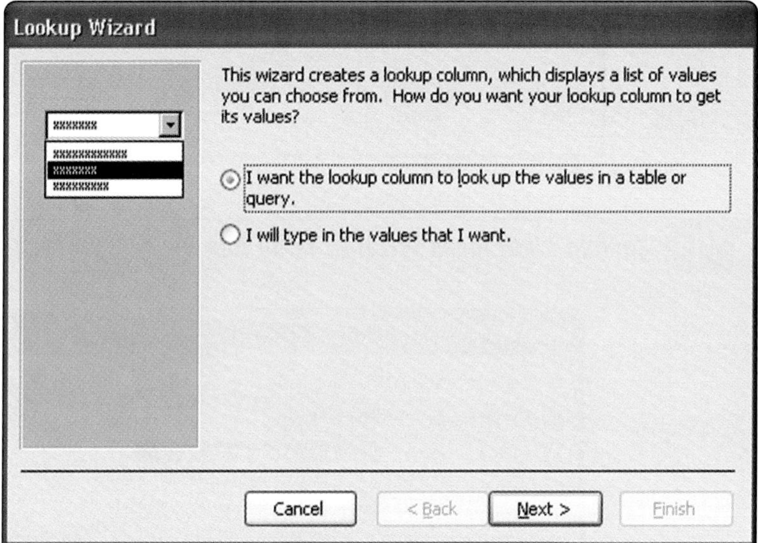

FIGURE 1.17 **Second Lookup Wizard Dialog Box**

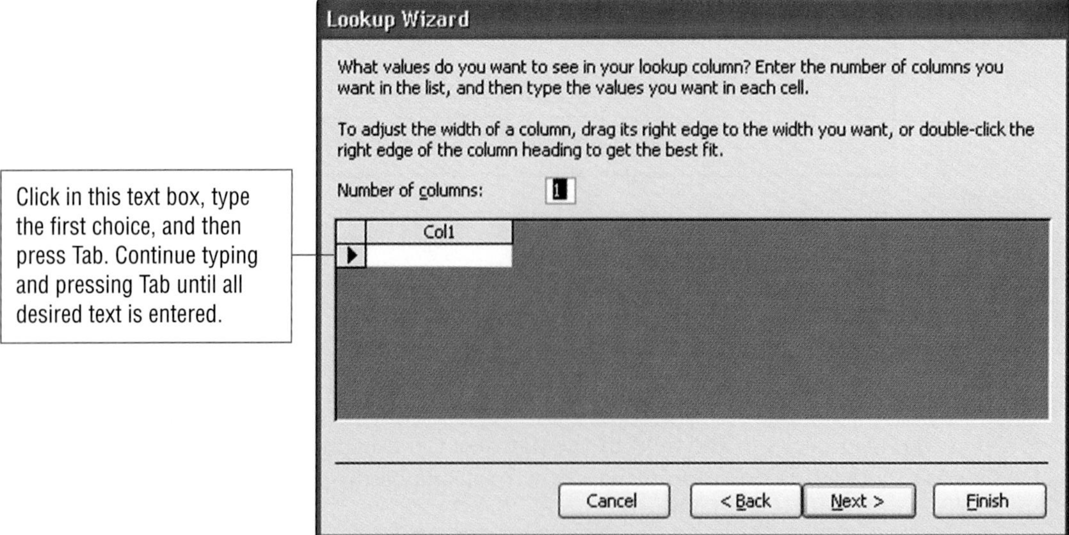

exercise 7

ADDING A FIELD TO AND DELETING A FIELD FROM THE EMPLOYEES TABLE

1. Open the **Premium** database file and then open the Employees database table.
2. Add the field *Telephone* to the table by completing the following steps:
   a. Click the down-pointing arrow at the right side of the View button on the Table Datasheet toolbar (first button from the left).
   b. At the drop-down list that displays, click *Design View*.
   c. Click anywhere in the text *Hire Date* that displays in the *Field Name* column. (You may need to scroll down the list to display this field.)
   d. Click the Insert Rows button on the Table Design toolbar.
   e. With the insertion point positioned in the new blank cell in the *Field Name* column, type **Telephone**.
   f. Press Tab (this moves the insertion point to the *Data Type* column).
   g. Select *50* that displays in the *Field Size* text box in the *Field Properties* section of the window and then type 14.
   h. Click the Save button to save the table. (You must save the table before using the Input Mask Wizard.)
   i. Click in the *Input Mask* text box in the *Field Properties* section of the window.
   j. Click the button containing the three black dots that displays to the right of the *Input Mask* text box.

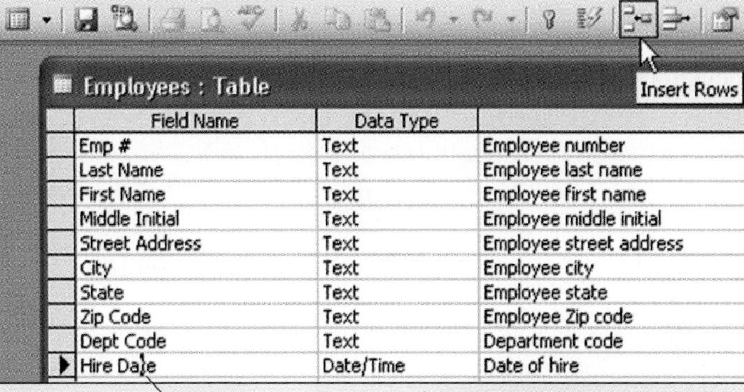

Step 2d
Insert Rows
Employees : Table
Field Name
Data Type
Emp #
Text
Employee number
Last Name
Text
Employee last name
First Name
Text
Employee first name
Middle Initial
Text
Employee middle initial
Street Address
Text
Employee street address
City
Text
Employee city
State
Text
Employee state
Zip Code
Text
Employee Zip code
Dept Code
Text
Department code
Hire Date
Date/Time
Date of hire
Step 2c

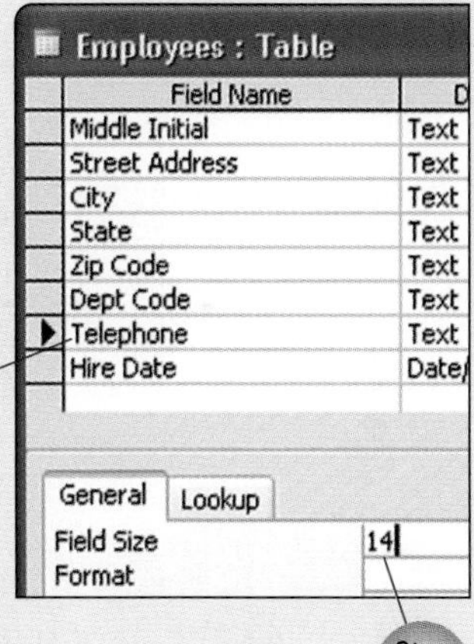

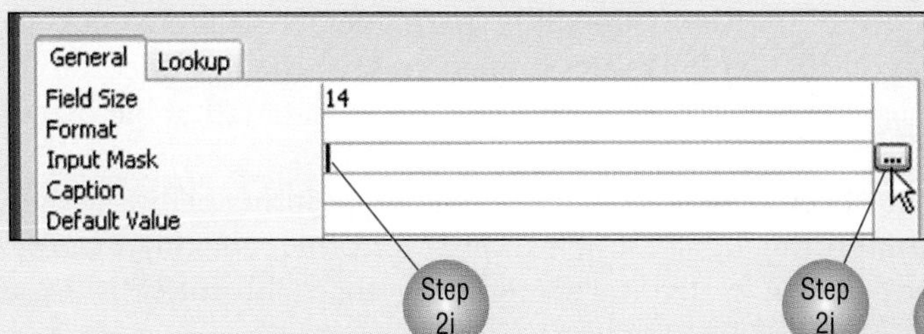

   k. At the first Input Mask Wizard dialog box, make sure *Phone Number* is selected in the *Input Mask* list box, and then click the Next button.

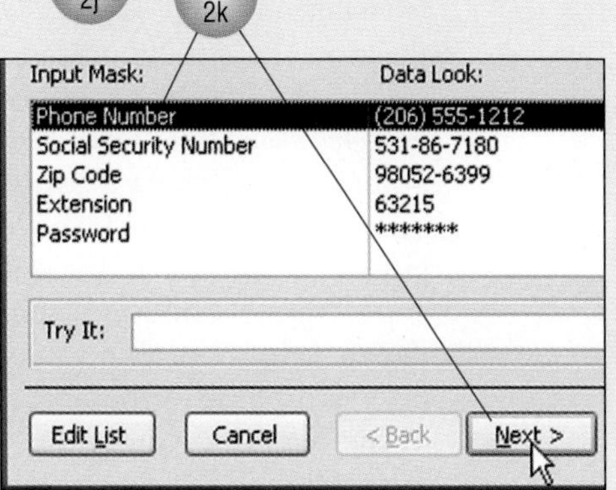

l. At the second Input Mask Wizard dialog box, click the down-pointing arrow at the right side of the *Placeholder character* text box, and then click # at the drop-down list.

Input Mask Wizard

Do you want to change the input mask?

Input Mask Name: Phone Number

Input Mask: !(999) 000-0000

What placeholder character do you want t

Placeholders are replaced as you enter da

Placeholder character:

Step 2l

m. Click the Next button.

n. At the third Input Mask Wizard dialog box, click the *With the symbols in the mask, like this* option.

o. Click the Next button.

p. At the fourth Input Mask Wizard dialog box, click the Finish button.

q. Click in the *Description* column in the *Telephone* row and then type **Employee home telephone number**.

3. Delete the *Hire Date* row by completing the following steps:
   a. Click anywhere in the text *Hire Date* that displays in the *Field Name* column.
   b. Click the Delete Rows button on the Table Design toolbar.

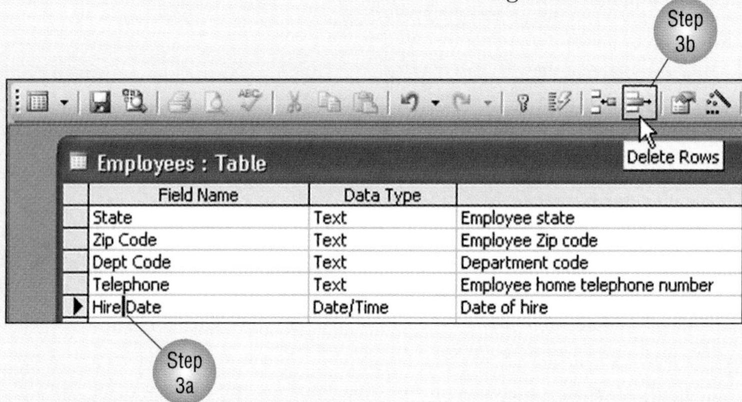

Field Name	Data Type	
State	Text	Employee state
Zip Code	Text	Employee Zip code
Dept Code	Text	Department code
Telephone	Text	Employee home telephone number
Hire Date	Date/Time	Date of hire

   c. At the message stating that the field will be permanently deleted, click Yes.
4. Click the Save button on the Table Design toolbar to save the modified table.
5. Add telephone numbers for the records in the Employees database table by completing the following steps:
   a. Change to the Datasheet view by clicking the down-pointing arrow at the right side of the View button on the Table Design toolbar and then clicking *Datasheet View*.
   b. Drag the scroll box on the horizontal scroll bar to the right until the *Telephone* field is visible.
   c. Position the arrow point at the left side of the first blank cell below the new *Telephone* field until the arrow pointer turns into a thick, white plus symbol and then click the left mouse button. (This selects the entire cell.)
   d. Type **4065556841** and then press the Down Arrow key. (This moves the insertion point to the next blank cell in the *Telephone* column.)

Employees : Table

Zip Code	Dept Code	Telephone
84302	HR	(406) 555-6841
84311	PA	
84325	HR	
84325	HR	
85901	PA	
86308	IS	

Step 5d

   e. Type **4065557454** and then press the Down Arrow key.

f. Type **4065553495** and then press the Down Arrow key.
g. Type **4065557732** and then press the Down Arrow key.
h. Type **4065550926** and then press the Down Arrow key.
i. Type **4065554509** and then press the Down Arrow key.

6. Click the Save button again on the Table Datasheet toolbar to save the database table.
7. Add the field *Employee Category* and use the Lookup Wizard to specify field choices by completing the following steps:
   a. Change to the Design view by clicking the down-pointing arrow at the right side of the View button on the Table Design toolbar and then clicking *Design View*.
   b. Click anywhere in the text *Dept Code* that displays in the *Field Name* column.
   c. Click the Insert Rows button on the Table Design toolbar.
   d. With the insertion point positioned in the new blank cell in the *Field Name* column, type **Employee Category**.
   e. Press Tab (this moves the insertion point to the *Data Type* column).
   f. Click the down-pointing arrow at the right side of the text box, and then click *Lookup Wizard* at the drop-down list.

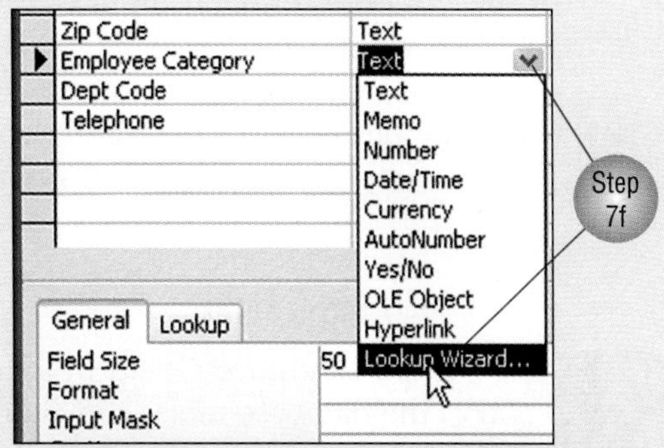

   g. At the first Lookup Wizard dialog box, click the *I will type in the values that I want* option, and then click the Next button.
   h. At the second Lookup Wizard dialog box, click in the blank text box below *Col1*, type **Salaried**, and then press Tab.
   i. Type **Hourly** and then press Tab.
   j. Type **Temporary**.
   k. Click the Next button.
   l. At the third Lookup Wizard dialog box, click the Finish button.
   m. Click in the *Description* column in the *Employee Category* row, and then type **Employee category**.

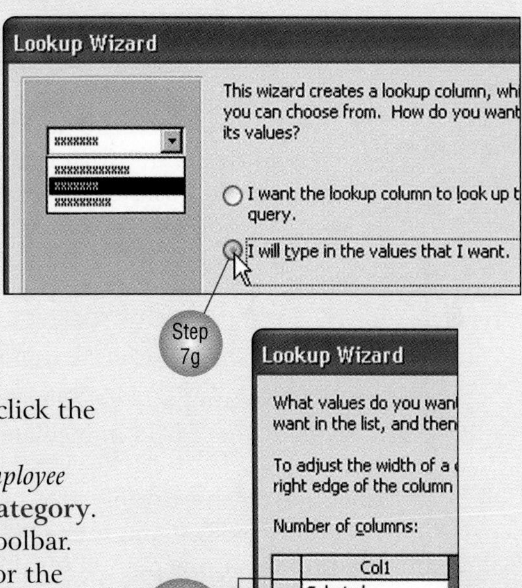

8. Click the Save button on the Table Design toolbar.
9. Insert information in the *Employee Category* for the records by completing the following steps:
   a. Change to the Datasheet view by clicking the down-pointing arrow at the right side of the View button on the Table Design toolbar and then clicking *Datasheet View*.
   b. Click in the first blank cell below the new *Employee Category* field.
   c. Click the down-pointing arrow at the right side of the cell and then click *Hourly* at the drop-down list.
   d. Click in next blank cell in the *Employee Category*, click the down-pointing arrow, and then click *Salaried* at the drop-down list.

e. Continue entering information in the *Employee Category* by completing similar steps. Type the following in the specified records:

Third record	=	Hourly
Fourth record	=	Hourly
Fifth record	=	Temporary
Sixth record	=	Salaried

10. Click the Save button again on the Table Datasheet toolbar.
11. Print the table in landscape orientation with .5-inch left and right margins. (Change to the *Landscape* orientation at the Page Setup dialog box with the Page tab selected, and then change to .5-inch left and right margins at the Page Setup dialog box with the Margins tab selected. [You must make the changes in this order.])
12. Close the Employees table and then close the **Premium** database file.

Moving a Field

Move a Field

1. Open table in Design view.
2. Select row to be moved.
3. Drag selected row to new position.

You can move a field in a database table to a different location. To do this, open the database table, and then change to the Design view. Position the arrow pointer on the gray button at the left side of the field you want moved until the arrow pointer turns into a right-pointing black arrow, and then click the left mouse button. This selects the entire row. Position the arrow pointer on the gray button at the left side of the selected row until it turns into the normal arrow pointer (white arrow pointing up and to the left). Hold down the left mouse button, drag the arrow pointer with the gray square attached until a thick gray line displays in the desired position, and then release the mouse button.

exercise 8

MOVING AND DELETING FIELDS IN THE EMPLOYEES TABLE

1. Open the **Premium** database file and then open the Employees database table.
2. Move the *Last Name* field immediately below the *Middle Initial* field by completing the following steps:
   a. Click the down-pointing arrow at the right of the View button on the Table Datasheet toolbar, and then click *Design View* at the drop-down list.
   b. Position the arrow pointer on the gray button (this color may vary) at the left side of the *Last Name* field until it turns into a right-pointing black arrow, and then click the left mouse button. (This selects the entire row.)
   c. Position the arrow pointer on the gray button at the left side of the selected row until it turns into the normal arrow pointer (white arrow pointing up and to the left).
   d. Hold down the left mouse button, drag the arrow pointer with the gray square attached until a thick gray line displays between the *Middle Initial* field and the *Street Address* field, and then release the mouse button.

Employees : Table

Field Name	Data Type
Emp #	Text
Last Name	Text
First Name	Text
Middle Initial	Text
Street Address	Text
City	Text
State	Text

Step 2d

3. Move the *Telephone* field above the *Dept Code* field by completing the following steps:
   a. Select the row containing the *Telephone* field.

b. Position the arrow pointer on the gray button at the left side of the selected row until it turns into the normal arrow pointer (white arrow pointing up and to the left).

c. Hold down the left mouse button, drag the arrow pointer above the *Dept Code* field, and then release the mouse button.

4. Delete the *Middle Initial* field and the data in the field by completing the following steps:
   a. Position the insertion point anywhere in the text *Middle Initial*.
   b. Click the Delete Rows button on the Table Design toolbar.
   c. At the message asking if you want to permanently delete the field and the data in the field, click Yes.
5. Click the Save button again on the Table Design toolbar to save the database table.
6. Click the View button on the Table Design toolbar to change to the Datasheet view.
7. Print the Employees database table in landscape orientation. (You will need to change to the *Landscape* orientation at the Page Setup dialog box with the Page tab selected.)
8. Close the Employees table and then close the **Premium** database file.

Sorting Records

The Table Datasheet toolbar contains two buttons you can use to sort data in records. Click the Sort Ascending button to sort from lowest to highest (or A-Z) on the field where the insertion point is located. Click the Sort Descending button to sort from highest to lowest (or Z-A).

Sort Records
1. Open table in Datasheet view.
2. Click Sort Ascending button or Sort Descending button.

exercise 9

SORTING RECORDS IN THE EMPLOYEES TABLE

1. Open the **Premium** database file and then open the Employees database table.
2. Sort records in ascending order by city by completing the following steps:
   a. Click in any city name in the database table.
   b. Click the Sort Ascending button on the Table Datasheet toolbar.
   c. Print the Employees database table in landscape orientation.
3. Sort records in descending order by employee number by completing the following steps:

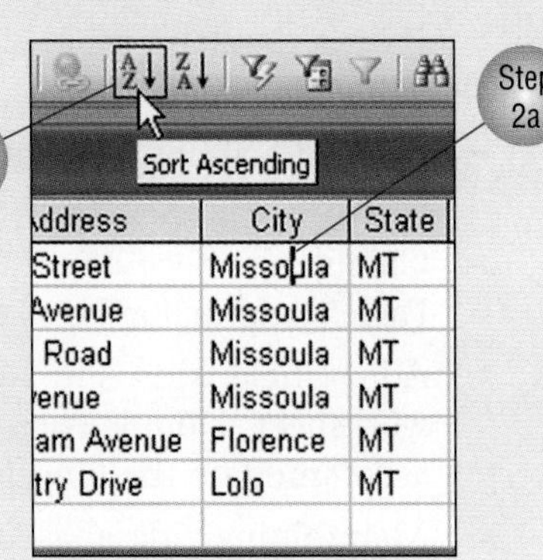

a. Click in any number in the *Emp #* field.
b. Click the Sort Descending button on the Table Datasheet toolbar.
c. Print the Employees database table in landscape orientation.

4. Click the Save button to save the database table.
5. Close the Employees table and then close the **Premium** database file.

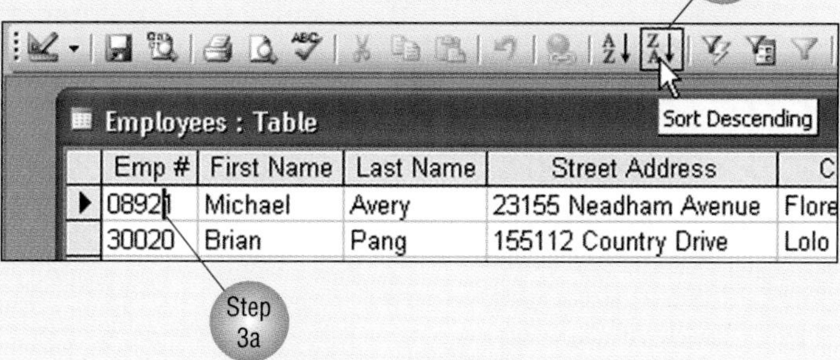

CHAPTER summary

- Microsoft Access is a database management system software program that will organize, store, maintain, retrieve, sort, and print all types of business data.
- Organize data in Access in related database tables in a database file.
- The first step in organizing data for a database table is determining fields. A field is one piece of information about a person, place, or item. All fields for one unit, such as an employee or customer, are considered a record.
- A field name should be unique and describe the contents of the field. It can contain up to 64 characters including letters, numbers, spaces, and some symbols.
- Part of the process of designing a database table is assigning a data type to each field, which helps maintain and manage data and helps identify what type of data is expected for the field. Data types include Text, Memo, Number, Currency, Date/Time, AutoNumber, and Yes/No.
- When assigning a data type, specific field sizes can be assigned to a field.
- Access automatically saves a database file on a periodic basis and also when the database file is closed.
- Open a database file when starting Access or open a database file at the Open dialog box.
- Enter data in a database table in the Datasheet view. Type data in a field, pressing Tab to move to the next field or pressing Shift + Tab to move to the previous field.
- Print a database table by opening the table and then clicking the Print button on the Table Datasheet toolbar.
- Change margins in a database table at the Page Setup dialog box with the Margins tab selected.
- Change the page orientation and paper size and specify the printer with options at the Page Setup dialog box with the Page tab selected.
- Adjust field widths in a database table in the same manner as column widths in an Excel worksheet. Double-click a column boundary to automatically adjust the width to accommodate the longest entry.
- Maintaining a database table can include adding and/or deleting records.

- Modifying a database table can include adding, moving, or deleting a field.
- Use the Input Mask Wizard to set a pattern for how data is entered in a field.
- Use the Lookup Wizard to confine data entered in a field to a specific list of items.
- Sort records in a database table in ascending order with the Sort Ascending button on the Table Datasheet toolbar or in descending order with the Sort Descending button.

FEATURES summary

FEATURE	BUTTON	MENU	KEYBOARD
New File task pane		File, New	Ctrl + N
Save As dialog box		File, Save As	Ctrl + S
Close table		File, Close	
Open dialog box		File, Open	Ctrl + O
Print dialog box		File, Print	
Send table to printer			Ctrl + P
Page Setup dialog box		File, Page Setup	
Add record to table		Insert, New Record	Ctrl + +
Delete record from table		Edit, Delete Record	
Switch to Design view		View, Design View	
Switch to Datasheet view		View, Datasheet View	
Add a field to a table		Insert, Rows	
Delete a field from a table		Edit, Delete Rows	
Input Mask			
Sort records in Ascending order		Records, Sort, Sort Ascending	
Sort records in Descending order		Records, Sort, Sort Descending	

CONCEPTS check

Completion: On a blank sheet of paper, indicate the correct term, symbol, or number for each description.

1. All fields for one unit, such as a customer, are considered to be this.
2. A field name can contain up to this number of characters.
3. Assign this data type to a field where more than 255 characters are needed.
4. Assign this data type to a field where you do not want calculations rounded off during a calculation.
5. You would probably assign this data type to a field that will contain telephone numbers.
6. In a field assigned the Yes/No data type, a check mark in the box in the field asking a yes/no question signifies this.
7. This view is used in a database table to define field names and assign data types.
8. This is the view used in a database table to enter data in fields.
9. Display this dialog box to change the page orientation.
10. This is the default left and right margin measurements for a database table.
11. Add a new record to a database table in this view.
12. Add a new field to a database table in this view.
13. Use this wizard to set a pattern for how data is entered in a field.
14. Use this wizard to confine data entered in a field to a specific list of items.
15. Click the Sort Ascending button on this toolbar to sort records in ascending order.
16. Suppose you work for an insurance company and have been asked by your supervisor to design a database table to keep track of client claims. This database table should include the following information: client number (assigned in a separate database table), the date of the claim, type of claim, and the amount of claim. Determine the fields you would use in this database table and the data type you would assign to each and write out that information.

SKILLS check

Assessment 1

1. Use Access to create a database file for a store that sells vitamins and other health aids. The database table you create will keep track of what vitamins are ordered for the store. (This table assumes that the database file contains at least two other tables—one table containing information on suppliers and the other containing information on products. You will learn more about how tables are related in Chapter 2.) Use the name of the store, HealthPlus, as the database file name, and name the database table Orders. (The table does not contain a primary key.) Create the following fields in the Orders database table, and assign the data type shown (you determine the Description):

Field Name		Data Type
Order #	=	Text (field size = 3)
Product Code	=	Text (field size = 2)
Supplier #	=	Text (field size = 2)
Date of Order	=	Date/Time
Amount of Order	=	Currency

2. Save the database table and name it Orders.
3. Change to the Datasheet view and then enter the following data:

Order #	=	214
Product Code	=	MT
Supplier #	=	10
Date of Order	=	4/5/2005
Amount of Order	=	$875.50

Order #	=	223
Product Code	=	PA
Supplier #	=	27
Date of Order	=	4/6/2005
Amount of Order	=	$1,005.45

Order #	=	241
Product Code	=	GS
Supplier #	=	10
Date of Order	=	4/8/2005
Amount of Order	=	$441.95

Order #	=	259
Product Code	=	AV
Supplier #	=	18
Date of Order	=	4/8/2005
Amount of Order	=	$772.00

4. Automatically adjust the width of fields.
5. Save the Orders database table again.
6. Print and then close the Orders table.

Assessment 2

1. With the **HealthPlus** database file open, open the Orders table and then add the following records (remember to do this in the Datasheet view):

Order #	=	262
Product Code	=	BC
Supplier #	=	27
Date of Order	=	4/9/2005
Amount of Order	=	$258.65

Order #	=	265
Product Code	=	VC
Supplier #	=	18
Date of Order	=	4/13/2005
Amount of Order	=	$1,103.45

2. Delete the record for order number 241.
3. Save the Orders database table and then print the table with a top margin of 2 inches.
4. Close the Orders database table.

Assessment 3

1. With the **HealthPlus** database file open, create a new table named Suppliers with the following fields and assign the data type shown (you determine the Description):

Field Name		**Data Type**
Supplier #	=	Text (field size = 2)
Supplier Name	=	Text (field size = 20)
Street Address	=	Text (field size = 30)
City	=	Text (field size = 20)
State	=	Text (field size = 2)
ZIP Code	=	Text (field size = 10) Use the Input Mask Wizard to specify a nine-digit ZIP Code. ***(Hint: At the first Input Mask Wizard dialog box, click* ZIP Code *in the* Input Mask *list box.)***

2. After creating and saving the database table with the fields shown above, enter the following data in the table (remember to do this in the Datasheet view):

Supplier #	=	10
Supplier Name	=	VitaHealth, Inc.
Street Address	=	12110 South 23rd
City	=	San Diego
State	=	CA
ZIP Code	=	97432-1567

Supplier #	=	18
Supplier Name	=	Mainstream Supplies
Street Address	=	312 Evergreen Building
City	=	Seattle
State	=	WA
ZIP Code	=	98220-2791

Supplier #	=	21
Supplier Name	=	LaVerde Products
Street Address	=	121 Vista Road
City	=	Phoenix
State	=	AZ
ZIP Code	=	86355-6014

Supplier #	=	27
Supplier Name	=	Redding Corporation
Street Address	=	554 Ninth Street
City	=	Portland
State	=	OR
ZIP Code	=	97466-3359

3. Automatically adjust the width of fields.
4. Save the Suppliers database table.
5. Change the page orientation to landscape and then print the table.
6. Close the Suppliers database table.

Assessment 4

1. With the **HealthPlus** database file open, open the Suppliers table.
2. Add the following fields and assign the data type as shown (remember to do this in the Design view):

Field Name		**Data Type**
Telephone	=	Text (field size = 14) Use the Input Mask Wizard to specify that the area code surrounded by parentheses is to be included in the telephone number.
E-mail Address	=	Text (field size = 30)
Supplier Type	=	Use the Lookup Wizard to create two categories for this field—*Wholesale* and *Retail*

3. Save the table, change to the Datasheet view, and then add the following information in the appropriate row (type the supplier telephone number, e-mail address, and insert the supplier type in the correct row).

Supplier = **LaVerde Product**
Telephone = **(602) 555-6775**
E-mail Address = **laverdep@emcp.net**
Supplier Type = *Wholesale*

Supplier = **VitaHealth, Inc.**
Telephone = **(619) 555-2388**
E-mail Address = **vitahealth@emcp.net**
Supplier Type = *Retail*

Supplier = **Redding Corporation**
Telephone = **(503) 555-6679**
E-mail Address = **redding@emcp.net**
Supplier Type = *Retail*

Supplier = **Mainstream Supplies**
Telephone = **(206) 555-9005**
E-mail Address = **mainsupplies@emcp.net**
Supplier Type = *Wholesale*

4. Automatically adjust the width of fields to accommodate the longest entry.
5. Save the Suppliers database table.
6. Change the page orientation to landscape and then print the table. (The table may print on two pages.)
7. Close the Suppliers database table.

Assessment 5

1. With the **HealthPlus** database file open, open the Orders table.
2. Change to the Design view and then move the fields around in the Orders database table so they are displayed in this order:

Order #
Date of Order
Amount of Order
Product Code
Supplier #

3. Save the table, change to the Datasheet view, and then sort the records in ascending order by *Supplier #*.
4. Save, print, and then close the Orders database table.
5. Close the **HealthPlus** database file.

CHAPTER challenge

You are the manager of Miles Music Mania, a small music store that specializes in CDs, DVDs, and Laserdiscs. Recently, the small store has increased its volume of merchandise requiring better organization and easier retrieval of information. You decide to create a database named **MilesMusicMania** that contains a table named Inventory with information pertaining to the inventory of CDs, DVDs and Laserdiscs. Create at least five fields, using at least three different data types. Add five records to the table.

As the manager of Miles Music Mania, customers approach you and are interested in learning more about the artists or bands. For quick and reliable answers, you decide to add another field to the Inventory table that includes a hyperlink to the artist's or band's Web site. Use the Help feature to learn more about hyperlink fields. Add a hyperlink field to the Inventory table created in the first part of the Chapter Challenge. Add a hyperlink to at least one of the records in the Inventory table. Save the table again.

Export the Inventory table created in the first part of the Chapter Challenge to Word. Once in Word, the information can be used to create a flyer showing the various types of merchandise sold at Miles Music Mania store. Add additional formatting, graphics, and information in Word. Save the flyer in Word as **MilesMusicManiaFlyer** and then print it.

CHAPTER 2

CREATING RELATIONSHIPS BETWEEN DATABASE TABLES

PERFORMANCE OBJECTIVES

Upon successful completion of Chapter 2, you will be able to:

- **Create a database table with a primary key and a foreign key**
- **Create a one-to-many relationship between database tables**

ACCESS

Access is a relational database program that allows you to create tables that have a relation or connection to each other within the same database file. In Chapter 1, you created a database table containing information on employees and another containing department information. With Access, you can connect these tables through a common field that appears in both tables.

In this chapter you will learn how to identify a primary key field in a database table that is unique to that table. In Access, data can be divided into logical groupings in database tables for easier manipulation and management. Duplicate information is generally minimized in database tables in the same database file. A link or relationship, however, should connect the database tables. In this chapter, you will define primary keys and define relationships between database tables.

Creating Related Tables

Generally, a database management system fits into one of two categories—either a file management system (also sometimes referred to as a ***flat file database***) or a relational database management system. In a file management system, data is stored without indexing and sequential processing. This type of system lacks flexibility in manipulating data and requires the same data to be stored in more than one place.

In a relational database management system, like Access, relationships are defined between sets of data allowing greater flexibility in manipulating data and eliminating data redundancy (entering the same data in more than one place). In exercises in this chapter, you will define relationships between tables in the insurance company database file. Because these tables will be related, information on a client does not need to be repeated in a table on claims filed. If you used a file management system to maintain insurance records, you would need to repeat the client information for each claim filed.

Determining Relationships

Taking time to plan a database file is extremely important. Creating a database file with related tables takes even more consideration. You need to determine how to break down the required data and what tables to create to eliminate redundancies. One idea to help you determine the necessary tables in a database file is to think of the word "about." For example, an insurance company database will probably need a table "about" clients, another "about" the type of coverage, another "about" claims, and so on. A table should be about only one subject, such as a client, customer, department, or supplier.

Along with deciding on the necessary tables for a database file, you also need to determine the relationship between tables. The ability to relate, or "join," tables is part of what makes Access a relational database system. Figure 2.1 illustrates the tables and fields that either are or will become part of the SouthwestInsurance database file. Notice how each table is about only one subject—clients, type of insurance, claims, or coverage.

FIGURE 2.1 ***SouthwestInsurance Database Tables***

Clients table
Client #
Client
Street Address
City
State
ZIP Code

Insurance table
License #
Client #
Insurance Code
Uninsured Motorist

Claims table
Claim #
Client #
License #
Date of Claim
Amount of Claim

Coverage table
Insurance Code
Type of Insurance

Some fields such as *Client #*, *License #*, and *Insurance Code* appear in more than one table. These fields are used to create a relationship between tables. For example, in Exercise 2 you will create a relationship between the Clients table and the Insurance table with the *Client #* field.

Creating relationships between tables tells Access how to bring the information in the database file back together again. With relationships defined, you can bring information together to create queries, forms, and reports. (You will learn about these features in future chapters.)

Creating a Primary Field

Specify a Primary Key
1. Open table in design view.
2. Click desired field.
3. Click Primary Key button.
4. Click Save button.

HINT

You must enter a value in the primary key field in every record.

Before creating a relationship between tables, you need to define the primary key in a table. In a database table, at least one field must be unique so that one record can be distinguished from another. A field (or several fields) with a unique value is considered a ***primary key***. When a primary key is defined, Access will not allow duplicate values in the primary field. For example, the *Client #* field in the Clients table must contain a unique number (you would not assign the same client number to two different clients). If you define this as the primary key field, Access will not allow you to type the same client number in two different records.

In a field specified as a primary key, Access expects a value in each record in the database table. This is referred to as ***entity integrity***. If a value is not entered in a field, Access actually enters a ***null value***. A null value cannot be given to a primary key field. Access will not let you close a database file containing a primary field with a null value.

To define a field as a primary key, open the database table, and then change to the Design view. Position the insertion point somewhere in the row containing the field you want as the primary key, and then click the Primary Key button on the Table Design toolbar. An image of a key is inserted at the beginning of the row identified as the primary key field. To define more than one field as a primary key, select the rows containing the fields you want as primary keys, and then click the Primary Key button on the Table Design toolbar.

Primary Key

Creating a Foreign Key

A primary key field in one table may be a foreign key in another. For example, if you define the *Client #* field in the Clients table as the primary key, the *Client #* field in the Insurance table will then be considered a ***foreign key***. The primary key field and the foreign key field form a relationship between the two tables. In the Clients table, each entry in the *Client #* field will be unique (it is the primary key), but the same client number may appear more than once in the *Client #* field in the Insurance table (such as a situation where a client has insurance on more than one vehicle).

Each table in Figure 2.1 contains a unique field that will be defined as the primary key. Figure 2.2 identifies the primary keys and also foreign keys.

FIGURE 2.2 ***Primary and Foreign Keys***

Clients table	**Insurance table**
Client # *(primary key)*	License # *(primary key)*
Client	Client # *(foreign key)*
Street Address	Insurance Code *(foreign key)*
City	Uninsured Motorist
State	
ZIP Code	

Continued on next page

Claims table
Claim # *(primary key)*
Client # *(foreign key)*
License # *(foreign key)*
Date of Claim
Amount of Claim

Coverage table
Insurance Code *(primary key)*
Type of Insurance

In Exercise 1, you will create another table for the SouthwestInsurance database file, enter data, and then define primary keys for the tables. In the section following Exercise 1, you will learn how to create relationships between the tables.

exercise 1

CREATING A TABLE AND DEFINING PRIMARY KEYS

(Note: Delete from your disk any database files you created in Chapter 1. In Step 1, you will copy the SouthwestInsurance database file from the CD that accompanies this textbook to your disk. You will then remove the read-only attribute from the SouthwestInsurance database file on your disk. You need to remove this attribute before you can make changes to the database file.)

1. Copy the **SouthwestInsurance** database file on the CD that accompanies this textbook to your disk, remove the read-only attribute, and then open the database file by completing the following steps:
   a. Insert the CD that accompanies this textbook into the drive.
   b. Copy the **SouthwestInsurance** database file from the CD to your disk.
   c. Remove the read-only attribute from the **SouthwestInsurance** database located on your disk by completing the following steps:
      1) In Access, display the Open dialog box with the drive active containing your disk.
      2) Click once on the **SouthwestInsurance** database file name.
      3) Click the Tools button on the Open dialog box toolbar, and then click Properties at the drop-down menu.
      4) At the SouthwestInsurance Properties dialog box with the General tab selected, click *Read-only* in the *Attributes* section to remove the check mark.
      5) Click OK to close the SouthwestInsurance Properties dialog box.

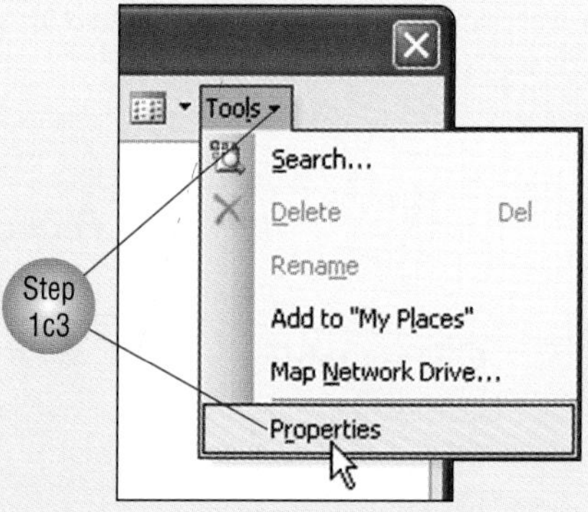

   d. Open the **SouthwestInsurance** database file.
2. At the SouthwestInsurance : Database window, create a new table by completing the following steps:
   a. Double-click *Create table in Design view* in the list box.
   b. At the Table1 : Table window, type the fields, assign the data types, and type the descriptions as shown below (for assistance, refer to Chapter 1, Exercise 1):

Field Name	Data Type	Description
License #	Text (Field Size = 7)	Vehicle license number
Client #	Text (Field Size = 4)	Client number
Insurance Code	Text (Field Size = 1)	Insurance code
Uninsured Motorist	Yes/No	Uninsured motorist coverage

(Note: To create the Yes/No data type for the* Uninsured Motorist *field, click the down-pointing arrow at the right side of the* Data Type *field, and then click* Yes/No *at the drop-down list.)

c. Specify the *License #* as the primary key by completing the following steps:
   1) Click anywhere in the text *License #* (in the top row).
   2) Click the Primary Key button on the Table Design toolbar.

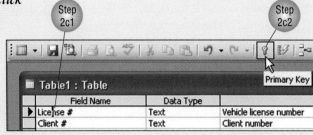

d. Save the database table by completing the following steps:
   1) Click the Save button on the Table Design toolbar.
   2) At the Save As dialog box, type **Insurance** in the *Table Name* text box, and then press Enter or click OK.

e. Close the Insurance table by clicking File and then Close or by clicking the Close button located in the upper right corner of the window.

3. Define primary keys for the other tables in the database file by completing the following steps:
   a. At the SouthwestInsurance : Database window, double-click *Claims* in the list box.
   b. With the Claims table open, click the View button on the Table Datasheet toolbar to switch to the Design view.
   c. Click anywhere in the text *Claim #,* and then click the Primary Key button on the Table Design toolbar.
   d. Click the Save button on the Table Design toolbar.
   e. Close the Claims table.
   f. At the SouthwestInsurance : Database window, double-click *Clients* in the list box.

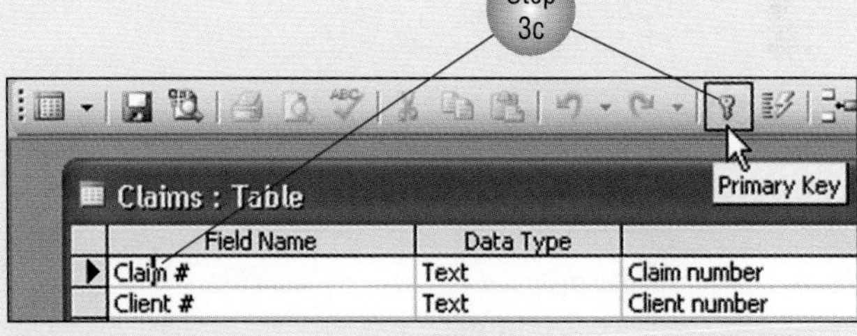

   g. With the Clients table open, click the View button on the Table Datasheet toolbar to switch to the Design view.
   h. Click anywhere in the text *Client #,* and then click the Primary Key button on the Table Design toolbar.
   i. Click the Save button on the Table Design toolbar.
   j. Close the Clients table.
   k. At the SouthwestInsurance : Database window, double-click *Coverage* in the list box.

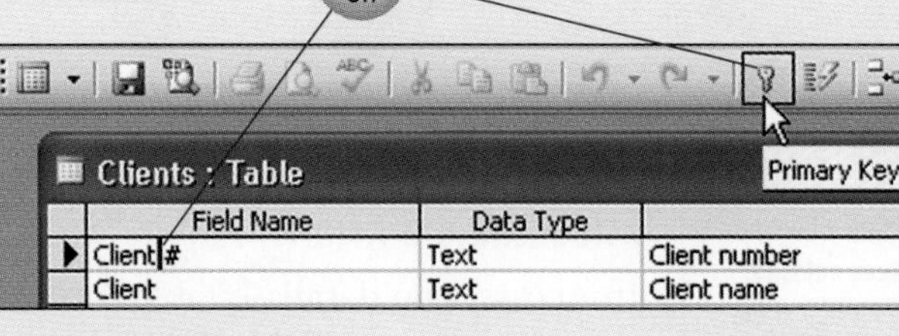

   l. With the Coverage table open, click the View button on the Table Datasheet toolbar to switch to the Design view.

m. Click anywhere in the text *Insurance Code* and then click the Primary Key button on the Table Design toolbar.
n. Click the Save button on the Table Design toolbar.
o. Close the Coverage table.

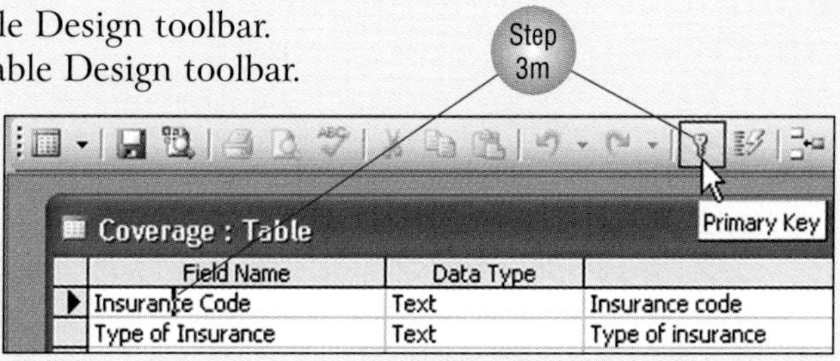

Step 3m

Primary Key

Coverage : Table

	Field Name	Data Type	
▶	Insurance Code	Text	Insurance code
	Type of Insurance	Text	Type of insurance

4. Open the Insurance table and then type the following data in the specified fields: (If the *Uninsured Motorist* field is Yes, insert a check mark in the field by pressing the spacebar. If the field is No, leave the check box blank.)

License # = 341 VIT
Client # = 3120
Insurance Code = F
Uninsured Motorist = Yes

License # = 776 ERU
Client # = 9383
Insurance Code = F
Uninsured Motorist = No

License # = 984 CWS
Client # = 7335
Insurance Code = L
Uninsured Motorist = Yes

License # = 877 BNN
Client # = 4300
Insurance Code = L
Uninsured Motorist = Yes

License # = 310 YTV
Client # = 3120
Insurance Code = F
Uninsured Motorist = Yes

Insurance : Table

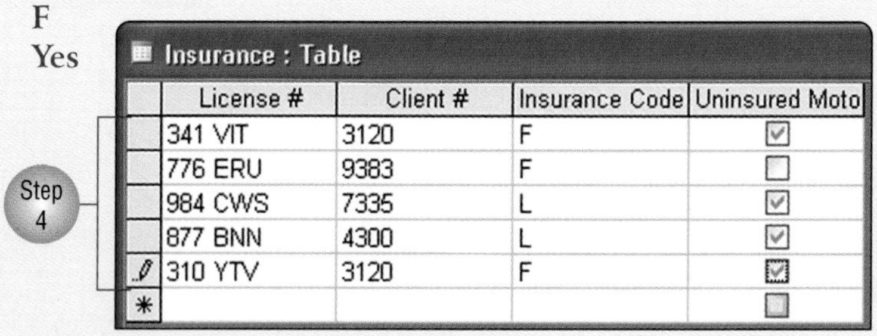

	License #	Client #	Insurance Code	Uninsured Moto
	341 VIT	3120	F	☑
	776 ERU	9383	F	☐
	984 CWS	7335	L	☑
	877 BNN	4300	L	☑
✎	310 YTV	3120	F	☑
*				☐

Step 4

5. Save and then close the Insurance table.
6. Close the **SouthwestInsurance** database file.

HINT

Defining a relationship between database tables is one of the most powerful features of a relational database management system.

Establishing a Relationship between Tables

In Access, one database table can be related to another, which is generally referred to as performing a ***join***. When database tables with a common field are joined, data can be extracted from both tables as if they were one large table. Another reason for relating tables is to ensure the integrity of the data. For example, in Exercise 2, you will create a relationship between the Clients database table and the Claims database table. The relationship that is established will ensure that a client cannot be entered in the Claims database table without first being entered in the Clients database table. This ensures that a claim is not processed on a person who is not a client of the insurance company. This type of relationship is called a one-to-many relationship, which means that one record in the Clients table will match zero, one, or many records in the Claims database table.

In a one-to-many relationship, the table containing the "one" is referred to as the ***primary table*** and the table containing the "many" is referred to as the ***related table***. Access follows a set of rules known as ***referential integrity***, which enforces consistency between related tables. These rules are enforced when data is updated in related database tables. The referential integrity rules ensure that a record added to a related table has a matching record in the primary table.

HINT

Access provides a Table Analyzer that will analyze your database tables and restructure them to better conform to relational theory. To use the Table Analyzer Wizard, click the Analyze button on the Database toolbar.

Creating a One-to-Many Relationship

A relationship is specified between existing tables in a database file. To create a one-to-many relationship, you would complete these basic steps:

1. Open the database file containing the tables to be related.
2. Click the Relationships button that displays at the right side of the Database toolbar; or click Tools and then Relationships. This displays the Show Table dialog box, as shown in Figure 2.3.
3. At the Show Table dialog box, each table that will be related must be added to the Relationships window. To do this, click the first database table name to be included, and then click Add. Continue in this manner until all necessary database table names have been added to the Relationships window and then click the Close button.
4. At the Relationships window, such as the one shown in Figure 2.4, use the mouse to drag the common field from the primary table (the "one") to the related table (the "many"). This causes the Edit Relationships dialog box to display as shown in Figure 2.5.
5. At the Edit Relationships dialog box, check to make sure the correct field name displays in the *Table/Query* and *Related Table/Query* list boxes and the relationship type at the bottom of the dialog box displays as *One-To-Many.*
6. Specify the relationship options by choosing *Enforce Referential Integrity*, as well as *Cascade Update Related Fields* and/or *Cascade Delete Related Records*. (These options are explained in the text after these steps.)
7. Click the Create button. This causes the Edit Relationships dialog box to close and the Relationships window to display showing the relationship between the tables. In Figure 2.6, the Clients box displays with a black line attached along with the number *1* (signifying the "one" side of the relationship). The black line is connected to the Claims box along with the infinity symbol ∞ (signifying the "many" side of the relationship). The black line, called the ***join line***, is thick at both ends if the enforce referential integrity option has been chosen. If this option is not chosen, the line is thin at both ends.
8. Click the Save button on the Relationship toolbar to save the relationship.
9. Close the Relationships window by clicking the Close button that displays at the right side of the Title bar.

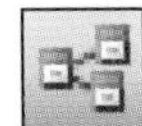

Relationships

Create a One-to-Many Relationship

1. Open database file.
2. Click Relationships button.
3. At Show Table dialog box, add tables to be related.
4. At Relationships window, drag "one" field from primary table to "many" field in related table.
5. At Edit Relationships dialog box, enforce referential integrity.
6. Click Create button.
7. Click Save button.

FIGURE

2.3 *Show Table Dialog Box*

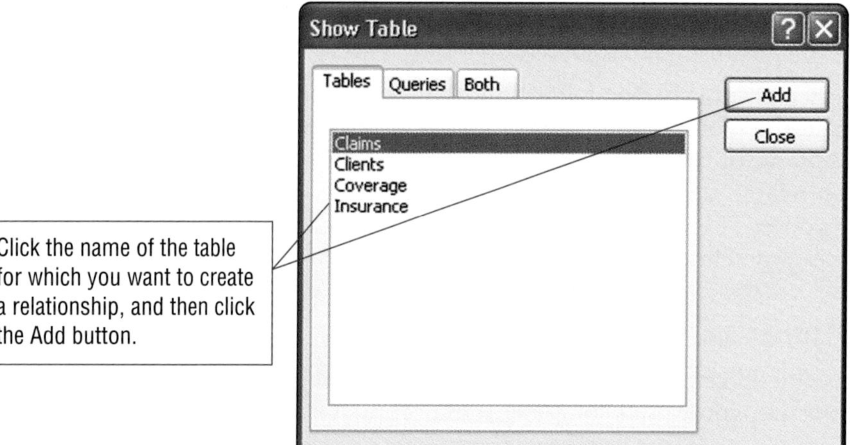

Show Table
Tables
Queries
Both
Add
Close
Claims
Clients
Coverage
Insurance
Click the name of the table for which you want to create a relationship, and then click the Add button.

FIGURE

2.4 *Relationships Window*

Insert in the Relationships window those tables for which you will create a relationship.

Relationships

Clients	Claims	Insurance	Coverage
Client #	Claim #	License #	Insurance Code
Client	Client #	Client #	Type of Insuranc
Street Addres	License #	Insurance Code	
City	Date of Claim	Uninsured Motori:	
State	Amount of Claim		

FIGURE 2.5 ***Edit Relationships Dialog Box***

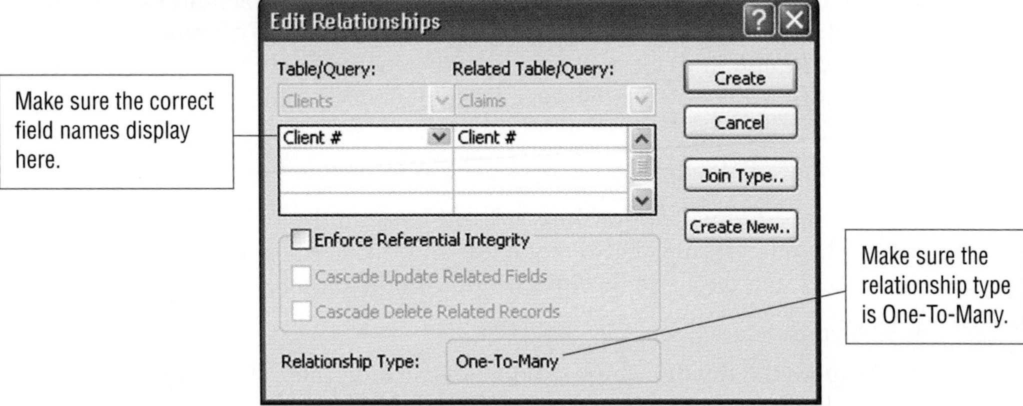

FIGURE 2.6 ***One-to-Many Relationship***

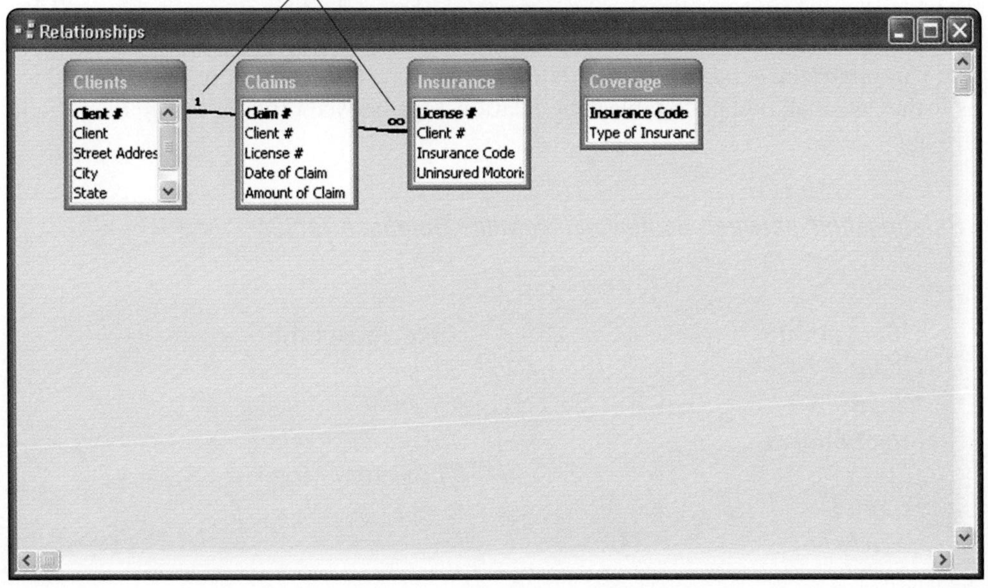

Specifying Referential Integrity

In Step 6, the referential integrity of the relationship was established. Choose *Enforce Referential Integrity* at the Edit Relationships dialog box to ensure that the relationships between records in related tables are valid. Referential integrity can be set if the field from the primary table is a primary key and the related fields have the same data type. When referential integrity is established, a value for the primary key must first be entered in the primary table before it can be entered in the related table.

HINT

Referential integrity makes sure that a record exists in the "one" database table before the record can be entered in the "many" database table.

If you select only *Enforce Referential Integrity* and the related table contains a record, you will not be able to change a primary key value or delete a primary key value in the primary table. If you choose *Cascade Update Related Fields*, you will be able to change a primary key value in the primary table and Access will automatically update the matching value in the related table. Choose *Cascade Delete Related Records* and you will be able to delete a record in the primary table and Access will delete any related records in the related table.

Print Database Relationships
1. Open database.
2. Click Relationships button.
3. Click File, Print Relationships.
4. Click Print button.
5. Click Close button.

Print

Printing Database Relationships

Access contains a Print Relationships Wizard you can use to print a report displaying the relationships between tables. To print a report of relationships between tables in a database file, you would complete these steps:

1. Open the database.
2. Display the Relationships window by clicking the Relationships button on the Database toolbar.
3. At the Relationships window, click File and then Print Relationships. (This displays the Relationships report in Print Preview.)
4. Click the Print button on the Print Preview toolbar to send the report to the printer.
5. Click the Close button to close Print Preview.

Relating Tables in the SouthwestInsurance Database File

The SouthwestInsurance database file contains the four tables shown in Figure 2.1. Each table contains data about something—clients, insurance, claims, and coverage. You can relate these tables so that data can be extracted from more than one table as if they were all one large table. The relationships between the tables are identified in Figure 2.7.

FIGURE 2.7 **Relationships between SouthwestInsurance Database Tables**

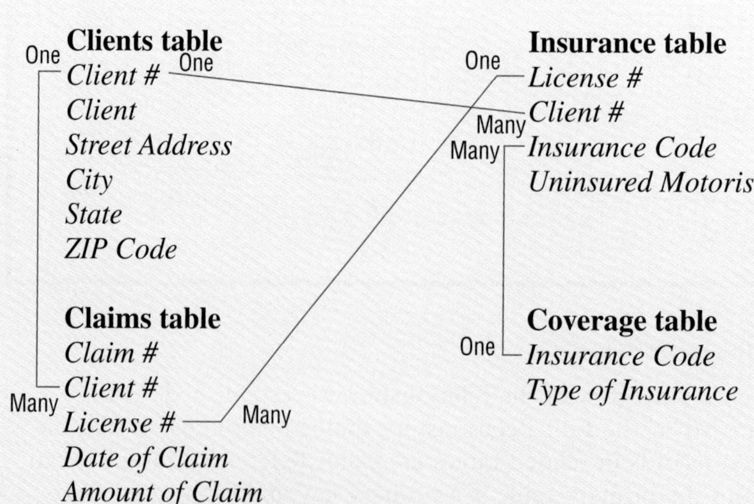

In the relationships shown in Figure 2.7, notice how the primary key is identified as the "one" and the foreign key is identified as the "many." Relate these tables so you can extract information from more than one table. For example, you can design a report about claims that contains information on claims as well as information on the clients submitting the claims.

exercise 2

CREATING A ONE-TO-MANY RELATIONSHIP BETWEEN TWO DATABASE TABLES

1. Create a one-to-many relationship between the Clients table and the Claims table by completing the following steps:
   a. Open the **SouthwestInsurance** database file.
   b. Click the Relationships button that displays toward the right side of the Database toolbar.

   c. At the Show Table dialog box, add the Clients and Claims tables to the Relationships window by completing the following steps:
      1) Click *Clients* in the list box and then click Add.
      2) Click *Claims* in the list box and then click Add.

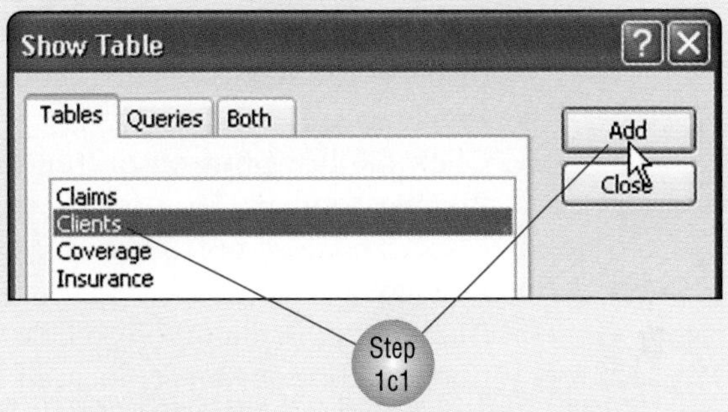

   d. Click the Close button to close the Show Table dialog box.
   e. At the Relationships window, drag the *Client #* field from the Clients table to the Claims table by completing the following steps:
      1) Position the arrow pointer on the *Client #* field that displays in the Clients box.
      2) Hold down the left mouse button, drag the arrow pointer (with a field icon attached) to the *Client #* field in the *Claims* box, and then release the mouse button. (This causes the Edit Relationships dialog box to display.)

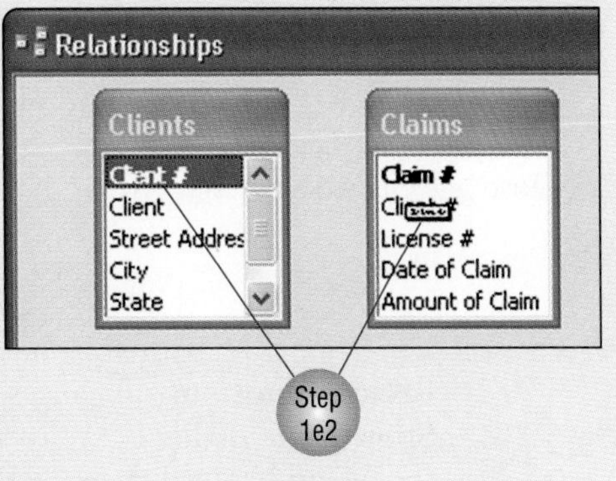

   f. At the Edit Relationships dialog box, make sure *Client #* displays in the *Table/Query* and *Related Table/Query* list boxes and the relationship type at the bottom of the dialog box displays as *One-To-Many*.
   g. Enforce the referential integrity of the relationship by completing the following steps:

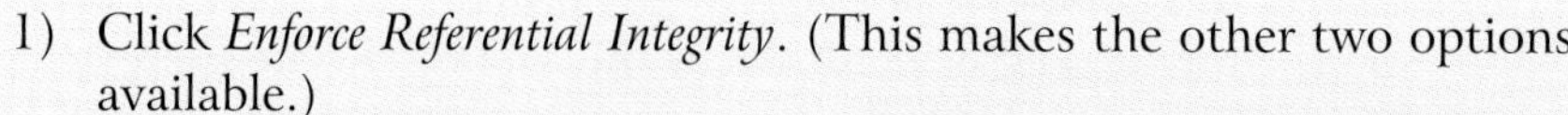

1) Click *Enforce Referential Integrity*. (This makes the other two options available.)
2) Click *Cascade Update Related Fields*.
3) Click *Cascade Delete Related Records*.

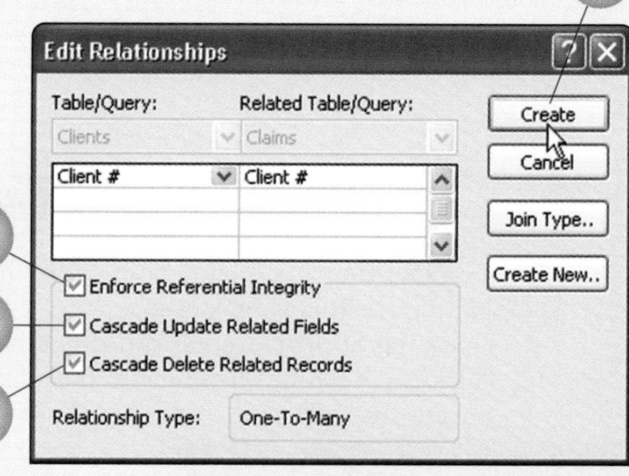

h. Click the Create button. (This causes the Edit Relationships dialog box to close and the Relationships window to display showing a thick black line connecting Clients to Claims. At the Clients side, a *1* will appear and an infinity symbol ∞ will display at the Claims side of the thick black line.)
i. Click the Save button on the Relationship toolbar to save the relationship.
j. Print the relationships by completing the following steps:
   1) At the Relationships window, click File and then Print Relationships. (This displays the Relationships report in Print Preview.)
   2) Click the Print button on the Print Preview toolbar.
   3) Click the Close button to close Print Preview.
   4) At the Report dialog box, click the Close button (contains an *X*) located in the upper right corner of the dialog box.
   5) At the message asking if you want to save changes to the design of the report, click No.

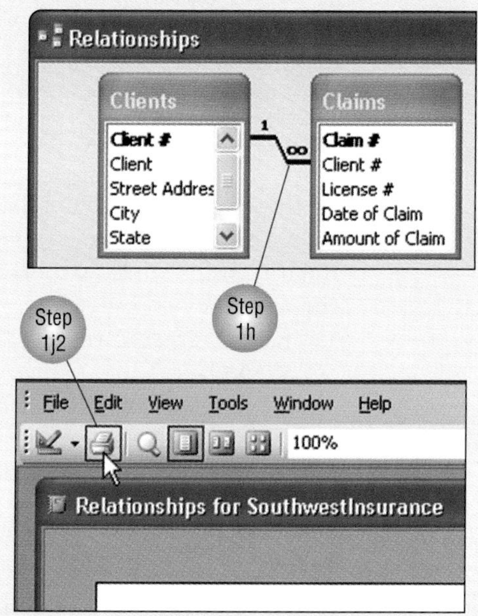

k. Close the Relationships window by clicking the Close button that displays at the right side of the Title bar.

2. Close the **SouthwestInsurance** database file.

Once a relationship has been established between tables, clicking the Relationships button causes the Relationships window to display (rather than the Show Table dialog box). To create additional relationships, click Relationships on the Menu bar and then click Show Table. This displays the Show Table dialog box where you can specify the tables you need for creating another relationship.

exercise 3 CREATING ADDITIONAL ONE-TO-MANY RELATIONSHIPS IN A DATABASE FILE

1. Open the **SouthwestInsurance** database file.
2. Create a one-to-many relationship between the Clients table and the Insurance table by completing the following steps:

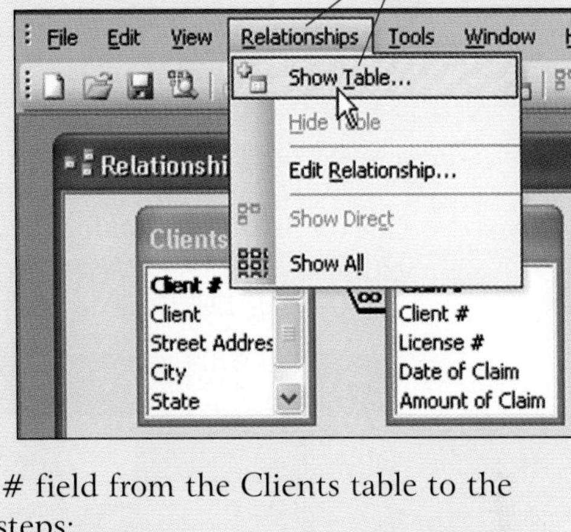

   a. Click the Relationships button that displays toward the right side of the Database toolbar.
   b. At the Relationships window, click Relationships on the Menu bar and then click Show Table at the drop-down menu.
   c. At the Show Table dialog box, click *Insurance* in the list box, and then click the Add button. (You do not need to add the Clients table because it was added in Exercise 2.)
   d. Click the Close button to close the Show Table dialog box.
   e. At the Relationships window, drag the *Client #* field from the Clients table to the Insurance table by completing the following steps:

      1) Position the arrow pointer on the *Client #* field that displays in the Clients box.
      2) Hold down the left mouse button, drag the arrow pointer (with a field icon attached), to the *Client #* field in the Insurance box, and then release the mouse button. (This causes the Edit Relationships dialog box to display.)

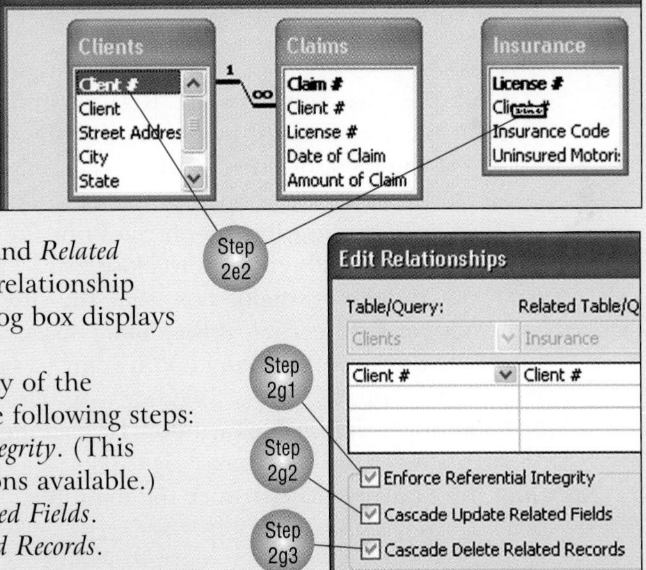

   f. At the Edit Relationships dialog box, make sure *Client #* displays in the *Table/Query* and *Related Table/Query* list boxes and the relationship type at the bottom of the dialog box displays as *One-To-Many*.
   g. Enforce the referential integrity of the relationship by completing the following steps:
      1) Click *Enforce Referential Integrity*. (This makes the other two options available.)
      2) Click *Cascade Update Related Fields*.
      3) Click *Cascade Delete Related Records*.
   h. Click the Create button. (This causes the Edit Relationships dialog box to close and the Relationships window to display showing a thick black line connecting Clients to Insurance. At the Clients side, a *1* will appear and an infinity symbol ∞ will display at the Insurance side of the thick black line.)

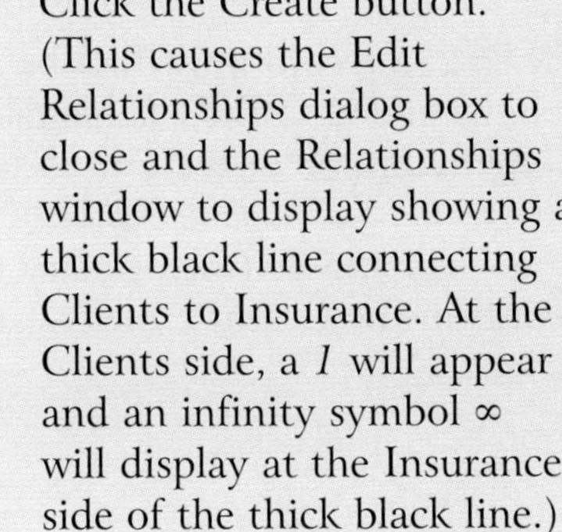

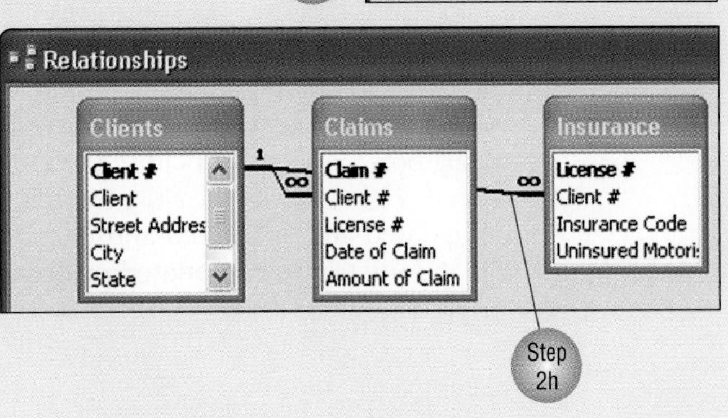

i. Click the Save button on the Relationship toolbar to save the relationship.
j. With the Relationships window still open, create the following one-to-many relationships by completing steps similar to those in Steps 2b through 2i:
   1) Create a relationship between *License #* in the Insurance table and the Claims table. (*License #* in the Insurance table is the "one" and *License #* in the Claims table is the "many.") At the Edit Relationships dialog box, be sure to choose *Enforce Referential Integrity*, *Cascade Update Related Fields*, and *Cascade Delete Related Records*.
   2) Add the Coverage table to the Relationships window and then create a relationship between *Insurance Code* in the Coverage table and the Insurance table. (*Insurance Code* in the Coverage table is the "one" and *Insurance Code* in the Insurance table is the "many.") At the Edit Relationships dialog box, be sure to choose *Enforce Referential Integrity*, *Cascade Update Related Fields*, and *Cascade Delete Related Records*.

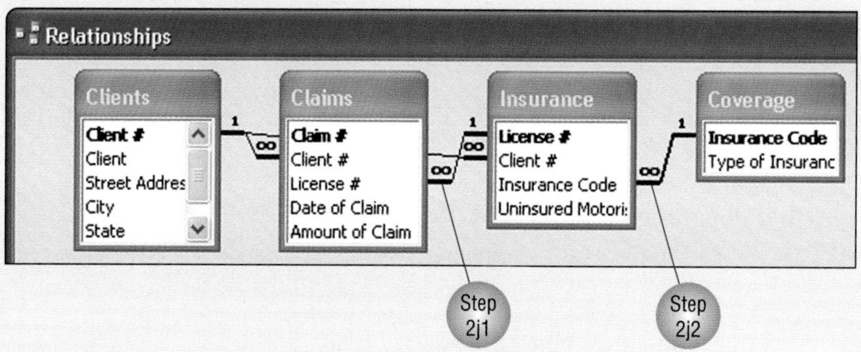

k. Click the Save button on the Relationship toolbar.
l. Print the relationships by completing the following steps:
   1) At the Relationships window, click File and then Print Relationships. (This displays the Relationships report in Print Preview.)
   2) Click the Print button on the Print Preview toolbar.
   3) Click the Close button to close Print Preview.
   4) At the Report dialog box, click the Close button (contains an *X*) located in the upper right corner of the dialog box.
   5) At the message asking if you want to save changes to the design of the report, click No.
m. Close the Relationships window by clicking the Close button that displays at the right side of the Title bar.

3. Close the **SouthwestInsurance** database file.

In the relationship established in Exercise 2, a record must first be added to the Clients table before a related record can be added to the Claims table. This is because you chose the *Enforce Referential Integrity* option at the Edit Relationships dialog box. Because you chose the two options *Cascade Update Related Fields* and *Cascade Delete Related Records*, records in the Clients table (the primary table) can be updated and/or deleted and related records in the Claims table (related table) will automatically be updated or deleted.

exercise 4

UPDATING FIELDS AND ADDING AND DELETING RECORDS IN RELATED DATABASE TABLES

1. Open the **SouthwestInsurance** database file.
2. Open the Clients table.
3. Change two client numbers in the Clients database (Access will automatically change it in the Claims table) by completing the following steps:
   a. Make sure the Clients : Table window displays in the Datasheet view.
   b. Click once in the *Client #* field for Paul Vuong containing the number *4300*.
   c. Change the number from *4300* to *4308*.
   d. Click once in the *Client #* field for Vernon Cook containing the number *7335*.
   e. Change the number from *7335* to *7325*.
   f. Click the Save button on the Table Datasheet toolbar.
   g. Close the Clients table.
   h. Open the Claims table. (Notice that the client numbers for Vernon Cook and Paul Vuong automatically changed.)
   i. Close the Claims table.
4. Open the Clients table, make sure the table displays in Datasheet view, and then add the following records at the end of the table:

Client #	=	**5508**
Client	=	**Martina Bentley**
Street Address	=	**6503 Taylor Street**
City	=	**Scottsdale**
State	=	**AZ**
ZIP Code	=	**85889**

Client #	=	**2511**
Client	=	**Keith Hammond**
Street Address	=	**21332 Janski Road**
City	=	**Glendale**
State	=	**AZ**
ZIP Code	=	**85310**

Clients : Table

Client #	Client
3120	Spenser Winters
4308	Paul Vuong
7325	Vernon Cook
9383	Elaine Hueneka

Step 3c Step 3e

Claims : Table

Claim #	Client #	License #
102394	9383	776 ERU
104366	7325	984 CWS
121039	4308	877 BNN
153001	9383	776 ERU

Step 3h

Clients : Table

Client #	Client	Street Address	City	State	Zip Code
3120	Spenser Winters	21329 132nd Street	Glendale	AZ	85310
4308	Paul Vuong	3451 South Varner	Glendale	AZ	85901
7325	Vernon Cook	22134 Cactus Drive	Phoenix	AZ	85344
9383	Elaine Hueneka	9088 Graham Road	Scottsdale	AZ	85889
5508	Martina Bentley	6503 Taylor Street	Scottsdale	AZ	85889
2511	Keith Hammond	21332 Janski Road	Glendale	AZ	85310

Step 4

5. With the Clients table still open, delete the record for Elaine Hueneka. At the message telling you that relationships that specify cascading deletes are about to cause records in this table and related tables to be deleted, click Yes.

Step 5

Delete Record

Clients : Table

	Client #	Client	Street Address	City	State	Zip Code
+	3120	Spenser Winters	21329 132nd Street	Glendale	AZ	85310
+	4308	Paul Vuong	3451 South Varner	Glendale	AZ	85901
+	7325	Vernon Cook	22134 Cactus Drive	Phoenix	AZ	85344
+	9383	Elaine Hueneka	9088 Graham Road	Scottsdale	AZ	85889
+	5508	Martina Bentley	6503 Taylor Street	Scottsdale	AZ	85889
+	2511	Keith Hammond	21332 Janski Road	Glendale	AZ	85310
*						

6. Save, print, and then close the Clients table.
7. Open the Insurance table, make sure the table displays in Datasheet view, and then add the following records at the end of the table:

License # = 422 RTW
Client # = 5508
Insurance Code = L
Uninsured Motorist = Yes

License # = 130 YWR
Client # = 5508
Insurance Code = F
Uninsured Motorist = No

License # = 795 GRT
Client # = 2511
Insurance Code = L
Uninsured Motorist = Yes

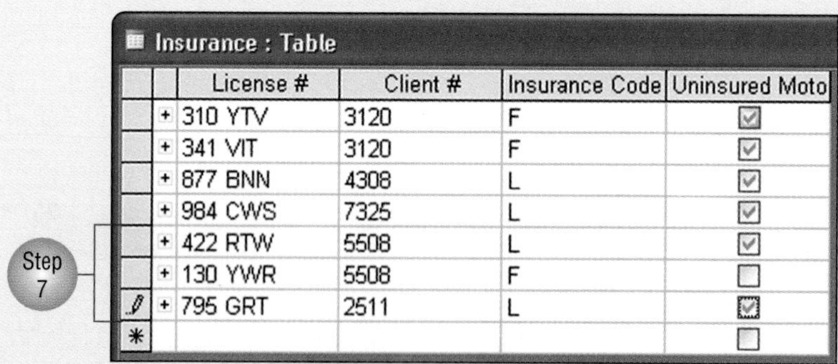

Insurance : Table

	License #	Client #	Insurance Code	Uninsured Moto
+	310 YTV	3120	F	☑
+	341 VIT	3120	F	☑
+	877 BNN	4308	L	☑
+	984 CWS	7325	L	☑
+	422 RTW	5508	L	☑
+	130 YWR	5508	F	☐
+	795 GRT	2511	L	☑
*				☐

Step 7

8. Save, print, and then close the Insurance table.

9. Open the Claims table, make sure the table displays in Datasheet view, and then add the following record:

Claim # = 130057
Client # = 2511
License # = 795 GRT
Date of Claim = 3/4/2005
Amount of Claim = $186.40

Claims : Table

Claim #	Client #	License #	Date of Claim	Amount of Claim
104366	7325	984 CWS	1/18/2005	$834.95
121039	4308	877 BNN	2/3/2005	$5,230.00
130057	2511	795 GRT	3/4/2005	$186.40
				$0.00

Step 9

10. Save and then print the Claims table.
11. With the Claims table still open, try to enter a record for a client who has not been entered in the Clients table by completing the following steps (Access will not allow this because of the one-to-many relationship that was established in Exercise 2):
    a. Add the following record to the Claims table:

    Claim # = 201221
    Client # = 5824
    License # = 640 TRS
    Date of Claim = 3/11/2005
    Amount of Claim = $895.25

    b. Click the Save button on the Table Datasheet toolbar.
    c. Click the Close button to close the Claims table. This causes a message to display telling you that the record cannot be added or changed because a related record is required in the Clients table. At this message, click OK.
    d. A message displays warning you that Access cannot save the table, that closing the object will cause the data changes you made to be lost, and asking if you want to close the database object. At this warning, click Yes.
12. Close the **SouthwestInsurance** database file.

Editing and Deleting a Relationship

Changes can be made to a relationship that has been established between database tables. The relationship can also be deleted. To edit a relationship, open the database file containing the tables with the relationship, and then click the Relationships button on the Database toolbar; or click Tools and then Relationships. This displays the Relationships window with the related database tables displayed in boxes. Position the arrow pointer on the thin portion of one of the black lines that connects the related tables and then click the *right* mouse button. This causes a shortcut menu to display. At this shortcut menu, click the left mouse button on Edit Relationship. This displays the Edit Relationships dialog box such as the one shown in Figure 2.5, where you can change the current relationship.

Edit a Relationship
1. Open database file.
2. Click Relationships button.
3. Right-click on black line connecting related tables.
4. Click Edit Relationship.
5. At Edit Relationship dialog box, make desired changes.
6. Click OK.

HINT

The Relationships window will display any relationship that has been defined between database tables.

To delete a relationship between tables, display the related tables in the Relationships window. Position the arrow pointer on the thin portion of the black line connecting the related tables, and then click the *right* mouse button. At the shortcut menu that displays, click the left mouse button on Delete. At the message asking if you are sure you want to permanently delete the selected relationship from your database, click Yes.

Displaying Related Records in a Subdatasheet

QUICK STEPS

Delete a Relationship
1. Open database file.
2. Click Relationships button.
3. Right-click on black line connecting related tables.
4. Click Delete.
5. Click Yes.

When a relationship is established between tables, you can view and edit fields in related tables with a subdatasheet. Figure 2.8 displays the Clients database table with the subdatasheet displayed for the client Spenser Winters. The subdatasheet displays the fields in the Insurance table related to Spenser Winters. Use this subdatasheet to view information and also to edit information in the Clients table a well as the Insurance table. Changes made to fields in a subdatasheet affect the table and any related table.

A plus symbol (+) displays before each record in the Clients table shown in Figure 2.8. Access automatically inserts plus symbols before each record in a table that is joined to another table by a one-to-many relationship.

FIGURE 2.8 ***Table with Subdatasheet Displayed***

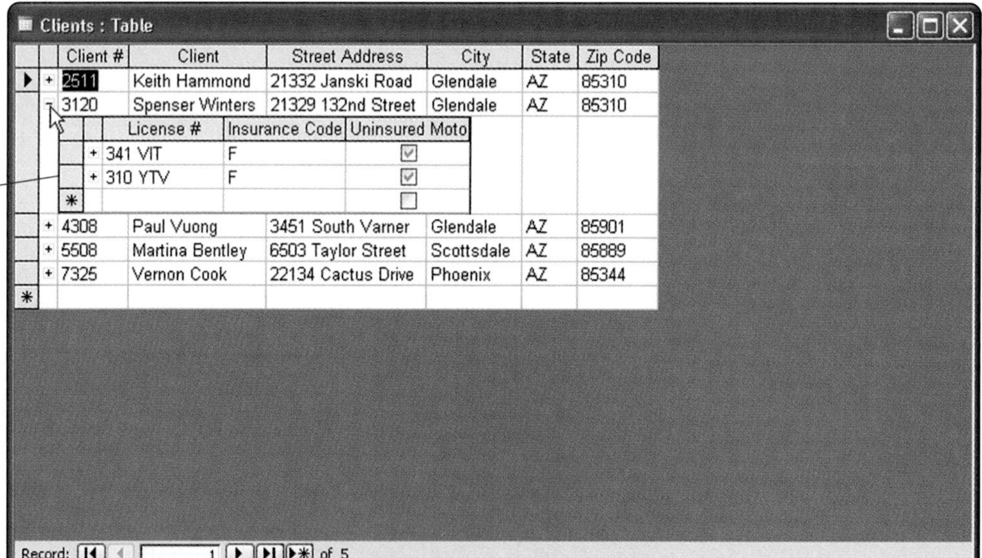

Subdatasheet
Clients : Table
Client # | Client | Street Address | City | State | Zip Code
2511 | Keith Hammond | 21332 Janski Road | Glendale | AZ | 85310
3120 | Spenser Winters | 21329 132nd Street | Glendale | AZ | 85310
License # | Insurance Code | Uninsured Moto
341 VIT | F
310 YTV | F
4308 | Paul Vuong | 3451 South Varner | Glendale | AZ | 85901
5508 | Martina Bentley | 6503 Taylor Street | Scottsdale | AZ | 85889
7325 | Vernon Cook | 22134 Cactus Drive | Phoenix | AZ | 85344
Record: 1 of 5

QUICK STEPS

Display Subdatasheet
1. Open database table in Datasheet view.
2. Click plus symbol at left of desired record.
3. At Insert Subdatasheet dialog box, click desired table.
4. Click OK.

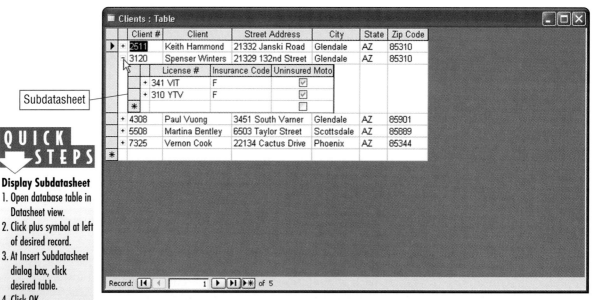

To create a subdatasheet, display the table that is the "one" in the one-to-many relationship. Click the plus symbol preceding the record for which you want to display fields in a related table. This displays the Insert Subdatasheet dialog box shown in Figure 2.9. At this dialog box, click the desired table in the list box, and then click OK. The subdatasheet is inserted below the record and contains fields from the related table. To remove the subdatasheet, click the minus sign preceding the record. (The plus symbol turns into the minus symbol when a subdatasheet displays.)

FIGURE 2.9 ***Insert Subdatasheet Dialog Box***

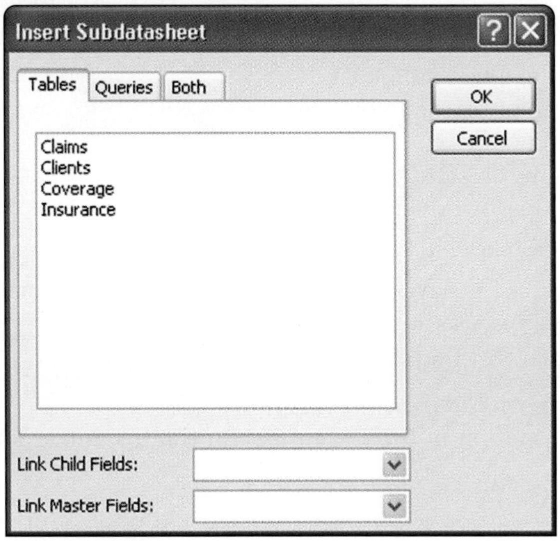
Insert Subdatasheet
Tables
Queries
Both
OK
Cancel
Claims
Clients
Coverage
Insurance
Link Child Fields:
Link Master Fields:

Specify a different subdatasheet in a table by clicking the Insert option on the Menu bar and then clicking Subdatasheet. This displays the Insert Subdatasheet dialog box shown in Figure 2.9 where you can specify the desired table.

exercise 5 VIEWING AND EDITING A SUBDATASHEET

1. Open the **SouthwestInsurance** database file.
2. Open the Clients table.
3. Display a subdatasheet with fields in the Claims table by completing the following steps:
   a. Click the plus symbol that displays at the left side of the first row (the row for Keith Hammond).
   b. At the Insert Subdatasheet dialog box, click *Claims* in the list box, and then click OK.

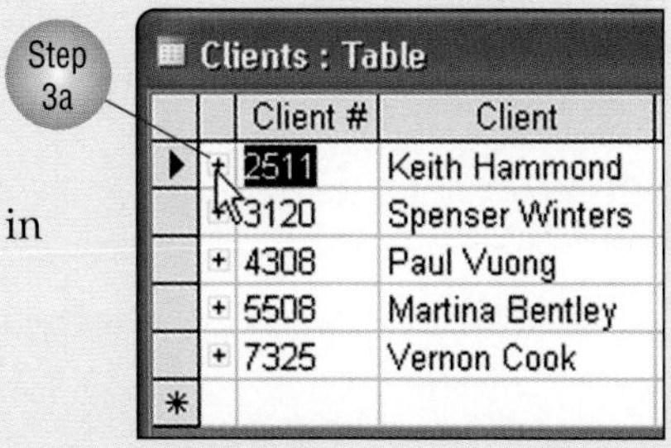
Step 3a
Clients : Table
Client #
Client
2511
Keith Hammond
3120
Spenser Winters
4308
Paul Vuong
5508
Martina Bentley
7325
Vernon Cook

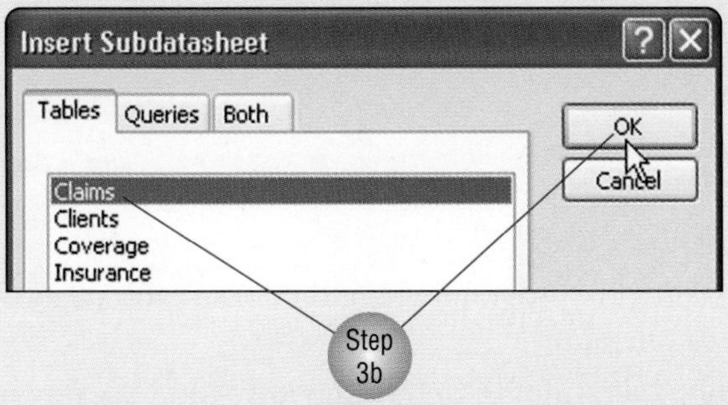
Insert Subdatasheet
Tables
Queries
Both
OK
Cancel
Claims
Clients
Coverage
Insurance
Step 3b

4. Display subdatasheets for each of the remaining records by clicking the plus symbol that displays before each of the remaining four rows.

5. Remove subdatasheets for each record by clicking the minus symbol that displays before each record.
6. Suppose that the client, Vernon Cook, has moved to a new address and purchased insurance for a new car. Display the Insurance subdatasheet and make changes to fields in the Clients table and the Insurance table by completing the following steps: 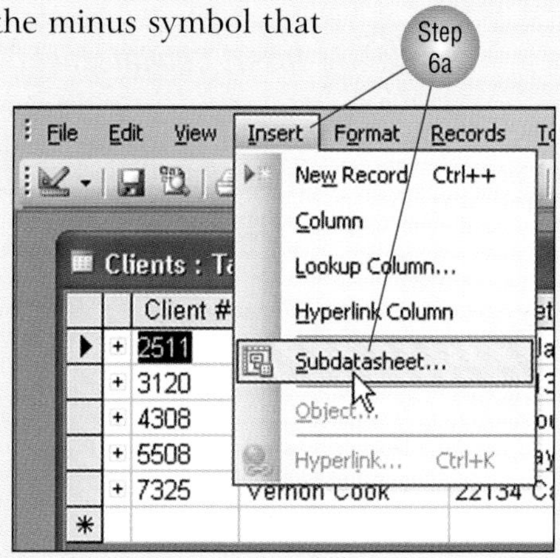
   a. Click Insert on the Menu bar, and then click Subdatasheet at the drop-down menu.
   b. At the Insert Subdatasheet dialog box, click *Insurance* in the list box, and then click OK.
   c. Click the plus symbol at the beginning of the row for Vernon Cook.
   d. Change his street address from *22135 Cactus Drive* to *1230 South Mesa*.
   e. Change his ZIP Code from *85344* to *86201*.
   f. Add the following information in the second row in the Insurance subdatasheet:

      License # = 430 DWT
      Insurance Code = F
      Uninsured Motorist = Yes

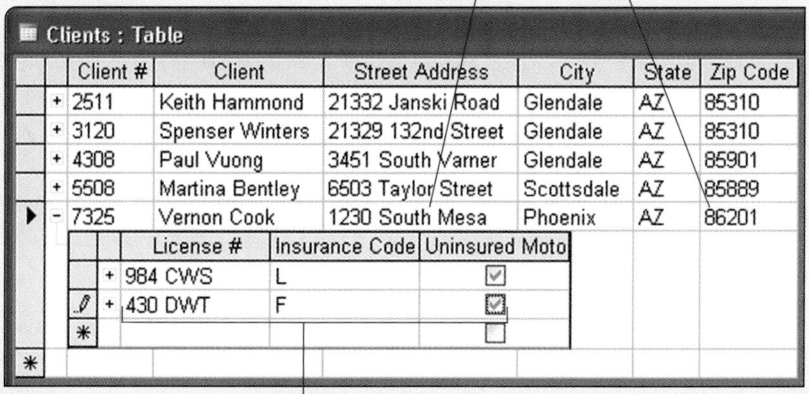

   g. Click the Save button on the Table Datasheet toolbar.
   h. Close the Clients table.
7. Open the Clients table, print it, and then close it.
8. Open the Insurance table, print it, and then close it.
9. Close the **SouthwestInsurance** database table.

	Client #	Client	Street Address	City	State	Zip Code
+	2511	Keith Hammond	21332 Janski Road	Glendale	AZ	85310
+	3120	Spenser Winters	21329 132nd Street	Glendale	AZ	85310
+	4308	Paul Vuong	3451 South Varner	Glendale	AZ	85901
+	5508	Martina Bentley	6503 Taylor Street	Scottsdale	AZ	85889
-	7325	Vernon Cook	1230 South Mesa	Phoenix	AZ	86201

	License #	Insurance Code	Uninsured Moto
+	984 CWS	L	☑
+	430 DWT	F	☑
*			☐

CHAPTER summary

- Access is a relational database software program where database tables can be created that have a relation or connection to one another.
- When planning a database table, take time to determine how to break down the required data and what relationships will need to be defined to eliminate data redundancies.
- In a database table there must be at least one field that is unique so that one record can be distinguished from another. A field with a unique value is considered a primary key.

- In a field defined as a primary key, duplicate values are not allowed in the primary field and Access also expects a value in each record in the primary key field.
- Define a primary key field with the Primary Key button on the Table Design toolbar.
- A primary key field included in another database table is referred to as a foreign key. Unlike a primary key field, a foreign key field can contain duplicate data.
- In Access, one database table can be related to another by performing a join. When database tables that have a common field are joined, data can be extracted from both tables as if they were one large table.
- A one-to-many relationship can be created between database tables in a database file. In this relationship, a record must be added to the "one" database table before it can be added to the "many" database table.
- A relationship between tables can be edited and/or deleted.
- Access contains a Print Relationships Wizard you can use to print a report displaying the relationships between tables.
- When a relationship is established between tables, you can view and edit fields in related tables with a subdatasheet.
- To display a subdatasheet, display the Insert Subdatasheet dialog box (by clicking the plus symbol at the beginning of a record or by clicking Insert and then Subdatasheet), click the desired table in the list box, and then click OK.
- Turn off the display of a subdatasheet by clicking the minus symbol at the beginning of a record.

FEATURES summary

FEATURE	BUTTON	MENU
Identify primary key		Edit, Primary Key
Relationships window		Tools, Relationships
Edit Relationships dialog box		Relationships, Edit Relationships
Show Table dialog box		Relationships, Show Table
Print database relationships		File, Print Relationships, Print
Insert Subdatasheet dialog box		Insert, Subdatasheet

CONCEPTS check

Completion: On a blank sheet of paper, indicate the correct term, symbol, or character for each description.

1. A primary key field must contain unique data while this type of key field can contain duplicate data.
2. In Access, one database can be related to another, which is generally referred to as performing this.
3. In a one-to-many relationship, the table containing the "one" is referred to as this.
4. In a one-to-many relationship, the table containing the "many" is referred to as this.
5. In a one-to-many relationship, Access follows a set of rules that enforces consistency between related tables and is referred to as this.
6. In related tables, this number displays near the black line next to the primary table.
7. In related tables, this symbol displays near the black line next to the related table.
8. The black line that connects related tables is referred to as this.
9. Click this symbol at the beginning of a record in a related table to display the Insert Subdatasheet dialog box.
10. Turn off the display of a subdatasheet by clicking this symbol that displays at the beginning of the record.
11. Suppose you have created a database table named Committees within the database file named Members. The Committees table contains a field named *Member #* that you decide should be identified as the primary key field. List the steps you would complete to identify *Member #* as the primary key field (you are beginning at a blank Access screen).
12. List the steps you would complete to create a one-to-many relationship between the Member Information table and the Committees table in the Members database file. The primary key field in the Member Information table is *Member #*. (You are beginning at the Members : Database window.)

SKILLS check

Assessment 1

1. Use Access to create a database for keeping track of books. Name the database file **Books**. Name the first database table you create Author Information and include the following fields in the table (you determine the data type, field size, and description):

    Field Name
    Author # (primary key)
    First Name
    Last Name
    Middle Initial

2. After creating the database table with the fields shown above and defining the primary key, save the table. Switch to Datasheet view and then enter the following data in the table:

Author # = 1
First Name = Branson
Last Name = Walters
Middle Initial = A.

Author # = 2
First Name = Christiana
Last Name = Copeland
Middle Initial = M.

Author # = 3
First Name = Shirley
Last Name = Romero
Middle Initial = E.

Author # = 4
First Name = Jeffrey
Last Name = Fiedler
Middle Initial = R.

3. Automatically adjust the width of columns.
4. Save, print, and then close the Author Information table.
5. At the **Books** database file, create another table with book information with the following fields (you determine the data type, field size, and description):

    Field Name
    ISBN (primary key)
    Author #
    Title
    Category Code
    Price

6. After creating the database table with the fields shown above and defining the primary key, save the table and name it Book Information. Switch to Datasheet view and then enter the following data in the table:

ISBN = 12-6543-9008-7
Author # = 4
Title = Today's Telecommunications
Category Code = B
Price = $34.95

ISBN = 09-5225-5466-6
Author # = 2
Title = Marketing in the Global Economy
Category Code = M
Price = $42.50

ISBN = 23-9822-7645-0
Author # = 1
Title = International Business Strategies
Category Code = B
Price = $45.00

ISBN = 08-4351-4890-3
Author # = 3
Title = Technological Advances
Category Code = B
Price = $36.95

7. Automatically adjust the width of columns (to accommodate the longest entry).
8. Save, print, and then close the Book Information table.
9. At the **Books** database file, create another table with category information with the following fields (you determine the data type, field size, and description):

Field Name
Category Code (primary key)
Category

10. After creating the database table with the fields shown above and defining the primary key, save the table and name it Category. Switch to Datasheet view and then enter the following data in the table:

Category Code = B
Category = Business

Category Code = M
Category = Marketing

11. Save, print, and then close the Category table.
12. Close the **Books** database file.

Assessment 2

1. Open the **Books** database file and then create the following relationships:
   a. Create a one-to-many relationship with the *Author #* field in the Author Information table the "one" and the *Author #* field in the Book Information table the "many." (At the Edit Relationships dialog box, choose *Enforce Referential Integrity*, *Cascade Update Related Fields*, and *Cascade Delete Related Records*.)
   b. Create a one-to-many relationship with the *Category Code* field in the Category table the "one" and the *Category Code* field in the Book Information table the "many." (At the Edit Relationships dialog box, choose *Enforce Referential Integrity*, *Cascade Update Related Fields*, and *Cascade Delete Related Records*.)
2. Print the relationships.
3. After creating, saving, and printing the relationships, add the following record to the Author Information table:

Author # = 5
First Name = Glenna
Last Name = Zener-Young
Middle Initial = A.

4. Adjust the column width for the *Last Name* field.
5. Save, print, and then close the Author Information table.
6. Add the following records to the Book Information table:

ISBN # = 23-8931-0084-7
Author # = 2
Title = Practical Marketing Strategies
Category = M
Price = $28.50

ISBN #	=	87-4009-7134-6
Author #	=	5
Title	=	Selling More
Category	=	M
Price	=	$40.25

7. Save, print, and then close the Book Information table.
8. Close the **Books** database file.

CHAPTER challenge

You are the librarian at Lacy's Literacy Center. To help maintain accurate records of the books and members, you decide to create a database named **Lacy'sLiteracyCenter**. The database will include two tables: one for book information (name of book, type of book, date checked out, etc.) and one for member information (member number, name, address, phone number, etc.). Include at least five fields for each table. Determine the appropriate data types and primary and foreign keys for each of the tables. Create a relationship between the two tables. Add two records to each of the tables.

Since many records will be added to each of the tables, creating a form will allow for easier and quicker data entry. Use the Help feature to learn how to create a form using the wizard. Use the member table in the database created in the first part of the Chapter Challenge to create a form that includes all of the fields in that table. Save the form as Member Form. Add three more records (members) using the Member Form.

In Word, create a short letter that will be sent to members informing them of the book signing that will take place next month. Use the members in the member table created in the first part of the Chapter Challenge and merge them with the letter created in Word. Save the main document as **BookSigning**. Merge and then print only one letter.

CHAPTER 3

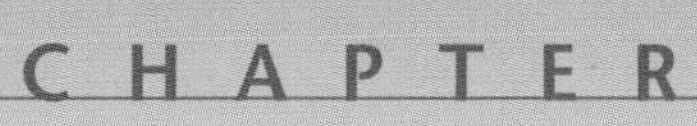

USING WIZARDS AND HELP

PERFORMANCE OBJECTIVES

Upon successful completion of Chapter 3, you will be able to:

- **Create a database table using the Table Wizard**
- **Complete a spelling check on data in a table**
- **Find specific records in a table**
- **Find specific data in a table and replace with other data**
- **Back up a database file**
- **Compact and repair a database file**
- **Use the Help feature**

ACCESS

Access, like other programs in the Microsoft Office suite, contains a variety of wizards you can use to design and create database tables, reports, forms, and so on. In this chapter, you will learn how to use the Table Wizard to prepare a database table. Access contains a spelling check feature as well as a find and replace feature. Use the spelling checker to find misspelled words in a table, and use the find and replace feature to find specific records in a table or find specific data in a table and replace with other data. As you continue working with a database file, consider compacting and repairing the file to optimize performance and back up the file to protect your data from accidental loss or hardware failure. Microsoft Office contains an on-screen reference manual containing information on features and commands for each program within the suite. In this chapter, you will learn to use the Help feature to display information about Access.

Creating a Database Table Using the Table Wizard

HINT

Before using the Table Wizard, you must create the database file into which you will save the table.

Access contains a Table Wizard you can use to design a database table. The wizard helps you design a table by offering possible field choices with data types already assigned. If the Table Wizard does not offer the exact field name you require, you can edit a field name to personalize it.

HINT

Choose the table that most closely matches the type of data you are managing.

HINT

Each field offered by the Table Wizard has the appropriate data type assigned to it.

To use the Table Wizard, create a new database file. At the new database window, double-click the *Create table by using wizard* option in the list box. This displays the first Table Wizard dialog box shown in Figure 3.1. At this window, specify whether the table is designed for a business or personal use, choose a sample table from the *Sample Tables* list box, and choose the desired fields.

At the second Table Wizard dialog box, shown in Figure 3.2, type a name for the table and then specify if you want the wizard to set the primary key or if you want to set it. At the third Table Wizard dialog box, shown in Figure 3.3, specify what you want to do after the wizard creates the table—modify the table design, enter data directly into the table, or enter data into the table using a form the wizard creates.

FIGURE 3.1 ***First Table Wizard Dialog Box***

FIGURE 3.2 ***Second Table Wizard Dialog Box***

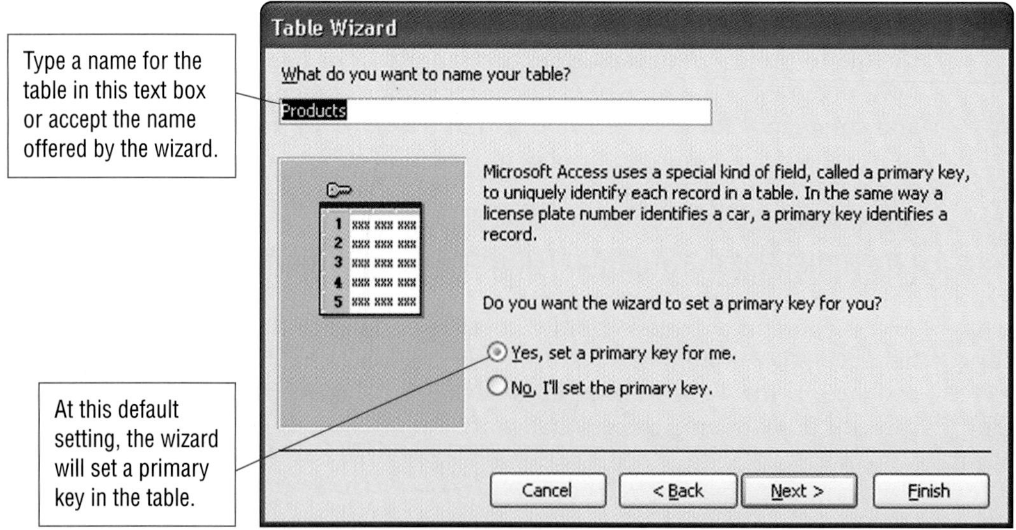

FIGURE

3.3 Third Table Wizard Dialog Box

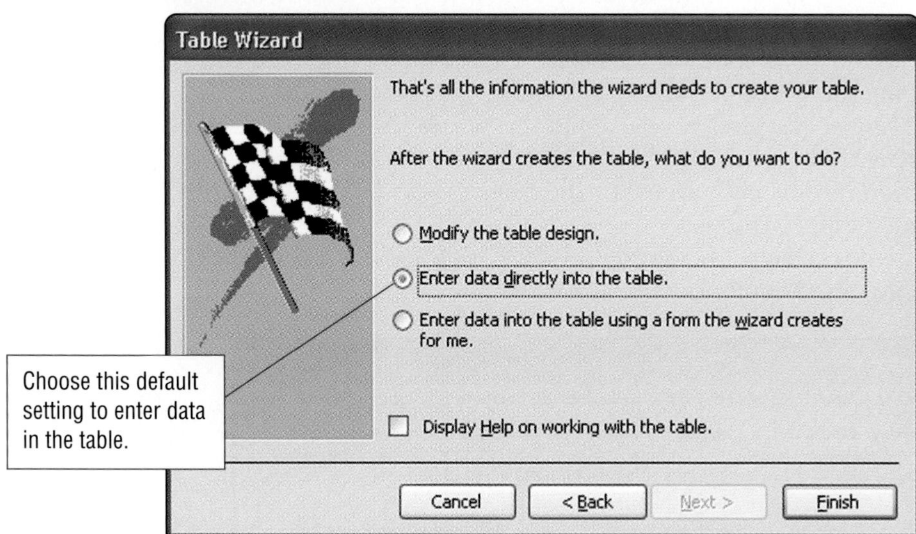
Table Wizard
That's all the information the wizard needs to create your table.
After the wizard creates the table, what do you want to do?
Modify the table design.
Enter data directly into the table.
Enter data into the table using a form the wizard creates for me.
Display Help on working with the table.
Cancel
< Back
Next >
Finish
Choose this default setting to enter data in the table.

QUICK STEPS

Create a Table Using the Table Wizard

1. At blank screen, click New button.
2. Click Blank database hyperlink.
3. Type database file name.
4. Press Enter.
5. Double-click *Create table by using wizard.*
6. Click desired sample table.
7. Insert desired fields in *Fields in my new table* list box.
8. Click Next button.
9. At second wizard dialog box, click Next.
10. At third wizard dialog box, click Finish.
11. Enter data into fields in table.

exercise 1

USING A TABLE WIZARD TO CREATE A DATABASE FILE

1. Create a database table for information on products used in MedSafe Clinic by completing the following steps:
   a. Start at the blank Access window and then click the New button on the Database toolbar or click File and then New. (This displays the New File task pane.)
   b. At the New File task pane, click the Blank database hyperlink.
   c. At the File New Database dialog box, make sure the proper drive is selected, type **MedSafeClinic** in the *File name* text box, and then press Enter or click the Create button.
   d. At the MedSafeClinic : Database window, double-click *Create table by using wizard* in the list box.

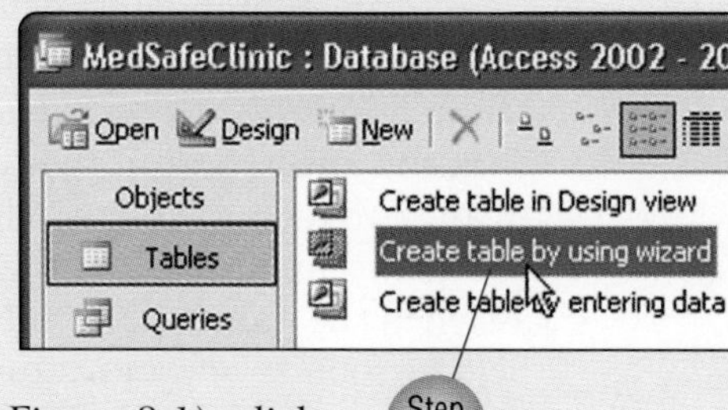
MedSafeClinic : Database (Access 2002 - 20
Open
Design
New
Objects
Tables
Queries
Create table in Design view
Create table by using wizard
Create table by entering data
Step 1d

   e. At the first Table Wizard dialog box (refer to Figure 3.1), click *Products* in the *Sample Tables* list box. (This changes the fields in the *Sample Fields* list box.)
   f. Choose some of the sample fields in the *Sample Fields* list box and add them to the *Fields in my new table* list box by completing the following steps:
      1) With *ProductID* already selected in the *Sample Fields* list box, click the button containing the greater than symbol (>) that displays between the *Sample Fields* list box and the *Fields in my new table* list box. (This inserts *ProductID* in the *Fields in my new table* list box and also selects *ProductName* in the *Sample Fields* list box.)

2) With *ProductName* selected in the *Sample Fields* list box, click the button containing the > symbol. (This adds *ProductName* to the *Fields in my new table* list box.)
3) Click once on *SupplierID* in the *Sample Fields* list box, and then click the button containing the > symbol.
4) Click once on *UnitsInStock* in the *Sample Fields* list box, and then click the button containing the > symbol.
5) With *UnitsOnOrder* already selected in the *Sample Fields* list box, click the button containing the > symbol.
6) With *UnitPrice* already selected in the *Sample Fields* list box, click the button containing the > symbol.
7) With *ReorderLevel* already selected in the *Sample Fields* list box, click the button containing the > symbol.

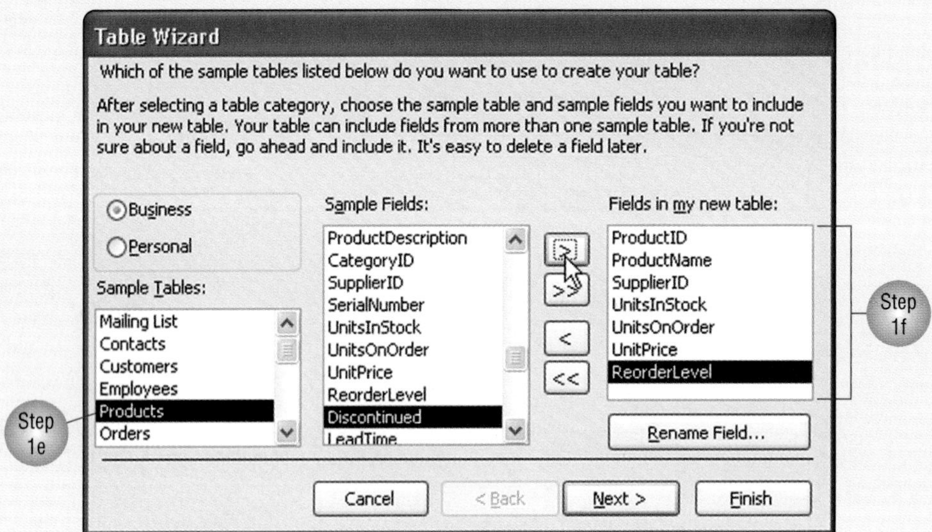

g. Click the Next button located at the bottom of the dialog box.
h. At the second Table Wizard dialog box (refer to Figure 3.2), the wizard offers the name *Products* for the table name and also will set a primary key for the table. These choices are appropriate so click the Next button at the bottom of the dialog box.
i. At the third Table Wizard dialog box (refer to Figure 3.3), the wizard has already selected *Enter data directly into the table*. This is appropriate for this exercise, so click the Finish button that displays at the bottom right corner of the dialog box.
j. At the Products : Table window shown in Figure 3.4, notice that *AutoNumber* automatically displays in the *Product ID* field. This is because the Table Wizard assigned the data type AutoNumber to the field. (Access will insert a *1* in this field as soon as you move to the second field in the *Product ID* field.) Press Tab to move the insertion point to the next field *(Product Name)*.
k. Type the following in the specified fields (do not type anything in the *Product ID* field; simply press the Tab key and let Access insert the number):

Product Name = Latex gloves
Supplier ID = 3
Units In Stock = 243
Units On Order = 0
Unit Price = 0.50
Reorder Level = 200

Product Name = Syringes
Supplier ID = 1
Units In Stock = 58
Units On Order = 75
Unit Price = 0.35
Reorder Level = 75

Product Name = 1-inch gauze pads
Supplier ID = 4
Units In Stock = 144
Units On Order = 0
Unit Price = 0.05
Reorder Level = 125

Product Name = Tongue depressors
Supplier ID = 1
Units In Stock = 85
Units On Order = 100
Unit Price = 0.03
Reorder Level = 100

Products : Table

Product ID	Product Name	Supplier ID	Units In Stock	Units On Order	Unit Price	Reorder Level
1	Latex gloves	3	243	0	$0.50	200
2	Syringes	1	58	75	$0.35	75
3	1-inch gauze pa	4	144	0	$0.05	125
4	Tongue depress	1	85	100	$0.03	100
(AutoNumber)						

l. Automatically adjust the column widths for all columns containing data.
m. After entering the data and adjusting the column widths, click the Save button on the Table Datasheet toolbar.

2. Change the page orientation to landscape, and then print the Products table.
3. Close the Products table.
4. Close the **MedSafeClinic** database file.

FIGURE 3.4 ***Products : Table Window***

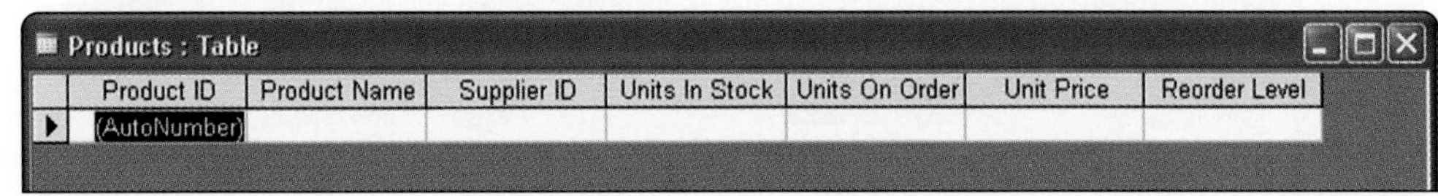

Products : Table

Product ID	Product Name	Supplier ID	Units In Stock	Units On Order	Unit Price	Reorder Level
(AutoNumber)						

In Exercise 1, Step 1f, you added fields to the *Fields in my new table* list box by selecting the desired field in the *Sample Fields* list box and then clicking the button containing the greater than symbol (>). Other buttons display by the button containing the greater than symbol. Click the button containing two greater than symbols (>>) and all fields in the *Sample Fields* list box are inserted in the *Fields in my new table* list box. If you want to remove a field from the *Fields in my new table* list box, select the field, and then click the button containing the less than symbol (<). Click the button containing two less than symbols (<<) to remove all fields from the *Fields in my new table* list box.

HINT

Rename a field by clicking the field in the *Fields in my new table* list box, clicking the Rename Field button, typing the new name, and then clicking OK.

The MedSafeClinic database file created in Exercise 1 contains only one table. Use the Table Wizard to create other tables within the same database file. In Exercise 2, you will use the Table Wizard to create a table containing information about suppliers used by MedSafeClinic.

When a second or subsequent table is created in a database file using the Table Wizard, a relationship can be created between database tables. In Exercise 2, you will be creating a one-to-many relationship using the Table Wizard. The Suppliers table you create in Exercise 2 will be identified as the "one" and the Products table you created in Exercise 1 will be identified as the "many."

exercise 2

CREATING ANOTHER TABLE AND RELATING TABLES USING THE TABLE WIZARD

1. Create a database table for suppliers used by MedSafeClinic by completing the following steps:
   a. At the blank Access window, click the Open button on the Database toolbar; or click File and then Open.
   b. At the Open dialog box, double-click ***MedSafeClinic*** in the list box.
   c. At the MedSafeClinic : Database window, double-click *Create table by using wizard* in the list box.
   d. At the first Table Wizard dialog box (refer to Figure 3.1), click *Suppliers* in the *Sample Tables* list box. (You will need to scroll down the list.)
   e. Add the following fields in the *Sample Fields* list box to the *Fields in my new table* list box (for help, refer to Exercise 1, Step 1f):

      SupplierID
      SupplierName
      Address
      City
      StateOrProvince
      PostalCode ***(Note: This is in a different order than shown in the*** **Sample Fields** ***list box.)***
      PhoneNumber
      EmailAddress

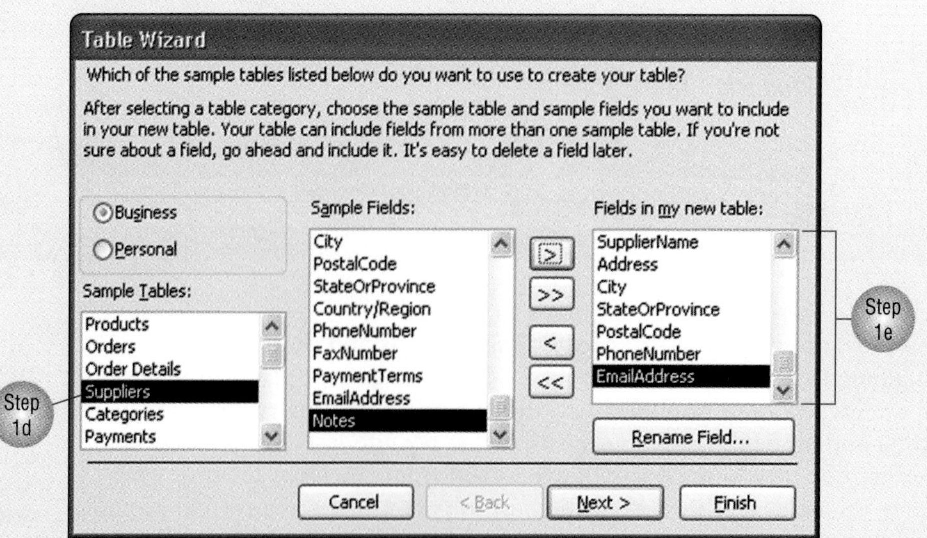

f. After inserting the fields above in the *Fields in my new table* list box, click the Next button located at the bottom of the dialog box.

g. At the second Table Wizard dialog box, the wizard offers the name *Suppliers* for the database table name and also will set a primary key for the table. These choices are appropriate so click the Next button at the bottom of the dialog box.

h. At the third Table Wizard dialog box shown in Figure 3.5, create a one-to-many relationship between Suppliers (the "one") and Products (the "many") by completing the following steps:

    1) Click the Relationships button that displays toward the bottom right side of the dialog box.

    2) At the Relationships dialog box shown in Figure 3.6, click the option button that displays before the *One record in the 'Suppliers' table will match many records in the 'Products' table* option.

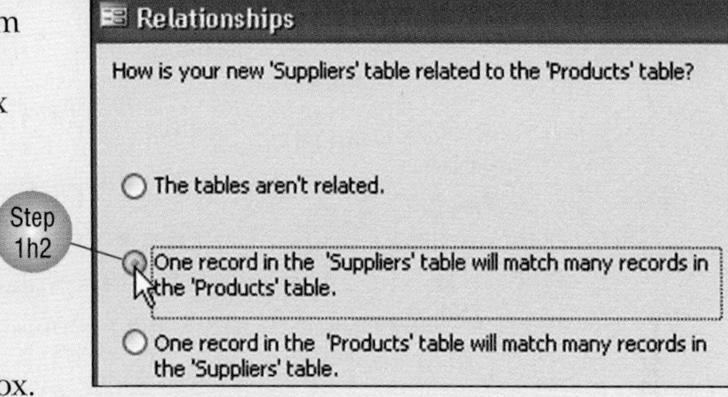
Relationships
How is your new 'Suppliers' table related to the 'Products' table?
The tables aren't related.
Step 1h2
One record in the 'Suppliers' table will match many records in the 'Products' table.
One record in the 'Products' table will match many records in the 'Suppliers' table.

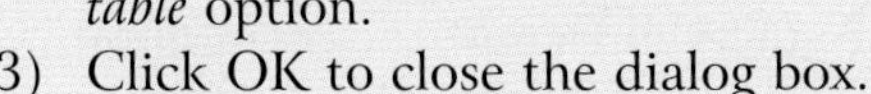

    3) Click OK to close the dialog box.

i. At the Table Wizard dialog box, click Next.

j. At the Table Wizard dialog box telling you that the wizard has all of the information it needs to create the table, make sure *Enter data directly into the table* is selected, and then click Finish.

k. At the Suppliers : Table window, type the following in the specified fields (the table wizard will automatically insert a number in the *Supplier ID* field):

Supplier Name	=	Robicheaux Suppliers
Address	=	3200 Linden Drive
City	=	Baton Rouge
State/Province	=	LA
Postal Code	=	70552
Phone Number	=	(318) 555-3411
E-mail Address	=	robi@emcp.net

Supplier Name	=	Quality Medical Supplies
Address	=	211 South Fourth Avenue
City	=	Tampa
State/Province	=	FL
Postal Code	=	33562
Phone Number	=	(813) 555-8900
E-mail Address	=	qms@emcp.net

Supplier Name	=	Peachtree Medical Supplies
Address	=	764 Harmon Way
City	=	Atlanta
State/Province	=	GA
Postal Code	=	73780
Phone Number	=	(404) 555-6474
E-mail Address	=	peachmed@emcp.net

Supplier Name	=	Lafferty Company
Address	=	12031 Ruston Way
City	=	Atlanta
State/Province	=	GA
Postal Code	=	73125
Phone Number	=	(404) 555-8225
E-mail Address	=	lafferty@emcp.net

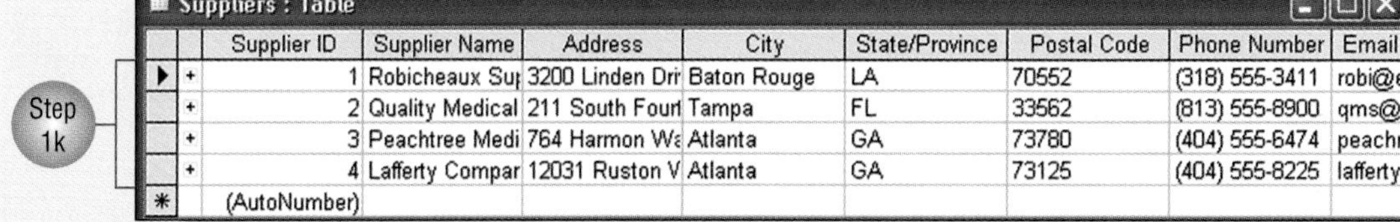

Supplier ID	Supplier Name	Address	City	State/Province	Postal Code	Phone Number	Email
1	Robicheaux Su	3200 Linden Dri	Baton Rouge	LA	70552	(318) 555-3411	robi@e
2	Quality Medical	211 South Fourt	Tampa	FL	33562	(813) 555-8900	qms@
3	Peachtree Medi	764 Harmon Wa	Atlanta	GA	73780	(404) 555-6474	peachr
4	Lafferty Compar	12031 Ruston V	Atlanta	GA	73125	(404) 555-8225	laffertyı
(AutoNumber)							

l. Automatically adjust the column widths for all columns containing data.
m. Click the Save button on the Table Datasheet toolbar to save the Suppliers table.

2. Change the page orientation to landscape, change the left and right margins to .3 inch, and then print the Suppliers table. (Make sure you change the orientation before changing the margins.)
3. Close the Suppliers table.
4. Close the **MedSafeClinic** database file.

FIGURE 3.5 ***Third Table Wizard Dialog Box***

Table Wizard

Is your new table related to any other tables in your database? Related tables have matching records. Usually, your new table is related to at least one other table in the current database.

In some cases, the wizard will create table relationships for you. The list below shows how your new table is related to existing tables. To change how a table is related, select a table in the list and click Relationships.

My new 'Suppliers' table is ...

not related to 'Products'

Relationships...

Cancel | < Back | Next > | Finish

Click this button to display the Relationships dialog box.

FIGURE

3.6 *Relationships Dialog Box*

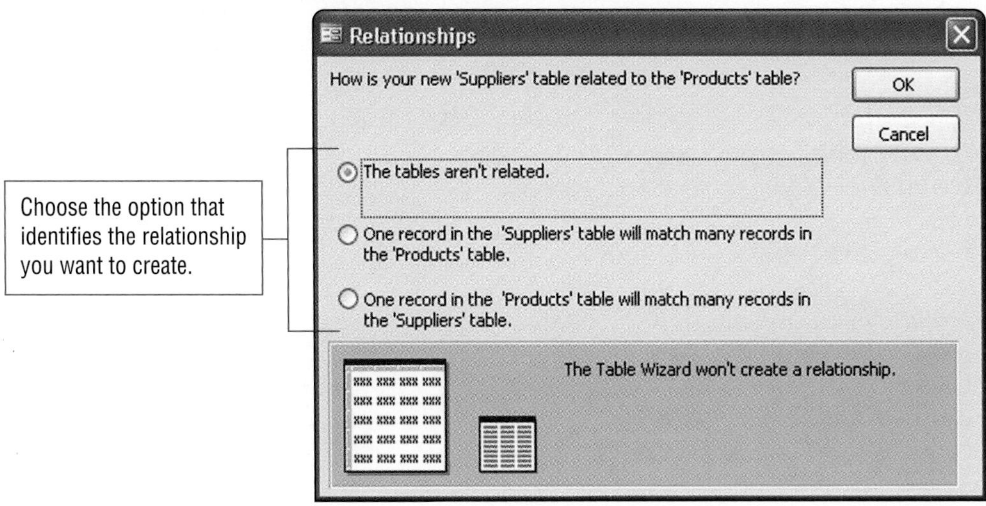
Choose the option that identifies the relationship you want to create.
Relationships
How is your new 'Suppliers' table related to the 'Products' table?
OK
Cancel
The tables aren't related.
One record in the 'Suppliers' table will match many records in the 'Products' table.
One record in the 'Products' table will match many records in the 'Suppliers' table.
The Table Wizard won't create a relationship.

In Exercise 2, a one-to-many relationship was created between the Suppliers and Products database tables. In this relationship, a record for a supplier must first be created in the Suppliers table before the supplier number can be used in a record in the Products table. In Exercise 3, you will add a new supplier to the Suppliers table and then use that supplier in a record in the Products table.

exercise 3

ADDING RECORDS TO THE SUPPLIERS AND PRODUCTS DATABASE TABLES

1. Open the **MedSafeClinic** database file.
2. Open the Suppliers table.
3. With Suppliers open in Datasheet view, add the following record at the end of the table:

Supplier Name	=	National Products
Address	=	2192 Second Street
City	=	Little Rock
State/Province	=	AR
Postal Code	=	72203
Phone Number	=	(501) 555-0551
E-mail Address	=	natprod@emcp.net

Suppliers : Table

Supplier ID	Supplier Name	Address	City	State/Province	Postal Code	Phone
1	Robicheaux Suppliers	3200 Linden Drive	Baton Rouge	LA	70552	(318) 5
2	Quality Medical Supplies	211 South Fourth Avenue	Tampa	FL	33562	(813) 5
3	Peachtree Medical Supplies	764 Harmon Way	Atlanta	GA	73780	(404) 5
4	Lafferty Company	12031 Ruston Way	Atlanta	GA	73125	(404) 5
5	National Products	2192 Second Street	Little Rock	AR	72203	(501) 5
utoNumber)						

Step 3

4. Save the Suppliers table.

5. Change the page orientation to landscape, change the left and right margins to .3 inch, and then print the Suppliers table. (Make sure you change the orientation before changing the margins.)
6. Close the Suppliers table.
7. Open the Products table and then add the following records at the end of the table:

Product Name	=	Cotton swabs
Supplier ID	=	5
Units In Stock	=	1345
Units On Order	=	1000
Unit Price	=	0.03
Reorder Level	=	1500

Product Name	=	Thermometer covers
Supplier ID	=	2
Units In Stock	=	414
Units On Order	=	250
Unit Price	=	0.02
Reorder Level	=	450

8. Delete the record for tongue depressors.

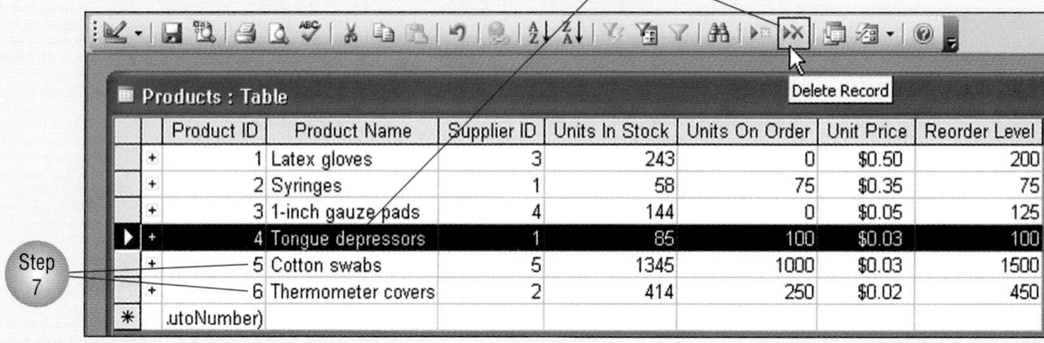

Product ID	Product Name	Supplier ID	Units In Stock	Units On Order	Unit Price	Reorder Level
1	Latex gloves	3	243	0	$0.50	200
2	Syringes	1	58	75	$0.35	75
3	1-inch gauze pads	4	144	0	$0.05	125
4	Tongue depressors	1	85	100	$0.03	100
5	Cotton swabs	5	1345	1000	$0.03	1500
6	Thermometer covers	2	414	250	$0.02	450
utoNumber)						

9. Adjust the column width for *Product Name*.
10. Save the Products table.
11. Change the page orientation to landscape and then print the Products table.
12. Close the Products table.
13. Close the **MedSafeClinic** database file.

Completing a Spelling Check

HINT

You can also begin spell checking by clicking Tools and then Spelling or by pressing F7.

The spelling checker feature in Access finds misspelled words and offers replacement words. It also finds duplicate words and irregular capitalizations. When you spell check an object in a database file such as a table, the spelling checker compares the words in your table with the words in its dictionary. If a match is found, the word is passed over. If no match is found for the word, the spelling checker selects the word and offers replacement suggestions.

Spelling

To complete a spelling check, open the desired database table in Datasheet view, and then click the Spelling button on the Table Datasheet toolbar. If the spelling checker does not find a match for a word in your table, the Spelling dialog box displays with replacement options. Figure 3.7 displays the Spelling dialog box with the word *Montain* selected and possible replacements displayed in the *Suggestions* list box. At the Spelling dialog box, you can choose to ignore the word (for example, if the spelling checker has selected a proper name), change to one of the replacement options, or add the word to the dictionary or AutoCorrect feature. You can also complete a spelling check on other objects in a database file such as a query, form, or report. (You will learn about these objects in future chapters.)

QUICK STEPS

Complete a Spelling Check
1. Open database table in Datasheet view.
2. Click Spelling button.
3. Change or ignore spelling as needed.
4. Click OK.

FIGURE 3.7 ***Spelling Dialog Box***

The spelling checker selects this word in the table and offers this selection.

Finding and Replacing Data

If you need to find a specific entry in a field in a database table, consider using options at the Find and Replace dialog box with the Find tab selected as shown in Figure 3.8. Display this dialog box by clicking the Find button on the Table Datasheet toolbar or by clicking Edit and then Find. At the Find and Replace dialog box, enter the data for which you are searching in the *Find What* text box. By default, Access will look in the specific column where the insertion point is positioned. Click the Find Next button to find the next occurrence of the data or click the Cancel button to remove the Find and Replace dialog box.

QUICK STEPS

Find Data
1. Open database table in Datasheet view.
2. Click Find button.
3. Type data in *Find What* text box.
4. Click Find Next button.
5. Continue clicking Find Next button until entire table is searched.

Find

FIGURE 3.8 ***Find and Replace Dialog Box with Find Tab Selected***

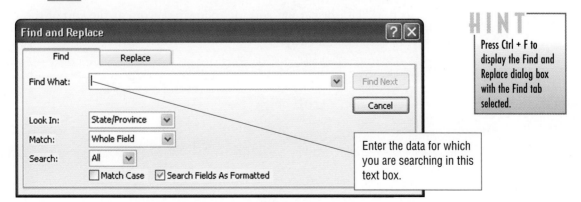

Find and Replace
Find | Replace
Find What:
Find Next
Cancel
Look In: State/Province
Match: Whole Field
Search: All
Match Case
Search Fields As Formatted

Enter the data for which you are searching in this text box.

HINT
Press Ctrl + F to display the Find and Replace dialog box with the Find tab selected.

Find and Replace Data

1. Open database table in Datasheet view.
2. Click Edit, Replace.
3. Type find data in *Find What* text box.
4. Type replace data in *Replace With* text box.
5. Click Find Next button.
6. Click Replace button or Find Next button.

The *Look In* option defaults to the column where the insertion point is positioned. You can choose to look in the entire table by clicking the down-pointing arrow at the right side of the option and then clicking the table name at the drop-down list. The *Match* option has a default setting of *Whole Field*. You can change this to *Any Part of Field* or *Start of Field*. The *Search* option has a default setting of *All*, which means that Access will search all data in a specific column. This can be changed to *Up* or *Down*. If you want to find data that contains specific uppercase and lowercase letters, insert a check mark in the *Match Case* check box. By default, Access will search fields as they are formatted.

You can use the Find and Replace dialog box with the Replace tab selected as shown in Figure 3.9 to search for specific data and replace with other data. Display this dialog box by clicking the Find button on the Table Datasheet toolbar and then clicking the Replace tab. Or you can display this dialog box by clicking Edit and then Replace.

FIGURE 3.9 **Find and Replace Dialog Box with Replace Tab Selected**

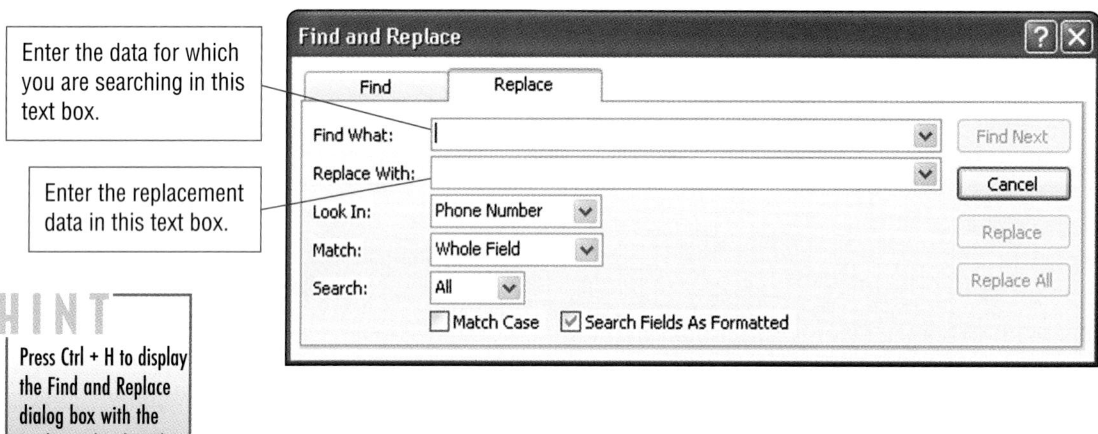

HINT

Press Ctrl + H to display the Find and Replace dialog box with the Replace tab selected.

exercise 4

CHECKING THE SPELLING AND FINDING SPECIFIC DATA

1. Open the **MedSafeClinic** database file.
2. Open the Suppliers table.
3. With Suppliers open in Datasheet view, add the following record at the end of the table. (Type the misspelled words as shown below. You will correct the spelling in a later step.)

Supplier Name	=	Blue Montain Supplies
Address	=	9550 Unaversity Avenue
City	=	Little Rock
State/Province	=	AR
Postal Code	=	72209
Phone Number	=	(501) 555-4400
E-mail Address	=	bluemtn@emcp.net

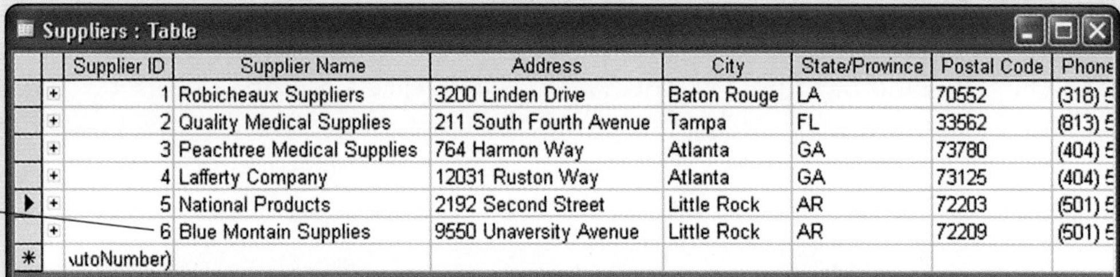

Supplier ID	Supplier Name	Address	City	State/Province	Postal Code	Phone
1	Robicheaux Suppliers	3200 Linden Drive	Baton Rouge	LA	70552	(318) 5
2	Quality Medical Supplies	211 South Fourth Avenue	Tampa	FL	33562	(813) 5
3	Peachtree Medical Supplies	764 Harmon Way	Atlanta	GA	73780	(404) 5
4	Lafferty Company	12031 Ruston Way	Atlanta	GA	73125	(404) 5
5	National Products	2192 Second Street	Little Rock	AR	72203	(501) 5
6	Blue Montain Supplies	9550 Unaversity Avenue	Little Rock	AR	72209	(501) 5
utoNumber)						

4. Save the Suppliers table.
5. Complete a spelling check on the table by completing the following steps:
   a. With the Suppliers table open in Datasheet view, click in the first entry in the *SupplierID* column.
   b. Click the Spelling button on the Table Datasheet toolbar.
   c. The spelling checker selects the name *Robicheaux*. This is a proper name, so click the Ignore button to tell the spelling checker to leave the name as written.

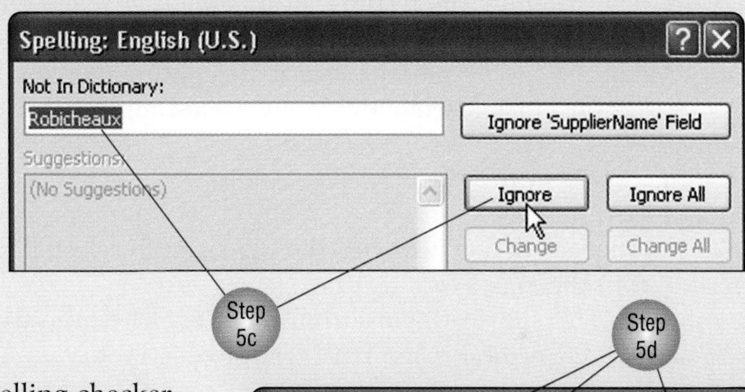

   d. The spelling checker selects *Montain*. The proper spelling *(Mountain)* is selected in the *Suggestions* list box, so click the Change button.
   e. The spelling checker selects *Unaversity*. The proper spelling *(University)* is selected in the *Suggestions* list box, so click the Change button.
   f. At the message telling you that the spelling check is complete, click the OK button.
6. Find any records containing the two-letter state abbreviation *GA* by completing the following steps:
   a. Click in the first entry in the *State/Province* column.
   b. Click the Find button on the Table Datasheet toolbar.

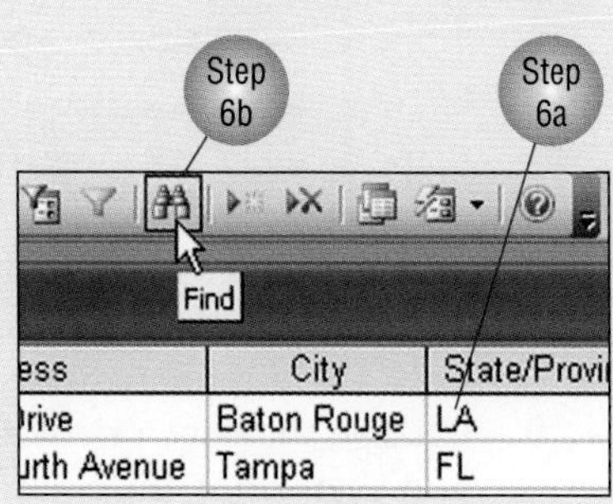

c. At the Find and Replace dialog box with the Find tab selected, type **GA** in the *Find What* text box.
d. Click the Find Next button. (Access finds and selects the first occurrence of *GA*. If the Find and Replace dialog box covers the data, drag the dialog box to a different location on the screen.)

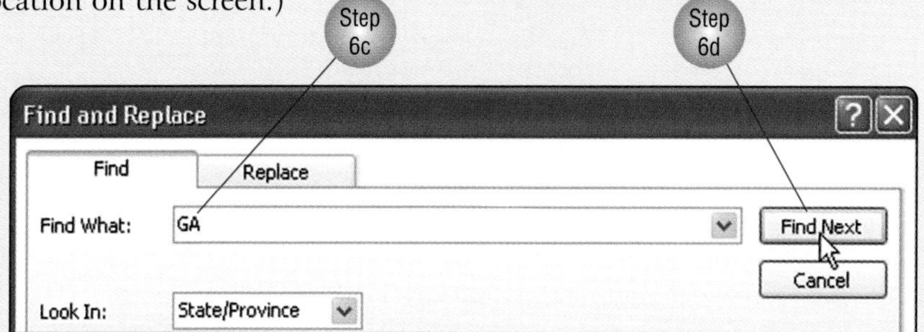

e. Continue clicking the Find What button until a message displays telling you that Access has finished searching the records. At this message, click OK.
f. Click the Cancel button to close the Find and Replace dialog box.

7. Suppose Quality Medical Supplies has changed its telephone number. Complete the following steps to find the current telephone number and replace it with the new telephone number:
   a. Click in the first entry in the *Phone Number* column.
   b. Click Edit and then Replace.
   c. At the Find and Replace dialog box with the Replace tab selected, type **(813) 555-8900** in the *Find What* text box.
   d. Press the Tab key. (This moves the insertion point to the *Replace With* text box.)
   e. Type **(863) 555-2255** in the *Replace With* text box.
   f. Click the Find Next button.
   g. When Access selects the telephone number *(813) 555-8900*, click the Replace button.

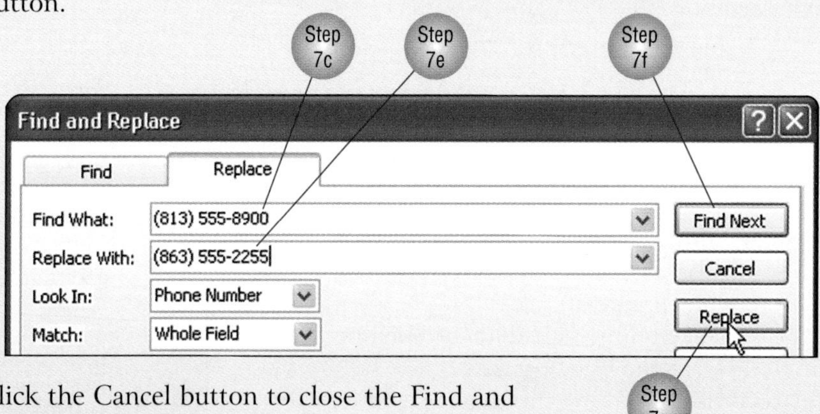

   h. Click the Cancel button to close the Find and Replace dialog box.
8. Save the Suppliers table.
9. Change the page orientation to landscape, change the left and right margins to .3 inch, and then print the Suppliers table.
10. Close the Suppliers table.
11. Close the **MedSafeClinic** database file.

Backing Up a Database File

Back up a database file on a consistent basis to protect the data in the file from accidental loss or from any hardware failure. To back up a database file, click File and then Back Up Database. This displays the Save Backup As dialog box. At this dialog box, navigate to the desired folder or drive, type a name for the database file, and then press Enter or click the Save button.

QUICK STEPS

Backup Database File
1. Open database file.
2. Click File, Back Up Database.
3. Type file name.
4. Click Save button.

Compacting and Repairing a Database File

To optimize performance of your database file, compact and repair the file on a consistent basis. As you work with a database file, data in the file can become fragmented causing the amount of space the database file takes on the disk or in the folder to be larger than necessary.

To compact and repair a database file, open the database file, click Tools, point to Database Utilities, and then click Compact and Repair Database. As the database file is compacting and repairing, a message displays on the Status bar indicating the progress of the procedure. When the procedure is completed, close the database file.

You can tell Access to compact and repair a database file each time you close the file. To do this, click Tools and then Options. At the Options dialog box, click the General tab and then click the *Compact on Close* option shown in Figure 3.10.

HINT

Before compacting and repairing a database file in a multi-user environment, make sure that no other user has the database file open.

QUICK STEPS

Compact and Repair Database File
1. Open database file.
2. Click Tools, Database Utilities, Compact and Repair Database.

FIGURE 3.10 ***Options Dialog Box with General Tab Selected***

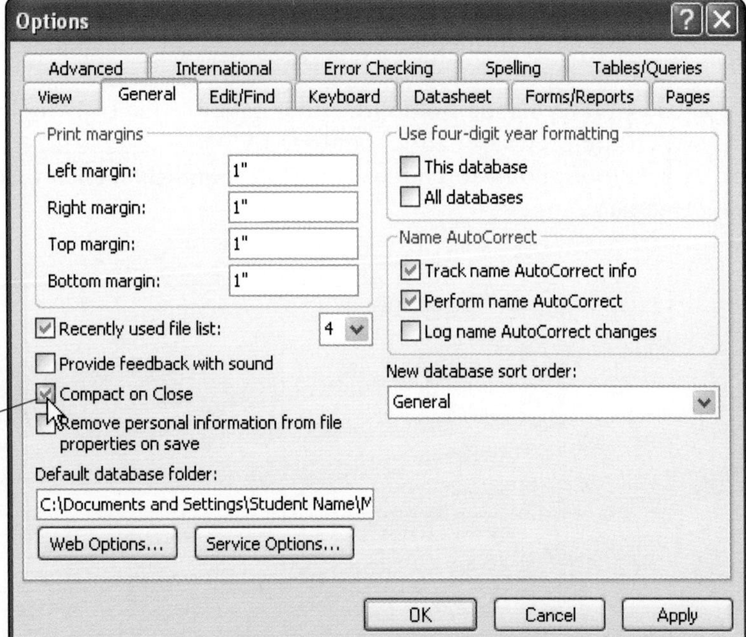

If you want Access to compact and repair a database file each time it is closed, insert a check mark in this check box.

exercise 5

BACK UP AND COMPACT AND REPAIR A DATABASE FILE

1. Open the **MedSafeClinic** database file located on your disk.
2. Create a backup of the MedSafeClinic database file. To do this, complete the following steps:
   a. Click File and then Back Up Database.
   b. At the Save Backup As dialog box, type **MSCBackup10-01-2005** in the *File name* text box. (This file name assumes that the date is October 1, 2005. You do not have to use the date in the file name but it does help when using the backup feature to archive database files.)
   c. Click the Save button.

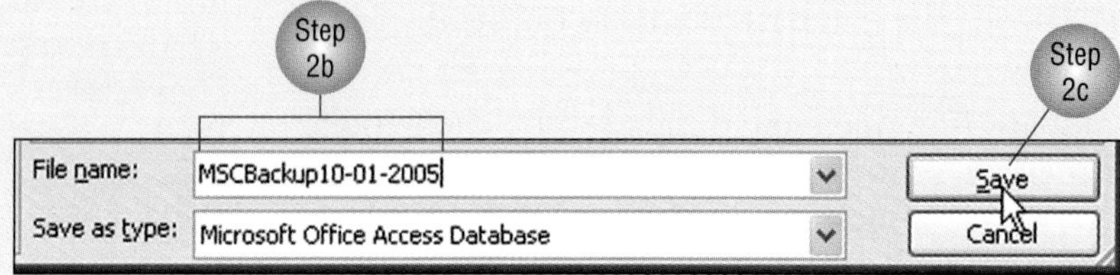

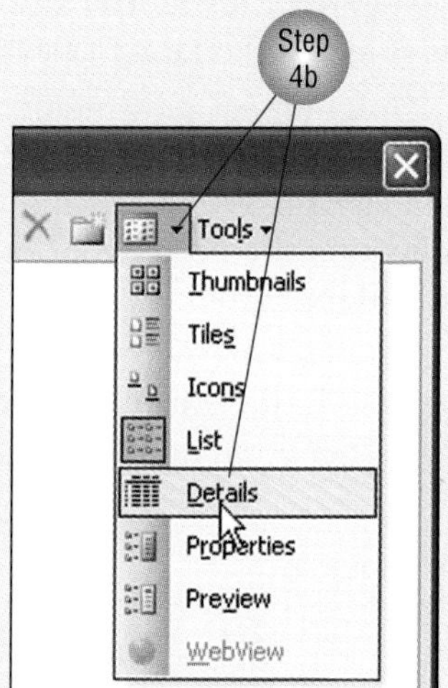

3. Close the **MedSafeClinic** database file.
4. Determine the current size of the **MedSafeClinic** database file (to compare to the size after compacting and repairing) by completing the following steps:
   a. At the blank Access screen, click the Open button on the Database toolbar.
   b. At the Open dialog box, click the down-pointing arrow at the right side of the Views button and then click *Details* at the drop-down list.
   c. Display the drive (or folder) where your **MedSafeClinic** database file is located and then check the size of the file.
   d. Close the Open dialog box.
5. Compact and repair the **MedSafeClinic** database file by completing the following steps:
   a. Open the **MedSafeClinic** database file.
   b. Click Tools, point to Database Utilities, and then click Compact and Repair Database.

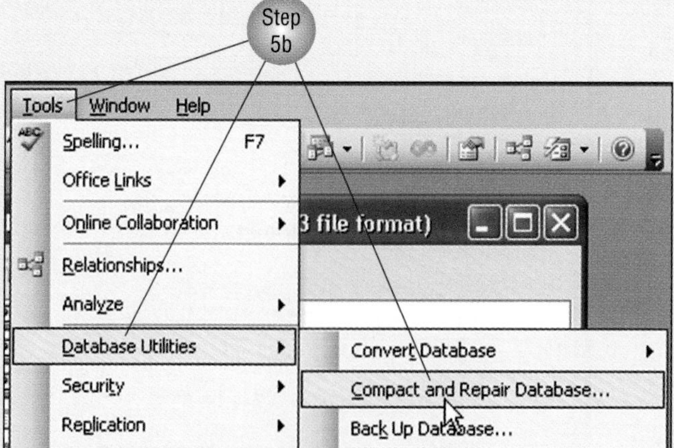

   c. When the compact and repair procedure is completed, close the **MedSafeClinic** database file.

6. Determine the size of the compacted and repaired **MedSafeClinic** database file by completing the following steps:
   a. Click the Open button on the Database toolbar.
   b. At the Open dialog box, make sure the details display in the list box and then look at the size of the **MedSafeClinic** database file and compare this size to the previous size. (Notice that the size of the compacted and repaired **MedSafeClinic** database file is the same size as the **MSCBackup10-01-2005** database file. The backup database file was automatically compacted and repaired when saved.)
   c. Return the display back to a list by clicking the down-pointing arrow at the right side of the Views button and then clicking *List* at the drop-down list.
   d. Close the Open dialog box.

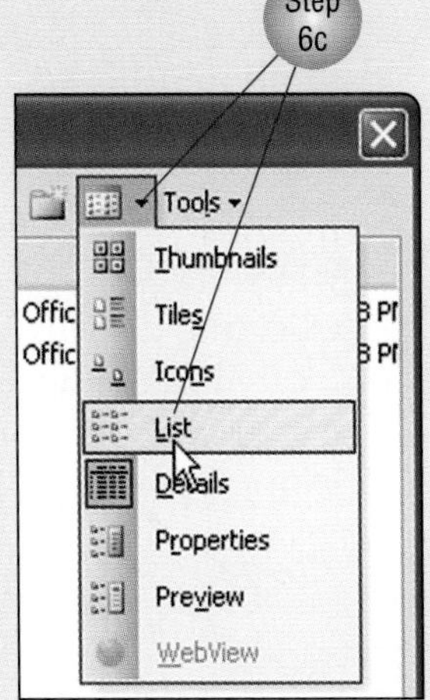

Using Help

The Access Help feature is an on-screen reference manual containing information about all Access features and commands. The Access Help feature is similar to the Windows Help and the Help features in Word, PowerPoint, and Access. Get help using the *Ask a Question* text box on the Menu bar or with options at the Access Help task pane.

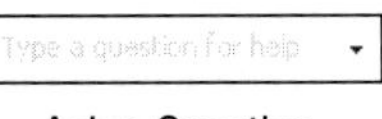

Ask a Question

Use Ask a Question Box
1. Click in *Ask a Question* text box.
2. Type help question.
3. Press Enter.

Getting Help Using the *Ask a Question* Text Box

Click the text inside the *Ask a Question* text box located at the right side of the Menu bar (this removes the text), type a help question, and then press Enter. A list of topics matching key words in your question displays in the Search Results task pane.

exercise 6

GETTING HELP USING THE *ASK A QUESTION* TEXT BOX

1. At a blank Access screen, click the text inside the *Ask a Question* text box located at the right side of the Menu bar.
2. Type **How do I create an Input Mask?**.
3. Press the Enter key.
4. At the Search Results task pane, click the Create an input mask hyperlink.
5. At the Microsoft Office Access Help window, click the Create an input mask (MDB) hyperlink.

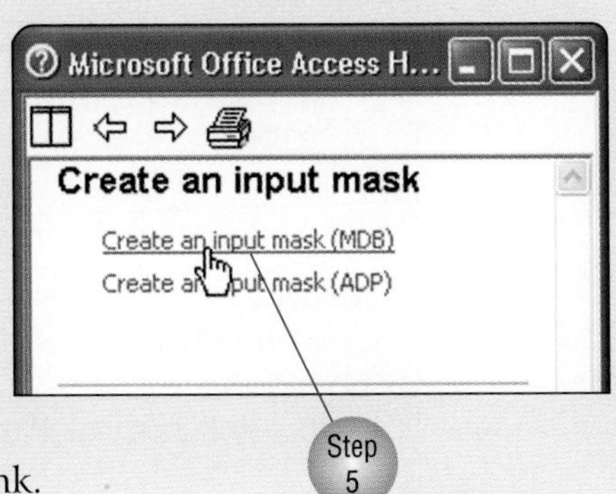

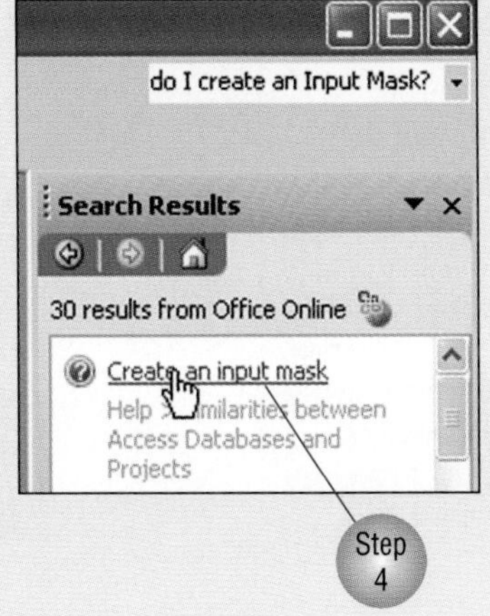

6. Click the Create an input mask for a field in table Design view hyperlink.
7. Click the Show All hyperlink that displays in the upper right corner of the window and then read the information that displays in the window.
8. Click the Close button (contains an *X*) located in the upper right corner of the Microsoft Office Access Help window.
9. Close the Search Results task pane.

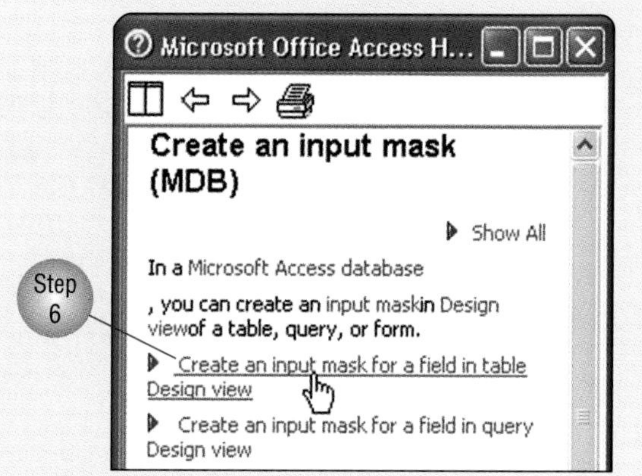

Microsoft Office Access Help

HINT

Press F1 to display the Access Help task pane .

Getting Help from the Access Help Task Pane

You can type a question in the *Ask a Question* text box or type a question or topic in the Access Help task pane. Display this task pane, shown in Figure 3.11, by clicking the Microsoft Office Access Help button on the Standard toolbar or by clicking Help on the Menu bar and then clicking Microsoft Office Access Help at the drop-down menu.

FIGURE 3.11 ***Access Help Task Pane***

Use Help Feature
1. Click Microsoft Office Access Help button.
2. Type help question.
3. Press Enter.

Type in this text box the word, topic, or phrase on which you want help.

HINT

Click Help, About Microsoft Office Access, and then click the System Info button to display information about your computer such as your processor type, operating system, memory, and hard disk space.

In the Access Help task pane, type a topic, feature, or question in the *Search for* text box and then press Enter or click the Start searching button (button containing white arrow on green background). Topics related to the topic, feature, or question display in the Search Results task pane. Click a topic in the results list box and information about that topic displays in the Microsoft Office Access Help window. If the window contains a Show All hyperlink in the upper right corner, click this hyperlink and the information expands to show all help information related to the topic. When you click the Show All hyperlink, it becomes the Hide All hyperlink.

(Note: If the Office Assistant displays when you click the Microsoft Office Access Help button, turn off the display of the Office Assistant. To do this, click the Options button in the yellow box above the Office Assistant. At the Office Assistant dialog box, click the **Use the Office Assistant** ***option to remove the check mark from the check box, and then click OK.)***

exercise 7

GETTING HELP

1. At a blank Access screen, display information on increasing row height in a table. To begin, click the Microsoft Office Access Help button on the Standard toolbar. (This displays the Access Help task pane.)
2. Type **How do I increase the row height in a table datasheet?** in the *Search for* text box and then press Enter.
3. At the Search Results task pane, click the Resize a column or row hyperlink. (This displays the Microsoft Office Access Help window.)
4. Click the Show All hyperlink that displays in the upper right corner of the window.
5. Read the information about resizing a column or row. (You will need to scroll down the window to display all of the information.)
6. Click the Close button to close the Microsoft Office Access Help window.
7. Close the Search Results task pane.

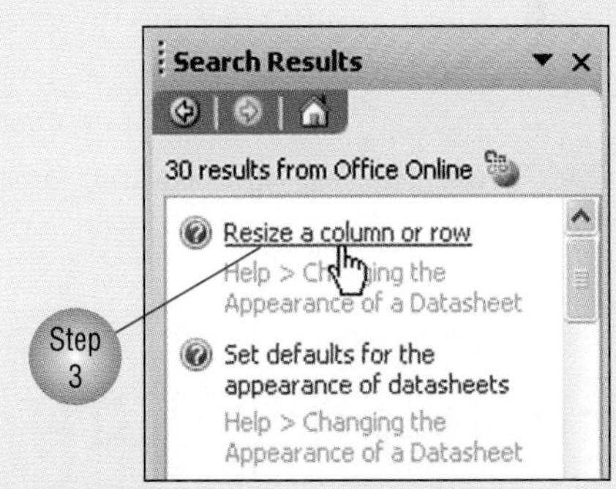

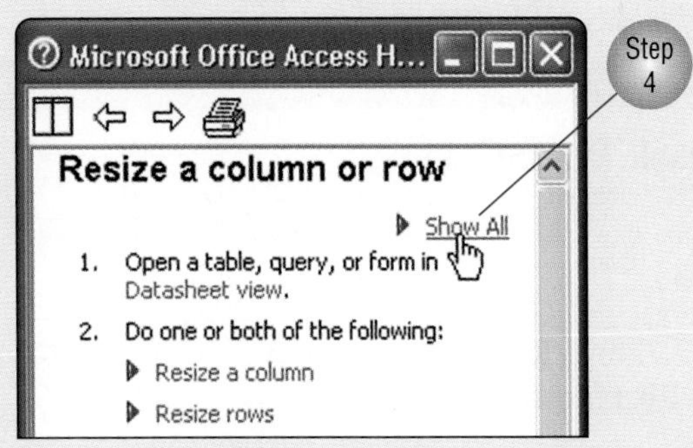

CHAPTER summary

- Access contains a Table Wizard that helps create database tables.
- The Table Wizard offers possible field choices with data types already assigned.
- When a second or subsequent table is created in a database file using the Table Wizard, a relationship can be created between the tables.

- Use the spelling checker to find misspelled words in a table.
- The spelling checker compares the words in a table with words in its dictionary. If a match is found, the word is passed over. If no match is found, the spelling checker will select the word and offer possible replacements.
- Begin the spelling checker by clicking the Spelling button on the Table Datasheet toolbar.
- Use options at the Find and Replace dialog box with the Find tab selected to search for specific field entries in a table. Display this dialog box by clicking the Find button on the Table Datasheet toolbar or by clicking Edit and then Find.
- Use options at the Find and Replace dialog box with the Replace tab selected to search for specific data and replace with other data. Display this dialog box by clicking Edit and then Replace.
- Back up a database file on a consistent basis to protect the data in the file from accidental loss or from any hardware failure. To back up a database file, click File and then Back Up Database.
- Compact and repair a database file to optimize the performance of the file. Compact and repair a database file by clicking Tools, pointing to Database Utilities, and then clicking Compact and Repair Database.
- Get help by typing a question in the *Ask a Question* text box located at the right side of the Menu bar.
- Display the Access Help task pane by clicking the Microsoft Office Access Help button on the Standard toolbar or by clicking Help and then Microsoft Office Access Help.

FEATURES summary

FEATURE	BUTTON	MENU	KEYBOARD
Table Wizard		Insert, Table, Table Wizard	
Spelling checker		Tools, Spelling	F7
Find and Replace dialog box with Find tab selected		Edit, Find	Ctrl + F
Find and Replace dialog box with Replace tab selected		Edit, Replace	Ctrl + H
Save Backup As dialog box		File, Back Up Database	
Compact and repair database		Tools, Database Utilities, Compact and Repair Database	
Access Help task pane		Help, Microsoft Office Access Help	F1

CONCEPTS check

Completion: On a blank sheet of paper, indicate the correct term, symbol, or character for each description.

1. Click this button at the first Table Wizard dialog box to add *all* of the selected fields in the *Sample Fields* list box to the *Fields in my new table* list box.
2. Click this button at the first Table Wizard dialog box to remove *all* of the fields in the *Fields in my new table* list box.
3. When a second or subsequent table is created in a database file using the Table Wizard, this can be created between the database tables.
4. Click this button on the Table Datasheet toolbar to begin the spelling checker.
5. Click this button on the Table Datasheet toolbar to display the Find and Replace dialog box with the Find tab selected.
6. Use options at the Find and Replace dialog box with this tab selected to search for specific data and replace with other data.
7. Click File and then Back Up Database and this dialog box displays.
8. To compact and repair a database file, click this option on the Menu bar, point to Database Utilities, and then click Compact and Repair Database.
9. Type a help question inside this box located at the right side of the Menu bar.
10. Click this hyperlink at the Microsoft Office Access Help window to display all information in the window.

SKILLS check

Assessment 1

1. Use the Table Wizard to create two tables in a database file named **LaffertyCompany**. Create the first table with the following specifications:
   a. At the first Table Wizard dialog box, click *Employees* in the *Sample Tables* list box.
   b. Insert the following fields located in the *Sample Fields* list box to the *Fields in my new table* list box:

      EmployeeID
      FirstName
      MiddleName
      LastName
      Title
      Extension

   c. At the second Table Wizard dialog box, accept the table name of *Employees* offered by the wizard and let the wizard set the primary key.
   d. At the third Table Wizard dialog box, leave *Enter data directly into the table* selected, and then click Finish.

e. Type the following data in the specified fields (the *Employee ID* field will automatically be assigned a number):

First Name	=	Samantha
Middle Name	=	Lee
Last Name	=	Murray
Title	=	Account Manager
Extension	=	412

First Name	=	Ralph
Middle Name	=	Edward
Last Name	=	Sorrell
Title	=	Director
Extension	=	432

First Name	=	Cheryl
Middle Name	=	Janet
Last Name	=	Plaschka
Title	=	Assistant Director
Extension	=	549

First Name	=	Brandon
Middle Name	=	Michael
Last Name	=	Perrault
Title	=	Administrative Assistant
Extension	=	653

First Name	=	Leland
Middle Name	=	John
Last Name	=	Nitsche
Title	=	Account Manager
Extension	=	894

f. Complete a spelling check on the table. (Assume proper names are spelled correctly.)
g. Adjust the column widths.
h. Save the Employees table.
i. Change the orientation to landscape and then print the table.
j. Close the Employees table.

2. Create a second table with the following specifications:
   a. At the first Table Wizard dialog box, click *Expenses* in the *Sample Tables* list box. (You will need to scroll down the list to display *Expenses*.)
   b. Insert the following fields located in the *Sample Fields* list box to the *Fields in my new table* list box:

      ExpenseID
      EmployeeID
      ExpenseType
      PurposeofExpense
      AmountSpent
      DateSubmitted

   c. At the second Table Wizard dialog box, accept the table name of *Expenses* offered by the wizard and let the wizard set the primary key.

d. At the third Table Wizard dialog box, create a one-to-many relationship where one record in the Employees table will match many records in the Expenses table. ***(Hint: You must click the Relationships button at the third Table Wizard dialog box.)***
e. At the fourth Table Wizard dialog box, leave *Enter data directly into the table* selected, and then click Finish.
f. Type the following data in the specified fields (the *Expense ID* field will automatically be assigned a number):

Employee ID = 1
Expense Type = Travel
Purpose of Expense = Marketing Conference
Amount Spent = $215.75
Date Submitted = 2/4/05

Employee ID = 2
Expense Type = Lodging
Purpose of Expense = Finance Conference
Amount Spent = $568.50
Date Submitted = 2/10/05

Employee ID = 3
Expense Type = Travel
Purpose of Expense = Management Workshop
Amount Spent = $422.70
Date Submitted = 2/12/05

Employee ID = 1
Expense Type = Business Dinner
Purpose of Expense = Customer Relations
Amount Spent = $124.90
Date Submitted = 2/16/05

Employee ID = 4
Expense Type = Printing
Purpose of Expense = Promotional Literature
Amount Spent = $96.00
Date Submitted = 2/18/05

Employee ID = 1
Expense Type = Travel
Purpose of Expense = Customer Contact
Amount Spent = $184.35
Date Submitted = 2/19/05

g. Complete a spelling check on the table.
h. Adjust the column widths.
i. Save the Expenses table.
j. Change the orientation to landscape and then print the table.
k. Close the Expenses table.

Assessment 2

1. Open the **Employees** table in the LaffertyCompany database file and then add the following records:

First Name	=	Laurie
Middle Name	=	Jean
Last Name	=	Noviello
Title	=	Account Manager
Extension	=	568

First Name	=	Roderick
Middle Name	=	Earl
Last Name	=	Lobdell
Title	=	Assistant Director
Extension	=	553

2. Delete the record for Leland John Nitsche.
3. Save the Employees table and then print the table in landscape orientation.
4. Close the Employees table.
5. Open the Expenses table and then add the following records:

Employee ID	=	4
Expense Type	=	Printing
Purpose of Expense	=	Product Brochure
Amount Spent	=	$510.00
Date Submitted	=	2/22/05

Employee ID	=	5
Expense Type	=	Travel
Purpose of Expense	=	Customer Contact
Amount Spent	=	$75.20
Date Submitted	=	2/23/05

6. Save the Expenses table.
7. Print the Expenses table in landscape orientation.
8. Close the Expenses table.

Assessment 3

1. Open the Employees table in the **LaffertyCompany** database file.
2. Make the following changes:
   a. Click in the first entry of the *Last Name* column and then find the one occurrence of *Noviello* and replace with *Orson*.
   b. Click in the first entry of the *Title* column and then find all occurrences of *Account Manager* and replace with *Sales Director*.
3. Save the Employees table and then print the table in landscape orientation.
4. Close the Employees table.
5. Compact and repair the **LaffertyCompany** database file.
6. Close the **LaffertyCompany** database file.

Assessment 4

1. In Chapter 2, you learned to create a one-to-many relationship between database tables. In Access, a many-to-many relationship can also be created between database tables. Use the Access Help feature to read and print information on creating a many-to-many relationship between database tables.
2. After reading the information, open Microsoft Word, and then create a memo to your instructor and include the following:
   a. Description of a many-to-many relationship.
   b. Steps to create a many-to-many relationship.
   c. At least one example of a situation in which a many-to-many relationship would be useful.
3. Save the Word document and name it **sac3sc04**.
4. Print and then close **sac3sc04**.

CHAPTER challenge

Create a database named **(Yourlastname) Household** using a personal sample table from the wizard. Select your own fields from the sample field list. Set a primary key (if necessary). Use appropriate data types and input masks. Add at least five records to the table. Sort the table in ascending order. Save and print the table.

Once a table has been created, printing a copy of the table's design properties can be very beneficial. Use the Help feature to learn about printing the design characteristics of a table. Then print the design properties of the table that was created in the first part of the Chapter Challenge.

You have talked with your friend Judy about the database you created, and she would like to see what you have done in Access. Since she lives 500 miles away, you decide to e-mail her the table. Judy does not have Access, but does have a word processing application. Export the table created in the first part of the Chapter Challenge as an rtf file, so that Judy can view it with her application.

CHAPTER 4

PERFORMING QUERIES AND FILTERING RECORDS

PERFORMANCE OBJECTIVES

Upon successful completion of Chapter 4, you will be able to:

- **Design a query to extract specific data from a database table**
- **Use the Simple Query Wizard to extract specific data from a database table**
- **Create a calculated field**
- **Use aggregate functions in queries**
- **Create crosstab, duplicate, and unmatched queries**
- **Filter data in records by selection and by form**

ACCESS

One of the primary uses of a database file is to extract specific information from the database. A company might need to know such information as: How much inventory is currently on hand? What products have been ordered? What accounts are past due? What customers live in a particular city? This type of information can be extracted from a database table by completing a query. You will learn how to perform a variety of queries on database tables in this chapter.

Access provides a Filter By Selection button and a Filter By Form button, which you can use to temporarily isolate specific records in a database table. Like a query, a filter lets you select specific field values from a database table. You will learn to use these two buttons to isolate specific data in tables.

Performing Queries

Being able to extract (pull out) specific data from a database table is one of the most important functions of a database. Extracting data in Access is referred to as performing a "query." The word ***query*** means to ask a question. Access provides several methods for performing a query. You can design your own query, use a Simple Query Wizard, or use complex query wizards. In this chapter, you will learn to design your own query, use the Simple Query Wizard, use aggregate functions in a query, and use the Crosstab, Find Duplicates, and Unmatched query wizards.

Design a Query
1. Open database file.
2. Click Queries button.
3. Double-click *Create query in Design view.*
4. At Show Table dialog box, select table(s).
5. At select query window, drag fields to desired location.
6. Click Run button.
7. Save query.

Designing a Query

Designing a query consists of identifying the table from which you are gathering data, the field or fields from which the data will be drawn, and the criteria for selecting the data. To design a query and perform the query, you would follow these basic steps:

1. Open the database file.
2. At the database file dialog box, click the Queries button on the Objects bar shown in Figure 4.1.
3. Double-click *Create query in Design view* in the list box.
4. At the Show Table dialog box with the Tables tab selected as shown in Figure 4.2, select the table you want included in the query, and then click the Add button. Add any other tables required for the query. When all tables have been added, click the Close button.
5. At the Query1 : Select Query window shown in Figure 4.3, use the mouse to drag the first field to be included in the query from the table box in the top of the dialog box to the first empty *Field* text box. If more than one field is to be included in the query, continue dragging field names from the box in the top to the *Field* text boxes.
6. To establish a criterion, click inside the *Criteria* text box in the column containing the desired field name, and then type the criterion.
7. With the fields and criteria established, click the Run button located on the Query Design toolbar.
8. Access searches the specified table for records that match the criteria and then displays those records in the Query1 : Select Query window.
9. If the query will be used in the future, save the query and name it. If you do not need the query again, close the Query1 : Select Query window without saving it.

Run

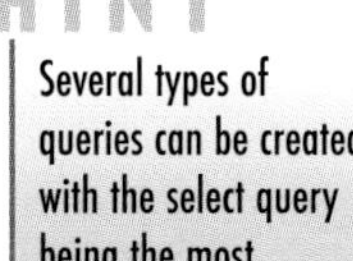

Several types of queries can be created, with the select query being the most common.

FIGURE 4.1 **Objects Bar**

FIGURE 4.2 *Show Table Dialog Box*

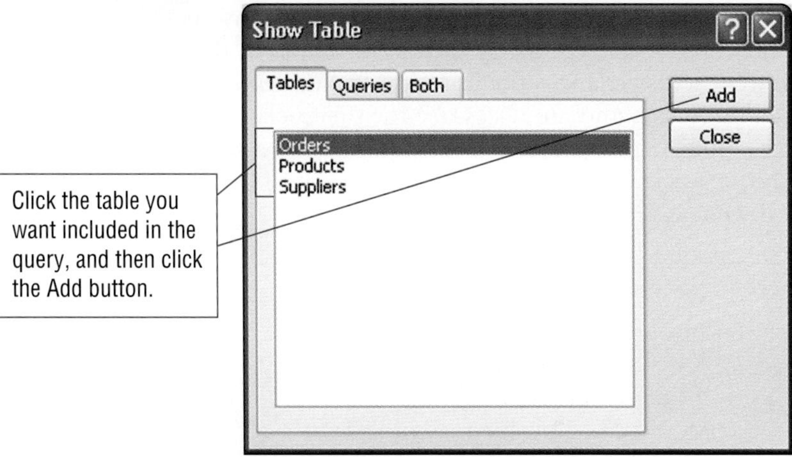

FIGURE 4.3 *Query1 : Select Query Window*

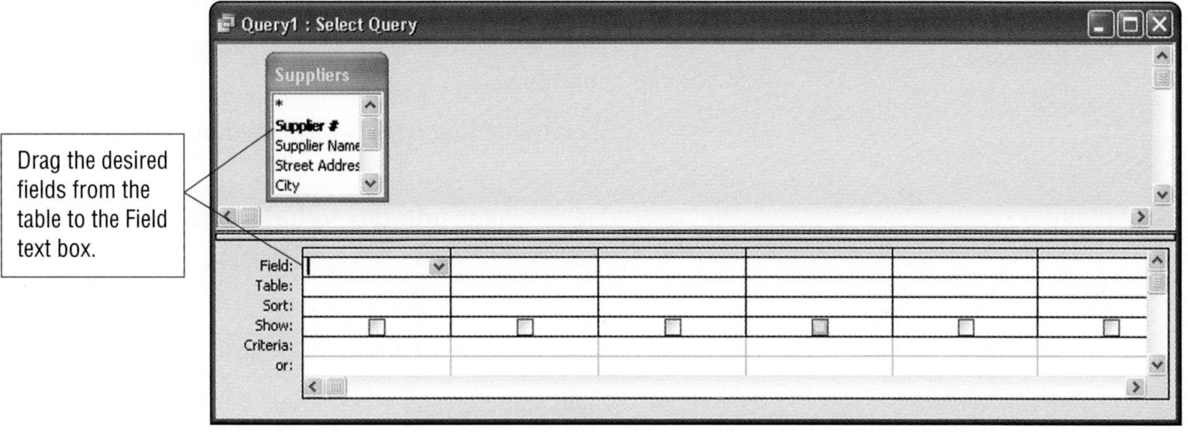

In Step 4, the mouse is used to drag fields from the table box in the top of the dialog box to the first empty *Field* text box in the lower part of the dialog box. As an example, suppose you wanted to find out how many purchase orders were issued on a specific date. To do this, you would drag the *PurchaseOrderID* field from the table to the first *Field* text box, and then drag the *OrderDate* field from the table to the second *Field* text box. In this example, both fields are needed so the purchase order ID is displayed along with the specific order date. After dragging the fields, you would then insert the criterion. The criterion for this example would be something like *#1/15/2005#*. After the criterion is inserted, click the Run button on the Query Design toolbar and the results of the query are displayed on the screen.

Establishing Query Criteria

A query does not require that specific criteria are established. In the example described above, if the criterion for the date was not included, the query would "return" (***return*** is the term used for the results of the query) all Purchase Order numbers with the dates. While this information may be helpful, you could easily

HINT
Limit the query results by specifying criteria.

HINT

Include only those fields in a query for which you want to enter criteria or fields which you want to display.

find this information in the table. The value of performing a query is to extract specific information from a table. To do this, you must insert a criterion like the one described in the example.

Access makes writing a criterion fairly simple because it inserts the necessary symbols in the criterion. If you type a city such as *Vancouver* in the *Criteria* text box and then press Enter, Access changes the criterion to *"Vancouver"*. The quotation marks are inserted by Access and are necessary for the query to run properly. You can either let Access put the proper symbols in the *Criteria* text box, or you can type the criterion with the symbols. Table 4.1 shows some criteria examples including what is typed and what is returned.

TABLE 4.1 ***Criteria Examples***

Typing this criterion	*Returns this*
"Smith"	Field value matching *Smith*
"Smith" or "Larson"	Field value matching either *Smith* or *Larson*
Not "Smith"	Field value that is not *Smith* (the opposite of "Smith")
"S*"	Field value that begins with *S* and ends in anything
"*s"	Field value that begins with anything and ends in *s*
"[A-D]*"	Field value that begins with *A* through *D* and ends in anything
#01/01/2005#	Field value matching the date 01/01/2005
< #04/01/2005#	Field value less than (before) 04/01/2005
> #04/01/2005#	Field value greater than (after) 04/01/2005
Between #01/01/2005 And #03/31/2005	Any date between 01/01/2005 and 03/31/2005

Establish Query Criteria

1. At select query window, click in desired *Criteria* text box.
2. Type criteria and then press Enter.
3. Click Run button.

In Table 4.1, notice the quotation marks surrounding field values (such as "Smith"). If you do not type the quotation marks when typing the criterion, Access will automatically insert them. The same is true for the pound symbol (#). Notice in Table 4.1 that the pound symbol (#) was used around dates. If you do not type the pound symbol around a date, Access will automatically insert the symbols. Access automatically inserts the correct symbol when you press the Enter key after typing the query criteria.

In the criteria examples, the asterisk was used as a wild card indicating any character. This is consistent with many other software applications where the asterisk is used as a wildcard character. The less than and greater than symbols were used in two of the criteria examples. These symbols can be used for fields containing numbers, values, dates, amounts, and so forth. In the next several exercises, you will be designing queries to extract specific information from different database tables in database files.

exercise 1

PERFORMING QUERIES ON DATABASE TABLES

(Note: Delete from your disk any database files you created in Chapter 3.)

1. Copy the **OutdoorOptions** database file from the CD that accompanies this textbook to your disk. Remove the read-only attribute from the **OutdoorOptions** database file.
2. Open the **OutdoorOptions** database file.
3. Extract records of those suppliers located in Vancouver by completing the following steps:
   a. Click the Queries button on the Objects bar.
   b. Double-click *Create query in Design view* in the list box.
   c. At the Show Table dialog box with the Tables tab selected (see Figure 4.2), click *Suppliers* in the list box, click the Add button, and then click the Close button.
   d. Drag fields from the table box to the *Field* text boxes by completing the following steps:
      1) Position the arrow pointer on the *Supplier Name* field in the table list box located toward the top of the window, hold down the left mouse button, drag the field icon to the first *Field* text box in the lower portion of the window, and then release the mouse button. (When you release the mouse button, Access automatically inserts the table name *Suppliers* in the *Table* text box and inserts a check mark in the *Show* check box.)
      2) Drag the *Street Address* field in the table list box to the next *Field* text box (to the right of *Supplier Name*).
      3) Drag the *City* field in the table list box to the next *Field* text box (to the right of *Street Address*).
      4) Drag the *Province* field in the table list box to the next *Field* text box (to the right of *City*).
      5) Drag the *Postal Code* field in the table list box to the next *Field* text box (to the right of *Province*).

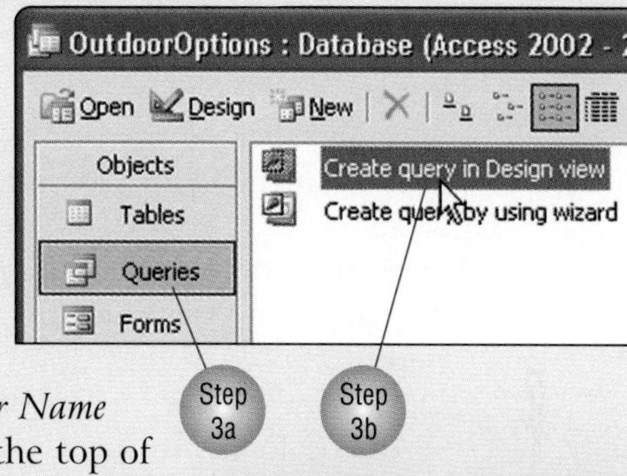

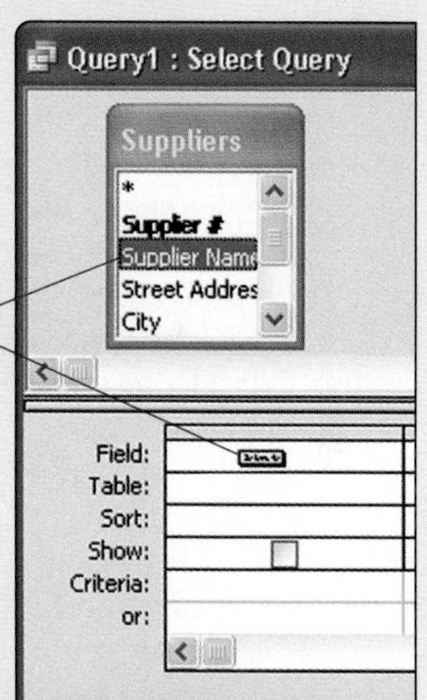

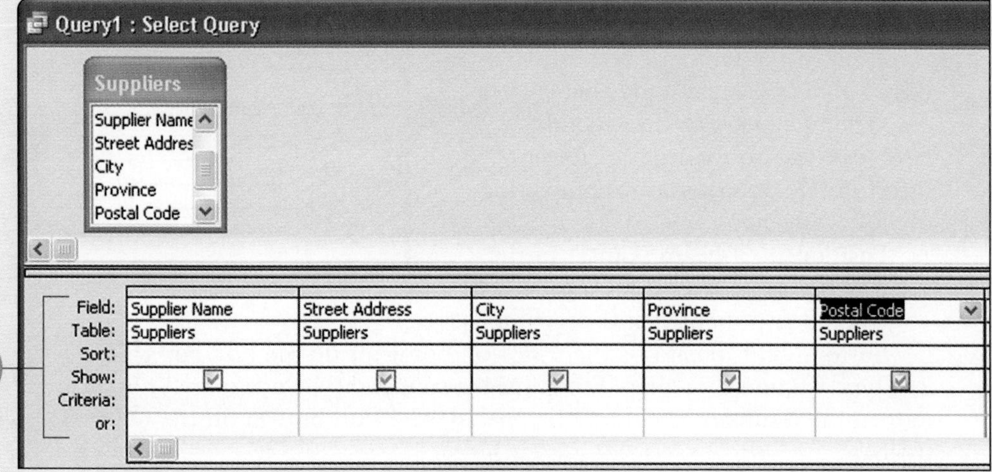

e. Insert the criterion text telling Access to display only those suppliers located in Vancouver by completing the following steps:
   1) Position the I-beam pointer in the *Criteria* text box in the *City* column and then click the left mouse button. (This positions the insertion point inside the text box.)
   2) Type **Vancouver** and then press Enter. (This changes the criteria to "Vancouver".)

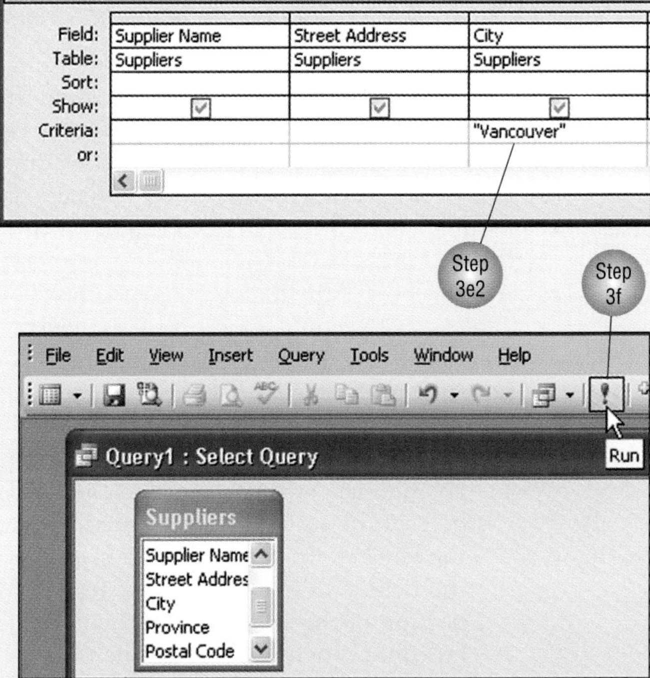

f. Return the results of the query by clicking the Run button on the Query Design toolbar.
g. Save the results of the query by completing the following steps:
   1) Click the Save button on the Query Datasheet toolbar.
   2) At the Save As dialog box, type **VancouverQuery** and then press Enter or click OK.
h. Print the results of the query by clicking the Print button on the Query Datasheet toolbar.
i. Close VancouverQuery.

4. Extract those product records with units on order greater than zero by completing the following steps:
   a. At the OutdoorOptions : Database window, double-click *Create query in Design view*.
   b. At the Show Table dialog box, click *Products* in the list box, click the Add button, and then click the Close button.
   c. At the Query1 : Select Query window, drag the *Product* field from the table list box to the first *Field* text box.
   d. Scroll down the table list box until *Units on Order* displays and then drag *Units on Order* to the second *Field* text box (to the right of *Product*).
   e. Insert the query criteria by completing the following steps:
      1) Position the I-beam pointer in the *Criteria* text box in the *Units on Order* column and then click the left mouse button. (This positions the insertion point inside the text box.)
      2) Type **>0** and then press Enter. (Make sure you type a zero and not a capital *O*.)

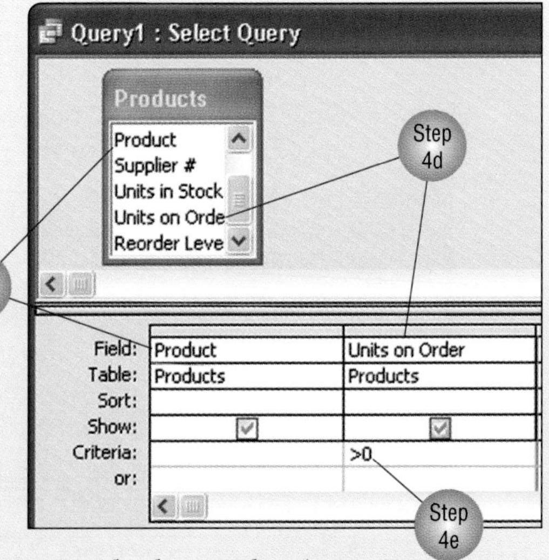

   f. Return the results of the query by clicking the Run button on the Query Design toolbar.

g. Save the query and name it UnitsOnOrderQuery.
h. Print the results of the query by clicking the Print button on the Query Datasheet toolbar.
i. Close UnitsOnOrderQuery.

5. Extract those orders greater than $1,500 by completing the following steps:
   a. At the OutdoorOptions : Database window, double-click *Create query in Design view*.
   b. At the Show Table dialog box, click *Orders* in the list box, click the Add button, and then click the Close button.
   c. At the Query1 : Select Query window, drag the *Order #* field from the table list box to the first *Field* text box.
   d. Drag the *Product #* field to the second *Field* text box (to the right of *Order #*).
   e. Scroll down the table list box until *Amount* is visible and then drag the *Amount* field to the third *Field* text box (to the right of *Product #*).
   f. Insert the query criteria by completing the following steps:
      1) Position the I-beam pointer in the *Criteria* text box in the *Amount* column and then click the left mouse button. (This positions the insertion point inside the text box.)
      2) Type >1500 and then press Enter. (Make sure you type zeros and not capital Os.)

Field:	Order #	Product #	Amount
Table:	Orders	Orders	Orders
Sort:			
Show:	☑	☑	☑
Criteria:			>1500
or:			

Step 5f2

   g. Return the results of the query by clicking the Run button on the Query Design toolbar.
   h. Save the query and name it OrdersOver$1500Query.
   i. Print the results of the query by clicking the Print button on the Query Datasheet toolbar.
   j. Close OrdersOver$1500Query.
6. Close the **OutdoorOptions** database file.

In Exercise 1, you performed several queries on specific database tables. A query can also be performed on fields from more than one table. In Exercise 2, you will be performing queries on related database tables.

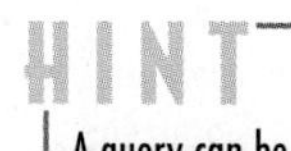

HINT

A query can be performed on two or more tables that are joined in a relationship.

exercise 2

PERFORMING A QUERY ON RELATED DATABASE TABLES

1. Open the **OutdoorOptions** database file.
2. Extract information on products ordered between February 20 and February 28, 2005, and include the supplier's name by completing the following steps:
   a. Click the Queries button on the Objects bar.
   b. Double-click *Create query in Design view*.
   c. At the Show Table dialog box, click *Products* in the list box and then click the Add button.
   d. Click *Suppliers* in the Show Table dialog box list box and then click the Add button.
   e. Click *Orders* in the list box, click the Add button, and then click the Close button.

f. At the Query1 : Select Query window, drag the *Product* field from the Products table list box to the first *Field* text box.
g. Drag the *Supplier Name* field from the Suppliers table list box to the second *Field* text box.
h. Drag the *Order Date* field from the Orders table list box to the third *Field* text box. (You will need to scroll down the list box to display the *Order Date* field.)
i. Insert the query criteria by completing the following steps:
   1) Position the I-beam pointer in the *Criteria* text box in the *Order Date* column and then click the left mouse button. (This positions the insertion point inside the text box.)
   2) Type **Between 2/20/2005 And 2/28/2005** and then press Enter. (Make sure you type zeros and not capital *O*s.)
j. Return the results of the query by clicking the Run button on the Query Design toolbar.
k. Save the query and name it Feb20-28OrdersQuery.
l. Print and then close the query.
3. Close the **OutdoorOptions** database file.

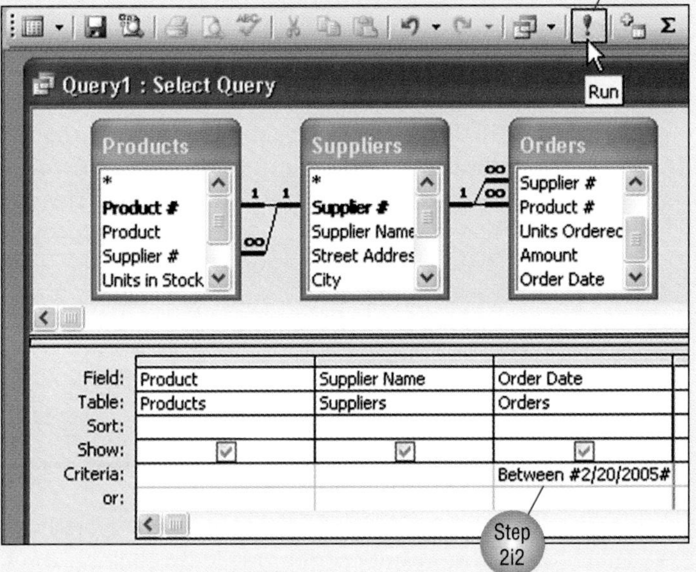

QUICK STEPS

Sort Fields in Query
1. At select query window, click in *Sort* text box.
2. Click down arrow in *Sort* text box.
3. Click *Ascending* or *Descending*.

Sorting Fields in a Query

When designing a query, the sort order of a field or fields can be specified. Notice in Figure 4.3 that a *Sort* text box displays. Click inside one of the columns in the *Sort* text box and a down-pointing arrow displays at the right of the field. Click this down-pointing arrow and a drop-down list displays with the choices *Ascending*, *Descending*, and *(not sorted)*. Click Ascending to sort from lowest to highest or click Descending to sort from highest to lowest.

exercise 3 PERFORMING A QUERY ON RELATED TABLES AND SORTING IN ASCENDING ORDER

1. Open the **OutdoorOptions** database file.
2. Extract information on orders less than $1,500 by completing the following steps:
   a. Click the Queries button on the Objects bar.
   b. Double-click *Create query in Design view*.
   c. At the Show Table dialog box, click *Products* in the list box and then click the Add button.
   d. Click *Orders* in the list box, click the Add button, and then click the Close button.
   e. At the Query1 : Select Query window, drag the *Product #* field from the Products table list box to the first *Field* text box.

f. Drag the *Supplier #* field from the Products table list box to the second *Field* text box.
g. Drag the *Units Ordered* field from the Orders table list box to the third *Field* text box.
h. Drag the *Amount* field from the Orders table list box to the fourth *Field* text box.
i. Insert the query criterion by completing the following steps:
   1) Position the I-beam pointer in the *Criteria* text box in the *Amount* column and then click the left mouse button.
   2) Type **<1500** and then press Enter. (Make sure you type a zero and not a capital *O*.)

Field:	Product #	Supplier #	Units Ordered	Amount
Table:	Products	Orders	Orders	Orders
Sort:				
Show:	☑	☑	☑	☑
Criteria:				<1500
or:				

Step 2i2

j. Sort the *Amount* field values from lowest to highest by completing the following steps:
   1) Position the insertion point in the *Sort* text box in the *Amount* column, and then click the left mouse button. (This will cause a down-pointing arrow to display at the right side of the text box.)
   2) Click the down-pointing arrow at the right side of the *Sort* text box and then click *Ascending*.

Step 2j1

Units Ordered	Amount
Orders	Orders
	Ascending / Descending / (not sorted)

Step 2j2

k. Return the results of the query by clicking the Run button on the Query Design toolbar.
l. Save the query and name it OrdersLessThan$1500Query.
m. Print and then close the query.

3. Close the **OutdoorOptions** database file.

Performing a Query with the Simple Query Wizard

The Simple Query Wizard provided by Access guides you through the steps for preparing a query. To use this wizard, open the database file, click the Queries button on the Objects bar, and then double-click the *Create query by using wizard* option in the list box. Or, click the New button and then, at the New Query dialog box, double-click *Simple Query Wizard* in the list box. At the first Simple Query Wizard dialog box, as shown in Figure 4.4, specify the database table(s) in the *Tables/Queries* list box. After specifying the database table, insert the fields you want included in the query in the *Selected Fields* list box, and then click the Next button.

HINT

Use the Simple Query Wizard to walk you through the steps for preparing a query.

Create Query with Simple Query Wizard
1. Open database file.
2. Click Queries button.
3. Double-click *Create query by using wizard.*
4. Follow query steps.

OR

1. Click the New button.
2. At New Query dialog box, double-click *Simple Query Wizard.*
3. Follow query steps.

FIGURE 4.4 ***First Simple Query Wizard Dialog Box***

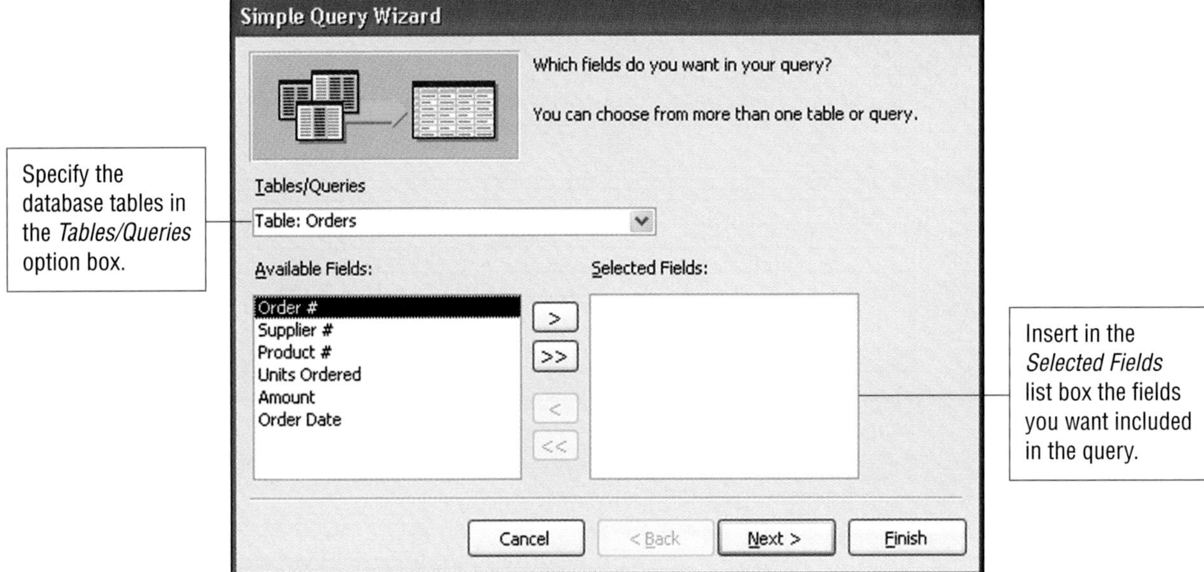
Simple Query Wizard
Which fields do you want in your query?
You can choose from more than one table or query.
Tables/Queries
Table: Orders
Available Fields:
Selected Fields:
Order #
Supplier #
Product #
Units Ordered
Amount
Order Date
Cancel
< Back
Next >
Finish
Specify the database tables in the Tables/Queries option box.
Insert in the Selected Fields list box the fields you want included in the query.

At the second Simple Query Wizard dialog box, specify whether you want a detail or summary query, and then click the Next button. At the third (and last) Simple Query Wizard dialog box, shown in Figure 4.5, type a name for the completed query or accept the name provided by the wizard. At this dialog box, you can also specify that you want to open the query to view the information or modify the query design. If you want to extract specific information, be sure to choose the *Modify the query design* option. After making any necessary changes, click the Finish button.

FIGURE 4.5 ***Last Simple Query Wizard Dialog Box***

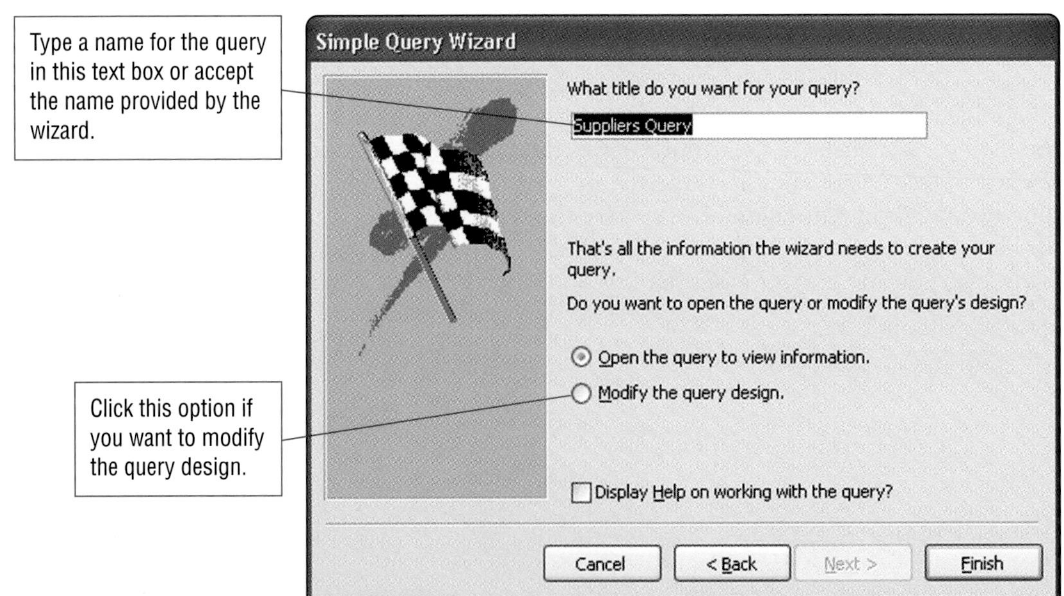
Simple Query Wizard
What title do you want for your query?
Suppliers Query
That's all the information the wizard needs to create your query.
Do you want to open the query or modify the query's design?
Open the query to view information.
Modify the query design.
Display Help on working with the query?
Cancel
< Back
Next >
Finish
Type a name for the query in this text box or accept the name provided by the wizard.
Click this option if you want to modify the query design.

If you do not modify the query design in the last Simple Query Wizard dialog box, the query displays all records for the fields identified in the first Simple Query Wizard dialog box. In Exercise 4 you will be performing a query without modifying the design, and in Exercise 5 you will be modifying the query design.

exercise 4

PERFORMING A QUERY WITH THE SIMPLE QUERY WIZARD

1. Open the **OutdoorOptions** database file.
2. Perform a query with the Simple Query Wizard by completing the following steps:
    a. Click the Queries button on the Objects bar.
    b. Double-click the *Create query by using wizard* option in the list box.
    c. At the first Simple Query Wizard dialog box, click the down-pointing arrow at the right of the *Tables/Queries* text box, and then click *Table: Suppliers*. 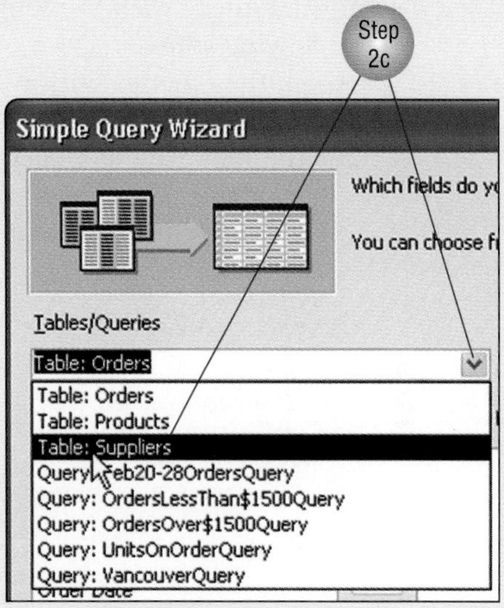
    d. With *Supplier #* selected in the *Available Fields* list box, click the button containing the greater than symbol. (This inserts the *Supplier #* field in the *Selected Fields* list box.)
    e. With *Supplier Name* selected in the *Available Fields* list box, click the button containing the greater than symbol.
    f. Click the down-pointing arrow at the right of the *Tables/Queries* text box, and then click *Table: Orders*.
    g. Click *Product #* in the *Available Fields* list box, and then click the button containing the greater than symbol.
    h. Click *Amount* in the *Available Fields* list box, and then click the button containing the greater than symbol. 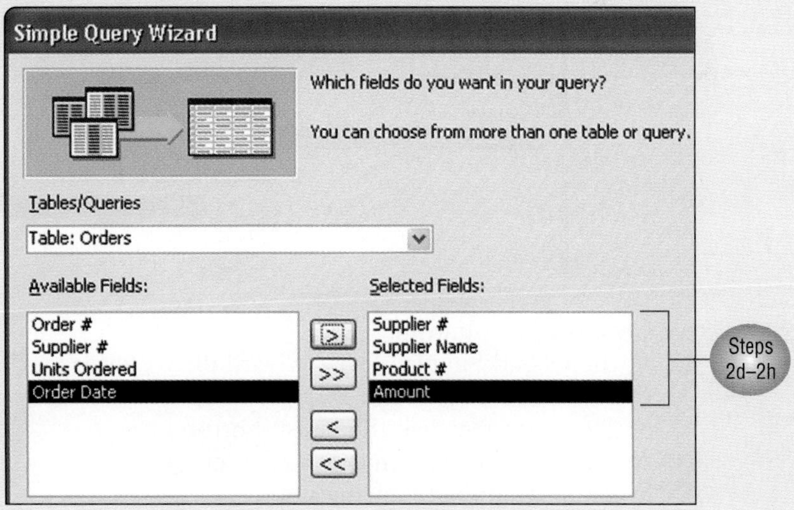
    i. Click the Next button.
    j. At the second Simple Query Wizard dialog box, click the Next button.
    k. At the last Simple Query Wizard dialog box, click the Finish button. (The wizard will automatically save the query with the name Supplies Query.)
3. When the results of the query display, print the results.
4. Close the Suppliers Query : Select Query window.
5. Close the **OutdoorOptions** database file.

To extract specific information when using the Simple Query Wizard, tell the wizard that you want to modify the query design. This displays a dialog box where you can insert query criteria.

exercise 5

PERFORMING AND MODIFYING A QUERY WITH THE SIMPLE QUERY WIZARD

1. Open the **OutdoorOptions** database file.
2. Perform a query with the Simple Query Wizard and modify the query by completing the following steps:
   a. Click the Queries button on the Objects bar.
   b. Double-click the *Create query by using wizard* option in the list box.
   c. At the first Simple Query Wizard dialog box, click the down-pointing arrow at the right of the *Tables/Queries* text box, and then click *Table: Suppliers*.
   d. Insert the following fields in the *Selected Fields* list box:

      Supplier Name
      Street Address
      City
      Province
      Postal Code

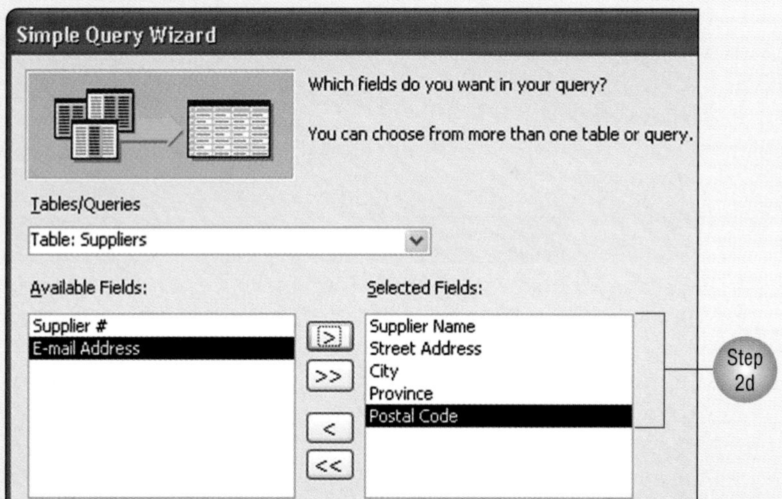

   e. Click the Next button.
   f. At the second Simple Query Wizard dialog box, type **SuppliersNotVancouver** in the *What title do you want for your query?* text box, click the *Modify the query design* option, and then click the Finish button.
   g. At the SuppliersNotVancouver : Select Query window, insert the query criterion by completing the following steps:
      1) Click in the *Criteria* text box in the *City* column.
      2) Type **Not Vancouver** and then press Enter.
   h. Specify that the fields are to be sorted in ascending order by Postal Code by completing the following steps:
      1) Click in the *Sort* text box in the *Postal Code* column (you may need to scroll to see this column).
      2) Click the down-pointing arrow that displays at the right side of the text box and then click *Ascending*.

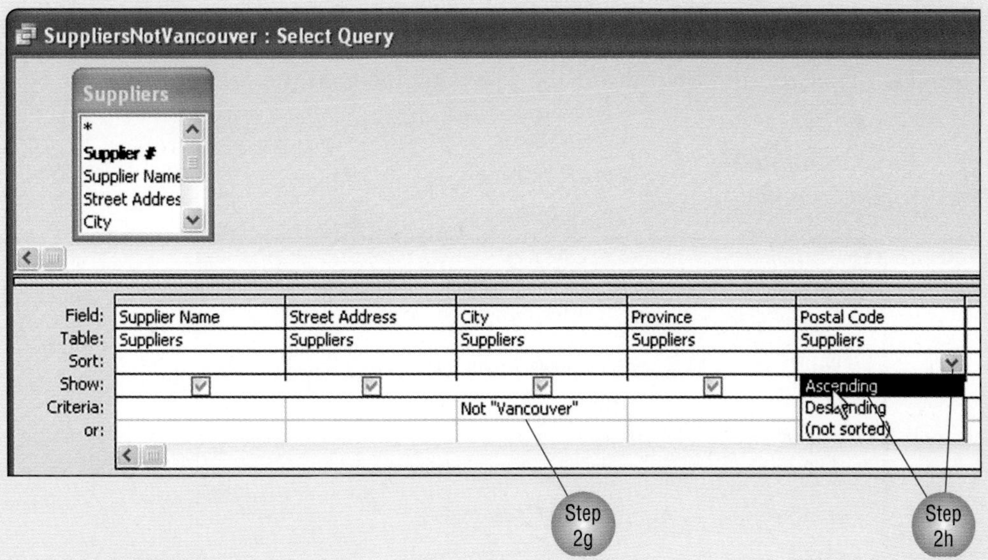

i. Click the Run button on the Query Design toolbar. (Those suppliers not situated in Vancouver will display and the records will display in ascending order by Postal Code.)
j. With the results of the query displayed, print the query.
k. Click the Save button to save the query.
l. Close the query.
3. Close the **OutdoorOptions** database file.

Creating a Calculated Field

A calculated control uses a mathematical equation to determine the contents that are displayed in the control object. In a query, you can insert a calculated field that performs mathematical equations. Insert a calculated field in the *Fields* text box when designing a query. To insert a calculated field, click in the desired *Field* text box. Type the desired field name followed by a colon and then type the equation. For example, to multiply Unit Price by Units Ordered and name the field *Total Amount*, you would type **Total Amount:[Unit Price]*[Units Ordered]** in the *Field* text box.

exercise 6

CREATING A CALCULATED FIELD IN A QUERY

1. Open the **OutdoorOptions** database file.
2. Perform a query with the Simple Query Wizard and modify the query by completing the following steps:
   a. Click the Queries button on the Objects bar.
   b. Double-click the *Create query by using wizard* option in the list box.
   c. At the first Simple Query Wizard dialog box, click the down-pointing arrow at the right of the *Tables/Queries* text box, and then click *Table: Suppliers*.

d. Insert the *Supplier Name* field in the *Selected Fields* list box.
e. Click the down-pointing arrow at the right of the *Tables/Queries* text box, click *Table: Products*, and then insert the following fields in the *Selected Fields* list box:

Product
Units in Stock
Units on Order

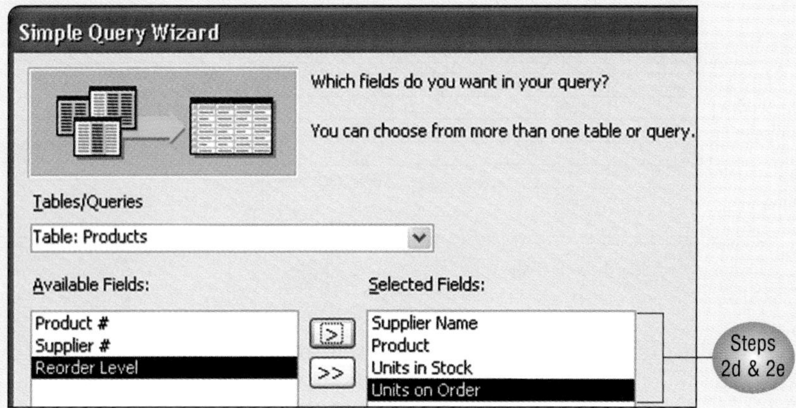

f. Click the Next button.
g. At the second Simple Query Wizard dialog box, click the Next button.
h. At the last Simple Query Wizard dialog box, type **StockTotals** in the *What title do you want for your query?* text box, click the *Modify the query design* option, and then click the Finish button.
i. At the StockTotals : Select Query window, insert a calculated field that calculates the total number of units by completing the following steps:
   1) Click in the fifth *Field* text box.
   2) Type **Total:[Units in Stock]+[Units on Order]** and then press Enter.

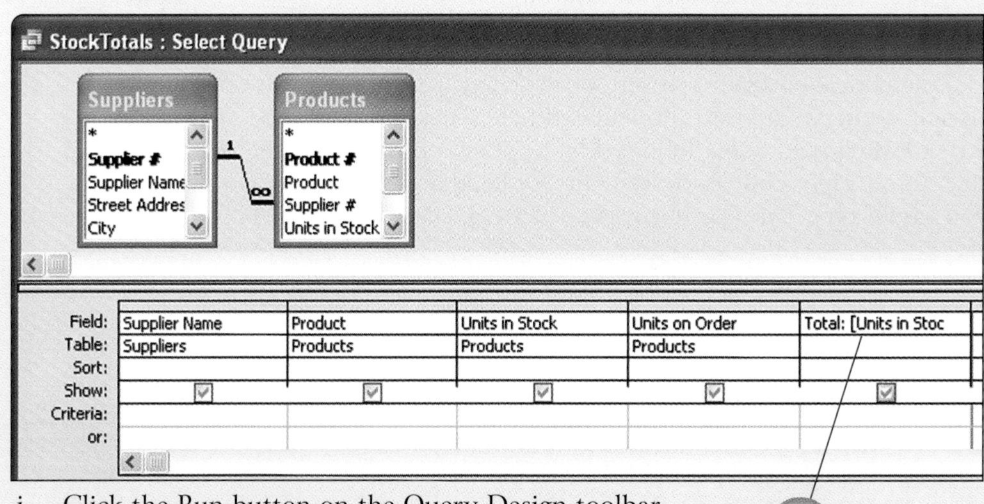

j. Click the Run button on the Query Design toolbar. (All records will display with the total of the units in stock and on order displayed.)
k. With the results of the query displayed, print the query.
l. Click the Save button to save the query.
m. Close the query.
3. Close the **OutdoorOptions** database file.

exercise 7

CREATING A CALCULATED FIELD IN A QUERY THAT CALCULATES UNIT PRICE

1. Open the **OutdoorOptions** database file.
2. Perform a query with the Simple Query Wizard and modify the query by completing the following steps:
   a. Click the Queries button on the Objects bar.
   b. Double-click the *Create query by using wizard* option in the list box.
   c. At the first Simple Query Wizard dialog box, click the down-pointing arrow at the right of the *Tables/Queries* text box, and then click *Table: Suppliers*.
   d. Insert the *Supplier Name* field in the *Selected Fields* list box.
   e. Click the down-pointing arrow at the right of the *Tables/Queries* text box, click *Table: Orders*, and then insert the following fields in the *Selected Fields* list box:

      Order #
      Units Ordered
      Amount

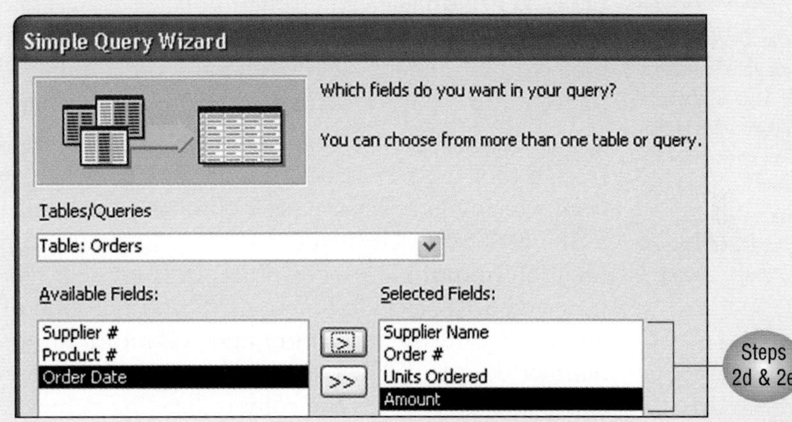

   f. Click the Next button.
   g. At the second Simple Query Wizard dialog box, click the Next button.
   h. At the last Simple Query Wizard dialog box, type **UnitPrices** in the *What title do you want for your query?* text box, click the *Modify the query design* option, and then click the Finish button.
   i. At the UnitPrices : Select Query window, insert a calculated field that calculates the unit price by completing the following steps:
      1) Click in the fifth *Field* text box.
      2) Type **Unit Price:[Amount]/[Units Ordered]** and then press Enter.

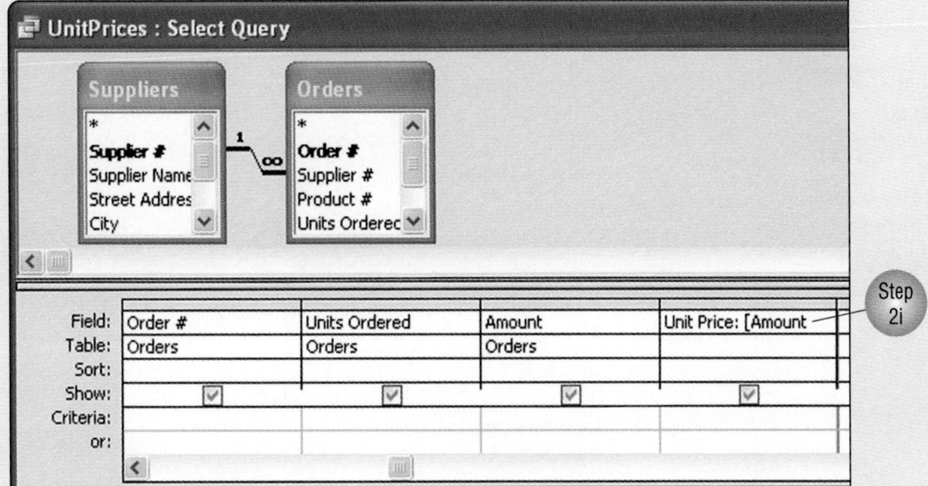

j. Click the Run button on the Query Design toolbar. (All records will display with the unit price calculated for each order.)

k. Save, print, and then close the query.

3. Close the **OutdoorOptions** database file.

Designing Queries with Aggregate Functions

QUICK STEPS

Design Query with Aggregate Function

1. At select query window, click the Totals button.
2. Click the down-pointing arrow in *Group By* list box.
3. Click desired aggregate function.

An aggregate function such as Sum, Avg, Min, Max, or Count can be included in a query to calculate statistics from numeric field values of all the records in the table. When an aggregate function is used, Access displays one row in the query results datasheet with the formula result for the function used. For example, in a table with a numeric field containing the annual salary amounts, you could use the Sum function to calculate the total of all salary amount values.

To display the aggregate function list, click the Totals button on the Query Design toolbar. Access adds a Total row to the design grid with a drop-down list from which you select the desired function. Access also inserts the words *Group By* in the list box. Click the down-pointing arrow and then click the desired aggregate function from the drop-down list. In Exercise 8, you will create a query in Design view and use aggregate functions to find the total of all order amounts, the average order amount, the maximum and the minimum order amount, and the total number of orders. The completed query will display as shown in Figure 4.6. Access automatically chooses the column heading names.

FIGURE 4.6 **Query Results for Exercise 8**

Access automatically chose the column heading names.

The aggregate functions calculated the order amounts in the *Amount* column in the Orders table.

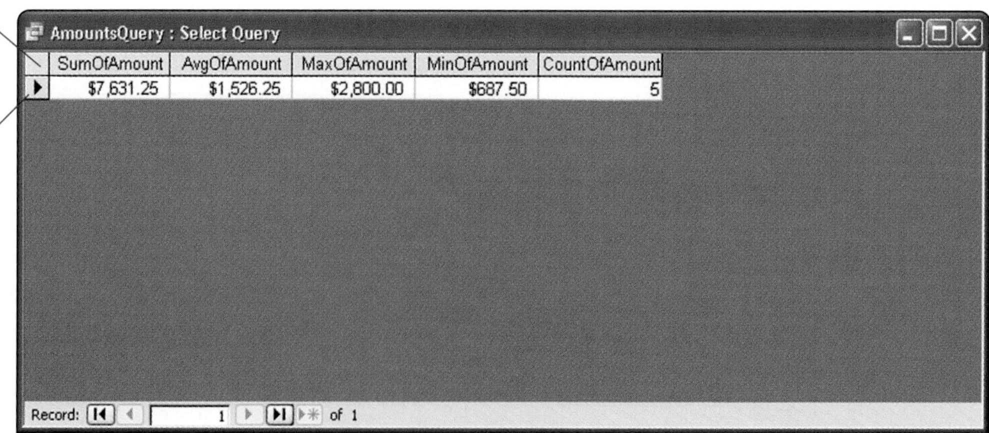

exercise 8

USING AGGREGATE FUNCTIONS IN A QUERY

1. Open the **OutdoorOptions** database file.
2. Determine the total, average, minimum, and maximum order amounts as well as the total number of orders. To begin, click the Queries button on the Objects bar.
3. Double-click *Create query in Design view*.
4. At the Show Table dialog box, click *Orders* in the list box, click the Add button, and then click the Close button.
5. Drag the *Amount* field from the Orders table list box (you will need to scroll down the list box to display this field) to the first *Field* text box.
6. Drag the *Amount* field to the second, third, fourth, and fifth *Field* text boxes.

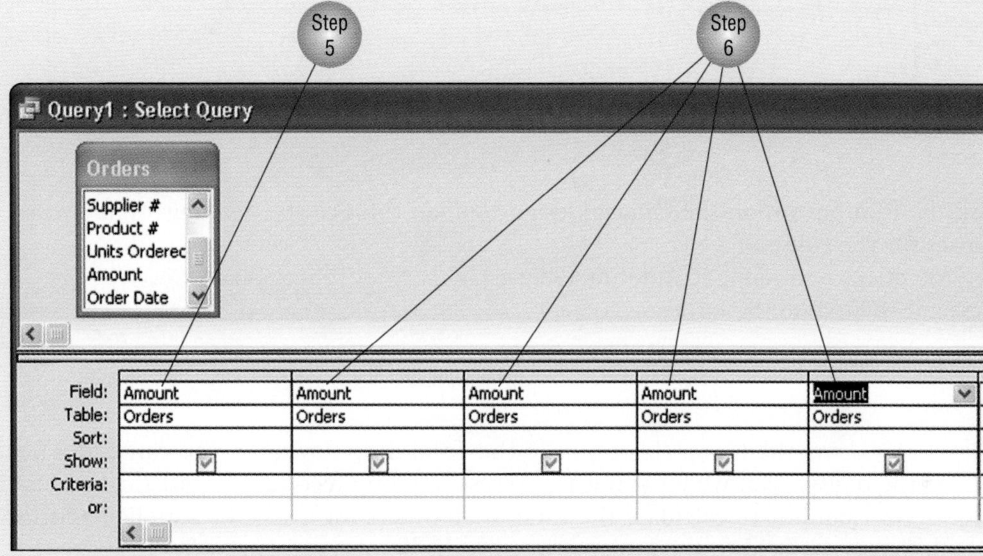

7. Click the Totals button on the Query Design toolbar. (This adds a *Total* row to the design grid between *Table* and *Sort* with the default option of *Group By*.)
8. Specify a Sum function for the first *Group By* list box by completing the following steps:
   a. Click in the first *Group By* option box in the *Total* row.
   b. Click the down-pointing arrow that displays at the right side of the list box.
   c. Click *Sum* at the drop-down list.

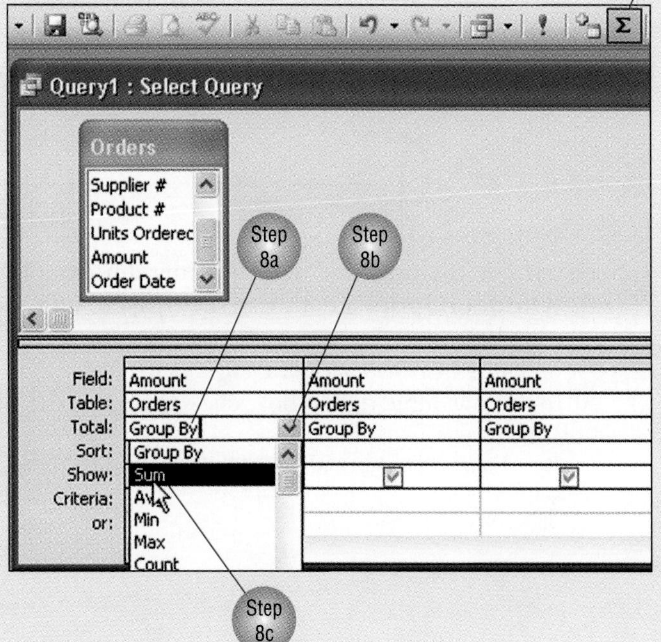

9. Complete steps similar to those in Step 8 to insert *Avg* in the second *Group By* list box in the *Total* row.
10. Complete steps similar to those in Step 8 to insert *Max* in the third *Group By* list box in the *Total* row.
11. Complete steps similar to those in Step 8 to insert *Min* in the fourth *Group By* list box in the *Total* row.
12. Complete steps similar to those in Step 8 to insert *Count* in the fifth *Group By* list box in the *Total* row.

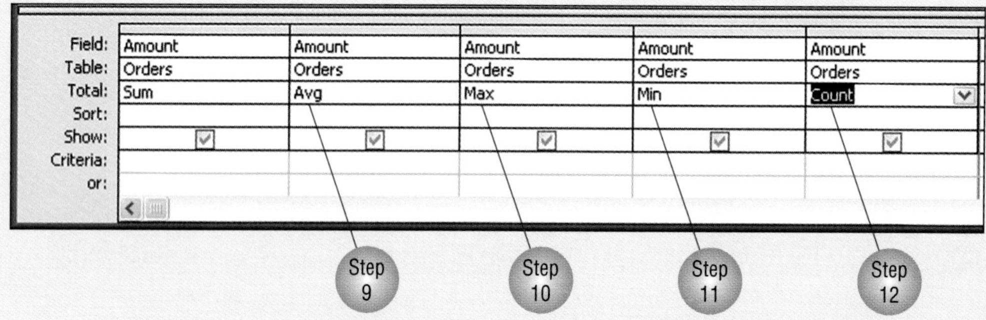

13. Click the Run button on the Query Design toolbar. (Notice the headings that Access chooses for the columns.)
14. Save the query and name it AmountsQuery.
15. Print and then close the query.

Using the *Group By* option in the Total drop-down list you can add a field to the query upon which you want Access to group records for statistical calculations. For example, to calculate the total of all orders for a specific supplier, add the *Supplier #* field to the design grid with the Total set to *Group By*. In Exercise 9, you will create a query in Design view and use aggregate functions to find the total of all order amounts and the average order amounts grouped by the supplier number.

exercise 9

USING AGGREGATE FUNCTIONS AND GROUPING RECORDS

1. Determine the total and average order amounts for each supplier. To begin, make sure the **OutdoorOptions** database file is open, and then click the Queries button on the Objects bar.
2. Double-click *Create query in Design view*.
3. At the Show Table dialog box, click *Orders* in the list box, and then click the Add button.
4. Click *Suppliers* in the list box, click the Add button, and then click the Close button.

5. Drag the *Amount* field from the Orders table list box to the first *Field* text box.
6. Drag the *Amount* field from the Orders table list box to the second *Field* text box.
7. Drag the *Supplier #* field from the Orders table list box to the third *Field* text box.
8. Drag the *Supplier Name* field from the Suppliers table to the fourth *Field* text box.
9. Click the Totals button on the Query Design toolbar.

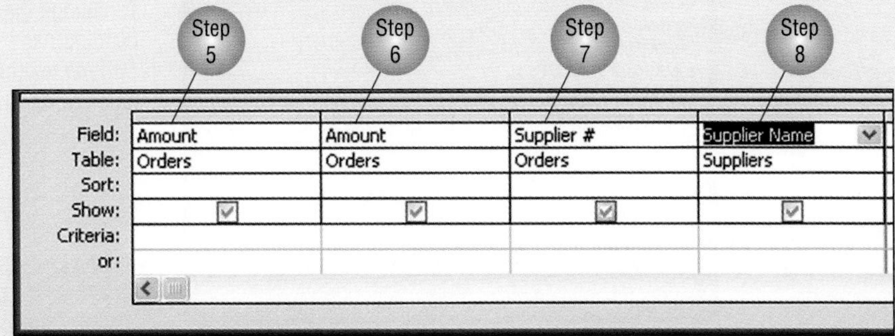

10. Click in the first *Group By* option box in the *Total* row, click the down-pointing arrow, and then click *Sum* at the drop-down list.
11. Click in the second *Group By* option box in the *Total* row, click the down-pointing arrow, and then click *Avg* at the drop-down list.
12. Make sure *Group By* displays in the third and fourth *Group By* option boxes.

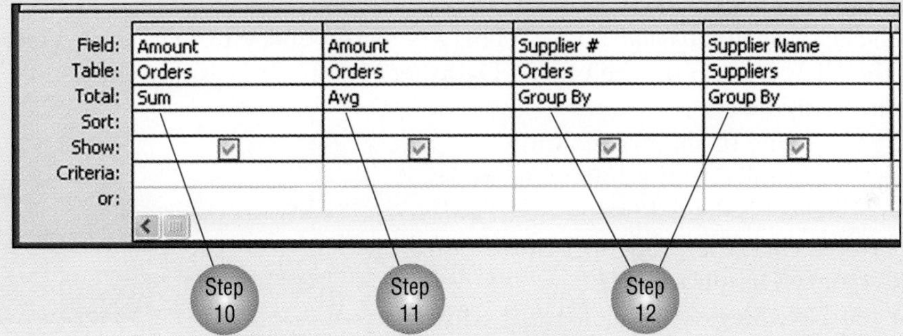

13. Click the Run button on the Query Design toolbar.
14. Save the query and name it SupplierAmountsQuery.
15. Print and then close the query.

Changing Query Column Headings

When you ran the queries in Exercises 8 and 9, Access chose the query column heading names for the columns containing aggregate functions. You can create your own headings. To do this, click in the *Field* text box, and then click the Properties button on the Query Design toolbar. This displays the Field Properties dialog box with the General tab selected as shown in Figure 4.7. At this dialog box, click in the *Caption* text box, and then type the desired column heading name.

FIGURE 4.7 ***Field Properties Dialog Box with General Tab Selected***

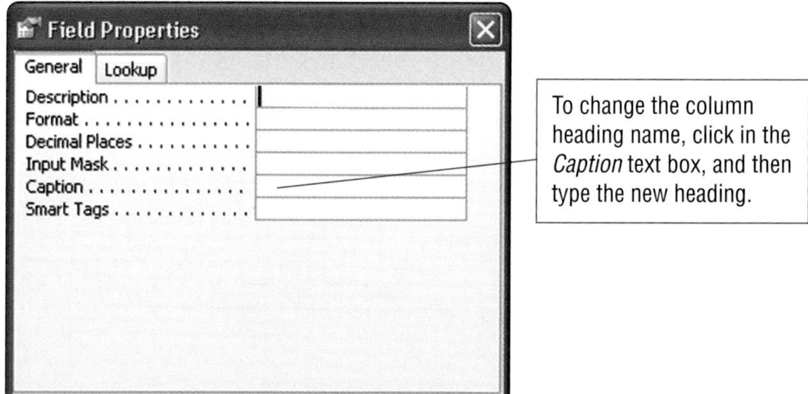

exercise 10

CHANGING QUERY COLUMN HEADING NAMES

1. Change two of the query column heading names in SupplierAmountsQuery. To begin, make sure the **OutdoorOptions** database file is open, and then click the Queries button on the Objects bar.
2. Double-click *SupplierAmountsQuery*. (This opens the query in Datasheet view.)
3. Click the View button on the Query Datasheet toolbar to display the query in Design view.
4. Change the name of the first column heading by completing the following steps:
   a. With *Amount* selected in the first *Field* text box, click the Properties button on the Query Design toolbar.
   b. At the Field Properties dialog box with the General tab selected, click in the *Caption* text box, and then type **Total Amount**.
   c. Click the Close button (located in the upper right corner of the dialog box).

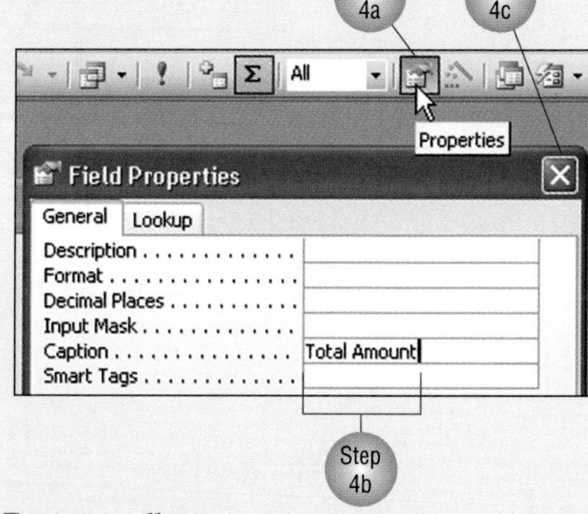

5. Change the name of the second column heading by completing the following steps:
   a. Click in the second *Field* text box.
   b. Click the Properties button on the Query Design toolbar.
   c. At the Field Properties dialog box with the General tab selected, click in the *Caption* text box, type **Average Order**, and then click the Close button.
6. Click the View button on the Query Design toolbar to change to the Datasheet view and then notice the column headings you created.
7. Save, print, and then close the query.
8. Close the **OutdoorOptions** database file.

Step 6

SupplierAmountsQuery : Select Query

Total Amount	Average Order	Supplier #	Supplier Name
$1,787.50	$893.75	68	Freedom Corporation
$2,800.00	$2,800.00	70	Rosewood, Inc.
$3,043.75	$1,521.88	99	KL Distributions

Creating a Crosstab Query

A crosstab query calculates aggregate functions such as Sum and Avg in which field values are grouped by two fields. A wizard is included that guides you through the steps to create the query. The first field selected causes one row to display in the query results datasheet for each group. The second field selected displays one column in the query results datasheet for each group. A third field is specified which is the numeric field to be summarized. The intersection of each row and column holds a value which is the result of the specified aggregate function for the designated row and column group.

Create a crosstab query from fields in one table. If you want to include fields from more than one table, you must first create a query containing the desired fields, and then create the crosstab query. For example, in Exercise 11, you will create a new query that contains fields from each of the three tables in the Outdoor Options database file. Using this query, you will use the Crosstab Query Wizard to create a query that summarizes the order amounts by supplier name and by product ordered. Figure 4.8 displays the results of that crosstab query. The first column displays the supplier names, the second column displays the total of amounts for each supplier, and the remaining columns display the amounts by suppliers for specific items.

QUICK STEPS

Create a Crosstab Query

1. Open database file.
2. Click Queries button.
3. Click New button.
4. Double-click *Crosstab Query Wizard.*
5. Complete wizard steps.

HINT

You can also create your own crosstab query in query Design view.

FIGURE 4.8 ***Crosstab Query Results for Exercise 11***

In this query, the order amounts are grouped by supplier name and by individual product.

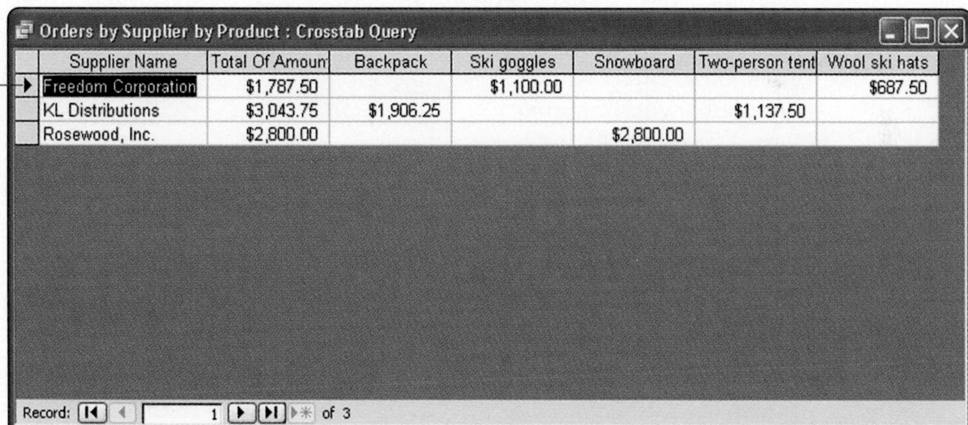

Orders by Supplier by Product : Crosstab Query
Supplier Name | Total Of Amoun | Backpack | Ski goggles | Snowboard | Two-person tent | Wool ski hats
Freedom Corporation | $1,787.50 | | $1,100.00 | | | $687.50
KL Distributions | $3,043.75 | $1,906.25 | | | $1,137.50 |
Rosewood, Inc. | $2,800.00 | | | $2,800.00 | |
Record: 1 of 3

exercise 11 CREATING A CROSSTAB QUERY

1. Open the **OutdoorOptions** database file.
2. Create a query containing fields from the three tables by completing the following steps:
   a. Click the Queries button on the Objects bar.
   b. Double-click *Create query in Design view.*
   c. At the Show Table dialog box, click *Orders* in the list box and then click the Add button.
   d. Click *Products* in the list box and then click the Add button.

e. Click *Suppliers* in the list box, click the Add button, and then click the Close button.
f. Drag the following fields to the specified *Field* text boxes:
   1) From the Orders table, drag the *Product #* field to the first *Field* text box.
   2) From the Products table, drag the *Product* field to the second *Field* text box.
   3) From the Orders table, drag the *Units Ordered* field to the third *Field* text box.
   4) From the Orders table, drag the *Amount* field to the fourth *Field* text box.
   5) From the Suppliers table, drag the *Supplier Name* field to the fifth *Field* text box.
   6) From the Orders table, drag the *Order Date* field to the sixth *Field* text box.

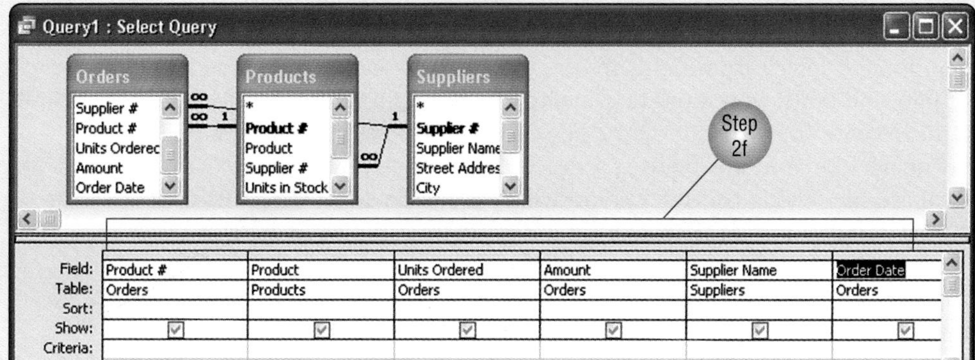

g. Click the Run button to run the query.
h. Save the query and name it Items Ordered.
i. Close the query.

3. Create a crosstab query that summarizes the orders by supplier name and by product ordered by completing the following steps:
   a. At the OutdoorOptions : Database window, make sure the Queries button is selected on the Objects bar, and then click the New button on the window toolbar.
   b. At the New Query dialog box, double-click *Crosstab Query Wizard* in the list box.
   c. At the first Crosstab Query Wizard dialog box, click the *Queries* option in the *View* section, and then click *Query: Items Ordered* in the list box.

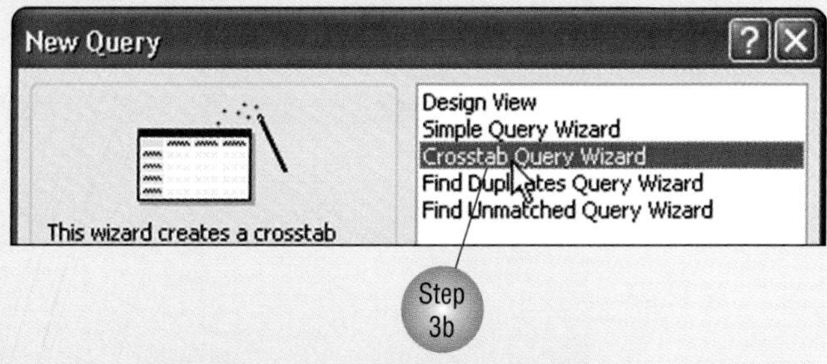

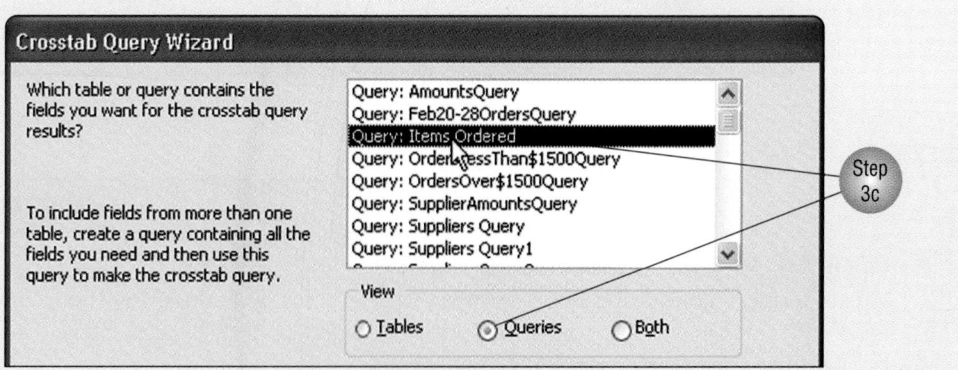

   d. Click the Next button.

e. At the second Crosstab Query Wizard dialog box, click *Supplier Name* in the *Available Fields* list box, and then click the button containing the greater than (>) symbol. (This inserts *Supplier Name* in the *Selected Fields* list box and specifies that you want *Supplier Name* for the row headings.) 
f. Click the Next button.
g. At the third Crosstab Query Wizard dialog box, click *Product* in the list box. (This specifies that you want *Product* for the column headings.) 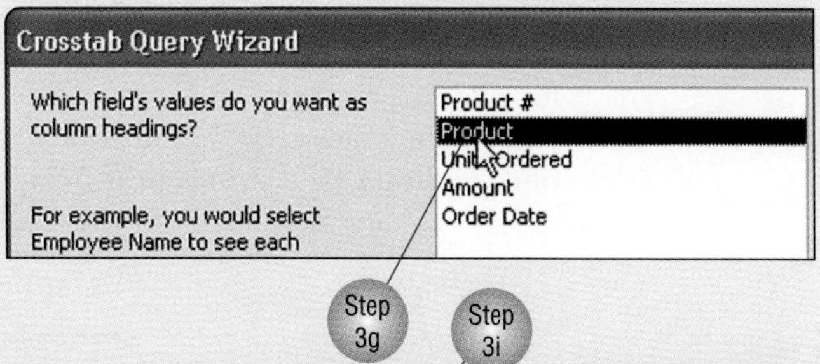
h. Click the Next button.
i. At the fourth Crosstab Query Wizard dialog box, click *Amount* in the *Fields* list box, and click *Sum* in the *Functions* list box. 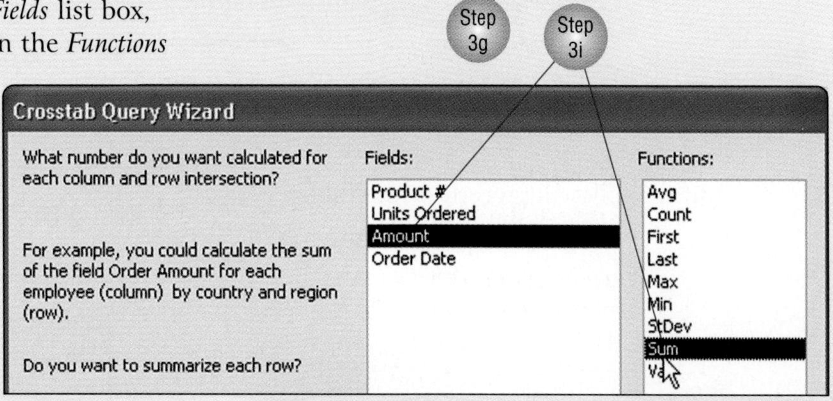
j. Click the Next button.
k. At the fifth Crosstab Query Wizard dialog box, type **Orders by Supplier by Product** in the *What do you want to name your query?* text box. 
l. Click the Finish button.

4. At the Orders by Supplier by Product query window, change the page orientation to landscape and then print the query by clicking the Print button on the Query Datasheet toolbar.
5. Close the query, and then close the **OutdoorOptions** database file.

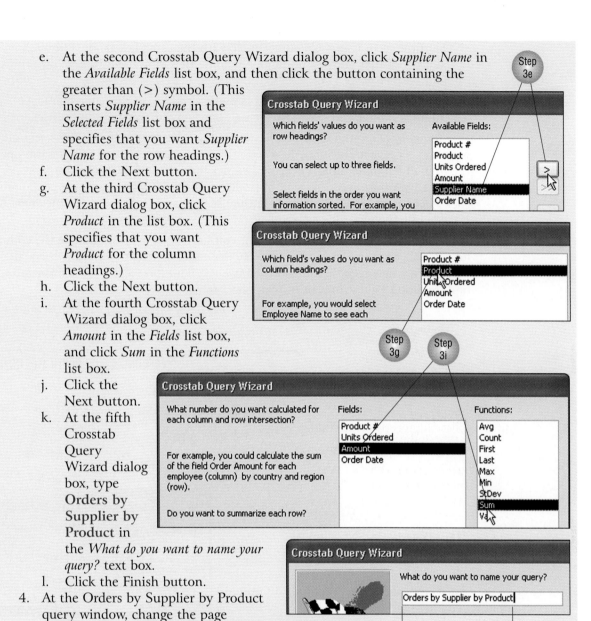

Creating a Find Duplicates Query

Use the find duplicates query to search a specified table or query for duplicate field values within a designated field or fields. Create this type of query, for example, if you suspect a record, such as a product record has inadvertently been entered twice under two different product numbers. A find duplicates query has many applications. A few other examples of how you can use a find duplicates query include:

- Find the records in an Orders table with the same customer number so that you can identify your loyal customers.

QUICK STEPS

Create a Find Duplicates Query
1. Open database file.
2. Click Queries button.
3. Click New button.
4. Double-click *Find Duplicates Query Wizard.*
5. Complete wizard steps.

- Find the records in a Customer table with the same last name and mailing address so that you send only one mailing to a household to save on printing and postage costs.
- Find the records in an Employee Expenses table with the same employee number so that you can see which employee is submitting the most claims.

Access provides the Find Duplicates Query Wizard that builds the select query based on the selections made in a series of dialog boxes. To use this wizard, open the desired database table, click the Queries button on the Objects bar, and then click the New button on the window toolbar. At the New Query dialog box, double-click *Find Duplicates Query Wizard* in the list box, and then complete the steps provided by the wizard.

In Exercise 12, you will assume that you have been asked to update the address for a supplier in the OutdoorOptions database file. Instead of updating the address, you create a new record. You will then use the Find Duplicates Query Wizard to find duplicate field values in the Suppliers table.

exercise 12 — CREATING A FIND DUPLICATES QUERY

1. Open the **OutdoorOptions** database file.
2. Click the Tables button on the Objects bar and then open the Suppliers table.
3. Add the following record to the table:

Supplier #	=	29
Supplier Name	=	Langley Corporation
Street Address	=	805 First Avenue
City	=	Burnaby
Province	=	BC
Postal Code	=	V5V 9K2
E-mail Address	=	langley@emcp.net

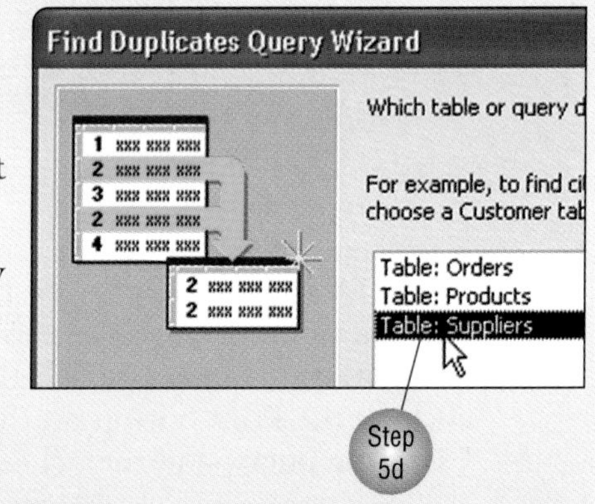

4. Close the Suppliers table.
5. Use the Find Duplicates Query Wizard to find any duplicate supplier names by completing the following steps:
   a. Click the Queries button on the Objects bar.
   b. Click the New button on the window toolbar.
   c. At the New Query dialog box, double-click *Find Duplicates Query Wizard*.
   d. At the first wizard dialog box, click *Table: Suppliers* in the list box.
   e. Click the Next button.
   f. At the second wizard dialog box, click *Supplier Name* in the *Available fields* list box, and then click the button containing the greater than (>) symbol. (This moves the *Supplier Name* field to the *Duplicate-value fields* list box.)
   g. Click the Next button.

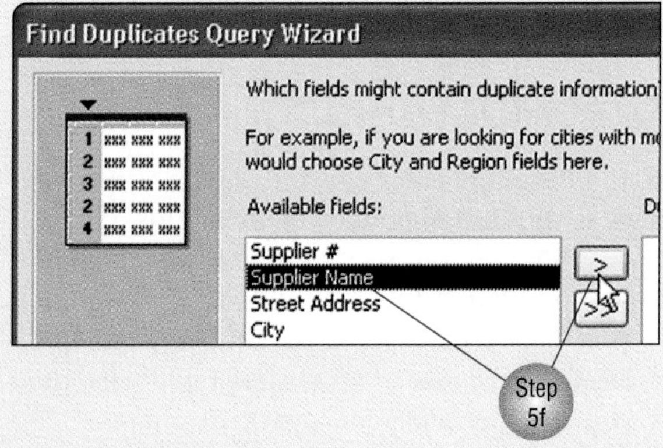

h. At the third wizard dialog box, click the button containing the two greater than (>>) symbols. (This moves all the fields to the *Additional query fields* list box. You are doing this because if you find a duplicate supplier name, you want to view all the fields to determine which record is accurate.)

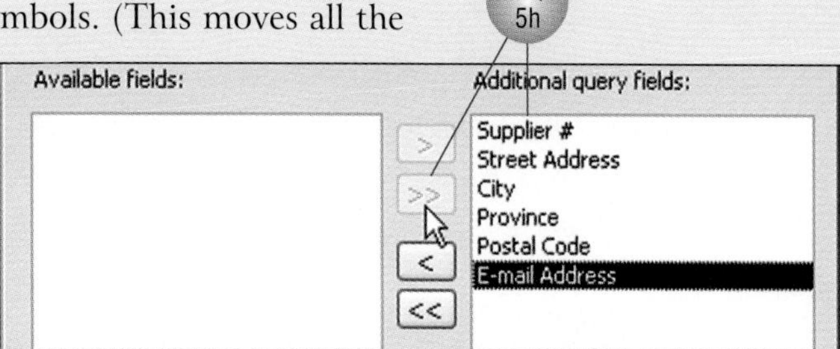

i. Click the Next button.

j. At the fourth (and last) wizard dialog box, type **DuplicateSuppliers** in the *What do you want to name your query?* text box.

k. Click the Finish button.

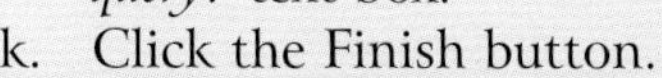

l. Change the orientation to landscape and then print the DuplicateSuppliers query.

Find Duplicates Query Wizard

What do you want to name your query?

DuplicateSuppliers

Step 5j

6. As you look at the query results, you realize that an inaccurate record was entered for Langley so you decide to delete one of the records. To do this, complete the following steps:

a. With the DuplicateSuppliers query open, position the mouse pointer in the record selector bar next to the first record (the one with a supplier number of *29*) until the pointer changes to a right-pointing black arrow, and then click the left mouse button. (This selects the entire row.)

b. Click the Delete Record button on the Query Datasheet toolbar.

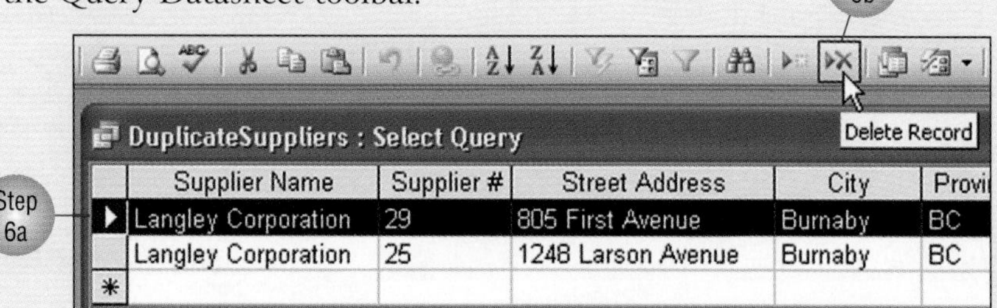

Supplier Name	Supplier #	Street Address	City	Provi
Langley Corporation	29	805 First Avenue	Burnaby	BC
Langley Corporation	25	1248 Larson Avenue	Burnaby	BC

c. At the message asking you to confirm, click the Yes button.

d. Close the DuplicateSuppliers query.

7. Change the street address for Langley Corporation by completing the following steps:

a. Click the Tables button on the Objects bar.

b. Double-click the *Suppliers* table.

c. With the Suppliers table open in Datasheet view, change the address for Langley Corporation from *1248 Larson Avenue* to *805 First Avenue*. Leave the other fields as displayed.

d. Close the Suppliers table.

8. Close the **OutdoorOptions** database file.

In Exercise 12, you used the Find Duplicates Query Wizard to find records containing the same field. In Exercise 13, you will use the Find Duplicates Query Wizard to find information on the suppliers you order from the most. You could use this information to negotiate for better prices or to ask for discounts.

exercise 13

FINDING DUPLICATE ORDERS

1. Open the **OutdoorOptions** database file.
2. Create a query with the following fields (in the order shown) from the specified tables:

Order #	=	Orders table
Supplier #	=	Orders table
Supplier Name	=	Suppliers table
Product #	=	Orders table
Units Ordered	=	Orders table
Amount	=	Orders table
Order Date	=	Orders table

3. Run the query.
4. Save the query with the name SupplierOrders and then close the query.
5. Use the Find Duplicates Query Wizard to find the suppliers you order from the most by completing the following steps:
   a. Click the Queries button on the Objects bar.
   b. Click the New button on the window toolbar.
   c. At the New Query dialog box, double-click *Find Duplicates Query Wizard*.
   d. At the first wizard dialog box, click *Queries* in the *View* section, and then double-click *Query: SupplierOrders*.
   e. Click the Next button.
   f. At the second wizard dialog box, click *Supplier #* in the *Available fields* list box and then click the button containing the greater than (>) symbol.

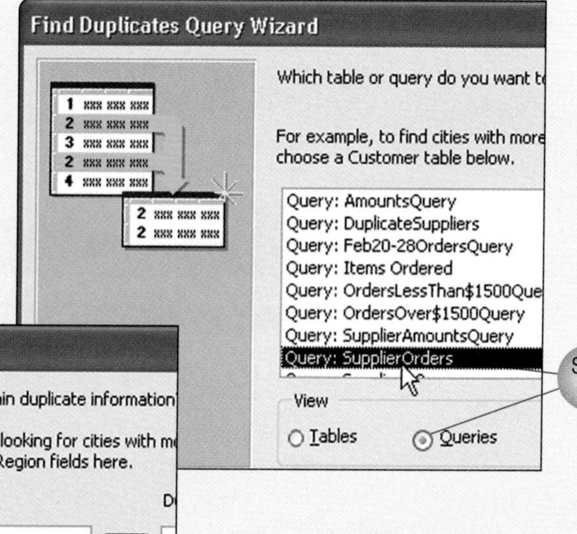

   g. Click the Next button.
   h. At the third wizard dialog box, click the button containing the two greater than (>>) symbols. (This moves all the fields to the *Duplicate-value fields* list box.)
   i. Click the Next button.

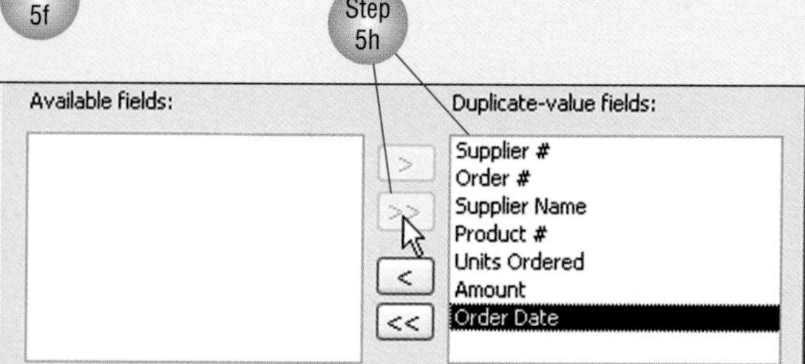

j. At the fourth (and last) wizard dialog box, type **DuplicateSupplierOrders** in the *What do you want to name your query?* text box.

k. Click the Finish button.

l. Print the DuplicateSupplierOrders query.

6. Close the query, and then close the **OutdoorOptions** database file.

Creating an Unmatched Query

Create a find unmatched query to compare two tables and produce a list of the records in one table that have no matching record in the other related table. This type of query is useful to produce lists such as customers who have never placed an order or an invoice with no payment record. Access provides the Find Unmatched Query Wizard that builds the select query by guiding you through a series of dialog boxes.

In Exercise 14, you will use the Find Unmatched Query Wizard to find all products that have no units on order. This information is helpful because it indicates which products are not selling and might need to be discontinued or returned. To use the Find Unmatched Query Wizard, open the database file, and then click the Queries button on the Objects bar. At the New Query dialog box, click the New button on the window toolbar, and then double-click *Find Unmatched Query Wizard* in the list box.

Create an Unmatched Query

1. Open database file.
2. Click Queries button.
3. Click New button.
4. Double-click *Find Unmatched Query Wizard.*
5. Complete wizard steps.

exercise 14

CREATING A FIND UNMATCHED QUERY

1. Open the **OutdoorOptions** database file.
2. Use the Find Unmatched Query Wizard to find all products that do not have any units on order by completing the following steps:
   a. Click the Queries button on the Objects bar.
   b. Click the New button on the window toolbar.
   c. At the New Query dialog box, double-click *Find Unmatched Query Wizard.*
   d. At the first wizard dialog box, click *Table: Products* in the list box. (This is the table containing the fields you want to see in the query results.)
   e. Click the Next button.
   f. At the second wizard dialog box, make sure *Table: Orders* is selected in the list box. (This is the table containing the related records.)
   g. Click the Next button.

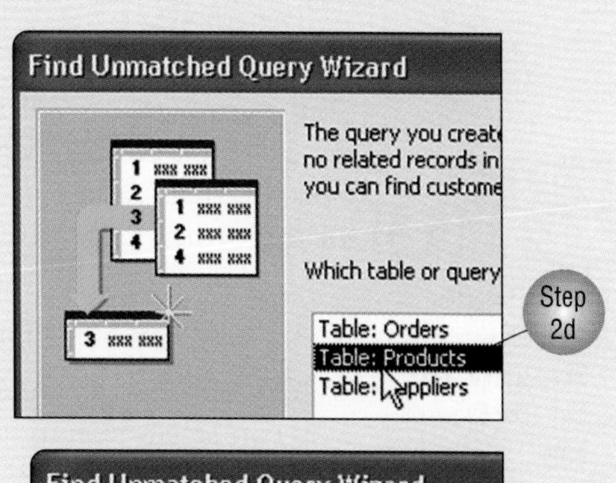

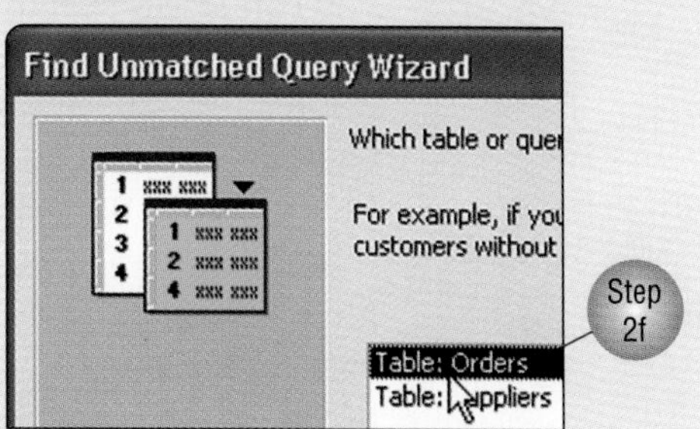

h. At the third wizard dialog box, make sure *Product #* is selected in the *Fields in 'Products'* list box and in the *Fields in 'Orders'* list box.

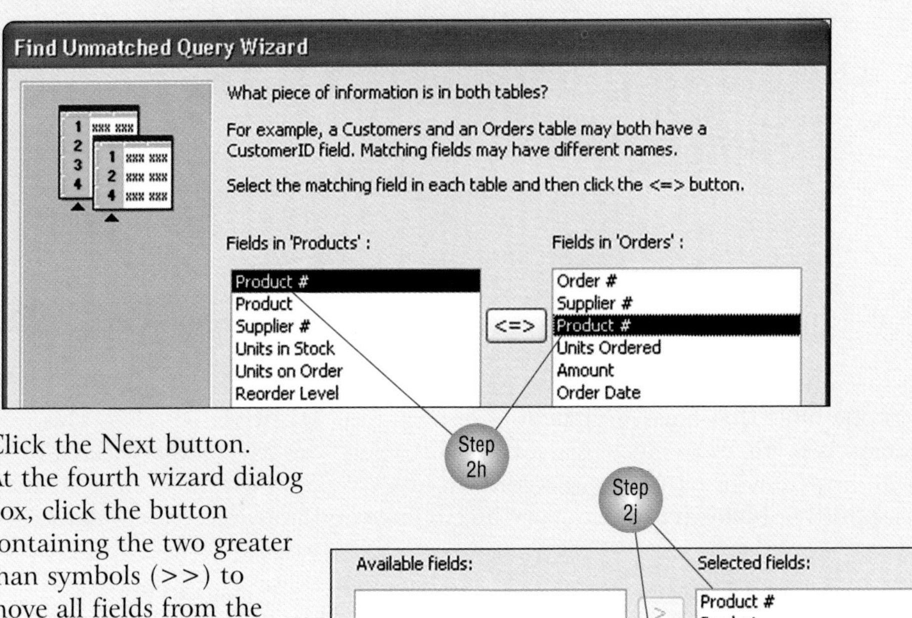

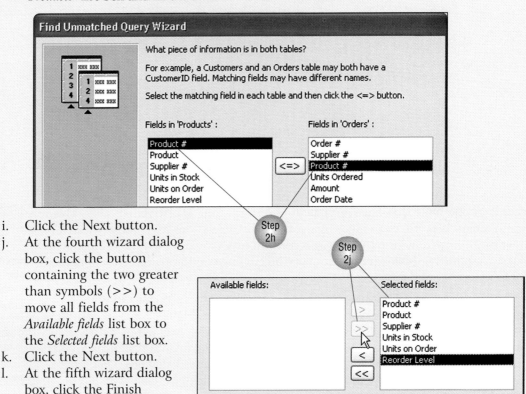

i. Click the Next button.

j. At the fourth wizard dialog box, click the button containing the two greater than symbols (>>) to move all fields from the *Available fields* list box to the *Selected fields* list box.

k. Click the Next button.

l. At the fifth wizard dialog box, click the Finish button. (Let the wizard determine the query name: *Products Without Matching Orders*.)

3. Print and then close the Products Without Matching Orders query.

Filtering Data

You can place a set of restrictions, called a ***filter***, on records in a database table or form to temporarily isolate specific records. A filter, like a query, lets you select specific field values in a database table or form. Data can be filtered by selection or by form.

QUICK STEPS

Filter by Selection
1. Open database table.
2. Select specific data.
3. Click Filter By Selection button.

Filter By Selection

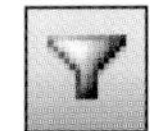
Apply Filter

Using Filter By Selection

With the Filter By Selection button that displays on the Table Datasheet toolbar, you can select specific data in a field and then tell Access to display only those records containing the selected data. For example, if you want to display only those records for a specific supplier number, select the supplier number in the appropriate database table, and then click the Filter By Selection button on the Table Datasheet toolbar. Only those records matching the selected data are displayed on the screen.

The Table Datasheet toolbar contains a button named Apply Filter. When a filter is applied by selection, this button changes to Remove Filter (and also displays with a blue border). If you want to remove the filter and display the original data in the database table, click the Remove Filter button on the Table Datasheet toolbar.

exercise 15

USING FILTER BY SELECTION TO DISPLAY SPECIFIC DATA IN A DATABASE TABLE

1. Open the **OutdoorOptions** database file.
2. At the OutdoorOptions : Database window, click the Tables button on the Objects bar.
3. Open the Products database table by double-clicking *Products* in the list box.
4. Use the Filter By Selection button to display only those records with no units on order by completing the following steps:
   a. Select a 0 (zero) in one of the fields in the *Units on Order* column.
   b. Click the Filter By Selection button on the Table Datasheet toolbar. (This displays only those records with no units on order.)
   c. Sort the records in ascending order by the supplier number by completing the following steps:
      1) Click in any field in the *Supplier #* column.
      2) Click the Sort Ascending button on the Table Datasheet toolbar.
   d. Print the database table.
   e. After printing the table, click the Remove Filter button on the Table Datasheet toolbar (this redisplays all records in the database table).
5. Close the Products database table without saving the changes to the design.
6. Open the Suppliers database table by double-clicking *Suppliers* in the list box.
7. Use the Filter By Selection button to display only those records of suppliers in Burnaby by completing the following steps:
   a. Select *Burnaby* in one of the fields in the *City* column.
   b. Click the Filter By Selection button on the Table Datasheet toolbar.
   c. Print the database table in landscape orientation.
   d. After printing the table, click the Remove Filter button on the Table Datasheet toolbar (this redisplays all records in the database table).
8. Close the Suppliers database table without saving changes to the design.
9. Close the **OutdoorOptions** database file.

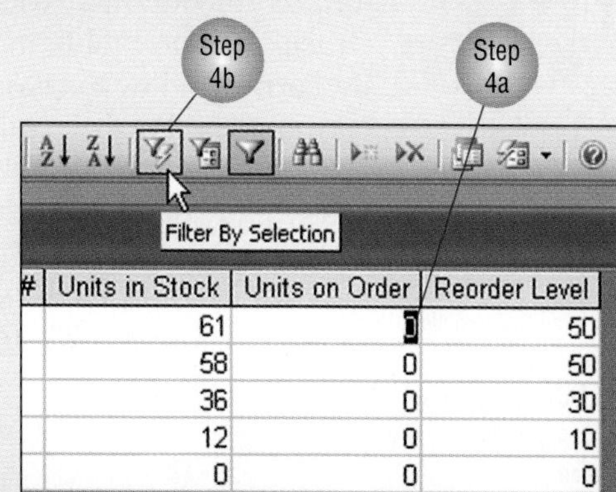

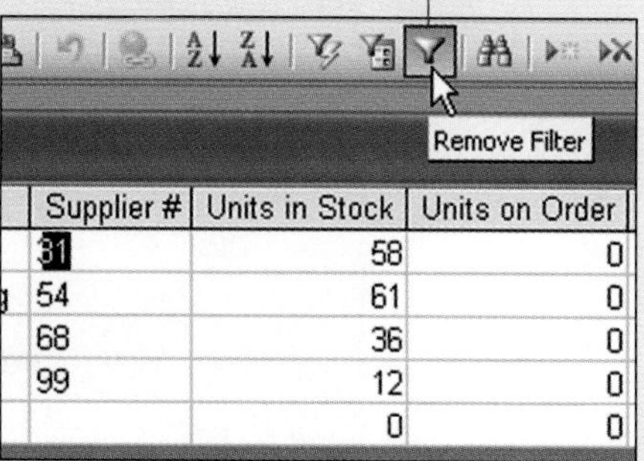

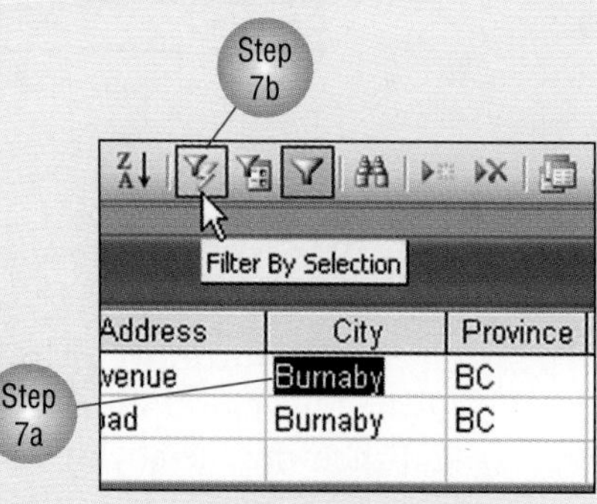

Filter By Form

Filter by Form
1. Open database table.
2. Click Filter By Form button.
3. Click in desired field.
4. Click the down-pointing arrow in field.
5. Click desired option.
6. Click Apply Filter button.

Using Filter By Form

The Table Datasheet toolbar contains a Filter By Form button that, when clicked, displays the database table with a blank record. You set the values you want filtered records to contain at this blank record. Figure 4.9 shows a blank record for the Orders database table in the OutdoorOptions database file. At the Orders : Filter By Form window displayed in Figure 4.9, notice that two tabs display toward the bottom. The Look for tab is active by default and tells Access to look for whatever data you insert in a field. To display only those records for supplier number 68, you would click inside the *Supplier #* field. This causes a down-pointing arrow to display. Click this down-pointing arrow and then click *68* at the drop-down list. To filter the records, click the Filter By Form button on the Table Datasheet toolbar and only those records for supplier number 68 are displayed on the screen.

FIGURE 4.9 ***Orders: Filter By Form Window***

Click in the desired field, click the down-pointing arrow, and then click the desired item.

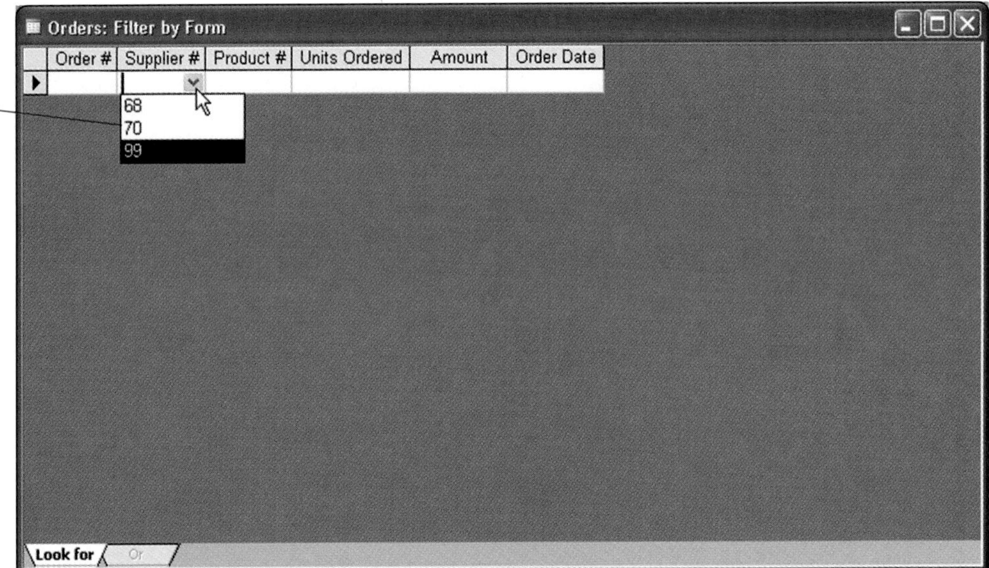

exercise 16 USING FILTER BY FORM TO DISPLAY SPECIFIC RECORDS

1. Open the **OutdoorOptions** database file.
2. At the OutdoorOptions : Database window, click the Tables button on the Objects bar, and then double-click *Orders* in the list box.
3. Use the Filter By Form button to display only those records containing supplier number 68 in the *Supplier #* field by completing the following steps:
   a. Click the Filter By Form button on the Table Datasheet toolbar.
   b. At the blank record, click in the *Supplier #* field.

c. Click the down-pointing arrow at the right side of the *Supplier #* field and then click *68* at the drop-down list.

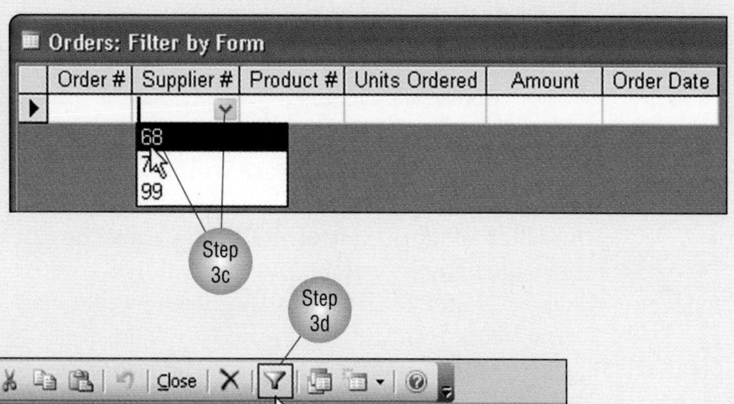

d. Click the Apply Filter button on the Table Datasheet toolbar.

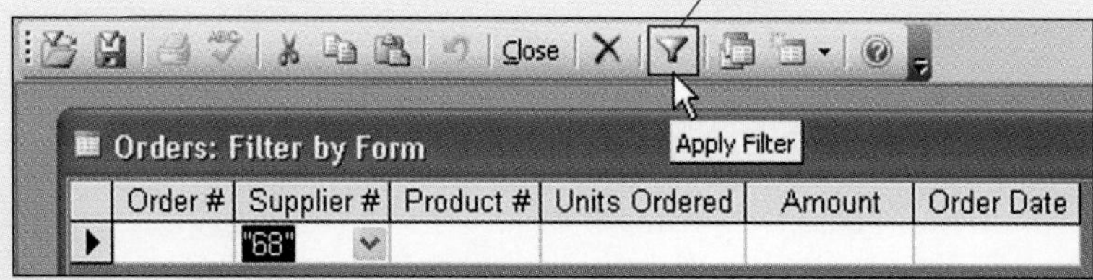

e. Print the records.

4. Close the Orders : Table window without saving the changes to the design.
5. At the OutdoorOptions : Database window, double-click *Products* in the list box.
6. Use the Filter By Form button to display only those records containing supplier number 99 in the *Supplier #* field by completing the following steps:
   a. Click the Filter By Form button on the Table Datasheet toolbar.
   b. At the blank record, click in the *Supplier #* field.
   c. Click the down-pointing arrow at the right side of the *Supplier #* field and then click *99* at the drop-down list.
   d. Click the Apply Filter button on the Table Datasheet toolbar.
   e. Print the records.

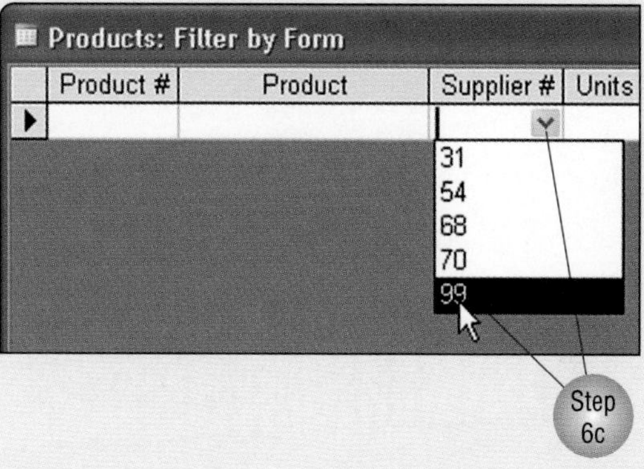

7. Close the Products : Table window without saving the changes to the design.
8. Close the **OutdoorOptions** database file.

A tab displays at the bottom of the Orders: Filter By Form window shown in Figure 4.6 with the word *Or*. Click this tab if you want to filter on two field values. When you click the Or tab, another blank record displays below the first one. As an example of when you would use the Or tab, suppose you wanted to display only those records for supplier # 68 *or* supplier # 31. You would insert *68* in the *Supplier #* field of the first blank record, click the Or button, and then insert *31* in the *Supplier #* field in the second blank record. As another example, in a database table containing suppliers' addresses, you could display only those records for suppliers located in Vancouver *or* Port Moody.

HINT
Data can be filtered on two field values.

exercise 17

USING FILTER BY FORM TO FILTER ON TWO FIELD VALUES

1. Open the **OutdoorOptions** database file.
2. At the OutdoorOptions : Database window, click the Tables button on the Objects bar, and then double-click *Suppliers* in the list box.
3. Use the Filter By Form button to display only those records for suppliers in Port Moody *or* Burnaby by completing the following steps:
   a. Click the Filter By Form button on the Table Datasheet toolbar.
   b. At the blank record, click in the *City* field.
   c. Click the down-pointing arrow at the right side of the *City* field, and then click *Port Moody* at the drop-down list.
   d. Click the Or tab located toward the bottom of the Suppliers : Filter by Form window.
   e. At the new blank record, click the down-pointing arrow at the right side of the *City* field, and then click *Burnaby* at the drop-down list.
   f. Click the Apply Filter button on the Table Datasheet toolbar.
   g. Print the records in landscape orientation.
4. Close the Suppliers : Table window without saving the changes to the design.
5. Close the **OutdoorOptions** database file.

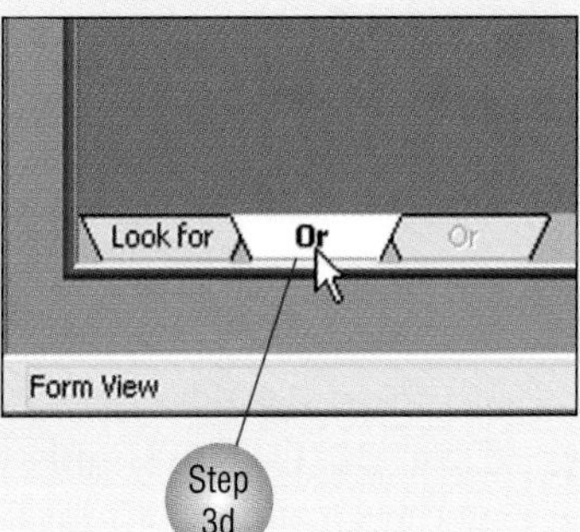

CHAPTER summary

- Being able to extract specific information is one of the most important functions of a database. Data can be extracted from an Access database file by performing a query, which can be done by designing a query or using the Simple Query Wizard.
- Designing a query consists of identifying the database table, the field or fields from which the data will be drawn, and the criteria for selecting the data.
- During the designing of a query, write the criterion (or criteria) for extracting the specific data. Access inserts any necessary symbols in the criterion when the Enter key is pressed.
- In a criterion, quotation marks surround field values and pound symbols (#) surround dates. The asterisk (*) can be used as a wildcard symbol.
- A query can be performed on fields within one database table or on fields from related database tables.
- When designing a query, you can specify the sort order of a field or fields.
- The Simple Query Wizard guides you through the steps for preparing a query. A query designed by the Simple Query Wizard can be modified.
- A calculated field can be inserted in a *Field* text box when designing a query.

- Include an aggregate function such as Sum, Avg, Min, Max, or Count to calculate statistics from numeric field values. Click the Totals button on the Query Design toolbar to display the aggregate function list.
- Use the *Group By* option in the Total drop-down list to add a field to a query upon which you want Access to group records for statistical calculations.
- Create a crosstab query to calculate aggregate functions such as Sum and Avg in which fields are grouped by two fields. Create a crosstab query from fields in one table. If you want to include fields from more than one table, create a query first, and then create the crosstab query.
- Use the find duplicates query to search a specified table or query for duplicate field values within a designated field or fields.
- Create a find unmatched query to compare two tables and produce a list of the records in one table that have no matching record in the other related table.
- A set of restrictions, called a filter, can be set on records in a database table or form. A filter lets you select specific field values.
- Filter specific data in a field with the Filter By Selection button that displays on the Table Datasheet toolbar.
- Click the Filter By Form button on the Table Datasheet toolbar and a blank record is displayed. Set the values you want filtered records to contain at this blank record.
- When a filter is done by selection or by form, the Apply Filter button on the Table Datasheet toolbar changes to Remove Filter.

FEATURES summary

FEATURE	BUTTON	MENU
New Query dialog box	New	Insert, Query
Simple Query Wizard		Insert, Query, Simple Query Wizard
Run a query	!	Query, Run
Add Total row to Design grid	Σ	View, Totals
Crosstab Query Wizard		Insert, Query, Crosstab Wizard
Find Duplicates Query Wizard		Insert, Query, Find Duplicates Query Wizard
Find Unmatched Query Wizard		Insert, Query, Find Unmatched Query Wizard
Filter by selection		Records, Filter, Filter By Selection
Filter by form		Records, Filter, Filter By Form

CONCEPTS check

Completion: On a blank sheet of paper, indicate the correct term, symbol, or command for each description.

1. A query can be performed by designing your own query or using this wizard.
2. This is the term used for the results of the query.
3. This is the symbol Access will automatically insert around a field value when establishing criteria for a query.
4. This is the symbol Access will automatically insert around a date when establishing criteria for a query.
5. Use this symbol when establishing criteria to indicate a wildcard character.
6. This is the criterion you would type to return field values greater than $500.
7. This is the criterion you would type to return field values that begin with the letter *L*.
8. This is the criterion you would type to return field values that are not in Oregon.
9. This type of function, such as Sum, Avg, Min, Max, or Count can be included in a query to calculate statistics from numeric field values of all the records in the table.
10. With this option from the Total drop-down list, you can add a field to the query upon which you want Access to group records for statistical calculations.
11. This type of query calculates aggregate functions in which field values are grouped by two fields.
12. Use this type of query to compare two tables and produce a list of the records in one table that have no matching record in the other related table.
13. A set of restrictions placed on records in a database table or form is referred to as this.
14. Click this button on the Table Datasheet toolbar to display only those records containing the selected data.
15. Click this tab, located at the bottom of the Filter By Form dialog box, to filter on two field values.
16. List the steps you would complete to display only those records with order dates between February 15, 2005, and February 20, 2005, in the Orders database table located in the OutdoorOptions database file.

SKILLS check

Assessment 1

1. Copy the **LegalServices** database file from the CD that accompanies this textbook to your disk. Remove the read-only attribute from the **LegalServices** database file.
2. Open the **LegalServices** database file.
3. Design the following queries on data in the **LegalServices** database file:
   a. Extract records from the Billing database table with the following specifications:
      1) Include the fields *Billing #*, *Client ID*, and *Category* in the query.
      2) Extract those records with the SE category.
      3) Save the query and name it SECategoryBillingQuery.
      4) Print and then close the query.
   b. Extract records from the Billing database table with the following specifications:
      1) Include the fields *Billing #*, *Client ID*, and *Date*.

2) Extract those records in the *Date* field with dates between 6/7/2005 and 6/9/2005.
3) Save the query and name it June7-9BillingQuery.
4) Print and then close the query.

c. Extract records from the Clients database table with the following specifications:
1) Include the fields *First Name*, *Last Name*, and *City*.
2) Extract those records with any city other than Kent in the *City* field.
3) Save the query and name it KentClientsQuery.
4) Print and then close the query.

Assessment 2

1. With the **LegalServices** database file open, perform a query by extracting information from two tables with the following specifications:
   a. Include the fields *Billing #*, *Client ID*, *Date*, and *Rate #* from the Billing database table.
   b. Include the field *Rate* from the Rates database table.
   c. Extract those records with a rate number greater than 2.
   d. Save the query and name it RateGreaterThan2Query.
   e. Print and then close the query.
2. Extract information from three tables with the following specifications:
   a. Include the field *Attorney* from the Attorneys database table.
   b. Include the fields *First Name* and *Last Name* from the Clients database table.
   c. Include the fields *Attorney ID*, *Date,* and *Hours* from the Billing database.
   d. Extract those records with an Attorney ID of 12.
   e. Save the query and name it AttorneyQuery.
   f. Print and then close the query.

Assessment 3

1. With the **LegalServices** database file open, use the Simple Query Wizard to extract specific information from three tables with the following specifications:
   a. At the first Simple Query Wizard dialog box, include the following fields:

      From the Attorneys table: *Attorney ID* and *Attorney*
      From Categories table: *Category Name*
      From Billing table: *Hours*

   b. At the second Simply Query Wizard dialog box, click Next.
   c. At the third Simple Query Wizard dialog box, click the *Modify the query design* option, and then click the Finish button.
   d. At the query window, insert *14* in the *Criteria* text box in the *Attorney ID* column.
   e. Run the query.
2. Save the query with the default name.
3. Print and then close the query.

Assessment 4

1. With the **LegalServices** database file open, create a query in Design view with the Billing table. Drag the *Hours* field from the Billing table to the first, second, third, fourth, and fifth *Field* text boxes.
2. Click the Totals button on the Query Design toolbar.
3. Insert *Sum* in the first *Group By* list box in the *Total* row.
4. Insert *Avg* in the second *Group By* list box in the *Total* row.

5. Insert *Min* in the third *Group By* list box in the *Total* row.
6. Insert *Max* in the fourth *Group By* list box in the *Total* row.
7. Insert *Count* in the fifth *Group By* list box in the *Total* row.
8. Run the query.
9. Save the query and name it HoursAmountQuery.
10. Print and then close the query.

Assessment 5

1. With the **LegalServices** database file open, create a query in Design view with the following specifications:
   a. Add the Attorneys table and the Billing table to the query window.
   b. Drag the *Attorney* field from the Attorneys table to the first *Field* text box.
   c. Drag the *Attorney ID* field from the Billing table to the second *Field* text box.
   d. Drag the *Hours* field from the Billing table to the third *Field* text box.
2. Click the Totals button on the Query Design toolbar.
3. Insert *Sum* in the third *Group By* list box in the *Hours* column (in the *Total* row).
4. Run the query.
5. Save the query and name it AttorneyHours.
6. Print and then close the query.

Assessment 6

1. With the **LegalServices** database file open, create a query in Design view with the following specifications:
   a. Add the Attorneys, Clients, Categories, and Billing tables to the query window.
   b. Drag the *Attorney* field from the Attorneys table to the first *Field* text box.
   c. Drag the *Client ID* field from the Clients table to the second *Field* text box.
   d. Drag the *Category Name* field from the Categories table to the third *Field* text box.
   e. Drag the *Hours* field from the Billing table to the fourth *Field* text box.
   f. Run the query.
   g. Save the query and name it AttorneyClientHours.
   h. Print and then close the query.
2. Create a crosstab query that summarizes the hours by attorney by category with the following specifications:
   a. At the first Crosstab Query Wizard dialog box, click the *Queries* option in the *View* section, and then click *Query: AttorneyClientHours* in the list box.
   b. At the second Crosstab Query Wizard dialog box, click *Attorney* in the *Available Fields* list box, and then click the button containing the greater than (>) symbol.
   c. At the third Crosstab Query Wizard dialog box, click *Category Name* in the list box.
   d. At the fourth Crosstab Query Wizard dialog box, click *Hours* in the *Fields* list box, and click *Sum* in the *Functions* list box.
   e. At the fifth Crosstab Query Wizard dialog box, type **Hours by Attorney by Category** in the *What do you want to name your query?* text box.
3. Change the page orientation to landscape and then print and then close the Hours by Attorney by Category query.

Assessment 7

1. With the **LegalServices** database file open, use the Find Duplicates Query Wizard to find those clients with the same last name with the following specifications:
   a. At the first wizard dialog box, click *Table: Clients* in the list box.
   b. At the second wizard dialog box, click *Last Name* in the *Available fields* list box, and then click the button containing the greater than (>) symbol.

c. At the third wizard dialog box, click the button containing the two greater than (>>) symbols.
d. At the fourth wizard dialog box, name the query DuplicateLastNames.

2. Change the page orientation to landscape and then print and then close the query.

Assessment 8

1. With the **LegalServices** database file open, use the Find Unmatched Query Wizard to find all clients who do not have any billing hours with the following specifications:
   a. At the first wizard dialog box, click *Table: Clients* in the list box.
   b. At the second wizard dialog box, click *Table: Billing* in the list box.
   c. At the third wizard dialog box, make sure *Client ID* is selected in the *Fields in 'Clients'* list box and in the *Fields in 'Billing'* list box.
   d. At the fourth wizard dialog box, click the button containing the two greater than symbols (>>) to move all fields from the *Available fields* list box to the *Selected fields* list box.
   e. At the fifth wizard dialog box, click the Finish button. (Let the wizard determine the query name: *Clients Without Matching Billing*.)
2. Change the page orientation to landscape and then print and then close the Clients Without Matching Billing query.

Assessment 9

1. With the **LegalServices** database file open, open the Clients database table and then use the Filter By Selection button on the Table Datasheet toolbar to display the following records:
   a. Display only those records of clients who live in Renton. When the records of clients in Renton display, change the page orientation to landscape, print the results, and then click the Remove Filter button.
   b. Display only those records of clients with the Zip Code of 98033. When the records of clients with the Zip Code 98033 display, change the page orientation to landscape, print the results, and then click the Remove Filter button.
2. Close the Clients database table without saving the changes.
3. Open the Billing database table, and then use the Filter By Selection button on the Table Datasheet toolbar to display the following records:
   a. Display only those records with a Category of CC. Print the CC records and then click the Remove Filter button.
   b. Display only those records with an Attorney ID of 12. Print the records, and then click the Remove Filter button.
4. Close the Billing database table without saving the changes.

Assessment 10

1. With the **LegalServices** database file open, open the Clients database table, and then use the Filter By Form button to display clients in Auburn or Renton. (Be sure to use the Or tab at the very bottom of the table.) Change the page orientation to landscape, print the table, and then click the Remove Filter button.
2. Close the Clients database table without saving the changes.
3. Open the Billing database table, and then use the Filter By Form button to display categories G or P. Print the table and then click the Remove Filter button.
4. Close the Billing database table without saving the changes.
5. Close the **LegalServices** database file.

Assessment 11

1. Use the Access Help feature to learn how to hide fields in a query's result.
2. After reading the information on hiding fields, complete the following steps:
    a. Open the **LegalServices** database file.
    b. Design the following query:
        1) At the Show Table dialog box, add the Billing table, the Clients table, and the Rates table.
        2) At the Query1 : Select Query window, drag the following fields to *Field* text boxes:

            Clients table:
                First Name
                Last Name
            Billing table:
                Hours
            Rates table:
                Rate

        3) Insert in the fifth *Field* text box the calculated field *Total:[Hours]*[Rate]*.
        4) Hide the *Hours* and the *Rate* fields.
    c. Run the query.
    d. Print the query and then close it without saving it.
3. Close the **LegalServices** database file.

CHAPTER challenge

You are a sales associate for a small boutique named Gigi's Gifts and Things. A shipment of items has just arrived. Prices need to be determined for each of the items. You have been asked by the manager to use the store's database, named **Gigi'sGifts**, to help with this process. You decide to create a query, based on the Inventory table. Include the *Item* and *Cost* fields in the query. In addition, create a calculated field that determines the selling price of each item. Assume a 65% markup for each item. Be sure the *Cost* field doesn't show when the query is run. Save the query as Selling Price.

When a calculated field is created in a query, no formatting is applied to the new field. Use the Help feature to learn about formatting fields in a query. Then use the Selling Price query created in the first part of the Chapter Challenge and format the Selling Price field to currency. Save the query again.

The prices of the new items will be posted to Gigi's Gifts and Things Web site. Prepare the query created and used in the first two parts of the Chapter Challenge for the Web site by exporting it as an HTML file. Save the HTML file as **Gigi'sInventory**.

WORK IN Progress

Creating Database Tables, Queries, and Filters

ASSESSING proficiencies

In this unit, you have learned to design and create database files, modify data in tables, and create a one-to-many relationship between database tables. You also learned how to create a database table using the Table Wizard, perform queries on data in tables, and filter records in a table.

Assessment 1

1. Use Access to create database tables for Cornerstone Catering. Name the database file **Cornerstone**. Create a database table named Employees that includes the following fields (you determine the data type, field size, and description):

   Employee # (primary key)
   First Name
   Last Name
   Cell Phone Number (Consider using the Input Mask Wizard for this field.)

2. After creating the database table, save the table. Switch to Datasheet view and then enter the following data in the appropriate fields:

   Employee #: 10
   First Name: Erin
   Last Name: Jergens
   Cell Phone Number: (505) 555-3193

   Employee #: 14
   First Name: Mikio
   Last Name: Ogami
   Cell Phone Number: (505) 555-1087

   Employee #: 19
   First Name: Martin
   Last Name: Vaughn
   Cell Phone Number: (505) 555-4461

   Employee #: 21
   First Name: Isabelle
   Last Name: Baptista
   Cell Phone Number: (505) 555-4425

   Employee #: 24
   First Name: Shawn
   Last Name: Kettering
   Cell Phone Number: (505) 555-3885

   Employee #: 26
   First Name: Madison
   Last Name: Harris
   Cell Phone Number: (505) 555-2256

3. Automatically adjust the column widths.
4. Save, print, and then close the Employees database table.
5. Create a database table named Plans that includes the following fields (you determine the data type, field size, and description):

   Plan Code (primary key)
   Plan

6. After creating the database table, save it and name it Plans. Switch to Datasheet view and then enter the following data in the appropriate fields:

   Plan Code: A
   Plan: Sandwich Buffet

   Plan Code: B
   Plan: Cold Luncheon Buffet

   Plan Code: C
   Plan: Hot Luncheon Buffet

   Plan Code: D
   Plan: Combination Dinner

7. Automatically adjust the column widths.
8. Save, print, and then close the Plans database table.
9. Create a database table named Prices that includes the following fields (you determine the data type, field size, and description [except as shown]):

   Price Code (primary key)
   Price Per Person (identify this data type as Currency)

10. After creating the database table, save the table. Switch to Datasheet view and then enter the following data in the appropriate fields:

    Price Code: 1
    Price Per Person: $11.50

    Price Code: 2
    Price Per Person: $12.75

    Price Code: 3
    Price Per Person: $14.50

    Price Code: 4
    Price Per Person: $16.00

    Price Code: 5
    Price Per Person: $18.50

11. Automatically adjust the column widths.
12. Save, print, and then close the Prices database table.
13. Create a database table named Clients that includes the following fields (you determine the data type, field size, and description):

    Client # (primary key)
    Client Name
    Street Address
    City
    State
    ZIP Code
    Telephone (Consider using the Input Mask Wizard for this field.)

14. After creating the database table, save the table. Switch to Datasheet view and then enter the following data in the appropriate fields:

    Client #: 104
    Client Name: Sarco Corporation
    Street Address: 340 Cordova Road
    City: Santa Fe
    State: NM
    ZIP Code: 87510
    Telephone: (505) 555-3880

    Client #: 155
    Client Name: Creative Concepts
    Street Address: 1046 Market Street
    City: Los Alamos
    State: NM
    ZIP Code: 87547
    Telephone: (505) 555-1200

    Client #: 218
    Client Name: Allenmore Systems
    Street Address: 7866 Second Street

    Client #: 286
    Client Name: Sol Enterprises
    Street Address: 120 Cerrillos Road

City: **Espanola**
State: **NM**
ZIP Code: **87535**
Telephone: **(505) 555-3455**

City: **Santa Fe**
State: **NM**
ZIP Code: **87560**
Telephone: **(505) 555-7700**

15. Automatically adjust the column widths.
16. Save, print, and then close the Clients database table.
17. Create a database table named Events that includes the following fields (you determine the data type, field size, and description [except as shown]):

    Event # (primary key; identify this data type as AutoNumber)
    Client #
    Employee #
    Date (identify this data type as Date/Time)
    Plan Code
    Price Code
    Number of People (identify this data type as Number)

18. After creating the database table, save the table. Switch to Datasheet view and then enter the following data in the appropriate fields:

    Event #: (AutoNumber)
    Client #: **218**
    Employee #: **14**
    Date: **7/1/2005**
    Plan Code: **B**
    Price Code: **3**
    Number of People: **250**

    Event #: (AutoNumber)
    Client #: **104**
    Employee #: **19**
    Date: **7/2/2005**
    Plan Code: **D**
    Price Code: **5**
    Number of People: **120**

    Event #: (AutoNumber)
    Client #: **155**
    Employee #: **24**
    Date: **7/8/2005**
    Plan Code: **A**
    Price Code: **1**
    Number of People: **300**

    Event #: (AutoNumber)
    Client #: **286**
    Employee #: **10**
    Date: **7/9/2005**
    Plan Code: **C**
    Price Code: **4**
    Number of People: **75**

    Event #: (AutoNumber)
    Client #: **218**
    Employee #: **14**
    Date: **7/10/2005**
    Plan Code: **C**
    Price Code: **4**
    Number of People: **50**

    Event #: (AutoNumber)
    Client #: **104**
    Employee #: **10**
    Date: **7/12/2005**
    Plan Code: **B**
    Price Code: **3**
    Number of People: **30**

19. Automatically adjust the column widths.
20. Save, print, and then close the Events database table.

Assessment 2

1. With the **Cornerstone** database file open, create the following one-to-many relationships enforcing referential integrity and cascading fields and records:
    a. *Client #* in the Clients table is the "one" and *Client #* in the Events table is the "many."

b. *Employee #* in the Employees table is the “one” and *Employee #* in the Events table is the “many.”
c. *Plan Code* in the Plans table is the “one” and *Plan Code* in the Events table is the “many.”
d. *Price Code* in the Prices table is the “one” and *Price Code* in the Events table is the “many.”

2. Save and then print the relationships.
3. Close the report and the Relationships window.

Assessment 3

1. With the **Cornerstone** database file open, open the Plans database table in Datasheet view and then add the following record at the end of the table:

   Plan Code: **E**
   Plan: **Hawaiian Luau Buffet**

2. Save, print, and then close the Plans database table.
3. Open the Events database table in Datasheet view and then add the following record at the end of the table:

   Event #: (AutoNumber)
   Client #: **104**
   Employee #: **21**
   Date: **7/16/2005**
   Plan Code: **E**
   Price Code: **5**
   Number of People: **125**

4. Save, print, and then close the Events database table.

Assessment 4

1. With the **Cornerstone** database file open, perform a query by extracting records from the Events database table with the following specifications:
   a. Include the fields *Client #*, *Date*, and *Plan Code*.
   b. Extract those records with a Plan Code of C.
   c. Save the query and name it PlanCodeC.
   d. Print and then close the query.
2. Extract records from the Clients database table with the following specifications:
   a. Include the fields *Client Name*, *City*, and *Telephone*.
   b. Extract those records with a city of Santa Fe.
   c. Save the query and name it SantaFeClients.
   d. Print and then close the query.
3. Extract information from two tables with the following specifications:
   a. From the Clients table, include the fields *Client Name* and *Telephone*.
   b. From the Events table, include the field *Date*, *Plan Code*, and *Number of People*.
   c. Extract those records with a date between July 10 and July 25, 2005.
   d. Save the query and name it July10-25Events.
   e. Print and then close the query.

Assessment 5

1. With the **Cornerstone** database file open, create a query in Design view with the Events table and the Prices table, and drag the following fields to the specified locations:
   a. Drag *Event #* from the *Events* table to the first *Field* text box.
   b. Drag *Date* from the *Events* table to the second *Field* text box.
   c. Drag *Number of People* from the *Events* table to the third *Field* text box.
   d. Drag *Price Per Person* from the *Prices* table to the fourth *Field* text box.
2. Insert the following calculated field entry in the fifth *Field* text box: **Amount:[Number of People]*[Price Per Person]**.
3. Run the query.
4. Save the query and name it EventAmounts.
5. Print and then close the query.

Assessment 6

1. With the **Cornerstone** database file open, create a query in Design view using the EventAmounts query with the following specifications:
   a. At the Cornerstone : Database window with Queries selected in the Objects bar, double-click *Create query in Design view*.
   b. At the Show Tables dialog box, click the Queries tab.
   c. Double-click *EventAmounts* in the list box, and then click the Close button.
   d. Drag the *Amount* field to the first, second, third, and fourth *Field* text boxes.
   e. Click the Totals button on the Query Design toolbar.
   f. Insert *Sum* in the first *Group By* list box in the *Total* row.
   g. Insert *Avg* in the second *Group By* list box in the *Total* row.
   h. Insert *Min* in the third *Group By* list box in the *Total* row.
   i. Insert *Max* in the fourth *Group By* list box in the *Total* row.
2. Run the query.
3. Save the query and name it AmountTotals.
4. Print and then close the query.

Assessment 7

1. With the **Cornerstone** database file open, create a query in Design view using the Employees table, the Clients table, the Events table, and the EventAmounts query with the following specifications:
   a. At the Cornerstone : Database window with Queries selected in the Objects bar, double-click *Create query in Design view*.
   b. At the Show Tables dialog box, click *Employees* and then click the Add button.
   c. Click *Clients* and then click the Add button.
   d. Click *Events* and then click the Add button.
   e. Click the Queries tab, click *EventAmounts* in the list box, click the Add button, and then click the Close button.
   f. Drag the *Last Name* field from the Employees table to the first *Field* text box.
   g. Drag the *Client Name* field from the Clients table to the second *Field* text box.
   h. Drag the *Amount* field from the EventAmounts query to the third *Field* text box.

i. Drag the *Date* field from the Events table to the fourth *Field* text box.

2. Run the query.
3. Save the query and name it EmployeeEvents.
4. Close the query.
5. Using the Crosstab Query Wizard, create a query that summarizes the total amount of events by employee by client using the following specifications:
   a. At the first Crosstab Query Wizard dialog box, click the *Queries* option in the *View* section, and then click *Query: EmployeeEvents* in the list box.
   b. At the second Crosstab Query Wizard dialog box, click *Last Name* in the *Available Fields* list box, and then click the button containing the greater than (>) symbol.
   c. At the third Crosstab Query Wizard dialog box, make sure *Client Name* is selected in the list box.
   d. At the fourth Crosstab Query Wizard dialog box, make sure *Amount* is selected in the *Fields* list box, and then click *Sum* in the *Functions* list box.
   e. At the fifth Crosstab Query Wizard dialog box, type **Amounts by Employee by Client** in the *What do you want to name your query?* text box.
6. Print and then close the Amounts by Employee by Client query.

Assessment 8

1. With the **Cornerstone** database file open, use the Find Duplicates Query Wizard to find employees who are responsible for at least two events with the following specifications:
   a. At the first wizard dialog box, click *Table: Events* in the list box.
   b. At the second wizard dialog box, click *Employee #* in the *Available fields* list box, and then click the button containing the greater than (>) symbol.
   c. At the third wizard dialog box, move the *Date* field and the *Number of People* field from the *Available fields* list box to the *Additional query fields* list box.
   d. At the fourth wizard dialog box, name the query *DuplicateEvents*.
2. Print and then close the DuplicateEvents query.

Assessment 9

1. With the **Cornerstone** database file open, use the Find Unmatched Query Wizard to find any employees who do not have an upcoming event scheduled with the following specifications:
   a. At the first wizard dialog box, click *Table: Employees* in the list box.
   b. At the second wizard dialog box, click *Table: Events* in the list box.
   c. At the third wizard dialog box, make sure *Employee #* is selected in the *Fields in 'Employees'* list box and in the *Fields in 'Events'* list box.
   d. At the fourth wizard dialog box, click the button containing the two greater than symbols (>>) to move all fields from the *Available fields* list box to the *Selected fields* list box.
   e. At the fifth wizard dialog box, click the Finish button. (Let the wizard determine the query name: *Employees Without Matching Events*.)
2. Print and then close the Employees Without Matching Events query.

Assessment 10

1. With the **Cornerstone** database file open, open the Events database table, and then use the Filter By Selection button on the Table Datasheet toolbar to display the following records:
   a. Display only those records with an Employee # of 14. When the records display, print the results, and then click the Remove Filter button.
   b. Display only those records with a Price Code of 4. When the records display, print the results, and then click the Remove Filter button.
2. Close the Events database table without saving the changes.
3. Open the Clients database table and then use the Filter By Form button to display clients in Espanola or Los Alamos. (Be sure to use the Or tab at the very bottom of the table.) Print the results and then click the Remove Filter button.
4. Close the Clients database table without saving the changes.
5. Open the Events database table and then use the Filter By Form button to display Plan Code A or C. Print the results and then click the Remove Filter button.
6. Close the Events database table without saving the changes.
7. Close the **Cornerstone** database file.

WRITING activities

The following activities give you the opportunity to practice your writing skills along with demonstrating an understanding of some of the important Access features you have mastered in this unit. Use correct grammar, appropriate word choices, and clear sentence constructions.

Activity 1

The manager of Cornerstone Catering has asked you to add information to the **Cornerstone** database file on employee payroll. You need to create another database table that will contain information on payroll. The manager wants the database table to include the following (you determine the appropriate data type, field size, and description):

Employee #: 10
Status: **Full-time**
Monthly Salary: $2,850

Employee #: 14
Status: **Part-time**
Monthly Salary: $1,500

Employee #: 19
Status: **Part-time**
Monthly Salary: $1,400

Employee #: 21
Status: **Full-time**
Monthly Salary: $2,500

Employee #: 24
Status: **Part-time**
Monthly Salary: $1,250

Employee #: 26
Status: **Part-time**
Monthly Salary: $1,000

Print and then close the payroll database table. Open Word and then write a report to the manager detailing how you created the database table. Include a title for the report, steps on how the database table was created, and any other pertinent information. Save the completed report and name it **sau1act01**. Print and then close **sau1act01**.

INTERNET project

Vehicle Search

In this activity you will search the Internet for information on different vehicles before doing actual test drives. Learning about a major product, such as a vehicle, can increase your chances of finding a good buy, can potentially guide you away from a poor purchase, and can help speed up the process of narrowing the search to the type of vehicle that will meet your needs. Before you begin, list the top five criteria you would look for in a vehicle. For example, it must be a 4-door vehicle, needs to be 4-wheel drive, and so on.

Using key search words, find at least two Web sites that list vehicle reviews. Use the search engines provided within the different review sites to find vehicles that fulfill the criteria you listed to meet your particular needs. Create a database file in Access and create a table in that file that will contain the results from your vehicle search. Design the table keeping in mind what type of data you need to record for each vehicle that meets your requirements. Include at least the make, model, year, price, description, and special problems in the table. Also, include the ability to rate the vehicle as poor, fair, good, or excellent. You will decide on the rating of each vehicle depending on your findings.

JOB study

Mobile Home Park Project

In this activity you are working in the office of a large mobile home park. The manager of the part has asked you to find a way to document information about the people living in the park so that she can better meet their needs. For example, when road work has to be done, she would like to know which patrons would have difficulty parking their cars a long distance from their homes. When utility workers are scheduled to be in the park, she would like to notify the children's parents of any potentially dangerous situations.

The mobile home lots are numbered 1 through 200 and each is rated by size and location for rent as either standard or premium. The manager has asked you to record for each lot number, the names and phone numbers of the residents, whether or not it is a premium lot, whether or not any disabled individuals live in the home, the number of children living in the home, and the date the individuals occupied the lot. Create a database file and a table within the file to store the information. Enter 10 records to test the table. (Make up the data for the table.) Create a query for all lots where children live and another query for all lots with disabled individuals. For each query, provide the residents' names and phone numbers, and then print the results. The queries should be saved with appropriate names for later use.

SPECIALIST

MICROSOFT®

ACCESS

Unit 2: Creating Forms and Reports

- Creating Forms
- Creating Reports, Mailing Labels, and Charts
- Importing and Exporting Data
- Creating Web Pages and Using Database Wizards

MICROSOFT ACCESS 2003

MICROSOFT OFFICE ACCESS 2003 SPECIALIST SKILLS – UNIT 2

Reference No.	Skill	Pages
AC03S-1-1	**Create database using a Database Wizard**	**S243-S251**
AC03S-1-8	Create forms	
	Create a form using AutoForm	S142-S145
	Create a form using the Form Wizard	S145-S151
	Create a form with related database tables	S150-S151
	Create a form in Design view	S151-S164
AC03S-1-9	Add and modify form controls and properties	
	Add, move, resize, format, and align control objects	S152-S164
	Add a calculated control	S161-S164
AC03S-1-10	Create reports	
	Create a report using AutoReport	S172
	Create a report using the Report Wizard	S172-S178
	Create a report with related database tables	S178-S179
	Create a report in Design view	S179-S194
AC03S-1-11	Add and modify report control properties	S181-S185
AC03S-1-12	Create a data access page	S237-S243
AC03S-2	**Entering Data**	
AC03S-2-2	Find and move among records	
	Navigating to specific records	S142-S143
AC03S-2-3	Import data to Access	
	Import data to a new table	S221-S222
	Link data to a new table	S223-S224
AC03S-3	**Organizing Data**	
AC03S-3-2	Modify form layout	
	Move, resize, format, and align form control objects	S151-S158
	Add a form header and form footer	S159-S161
AC03S-3-3	Modify report layout and page setup	
	Move, resize, and add customize control objects	S181-S185
	Add a report header and report footer	S181-S185
AC03S-4	**Managing Databases**	
AC03S-4-1	Identify and modify object dependencies	S226-S230
AC03S-4-2	View objects and object data in other views	
	View objects and object dependencies	S226-S230
	Use PivotTable view	S194-S199
	Use PivotChart view	S199-S202
AC03S-4-3	Print database objects and data	
	Print a form	S142-S143
AC03S-4-4	Export data from Access	
	Export data to Excel	S209-S212
	Export data to Word	S212-S221

CHAPTER 5

CREATING FORMS

PERFORMANCE OBJECTIVES

Upon successful completion of Chapter 5, you will be able to:

- **Create a form using AutoForm**
- **Create a form using the Form Wizard**
- **Create a form with fields from related database tables**
- **Create a form in Design view**
- **Move, resize, format, and align control objects**
- **Use fields to add controls**
- **Add controls using buttons on the Toolbox**
- **Add a Form Header and Form Footer to a form**
- **Add a calculated control to a form**

ACCESS

In this chapter, you will learn to create a form from database tables, improving the data display and making data entry easier. Access offers several methods for presenting data on the screen for easier data entry. You can create a form using the AutoForm and the Form Wizard. You can also create a form in Design view and then edit control objects in the form.

Creating a Form

HINT
Use a form to easily enter, edit, and/or view data.

HINT
A form allows you to focus on a single record at a time.

Access offers a variety of options for presenting data in a more easily read and attractive format. When entering data in a database table at the Datasheet view, multiple records are displayed at the same time. If a record contains several fields, you may not be able to view all fields within a record at the same time. If you create a form, generally all fields for a record are visible at one time.

Several methods are available for creating a form. In this section, you will learn how to use AutoForm to insert existing data into a form, use the Form Wizard to create a form, and use the Form Wizard to create a form with fields from related database tables.

HINT
After creating a form, save it before working with it.

New Object

Creating a Form Using AutoForm

Data in a database table can be viewed, added, or edited in the Datasheet view. You can perform these functions on data inserted in a form. The advantage to a form is that the functions are generally easier to perform because the data is easier to read. Access offers the AutoForm feature, which automatically copies data in a database table and creates a form. To use the AutoForm feature, click the down-pointing arrow at the right side of the New Object button on the Database toolbar, and then click AutoForm at the drop-down list. The AutoForm automatically creates a form and inserts it on the screen.

In Exercise 1, you will be using AutoForm to create a form for data contained in the Orders table, which is part of the OutdoorOptions database file. When AutoForm creates the form, the first record will display as shown in Figure 5.1.

FIGURE 5.1 ***Form Created from Data in Orders Table***

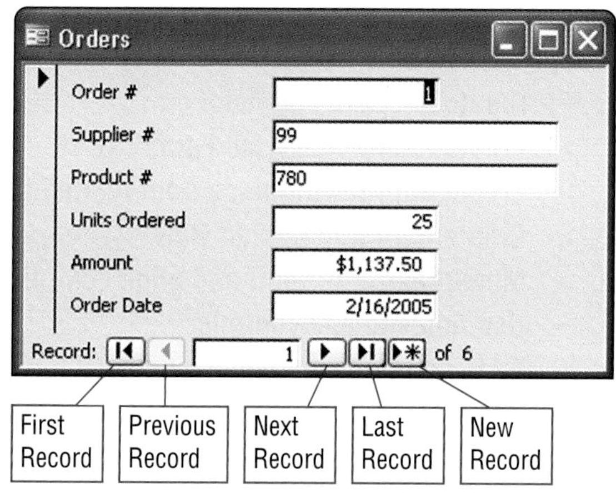

QUICK STEPS

Create a Form Using AutoForm
1. Open database file.
2. Click desired table.
3. Click down-pointing arrow at right of New Object button.
4. Click AutoForm.

HINT
You can use the keyboard to display specific records. Press Page Down to move forward a single record or press Page Up to move back a single record. Press Ctrl + Home to display the first record or press Ctrl + End to display the last record.

Navigation buttons display along the bottom of the first Orders record. The function each button performs is shown in Figure 5.1. Using these navigation buttons, you can display the first record in the database table, the previous record, the next record, the last record, and a new record.

Sorting Records

In Chapter 1, you learned about the Sort Ascending and Sort Descending buttons on the Table Datasheet toolbar. These buttons are also available on the Formatting (Form/Report) toolbar. Display a form in Form view and then click in the field on which you want to sort. Click the Sort Ascending button to sort the records in ascending alphabetic or numeric order (A-Z or lowest number to highest number). Click the Sort Descending button to sort the records in descending alphabetic or numeric order (Z-A or highest number to lowest number).

QUICK STEPS

Print Specific Record
1. Display form.
2. Click File, Print.
3. Click *Selected Record(s)*.
4. Click OK.

Printing a Form

Print a form in the same manner as a database table. If desired, changes can be made to the page margins and/or page orientation at the Page Setup dialog box. To display this dialog box, click File and then Page Setup. Print all records in the form by clicking the Print button on the Database toolbar. If you want to print a specific record, display the desired record, and then display the Print dialog box by clicking File and then Print. At the Print dialog box, click the *Selected Record(s)* option, and then click OK.

exercise 1

CREATING A FORM WITH THE PRODUCTS DATABASE FILE

(Note: Delete any database files from your disk.)

1. Copy the **OutdoorOptions** database file from the CD that accompanies this textbook to your disk. Remove the read-only attribute from the **OutdoorOptions** database file.
2. Open the **OutdoorOptions** database file.
3. Use the AutoForm feature to create a form with the data in the Orders table by completing the following steps:
   a. At the OutdoorOptions : Database window, click *Orders* in the list box.
   b. Click the down-pointing arrow at the right of the New Object button on the Database toolbar.
   c. At the drop-down list that displays, click the AutoForm option.
   d. When the first record displays in Form view, click in the *Product #* field and then click the Sort Ascending button on the Form View toolbar.
   e. Display the next record by clicking the button toward the bottom of the Orders dialog box (see Figure 5.1) that contains a right-pointing arrow.
   f. Practice displaying different records using the navigation buttons along the bottom of the Orders dialog box.

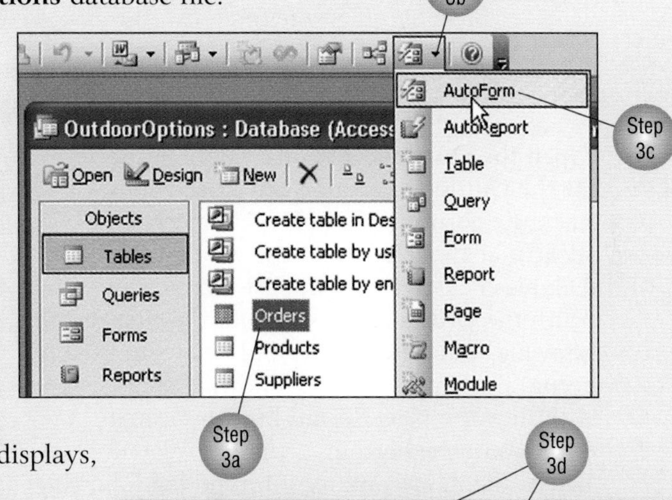

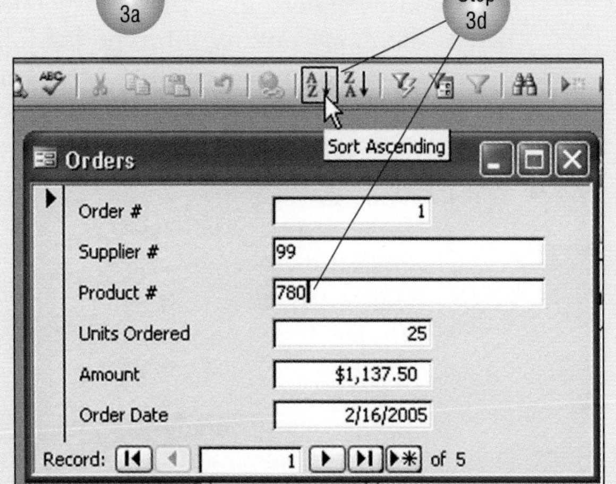

4. Save the form by completing the following steps:
   a. Click the Save button on the Form View toolbar.
   b. At the Save As dialog box, with *Orders* inserted in the *Form Name* text box, click OK.
5. Print all records in the form by clicking the Print button on the Form View toolbar.
6. Close the Orders form.
7. Close the **OutdoorOptions** database file.

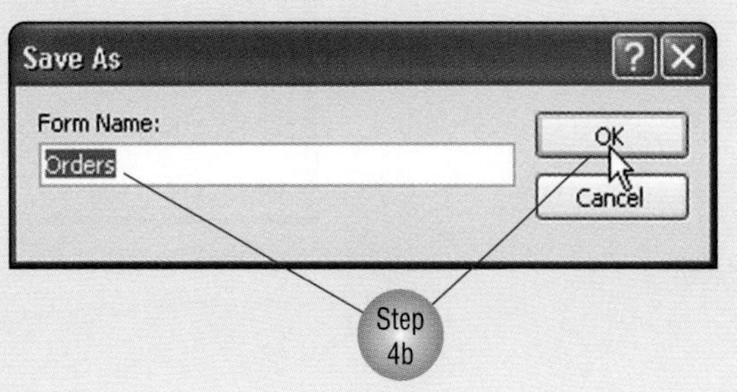

Adding/Deleting Records

New Record

Delete Record

Navigate through records in a form using the navigation buttons that display along the bottom of the form, as shown in Figure 5.1. Add a new record to the form by clicking the New Record button that displays along the bottom of the form and contains a right-pointing arrow followed by an asterisk. You can also add a new record to a form by clicking the New Record button on the Form View toolbar that displays toward the top of the screen.

To delete a record, display the record, and then click the Delete Record button on the Form View toolbar. At the message telling you that the record will be deleted permanently, click Yes.

exercise 2

ADDING AND DELETING RECORDS IN A FORM

1. Open the **OutdoorOptions** database file.
2. At the OutdoorOptions : Database window, click the Forms button on the Objects bar located at the left side of the window.
3. Double-click *Orders* in the list box.
4. With the Orders form open and the first record showing, add new records and delete an existing record by completing the following steps:
   a. Click the New Record button located toward the bottom of the first record.
   b. At the new blank record, type the following information in the specified fields (move to the next field by pressing Tab or Enter; move to the previous field by pressing Shift + Tab):

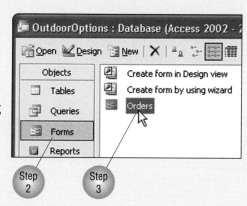

Order #	=	(automatically inserted)
Supplier #	=	54
Product #	=	103
Units Ordered	=	10
Amount	=	$573.25
Order Date	=	2/22/2005

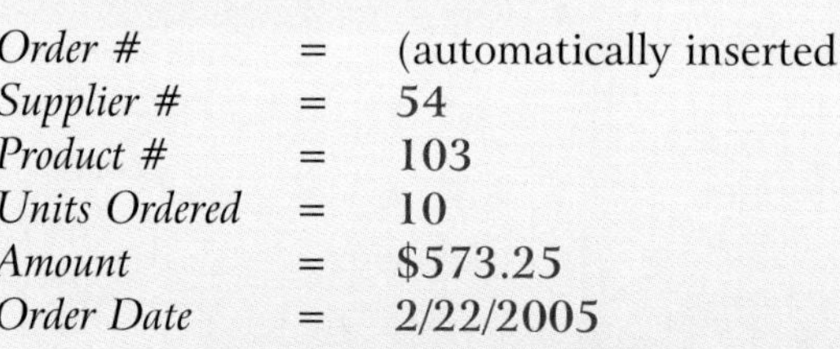

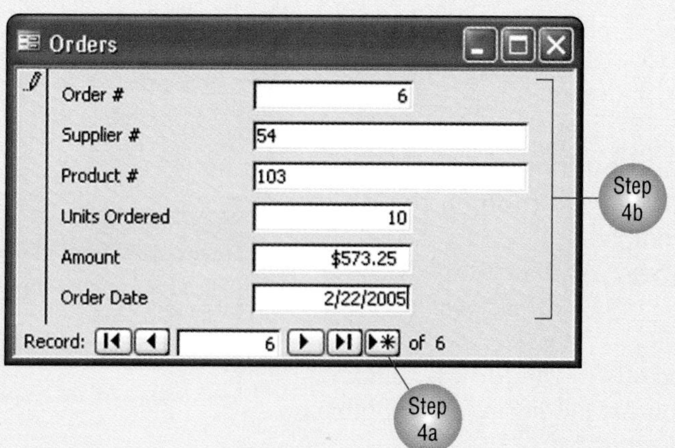

c. After typing the information for the new record, press the Tab key to display the next new record (you can also click the New Record button), and then type the following information in the specified fields:

Order #	=	(automatically inserted)
Supplier #	=	99
Product #	=	647
Units Ordered	=	5
Amount	=	$325.00
Order Date	=	2/22/2005

d. Delete the second record by completing the following steps:
   1) Click the button toward the bottom of the record that displays with a left-pointing arrow until Record 2 displays.
   2) With Record 2 displayed, click the Delete Record button on the Form View toolbar.
   3) At the message telling you that you will not be able to undo the delete operation, click Yes.

e. Click the Save button on the Form View toolbar.

f. Print all records in the form by clicking the Print button on the Form View toolbar.

g. Close the Orders form.

5. Close the **OutdoorOptions** database file.

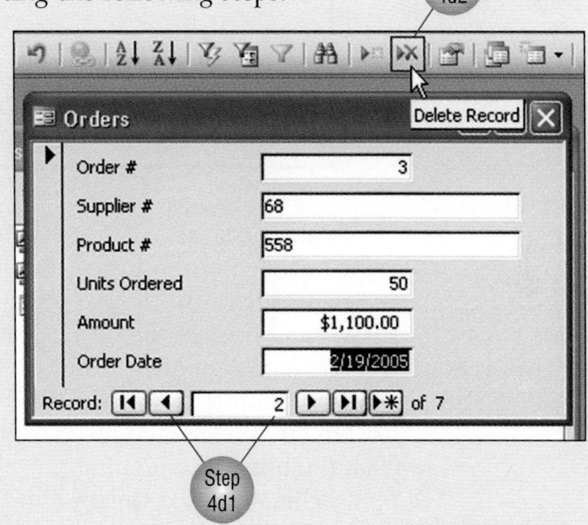

Creating a Form Using the Form Wizard

Access offers a Form Wizard that will guide you through the creation of a form. The Form Wizard offers more formatting choices than the AutoForm feature. To create a form using the Form Wizard, open the database file containing the table for which you want to create a form. At the database window, click the Forms button on the Objects bar, and then click the New button on the window toolbar. At the New Form dialog box shown in Figure 5.2, double-click *Form Wizard* in the list box and the first Form Wizard dialog box displays as shown in Figure 5.3.

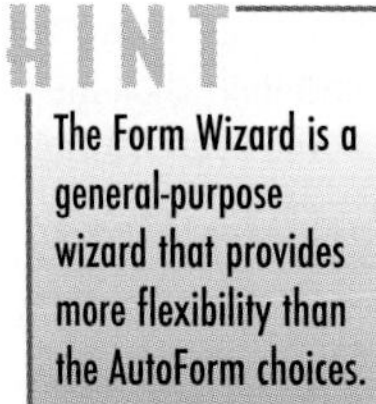

HINT
The Form Wizard is a general-purpose wizard that provides more flexibility than the AutoForm choices.

Create a Form Using Form Wizard
1. Open database file.
2. Click Forms button on Objects bar.
3. Click New button.
4. Double-click *Form Wizard.*
5. Choose desired options at each of the Form Wizard dialog boxes.

FIGURE

5.2 ***New Form Dialog Box***

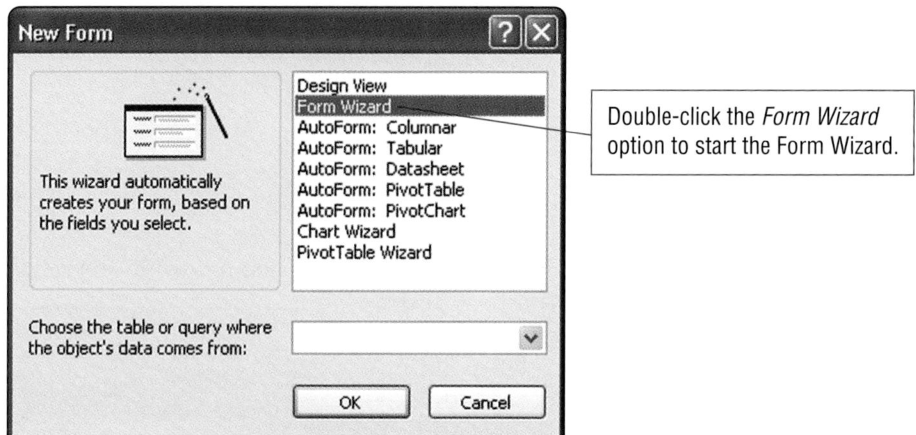

HINT

The Form Wizard automates the creating of a form and lets you specify some or all of the fields to be used in the form.

At the first Form Wizard dialog box, specify the table and then the fields you want included in the form. To select the table, click the down-pointing arrow at the right side of the *Tables/Queries* text box, and then click the desired table. Select the desired field in the *Available Fields* list box, click the button containing the greater than symbol (>), and the field is inserted in the *Selected Fields* list box. Continue in this manner until all desired fields are inserted in the *Selected Fields* list box. If you want to insert all fields into the *Selected Fields* list box at one time, click the button containing the two greater than symbols (>>). After specifying fields, click the Next button.

FIGURE

5.3 ***First Form Wizard Dialog Box***

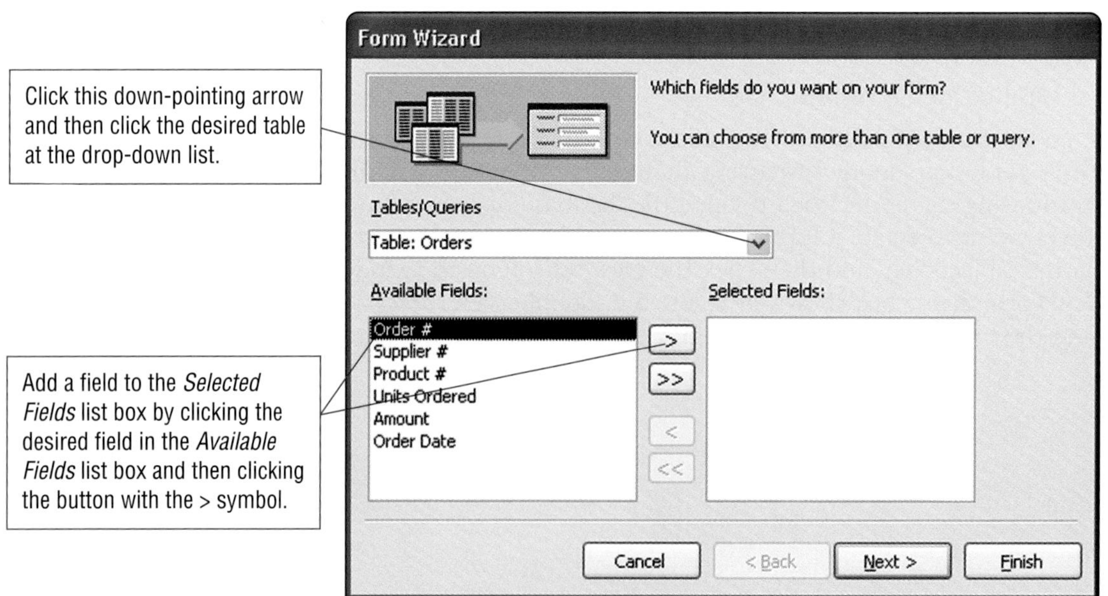

At the second Form Wizard dialog box, shown in Figure 5.4, specify the layout for the records. You can choose from *Columnar*, *Tabular*, *Datasheet*, and *Justified* (with *Columnar* the default). After choosing the layout, click the Next button.

FIGURE

5.4 Second Form Wizard Dialog Box

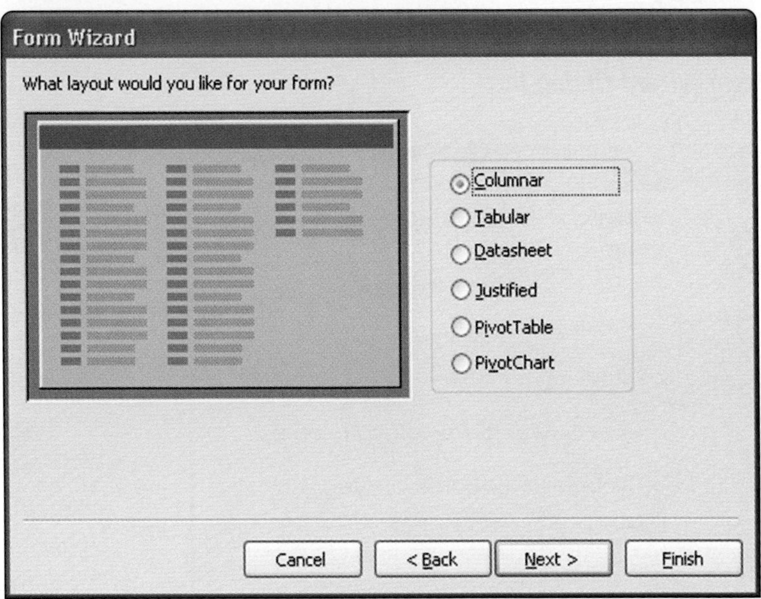

One of the advantages offered by the Form Wizard is the ability to choose from a variety of formats. At the third Form Wizard dialog box, shown in Figure 5.5, you choose a format style, such as *Blends*, *Blueprint*, *Expedition*, *Industrial*, and so forth. Click a format style and the results of the style are shown in the preview box. After selecting the desired format style, click the Next button.

FIGURE

5.5 Third Form Wizard Dialog Box

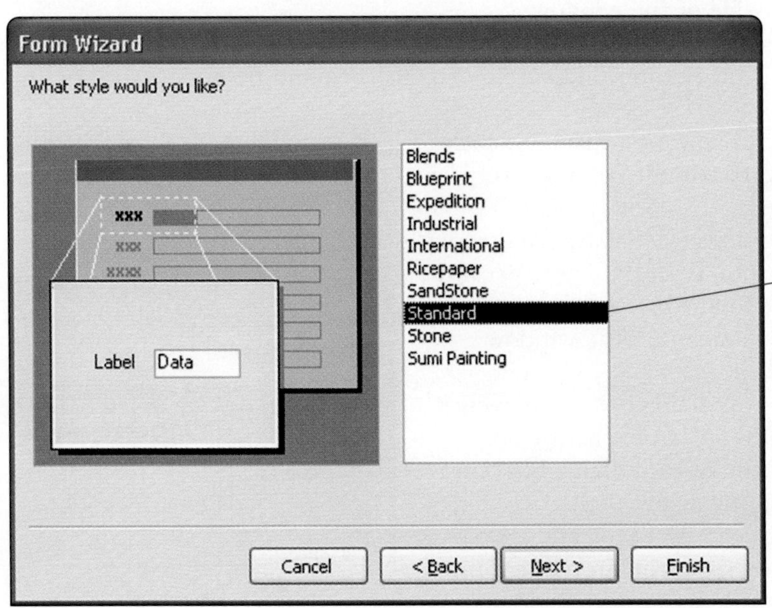

Click the desired format with options in the list box and then preview the format in the preview box at the left side of the dialog box.

At the last Form Wizard dialog box, shown in Figure 5.6, the Form Wizard offers a title for the form and also provides the option *Open the form to view or enter information*. Make any necessary changes in this dialog box and then click the Finish button.

FIGURE 5.6 ***Fourth Form Wizard Dialog Box***

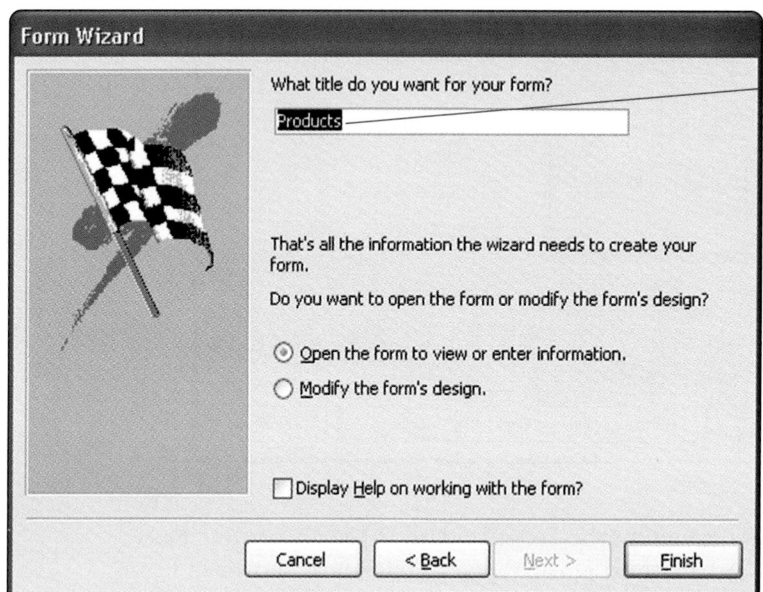

Type a title for the form in this text box or accept the default name provided by the wizard.

exercise 3

CREATING A FORM USING THE FORM WIZARD

1. Open the **OutdoorOptions** database file.
2. At the OutdoorOptions : Database window, click the Forms button on the Objects bar located at the left side of the window.
3. Delete the Orders form you created in Exercise 1 by completing the following steps:
   a. Position the arrow pointer on *Orders* in the list box and then click the *right* mouse button.
   b. At the shortcut menu that displays, click Delete using the left mouse button.
   c. At the question asking if you want to permanently delete the form, click Yes.
4. At the OutdoorOptions : Database window with the Forms button selected, create a form with the Form Wizard by completing the following steps:
   a. Click the New button on the window toolbar.
   b. At the New Form dialog box, double-click the *Form Wizard* option in the list box.
   c. At the first Form Wizard dialog box, click the down-pointing arrow at the right side of the *Tables/Queries* text box, and then click *Table: Products* at the drop-down list.

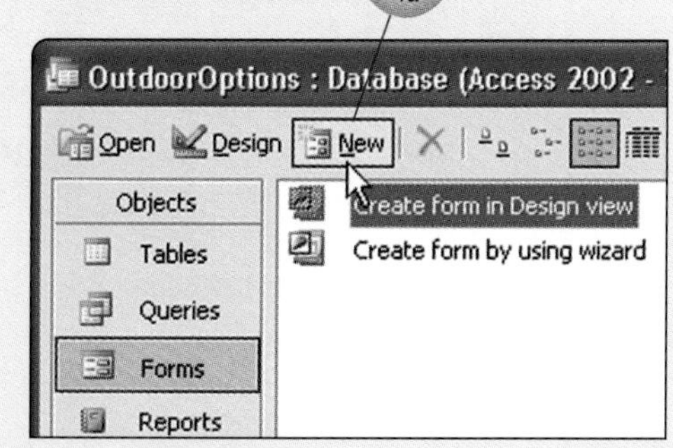

d. Specify that you want all fields included in the form by clicking the button containing the two greater than symbols (>>).
e. Click the Next button.
f. At the second Form Wizard dialog box, click the Next button. (This leaves the layout at the default of *Columnar*.)
g. At the third Form Wizard dialog box, click the *International* option in the list box.

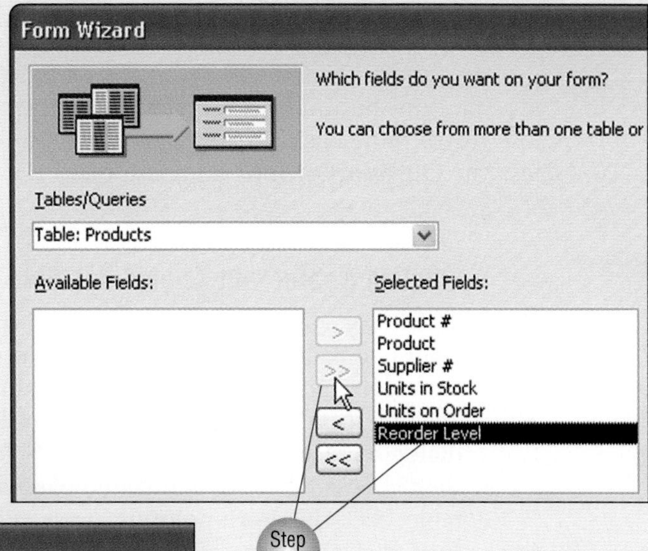

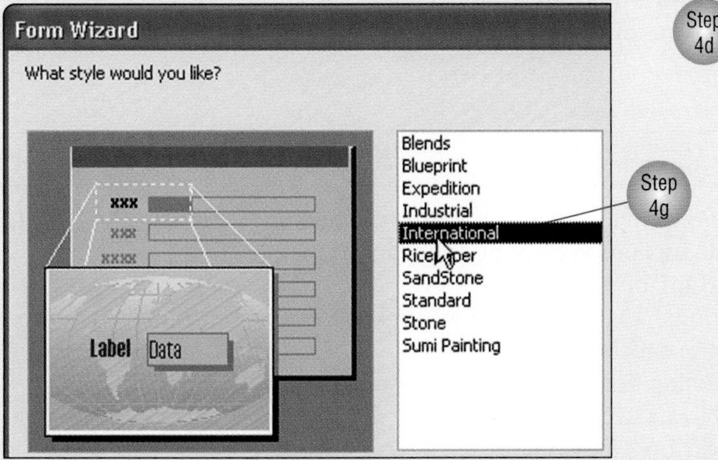

h. Click the Next button.
i. At the fourth Form Wizard dialog box, leave the options at the default, and then finish the form by clicking the Finish button.

5. When the first record is shown in the form, click the New Record button, and then add the following records:

Product #	=	448
Product	=	Canteen kit
Supplier #	=	54
Units in Stock	=	41
Units on Order	=	50
Reorder Level	=	50
Product #	=	302
Product	=	Pocket warmer
Supplier #	=	31
Units in Stock	=	13
Units on Order	=	15
Reorder Level	=	15

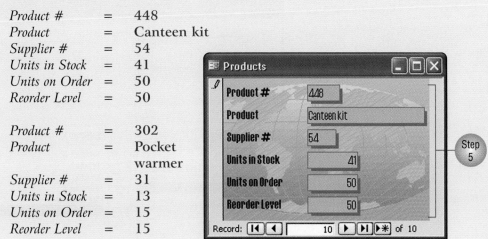

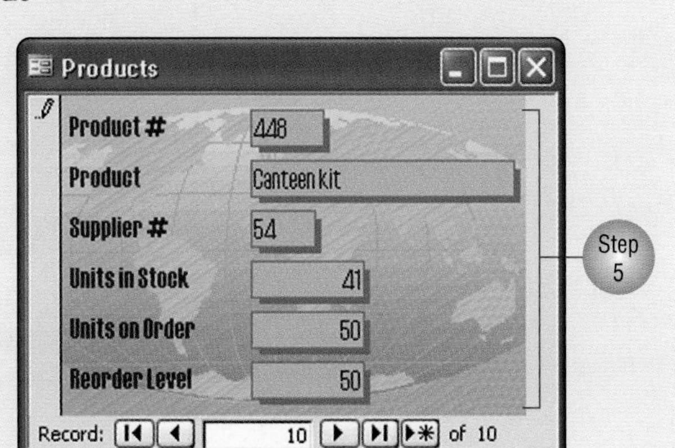

6. Delete the record containing information on ski goggles. (At the warning message, click Yes.)
7. Click the Save button on the Form View toolbar.
8. Click the Print button to print all records in the form.
9. Close the form by clicking the Close button in the upper right corner of the record.
10. Close the **OutdoorOptions** database file.

Creating a Form with Related Database Tables

The forms you have created so far in this chapter have included all of the fields from one database table. Forms can also be created with fields from tables that are connected by a one-to-many relationship. You can use the Form Wizard to create a form with fields from related database tables. At the first Form Wizard dialog box (see Figure 5.3), choose fields from the selected database table and then choose fields from a related database table. To change to the related database table, click the down-pointing arrow at the right of the *Tables/Queries* text box, and then click the name of the desired database table.

exercise 4

CREATING A FORM WITH RELATED DATABASE TABLES

1. Create a form that includes fields from the Products database table and fields from the Suppliers database table by completing the following steps:
   a. Open the **OutdoorOptions** database file.
   b. At the OutdoorOptions : Database window, click the Forms button on the Objects bar.
   c. Click the New button on the window toolbar.
   d. At the New Form dialog box, double-click *Form Wizard* in the list box.
   e. At the first Form Wizard dialog box, click the down-pointing arrow at the right of the *Tables/Queries* text box, and then click *Table: Products*.
   f. Complete the following steps to insert fields in the *Selected Fields* list box:
      1) With *Product #* selected in the *Available Fields* list box, click the button containing the greater than symbol (>).
      2) With *Product* selected in the *Available Fields* list box, click the button containing the greater than symbol (>).
      3) Click *Units in Stock* in the *Available Fields* list box and then click the button containing the greater than symbol (>).
      4) Click the down-pointing arrow at the right of the *Table/Queries* text box and then click *Table: Suppliers*.

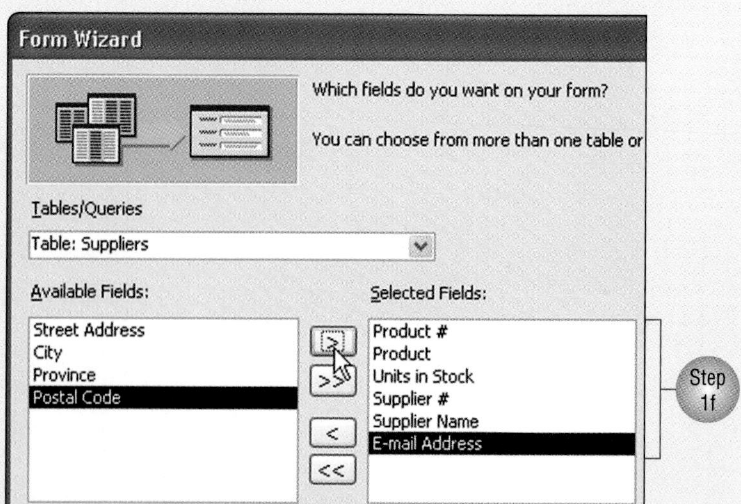

5) With *Supplier #* selected in the *Available Fields* list box, click the button containing the greater than symbol (>).
6) With *Supplier Name* selected in the *Available Fields* list box, click the button containing the greater than symbol (>).
7) Click *E-mail Address* in the *Available Fields* list box and then click the button containing the greater than symbol (>).
8) Click the Next button.

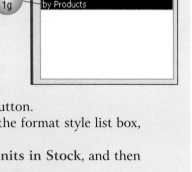

g. At the second Form Wizard dialog box, make sure *by Products* is selected in the list box that displays in the upper left corner of the dialog box, and then click the Next button.
h. At the third Form Wizard dialog box, click the Next button.

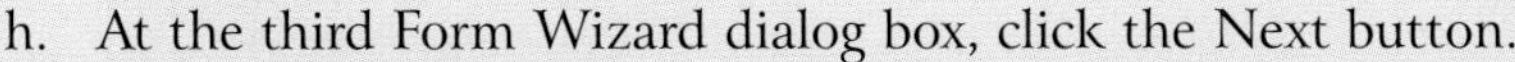

i. At the fourth Form Wizard dialog box, click *Blends* in the format style list box, and then click the Next button.
j. At the fifth Form Wizard dialog box, type the name **Units in Stock**, and then click the Finish button.

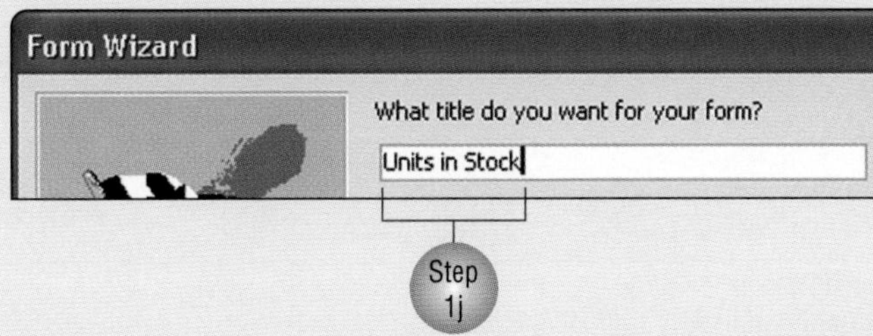

2. When the first record displays, print the record by displaying the Print dialog box, clicking *Selected Record(s)* in the *Print Range* section, and then clicking OK.
3. Close the form by clicking the Close button.
4. Close the **OutdoorOptions** database file.

Creating a Form in Design View

A form is comprised of a series of controls, which are objects that display titles or descriptions, accept data, or perform actions. In the forms you created in this chapter, the AutoForm feature or the Form Wizard created the controls for the form using fields from the tables. Another method for creating a form is to use the Design view. To display the Design view, as shown in Figure 5.7, click the Forms button on the Objects bar, and then double-click the *Create form in Design view* option in the list box. In the Design view, you can use fields from a table to create controls in the Design grid and you can also add controls with buttons on the Toolbox palette. The Toolbox palette, shown in Figure 5.7, appears automatically in the Design view.

QUICK STEPS

Create a Form in Design View

1. Open database file.
2. Click Forms button.
3. Double-click *Create form in Design view.*
4. Click Properties button.
5. Click Form properties sheet All tab.
6. Click in *Record Source* text box.
7. Click down-pointing arrow and then click desired table.
8. Drag desired fields from field list box to Design grid.

FIGURE

5.7 *Form in Design View*

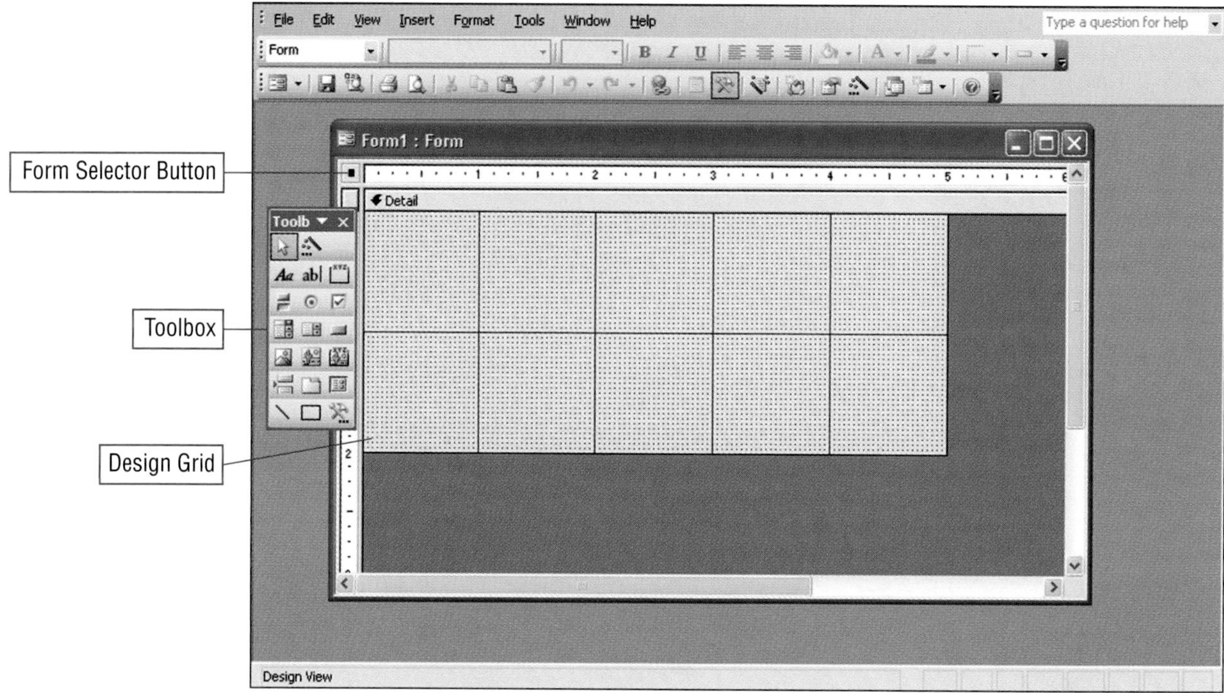

HINT

You can also display the Form properties sheet by right-clicking the Form1 : Form title bar and then clicking Properties or by double-clicking the Form selector button that displays in the upper left corner of the Design window.

Form Selector

A form in Design view contains three sections—Form Header, Detail, and Form Footer. The Detail section is the only section that displays by default. (You will learn more about the Form Header and Form Footer sections later in this chapter.) The Detail section of the form in Design view is set up as a grid. Use the rulers along the top and left side of the section and the lines and dots that make up the grid to precisely position fields and controls.

Using Fields to Add Controls

Associate a table with the form to use fields to create controls. To associate a table, click the Properties button on the Form Design toolbar. This displays the Form properties sheet. At the Form properties sheet, click the All tab, and then click in the Record Source text box. Click the down-pointing arrow that displays at the right side of the text box and then click the desired table. This displays the table fields in a field list box. (If the field list box does not display, click the Field List button on the Form Design toolbar.) Using the mouse, drag the desired field from the field list box to the Design grid.

Moving Control Objects

When a field is moved to the Design grid, a label control containing the field name and a text box control used to accept data are placed adjacent to each other on the grid. The label control containing the field name is included for descriptive purposes so that the user knows which data to type into the corresponding text box.

The label control and its corresponding text box control for a field can be moved individually or together to another location on the form. To move the two control objects together, click one of the objects. This inserts eight sizing handles around the object you clicked with a large black handle displaying in the upper left corner as shown in Figure 5.8. The adjacent object displays with one large black sizing handle in the upper left corner. Position the arrow pointer on the border of the control object containing the eight sizing handles (on the border, not on a sizing handle) until the pointer turns into a hand. Hold down the left mouse button and then drag the objects to the desired position. Move multiple control objects at the same time by holding down the Shift key while clicking each object. You can also select multiple control objects by drawing a border around the desired control objects.

FIGURE 5.8 ***Selected Control Object***

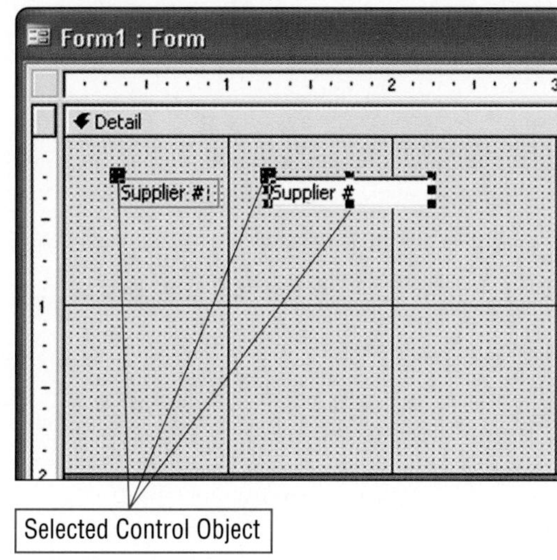

To move a control object separately from the adjacent object, position the mouse pointer on the large black handle that displays in the upper left corner of the object, hold down the left mouse button, and then drag the object to the desired position.

Resizing Control Objects

Increase or decrease the size of a selected control object using the sizing handles that display around the object. Drag the middle sizing handles at the left or right edge to make the control wider or narrower; drag the middle sizing handles at the top or bottom to make the control taller or shorter; and use the corner sizing handles to resize the object both horizontally and vertically at the same time.

Formatting Control Objects

Customize the formatting of selected control objects with options at the properties sheet. (The name of the properties sheet will vary depending on what is selected.) With the All tab selected, all formatting options are available. Click the Format tab to display only formatting options such as options to change the font size, font style, font color, foreground color, background color, and caption. Click in a text box for some options and a button containing three black dots displays at the right side. Click this button to display additional formatting choices.

Aligning Control Objects

Control objects inserted in the Design grid align with horizontal and vertical lines in the grid. This is because the Snap to Grid effect is on by default. Even with the Snap to Grid effect on, you may want to control the alignment of control objects. To align control objects, select the desired objects, and then click the Format option on the Menu bar. At the drop-down menu that displays, point to the Align option, and then click the desired alignment at the side menu.

exercise 5

CREATING AND FORMATTING A FORM IN DESIGN VIEW

1. Open the **OutdoorOptions** database file.
2. At the OutdoorOptions : Database window, click the Forms button on the Objects bar.
3. Create a form in Design view by completing the following steps:
   a. Double-click the *Create form in Design view* option in the list box.

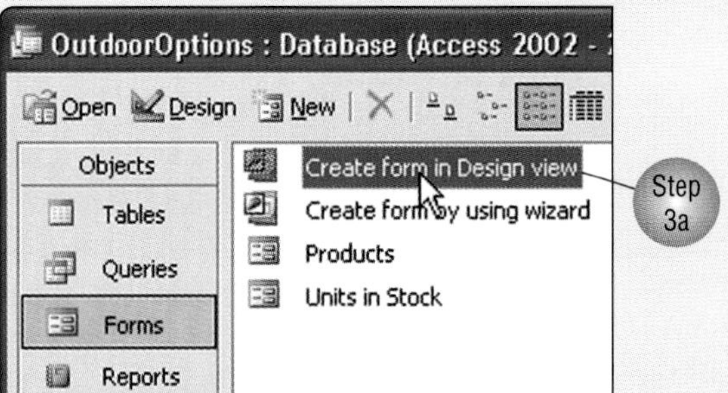

   b. At the Design window, click the Properties button on the Form Design toolbar.
   c. At the Form properties sheet, click the All tab.
   d. At the Form properties sheet with the All tab selected, click in the *Record Source* text box, and then click the down-pointing arrow that displays at the right side of the text box.
   e. At the drop-down list that displays, click *Suppliers*.

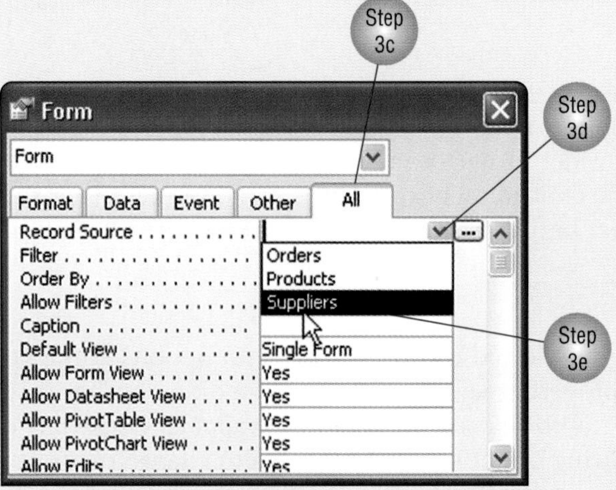

f. Drag the *Supplier #* field from the field list box to the Design grid to the approximate location shown below. (You will be aligning the control objects later in this exercise.)
g. Drag the remaining fields from the field list box to the Design grid to the approximate locations shown below. (You will be formatting the control objects later in this exercise.)
h. Align the control objects by completing the following steps:
    1) With the mouse, draw a border around all control objects located in the first column. (This selects the control objects.)

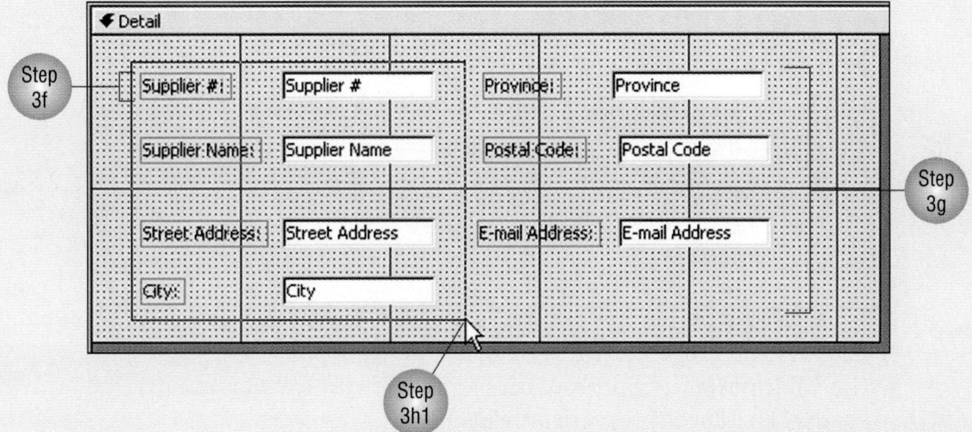

    2) With the control objects selected, click Format on the Menu bar, point to Align, and then click Right at the side menu.
    3) With the mouse, draw a border around all control objects located in the second column.
    4) Click Format on the Menu bar, point to Align, and then click Right at the side menu.
    5) If the control objects are not positioned in the locations shown in Figure 5.9, select and then drag the object to the desired position.
i. Change the *Supplier #:* caption by completing the following steps:
    1) Click the *Supplier #:* label control object (displays with a gray background).
    2) Click in the *Caption* text box in the Label properties sheet. (The Form properties sheet became the Label properties sheet when the label control object was selected.) (You may need to scroll up the list to display the *Caption* text box.)
    3) Edit the text in the *Caption* text box so it displays as *Supplier Number:*.

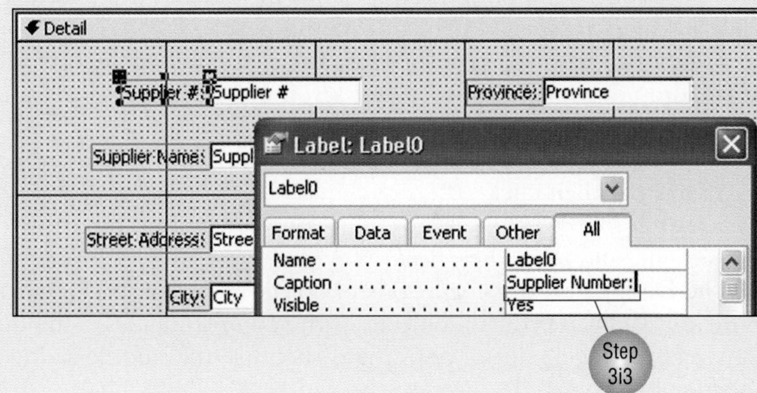

4) Click anywhere in the Design grid outside a control object to deselect the object.

j. Format the label control objects by completing the following steps:
   1) Click the *Supplier Number* label control object (displays with a gray background).
   2) Hold down the Shift key, and then click each of the remaining label control objects (objects that display with a gray background).

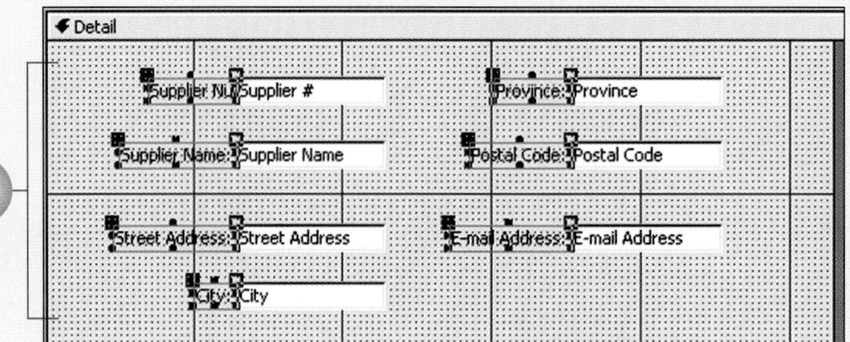

   3) Click in the *Fore Color* text box in the Multiple selection properties sheet. (The Label properties sheet became the Multiple selection properties sheet when you selected the labels.) (You will need to scroll down the list to display the *Fore Color* text box.)
   4) Click the button containing three black dots that displays at the right side of the text box.

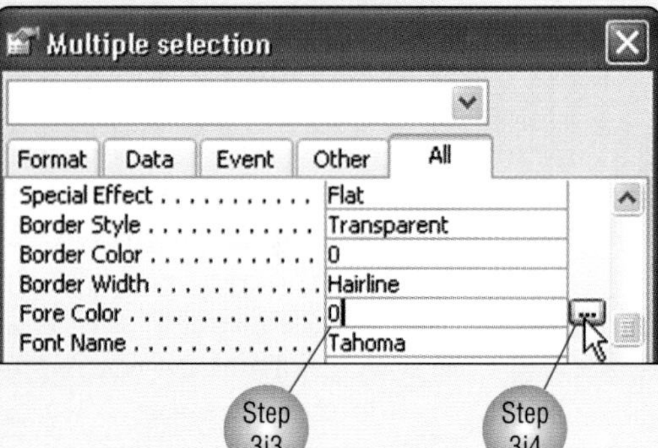

   5) At the color palette that displays, click the Turquoise color (fifth color from the left in the top row), and then click OK to close the palette. (The color will not be visible in the Design grid until you choose another option.)
   6) Click in the *Back Color* text box, and then click the button containing three black dots.
   7) At the color palette that displays, click the Blue color (sixth color from the left in the fourth row from the top), and then click OK to close the palette.
   8) Click in the *Font Name* text box in the properties sheet, and then click the down-pointing arrow that displays at the right side of the text box.
   9) At the drop-down list that displays, scroll up the list to display *Arial* and then click *Arial*.
   10) Click in the *Font Size* text box, click the down-pointing arrow that displays at the right, and then click *10*.
   11) Click in the *Font Weight* text box, click the down-pointing arrow that displays at the right, and then click *Bold*.

k. Click in the Design grid outside a control object to deselect the objects.

l. Resize each of the label control objects so the complete label name displays. (To do this, select the label control object and then use the middle sizing handle at the left side of the object to increase the width.)

m. Format the text control objects by completing the following steps:
   1) Click the *Supplier Number* text control object (contains a white background).
   2) Hold down the Shift key and then click each of the remaining text control objects (objects that display with a white background).

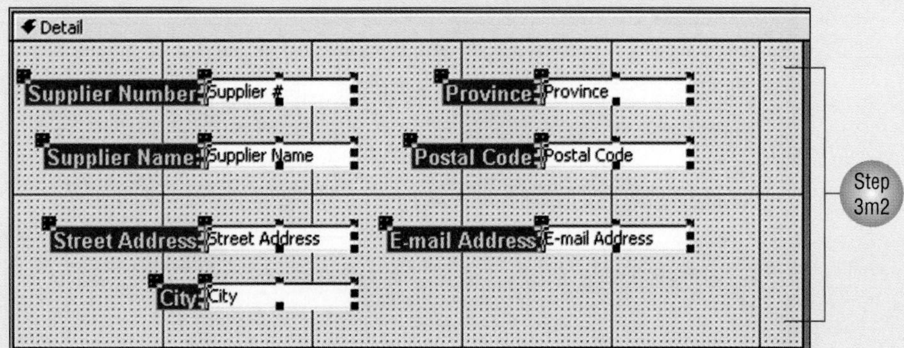

   3) Click in the *Fore Color* text box in the Multiple selection properties sheet, click the button containing three black dots, click the Blue color (sixth color from the left in the fourth row), and then click OK.
   4) Click in the *Back Color* text box, click the button containing three black dots, click the Turquoise color (fifth color from the left in the top row), and then click OK.
   5) Click in the *Font Name* text box, click the down-pointing arrow that displays at the right, and then click *Arial* at the drop-down list. (You will need to scroll up the list to display *Arial*.)
   6) Click in the *Font Size* text box, click the down-pointing arrow that displays at the right, and then click *10*.
   7) Click in the *Font Weight* text box, click the down-pointing arrow that displays at the right, and then click *Bold*.

n. Click in the Design grid outside a control object to deselect the objects.

4. Close the properties sheet. (To do this, click the Close button that displays in the upper right corner of the sheet [contains an *X*].)
5. View the form in Form view by clicking the View button on the Form Design toolbar.
6. Save the form and name it Suppliers Form.
7. Print the currently displayed form by completing the following steps:
   a. Click File and then Print.
   b. At the Print dialog box, click the *Selected Record(s)* option in the *Print Range* section.
   c. Click OK.
8. Close the Suppliers Form form.
9. Close the **OutdoorOptions** database file.

FIGURE

5.9 ***Exercise 5***

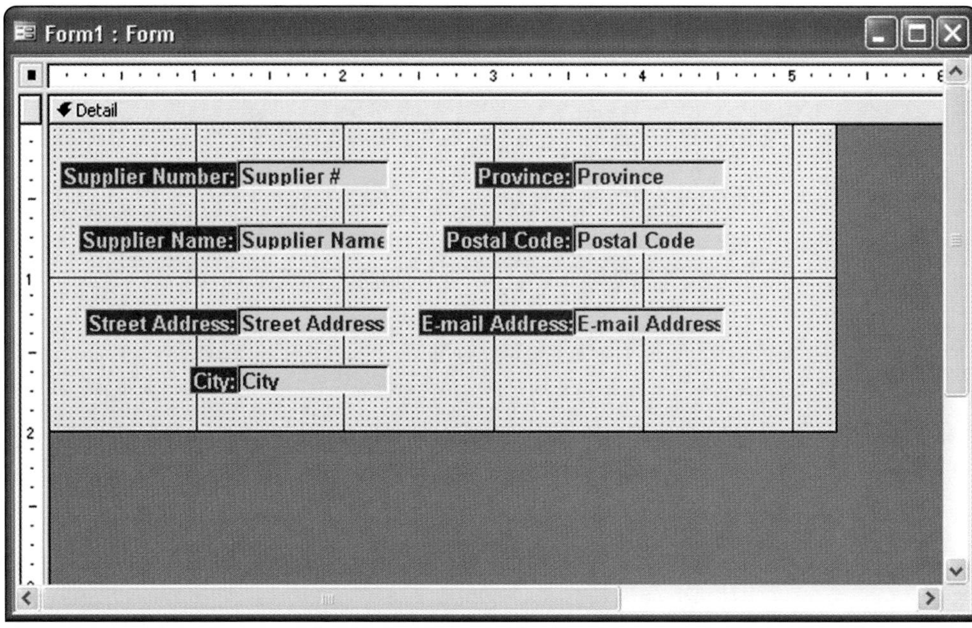

Adding Controls Using the Toolbox

The Toolbox is a palette of control object buttons that automatically appears when a form is displayed in Design view. With the buttons on this Toolbox, shown in Figure 5.10, you can add and modify controls in the form. (Figure 5.10 identifies a few of the buttons on the toolbar.) To add a control in Design view, click the desired button on the Toolbox. This causes the mouse pointer to change to a crosshair pointer with an icon attached. The icon that displays will vary depending on the control object button selected. Move the pointer to the position on the form where you want to place the object and then drag to create the object. Use the sizing handles that display around the control to increase or decrease the size.

FIGURE

5.10 ***Toolbox Buttons***

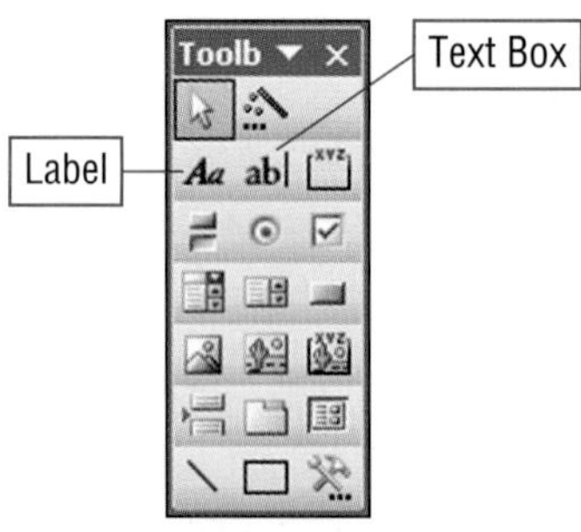

Adding a Form Header and Form Footer

A form in Design view can contain up to three sections—Detail, Form Header, and Form Footer. The Detail section is the only section that displays by default. You created a form in Exercise 5 in the Detail section of the form. A Form Header displays at the top of the form in Form view and at the beginning of a printout started from the Form view screen. A Form Footer appears at the bottom of the form in Form view and at the end of a printout started from the Form view screen.

Add Form Header and Form Footer to Form

1. Open form in Design view.
2. Click View, Form Header/Footer.

Display a Form Header and Form Footer by clicking View on the Menu bar and then clicking Form Header/Footer. Another method is to right-click on the Form 1 : Form title bar and then click Form Header/Footer at the shortcut menu. Use the same methods for turning off the display of a Form Header and Form Footer.

To insert text in a Form Header or Form Footer use the Label button on the Toolbox. Click the Label button and then draw the label in the Form Header or Form Footer. Type text inside the label control object and apply the desired formatting.

Label

Apply formatting to a Form Header with options at the FormHeader properties sheet. Display this sheet by right-clicking the Form Header gray border bar and then clicking Properties at the shortcut menu. Complete similar steps to display the FormFooter properties sheet.

exercise 6

ADDING A FORM HEADER AND FORM FOOTER TO A FORM

1. Open the **OutdoorOptions** database file.
2. If necessary, click the Forms button on the Objects bar.
3. Double-click *Suppliers Form* in the list box.
4. Add and modify a Form Header and Form Footer in Design view by completing the following steps:
   a. Change to the Design view by clicking the View button on the Form View toolbar.
   b. Add and modify a Form Header by completing the following steps:
      1) Right-click on the Suppliers Form : Form title bar and then click Form Header/Footer at the shortcut menu.
      2) Increase the height of the Form Header section by positioning the pointer at the top of the gray Detail border line until the pointer changes to a black vertical line with an up- and down-pointing arrow, and then drag the mouse down to the approximate height shown at the right.
      3) Click the Label button on the Toolbox. (If the Toolbox is not displayed, click the Toolbox button on the Form Design toolbar.)

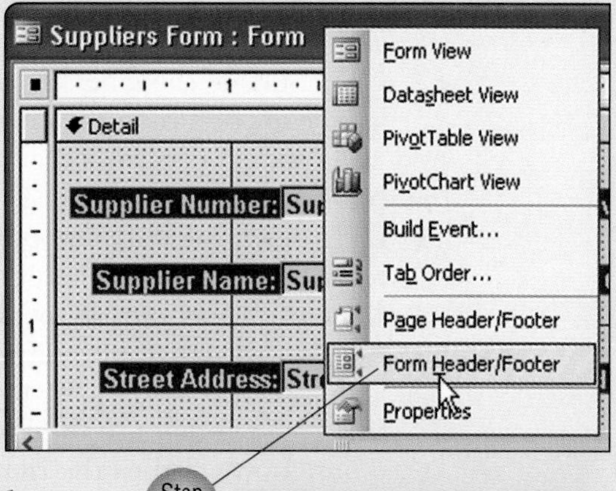

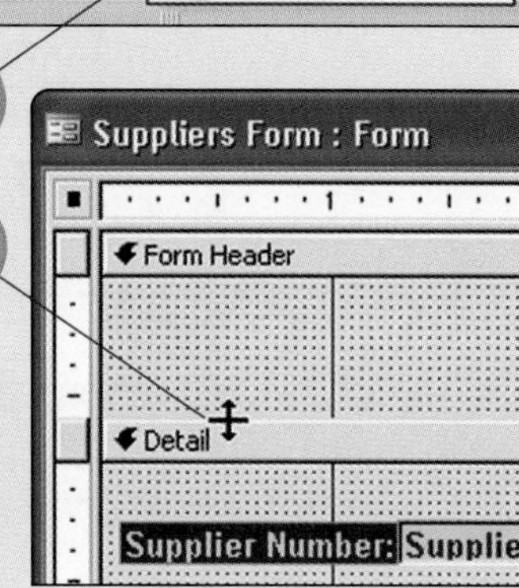

4) Position the crosshair pointer with the label icon attached to it at the top left edge of the first black gridline in the Form Header section, drag the mouse down to the approximate height and width shown below, and then release the mouse button.

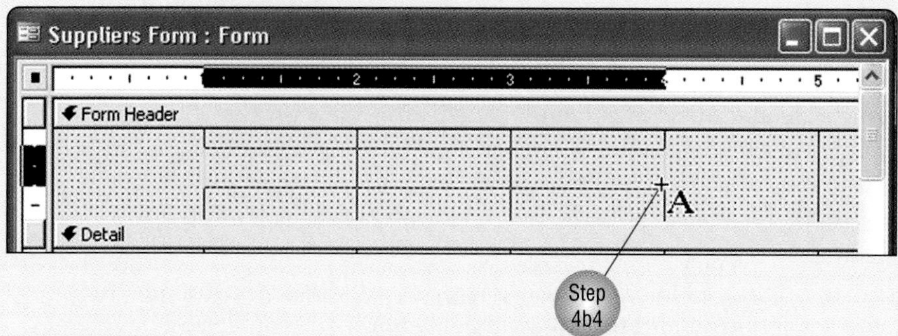

5) A label box will appear with the insertion point automatically positioned in the top left edge of the box. Type **OutdoorOptions Suppliers Form** and then click outside the box.
6) Click once on the label control object to select it.
7) Click the Properties button on the Form Design toolbar.
8) Click the Format tab at the Label properties sheet.
9) Click in the *Font Name* text box (you will need to scroll down the Format list box to display this text box), click the down-pointing arrow at the right, and then click *Arial* at the drop-down menu. (You will need to scroll up the drop-down menu to display *Arial*.)
10) Click in the *Font Size* text box, click the down-pointing arrow at the right, and then click *14* at the drop-down menu.
11) Click in the *Font Weight* text box, click the down-pointing arrow at the right, and then click *Bold* at the drop-down menu.
12) Click outside the label control box. (Increase the height and width of the label control box so the entire title displays.)

c. Add and modify a Form Footer by completing the following steps:
   1) Drag down the bottom border of the form to display the Form Footer section.
   2) Click the Label button on the Toolbox.
   3) Position the crosshair pointer with the label icon attached to it at the top left edge of the first black gridline in the Form Footer section, drag the mouse down and to the right to the approximate height and width shown at the right, and then release the mouse button.

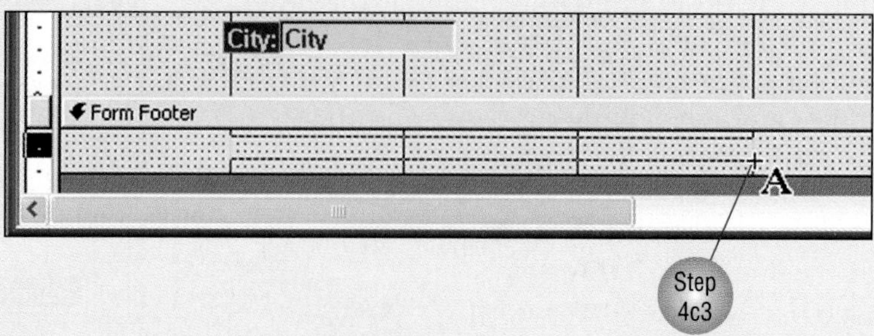

4) A label box will appear with the insertion point automatically positioned in the box. Type **Suppliers Form designed by Student Name** (type your name instead of *Student Name*), and then click outside the box.
5) Click once on the label control object to select it. (The Label properties sheet should be visible. If it is not visible, click the Properties button on the Form Design toolbar.)
6) If necessary, click the Format tab at the Label properties sheet.
7) Make the following changes:
    a) Change the font name to Arial.
    b) Change the font size to 10.
    c) Change the font weight to bold.
8) Click outside the label control box.
9) If necessary, increase the height and width of the label control box so the entire footer displays.

5. Close the properties sheet. (To do this, click the Close button that displays in the upper right corner of the sheet [contains an *X*].)
6. View the form in Form view by clicking the View button on the Form Design toolbar.
7. Click the Save button to save the form.
8. Click the New Record button that displays along the bottom of the form.

9. Add the following record:

Supplier Number	=	**44**
Supplier Name	=	**Everwear Supplies**
Street Address	=	**4500 Second Avenue**
City	=	**Vancouver**
Province	=	**BC**
Postal Code	=	**V2V 6K2**
E-mail Address	=	**everwear@emcp.net**

10. Print the currently displayed record.
11. Close the Suppliers Form form.
12. Close the **OutdoorOptions** database file.

Adding a Calculated Control

A calculated control uses a mathematical equation to determine the contents that are displayed in the control object. Insert a calculated control field in Design view by creating a text box control object and then entering the mathematical equation in the text box. A calculated field is used to perform mathematical operations on existing fields, but it does not exist in the table associated with the form. In Exercise 7, you will create a calculated control in a form that divides the order amount by the number of units.

HINT
Press Ctrl + Enter to begin a new line in a text box.

Type a mathematical expression in a calculated control box. Begin the expression with the equals sign (=) and insert square brackets around field names. Use mathematical operators such as +, -, *, and / to perform calculations.

exercise 7

CREATING A FORM IN DESIGN VIEW AND ADDING A CALCULATED CONTROL

1. Open the **OutdoorOptions** database file.
2. At the OutdoorOptions : Database window, if necessary, click the Forms button on the Objects bar.
3. Create a form in Design view by completing the following steps:
   a. Double-click the *Create form in Design view* option in the list box.
   b. At the Design grid, click the Properties button on the Form Design toolbar.
   c. At the Form properties sheet, click the All tab.
   d. Click in the *Record Source* text box, click the down-pointing arrow at the right, and then click *Orders* at the drop-down list.
   e. Drag the fields in the field list box to the Design grid to the approximate locations shown below.

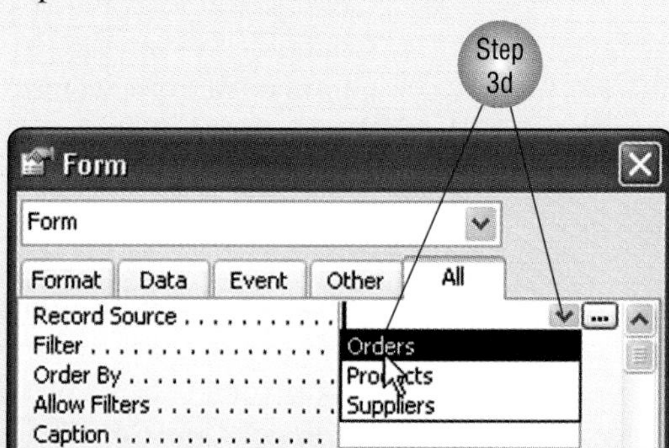

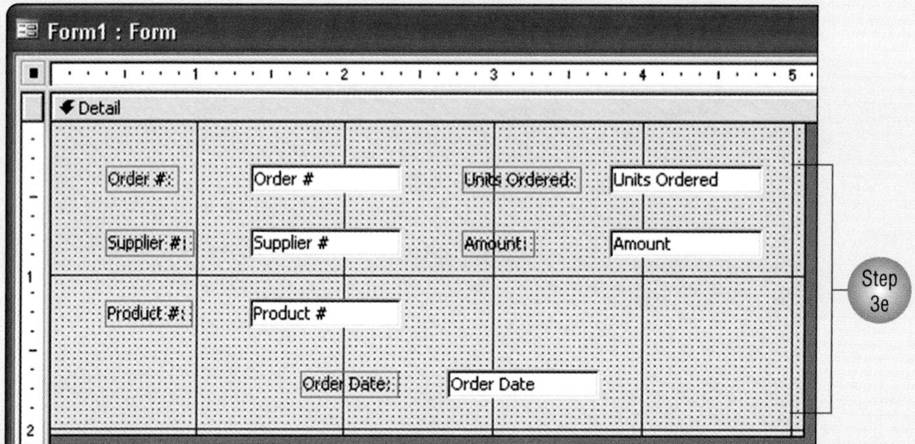

   f. Select the three label and text box control objects at the left side of the Design grid and then align them at the right.
   g. Select the two label and text box control objects at the right side of the Design grid and then align them at the right.
   h. Select the label and text box control objects located at the bottom of the design grid and align them at the right. (This moves the label control object next to the text box control object.)
   i. Add a calculated control field by completing the following steps:
      1) Click the Text Box button on the Toolbox. (If the Toolbox is not visible, click the Toolbox button on the Form Design toolbar.)

2) Position the crosshair pointer with the text box icon attached below the *Amount* text box control and then drag the outline of a box approximately the same size as the text box control above it. 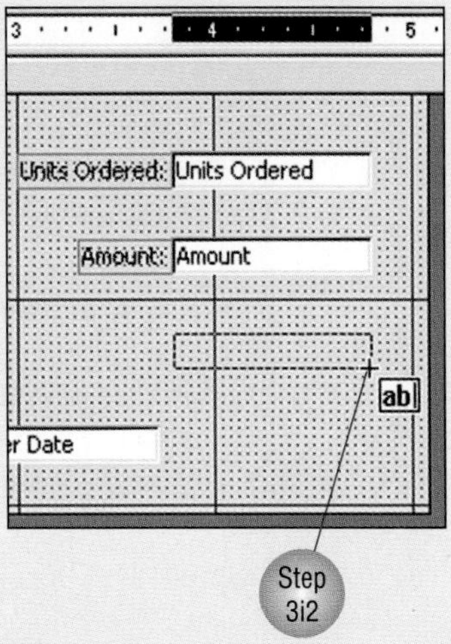
3) Click in the text box control (which currently displays *Unbound*), type **=[Amount]/[Units Ordered]**, and then click outside the control to deselect it.
4) Click the label control object adjacent to the text box control (which currently displays *Text6:* [your number may vary]) to select it.
5) Click the label control object again to position the insertion point inside the label box.
6) Delete the current entry, type **Unit Price:**, and then click outside the label control to deselect it.
7) Move and/or size the calculated control and the label control to align them with the fields displayed above.

Step 3i2

j. Click the View button on the Form Design toolbar to display the form in Form view. Notice the Unit Price amount displays aligned at the left edge of the control. Change the format properties for the calculated control by completing the following steps:
1) Click the View button on the Form View toolbar.
2) Click the text box calculated control to select it.
3) At the Text Box properties sheet, click the Format tab.
4) Click in the *Format* text box (you may need to scroll up to display this text box), click the down-pointing arrow at the right, and then click *Currency* at the drop-down list. 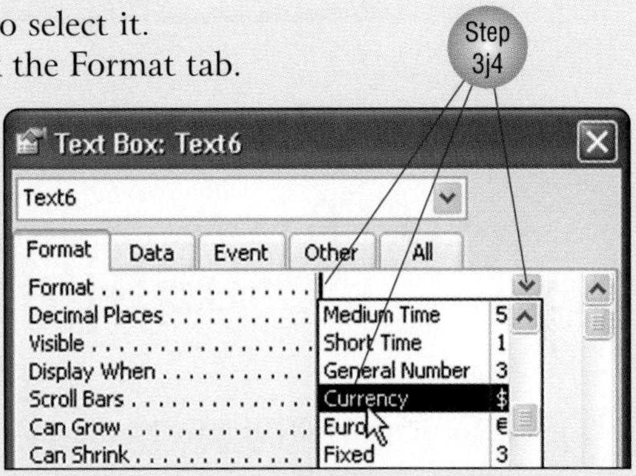
5) Click in the *Text Align* text box (you will need to scroll down the list to display this text box), click the down-pointing arrow at the right, and then click *Right* at the drop-down list.
6) Close the Text Box properties sheet.

Step 3j4

4. View the form in Form view by clicking View button on the Form Design toolbar. Your form should look similar to what you see in Figure 5.11.
5. Save the form and name it Orders Form.
6. Print the first record.
7. Close the Orders Form form.
8. Close the **OutdoorOptions** database file.

FIGURE 5.11 **Exercise 7**

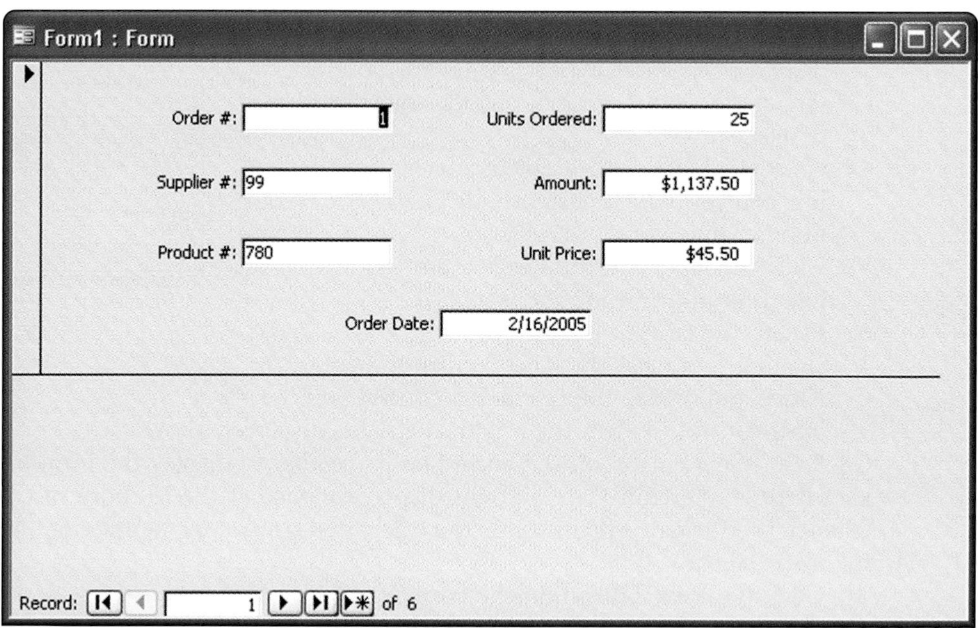

CHAPTER summary

- A form generally improves the ease with which data is entered into a database table. A form can be created with the AutoForm feature and also with the Form Wizard.
- A record in a form displays with navigation buttons that are used to display various records in the form.
- Print a form in the same manner as a database table. Changes can be made to the page margins and/or page orientation at the Page Setup dialog box.
- Add a new record to a form by clicking the New Record button on the Form View toolbar or by clicking the button at the bottom of the record that displays with a right-pointing arrow followed by an asterisk.
- Delete a record by displaying the record and then clicking the Delete Record button on the Form View toolbar.
- The Form Wizard walks you through the steps for creating a form and lets you specify the fields you want included in the form, a layout for the records, the desired formatting, and a name for the form.
- A form can be created with fields from tables that are connected by a one-to-many relationship.

- A form is comprised of a series of controls, which are objects that display titles or descriptions, accept data, or perform actions.
- In Design view, you can use fields from a table to create controls in the Design grid and also add controls with buttons on the Toolbox palette.
- Associate a table with the form to use fields to create controls.
- Move control objects in the Design grid. A label control and its corresponding text box control for a field can be moved individually or together.
- Use the sizing handles around a selected control object to change the size of the object.
- Customize control objects with options at the properties sheet.
- To align control objects in the Design grid, select the objects, click Format, point to Align, and then click the desired alignment at the side menu.
- To add a control using a button on the Toolbox, click the button, move the pointer to the position on the form where you want to place the object, and then drag to create the object.
- Turn on the display of the Form Header and the Form Footer by clicking View and then Form Header/Footer.
- A Form Header displays at the top of the form in Form view and at the beginning of a printout started from the Form view screen.
- A Form Footer displays at the bottom of the form in Form view and at the end of a printout started from the Form view screen.
- A calculated control uses a mathematical equation to determine the contents that are displayed in the control object. A calculated field is used to perform mathematical operations on existing fields, but it does not exist in the table associated with the form.

FEATURES summary

FEATURE	BUTTON	MENU	KEYBOARD
New Form dialog box	New	Insert, Form	
Begin Form Wizard		Insert, Form, Form Wizard	
Properties sheet		View, Properties	Alt + Enter
Toolbox		View, Toolbox	

CONCEPTS check

Completion: On a blank sheet of paper, indicate the correct term, symbol, or command for each description.

1. To create a form with the AutoForm feature, open the database file, click the database table in the list box, and then click this button on the Database toolbar.
2. Use these buttons, which appear along the bottom of a record in a form, to display the first record in the form, the previous record, the next record, or the last record.
3. Click this button on the Form View toolbar to add a new record to the form.
4. Click this button on the Form View toolbar to delete a record from the form.
5. In the form Design view, add controls with buttons on this palette.
6. This section of the form in Design view is set up as a grid.
7. This appears at the bottom of the form in Form view and at the end of a printout started from the Form view screen.
8. This type of control uses a mathematical equation to determine the contents that are displayed in the control object.

SKILLS check

Assessment 1

1. Open the **OutdoorOptions** database file.
2. Use the AutoForm feature to create a form with the data in the Suppliers database table.
3. After creating the form, add the following records to the Suppliers form:

   Supplier # = 12
   Supplier Name = Seaside Suppliers
   Street Address = 4120 Shoreline Drive
   City = Vancouver
   Province = BC
   Postal Code = V2V 8K4
   E-mail Address = seaside@emcp.net

   Supplier # = 34
   Supplier Name = Carson Company
   Street Address = 120 Plaza Center
   City = Vancouver
   Province = BC
   Postal Code = V2V 1K6
   E-mail Address = carson@emcp.net

4. Delete the record containing information on Manning, Inc.
5. Save the form with the name offered by Access (Suppliers).
6. Print and then close the Suppliers form.
7. Close the **OutdoorOptions** database file.

Assessment 2

1. Open the **OutdoorOptions** database file.
2. At the OutdoorOptions : Database window, click the Forms button on the Objects bar.
3. Delete the Suppliers form that displays in the list box. (For assistance, refer to Exercise 3, Step 3.)
4. Create a form for the Suppliers database table using the Form Wizard. Use all of the fields in the Suppliers database table to create the form. You determine the format style. Name the form *Suppliers*.
5. When the Form Wizard is finished, add the following record:

Supplier #	=	**50**
Supplier Name	=	**Binder Corporation**
Street Address	=	**9033 East 32nd**
City	=	**Vancouver**
Province	=	**BC**
Postal Code	=	**V2V 3K2**
E-mail Address	=	**binder@emcp.net**

6. Delete the record containing information on Langley Corporation.
7. Save the Suppliers form.
8. Print the Suppliers form and then close the form.
9. Close the **OutdoorOptions** database file.

Assessment 3

1. Open the **OutdoorOptions** database file.
2. Create a form from two related database tables using the Form Wizard with the following specifications:
   a. At the first Form Wizard dialog box, insert the following fields in the *Selected Fields* list box:

      From the Products database table:
      - *Product #*
      - *Product*
      - *Units on Order*

      From the Suppliers database table:
      - *Supplier #*
      - *Supplier Name*
      - *Street Address*
      - *City*
      - *Province*
      - *Postal Code*

   b. Do not make any changes at the second Form Wizard dialog box.
   c. Do not make any changes at the third Form Wizard dialog box.
   d. You determine the format style at the fourth Form Wizard dialog box.
   e. At the fifth Form Wizard dialog box, type the name **Units on Order**.
   f. When the first record displays, print the form.
   g. Close the record that displays.
3. Close the **OutdoorOptions** database file.

Assessment 4

1. Open the **OutdoorOptions** database file.
2. Open the Orders table and then make the following changes:
   a. Display the table in Design view.
   b. Insert a row above *Order Date.*
   c. Specify the following for the new row:

      Field Name = *Unit Price*
      Data Type = *Currency*
      Description = *Unit price*

   d. Save the table.
   e. Change to the Datasheet view and then enter the following unit price in the specified order number record:

      Order #4 = 72.25
      Order #5 = 112.00

   f. Save and then close the table.
3. Create a form by design with the following specifications:
   a. Create a form by design with all of the fields in the Orders table *except* the *Amount* field. (You determine the location of the fields in the Design grid.)
   b. Add a calculated control that contains *[Unit Price]*[Units Ordered]* in the text box control (the box that contains the word *Unbound*) and *Amount* in the label control (the box that contains the word *Text* followed by a number). Change the format of the text box calculated control to *Currency*.
   c. Apply formatting of your choosing to the label and text box control objects. (Change at least the font name, fore color, and back color.)
   d. Add the Form Header *OutdoorOptions – Orders Form*. Change the font name, font size, and font weight of the Form Header. (You determine the font, size, and weight.)
   e. Add the Form Footer *Order Totals*. Change the font name, font size, and font weight of the Form Footer. (You determine the font, size, and weight.)
   f. Save the form and name it Order Totals.
   g. Change to the Form view.
   h. Print the currently displayed record.
4. Close the Order Totals form.
5. Close the **OutdoorOptions** database file.

Assessment 5

1. The New Form dialog box contains a number of options for creating a form. In this chapter, you have used the Form Wizard to prepare forms. Experiment with two other options available at the New Form dialog box—*AutoForm: Columnar* and *AutoForm: Tabular*.
2. After experimenting with these two wizards, open the **OutdoorOptions** database file and then complete the following:
   a. Use the AutoForm: Columnar option to create a form with all of the fields in the Suppliers database table. Print the first record that displays and then close the form.
   b. Use the AutoForm: Tabular option to create a form with all of the fields in the Products database table. Print the first record that displays and then close the form.
3. Close the **OutdoorOptions** database file.

CHAPTER challenge

You are the office manager at Tri-State Vision Care Center. The Center houses several optometrists and ophthalmologists. To maintain patients' billing records, you decide to create a database named **Tri-StateVisionCare** to automate this process. Create two tables in the database. One table named Patients will be created for patient information, such as *Patient ID*, *Name*, *Address*, *Phone Number*, etc. Another table named Patient Billing will be created for patient billing and should include fields such as *Patient ID*, *Date of Visit*, *Doctor's Name*, *Method of Payment*, and *Fees Rendered*. Create and format a form (with a title) for each of the tables so others working in the office can easily and quickly add records. Add an additional calculated control to the Patient Billing form called Total Due that displays the total due when a 5% tax has added to fees rendered. Once the forms are complete, add at least five records to each of them.

You are looking for ways to improve the efficiency of entering records in the forms created in the first part of the Chapter Challenge. One method is through the use of combo boxes. Use the Help feature to learn more about combo boxes. Then create combo boxes for the *Doctor's Name* field and *Method of Payment* field in the Patient Billing form created in the first part of the Chapter Challenge. Save the form again.

All billing information from the Tri-State Vision Care Center is sent to headquarters every month. The billing department at headquarters is using Excel and wants all information sent in an Excel format. Export the Patient Billing table created in the first part of the Chapter Challenge to Excel so that it will be ready to send to headquarters. Save the Excel file with the same name as the table.

CHAPTER 6

CREATING REPORTS, MAILING LABELS, AND CHARTS

PERFORMANCE OBJECTIVES

Upon successful completion of Chapter 6, you will be able to:

- **Create a report using AutoReport**
- **Create a report using the Report Wizard**
- **Create a report in Design view**
- **Add a Report Header and Report Footer**
- **Create mailing labels using the Label Wizard**
- **Create a chart using the Chart Wizard**
- **Summarize data using PivotTable View and PivotChart View**

ACCESS

In this chapter, you will learn how to prepare reports from data in a database table using the AutoReport feature and also the Report Wizard. A report lets you specify how data will appear when printed. You will also learn how to create mailing labels using the Label Wizard, how to create a chart with the Chart Wizard, and how to summarize data using the PivotTable View and PivotChart View.

Creating Reports

HINT

Create a report to control what data appears on the page when printed.

The primary purpose for inserting data in a form is to improve the display of the data and to make data entry easier. Data can also be inserted in a report. The purpose for this is to control what data appears on the page when printed. Reports generally answer specific questions (queries). For example, a report could answer the question *What customers have submitted claims?* or *What products do we currently have on order?* Access includes the AutoReport feature that automatically creates a report based on data in a table and also the Report Wizard that walks you through the process of creating a report. Like the Form Wizard, you specify fields, format style, and the report name when creating a report.

Create a Report Using AutoForm
1. Open database file.
2. Click desired table.
3. Click down-pointing arrow at the right of New Object button.
4. Click AutoReport.

Creating a Report Using AutoReport

The AutoReport feature automatically creates a plainly formatted report in a columnar arrangement. To use the AutoReport feature, select the desired table, click the down-pointing arrow at the right side of the New Object button on the Database toolbar, and then click AutoReport at the drop-down list.

exercise 1

CREATING A REPORT USING AUTOREPORT

(Note: Delete any database files from your disk.)

1. Copy the **OutdoorOptions** database file from the CD that accompanies this textbook to your disk. Remove the read-only attribute from the **OutdoorOptions** database file.
2. Open the **OutdoorOptions** database file.
3. At the OutdoorOptions : Database window, click the Tables button on the Objects bar.
4. Create and print a report using AutoReport by completing the following steps:
   a. Click *Suppliers* in the list box to select the Suppliers table.
   b. Click the down-pointing arrow at the right side of the New Object button on the Database toolbar.
   c. At the drop-down list that displays, click *AutoReport*.
   d. When the report displays in Print Preview, view the report, and then click the Print button on the Print Preview toolbar.
   e. Click the Close button at the right side of the Suppliers title bar.
   f. At the message asking if you want to save the changes to the design of the report, click the No button.
5. Close the **OutdoorOptions** database file.

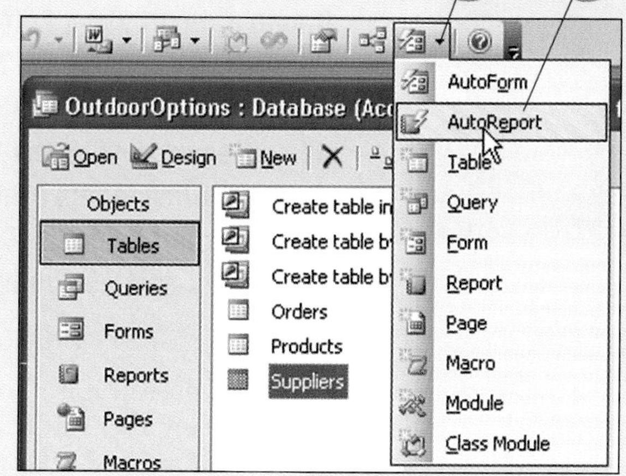

Creating a Report Using the Report Wizard

HINT
The second Report Wizard dialog box only opens if you select fields from more than one table.

To create a report using the Report Wizard, open the database file, click the Reports button on the Objects bar, and then click the New button. At the New Report dialog box, double-click *Report Wizard* in the list box. The first Report Wizard dialog box is similar to the first Form Wizard dialog box. Choose the desired table with options from the *Tables/Queries* text box. Specify the fields you want included in the report by inserting them in the *Selected Fields* list box and then clicking the Next button.

At the second Report Wizard dialog box, shown in Figure 6.1, you can increase or decrease the priority level of fields in the report. To increase the priority level, click the desired field name in the list box at the left side of the dialog box, and then click the button containing the greater than symbol (>). To decrease the priority level, click the desired field, and then click the button containing the less than symbol (<). This changes the sample information displayed at the right side of the dialog box. After specifying the field levels, click the Next button.

Create a Report Using Report Wizard

1. Open database file.
2. Click Reports button on Objects bar.
3. Click New button.
4. Double-click *Report Wizard.*
5. Choose desired options at each of the Report Wizard dialog boxes.

FIGURE 6.1 ***Second Report Wizard Dialog Box***

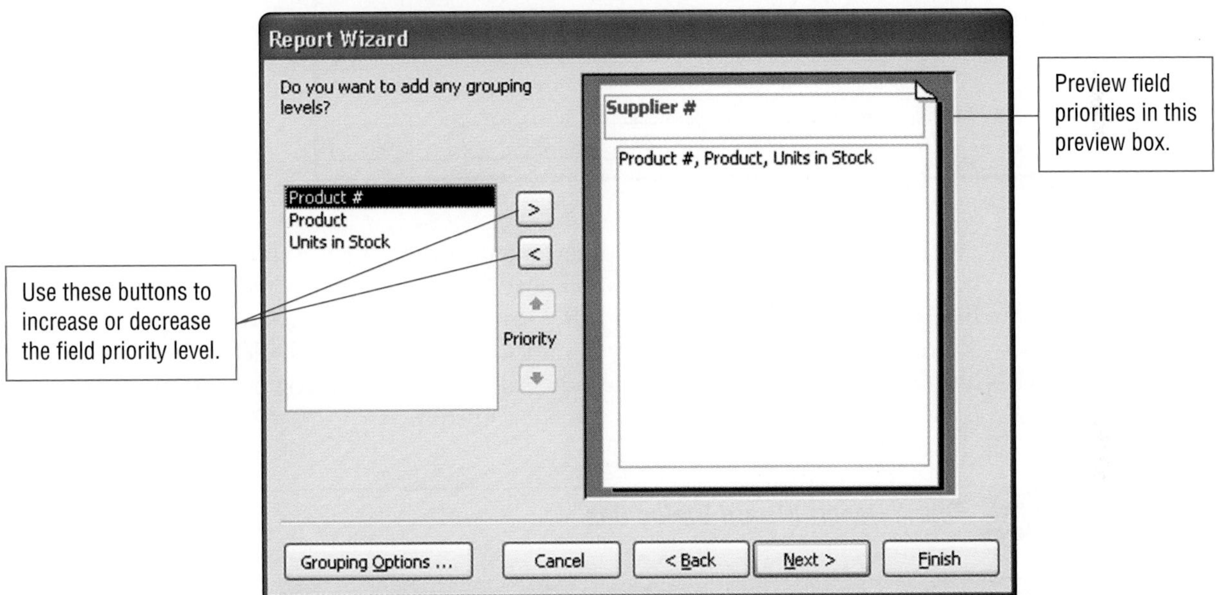

You can specify the order in which records are displayed in the report at the third Report Wizard dialog box shown in Figure 6.2. To specify a sort order, click the down-pointing arrow at the right of the text box preceded by a number 1, and then click the field name. The default sort is done in ascending order. This can be changed to descending by clicking the button that displays at the right side of the text box. After identifying the sort order, click the Next button.

FIGURE 6.2 **Third Report Wizard Dialog Box**

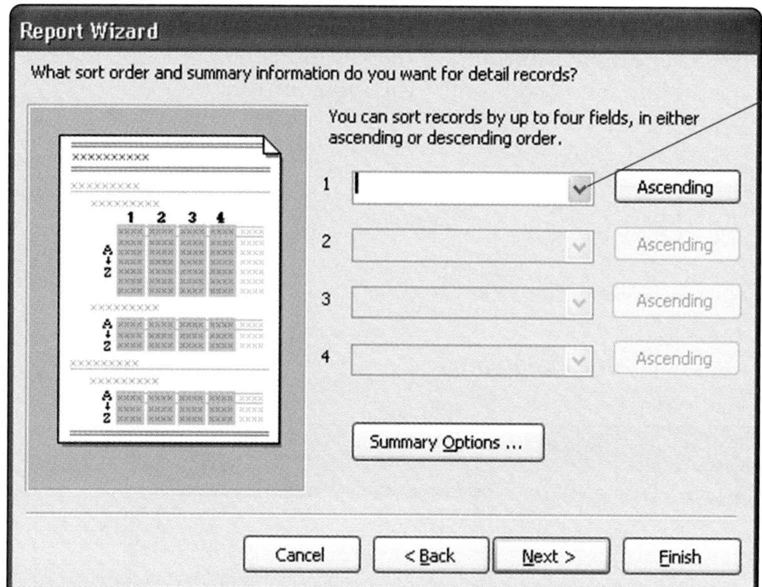

Specify a sort order by clicking this down-pointing arrow and then clicking the desired field name.

The layout of the report is determined in the fourth Report Wizard dialog box shown in Figure 6.3. You can choose from a variety of layouts such as *Stepped*, *Block*, *Outline 1*, *Outline 2*, *Align Left 1*, and *Align Left 2*. Click a layout option and a sample of the layout is displayed on the sample page at the left side of the dialog box. The page orientation can also be selected at this dialog box. After choosing a layout and/or orientation, click the Next button.

FIGURE 6.3 **Fourth Report Wizard Dialog Box**

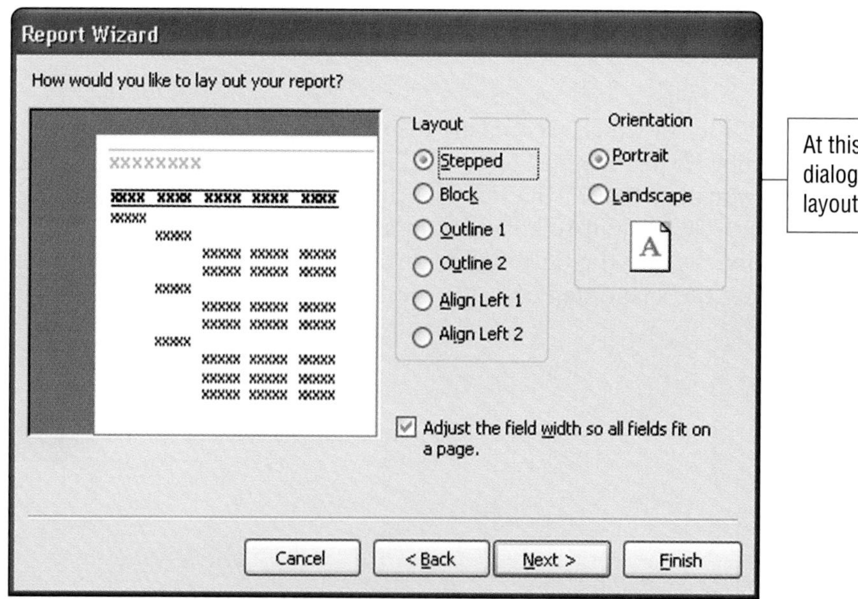

At this Report Wizard dialog box, choose a layout and orientation.

The Report Wizard offers several report styles at the fifth Report Wizard dialog box shown in Figure 6.4. Click a report style and the wizard will display a sample at the left side of the dialog box. Click the Next button to display the sixth Report Wizard dialog box.

FIGURE 6.4 **Fifth Report Wizard Dialog Box**

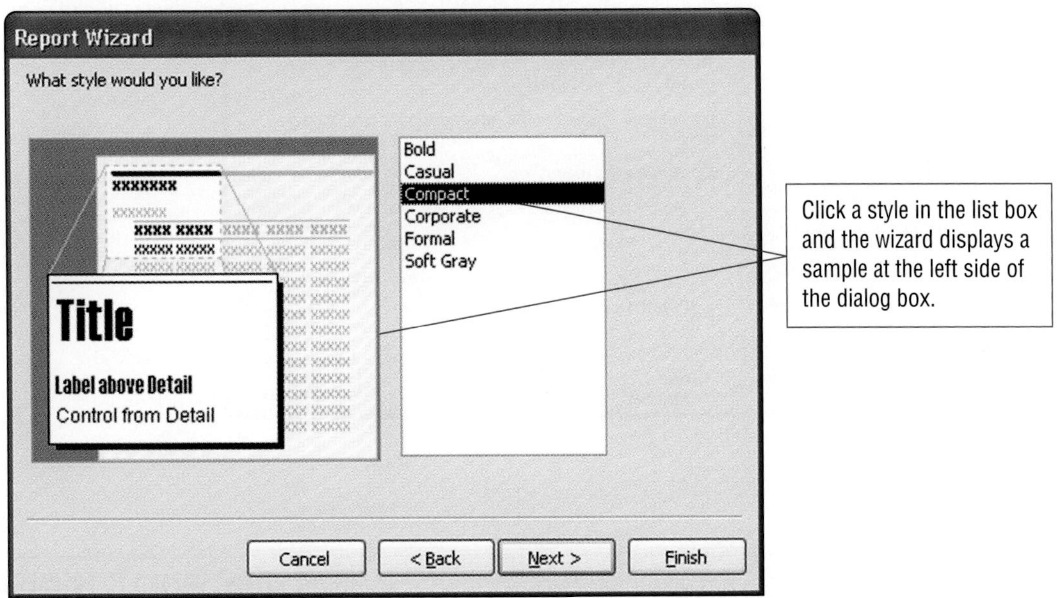

At the sixth Report Wizard dialog box, shown in Figure 6.5, type a name for the report, and then click Finish. Creating the report may take a few moments. When the report is finished, it displays on the screen in Print Preview. In Print Preview, you can change the percentage of display of data and also send the report to the printer. To print the report, click the Print button on the Print Preview toolbar. After viewing and/or printing the report, close Print Preview by clicking the Close button.

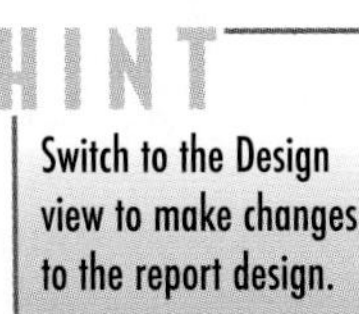

HINT

Switch to the Design view to make changes to the report design.

FIGURE

6.5 **Sixth Report Wizard Dialog Box**

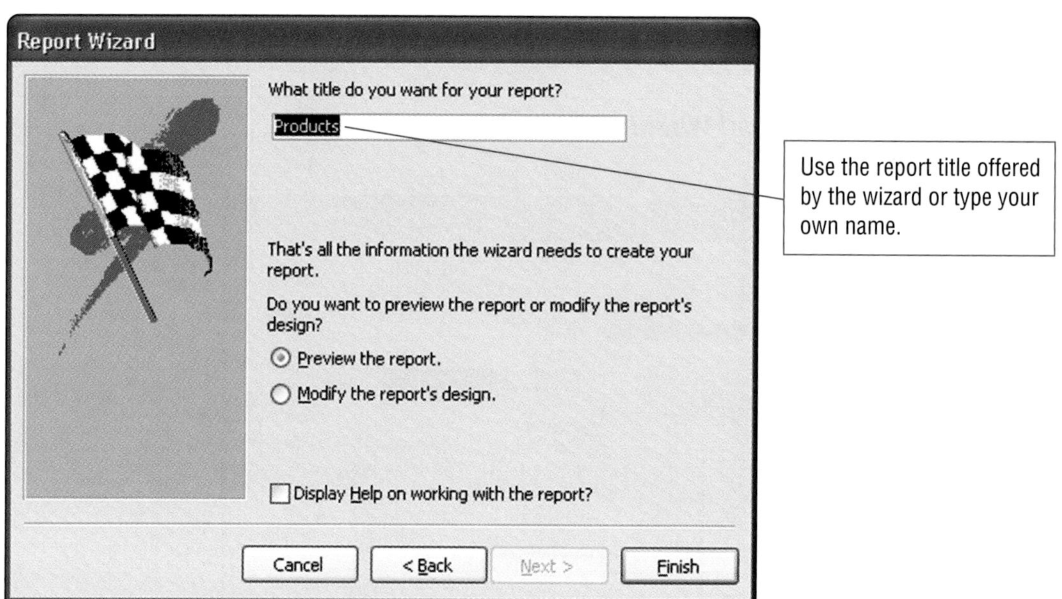

exercise 2

USING THE REPORT WIZARD TO PREPARE A REPORT

1. Open the **OutdoorOptions** database file.
2. At the OutdoorOptions : Database window, click the Reports button on the Objects bar.
3. Create a report with the Report Wizard by completing the following steps:
   a. Click the New button on the window toolbar.
   b. At the New Report dialog box, double-click the *Report Wizard* option in the list box.
   c. At the first Report Wizard dialog box, click the down-pointing arrow at the right side of the *Tables/Queries* text box, and then click *Table: Products* at the drop-down list.
   d. Insert the following fields in the *Selected Fields* list box:

      Product #
      Product
      Supplier #
      Units in Stock

   e. After inserting the fields, click the Next button.

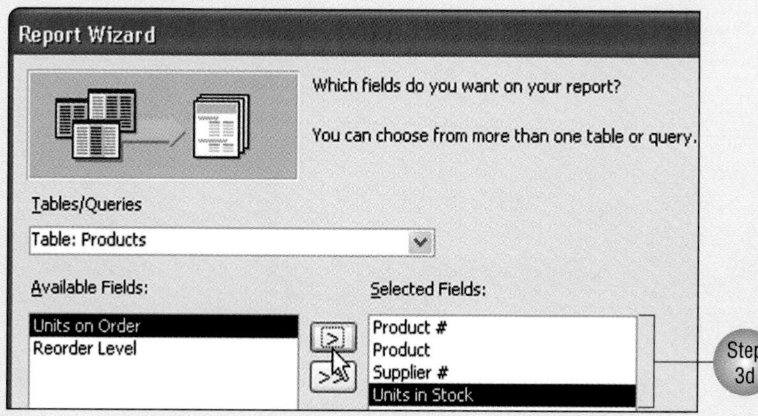

f. At the second Report Wizard dialog box, decrease and increase priority levels by completing the following steps:
   1) Click the button to the right of the list box that displays with a less than symbol (<). (This decreases the priority level of the *Supplier #* field.)
   2) Click *Product* in the list box that displays at the left side of the dialog box, and then click the button to the right of the list box that displays with a greater than symbol (>). (This increases the priority level of the *Product* field.)

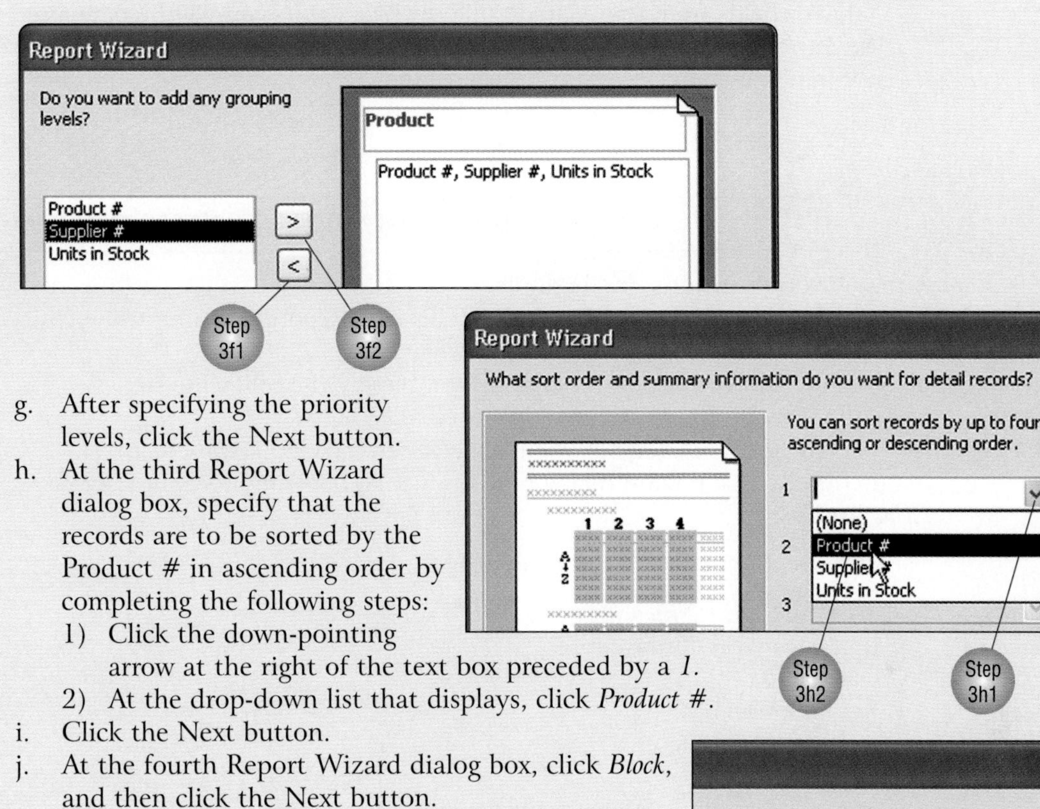

g. After specifying the priority levels, click the Next button.
h. At the third Report Wizard dialog box, specify that the records are to be sorted by the Product # in ascending order by completing the following steps:
   1) Click the down-pointing arrow at the right of the text box preceded by a *1*.
   2) At the drop-down list that displays, click *Product #*.
i. Click the Next button.
j. At the fourth Report Wizard dialog box, click *Block*, and then click the Next button.
k. At the fifth Report Wizard dialog box, click *Compact* in the list box, and then click the Next button.

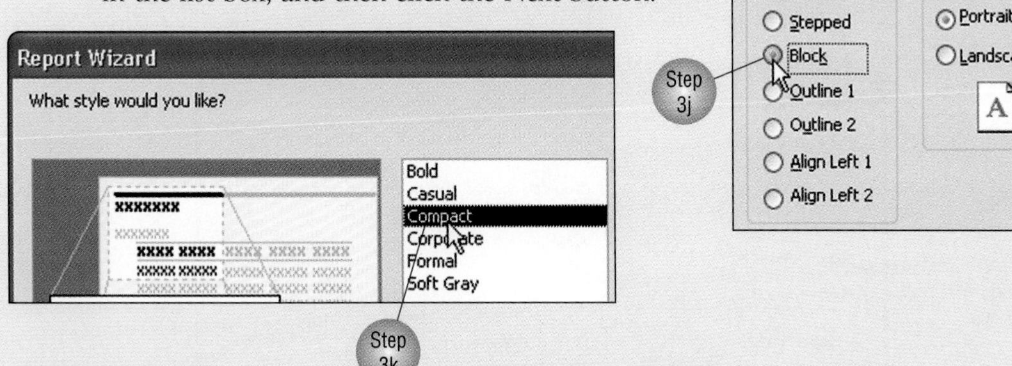

l. At the sixth Report Wizard dialog box, click the Finish button.
m. When the report displays in Print Preview, view the report, and then click the Print button that displays on the Print Preview toolbar.
n. Click the Close button at the right side of the Products title bar.

4. Close the **OutdoorOptions** database file.

Preparing a Report Based on Two Database Tables

In the previous chapter on creating forms, you learned to create a form with fields from related database tables. Fields from related database tables can also be used to create a report. The steps to prepare a report with fields from two database tables are basically the same as those you completed in Exercise 2. The only difference is that an additional Report Wizard dialog box displays during the steps asking you to specify whether the fields should be grouped by the fields from the primary table or fields from the related table. In Exercise 3, you will prepare a report with fields from the Products database table and also the Suppliers table. These tables are joined by a one-to-many relationship.

exercise 3

PREPARING A REPORT WITH FIELDS FROM TWO DATABASE TABLES

1. Open the **OutdoorOptions** database file.
2. At the OutdoorOptions : Database window, click the Reports button on the Objects bar.
3. Create a report with the Report Wizard by completing the following steps:
   a. Click the New button on the window toolbar.
   b. At the New Report dialog box, double-click *Report Wizard* in the list box.
   c. At the first Report Wizard dialog box, insert the following fields in the *Selected Fields* list box:

      From the Suppliers database table:

      Supplier Name
      Street Address
      City
      Province
      Postal Code

      From the Products database table:

      Product
      Product #

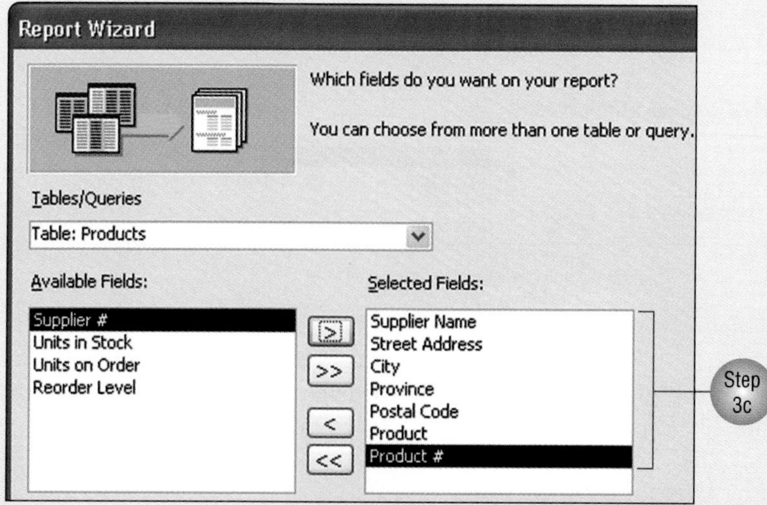

d. After inserting the fields, click the Next button.
e. At the second Report Wizard dialog box, make sure *by Suppliers* is selected in the list box in the upper left corner, and then click the Next button.
f. At the third Report Wizard dialog box, increase the priority level of the *Supplier Name* field. To do this, make sure *Supplier Name* is selected in the list box, and then click the button containing the greater than symbol (>).

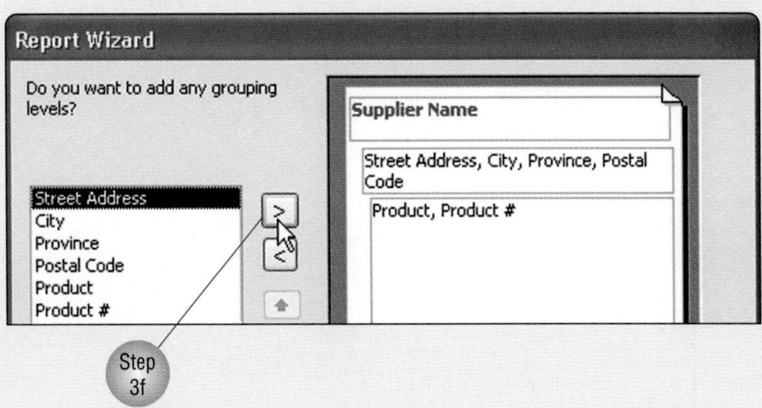

g. Click the Next button.
h. At the fourth Report Wizard dialog box, click the Next button. (Do not specify a sort order.)
i. At the fifth Report Wizard dialog box, click *Align Left 1*, and then click the Next button.
j. At the sixth Report Wizard dialog box, click *Corporate* in the list box, and then click the Next button.
k. At the seventh Report Wizard dialog box, click the Finish button.
l. When the report displays in Print Preview, view the report, and then click the Print button that displays on the Print Preview toolbar.
m. Click the Close button (displays with an *X*) that displays at the right side of the Suppliers title bar.

4. Close the **OutdoorOptions** database file.

Creating a Report in Design View

A report, like a form, is comprised of a series of controls, which are objects that display titles or descriptions, accept data, or perform actions. In the reports you created in this chapter, the Report Wizard created the controls for the report using fields from the tables. A report, like a form, can be created in Design view. To display the report Design view, click the Reports button on the Objects bar, and then double-click *Create report in Design view*.

A report can include up to five sections including Report Header, Page Header, Detail, Page Footer, and Report Footer. These five sections are identified in the sample report shown in Figure 6.6.

QUICK STEPS

Create a Report in Design View

1. Open database file.
2. Click Reports button.
3. Double-click *Create report in Design view.*
4. Click Properties button.
5. Click Report properties sheet All tab.
6. Click in *Record Source* text box.
7. Click down-pointing arrow and then click desired table.
8. Drag desired fields from field list box to Design grid.

FIGURE 6.6 ***Sample Report***

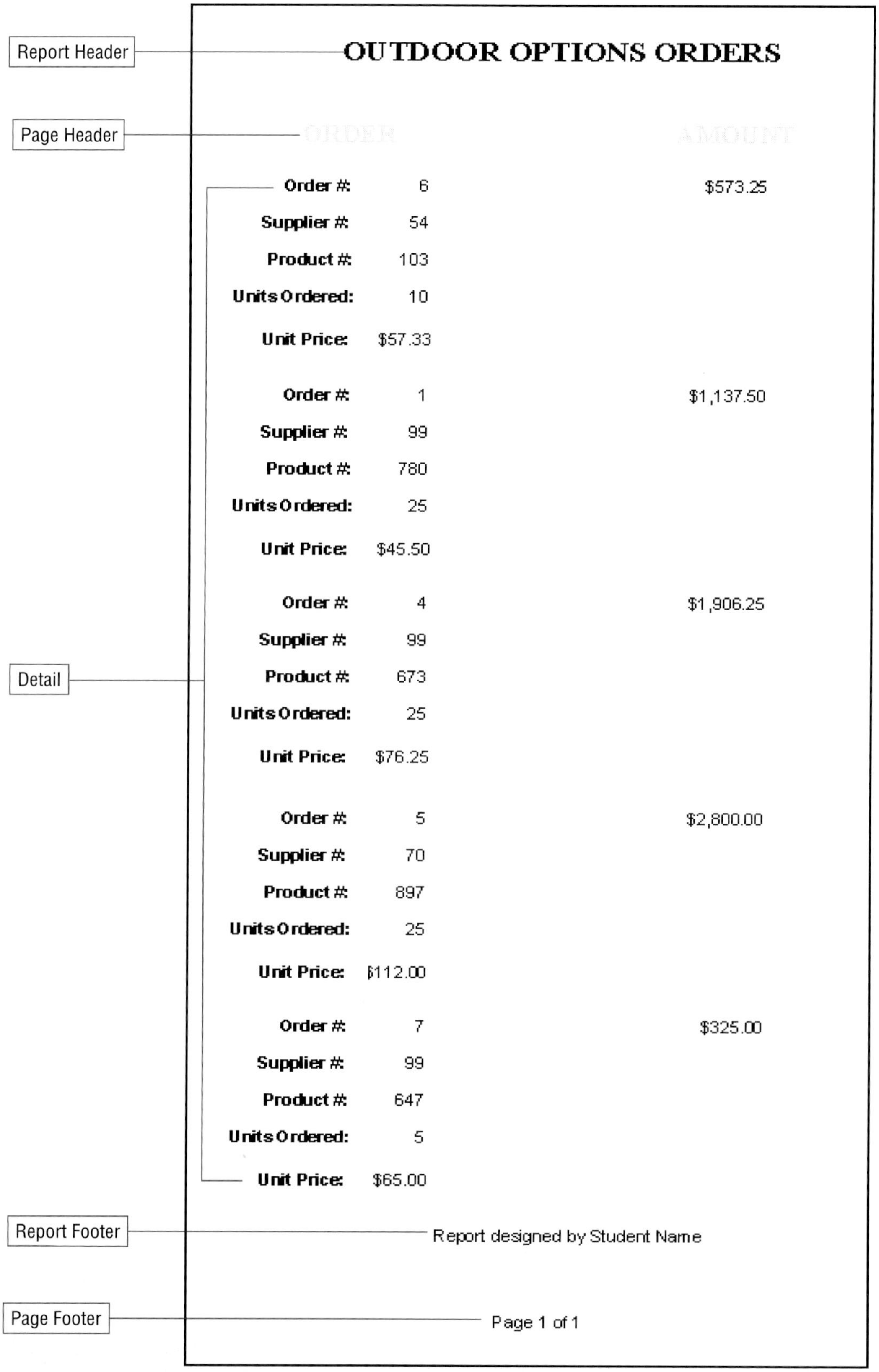

Report Header — **OUTDOOR OPTIONS ORDERS**

Page Header — ORDER | AMOUNT

Detail

Order #:	6	$573.25
Supplier #:	54	
Product #:	103	
Units Ordered:	10	
Unit Price:	$57.33	
Order #:	1	$1,137.50
Supplier #:	99	
Product #:	780	
Units Ordered:	25	
Unit Price:	$45.50	
Order #:	4	$1,906.25
Supplier #:	99	
Product #:	673	
Units Ordered:	25	
Unit Price:	$76.25	
Order #:	5	$2,800.00
Supplier #:	70	
Product #:	897	
Units Ordered:	25	
Unit Price:	$112.00	
Order #:	7	$325.00
Supplier #:	99	
Product #:	647	
Units Ordered:	5	
Unit Price:	$65.00	

Report Footer — Report designed by Student Name

Page Footer — Page 1 of 1

The Report Header generally includes the title of the report and/or the company logo. The Page Header appears at the top of each page and generally includes column headings identifying the data in the report. The Detail section of the report contains the data from the table. The Page Footer appears at the bottom of each page and might include information such as the page number. The Report Footer appears on the last page of the report and might include information such as the person designing the report.

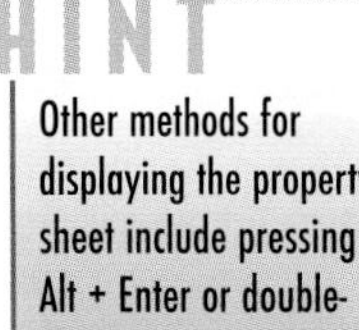

HINT

Other methods for displaying the property sheet include pressing Alt + Enter or double-clicking the control.

Using Fields to Add Controls

To add fields to a report in Design view, associate the report with the desired table. To do this, click the Properties button on the Report Design toolbar. This displays the Report properties sheet. At the Report properties sheet, click the All tab, and then click in the *Record Source* text box. Click the down-pointing arrow that displays at the right side of the text box, and then click the desired table. This displays the table fields in a field list box. Using the mouse, drag the desired field from the field list box to the Design grid.

HINT

Display Help on a property by clicking in the property and then pressing F1.

Moving, Resizing, and Customizing Control Objects

The steps to move, resize, and/or customize control objects in report Design view are the same as the steps to remove, resize, and/or customize control objects in form Design view. Select an object and then either move the individual object or move the label control object and the text box control object together. Customize control objects with options at the properties sheet. (The name of the properties sheet will vary depending on what is selected.)

When a field is added to the report in Design view, a label control containing the field name and a text box control used to accept data are placed adjacent to each other. The label control containing the field name is included for descriptive purposes so that the user knows which data to type into the corresponding text box. In a report, a column heading is generally included in the Page Header describing the data and, therefore, some label control objects may not be needed.

Adding Controls Using the Toolbox

Add controls to the report using buttons on the Toolbox. To add a control in Design view, click the desired button on the Toolbox. This causes the mouse pointer to change to a crosshair pointer with an icon attached. The icon that displays will vary depending on the control object button selected. Move the pointer to the position on the form where you want to place the object and then drag to create the object. Use the sizing handles that display around the control to increase or decrease the size.

Adding a Report Header and Report Footer

The Design view, by default, displays the Detail section and the Page Header and Page Footer. To add a Report Header and/or Report Footer to a report, click View on the Menu bar and then click Report Header/Footer. Another method is to right-click on the Report 1 : Report title bar, and then click Report Header/Footer at the shortcut menu. Use the same methods to turn off the display of a Report Header and Report Footer.

Add Report Header and Report Footer
1. Open report in Design view.
2. Click View, Report Header/Footer.

To insert text in a Page Header, Report Header, Page Footer, or Report Footer, use the Label button on the Toolbox. Click the Label button and then draw the label in the desired section. Type text inside the label control object and apply the desired formatting.

exercise 4

CREATING, CUSTOMIZING, AND FORMATTING A REPORT IN DESIGN VIEW

1. Open the **OutdoorOptions** database file.
2. At the OutdoorOptions : Database window, click the Reports button on the Objects bar.
3. Create the report shown in Figure 6.7 in Design view by completing the following steps:
   a. Double-click the *Create report in Design view* option in the list box.
   b. At the Design grid, click the Properties button on the Report Design toolbar.
   c. At the Report properties sheet, click the All tab.
   d. At the Report properties sheet with the All tab selected, click in the *Record Source* text box, and then click the down-pointing arrow that displays at the right side of the text box.
   e. At the drop-down list that displays, click *Orders*.
   f. Drag the *Order #* field from the field list box to the Design grid to the approximate location shown below.
   g. Drag the other fields (*Supplier #*, *Product #*, *Units Ordered*, and *Amount*) from the field list box to the Design grid in the approximate locations shown below.

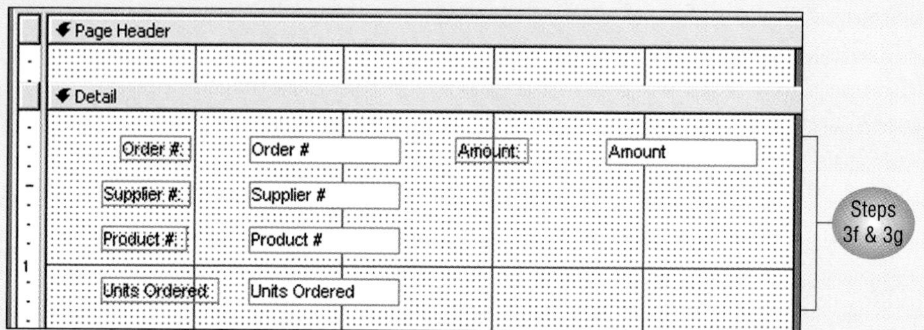

   h. Delete the label control object for the Amount. (The label control object contains *Amount* with a transparent background [gray dots from the grid show through].)
   i. Insert a calculated control field by completing the following steps:
      1) Click the Text Box button on the Toolbox. (If the Toolbox is not visible, click the Toolbox button on the Report Design toolbar.)
      2) Position the crosshair pointer with the text box icon attached below the Units Ordered text box control and then drag the outline of a box approximately the same size as the text box control above.
      3) Click in the text box control (which currently displays *Unbound*) and type **=[Amount]/[Units Ordered]**.
      4) Click outside the box, and then click the text box control to select it.

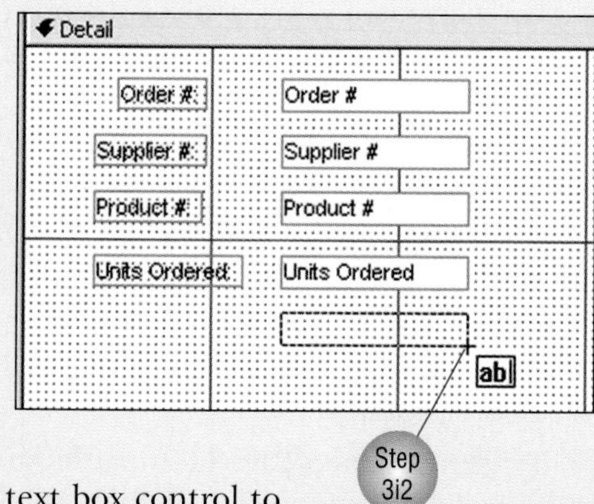

5) With the text box control selected, click in the *Format* text box in the Text Box properties sheet (you may need to scroll up to display the *Format* text box), click the down-pointing arrow, and then click *Currency* at the drop-down list.
6) Click outside the text box control to deselect it.

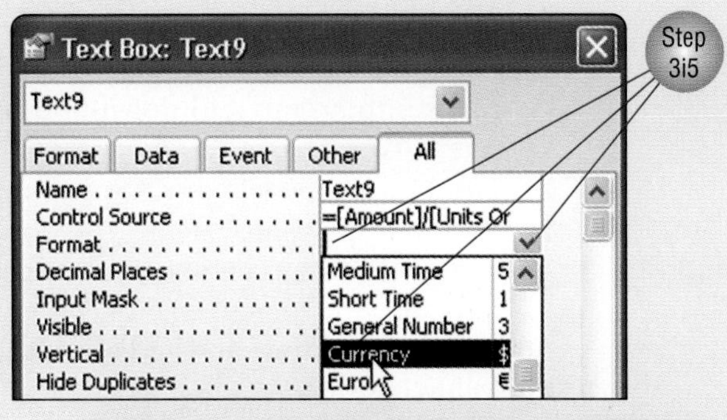

j. Change the caption in the new label control box by completing the following steps:
   1) Click the label control box to select it (contains *Text #* [where a number displays in place of the # symbol]).
   2) Click in the *Caption* text box located in the Label properties sheet. (You may need to scroll up to display the *Caption* text box.)
   3) Delete the text currently displayed in the *Caption* text box and then type **Unit Price:**.

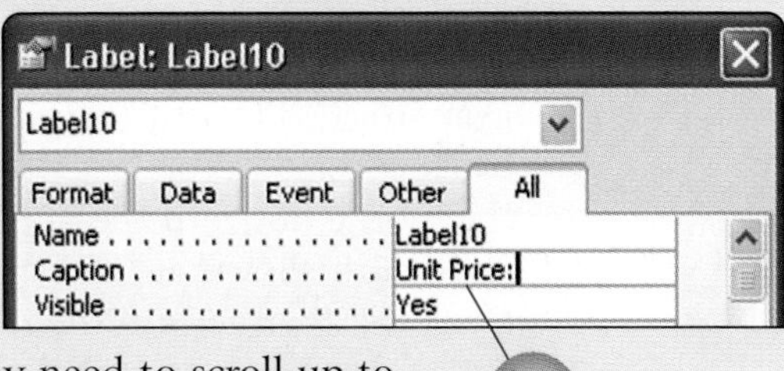

k. Decrease the size of the text box controls as shown at the right.
l. Select the label control objects at the left side of the Design grid (just the label control objects—not the text box control objects) and then align them at the right.

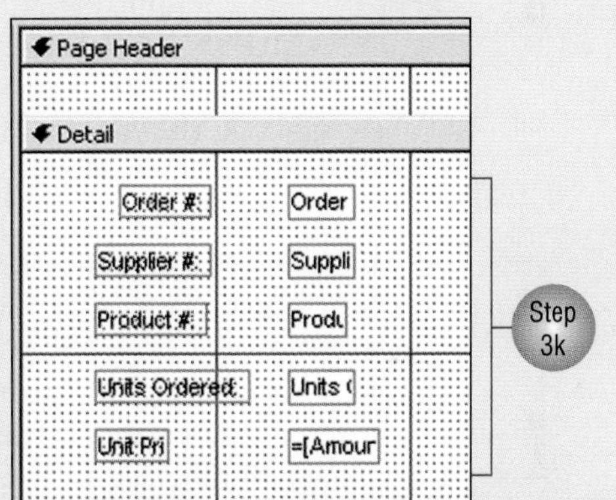

m. With the label object control boxes still selected, change the font weight to bold.
n. With the label object control boxes still selected, change the text alignment to right. To do this, click in the *Text Align* text box in the Multiple selection properties sheet (you may need to scroll down the list to display this text box), click the down-pointing arrow, and then click *Right* at the drop-down list.
o. With the label object control boxes still selected, position the mouse pointer on one of the selected boxes and then click the right mouse button. At the shortcut menu that displays, point to Size, and then click To Fit at the side menu.

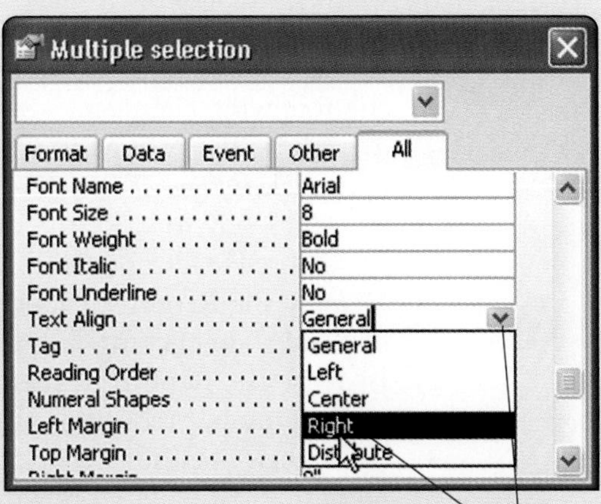

p. Select all of the text box control objects (contain a white background) and then click in the *Text Align* text box in the Multiple selection properties sheet. Click the down-pointing arrow at the right side of the text box and then click *Right* at the drop-down list.
q. Decrease the height of the Detail section by completing the following steps:

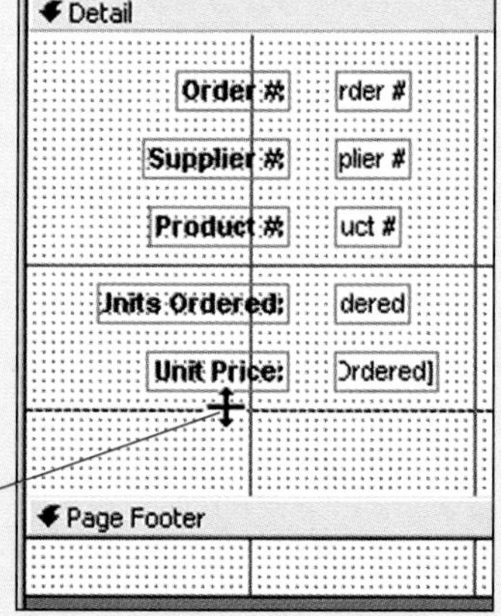

1) Position the mouse pointer on the top of the gray bar containing the text *Page Footer* until the pointer turns into an up- and down-pointing arrow with a line between.
2) Hold down the left mouse button, drag up until the border displays just below the bottom label and text box control objects, and then release the mouse button.

r. Add column headings in the Page Header by completing the following steps:
   1) Click the Label button on the Toolbox.
   2) Position the crosshair pointer with the label icon attached to it at the top left edge of the first black gridline in the Page Header section, drag the mouse down to the approximate height and width shown at the right (and in Figure 6.7), and then release the mouse button.
   3) Type **ORDER** in the label control box, and then click outside the box.
   4) Use the Label button on the Toolbox to create the AMOUNT label shown in Figure 6.7.
   5) Select the two labels and then apply the following formatting:
      a) Change the font name to Times New Roman.
      b) Change the font size to 12.
      c) Change the font weight to bold.
      d) Change the fore color to Dark Teal (fourth color from the left in the third row from the top).
   6) Increase the size of the label control boxes so the entire text displays in each label.

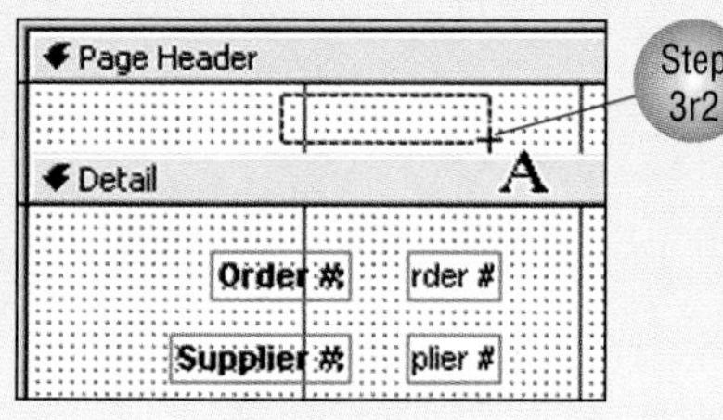

s. Insert page numbering in the Page Footer by completing the following steps:
   1) Click Insert and then Page Numbers.
   2) At the Page Numbers dialog box, make the following changes:
      a) Click *Page N of M* in the *Format* section.
      b) Click *Bottom of Page [Footer]* in the *Position* section.
      c) Click OK to close the dialog box.

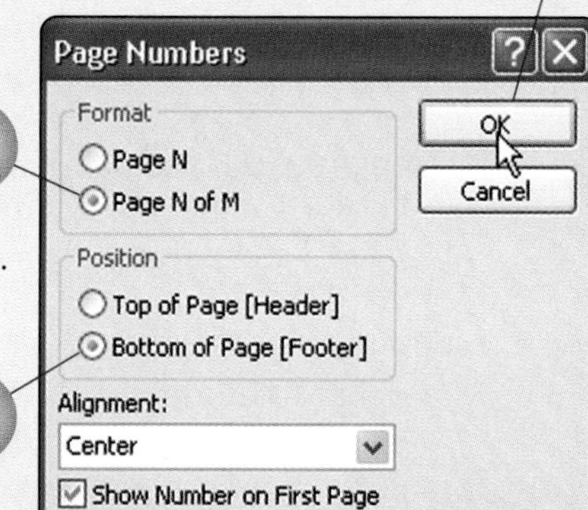

t. Add a Report Header by completing the following steps:
   1) Display the Report Header and Report Footer by clicking View on the Menu bar and then clicking Report Header/Footer.
   2) Increase the Report Header section by about .5 inch by dragging down the top of the gray bar (contains the words *Page Header*).
   3) Click the Label button on the Toolbox.
   4) Drag to create a label box inside the Report Header that is large enough to hold the title shown in Figure 6.7.
   5) Type the text **OUTDOOR OPTIONS ORDERS** inside the label, and then click outside the box.
   6) Click the label control box and then apply the following formatting:
      a) Change the font name to Times New Roman.
      b) Change the font size to 14.

c) Change the font weight to bold.
d) Change the fore color to Dark Teal (the fourth color from the left in the third row from the top).

7) Click outside the label box to deselect it.

u. Add a Report Footer by completing the following steps:
1) Increase the height of the Report Footer section by about .5 inch. (To do this, drag down the bottom edge of the Report Footer section.)
2) Click the Label button on the Toolbox and then draw a label box inside the Report Footer large enough to hold the text shown in Figure 6.7.
3) Type the text **Report designed by Student Name** (insert your name instead of *Student Name*).

4. Close the properties sheet. (To do this, click the Close button that displays in the upper right corner of the sheet.)
5. View the report in Print Preview by clicking the View button on the Report Design toolbar.
6. Check the headings *ORDERS* and *AMOUNT* and make sure the headings display approximately centered over the information in columns. (If they do not, change to Design view, move the heading or headings to the desired location, and then change back to Print Preview.)
7. Print the report by clicking the Print button on the Print Preview toolbar.
8. Click the View button to return to the Design view.
9. In Design view, save the report and name it Orders Report.
10. Close Orders Report.
11. Close the **OutdoorOptions** database file.

FIGURE 6.7 ***Exercise 4***

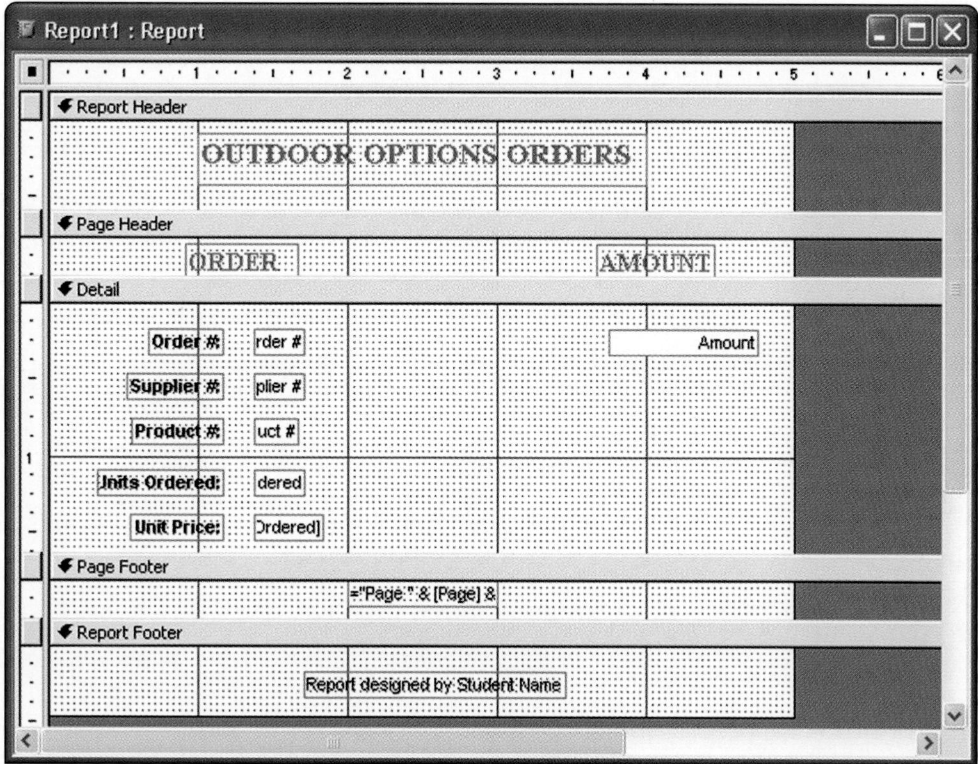

Preparing Mailing Labels

HINT
Use the Label Wizard to create mailing labels easily.

Access includes a Mailing Label Wizard that walks you through the steps for creating mailing labels with fields in a database table. To create mailing labels, open the database file, click the Reports button on the Objects bar, and then click the New button. This displays the New Report dialog box. At this dialog box, specify the database table where the information for creating the mailing labels is located, and then double-click *Label Wizard* in the list box. At the first Label Wizard dialog box shown in Figure 6.8, specify the label size, units of measure, and the label type, and then click the Next button.

FIGURE 6.8 **First Label Wizard Dialog Box**

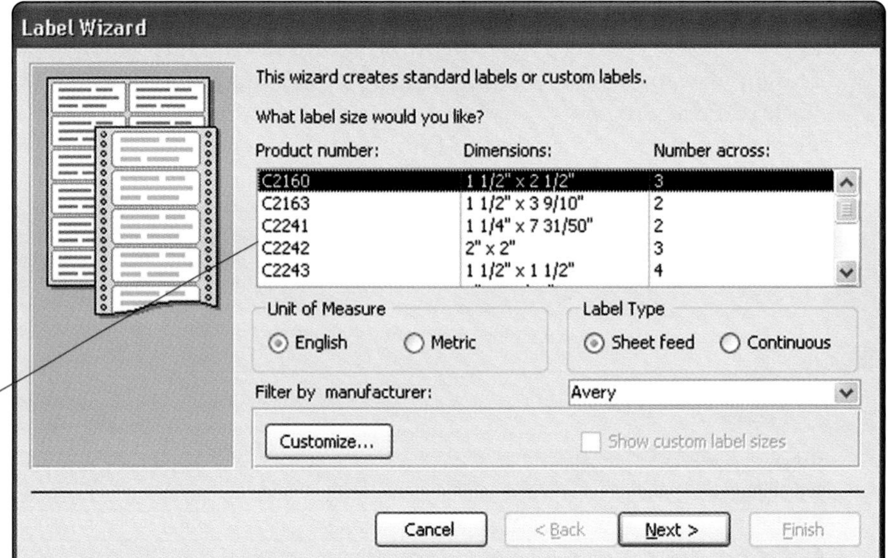

Scroll through this list box and choose the desired label.

Create Mailing Labels Using Label Wizard
1. Open database file.
2. Click Reports button on Objects bar.
3. Click New button.
4. Specify desired table.
5. Double-click *Label Wizard.*
6. Choose desired options at each of the Label Wizard dialog boxes.

At the second Label Wizard dialog box shown in Figure 6.9, specify the font name, size, weight, and color, and then click the Next button.

FIGURE 6.9 ***Second Label Wizard Dialog Box***

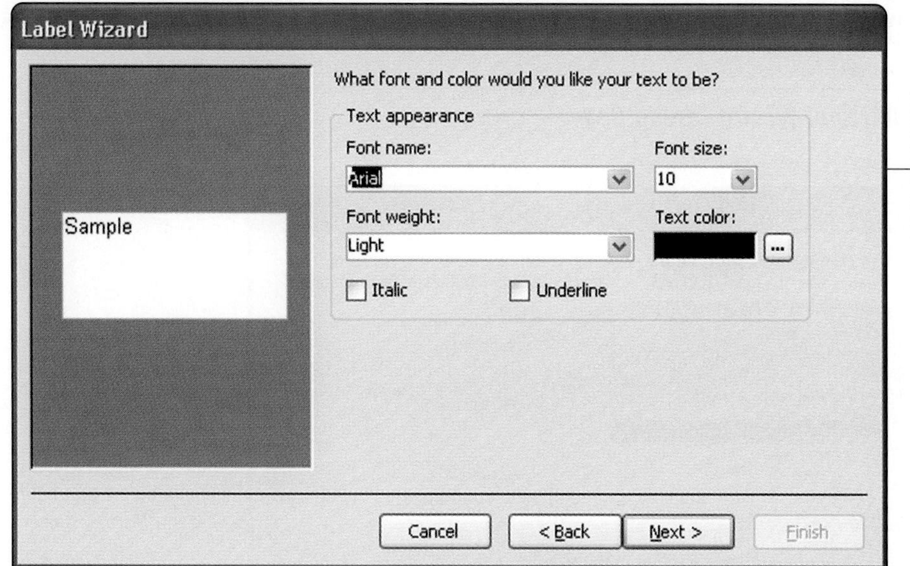

Specify the fields you want included in the mailing labels at the third Label Wizard dialog box shown in Figure 6.10. To do this, select the field in the *Available fields* list box, and then click the button containing the greater than symbol (>). This moves the field to the Prototype label. Insert the fields in the Prototype label as you want the text to display on the label. After inserting the fields in the Prototype label, click the Next button.

FIGURE 6.10 ***Third Label Wizard Dialog Box***

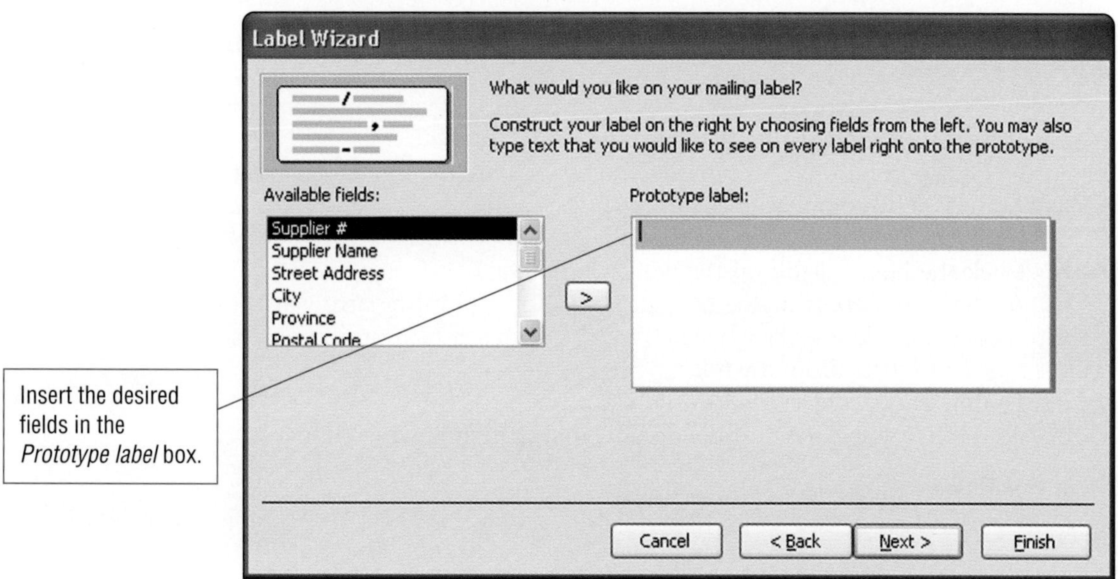

At the fourth Label Wizard dialog box, shown in Figure 6.11, you can specify a field from the database file by which the labels are sorted. If you want the labels sorted (for example, by last name, postal code, and so on.), insert the field by which you want the fields sorted in the *Sort by* list box, and then click the Next button.

FIGURE 6.11 **Fourth Label Wizard Dialog Box**

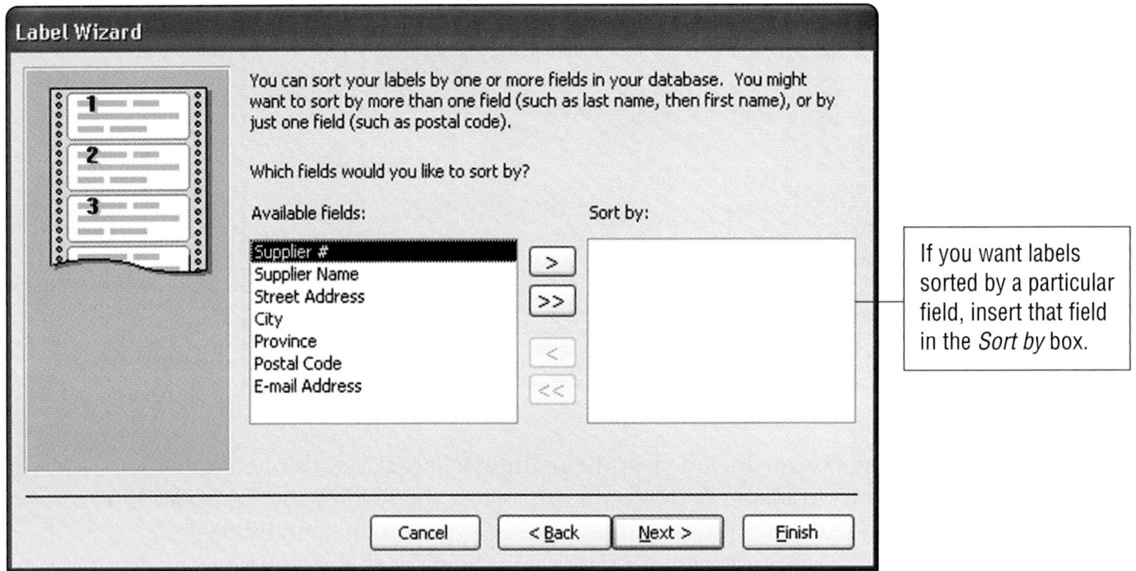
Label Wizard
You can sort your labels by one or more fields in your database. You might want to sort by more than one field (such as last name, then first name), or by just one field (such as postal code).
Which fields would you like to sort by?
Available fields:
Sort by:
Supplier #
Supplier Name
Street Address
City
Province
Postal Code
E-mail Address
Cancel
< Back
Next >
Finish
If you want labels sorted by a particular field, insert that field in the Sort by box.

At the last Label Wizard dialog box, type a name for the label file, and then click the Finish button. After a few moments, the labels display on the screen in Print Preview. Print the labels and/or close Print Preview.

exercise 5 PREPARING MAILING LABELS

1. Open the **OutdoorOptions** database file.
2. At the OutdoorOptions : Database window, prepare mailing labels with supplier names and addresses by completing the following steps:
   a. Click the Reports button on the Objects bar.
   b. Click the New button on the window toolbar.
   c. At the New Report dialog box, click the down-pointing arrow at the right of the *Choose the table or query where the object's data comes from* option box, and then click *Suppliers* at the drop-down list.
   d. Double-click *Label Wizard* in the list box.
   e. At the first Label Wizard dialog box, make the following changes:

1) Click *English* in the *Unit of Measure* section. (Skip this step if *English* is already selected.)
2) Click the down-pointing arrow at the right side of the *Filter by manufacturer* option, and then click *Avery* at the drop-down list. (Skip this step if *Avery* is already selected.)
3) Make sure *C2160* is selected in the *Product number* list box.
4) Click the Next button.

f. At the second Label Wizard dialog box (see Figure 6.9), change the font size to 10, and then click the Next button.

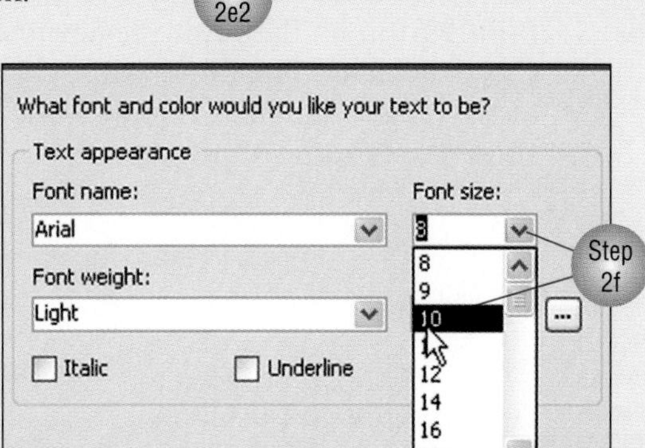

g. At the third Label Wizard dialog box, complete the following steps to insert the fields in the Prototype label:
1) Click *Supplier Name* in the *Available fields* list box, and then click the button containing the greater than symbol (>).
2) Press the Enter key (this moves the insertion point down to the next line in the Prototype label).
3) With *Street Address* selected in the *Available fields* list box, click the button containing the greater than symbol (>).
4) Press the Enter key.
5) With *City* selected in the *Available fields* list box, click the button containing the greater than symbol (>).
6) Type a comma (,) and then press the spacebar.
7) With *Province* selected in the *Available fields* list box, click the button containing the greater than symbol (>).
8) Press the Enter key.
9) With *Postal Code* selected in the *Available fields* list box, click the button containing the greater than symbol (>).

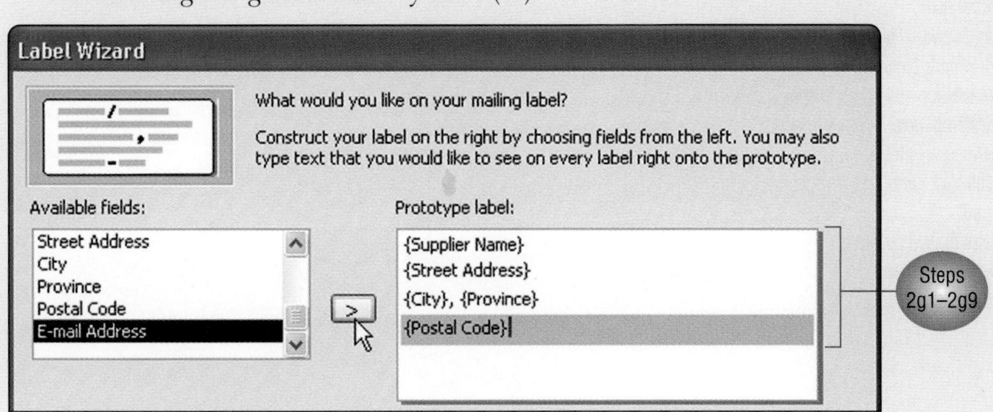

10) Click the Next button.

h. At the fourth Label Wizard dialog box, sort by postal code. To do this, click *Postal Code* in the *Available fields* list box and then click the button containing the greater than symbol (>).

i. Click the Next button.

j. At the last Label Wizard dialog box, click the Finish button. (The Label Wizard automatically names the label file Labels Suppliers.)

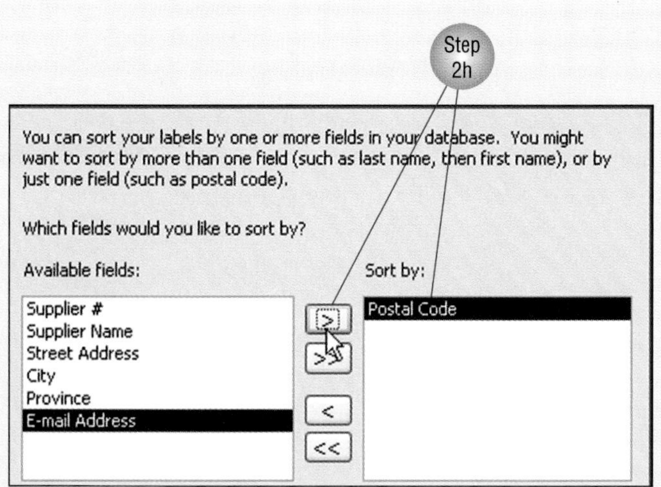

Step 2h
You can sort your labels by one or more fields in your database. You might want to sort by more than one field (such as last name, then first name), or by just one field (such as postal code).
Which fields would you like to sort by?
Available fields:
Supplier #
Supplier Name
Street Address
City
Province
E-mail Address
Sort by:
Postal Code

3. Print the labels by clicking the Print button on the Print Preview toolbar.
4. Close the labels file. (To do this, click the Close button that displays at the right side of the Labels Suppliers : Report title bar.)
5. Close the **OutdoorOptions** database file.

HINT

Create a chart with data from a database table to provide a visual display of data.

HINT

The Chart Wizard is shared by Microsoft Office applications.

QUICK STEPS

Create Chart Using Chart Wizard

1. Open database file.
2. Click Reports button on Objects bar.
3. Click New button.
4. Specify desired table.
5. Double-click *Chart Wizard.*
6. Choose desired options at each of the Chart Wizard dialog boxes.

Creating a Chart

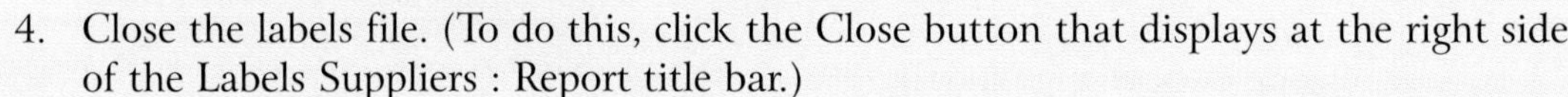

Access includes a Chart Wizard you can use to display data more visually than a table, form, or report. Use the Chart Wizard to create a chart with data from a database table. To create a chart with the Chart Wizard, open the database file, and then click either the Forms button or the Reports button on the Objects bar. Specify the database table containing the fields to be included in the chart and then double-click the *Chart Wizard* option in the list box. This displays the first Chart Wizard dialog box, shown in Figure 6.12.

FIGURE 6.12 ***First Chart Wizard Dialog Box***

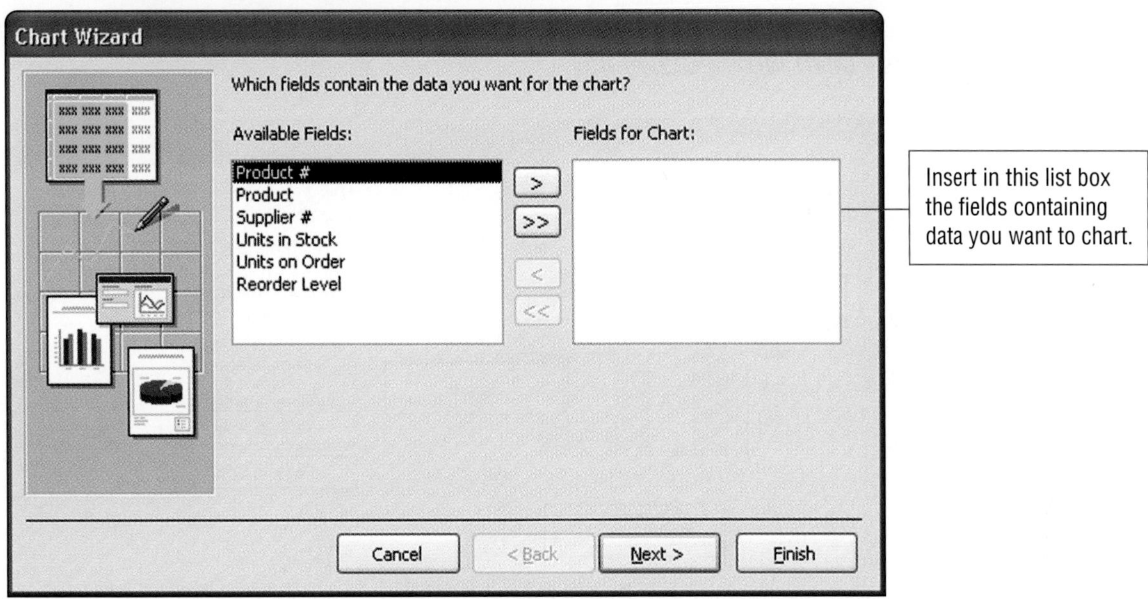

At the first Chart Wizard dialog box, insert the fields you want included in the chart in the *Fields for Chart* list box. The first field inserted in the *Fields for Chart* list box will be used by the Chart Wizard as the x-axis in the chart. After inserting the fields, click the Next button. This displays the second Chart Wizard dialog box, shown in Figure 6.13.

FIGURE 6.13 ***Second Chart Wizard Dialog Box***

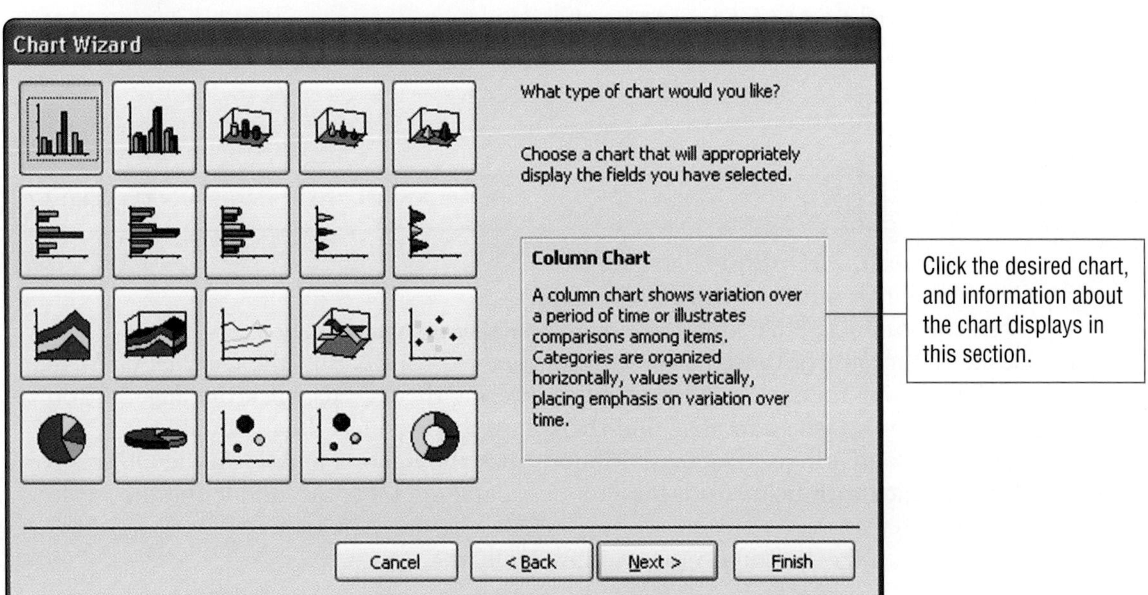

Choose the chart type at the second Chart Wizard dialog box. To do this, click the icon representing the desired chart, and then click the Next button. This displays the third Chart Wizard dialog box, shown in Figure 6.14.

FIGURE 6.14 ***Third Chart Wizard Dialog Box***

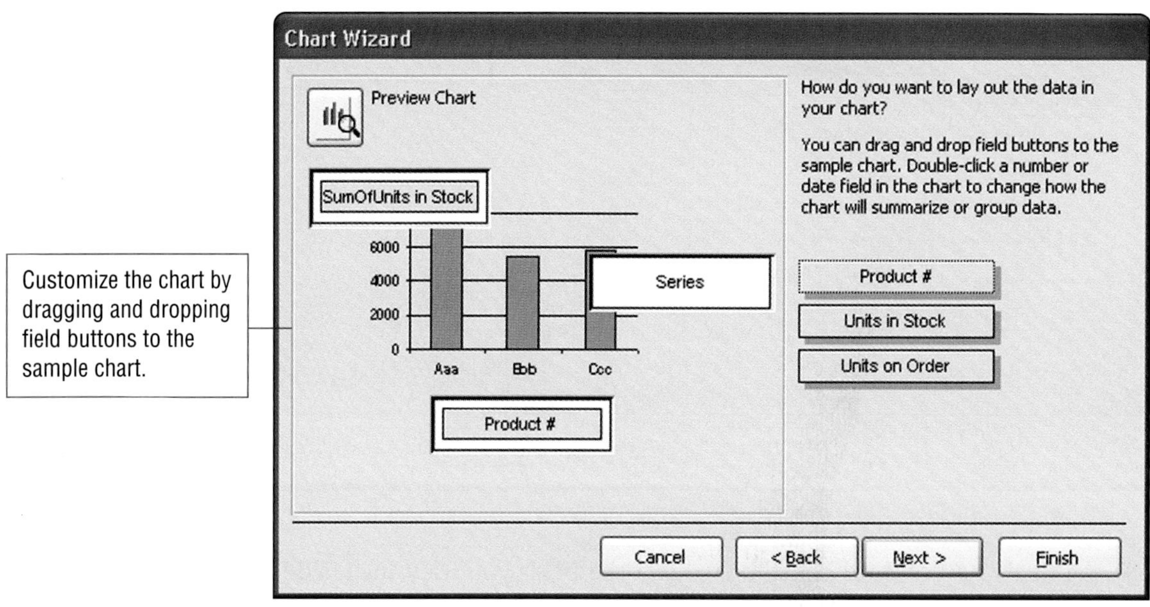

At the third Chart Wizard dialog box, specify how you want labels to appear in the chart. To do this, double-click a label in the preview chart. At the drop-down list that displays, click the desired label option. At this dialog box, you can also add another field to the chart. For example, in Exercise 6, you will be charting Units on Order as well as Units in Stock. To do this, you will drag the desired field from the right side of the dialog box to the appropriate location in the preview chart. When all changes have been made, click the Next button. At the fourth, and last, Chart Wizard dialog box, type a name for the chart, and then click the Finish button.

exercise 6 CREATING A CHART

1. Open the **OutdoorOptions** database file.
2. Click the Tables button on the Objects bar.
3. Open the Products table by double-clicking *Products* in the list box.
4. Delete the records of those products where zero *(0)* displays in the *Units on Order* field (at the warning message, click Yes). After deleting the records, click the Save button on the Table Datasheet toolbar, and then close the Products database table.
5. At the OutdoorOptions : Database window, click the Reports button on the Objects bar.
6. Create a chart with fields from the Products database table by completing the following steps:
   a. Click the New button on the window toolbar.

b. At the New Report dialog box, click the down-pointing arrow at the right of the *Choose the table or query where the object's data comes from* option, and then click *Products*.
c. Double-click *Chart Wizard* in the list box.
d. At the first Chart Wizard dialog box, complete the following steps:
   1) With *Product #* selected in the *Available Fields* list box, click the button containing the greater than symbol (>).
   2) Click *Units in Stock* in the *Available Fields* list box and then click the button containing the greater than symbol (>).
   3) With *Units on Order* selected in the *Available Fields* list box, click the button containing the greater than symbol (>).
   4) Click the Next button.

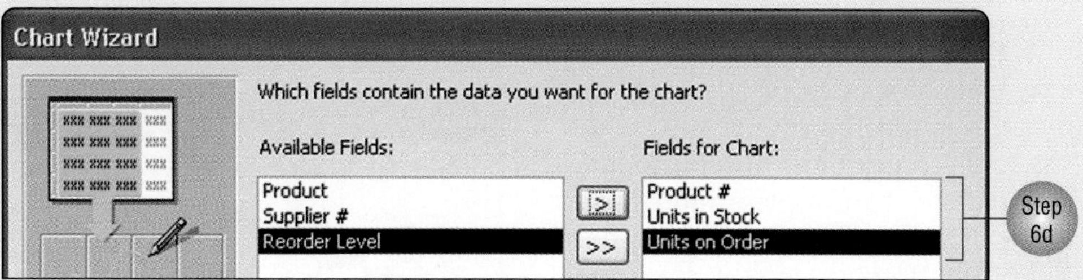

e. At the second Chart Wizard dialog box, click the Next button.
f. At the third Chart Wizard dialog box, complete the following steps:
   1) Position the arrow pointer on the Units on Order button at the right side of the dialog box, hold down the left mouse button, drag the outline of the button to the bottom of the *SumOfUnits in Stock* field that displays in the preview chart, and then release the left mouse button.

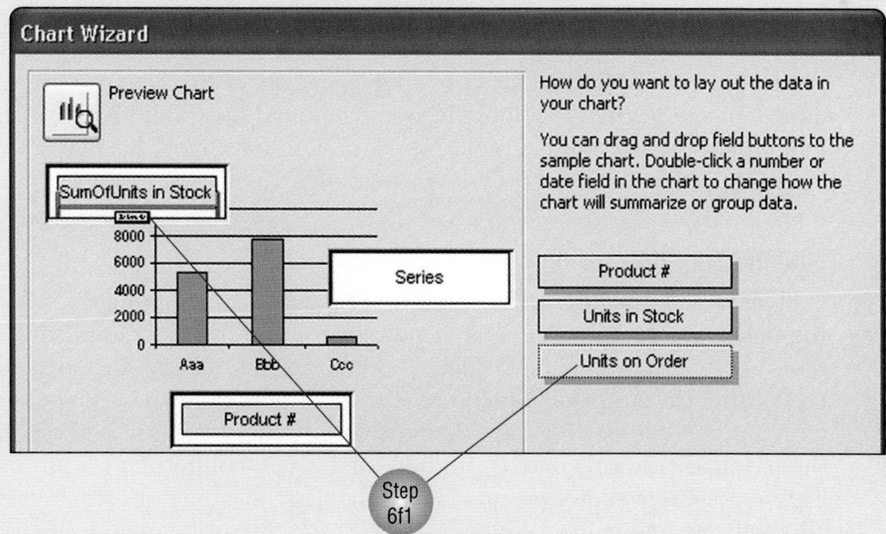

   2) Double-click the *SumOfUnits in Stock* field that displays in the preview chart.

3) At the Summarize dialog box, double-click *None* in the list box. (This changes *SumOfUnits in Stock* to *Units in Stock*. By default, the Chart Wizard will sum the number of units in stock. Changing the field to *Units in Stock* tells the Chart Wizard to simply display the number of units in stock and not the sum.)

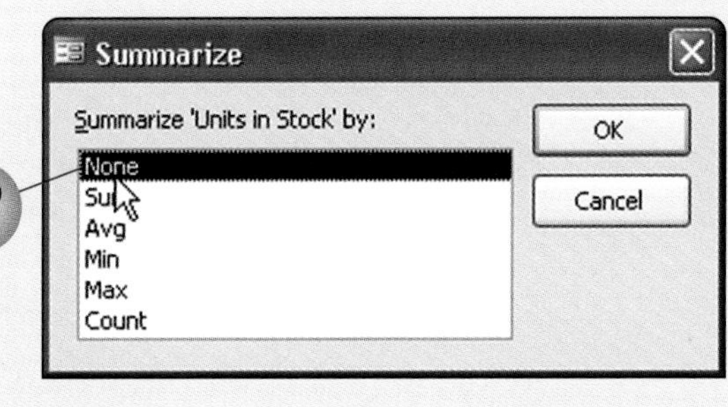

4) Double-click the *SumOfUnits on Order* field that displays in the preview chart.
5) At the Summarize dialog box, double-click *None* in the list box. (This changes *SumOfUnits on Order* to *Units on Order*.)
6) Click the Next button.

g. At the fourth Chart Wizard dialog box, type **Product Units**, and then click the Finish button.

7. With the chart displayed in Print Preview, print the chart by clicking the Print button on the Print Preview toolbar.
8. After the chart is printed, click the Close button that displays at the right side of the Report1 : Report title bar. At the message asking if you want to save the changes to the design of the report, click No.
9. Close the **OutdoorOptions** database table.

Summarizing Data By Changing Views

Access provides additional views in a table and query that you can use to summarize data. Change to the PivotTable view to create a PivotTable that is an interactive table that organizes and summarizes data. Use the PivotChart view to create a PivotChart that summarizes data in a graph.

Display PivotTable View
1. Open table or query.
2. Click View, PivotTable View.

HINT
Dimmed text in each section of the PivotTable layout describes the type of fields that should be dragged and dropped.

Summarizing Data Using PivotTable View

A PivotTable is an interactive table that organizes and summarizes data based on the fields you designate for row headings, column headings, and source record filtering. Aggregate functions such as Sum, Avg, and Count are easily added to the table using the AutoCalc button on the PivotTable toolbar. A PivotTable provides more options for viewing data than a crosstab query because you can easily change the results by filtering data by an item in a row, a column, or for all source records. This interactivity allows you to analyze the data for numerous scenarios. PivotTables are easily created using a drag-and-drop technique in PivotTable View.

To create a PivotTable, open a table or query in Datasheet view, click View, and then click PivotTable View. (You can also click the down-pointing arrow at the right of the View button on the table or query toolbar, and then click PivotTable View.) This changes the datasheet to PivotTable layout with four sections and a PivotTable Field List box. Dimmed text in each section describes the types of fields that should be dragged and dropped. Figure 6.15 displays the PivotTable layout you will be using in Exercise 7.

FIGURE 6.15 **PivotTable Layout**

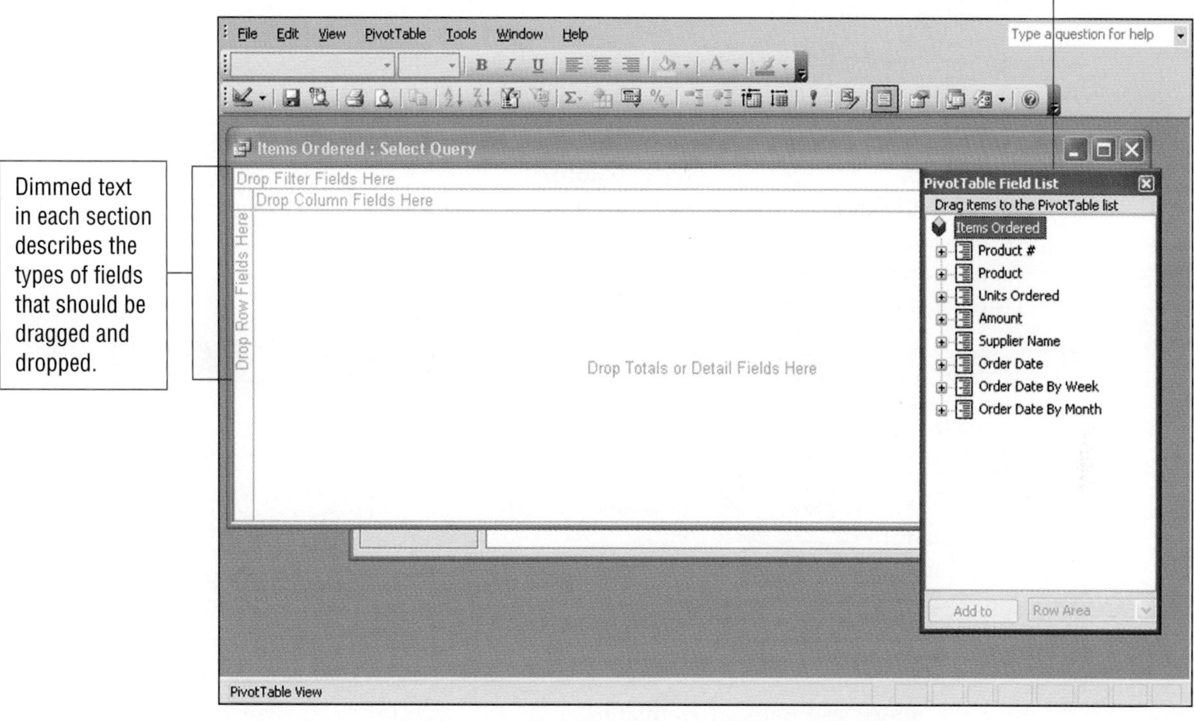

Drag the fields from the PivotTable Field List box to the desired locations in the PivotTable layout. The dimmed text in the PivotTable layout identifies the field that should be dropped in the location. In Exercise 7, you will drag the *Supplier Name* field to the Row field section, the *Product* field to the Column field section, the *Amount* field to the Totals or Details field section, and the *Order Date* to the Filter section. The PivotTable will then display as shown in Figure 6.16.

FIGURE 6.16 **PivotTable for Exercise 7**

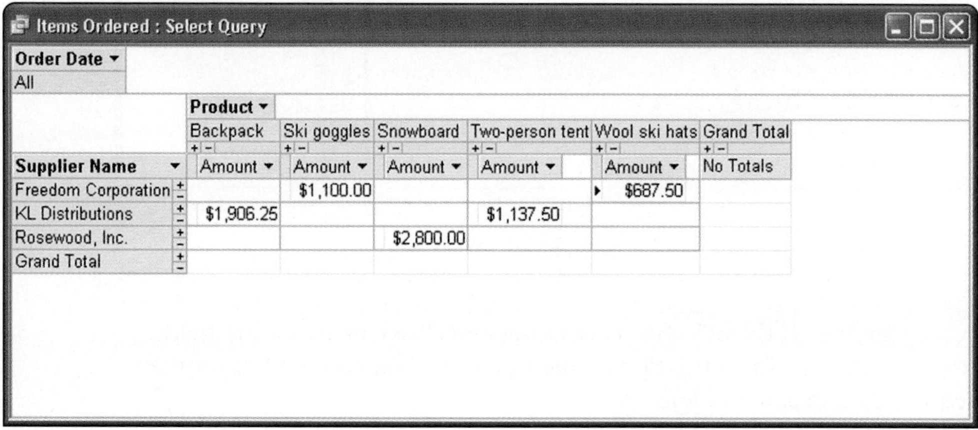

Supplier Name	Backpack	Ski goggles	Snowboard	Two-person tent	Wool ski hats	Grand Total
	Amount	Amount	Amount	Amount	Amount	No Totals
Freedom Corporation		$1,100.00			$687.50	
KL Distributions	$1,906.25			$1,137.50		
Rosewood, Inc.			$2,800.00			
Grand Total						

exercise 7

SUMMARIZING DATA IN PIVOTTABLE VIEW

1. Open the **OutdoorOptions** database table.
2. Click the Queries button on the Objects bar and then create a new query in Design view with the following specifications:
   a. Add the Orders, Products, and Suppliers tables to the design grid.
   b. Add the following fields from the specified tables:

Product #	=	Orders table
Product	=	Products table
Units Ordered	=	Orders table
Amount	=	Orders table
Supplier Name	=	Suppliers table
Order Date	=	Orders table

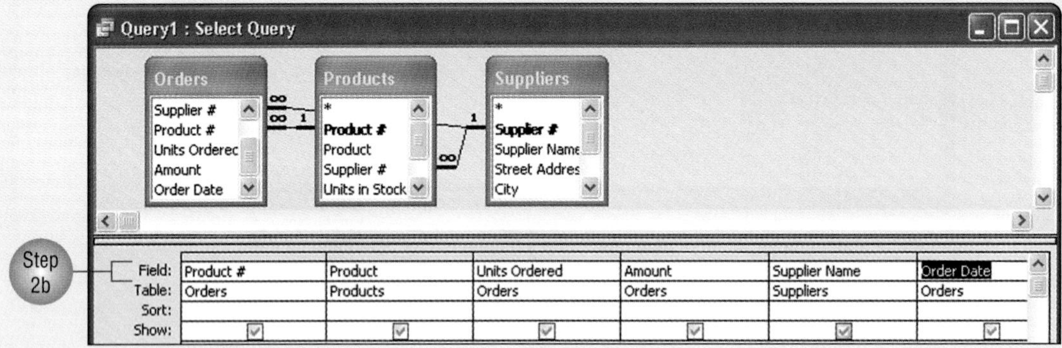

   c. Save the query and name it Items Ordered.
   d. Run the query.
3. Click View and then PivotTable View.
4. At the PivotTable layout, drag and drop the *Supplier Name* field to the Row field section by completing the following steps:
   a. Position the mouse pointer on the *Supplier Name* field in the PivotTable Field List box.
   b. Hold down the left mouse button, drag to the dimmed text *Drop Row Fields Here* located at the left side of the query window, and then release the mouse button.

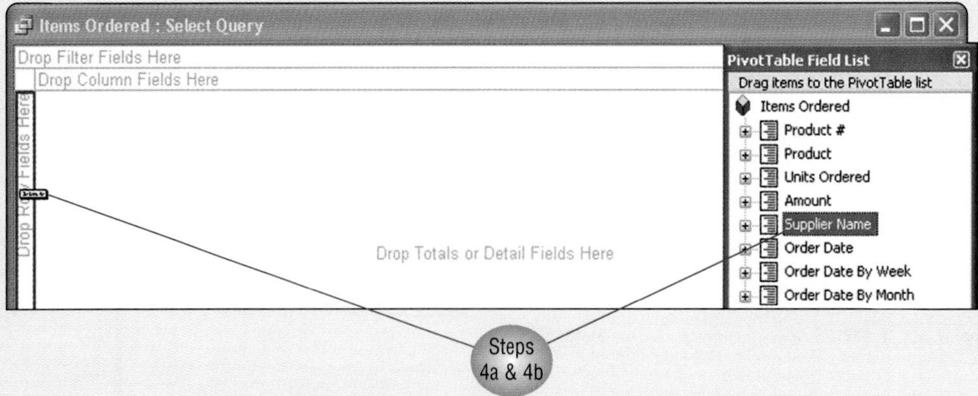

5. Complete steps similar to those in Step 4 to drag and drop the following fields:
   a. Drag the *Product* field from the PivotTable Field List box and drop it on the dimmed text *Drop Columns Fields Here*.

b. Drag the *Amount* field from the PivotTable Field List box and drop it on the dimmed text *Drop Totals or Detail Fields Here*.

c. Drag the *Order Date* field from the PivotTable Field List box and drop it on the dimmed text *Drop Filter Fields Here*.

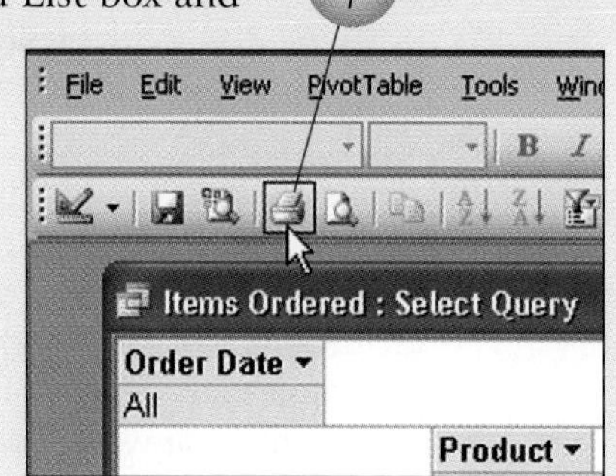

6. Remove the PivotTable Field List box from the screen by clicking the Field List button on the PivotTable toolbar. (Your PivotTable should look like the PivotTable shown in Figure 6.16.)
7. Click the Print button to print the query in PivotTable view.
8. Click View and then Datasheet View to return the query to the Datasheet view.
9. Close the query. At the message asking if you want to save the changes, click Yes.
10. Close the **OutdoorOptions** database table.

When you create a PivotTable in a query or table, it becomes a part of and is saved with the table or query. The next time you open the table or query, display the PivotTable by clicking View and then PivotTable. If you make changes to data in fields that are part of the table or query (and PivotTable), the data is automatically updated in the table or query.

The power of a PivotTable is the ability to analyze data for numerous scenarios. For example, in the PivotTable you created in Exercise 7, you can display orders for a specific date or isolate a specific supplier. Use the plus and minus symbols that display in a row or column heading to show (plus symbol) or hide (minus symbol) data. Use the down-pointing arrow (called the *filter* arrow) that displays in a field to display specific data in the field. You can also use buttons on the PivotTable toolbar to perform actions such as filtering data and performing calculations on data.

exercise 8

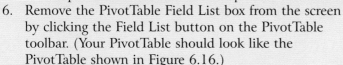

ANALYZING DATA IN PIVOTTABLE VIEW

1. Open the **OutdoorOptions** database table.
2. Click the Tables button on the Objects bar, open the Orders table, and then add the following records:

Order #	=	(AutoNumber)
Supplier #	=	68
Product #	=	558
Units Ordered	=	25
Amount	=	$550
Order Date	=	2/28/2005

Order #	=	(AutoNumber)
Supplier #	=	70
Product #	=	897
Units Ordered	=	10
Amount	=	$1,120
Order Date	=	2/28/2005

3. Close the Orders table.
4. Click the Queries button on the Objects bar and then double-click the *Items Ordered* query in the list box.
5. With the query open, click View and then PivotTable View. (Notice the PivotTable reflects the two new order records you inserted in the Orders table.)
6. Display only items ordered on February 28 by completing the following steps:
   a. Click the filter arrow (down-pointing arrow) at the right of the *Order Date* field (located in the upper left corner of the query window).
   b. At the drop-down list that displays, click the *(All)* check box to remove the check mark before each date.
   c. Click the check box to the left of *2/28/2005*.
   d. Click the OK button.
   e. Click the Print button on the PivotTable toolbar.
   f. Redisplay all items by clicking the filter arrow at the right of the *Order Date* field, clicking the check box to the left of *(All)*, and then clicking OK.

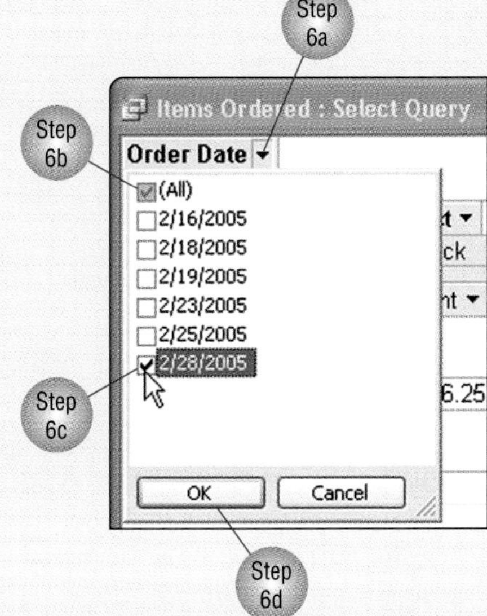

7. Display only those order amounts for Freedom Corporation by completing the following steps:
   a. Click the filter arrow at the right of the *Supplier Name* field.
   b. At the drop-down list, click the *(All)* check box to remove the check mark before each supplier name.
   c. Click the check box to the left of *Freedom Corporation*.
   d. Click the OK button.
   e. Click the Print button on the PivotTable toolbar.
   f. Redisplay all supplier names by clicking the filter arrow at the right of the *Supplier Name* field, clicking the check box to the left of *(All)*, and then clicking OK.

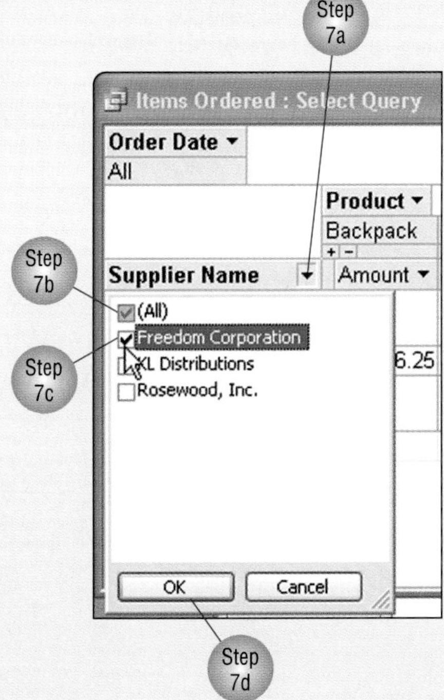

8. Display subtotals and totals of order amounts by completing the following steps:
   a. Position the mouse pointer on any *Amount* column heading until the pointer displays with a four-headed arrow attached and then click the left mouse button. (This displays all the *Amount* column headings and amounts with a light blue background.)

b. Click the AutoCalc button on the PivotTable toolbar, and then click *Sum* at the drop-down list. (This inserts subtotals and totals in the PivotTable.)

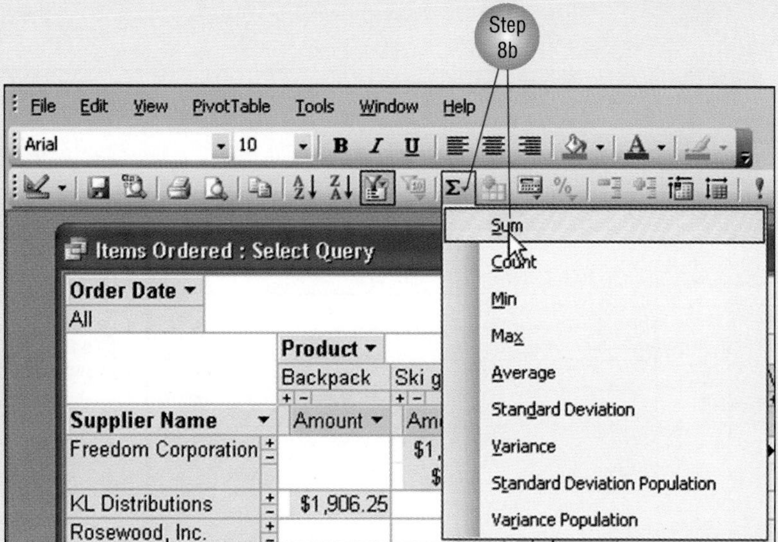

9. Change the page orientation to landscape and then print the PivotTable.
10. Close the PivotTable. (At the message asking if you want to save the changes, click Yes.)
11. Close the **OutdoorOptions** database table.

Summarizing Data Using PivotChart View

A PivotChart performs the same function as a PivotTable with the exception that the source data is displayed in a graph instead of a table. A chart is created by dragging fields from the Chart Field List box to the Filter, Data, Category, and Series sections of the chart. As with a PivotTable, the PivotChart can be easily altered using the filter arrows.

To create a PivotChart, open a table or query in Datasheet view, click View, and then click PivotChart View (or click the down-pointing arrow at the right of the View button, and then click PivotChart View). This changes the datasheet to PivotChart layout with four sections and a Chart Field List box. Dimmed text in each section describes the types of fields that should be dragged and dropped. Figure 6.17 displays the PivotChart layout you will be using in Exercise 9.

Display PivotChart View

1. Open table or query.
2. Click View, PivotChart View.

HINT

A PivotTable is dynamically linked to a PivotChart. Changes made to the filter settings in PivotChart view are also updated in PivotTable view.

FIGURE 6.17 ***PivotChart Layout***

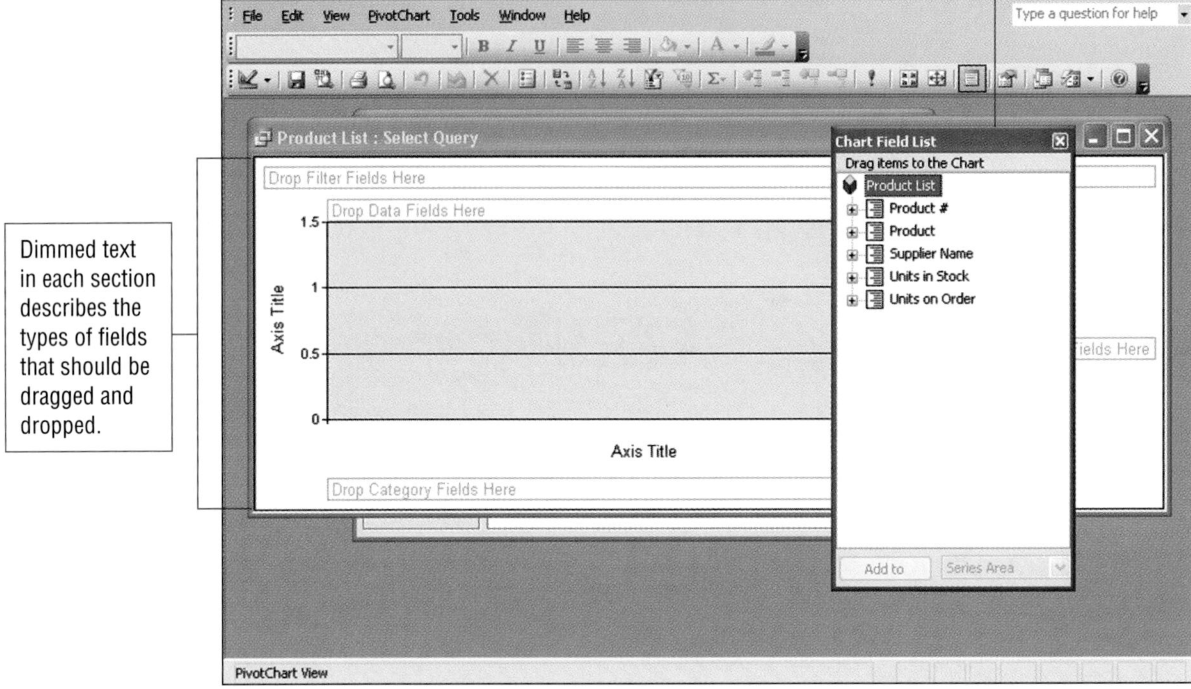

Drag the fields from the Chart Field List box to the desired locations in the PivotChart layout. The dimmed text in the PivotChart layout identifies the field that should be dropped in the location. In Exercise 9, you will drag the *Supplier Name* field to the Row field section, the *Product* field to the Column field section, the *Amount* field to the Totals or Details field section, and the *Order Date* to the Filter section. The PivotTable will then display as shown in Figure 6.18.

When you create a PivotChart, Access automatically creates a PivotTable. View a PivotTable based on a PivotChart by clicking View and then PivotTable.

FIGURE 6.18 ***PivotChart for Exercise 9***

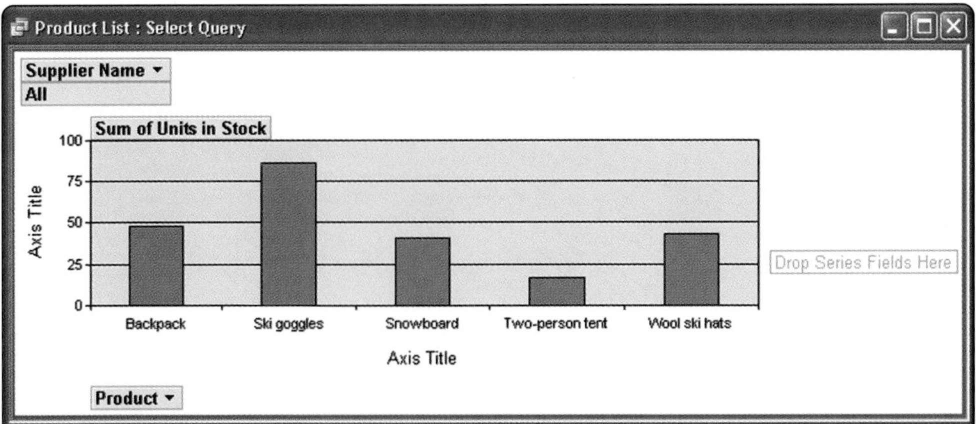

exercise 9

SUMMARIZING DATA USING PIVOTCHART VIEW

1. Open the **OutdoorOptions** database table.
2. Click the Queries button on the Objects bar and then create a new query in Design view with the following specifications:
   a. Add the Products and Suppliers tables to the design grid.
   b. Add the following fields from the specified tables:

Product #	=	Products table
Product	=	Products table
Supplier Name	=	Suppliers table
Units in Stock	=	Products table
Units on Order	=	Products table

   c. Save the query and name it Product List.
   d. Run the query.
3. Click View and then PivotChart view.
4. At the PivotChart layout, drag and drop the following fields:
   a. Drag the *Supplier Name* field from the Chart Field List box and drop it on the dimmed text *Drop Filter Fields Here*.

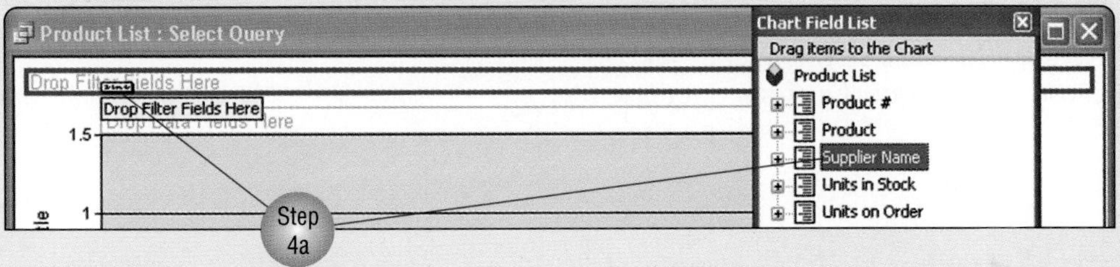

   b. Drag the *Product* field from the Chart Field List box and drop it on the dimmed text *Drop Category Fields Here*.
   c. Drag the *Units in Stock* field from the Chart Field List box and drop it on the dimmed text *Drop Data Fields Here*.
5. Remove the Chart Field List box from the screen by clicking the Field List button on the PivotTable toolbar. (Your PivotChart should look like the PivotChart shown in Figure 6.18.)
6. Click the Print button to print the query in PivotChart view.
7. Display specific items on order by completing the following steps:
   a. Click the filter arrow at the right of the *Product* field (located in the lower left corner of the query window).
   b. At the drop-down list that displays, click the *(All)* check box to remove the check mark before each date.
   c. Click the check box to the left of *Ski goggles*.
   d. Click the check box to the left of *Snowboard*.
   e. Click the check box to the left of *Wool ski hats*.
   f. Click the OK button.

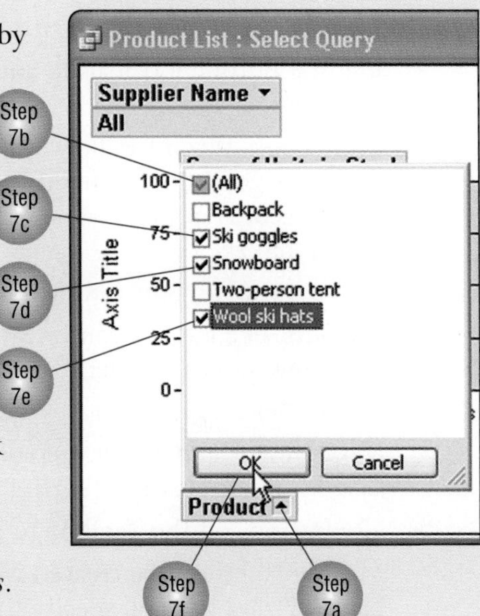

    g. Click the Print button on the PivotChart toolbar.
    h. Redisplay all items by clicking the filter arrow at the right of the *Product* field, clicking the check box to the left of *(All)*, and then clicking OK.
8. Display only those products ordered from KL Distributions by completing the following steps:
    a. Click the filter arrow at the right of the *Supplier Name* field.
    b. At the drop-down list, click the *(All)* check box to remove the check mark before each supplier name.
    c. Click the check box to the left of *KL Distributions*.
    d. Click the OK button.
    e. Click the Print button on the PivotChart toolbar.
    f. Redisplay all supplier names by clicking the filter arrow at the right of the *Supplier Name* field, clicking the check box to the left of *(All)*, and then clicking OK.
9. Click View and then PivotTable View to display the chart as a PivotTable.
10. Click the Print button on the PivotTable toolbar.
11. Click View and then Datasheet View to return the query to the Datasheet view.
12. Save and then close the query.
13. Close the **OutdoorOptions** database file.

CHAPTER summary

- Data in a database table can be inserted in a report, which lets you control how the data appears on the page when printed.
- Use the AutoReport feature automatically to create a plainly formatted report in a columnar arrangement.
- The Report Wizard walks you through the steps for creating a report and lets you specify the fields you want included in the report, the level of fields in the report, the order in which records display in the report, the layout of the report, the report style, and a name for the report.
- Like a form, a report can be created with fields from related database tables.
- A report, like a form, can be created in Design view. A report includes up to five sections including Report Header, Page Header, Detail, Page Footer, and Report Footer.
- To add fields to a report in Design view, associate the report with the desired table.
- Move, resize, and customize control objects in the report Design view in the same manner as control objects in the form Design view.
- Use buttons on the Toolbox to add controls to a report in Design view.
- Mailing labels can be created with data in a database table using the Label Wizard. The Label Wizard lets you specify the label type; the fields you want included in the labels; the font name, size, weight, and color; a sorting order; and a name for the mailing label file.

- A chart can be created with specific fields in a database table using the Chart Wizard. The Chart Wizard lets you specify the fields you want included in the chart, the chart type, how labels will appear in the chart, and the name for the chart file.
- Change to the PivotTable view to create a PivotTable that is an interactive table that organizes and summarizes data. Change to the PivotChart view to create a PivotChart that summarizes data in a graph.
- To create a PivotTable, open a table or query, click View, and then click PivotTable View. At the PivotTable layout, drag the fields to the desired locations.
- To create a PivotChart, open a table or query, click View, and then click PivotChart View. At the PivotChart layout, drag the fields to the desired locations.

FEATURES summary

FEATURE	BUTTON	MENU
Display New Report dialog box	New	
Begin Report Wizard		Insert, Report, Report Wizard
Begin Label Wizard		Insert, Report, specify table, double-click *Label Wizard*
Begin Chart Wizard		Insert, Report, specify table, double-click *Chart Wizard*
Display table or query in PivotTable view		View, PivotTable View
Display table or query in PivotChart view		View, PivotChart View

CONCEPTS check

Completion: On a blank sheet of paper, indicate the correct term, symbol, or command for each description.

1. Click the down-pointing arrow at the right side of this button to display the AutoReport option.
2. Use this to guide you through the steps for creating a report.
3. When all of the steps in the Report Wizard are completed, the report displays in this view.

4. This appears at the top of each page of a report and generally includes information such as column headings identifying the data in the report.
5. Use these to increase or decrease the size of a selected control object.
6. To create a chart with the Chart Wizard, open the database file, and then click either the Forms button or this button on the Objects bar.
7. When creating a chart with the Chart Wizard, the first field inserted in the *Fields for Chart* list box will be used as this axis in the chart.
8. Display a table or query in this view to summarize data based on the fields you designate for row headings, column headings, and source record filtering.
9. Suppose you are using the Report Wizard with the OutdoorOptions database file to show information on what products are currently on order, from what company, and the e-mail address of the companies. At the first Report Wizard step, what fields would you insert from the Products database table and what fields would you insert from the Suppliers database table?
10. When using the Chart Wizard, write the fields in the Products database table (in the OutdoorOptions database file) you would use to create a chart that shows thé reorder level for products.

SKILLS check

(Note: Copy the Hilltop database file from the CD that accompanies this textbook to your disk and then remove the read-only attribute from the database file. Before completing the following assessments, consider deleting the OutdoorOptions database file from your disk.)

Assessment 1

1. Open the **Hilltop** database file.
2. Click the Tables button on the Objects bar.
3. Use AutoReport to create a report with the Inventory table.
4. When the report displays in Print Preview, print the report.
5. Close the report without saving it.

Assessment 2

1. With the **Hilltop** database file open, create a report using the Report Wizard with the following specifications:
   a. At the first Report Wizard dialog box, insert the following fields in the *Selected Fields* list box:

      From the Equipment database table:

      Equipment

      From the Inventory database table:

      Purchase Date
      Purchase Price
      Available Hours

   b. At the second Report Wizard dialog box, make sure *Equipment* is selected, and then click the button containing the greater than symbol (>).
   c. Do not make any changes at the third Report Wizard dialog box.

d. At the fourth Report Wizard dialog box, choose the *Align Left 1* option.
e. At the fifth Report Wizard dialog box, choose the *Soft Gray* option.
f. At the last Report Wizard dialog box, click the Finish button. (This accepts the default report name of Equipment.)
g. When the report displays in Print Preview, print the report.

2. Close the report.

Assessment 3

1. With the **Hilltop** database file open, create a report using the Report Wizard with the following specifications:
   a. At the first Report Wizard dialog box, insert the following fields in the *Selected Fields* list box:

      From the Customers database table:

      Customer

      From the Invoices database table:

      Date
      Hours

      From the Equipment database table:

      Equipment

      From the Rates database table:

      Rate

   b. At the second Report Wizard dialog box, make sure *by Customers* is selected.
   c. Do not make any changes at the third Report Wizard dialog box.
   d. Do not make any changes at the fourth Report Wizard dialog box.
   e. At the fifth Report Wizard dialog box, choose the *Block* option.
   f. At the sixth Report Wizard dialog box, choose the *Casual* option.
   g. At the last Report Wizard dialog box, name the report Rentals.
   h. When the report displays in Print Preview, print the report.
2. Close the report.

Assessment 4

1. With the **Hilltop** database file open, use the Label Wizard to create mailing labels (you determine the label type) with the customer names and addresses and sorted by customer names. Name the mailing label report Customer Mailing Labels.
2. Print the mailing labels.
3. Close the mailing labels report.

Assessment 5

1. With the **Hilltop** database file open, create a query in Design view with the following specifications:
   a. Add the Invoices, Customers, Equipment, and Rates tables to the design grid.
   b. Add the following fields from the specified tables:

Date	=	Invoices table
Customer	=	Customers table
Equipment	=	Equipment table

Hours	=	Invoices table
Rate	=	Rates table

   c. Click in the sixth *Field* text and then insert a calculation to total the rental hour amounts by typing **Total: [Hours]*[Rate]**. (Press the Tab key to move to the next field.)
   d. Run the query.
   e. Save the query and name it RentalTotals.
2. Display the query in PivotTable view.
3. At the PivotTable layout, drag and drop the fields as follows:
   a. Drag the *Equipment* field to the *Drop Row Fields Here* section.
   b. Drag the *Customer* field to the *Drop Column Fields Here* section.
   c. Drag the *Total* field to the *Drop Totals or Detail Fields Here* section.
   d. Drag the *Date* field to the *Drop Filter Fields Here* section.
4. Remove the PivotTable Field List box from the screen.
5. Click the Print button to print the query in PivotTable view. (Numbers in the thousands will print as number symbols.)
6. In the *Date* field, display only equipment rentals for May 1, 2005.
7. Print the PivotTable and then redisplay all rental dates.
8. In the *Equipment* field, display records only for the Hydraulic Pump and Pressure Sprayer.
9. Print the PivotTable and then redisplay all equipment.
10. Switch to Datasheet view, save the query, and then close the query.

Assessment 6

1. With the **Hilltop** database file open, click the Queries button on the Objects bar and then create a query in Design view with the following specifications:
   a. Add the Equipment, Customers, and Invoices tables to the design grid.
   b. Add the following fields from the specified tables:

Equipment	=	Equipment table
Customer	=	Customers table
Hours	=	Invoices table

   c. Run the query.
   d. Save the query and name it CustomerHours.
2. Click View and then PivotChart View.
3. At the PivotChart layout, drag and drop the following fields:
   a. Drag the *Equipment* field to the *Drop Filter Fields Here* section.
   b. Drag the *Customer* field to the *Drop Category Fields Here* section.
   c. Drag the *Hours* field to the *Drop Data Fields Here* section.
4. Remove the Chart Field List box from the screen.
5. Click the Print button to print the query in PivotChart view.
6. In the *Equipment* field, display only *Backhoe*, print the PivotChart, and then redisplay all equipment.
7. In the *Customer* field, display only *Allied Builders* and *Cascade Enterprises*, print the PivotChart, and then redisplay all customers.
8. Click the Save button to save the PivotChart.
9. Switch to Datasheet view and then close the query.
10. Close the **Hilltop** database file.

Assessment 7

1. The New Report dialog box contains options for creating a form. In this chapter, you have used the Report Wizard to prepare forms. Experiment with two other options available at the New Report dialog box—AutoReport: Columnar and AutoReport: Tabular.
2. After experimenting with these two wizards, open the **Hilltop** database file and then complete the following:
   a. Use the AutoReport: Columnar option to create a report with all of the fields in the Inventory database table. Print the report that displays and then close the report.
   b. Use the AutoReport: Tabular option to create a report with all of the fields in the Customers database table. Print the report that displays and then close the report.
3. Close the **Hilltop** database file.

CHAPTER challenge

You are the office manager at Tri-State Vision Care Center. The Center houses several optometrists and ophthalmologists. Use the **Tri-StateVisionCare** database created in the Chapter 5 Chapter Challenge. (If you have not already created it, create the two tables described in the first part of the Chapter Challenge in Chapter 5 and add at least three records to each table. Creating the form at this time will not be necessary. Patients are contacted by phone two to three days prior to the appointment to remind them of the upcoming appointment. You believe that having a patient phone list for this process would be helpful. One way to prepare a phone list is through the creation of a report. You will create a report based on the Patients table that includes the patient's first and last name and the telephone number. Sort the list by last name in ascending order. Save the report as Phone List. Also, prepare mailing labels for each of the patients for use when sending out letters. Save and print the labels.

To visually enhance the report, you decide to add a graphic. Use the Help feature to learn more about adding a picture or graphic to a report. Then add an appropriate picture or graphic to the phone list created in the first part of the Chapter Challenge. Save the report again and print it.

Create a business letter in Word that will be sent to patients thanking them for choosing Tri-State Vision Care Center for their eye care. Include any other information in the body of the letter that you feel appropriate. Save the main document of the letter as **ThankYou**. Merge this letter with the Patients table used in the first part of the Chapter Challenge. After merging, print one copy of the letter.

7

IMPORTING AND EXPORTING DATA

PERFORMANCE OBJECTIVES

Upon successful completion of Chapter 7, you will be able to:

- **Export Access data to Excel**
- **Export Access data to Word**
- **Merge Access data with a Word document**
- **Import data to a new table**
- **Link data to a new table**
- **Use the Office Clipboard**
- **Display database contents**
- **View object dependencies**

Microsoft Office 2003 is a suite of programs that allows easy data exchange between programs. In this chapter you will learn how to export data from Access to Excel and Word, merge Access data with a Word document, import and link data to a new table, and copy and paste data between programs. You will also learn how to display database contents and view database object dependencies.

HINT

Data exported from Access to Excel is automatically saved as an Excel workbook with the *.xls* extension.

Using OfficeLinks

OfficeLinks

One of the advantages of a suite of programs like Microsoft Office is the ability to exchange data from one program to another. Access, like the other programs in the suite, offers a feature to export data from Access into Word and/or Excel. Exporting data can be easily accomplished with the OfficeLinks button on the Database toolbar.

HINT

You can export a datasheet as unformatted data to Excel or other spreadsheet programs.

Exporting Data to Excel

Access data saved in a table, form, or report can be exported to Excel. Use an option from the OfficeLinks drop-down list to export data from Access to Excel. The data is saved as an Excel file in the folder where Access is installed. Excel is automatically started when the file is opened.

QUICK STEPS

Export Data to Excel
1. Click the desired table, query, form, or report.
2. Click down-pointing arrow on OfficeLinks button.
3. Click Analyze It with Microsoft Office Excel.

To export data to Excel, open the database file, and then click the name of the database table, query, form, or report you want saved in Excel. With the file selected, click the down-pointing arrow at the right side of the OfficeLinks button on the Database toolbar, and then click Analyze It with Microsoft Office Excel at the drop-down list. The data is converted to an Excel worksheet, Excel is opened, and the data is displayed in a worksheet. The worksheet is automatically saved with the same name as the name in the database file, except the Excel extension of *.xls* is added to the name.

exercise 1

SAVING A DATABASE TABLE AS AN EXCEL WORKSHEET

(Note: Delete any database files from your disk.)

1. Copy the **Hilltop** database file from the CD that accompanies this textbook to your disk and then remove the read-only attribute.
2. Open the **Hilltop** database file and then click the Tables button on the Objects bar.
3. Save the Invoices database table as an Excel worksheet and format the worksheet by completing the following steps:
    a. Click once on *Invoices* in the list box. (This selects the database table.)
    b. Click the down-pointing arrow at the right side of the OfficeLinks button on the Database toolbar.
    c. At the drop-down list that displays, click Analyze It with Microsoft Office Excel.

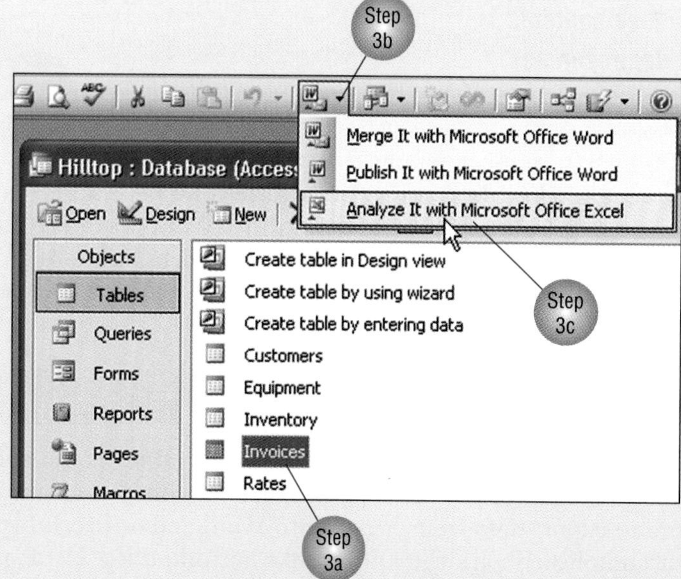

    d. When the data displays on the screen in Excel as a worksheet, make the following changes:
        1) Select cells A1 through F15.
        2) Click Format on the Menu bar and then click AutoFormat.
        3) At the AutoFormat dialog box, double-click the *Classic 2* autoformat.

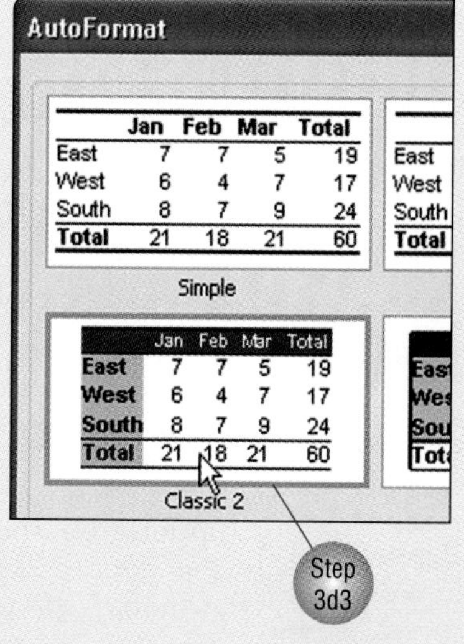

4) With cells A1 through F15 still selected, click the Center button on the Formatting toolbar.
5) Deselect the cells.

e. Click the Save button on the Standard toolbar.
f. Click the Print button on the Standard toolbar.
g. Close the worksheet and then exit Excel.

4. Close the **Hilltop** database file.

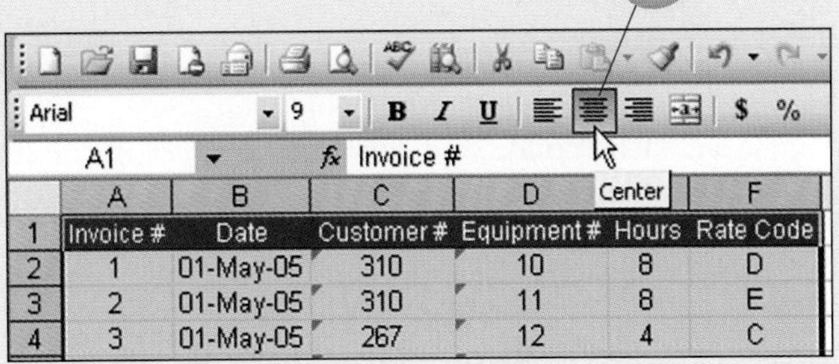

When you use the Analyze It with Microsoft Office Excel option from the OfficeLinks drop-down list, the table becomes an Excel worksheet. All Excel editing capabilities are available for changing or modifying the worksheet. A form can also be converted to a worksheet with the Analyze It with Microsoft Office Excel option.

exercise 2

SAVING A FORM AS AN EXCEL WORKSHEET

1. Open the **Hilltop** database file.
2. Create a form with fields in the Inventory table by completing the following steps:
   a. At the Hilltop : Database window, click the Forms button on the Objects bar.
   b. Double-click *Create form by using wizard*.
   c. At the first Form Wizard dialog box, click the down-pointing arrow at the right of the *Tables/Queries* option box, and then click *Table: Inventory* at the drop-down list. Click the button containing the two greater than symbols (>>) to insert all of the *Available Fields* in the *Selected Fields* list box.
   d. After entering the fields, click the Next button.
   e. At the second Form Wizard dialog box, click the Next button.
   f. At the third Form Wizard dialog box, click *Blueprint* in the format style list box, and then click the Next button.

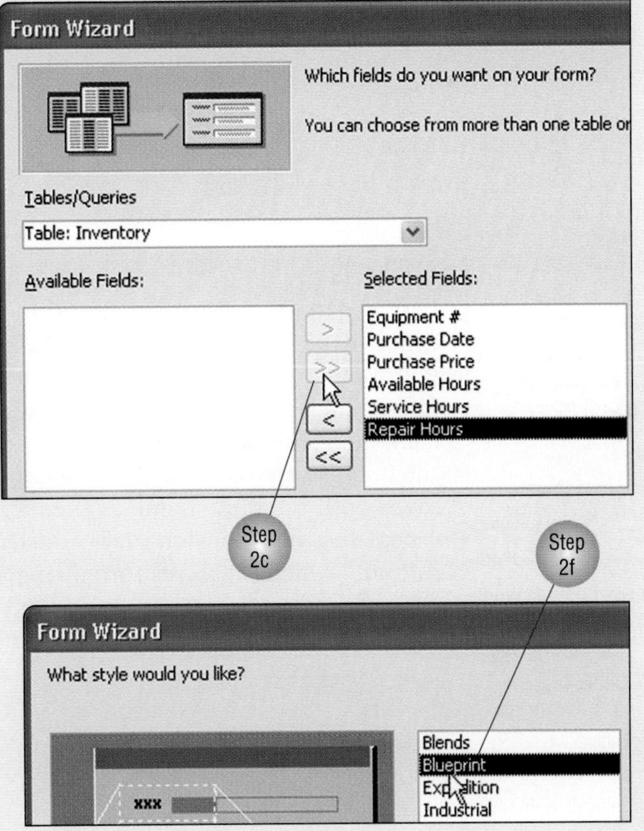

g. At the fourth Form Wizard dialog box, type **Equipment Inventory**, and then click the Finish button.
h. When the first record displays, click the Close button.

3. Save the Equipment Inventory form as an Excel worksheet and format the worksheet by completing the following steps:
   a. Click once on *Equipment Inventory* in the list box. (This selects the form.)
   b. Click the down-pointing arrow at the right side of the OfficeLinks button on the Database toolbar.
   c. At the drop-down list that displays, click Analyze It with Microsoft Office Excel.
   d. When the data displays on the screen in Excel as a worksheet, make the following changes:
      1) Select cells A1 through F11.
      2) Click Format on the Menu bar, and then click AutoFormat.
      3) At the AutoFormat dialog box, double-click the *Colorful 1* autoformat.
      4) Select cells A2 through B11 and then click the Center button on the Formatting toolbar.
      5) Select cells D2 through F11 and then click the Center button on the Formatting toolbar.
      6) Deselect the cells.
   e. Click the Save button on the Standard toolbar.
   f. Print and then close the worksheet.
   g. Exit Excel.
4. Close the **Hilltop** database file.

HINT

Data exported from Access to Word is automatically saved in the *rft* (rich-text format) file format.

Exporting Data to Word

Export data from Access to Word in the same manner as exporting to Excel. To export data to Word, open the database file, select the table, query, form, or report you want to export to Word, and then click the down-pointing arrow on the OfficeLinks button on the Database toolbar. At the drop-down list that displays, click Publish It with Microsoft Office Word. Word is automatically opened and the data is inserted in a Word document. The Word document is automatically saved with the same name as the database table, form, or report you selected, except the file extension *.rtf* is added to the name. An *rtf* file is saved in "rich-text format," which preserves formatting such as fonts and styles. A document saved with the *.rtf* extension can be opened with Microsoft Word and other Windows word processing or desktop publishing programs.

Export Data to Word
1. Click the desired table, query, form, or report.
2. Click down-pointing arrow on OfficeLinks button.
3. Click Publish It with Microsoft Office Word.

exercise 3

SAVING A DATABASE TABLE AS A WORD TABLE

1. Open the **Hilltop** database file.
2. At the Hilltop : Database window, click the Tables button on the Objects bar.
3. Save the Invoices database table as a Word table and then add additional text to the Word document by completing the following steps:
   a. Click once on *Invoices* in the list box.
   b. Click the down-pointing arrow at the right side of the OfficeLinks button on the Database toolbar.
   c. At the drop-down list that displays, click Publish It with Microsoft Office Word.
   d. When the data displays on the screen in Word as a table, add text to the document (not the table) by completing the following steps:
      1) Press the Enter key three times. (This inserts blank lines above the table.)
      2) Move the insertion point to the beginning of the document, turn on bold, type **TRANSACTIONS: 05/01/2005 - 05/03/2005**, and then turn off bold.
      3) Press the Enter key twice, and then type the following text:

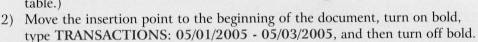

      The following table displays the rentals that occurred between May 1, 2005, and May 3, 2005.

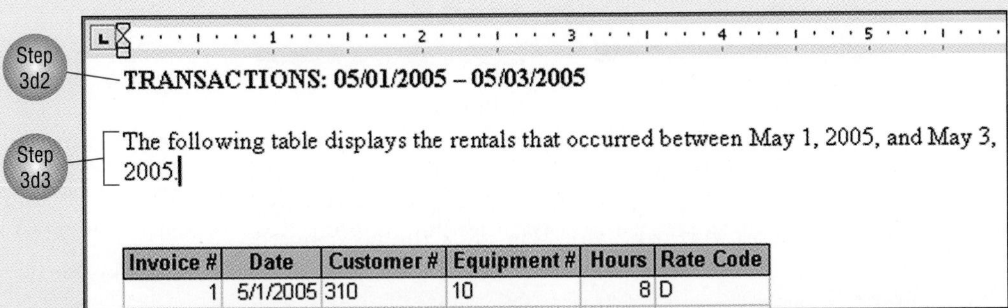

TRANSACTIONS: 05/01/2005 – 05/03/2005

The following table displays the rentals that occurred between May 1, 2005, and May 3, 2005.

Invoice #	Date	Customer #	Equipment #	Hours	Rate Code
1	5/1/2005	310	10	8	D

   e. Click the Save button on the Standard toolbar.
   f. Print the document.
   g. Close the document and then exit Word.
4. Close the **Hilltop** database file.

exercise 4

SAVING A REPORT AS A WORD DOCUMENT

1. Open the **Hilltop** database file.
2. At the Hilltop : Database window, click the Reports button on the Objects bar.
3. Create a report with the Report Wizard by completing the following steps:
   a. Click the New button on the window toolbar.
   b. At the New Report dialog box, double-click *Report Wizard* in the list box.
   c. At the first Report Wizard dialog box, insert the following fields in the *Selected Fields* list box:

      From the Customers table:

         Customer

      From the Equipment table:

         Equipment

      From the Invoices table:

         Date
         Hours

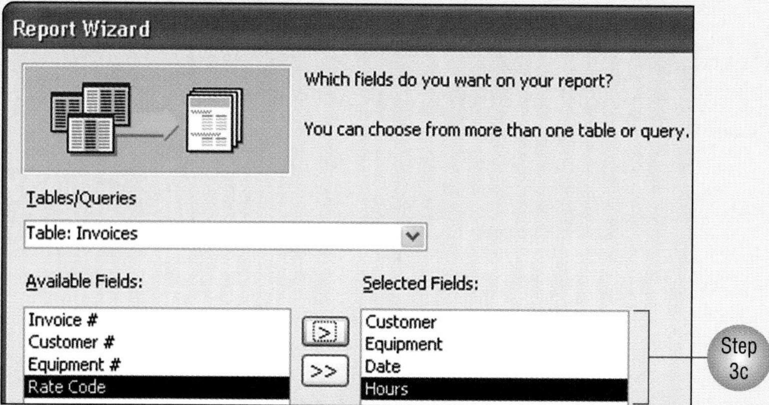

   d. After inserting the fields, click the Next button.
   e. At the second Report Wizard dialog box, make sure *by Customers* is selected in the list box in the upper left corner, and then click the Next button.
   f. At the third Report Wizard dialog box, click the Next button.
   g. At the fourth Report Wizard dialog box, click the Next button.
   h. At the fifth Report Wizard dialog box, click *Align Left 1*, and then click the Next button.
   i. At the sixth Report Wizard dialog box, click *Corporate* in the list box, and then click the Next button.
   j. At the seventh Report Wizard dialog box, type **Customer Report**, and then click the Finish button.
   k. When the report displays in Print Preview, view the report, and then click the Print button that displays on the Print Preview toolbar.
   l. Click the Close button that displays at the right side of the Customer Report title bar.

4. Save the Customer Report as a Word document by completing the following steps:
   a. Click once on *Customer Report* in the list box.
   b. Click the down-pointing arrow at the right side of the OfficeLinks button on the Database toolbar.
   c. At the drop-down list that displays, click Publish It with Microsoft Office Word.

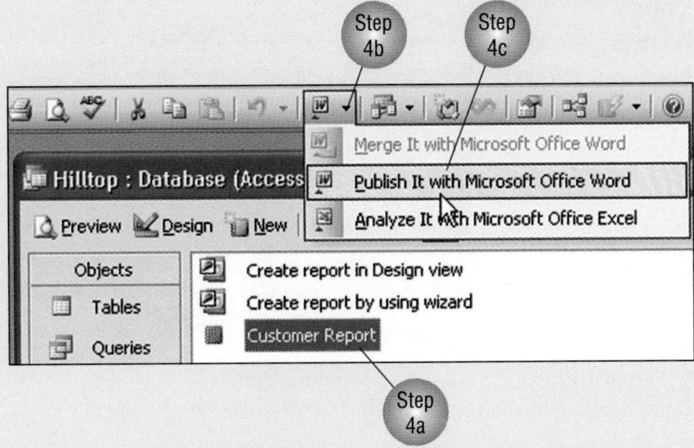

   d. When the data displays on the screen in Word, print the report by clicking the Print button on the Standard toolbar.
   e. Click the Save button (to save the document with the default name of Customer Report).
   f. Close the document and then exit Word.
5. Close the **Hilltop** database file.

Merging Access Data with a Word Document

Data from an Access database table can be merged with a Word document. When merging data in an Access table with a Word document, the data in the Access table is considered the data source and the Word document is considered the main document. When the merge is completed, the merged documents display in Word.

When merging Access data, you can either type the text in the main document or merge Access data with an existing Word document. In Exercise 5, you will merge Access data with an existing Word document and in Exercise 6, you will type the main document.

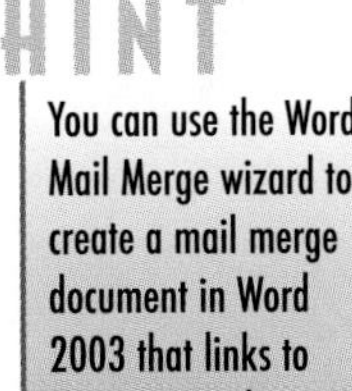

You can use the Word Mail Merge wizard to create a mail merge document in Word 2003 that links to Access 2003 data.

Merge Data with Word

1. Click the desired table or query.
2. Click down-pointing arrow on OfficeLinks button.
3. Click Merge It with Microsoft Office Word.
4. Make desired choices at each of the wizard dialog boxes.

exercise 5

MERGING ACCESS DATA WITH A WORD DOCUMENT

1. Open the **Hilltop** database file.
2. At the Hilltop : Database window, click the Tables button on the Objects bar.
3. Merge data in the Customers database table with a Word document by completing the following steps:
   a. Click once on *Customers* in the list box.
   b. Click the down-pointing arrow at the right side of the OfficeLinks button on the Database toolbar.
   c. At the drop-down list that displays, click Merge It with Microsoft Office Word.
   d. At the Microsoft Word Mail Merge Wizard dialog box, make sure *Link your data to an existing Microsoft Word document* is selected, and then click OK.
   e. At the Select Microsoft Word Document dialog box, make the AccessChapter07S folder on your disk the active folder, and then double-click the document named ***HilltopLetter***.
   f. Click the Maximize button located at the right side of the HilltopLetter title bar.
   g. Press the Down Arrow key six times (not the Enter key), and then type the current date.
   h. Press the Down Arrow key five times, and then insert fields for merging from the Customers database table by completing the following steps:
      1) Click the Insert Merge Fields button located toward the left side of the Merge toolbar.
      2) At the Insert Merge Field dialog box, double-click *Customer* in the *Fields* list box. (This inserts the *«Customer»* field in the document.)
      3) Click the Close button to close the Insert Merge Field dialog box.
      4) Press Enter, click the Insert Merge Fields button, and then double-click *Street Address* in the *Fields* list box of the Insert Merge Field dialog box.
      5) Click the Close button to close the dialog box.
      6) Press Enter, click the Insert Merge Fields button, and then double-click *City* in the *Fields* list box.

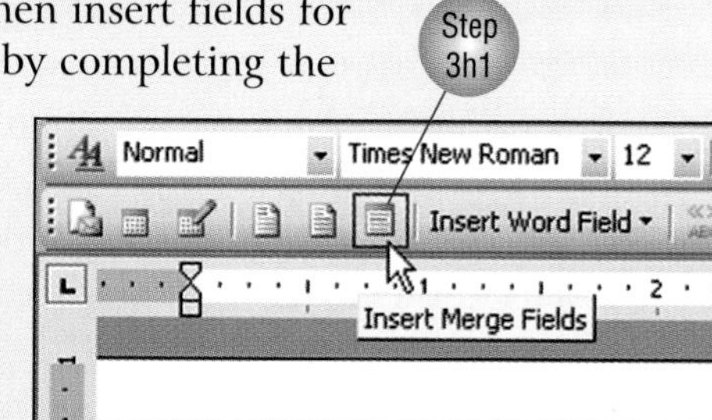

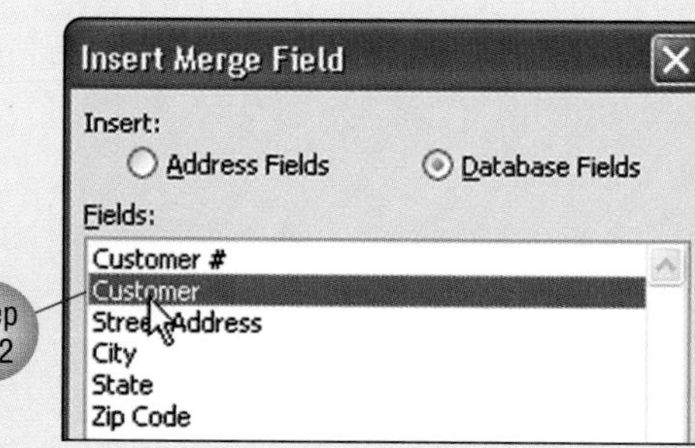

7) Click the Close button to close the dialog box.
8) Type a comma (,) and then press the spacebar.
9) Click the Insert Merge Fields button and then double-click *State* in the *Fields* list box.
10) Click the Close button to close the dialog box.
11) Press the spacebar, click the Insert Merge Fields button, and then double-click *Zip Code* in the *Fields* list box.
12) Click the Close button to close the dialog box.
13) Replace the letters *XX* that display toward the bottom of the letter with your initials.

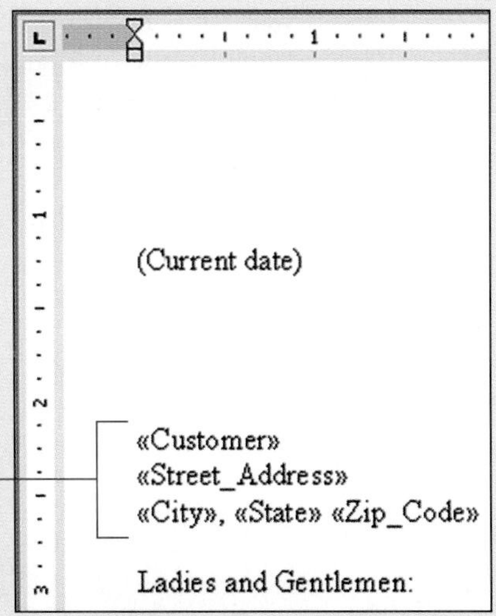

i. Click the Merge to New Document button located toward the right side of the Merge toolbar.
j. At the Merge to New Document dialog box, make sure *All* is selected, and then click OK.
k. When the merge is completed, save the new document as **Wordsac7x05** in the AccessChapter07S folder on your disk.
l. Print just the first two pages (two letters) of **Wordsac7x05**.
m. Close **Wordsac7x05** and then close HilltopLetter, without saving the changes.
n. Exit Word.

4. Close the **Hilltop** database file.

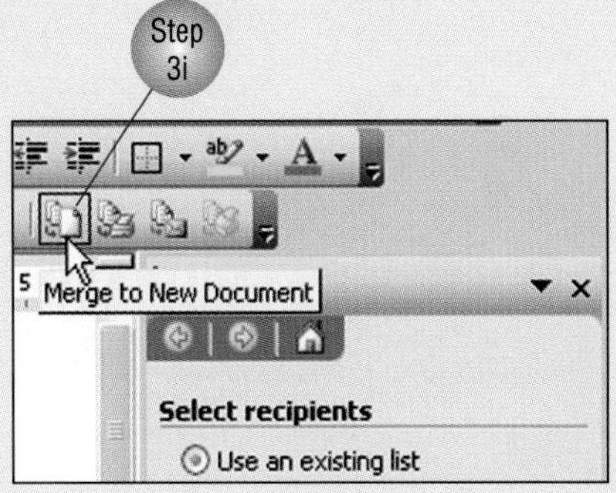

exercise 6

MERGING ACCESS DATA WITH A NEW WORD DOCUMENT

1. Open the **Hilltop** database file.
2. At the Hilltop : Database window, click the Tables button on the Objects bar.
3. Merge data in the Customers database table to a new Word document by completing the following steps:
   a. Click once on *Customers* in the list box.
   b. Click the down-pointing arrow at the right side of the OfficeLinks button on the Database toolbar.
   c. At the drop-down list that displays, click Merge It with Microsoft Office Word.
   d. At the Microsoft Word Mail Merge Wizard dialog box, click the *Create a new document and then link the data to it* option, and then click OK.

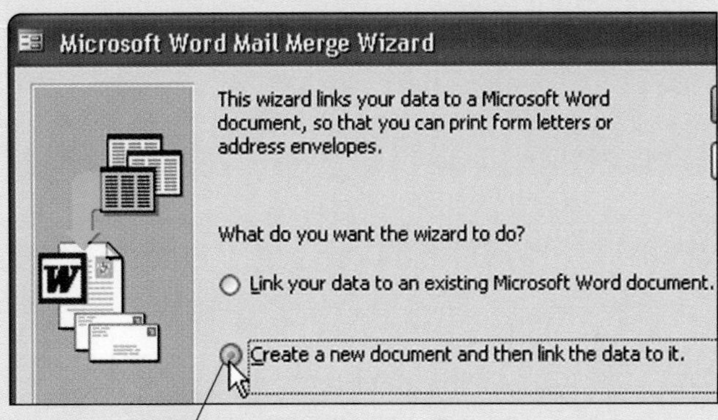

e. Click the Maximize button located at the right side of the Document1 title bar.
f. Complete the following steps to type text and insert fields in the blank Word document:
   1) Press Enter six times.
   2) Type the current date.
   3) Press Enter five times.
   4) Insert the following fields at the left margin in the order shown below (start by clicking the Insert Merge Fields button located toward the left side of the Mail Merge toolbar).

      «Customer»
      «Street_Address»
      «City», «State» «Zip_Code»

   5) Press Enter twice, and then type the salutation **Ladies and Gentlemen:**.
   6) Press Enter twice, and then type the following paragraph of text. (After typing the Hilltop e-mail address, Word will convert it to a hyperlink. Immediately click the Undo button to remove the hyperlink and then continue typing the remainder of the paragraph.)

      We have installed a new computer system for receiving rental equipment requests electronically. If you are interested in requesting equipment online, you may contact us at hilltop@emcp.com or visit our Web site at www.hilltop.emcp.com. If you need assistance with an online request, please contact us at (303) 555-9066.

   7) Press Enter twice, and then type the following complimentary close (at the left margin):

      Sincerely,

      Lou Galloway
      Manager

      XX:Wordsac7x06

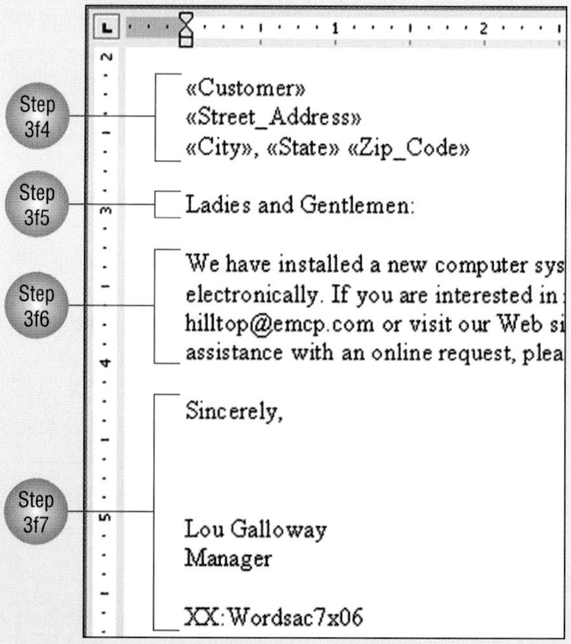

g. Click the Merge to New Document button located toward the right side of the Merge toolbar.
h. At the Merge to New Document dialog box, make sure *All* is selected, and then click OK.
i. When the merge is completed, save the new document as **Wordsac7x06** in the AccessChapter07S folder on your disk.
j. Print the first two pages (two letters) of **Wordsac7x06**.
k. Close **Wordsac7x06**.
l. Save the main document as **WordHilltopLetter** in the AccessChapter07S folder on your disk and then close **WordHilltopLetter**.
m. Exit Word.

4. Close the **Hilltop** database file.

Merging Query Data with a Word Document

A query performed in Access can be saved, and then data from that query can be merged with a Word document. To do this, you would open the database file, complete the query, and then save the query. With the query name selected in the database file, you would click the OfficeLinks button on the Database toolbar and then click the Merge It with Microsoft Office Word option. You would specify whether you want to merge with an existing Word document or create a new document and then insert the appropriate fields.

exercise 7

PERFORMING A QUERY AND THEN MERGING WITH A WORD DOCUMENT

1. Open the **Hilltop** database file.
2. Perform a query with the Simple Query Wizard and modify the query by completing the following steps:
   a. Click the Queries button on the Objects bar.
   b. Double-click *Create query by using wizard* in the list box.
   c. At the first Simple Query Wizard dialog box, click the down-pointing arrow at the right of the *Tables/Queries* text box, and then click *Table: Customers*.
   d. Click the button containing the two greater than symbols (>>) to insert all of the fields in the *Selected Fields* list box.

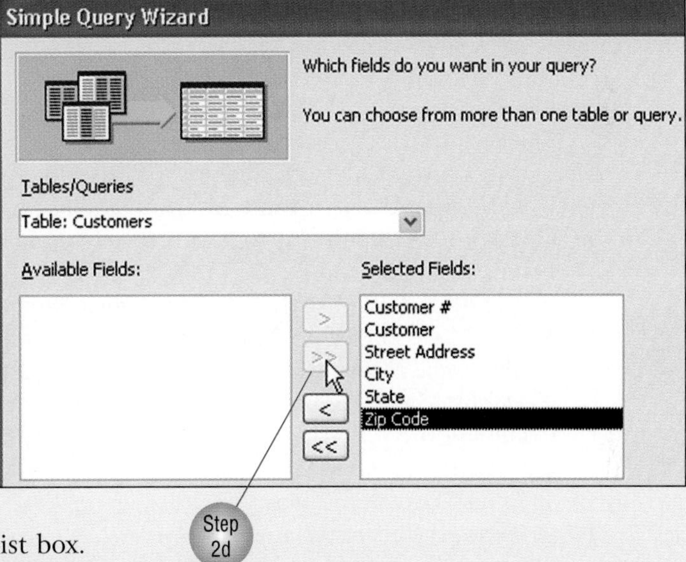

   e. Click the Next button.
   f. At the second Simple Query Wizard dialog box, click the *Modify the query design* option, and then click the Finish button.
   g. At the Customers Query : Select Query window, insert the query criterion by completing the following steps:
      1) Click in the *Criteria* text box in the *City* column.
      2) Type Denver and then press Enter.

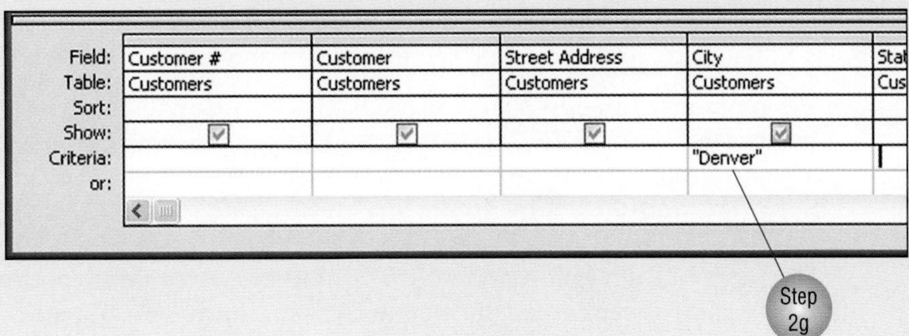

h. Click the Run button on the Query Design toolbar. (Those customers located in Denver will display.)

i. Save the query as Denver Query by completing the following steps:
   1) Click File and then Save As.
   2) At the Save As dialog box, type **Denver Query**, and then press Enter or click OK.

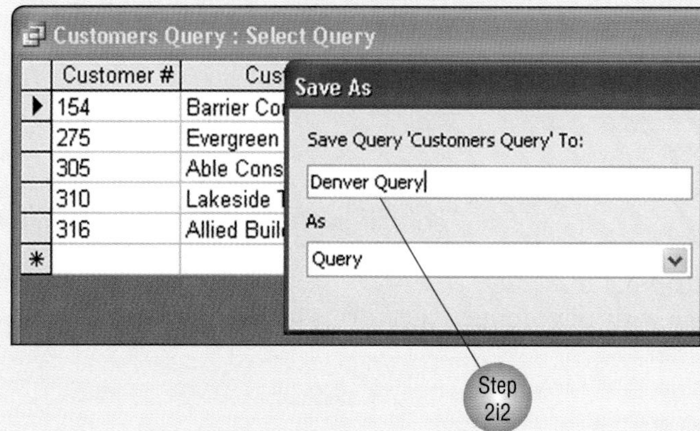

j. Close the Denver Query by clicking the Close button at the right side of the Query title bar.

3. Merge the Denver Query to a new Word document by completing the following steps:
   a. Click *Denver Query* in the Hilltop : Database window list box.
   b. Click the down-pointing arrow at the right side of the OfficeLinks button on the Database toolbar.
   c. At the drop-down list that displays, click Merge It with Microsoft Office Word.
   d. At the Microsoft Word Mail Merge Wizard dialog box, click the *Create a new document and then link the data to it* option, and then click OK.
   e. Click the Maximize button located at the right side of the Document1 title bar.
   f. Complete the following steps to type text and insert fields in the blank Word document:
      1) Press Enter six times.
      2) Type the current date.
      3) Press Enter five times.
      4) Insert the following fields at the left margin in the order shown below (start by clicking the Insert Merge Fields button at the left side of the Mail Merge toolbar).

         «Customer»
         «Street_Address»
         «City», «State» «Zip_Code»

      5) Press Enter twice, and then type the salutation **Ladies and Gentlemen:**.
      6) Press Enter twice, and then type the following paragraphs of text.

         We have just opened a new branch office in downtown Denver to better serve our Denver customers. The branch office hours are 7:30 a.m. to 7:00 p.m. Monday through Friday, 8:00 a.m. to 5:00 p.m. Saturday, and 9:00 a.m. to 3:30 p.m. Sunday.

         Our new branch is located at 7500 Alameda Avenue. Stop by during the next two weeks and receive a 10% discount on your next equipment rental.

7) Press Enter twice, and then type the following complimentary close (at the left margin):

Sincerely,

Lou Galloway
Manager

XX:Wordsac7x07

g. Click the Merge to New Document button located toward the right side of the Mail Merge toolbar.
h. At the Merge to New Document dialog box, make sure *All* is selected, and then click OK.
i. When the merge is completed, save the new document as **Wordsac7x07** in the AccessChapter07S folder on your disk.
j. Print and then close **Wordsac7x07**.
k. Save the main document and name it **WordBranchLetter**.
l. Close **WordBranchLetter** and then exit Word.

4. Close the **Hilltop** database file.

Importing and Linking Data to a New Table

In this chapter, you learned how to export Access data to Excel and Word. Data from other programs, such as Excel and Word, can also be imported into an Access table. For example, you can import data from an Excel worksheet and create a new table in a database file. Data in the original program is not connected to the data imported into an Access table. If you make changes to the data in the original program, those changes are not reflected in the Access table. If you want the imported data connected to the original program, link the data.

Importing Data to a New Table

To import data, open the database file, click File, point to Get External Data, and then click Import. At the Import dialog box that displays, double-click the desired file name. This activates the Import Wizard and displays the first Wizard dialog box. The appearance of the dialog box varies depending on the file selected. Complete the steps of the Import Wizard specifying information such as the range of data, whether or not the first row contains column headings, whether you want to store the data in a new table or store it in an existing table, the primary key, and the name of the table.

Import Data to a New Table
1. Open database file.
2. Click File, Get External Data, Import.
3. Double-click desired file name.
4. Make desired choices at each of the wizard dialog boxes.

exercise 8

IMPORTING AN EXCEL WORKSHEET INTO AN ACCESS TABLE

(Note: Before completing this exercise, open Excel and then open** ExcelWorksheet01 **[located in your AccessChapter07S folder]. Save the worksheet with Save As and name it** Excelsac7**. Close** Excelsac7 **and then exit Excel.)

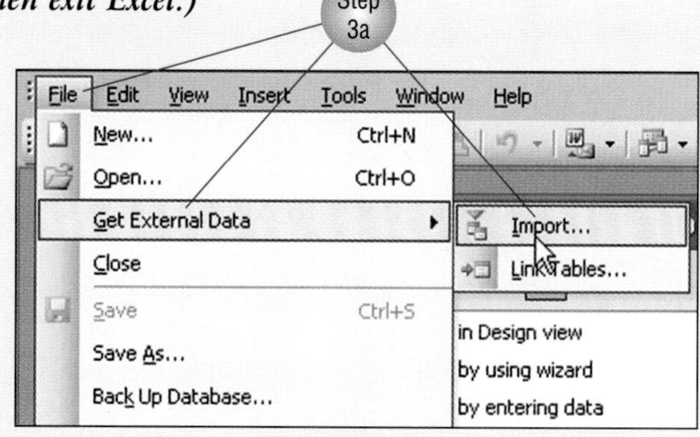

1. Copy the **SouthwestInsurance** database file from the CD that accompanies this textbook to your disk and then remove the read-only attribute.
2. Open the **SouthwestInsurance** database file and click the Tables button on the Objects bar.
3. Import an Excel worksheet into a new table in the **SouthwestInsurance** database file by completing the following steps:
   a. Click File, point to Get External Data, and then click Import.
   b. At the Import dialog box, make the AccessChapter07S folder on your disk the active folder.
   c. Change the *Files of type* option to *Microsoft Excel*.
   d. Double-click ***Excelsac7*** in the list box.
   e. At the first Import Spreadsheet Wizard dialog box, click the Next button.
   f. At the second Import Spreadsheet Wizard dialog box, make sure the *First Row Contains Column Headings* option contains a check mark, and then click the Next button.
   g. At the third Import Spreadsheet Wizard dialog box, make sure the *In a New Table* option is selected, and then click the Next button.
   h. At the fourth Import Spreadsheet Wizard dialog box, click the Next button.
   i. At the fifth Import Spreadsheet Wizard dialog box, click the *Choose my own primary key* option (this inserts *Policy #* in the text box located to the right of the option), and then click the Next button.
   j. At the sixth Import Spreadsheet Wizard dialog box, type **Policies** in the *Import to Table* text box, and then click the Finish button.
   k. At the message saying the data was imported, click OK.
4. Open the new Policies table in Datasheet view.
5. Print and then close the Policies table.
6. Close the **SouthwestInsurance** database file.

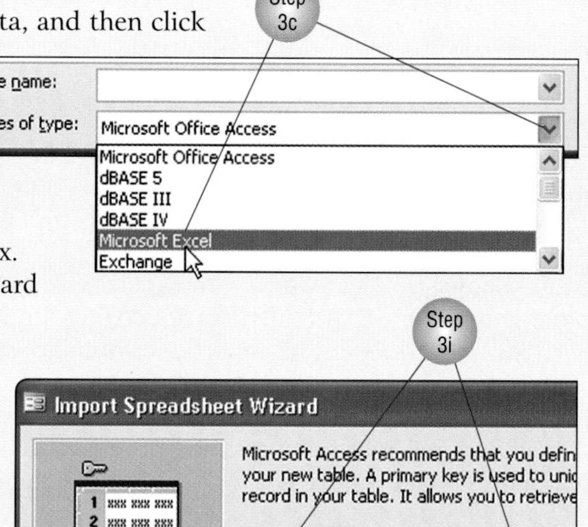

Linking Data to a New Table

Imported data is not connected to the source program. If you want the data to be connected, link the data. When the data is linked, changes made to the data in the source program are reflected in the data in the destination program and changes made in the destination program are reflected in the source program.

To link data to a new table, open the database file, click File, point to Get External Data, and then click Link Tables. At the Link dialog box, double-click the desired file name. This activates the Link Wizard and displays the first Wizard dialog box. Complete the steps of the Link Wizard specifying the same basic information as the Import Wizard.

HINT

Linked data is not copied into a new table but remains within the original database file.

QUICK STEPS

Link Data to a New Table

1. Open database file.
2. Click File, Get External Data, Link Tables.
3. Double-click desired file name.
4. Make desired choices at each of the wizard dialog boxes.

exercise 9

LINKING AN EXCEL WORKSHEET WITH AN ACCESS TABLE

1. Open the **SouthwestInsurance** database file and then click the Tables button on the Objects bar.
2. Link an Excel worksheet with a new table in the **SouthwestInsurance** database file by completing the following steps:
   a. Click File, point to Get External Data, and then click Link Tables.
   b. At the Link dialog box, make sure the AccessChapter07S folder on your disk is the active folder, and then change the *Files of type* option to *Microsoft Excel*.
   c. Double-click ***Excelsac7***.
   d. At the first Link Spreadsheet Wizard dialog box, make sure *Show Worksheets* is selected, and that *Sheet1* is selected in the list box, and then click the Next button.
   e. At the second Link Spreadsheet Wizard dialog box, make sure the *First Row Contains Column Headings* option contains a check mark, and then click the Next button.
   f. At the third Link Spreadsheet Wizard dialog box, type **Linked Policies** (in the *Linked Table Name* text box), and then click the Finish button.
   g. At the message stating the linking is finished, click OK.
3. Open the new Linked Policies table in Datasheet view.

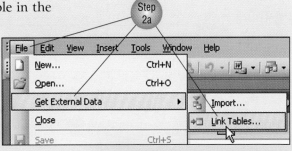

4. Change the number *745* in the *Premium* column to *850*.
5. Add the following new record in the specified fields:

   Policy # = 227-C-28
   Client # = 3120
   Premium = 685

6. Save, print, and then close the Linked Policies table.
7. Open Excel and then open **Excelsac7**. Notice that the information in this table contains the changes made to the Linked Policies table in Access.
8. Close **Excelsac7** and then exit Excel.
9. In Access, close the **SouthwestInsurance** database file.

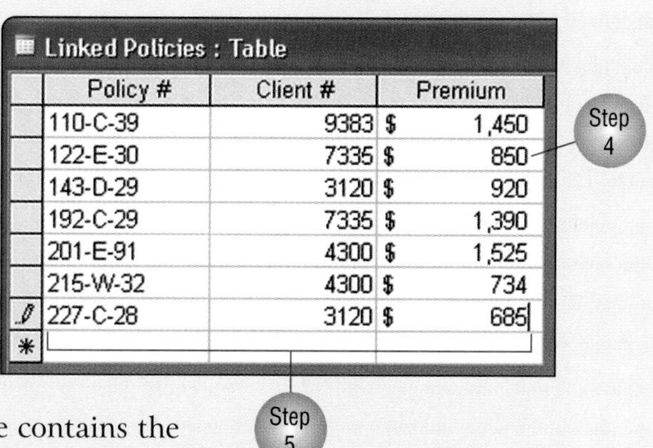

Linked Policies : Table
Policy # | Client # | Premium
110-C-39 | 9383 | $ 1,450
122-E-30 | 7335 | $ 850
143-D-29 | 3120 | $ 920
192-C-29 | 7335 | $ 1,390
201-E-91 | 4300 | $ 1,525
215-W-32 | 4300 | $ 734
227-C-28 | 3120 | $ 685
Step 4
Step 5

QUICK STEPS

Display Clipboard Task Pane
1. Open database file.
2. Click Edit, Office Clipboard.

Using the Office Clipboard

Use the Office Clipboard to collect and paste multiple items. You can collect up to 24 different items in Access or other programs in the Office suite and then paste the items in various locations. To copy and paste multiple items, display the Clipboard task pane shown in Figure 7.1 by clicking Edit and then Office Clipboard.

FIGURE 7.1 ***Clipboard Task Pane***

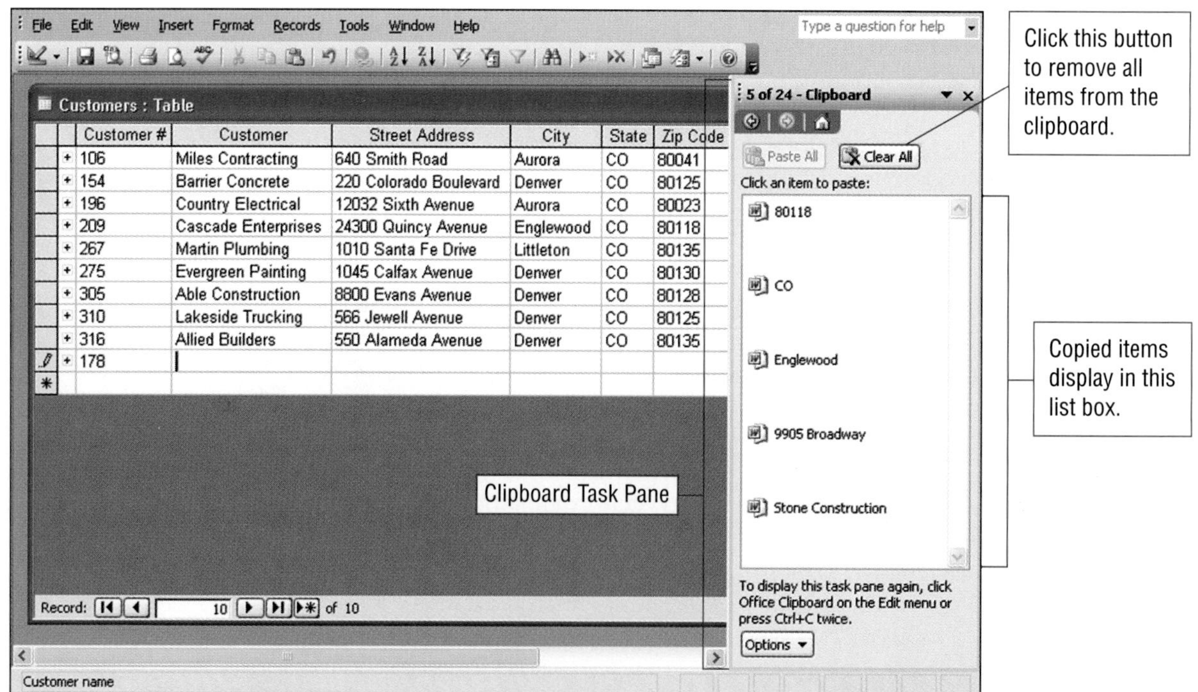

Select data or an object you want to copy and then click the Copy button on the toolbar. Continue selecting text or items and clicking the Copy button. To insert an item from the Clipboard task pane into a field in an Access table, make the desired field active, and then click the button in the Clipboard task pane representing the item. If the copied item is text, the first 50 characters display. When all desired items are inserted, click the Clear All button to remove any remaining items from the Clipboard task pane.

You can copy data from one table to another in an Access database file or from a file in another program to an Access database file. In Exercise 10, you will copy data from a Word document and paste it into a database table. Data can also be collected from documents in other programs such as PowerPoint and Excel.

exercise 10

COLLECTING DATA IN WORD AND PASTING IT IN AN ACCESS DATABASE TABLE

1. In Access, open the **Hilltop** database file.
2. Open the Customers table in Datasheet view.
3. Copy data from Word and paste it into the Customers table by completing the following steps:
   a. Open Word, make the AccessChapter07S folder on your disk the active folder, and then open **HilltopCustomers**.
   b. Display the Clipboard task pane by clicking Edit and then Office Clipboard.
   c. Select the first company name, *Stone Construction*, and then click the Copy button on the Standard toolbar.

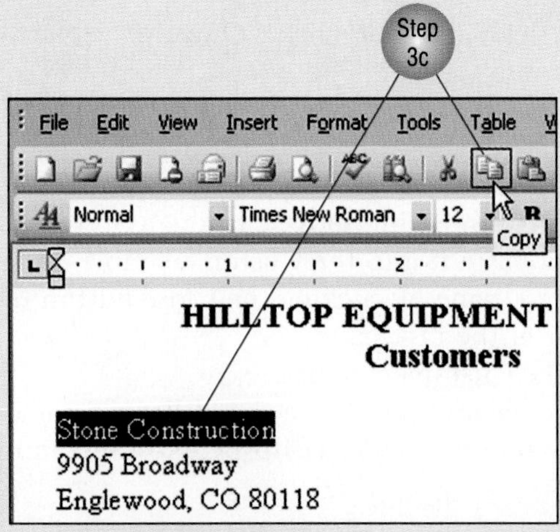

   d. Select the street address, *9905 Broadway*, and then click the Copy button.
   e. Select the city, *Englewood*, and then click the Copy button.
   f. Select the state, *CO*, and then click the Copy button.
   g. Select the Zip Code, *80118*, and then click the Copy button.
   h. Click the button on the Taskbar representing the Access Customers table. (Make sure you are in Datasheet view.)

i. Click in the first empty cell in the *Customer #* field, and then type 178.
j. Display the Clipboard task pane by clicking Edit, and then Office Clipboard.
k. Click in the first empty cell in the *Customer* field, and then click *Stone Construction* in the Clipboard task pane.

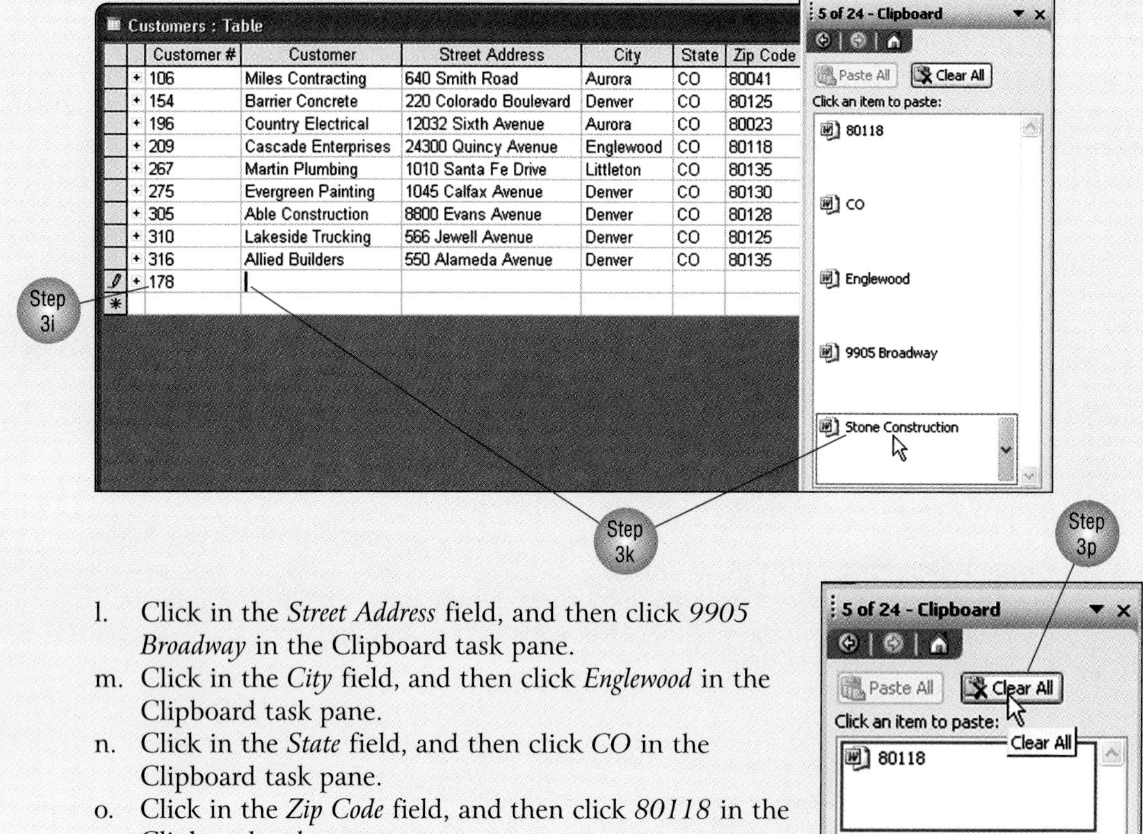
Customers : Table

Customer #	Customer	Street Address	City	State	Zip Code
106	Miles Contracting	640 Smith Road	Aurora	CO	80041
154	Barrier Concrete	220 Colorado Boulevard	Denver	CO	80125
196	Country Electrical	12032 Sixth Avenue	Aurora	CO	80023
209	Cascade Enterprises	24300 Quincy Avenue	Englewood	CO	80118
267	Martin Plumbing	1010 Santa Fe Drive	Littleton	CO	80135
275	Evergreen Painting	1045 Calfax Avenue	Denver	CO	80130
305	Able Construction	8800 Evans Avenue	Denver	CO	80128
310	Lakeside Trucking	566 Jewell Avenue	Denver	CO	80125
316	Allied Builders	550 Alameda Avenue	Denver	CO	80135
178					

l. Click in the *Street Address* field, and then click *9905 Broadway* in the Clipboard task pane.
m. Click in the *City* field, and then click *Englewood* in the Clipboard task pane.
n. Click in the *State* field, and then click *CO* in the Clipboard task pane.
o. Click in the *Zip Code* field, and then click *80118* in the Clipboard task pane.
p. Click the Clear All button on the Clipboard task pane.

4. Complete steps similar to those in Steps 3c through 3p to copy the information for Laughlin Products and paste it into the Customers table. (The Customer # is 225.)
5. Close the Clipboard task pane by clicking the Close button (contains an *X*) located in the upper right corner of the task pane.
6. Save and then print the Customers table.
7. Close the Customers table and then close the **Hilltop** database file.
8. Make Word the active program, close **HilltopCustomers**, and then exit Word.

Viewing Objects and Object Dependencies

As you have learned throughout this book, the structure of a database is comprised of table, query, form, and report objects. Tables are related to other table(s) by creating relationships. Queries, forms, and reports draw the source data from records in the tables to which they have been associated and forms and reports can include subforms and subreports which further expand the associations between objects. A database with a large number of interdependent objects is more complex to work with. Viewing a list of the objects within a database and viewing the dependencies between objects can be beneficial to ensure an object is not deleted or otherwise modified causing an unforeseen effect on another object. Access provides two features that provide information on objects—database properties and the Object Dependencies task pane.

Displaying Database Contents

Display Properties Dialog Box
1. Open database file.
2. Click File, Database Properties.

The database Properties dialog box contains information about the database file. Display the Properties dialog box by opening the database file, clicking File, and then clicking Database Properties. Click each tab at the dialog box to display different information about the database file. Click the Contents tab and information displays about the contents of the database file including all objects such as tables, queries, forms, and reports. Figure 7.2 displays the Properties dialog box for the Hilltop database file.

FIGURE 7.2 ***Hilltop Properties Dialog Box with Contents Tab Selected***

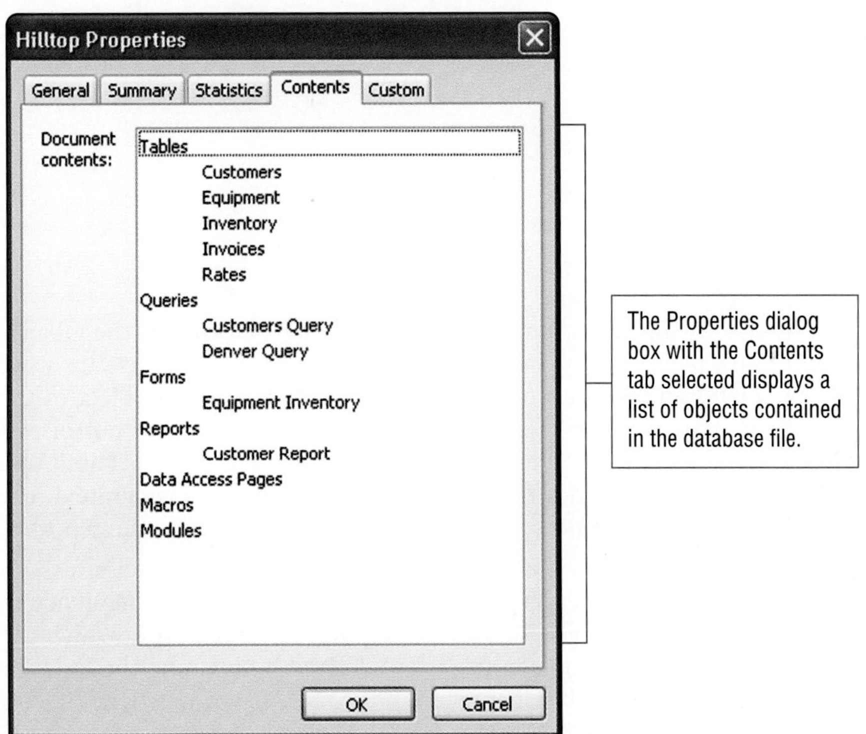

Viewing Object Dependencies

Display the structure of a database table, including tables, queries, forms, and reports objects as well as relationships at the Object Dependencies task pane. Display this task pane by opening the database file, clicking View, and then clicking Object Dependencies. The Object Dependencies task pane in Figure 7.3 displays the objects for the Hilltop database file.

FIGURE 7.3 **Object Dependencies Task Pane**

Display Object Dependencies Task Pane
1. Open database file.
2. Click desired table.
3. Click View, Object Dependencies.

Clicking an object name in the Object Dependencies task pane opens the object in Design view so that you can remove the dependency by deleting bound fields, controls, or otherwise changing the source from which the data is obtained.

By default, *Objects that depend on me* is selected in the Object Dependencies task pane and the list box displays the names of objects for which the Employee Dates and Salaries table is the source. Next to each object in the task pane list is an expand button (plus symbol). Clicking the expand button will show objects dependent at the next level. For example, if a query is based upon the Employee Dates and Salaries table and the query is used to generate a report, clicking the expand button next to the query name would show the report name.

Clicking an object name in the Object Dependencies task pane opens the object in Design view so that you can remove the dependency by deleting bound fields, controls, or otherwise changing the source from which the data is obtained. Relationships between tables are deleted by opening the Relationships window (as you learned in Chapter 2).

exercise 11

VIEWING DATABASE CONTENTS AND OBJECT DEPENDENCIES

1. Open the **Hilltop** database file.
2. Display file properties by completing the following steps:
   a. Click File and then Database Properties.
   b. At the Hilltop Properties dialog box, click the General tab.
   c. Read the information that displays in the dialog box, and then click the Summary tab.

d. Read the information that displays in the dialog box and then click the Statistics tab.
e. Read the information that displays in the dialog box and then click the Contents tab. Notice that the list box displays all objects in the database file.
f. Click the Cancel button to remove the Hilltop Properties dialog box.

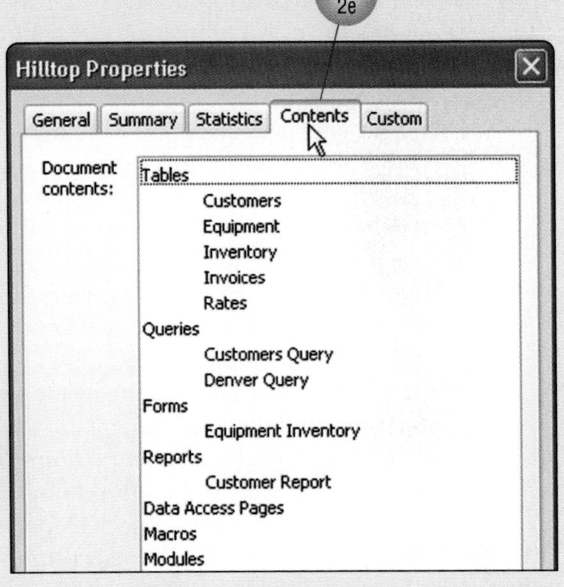

3. Display the structure of the database file by completing the following steps:
   a. At the Hilltop database file window, click the Tables button on the Objects bar.
   b. Click once on the *Customers* table name.
   c. Click View and then Object Dependencies. (If a message displays telling you that the dependency information needs to be updated, click OK. The Object Dependencies task pane displays. By default, *Objects that depend on me* is selected and the task pane lists the names of objects for which the Customers table is the source. Next to each object in the task pane list is an expand button (plus symbol). Clicking the expand button will show objects dependent at the next level.
   d. Click the expand button (plus symbol) to the left of *Invoices* in the Tables section. (This displays the tables, queries, and reports that are dependent on the Invoices table. See figure at the far right.)
   e. Click the *Objects that I depend on* option located toward the top of the Object Dependencies task pane.
   f. Click the *Invoices* table in the Hilltop : Database window. 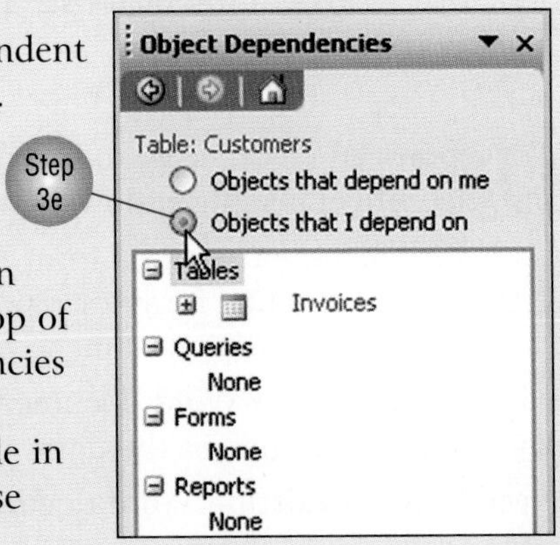
   g. Click View and then Object Dependencies. (This displays the objects dependent on the Invoices table. The Object Dependencies task pane does not automatically update when you click a different table name. To update the task pane, you must click View and then Object Dependencies.)
   h. Click the *Objects that depend on me* option located toward the top of the Object Dependencies task pane. Notice the objects that are dependent on the Invoices table.

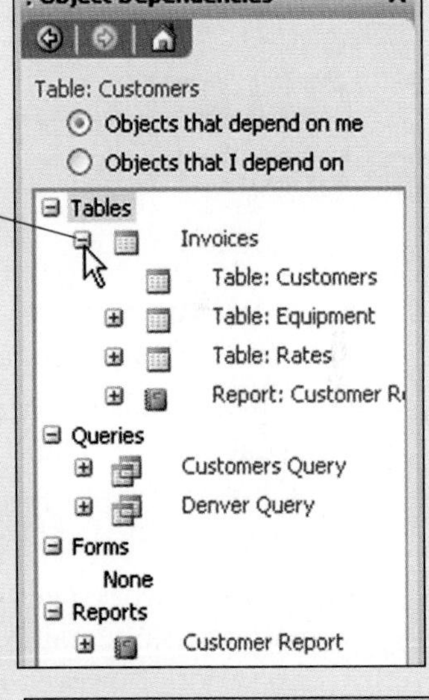

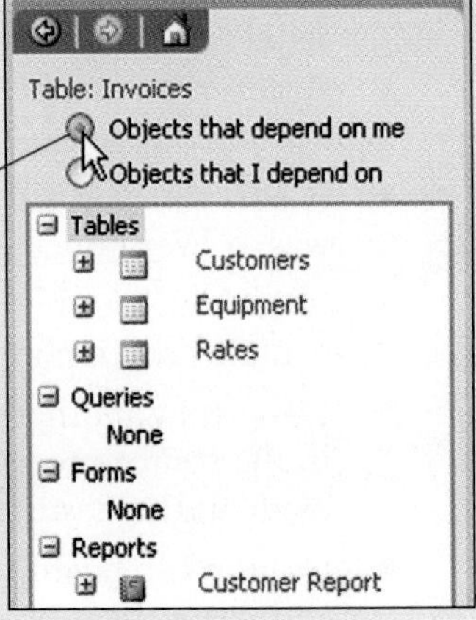

i. Close the Object Dependencies task pane.

4. Delete the relationship between the Invoices table and the Rates table by completing the following steps:
   a. Click the Relationships button on the Database toolbar.
   b. Right-click the black join line between the Invoices and Rates tables.
   c. At the shortcut menu that displays, click Delete.
   d. At the message asking if you are sure you want to permanently delete the relationship, click Yes.
   e. Close the Relationships window.

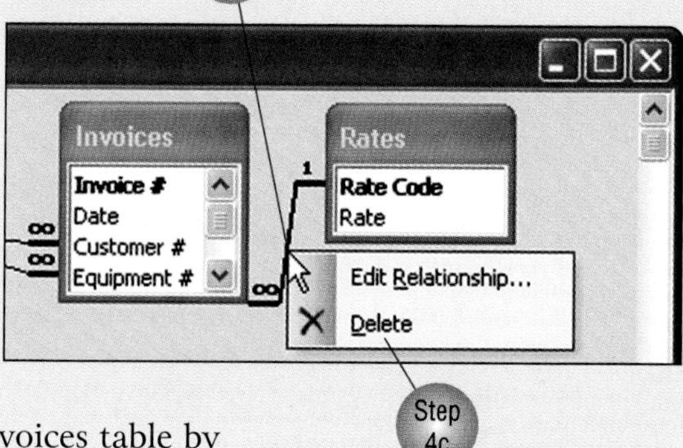

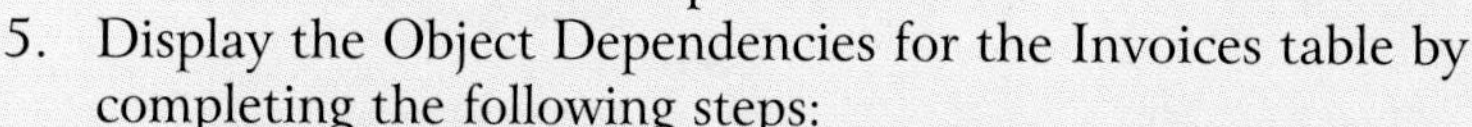

5. Display the Object Dependencies for the Invoices table by completing the following steps:
   a. Click once on the *Invoices* table in the Hilltop: Database window with the Tables button selected on the Objects bar.
   b. Click View and then Object Dependencies. (Notice that the Rates table is no longer listed in the Tables section of the Object Dependencies task pane.)
6. Close the Object Dependencies task pane.
7. Close the **Hilltop** database file.

CHAPTER summary

- A database table, form, or report can be exported to Excel with the Analyze It with Microsoft Office Excel option at the OfficeLinks drop-down list.
- When data is exported to Excel, the data becomes an Excel worksheet with all Excel editing capabilities available.
- A database table, form, or report can be exported to Word with the Publish It with Microsoft Office Word option from the OfficeLinks drop-down list.
- An Excel worksheet or a Word document created from Access data is automatically saved with the same name as the database table, form, or report selected. A different file extension, however, is added to the document name.
- Access data can be used to merge with a Word document. Access uses the data from the database table as the data source and merges the data with a Word document.
- Access data can be merged with an existing Word document or merged with a new document.
- A query performed in Access can be saved, and then data from that query can be merged with a Word document.
- Data from another program can be imported into an Access database table. Access contains an Import Wizard that guides you through the importing data steps.
- Data from another program can be linked to an Access table. Changes made to the data in the source program are reflected in the data in the destination program and changes made in the destination program are reflected in the source program.
- Use the Clipboard task pane to collect up to 24 different items in Access or other programs and paste them in various locations.

- The database Properties dialog box contains information about the open database file. Display this dialog box by clicking File and then Database Properties.
- Display the structure of a database table at the Object Dependencies task pane. Display this task pane by opening a database file, clicking a table name, clicking View, and then clicking Object Dependencies.

FEATURES summary

FEATURE	BUTTON	MENU
OfficeLinks drop-down list		Tools, Office Links
Import Wizard		File, Get External Data, Import
Link Wizard		File, Get External Data, Link Tables
Clipboard task pane		Edit, Office Clipboard
Properties dialog box		File, Database Properties
Object Dependencies task pane		View, Object Dependencies

CONCEPTS check

Completion: On a blank sheet of paper, indicate the correct term, symbol, or command for each description.

1. Click this option from the OfficeLinks drop-down list to export the selected database table, form, or report to Excel.
2. Click this option from the OfficeLinks drop-down list to export the selected database table, form, or report to Word.
3. Click this option from the OfficeLinks drop-down list to merge Access data with a Word document.
4. Access data exported to Excel is saved with this file extension.
5. Access data exported to Word is saved with this file extension.
6. If you want imported data connected to the original program, do this to the data.
7. Display this task pane to collect up to 24 different items in Access or other programs and then paste them in various locations.
8. Click this option on the Menu bar, and then click Database Properties to display the Properties dialog box.
9. This task pane displays the structure of a table including the objects that are dependent on the table and upon which the table is dependent.

SKILLS check

Assessment 1

1. Copy the database file named **LegalServices** from the CD that accompanies this textbook to your disk. Remove the read-only attribute from the **LegalServices** database file.
2. Open the **LegalServices** database file.
3. Create a form named Billing using the Form Wizard with the following fields:

   From the Billing table:

   Billing #
   Client ID
   Date
   Hours

   From the Rates table:

   Rate

4. When the form displays, close it.
5. At the LegalServices : Database window, create an Excel worksheet with the Billing form.
6. Make the following changes to the *Billing* worksheet:
   a. Select cells A1 through E22 and then apply the Classic 2 autoformat.
   b. Select cells A1 through E1 and then click the Center button on the Formatting toolbar.
   c. Select cells A2 through B22 and then click the Center button on the Formatting toolbar.
   d. Save the *Billing* worksheet.
   e. Print and then close the *Billing* worksheet.
   f. Exit Excel.
7. Close the **LegalServices** database file.

Assessment 2

1. Open the **LegalServices** database file.
2. Create a report named Client Billing using the Report Wizard with the following fields:

   From the Clients table:

   First Name
   Last Name

   From the Billing table:

   Date
   Hours

   From the Rates table:

   Rate

3. When the report displays, print and then close the report.

4. At the LegalServices : Database window, create a Word document with the Client Billing report form. In the Word document, add the following text *above* the report data:

   LEGAL SERVICES
   330 Jackson Street
   Kent, WA 98043
   (253) 555-3490

   CLIENT BILLING INFORMATION

5. Select the text you just typed and then apply a typeface, type size, and font color that closely matches the existing text in the report.
6. Save the Word document with Save As and name it **Wordsac7Report**.
7. Print **Wordsac7Report**, close it, and then exit Word.
8. Close the **LegalServices** database file.

Assessment 3

1. Open the **LegalServices** database file.
2. Merge data in the Clients database table to a new Word document using the Merge It with Microsoft Office Word option from the OfficeLinks drop-down list.
3. Click the Maximize button located at the right side of the Document1 title bar.
4. Compose a letter with the following elements:
   a. Press Enter six times, type the current date, and then press Enter five times.
   b. Insert the proper field names for the inside address. ***(Hint: Use the Insert Merge Fields button on the Mail Merge toolbar.)***
   c. Insert a proper salutation.
   d. Compose a letter to clients that includes the following information:

      The last time you visited our offices, you may have noticed how crowded we were. To alleviate the overcrowding we are leasing new offices in the Meridian Building and will be moving in at the beginning of next month.

      Stop by and see our new offices at our open house planned for the second Friday of next month. Drop by any time between 2:00 and 5:30 p.m. We look forward to seeing you.

   e. Include an appropriate complimentary close for the letter. Use the name and title *Marjorie Shaw, Senior Partner* for the signature and add your reference initials and the document name (**Wordsac7sc03**).
5. Merge to a new document and then save the document with the name **Wordsac7sc03**.
6. Print only the first two letters in the document and then close **Wordsac7sc03**.
7. Close the main document without saving it and then exit Word.
8. Close the **LegalServices** database table.

Assessment 4

1. Open the **LegalServices** database file.
2. Extract records from the Clients database table of those clients located in Kent and then name the query Kent Query.
3. Merge the Kent Query to a new Word document using the Merge It with Microsoft Office Word option from the OfficeLinks drop-down list.

4. Click the Maximize button located at the right side of the Document1 title bar.
5. Compose a letter with the following elements:
   a. Press Enter six times, type the current date, and then press Enter five times.
   b. Insert the proper field names for the inside address.
   c. Insert a proper salutation.
   d. Compose a letter to clients that includes the following information:

      The City of Kent Municipal Court has moved from 1024 Meeker Street to a new building located at 3201 James Avenue. All court hearings after the end of this month will be held at the new address. If you need directions to the new building, please call our office.

   e. Include an appropriate complimentary close for the letter. Use the name *Thomas Zeiger* and the title *Attorney* in the complimentary close and add your reference initials and the document name (**Wordsac7sc04**).
6. Merge to a new document and then save the document with the name **Wordsac7sc04**.
7. Print only the first two letters in the document and then close **Wordsac7sc04**.
8. Close the main document without saving it and then exit Word.
9. Close the **LegalServices** database table.

Assessment 5

1. Open the **LegalServices** database file and click the Tables button on the Objects bar.
2. Import **ExcelWorksheet02** into a new table named Cases. (Use the Import Spreadsheet Wizard to do this.)
3. Open the Cases table in Datasheet view.
4. Print and then close the Cases table.
5. Close the **LegalServices** database file.

Assessment 6

1. Open the **LegalServices** database table.
2. Use the Access Help feature to learn how to change the font, font style, size, and color in a datasheet.
3. Open the Clients table and then make the following changes:
   a. Change the font to Times New Roman.
   b. Change the font size to 9.
   c. Change the font color to Maroon.
4. Change the page orientation to landscape and then print the table in datasheet view.
5. Close the table without saving the changes.
6. Close the **LegalServices** database table.

CHAPTER challenge

You work in the customer relations department at Molly's Museum and Memories. Currently, a simple tracking system of customers is being used and maintained in Excel. The information is very beneficial, but you see where it could be more easily managed if it were in Access. Import the worksheet named *Tracking* in the Excel file named **Molly'sMuseum** into a new database table named **Molly's Museum and Memories**. ***(Hint: Prepare the Excel file for import.)*** Do not import the *Distance Traveled* field. Use the *Customer Number* field as the primary key. Once the table has been imported, be sure to assign appropriate data types to each field.

Once tables have been created in Access, renaming the tables to better identify the information in the table may be necessary. Use the Help feature to learn about renaming tables. Then rename the Tracking table imported in the first part of the Chapter Challenge to Statistics.

You decide that the information being gathered in the Statistics table may be of interest to others. To share the information with others, you will post it to the museum's intranet on a monthly basis and possibly to the museum's Web site. Export the Statistics table as an HTML file to prepare it for posting. Save the HTML file as **Statistics**.

CHAPTER 8

CREATING WEB PAGES AND USING DATABASE WIZARDS

PERFORMANCE OBJECTIVES

Upon successful completion of Chapter 8, you will be able to:

- **Save a table as a Web page**
- **Apply a theme to a Web page**
- **Create hyperlinks in a Web page**
- **Create a database with sample data using a Database Wizard**
- **Manipulate data within the database file**

ACCESS

In previous chapters, you learned to use wizards to organize fields in a variety of formats including queries, forms, reports, mailing labels, and charts. Access also includes a wizard that walks you through the steps for creating a data access page along with a number of database wizards you can use to create an entire database file. In this chapter, you will use the Page Wizard to create a data access page from data in a table and you will also create a database file using a database wizard.

Creating a Data Access Page

HINT

A data access page is stored in a separate file in HTML format.

Make Access data available for viewing on the Internet or on a company's intranet by saving the data as a data access page. A data access page is a special type of Web page designed for viewing and working with data from the Internet or intranet. Data saved as a Web page can be viewed in the default browser, formatting can be applied to the Web page, and hyperlinks can be inserted in the Web page.

Saving a Table as a Web Page

HINT

Other users on the Internet or on a company intranet can work with a data access page.

Access contains a wizard that walks you through the steps for creating a data access page. To use this wizard, open the desired database file, click the Pages button on the Objects bar, and then double-click *Create data access page by using wizard* in the list box. Complete the Page Wizard steps to create the data access page. The Page Wizard steps are similar to the wizard steps for creating a form or report.

Save a Table as a Web Page
1. Open database file.
2. Click Page button on Objects bar.
3. Double-click *Create data access page by using wizard.*
4. Complete Page Wizard steps.

When you create a data access page, the Page Wizard specifies a folder and subfolders for Web page files. This is because a Web page generally consists of a variety of items that are inserted in individual files. For example, each bullet image and clip art image or picture in a Web page is saved in a separate image file. Inserting all of these files into folders makes it easier for you to take this information to another location. For example, you can copy the contents of a Web page folder and all of its subfolders to another computer or onto a disk.

Another method for creating a data access page is to create the page in Design view. To do this, open the desired database file, click the Pages button on the Objects bar, and then double-click *Create data access page in Design view*. This displays the Design grid where you can create the form with the desired objects. Use the Toolbox to add control objects to the grid. With buttons on the Toolbox, you can also add Web page features such as hyperlinks and scrolling text.

Applying a Theme to a Web Page

Some interesting and colorful formatting can be applied to a Web page with options at the Theme dialog box shown in Figure 8.1. To display this dialog box, click Format, and then click Theme. Click a theme in the *Choose a Theme* list box and a preview displays at the right side. Click OK to close the dialog box and apply the theme to the page. (You can also double-click a theme at the Theme dialog box.)

FIGURE 8.1 ***Theme Dialog Box***

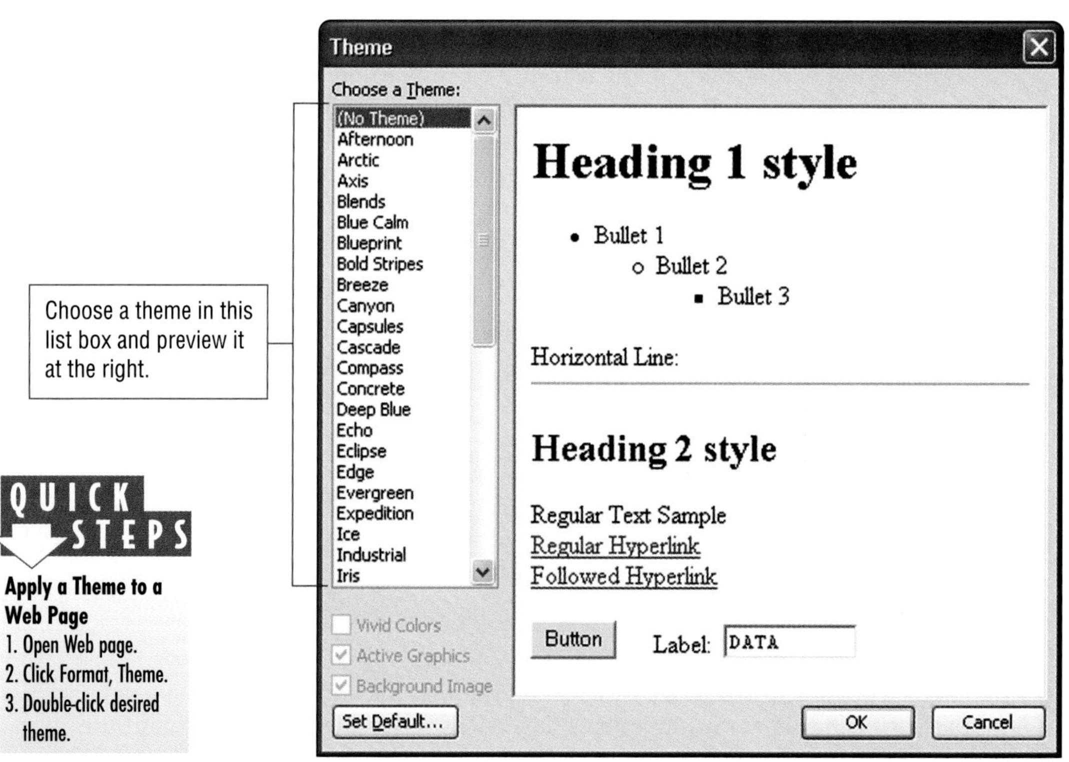

Apply a Theme to a Web Page
1. Open Web page.
2. Click Format, Theme.
3. Double-click desired theme.

Previewing a Web Page in Web Page Preview

When creating a Web page, you may want to preview it in your default Web browser. Depending on the browser you are using, some of the formatting may not display in the browser. To preview a Web page in your default Web browser, click File and then Web Page Preview.

exercise 1

SAVING A TABLE AS A WEB PAGE

(Note: Delete any database files from your disk.)

1. Copy the **OutdoorOptions** database file from the CD that accompanies this textbook to your disk and then remove the read-only attribute from **OutdoorOptions**.
2. Create a Web page by completing the following steps:
   a. At the OutdoorOptions : Database window, click the Pages button on the Objects bar.
   b. Double-click *Create data access page by using wizard* in the list box.

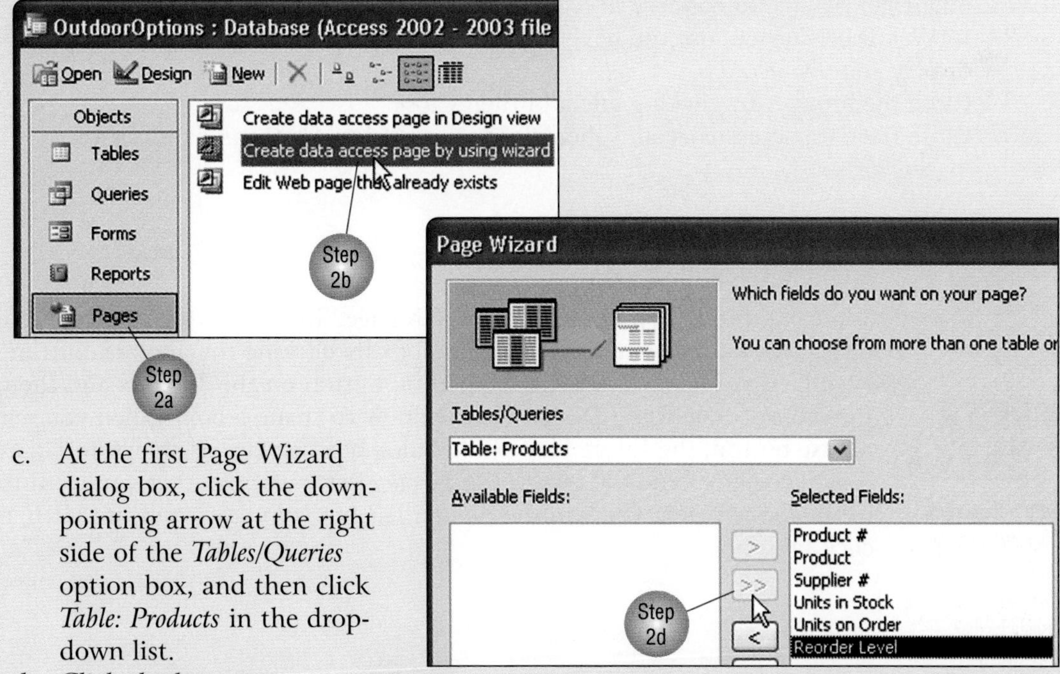

   c. At the first Page Wizard dialog box, click the down-pointing arrow at the right side of the *Tables/Queries* option box, and then click *Table: Products* in the drop-down list.
   d. Click the button containing the greater than symbols (>>) (this inserts all of the fields in the *Selected Fields* list box).
   e. Click the Next button.
   f. At the second Page Wizard dialog box, click the button containing the less than symbol (<) to reduce the priority of *Supplier #*.

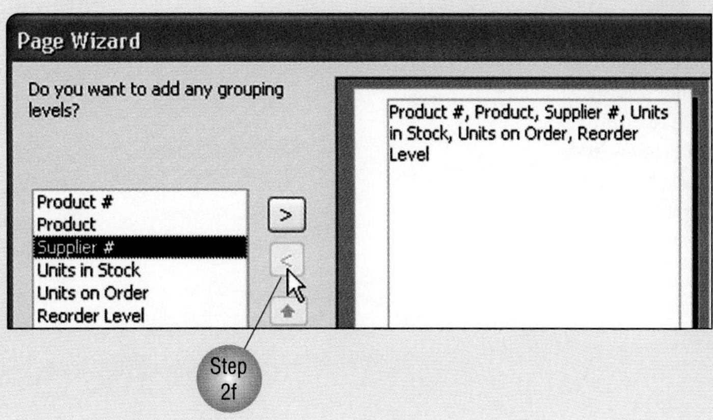

g. Click the Next button.
h. At the third Page Wizard dialog box, click the Next button.
i. At the fourth Page Wizard dialog box, make sure the *Modify the page's design* option is selected, and then click the Finish button. (The completed data access page displays on the screen in Design view.)

3. Click the text *Click here and type title text*, and then type **Outdoor Options – Products**.
4. Apply a theme to the page by completing the following steps:
   a. Click Format and then Theme.
   b. At the Theme dialog box, click *Blends* in the *Choose a Theme* list box, and then click OK.
5. Click the View button to change to the Page view.
6. Save the access data page and name it **ProductsWebPage**.
7. Make sure you are connected to the Internet and then view the page in the default Web browser by clicking File and then Web Page Preview. (If you are not connected to the Internet, a message may display telling you that the page might not be able to connect to data. At this message, click OK.)
8. In Web Page Preview, use the navigation buttons along the bottom of the form to display various records.
9. Close the browser by clicking File and then Close.
10. Close the data access page and then close the **OutdoorOptions** database file.

Toolbox

Create a Hyperlink
1. Open Web page in Design view.
2. Click Toolbox button to display Toolbox.
3. Click Hyperlink button on Toolbox.
4. Drag to create hyperlink text box.
5. At Insert Hyperlink dialog box, type desired text in *Text to display* text box, type Web address in the *Address* text box, then click OK.

Creating Hyperlinks

You can create a hyperlink in your Web page. To do this, display the Web page in Design view and then display the Toolbox by clicking the Toolbox button on the Page Design toolbar. Click the Hyperlink button on the Toolbox and then, using the mouse, drag in the Design view window to create a box. When you release the mouse button, the Insert Hyperlink dialog box displays as shown in Figure 8.2. At this dialog box, type the text in the *Text to display* text box that you want to display in the Design view. Click in the *Address text* box, type the Web site URL, and then click OK.

FIGURE

8.2 ***Insert Hyperlink Dialog Box***

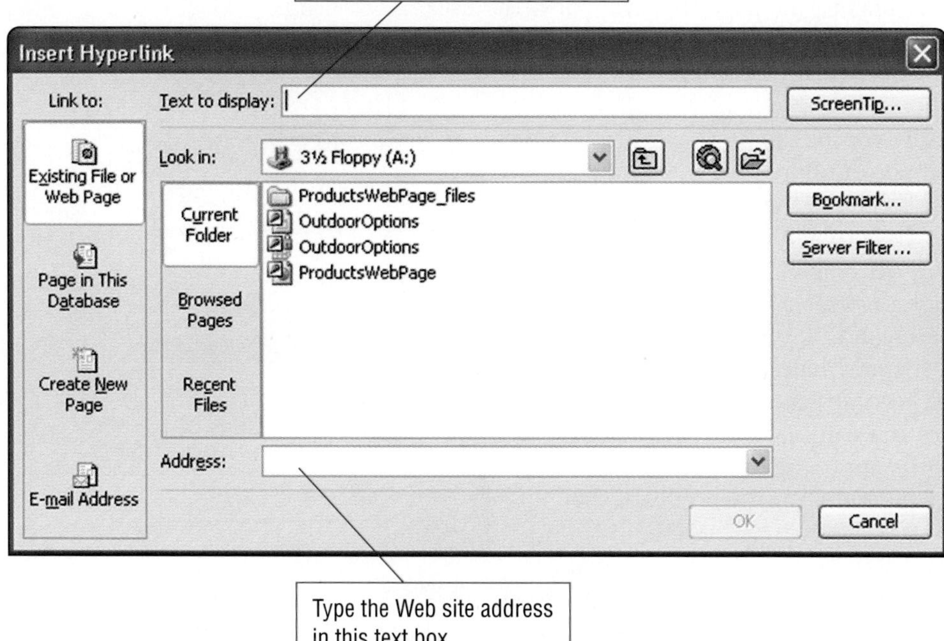

Another method for creating a hyperlink is to type the URL in a label in the Design view. When you type the complete URL, Access automatically converts the URL to a hyperlink and changes the color of the URL.

HINT

A hyperlink is a pointer from one object to another. A hyperlink generally points to a Web page but it can also point to a file, a program, a picture, or an e-mail address.

exercise 2

SAVING A TABLE AS A WEB PAGE

1. Open the **OutdoorOptions** database file.
2. Create a Web page by completing the following steps:
   a. At the OutdoorOptions : Database window, click the Pages button on the Objects bar.
   b. Double-click *Create data access page by using wizard* in the list box.
   c. At the first Page Wizard dialog box, click the down-pointing arrow at the right side of the *Tables/Queries* option box, and then click *Table: Suppliers* at the drop-down list.
   d. Click the button containing the two greater than symbols (>>). (This inserts all of the fields in the *Selected Fields* list box.)
   e. Click the Next button.
   f. At the second Page Wizard dialog box, click the Next button.
   g. At the third Page Wizard dialog box, click the Next button.
   h. At the fourth Page Wizard dialog box, make sure the *Modify the page's design* option is selected, and then click the Finish button. (The completed data access page displays on the screen in Design view.)

3. Click the text *Click here and type title text*, and then type **OUTDOOR OPTIONS**. (You may need to drag up the top of the data access page window to see this text.)
4. Apply a theme to the page by completing the following steps:
   a. Click Format and then Theme.
   b. At the Theme dialog box, click *Blends* in the *Choose a Theme* list box, and then click OK.
5. Add two hyperlinks to the page that will allow the user to jump to the Parks Canada site and the United States National Park Service site by completing the following steps:

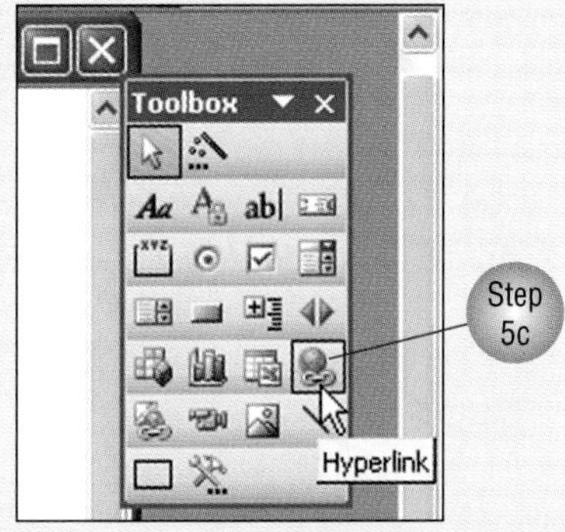

   a. Increase the size of the page window by dragging down the bottom border of the window. (This gives you space to create the hyperlinks.)
   b. Click the Toolbox button on the Page Design toolbar to turn on the display of the Toolbox. (Skip this step if the Toolbox is already displayed.)
   c. Click the Hyperlink button on the Toolbox.
   d. Position the crosshair pointer with the hyperlink icon attached to it toward the bottom of the window. Drag the mouse down to the approximate height and width shown at the right and then release the mouse button.
   e. At the Insert Hyperlink dialog box, make the following changes:
      1) Click in the *Text to display* text box, and then type **Parks Canada**.
      2) Click in the *Address* text box, and then type **http://parkscanada.gc.ca**.
      3) Click OK.
   f. Click the Hyperlink button on the Toolbox.
   g. Position the crosshair pointer with the hyperlink icon attached to it to the right of the Parks Canada hyperlink, and then drag to create a box.
   h. At the Insert Hyperlink dialog box, make the following changes:
      1) Click in the *Text to display* text box, and then type **National Parks Service**.
      2) Click in the *Address* text box, and then type **http://www.nps.gov**.
      3) Click OK.

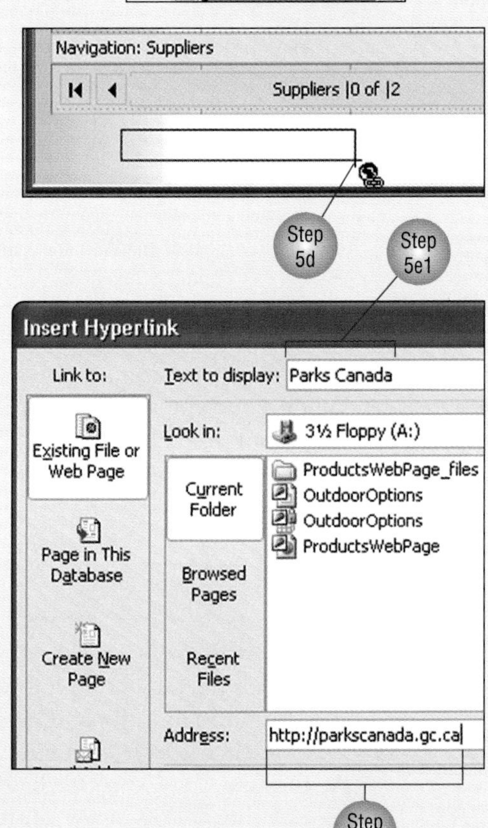

6. Click the View button to change to the Page view.
7. Save the access data page and name it **SuppliersWebPage**.
8. View the page in the default Web browser by clicking File and then Web Page Preview.
9. In Web Page Preview, complete the following steps:
   a. Click the Parks Canada hyperlink.
   b. At the Parks Canada home page, navigate to a particular page that interests you.
   c. Close the page by clicking File and then Close.
   d. At the Suppliers Web Page, click the National Parks Service hyperlink.

e. At the National Parks Service home page, navigate to a particular page that interests you.
f. Close the page by clicking File and then Close.
10. Close the browser by clicking File and then Close.
11. Close the data access page, and then close the **OutdoorOptions** database file.

Creating a Database with a Wizard

Create a Database Using a Wizard
1. Click New button.
2. Click On my computer hyperlink at New File task pane.
3. Click Databases tab at Templates dialog box.
4. Double-click desired template.
5. Complete database wizard steps.

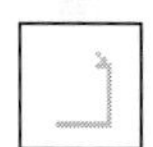

New Database

Access provides numerous database wizards you can use to create database files. These wizards include all of the fields, formatting, tables, and reports needed to manage data. Most of the work of creating the database file is done for you by the wizard. In Exercise 3, you will be using the Contact Management Database Wizard to create a contact management database file.

To see a list of available database wizards, click the New button on the Database toolbar (first button from the left). This displays the New File task pane. Click the On my computer hyperlink in the New File task pane and the Templates dialog box displays. Click the Databases tab and the dialog box displays as shown in Figure 8.3.

FIGURE 8.3 **Templates Dialog Box with Databases Tab Selected**

If your dialog box displays with fewer wizards than what you see in Figure 8.3, not all components of the Access program were installed. You may need to run the Microsoft Installation process again to include the database wizards.

HINT
Choose the wizard that creates the database that most closely meets your needs.

At the Templates dialog box with the Databases tab selected, double-click the desired wizard. This displays the File New Database dialog box. At this dialog box, type a new name for the database or accept the default name provided by Access, and then press Enter or click Create.

After a few moments, the first Database Wizard dialog box displays as shown in Figure 8.4. This dialog box shows information about the Contact Management database you will create in Exercise 3. Depending on the database you choose, this information will vary. After reading the information in the dialog box, click the Next button.

FIGURE 8.4 ***First Database Wizard Dialog Box (for Contact Management)***

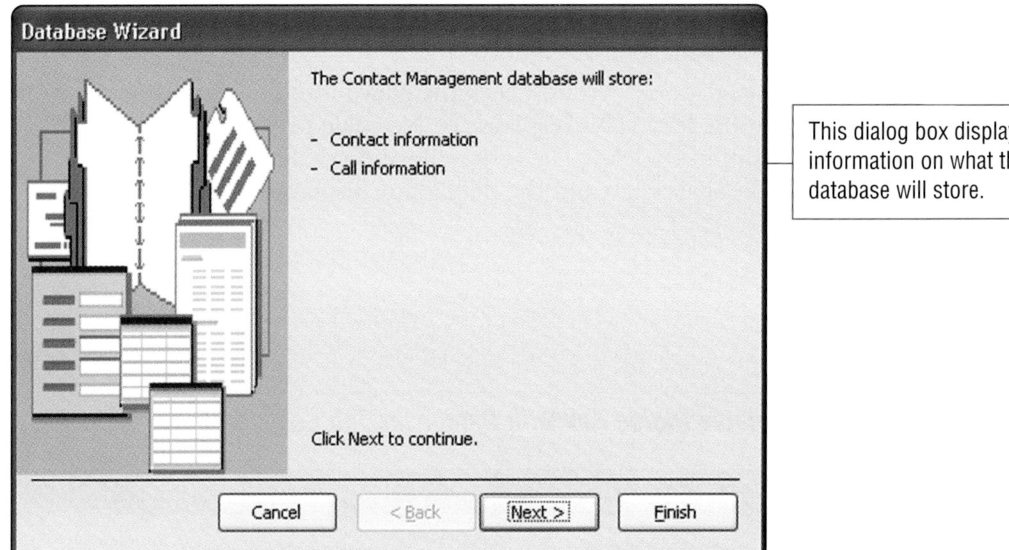

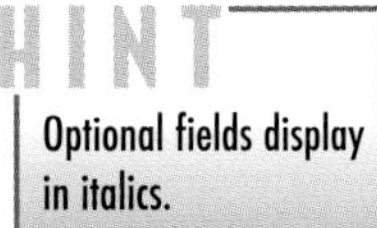

At the second Database Wizard dialog box, shown in Figure 8.5, notice how the wizard provides predesigned tables displayed in the *Tables in the database* list box and also fields displayed in the *Fields in the table* list box. Most field names in the *Fields in the table* list box are preceded by a check mark. Some database tables may include fields in the *Fields in the table* list box that display in italics with no check mark in the check box. These are additional fields that are not included as part of the table. If you want one of these extra fields included in a table, click the check box to insert a check mark. When all changes are made to this dialog box, click the Next button.

FIGURE

8.5 Second Database Wizard Dialog Box

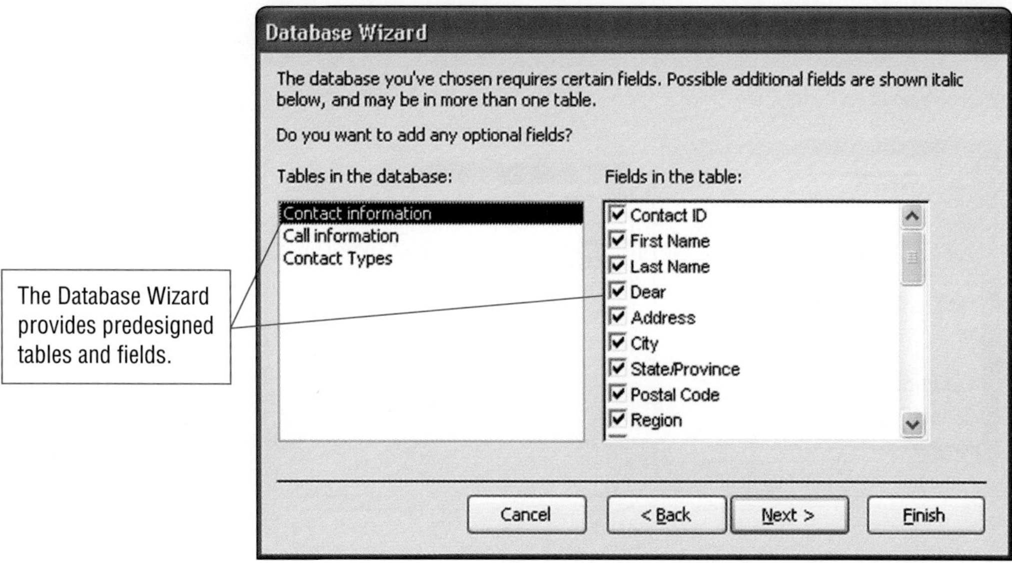

Choose a screen display at the third Database Wizard dialog box, shown in Figure 8.6. A sample displays at the left side of the dialog box. After choosing the screen display, click the Next button.

FIGURE

8.6 Third Database Wizard Dialog Box

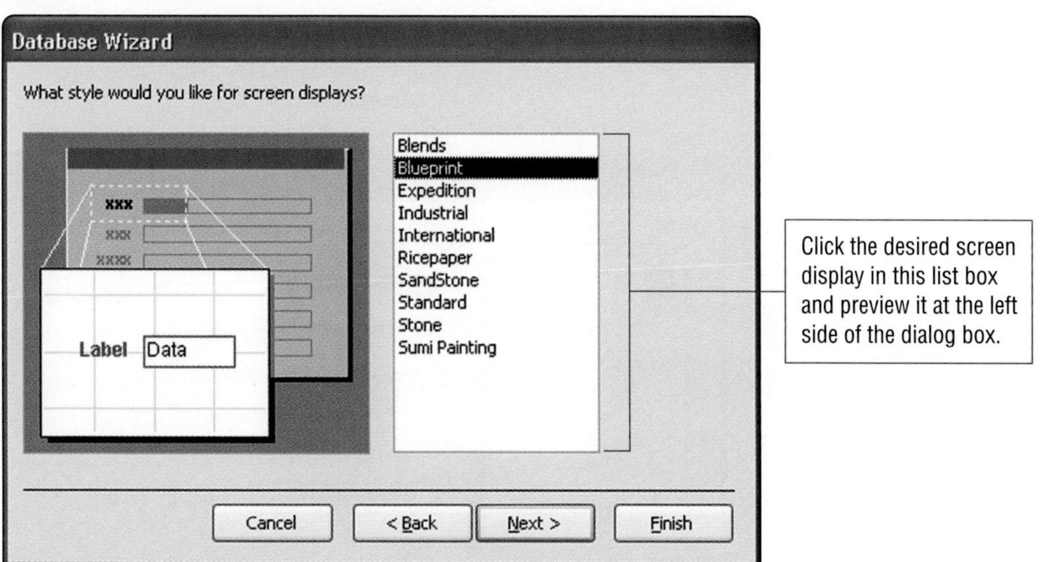

The fourth Database Wizard dialog box, shown in Figure 8.7, asks you to choose a style for printed reports. Like the previous dialog box, a sample displays at the left side of the dialog box. After choosing the style, click the Next button.

FIGURE

8.7 *Fourth Database Wizard Dialog Box*

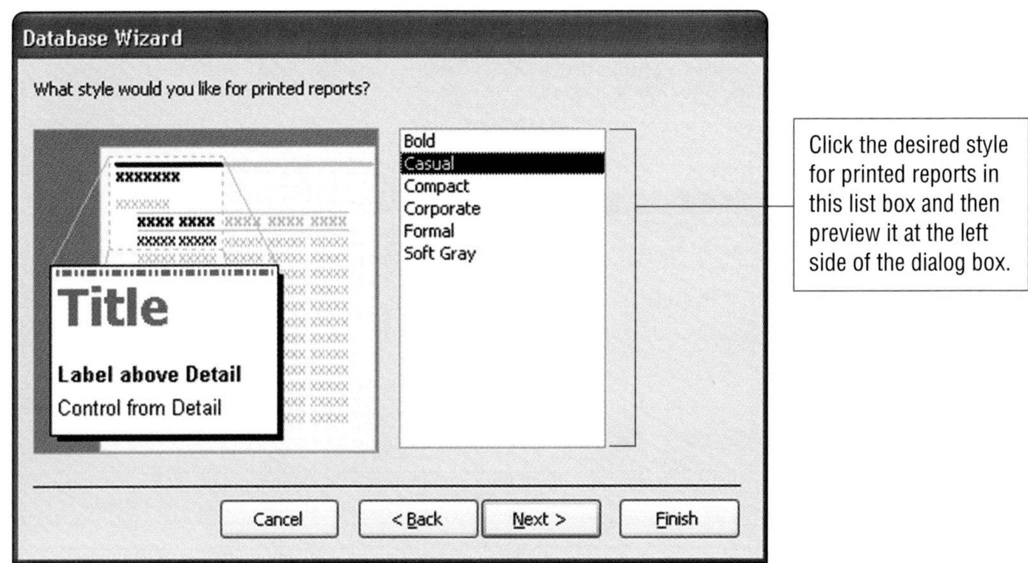

Type a name for the database or accept the default at the fifth Database Wizard dialog box shown in Figure 8.8. At this dialog box, you can also choose to include a picture in all reports. After making these decisions, click the Next button.

FIGURE

8.8 *Fifth Database Wizard Dialog Box*

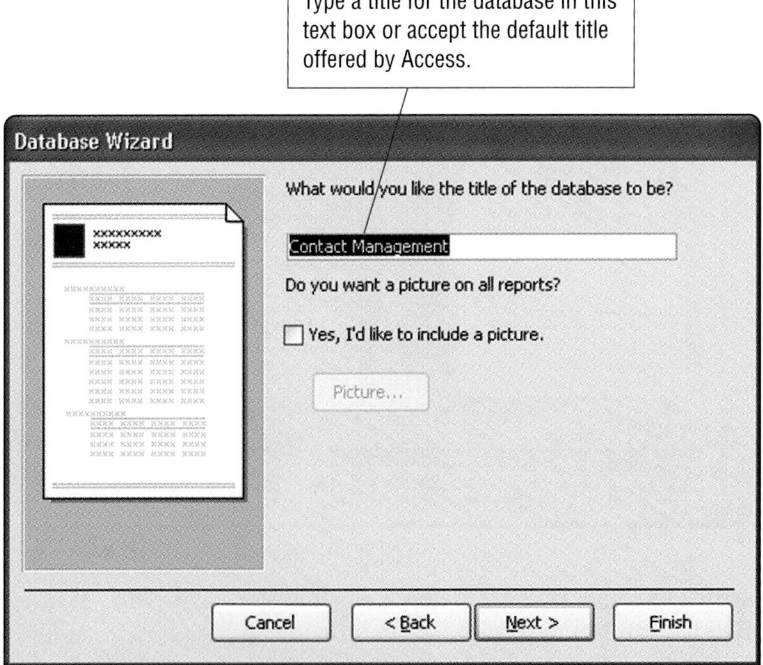

The sixth (and last) Database Wizard dialog box tells you that the wizard has all of the information it needs to build the database. By default, the database will start when the database is completed. Remove the check mark from this option if you do not want the database to start when completed. Click the Finish button and the wizard builds the database. This process can take several minutes.

When the database is completed, a Main Switchboard displays as shown in Figure 8.9, and the Database window is minimized and displays in the bottom left corner of the Access window. With options on the Switchboard, you can choose to enter or view products, enter or view other information in the database, preview reports, change the switchboard items, or exit the database. The Switchboard is intended for people who use the database rather than work on the design of the database. To bypass the Switchboard, click the Minimize button located in the upper right corner of the Switchboard title bar. Display the Database window by clicking the Maximize button located on the Database title bar.

Minimize

Maximize

FIGURE 8.9 **Main Switchboard**

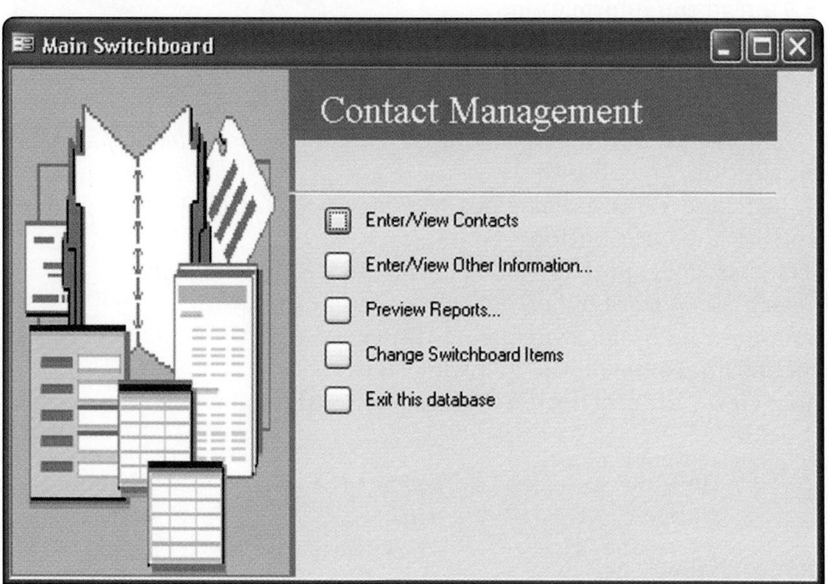

In Exercise 3, you will be creating a contact management database. When the database is completed, you will enter two records and then view some of the different database tables and forms contained in the database.

exercise 3

CREATING A CONTACT MANAGEMENT DATABASE WITH A WIZARD

(Before beginning Exercise 3, delete the OutdoorOptions database file from your disk.)

1. Create a contact management database by completing the following steps:
   a. At the blank Access screen, click the New button on the Database toolbar.
   b. Click the On my computer hyperlink in the New File task pane.
   c. At the Templates dialog box, click the Databases tab.
   d. Double-click *Contact Management* in the list box.
   e. At the File New Database dialog box, type **Contacts**, and then press Enter or click the Create button.
   f. At the first Database Wizard dialog box (see Figure 8.4), read the information, and then click the Next button.

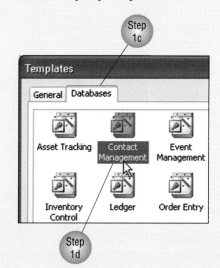

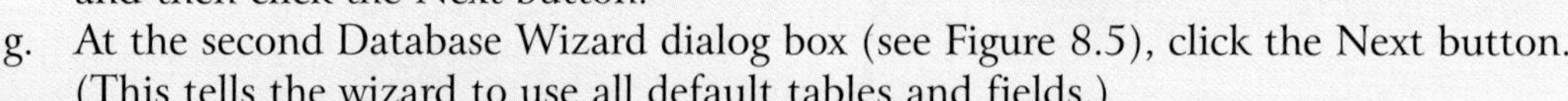

   g. At the second Database Wizard dialog box (see Figure 8.5), click the Next button. (This tells the wizard to use all default tables and fields.)
   h. At the third Database Wizard dialog box (see Figure 8.6), click *Blueprint* in the list box, and then click the Next button.
   i. At the fourth Database Wizard dialog box (see Figure 8.7), click *Casual* in the list box, and then click the Next button.
   j. At the fifth Database Wizard dialog box (see Figure 8.8), click Next.
   k. At the sixth Database Wizard dialog box, click the Finish button.
   l. After a few minutes, the Main Switchboard displays.
2. At the Main Switchboard, complete the following steps:
   a. Click the Enter/View Contacts button and then enter the following information in the specified fields:

First Name	=	**Robin**	*Contact ID*	=	(AutoNumber)
Last Name	=	**Osborn**	*Title*	=	**Manager**
Company	=	**Westside Storage**	*Work Phone*	=	**(612) 555-4550**
Dear	=	**Ms. Osborn**	*Work Extension*	=	**245**
Address	=	**403 West 22nd**	*Mobile Phone*	=	**(612) 555-1209**
City	=	**St. Cloud**	*Fax Number*	=	**(612) 555-4590**
State/Province	=	**MN**			
Postal Code	=	**55200**			
Country/Region	=	**U.S.A.**			

   b. Click the 2 button that displays toward the bottom of the record. (This displays page 2 of the record.) Enter the following information in the specified fields:

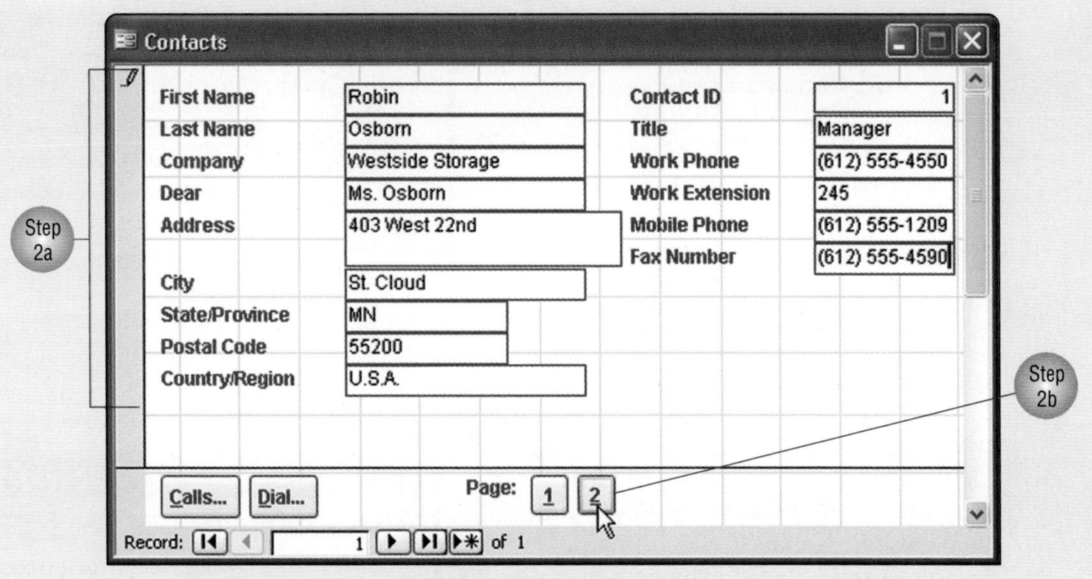

Contact Name = (Access automatically inserts *Robin Osborn*)
Contact Type = (skip this field)
Email Name = rosborn@emcp.net
Referred By = Samuel Eldred
Notes = (skip this field)

c. Click the New Record button, click the 1 button, and then type the following information in the specified fields:

First Name = Carol
Last Name = Hoyt
Company = Hoyt Construction
Dear = Ms. Hoyt
Address = 900 North 21st
City = St. Cloud
State/Province = MN
Postal Code = 55200
Country/Region = U.S.A.
Contact ID = (AutoNumber)
Title = Owner
Work Phone = (612) 555-4322
Work Extension = 10
Mobile Phone = (612) 555-4100
Fax Number = (612) 555-4201

d. Click the 2 button that displays toward the bottom of the record. (This displays page 2 of the record.) Enter the following information in the specified fields:

Contact Name = (Access automatically inserts *Carol Hoyt*)
Contact Type = (skip this field)
Email Name = choyt@emcp.net
Referred By = Jared Snyder
Notes = (skip this field)

3. Click the Save button on the toolbar to save the records.
4. Close the Contacts form.
5. Close the Main Switchboard and display the Contacts : Database window by completing the following steps:
   a. With the Main Switchboard displayed, click the Close button that displays at the right side of the dialog box title bar. (This closes the Main Switchboard and displays the minimized Contacts.)

b. Click the Restore button on the minimized Contacts title bar. (This displays the Contacts : Database window with the Forms button selected.)

6. View various tables, forms, and reports in the database file by completing the following steps:
   a. Click the Tables button on the Objects bar.
   b. Double-click *Calls* in the list box (this opens the Calls table), look at the fields in the table, and then close the table.
   c. Double-click *Contact Types* in the list box, look at the fields in the table, and then close the table.
   d. Double-click *Contacts* in the list box, look at the fields in the table, and then close the table.
   e. Click the Forms button on the Objects bar.
   f. Double-click *Contacts* in the list box, look at the layout of the form, and then close the form.
   g. Click the Reports button on the Objects bar.
   h. Double-click *Alphabetical Contact Listing* in the list box.
   i. When the report displays, print it by clicking the Print button.
   j. Close the report.

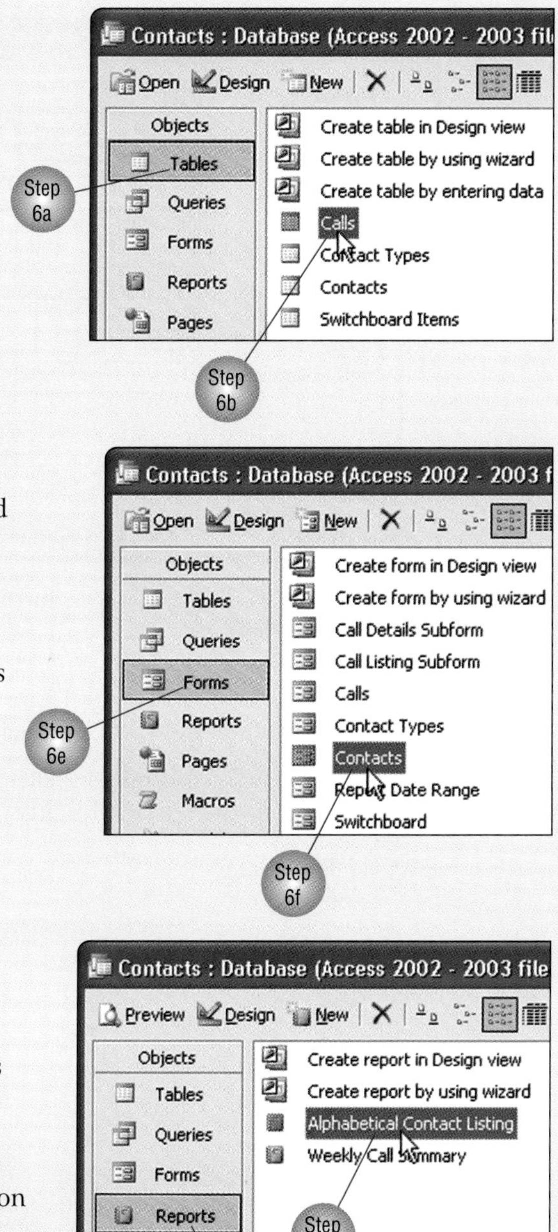

7. Investigate the relationship between tables created by the wizard by completing the following steps:
   a. With the Contacts : Database window displayed, click the Relationships button on the Database toolbar.
   b. At the Relationships window, notice the one-to-many relationship created by the wizard. View information about the relationship by completing the following steps:
      1) Position the arrow pointer on the black join line connecting *ContactID* in the Contacts table with *ContactID* in the Calls table and then click the *right* mouse button.

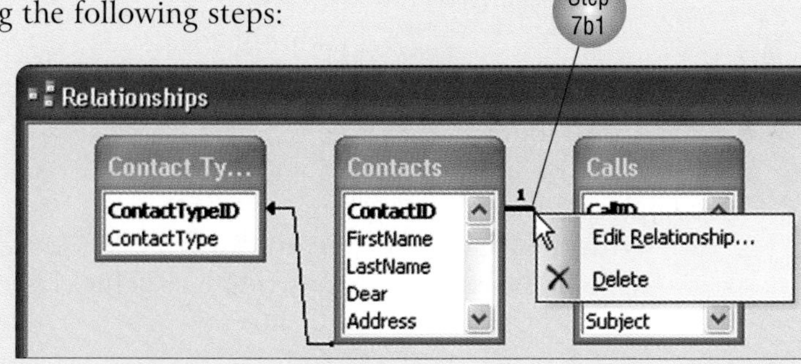

2) At the shortcut menu that displays, click Edit Relationship. This displays the Edit Relationships dialog box, which displays information on the type of relationship created between the tables.
3) After viewing the information in the Edit Relationships dialog box, click the Cancel button.

c. Click the Close button at the right side of the Relationships window title bar.

8. Close the **Contacts** database file.

Viewing a database file created by the database wizard provides you with an example of what can be included in a database file. Consider using some of the other wizards displayed in the Templates dialog box with the Databases tab selected. Each database is set up differently with different tables, forms, and reports. The sample Contacts database you created in Exercise 3 is fairly large—it will probably occupy over 1,000 kilobytes of space on your disk. For this reason, you will delete the Contacts database table.

exercise 4

DELETING THE CONTACTS DATABASE FILE

1. At the blank Access screen, click the Open button on the Database toolbar.
2. At the Open dialog box, click ***Contacts*** in the list box, and then click the Delete button on the dialog box toolbar.
3. At the message asking if you are sure you want to delete the database file, click Yes.
4. Click Cancel to close the Open dialog box.

CHAPTER summary

- Make Access data available for viewing on the Internet or on a company's intranet by saving the data as a data access page.
- Data saved as a Web page can be viewed in the default browser, formatting can be applied to a data access page, and hyperlinks can be inserted.
- Apply theme formatting to a Web page with options at the Theme dialog box.
- Preview a Web page in the default browser by clicking File and then Web Page Preview.
- One method for displaying the Insert Hyperlink dialog box is to click the Hyperlink button on the Toolbox and then drag to create a box.
- Access provides numerous database wizards that will create a variety of database files including all of the fields, formatting, tables, and reports needed to manage the data.
- Database wizards are displayed in the Templates dialog box with the Databases tab selected.
- A database file created with a wizard can be modified.

FEATURES summary

FEATURE	BUTTON	MENU	KEYBOARD
New File task pane		File, New	Ctrl + N
Templates dialog box		File, New, On my computer	
Theme dialog box		Format, Theme	
Preview Web page		File, Web Page Preview	
Hyperlink dialog box		Insert, Hyperlink	Ctrl + K

CONCEPTS check

Completion: On a blank sheet of paper, indicate the correct term, symbol, or command for each description.

1. Make Access data available for viewing on the Internet or on a company's intranet by saving the data as this.
2. Review a Web page in the default browser by clicking File and then this.
3. Display a list of database wizards by displaying the Templates dialog box with this tab selected.
4. To display the New File task pane, click this button on the Database toolbar.
5. When a database wizard is done creating a database, this displays giving you options for entering or viewing information in the database, previewing reports, changing items, or exiting the database.
6. Delete a database file at this dialog box.
7. List the steps you would complete to create a sample database with the Ledger Database Wizard.

SKILLS check

Assessment 1

1. Copy the **Hilltop** database file from the CD that accompanies this textbook to your disk and then remove the read-only attribute from **Hilltop**.
2. Create a Web page using the data access Page Wizard with the fields from the Inventory table. (You determine the title of the page.)
3. Apply a theme of your choosing to the page.
4. Change to the Page view.
5. Save the data access page and name it **InventoryWebPage**.
6. View the page in the default Web browser, use navigation buttons along the bottom of the window to display various records, and then close the browser.
7. Close the data access page and then close the **Hilltop** database file.

Assessment 2

1. Open the **Hilltop** database file.
2. Create a Web page using the data access Page Wizard with the fields from the Customers table. (You determine the title of the page.)
3. Apply a theme of your choosing to the page.
4. Add a hyperlink to the page that will allow the user to jump to the City of Denver Web site at www.denvergov.org. (You determine the location of the hyperlink.)
5. Add a hyperlink to the page that will allow the user to jump to the State of Colorado Web site at www.state.co.us. (You determine the location of the hyperlink.)
6. Change to the Page view.
7. Save the access data page and name it **CustomersWebPage**.
8. View the page in the default Web browser, use navigation buttons along the bottom of the window to display various records, and then click each hyperlink to jump to the specified Web site.
9. Close the browser, close the data access page, and then close the **Hilltop** database file.

Assessment 3

1. Use the Expenses Database Wizard to create a database with the following specifications:
   a. At the File New Database dialog box, type **Expenses** as the database file name.
   b. At the third Database Wizard dialog box, you determine the type of screen display.
   c. At the fourth Database Wizard dialog box, you determine the style for reports.
2. When the database file is completed and the Main Switchboard displays, enter information on expenses for one employee by completing the following steps:
   a. Click the Enter/View Expense Reports by Employee button that displays in the Main Switchboard.
   b. At the Expense Reports by Employee dialog box, type the following in the specified fields (you will be skipping many of the fields):

      First Name = **Nina**
      Last Name = **Schueller**
      Title = **Manager**
      Employee # = **210**

   c. Click the Expense Report Form button that displays in the lower left corner of the dialog box.

d. At the Expense Reports dialog box, type the following in the specified fields (you will be skipping fields):

Exp Rpt Name	=	Marketing Seminar
Exp Rpt Descr	=	Two-day Marketing Seminar
Dept Charged	=	Marketing Department
Date Submitted	=	5/14/05

e. Create three expense categories by completing the following steps:
   1) Double-click in the first box below the *Expense Category* heading (located toward the bottom of the dialog box). (This displays the Expense Categories dialog box.)
   2) At the Expense Categories dialog box, enter the following three records:

Expense Category	=	Airfare
Expense Account#	=	10
Expense Category	=	Meals
Expense Account#	=	20
Expense Category	=	Lodging
Expense Account#	=	30

f. After entering the third record, click the Close button to close the Expense Categories dialog box.
g. At the Expense Reports dialog box, enter the following in the specified fields (located toward the bottom of the dialog box):

Expense Date	=	05/10/05
Expense Category	=	Airfare
Description	=	Airline ticket
Amount	=	850
Expense Date	=	05/11/05
Expense Category	=	Meals
Description	=	Daily meals
Amount	=	52
Expense Date	=	05/12/05
Expense Category	=	Meals
Description	=	Daily meals
Amount	=	48
Expense Date	=	05/12/05
Expense Category	=	Lodging
Description	=	Hotel
Amount	=	220

h. Click the Preview Report button located in the lower left corner of the dialog box.
i. When the report displays, print the report by clicking the Print button on the Print Preview toolbar.
j. Close the Expense Report report.
k. Close the Expense Reports form.
l. Close the Expense Reports by Employee form.

3. View the relationships between tables by completing the following steps:
   a. Close the Main Switchboard.
   b. Click the Restore button on the minimized **Expenses** database file.
   c. With the Expenses : Database window displayed, click the Relationships button on the Database toolbar.
   d. After viewing the relationships between tables, click the Close button to close the Relationships window.
   e. Display a few tables and forms to see how the data is organized.
4. Close the **Expenses** database file.
5. Delete the **Expenses** database file.

Assessment 4

1. You can get help for Microsoft Office 2003 programs, such as Access, using the Help feature. Assistance is also available from resources on the Web. Use the Access Help feature to learn about the Help resources available on the Web.
2. After reading the information on Web resources, make sure you are connected to the Internet and then visit at least one Web site that provides information on Microsoft Office 2003. Print at least one page from a site you visit.
3. Create a Word document explaining the resources available. Save the document and name it **WebResources**. Print and then close **WebResources**.

CHAPTER challenge

You work in the business department at a large computer corporation, Computers R Us. Sales representatives from various departments within the corporation are responsible for completing their own expense reports. To ensure consistency and increase efficiency, you decide to create a database that contains expense reports that could be used by these sales reps. Create a new database based on the Expenses Wizard. Choose appropriate fields for each of the tables and select styles and formats of your own. Enter information about yourself in the expense report and then print it. To give sales reps easier access to these forms, you decide to post the expense report to the company's intranet. To do this, you will create a data access page based on the Expense Reports table. Format the data page so that it is attractive and easily understood.

In the database created in the first part of the Chapter Challenge, a switchboard was generated as well. You decide that one of the titles on the switchboard could be better identified. Use the Help feature to learn about customizing switchboards. Then customize the switchboard created in the Expenses database by changing the text of item 4, "Change Switchboard Items" to "Modify Switchboard Items".

One of the supervisors has requested an expense report for a particular sales rep in the software department. Send the expense report created in the first part of the Chapter Challenge as an attachment to the supervisor (your professor). Provide the necessary information in the subject line and in the message of the e-mail.

Client #: 4419
Lorena Hearron
3112 96th Street East
Philadelphia, PA 19132
(215) 555-3281
Date of Birth: 07/02/1984
Diagnosis ID: AD

Client #: 1103
Raymond Mandato
631 Garden Boulevard
Jenkintown, PA 19209
(215) 555-0957
Date of Birth: 09/20/1974
Diagnosis ID: MDD

3. Adjust the column widths and then save the Clients database table.
4. Change the page orientation to landscape, print, and then close the Clients database table.
5. Create a database table named Diagnoses that includes the following fields (you determine the data type, field size, and description):

   Diagnosis ID (primary key)
   Diagnosis

6. After creating the database table, save it, switch to Datasheet view, and then enter the following data in the appropriate fields:

   Diagnosis ID = AD
   Diagnosis = Adjustment Disorder

   Diagnosis ID = MDD
   Diagnosis = Manic-Depressive Disorder

   Diagnosis ID = OCD
   Diagnosis = Obsessive-Compulsive Disorder

   Diagnosis ID = SC
   Diagnosis = Schizophrenia

7. Adjust the column widths, print, and then close the table.
8. Create a database table named Fees that includes the following fields (you determine the data type, field size, and description):

   Fee Code (primary key)
   Hourly Fee

9. After creating the database table, save it, switch to Datasheet view, and then enter the following data in the appropriate fields:

   Fee Code = A
   Hourly Fee = $75.00

   Fee Code = B
   Hourly Fee = $80.00

   Fee Code = C
   Hourly Fee = $85.00

   Fee Code = D
   Hourly Fee = $90.00

   Fee Code = E
   Hourly Fee = $95.00

   Fee Code = F
   Hourly Fee = $100.00

Fee Code	=	G
Hourly Fee	=	$105.00
Fee Code	=	H
Hourly Fee	=	$110.00

10. Save, print, and then close the Fees table.
11. Create a database table named Employees that includes the following fields (you determine the data type, field size, and description):

    Provider # (primary key)
    Provider Name
    Title
    Extension

12. After creating the database table, save it, switch to Datasheet view, and then enter the following data in the appropriate fields:

    Provider #: 29
    Provider Name: James Schouten
    Title: Psychologist
    Extension: 399

    Provider #: 15
    Provider Name: Lynn Yee
    Title: Child Psychologist
    Extension: 102

    Provider #: 33
    Provider Name: Janice Grisham
    Title: Psychiatrist
    Extension: 11

    Provider #: 18
    Provider Name: Craig Chilton
    Title: Psychologist
    Extension: 20

13. Adjust the column widths and then save the Employees database table.
14. Print and then close the Employees database table.
15. Create a database table named Billing that includes the following fields (you determine the data type, field size, and description):

    Billing # (primary key; identify the data type as *AutoNumber*)
    Client #
    Date of Service
    Insurer
    Provider #
    Hours
    Fee Code

16. After creating the database table, save it, switch to Datasheet view, and then enter the following data in the appropriate fields:

    Client #: 4419
    Date of Service: 03/01/2005
    Insurer: Health Plus
    Provider #: 15
    Hours: 2
    Fee Code: B

    Client #: 1831
    Date of Service: 03/01/2005
    Insurer: Self
    Provider #: 33
    Hours: 1
    Fee Code: H

    Client #: 3219
    Date of Service: 03/02/2005
    Insurer: Health Plus
    Provider #: 15
    Hours: 1
    Fee Code: D

    Client #: 2874
    Date of Service: 03/02/2005
    Insurer: Penn-State Health
    Provider #: 18
    Hours: 2
    Fee Code: C

Client #: 4419
Date of Service: 03/03/2005
Insurer: Health Plus
Provider #: 15
Hours: 1
Fee Code: A

Client #: 1103
Date of Service: 03/04/2005
Insurer: Penn-State Health
Provider #: 18
Hours: 0.5
Fee Code: A

Client #: 1831
Date of Service: 03/04/2005
Insurer: Self
Provider #: 33
Hours: 1
Fee Code: H

Client #: 2874
Date of Service: 03/04/2005
Insurer: Penn-State Health
Provider #: 18
Hours: 0.5
Fee Code: C

17. Adjust the column widths and then save the Billing database table.
18. Print and then close the Billing database table.

Assessment 2

1. With the **LancasterClinic** database file open, create the following one-to-many relationships (enforcing referential integrity and cascading fields and records):
   a. *Client #* in the Clients table is the "one" and *Client #* in the Billing table is the "many."
   b. *Diagnosis ID* in the Diagnoses table is the "one" and *Diagnosis ID* in the Clients table is the "many."
   c. *Provider #* in the Employees table is the "one" and *Provider #* in the Billing table is the "many."
   d. *Fee Code* in the Fees table is the "one" and *Fee Code* in the Billing table is the "many."
2. Use the AutoForm feature to create a form with the data in the Clients database table.
3. After creating the form, add the following record to the Clients form:

   Client #: 1179
   Timothy Fierro
   1133 Tenth Southwest
   Philadelphia, PA 19178
   (215) 555-5594
   Date of Birth: 12/07/1987
   Diagnosis ID: AD

4. Save the form as Clients, print the form, and then close the form.
5. Add the following records to the Billing database table:

   Client #: 1179
   Date of Service: 03/08/2005
   Insurer: Health Plus
   Provider #: 15
   Hours: 0.5
   Fee Code: C

   Client #: 1831
   Date of Service: 03/09/2005
   Insurer: Self
   Provider #: 33
   Hours: 1
   Fee Code: H

6. Save and then print the Billing database table.
7. Close the Billing database table.

Assessment 3

1. With the **LancasterClinic** database file open, create a form with fields from related database tables using the Form Wizard with the following specifications:
   a. At the first Form Wizard dialog box, insert the following fields in the *Selected Fields* list box:

      From the Clients database table:

      Client #
      Date of Birth
      Diagnosis ID

      From the Billing database table:

      Insurer
      Provider #

   b. Do not make any changes at the second Form Wizard dialog box.
   c. Do not make any changes at the third Form Wizard dialog box.
   d. You determine the format style at the fourth Form Wizard dialog box.
   e. At the fifth Form Wizard dialog box, type the name **ProviderInformation**.
2. When the first record displays, print the form.
3. Close the record that displays.

Assessment 4

1. With the **LancasterClinic** database file open, create a query in Design view with the following specifications:
   a. Add the Billing, Employees, and Clients tables to the design grid.
   b. Add the following fields from the specified tables:

Date of Service	=	Billing table
Provider #	=	Employees table
Client #	=	Clients table
Hours	=	Billing table

   c. Run the query.
   d. Save the query and name it ProviderHours.
2. Display the query in PivotTable view.
3. At the PivotTable layout, drag and drop the fields as follows:
   a. Drag the *Provider #* field to the *Drop Row Fields Here* section.
   b. Drag the *Client #* field to the *Drop Column Fields Here* section.
   c. Drag the *Hours* field to the *Drop Totals or Detail Fields Here* section.
   d. Drag the *Date of Service* field to the *Drop Filter Fields Here* section.
4. Remove the PivotTable Field List box from the screen.
5. Click the Print button to print the query in PivotTable view.
6. In the *Provider #* field, display only the hours for provider number 15.
7. Print the PivotTable and then redisplay all providers.
8. In the *Date of Service* field, display only hours for provider hours for March 1, 2005.
9. Print the PivotTable and then redisplay all rental dates.
10. Switch to Datasheet view, save, and then close the query.

Assessment 5

1. Open the **LancasterClinic** database file.
2. Use the Label Wizard to create mailing labels (you determine the label type) with the client names and addresses and sorted by ZIP Code. Name the mailing label file **ClientMailingLabels**.
3. Print the mailing labels.
4. Close the mailing labels file and then close the **LancasterClinic** database file.

Assessment 6

1. Open the **LancasterClinic** database file.
2. Create an Excel worksheet with the Billing database table, with the following specifications:
   a. In Excel, select the cells in the worksheet containing data and then apply an autoformat of your choosing.
   b. Print the worksheet centered horizontally and vertically on the page.
   c. Save the worksheet. (Excel will automatically name it **Billing**.)
3. Exit Excel.
4. Close the **LancasterClinic** database file.

Assessment 7

1. Open the **LancasterClinic** database file.
2. Merge data in the Clients database table to a blank Word screen. ***(Hint: Use the Merge It with Microsoft Office Word option from the OfficeLinks drop-down menu.)*** You determine the fields to use in the inside address and an appropriate salutation. Type March 10, 2005 as the date of the letter and type the following text in the body of the document:

   > **The building of a new wing for the Lancaster Clinic will begin April 1, 2005. We are excited about this new addition to our clinic. With the new facilities, we will be able to offer additional community and group services along with enhanced child-play therapy treatment.**
   >
   > **During the construction, the main entrance will be moved to the north end of the building. Please use this entrance until the construction of the wing is completed. We apologize in advance for any inconvenience this causes you.**

   Include an appropriate complimentary close for the letter. Use the name and title *Marianne Lambert, Clinic Director* for the signature and add your reference initials and the document name (Wordsau2pa07).
3. Merge to a new document and then save the document with the name **Wordsau2pa07**.
4. Print the first two letters of the document and then close **Wordsau2pa07**.
5. Save the main document as **ConstructionLetter** and then close **ConstructionLetter**.
6. Exit Word and then close the **LancasterClinic** database file.

Assessment 8

1. Open the **LancasterClinic** database file.
2. Click the Tables button on the Objects bar.
3. Import **ExcelWorksheet03** into a new table named StaffHours. (Use the Import Spreadsheet Wizard to do this.)
4. Open the StaffHours table in Datasheet view.
5. Print and then close the StaffHours table.
6. Use the Form Wizard to create a form with the following specifications:
   a. Use all of the fields from the StaffHours table.
   b. You determine the layout and the style of the form.
   c. Name the form StaffWages.
   d. When the form is completed, change to Design view and add the following:
      1) Add a calculated control that multiplies the Hours by the Rate. (Name this calculated control Wages.)
      2) Format the calculated control text box so that the format is changed to *Currency* and the decimal places option is set to 2.
      3) Insert the company name, *Lancaster Clinic*, in the Form Header and increase the size of the company name (you determine the size).
      4) Make any other changes you feel are necessary to create an attractive form.
   e. Change to the Form view.
   f. Print only the first record in the form.
   g. Close the StaffWages form.
7. Close the **LancasterClinic** database file.

Assessment 9

1. Open the **LancasterClinic** database file.
2. Create a Web page using the data access Page Wizard with the fields from the Billing table. (You determine the title of the page.)
3. Apply a theme of your choosing to the page.
4. Change to the Page view.
5. Save the data access page and name it **BillingWebPage**.
6. View the page in the default Web browser, use navigation buttons along the bottom of the window to display various records, and then close the browser.
7. Close the data access page and then close the **LancasterClinic** database file.

WRITING activities

The following activities give you the opportunity to practice your writing skills along with demonstrating an understanding of some of the important Access features you have mastered in this unit. Use correct grammar, appropriate word choices, and clear sentence constructions.

Activity 1

The director at Lancaster Clinic has asked you to add information to the **LancasterClinic** database file on insurance companies contracted by the clinic. You need to create another database table that will contain information on insurance companies. The director wants the database table to include the insurance company name, address, city, state, and ZIP Code along with a telephone number and a name of a representative. You determine the field names, data types, field sizes, and description for the database table and then include the following information (in the appropriate fields):

Health Plus
4102 22nd Street
Philadelphia, PA 19166
(212) 555-0990
Representative: Byron Tolleson

Penn-State Health
5933 Lehigh Avenue
Philadelphia, PA 19148
(212) 555-3477
Representative: Tracey Pavone

Quality Medical
51 Cecil B. Moore Avenue
Philadelphia, PA 19168
(212) 555-4600
Representative: Lee Stafford

Delaware Health
4418 Front Street
Philadelphia, PA 19132
(212) 555-6770
Representative: Melanie Chon

Print the insurance company database table. Create a form with the insurance company database table and then print the form.

Open Word and then write a report to the clinic director detailing how you created the database table. Include a title for the report, steps on how the database table was created, and any other pertinent information. Save the completed report and name it **sau2act01**. Print and then close **sau2act01**.

Activity 2

Merge data in the insurance company database table to a blank Word screen. You determine the fields to use in the inside address and an appropriate salutation. Compose a letter to the insurance companies informing them that Lancaster Clinic is providing mental health counseling services to people with health insurance through their company. You are sending an informational brochure about Lancaster Clinic and are requesting information from the insurance companies on services and service limitations. Include an appropriate complimentary close for the letter. Use the name and title *Marianne Lambert, Clinic Director* for the signature and add your reference initials. When the merge is completed, name the document containing the merged letters **sau2act02**. Print the first two letters in the merged document and then close **sau2act02**. Close the main document without saving it and then exit Word. Close the insurance company database table and then close the **LancasterClinic** database file.

INTERNET project

Health Information Search

In this activity, you will search the Internet for information on a health concern or disease that interests you. You will be looking for specific organizations, interest groups, or individuals who are somehow connected to the topic you have chosen. It may be an organization that raises money to support research, it may be a support group that posts information or answers questions, or you may find information about clinics or doctors who specialize in your topic. Try to find at least ten different groups that support the health concern you are researching.

Record information about the organizations you found in your database. Create a database file in Access and create a table in that file to store the results of your search. Design the table so that you can store the name, address, phone number, and Web address of the organizations you find. You will also want to identify the connection the group has to your topic (supports research, interest group, treats patients, etc.). Create a report to summarize your findings. In Microsoft Word, create a letter that could be used to write for further information about the organization. Then use the names and addresses in your database to merge with the letter. Select and then print the first two letters that result from the merge. Finally, write a paragraph describing information you found out about the health concern while searching the Web that you previously did not know.

JOB study

City Improvement Projects

In this activity, you are working with the city council in your area to keep the public informed of the progress being made on improvement projects throughout the city. These projects are paid for through tax dollars voted on by the public, and the city council feels that an informed public leads to a good voter turnout when it is time to make more improvements.

Your job is to create a database file and a table in the database that will store the following information for each project: a project ID number, a description of the project, the budgeted dollar amount to be spent, the amount spent so far, the amount of time allocated to the project, and the amount of time spent so far. Enter five city improvement projects into the table (sample data created by you). Create a query based on the table that calculates the percent of budgeted dollars spent so far and the percent of budgeted time spent so far. Generate a report that will include a chart showing the percentages of dollars and time spent so far for each project. Finally, save the report as a Web page to be viewed by the public. Include an attractive theme and a link to your city's home Web site (or a city of your choice).

INDEX

SPECIALIST

MICROSOFT® POWERPOINT

Being an effective communicator is one of the most marketable job skills you can possess. Whether your audience is a few colleagues in a small meeting room or a larger gathering in a conference center, you can enhance your message through the use of visual aids created with presentation software. Microsoft PowerPoint 2003 is the presentation graphics program included in the Microsoft Office 2003 suite. Content created in PowerPoint can be projected through a computer to a large screen or output in various formats, including slides, transparencies, or hard copy.

Organizing Information

Microsoft PowerPoint offers several views in which you can organize the content of your topic. Each view is suited for specific tasks, but you can choose to work in the view in which you are most comfortable. For example, use Normal View with the Outline tab selected if you have a lot of typing to do. Switch to Slide Sorter View to rearrange several slides by dragging slide miniatures to new positions in the presentation. Use Notes Page View to add speaker notes to your slides. Insert and position graphics in Normal View with the Slides tab selected. Preview the presentation in Slide Show View.

Organize your content and slides in the various views available in Microsoft PowerPoint.

SPECIALIST

Making PowerPoint Work for YOU!

Changing a format or color used in a design template is made easier with the use of *slide masters*. Open a slide in Slide Master View to make global changes—changes you want applied to all slides. Changes can be made before or after content has been added. A slide master can also be used to add a graphic object, such as a company logo, to the same position in each slide. Use slide masters whenever possible to reduce the number of steps needed to make changes to all slides in a presentation.

Analyzing Information

In today's global workplace, it is very common for two or more people to collaborate on a presentation. PowerPoint includes the ability to send a presentation for review by others either by e-mail or by placing copies of the presentation on a network share folder. Use options on the Reviewing toolbar to add, edit, and delete comments, and accept and reject changes made by multiple authors. As an alternative, use the compare and merge presentations option to combine changes made in two copies of a presentation.

Editing slides by rearranging the progression of content is easily accomplished using a drag and drop technique in either Slide Sorter View or Outline View. Use the Spelling feature to help find common misspellings. Everyone remembers the speaker with the slides that had typos. Make sure your audience remembers you for the brilliant insight you gave about your topic and not for the typing errors!

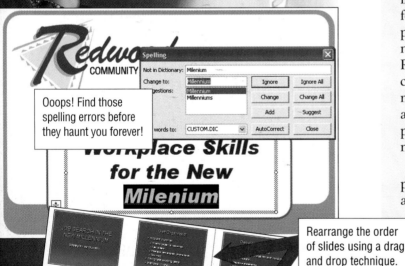

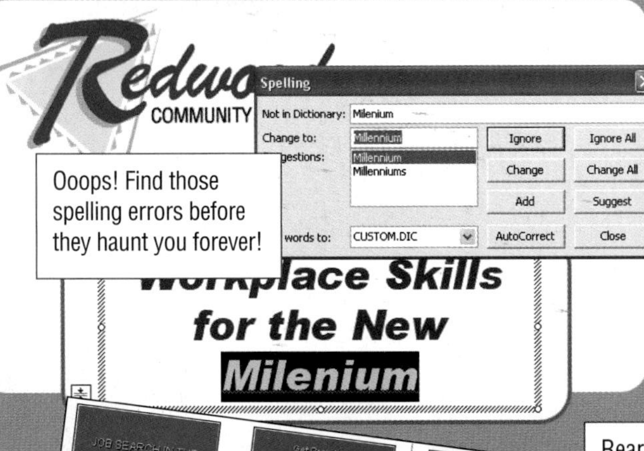

Use the Rehearse Timings feature to set up a self-running presentation that has to synchronize times in which to advance slides. Turn on the Rehearsal toolbar in Slide Sorter View and with the timer turned on, use the buttons on the toolbar to set the appropriate amount of time each slide should display on the screen.

Presenting Information

Creating an eye-catching, thought-provoking presentation has never been easier. Microsoft PowerPoint includes several professionally designed templates that you can easily apply to your content. You don't have to be knowledgeable about choosing complementary colors or scaling font sizes for readability to create a background or interesting bullet style—templates have all of these features incorporated for you. Open the Slide Design task pane and then browse the reduced-size template previews until you find one that intrigues you. Click the template style and it is instantly applied to your presentation. Want to preview more designs? Click the template that says *Design Templates on Microsoft Office Online* to browse the Web site where additional templates can be downloaded. This site is constantly updated, so check back often for creative new offerings.

No one wants to sit and watch a presentation that is filled only with text, text, and more text! Add interest to your presentation by inserting objects such as clip art, pictures, photographs, movies, sounds, and more. Display the Clip Art task pane and search both your computer's media Gallery and the Microsoft Office Online Gallery for the right media clip to spruce up that text-only slide.

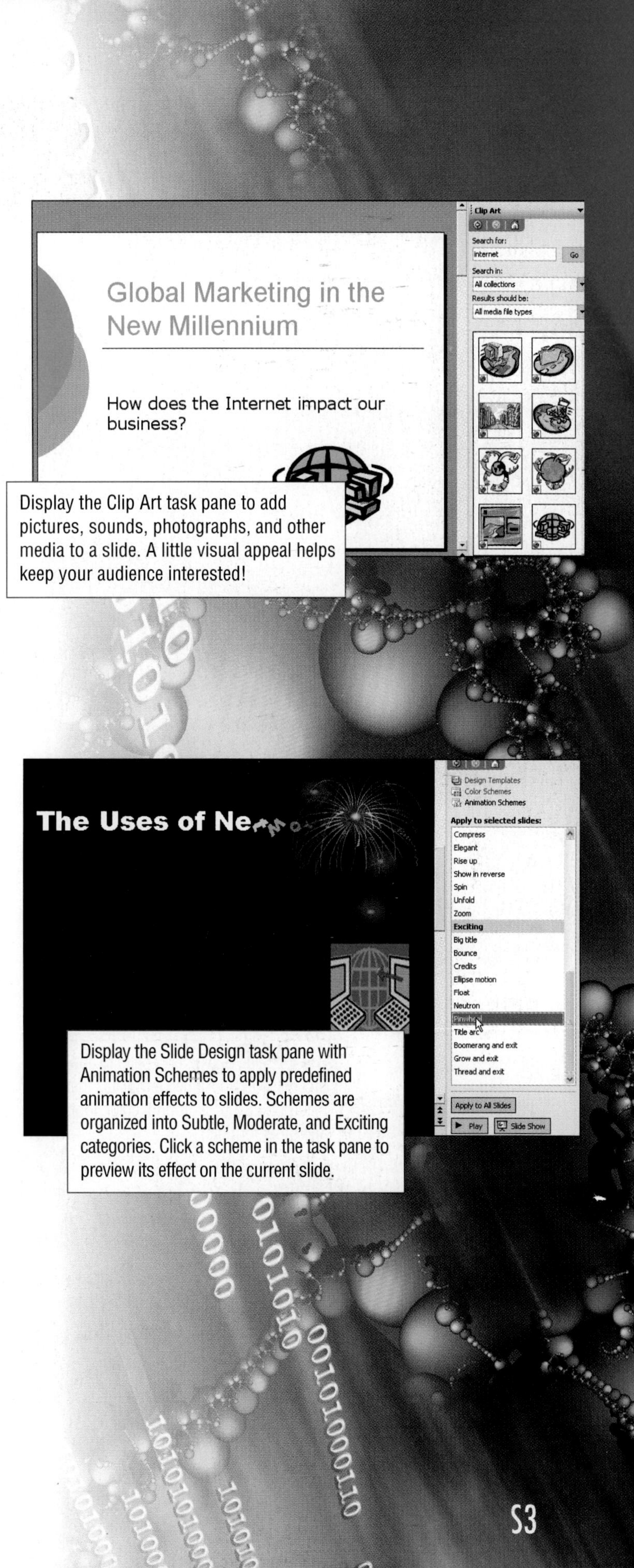

Display the Clip Art task pane to add pictures, sounds, photographs, and other media to a slide. A little visual appeal helps keep your audience interested!

Display the Slide Design task pane with Animation Schemes to apply predefined animation effects to slides. Schemes are organized into Subtle, Moderate, and Exciting categories. Click a scheme in the task pane to preview its effect on the current slide.

Global Marketing in the New Millennium
How does the Internet impact our business?
Global Marketing in the New Millennium
How does the Internet impact our business?
Global Marketing in the New Millennium
How does the Internet impact our business?
Global Marketing in the New Millennium
How does the Internet impact our business?

Use the Slide Design task pane to apply professionally designed templates that incorportate a background, color, font, and other formats.

After adding clip art or photographs to your slides, consider adding animation effects to maintain audience interest, create focus, or signal changes in content. Microsoft PowerPoint includes animation schemes that provide preset effects to simplify the process. Animation can be applied to all slides or individual slides within the presentation.

Set up your slide show presentation by creating a custom show. Add or modify action buttons to control slide progression or hide slides that you do not want the audience to view. On the day you are to deliver your presentation, use the slide show features to advance slides and use the pointer options to focus attention on a slide element by drawing with a ballpoint pen, felt tip pen, or highlighter.

Get started and have fun learning to use Microsoft PowerPoint. You will soon be amazing audiences with your ability to produce effective and visually appealing presentations that help make your point!

SPECIALIST

MICROSOFT®

POWERPOINT

UNIT 1: Creating and Formatting PowerPoint Presentations

Benchmark MICROSOFT® POWERPOINT 2003

MICROSOFT OFFICE POWERPOINT 2003 SPECIALIST SKILLS – UNIT 1

Reference No.	Skill	Pages
PP03S-1	**Creating Content**	
PP03S-1-1	Create new presentations from templates	
	Create a presentation using a design template	S9-S13
	Create a presentation using the AutoContent Wizard	S27-S28
	Create a blank presentation	S73-S75
PP03S-1-2	Insert and edit text-based content	
	Insert, edit, and delete text in slides	S39-S42
	Rearrange text in slides	S42-S47
	Complete a spelling check	S43-S45
	Use Thesaurus	S43-S45
PP03S-1-4	Insert pictures, shapes and graphics	
	Insert and format objects, autoshapes, and text boxes	S91-S103
	Insert clip art images	S103-S107
	Insert a bitmapped image	S110-S111
PP03S-2	**Formatting Content**	
PP03S-2-1	Format text-based content	
	Change text font typeface, style, size and color	S61-S67
	Increase/decrease paragraphs spacing	S63-S67
	Change text alignment	S61-S62, S95
	Change alignment of text in columns	S97, S100-S101
PP03S-2-2	Format pictures, shapes and graphics	
	Select, move, copy, delete, size, and format objects, autoshapes, and text boxes	S91-S103
	Format images using buttons on the Picture toolbar	S108-S109
PP03S-2-3	Format slides	
	Apply a design template	S11-S12, S16
	Change the design template	S72
	Choose a slide layout	S13, S16
	Format and customize slide color scheme and background color	S69-S72
	Modify page setup	S14, S18
PP03S-2-4	Apply animation schemes	
	Apply an animation scheme	S111-S112
	Customize an animation scheme	S112-S114
PP03S-2-5	Apply slide transitions	S24-S27
PP03S-2-7	Work with masters	
	Format a slide master and title master	S64-S67
	Arrange placeholders on slide	S42, S46
	Apply more than one design template and work with multiple slide masters	S67-S69
	Insert headers and footers	S78-S80
PP03S-4	**Managing and Delivering Presentations**	
PP03S-4-1	Organize a presentation	
	Insert, delete, copy, and move slides	S48-S51
	View a presentation in Normal, Slide Sorter, Notes Page and Slide Show views	S18-S19, S22-S24
	Display rulers, guide lines, and grid lines	S98-S103
PP03S-4-2	Set up slide shows for delivery	
	Hide and unhide slides	S81-S83
PP03S-4-4	Deliver presentations	
	Run a slide show	S19-S24
	Use the pen and highlighter when running a presentation	S21-S24
	Run a show automatically	S26-S27
PP03S-4-5	Prepare presentations for remote delivery	
PP03S-4-6	Save and publish presentations	
	Save a presentation	S15, S17-S18
	Save a presentation with a different name	S25
PP03S-4-7	Print slides, outlines, handouts, and speaker notes	
	Print a presentation	S14
	Print a presentation as handouts	S18
	Print a presentation as an outline	S22
	Print a presentation as notes pages	S31
	Print speakers notes	S81-S82
	Preview a presentation	S48-S51

1

PREPARING A POWERPOINT PRESENTATION

PERFORMANCE OBJECTIVES

Upon successful completion of Chapter 1, you will be able to:

- **Plan a PowerPoint presentation**
- **Create a PowerPoint presentation**
- **Print a PowerPoint presentation**
- **Save, open, and close presentations**
- **View a presentation**
- **Run a presentation**
- **Add transitions and sound effects to a presentation**
- **Run a slide show automatically**
- **Prepare a presentation in Outline view**
- **Delete a presentation**

During a presentation, the person doing the presenting may use visual aids to strengthen the impact of the message as well as help organize the presentation. Visual aids may include transparencies, slides, photographs, or an on-screen presentation. With Microsoft's PowerPoint program, you can easily create visual aids for a presentation and then print copies of the aids as well as run the presentation. PowerPoint is a presentation graphics program that you can use to organize and present information.

PowerPoint provides a variety of output capabilities for presentations. A presentation prepared in PowerPoint can be run directly on the computer. In addition, black and white overheads can be created by printing slides on transparencies; or, color transparencies can be created if you have access to a color printer. Slides can be created in PowerPoint and then sent to a film processing company to be converted to 35mm slides. Also, printouts of slides can be made for use as speaker's notes, audience handouts, or outline pages.

Planning a Presentation

With PowerPoint, you can create slides for an on-screen presentation, or for an overhead or slide projector. You can also print handouts of the presentation, print an outline, or print the entire presentation. When planning a presentation, first define the purpose of the presentation. Is the intent to inform? educate? sell? motivate? and/or entertain? Additionally, consider the audience who will be listening to and watching the presentation. Determine the content of the presentation and also the medium that will be used to convey the message. Will a computer be used to display the slides of a presentation or will overhead transparencies be created from the slides? Some basic guidelines to consider when preparing the content of the presentation include:

- **Determine the main purpose of the presentation.** Do not try to cover too many topics—this may strain the audience's attention or cause confusion. Identifying the main point of the presentation will help you stay focused and convey a clear message to the audience.
- **Determine the output.** Is the presentation going to be presented in PowerPoint? Will slides be used? Or will black and white or color transparencies be made for an overhead? To help decide the type of output needed, consider the availability of equipment, the size of the room where the presentation will be made, and the number of people who will be attending the presentation.
- **Show one idea per slide.** Each slide in a presentation should convey only one main idea. Too many thoughts or ideas on a slide may confuse the audience and cause you to stray from the purpose of the slide. Determine the specific message you want to convey to the audience and then outline the message to organize ideas.
- **Maintain a consistent layout.** A consistent layout and color scheme for slides in a presentation will create continuity and cohesiveness. Do not get carried away by using too many colors and too many pictures or other graphic elements.
- **Keep slides easy to read and uncluttered.** Keep slides simple and easy for the audience to read. Keep words and other items such as bullets to a minimum. If the presentation is done with 35mm slides, consider using a dark background color for slides. Use a light background color when creating overhead transparencies.
- **Determine the output needed.** Will you be providing audience members with handouts? If so, will these handouts consist of a printing of each slide? an outline of the presentation? a printing of each slide with space for taking notes?

Creating a PowerPoint Presentation

PowerPoint provides several methods for creating a presentation. You can use PowerPoint's AutoContent Wizard, which asks questions and then chooses a presentation layout based on your answers. You can also create a presentation using predesigned templates. PowerPoint's templates provide a variety of formatting options for slides. If you want to apply your own formatting to slides, you can choose a blank presentation. The steps you follow to create a presentation will vary depending on the method you choose, but will probably follow these basic steps:

1. Open PowerPoint.
2. Choose the desired slide layout.
3. Choose a design template.
4. Type the text for each slide, adding additional elements as needed such as graphic images.
5. Save the presentation.
6. Print the presentation as slides, handouts, notes pages, or an outline.
7. Run the presentation.
8. Close the presentation.
9. Exit PowerPoint.

Understanding the PowerPoint Window

When you chose the specific type of presentation you want to create, you are presented with the PowerPoint window in the Normal view. What displays in the window will vary depending on the type of presentation you are creating. However, the PowerPoint window contains some consistent elements as shown in Figure 1.1. The PowerPoint window elements are described following the figure.

In Figure 1.1, the Standard and Formatting toolbars are displayed as two separate toolbars. When you start PowerPoint, the Standard and Formatting toolbars may appear together on the same row. In this case, you will notice two buttons on the toolbar containing a small horizontal line with a down-pointing triangle below the line. These are the Toolbar Options buttons and are used to access the Standard and Formatting toolbar buttons that are not visible. The Toolbar Options button approximately halfway across the toolbar provides access to additional Standard toolbar buttons, while the Toolbar Options button at the right side of the toolbar provides access to additional Formatting toolbar buttons. Click the Toolbar Options button to display a palette of additional buttons.

Toolbar Options

To set up PowerPoint so that the Standard and Formatting toolbars are separate as shown in Figure 1.1, click the Toolbar Options button (either one), and then click Show Buttons on Two Rows at the drop-down list.

FIGURE 1.1 *PowerPoint Window*

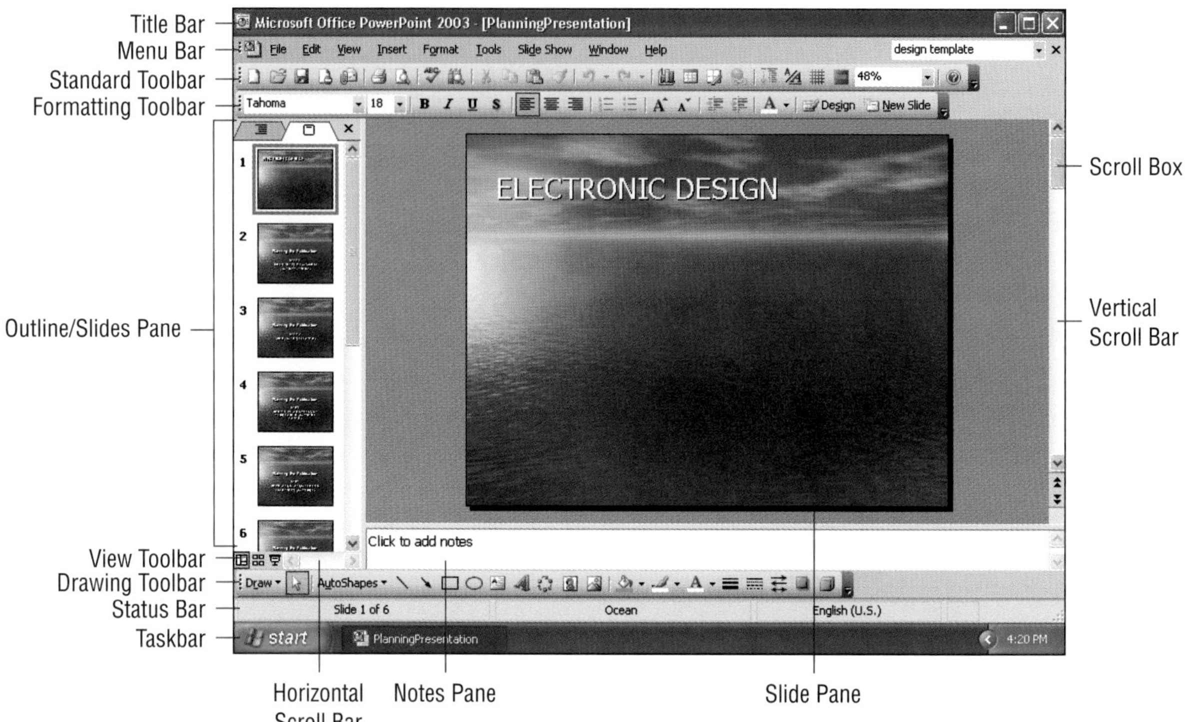

The PowerPoint window contains many elements that are similar to other Microsoft Office programs such as Word and Excel. For example, the PowerPoint window, like the Word window, contains a Title bar, Menu bar, Standard and Formatting toolbars, scroll bars, and a Status bar. The elements of the PowerPoint window include:

- **Title bar:** This bar displays the program name, a presentation title, a control menu, the Close button, and the Minimize and Restore buttons for resizing the window.
- **Menu bar:** PowerPoint commands are grouped into options that display on the Menu bar. For example, options for formatting slides can be found at the Format drop-down menu.
- **Standard toolbar:** This toolbar contains buttons for the most frequently used commands in PowerPoint such as cutting, copying, and pasting text; inserting hyperlinks, tables, and charts; and changing the Zoom display.
- **Formatting toolbar:** Frequently used commands for formatting a PowerPoint presentation are grouped onto the Formatting toolbar. This toolbar contains options such as changing typeface and size, increasing and decreasing type size, adding typestyles such as bold and italics, changing paragraph alignment, and displaying the Slide Design task pane.
- **Drawing toolbar:** With buttons on the Drawing toolbar, you can draw objects such as lines, arcs, and shapes. Buttons on this toolbar also contain options for adding attributes to objects such as color, shading, and shadow.

- **Outline/Slides pane:** The pane at the left side of the screen contains two tabs—Outline and Slides. With the Outline tab selected, the contents of a presentation display in the pane. With the Slides tab selected, a slide miniature displays in the pane.
- **Slide pane:** The Slide pane is where slides are created and displayed. Here you can see how text looks on each slide and add elements such as clip art images, hyperlinks, and animation effects.
- **Notes pane:** Add notes to a presentation in the Notes pane.
- **Vertical scroll bar:** Use the vertical scroll bar to display specific slides in a presentation. The small box located on the vertical scroll bar is called the ***scroll box***. Drag the scroll box on the vertical scroll bar and a yellow box displays specifying the slide number within the presentation. Use the scroll box to move quickly to a specific slide.
- **Horizontal scroll bar:** The Outline/Slides pane contains a horizontal scroll bar you can use to shift text left or right in the pane.
- **View toolbar:** The View toolbar, located at the left side of the horizontal scroll bar, contains buttons for changing the presentation view. For example, you can view individual slides, view several slides at once, view slide information as an outline, and also run the presentation.
- **Status bar:** Messages about PowerPoint features display in the Status bar, which is located toward the bottom of the PowerPoint window. The Status bar also displays information about the view.

Slide Design

HINT

Design templates provided by PowerPoint were designed by professional graphic artists who understand the use of color, space, and design.

PowerPoint, like other Microsoft Office programs, provides ScreenTips for buttons on toolbars. Position the arrow pointer on a button on any of the PowerPoint toolbars, and a ScreenTip displays (after approximately one second) for the button.

QUICK STEPS

Choose a Design Template

1. At PowerPoint window, click Slide Design button on Formatting toolbar.
2. Click desired template design in Slide Design task pane.

Creating a Presentation Using a Design Template

PowerPoint provides a variety of predesigned templates you can use when creating slides for a presentation. These predesigned templates include formatting such as color, background, fonts, and so on. To choose a template, click the Slide Design button on the Formatting toolbar. This displays the available templates in the Slide Design task pane that displays at the right side of the screen as shown in Figure 1.2. Position the mouse pointer on a thumbnail of a template and the name of the template displays in a yellow box.

HINT

With options at the Slide Design task pane, you can install additional PowerPoint templates.

After choosing the desired template, choose a slide layout. PowerPoint provides a number of slide layouts you can display by clicking Format on the Menu bar and then clicking Slide Layout. This displays the available layouts in the Slide Layout task pane shown in Figure 1.3. You can also display layouts by clicking the Other Task Panes button (contains the name of the task pane and a down-pointing arrow) located in the upper right corner of the current task pane and then clicking Slide Layout at the drop-down list.

New Slide

Save

After choosing a slide layout, type the desired text and/or insert the desired elements in the slide. To create another slide, click the New Slide button on the Formatting toolbar, click the desired layout in the Slide Layout task pane, and then type the text in the slide or insert the desired elements.

HINT

Use the Blank Presentation template if you want complete control over the presentation design.

When all slides have been completed, save the presentation by clicking the Save button on the Standard toolbar. At the Save As dialog box, type a name for the presentation and then click the Save button or press Enter.

FIGURE

1.2 Slide Design Task Pane

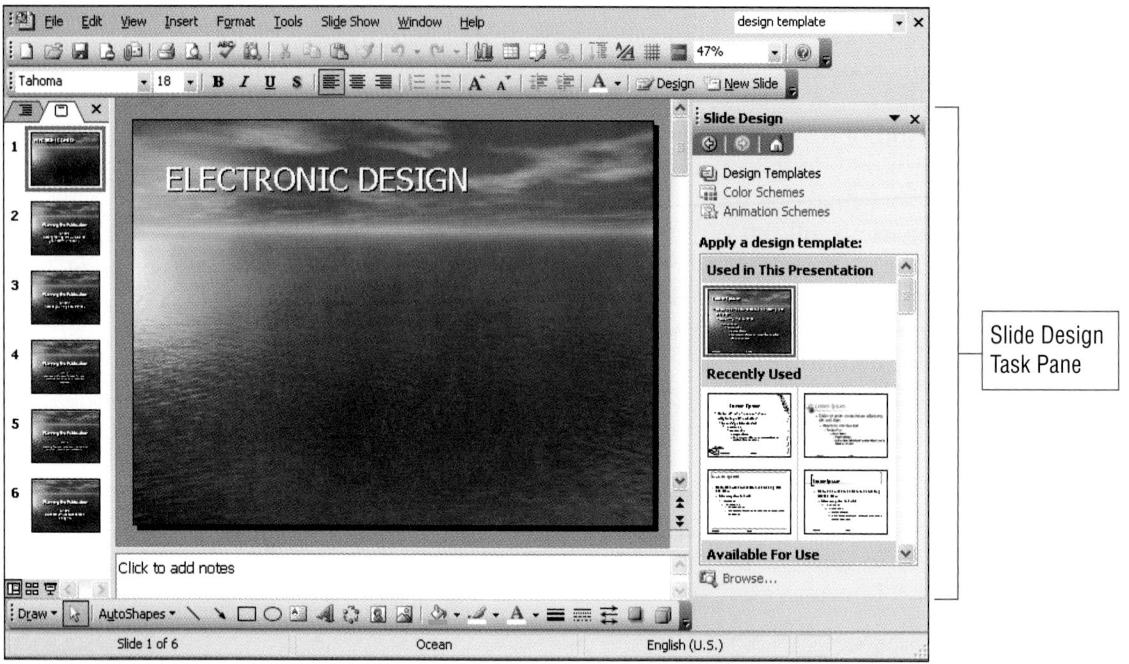

FIGURE

1.3 Slide Layout Task Pane

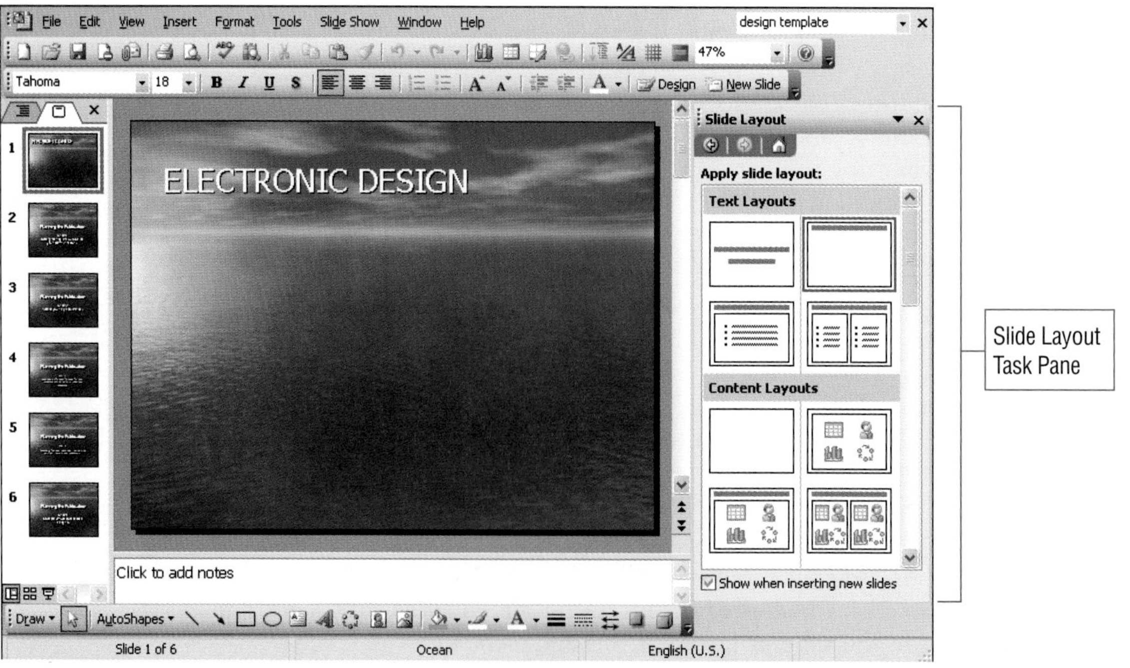

Displaying and Maneuvering in Task Panes

As you use various PowerPoint features, a task pane may display at the right side of the screen. The name of the task pane varies depending on the feature. For example, when you click the Slide Design button on the Formatting toolbar, the Slide Design task pane displays. If you click Format on the Menu bar and then click Slide Layout, the Slide Layout task pane displays. A task pane presents features to help you easily identify and use more of the program.

As you learn more features in PowerPoint, the options in the task pane as well as the task pane name may change. Maneuver within various task panes with buttons on the task pane toolbar. Click the Back button (contains a left-pointing arrow) on the toolbar to display the previous task pane or click the Forward button (contains a right-pointing arrow) to display the next task pane. Click the Home button to return to the Getting Started task pane. You can also maneuver within various task panes by clicking the Other Task Panes button (contains the name of the task pane and a down-pointing arrow) and then clicking the desired task pane at the drop-down list. You can control whether the display of the task pane is on or off by clicking View and then Task Pane. You can also close the task pane by clicking the Close button (contains an *X*) located in the upper right corner of the task pane.

The task pane can be docked and undocked. By default, the task pane is docked at the right side of the screen. Undock (move) the task pane by positioning the mouse pointer to the left of the task pane name, holding down the left mouse button (mouse pointer turns into a four-headed arrow), and then dragging the task pane to the desired location. If you undock the task pane, you can dock it back at the right side of the screen by double-clicking to the left of the task pane name.

Inserting a New Slide

Create a new slide in a presentation by clicking the New Slide button on the Formatting toolbar. This displays the Slide Layout task pane at the right side of the screen. Click the desired layout in the Slide Layout task pane and then insert the desired data in the slide. The new slide is inserted after the selected slide.

Insert a New Slide
1. Click New Slide button on Formatting toolbar.
2. Click desired layout at Slide Layout task pane.

Choosing a Slide Layout

A variety of slide layout options are available at the Slide Layout task pane. This task pane displays when you click Format and then Slide Layout or click the New Slide button on the Formatting toolbar. Position the mouse pointer on a slide layout and the name of the layout displays in a yellow box.

HINT
Slide layouts make arranging elements in a slide easier.

When you position the mouse pointer on a slide layout, the name of the layout displays along with a down-pointing arrow at the right side of the layout. Click this arrow and a drop-down list displays with options for applying the layout to selected slides, reapplying a master style, or inserting a new slide.

HINT
Scroll down the *Apply slide layout* list box to view additional slide layouts.

The slide layouts in the Slide Layout task pane contain placeholders. A placeholder is a location on the slide where information is entered or inserted. For example, many slides contain a title placeholder. Click in this placeholder and then type the title of the slide. When text is entered into a placeholder, the placeholder turns into a text object.

QUICK STEPS

Print a Presentation

1. Click File, Print.
2. Click down-pointing arrow at right of *Print what* option.
3. Click desired printing option.
4. Click OK.

Printing a Presentation

A presentation can be printed in a variety of formats. You can print each slide on a separate piece of paper; print each slide at the top of the page, leaving the bottom of the page for notes; print up to nine slides or a specific number of slides on a single piece of paper; or print the slide titles and topics in outline form. Use the *Print what* option at the Print dialog box to specify what you want printed.

To display the Print dialog box, shown in Figure 1.4, click File and then Print. At the Print dialog box, click the down-pointing arrow at the right side of the *Print what* text box, and then click the desired printing format.

FIGURE 1.4 ***Print Dialog Box***

HINT Printing a hard copy of your presentation and distributing it to your audience helps reinforce your message.

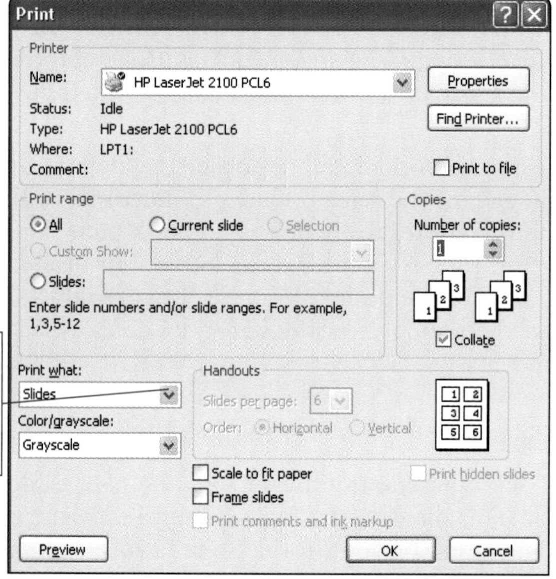

Click this down-pointing arrow to display a list of printing options.

Expanding Drop-Down Menus

When you open PowerPoint, the menus display a limited selection of basic commands called ***first rank options***. At the bottom of each menu is a down-pointing double arrow. Click this double arrow to expand the drop-down menu and display additional options, known as ***second rank options***. Or, allow the mouse pointer to rest on the menu option for approximately five seconds and the menu will expand to show all options. Second rank options display with a lighter gray background.

As you create and edit presentations, the commands you use most often are stored as personalized options and display on the drop-down menus when you select them. Expand the menu if an option you require does not appear on the menu. Second rank options become first rank options after you use them once.

To disable the personalized menu feature and display all menu options, click Tools and then Customize. At the Customize dialog box, click the Options tab. Click the *Always show full menus* option to insert a check mark in the check box and then click the Close button to close the dialog box.

HINT At the Page Setup dialog box, you can change the page width and height, and choose the page orientation – Portrait or Landscape. Display this dialog box by clicking File and then Page Setup.

The instructions in this book assume that the personalized menu feature has been disabled. If the computer you are using has this feature enabled, you may need to expand the drop-down menus to find the required options.

Saving a Presentation

After creating a presentation, save it by clicking File and then Save or by clicking the Save button on the Standard toolbar. This displays the Save As dialog box. By default, a PowerPoint presentation is saved to the *My Documents* folder. To save a presentation onto your data disk, you will need to change the active folder. To change to a data disk that is located in drive A, click the down-pointing arrow at the right of the *Save in* text box, and then click *3½ Floppy (A:)*. After changing the default folder, type the presentation name in the *File name* text box, and then click the Save button or press Enter.

Save a Presentation

1. Click Save button on Standard toolbar.
2. Navigate to desired folder or drive.
3. Type presentation name in *File name* text box.
4. Click Save button.

Closing a Presentation

After creating, viewing, and/or printing a presentation, close the presentation. To do this, click the Close Window button at the right side of the Menu bar or click File and then Close. If any changes were made to the presentation that were not saved, you will be asked if you want to save the changes.

Completing Computer Exercises

At the end of sections within chapters and at the end of chapters, you will be completing hands-on exercises at the computer. These exercises will provide you with the opportunity to practice the presented functions and commands. The skill assessment exercises at the end of each chapter include general directions. If you do not remember how to perform a particular function, refer to the text in the chapter.

Copying Presentations

In some exercises in each chapter, you will be opening a presentation provided with this textbook. Before beginning each chapter, copy the chapter folder from the CD that accompanies this textbook to a floppy disk (or other folder). Steps on how to copy a folder from the CD to your floppy disk are printed on the inside of the back cover of this textbook.

Changing the Default Folder

In this chapter and the other chapters in this textbook, you will be saving presentations onto a disk (or other folder). To save presentations to and open presentations from the chapter folder on your disk, you will need to specify the chapter folder on your disk as the default folder. Once you specify the chapter folder on your disk, PowerPoint uses this as the default folder until you exit the PowerPoint program. The next time you open PowerPoint, you will again need to specify the chapter folder on your disk as the default folder.

Change the default folder at the Open dialog box or the Save As dialog box. To change the folder to the PowerPointChapter01S folder on the disk in drive A at the Open dialog box, you would complete the following steps:

1. Click the Open button on the Standard toolbar (the second button from the left); or click File and then Open.
2. At the Open dialog box, click the down-pointing arrow at the right side of the *Look in* option box.
3. From the drop-down list that displays, click *3½ Floppy (A:)*.
4. Double-click *PowerPointChapter01S* that displays in the list box.
5. Click the Cancel button in the lower right corner of the dialog box.

(Note: Before completing Exercise 1, copy to your disk the PowerPointChapter01S subfolder from the PowerPoint2003Specialist folder on the CD that accompanies this textbook. Steps on how to copy a folder are presented on the inside of the back cover of this textbook. Do this every time you start a chapter's exercises.)

exercise 1

CREATING AND PRINTING A PRESENTATION

1. Copy the PowerPointChapter01S folder from the CD that accompanies this textbook to your disk. For steps on how to copy the folder, please refer to the steps that are printed on the inside of the back cover of this textbook.
2. Prepare a presentation on the steps for planning a publication by completing the following steps:
   a. At the PowerPoint window, click the Slide Design button on the Formatting toolbar. (This displays the Slide Design task pane at the right side of the screen.)
   b. Scroll down the list of design templates in the *Apply a design template* list box until the Digital Dots template displays. (Position the mouse pointer on a template and, after approximately one second, the name of the template displays in a yellow box.)
   c. Click once on the Digital Dots template. (This applies the design template to the slide in the Slide pane with the Title Slide layout displayed.)
   d. Display slide layout options by clicking Format and then Slide Layout. (This displays the Slide Layout task pane.)
   e. Click the Title Only slide layout at the Slide Layout task pane. (Position the mouse pointer on a layout and after approximately one second the name of the layout displays in a yellow box.)
   f. On the slide, click anywhere in the text *Click to add title* and then type **ELECTRONIC DESIGN**.

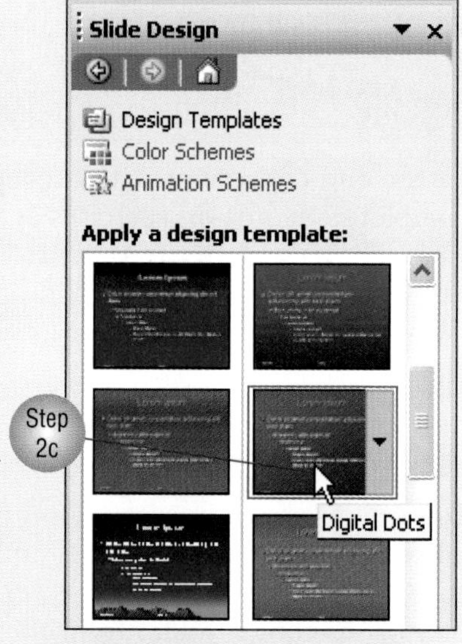

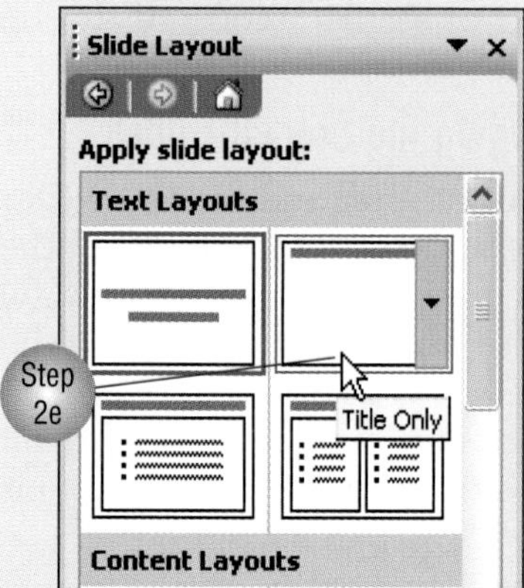

g. Click the New Slide button on the Standard toolbar. (This causes a new slide to display in the Slide pane.)
h. Click the Title Slide layout in the Slide Layout task pane. (The Title Slide layout should be the first layout from the left in the top row.)
i. At the slide, click anywhere in the text *Click to add title* and then type **Guidelines for Using Color**.
j. Click anywhere in the text *Click to add subtitle* and then type **Limit your use of color to two or three colors, including the color of the paper.** 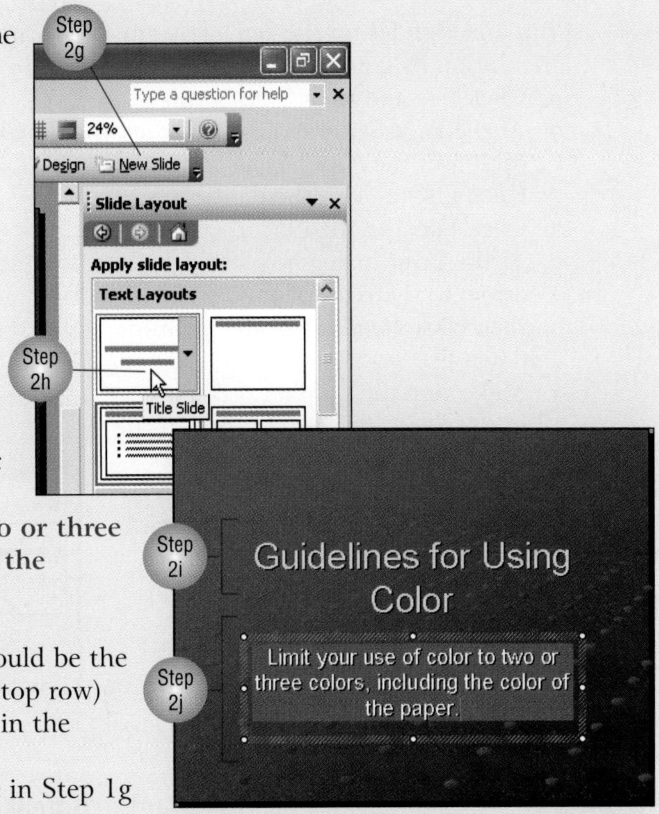
k. Click the New Slide button.
l. Click the Title Slide layout (should be the first layout from the left in the top row) in the *Apply slide layout* list box in the Slide Layout task pane.
m. Complete steps similar to those in Step 1g through 1j to create the following text:

Title	=	**Guidelines for Using Color**
Subtitle	=	**Do not let color overpower the words.**

n. Complete steps similar to those in 1g through 1j to create the following slides:

Slide 4	Title	=	**Guidelines for Using Color**
	Subtitle	=	**Use color to identify consistent elements.**
Slide 5	Title	=	**Guidelines for Using Color**
	Subtitle	=	**Do not set text in light colors because the text is too hard to read.**
Slide 6	Title	=	**Guidelines for Using Color**
	Subtitle	=	**Use color to communicate, not decorate.**

o. Click in the slide outside the selected area. (This should deselect the box containing the subtitle.)

3. Save the presentation by completing the following steps:
   a. Click the Save button on the Standard toolbar.
   b. At the Save As dialog box, click the down-pointing arrow to the right of the *Save in* text box, and then click *3½ Floppy (A:)*.
   c. Double-click the *PowerPointChapter01S* folder.
   d. Select the text in the *File name* text box, type sppc1x01 (for *Specialist PowerPoint Chapter 1 Exercise 1*), and then press Enter or click Save. (PowerPointChapter01S is now the default folder until you exit PowerPoint.)

4. Print all six slides on the same page in Landscape Orientation by completing the following steps:
   a. Click File and then Page Setup.
   b. At the Page Setup dialog box, click the *Landscape* option in the *Notes, handouts & outline* section.
   c. Click OK to close the dialog box.
   d. Click File and then Print.
   e. At the Print dialog box, click the down-pointing arrow to the right of the *Print what* option, and then click *Handouts* from the drop-down list.
   f. Make sure the number *6* displays in the *Slides per page* text box in the *Handouts* section of the dialog box. Click OK.
5. Sace the presentation by clicking the Save button on the Standard toolbar.
6. Close **sppc1x01** by clicking File and then Close.

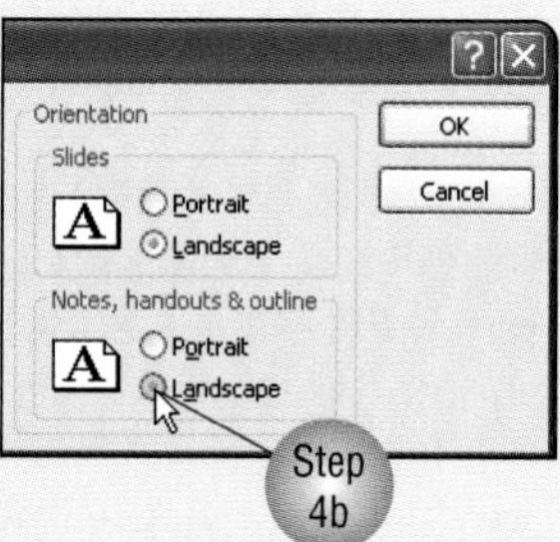

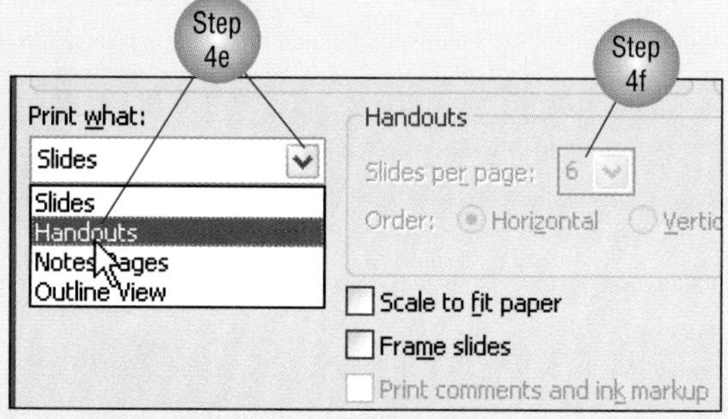

QUICK STEPS

Open a Presentation
1. Click Open button on Standard toolbar.
2. Navigate to desired folder or drive.
3. Double-click the presentation.

Open

Opening a Presentation Document

A saved presentation document can be opened at the Open dialog box. To display this dialog box, click File and then Open or click the Open button on the Standard toolbar. At the Open dialog box, double-click the desired presentation document in the list box.

HINT

Type and edit text in individual slides in Normal view.

HINT

Quickly and easily reorganize slides in Slide Sorter view.

Viewing a Presentation

PowerPoint provides a variety of viewing options for a presentation. The presentation view can be changed with options from the View drop-down menu or with viewing buttons that display on the View toolbar, shown in Figure 1.5, located at the left side of the horizontal scroll bar. The viewing choices include:

- **Normal View:** This is the default view and displays three panes—Outline/Slides, Slide, and Notes. With these three panes, you can work with all features in one place. This view is also referred to as tri-pane view.
- **Slide Sorter View:** Choosing the Slide Sorter view displays all slides in the presentation in slide miniatures. In this view, you can easily add, move, rearrange, and delete slides.
- **Notes Page View:** Change to the Notes Page view and an individual slide displays on a page with any added notes displayed below the slide.
- **Slide Show View:** Use the Slide Show view to run a presentation. When you choose this view, the slide fills the entire screen.

FIGURE

1.5 View Toolbar

Normal View
Slide Sorter View
Slide Show

Change the view using either buttons on the View toolbar or options from the View drop-down menu. To use the View toolbar, click the desired button. (The View toolbar does not contain a button for changing to the Notes Page view.) To use the View option on the Menu bar, click View, and then click the desired view from the drop-down menu. The View drop-down menu contains the Notes Page option. At the Notes Page view, the slide displays along with a space below the slide for inserting text. Click the text *Click to add text* that displays in the box below the slide and then type the desired note. When running the presentation, you can display any notes attached to a slide.

In the Normal view, change slides by clicking the Previous Slide or Next Slide buttons located at the bottom of the vertical scroll bar. You can also change to a different slide by using the mouse pointer on the scroll box on the vertical scroll bar. To do this, position the mouse pointer on the scroll box, hold down the left mouse button, drag up or down until a yellow box displays with the desired slide number, and then release the mouse button. The keyboard can also be used to change to a different slide. Press the Page Down key to display the next slide in the presentation or press the Page Up key to display the previous slide in the presentation.

Previous Slide

Next Slide

Running a Slide Show

Slides created in PowerPoint can be converted to 35mm slides or transparencies, or the computer screen can provide the output. An on-screen presentation saves the expense of producing slides, requires no projection equipment, and lets you use the computer's color capability. Several methods are available for running a slide show. You can run the slide show manually (you determine when to advance to the next slide), advance slides automatically, or set up a slide show to run continuously for demonstration purposes.

Run a Presentation

1. Click Slide Show button on View toolbar.
2. Click left mouse button to advance slides.

If you want to run a slide show manually, open the presentation, and then click the Slide Show button on the View toolbar, or click View and then Slide Show. Click the Slide Show button on the View toolbar and the presentation begins with the currently active slide. To begin a slide show on any slide, make the desired slide active and then click the Slide Show button. If you want to begin the presentation with the first slide, make sure it is the active slide before clicking the Slide Show button.

Slide Show

PowerPoint offers a wide variety of options for navigating through slides in a presentation. Figure 1.6 displays the Slide Show Help window that contains all the navigating options. In addition to the methods described in the Slide Show Help window, you can also navigate in a presentation using buttons on the Slide Show toolbar shown in Figure 1.7. To display this toolbar, run the presentation, and then move the mouse pointer. Click the right-pointing arrow button to display the next slide and click the left-pointing arrow button to display the previous slide. Click the slide icon button and a pop-up menu displays with the following options: *Next*, *Previous*, *Last Viewed*, *Go to Slide*, *Custom Show*, *Screen*, *Help*, *Pause*, and *End Show*. Use these options to navigate to a particular slide in the presentation, display the Slide Show Help window, and pause or end the show. Click the pen button and a pop-up menu displays with the following options: *Arrow*, *Ballpoint Pen*, *Felt Tip Pen*, *Highlighter*, *Ink Color*, *Eraser*, *Erase All Ink on Slide*, and *Arrow Options*.

FIGURE 1.6 **Slide Show Help Window**

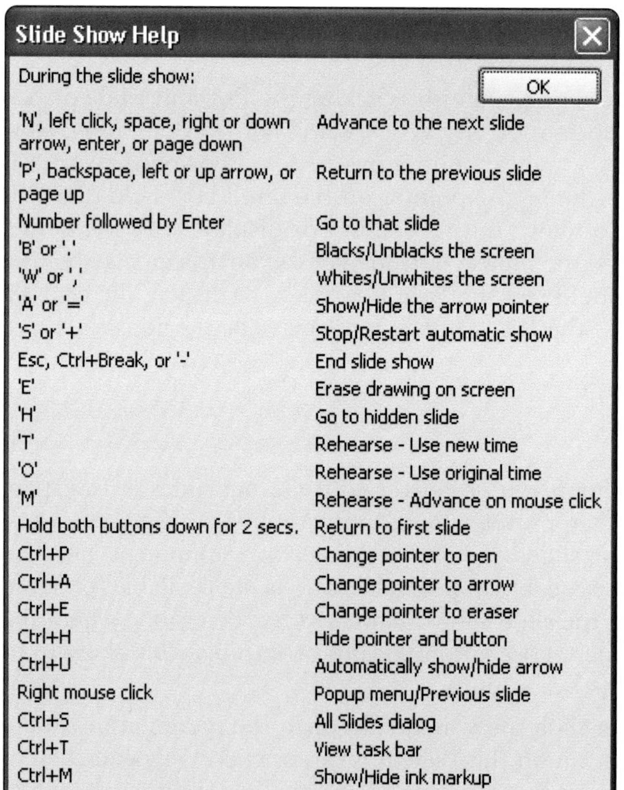

FIGURE 1.7 *Slide Show Toolbar*

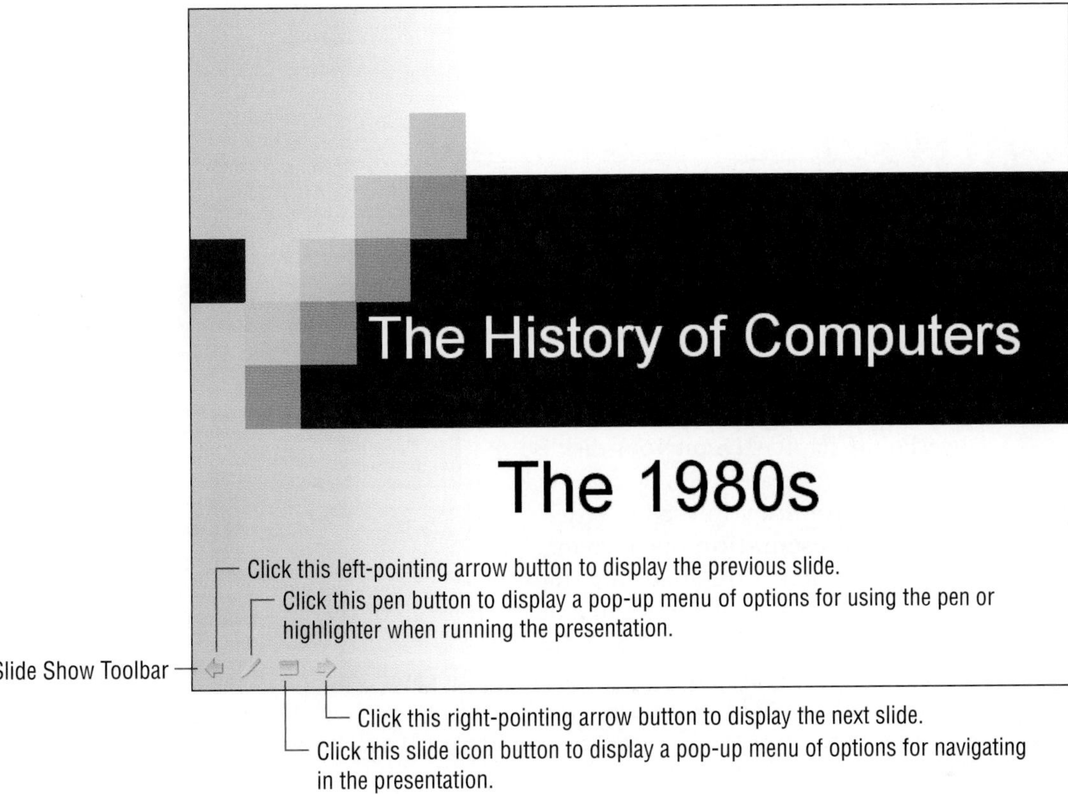
The History of Computers
The 1980s
Click this left-pointing arrow button to display the previous slide.
Click this pen button to display a pop-up menu of options for using the pen or highlighter when running the presentation.
Slide Show Toolbar
Click this right-pointing arrow button to display the next slide.
Click this slide icon button to display a pop-up menu of options for navigating in the presentation.

When running a presentation, the mouse pointer is set, by default, to be hidden automatically after three seconds of inactivity. The mouse pointer will appear again when you move the mouse. You can change this default setting by clicking the pen button on the Slide Show toolbar, pointing to Arrow Options, and then clicking Visible if you want the mouse pointer always visible or Hidden if you do not want the mouse to display at all as you run the presentation. The Automatic option is the default setting.

HINT

If you use the pen or highlighter on a slide when running a presentation, choose an ink color that is easily seen by the audience.

Using the Pen and Highlighter during a Presentation

Emphasize major points or draw the attention of the audience to specific items in a slide during a presentation using the pen or highlighter. To use the pen on a slide, run the presentation, and when the desired slide displays, move the mouse to display the Slide Show toolbar. Click the pen button and then click either *Ballpoint Pen* or *Felt Tip Pen*. The felt tip pen draws a thicker line than the ballpoint pen. When you click a pen option, the mouse pointer displays as a pen. Use the mouse to draw in the slide to emphasize a point or specific text. Change the pen ink color by clicking the pen button, pointing to Ink Color, and then clicking the desired color at the color palette. Follow similar steps to highlight specific text or items in a slide.

QUICK STEPS

Use Pen/Highlighter during Presentation

1. Run presentation.
2. Display desired slide.
3. Click pen button on Slide Show toolbar.
4. Click pen or highlighter option.
5. Drag to draw line or highlight text.

If you want to erase the marks you made with the pen, click the pen button and then click *Eraser*. This causes the mouse pointer to display as an eraser. Drag through an ink mark to remove it. To remove all ink marks at the same time, click the *Erase All Ink on Slide* option. When you are finished with the pen, click the *Arrow* option to return the mouse pointer to an arrow.

exercise 2

VIEWING, PRINTING, AND RUNNING A PRESENTATION

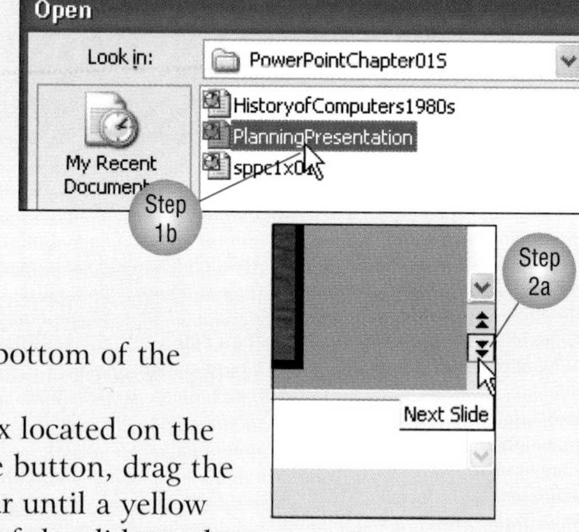

1. Open **PlanningPresentation** located in the PowerPointChapter01S folder on your disk by completing the following steps:
   a. At the PowerPoint window, click the Open button on the Standard toolbar.
   b. At the Open dialog box, make sure PowerPointChapter01S on your disk is the default folder, and then double-click ***PlanningPresentation*** in the list box.
2. With **PlanningPresentation** open, change the views by completing the following steps:
   a. Click the Next Slide button located at the bottom of the vertical scroll bar until Slide 6 is visible.
   b. Position the mouse pointer on the scroll box located on the vertical scroll bar, hold down the left mouse button, drag the scroll box to the top of the vertical scroll bar until a yellow box displays with *Slide: 1 of 6* and the title of the slide, and then release the mouse button.
   c. Change to the Notes Page view by clicking View on the Menu bar and then clicking Notes Page at the drop-down menu.
   d. Use the scroll box on the vertical scroll bar to display Slide 6.
   e. Change to the Slide Sorter view by clicking the Slide Sorter View button on the View toolbar.
   f. Double-click Slide 1. (This displays Slide 1 in Normal view.)
3. Print the presentation in Outline view by completing the following steps:
   a. Choose File and then Print.
   b. At the Print dialog box, change the *Print what* option to *Outline View*.
   c. Click OK or press Enter.
4. Run the slide presentation on the screen by completing the following steps:
   a. Make sure Slide 1 displays in the Slide pane.
   b. Click the Slide Show button on the View toolbar. (Slide 1 fills the entire screen.)
   c. After viewing Slide 1, click the left mouse button. (This causes Slide 2 to display.)
   d. Continue viewing and then clicking the left mouse button until all six slides have been viewed.

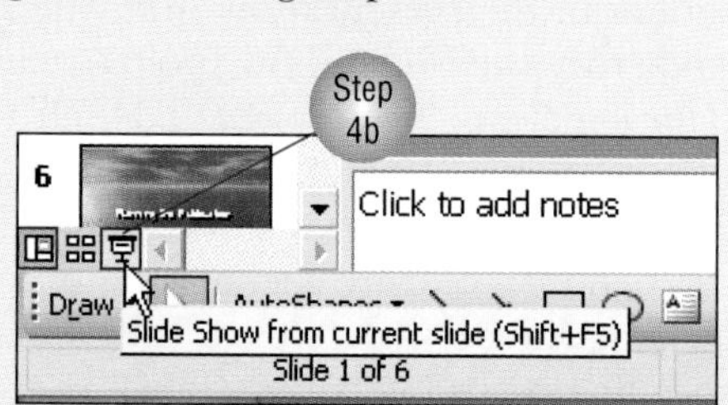

e. At the black screen with the message *End of slide show, click to exit.*, click the left mouse button. This returns the presentation to the Normal view.

5. Run the presentation beginning with Slide 3 by completing the following steps:
   a. Click the Slide Sorter View button on the View toolbar.
   b. Double-click Slide 3. (This displays Slide 3 in Normal view.)
   c. Click the Slide Show button on the View toolbar.
   d. After viewing Slide 3, click the left mouse button.
   e. Continue viewing slides until the black screen displays. At this screen, click the left mouse button.
6. Run the presentation and use the pen and highlighter to emphasize specific words in the slides by completing the following steps:
   a. Drag the scroll box to the top of the vertical scroll bar. (This displays Slide 1 in the Slide pane.)
   b. Click the Slide Show button on the View toolbar.
   c. When Slide 1 displays on the screen, click the left mouse button. (This displays Slide 2.)
   d. With Slide 2 displayed, use the felt tip pen to underline a word by completing the following steps:
      1) Move the mouse to display the Slide Show toolbar.
      2) Click the pen button on the Slide Show toolbar and then click Felt Tip Pen. (This turns the mouse pointer into a small circle.)
      3) Using the mouse, draw a circle around the text *STEP 1*.
      4) Draw a line below the word *identify*.
      5) Erase the pen markings by clicking the pen button on the Slide Show toolbar and then clicking Erase All Ink on Slide.
      6) Change the color of the ink by clicking the pen button, pointing to Ink Color, and then clicking the bright yellow color.
      7) Draw a yellow line below the word *identify*.
      8) Return the mouse pointer back to an arrow by clicking the pen button and then clicking Arrow at the pop-up menu.
   e. Click the right-pointing arrow button on the Slide Show toolbar to display the next slide. Continue clicking the button until Slide 5 displays (this slide contains STEP 4).
   f. Click the pen button and then click Highlighter at the pop-up menu. (This changes the mouse pointer to a light yellow rectangle.)
   g. Drag through the word *after* to highlight it.
   h. Click the left mouse button to display Slide 6 (this slide contains *STEP 5*) and use the highlighter to highlight the word *effective*.

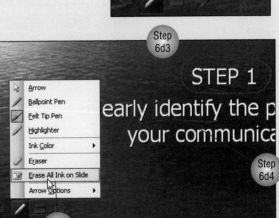

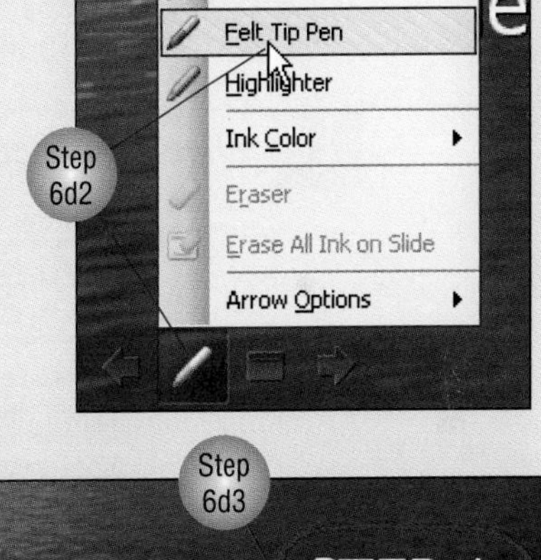

i. Return the mouse pointer back to an arrow by clicking the pen button and then clicking Arrow.
j. Click the left mouse button and then, at the black screen, click the left mouse button again.
k. At the message asking if you want to keep your ink annotations, click the Discard button.
7. Close **PlanningPresentation**.

Adding Transition and Sound Effects

Transition

Slide Transition

HINT

Make a presentation more appealing by adding effects such as transitions and sounds.

Interesting transitions and sounds can be applied to a presentation. A transition is how one slide is removed from the screen during a presentation and the next slide is displayed. Interesting transitions can be added such as blinds, boxes, checkerboards, covers, random bars, stripes, and wipes. To add transitions and sounds, open a presentation, and then display the Slide Transition task pane shown in Figure 1.8 by clicking Slide Show and then Slide Transition. You can also display this task pane by changing to the Slide Sorter view and then clicking the Slide Transition button on the Slide Sorter toolbar. The Slide Sorter toolbar displays at the right side of the Standard toolbar in Slide Sorter view. If the Slide Transition button is not visible, click the Toolbar Options button (contains a horizontal line with a down-pointing arrow below) that displays at the right side of the toolbar, and then click Transition at the drop-down list.

FIGURE 1.8 ***Slide Transition Task Pane***

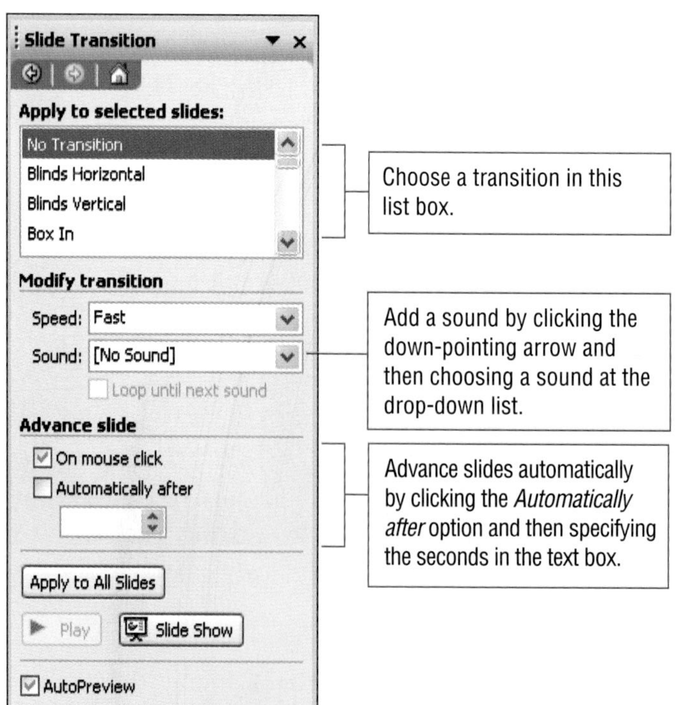

QUICK STEPS

Apply Transition to Slides

1. Click Slide Show, Slide Transition.
2. Click desired transition in the Slide Transition task pane.
3. Click Apply to All Slides button.

To add a transition effect, click the desired transition in the *Apply to selected slides* list box located in the Slide Transition task pane. When you click the desired transition, the transition effect displays in the slide in Normal view or in the selected slide miniature in Slide Sorter view. You can also display the transition effect by clicking the Play button located toward the bottom of the Slide Transition task pane. When a transition is added to a slide, a transition icon displays below the slide number in the Outline/Slides pane in Normal view or below the slide in Slide Sorter view.

As a slide is removed from the screen and another slide is displayed, a sound can be added. To add a sound, click the down-pointing arrow to the right of the *Sound* option box located in the *Modify transition* section of the Slide Transition task pane, and then click the desired sound at the drop-down list. You can choose from a list of sounds such as applause, bomb, breeze, camera, and much more.

Transition and sound effects apply by default to the currently displayed slide in Normal view or the selected slide in Slide Sorter view. If you want transition and sound to affect all slides in Normal view, click the Apply to All Slides button located toward the bottom of the Slide Transition task pane. In Slide Sorter view, select all slides by clicking Edit and then Select All or by pressing Ctrl + A, and then apply the desired transition and/or sound.

QUICK STEPS

Apply Sound Effect to Slides
1. Click Slide Show, Slide Transition.
2. Click down-pointing arrow at right of *Sound* option.
3. Click desired sound.
4. Click Apply to All Slides button.

exercise 3

ADDING TRANSITIONS AND SOUNDS TO A PRESENTATION

1. At the PowerPoint window, click the Open button on the Standard toolbar.
2. At the Open dialog box, make sure the PowerPointChapter01S folder on your disk is the active folder, and then double-click ***PlanningPresentation*** in the list box.
3. Save the presentation with Save As and name it **sppc1x03** by completing the following steps:
   a. Click File and then Save As.
   b. At the Save As dialog box, type sppc1x03 in the *File name* text box.
   c. Click Save or press Enter.
4. Add transition and sound effects by completing the following steps:
   a. Click Slide Show on the Menu bar and then click Slide Transition.
   b. At the Slide Transition task pane, click *Blinds Horizontal* in the *Apply to selected slides* list box.
   c. Click the down-pointing arrow at the right side of the *Sound* option box in the *Modify transition* section of the Slide Transition task pane and then click *Camera* at the drop-down list. (You will need to scroll down the list to display *Camera*.)
   d. Click the Apply to All Slides button located toward the bottom of the Slide Transition task pane.
5. Run the presentation by clicking the Slide Show button on the View toolbar and then clicking the left mouse button to advance each slide. (When the presentation is finished and the black screen displays with the message *End of slide show, click to exit.*, click the left mouse button or press the Esc key. This returns the presentation to the Normal view.)
6. Click the Save button on the Standard toolbar to save the presentation with the same name (**sppc1x03**).
7. Close the Slide Transition task pane and then close the presentation.

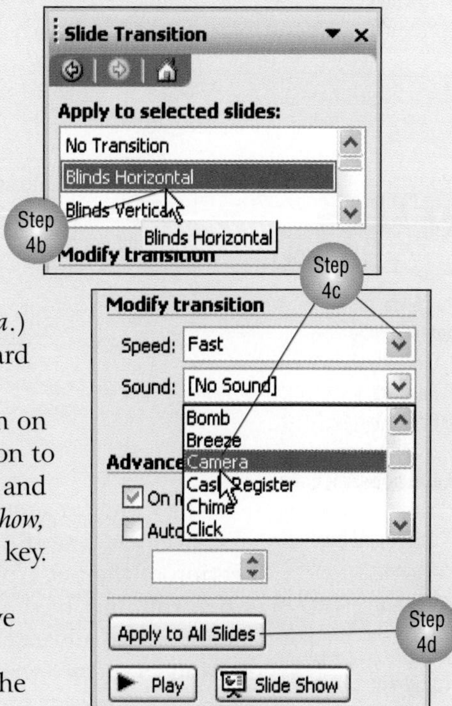

Running a Slide Show Automatically

Slides in a slide show can be advanced automatically after a specific number of seconds with options in the *Advance slide* section of the Slide Transition task pane. To automatically advance slides, click in the *Automatically after* check box and then insert the desired number of seconds in the text box. Change the time in the text box by clicking the up- or down-pointing arrows at the right side of the text box or by selecting any text in the text box and then typing the desired time. If you want the transition time to affect all slides in the presentation, click the Apply to All Slides button. In Slide Sorter view, the transition time displays below each affected slide.

HINT

Set automatic times for slides in a presentation if you do not want to manually control slides during a presentation.

To automatically run the presentation, make sure the first slide is selected, and then click the Slide Show button located towards the bottom of the task pane. (You can also click the Slide Show button on the View toolbar.) The first slide displays for the specified amount of time and then the next slide automatically displays.

In some situations, such as at a trade show or convention, you may want to prepare a self-running presentation. A self-running presentation is set up on a continuous loop and does not require someone to run the presentation. To design a self-running presentation, choose options at the Set Up Show dialog box shown in Figure 1.9. To display this dialog box, open a presentation, click Slide Show, and then click Set Up Show.

FIGURE 1.9 *Set Up Show Dialog Box*

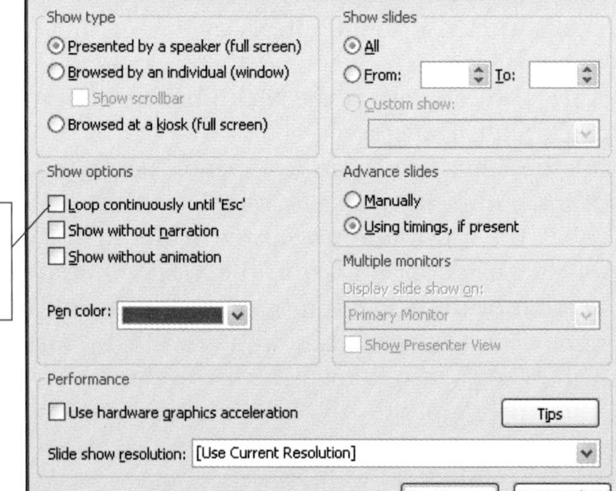

QUICK STEPS

Run Slide Show Automatically

1. Click Slide Show, Slide Transition.
2. Click *Automatically after* check box.
3. Click up-pointing arrow at right side of text box until desired time displays.
4. Click Slide Show, Set Up Show.
5. Click *Loop continuously until 'Esc'*.
6. Click OK.

Click the *Loop continuously until 'Esc'* option and the presentation runs over and over again until the Esc key is pressed. With other options in the *Show type* section of the Set Up Show dialog box, you can specify what a presentation shows when running. In the *Advance slides* section of the dialog box, specify whether the slides will be advanced manually or automatically. Use options in the *Show slides* section to specify whether options are to be applied to all slides or specific slides within the presentation.

exercise 4

PREPARING A SELF-RUNNING PRESENTATION

1. Open **HistoryofComputers1980s**. (This presentation is located in PowerPointChapter01S folder on your disk.)
2. Save the presentation with Save As in the PowerPointChapter01S folder on your disk and name it **sppc1x04**.
3. Add transition and sound effects and specify a time for automatically advancing slides by completing the following steps:
   a. Change to the Slide Sorter view.
   b. Click Slide Show and then Slide Transition.
   c. Select all slides by clicking Edit and then Select All. (You can also select all slides by pressing Ctrl + A.)
   d. At the Slide Transition task pane, click in the *Automatically after* check box. (This inserts a check mark.)
   e. Click the up-pointing arrow at the right side of the text box until *00:05* displays.
   f. Add a transition effect by clicking *Box Out* in the *Apply to selected slides* list box.
   g. Add a sound effect by clicking the down-pointing arrow to the right of the *Sound* option box in the *Modify transition* section of the task pane and then clicking *Laser* at the drop-down list.

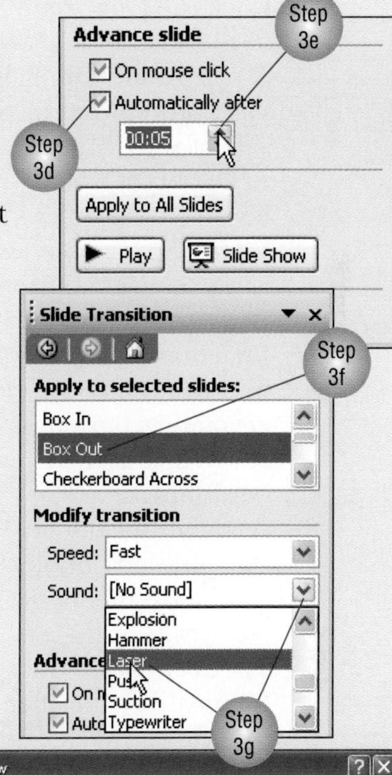

4. Set up the presentation to run continuously by completing the following steps:
   a. Click Slide Show and then Set Up Show.
   b. At the Set Up Show dialog box, click in the *Loop continuously until 'Esc'* check box to insert a check mark. (Make sure *All* is selected in the *Show slides* section and *Using timings, if present* is selected in the *Advance slides* section.)
   c. Click OK to close the dialog box.
5. Click Slide 1 to select it and then run the presentation continuously by clicking the Slide Show button in the Slide Transition task pane.
6. After viewing the presentation at least twice, press the Esc key on the keyboard.
7. Close the Slide Transition task pane.
8. Save and then close **sppc1x04**.

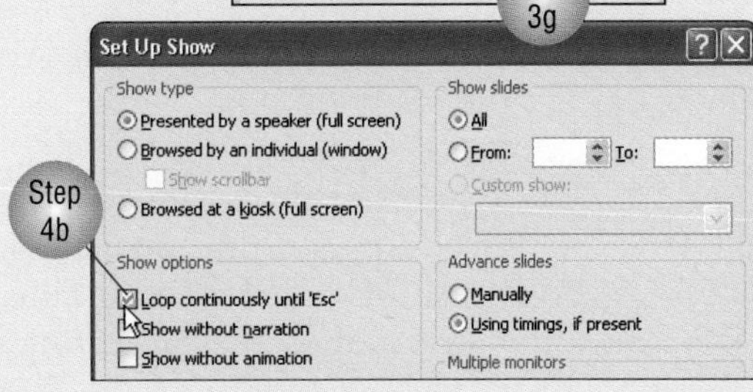

Planning a Presentation with the AutoContent Wizard

PowerPoint contains an AutoContent Wizard that will help you in the planning and organizing of a presentation. You respond to certain questions from the wizard and, on the basis of your responses, you are presented with slides containing information on how to organize the presentation. For example, suppose you are an employee of an investment firm and have been asked to prepare a presentation on a variable annuity fund. You can use the AutoContent Wizard for help on how to organize this presentation. You will be doing this in Exercise 5. The wizard provides additional information on other types of presentations. Consider printing the information for these other presentations.

exercise 5

GETTING HELP FROM THE AUTOCONTENT WIZARD

1. Prepare slides for helping organize a presentation to market and sell a service by completing the following steps:
   a. Make sure the task pane displays. (If not, click View and then Task Pane.)
   b. Click the Other Task Panes button (contains the name of the task pane and a down-pointing arrow) located toward the top of the task pane and then click *New Presentation* at the drop-down list.
   c. Click the <u>From AutoContent wizard</u> hyperlink located in the *New* section of the New Presentation task pane.
   d. At the AutoContent Wizard Start dialog box, click the Next button that displays toward the bottom right side of the dialog box.
   e. At the AutoContent Wizard Presentation type dialog box, click the Sales / Marketing button, and then click *Product/Services Overview* in the list box.

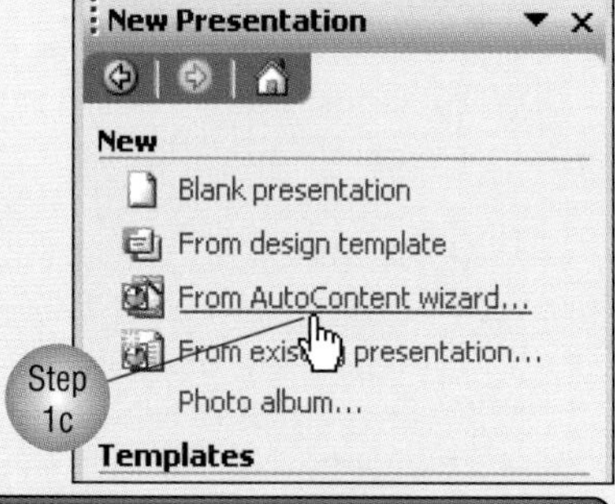

   f. Click the Next button.
   g. At the AutoContent Wizard Presentation style dialog box, make sure the *On-screen presentation* option is selected, and then click the Next button.
   h. At the AutoContent Wizard Presentation options dialog box, make the following changes:
      1) Click inside the *Presentation title* text box and then type **McCormack Funds**.
      2) Press the Tab key. (This moves the insertion point to the *Footer* text box.)
      3) Type **Variable Annuity Fund**.
      4) Click the Next button.

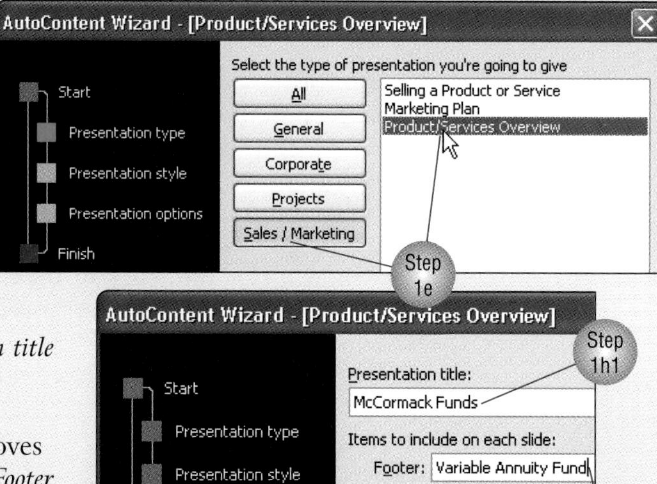

   i. At the AutoContent Wizard Finish dialog box, click the Finish button.
2. Save the presentation by completing the following steps:
   a. Click the Save button on the Standard toolbar.
   b. At the Save As dialog box, make sure PowerPointChapter01S is the default folder, type **sppc1x05** in the *File name* text box, and then press Enter or click Save.
3. Print the information on the slides provided by the wizard in Outline View by completing the following steps:
   a. Click File and then Print.
   b. At the Print dialog box, click the down-pointing arrow to the right of the *Print what* option, and then click *Outline View* at the drop-down list.
   c. Click OK.
4. Run the presentation. (Read the information on each slide provided by the wizard.)
5. Close the presentation. (If a dialog box displays asking if you want to save the changes, click Yes.)

Preparing a Presentation in the Outline/Slides Pane

In Exercise 1, you created a slide presentation using a PowerPoint template. With this method, a slide with formatting applied was presented in the Slide pane where you entered specific text. You can also enter text on a slide in the Outline/Slides pane with the Outline tab selected. Consider turning on the display of the Outlining toolbar when using the Outline/Slides pane to create slides. Turn on the Outlining toolbar by clicking View, pointing to Toolbars, and then clicking Outlining. The Outlining toolbar displays along the left side of the Outline/Slides pane. The buttons on the Outlining toolbar are described in Table 1.1.

TABLE 1.1 ***Outlining Toolbar Buttons***

Button	Name	Function
	Promote	Moves insertion point along with any text to the previous tab stop to the left
	Demote	Moves insertion point along with any text to the next tab stop to the right
	Move Up	Moves insertion point along with any text up to the previous line
	Move Down	Moves insertion point along with any text down to the next line
	Collapse	Displays only the titles of the slides
	Expand	Displays all levels of the slides
	Collapse All	Displays only the titles of the slides
	Expand All	Displays titles and body text for all slides (also available on the Standard toolbar)
	Summary Slide	Creates a summary slide of presentation based on titles of slides you select
	Show Formatting	Displays all character formatting (also available on the Standard toolbar)

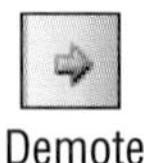
Demote

Promote

To create a slide in the Outline/Slides pane, click in the pane and then type the text. Press the Tab key or click the Demote button on the Outlining toolbar to move the insertion point to the next tab stop. This moves the insertion point and also changes the formatting. The formatting will vary depending on the design template you chose in the Slide Design task pane. Press Shift + Tab or click the Promote button on the Outlining toolbar to move the insertion point to the previous tab stop and change the formatting. Moving the insertion point back to the left margin will begin another slide. Slides are numbered at the left side of the screen and are followed by a slide icon.

exercise 6

PREPARING A PRESENTATION IN THE OUTLINE/SLIDES PANE

1. Create a presentation in the Outline/Slides pane by completing the following steps:
   a. With PowerPoint open and a blank screen displayed, click the New button on the Standard toolbar (first button from the left).
   b. Click Format and then Slide Design.
   c. Click *Edge* in the *Apply a design template* list box. (You will need to scroll down the list to display this design template. Position the arrow pointer on a design template to display the name.)
   d. Display the Outlining toolbar by clicking View, pointing to Toolbars, and then clicking Outlining.
   e. Click the Outline tab in the Outline/Slides pane.
   f. Click immediately right of the Slide 1 icon in the Outline/Slides pane, type the first slide title shown in Figure 1.10 *(Computer Technology)*, and then press Enter.
   g. Type the second slide title shown in Figure 1.10 *(The Motherboard)* and then press Enter.
   h. Click the Demote button on the Outlining toolbar or press Tab, type the text after the first bullet in Figure 1.10 *(Buses)*, and then press Enter.
   i. Continue typing the text as it displays in Figure 1.10. Click the Demote button or press Tab to move the insertion point to the next tab stop. Click the Promote button or press Shift + Tab to move the insertion back to a previous tab stop.
   j. Click the Collapse All button on the Outlining toolbar. (This displays only the title of each slide.)
   k. Click the Expand All button on the Outlining toolbar.
2. Save the presentation by completing the following steps:
   a. Click the Save button on the Standard toolbar.
   b. At the Save As dialog box, make sure the PowerPointChapter01S folder on your disk is the active folder.
   c. Type sppc1x06 in the *File name* text box and then press Enter.

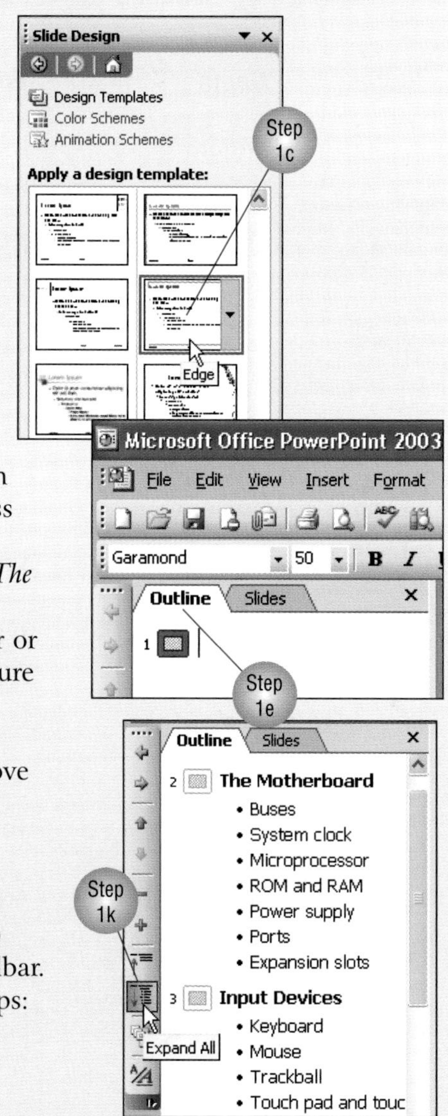

3. View the slides by clicking the Slide Sorter View button on the View toolbar.
4. Print the four slides as notes pages by displaying the Print dialog box and then changing the *Print what* option to *Notes Pages*.
5. Close the presentation.

FIGURE 1.10 **Exercise 6**

1 Computer Technology
2 The Motherboard
- Buses
- System clock
- Microprocessor
- ROM and RAM
- Power supply
- Ports
- Expansion slots

3 Input Devices
- Keyboard
- Mouse
- Trackball
- Touch pad and touch screen
- Pen and tablet
- Joystick
- Scanner

4 Output Devices
- Monitor
- Printer
  - Dot matrix
  - Laser
  - Ink jet
- Speakers

Deleting a Presentation

File management tasks in PowerPoint can be performed at the Open or Save As dialog box. To delete a PowerPoint presentation, display the Open dialog box, click the presentation you want deleted, and then click the Delete button on the dialog box toolbar. At the message asking if you are sure you want to delete the presentation, click the Yes button.

Delete

Delete a Presentation
1. Click Open button on Standard toolbar.
2. Navigate to desired folder or drive.
3. Click the presentation.
4. Click Delete button.
5. Click Yes.

exercise 7

DELETING A POWERPOINT PRESENTATION

1. Delete a presentation from the PowerPointChapter01S folder on your disk by completing the following steps:
   a. With PowerPoint open, display the Open dialog box by clicking the Open button on the Standard toolbar.
   b. At the Open dialog box, make sure the PowerPointChapter01S folder on your disk is the active folder.
   c. Click ***sppc1x05*** in the list box to select it.
   d. Click the Delete button on the dialog box toolbar.
   e. At the dialog box asking if you are sure you want to delete the presentation, click Yes.
   f. At the Open dialog box, delete **sppc1x04** by completing steps similar to those in Steps 1c through 1e.
2. Close the Open dialog box.

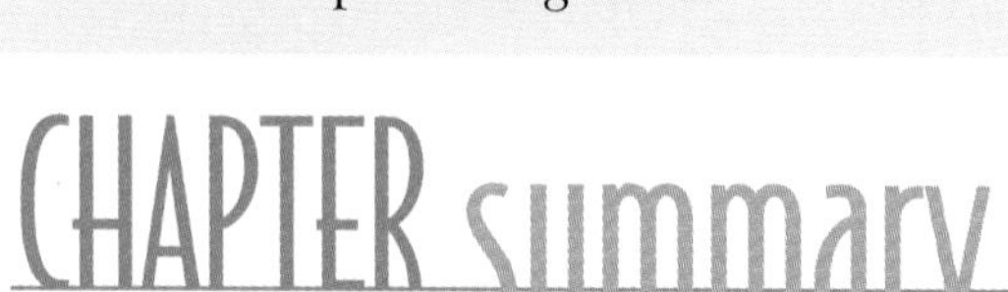

CHAPTER summary

- PowerPoint is a software program you can use to create slides for an on-screen presentation or for an overhead or slide projector. In PowerPoint, you can print handouts of the presentation, print an outline, or print the entire presentation.
- Before creating a presentation in PowerPoint, plan the presentation by defining the purpose and determining the content and medium.
- The PowerPoint window contains the following elements: Title bar, Menu bar, Standard toolbar, Formatting toolbar, Drawing toolbar, Outline/Slides pane, Slide pane, Notes pane, scroll bars, View toolbar, and Status bar.
- PowerPoint includes a variety of preformatted design templates you can use for creating a presentation. Click the Slide Design button on the Standard toolbar and the Slide Design task pane displays with design templates.
- Choose a slide layout at the Slide Layout task pane. Display this task pane by clicking Format on the Menu bar and then clicking Slide Layout. Slide layouts contain placeholders, which are locations on the slide where information is entered or inserted.
- Click the New Slide button on the Formatting toolbar to insert a new slide in a presentation.
- With options at the Print dialog box, you can print presentations with each slide on a separate piece of paper; each slide at the top of the page, leaving room for notes; all or a specific number of slides on a single piece of paper; or slide titles and topics in outline form.
- Save a presentation by clicking the Save button on the Formatting toolbar, typing a name for the presentation, and then pressing Enter or clicking the Save button.

- Close a PowerPoint presentation by clicking File and then Close or by clicking the Close Window button at the right side of the Menu bar.
- Open a presentation by clicking the Open button on the Standard toolbar and then double-clicking the desired presentation.
- View a presentation in one of the following four views: Normal view, which is the default and displays three panes—Outline/Slides, Slide, and Notes; Slide Sorter view, which displays all slides in the presentation in slide miniatures; Notes Page view, which displays an individual slide with any added notes displayed below the slide; and Slide Show view, which runs the presentation.
- A slide show can be run manually, where you determine when to advance to the next slide; automatically, where PowerPoint advances the slides; or continuously, for demonstration purposes.
- Use the pen or highlighter during a presentation to emphasize major points or draw the attention of the audience to specific items on a slide. Change the mouse pointer to a pen or highlighter by clicking the pen button on the Slide View toolbar and then clicking the desired item.
- Enhance a presentation by adding transitions (how one slide is removed from the screen and replaced with the next slide) and sound. Add transitions and sound to a presentation with options at the Slide Transition task pane.
- In Slide Sorter view, select all slides by clicking Edit and then Select All or by pressing Ctrl + A.
- Use options at the Slide Transition task pane to automatically advance slides after a specific number of seconds when running a presentation.
- Create a self-running presentation with options at the Set Up Show dialog box.
- Use PowerPoint's AutoContent Wizard to help in the planning and organizing of a presentation.
- You can enter text on a slide in the Outline/Slides pane. Use buttons on the Outlining toolbar to promote, demote, move up, or move down text on the slide and collapse and expand text on slides.
- Delete a presentation at the Open dialog box by clicking the presentation file name and then clicking the Delete button on the dialog box toolbar. Click Yes at the confirm message.

FEATURES summary

FEATURE	BUTTON	MENU	KEYBOARD
Slide Design task pane	Design	Format, Slide Design	
Slide Layout task pane	Layout	Format, Slide Layout	
Insert new slide	New Slide	Insert, New Slide	Ctrl + M
Print presentation			
Print dialog box		File, Print	Ctrl + P
Save As dialog box		File, Save As	Ctrl + S

FEATURE	BUTTON	MENU	KEYBOARD
Close presentation	✕	File, Close Window	Ctrl + F4
Open dialog box		File, Open	Ctrl + O
Run presentation		View, Slide Show	F5
Slide Transition task pane	Transition	Slide Show, Slide Transition	
Set Up Show dialog box		Slide Show, Set Up Show	
Outlining toolbar		View, Toolbars, Outlining	

CONCEPTS check

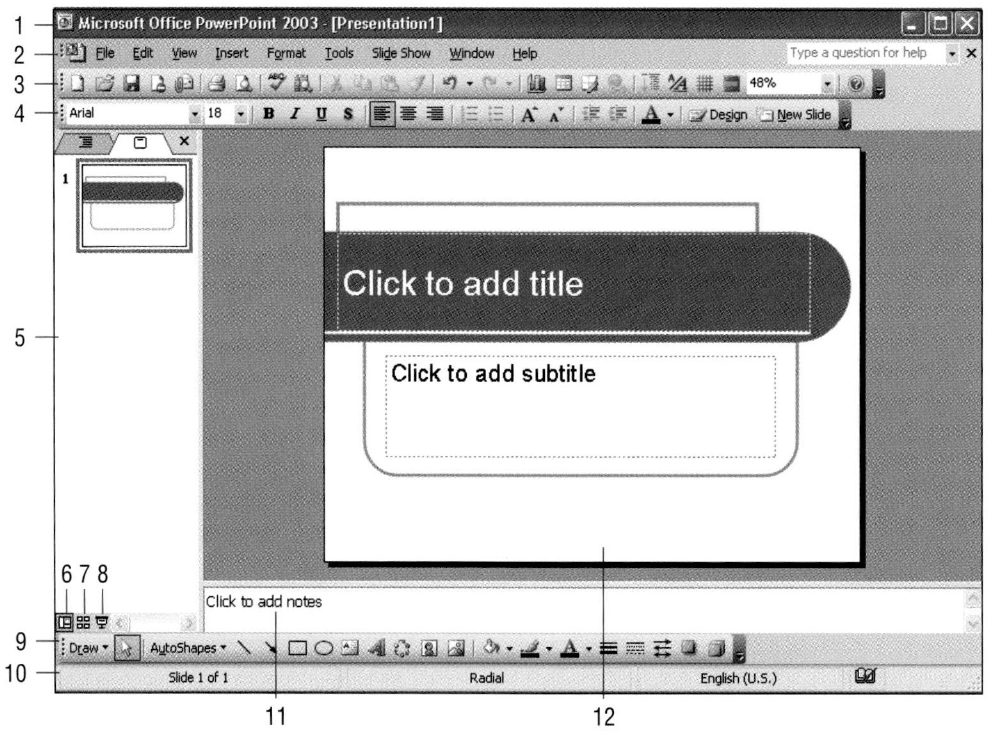

Identifying: Look at the PowerPoint screen shown above. This screen contains numbers with lines pointing to specific items. On a blank sheet of paper, write the name of the item that corresponds with each number in the PowerPoint screen.

Completion: On a blank sheet of paper, indicate the correct term, symbol, or command for each description.

1. Click this button on the View toolbar to run a presentation.
2. Click this button on the View toolbar to display all slides in the presentation in slide miniatures.
3. While running a presentation, click this button on the mouse to display the previous slide.
4. If a presentation contains six slides, click this option at the *Print what* drop-down list at the Print dialog box to print all of the slides on the same page.
5. This term refers to how one slide is removed from the screen and replaced with the next slide.
6. To display the Slide Transition task pane, click this option on the Menu bar, and then click Slide Transition.
7. Click this button on the Outlining toolbar to move the insertion point to the next tab stop.
8. Click this button on the Outlining toolbar to move the insertion point to the previous tab stop.

SKILLS check

Assessment 1

1. Create a presentation with the text shown in Figure 1.11 by completing the following steps:
   a. With PowerPoint open, click the New button on the Standard toolbar (first button from the left).
   b. Click the Slide Design button on the Formatting toolbar.
   c. Click the *Watermark* design template in the *Apply a design template* list box. (You will need to scroll toward the end of the list box to display this template.)
   d. Display the Slide Layout task pane by clicking Format and then Slide Layout.
   e. At the slide, click anywhere in the text *Click to add title*, and then type **DEDUCTIBLE INCOME**.
   f. Click anywhere in the text *Click to add subtitle* and then type **Exceptions to Deductible Income**.
   g. Click the New Slide button located on the Formatting toolbar.
   h. Click the Title Slide layout in the Slide Layout task pane and then create the second slide with the text shown in Figure 1.11.
   i. Create the remaining slides as shown in Figure 1.11 by completing steps similar to those in Steps 1g and 1h.
2. Save the presentation in the PowerPointChapter01S folder on your disk and name the presentation **sppc1sc01**.
3. Run the presentation.
4. Print all of the slides on one page as handouts.
5. Close the Slide Layout task pane and then close the presentation.

FIGURE 1.11 ***Assessment 1***

Slide 1	Title	=	DEDUCTIBLE INCOME
	Subtitle	=	Exceptions to Deductible Income
Slide 2	Title	=	EXCEPTION 1
	Subtitle	=	Any cost of living increase if increase becomes effective while disabled
Slide 3	Title	=	EXCEPTION 2
	Subtitle	=	Reimbursement for hospital, medical, or surgical expense
Slide 4	Title	=	EXCEPTION 3
	Subtitle	=	Reasonable attorney's fees incurred in connection with a claim for deductible income
Slide 5	Title	=	EXCEPTION 4
	Subtitle	=	Benefits from any individual disability insurance policy
Slide 6	Title	=	EXCEPTION 5
	Subtitle	=	Group credit or mortgage disability insurance benefits

Assessment 2

1. Open **sppc1sc01**.
2. Save the presentation with Save As in the PowerPointChapter01S folder on your disk and name the presentation **sppc1sc02**.
3. Make the following changes to the presentation:
   a. Add the transition *Split Vertical Out* to all slides in the presentation.
   b. Add the cash register sound to all slides in the presentation.
4. Save the presentation again with the same name (**sppc1sc02**).
5. Run the presentation.
6. Close the Slide Transition task pane and then close the presentation.

Assessment 3

1. Create a presentation with the text shown in Figure 1.12. You determine the design template for the presentation and the layout for each slide. ***(Hint: Use the Title Slide layout for the first slide and the Title and Text layout for the remaining slides.)***
2. Save the completed presentation in the PowerPointChapter01S folder on your disk and name it **sppc1sc03**.
3. Print the presentation as an outline.
4. Print the presentation as individual slides.
5. Close the presentation.

FIGURE

1.12 Assessment 3

Slide 1	Title	=	PREPARING A COMPANY NEWSLETTER
	Subtitle	=	Planning and Designing the Layout
Slide 2	Title	=	Planning a Newsletter
	Bullets	=	♦ If a scanner is available, use pictures of different people from your organization in each issue. ♦ Distribute contributor sheets soliciting information from employees. ♦ Keep the focus of the newsletter on issues of interest to employees.
Slide 3	Title	=	Planning a Newsletter
	Bullets	=	♦ Make sure the focus is on various levels of employment; do not focus on top management only. ♦ Conduct regular surveys to see if your newsletter provides a needed source of information.
Slide 4	Title	=	Designing a Newsletter
	Bullets	=	♦ Maintain consistent elements from issue to issue such as: - Column layout - Nameplate formatting and location - Formatting of headlines - Use of color
Slide 5	Title	=	Designing a Newsletter
	Bullets	=	♦ Consider the following elements when designing a newsletter: - Focus - Balance - White space - Directional flow
Slide 6	Title	=	Creating a Newsletter Layout
	Bullets	=	♦ Choose paper size ♦ Choose paper weight ♦ Determine margins ♦ Specify column layout

TABLE 2.1 **Selecting Text**

To do this	*Perform this action*
Select text mouse pointer passes through	Click and drag mouse
Select entire word	Double-click word
Select entire paragraph	Triple-click anywhere in paragraph
Select entire sentence	Ctrl + click anywhere in sentence
Select all text in selected placeholder	Click Edit, Select All or press Ctrl + A

QUICK STEPS

Find Text
1. Click Edit, Find.
2. Type text for which you are searching.
3. Click Find Next button.

Finding and Replacing Text in Slides

Use the find feature to look for specific text in slides in a presentation and use the find and replace feature to look for specific text in slides in a presentation and replace with other text. Begin a find by clicking Edit and then Find. This displays the Find dialog box shown in Figure 2.1. You can also open the Find dialog box with the keyboard shortcut Ctrl + F. In the *Find what* text box, type the text you want to find and then click the Find Next button. Continue clicking this button until a message displays telling you that the search is complete. At this message, click OK.

FIGURE 2.1 **Find Dialog Box**

In this text box, type the text for which you are searching.

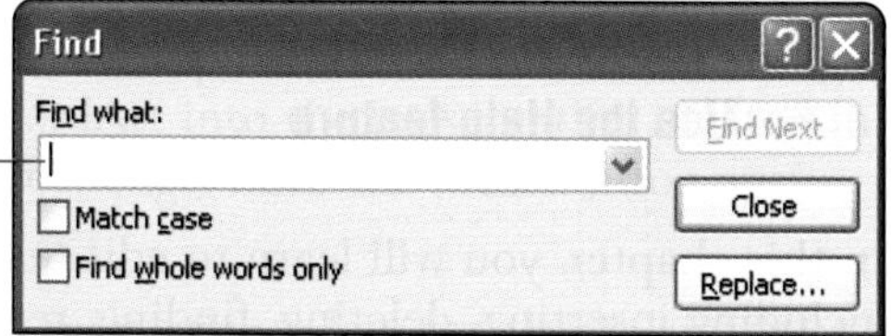

QUICK STEPS

Replace Text
1. Click Edit, Replace.
2. Type text for which you are searching.
3. Press Tab.
4. Type replacement text.
5. Click Replace All.

Use options at the Replace dialog box shown in Figure 2.2 to search for text and replace with other text. Display this dialog box by clicking Edit and then Replace, or with the keyboard shortcut Ctrl + H. Type the text you want to find in the *Find what* text box, press the Tab key, and then type the replacement text in the *Replace with* text box. Click the Find Next button to find the next occurrence of the text or click the Replace All button to replace all occurrences in the presentation.

FIGURE 2.2 **Replace Dialog Box**

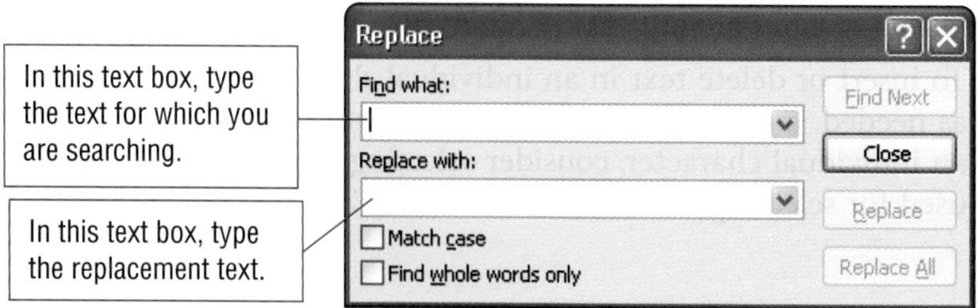

FIGURE

1.12 ***Assessment 3***

Slide 1	Title	=	PREPARING A COMPANY NEWSLETTER
	Subtitle	=	Planning and Designing the Layout
Slide 2	Title	=	Planning a Newsletter
	Bullets	=	• If a scanner is available, use pictures of different people from your organization in each issue. • Distribute contributor sheets soliciting information from employees. • Keep the focus of the newsletter on issues of interest to employees.
Slide 3	Title	=	Planning a Newsletter
	Bullets	=	• Make sure the focus is on various levels of employment; do not focus on top management only. • Conduct regular surveys to see if your newsletter provides a needed source of information.
Slide 4	Title	=	Designing a Newsletter
	Bullets	=	• Maintain consistent elements from issue to issue such as: - Column layout - Nameplate formatting and location - Formatting of headlines - Use of color
Slide 5	Title	=	Designing a Newsletter
	Bullets	=	• Consider the following elements when designing a newsletter: - Focus - Balance - White space - Directional flow
Slide 6	Title	=	Creating a Newsletter Layout
	Bullets	=	• Choose paper size • Choose paper weight • Determine margins • Specify column layout

Assessment 4

1. Open **sppc1sc03**.
2. Save the presentation with Save As in the PowerPointChapter01S folder on your disk and name the presentation **sppc1sc04**.
3. Make the following changes to the presentation:
   a. Add a transition of your choosing to each slide.
   b. Add a sound of your choosing to each slide.
   c. Specify that all slides advance automatically after five seconds.
   d. Set up the presentation as continuous.
4. Save and then run the presentation.
5. Close the presentation.

CHAPTER challenge

You work in the Admissions Office at the local university. You have been asked to create a PowerPoint presentation describing the process of enrolling for classes. The presentation will be used during the week of freshman orientation. Create at least five slides. Use an appropriate design template. Add transitions and sound effects. The presentation will be placed on a kiosk in the Student Center, therefore, set the slide show to run automatically. Save the presentation as **EnrollmentProcess**. Print the first slide of the presentation.

You would like to visually enhance the presentation by adding WordArt. Use the Help feature to learn about using WordArt. Then incorporate WordArt into the presentation created in the first part of the Chapter Challenge. Save the presentation again.

Some students may sign up late for classes and miss freshman orientation week. To ensure that students get the accurate information, you will prepare the presentation to be packaged for a CD. This will enable students to view the presentation even if they do not have PowerPoint.

CHAPTER 2

MODIFYING A PRESENTATION AND USING HELP

PERFORMANCE OBJECTIVES

Upon successful completion of Chapter 2, you will be able to:

- **Insert and delete text in slides**
- **Find and replace text in slides**
- **Rearrange text and placeholders in slides**
- **Complete a spelling check**
- **Use Thesaurus to look up synonyms for specific words**
- **Insert, copy, delete, and rearrange slides in a presentation**
- **Copy slides between presentations**
- **Preview a presentation**
- **Use the Help feature**

Chapter02S

PowerPoint

In this chapter, you will learn to edit text and slides in a PowerPoint presentation, including inserting, deleting, finding, replacing, and rearranging text within slides and inserting, copying, deleting, and rearranging slides within a presentation. You will also learn about a number of PowerPoint features including spell checking, Thesaurus, preview, and Help.

Editing Slides

You can edit text in slides in a PowerPoint presentation. For example, you can insert text into a slide or delete text from a slide. You can also search for specific text and replace it with other text; cut, copy, and paste text within and between slides; and complete a spelling check.

Inserting and Deleting Text in Slides

To insert or delete text in an individual slide, open the presentation, edit the text as needed, and then save the presentation again. If you want to delete more than an individual character, consider selecting the text first. Several methods can be used for selecting text as shown in Table 2.1.

TABLE 2.1 Selecting Text

To do this	Perform this action
Select text mouse pointer passes through	Click and drag mouse
Select entire word	Double-click word
Select entire paragraph	Triple-click anywhere in paragraph
Select entire sentence	Ctrl + click anywhere in sentence
Select all text in selected placeholder	Click Edit, Select All or press Ctrl + A

QUICK STEPS

Find Text
1. Click Edit, Find.
2. Type text for which you are searching.
3. Click Find Next button.

Finding and Replacing Text in Slides

Use the find feature to look for specific text in slides in a presentation and use the find and replace feature to look for specific text in slides in a presentation and replace with other text. Begin a find by clicking Edit and then Find. This displays the Find dialog box shown in Figure 2.1. You can also open the Find dialog box with the keyboard shortcut Ctrl + F. In the *Find what* text box, type the text you want to find and then click the Find Next button. Continue clicking this button until a message displays telling you that the search is complete. At this message, click OK.

FIGURE 2.1 Find Dialog Box

In this text box, type the text for which you are searching.

Find
Find what:
Match case
Find whole words only
Find Next
Close
Replace...

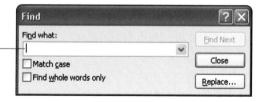

Replace Text
1. Click Edit, Replace.
2. Type text for which you are searching.
3. Press Tab.
4. Type replacement text.
5. Click Replace All.

Use options at the Replace dialog box shown in Figure 2.2 to search for text and replace with other text. Display this dialog box by clicking Edit and then Replace, or with the keyboard shortcut Ctrl + H. Type the text you want to find in the *Find what* text box, press the Tab key, and then type the replacement text in the *Replace with* text box. Click the Find Next button to find the next occurrence of the text or click the Replace All button to replace all occurrences in the presentation.

FIGURE 2.2 Replace Dialog Box

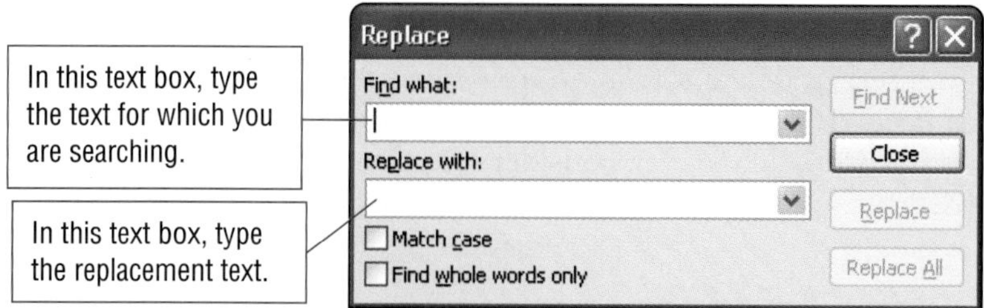

(Note: Before completing Exercise 1, delete the PowerPointChapter01S folder on your disk. Next, copy to your disk the PowerPointChapter02S subfolder from the PowerPoint2003Specialist folder on the CD that accompanies this textbook and then make PowerPointChapter02S the active folder.)

exercise 1

INSERTING, DELETING, FINDING AND REPLACING TEXT IN SLIDES

1. Open PowerPoint and then open PlanningPresentation from the PowerPointChapter02S folder on your disk.
2. Save the presentation with Save As in the PowerPointChapter02S folder on your disk and name the presentation **sppc2x01**.
3. Delete and insert text in slides by completing the following steps:
   a. In the Normal view, click the Next Slide button located at the bottom of the vertical scroll bar until Slide 5 displays.
   b. Edit Slide 5 by completing the following steps:
      1) Position the I-beam pointer on the sentence below *STEP 4* and then click the left mouse button. (This inserts a frame around the text.)
      2) Edit the sentence so it reads *Decide what steps you want readers to take after reading your message.* (Use deleting and inserting commands to edit this sentence.)

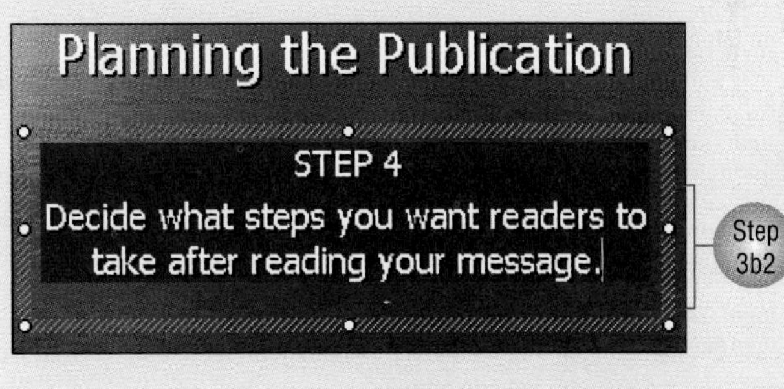

   c. Click the Next Slide button to display Slide 6.
   d. Edit Slide 6 in the Outline/Slides pane by completing the following steps:
      1) Click the Outline tab in the Outline/Slides pane.
      2) Click in the sentence below *STEP 5* and then edit the sentence so it reads *Collect and assess examples of effective designs.*
      3) Click the Slides tab.

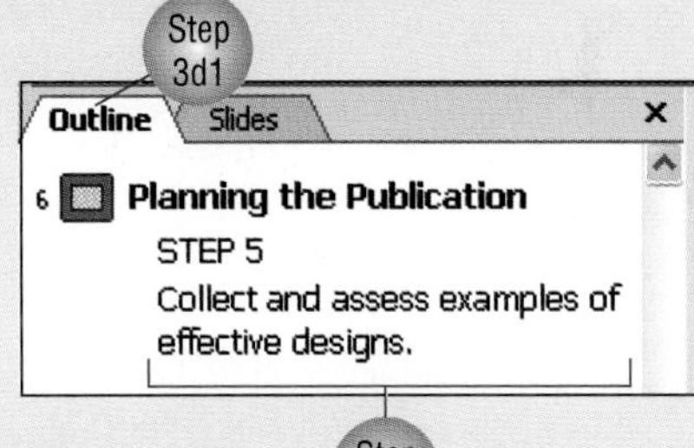

4. Find all occurrences of *Planning* in the presentation and replace with *Preparing* by completing the following steps:
   a. Display Slide 1 in the Slide pane.
   b. Click Edit and then Replace.
   c. At the Replace dialog box, type **Planning** in the *Find what* text box.
   d. Press the Tab key.
   e. Type **Preparing** in the *Replace with* text box.
   f. Click the Replace All button.
   g. At the message telling you that five replacements were made, click OK.
   h. Click the Close button to close the Replace dialog box.

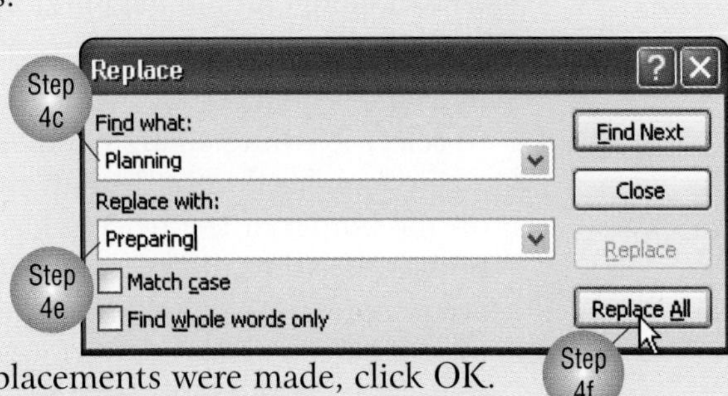

5. Find all occurrences of *Publication* and replace with *Newsletter* by completing steps similar to those in Step 4.
6. Save the presentation.

7. Print the six slides on one page. (Change the *Print what* option at the Print dialog box to *Handouts*.)
8. Close **sppc2x01**.

Rearranging Text in Slides

Cut

Paste

Copy

With buttons on the Standard toolbar or options on the Menu bar, you can cut, copy, delete, and/or paste text in slides. For example, to move text in a slide, click once in the placeholder containing the text to be moved, select the text, and then click the Cut button on the Standard toolbar. Position the insertion point where you want the text inserted and then click the Paste button on the Standard toolbar. You can also move text from one slide to another by selecting the text, clicking the Cut button, displaying the slide where you want the text inserted, and then clicking the Paste button. To copy text in or between slides, complete similar steps. Select the text to be copied, click the Copy button on the Standard toolbar, move the insertion point to the position where the text is to be copied, and then click the Paste button.

Rearranging Text in the Outline/Slides Pane

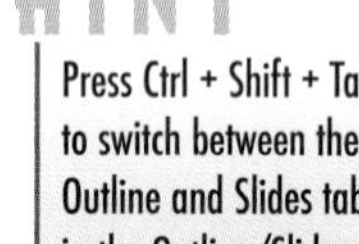

HINT
Press Ctrl + Shift + Tab to switch between the Outline and Slides tabs in the Outline/Slides pane.

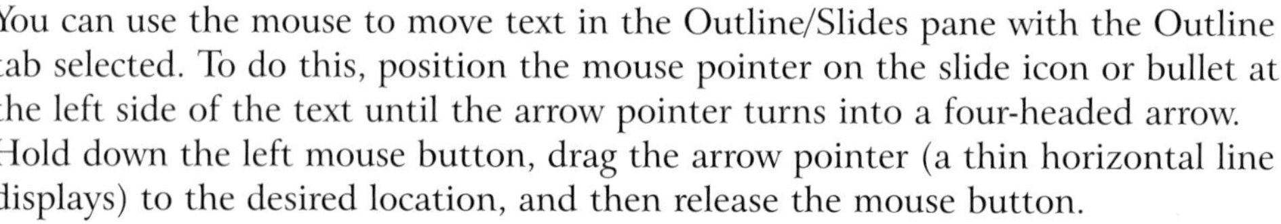

You can use the mouse to move text in the Outline/Slides pane with the Outline tab selected. To do this, position the mouse pointer on the slide icon or bullet at the left side of the text until the arrow pointer turns into a four-headed arrow. Hold down the left mouse button, drag the arrow pointer (a thin horizontal line displays) to the desired location, and then release the mouse button.

If you position the arrow pointer on the slide icon and then hold down the left mouse button, all of the text in the slide is selected. If you position the arrow pointer on the bullet and then hold down the left mouse button, all text following that bullet is selected.

Dragging selected text with the mouse moves the selected text to a new location in the presentation. You can also copy selected text. To do this, click the slide icon or click the bullet to select the desired text. Position the arrow pointer in the selected text, hold down the Ctrl key, and then the left mouse button. Drag the arrow pointer (displays with a light gray box and a plus sign attached) to the desired location, release the mouse button, and then release the Ctrl key.

Rearranging Placeholders in a Slide

Text in a slide is positioned inside a placeholder. A selected placeholder can be moved easily in a slide. To do this, click once in the placeholder (outside any text) to select it (white sizing handles should display around the placeholder). If white sizing handles do not display around the placeholder, position the arrow pointer on the border of the placeholder (small gray lines), and then click the left mouse button. Position the arrow pointer on the border around the placeholder until the arrow pointer displays with a four-headed arrow attached. Hold down the left mouse button, drag the outline of the placeholder to the desired position, and then release the mouse button.

Dragging a selected placeholder with the mouse moves the box. You can also copy a selected placeholder. To do this, hold down the Ctrl key while dragging the placeholder with the mouse. When the outline of the placeholder is in the desired position, release the mouse button, and then release the Ctrl key.

Sizing a Placeholder

Click a placeholder in a slide and sizing handles display around the placeholder. Use these sizing handles to increase or decrease the size of the placeholder. To increase or decrease the size, position the arrow pointer on one of the white sizing handles until the arrow pointer turns into a double-headed arrow. Hold down the left mouse button, drag the outline of the placeholder in to decrease the size or drag the outline out to increase the size, and then release the mouse button. You can increase or decrease the height and width of the placeholder at the same time by using the sizing handles that display in each corner of the selected placeholder.

HINT

Change the size of a selected placeholder by dragging a corner or side sizing handle.

Complete a Spelling Check

1. Click Spelling button.
2. Change or ignore words.
3. Click OK.

Completing a Spelling Check

When you create a presentation, consider performing a spelling check on text in slides. PowerPoint's spelling check feature compares words in a presentation with words in its dictionary. If a match is found, the word is passed over. If a match is not found, the spelling checker selects the word and offers replacement suggestions. To perform a spelling check on a PowerPoint presentation, click the Spelling button on the Standard toolbar or click Tools and then Spelling. Change or ignore selected text as required.

HINT

Press F7 to begin spell checking a presentation.

Spelling

Using Thesaurus

Use the Thesaurus feature to find synonyms, antonyms, and related words for a particular word. To use the Thesaurus, click on the word for which you want to display synonyms and antonyms, click Tools, and then click Thesaurus. This displays the Research task pane with information about the word where the insertion point is positioned. Figure 2.3 displays the Research task pane with synonyms and antonyms displayed for the word *efficiency*.

FIGURE 2.3 **Research Task Pane**

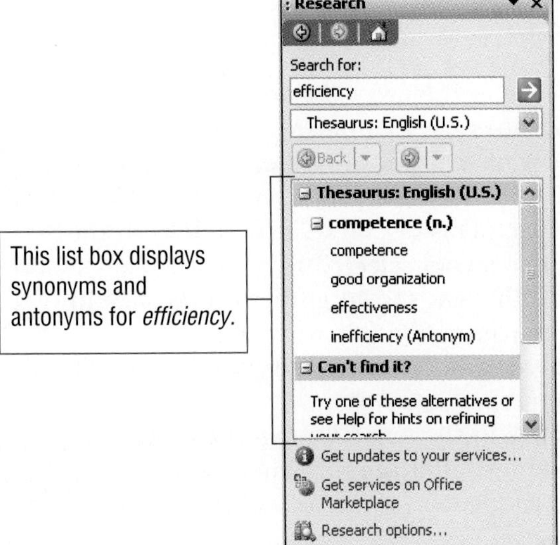

Hold down the Alt key and then click a word to display synonyms in the Research task pane.

QUICK STEPS

Replace Word with Synonym
1. Click word.
2. Click Tools, Thesaurus.
3. Click desired synonym in Research task pane.

Depending on the word you are looking up, the words in the Research task pane list box may display followed by *(n.)* for *noun*, *(adj.)* for *adjective*, or *(adv.)* for *adverb*. Antonyms may display in the list of related synonyms, generally at the end of the list of related synonyms and are followed by *(Antonym)*.

Display synonyms and antonyms for other words by typing the desired word in the *Search for* text box and then clicking the Start searching button (white arrow on green background). As you look up synonyms and antonyms for various words, you can display the list of synonyms and antonyms for the previous word by clicking the Previous search button (contains the word *Back* and a left-pointing arrow) located above the Research task pane list box (see Figure 2.3). Click the Next search button to display the next search in the sequence. You can also click the down-pointing arrow at the right side of the Next search button to display a list of words for which you have looked up synonyms and antonyms.

You can also use a shortcut menu option to display synonyms for a specific word. To do this, right-click on the desired word and then point to Synonyms at the shortcut menu. This displays a side menu of synonyms. Click the desired synonym and that synonym replaces the word where the insertion point is positioned.

(Note: By default, not all PowerPoint design templates are installed. Before completing Exercise 2, make sure the additional design templates are installed. [You can begin the installation by scrolling to the end of the* Apply a design template *list box and then clicking the option for installing additional templates.])

exercise 2 CREATING A PRESENTATION AND THEN REARRANGING TEXT IN SLIDES

1. Create the slides for a presentation as shown in Figure 2.4 by completing the following steps:
   a. At a blank PowerPoint screen, click the New button on the Standard toolbar.
   b. Click the Slide Design button on the Formatting toolbar.
   c. Click *Cascade* in the *Apply a design template* list box in the Slide Design task pane.
   d. At the slide, type the text for the first slide shown in Figure 2.4 by completing the following steps:
      1) At the slide, click anywhere in the text *Click to add title* and then type **Telecommunications System**.
      2) Click anywhere in the text *Click to add subtitle* and then type **Factors for Evaluating the Effectiveness of a Telecommunications System**.
   e. At the slide, click the New Slide button on the Formatting toolbar. (This displays a new slide with the Title and Text slide layout selected.)
   f. At the slide, type the text shown in the second slide in Figure 2.4 by completing the following steps:
      1) At the slide, click anywhere in the text *Click to add title* and then type **COST**.
      2) Click anywhere in the text *Click to add text* and then type the text after the first bullet in the second slide in Figure 2.4 (the text that begins *How does the cost of a new system compare...*).

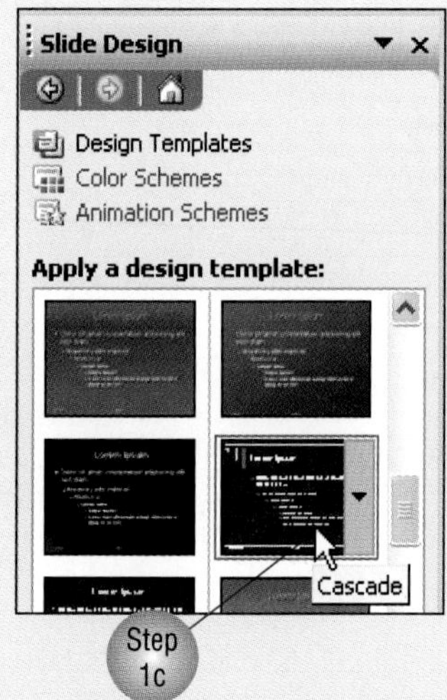

3) Type the text following the remaining bullets.
g. Click the New Slide button.
h. Continue creating the remaining slides in Figure 2.4 by completing steps similar to those in Steps 1e and 1f.

2. When all six slides have been created, make Slide 1 the active slide, and then perform a spelling check by clicking the Spelling button on the Standard toolbar. Change or ignore as required during the spelling check.
3. Use Thesaurus to replace a word with a synonym by completing the following steps:
   a. Make Slide 3 the active slide.
   b. Click in the word *effectiveness* located in the first bulleted item.
   c. Click Tools, and then Thesaurus. (This displays the Research task pane containing a list of synonyms for *effectiveness*.)
   d. Position the mouse pointer on the word *efficiency* in the Research task pane, click the down-pointing arrow that displays at the right side of the word, and then click *Insert* at the drop-down list. (This replaces the word *effectiveness* with the word *efficiency*.)
   e. Make Slide 4 the active slide.
   f. Right-click on the word *effectiveness* located in the first bulleted item.
   g. At the shortcut menu that displays, point to Synonyms, and then click *usefulness*.

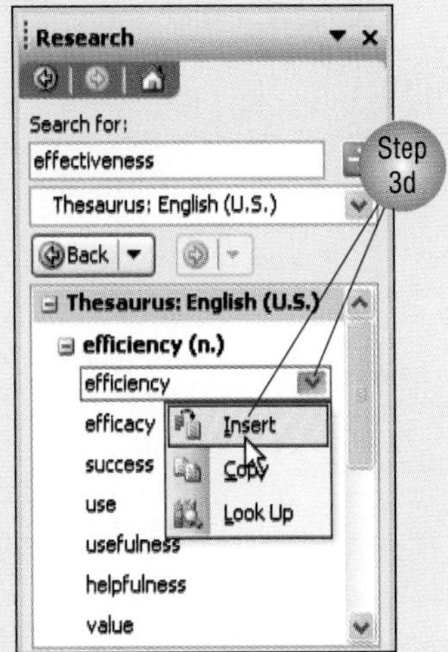

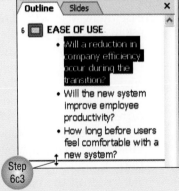

4. Save the presentation in the PowerPointChapter02S folder on your disk and name the presentation **sppc2x02**.
5. Print the six slides on one page.
6. Move and copy text within and between slides by completing the following steps:
   a. Make sure you are in Normal view.
   b. Click the Outline tab in the Outline/Slides pane.
   c. Move the first bulleted item in Slide 6 to the end of the list by completing the following steps:
      1) Scroll down the Outline/Slides pane until all of the Slide 6 text displays in the pane.
      2) Position the mouse pointer on the first bullet below *EASE OF USE* until it turns into a four-headed arrow.
      3) Hold down the left mouse button, drag the arrow pointer down until a thin horizontal line displays below the last bulleted item, and then release the mouse button.
      4) Click the Slides tab in the Outline/Slides pane.
   d. Copy a bulleted item from Slide 3 (*EFFICIENCY*) to Slide 5 (*TIME*) by completing the following steps:
      1) Display Slide 3 in the Slide pane.
      2) Click anywhere in the bulleted text. (This selects the placeholder containing the text.)

3) Position the mouse pointer on the last square bullet in Slide 3 until it turns into a four-headed arrow and then click the left mouse button. (This selects the text after the bullet.)

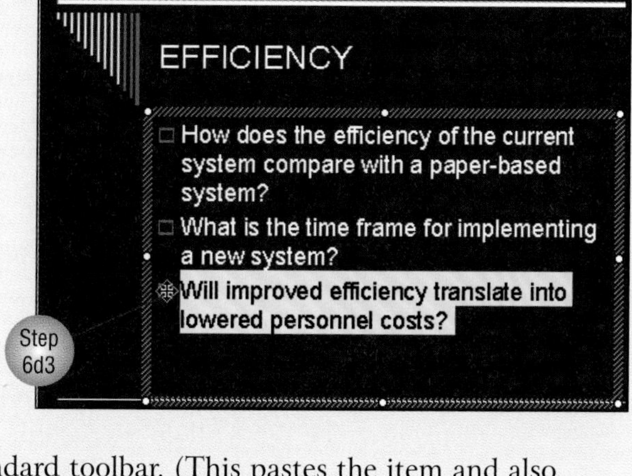

4) With the text selected, click the Copy button on the Standard toolbar.
5) Display Slide 5 in the Slide pane.
6) Position the I-beam pointer immediately after the question mark in the second bulleted item in Slide 5 and then click the left mouse button.
7) Press the Enter key. (This moves the insertion point down to the next line and inserts another bullet.)

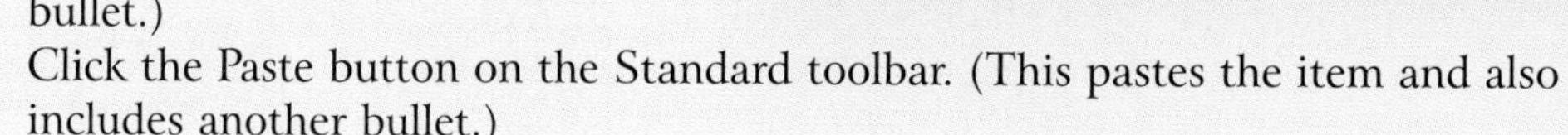

8) Click the Paste button on the Standard toolbar. (This pastes the item and also includes another bullet.)
9) Press the Backspace key twice to remove the extra bullet.

e. Move and size a placeholder in a slide by completing the following steps:
1) Display Slide 1 in the Slide pane.
2) Click anywhere in the subtitle text *Factors for Evaluating the Effectiveness of a Telecommunications System*. (This selects the placeholder containing the text.)

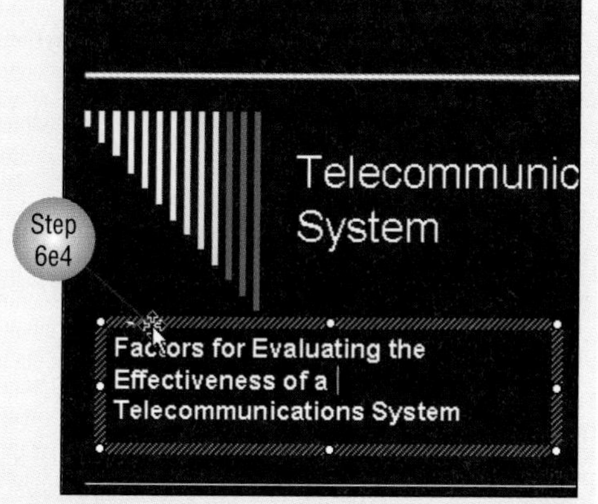

3) Position the arrow pointer on the border of the placeholder until the pointer turns into a four-headed arrow.
4) Hold down the left mouse button, drag the placeholder to the left as shown at the right, and then release the mouse button.
5) Increase the width of the box by completing the following steps:
   a) Position the mouse pointer on the middle sizing handle (white circle) at the right side of the placeholder until the pointer turns into a double-headed arrow pointing left and right.

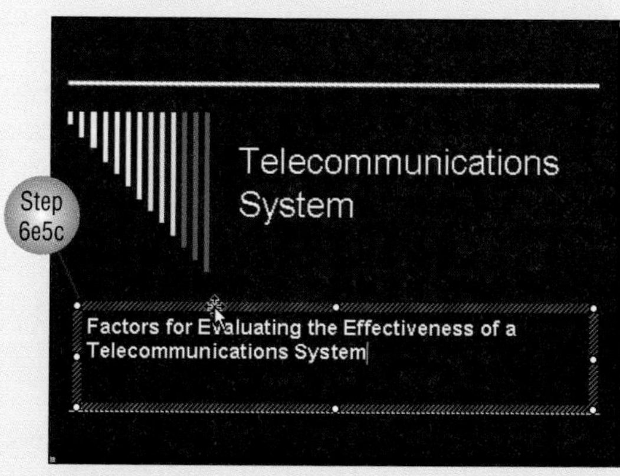

   b) Hold down the left mouse button, drag to the right so the right edge of the placeholder is approximately positioned at the end of the white line at the bottom of the slide, and then release the mouse button.
   c) Drag the box down and position it as shown at the right.
   d) Click outside the placeholder to deselect it.

7. Add a transition and sound of your choosing to all slides.

8. Save and then run the presentation.
9. Print the presentation in Outline view.
10. Close the presentation.

FIGURE 2.4 **Exercise 2**

Slide 1	Title	=	Telecommunications System
	Subtitle	=	Factors for Evaluating the Effectiveness of a Telecommunications System
Slide 2	Title	=	COST
	Bullets	=	• How does the cost of a new system compare with the cost of the current system? • What is the cost of maintaining the current system? • What will be the training costs of a new system?
Slide 3	Title	=	EFFICIENCY
	Bullets	=	• How does the effectiveness of the current system compare with a paper-based system? • What is the time frame for implementing a new system? • Will improved efficiency translate into lowered personnel costs?
Slide 4	Title	=	QUALITY
	Bullets	=	• How does the current system rank in terms of effectiveness? • What is the current quality of transmission? • Is the current system effective in producing the required internal and external documents?
Slide 5	Title	=	TIME
	Bullets	=	• How quickly can information be delivered? • What is the estimated training time for a new system? • What is the time frame for implementing a new system?
Slide 6	Title	=	EASE OF USE
	Bullets	=	• Will a reduction in company efficiency occur during the transition? • Will the new system improve employee productivity? • How long before users feel comfortable with a new system?

Organizing Slides

As you edit a presentation, you may need to reorganize slides and insert a new slide or delete an existing slide. Change to the Slide Sorter view to perform some reorganization activities such as moving, copying, and deleting slides.

Inserting and Deleting Slides

HINT
Press Ctrl + M to insert a new slide.

HINT
Press Ctrl + X to cut the selected slide or placeholder.

Delete a slide from a presentation by changing to the Slide Sorter view, clicking the slide you want to delete to select it, and then pressing the Delete key on the keyboard. You can also delete a slide in Normal view with the Slides tab selected in the Outline/Slides pane. To do this, click the slide miniature in the Outline/Slides pane, and then press the Delete key.

Insert a new slide in a presentation in the Normal view or the Slide Sorter view. To add a slide to a presentation in Normal view, click the New Slide button on the Formatting toolbar, click the desired slide layout in the Slide Layout task pane, and then type the text in the slide. To add a slide to a presentation in Slide Sorter view, click the slide that will immediately precede the new slide, click Insert, and then click New Slide. Double-click the new blank slide (this displays the slide in Normal view), click the desired slide layout in the Slide Layout task pane, and then type the text in the slide.

Copying a Slide

HINT
Press Ctrl + C to copy the selected slide or placeholder.

Slides in some presentations may contain similar text, objects, and formatting. Rather than create a new slide, consider copying a slide. To do this, display the presentation in either Slide Sorter view or in Normal view with the Slides tab selected in the Outline/Slides pane. Position the arrow pointer in the slide, hold down the Ctrl key and then the left mouse button. Drag to the location where you want the slide copied, release the mouse button, and then release the Ctrl key.

Copying a Slide between Presentations

HINT
Press Ctrl + V to paste the slide or placeholder.

You can copy slides between presentations as well as within a presentation. To copy a slide between presentations, click the slide you want to copy (either in Slide Sorter view or in Normal view with the Slides tab selected in the Outline/Slides pane) and then click the Copy button on the Standard toolbar. Open the presentation into which the slide is to be copied (in either Slide Sorter view or Normal view with the Slides tab selected in the Outline/Slides pane). Click in the location where you want the slide positioned and then click the Paste button. The copied slide will take on the template design of the presentation into which it is copied.

Rearranging Slides

Rearrange slides in the Slide Sorter view or in Normal view with the Slides tab selected in the Outline/Slides pane. To do this, position the arrow pointer on the slide to be moved, hold down the left mouse button, drag the arrow pointer (with a square attached) to the desired position, and then release the mouse button.

Previewing a Presentation

Print Preview

Before printing a presentation, consider previewing the presentation. To do this, click the Print Preview button on the Standard toolbar or click File and then Print Preview. This displays the active slide in the Print Preview window as it will appear when printed. Figure 2.5 displays the Planning Presentation in Print Preview. The display of your slide in Print Preview may vary depending on the selected printer. (For example, if you have a color printer selected, the slide displays in color in Print Preview. If you have a black and white laser printer selected, the slide displays as you see in Figure 2.5.) Use options on the Print Preview toolbar to display the next or previous slide, display the Print dialog box, specify how you want the presentation printed, change the Zoom (percentage of display), choose an orientation (portrait or landscape), and close Print Preview.

FIGURE 2.5 **Presentation in Print Preview**

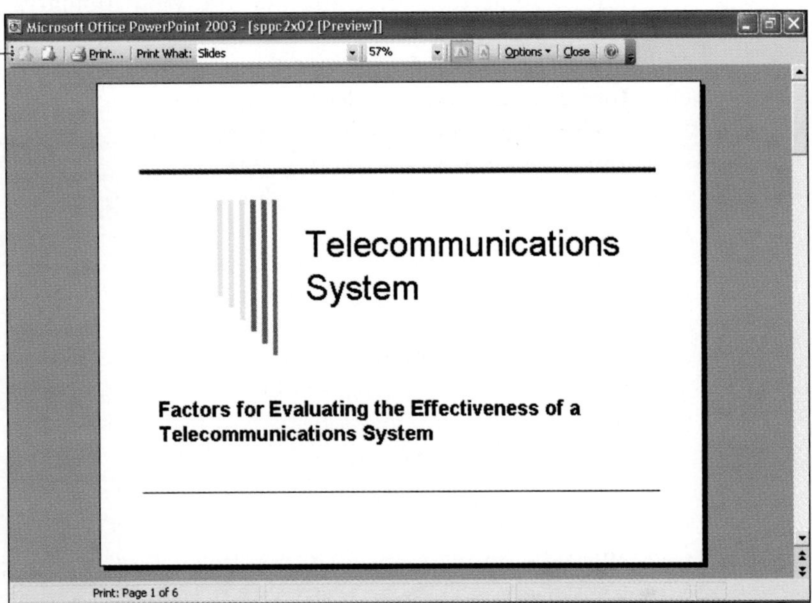

Previewing with the Color/Grayscale Button

Along with Print Preview, you can view your presentation in color, grayscale, or black and white with options from the Color/Grayscale button on the Standard toolbar. Click the Color/Grayscale button and a drop-down list displays with three options—Color, Grayscale, and Pure Black and White. Click the Color option to display your presentation. (This is the default setting.) Click the Grayscale option and the presentation displays in black and white and the Grayscale View shortcut menu displays. Click the Setting option on the Grayscale View shortcut menu and options display for changing the appearance of objects on the slides in the presentation. Click the Pure Black and White option and most objects in slides display in either black or white. The display of objects depends on the options you select with the Setting option on the Grayscale View shortcut menu.

Color/Grayscale

exercise 3

INSERTING, COPYING, AND REARRANGING SLIDES

1. Open **PlanningPresentation**.
2. Save the presentation with Save As in the PowerPointChapter02S folder on your disk and name the presentation **sppc2x03**.
3. Add a new slide to the presentation by completing the following steps:
   a. In Normal view, click the Next Slide button to display Slide 2 in the Slide pane.

b. Click the New Slide button on the Formatting toolbar. (This displays a new blank slide in the Slide pane and also displays the Slide Layout task pane.)
c. Click the Title Slide layout in the Slide Layout task pane.
d. Click anywhere in the text *Click to add title* and then type **Preparing the Newsletter**.
e. Click anywhere in the text *Click to add subtitle* and then type the following:
   1) Type **STEP 3** and then press Enter.
   2) Type **Determine the available budget for the publication.**

4. Add another new slide by completing the following steps:
   a. Click the Slide Sorter View button on the View toolbar.
   b. Click Slide 4 to select it.
   c. Click Insert on the Menu bar and then click New Slide at the drop-down menu.
   d. Double-click the new slide. (This changes the view from Slide Sorter view to Normal view.)
   e. Click the Title Slide layout in the Slide Layout task pane.
   f. Click anywhere in the text *Click to add title* and then type **Preparing the Newsletter**.
   g. Click anywhere in the text *Click to add subtitle* and then type the following:
      1) Type **STEP 5** and then press Enter.
      2) Type **Specify the layout of elements to be included in the newsletter.**

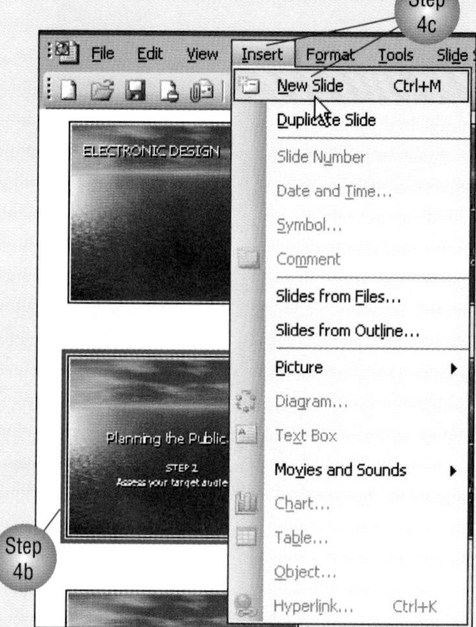

5. Delete Slide 2 by completing the following steps:
   a. Click the Slide Sorter View button on the View toolbar.
   b. Click Slide 2 to select it.
   c. Press the Delete key.
6. Move Slide 3 after Slide 5 by completing the following steps:
   a. In Slide Sorter view, position the mouse pointer in Slide 3, and then hold down the left mouse button.
   b. Drag the arrow pointer (with the gray square attached) between Slides 5 and 6 (a vertical black line displays between the slides) and then release the mouse button.

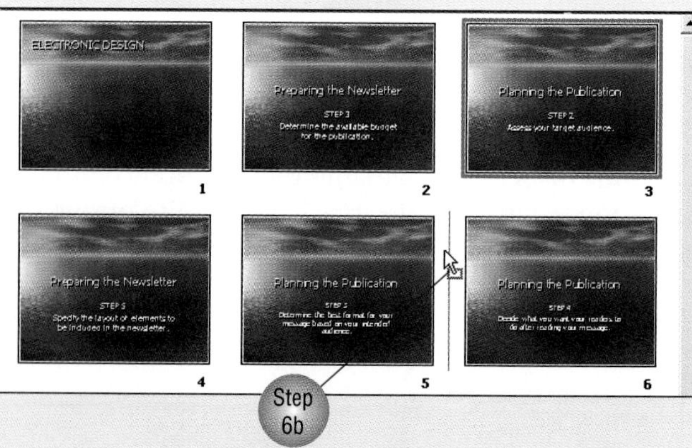

7. Complete steps similar to those in Step 6 to move Slide 7 between Slides 2 and 3.
8. Edit each slide so the step numbers are in sequential order.
9. Copy slides from a different presentation into the **sppc2x03** presentation by completing the following steps:
   a. Change to the Slide Sorter view.

b. Open **CompanyNewsletter** located in the PowerPointChapter02S folder on your disk.
c. With the **CompanyNewsletter** presentation open, change to the Slide Sorter view.
d. Click Slide 2, hold down the Shift key, and then click Slide 3. (This selects both slides.)
e. Click the Copy button on the Standard toolbar.
f. Click the button on the Taskbar representing **sppc2x03**.
g. Click to the right of the last slide in the presentation and then click the Paste button on the Standard toolbar.

10. Apply a transition and sound of your choosing to all slides in the presentation.
11. Save and then run the presentation.
12. Preview and then print the presentation by completing the following steps:
    a. Click the Print Preview button on the Standard toolbar.
    b. At the Print Preview window (with the first slide displayed), display the next slide by clicking the Next Page button on the Print Preview toolbar.
    c. Continue clicking the Next Page button until the last slide displays in the presentation.
    d. Click the down-pointing arrow to the right of the *Print What* option box on the Print Preview toolbar and then click *Handouts (9 slides per page)* at the drop-down list.
    e. Click the Print button on the Print Preview toolbar.
    f. At the Print dialog box, click OK.
    g. Click the Close button to close Print Preview.

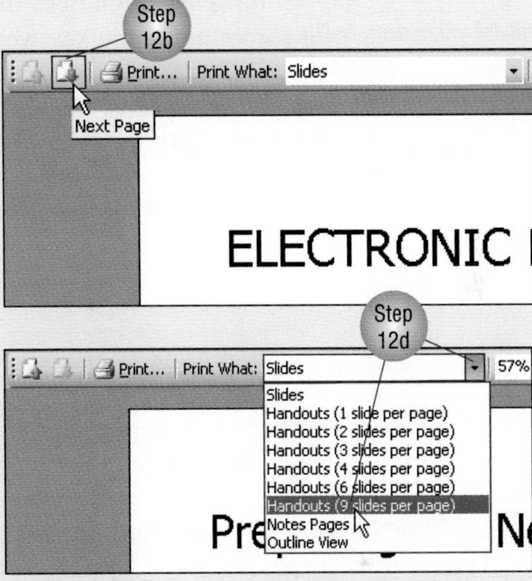

13. Change to the Normal view and then display the presentation in grayscale by completing the following steps:
    a. Click the Color/Grayscale button on the Standard toolbar.
    b. At the drop-down list that displays, click the Grayscale option. (This displays the slide in grayscale and also displays the Grayscale View toolbar.)
    c. Click the Setting button on the Grayscale View toolbar.
    d. At the drop-down list that displays, click Light Grayscale. (Notice the changes to the slide.)
    e. Click the Setting button on the Grayscale View toolbar and then click Inverse Grayscale at the drop-down list. (Notice the changes to the slide.)
    f. Experiment with a few other options from the Setting drop-down list.
    g. Click the Close Grayscale View button to turn off the display of the Grayscale View toolbar.
14. Close **sppc2x03** without saving the changes.
15. Close **CompanyNewsletter**.

Using Help

Type a question for help

Ask a Question

PowerPoint's Help feature is an on-screen reference manual containing information about all PowerPoint features and commands. PowerPoint's Help feature is similar to the Windows Help and the Help features in Word, Excel, and Access. Get help using the *Ask a Question* text box on the Menu bar or with options at the PowerPoint Help task pane.

QUICK STEPS

Use *Ask a Question* Text Box

1. Click in Ask a Question text box.
2. Type help question.
3. Press Enter.

Getting Help Using the *Ask a Question* text Box

Click the text inside the *Ask a Question* text box located at the right side of the Menu bar (this removes the text), type a help question, and then press Enter. A list of topics matching key words in your question displays in the Search Results task pane. Click a topic in the Search Results task pane list box and information about that topic displays in the Microsoft Office PowerPoint Help window. If the window contains a Show All hyperlink in the upper right corner, click this hyperlink and the information expands to show all help information related to the topic. When you click the Show All hyperlink, it becomes the Hide All hyperlink.

exercise 4

GETTING HELP USING THE *ASK A QUESTION* TEXT BOX

1. At a clear PowerPoint screen, click the text inside the *Ask a Question* text box located at the right side of the Menu bar.
2. Type **How do I choose a design template?**.
3. Press the Enter key.
4. At the Search Results task pane, click the Create a presentation using a design template hyperlink in the list box.
5. When the Microsoft Office PowerPoint Help window displays, click the *Show All* hyperlink that displays in the upper right corner of the window. (This displays all the information available related to the topic.)
6. Read the information contained in the window, and then click the Close button (contains an *X*) located in the upper right corner of the Microsoft Office PowerPoint Help window.
7. Close the Search Results task pane.

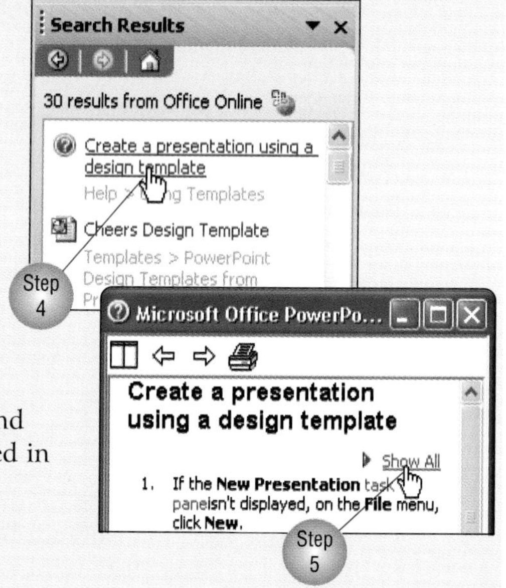

QUICK STEPS

Use Help Feature

1. Click Microsoft Office PowerPoint Help button.
2. Type help question.
3. Press Enter.

Getting Help from the PowerPoint Help Task Pane

You can type a question in the *Ask a Question* text box or type a question or topic in the PowerPoint Help task pane. Display this task pane by clicking the Microsoft Office PowerPoint Help button on the Standard toolbar, by clicking Help on the Menu bar and then clicking Microsoft Office PowerPoint Help at the drop-down menu, or by pressing the F1 function key.

In the PowerPoint Help task pane, type a topic, feature, or question in the *Search for* text box and then press Enter or click the Start searching button (button containing white arrow on green background). Topics related to the topic, feature, or question display in the Search Results task pane. Click a topic in the results list box and information about that topic displays in the Microsoft Office PowerPoint Help window.

Microsoft Office PowerPoint Help

(Note: If the Office Assistant displays when you click the Microsoft Office PowerPoint Help button, turn off the display of the Office Assistant. To do this, click the Options button in the yellow box above the Office Assistant. At the Office Assistant dialog box, click the* Use the Office Assistant *option to remove the check mark from the check box, and then click OK.)

exercise 5

GETTING HELP

1. At a clear PowerPoint screen, display information on applying a sound effect to a presentation. To begin, click the Microsoft Office PowerPoint Help button on the Standard toolbar. (This displays the PowerPoint Help task pane.)
2. Type How do I apply a sound effect? in the *Search for* text box and then press Enter.
3. Click the Add music or sound effects to a slide hyperlink in the results list box. (This displays the Microsoft Office PowerPoint Help window.)
4. Click the Show All hyperlink that displays in the upper right corner of the window.
5. Read the information about adding music or sound effects to a slide. (You will need to scroll down the window to display all of the information.)
6. Click the Close button to close the Microsoft Office PowerPoint Help window.
7. Close the Search Results task pane.

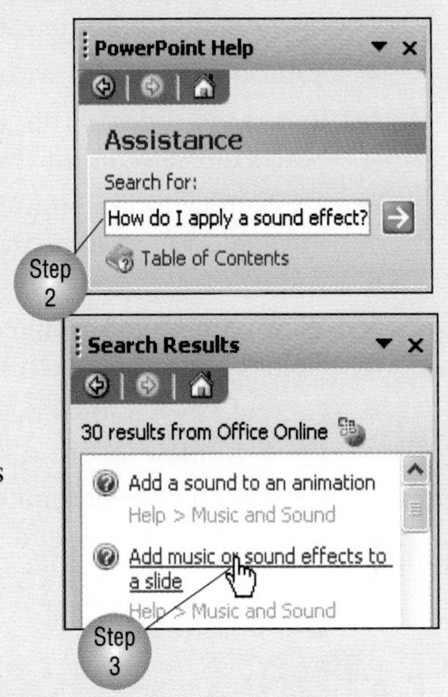

CHAPTER summary

- You can insert and/or delete text in an individual slide in a presentation. Click the placeholder containing the text you want to insert and/or delete. Select text you want to delete using options described in Table 2.1.
- Use the find feature to look for specific text in slides in a presentation and use the find and replace feature to search for specific text and replace with other text.
- Use Cut, Copy, and Paste buttons on the Standard toolbar to rearrange text in and between slides.
- You can use the mouse to move text within and between slides in the Outline/Slides pane with the Outline tab selected.
- Text in a slide is positioned in a placeholder. Move this placeholder by clicking the placeholder to select it, positioning the mouse pointer on the border until the pointer turns into a four-headed arrow. Hold down the left mouse button, drag the outline of the placeholder to the desired position, and then release the mouse button.

- Use the sizing handles that display around a selected placeholder to increase and/or decrease the size of the box.
- Click the Spelling button on the Standard toolbar to complete a spelling check on text in slides.
- Use the Thesaurus feature to find synonyms and/or antonyms for a word. To use Thesaurus, click the desired word, click Tools, and then click Thesaurus. This displays the Research task pane with a list of synonyms and antonyms. You can also right-click a word in a slide, point to Synonyms at the shortcut menu, and then click the desired synonym at the side menu.
- Delete a slide in Slide Sorter view or in Normal view with the Slides tab selected in the Outline/Slides pane by clicking the slide and then pressing the Delete key.
- Insert a new slide in Normal view by clicking the New Slide button on the Formatting toolbar. Insert a new slide in Slide Sorter view by clicking Insert and then New Slide.
- Copy a selected slide by clicking the slide, holding down the Ctrl key, dragging the outline of the slide to the new location, and then releasing the mouse button and the Ctrl key.
- You can copy slides within a presentation as well as between presentations.
- Rearrange slides within a presentation in Slide Sorter view or in Normal view with the Slides tab selected in the Outline/Slides pane.
- To see how a presentation will appear when printed, display the presentation in Print Preview. Use buttons on the Print Preview toolbar to display various slides, specify how you want the presentation printed, change the Zoom display, and choose an orientation.
- View a presentation in color, grayscale, or black and white with options on the Color/Grayscale button on the Standard toolbar.
- Get help by typing a question in the *Ask a Question* text box located at the right side of the Menu bar.
- Display the PowerPoint Help task pane by clicking the Microsoft Office PowerPoint Help button on the Standard toolbar or by clicking Help and then Microsoft Office PowerPoint Help.

FEATURES summary

FEATURE	BUTTON	MENU	KEYBOARD
Find dialog box		Edit, Find	Ctrl + F
Replace dialog box		Edit, Replace	Ctrl + H
Begin a spelling check		Tools, Spelling	F7
Research		Tools, Research	Shift + F7
Print Preview		File, Print Preview	
Color/Grayscale options		View, Color/Grayscale	
PowerPoint Help task pane		Help, Microsoft Office PowerPoint Help	F1

CONCEPTS check

Completion: On a blank sheet of paper, indicate the correct term, symbol, or command for each description.

1. Perform this action with the mouse to select an entire word.
2. Display the Replace dialog box by clicking this option on the Menu bar and then clicking Replace.
3. Copy a slide by holding down this key while dragging the slide.
4. Click a placeholder and these display around the box.
5. Click this button on the Standard toolbar to begin a spelling check.
6. Use this feature to find synonyms and antonyms for a specific word.
7. Click this button on the Standard toolbar to display a drop-down list with options for displaying the presentation in color, grayscale, or black and white.
8. The *Ask a Question* text box is located at the right side of this.
9. Click this button on the Standard toolbar to display the PowerPoint Help task pane.
10. Click this hyperlink located in the upper right corner of the Help window to expand the topics and display all of the information related to each topic.

SKILLS check

Assessment 1

1. Create a presentation with the text shown in Figure 2.6. You determine the design template and the slide layout.
2. After creating the presentation, complete a spelling check.
3. Use the Thesaurus to change the word *expansion* in Slide 7 to an appropriate synonym.
4. Save the presentation into the PowerPointChapter02S folder on your disk and name the presentation **sppc2sc01**.
5. Add a transition and sound of your choosing to each slide.
6. Run the presentation.
7. Print the slides as handouts with six slides per page.
8. Close the presentation.

FIGURE

2.6 Assessment 1

Slide 1	Title	=	TRENDS IN TELECOMMUNICATIONS
	Subtitle	=	Current and Future Trends
Slide 2	Title	=	Trend 1
	Subtitle	=	Continued movement toward the deregulation of telecommunications services
Slide 3	Title	=	Trend 2
	Subtitle	=	Continued expansion and enhancement of local and wide area networks
Slide 4	Title	=	Trend 3
	Subtitle	=	Movement toward integrated services digital networks
Slide 5	Title	=	Trend 4
	Subtitle	=	Movement toward standardization of data communication protocols
Slide 6	Title	=	Trend 5
	Subtitle	=	Increased use of wireless radio-based technology
Slide 7	Title	=	Trend 6
	Subtitle	=	Continued expansion of photonics (fiber optics)
Slide 8	Title	=	Trend 7
	Subtitle	=	Expansion of video teleconferencing
Slide 9	Title	=	Trend 8
	Subtitle	=	Increased power in electronic workstations
Slide 10	Title	=	Trend 9
	Subtitle	=	More sophisticated software
Slide 11	Title	=	Trend 10
	Subtitle	=	Continued growth of voice processing
Slide 12	Title	=	Trend 11
	Subtitle	=	Greater use of optical storage technologies

Assessment 2

1. Open **sppc2sc01**.
2. Save the presentation with Save As in the PowerPointChapter02S folder on your disk and name the presentation **sppc2sc02**.
3. Make the following edits to the presentation:
   a. Display the presentation in Slide Sorter view.
   b. Move Slide 2 between Slide 5 and Slide 6.
   c. Move Slide 10 between Slides 7 and 8.
   d. Renumber the trend numbers in the titles to reflect the correct order.
   e. Display Slide 4 in Slide view, delete the subtitle text, and then type Multimedia in integrated systems.
   f. Display Slide 8 in Slide view, delete the subtitle text, and then type Information as a strategic resource.
4. Save and then run the presentation.
5. Print the presentation as handouts with six slides per page.
6. Close the presentation.

Assessment 3

1. Create the presentation shown in Figure 2.7 using a design template of your choosing.
2. When the slides are completed, run a spelling check on the presentation.
3. Save the presentation in the PowerPointChapter02S folder on your disk and name the presentation **sppc2sc03**.
4. Run the presentation.
5. Print all four slides on one page.
6. Close the presentation.

FIGURE 2.7 ***Assessment 3***

Slide 1	Title	=	Electronic Design and Production
	Subtitle	=	Designing a Document
Slide 2	Title	=	Creating Balance
	Bullets	=	• Symmetrical balance—Balancing similar elements equally on a page (centered alignment) of the document • Asymmetrical balance—Balancing contrasting elements on a page of the document
Slide 3	Title	=	Creating Focus
	Bullets	=	• Creating focus with titles, headings, and subheads in a document • Creating focus with graphic elements in a document – Clip art – Watermarks – Illustrations

– Photographs
– Charts
– Graphs

Slide 4	Title	=	Providing Proportion
	Bullets	=	• Evaluating proportions in a document
			• Sizing graphic elements in a document
			• Using white space in a document

Assessment 4

1. Open **sppc2sc03**.
2. Save the presentation with Save As in the PowerPointChapter02S folder on your disk and name the presentation **sppc2sc04**.
3. Make the following changes to the presentation:
   a. Change to Slide Sorter view and then move Slide 3 between Slides 1 and 2.
   b. Move Slide 4 between Slides 2 and 3.
   c. Search for the word *document* and replace all occurences with the word *brochure*.
   d. Add a transition and sound of your choosing to each slide.
4. Save and then run the presentation.
5. Print all four slides on one page.
6. Close the presentation.

Assessment 5

1. A presentation created in PowerPoint can be sent to Word as an outline or as a handout. This might be useful if you want to format or enhance the presentation using Word tools and features. Use PowerPoint's Help feature to learn about how to send slide images to Word. ***(Hint: To get started, type*** *How do I send slides to Word?* ***in the* Ask a Question *text box and then press Enter. At the Search Results task pane, click the Send slides to Microsoft Word hyperlink.)***
2. After reading the Help information, open **sppc2sc03** and then send it to Word. (At the Send To Microsoft Office Word dialog box, you choose the layout.)
3. When the document displays in Word, print the document.
4. Close the Word document without saving it and then exit Word.

CHAPTER challenge

You are the office manager at the Employee/Employer Connection agency. One specific department in the agency is responsible for preparing individuals for the job search process. You have been asked to create a PowerPoint presentation that can be used as part of this preparation. The previous office manager had started a presentation for this purpose, but was unable to finish it. You reviewed the presentation and would like to use a couple of the slides in your presentation. Copy Slides 2-5 from the **JobAnalysis** presentation to your presentation. Arrange the slides in a logical order. Add at least five more slides. Apply an appropriate design template. Use transitions and sound effects. Run the spell check feature. Save the presentation as **JobSearch**.

Custom animation is a method of adding visual and sound effects to bulleted and other text items. Use the Help feature to learn about custom animation. Then apply custom animation to at least two slides of the **JobSearch** presentation created in the first part of the Chapter Challenge. Save the presentation again.

Some potential employees would like to review the presentation, but are unable to visit the agency. The agency does have a Web site. Therefore, publish the entire presentation as a Web page so that those seeking employment can access the presentation by logging on to the Web site. Save the Web page as **WebJobSearch**.

CHAPTER 3

FORMATTING SLIDES

PERFORMANCE OBJECTIVES

Upon successful completion of Chapter 3, you will be able to:

- **Format slides in a presentation**
- **Format a slide master and title master in a presentation**
- **Change slide color schemes, backgrounds, and design templates**
- **Create a presentation with the Blank Presentation template**
- **Format slides with Format Painter**
- **Format slides with bullets and numbers**
- **Insert the date and time, a header and footer, and page numbering in slides**
- **Create, format, and print speaker notes**

Chapter03S

PowerPoint

PowerPoint provides design templates that apply specific formatting to slides. You can further customize slides in a presentation by applying your own formatting. If you want formatting changes to affect all slides in a presentation, make the changes at the slide master. In this chapter, you will learn how to make formatting changes to slides, make formatting changes at a slide master, use the Format Painter to apply formatting, and insert headers and footers and speaker notes in slides.

Formatting a Presentation

PowerPoint provides a variety of design templates you can use to create a presentation. These templates contain formatting provided by the program. In some situations, the formatting provided by the template will be appropriate; in other situations you will want to change or enhance the formatting of a slide. Formatting can be applied to specific text in a slide or formatting can be applied to a placeholder.

Formatting Text in a Slide

Text formatting can include a variety of options such as changing fonts, changing font color, and changing paragraph alignment. The steps to change the formatting of a slide vary depending on the type of formatting desired. For example, to change the font of text in a slide, you would select the text first, and then change to the desired font. To change the alignment of a paragraph of text, you would position the insertion point on any character in the paragraph, and then choose the desired alignment.

The Formatting toolbar contains several buttons for applying formatting to text in a slide. The buttons, button names, and a description of what each button accomplishes is shown in Table 3.1.

TABLE 3.1 ***PowerPoint Formatting Toolbar Buttons***

Button	Name	Function
Arial	Font	Changes selected text to a different font
28	Font Size	Changes selected text to a different font size
B	Bold	Adds or removes bold formatting to or from selected text
I	Italic	Adds or removes italic formatting to or from selected text
U	Underline	Adds or removes underline formatting to or from selected text
S	Shadow	Adds or removes shadow formatting to or from selected text
	Align Left	Left-aligns text
	Center	Center-aligns text
	Align Right	Right-aligns text
	Numbering	Adds or removes numbers to or from selected text
	Bullets	Adds or removes bullets to or from selected text
A	Increase Font Size	Increases font size of selected text to next available larger size
A	Decrease Font Size	Decreases font size of selected text to next available smaller size
	Decrease Indent	Moves text to the previous tab stop (level)
	Increase Indent	Moves text to the next tab stop (level)
A	Font Color	Changes the font color of selected text
Design	Slide Design	Displays slide design templates in the Slide Design task pane
New Slide	New Slide	Inserts a new slide in a presentation

Choosing a Font

Design templates apply a font to text in slides. You may want to change this default to some other font for such reasons as changing the mood of a presentation, enhancing the visual appeal of slides, and increasing the readability of the text in slides. Change the font with the Font and Font Size buttons on the Formatting toolbar or at the Font dialog box. Display the Font dialog box shown in Figure 3.1 by clicking Format and then Font. Use options at the Font dialog box to choose a font, font style, font size, and to apply special effects to text in slides such as Shadow, Emboss, Superscript, and Subscript.

Fonts may be decorative or plain and generally fall into one of two categories—***serif*** or ***sans serif***. A serif is a small line at the end of a character stroke. A serif font is easier to read and is generally used for large amounts of text. A sans serif font does not have serifs (*sans* is French for *without*) and is generally used for titles and headings. Limit to two the number of fonts used in a slide.

Font, font size, style, and color of text are defined by the design template applied to the slides in the presentation.

Change Font
1. Select text.
2. Click Format, Font.
3. Choose the desired font, style, size, and color.
4. Click OK.

FIGURE 3.1 ***Font Dialog Box***

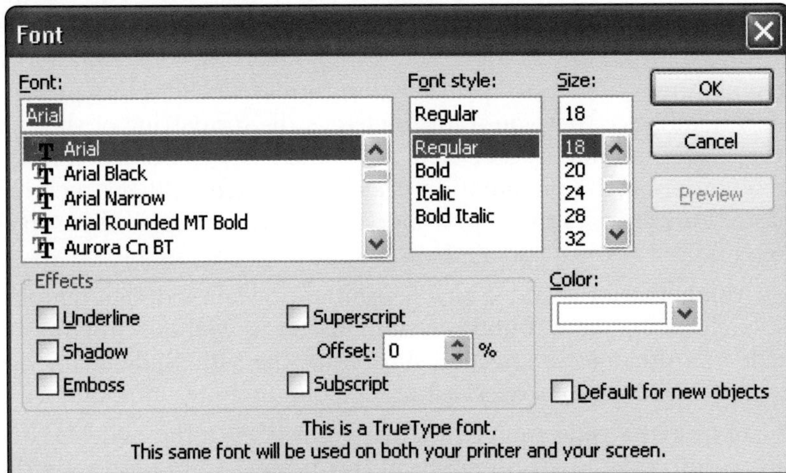

QUICK STEPS

Change Line Spacing
1. Select text.
2. Click Format, Line Spacing.
3. Type desired measurement in *Line spacing* text box.
4. Click OK.

QUICK STEPS

Increase/Decrease Spacing Before/After Paragraph
1. Select text.
2. Click Format, Line Spacing.
3. Type desired measurement in *Before Paragraph* or *After Paragraph* text box.
4. Click OK.

Increasing/Decreasing Spacing Before/After Paragraphs

If you want control over line spacing in text or the amount of spacing before or after paragraphs of text, use options from the Line Spacing dialog box shown in Figure 3.2. Display this dialog box by clicking Format and then Line Spacing. Change line spacing by increasing or decreasing the number in the *Line spacing* text box. Increase or decrease spacing before a paragraph by typing the desired line spacing measurement in the *Before paragraph* text box. Type a line spacing measurement in the *After paragraph* text box to control the amount of spacing after paragraphs. By default, the measurement used is Line spacing. This can be changed to *Points* by clicking the down-pointing arrow after the option box containing the word *Lines* and then clicking *Points* at the drop-down list. If text in paragraphs fills more than one line, increase or decrease spacing between paragraphs with the *Before paragraph* or *After paragraph* option rather than the *Line spacing* option.

FIGURE

3.2 ***Line Spacing Dialog Box***

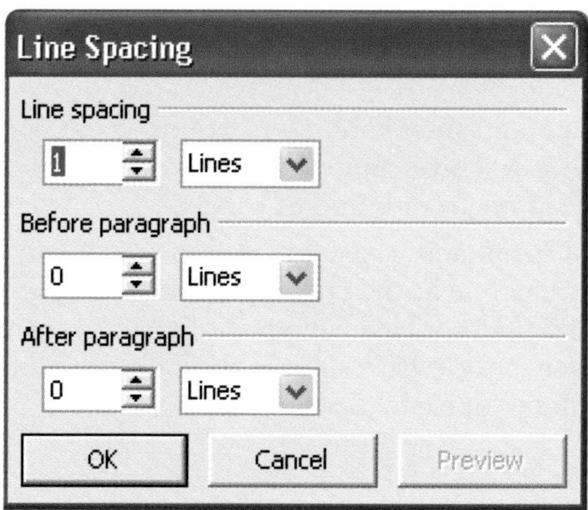

Formatting with a Slide Master

If you use a PowerPoint design template, you may choose to use the formatting provided by the template, or you may want to customize the formatting. If you customize formatting in a presentation, PowerPoint's slide master can be very helpful in reducing the steps needed to format all slides in a presentation. If you know in advance that you want to change the formatting of slides, display the slide master in Slide Master view, make the changes needed, and then create the presentation. If the presentation is already created, edit the presentation in a slide master. Any changes made to a slide master will affect all slides in the presentation.

A slide master is added to a presentation when a design template is applied. Generally, a template contains a slide master as well as a title master. Changes made to a title master affect all slides with the Title Slide layout applied. Changes made to a slide master affect all other slides in a presentation.

Display Slide Master
1. Hold down Shift key.
2. Click Normal View button on View toolbar.

To format a slide and/or title master, change to the Slide Master view. To do this, position the insertion point on the Normal View button on the View toolbar, hold down the Shift key (this causes the Normal View button to change to the Slide Master View button), and then click the left mouse button. You can also click View, point to Master, and then click Slide Master. This displays a slide master in the Slide pane as shown in Figure 3.3. A slide-title master pair also displays as slide miniatures at the left side of the window and a Slide Master View toolbar displays. Position the mouse pointer on the slide miniature and the name of the miniature displays in a yellow box above the miniature. Click the desired slide master miniature and then apply specific formatting to the slide master in the Slide pane. Switch between the slide-title master pair by clicking the desired miniature. When all changes have been made to the slide and title masters, click the Close Master View button on the Slide Master View toolbar or click the Normal View button on the View toolbar.

FIGURE

3.3 ***Slide Master View***

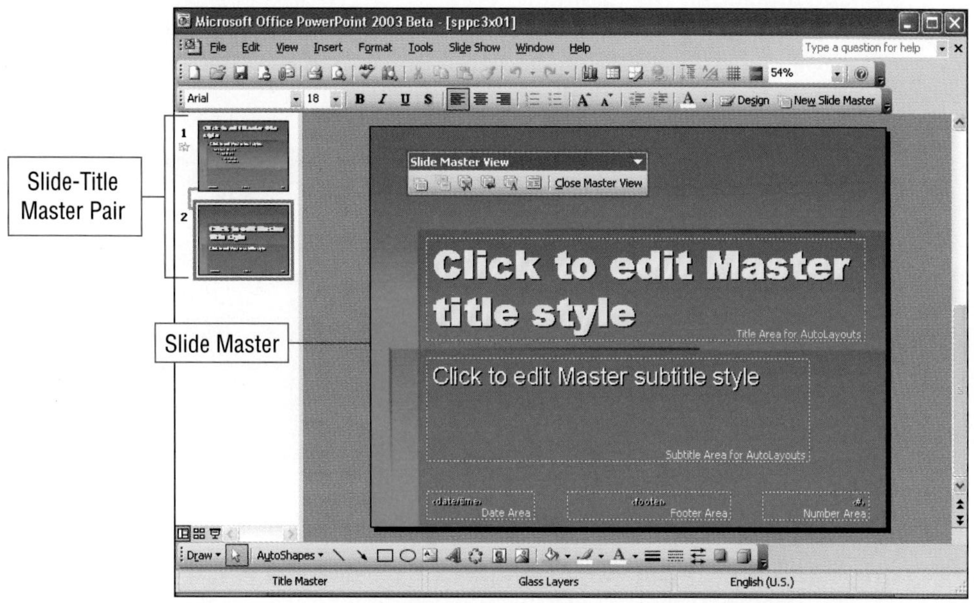

(Note: Before completing Exercise 1, delete the PowerPointChapter02S folder on your disk. Next, copy to your disk the PowerPointChapter03S subfolder from the PowerPoint2003Specialist folder on the CD that accompanies this textbook and then make PowerPointChapter03S the active folder.)

exercise 1

FORMATTING TEXT IN A PRESENTATION USING A SLIDE MASTER

1. Open NetworkingPresentation from the PowerPointChapter03S folder on your disk.
2. Save the presentation with Save As into the PowerPointChapter03S folder on your disk and name the presentation **sppc3x01**.
3. Add a slide by completing the following steps:
   a. Display Slide 4 in the Slide pane.
   b. Click the New Slide button on the Formatting toolbar.
   c. Click the Title Slide layout in the Slide Layout task pane.
   d. Click in the text *Click to add title* and then type **Designing a Network**.
   e. Click in the text *Click to add subtitle* and then type **Creating and Implementing the Network**.
4. Format the presentation using the slide master and the title master by completing the following steps:
   a. Display Slide 1 in Normal view.
   b. Position the arrow pointer on the Normal View button on the View toolbar, hold down the Shift key (the Normal View button turns into the Slide Master View button), and then click the left mouse button.

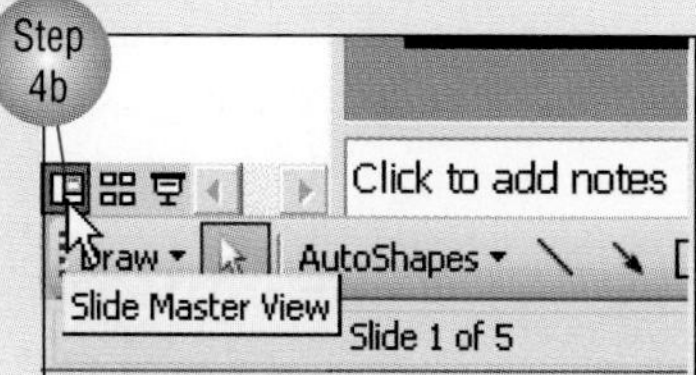

   c. With the Glass Layers Title Master slide miniature selected at the left side of the window and the title master slide displayed in the Slide pane, complete the following steps:

1) Click anywhere in the *Click to edit Master title style*. (This selects the text in the placeholder.)
2) Click Format and then Font.
3) At the Font dialog box, click *Bookman Old Style* in the *Font* list box. (You will need to scroll down the list of typefaces to display *Bookman Old Style*. If this typeface is not available, choose a similar serif typeface.)
4) Click *48* in the *Size* list box. (You may need to scroll up this list box to display *48*.)
5) Click the down-pointing arrow at the right of the *Color* option box.
6) At the color palette, click the white color (second color from the left).
7) Click OK to close the Font dialog box.
8) Click anywhere in the text *Click to edit Master subtitle style*. (This selects the text in the placeholder.)
9) Click the down-pointing arrow at the right side of the Font button on the Formatting toolbar and then click *Bookman Old Style* at the drop-down list.
10) Click the down-pointing arrow at the right side of the Font Size button on the Formatting toolbar and then click *28* at the drop-down list.

d. Click the Glass Layers Slide Master miniature (the top miniature) located at the left side of the window.

e. Change the font and color of the text after bullets by completing the following steps:

1) Click anywhere in the text *Click to edit Master title style*.
2) Change the font to 48-point Bookman Old Style and the font color to white by completing steps similar to those in Steps 4c2 through 4c7.
3) Click anywhere in the text *Click to edit Master text styles*. (This selects the text after the first bullet.)
4) Click Format and then Font.
5) At the Font dialog box, click *Bookman Old Style* in the *Font* list box.
6) Click the down-pointing arrow at the right of the *Color* option box.
7) Click the More Colors option that displays at the bottom of the palette.
8) At the Colors dialog box with the Standard tab selected, click the light blue color shown above.

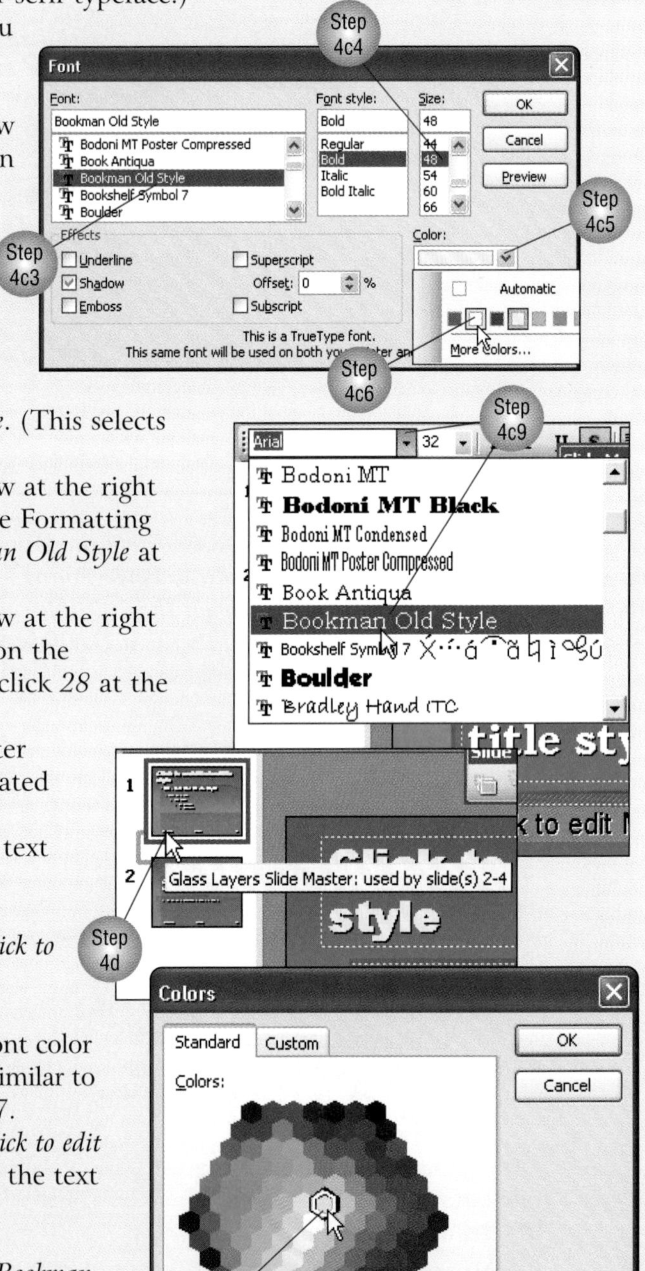

9) Click OK to close the Colors dialog box.
10) Click OK to close the Font dialog box.

f. Click the Close Master View button on the Slide Master View toolbar. (This displays Slide 1 with the formatting applied.)
g. Click the Slide Sorter View button on the View toolbar to see how the slides display with the ncw formatting.

5. Center the text in the title placeholder and move the placeholder by completing the following steps:
   a. At the Slide Sorter view, double-click Slide 1.
   b. Click in the placeholder containing the text *NETWORKING*. (This selects the placeholder.)
   c. Click the Center button on the Formatting toolbar. (This centers the text horizontally in the placeholder.)
   d. With the placeholder still selected, position the arrow pointer on the placeholder border until a four-headed arrow displays attached to the arrow pointer.
   e. Hold down the left mouse button, drag the outline of the placeholder until it is centered horizontally and vertically on the slide, and then release the mouse button.

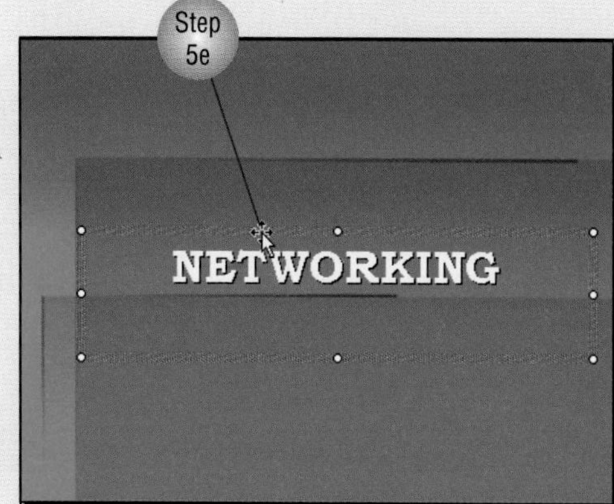

6. Decrease the line spacing between paragraphs for the text in Slide 2 by completing the following steps:
   a. Click the Next Slide button to display Slide 2.
   b. Click in the placeholder containing the bulleted text.
   c. Select the bulleted paragraphs of text.
   d. Click Format and then Line Spacing.
   e. At the Line Spacing dialog box, click the down-pointing arrow at the right of the *Line spacing* text box (contains the number *1*) until *0.9* displays in the text box.
   f. Click OK to close the dialog box.
   g. Deselect the text.

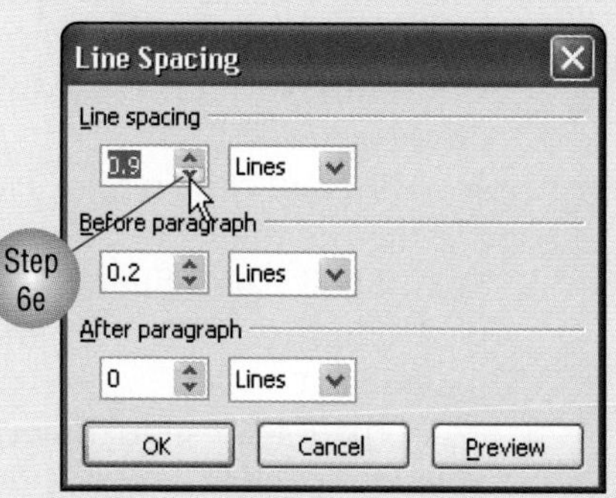

7. Add a transition and sound of your choosing to each slide.
8. Save and then run the presentation.
9. Print the presentation as handouts with all slides printed on one page.
10. Close the presentation.

Applying More than One Design Template to a Presentation

Each design template applies specific formatting to slides. You can apply more than one design template to slides in a presentation. To do this, select the specific slides and then choose the desired design template. The design template is applied only to the selected slides. If you apply more than one design template to a presentation, multiple slide masters will display in the Slide Master view. For example, if two design templates are applied to a presentation, two slide-title master pairs will display—one pair for each design template. Use these slide-title master pairs to specify the formatting for each design template.

HINT
If you change the design template for an existing presentation, check to see how the new design formatting affects text and objects in slides. You may need to make some adjustments.

exercise 2

APPLYING MORE THAN ONE TEMPLATE TO A PRESENTATION

1. Open **PlanningPresentation**.
2. Save the presentation in the PowerPointChapter03S folder on your disk and name the presentation **sppc3x02**.
3. Copy slides from the **CompanyNewsletter** presentation into the current presentation by completing the following steps:
   a. Make sure Normal view is selected and the Slides tab is selected in the Outline/Slides pane.
   b. Open **CompanyNewsletter** located in the PowerPointChapter03S folder on your disk.
   c. With the **CompanyNewsletter** presentation open, make sure the Slides tab is selected in the Outline/Slides pane.
   d. Click Slide 2 in the Outline/Slides pane, hold down the Shift key, and then click Slide 3. (This selects both slides.)
   e. Click the Copy button on the Standard toolbar.
   f. Click the button on the Taskbar representing **sppc3x02**.
   g. Click below Slide 6 in the Outline/Slides pane.
   h. Click the Paste button on the Standard toolbar. (The pasted slides take on the design template of the current presentation.)
   i. Click the button on the Taskbar representing **CompanyNewsletter** and then close **CompanyNewsletter**. (Make sure **sppc3x02** displays on the screen.)

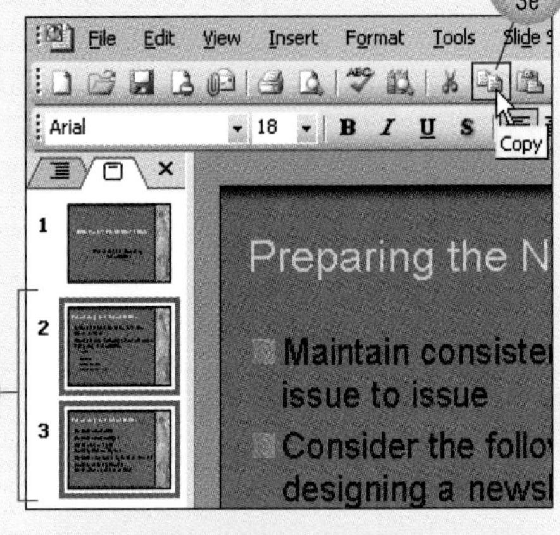

4. Apply a different design template to the pasted slides by completing the following steps:
   a. With Slide 7 and Slide 8 selected in the Outline/Slides pane, click the Slide Design button on the Formatting toolbar.
   b. Click the *Radial* slide design in the *Apply a design template* list box. (You will need to scroll down the list to display this template.)

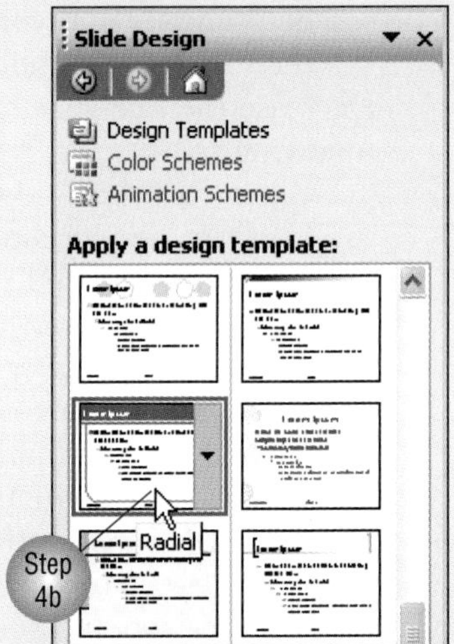

5. Format the slides using the slide-title master pairs by completing the following steps:
   a. Hold down the Shift key and then click the Normal View button (the button name changes to Slide Master View with the Shift key down).
   b. Click the Ocean Title Master slide miniature located at the left side of the window (second slide miniature from the top).
   c. Click anywhere in the text *Click to edit Master subtitle style*. (This selects the text.)
   d. Change the font by completing the following steps:

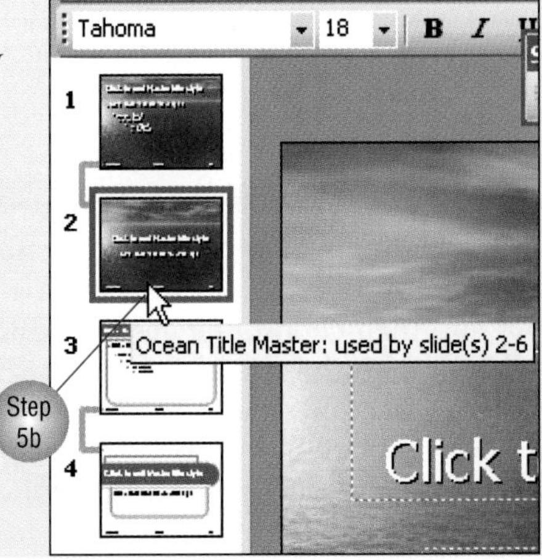

1) Click Format and then Font.
2) At the Font dialog box, click *Times New Roman* in the *Font* list box.
3) Click *Bold* in the *Font style* list box.
4) Click *36* in the *Size* list box.
5) Click the down-pointing arrow at the right of the *Color* option and then click the More Colors option at the palette.
6) At the Colors dialog box with the Standard tab selected, click a light blue color of your choosing and then click OK.
7) Click OK to close the Font dialog box.

e. Click the Radial Slide Master slide miniature located at the left side of the window (third slide miniature from the top).
f. Select the first and second bulleted text (this is the text *Click to edit Master text styles* and *Second level*).
g. Change the font by completing the following steps:
1) Click Format and then Font.
2) At the Font dialog box, click *Times New Roman* in the *Font* list box. (You will need to scroll down this list to display *Times New Roman*.)
3) Click *Bold* in the *Font style* list box.
4) Click the down-pointing arrow at the right of the *Color* option and then click the blue color that is the last color at the right.
5) Click OK to close the Font dialog box.

h. Click the Normal View button on the View toolbar.

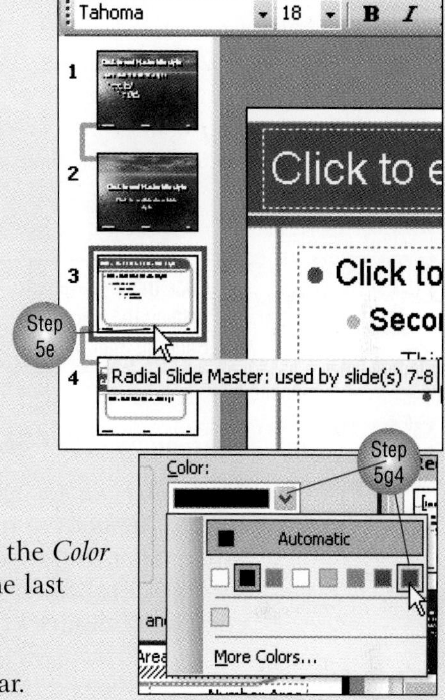

6. Add a transition and sound of your choosing to all slides in the presentation.
7. Save and then run the presentation.
8. Print the presentation as handouts with nine slides per page.
9. Close the presentation.

Formatting the Slide Color Scheme

PowerPoint design templates provide interesting and varied formatting effects and save time when preparing a presentation. Some of the formatting applied to slides by the design template can be customized. For example, the color scheme and background of slides can be changed.

A design template includes a default color scheme consisting of eight colors. Colors are chosen for the background, accents, text, fills, shadows, title text, and hyperlinks. Additional color schemes are available for design templates. To choose another color scheme for a design template, display the Slide Design task pane. Click the Color Schemes hyperlink located toward the top of the task pane and then click the desired scheme. Figure 3.4 shows the Slide Design task pane with color schemes displayed for NetworkingPresentation.

Display Color Schemes
1. Click Slide Design button.
2. Click Color Schemes hyperlink in Slide Design task pane.

FIGURE 3.4 ***Slide Design Task Pane with Color Schemes Displayed***

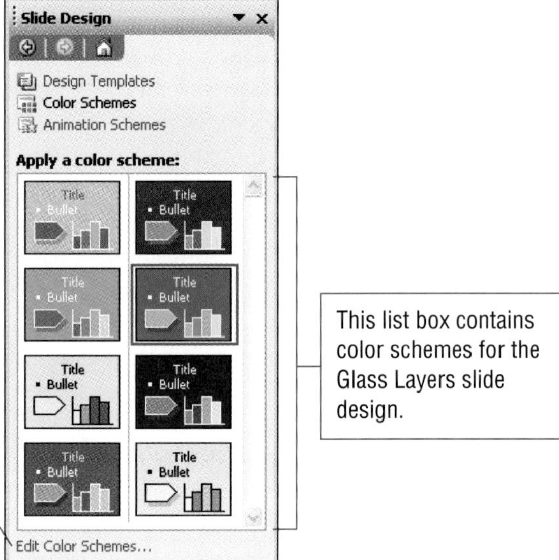

Click this hyperlink to display the Edit Color Scheme dialog box.

Customize Color Scheme

1. Click Edit Color Schemes hyperlink in Slide Design task pane.
2. Make desired changes at Edit Color Scheme dialog box.
3. Click OK.

Customizing the Color Scheme

Customize a color scheme by clicking the Edit Color Schemes hyperlink located toward the bottom of the task pane. This displays the Edit Color Scheme dialog box, similar to the one shown in Figure 3.5. Click an option in the *Scheme colors* section and then click the Change Color button. At the dialog box that displays, choose the desired color, and then click OK.

FIGURE 3.5 ***Edit Color Scheme Dialog Box***

Change color for a specific item by clicking the box preceding the desired item in this section and then clicking the Change Color button. At the dialog box that displays, choose the desired color.

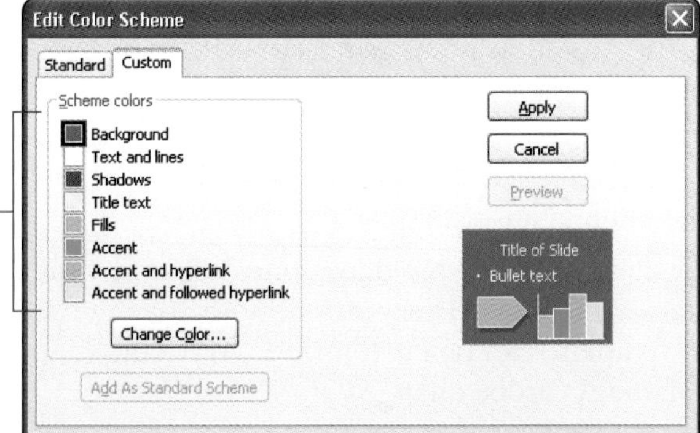

HINT

Create a custom fill for the slide background with options at the Fill Effects dialog box.

QUICK STEPS

Change Background Color

1. Click Format, Background.
2. Make desired changes at Background dialog box.
3. Click OK.

Changing Background Color

Background color can be changed with options at the Edit Color Scheme dialog box or at the Background dialog box shown in Figure 3.6. Display this dialog box by clicking Format and then Background. At the Background dialog box, click the down-pointing arrow at the right of the *Background fill* option box and then click the desired color at the drop-down list. Click the Apply button to apply the background color to the active slide or click the Apply to All button to apply the background color to all slides.

FIGURE

3.6 **Background Dialog Box**

exercise 3

FORMATTING SLIDE COLOR SCHEMES

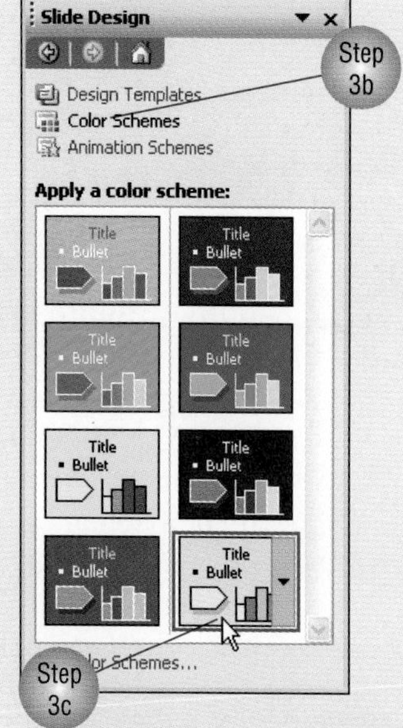

1. Open **NetworkingPresentation**.
2. Save the presentation with Save As and name it **sppc3x03**.
3. Change the color scheme by completing the following steps:
   a. With the presentation displayed in Normal view, click the Slide Design button on the Formatting toolbar.
   b. Click the Color Schemes hyperlink located toward the top of the task pane.
   c. Click the last color scheme option in the bottom row (the color scheme shown at the right).
4. Print the presentation as handouts with four slides per page.
5. Customize the slide color scheme by completing the following steps:
   a. Click the Edit Color Schemes hyperlink located toward the bottom of the Slide Design task pane.
   b. At the Edit Color Scheme dialog box with the Custom tab selected, click *Text and lines* in the *Scheme colors* section.
   c. Click the Change Color button.
   d. At the Text and Line Color dialog box, click a medium blue color of your choosing and then click OK.
   e. At the Edit Color Scheme dialog box, click *Title text* in the *Scheme colors* section.
   f. Click the Change Color button.
   g. At the Title Text Color dialog box, click a dark blue color of your choosing and then click OK.
   h. Click the Apply button to apply the color changes and to close the Edit Color Scheme dialog box.
6. Print the presentation as handouts with four slides per page.
7. Customize the background of the slide color scheme by completing the following steps:
   a. Click Format and then Background.

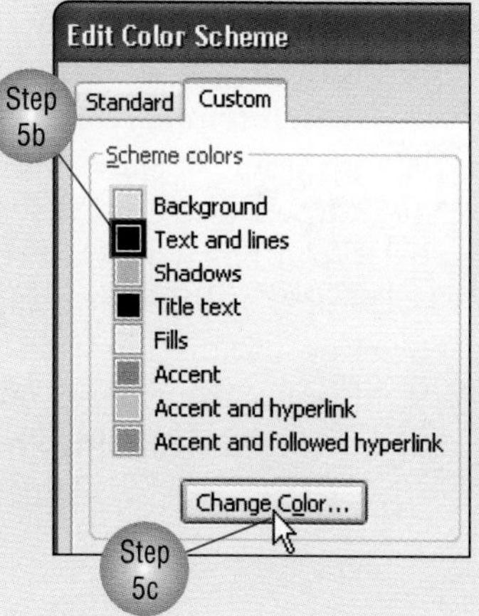

b. At the Background dialog box, click the down-pointing arrow at the right side of the *Background fill* option box, and then click *More Colors* at the palette.
c. At the Colors dialog box with the Standard tab selected, click a light green color of your choosing, and then click the OK button.
d. Click the Apply to All button at the Background dialog box.
8. Print the presentation as handouts with four slides per page.
9. Save, run, and then close the presentation.

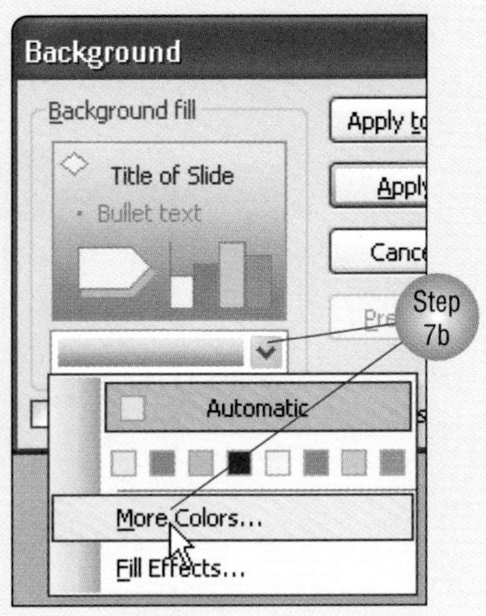

Changing the Design Template

When preparing presentations for this and previous chapters, you have first chosen a design template and then created each slide. A different design template can be applied to an existing presentation. To do this, click the Slide Design button on the Formatting toolbar and then click the desired template in the Slide Design task pane.

exercise 4 CHANGING THE DESIGN TEMPLATE

1. Open **PlanningPresentation**.
2. Choose a different design template for the presentation by completing the following steps:
   a. Click the Slide Design button on the Formatting toolbar.
   b. If color schemes display in the task pane, click the Design Templates hyperlink to display slide design templates.
   c. Click the *Layers* slide design in the *Apply a design template* list box in the Slide Design task pane. (You will need to scroll down the list to display this template.)
3. Run the presentation to see how it appears with the new design template applied.
4. Print all six slides on one page.
5. Close **PlanningPresentation** without saving the changes.
6. Open **NetworkingPresentation**.
7. Apply a different design template of your choosing to this presentation.
8. Run the presentation to see how it appears with the new design template applied.
9. Print all four slides on the same page.
10. Close **NetworkingPresentation** without saving the changes.

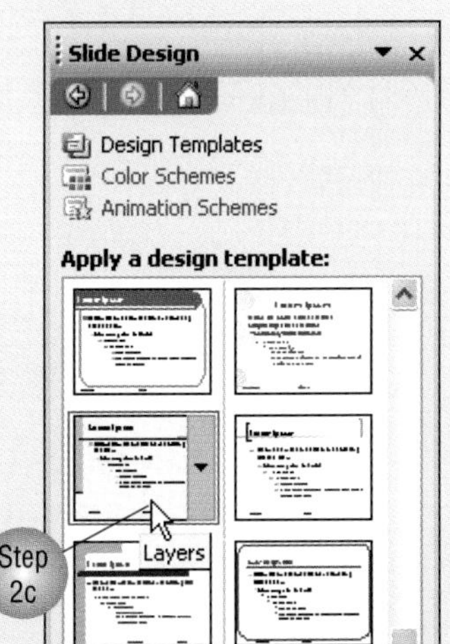

Formatting with Format Painter

If you create a blank presentation and decide to apply your own formatting, consider using the Format Painter. Use Format Painter to apply the same formatting in more than one location in a slide or slides. To use the Format Painter, apply the desired formatting to text, position the insertion point anywhere in the formatted text, and then double-click the Format Painter button on the Standard toolbar. Using the mouse, select the additional text to which you want the formatting applied. After applying the formatting in the desired locations, click the Format Painter button to deactivate it. If you need to apply formatting in only one other location, click the Format Painter button once. The first time you select text, the formatting is applied and the Format Painter is deactivated.

Format with Format Painter
1. Click text containing desired formatting.
2. Double-click Format Painter button.
3. Select text.
4. Click Format Painter button.

Creating a Blank Presentation

Many of the presentations you have created in this and previous chapters have been based on a design template. You can also create a blank presentation and then apply your own formatting or apply a design template. To create a blank presentation, click the New button on the Standard toolbar. This displays an unformatted slide in the Slide pane. You can also create a blank presentation by displaying the New Presentation task pane and then clicking the Blank presentation hyperlink.

New

exercise 5 — CREATING AND FORMATTING A BLANK PRESENTATION

1. At the blank PowerPoint window, click the New button on the Standard toolbar. (This displays an unformatted slide in the Slide pane and also displays the Slide Layout task pane.)
2. In the unformatted slide that displays in the Slide pane, type the title and subtitle for Slide 1 as shown in Figure 3.7.
3. Create the remaining slides shown in Figure 3.7 using the Title and Text slide layout for Slides 2 through 5. When typing the bulleted text, press the Tab key to move (demote) the insertion point to the next tab stop or press Shift + Tab to move (promote) the insertion point to the previous tab stop.
4. Save the presentation and name it **sppc3x05**.
5. Print the presentation as handouts with six slides per page. (The presentation contains only five slides.)
6. Suppose you are going to print transparencies for the slides in this presentation. To do this, apply a design template with a light background by completing the following steps:
   a. Click the Slide Design button on the Formatting toolbar.
   b. Click *Blends* in the *Apply a design template* list box. (You will need to scroll down the list to display this template.)

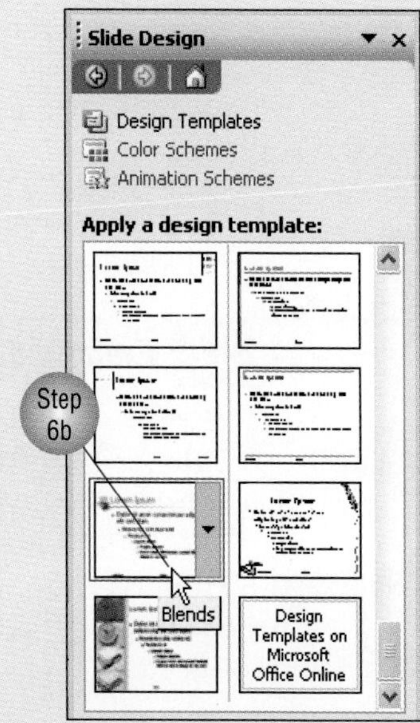

7. Change the font style and color of the terms using Format Painter by completing the following steps:
   a. Display Slide 4 in the Slide pane.
   b. Select the term *Balance:* (be sure to select the colon).

c. Display the Font dialog box, change the font style to bold, change the color to the red that follows the color scheme, and then close the dialog box.
d. Deselect *Balance:* and then click anywhere in *Balance:*.
e. Double-click the Format Painter button on the Standard toolbar.

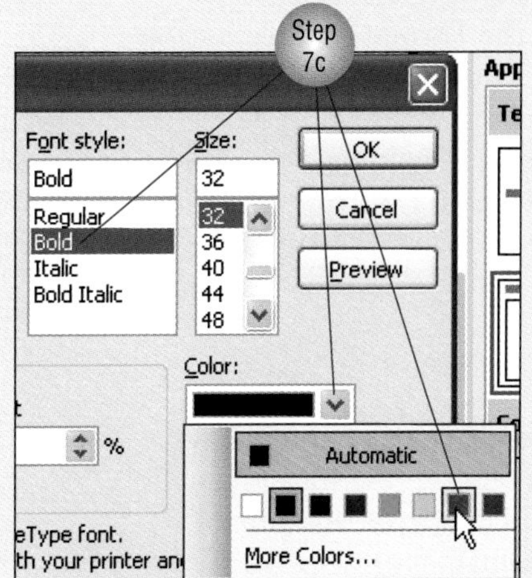

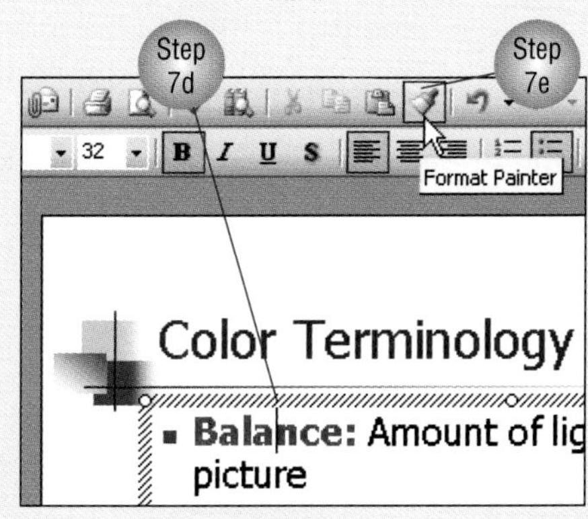

f. Using the mouse, select *Color Wheel:*. (The pointer displays as an I-beam with a paintbrush attached.)
g. Using the mouse, select each of the other terms in Slide 4 (*Contrast:*, *Gradient:*, *Hue:*).
h. Display Slide 5 and then use the mouse to select each of the terms (including the colon) in the slide.
i. Click the Format Painter button to deactivate it.
j. Deselect the text.

8. Print only Slide 4 by completing the following steps:
   a. Display Slide 4 in the Slide pane.
   b. Click File and then Print.
   c. At the Print dialog box, click the *Current slide* option in the *Print range* section.
   d. Click OK.
9. Save, run, and then close the presentation.

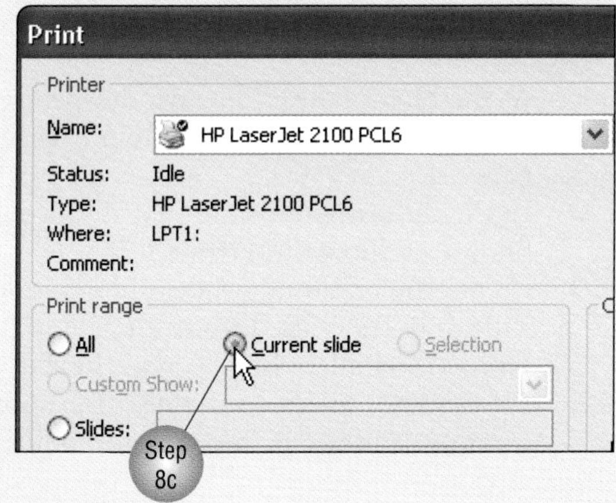

FIGURE 3.7 **Exercise 5**

Slide 1	Title	=	COMPANY PUBLICATIONS
	Subtitle	=	Using Color in Publications
Slide 2	Title	=	Communicating with Color
	Bullets	=	• Color in a publication can: – Elicit feelings

– Emphasize important text
– Attract attention
- Choose one or two colors
- Use “spot color” by using color only in specific areas

Slide 3 Title = Printing the Publication
Bullets =
- Print all copies on a color printer
- Print on a color printer and duplicate with a color photocopier
- Print on colored paper
- Print on specialty paper

Slide 4 Title = Color Terminology
Bullets =
- Balance: Amount of light and dark in a picture
- Color Wheel: Device used to illustrate color relationships
- Contrast: Amount of gray in a color
- Gradient: Gradual varying of color
- Hue: Variation of a color such as green-blue

Slide 5 Title = Color Terminology
Bullets =
- Pixel: Each dot in a picture or graphic
- Resolution: The number of dots that make up an image on a screen or printer
- Reverse: Black background on white foreground or white type against a colored background
- Saturation: Purity of a color

Formatting with Bullets and Numbers

Each design template contains a Title and Text slide layout containing bullets. The appearance and formatting of the bullets in this slide layout varies with each template. You can choose to use the bullet provided by the design template or you can insert different bullets and also change to numbering.

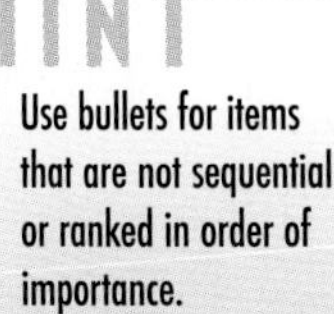

HINT
Use bullets for items that are not sequential or ranked in order of importance.

Changing Bullets

Customize bullets with options at the Bullets and Numbering dialog box with the Bulleted tab selected as shown in Figure 3.8. Display this dialog box by clicking in a bulleted list placeholder, clicking Format, and then clicking Bullets and Numbering. At the Bullets and Numbering dialog box, choose one of the predesigned bullets from the list box, change the size of the bullets by percentage in relation to the text size, change the bullet color, and display bullet pictures and characters.

Change Bullets
1. Select bulleted text.
2. Click Format, Bullets and Numbering.
3. At Bullets and Numbering dialog box, make desired changes.
4. Click OK.

FIGURE 3.8 **Bullets and Numbering Dialog Box with Bulleted Tab Selected**

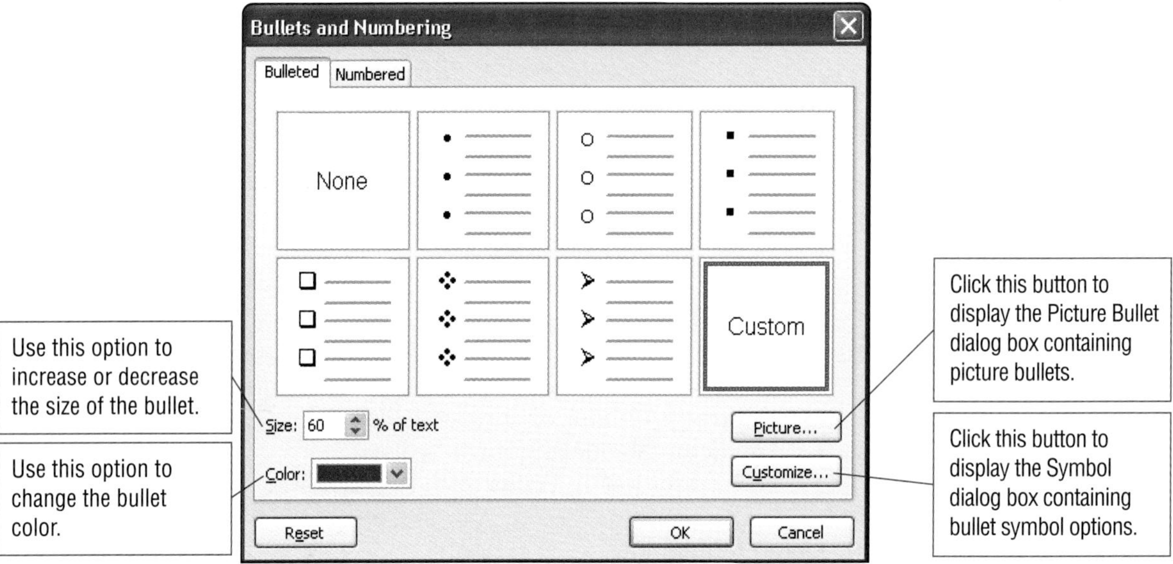
Bullets and Numbering
Bulleted
Numbered
None
Custom
Size: 60 % of text
Color:
Picture...
Customize...
Reset
OK
Cancel
Use this option to increase or decrease the size of the bullet.
Use this option to change the bullet color.
Click this button to display the Picture Bullet dialog box containing picture bullets.
Click this button to display the Symbol dialog box containing bullet symbol options.

HINT

If you increase the size of bullets, you may need to increase paragraph indention or spacing between paragraphs.

Click the Picture button located toward the bottom of the dialog box and the Picture Bullet dialog box displays. Click the desired bullet in the list box and then click OK. Click the Customize button located toward the bottom of the Bullets and Numbering dialog box and the Symbol dialog box displays. Choose a symbol bullet option at the Symbol dialog box and then click OK.

Inserting Numbering

Numbering

A bulleted list can easily be changed to numbers. To do this, select the bulleted list and then click the Numbering button on the Formatting toolbar. You can also change to numbering by selecting the list and then displaying the Bullets and Numbering dialog box with the Numbered tab selected. At this dialog box, choose the desired numbering style, and then click OK.

exercise 6 CHANGING BULLETS AND APPLYING NUMBERING

1. Open **sppc3x05**.
2. Save the presentation with Save As and name it **sppc3x06**.
3. Change the first-level bullets in Slides 2 through 5 by completing the following steps:
   a. Display Slide 2 in the Slide pane.
   b. Hold down the Shift key and then click the Slide Master View button on the View toolbar.
   c. Click in the text *Click to edit Master text styles*.
   d. Click Format and then Bullets and Numbering.
   e. At the Bullets and Numbering dialog box with the Bulleted tab selected, click the up-pointing arrow at the right side of the *Size* option until *85* displays in the text box.
   f. Click the Picture button located toward the bottom of the dialog box.

g. At the Picture Bullet dialog box, click the first bullet option from the left in the third row (gold, square bullet).
h. Click OK to close the Picture Bullet dialog box and the Bullets and Numbering dialog box.
i. Click the Normal View button. (This removes the slide master.)

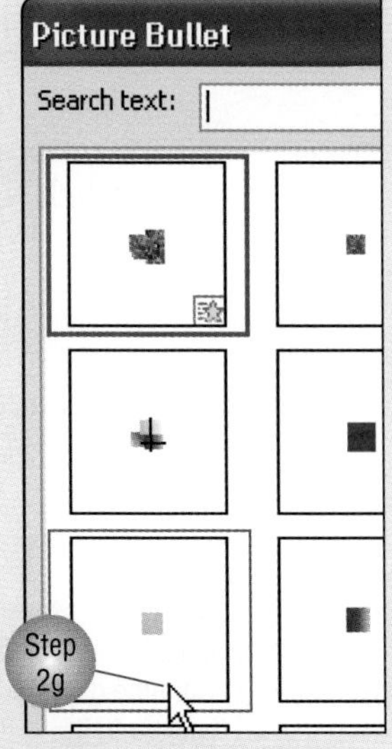

4. Print only Slide 2.
5. Change the second-level bullets in Slide 2 by completing the following steps:
   a. Make sure Slide 2 is displayed in Slide view.
   b. Hold down the Shift key and then click the Slide Master View button on the View toolbar.
   c. Click in the text *Second level*.
   d. Click Format and then Bullets and Numbering.
   e. At the Bullets and Numbering dialog box with the Bulleted tab selected, click the up-pointing arrow at the right side of the *Size* option until *70* displays in the text box.
   f. Click the Customize button located toward the bottom of the dialog box.
   g. At the Symbol dialog box, click the pen image (first image [in the second square] from the left in the top row).
   h. Click OK to close the Symbol dialog box.
   i. Click OK to close the Bullets and Numbering dialog box.
   j. Click the Normal View button. (This removes the slide master.)
6. Print only Slide 2.
7. Save the presentation with the same name (**sppc3x06**).
8. Change the first-level bullets to numbers in Slides 2 through 5 by completing the following steps:
   a. Make sure Slide 2 displays in the Slide pane.
   b. Hold down the Shift key and then click the Slide Master View button on the View toolbar.
   c. Click in the text *Click to edit Master text styles*.
   d. Click the Numbering button on the Formatting toolbar.
   e. Change the color of the numbers by completing the following steps:
      1) Click Format and then Bullets and Numbering.
      2) At the Bullets and Numbering dialog box, make sure the Numbered tab is selected.
      3) Click the down-pointing arrow at the right side of the *Color* option and then click the green color that follows the color scheme.
      4) Click OK to close the dialog box.
   f. Click the Normal View button. (This removes the slide master.)

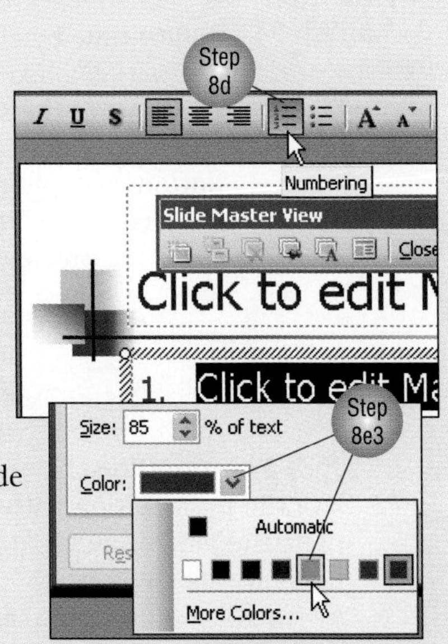

9. Save the presentation.
10. Display Slide 1 and then run the presentation.
11. Print all five slides on one page.
12. Close the presentation.

Inserting Headers and Footers in a Presentation

Insert information that you want to appear at the top or bottom of each slide or on note and handout pages with options at the Header and Footer dialog box. Click View and then Header and Footer to display the Header and Footer dialog box shown in Figure 3.9.

FIGURE 3.9 ***Header and Footer Dialog Box with Slide Tab Selected***

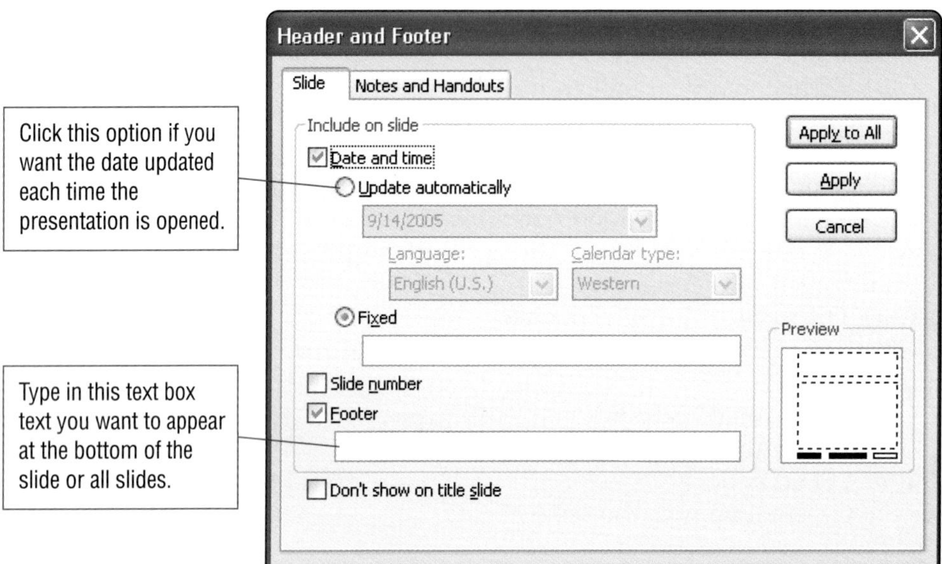

QUICK STEPS

Insert Header/Footer
1. Click View, Header and Footer.
2. Click Slide tab.
3. Make desired changes.
4. Click OK.

Include the date and time as fixed or automatic. To include a fixed date and time, click in the *Fixed* text box and then type the desired text. If you want the date and/or time inserted and then automatically updated when the presentation is opened, click the *Update automatically* option. Specify the format for the date and/or time by clicking the down-pointing arrow at the right side of the *Update automatically* text box and then clicking the desired format at the drop-down list. If you want the slide number inserted in a presentation, click the *Slide number* check box. Type any footer text desired in the *Footer* text box. Click the Apply button to apply the element(s) to the current slide. If you want the element(s) inserted in all slides, click the Apply to All button. Elements added to a slide or slides are previewed in the *Preview* section of the dialog box.

exercise 7 INSERTING THE DATE, TIME, SLIDE NUMBER, AND A FOOTER IN A PRESENTATION

1. Open **PlanningPresentation**.
2. Save the presentation with Save As and name it **sppc3x07**.
3. Insert the date, time, slide number, and footer text into the presentation by completing the following steps:
   a. Click View and then Header and Footer.
   b. At the Header and Footer dialog box with the Slide tab selected, make sure a check mark displays in the *Date and time* check box.

c. Click the *Update automatically* option.
d. Click the down-pointing arrow at the right side of the *Update automatically* text box and then click the option that displays the date in numbers followed by the time (i.e., 09/14/2005 6:47 PM).
e. Click the *Slide number* option to insert a check mark in the check box.
f. Click in the *Footer* text box and then type **Electronic Design**.
g. Click the Apply to All button.

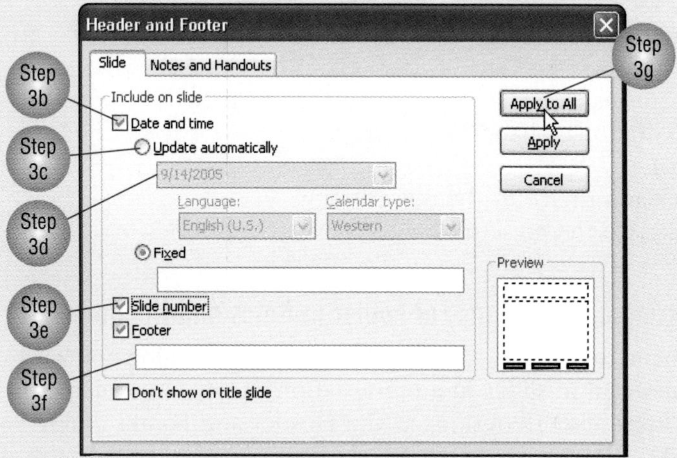

4. Save the presentation and then run the presentation to see how the footer text displays in the slides.
5. Print all six slides on one page.
6. Close the presentation.

Inserting Information in the Footer Area of a Slide Master

You can include footer information in slides by typing the information in the slide master. To insert information in the Footer area of a slide master, display the Slide Master view, click in the desired section of the slide master, and then type or insert the desired information. Apply the desired formatting to the footer text at the Slide Master view.

exercise 8

INSERTING INFORMATION IN THE FOOTER AREA OF A SLIDE MASTER

1. Open **sppc3x05**.
2. Save the presentation with Save As and name it **sppc3x08**.
3. Insert and format a footer in the Slide Master by completing the following steps:
   a. Hold down the Shift key and then click the Slide Master View button on the View toolbar.
   b. Click the Blends Slide Master miniature (the top miniature) located at the left side of the window.
   c. Click the text <footer> in the Footer Area of the slide master.

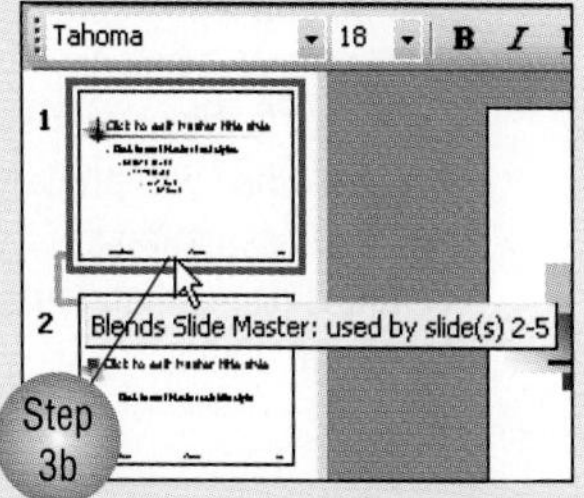

d. Type Using Colors in Publications.

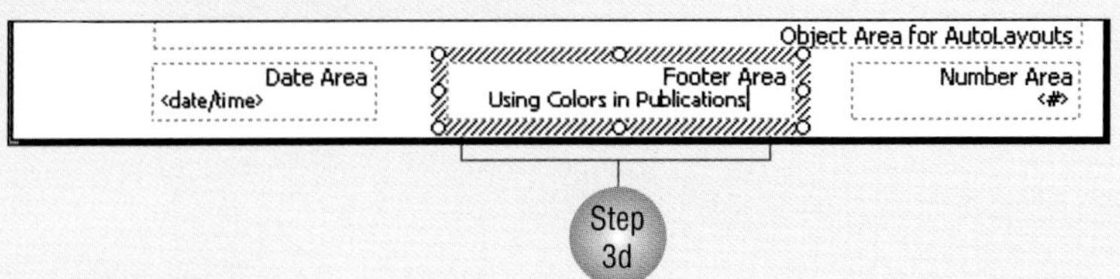

e. Select *Using Colors in Publications* and then change the font size to *12* and turn on bold.

f. Click the Normal View button on the View toolbar.

4. Print the presentation as handouts with six slides per page. (The footer text does not print on Slide 1.)
5. Display Slide 1 and then run the presentation.
6. Save and then close the presentation.

QUICK STEPS

Insert Header/Footer in Notes and Handouts

1. Click View, Header and Footer.
2. Click Notes and Handouts tab.
3. Make desired changes.
4. Click OK.

Inserting a Header and/or Footer in Notes and Handouts

Elements selected at the Header and Footer dialog box with the Slide tab selected are inserted in slides in a presentation. If you want elements inserted in notes or handouts, choose options at the Header and Footer dialog box with the Notes and Handouts tab selected as shown in Figure 3.10. At this dialog box, choose to insert the date and/or time fixed or automatically, include a header and/or footer, and include page numbering. Choices made at this dialog box print when the presentation is printed as notes pages, handouts, or an outline.

FIGURE 3.10 ***Header and Footer Dialog Box with Notes and Handouts Tab Selected***

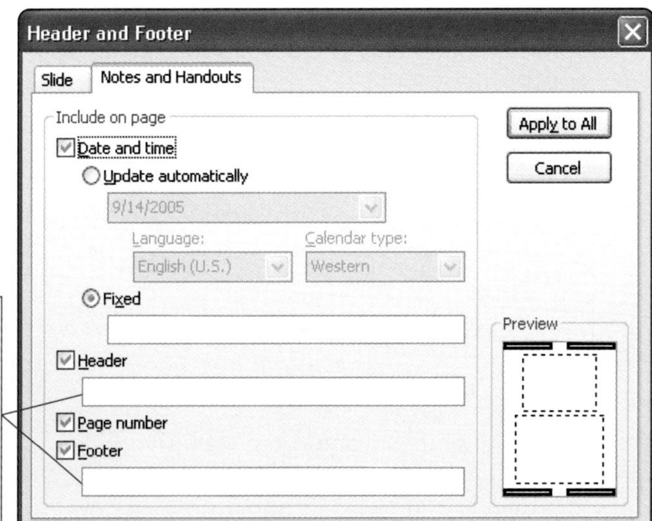

Adding Speaker Notes

If you are going to give your presentation in front of an audience, consider creating speaker notes for some or all of the slides. Create speaker notes containing additional information about the slide that will help you during the presentation. Speaker notes do not display on a slide when the presentation is running. Speaker notes print when the *Notes Pages* option is selected at the Print dialog box.

To insert speaker notes, display slides in the Normal view, click in the Notes pane, and then type the information. Another method for inserting speaker notes is to display the presentation in Notes Page view. To do this, click View and then Notes Page. This displays the active slide with a text box below. Click inside the text box and then type the speaker note information. Format speaker notes in the normal manner. For example, you can change the font, change the text alignment, and insert bullets or numbering.

QUICK STEPS

Add Speaker Notes

1. Display presentation in Normal view.
2. Click in Notes pane.
3. Type note.

You can create and/or display speaker notes while a presentation is running. To do this, run the presentation, and then display the desired slide. Move the mouse to display the Slide Show toolbar. Click the slide icon button on the Slide Show toolbar, point to Screen, and then click Speaker Notes. This displays the Speaker Notes dialog box. View, type, or edit text at this dialog box and then click the Close button.

Hiding Slides

A presentation you create may be presented to a number of different groups or departments. In some situations, you may want to hide specific slides in a presentation depending on the audience. To hide a slide in a presentation, click the slide miniature in the Outline/Slides pane, click Slide Show, and then click Hide Slide. When a slide is hidden, a square with a slash through it displays over the slide number in the Outline/Slides pane. The slide is visible in the Outline/Slides pane in Normal view and also in the Slide Sorter view. To remove the hidden icon and redisplay the slide when running a presentation, click the slide miniature in the Outline/Slides pane, click Slide Show, and then click Hide Slide.

Hide Slide

1. Make slide active.
2. Click Slide Show, Hide Slide.

exercise 9

INSERTING A HEADER, FOOTER, AND THE DATE IN NOTES AND HANDOUTS

1. Open **PlanningPresentation**.
2. Save the presentation with Save As and name it **sppc3x09**.
3. Copy slides from another presentation into **sppc3x09** by completing the following steps:
   a. Open **CompanyNewsletter**. (Make sure the Normal view is selected.)
   b. Click the Slide 2 miniature in the Outline/Slides pane.
   c. Hold down the Shift key and then click the Slide 3 miniature.
   d. Click the Copy button on the Standard toolbar.
   e. Close **CompanyNewsletter**.
   f. Click below the Slide 6 miniature in the Outline/Slides pane and then click the Paste button.

4. Insert a header and footer, the date, and page numbering in notes and handouts by completing the following steps:
   a. Click View and then Header and Footer.
   b. At the Header and Footer dialog box, click the Notes and Handouts tab.
   c. At the Header and Footer dialog box with the Notes and Handouts tab selected, click the *Update automatically* option. (Check to make sure the current date displays in the *Update automatically* text box. If not, click the down-pointing arrow at the right side of the text box, and then click the desired date style at the drop-down list.)

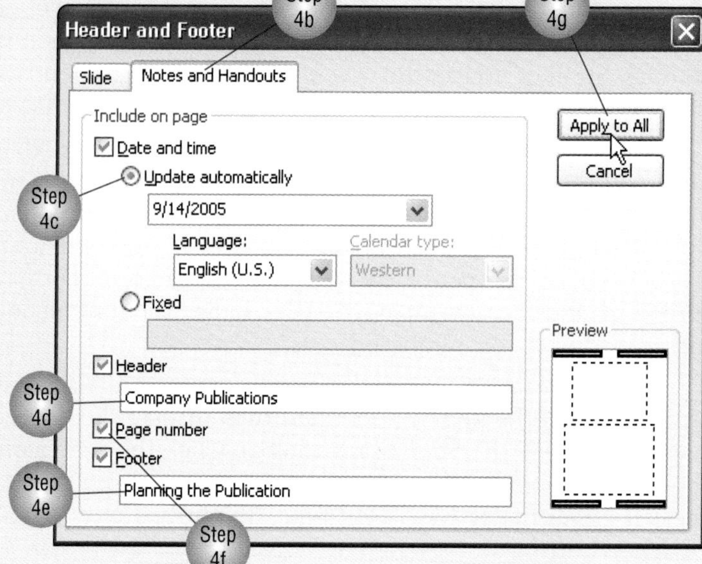

   d. Click in the *Header* text box and then type **Company Publications**.
   e. Click in the *Footer* text box and then type **Planning the Publication**.
   f. Make sure a check mark displays in the *Page number* check box.
   g. Click the Apply to All button.
5. Add and format speaker notes by completing the following steps:
   a. Display Slide 2 in the Slide pane.
   b. Click in the Notes pane. (This pane displays below the slide and contains the text *Click to add notes*.)
   c. Click the Bold button on the Formatting toolbar and then click the Center button.
   d. Type **Distribute publication examples.**, press Enter, and then type **Compare examples 1 and 2.**
   e. Display Slide 4 in the Slide pane.
   f. Click in the Notes pane.
   g. Click the Bold button on the Formatting toolbar and then click the Center button.
   h. Type **Elicit comments from participants regarding current corporate publications.**, press Enter, and then type **Ask what changes individuals would like to make.**
6. Print Slides 2 and 4 as notes pages by completing the following steps:
   a. Display the Print dialog box.
   b. Click the down-pointing arrow to the right of the *Print what* option and then click *Notes Pages* at the drop-down list.
   c. Click the *Slides* option box and then type **2,4**.
   d. Click OK. (This prints each slide [Slides 2 and 4] toward the top of the page on a separate piece of paper with the header, footer, date, page number, and speaker notes included.)

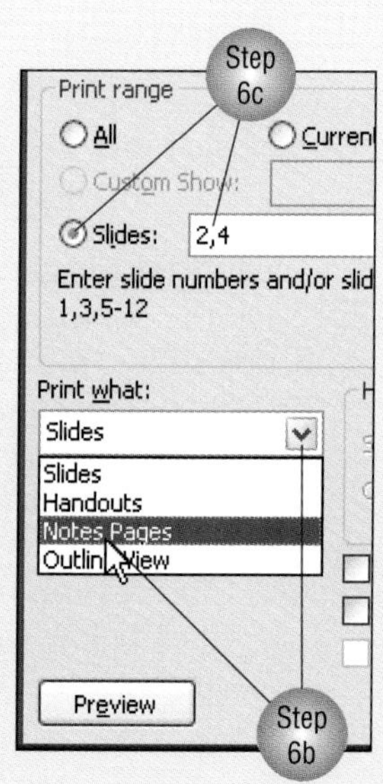

7. Run the presentation by completing the following steps:

a. Make Slide 1 the active slide.
b. Click the Slide Show button on the View toolbar.
c. When the first slide displays on the screen, click the left mouse button.
d. At the second slide, move the mouse to display the Slide Show toolbar.
e. Click the slide icon button on the Slide Show toolbar, point to Screen, and then click Speaker Notes.
f. After viewing the note in the Speaker Notes dialog box, click the Close button.
g. Run the rest of the presentation.

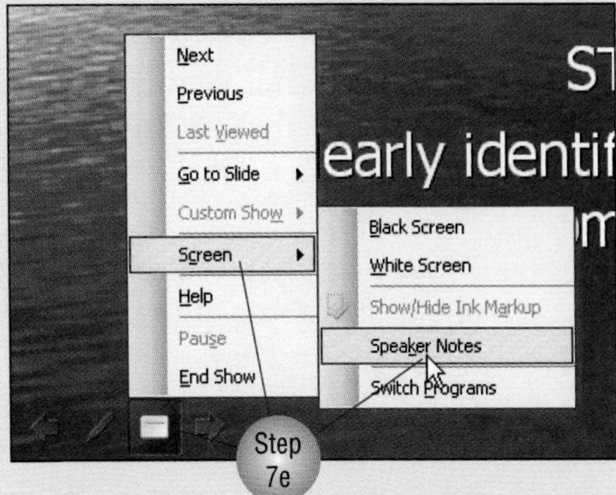

8. Hide slides by completing the following steps:
   a. Make sure the presentation displays in Normal view.
   b. Click the Slide 7 miniature in the Outline/Slides pane.
   c. Hold down the Shift key and then click the Slide 8 miniature in the Outline/Slides pane.
   d. Click Slide Show and then click Hide Slide. (Notice the hide slide icon that displays around the Slide 7 and Slide 8 numbers in the Outline/Slides pane.)

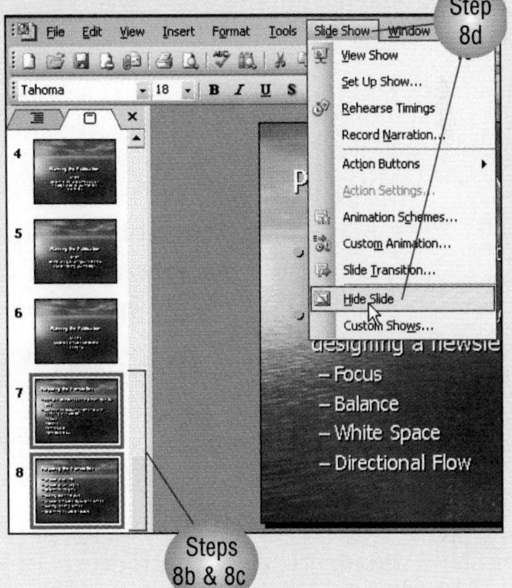

9. Make Slide 1 the active slide and then run the presentation. (Notice that Slide 7 and Slide 8 do not display.)
10. Remove the hide slide icons by completing the following steps:
    a. Click the Slide 7 miniature in the Outline/Slides pane.
    b. Hold down the Shift key and then click the Slide 8 miniature in the Outline/Slides pane.
    c. Click Slide Show and then click Hide Slide.
11. Save the presentation.
12. Print the presentation with all eight slides on one page.
13. Close the presentation.

CHAPTER summary

- Formatting such as changing fonts, changing font color, and changing paragraph alignment can be applied to text in slides.
- The Formatting toolbar contains several buttons you can use to apply formatting to text in slides.
- Change the font of selected text with options at the Font dialog box or with the Font and Font Size buttons on the Formatting toolbar.
- Increase or decrease line spacing or the spacing before or after paragraphs with options at the Line Spacing dialog box.

- Generally, a template contains a slide master as well as a title master. Changes made to a title master affect all slides with the Title Slide layout applied. Changes made to the slide master affect all other slides in a presentation.
- Change to the Slide Master view by holding down the Shift key and clicking the Slide Master View button on the View toolbar. (The Normal View button changes to the Slide Master View button when you hold down the Shift key.)
- In Slide Master view, a slide master displays in the Slide pane along with a slide-title master pair that display, as slide miniatures at the left side of the window. Click the desired slide master miniature and then apply specific formatting to the slide master in the Slide pane.
- You can apply more than one design template to slides in a presentation. If more than one design template is applied to slides, multiple slide-title master pairs will display in the Slide Master view.
- A design template includes a default color scheme. Click the Color Schemes hyperlink located toward the bottom of the Slide Design task pane and a number of additional color schemes display in the task pane.
- Click the Edit Color Schemes hyperlink in the task pane to display the Edit Color Scheme dialog box. Use options at this dialog box to change color for specific items.
- Change the background color of a design template with options at the Background dialog box.
- You can apply a different design template to an existing presentation.
- Create a presentation with little formatting using the Blank Presentation template. To create a blank presentation, click the New button on the Standard toolbar or click the Blank presentation hyperlink in the New Presentation task pane.
- Use Format Painter to apply the same formatting to more than one location in a slide or slides.
- Customize bullets with options at the Bullets and Numbering dialog box with the Bulleted tab selected.
- Click the Picture button located toward the bottom of the Bullets and Numbering dialog box to display the Picture Bullet dialog box that contains bullet images. Click the Customize button at the dialog box to display the Symbol dialog box containing symbol options for bullets.
- Apply numbering to selected text by clicking the Numbering button on the Formatting toolbar or with options at the Bullets and Numbering dialog box with the Numbered tab selected.
- Insert elements in a slide or slides such as the date and time, slide number, and a footer with options at the Header and Footer dialog box with the Slide tab selected.
- You can create a footer for slides in the Footer Area of a slide master.
- Insert elements in notes and handouts such as the date and time, page number, and a header and footer with options from the Header and Footer dialog box with the Notes and Handouts tab selected.
- Insert speaker notes in the Notes pane that displays below the Slide pane in Normal view.
- Hide slides you do not want to appear when running a presentation by selecting the slide(s), clicking Slide Show, and then clicking Hide Slide.

FEATURES summary

Note: No buttons are included in this table because they are available only on customized toolbars.

FEATURE	MENU
Font dialog box	Format, Font
Line Spacing dialog box	Format, Line Spacing
Slide Master view	View, Master, Slide Master
Color scheme options	Click Color Schemes hyperlink in Slide Design task pane
Edit Color Scheme dialog box	Click Edit Color Schemes hyperlink in Slide Design task pane
Background dialog box	Format, Background
Header and Footer dialog box	View, Header and Footer
Hide a slide	Slide Show, Hide Slide

CONCEPTS check

Completion: On a blank sheet of paper, indicate the correct term, symbol, or command for each description.

1. Display the Font dialog box by clicking this option on the Menu bar and then clicking Font at the drop-down menu.
2. Increase spacing before and after paragraphs with options at this dialog box.
3. Display the Slide Master view by holding down this key while clicking the Normal View button on the View toolbar.
4. Display additional color schemes for a design template by clicking this hyperlink in the Slide Design task pane.
5. Customize a color scheme with options at this dialog box.
6. Use this button on the Standard toolbar to apply formatting to more than one location in a slide or slides.
7. Click this button at the Bullets and Numbering dialog box to display the Symbol dialog box.
8. Change a selected bulleted list to numbers by clicking this button on the Formatting toolbar.
9. Insert information you want to appear at the top or bottom of each slide or on note and handout pages with options at this dialog box.
10. Click in this pane in the Normal view to add speaker notes to a slide.
11. Hide a slide by selecting the slide, clicking this option on the Menu bar, and then clicking Hide Slide.

SKILLS check

Assessment 1

1. Create a presentation with the text shown in Figure 3.11 using the Axis design template. Choose the appropriate layout for each slide.
2. When all of the slides are created, complete a spelling check on the presentation.
3. Add a transition and sound of your choosing to each slide.
4. Save the presentation and name it **sppc3sc01**.
5. Run the presentation.
6. Print all of the slides on one page.
7. Close the presentation.

FIGURE 3.11 ***Assessment 1***

Slide 1	Title	=	BENEFITS PROGRAM
	Subtitle	=	Changes to Plans
Slide 2	Title	=	INTRODUCTION
	Bullets	=	• Changes made for 2005
			• Description of eligibility
			• Instructions for enrolling new members
			• Overview of medical and dental coverage
Slide 3	Title	=	INTRODUCTION
	Bullets	=	• Expanded enrollment forms
			• Glossary defining terms
			• Telephone directory
			• Pamphlet with commonly asked questions
Slide 4	Title	=	WHAT'S NEW
	Bullets	=	• New medical plan
			• Changes in monthly contributions
			• Paying with pretax dollars
			• Contributions toward spouse's coverage

Slide 5	Title	=	COST SHARING
	Bullets	=	• Increased deductible • New coinsurance amount • Higher coinsurance amount for retail prescription drugs • Co-payment for mail-order medicines • New stop loss limit

Assessment 2

1. Open **sppc3sc01**.
2. Save the presentation with Save As and name it **sppc3sc02**.
3. Make the following changes to the presentation:
   a. Change to the Slide Master view.
   b. Click the Axis Title Master slide miniature (the bottom miniature).
   c. Click in the text *Click to edit Master title style* and then click the Italic button on the Formatting toolbar.
   d. Click the Axis Slide Master slide miniature (the top miniature).
   e. Click anywhere in the text *Click to edit Master title style* and then click the Italic button on the Formatting toolbar.
   f. Increase line spacing for the bulleted text by completing the following steps:
      1) Click anywhere in the text *Click to edit Master text styles*.
      2) Display the Line Spacing dialog box.
      3) Change the *Line spacing* to *1.3*.
      4) Close the Line Spacing dialog box.
   g. Click the Normal View button.
   h. Change the background color for all slides. (Make sure you choose a complementary color.)
4. Save and then run the presentation.
5. Print all of the slides on one page.
6. Close the presentation.

Assessment 3

1. Open **sppc3sc02**.
2. Save the presentation with Save As and name it **sppc3sc03**.
3. Make the following changes to the presentation:
   a. Apply a different design template of your choosing.
   b. Insert the current date and slide number on all slides in the presentation. (Make sure the *Don't show on title slide* option at the Header and Footer dialog box does not contain a check mark.)
   c. Change the bullets in Slide 2 to numbers.
4. Save and then run the presentation.
5. Print all of the slides on one page.
6. Close the presentation.

Assessment 4

1. Open **JobSearchPresentation**. (This presentation is located in the PowerPointChapter03S folder on your disk.)
2. Save the presentation with Save As and name it **sppc3sc04**.
3. Make the following change to the presentation:
   a. Create the header *Professional Employment Services*, the footer *Job Search Strategies*, and insert the date and page number for notes and handouts. (Make sure the *Don't show on title slide* option at the Header and Footer dialog box with the Slide tab selected does not contain a check mark.)
   b. Display Slide 2 in Normal view and then add the speaker note *Refer participants to visual aids*.
   c. Display Slide 5 in Normal view and then add the speaker note *Provide participants with an example of a contact list.*
4. Add a transition and sound of your choosing to all slides in the presentation.
5. Save and then run the presentation.
6. Print Slides 2 and 5 as notes pages.
7. Close the presentation.

Assessment 5

1. Slides in a presentation generally display and print in landscape orientation. This orientation can be changed to portrait. Use PowerPoint's Help feature to learn about slide orientations and how to change the orientation.
2. Open **JobSearchPresentation**.
3. Change the orientation of all slides in the presentation from landscape to portrait.
4. Print all slides on one page.
5. Close the **JobSearchPresentation** without saving the changes.

CHAPTER challenge

You own a small travel agency, Tia's Travel. On the first Saturday of each month, you will be holding a short seminar providing an overview of vacation planning. Prepare a presentation named **PlanforFun** that includes at least 10 slides. Using the slide master, change the first-level bullets to appear as airplanes (or a symbol associated with travel). Include a footer that includes the name of the presentation and the date on each slide. Apply a background or design template. Add transitions, sounds, and so on, to add variety to the presentation. Create speaker notes for at least two of the slides. Save the presentation again. Print only the slides that have speaker notes.

Another way to add variety to a presentation is through the use of Clip art and pictures. Use the Help feature to learn how to find and insert Clip art and pictures into a presentation. Then add at least two different pieces of Clip art or pictures to the **PlanforFun** presentation created in the first part of the Chapter Challenge. Save the presentation again.

After conducting the first seminar, one of the participants e-mails you and asks if the presentation could be e-mailed to her. E-mail the presentation as an attachment to the "participant" (your professor). Be sure to include appropriate information in the subject line and in the body of the message.

CHAPTER 4

ADDING VISUAL APPEAL AND ANIMATION TO PRESENTATIONS

PERFORMANCE OBJECTIVES

Upon successful completion of Chapter 4, you will be able to:

- **Format placeholders**
- **Draw objects and autoshapes with buttons on the Drawing toolbar**
- **Select, delete, move, copy, size, and format objects**
- **Create a text box and wrap text within an autoshape**
- **Display rulers, guide lines, and grid lines**
- **Insert clip art images in a presentation**
- **Size, move, and format clip art images**
- **Insert a bitmap graphic in a slide**
- **Add an animation scheme to slides**
- **Add a build to slides**

Add visual appeal to slides in a presentation by including shapes, objects, and autoshapes and by inserting clip art images or pictures. With buttons on the Drawing toolbar, you can format and customize placeholders in slides, draw objects, and create autoshapes. Insert clip art images in a slide with options at the Clip Art task pane or at the Select Picture dialog box. Add an animation scheme to a presentation to add visual interest to your presentation as well as create focus on specific items. In this chapter you will learn a number of features for adding visual appeal and animation to presentations.

Formatting with Buttons on the Drawing Toolbar

Slides in a presentation contain placeholders where specific text or objects are inserted. The formatting applied to placeholders in a design template will vary depending on the template selected. These placeholders can be customized by changing such items as the background color or adding a border or shadow. These types of changes can be made with buttons on the Drawing toolbar. The Drawing toolbar displays toward the bottom of the PowerPoint window (above the Status bar). Table 4.1 describes the buttons on the Drawing toolbar.

TABLE 4.1 PowerPoint Drawing Toolbar Buttons

Button	Name	Function
Draw	Draw	Display a drop-down menu with options for grouping and positioning drawings.
	Select Objects	Select text or objects.
AutoShapes	AutoShapes	Display a palette of shapes that can be drawn in a document. (To draw a shape circumscribed within a perfect square, hold down the Shift key while drawing the shape.)
	Line	Draw a line in a document.
	Arrow	Insert a line with an arrowhead. (To draw at 15-degree angles, hold down the Shift key.)
	Rectangle	Draw a rectangle in a document. (To draw a perfect square, hold down the Shift key while drawing the shape.)
	Oval	Draw an oval in a document. (To draw a perfect circle, hold down the Shift key while drawing the shape.)
	Text Box	Create a text box. (To add text that does not wrap, click the button, click in the document, and then type the text. To add text that does wrap, click the button, drag to create a box, and then type the text.)
	Insert WordArt	Insert a Microsoft Office drawing object.
	Insert Diagram or Organization Chart	Insert and customize a predesigned diagram or organizational chart.
	Insert Clip Art	Display the Clip Art task pane.
	Insert Picture	Display Insert Picture dialog box containing pictures you can insert in the document.
	Fill Color	Fill selected object with a color, pattern, texture, or shaded fill.
	Line Color	Change color of selected line.
A	Font Color	Format selected text with a color.
	Line Style	Change thickness of selected line or change it to a compound line.
	Dash Style	Change style of selected line, arc, or border to dashed.

Button	Name	Function
	Arrow Style	Add arrowheads to a selected line, arc, or open free-form.
	Shadow Style	Add or remove an object shadow.
	3-D Style	Add or remove a 3-D effect.

Drawing an Object

Line

Arrow

Rectangle

Oval

With buttons on the Drawing toolbar, you can draw a variety of shapes such as circles, squares, rectangles, ovals, and draw straight lines, free-form lines, and lines with arrowheads. If you draw a shape with the Line button or the Arrow button, the shape is considered a ***line drawing***. If you draw a shape with the Rectangle or Oval button, the shape is considered an ***enclosed object***. If you want to draw the same shape more than once, double-click the shape button on the Drawing toolbar. After drawing the shapes, click the button again to deactivate it.

Use the Rectangle button on the Drawing toolbar to draw a square or rectangle in a document. If you want to draw a square, hold down the Shift key while drawing the shape. The Shift key keeps all sides of the drawn object equal. Use the Oval button to draw a circle or an oval object. To draw a circle, hold down the Shift key while drawing the object.

Creating AutoShapes

Auto Shapes

With options from the AutoShapes button, you can choose from a variety of predesigned shapes. Click the AutoShapes button and a pop-up menu displays. Point to the desired menu option and a side menu displays. This side menu will offer autoshape choices for the selected option. For example, if you point to the Basic Shapes option, a number of shapes such as a circle, square, triangle, box, stop sign, and so on display at the right side of the pop-up menu. Click the desired shape and the mouse pointer turns into crosshairs. Position the crosshairs in the document screen, hold down the left mouse button, drag to create the shape, and then release the button. You can also use an autoshape to draw connector lines between objects. To draw a connector line, choose the desired autoshape, position the mouse pointer on the first object until the pointer turns into a connector pointer, click the left mouse button, and then click the second object.

QUICK STEPS

Create an Autoshape

1. Click Autoshapes button on Drawing toolbar.
2. Point to desired autoshape category.
3. Click desired autoshape.
4. Drag in slide to draw autoshape.

Selecting an Object

After an object has been created, you may decide to make changes to the object or delete the object. To do this, the object must be selected. To select an enclosed object, position the mouse pointer anywhere inside the object (the mouse pointer displays with a four-headed arrow attached) and then click the left mouse button. To select a line, position the mouse pointer on the line until the pointer displays with a four-headed arrow attached, and then click the left mouse button. When an object is selected, it displays surrounded by white sizing handles. Once an object is selected, it can be edited (such as by changing the fill and the line), it can be moved, or it can be deleted.

HINT

Many autoshapes have an adjustment handle you can use to change the most prominent feature of the autoshape.

Select Objects

Select Multiple Items
1. Click Select Objects button on Drawing toolbar.
2. Drag to outline desired objects.

If a slide contains more than one object, you can select several objects at once using the Select Objects button on the Drawing toolbar. To do this, click the Select Objects button, position the crosshairs in the upper left corner of the area containing the objects, hold down the left mouse button, drag the outline to the lower right corner of the area containing the objects, and then release the mouse button. You can also select more than one object by holding down the Shift key as you click each object.

Each object in the selected area displays surrounded by white sizing handles. Objects in the selected area are connected. For example, if you move one of the objects in the selected area, the other objects move relatively.

Deleting, Moving, and Copying an Object

Copy Object
1. Click object.
2. Hold down Ctrl key.
3. Drag object to desired location.

Delete an object you have drawn by selecting the object and then clicking the Delete key. Move an object by selecting it, positioning the mouse pointer inside the object (mouse pointer displays with a four-headed arrow attached), holding down the left mouse button, and then dragging the outline of the object to the new location. If you select more than one object, moving one of the objects will move the other objects. Moving an object removes the object from its original position and inserts it into a new location. If you want the object to stay in its original location and an exact copy to be inserted in a new location, use the Ctrl key while dragging the object.

Sizing an Object

Size Object
1. Click object.
2. Drag sizing handle.

With the sizing handles that appear around an object when it is selected, the size of the object can be changed. To change the size of the object, select it, and then position the mouse pointer on a sizing handle until it turns into a double-headed arrow. Hold down the left mouse button, drag the outline of the shape toward or away from the center of the object until it is the desired size, and then release the mouse button.

Formatting Objects

Fill Color

Line Color

With buttons on the Drawing toolbar you can add fill color and/or shading to an object, change the line style, and change the line color. Click the down-pointing arrow at the right side of the Fill Color or Line Color button and a palette of color choices displays. Choose a color at this palette or click an option to display more fill or line colors and fill or line patterns.

(Note: Before completing Exercise 1, delete the PowerPointChapter03S folder on your disk. Next, copy to your disk the PowerPointChapter04S subfolder from the PowerPoint2003Specialist folder on the CD that accompanies this textbook and then make PowerPointChapter04S the active folder.)

exercise 1

CREATING A PRESENTATION AND FORMATTING OBJECTS USING A MASTER SLIDE

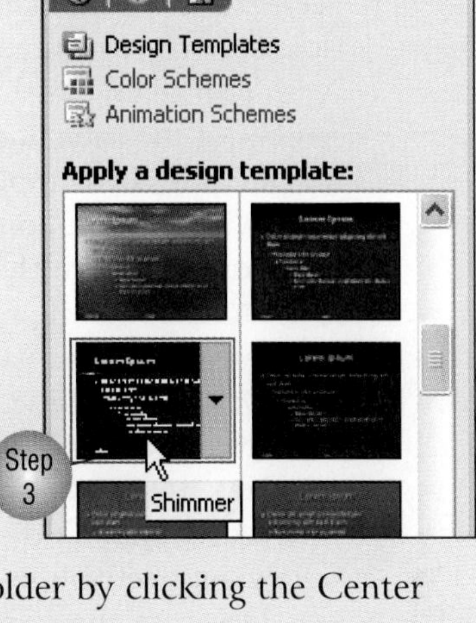

1. Prepare the presentation on enhanced services for McCormack Financial Services shown in Figure 4.1. Begin at a blank PowerPoint screen and then click the New button on the Standard toolbar.
2. Click the Slide Design button on the Formatting toolbar.
3. Click *Shimmer* in the *Apply a design template* list box in the Slide Design task pane.
4. Create a title master slide for the presentation by completing the following steps:
   a. Position the arrow pointer on the Normal View button on the View toolbar, hold down the Shift key, and then click the left mouse button.
   b. With the Shimmer Title Master slide displayed, click anywhere in the text *Click to edit Master title style.* (This selects the text in the placeholder.)
   c. Change the horizontal alignment of text in the placeholder by clicking the Center button on the Formatting toolbar.
   d. With the text in the placeholder still selected, add fill color by completing the following steps:
      1) Click the down-pointing arrow at the right side of the Fill Color button on the Drawing toolbar.
      2) At the drop-down menu that displays, click the second color from the right (light yellow).

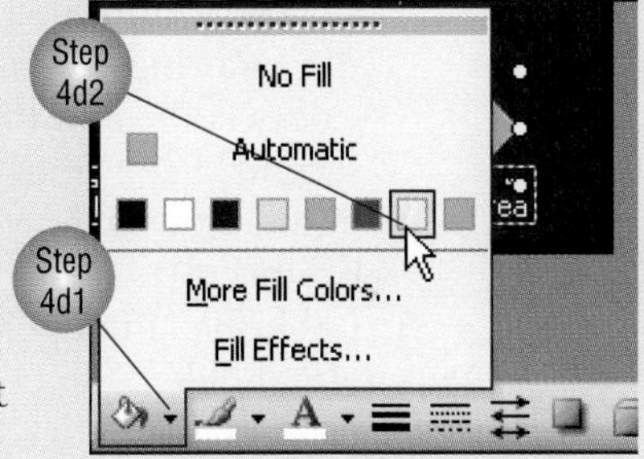

   e. With the text in the placeholder still selected, click the down-pointing arrow at the right side of the Font Color button on the Drawing toolbar and then click the dark blue color (third color from the left) at the drop-down menu that displays.
   f. Click in the text *Click to edit Master subtitle style* and then click the Center button on the Formatting toolbar.
   g. Draw and then copy diamond shapes in the upper left and lower right corners of the slide by completing the following steps:
      1) Click the AutoShapes button on the Drawing toolbar, point to Basic Shapes, and then click the diamond shape (last shape in the top row).
      2) Hold down the Shift key (this draws the diamond circumscribed in a square) and then position the arrow pointer (displays as a crosshair) in the upper left corner of the slide.
      3) With the Shift key still down, hold down the left mouse button, drag the mouse down and to the right until the diamond is about .5 inch tall, release the mouse button, and then release the Shift key. (If you do not like the size or position of the diamond, delete it. To do this, make sure the diamond is selected, and then press the Delete key.)

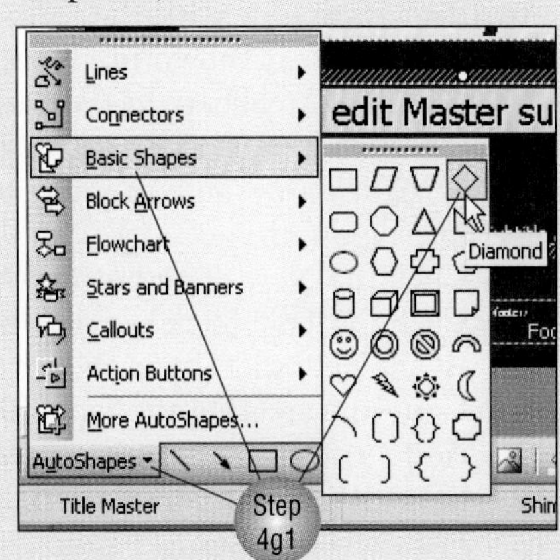

4) Click the Fill Color button on the Drawing toolbar to change the diamond fill color to light yellow.
5) If you need to move the diamond, make sure it is selected, position the arrow pointer inside the selected area, hold down the left mouse button, drag to the desired position, and then release the mouse button.

h. When the diamond is positioned in the desired location, copy it three times (you should end up with four diamond shapes—two in the upper left corner of the slide and two in the lower right corner of the slide) by completing the following steps:

1) With the diamond selected, position the arrow pointer inside the selected box.
2) Hold down the Ctrl key and the left mouse button.
3) Drag the outline to the desired position, then release the mouse button and then the Ctrl key. Repeat these steps to create the third and fourth diamond shapes. (See slide below.)

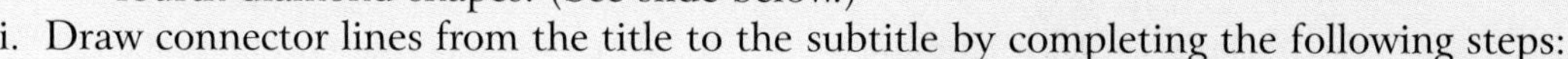

i. Draw connector lines from the title to the subtitle by completing the following steps:

1) Decrease the size of the subtitle place holder and move it so it appears as shown at the right.
2) Click the AutoShapes button on the Drawing toolbar, point to Connectors, and then click the second shape from the left in the middle row (Elbow Arrow Connector).
3) Click the left edge of the title placeholder.
4) Click the left edge of the subtitle placeholder.
5) Click the AutoShapes button, point to Connectors, and then click the Elbow Arrow Connector.
6) Click the right edge of the title placeholder.
7) Click the right edge of the subtitle placeholder.

5. Click the Normal View button on the View toolbar. (This removes the master slide and displays a slide with the formatted elements.)
6. Type the text shown in Figure 4.1 by completing the following steps:
   a. Click anywhere in the text *Click to add title*.
   b. Type **McCormack Annuity Funds**.
   c. Click anywhere in the text *Click to add subtitle*.
   d. Type **Enhanced Services**.
7. Click the New Slide button on the Formatting toolbar.
8. Click the Title Slide layout in the *Apply slide layout* section of the Slide Layout task pane.
9. At the new slide, type the text shown in the second slide in Figure 4.1.
10. Continue creating the remaining four slides shown in Figure 4.1.
11. Add a transition and sound of your choosing to all slides.
12. Save the presentation and name it **sppc4x01** and then run the presentation.
13. Print all six slides as handouts on one page and then close the presentation.

FIGURE

4.1 Exercise 1

Slide 1	Title	=	McCormack Annuity Funds
	Subtitle	=	Enhanced Services
Slide 2	Title	=	Enhanced Services
	Subtitle	=	Set up future accumulations transfers
Slide 3	Title	=	Enhanced Services
	Subtitle	=	Receive automatic statement confirmation
Slide 4	Title	=	Enhanced Services
	Subtitle	=	Faster cash withdrawals
Slide 5	Title	=	Enhanced Services
	Subtitle	=	Personal service from 8 a.m. to 11 p.m. weekdays
Slide 6	Title	=	Enhanced Services
	Subtitle	=	Multiple transfers made with one telephone call

Creating a Text Box

Text Box

With the Text Box button on the Drawing toolbar, you can create a box and then insert text inside the box. Text inside a box can be formatted in the normal manner. For example, you can change the font, alignment, or indent of the text.

HINT

Use a text box to place text anywhere in a slide.

Changing Tabs in a Text Box

Inside a text box, you may want to align text in columns. A text box, by default, contains left alignment tabs. You can display these default tabs by turning on the display of the Ruler by clicking View and then Ruler. The default left alignment tabs display as light gray marks along the bottom of the horizontal ruler.You can change these default left alignment tabs. Four types of tabs are available: left, center, right, and decimal. To change to a different tab alignment, click the Alignment button located at the left side of the horizontal ruler. Display the desired tab alignment symbol and then click at the desired position on the horizontal ruler. When you set a tab on the horizontal ruler, any default tabs to the left of the new tab are deleted.

Create Text Box
1. Click Text Box button on Drawing toolbar.
2. Click in slide or drag to create box.

Wrapping Text in an Autoshape

A text box can be drawn inside an autoshape. You can also click the Text Box button on the Drawing toolbar and then click in the autoshape. This positions the insertion point inside the shape where you can type text. If you want text to wrap within the autoshape, click Format and then AutoShape. At the Format AutoShape dialog box, click the Text Box tab. This displays the dialog box as shown in Figure 4.2. At this dialog box, choose the *Word wrap text in AutoShape* option. Choose the *Resize AutoShape to fit text* option if you want the size of the autoshape to conform to the text. Rotate text in a text box by choosing the *Rotate text within AutoShape by 90°* option.

FIGURE 4.2 ***Format AutoShape Dialog Box with Text Box Tab Selected***

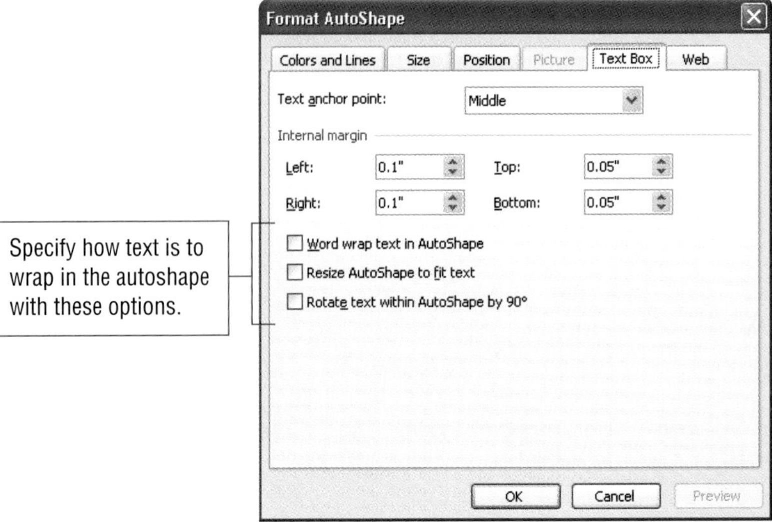

Displaying Ruler, Guide Lines, and Grid Lines

To help position elements such as shapes and images on a slide, consider displaying horizontal and vertical rulers, guide lines, and/or grid lines as shown in Figure 4.3. To turn on the rulers, click View and then Ruler. This displays a horizontal ruler above the slide in the Slide pane and a vertical ruler at the left side of the slide (see Figure 4.3).

FIGURE 4.3 ***Rulers, Guide Lines, and Grid Lines***

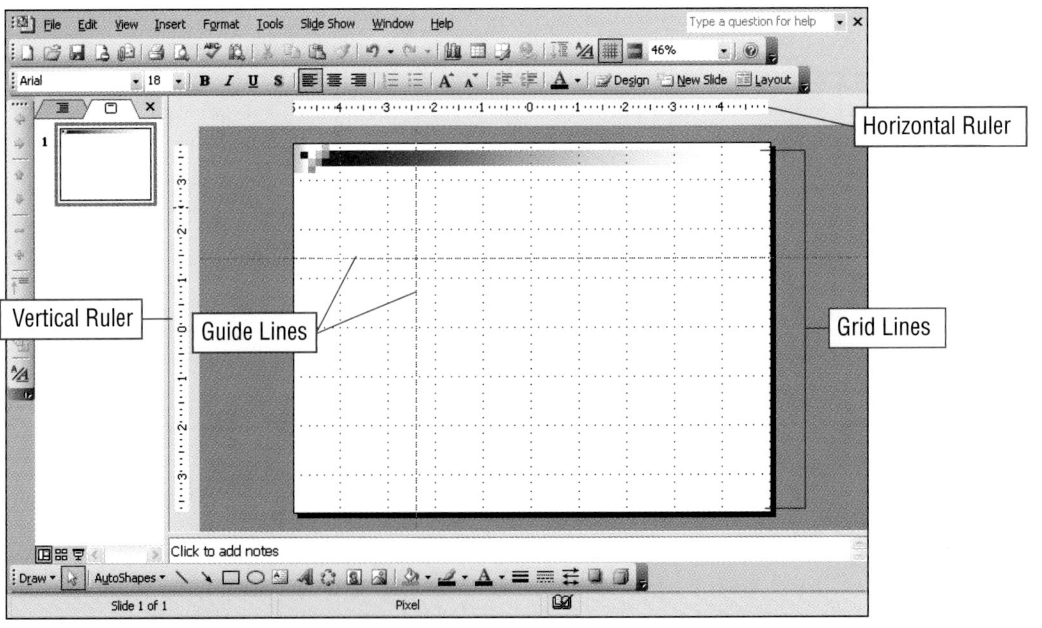

Turn on guide lines to help position objects on the slide. Guide lines are horizontal and vertical dashed lines that display on the slide in the Slide pane as shown in Figure 4.3. To turn on the guide lines, display the Grid and Guides dialog box shown in Figure 4.4. Display this dialog box by clicking View and then Grid and Guides or by clicking the Draw button on the Drawing toolbar and then clicking Grid and Guides. At the dialog box, insert a check mark in the *Display drawing guides on screen* check box. By default, the horizontal and vertical guide lines intersect in the middle of the slide. You can move these guide lines by dragging a line with the mouse. As you drag the line, a measurement displays next to the mouse pointer. Guide lines and grid lines display on the slide but do not print.

Display Guide Lines

1. Click View, Grid and Guides.
2. Click *Display drawing guides on screen* check box.
3. Click OK.

FIGURE 4.4 ***Grid and Guides Dialog Box***

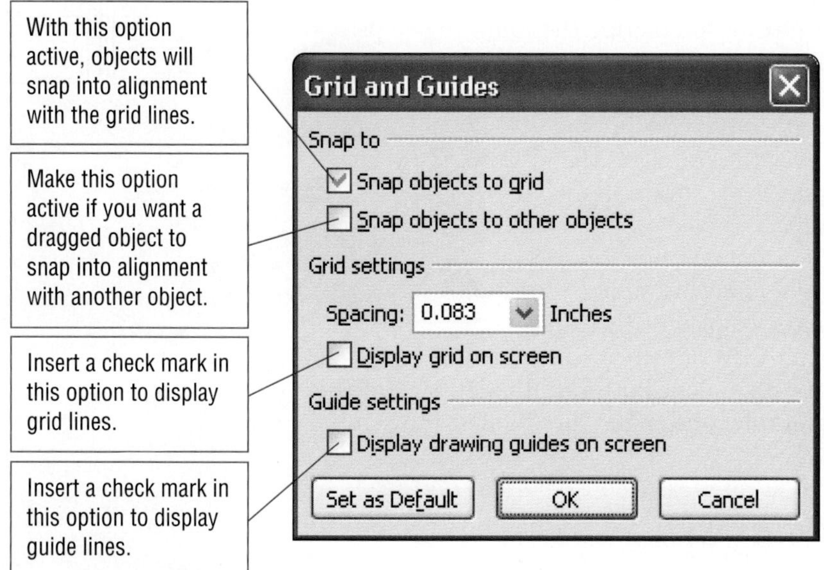
With this option active, objects will snap into alignment with the grid lines.
Make this option active if you want a dragged object to snap into alignment with another object.
Insert a check mark in this option to display grid lines.
Insert a check mark in this option to display guide lines.
Grid and Guides
Snap to
Snap objects to grid
Snap objects to other objects
Grid settings
Spacing: 0.083 Inches
Display grid on screen
Guide settings
Display drawing guides on screen
Set as Default
OK
Cancel

Another feature for helping you align objects on a slide is the grid. The grid is a set of intersecting lines that display on the slide in the Slide pane as shown in Figure 4.3. Turn on the grid by clicking the Show/Hide Grid button on the Standard toolbar, or displaying the Grid and Guides dialog box and then inserting a check mark in the *Display grid on screen* check box. The horizontal and vertical spacing between the gridlines is 0.083 inch by default. You can change this measurement with the *Spacing* option at the Grid and Guides dialog box.

As you drag or draw an object on the slide, it is pulled into alignment with the nearest intersection of gridlines. This is because the *Snap objects to grid* option at the Grid and Guides dialog box is active by default. If you want to precisely position an object, you can remove the check mark from the *Snap objects to grid* to turn the feature off or you can hold down the Alt key while dragging an object. If you want an object to be pulled into alignment with another object, insert a check mark in the *Snap objects to other objects* check box.

QUICK STEPS

Display Grid

1. Click Show/Hide Grid button.

OR

1. Click View, Grid and Guides.
2. Click *Display grid on screen* check box.
3. Click OK.

Show/Hide Grid

HINT

If you want to precisely position an object, hold down the Alt key while dragging the object.

exercise 2

CREATING TEXT BOXES AND AUTOSHAPES

1. Open **sppc4x01**.
2. Save the presentation with Save As and name it **sppc4x02**.
3. Create the slide shown in Figure 4.5 by completing the following steps:
   a. Display Slide 6. (This is the last slide in the presentation.)
   b. Click the New Slide button on the Formatting toolbar.
   c. Click the Title Only layout in the *Apply slide layout* section of the Slide Layout task pane.
   d. Click the text *Click to add title* and then type **Contact Personnel**.
   e. Click the Center button on the Formatting toolbar.
   f. Draw a text box by completing the following steps:
      1) Click the Text Box button on the Drawing toolbar.
      2) Position the crosshairs in the slide, below the title, and then drag to draw a text box as shown at the right.

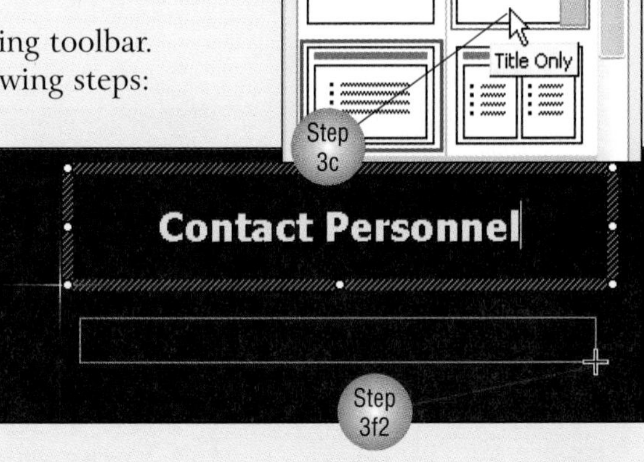

   g. Change tabs in the text box by completing the following steps:
      1) Turn on the display of the Ruler by clicking View and then Ruler.
      2) Check the alignment button at the left side of the horizontal ruler and make sure the left tab symbol displays.
      3) Position the tip of the mouse pointer on the horizontal ruler below the 0.5-inch mark and then click the left mouse button.
      4) Click once on the Alignment button to display the Center alignment symbol.
      5) Click on the horizontal ruler immediately below the 4-inch mark on the horizontal ruler.
      6) Click once on the Alignment button to display the Right alignment symbol.
      7) Click on the horizontal ruler immediately below the 7.5-inch mark.
   h. Type the text in the text box as shown in the slide in Figure 4.5. Make sure you press the Tab key before typing text in the first column (this moves the insertion point to the first tab, which is a left alignment tab).
   i. When you are done typing the text in the text box, change the font size of the text by completing the following steps:
      1) Make sure the text box is selected.
      2) Press Ctrl + A. (This selects all text in the text box.)
      3) Click the down-pointing arrow at the right side of the Font Size button on the Formatting toolbar, and then click *20*.
   j. Click outside the text box to deselect it.

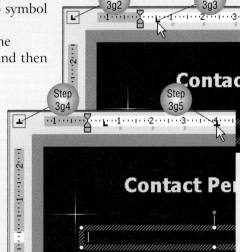

4. Create the slide shown in Figure 4.6 by completing the following steps:
   a. Make sure Slide 7 is the active slide. (This is the last slide in the presentation.)
   b. Click the New Slide button on the Formatting toolbar.
   c. Click the Title Only layout in the *Apply slide layout* section of the Slide Layout task pane.
   d. Click the text *Click to add title* and then type **Enhanced Services Features**.
   e. Click the Center button on the Formatting toolbar.
   f. Make sure the horizontal and vertical rulers are visible.
   g. Turn on the display of the guide lines by completing the following steps:
      1) Click the Draw button on the Drawing toolbar and then click Grid and Guides at the drop-down menu.
      2) At the Grid and Guides dialog box, insert a check mark in the *Display drawing guides on screen* option.
      3) Make sure the *Snap objects to grid* check box contains a check mark.
      4) Click OK.
      5) At the slide, drag the vertical guide line to the left until the measurement displays as *4.00*.
      6) Drag the horizontal guide line up until the measurement displays as *0.75*.

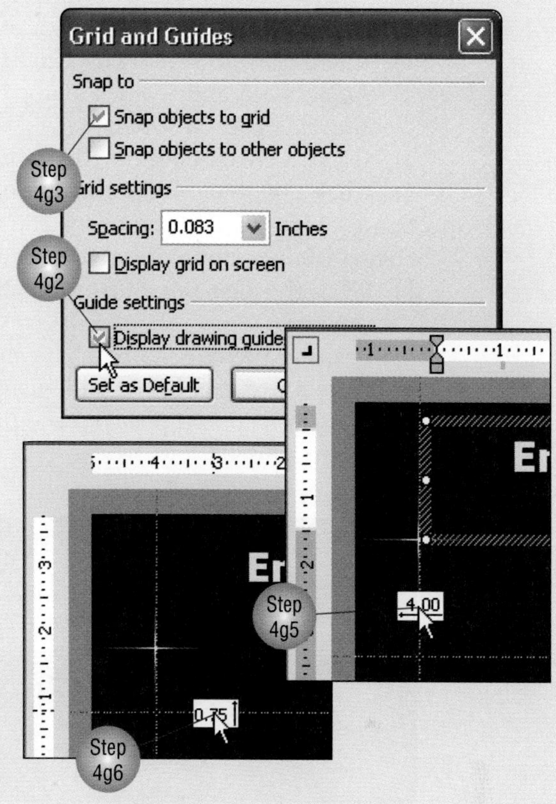

   h. Draw the diamond at the left by completing the following steps:
      1) Click the AutoShapes button on the Drawing toolbar, point to Basic Shapes, and then click Diamond.
      2) Hold down the Shift key and then draw the diamond the approximate size shown in Figure 4.6. After drawing the diamond, drag it so the left side of the diamond is aligned with the vertical guide line and the top of the diamond is aligned with the horizontal guide line.
      3) Insert the text and wrap the text in the autoshape by completing the following steps:
         a) Click the Text Box button on the Drawing toolbar.
         b) Click inside the diamond shape.
         c) Click Format and then AutoShape.
         d) At the Format AutoShape dialog box, click the Text Box tab.
         e) At the Format AutoShape dialog box with the Text Box tab selected, click the *Word wrap text in AutoShape* option. (This inserts a check mark.)
         f) Click OK to close the dialog box.
         g) Change the font size to 20, turn on bold, and change the font color to black.

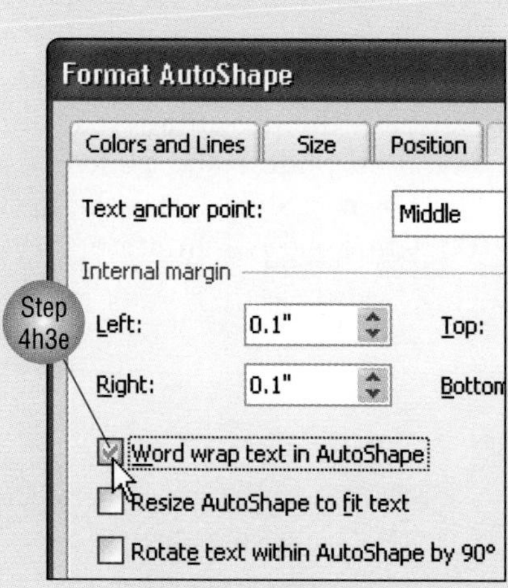

h) Type the text **Personal Service**. (Make sure the word *Personal* is not split between two lines. If it is, increase the size of the diamond.)

i. Copy the diamond to the right two times. (Align the top of the copied diamonds with the horizontal guide line.)

j. Select the text in the middle diamond and then type **Easy to Use**.

k. Select the text in the diamond at the right and then type **Fast and Accurate**.

l. Turn off the guide lines and turn on grid lines by completing the following steps:

1) Click View and then Grid and Guides.

2) At the Grid and Guides dialog box, remove the check mark from the *Display drawing guides on screen*.

3) Insert a check mark in the *Display grid on screen* check box.

4) Click OK to close the dialog box.

m. Draw a text box and then type the text located toward the bottom of the slide in Figure 4.6 by completing the following steps:

1) Click the Text Box button on the Drawing toolbar.

2) Position the crosshairs in the slide and then draw a text box in the slide using the grid lines to help you position the text box (see figure below).

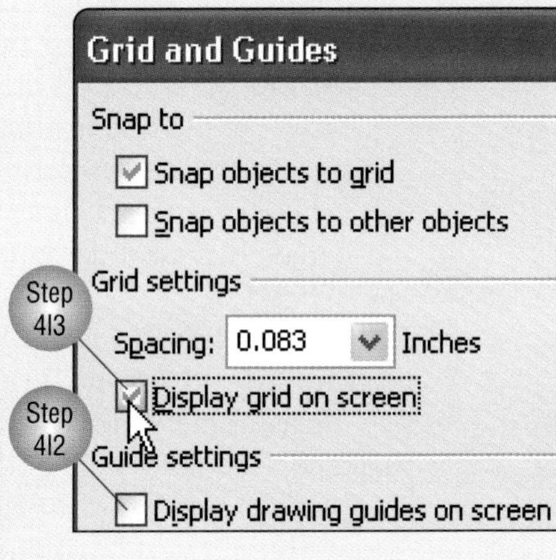

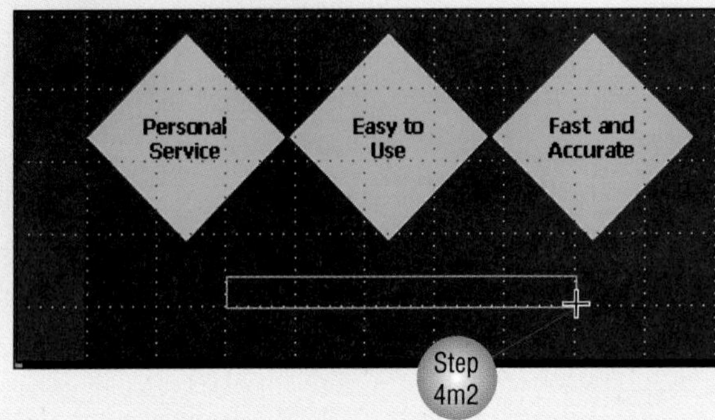

3) Click the Center button on the Formatting toolbar.

4) Turn on bold and then turn on italics.

5) Type **Quality Services for Our Customers**.

6) Click outside the text box to deselect it.

5. Click View and then Ruler to turn off the display of the horizontal and vertical rulers.
6. Turn off the display of the grid lines by clicking the Show/Hide Grid button on the Standard toolbar.
7. Save the presentation again with the same name.
8. Print Slide 7 and Slide 8.
9. Display Slide 1 and then run the presentation.
10. Close the presentation.

FIGURE 4.5 *Slide 7, Exercise 2*

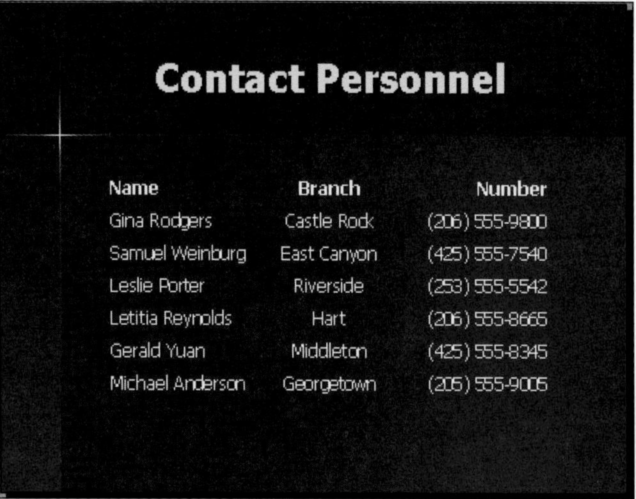

FIGURE 4.6 *Slide 8, Exercise 2*

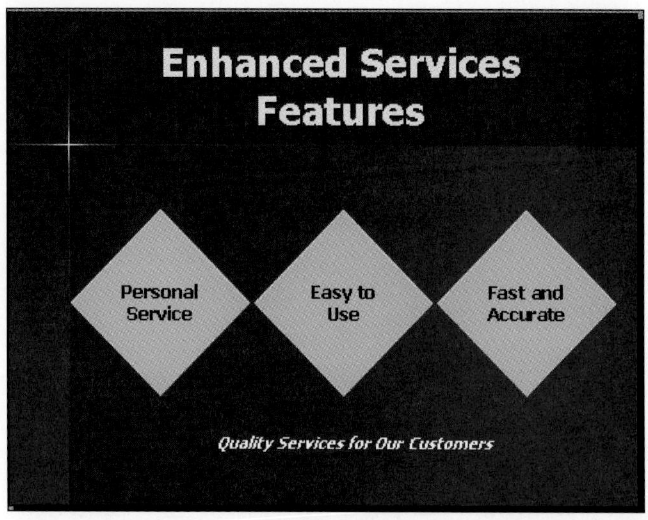

Inserting Images in a Presentation

Microsoft Office includes a gallery of media images that can be inserted in a presentation such as clip art, photographs, and movie images, as well as sound clips. To insert an image in a slide, click the Insert Clip Art button on the Drawing toolbar or click Insert, point to Picture, and then click Clip Art. This displays the Clip Art task pane at the right side of the screen as shown in Figure 4.7. To view all picture, sound, and motion files, make sure no text displays in the *Search for* text box at the Clip Art task pane, and then click the Go button.

Insert Clip Art

HINT
If you want the same image on every slide, insert it on the slide master.

FIGURE

4.7 ***Clip Art Task Pane***

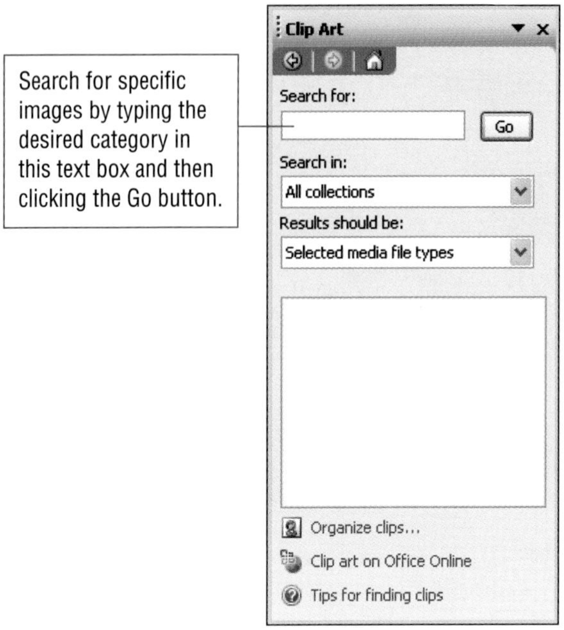

HINT

Preview a clip art image and display properties by moving the pointer over the image, clicking the arrow that displays, and then clicking Preview/Properties.

QUICK STEPS

Insert Image in Slide

1. Click Insert Clip Art button on Drawing toolbar.
2. Type desired topic and then click Go button.
3. Click desired image.

Another method for inserting an image in a slide is to choose a slide layout containing a Content placeholder. A content placeholder displays with six images. These images represent buttons. For example, click the button containing the image of a person and the Select Picture dialog box displays as shown in Figure 4.8. To search for specific images, type a topic or category in the *Search text* box and then click the Go button.

FIGURE

4.8 ***Select Picture Dialog Box***

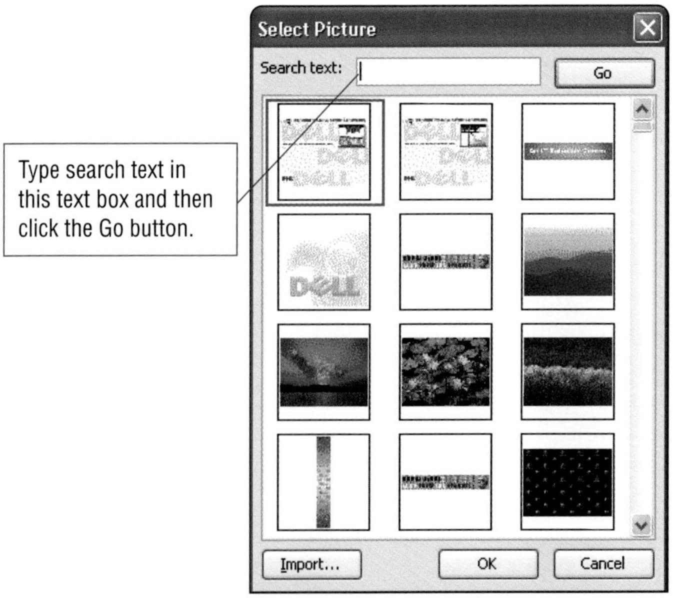

Narrowing a Search

By default (unless it has been customized), the Clip Art task pane looks for all media images and sound clips found in all locations. You can narrow the search to specific locations and to specific images. The *Search in* option at the Clip Art task pane has a default setting of *All collections*. This can be changed to *My Collections*, *Office Collections*, and *Web Collections*. The *Results should be* option has a default setting of *Selected media file types*. Click the down-pointing arrow at the right side of this option to display media types. To search for a specific media type, remove the check mark before all options at the drop-down list except for the desired type. For example, if you are searching only for photograph images, remove the check mark before Clip Art, Movies, and Sound.

HINT
For additional clip art images, consider buying a commercial package of images.

If you are searching for specific images, click in the *Search for* text box, type the desired word, and then click the Go button. For example, if you want to find images related to computers, click in the *Search for* text box, type **computer**, and then click the Go button. Clip art images related *computer* display in the viewing area of the task pane. If you are connected to the Internet, Word will search for images at the Microsoft Office Online Clip Art and Media Web site matching the topic.

Sizing an Image

Size an image in a slide using the sizing handles that display around a selected image. To change the size of an image, click in the image to select it, and then position the mouse pointer on a sizing handle until the pointer turns into a double-headed arrow. Hold down the left mouse button, drag the sizing handle in or out to decrease or increase the size of the image, and then release the mouse button.

Use the middle sizing handles at the left or right side of the image to make the image wider or thinner. Use the middle sizing handles at the top or bottom of the image to make the image taller or shorter. Use the sizing handles at the corners of the image to change both the width and height at the same time. To deselect an image, click anywhere in the slide outside the image.

Moving and Deleting an Image

To move an image, select the image, and then position the mouse pointer inside the image until the pointer turns into a four-headed arrow. Hold down the left mouse button, drag the image to the desired position, and then release the mouse button. Rotate an image by positioning the mouse pointer on the green, round rotation handle until the pointer displays as a circular arrow. Hold down the left mouse button, drag in the desired direction, and then release the mouse button. Delete a clip art image by selecting the image and then pressing the Delete key.

Changing the Slide Layout

When preparing a presentation, you choose a slide layout containing placeholders that most closely matches the type of information you want to insert on the slide. If you decide you want to add information or rearrange information on an existing slide, you can choose a different slide layout. For example, in Exercise 3, you will choose the Title and Text slide layout to create a slide and then change to the Title, Text, and Content slide layout to insert a clip art image. To change a slide layout, display the specific slide in the Slide pane, display the Slide Layout task pane, and then click the desired layout in the list box.

Change Slide Layout
1. Display specific slide.
2. Click Format, Slide Layout.
3. Click desired layout.

exercise 3

INSERTING AND SIZING A CLIP ART IMAGE IN A SLIDE

1. Open **NetworkingPresentation**.
2. Save the presentation with Save As and name it **sppc4x03**.
3. Insert a clip art image in Slide 4 as shown in Figure 4.9 by completing the following steps:
   a. Make sure Normal view is selected and then display Slide 4 in the Slide pane.
   b. Click the Insert Clip Art button on the Drawing toolbar.
   c. At the Clip Art task pane, click in the *Search for* text box.
   d. Type **computer** and then click the Go button.
   e. Click the image shown in Figure 4.9 (below to the right). (If this clip art image is not available, click another image that interests you.)
   f. With the image selected (white sizing handles display around the image), position the mouse pointer on the bottom right sizing handle until it turns into a diagonally pointing two-headed arrow.
   g. Hold down the left mouse button, drag away from the image to increase the size until the image is approximately the size shown in Figure 4.9, and then release the mouse button.
   h. Move the image so it is positioned as shown in Figure 4.9. To do this, position the mouse pointer on the selected image, hold down the left mouse button, drag to the desired position, and then release the mouse button.
   i. Click outside the image to deselect it.

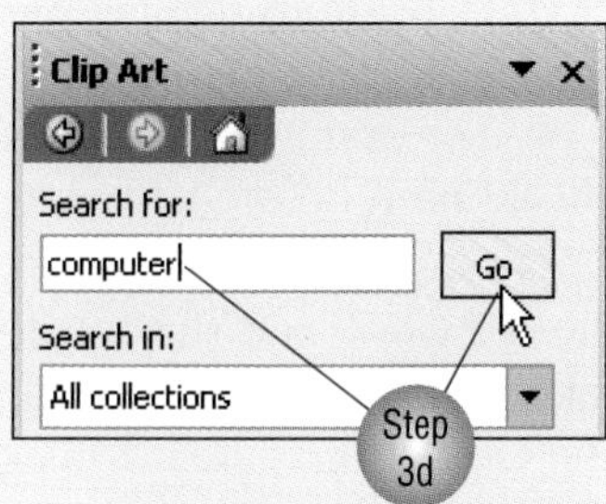

4. Create a new Slide 5 as shown in Figure 4.10 by completing the following steps:
   a. With Slide 4 displayed in the Slide pane, click the New Slide button on the Formatting toolbar. (This displays a new slide with the Title and Text layout selected.)
   b. Click in the text *Click to add title* and then type **Using Modems**.
   c. Click in the text *Click to add text* and then type the bulleted text shown in Figure 4.10.
   d. Change the slide layout by clicking the *Title, Text, and Content* slide layout in the Slide Layout task pane. (You will need to scroll down the list to display this layout.)
   e. Insert the image shown in Figure 4.10 by completing the following steps:
      1) Click the Insert Clip Art button that displays in the content placeholder in the slide.

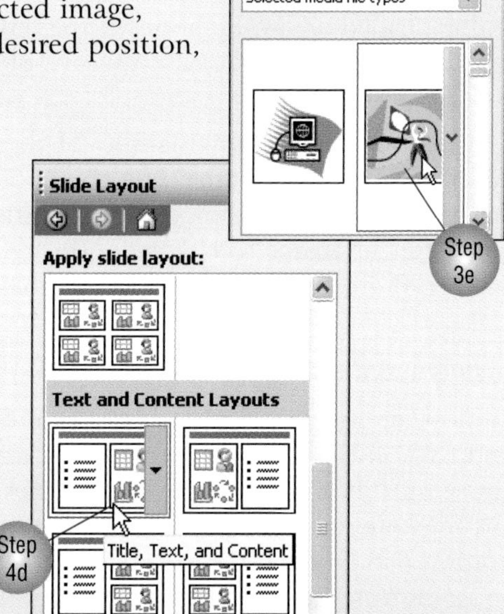

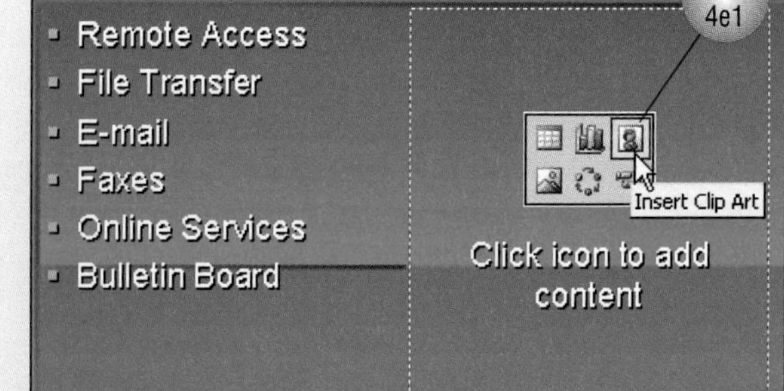

2) At the Select Picture dialog box, type **telephone** in the *Search for* text box and then click the Go button.
3) Click the image shown in Figure 4.10 (and at the right) and then click OK.
4) Increase the size of the image and then move the image so it displays as shown in Figure 4.10.
5) Deselect the image.

5. Save the presentation again with the same name.
6. Display Slide 1 in the Slide pane and then run the presentation.
7. Print all five slides as handouts on one page.
8. Close the presentation.

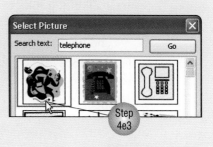

FIGURE 4.9 **Slide 4, Exercise 3**

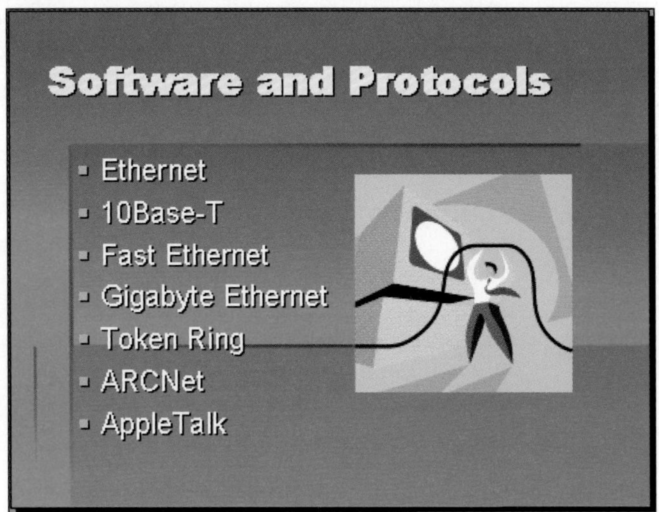

FIGURE 4.10 **Slide 5, Exercise 3**

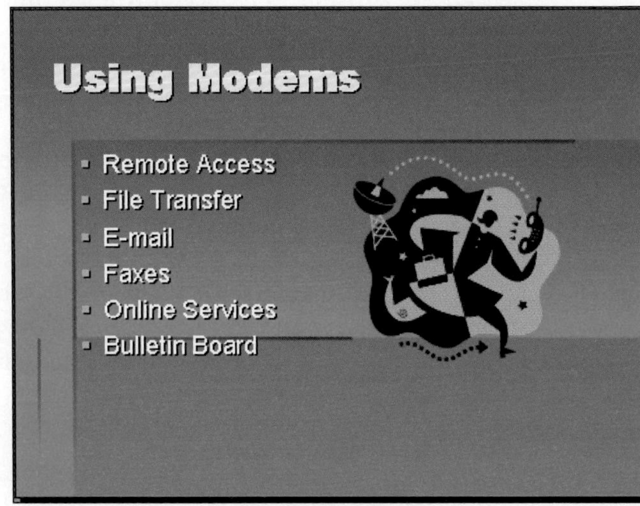

Formatting Images with Buttons on the Picture Toolbar

You can format images in a variety of ways. Formatting might include adding fill color and border lines, increasing or decreasing the brightness or contrast, choosing a wrapping style, and cropping the image. Format an image with buttons on the Picture toolbar or options at the Format Picture dialog box. Display the Picture toolbar by clicking an image or by right-clicking an image and then clicking Show Picture Toolbar at the shortcut menu. Table 4.2 identifies the buttons on the Picture toolbar.

TABLE 4.2 **Picture Toolbar Buttons**

Button	Name	Function
	Insert Picture	Display the Insert Picture dialog box with a list of subfolders containing additional images.
	Color	Display a drop-down list with options for controlling how the image displays. Options include Automatic, Grayscale, Black & White, and Washout.
	More Contrast	Increase contrast of the image.
	Less Contrast	Decrease contrast of the image.
	More Brightness	Increase brightness of the image.
	Less Brightness	Decrease brightness of the image.
	Crop	Crop image so only a specific portion of the image is visible.
	Rotate Left 90°	Rotate the image 90 degrees to the left.
	Line Style	Insert a border around the image and specify the border line style.
	Compress Pictures	Reduce resolution or discard extra information to save room on the hard drive or to reduce download time.
	Recolor Picture	Display Recolor Picture dialog box with options for changing the colors of the selected image.
	Format Picture	Display Format Picture dialog box with options for formatting the image. Tabs in the dialog box include Colors and Lines, Size, Position, Wrapping, and Picture.
	Set Transparent Color	This button is not active. (When an image contains a transparent area, the background color or texture of the page shows through the image. Set transparent color in Microsoft Photo Editor.)
	Reset Picture	Reset image to its original size, position, and color.

exercise 4 CUSTOMIZING IMAGES

1. Open **sppc4x03**.
2. Save the presentation with Save As and name it **sppc4x04**.
3. Format the clip art image in Slide 4 by completing the following steps:
   a. Display Slide 4 in the Slide pane.
   b. Click the clip art image to select.
   c. Click the Format Picture button on the Picture toolbar. (If the Picture toolbar is not visible, click View, point to Toolbars, and then click Picture.)
   d. At the Format Picture dialog box, click the Size tab.
   e. Select the current measurement in the *Height* text box (in the *Size and rotate* section) and then type 4.
   f. Click OK to close the dialog box.
   g. Click the Less Contrast button on the Picture toolbar three times.
   h. Click outside the image to deselect it.

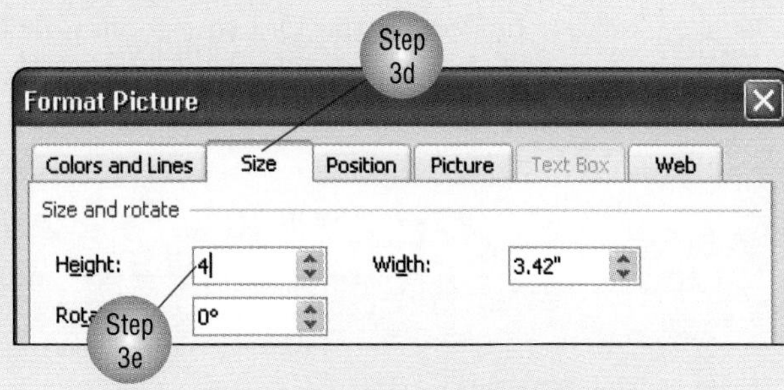

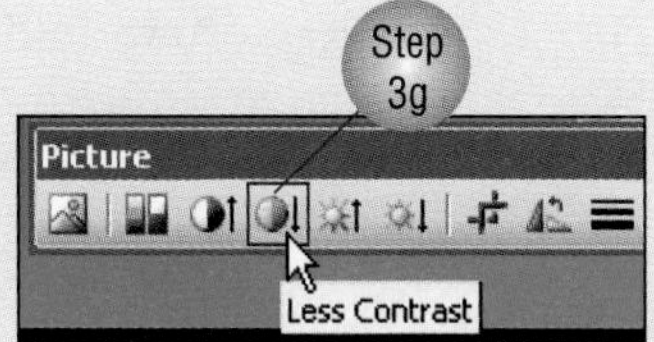

4. Format the clip art image in Slide 5 by completing the following steps:
   a. Display Slide 5 in the Slide pane.
   b. Click the clip art image to select it. (Make sure the Picture toolbar displays.)
   c. Click the Recolor Picture button on the Picture toolbar.
   d. At the Recolor Picture dialog box, click the down-pointing arrow at the right side of the first button below the *New* section (contains the color black).
   e. At the color palette that displays, click the third color from the left (see figure at right).
   f. Click the down-pointing arrow at the right side of the second button below the *New* section (contains the color blue).
   g. At the color palette, click the light yellow color.
   h. Click OK to close the Recolor Picture dialog box.
   i. Click outside the image to deselect it.

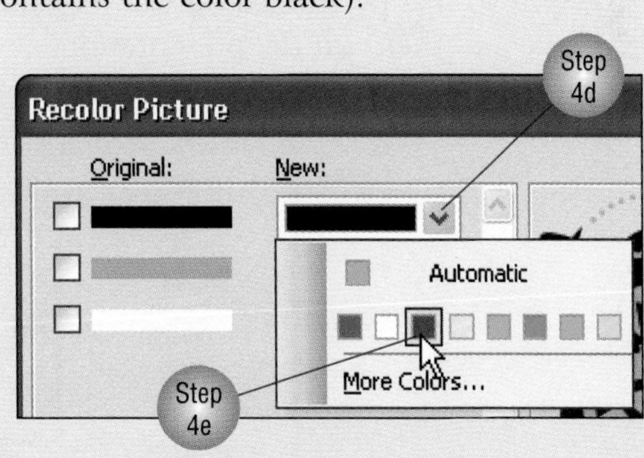

5. Save the presentation again with the same name.
6. Display Slide 1 in the Slide pane and then run the presentation.
7. Print all five slides as handouts on one page.
8. Close the presentation.

Adding Bitmapped Graphics to a Slide

PowerPoint recognizes a variety of picture formats dependent on the graphic filters installed with your program. Basically, pictures fall into one of two file categories—bitmaps and metafiles. Most clip art images are saved in a metafile format (named with a *.wmf* extension). Metafiles can be edited in PowerPoint, while bitmap files cannot. However, bitmaps can be edited in Microsoft Paint, Microsoft Photo Editor, or the program in which they were created. Pictures created in bitmap format are made from a series of small dots that form shapes and lines. Many scanned pictures are bitmapped. Bitmaps cannot be converted to drawing objects, but they can be scaled, sized, and moved.

Insert a bitmap image in a PowerPoint presentation by clicking the Insert Picture button on the Drawing toolbar or by clicking Insert, pointing to Picture, and then clicking From File. At the Insert Picture dialog box, change to the folder containing the bitmap image, and then double-click the desired image in the list box.

exercise 5

INSERTING A BITMAP GRAPHIC IN A SLIDE

1. Open **WaterfrontPresentation**. (This presentation is located in the PowerPointChapter04S folder on your disk.)
2. Save the presentation with Save As and name the presentation **sppc4x05**.
3. Insert a bitmap graphic into Slide 1 by completing the following steps:
   a. Display Slide 1 in the Slide pane.
   b. Click the Insert Picture button on the Drawing toolbar.
   c. At the Insert Picture dialog box, change the *Look in* option to the PowerPointChapter04S folder on your disk.
   d. Double-click the *Waterfrnt* bitmap image in the list box.
   e. With the bitmap image inserted in the slide, increase the size of the image and move it so it is positioned on the slide as shown in Figure 4.11.
4. Save and then run the presentation.

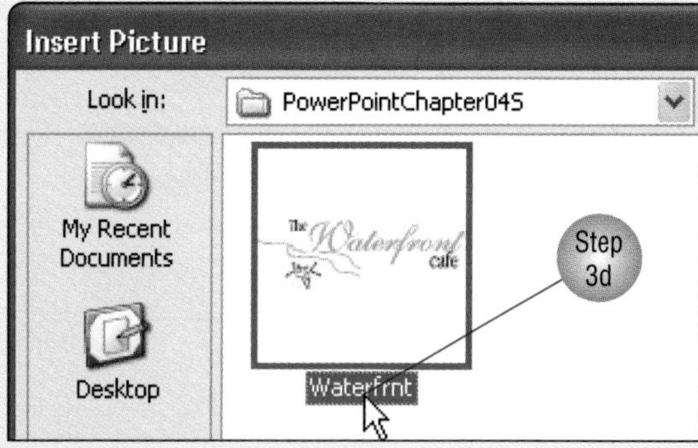

5. Print the slides on one page.
6. Close the presentation.

FIGURE 4.11 *Slide 1, Exercise 5*

HINT

Enhance the impact of your presentation with animation schemes and effects.

Adding Animation Effects to a Presentation

You can animate objects in a slide to add visual interest to your presentation as well as create focus on specific items. PowerPoint includes preset animation schemes you can apply to objects in a presentation. Display these preset animation schemes by clicking Slide Show on the Menu bar and then clicking Animation Schemes at the drop-down list. This displays animation schemes in the Slide Design task pane as shown in Figure 4.12. You can also display the animation schemes by clicking the Animation Schemes hyperlink located toward the top of the Slide Design task pane.

QUICK STEPS

Add Animation Effect to All Slides

1. Click Slide Show, Animation Schemes.
2. Click desired animation scheme in Slide Design task pane.
3. Click Apply To All Slides button.

FIGURE 4.12 *Animation Schemes in Slide Design Task Pane*

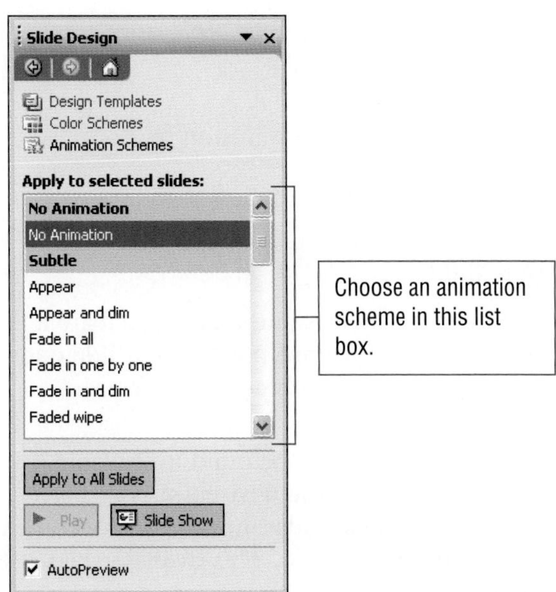

Choose an animation scheme in this list box.

Click the desired animation scheme in the *Apply to selected slides* list box. Animation schemes are grouped into three categories—Subtle, Moderate, and Exciting. When you click an animation effect, the effect displays in the slide in the Slide pane. You can preview the animation again by clicking the Play button located toward the bottom of the Slide Design task pane. If you want the animation scheme to affect all slides in the presentation click the Apply to All Slides button located toward the bottom of the task pane. Apply an animation scheme to individual slides by selecting the slides first and then choosing an animation scheme.

When an animation scheme is applied to a slide, objects will appear on the slide in a specific order. When running the presentation, the slide will display on the screen followed by the slide title. To display any subtitles or bulleted text, click the mouse button. The animation scheme controls how much text displays when the mouse is clicked. If your slide contains bulleted text, clicking the left mouse button when running the presentation will cause the first bulleted item to display. Click the left mouse button again to display the next bulleted item, and so on.

exercise 6

ADDING ANIMATION SCHEME TO A PRESENTATION

1. Open **sppc4x01**.
2. Save the presentation with Save As and name it **sppc4x06**.
3. Add an animation scheme to each slide by completing the following steps:
   a. Make sure Normal view is selected and Slide 1 displays in the Slide pane.
   b. Click Slide Show on the Menu bar and then click Animation Schemes at the drop-down menu. (This displays animation effects in the Slide Design task pane.)
   c. Scroll to the end of the *Apply to selected slides* list box and then click *Pinwheel*.
   d. Click the Apply to All Slides button located toward the bottom of the Slide Design task pane.
4. Run the presentation. Click the left mouse button to display objects in the slide.
5. Save and then close the presentation.

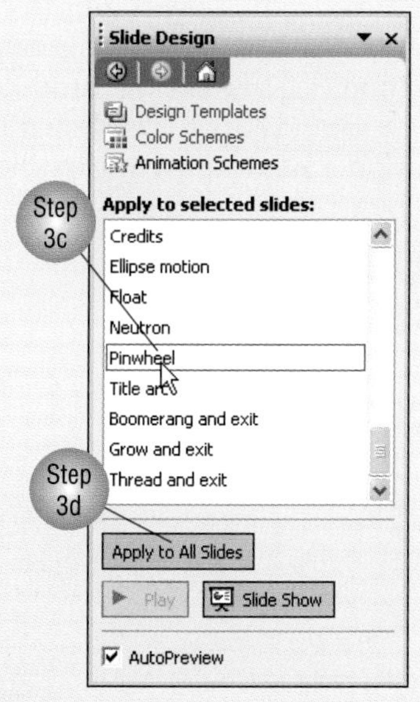

Customizing a Build

The preset animation schemes automatically create a ***build*** with objects on the slide. A build displays important points on a slide one point at a time, and is useful for keeping the audience's attention focused on the point being presented rather than reading ahead.

HINT
Add a build to bulleted items to focus the attention of the audience on a specific item.

You can further customize the build in the animation scheme by causing a previous point to dim when the next point is displayed on the slide. To customize an animation scheme, click Slide Show on the Menu bar and then click Custom Animation at the drop-down list. This displays the Custom Animation task pane as shown in Figure 4.13.

FIGURE

4.13 Custom Animation Task Pane

To add a dim effect to bulleted items, you would click the placeholder containing the bulleted text and then click the Add Effect button located toward the top of the Custom Animation task pane. At the drop-down menu that displays, point to Entrance, and then click the desired effect in the side menu. This causes a box to display in the Custom Animation task pane list box containing a number, an image of a mouse, and a down-pointing arrow. Click the down-pointing arrow and then click Effect Options at the drop-down menu. At the dialog box that displays, click the down-pointing arrow at the right of the *After animation* option box and then click the desired color.

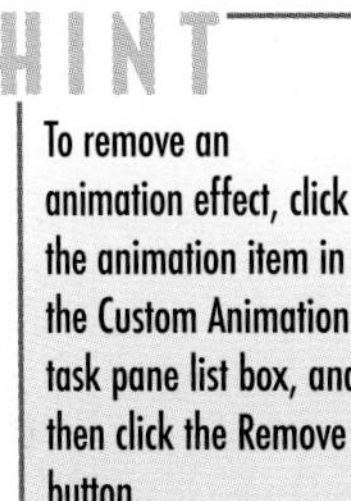

HINT

To remove an animation effect, click the animation item in the Custom Animation task pane list box, and then click the Remove button.

exercise 7

CUSTOMIZING A BUILD FOR A PRESENTATION

1. Open **NetworkingPresentation**.
2. Save the presentation with Save As and name it **sppc4x07**.
3. Display the Custom Animation task pane by clicking Slide Show on the Menu bar and then clicking Custom Animation at the drop-down list.
4. Add an animation scheme to the title of Slide 1 by completing the following steps:
   a. Make sure Normal view is selected and Slide 1 displays in the Slide pane.
   b. Click in the text *NETWORKING* to select the placeholder.
   c. Click the Add Effect button located toward the top of the Custom Animation task pane, point to Entrance, and then click 2. Box at the drop-down menu.

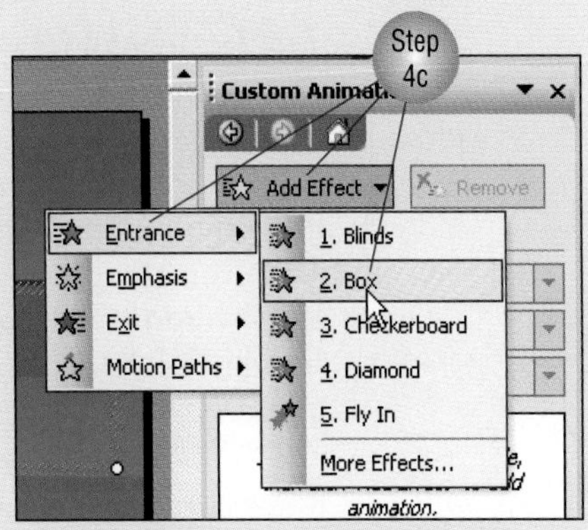

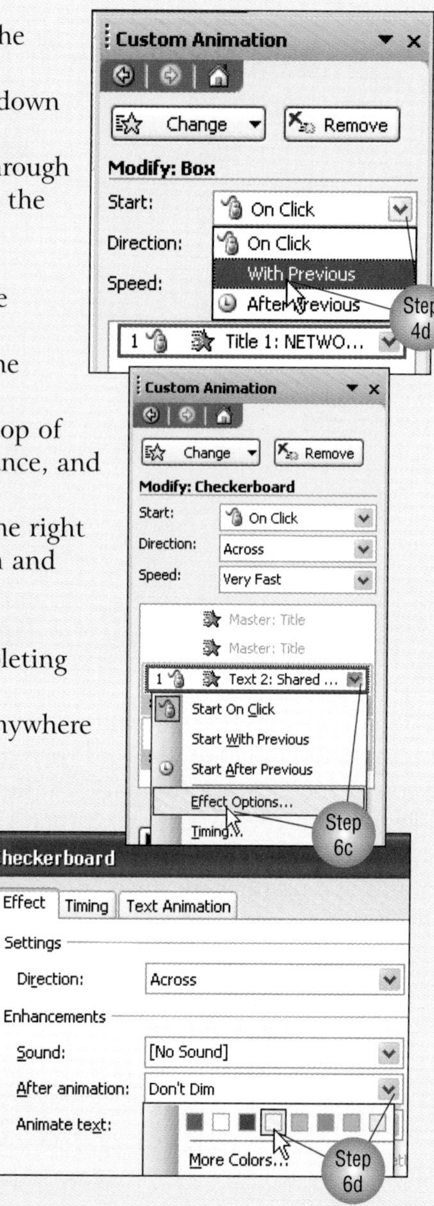

   d. Click the down-pointing arrow that displays at the right side of the *Start* option in the *Modify: Box* section and then click *With Previous* at the drop-down list.
5. Apply the same animation to the titles in Slides 2 through 4 using the Glass Layers Slide Master by completing the following steps:
   a. Display Slide 2 in the Slide pane.
   b. Hold down the Shift key and then click the Slide Master View button.
   c. Click in the text *Click to edit Master title style* in the slide master.
   d. Click the Add Effect button located toward the top of the Custom Animation task pane, point to Entrance, and then click 2. Box at the drop-down list.
   e. Click the down-pointing arrow that displays at the right side of the *Start* option in the *Modify: Box* section and then click *With Previous* at the drop-down list.
   f. Click the Normal View button.
6. Add a build to the bulleted items in Slide 2 by completing the following steps:
   a. With Slide 2 displayed in the Slide pane, click anywhere in the bulleted text.
   b. Click the Add Effect button located toward the top of the Custom Animation task pane, point to Entrance, and then click 3. Checkerboard at the side menu.
   c. Click the down-pointing arrow at the right of the box in the Custom Animation task pane list box and then click Effect Options at the drop-down menu.
   d. At the Checkerboard dialog box with the Effect tab selected, click the down-pointing arrow at the right of the *After animation* option box and then click the light yellow color.
   e. Click OK to close the dialog box.
7. Display Slide 3 in the Slide pane and then complete steps similar to those in Step 6 to add a build to the bulleted text.
8. Display Slide 4 in the Slide pane and then complete steps similar to those in Step 6 to add a build to the bulleted text.
9. Save and then run the presentation. (As you run the presentation, notice how the a bulleted item is dimmed when you advance to the next item.)
10. Close the presentation.

CHAPTER summary

- Use buttons on the Drawing toolbar to draw a variety of shapes and lines and to apply formatting to a drawn object.
- A shape drawn with the Line or Arrow buttons is considered a line drawing. A shape drawn with the Rectangle or Oval buttons is considered an enclosed object.
- A variety of predesigned shapes is available from the AutoShapes button on the Drawing toolbar.
- To select an enclosed object, position the mouse pointer inside the object and then click the left mouse button. To select a line, position the mouse pointer on the line until the pointer turns into an arrow with a four-headed arrow attached, and then click the left mouse button.
- To select several objects at once, click the Select Objects button and then draw a border around the objects. You can also select more than one object by holding down the Shift key and then clicking each object.
- To delete an object, select it, and then press the Delete key. To move an object, select it, and then drag it to the desired location. To copy an object, select it, and then hold down the Ctrl key while dragging the object.
- Use the sizing handles that display around a selected object to increase or decrease the size of the object.
- Apply formatting to an object such as fill color, shading, line color, and shadows with buttons on the Drawing toolbar.
- Create a text box in a slide by clicking the Text Box button on the Drawing toolbar and then drawing the box in the slide.
- A text box can be drawn inside an autoshape. Choose a text wrapping style for text inside an autoshape with options at the Format AutoShape dialog box with the Text Box tab selected.
- To help position objects on a slide, turn on the display of the rulers, guide lines, and/or grid lines.
- Click View and then Rulers to turn on/off the display of the horizontal and vertical rulers.
- Turn on/off guide lines and/or grid lines with options at the Grid and Guides dialog box. Turn on/off the display of grid lines with the Show/Hide Grid button on the Standard toolbar.
- Insert an image in a slide with options at the Clip Art task pane or the Select Picture dialog box.
- With options at the Clip Art task pane, you can narrow the search for images to specific locations and to specific images.
- Format a clip art image with buttons on the Picture toolbar.
- Pictures fall into one of two basic file categories—bitmaps and metafiles. Most clip art images are saved in a metafile format. Insert a bitmap image in a slide by displaying the Insert Picture dialog box, and then double-clicking the desired image.
- Animate objects in slides to add visual interest and create focus on specific items in a presentation.
- PowerPoint includes preset animation schemes. Display animation schemes in the Slide Design task pane by clicking Slide Show on the Menu bar and then clicking Animation Schemes or by clicking the Animation Schemes hyperlink located toward the top of the Slide Design task pane.

- Customize animation with options at the Custom Animation task pane. Display this task pane by clicking Slide Show on the Menu bar and then clicking Custom Animation.

FEATURES summary

FEATURE	BUTTON	MENU
Format AutoShape dialog box		Format, AutoShape
Grid and Guides dialog box		View, Grid and Guides
Grid lines		
Clip Art task pane		Insert, Picture, Clip Art
Format Picture dialog box		Format, Picture
Recolor Picture dialog box		
Insert Picture dialog box		Insert, Picture, From File
Animation schemes		Slide Show, Animation Schemes
Custom Animation task pane		Slide Show, Custom Animation

CONCEPTS check

Completion: On a blank sheet of paper, indicate the correct term, command, or number for each discription.

1. A variety of predesigned shapes is available with options from this button on the Drawing toolbar.
2. Change the size of a selected object using these items that display around a selected object.
3. Choose a text wrapping style for text inside an autoshape with options at the Format AutoShape dialog box with this tab selected.
4. Display guide lines and/or grid lines with options at this dialog box.
5. Insert an image in a slide with options at this task pane.
6. Select a clip art image in a slide and this toolbar displays containing buttons for formatting the image.
7. Change the colors of a selected clip art image with options at this dialog box.
8. Pictures generally fall into one of two file categories—metafiles and this.
9. Click Slide Show and then Animation Schemes and preset animation schemes display in this task pane.
10. Animation schemes are grouped into three categories—Subtle, Moderate, and this.
11. Customize an animation scheme with options at this task pane.

SKILLS check

Assessment 1

1. Open **sppc4x01**.
2. Save the presentation with Save As and name it **sppc4sc01**.
3. Change to the Slide Master view and then make the following changes:
   a. With the Shimmer Title Master slide miniature selected at the left side of the screen, click anywhere in the text *Click to edit Master title style*, and then change the fill color to the light blue that follows the scheme of the design template.
   b. Select and then delete each of the four diamond shapes.
   c. Using the 5-Point Star autoshape (click AutoShapes, point to Stars and Banners, click the 5-Point Star autoshape), draw a small star in the upper left corner of the slide master. (When you release the mouse button, the star should fill with the same light blue color you chose in Step 3a.)
   d. Copy the star to the right two times. (You should have a total of three stars in the upper left corner of the slide all containing light blue fill.)
   e. Click the Normal View button to remove the slide master.
4. Create a new Slide 7 that displays as shown in Figure 4.14 with the following specifications:
   a. Create the new slide with the Title Only slide layout.
   b. Center align the title *Enhanced Services Launch Date*.
   c. Turn on the display of the grid and/or guide lines to help you position the text box and the arrows.
   d. Use the Text Box button on the Drawing toolbar to draw a text box for the text *May 1, 2005*. Set the text in 28-point size, turn on bold, and change the alignment to center.
   e. Use the Right Arrow autoshape (AutoShapes, Block Arrows, Right Arrow) to draw the arrow at the left side. Use the Left Arrow autoshape (AutoShapes, Block Arrows, Left Arrow) to draw the arrow at the right.
   f. Turn off the display of the grid and/or guide lines.
5. Save and then run the presentation.
6. Print all of the slides as handouts on one page.
7. Print only Slide 7.
8. Close the presentation.

FIGURE

4.14 ***Slide 7, Assessment 1***

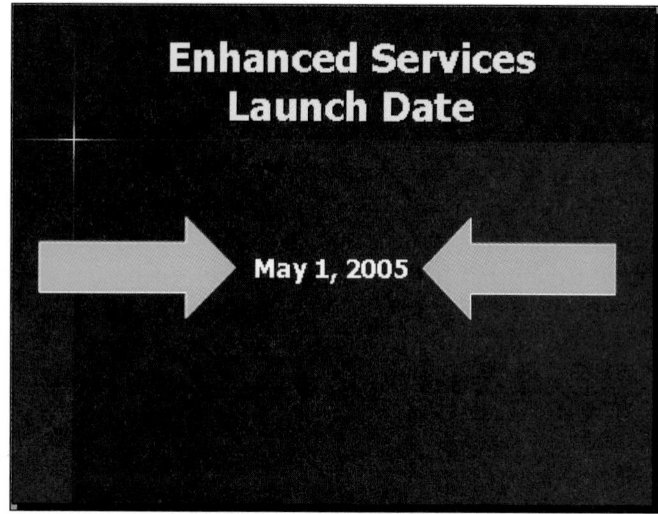

Assessment 2

1. Open **WaterfrontPresentation**.
2. Save the presentation with Save As and name it **sppc4sc02**.
3. Make the following changes to the presentation:
   a. Delete Slide 1.
   b. Apply the *Ripple* design template to the presentation.
   c. Check each slide and make any needed adjustments (repositioning elements, and so on).
   d. Insert a clip art image in Slide 3 related to *restaurant* or *food*. You determine the size and position of the image. Recolor the image so it follows the color scheme of the design template.
   e. Insert another clip art image in Slide 4 related to *restaurant* or *food* (use a different image from the one you chose for Slide 3). You determine the size and position of the image. Recolor the image so it follows the color scheme of the design template.
   f. Apply an animation scheme of your choosing to all slides in the presentation.
4. Save and then run the presentation.
5. Print all four slides as handouts on one page.
6. Close the presentation.

Assessment 3

1. Open **JobSearchPresentation**.
2. Save the presentation with Save As and name it **sppc4sc03**.
3. Make the following changes to the presentation:
   a. Apply the *Radial* design template to the presentation.
   b. Display color schemes for the Radial design template and then choose a color scheme other than the default.
   c. Add an animation scheme of your choosing to the title of Slide 1. ***(Hint: Refer to Exercise 7, Steps 3 and 4.)***
   d. Add an animation scheme of your choosing to the subtitle of Slide 1. ***(Hint: Refer to Exercise 7, Step 4.)***
   e. Apply the same animation scheme to the titles in Slides 2 through 9 in Slide Master view using the Radial Slide Master. ***(Hint: Refer to Exercise 7, Step 5.)***

f. Add a build to the bulleted items in Slide 2. You determine the Entrance animation and also the After animation color. ***(Hint: Refer to Exercise 7, Step 6.)***
g. Apply the same build to the bulleted items in Slides 3 through 9.

4. Save the presentation and then print all nine slides as handouts on one page.
5. Run the presentation. (Make sure the animation and builds function properly.)
6. Close the presentation.

Assessment 4

1. Use PowerPoint's Help feature to learn about adding music or sound effects to a slide. Learn specifically how to insert a sound from the Clip Organizer.
2. Open **NetworkingPresentation**.
3. Save the presentation with Save As and name it **sppc4sc04**.
4. Insert a sound clip of your choosing from the Clip Organizer into Slide 1.
5. Run the presentation and make sure you hear the sound you inserted in Slide 1.
6. Save and then print **sppc4sc04**.

CHAPTER challenge

You are a representative for a local credit corporation and have been asked to make a presentation for a business class at the local community college. The professor of the business course has asked that you address the use of credit cards. Include at least 10 slides in the presentation. Create the presentation to be visually appealing using at least three different features learned in Chapter 4 and any additional features learned in previous chapters. Save the presentation as **CreditCards**.

Pictures can visually enhance the appearance of the presentations. A creative way to incorporate a picture into a presentation is through a background. Use the Help feature to learn how to insert a picture as a background on a slide in a presentation. Then insert a picture as a background in the presentation created in the first part of the Chapter Challenge. Save the presentation again.

The professor of the course really liked the presentation and has asked if you would save the presentation as a Word outline, so the students could use the information in a report that is due at the end of the semester. Save the presentation created and edited in the first two parts of the Chapter Challenge as a Word outline named **CreditCards**.

WORK IN Progress

Creating and Formatting PowerPoint Presentations

ASSESSING proficiency

In this unit, you have learned to create, print, save, close, open, view, run, edit, and format a PowerPoint presentation. You also learned how to add transition and sound to presentations, rearrange slides, customize presentations by changing the design template and color scheme, make global formatting changes with slide and title masters, add visual appeal to slides by inserting drawn objects and clip art images, and how to add animation and build to items in slides.

(Note: Before completing unit assessments, delete the PowerPointChapter04S folder on your disk. Next, copy to your disk the PowerPointUnit01S subfolder from the PowerPoint2003Specialist folder on the CD that accompanies this textbook and then make PowerPointUnit01S the active folder.)

Assessment 1

1. Create a presentation with the text shown in Figure U1.1 using the Pixel design template. Use the appropriate slide layout for each slide. After creating the slides, complete a spelling check on the text in slides.
2. Add a transition and sound of your choosing to all slides.
3. Save the presentation and name it **sppu1pa01**.
4. Run the presentation.
5. Print all six slides as handouts on one page.
6. Close the presentation.

Slide 1	Title	=	CORNERSTONE SYSTEMS
	Subtitle	=	Yearly Report
Slide 2	Title	=	Financial Review
	Bullets	=	• Net Revenues • Operating Income • Net Income • Return on Average Equity • Return on Average Asset

Slide 3	Title	=	Corporate Vision
	Bullets	=	• Expansion • Increased Productivity • Consumer Satisfaction • Employee Satisfaction • Market Visibility
Slide 4	Title	=	Consumer Market
	Bullets	=	• Travel • Shopping • Entertainment • Personal Finance • E-mail
Slide 5	Title	=	Industrial Market
	Bullets	=	• Finance • Education • Government • Manufacturing • Utilities
Slide 6	Title	=	Future Goals
	Bullets	=	• International Market • Acquisitions • Benefits Packages • Product Expansion

Figure U1.1 • Assessment 1

Assessment 2

1. Open **sppu1pa01**.
2. Save the presentation with Save As and name it **sppu1pa02**.
3. Make the following changes to Slide 2:
   a. Type **Net Income per Common Share** over *Net Income*.
   b. Delete *Return on Average Equity*.
4. Make the following changes to Slide 4:
   a. Delete *Shopping*.
   b. Type **Business Finance** between *Personal Finance* and *E-mail*.
5. Rearrange the slides in the presentation so they are in the following order (only the slide titles are shown below):
   Slide 1 = CORNERSTONE SYSTEMS
   Slide 2 = Corporate Vision
   Slide 3 = Future Goals
   Slide 4 = Industrial Market
   Slide 5 = Consumer Market
   Slide 6 = Financial Review
6. Increase spacing between bulleted items by completing the following steps:

a. Display the Pixel Slide Master in Slide Master view.
b. Click the text *Click to edit Master text styles*.
c. Display the Line Spacing dialog box, change the line spacing to 1.4, and then close the dialog box.
d. Return to the Normal view.

7. Apply a different color scheme to the presentation.
8. Save and then run the presentation.
9. Print all six slides as handouts on one page.
10. Close the presentation.

Assessment 3

1. Open **ArtworksPresentation**. (This presentation is located in the PowerPointUnit01S folder on your disk.)
2. Save the presentation with Save As and name it **sppu1pa03**.
3. Insert in Slide 1 the autoshape and text shown in Figure U1.2 with the following specifications:
   a. Use the Horizontal Scroll autoshape (AutoShapes, Stars and Banners, Horizontal Scroll) to create the banner autoshape. Make sure the banner fill color is the green color shown in Figure U1.2 that follows the design color scheme. (This should be the default fill color.)
   b. Insert a text box in the autoshape and then type the text Rainbow Artworks as shown in Figure U1.2 with the following specifications:
      1) Change the alignment to center.
      2) Change the font to 88-point Comic Sans MS bold. (If this font is not available, choose a similar font.)
      3) Change the font color to the medium blue that follows the design color scheme.
4. Change the font for slide titles on Slides 2 through 4 by completing the following steps:
   a. Display the Blends Title Master in Slide Master view.
   b. Click the text *Click to edit Master title style*.
   c. Change the alignment to center.
   d. Change the font to 44-point Comic Sans MS bold (or the font you chose in Step 3b2) and the font color to red (that follows the design color scheme).
   e. Click the text *Click to edit Master subtitle style*.
   f. Change the font to 28-point Comic Sans MS bold (or the font you chose in Step 3b2) and the font color to medium blue (that follows the design color scheme).
   g. Return to the Normal view.
5. Add a transition and sound of your choosing to all slides.
6. Save and then run the presentation.
7. Print all four slides as handouts on the same page.
8. Print only Slide 1.
9. Close the presentation.

Figure U1.2 • Slide 1, Assessment 3

Assessment 4

1. Open **JobSearchPresentation**. (This presentation is located in the PowerPointUnit01S folder on your disk.)
2. Save the presentation with Save As and name it **sppu1pa04**.
3. Make the following changes to the presentation:
   a. Change the design template. (Choose something appropriate for the subject matter.)
   b. Insert a clip art image in Slide 5 related to *telephone*, *people*, or *Internet*. You determine the size and position of the image. Recolor the image so it follows the color scheme of the design template.
   c. Insert a clip art image in Slide 6 related to *clock* or *time*. You determine the size and position of the element. Recolor the image so it follows the color scheme of the design template.
   d. Insert the current date and slide number on all slides in the presentation. (Make sure the *Don't show on title slide* option at the Header and Footer dialog box does not contain a check mark.)
   e. Create the header *Job Search Seminar*, the footer *Employment Strategies*, and insert the date and page number for notes and handouts.
   f. Add the speaker note *Handout list of Internet employment sites.* to Slide 5.
4. Apply an animation scheme of your choosing to all slides in the presentation.
5. Save and then run the presentation.
6. Print all nine slides as handouts on one page.
7. Print Slide 5 as notes pages.
8. Close the presentation.

Assessment 5

1. Open **MedicalPlansPresentation**. (This presentation is located in the PowerPointUnit01S folder on your disk.)
2. Save the presentation with Save As and name it **sppu1pa05**.
3. Make the following changes to the presentation:
   a. Insert a clip art image in Slide 3 related to *medicine*. You determine the size and position of the image. Recolor the image so it follows the color scheme of the design template.
   b. Insert a clip art image in Slide 4 related to *buildings*. You determine the size and position of the image. Recolor the image so it follows the color scheme of the design template.
   c. Display the Custom Animation task pane and then use the Add Effect button in the task pane to apply an animation of your choosing to the title of Slide 1. (Refer to Chapter 4, Exercise 7, Step 4.)
   d. Apply the same animation to the titles in Slides 2 through 4 in Slide Master view using the Capsules Slide Master. (Refer to Chapter 4, Exercise 7, Step 5.)
   e. Add a build to the bulleted items in Slide 2. You determine the Entrance animation and also the After animation color. (Refer to Chapter 4, Exercise 7, Step 6.)
   f. Apply the same build to the bulleted items in Slides 3 and 4.
4. Save the presentation and then print all four slides as handouts on one page.
5. Run the presentation. (Make sure the animation and builds function properly.)
6. Close the presentation.

WRITING activity

The following activity gives you the opportunity to practice your writing skills along with demonstrating an understanding of some of the important PowerPoint features you have mastered in this unit. Use correct grammar, appropriate word choices, and clear sentence structure.

Activity 1

Using PowerPoint's Help feature, learn more about animating slides and then prepare a PowerPoint presentation with the information by completing the following steps:

1. Click in the *Ask a Question* text box, type **custom animation**, and then press Enter.
2. Click the Animate text and objects hyperlink in the Search Results task pane. (You will need to scroll down the list box to display the hyperlink.)
3. Click the Show All hyperlink in the upper right corner of the Help window and then print the information that displays.

4. Select the text *custom animation* in the *Ask a Question* text box, type **animation order**, and then press Enter.
5. Click the About timing animations hyperlink in the Search Results list box.
6. Click the Show All hyperlink and then print the information.
7. Read the information you printed on custom animation and animation order and then prepare a PowerPoint presentation with the following information:

Slide 1	=	Title of presentation and your name
Slide 2	=	Steps on how to apply a preset animation scheme
Slide 3	=	Steps on how to display the Custom Animation task pane
Slide 4	=	Explanation of the three options (*Entrance*, *Emphasis*, and *Exit*) available with the Add Effect button
Slide 5	=	Steps on changing the order of an animation

8. Save the completed presentation and name it **sppu1act01**.
9. Run the presentation.
10. Print all five slides as handouts on one page.
11. Close the presentation.

The presentation you customized in Assessment 5 contains clip art images on Slides 3 and 4. When you ran the presentation, the clip art image automatically displayed in the slide and then the title displayed. Using the information you learned about animation order, open the **sppu1pa05** presentation, change the animation order of objects on Slides 3 and 4 so the title displays first, followed by the clip art image, and then the bulleted items. Run the presentation to make sure the items animate in the proper order. Save the presentation with the same name.

Activity 2

1. Open Word and then open, print, and close **KeyLifeHealthPlan**. Looking at the printing of this document, create a presentation in PowerPoint that presents the main points of the plan. (Use bullets in the presentation.) Add a transition and build to the slides.
2. Save the presentation and name it **sppu1act02**.
3. Run the presentation.
4. Print the slides as handouts with six slides per page.
5. Close the presentation.

INTERNET project

Analyzing a Magazine Web Site

Make sure you are connected to the Internet and then explore the Time Magazine Web site at www.time.com. Discover the following information for the site:

- Magazine sections (i.e., *Nation, World, Business*, and so on.)
- The type of information presented in each section
- Services available
- Information on how to subscribe

Use the information you discovered about the Time Magazine Web site and create a PowerPoint presentation that presents the information in a clear, concise, and logical manner. Add formatting and enhancements to the presentation to make it more interesting. When the presentation is completed, save it and name it **TimeMagPres**. Run, print, and then close the presentation.

JOB study

Presenting Career Options

As a counselor in the university's Career Development office, you have been asked to give a presentation to a group of seniors. Research career paths (feel free to use the Internet) related to their field of study and create a PowerPoint presentation that explains your selections. You must "sell" your examples to the students and make them see why these are good choices. ***(Hint: You may want to use a wizard.)***

Your PowerPoint presentation should contain at least ten slides. You determine the design template. Edit the slide master layout for both the title and slide master layouts to feature a clip art image of someone performing a job similar to the one you have chosen. Include this image in the upper left corner on all your slides. Apply any formatting options you think are appropriate. Print the slides as handouts with six slides per page. Print an outline of your presentation.

SPECIALIST

MICROSOFT®

POWERPOINT

UNIT 2: Customizing and Enhancing Presentations

- Adding Visual Elements to a Presentation
- Sharing and Connecting Data
- Linking and Embedding Objects and Files
- Sharing Presentations

Benchmark MICROSOFT® POWERPOINT 2003

MICROSOFT OFFICE POWERPOINT 2003 SPECIALIST SKILLS – UNIT 2

Reference No.	Skill	Pages
PP03S-1	**Creating Content**	
PP03S-1-2	Insert and edit text-based content	
	Import text from Word	S166-S167
	Embed a Word table in a presentation	S189-S190
PP03S-1-3	Insert tables, charts and diagrams	
	Create and format organizational charts and diagrams	S136-S139
	Create and format a chart	S139-S145
	Create and format a table	S145-S148
PP03S-1-4	Insert pictures, shapes and graphics	
	Insert, size, move, and customize WordArt	S131-S136
	Insert and size a scanned image	S148-S149
PP03S-1-5	Insert objects	
	Embed and edit an Excel chart in a slide	S191-S192
	Link and edit an Excel chart to a presentation	S192-S194
	Add animated GIFs to a presentation	S149-S150
	Add and modify sound and video files	S151-S154
PP03S-2	**Formatting Content**	
PP03S-2-3	Format slides	
	Modify slide layout	S167
PP03S-2-6	Customize slide templates	
	Create and apply a custom template	S155-S156
PP03S-3	**Collaborating**	
PP03S-3-1	Track, accept and reject changes in a presentation	
	Send and edit a presentation for review	S211-S214
	Accept/reject changes from reviewers	S214-S217
PP03S-3-2	Add, edit and delete comments in a presentation	S217-S219
PP03S-3-3	Compare and merge presentations	S214-S217
PP03S-4	**Managing and Delivering Presentations**	
PP03S-4-1	Organize a presentation	
	Create hyperlinks	S176-S177
	Create a hyperlink using an action button	S174-S175
PP03S-4-2	Set up slide shows for delivery	
	Create, run, edit, and print a custom show	S200-S204
	Add action buttons	S172-S175
PP03S-4-3	Rehearse timing	S177-S179
PP03S-4-5	Prepare presentations for remote delivery	
	Use the Package for CD feature	S219-S221
PP03S-4-6	Save and publish presentations	
	Create a folder and select, copy, delete, and rename files and folders	S195-S200
	Save a presentation in a different file format	S171-S172, S212
	Save a presentation as a Web page	S222-S229
PP03S-4-8	Export a presentation to another Microsoft Office program	
	Export presentation to Microsoft Word	S170-S171

5

ADDING VISUAL ELEMENTS TO A PRESENTATION

PERFORMANCE OBJECTIVES

Upon successful completing of Chapter 5, you will be able to:

- **Create, size, move, modify, and format WordArt text**
- **Create and format an organizational chart**
- **Create and format a diagram**
- **Create, edit, and modify a chart**
- **Create and format a table**
- **Add a scanned image to a slide**
- **Add animated GIFs to slides**
- **Add sound and video effects to a presentation**
- **Create and apply a custom template**

A presentation consisting only of text slides may have important information in it that will be overlooked by the audience because a slide contains too much text. Adding visual elements, where appropriate, can help to deliver the message by adding interest and impact to the information. In this chapter, you will learn how to create visual elements on slides such as WordArt, organizational charts, diagrams, miscellaneous charts, and tables. You will also learn how to add scanned images, sound, video, and animated GIFs, which are multimedia effects that will make the delivery of your presentation a dynamic experience for your audience. This chapter also includes information on how to customize a design template and then save it as a template for future use.

Creating WordArt

HINT
Use WordArt to create interesting text effects in slides.

Insert Word Art

With the WordArt application, you can distort or modify text to conform to a variety of shapes. This is useful for creating company logos and headings. With WordArt, you can change the font, style, and alignment of text. You can also use different fill patterns and colors, customize border lines, and add shadow and three-dimensional effects. To insert WordArt in a slide, click the Insert WordArt button on the Drawing toolbar. You can also click Insert, point to Picture, and then click WordArt. This displays the WordArt Gallery shown in Figure 5.1.

FIGURE 5.1 *WordArt Gallery*

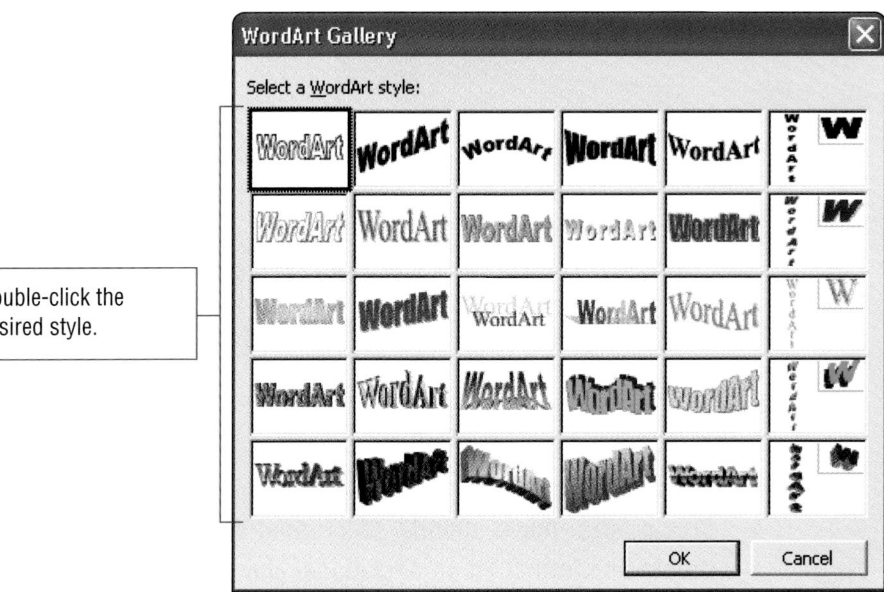

Double-click the desired style.

QUICK STEPS

Create WordArt

1. Click Insert WordArt button.
2. Double-click desired option.
3. Type WordArt text.
4. Click OK.

Entering Text

Double-click a WordArt choice at the WordArt Gallery and the Edit WordArt Text dialog box displays as shown in Figure 5.2. At the Edit WordArt Text dialog box, type the WordArt text and then click the OK button. At the Edit WordArt Text dialog box, you can change the font and/or size of text and also apply bold or italic formatting.

FIGURE 5.2 *Edit WordArt Text Dialog Box*

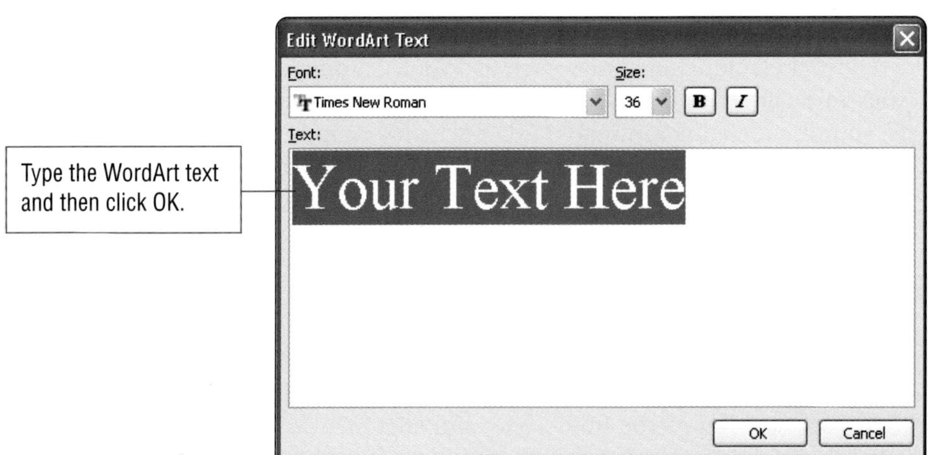

Type the WordArt text and then click OK.

Sizing and Moving WordArt

WordArt text is inserted in the workbook with the formatting selected at the WordArt Gallery. The WordArt text is surrounded by white sizing handles and the WordArt toolbar displays near the text. Use the white sizing handles to change the height and width of the WordArt text. Use the yellow diamond located at the bottom of the WordArt text to change the slant of the WordArt text. To do this, position the arrow pointer on the yellow diamond, hold down the left mouse button, drag to the left or right, and then release the mouse button.

To move WordArt text, position the arrow pointer on any letter of the WordArt text until the arrow pointer displays with a four-headed arrow attached. Hold down the left mouse button, drag the outline of the WordArt text box to the desired position, and then release the mouse button.

HINT Edit WordArt by double-clicking the WordArt text.

HINT Delete WordArt by clicking it and then pressing the Delete key.

(Note: Before completing Exercise 1, delete the PowerPointUnit01S folder on your disk. Next, copy to your disk the PowerPointChapter05S subfolder from the PowerPoint2003Specialist folder on the CD that accompanies this textbook and then make PowerPointChapter05S the active folder.)

exercise 1

INSERTING WORDART IN A SLIDE

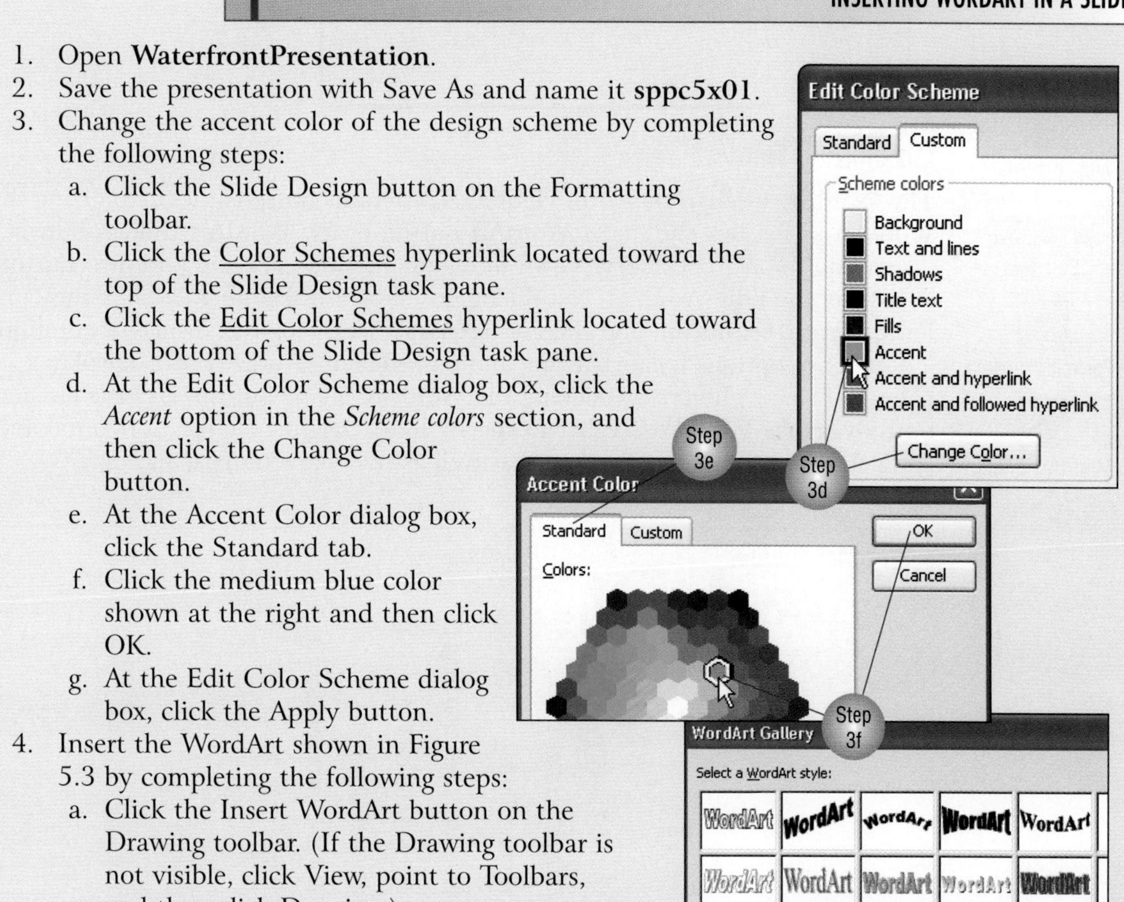

1. Open **WaterfrontPresentation**.
2. Save the presentation with Save As and name it **sppc5x01**.
3. Change the accent color of the design scheme by completing the following steps:
   a. Click the Slide Design button on the Formatting toolbar.
   b. Click the Color Schemes hyperlink located toward the top of the Slide Design task pane.
   c. Click the Edit Color Schemes hyperlink located toward the bottom of the Slide Design task pane.
   d. At the Edit Color Scheme dialog box, click the *Accent* option in the *Scheme colors* section, and then click the Change Color button.
   e. At the Accent Color dialog box, click the Standard tab.
   f. Click the medium blue color shown at the right and then click OK.
   g. At the Edit Color Scheme dialog box, click the Apply button.
4. Insert the WordArt shown in Figure 5.3 by completing the following steps:
   a. Click the Insert WordArt button on the Drawing toolbar. (If the Drawing toolbar is not visible, click View, point to Toolbars, and then click Drawing.)
   b. At the WordArt Gallery, double-click the fifth option from the left in the third row.

c. At the Edit WordArt Text dialog box, type **Waterfront Cafe** and then click OK.
d. Using the sizing handles that display around the selected WordArt text, increase the size of the WordArt so it is approximately the size shown in Figure 5.3.
e. Move the WordArt text so it is positioned approximately as shown in Figure 5.3.

5. Add a transition and sound of your choosing to all slides in the presentation.
6. Run the presentation.
7. Print only Slide 1.
8. Save and then close the presentation.

FIGURE 5.3 ***Slide 1, Exercise 1***

WordArt Gallery

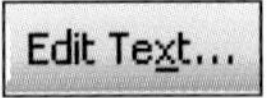

Edit Text

Format WordArt

WordArt Shape

Customizing WordArt

The WordArt toolbar, shown in Figure 5.4, contains buttons for customizing the WordArt text. Click the Insert WordArt button or the WordArt Gallery button to display the WordArt Gallery shown in Figure 5.1 and click the Edit Text button to display the Edit WordArt Text dialog box shown in Figure 5.2. Click the Format WordArt button and the Format WordArt dialog box displays containing a number of options for formatting and customizing WordArt text. Display a palette of shape choices by clicking the WordArt Shape button. Use the last four buttons on the WordArt toolbar to specify letter heights, change horizontal and vertical alignment of WordArt text, as well as the character spacing.

FIGURE 5.4 ***WordArt Toolbar***

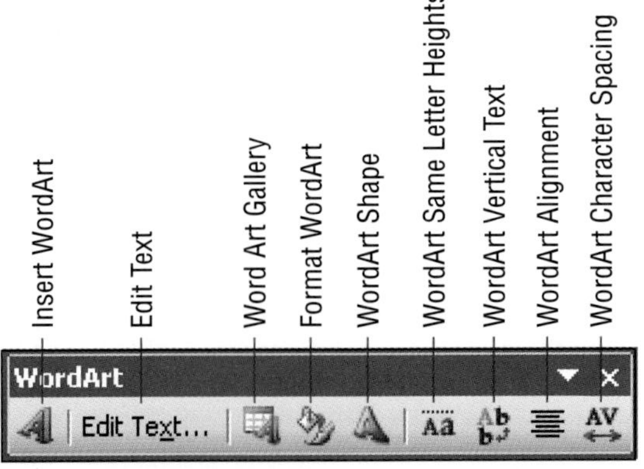

exercise 2

INSERTING AND FORMATTING WORDART IN A SLIDE

1. Open **ArtworksPresentation**.
2. Save the presentation with Save As and name it **sppc5x02**.
3. Insert WordArt in Slide 1 as shown in Figure 5.5 by completing the following steps:
   a. With Slide 1 displayed in the Slide pane, click the Insert WordArt button on the Drawing toolbar.
   b. At the WordArt Gallery, double-click the fourth option from the left in the third row.
   c. At the Edit WordArt Text dialog box, type **Rainbow Artworks** and then click OK.
   d. Click the WordArt Shape button on the WordArt toolbar and then click the first option from the left in the second row from the top (Arch Up [Curve]).
   e. Click the Format WordArt button on the WordArt toolbar.
   f. At the Format WordArt dialog box, click the Size tab.
   g. At the Format WordArt dialog box with the Size tab selected, select the current measurement in the *Height* text box and then type **7**.
   h. Select the current measurement in the *Width* text box and then type **6.5**.

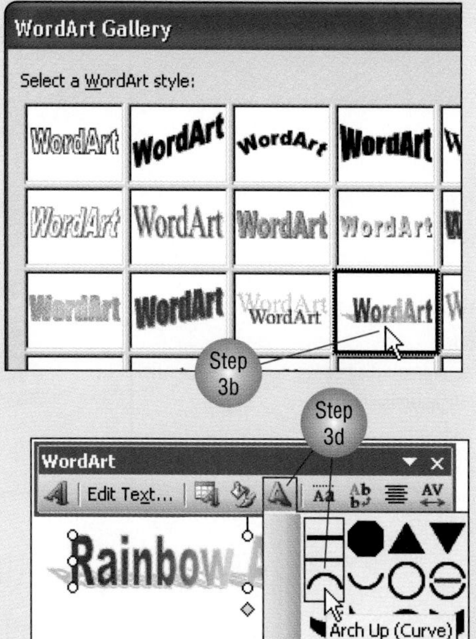

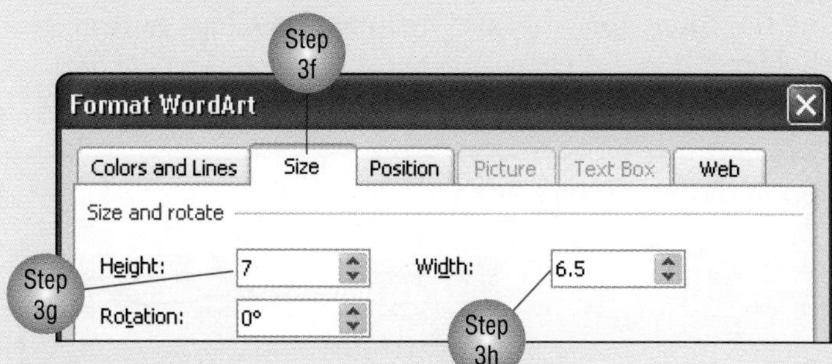

   i. Click OK to close the dialog box.
   j. Drag the WordArt text so it is positioned on the slide as shown in Figure 5.5.
4. Add an animation scheme of your choosing to the slides in the presentation. (The animation scheme will not apply to Slide 1 because the slide contains only WordArt.)
5. Run the presentation.
6. Print only Slide 1.
7. Save and then close the presentation.

FIGURE 5.5 ***Slide 1, Exercise 2***

Create Organization Chart

1. Click Insert Diagram or Organization Chart button.
2. Click organization chart option.
3. Click OK.
4. Customize organization chart.
5. Type text in organization chart boxes.

Insert Diagram or Organization Chart

Creating Organizational Charts and Diagrams

Use the Diagram Gallery to create organizational charts or other types of diagrams. Display the Diagram Gallery dialog box, shown in Figure 5.6, by clicking the Insert Diagram or Organization Chart button on the Drawing toolbar or by clicking Insert and then Diagram. You can also display the Diagram Gallery dialog box by choosing a slide layout containing a content placeholder and then clicking the Insert Diagram or Organization Chart button in the content placeholder.

FIGURE 5.6 ***Diagram Gallery Dialog Box***

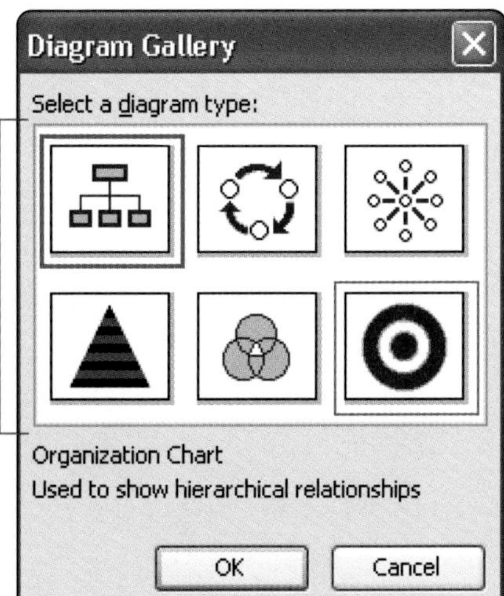

Click the desired chart or diagram in this list box.

HINT

Use an organizational chart to visually illustrate hieracrchical data.

HINT

Use a diagram to illustrate a concept and enhance the visual appeal of a document.

At the Diagram Gallery dialog box, click the desired option in the *Select a diagram type* list box and then click OK. If you click an organizational chart option, chart boxes appear in the slide and the Organization Chart toolbar displays. Use buttons on this toolbar to create additional boxes in the chart, specify the layout of the chart, expand or scale the chart, select specific elements in the chart, apply an autoformat to the chart, or specify a text wrapping option.

If you click a diagram option at the Diagram Gallery dialog box, the diagram is inserted in the slide and the Diagram toolbar displays. Use buttons on this toolbar to insert additional shapes; move shapes backward or forward or reverse the diagram; expand, scale, or fit the contents of the diagram; apply an autoformat to the diagram; or change the type of diagram (choices include Cycle, Radial, Pyramid, Venn, and Target).

Create a Diagram
1. Click Insert Diagram or Organization Chart button.
2. Click desired diagram.
3. Click OK.
4. Customize diagram options.
5. Type text in diagram boxes.

exercise 3 CREATING AND CUSTOMIZING AN ORGANIZATIONAL CHART AND A DIAGRAM

1. Open **sppc5x01**.
2. Save the presentation with Save As and name it **sppc5x03**.
3. Add a new Slide 6 containing an organizational chart as shown in Figure 5.7 by completing the following steps:
   a. Display Slide 5 in the Slide pane.
   b. Click the New Slide button on the Formatting toolbar.
   c. At the Slide Layout task pane, click the Title and Content slide layout.
   d. Click in the text *Click to add title* and then type **Executive Officers**.
   e. Click the Insert Diagram or Organization Chart button located in the middle of the slide in the content placeholder.
   f. At the Diagram Gallery dialog box, make sure the first option from the left in the top row is selected, and then click OK.
   g. Create the organizational chart shown in Figure 5.7 by completing the following steps:
      1) Click the Autoformat button on the Organization Chart toolbar.
      2) At the Organization Chart Style Gallery, double-click *Double Outline* in the *Select a Diagram Style* list box.

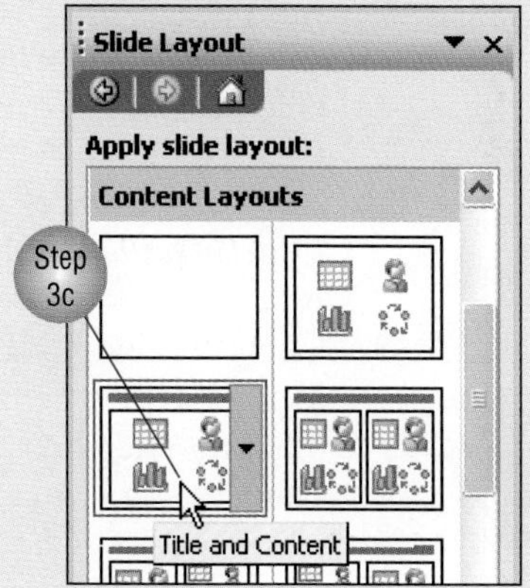

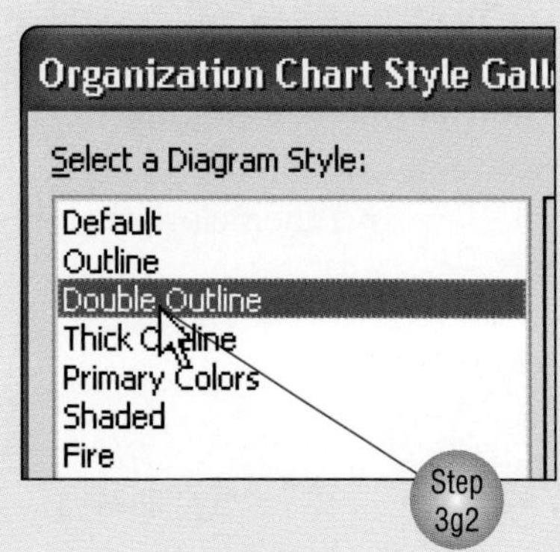

3) Click in the top box, type **Tanya Mitchell**, press Enter, and then type **Owner**.
4) Click in each of the remaining boxes and then type the text as shown in Figure 5.7.
5) After typing the text in all of the boxes, click the Fit Text button on the Organization Chart toolbar.

4. Add a new Slide 7 containing a diagram as shown in Figure 5.8 by completing the following steps:
   a. Click the New Slide button on the Formatting toolbar.
   b. At the Slide Layout task pane, click the Title and Content slide layout.
   c. Click in the text *Click to add title* and then type **Company Divisions**.
   d. Click the Insert Diagram or Organization Chart button located in the middle of the slide in the content placeholder.
   e. At the Diagram Gallery dialog box, click the middle diagram in the top row, and then click OK.

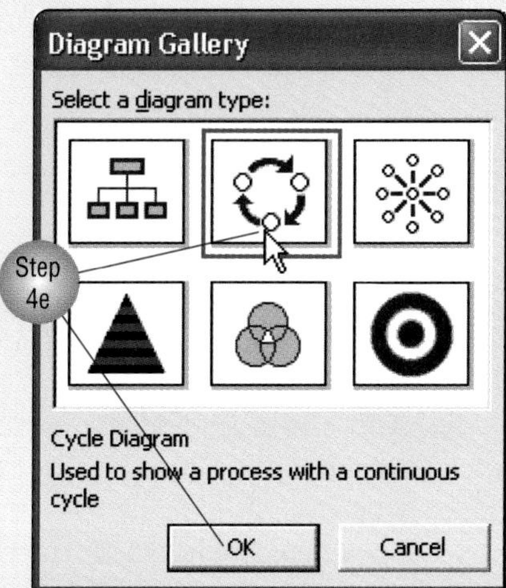

   f. Create the diagram shown in Figure 5.8 by completing the following steps:
      1) Click the AutoFormat button on the Diagram Chart toolbar.
      2) At the Diagram Style Gallery, double-click *Double Outline* in the *Select a Diagram Style* list box.
      3) Click the text *Click to add text* located at the right side of the diagram and then type **Dining Room**.
      4) Click the text *Click to add text* located at the left side of the diagram and then type **Catering**.
      5) Click the text *Click to add text* located at the bottom of the diagram and then type **Wine Cellar**.
      6) Select the text *Catering*, change the font size to 20, and turn on bold.
      7) Select the text *Dining Room*, change the font size to 20, and turn on bold.
      8) Select the text *Wine Cellar*, change the font size to *20*, and turn on bold.

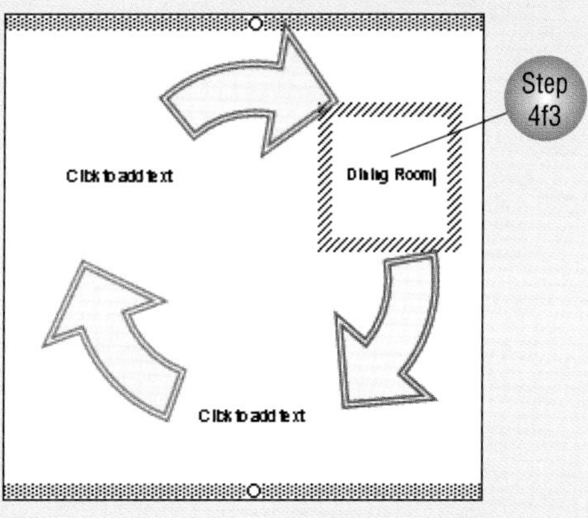

5. Run the presentation.
6. Print only Slides 6 and 7.
7. Save and then close the presentation.

FIGURE 5.7 *Slide 6, Exercise 3*

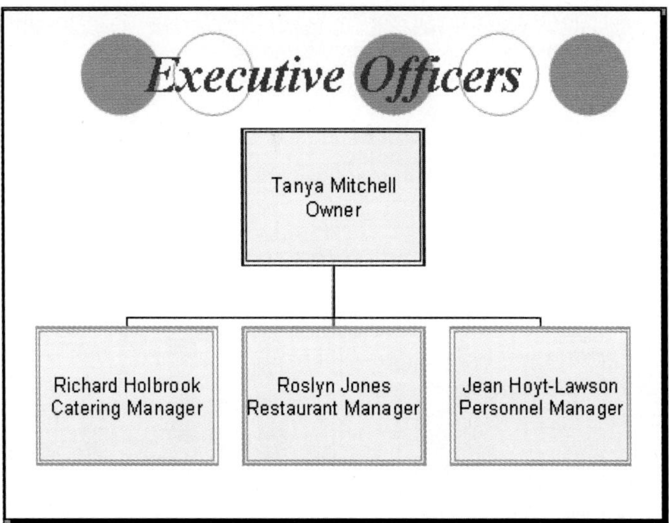

FIGURE 5.8 *Slide 7, Exercise 3*

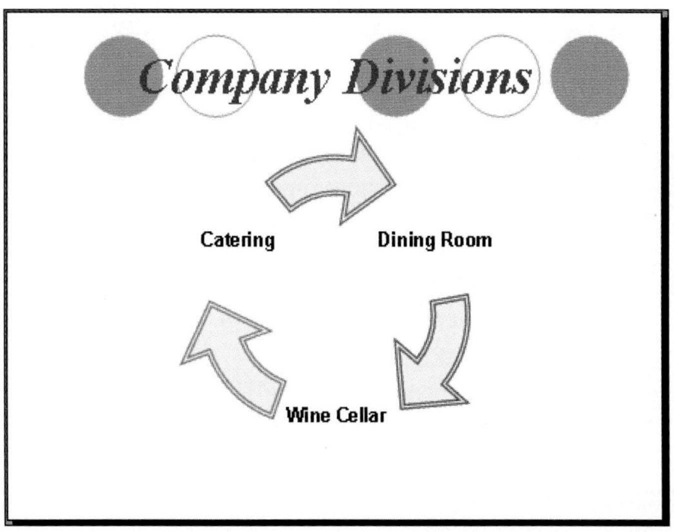

Creating a Chart

A chart is an effective way of visually presenting relationships between numerical data. The audience will be able to quickly grasp the largest expenditure, or the sales trend line, because the information is displayed in a graph format. Microsoft Office includes a feature called Microsoft Graph Chart you can use to create charts.

To add a chart to your presentation, insert a new slide with a slide layout that contains a content placeholder. Click the Insert Chart button in the content placeholder and a chart displays in the slide along with a datasheet as shown in Figure 5.9. You can also insert a chart by clicking the Insert Chart button on the Standard toolbar or by clicking Insert and then Chart.

QUICK STEPS

Create a Chart

1. Click Insert Chart button in slide content placeholder.
2. Delete text in datasheet.
3. Type desired data in datasheet.

Insert Chart

FIGURE 5.9 ***Chart and Datasheet***

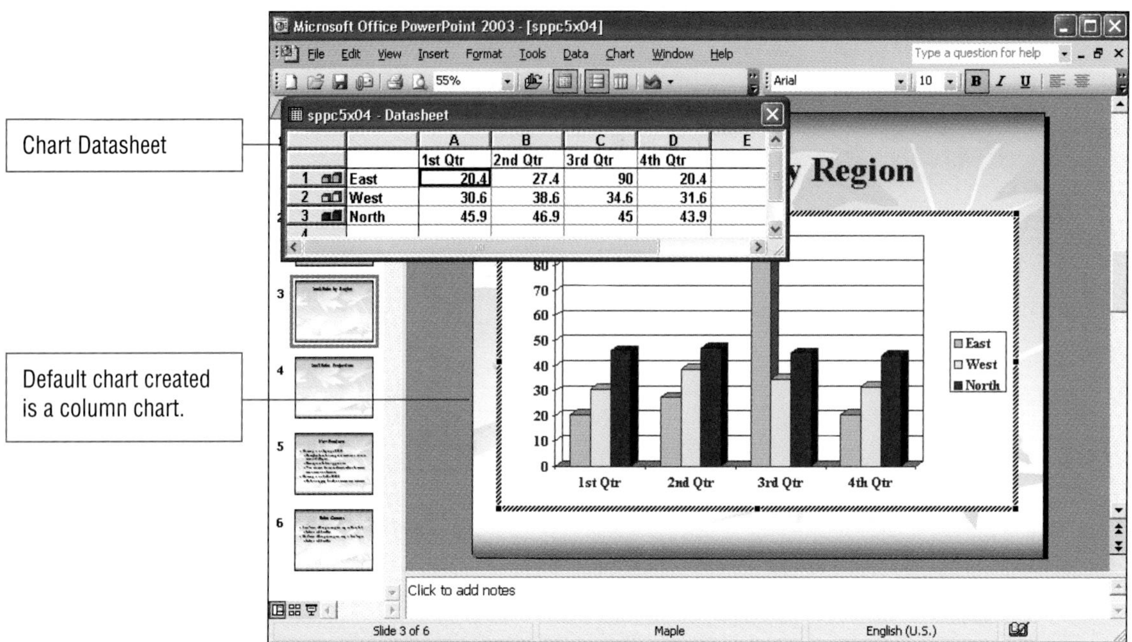

Editing the Datasheet

The datasheet is set up similarly to an Excel worksheet with columns and rows. Data is entered into a cell, which is the intersection of a column with a row. Each row in the datasheet represents a series in the chart as noted by the colored bars to the right of the row numbers. Type your data by clicking the required cell in the datasheet and then typing the correct label or value. Press Tab or use the arrow keys on the keyboard to move from cell to cell in the datasheet. As you make changes to the contents of the datasheet, the chart will update automatically. You can also clear the entire datasheet first and then type the data for the chart into an empty datasheet. To do this, select all of the cells in the datasheet, and then either press the Delete key or click Edit, point to Clear, and then click All.

Changing the Chart Type

HINT

Change to a chart type that is suited to the data. For example, a single series is best represented in a pie chart.

Once the correct data has been entered, you can modify the chart settings to suit your needs. You can choose from several standard chart types. Each chart category includes several subtypes. In addition to the standard chart types, PowerPoint includes some custom charts that are preformatted combinations of charts with various colors, patterns, gridlines, and other options. Select a custom chart at the Chart Type dialog box. Display this dialog box by clicking Chart on the Chart Menu bar and then clicking Chart Type at the drop-down menu. The standard chart types and a brief description of each are listed in Table 5.1.

TABLE 5.1 **Standard Chart Types**

Type	*Description*
Column	This is useful to compare related items and show changes over a period of time.
Bar	Similar to a column chart except the x-axis is displayed vertically and the y-axis is displayed horizontally.
Line	A line chart is useful to illustrate changes in values or to show trends over time.
Pie	Individual items are displayed as they relate to the sum of all of the items in a pie chart.
XY (Scatter)	Values are plotted as individual points in the chart. Each point is the intersection of the x and y values. XY charts are commonly used for scientific data.
Area	This chart is similar to a line chart with a solid color filling in the area of the chart below the line.
Doughnut	The doughnut chart illustrates each item as it relates to the sum of all of the items. It is used instead of a pie chart when more than one data series are to be graphed.
Radar	In this chart, the axis radiates from the center of the chart. Data is plotted along the axes radiating from the center and then lines are shown joining axis to axis.
Surface	Two sets of data can be illustrated topographically with peaks and valleys in a surface chart. Areas with the same color and pattern indicate similar values.
Bubble	Three values are required to create a bubble chart. Two of the values cause the bubble to be positioned on the chart similar to an XY chart. The third value affects the size of the bubble.
Stock	Stock prices are graphed according to their *high-low-close* prices. Graphing a particular stock is useful to see the beginning value, how much the value fluctuated, and the ending value.
Cylinder	This is the column or bar chart shown with a cylinder series instead of a rectangular bar.
Cone	This is the column or bar chart shown with a cone series instead of a rectangular bar.
Pyramid	This is the column or bar chart shown with a pyramid series instead of a rectangular bar.

exercise 4

ADDING A CHART, EDITING THE DATASHEET, AND CHANGING THE CHART TYPE

1. Open **ConferencePresentation** from the PowerPointChapter05S folder on your disk.
2. Save the presentation with Save As and name it **sppc5x04**.
3. Add a chart to the presentation, edit the datasheet, and change the chart type by completing the following steps:
   a. Display Slide 3 in the Slide pane.
   b. Click the Insert Chart button in the middle of the slide in the content placeholder.
   c. Delete the existing data in the datasheet by completing the following steps:

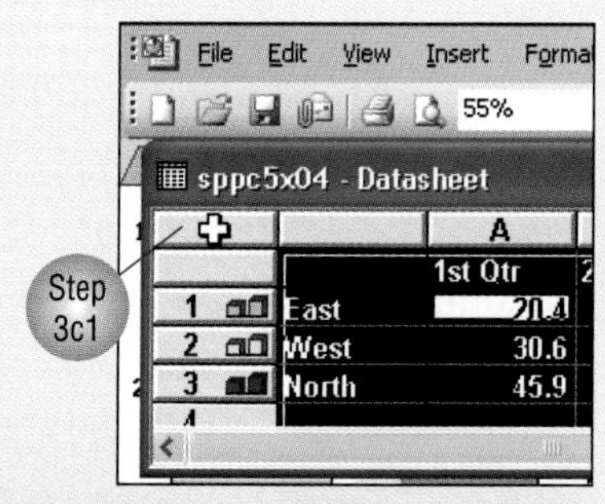

1) Click the Select All button at the top left corner of the datasheet. This button is located at the top of the row indicators and to the left of the column indicators.
2) Press the Delete key on the keyboard.

d. Type the data displayed below into the datasheet. Press the Tab key to move from one cell to the next. As you enter new data, the chart will update automatically to reflect the changes.

e. Change to a 3-D clustered bar chart by completing the following steps:
1) Click Chart and then Chart Type.
2) Click *Bar* in the *Chart type* list box.
3) Click the first sub-type in the second row in the *Chart sub-type* section.
4) Click OK.

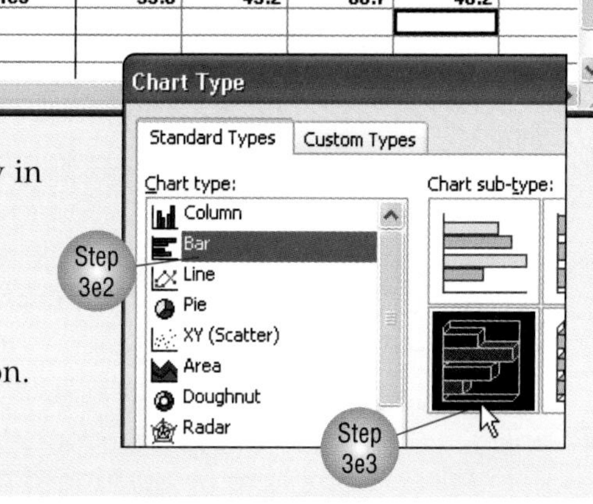

4. Click in an area on the slide outside the chart to deselect it.
5. Make Slide 1 active and then run the presentation.
6. Print only Slide 3.
7. Save and then close the presentation.

Modifying a Chart

The chart created in Exercise 4 needs more information added to it to make it more readily understood by the conference participants. You can tell by looking at the chart that the East region had the largest sales volume, but what do the values represent? Are the sales figures represented in thousands, millions, or billions? The legend in the chart created in Exercise 4 is not necessary since the slide title provides the same information.

Additional elements such as titles can be added to the chart, or, existing elements can be deleted or formatted by modifying the chart. Double-click a chart to edit it. The chart displays with a thick shaded border surrounding it, the datasheet window opens, and the chart options appear on the Menu bar and toolbar.

View Datasheet

Click the Close button (contains an *X*) on the datasheet title bar or click the View Datasheet button on the Chart Standard toolbar to remove the datasheet from the screen. The View Datasheet button on the toolbar is a toggle. Clicking it once will remove the datasheet; clicking it again will redisplay it.

HINT

Click a chart once to select it and then move or size it. Double-click a chart to edit the chart contents or elements.

Once a chart has been created on a slide, clicking the chart once will display eight white sizing handles around the chart. Drag the sizing handles to change the size of the chart. Press the Delete key to delete the chart from the slide. To move the chart, position the mouse pointer inside the chart until the four-headed move icon displays, and then drag the chart to the new location on the slide. Click in an area on the slide outside the chart to deselect it.

Adding Chart Titles

Three titles can be added to a chart: the Chart title, the Category title, and the Value title. To add a title to the chart, click Chart and then Chart Options, or right-click the chart and then click Chart Options at the shortcut menu. This opens the Chart Options dialog box with the Titles tab selected as displayed in Figure 5.10. Type the titles in the appropriate text boxes then click OK.

> **HINT**
> Right-click any of the chart elements to display a format dialog box for the selected element.

FIGURE 5.10 **Chart Options Dialog Box**

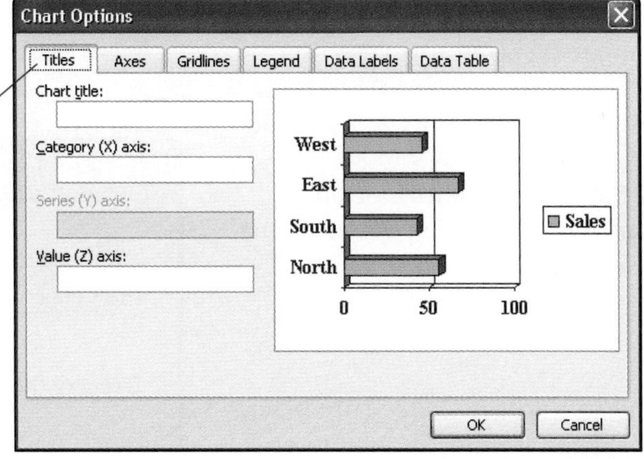

Formatting Chart Elements

A chart is comprised of several elements as shown in Figure 5.11. Double-clicking a chart element will open a dialog box with formatting options that are available for the selected element. You can also right-click the object and then click the desired option at the shortcut menu, or click to select the object and then use options from the Format or Chart menus on the Menu bar.

> **HINT**
> If you make a change to a chart element and do not like the results, immediately click the Undo button.

FIGURE 5.11 **Chart Elements**

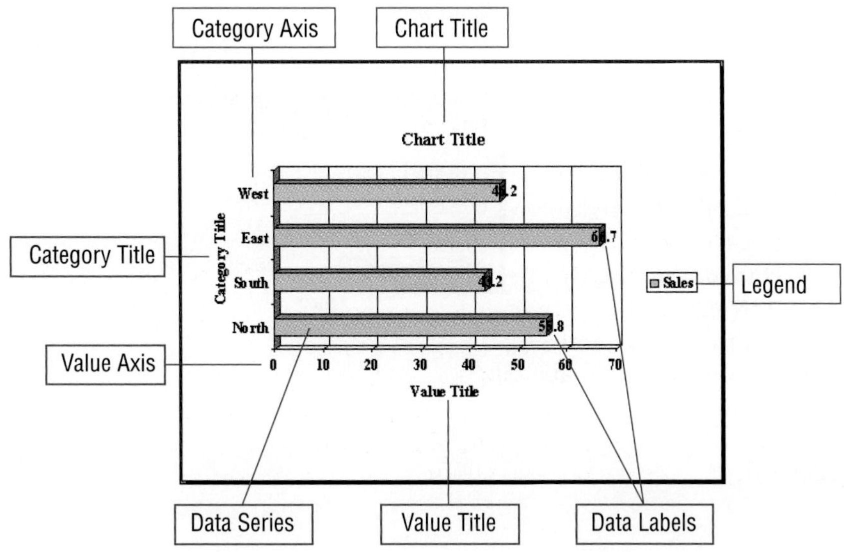

In Exercise 5 you will add a title to the axis displaying the dollar amounts, delete the legend, format the value axis to display the numbers in currency format, change the shape of the bars, and add value labels to the bars.

exercise 5 ENHANCING THE CHART

1. Open **sppc5x04**.
2. Save the presentation with Save As and name it **sppc5x05**.
3. Display Slide 3 in the Slide pane.
4. Double-click the chart to edit it.
5. Click the Close button (contains an *X*) on the datasheet title bar to remove it from the slide.
6. Add a value title by completing the following steps:
   a. Click Chart and then Chart Options.
   b. At the Chart Options dialog box with the Titles tab selected, click in the *Value (Z) axis* text box and then type **Sales in Millions.**
   c. Click OK.
7. Click the legend to select it. Make sure black sizing handles appear around the legend and then press the Delete key.
8. Change the format of the numbers in the value axis to Currency by completing the following steps:
   a. Point to the values along the bottom of the chart until a yellow box appears which reads *Value Axis*.
   b. Click the right mouse button and then click Format Axis at the shortcut menu.
   c. At the Format Axis dialog box, click the Number tab.
   d. Click *Currency* in the *Category* list box.
   e. Change the number in the *Decimal places* text box to zero (0).
   f. Click OK.
9. Change the shape of the bars in the chart by completing the following steps:
   a. Point to any of the bars in the chart, click the right mouse button, and then click Format Data Series at the shortcut menu.
   b. At the Format Data Series dialog box, click the Shape tab.
   c. Click the first shape in the second row (shape 4 in the *Bar shape* section).
   d. Click OK.

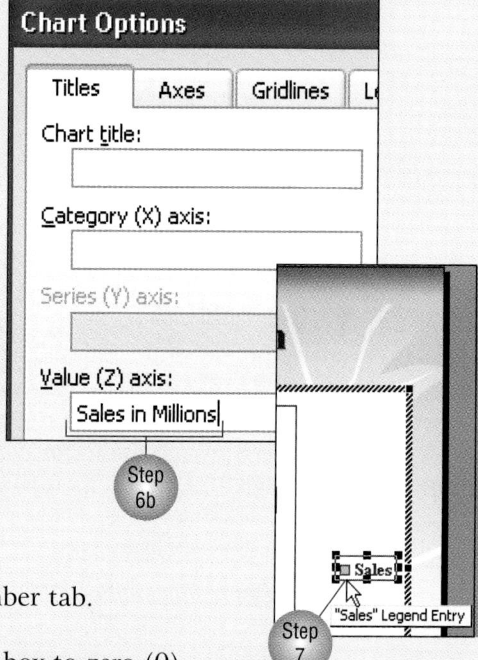

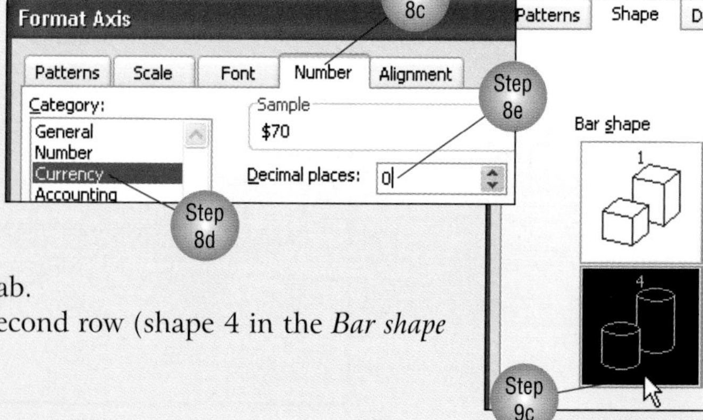

10. Add data labels to the chart and reposition the labels by completing the following steps:
    a. Click Chart and then Chart Options.
    b. At the Chart Options dialog box, click the Data Labels tab.
    c. Click in the *Value* check box in the *Label Contains* section to insert a check mark.
    d. Click OK.
    e. The values are placed at the end of the cylinders, but are partly obstructed from view by the cylinders. Move the values by completing the following steps:
        1) Point to the first value label and click the left mouse button. (This selects all of the value labels.)
        2) Click the left mouse button again and sizing handles appear around the first value label only.
        3) Point the mouse pointer at the border around the sizing handles and then drag the value label to the right of the cylinder until the entire value is visible.
    f. Repeat Steps 10e1 through 10e3 to move the remaining value labels.
11. Click in an area on the slide outside the chart to deselect it.
12. Make Slide 1 active and then run the presentation.
13. Print only Slide 3.
14. Save and then close the presentation.

Creating a Table

Tables are useful for numbers and lists where you want to present the data in column format. Each entry in a table is called a cell and can be formatted independently. If you want to arrange the content of a slide in columns and rows, insert a new slide with the slide layout that includes a content placeholder. Click the Insert Table button in the content placeholder and the Insert Table dialog box displays. At the Insert Table dialog box, type the number of columns, press the Tab key, type the number of rows, and then press Enter.

You can also insert a table using the Insert Table button on the Standard toolbar. Click the Insert Table button, drag the mouse down and to the right to select the desired number of columns and rows, and then click the left mouse button.

Insert Table

HINT

Use PowerPoint to create a table with simple formatting. For more complex formatting, consider creating the table in Word or Excel and then embedding it in a slide.

Entering Text in Cells in a Table

To enter text in the table, click in the desired cell and then type the text. Press the Tab key to move the insertion point to the next cell to the right. Press Shift + Tab to move the insertion point to the previous cell. If you want to insert a tab within a cell, press Ctrl + Tab. If you press the Tab key when the insertion point is positioned in the last cell in the table, a new row is automatically added to the bottom of the table.

Create a Table

1. Click Insert Table button in slide's content placeholder.
2. At Insert Table dialog box, specify number of rows and columns.
3. Click OK.
4. Type data in table cells.

CREATING A TABLE IN A SLIDE

1. Open **sppc5x05**.
2. Save the presentation with Save As and name it **sppc5x06**.
3. Display Slide 4 in the Slide pane.
4. Add a table to the slide and enter text into the cells by completing the following steps:
   a. Click the Insert Table button located in the middle of the slide in the content placeholder.
   b. At the Insert Table dialog box, press the Tab key. (This accepts the default of *2* in the *Number of columns* text box.)
   c. Type 5 in the *Number of rows* text box.
   d. Click OK or press Enter.
   e. Type the text as displayed in the table at the right. Press the Tab key to move to the next cell. Press Shift + Tab to move to the previous cell. Do not press Tab after typing the last cell entry.
   f. Click outside the table to deselect it.
5. Make Slide 1 active and then run the presentation.
6. Print only Slide 4.
7. Save and then close the presentation.

2003 Sales Projections

Region	In millions of dollars
North	68.3
South	55.2
East	77.8
West	59.9

Step 4e

Modifying a Table

Text in a table does not display in the Outline/Slides pane with the Outline tab selected.

Once a table has been created it can be resized and moved to another position on the slide. Click the table to select it and then use the sizing handles that display around the table to increase or decrease the size. To move the table, point to the border of the table until the mouse pointer displays with a four-headed arrow attached, and then drag the table to the desired position.

Use buttons on the Tables and Borders toolbar shown in Figure 5.12 to format a table. For example, you can insert and/or delete rows and columns from the table. To delete a column or row, select the cells in the column or row to be deleted, click the Table button on the Tables and Borders toolbar, and then click Delete Columns or Delete Rows. Insert a column or row by following a similar procedure. You can also use buttons on the toolbar to change the border style, width, and color and add fill color or effects to the table.

The Tables and Borders toolbar should appear automatically when you click inside a cell. If the toolbar has been closed, redisplay it by clicking View, pointing to Toolbars, and then clicking Tables and Borders.

FIGURE

5.12 Tables and Borders Toolbar

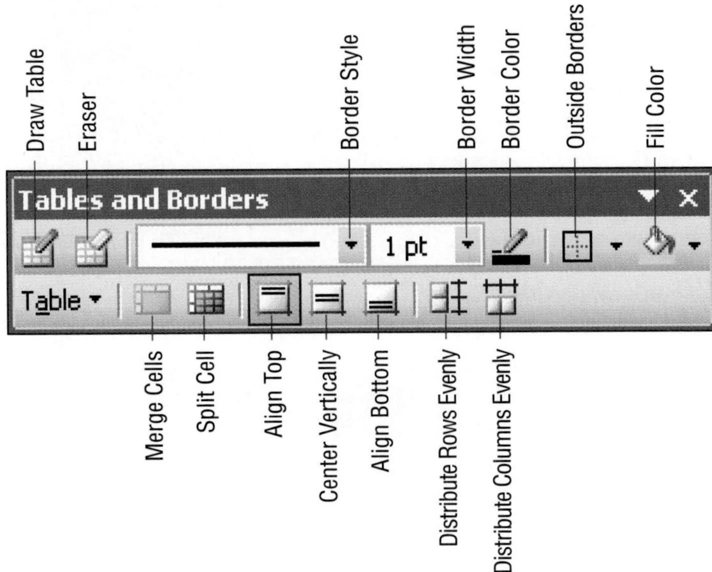

Adjust column widths by positioning the pointer on the column gridline until the pointer changes to a double vertical line with a left- and right-pointing arrow attached to it. Drag the column gridline to the left or right to decrease or increase the width. Other options available from the Table button on the Tables and Borders toolbar allow you to merge and split cells and apply borders and fill.

exercise 7

MODIFYING A TABLE

1. Open **sppc5x06**.
2. Save the presentation with Save As and name it **sppc5x07**.
3. Display Slide 4 in the Slide pane.
4. Modify the table by completing the following steps:
   a. Click the table to select it.
   b. Position the mouse pointer on the bottom right sizing handle until the pointer turns into a diagonally pointing double-headed arrow and then drag up and to the left approximately .5 inch.
   c. Position the mouse pointer on the gridline at the left edge of the table until the pointer turns into a double vertical bar with a left- and right-pointing arrow attached and then drag to the right approximately 1 inch.
   d. Delete the words *of dollars* from the second cell in the first row.
   e. Decrease the width of the second column by positioning the mouse pointer on the gridline at the right edge of the table until the pointer turns into a double vertical bar with a left- and right-pointing arrow attached, and then dragging to the left approximately 1 inch.
   f. Position the arrow pointer along the border of the table until the pointer displays with a four-headed arrow attached and then drag the table until it displays centered in the middle of the slide.

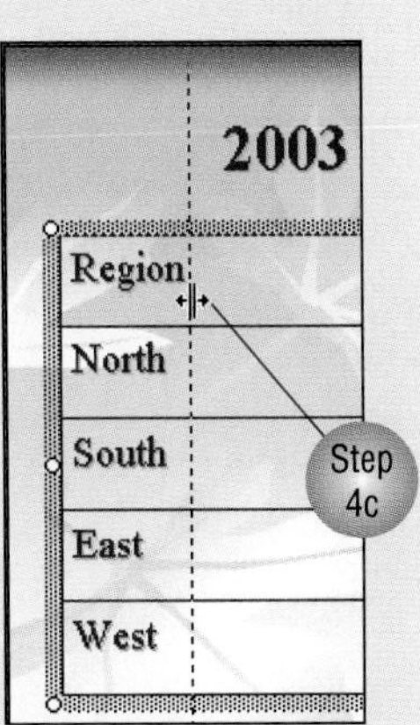

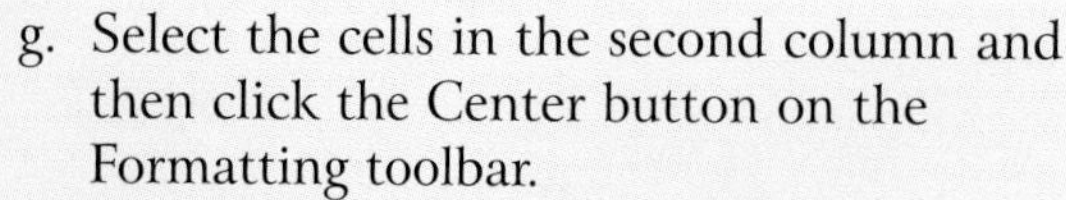

g. Select the cells in the second column and then click the Center button on the Formatting toolbar.
h. Select all of the cells in the table.
i. Click the down-pointing arrow on the Border Width button on the Tables and Borders toolbar and then click *4½ pt* at the drop-down list.
j. Click the Border Color button on the Tables and Borders toolbar and then click the fifth color (blue) from the left (see figure at right).
k. Click the down-pointing arrow at the right of the Outside Borders button on the Tables and Borders toolbar and then click the All Borders button (second button from the left in the top row).
l. Click the down-pointing arrow to the right of the Fill Color button on the Tables and Borders toolbar and then click the first color from the left (white).
m. Click twice outside the table to deselect it and change the pointer back to an arrow.

5. Make Slide 1 active and then run the presentation.
6. Print only Slide 4.
7. Save and then close the presentation.

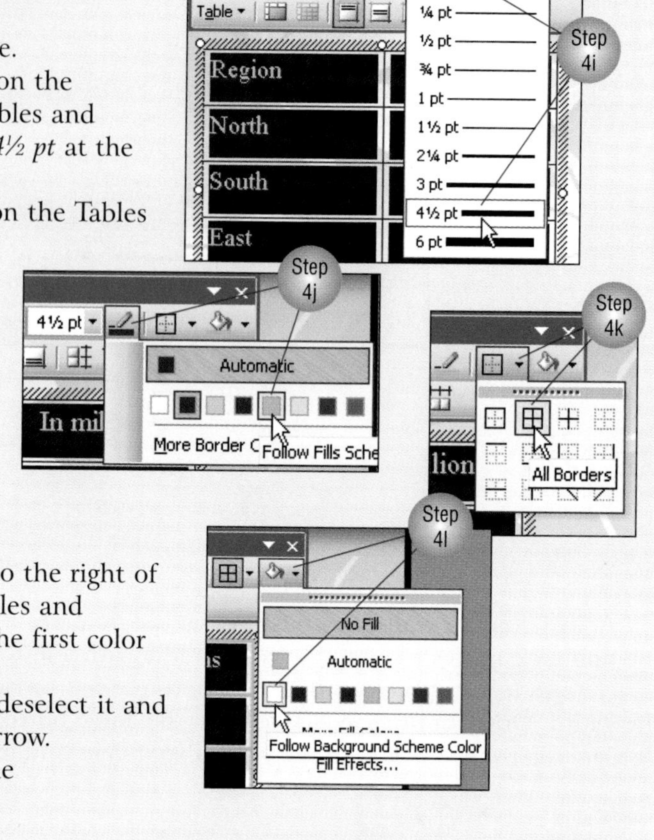

Inserting a Scanned Image

Insert Picture

QUICK STEPS

Insert Scanned Image or GIF

1. Click Insert Picture button.
2. Navigate to desired folder.
3. Double-click file name.

Many computer systems are sold today with color scanners as part of the multimedia package. PowerPoint contains a variety of filters that allow you to insert many popular graphic file formats into a presentation. Scanners can be used to capture pictures, logos, or other artwork you want inserted into a presentation. Scanned images are stored as files and can easily be placed on a slide. Once the image has been inserted, you can resize or move it around on the slide using the sizing handles.

To insert a scanned image, click the Insert Picture button on the Drawing toolbar (or click Insert, point to Picture, and then click From File). At the Insert Picture dialog box, navigate to the folder where the picture is stored, and then double-click the file name. This picture will be inserted in the current slide and white sizing handles will display around it. Move and resize the picture as required.

exercise 8

INSERTING SCANNED IMAGES

1. Open **SemesterPresentation**.
2. Save the presentation with Save As and name it **sppc5x08**.
3. Add a scanned logo to Slide 1 (shown in Figure 5.13) by completing the following steps:
   a. Display Slide 1 in the Slide pane.
   b. Click the Insert Picture button on the Drawing toolbar.
   c. At the Insert Picture dialog box, navigate to the Logos folder on the CD that accompanies this textbook, and then double-click the file named ***Redwood***.
   d. Resize the logo and reposition it in the slide as shown in Figure 5.13.
4. Insert a scanned picture as shown in Figure 5.13 by completing the following steps:
   a. Click the Insert Picture button on the Drawing toolbar.
   b. At the Insert Picture dialog box, navigate to the Pictures folder on the CD that accompanies this textbook, and then double-click the file named ***Building1***.
   c. Resize the picture and reposition it in the slide as shown in Figure 5.13.
5. Print only Slide 1.
6. Run the presentation.
7. Save and then close the presentation.

FIGURE 5.13 ***Slide 1, Exercise 8***

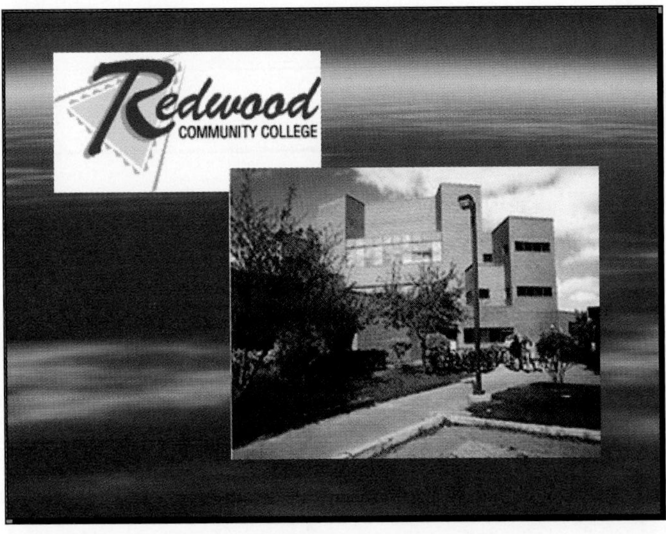

Adding Animated GIFs

GIF files are graphic files saved in *G*raphics *I*nterchange *F*ormat, which is a type of file format commonly used for graphics on Web pages. Animated GIFs are GIF files that have been programmed to display a series of images one on top of another that give the illusion of motion. If you surf the Internet you will see most Web sites have incorporated one or more animated GIFs on their pages to add interest and variety to their site.

HINT

You can move and size an animated GIF, but you have to edit and format it in an animated GIF editing program.

Animated GIFs do not display the motion until you display the slide in a slide show. To insert an animated GIF that you have stored as a file on disk, click the Insert Picture button on the Drawing toolbar (or click Insert, point to Picture, and then click From File). Navigate to the folder containing the GIF file and then double-click the file name. Once the GIF image has been placed in the slide it can be resized and moved using the sizing handles.

exercise 9

ADDING ANIMATED GIFS

1. Open **DesignPresentation**.
2. Save the presentation with Save As and name it **sppc5x09**.
3. Add an animated GIF from a file to Slide 1 as shown in Figure 5.14 by completing the following steps:
   a. Click the Insert Picture button on the Drawing toolbar.
   b. At the Insert Picture dialog box, navigate to the Pictures folder on the CD that accompanies this textbook, and then double-click the file named ***Banner***.
   c. Slightly increase the size of the image and then position it inside the circle at the upper left side of the slide as shown in Figure 5.14.
4. Run the presentation and notice the animation (the red circles move around the text) in the image you inserted.
5. Print only Slide 1.
6. Save and then close the presentation.

FIGURE 5.14 ***Slide 1, Exercise 9***

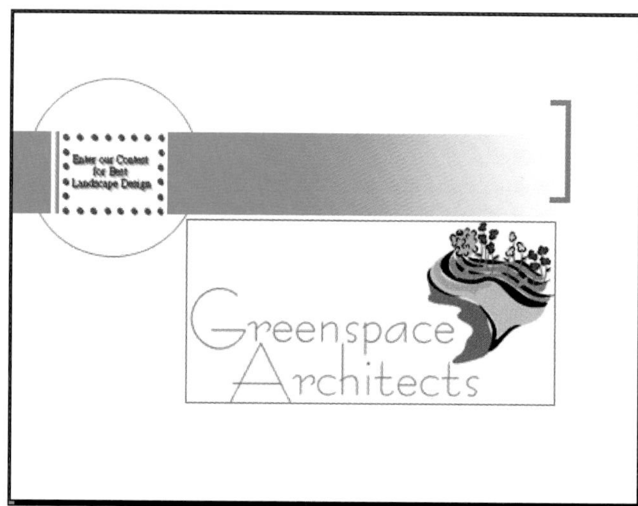

Adding Sound and Video

Adding sound and/or video effects to a presentation will turn a slide show into a true multimedia experience for your audience. Including a variety of elements in a presentation will stimulate interest in your presentation and keep the audience motivated.

To add a sound to your presentation, choose Insert, point to Movies and Sounds, and then click Sound from Clip Organizer or click Sound from File. Clicking Sound from Clip Organizer will display sound files in the Clip Art task pane. Click the desired sound to insert it in the active slide. If the sound you want to incorporate into your presentation is not part of the gallery but stored in a file on disk, click Sound from File. This displays the Insert Sound dialog box where you can navigate to the file's location and then double-click the sound to insert it in the active slide.

When a sound is inserted, you will be prompted with a message asking how you want the sound to start when the slide displays in the slide show. Click the Automatically button if you want the sound to begin when the slide displays or click the When Clicked button if you want the sound to begin when you click the sound icon.

Adding a video clip is a similar process to adding sound. Click Insert, point to Movies and Sounds, and then click either Movie from Clip Organizer or Movie from File.

Insert Sound File

1. Click Insert, Movies and Sounds, Sound from File.
2. Navigate to desired folder.
3. Double-click file name.

Insert Movie File

1. Click Insert, Movies and Sounds, Movie from File.
2. Navigate to desired folder.
3. Double-click file name.

exercise 10

ADDING SOUND AND VIDEO TO A PRESENTATION

1. Open **PotentialPresentation**.
2. Save the presentation with Save As and name it **sppc5x10**.
3. Add a movie clip and sound to the Slide 6 as shown in Figure 5.15 by completing the following steps:
   a. Display Slide 6 in the Slide pane.
   b. Click Insert, point to Movies and Sounds, and then click Movie from File.
   c. At the Insert Movie dialog box, navigate to the SoundandVideo folder on the CD that accompanies this textbook, and then double-click the file named ***Launch***.
   d. At the message asking how you want the movie to start, click the When Clicked button.
   e. Resize and position the movie on the slide as shown in Figure 5.15.
   f. Add a sound clip to Slide 6 that will automatically play by completing the following steps:
      1) Click Insert, point to Movies and Sounds, and then click Sound from File.
      2) At the Insert Sound dialog box, navigate to the SoundandVideo folder on the CD that accompanies this textbook, and then double-click the file named ***Greatfire***.
      3) At the message asking how you want the sound to start, click the Automatically button.
      4) Resize and position the sound icon as shown in Figure 5.15.
4. Display Slide 1 in the Slide pane and then run the presentation. When the last slide (Slide 6) displays, as soon as you hear the music, click the video image to begin the video. After viewing the video and listening to the music for about 30 seconds, end the slide show.

5. Sounds and videos can be set to loop continuously. The sound and/or video will continue playing over and over again until the slide show is ended. In this exercise, when the speaker has finished the presentation, he or she might choose to have the sound and video play for a few minutes until the audience has left the room. Change the video and sound in Slide 6 to loop continuously by completing the following steps:
   a. Display Slide 6 in the Slide pane.
   b. Right-click the video and then click Edit Movie Object at the shortcut menu.
   c. At the Movie Options dialog box, click *Loop until stopped* to insert a check mark, and then click OK.
   d. Right-click the sound icon and then click Edit Sound Object at the shortcut menu.
   e. At the Sound Options dialog box, click *Loop until stopped*, and then click OK.
   f. Deselect the sound icon.
6. Display Slide 1 and then run the presentation. When you reach Slide 6, click the video image when you hear the music. Watch the video and listen to the sound repeat a few times and then end the slide show.
7. Print only Slide 6.
8. Print the slides as handouts with all six slides on one page.
9. Save and then close the presentation.

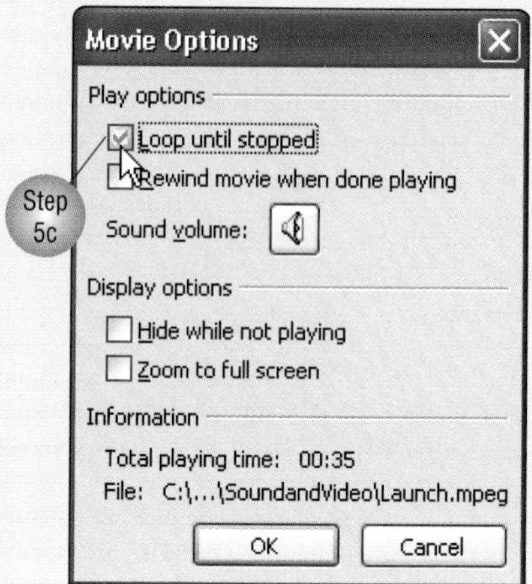

FIGURE 5.15 ***Slide 6, Exercise 10***

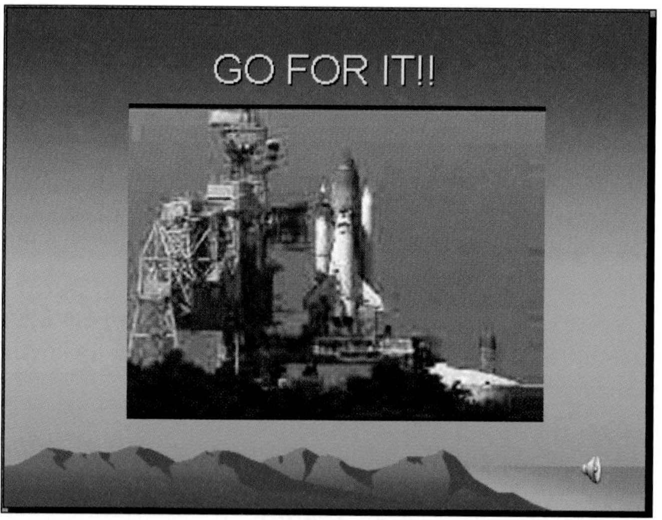

Playing a Sound throughout a Presentation

In Exercise 10, you inserted a sound object that played when a specific slide displayed. You can also insert a sound file in a presentation and have the sound continue through all slides in a presentation. Generally, you would add a sound for the entire presentation when setting up a self-running presentation. You learned how to prepare a self-running presentation in Chapter 1. To include a sound clip in a self-running presentation, insert the sound, right-click the sound icon, and then click Custom Animation. In the Custom Animation task pane, click the down-pointing arrow at the right of the sound file name in the list box, and then click Effect Options at the drop-down menu. At the Play Sound dialog box with the Effect tab selected as shown in Figure 5.16, click the *After* option, specify the number of slides in the presentation, and then click OK.

FIGURE 5.16 **Play Sound Dialog Box with Effect Tab Selected**

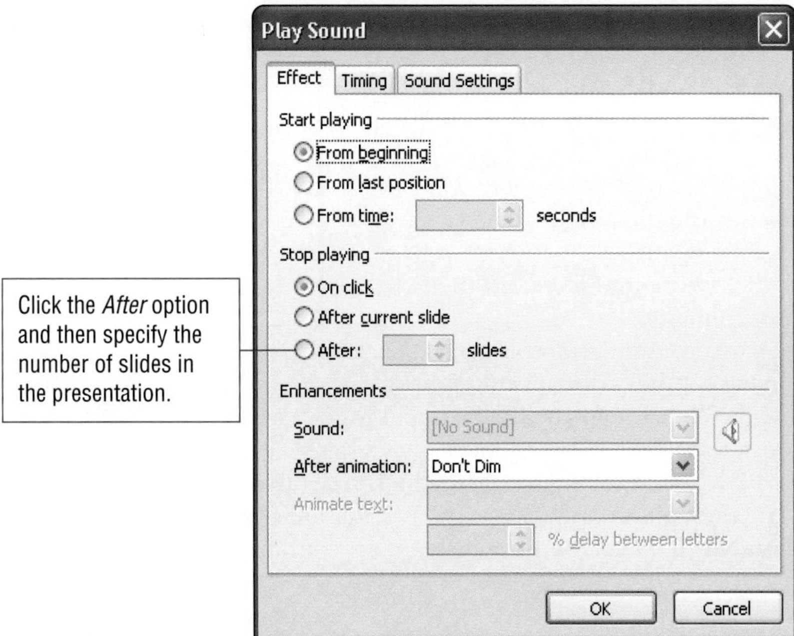

exercise 11

INSERTING SOUND AND PLAYING IT THROUGHOUT PRESENTATION

1. Open **JobSearchPresentation**.
2. Save the presentation with Save As and name it **sppc5x11**.
3. Suppose you are going to display this presentation at a trade show and you want to set it up as a self-running presentation. To do this, complete the following steps:
   a. Change to the Slide Sorter view.
   b. Click Slide Show and then Slide Transition.
   c. Select all slides by pressing Ctrl + A.
   d. In the Slide Transition task pane, click in the *Automatically after* option check box in the *Advance slide* section.
   e. Click the up-pointing arrow at the right side of the time box until *00:05* displays.

f. Add a transition effect by clicking *Shape Diamond* in the *Apply to selected slides* list box. (You will need to scroll down the list box to display this option.)
g. Click Slide Show and then Set Up Show.
h. At the Set Up Show dialog box, click in the *Loop continuously until 'Esc'* check box to insert a check mark. (Make sure *All* is selected in the *Show slides* section and *Using timings, if present* is selected in the *Advance slides* section.)
i. Click OK to close the dialog box.

4. To add more interest to the presentation, you decide to add a sound that plays throughout the presentation. To do this, complete the following steps:
   a. Change to the Normal view.
   b. Make Slide 1 the active slide.
   c. Click Insert, point to Movies and Sounds, and then click Sound from File.
   d. At the Insert Sound dialog box, navigate to the SoundandVideo folder on the CD that accompanies this textbook, and then double-click the file named ***Greenspace***.
   e. At the message asking how you want the sound to start, click the Automatically button.
   f. Right-click the sound icon and then click Custom Animation.
   g. In the Custom Animation task pane, click the down-pointing arrow at the right of the sound file name in the list box, and then click Effect Options at the drop-down menu.
   h. At the Play Sound dialog box with the Effect tab selected, click the *After* option and then type 9. (You are changing this number to *9* because the presentation contains nine slides.)
   i. Click OK.
   j. Move the sound icon down to the bottom right corner of the slide.
5. With Slide 1 the active slide, run the presentation by clicking the Slide Show button in the Custom Animation task pane.
6. After viewing the presentation at least twice, press the Esc key on the keyboard.
7. Close the Custom Animation task pane.
8. Save and then close the presentation.

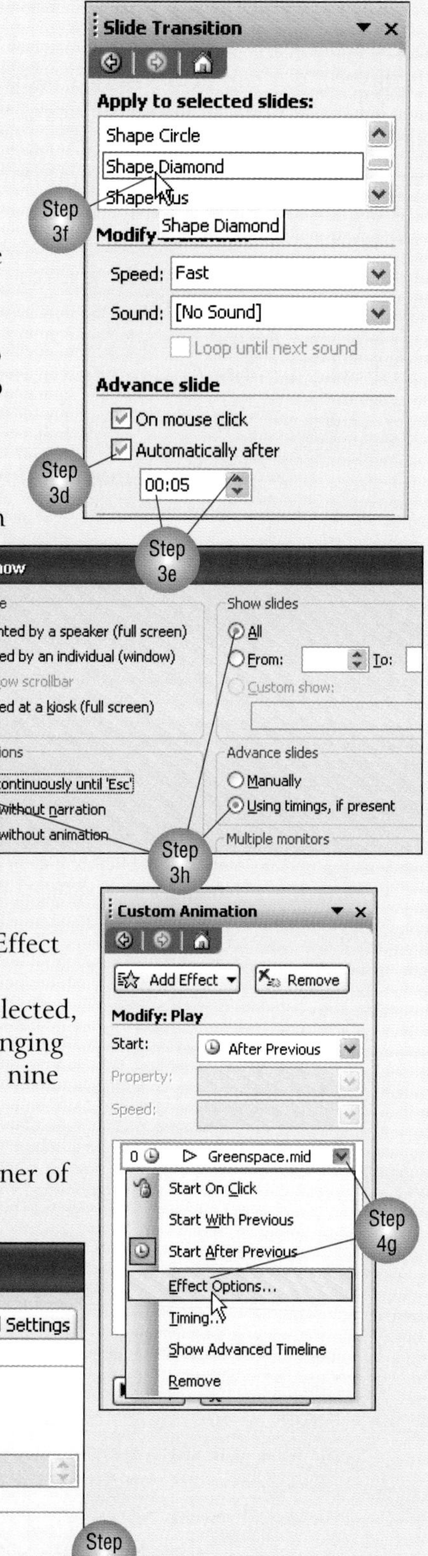

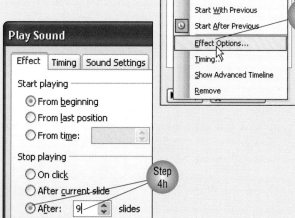

Creating and Applying a Custom Template

Create Custom Template
1. Display blank, unformatted slide.
2. Customize the slide as desired.
3. Click File, Save As.
4. Type template name in *File name* text box.
5. Change *Save as type* option to *Design Template.*
6. Change *Save in* option to desired folder.
7. Click Save button.

Each PowerPoint presentation is based on a template. The Slide Design task pane offers a number of design templates that apply specific formatting to slides in a presentation. If you customize a design template and then decide you want to use the customized template in the future, save it as a template.

To save a customized design as a design template, click File and then Save As. At the Save As dialog box, type a name for the template, click the down-pointing arrow at the right side of the *Save as type* option box, and then click *Design Template* at the drop-down list. Specify the location where you want the design template saved and then click the Save button.

exercise 12

CREATING AND APPLYING A CUSTOM DESIGN

1. At a blank PowerPoint screen, click the New button on the Standard toolbar. (This displays a blank, unformatted slide.)
2. Click the Slide Design button on the Formatting toolbar.
3. Click the *Crayons* design template in the *Apply a design template* list box at the Slide Design task pane.
4. Customize the design template by completing the following steps:
   a. Click the Color Schemes hyperlink located toward the top of the Slide Design task pane.
   b. Click the first color scheme option in the second row.
   c. Click the Edit Color Schemes hyperlink located toward the bottom of the Slide Design task pane.
   d. At the Edit Color Scheme dialog box, click the *Accent* option, and then click the Change Color button.
   e. At the Accent Color dialog box with the Standard tab selected, click a bright yellow color of your choosing, and then click OK.
   f. At the Edit Color Scheme dialog box, click the *Accent and followed hyperlink* option, and then click the Change Color button.
   g. At the Accent and Followed Hyperlink Color dialog box with the Standard tab selected, click a bright red color of your choosing, and then click OK.
   h. Click the Apply button at the Edit Color Scheme dialog box.

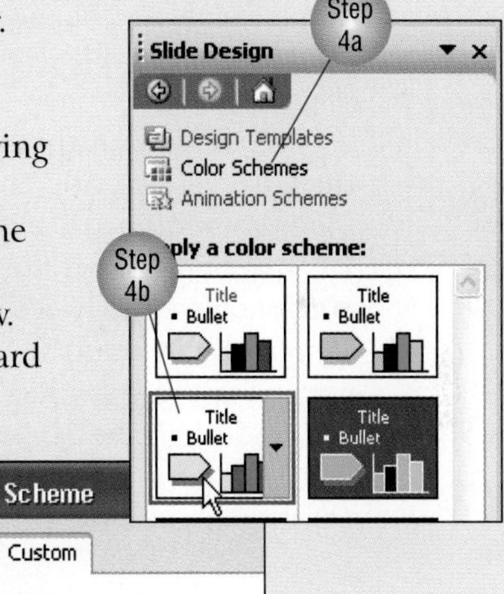

5. Save the customized design as a design template by completing the following steps:
   a. Click File and then Save As.
   b. At the Save As dialog box, type **ArtworksTemplate** in the *File name* text box.

c. Click the down-pointing arrow at the right side of the *Save as type* option box and then click *Design Template* at the drop-down list.
d. Change the *Save in* option to the PowerPointChapter05S folder on your disk.
e. Click the Save button.

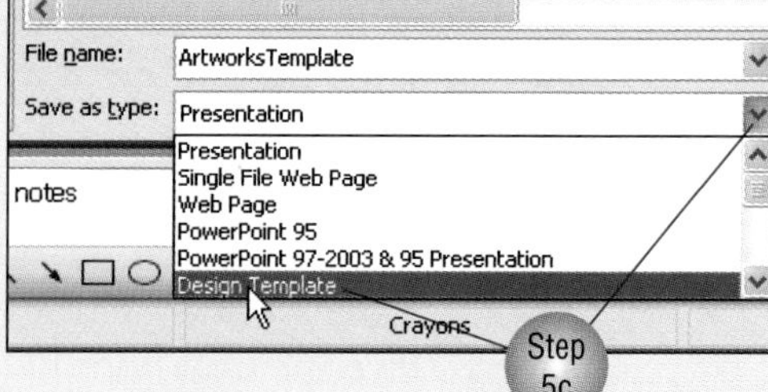

6. Close **ArtworksTemplate**.
7. Apply the ArtworksTemplate to the sppc5x02 presentation by completing the following steps:
   a. Open **sppc5x02**. (You saved this presentation in Exercise 2. If you did not complete Exercise 2, open **ArtworksPresentation**.)
   b. Save the presentation with Save As and name it **sppc5x12**.
   c. Apply the ArtworksTemplate by completing the following steps:
      1) If necessary, display the Slide Design task pane.
      2) Click the Design Templates hyperlink located toward the top of the Slide Design task pane.
      3) Click the Browse hyperlink located toward the bottom of the Slide Design task pane.
      4) At the Apply Design Template dialog box, change the *Look in* option to the PowerPointChapter05S folder on your disk.
      5) Double-click *ArtworksTemplate* in the list box. (This applies the customized template to the slides in the presentation.)
8. Make the following changes to the slides:
   a. With Slide 1 displayed in the Slide pane, click the *Rainbow Artworks* WordArt text to select it and then drag the WordArt so it is balanced in the slide.
   b. Display Slide 2 in the Slide pane, click to select the subtitle placeholder (contains the Goal 1 text), and then drag the placeholder up slightly so the text does not touch the wavy red line that is part of the design template.
   c. Display Slide 3 and then drag the subtitle placeholder up slightly so the text does not touch the wavy red line.
   d. Display Slide 4 and then drag the subtitle placeholder up slightly so the text does not touch the wavy red line.
9. Display Slide 1 in the Slide pane and then run the presentation.
10. Print the presentation as handouts with all four slides on one page.
11. Save and then close the presentation.

CHAPTER summary

- Use WordArt to create, distort, modify, and/or conform text to a variety of shapes.
- The WordArt Gallery contains a variety of predesigned WordArt styles.
- Size WordArt using the sizing handles that display around selected WordArt text and move selected WordArt by dragging it to the desired location using the mouse.
- Customize WordArt text with buttons on the WordArt toolbar and/or with options at the Format WordArt dialog box.
- Create organizational charts and diagrams with options at the Diagram Gallery. Use buttons on the Organization Chart toolbar to customize an organizational chart. Use buttons on the Diagram toolbar to customize a diagram.

- Add a chart to a slide to visually present relationships between numerical data. Use the Microsoft Graph Chart feature to create a variety of charts.
- Data for a chart is entered in the datasheet. When a new chart is created, a sample datasheet and chart display. Edit the datasheet to insert the values you want to plot on the graph.
- Double-click a chart to edit it. A chart is comprised of several chart elements that can be added, deleted, or formatted.
- Create a table on a slide when you want to present information in columns and/or rows. Each entry in a table is entered into a cell that can be formatted independently of the other cells.
- In a table, press the Tab key to move the insertion point to the next cell or press Shift + Tab to move the insertion point to the previous cell.
- Click a table to select it. You can resize, move, or delete a selected table.
- Use buttons on the Tables and Borders toolbar to customize and format cells in a table.
- Insert a scanned image or animated GIF by double-clicking the desired image at the Insert Picture dialog box. You can resize and/or move a scanned image or GIF on a slide.
- An animated GIF is a graphic file that displays motion when running a presentation.
- Sound and/or video effects can be added to a presentation that will play when running the presentation. You can configure a sound or video object to play continuously until the slide show is ended.
- To include a sound clip in a self-running presentation, insert the sound, right-click the sound icon, and then click Custom Animation. In the Custom Animation task pane, click the down-pointing arrow at the right of the sound file name in the list box, and then click Effect Options at the drop-down menu. At the Play Sound dialog box with the Effect tab selected, click the *After* option, specify the number of slides in the presentation, and then click OK.
- Save a customized template you want to use in the future as a design template. To do this, display the Save As dialog box, type a name for the customized template, change the *Save as type* option to *Design Template*, identify the *Save in* location, and then click Save.

FEATURES summary

FEATURE	BUTTON	MENU
WordArt Gallery		Insert, Picture, WordArt
Diagram Gallery		Insert, Diagram
Insert a chart		Insert, Chart
Insert table dialog box		Insert, Table
Insert Picture dialog box		Insert, Picture, From File
Insert Movie dialog box		Insert, Movies and Sounds, Movie from File
Insert Sound dialog box		Insert, Movies and Sounds, Sounds from File

CONCEPTS check

Completion: On a blank sheet of paper, indicate the correct term, symbol, or command for each description.

1. Click the Insert WordArt button on the Drawing toolbar and this displays.
2. Display a palette of shape choices by clicking this button on the WordArt toolbar.
3. Click this button on the Drawing toolbar to display the Diagram Gallery.
4. If you click an organizational chart option at the Diagram Gallery, this toolbar displays.
5. Use this Microsoft Office feature to create charts.
6. Click this button on the Chart Standard toolbar to remove the datasheet from the screen.
7. Three titles can be added to a chart: the Category title, the Value title, and this title.
8. Press this key in a table to move the insertion point to the next cell.
9. Use buttons on this toolbar to customize and format a table.
10. Insert a scanned image by double-clicking the desired image at this dialog box.
11. The initials *GIF* stand for this.
12. To save a customized design as a design template, change the *Save as type* option at the Save As dialog box to this.

SKILLS check

(Note: Due to the file size of the presentations you created in this chapter, you may want to delete from your disk some of the presentations that begin with **sppc5x** ***or you might want to save the Skills Check assessments on another disk.)***

Assessment 1

1. Open **CorporatePresentation**.
2. Save the presentation with Save As and name it **sppc5sc01**.
3. Create the WordArt on Slide 1 as shown in Figure 5.17 with the following specifications:
   a. At the WordArt Gallery, double-click the second option from the left in the second row.
   b. Change the shape of the WordArt to the Deflate shape (second shape from the left in the fourth row from the top).
   c. Display the Format WordArt dialog box with the Colors and Lines tab selected, change the *Color* option in the *Fill* section to dark blue/green that follows the color scheme of the design template.
   d. Size and move the WordArt so it displays on the slide as shown in Figure 5.17.
4. Create the organizational chart on Slide 3 as shown in Figure 5.18 with the following specifications:
   a. Display the Diagram Gallery and then choose the first option from the left in the top row.
   b. Display the Organization Chart Style Gallery dialog box and then double-click the *Outline* style.

c. Type the text in bold in the organizational chart boxes as shown in Figure 5.18.
d. Click the Fit Text button on the Organization Chart toolbar to better fit the text in the chart.

5. Create the diagram on Slide 4 as shown in Figure 5.19 with the following specifications:
   a. Display the Diagram Gallery and then choose the second option from the left in the top row.
   b. Type the text in the diagram as shown in Figure 5.19 and set the text in 18-point bold.
6. Add an animation scheme of your choosing to the presentation. (The animation scheme will not apply to Slide 1 because the slide contains only WordArt.)
7. Run the presentation beginning with Slide 1.
8. Print the presentation as handouts with all four slides on one page.
9. Save and then close the presentation.

FIGURE 5.17 ***Slide 1, Assessment 1***

FIGURE 5.18 ***Slide 3, Assessment 1***

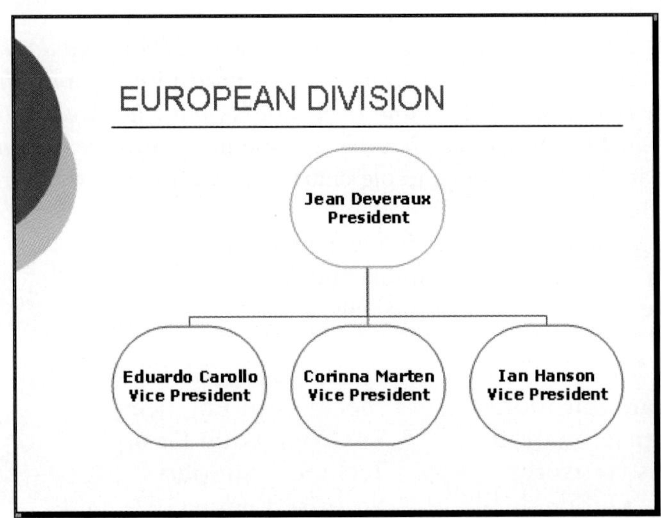

FIGURE

5.19 ***Slide 4, Assessment 1***

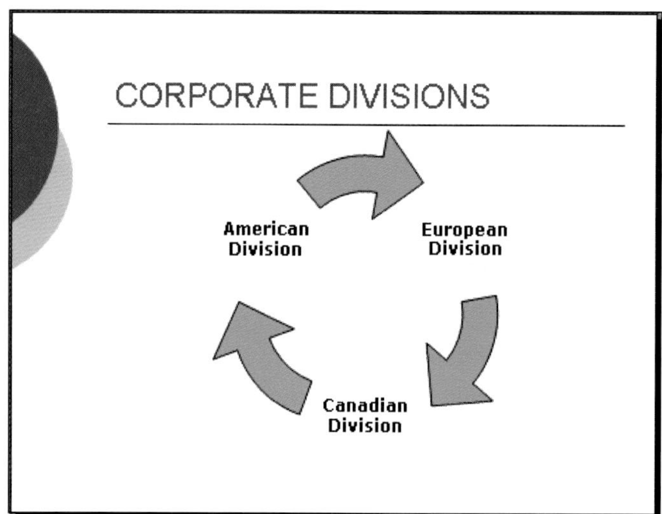

Assessment 2

1. Open **GreenspacePresentation**.
2. Save the presentation with Save As and name it **sppc5sc02**.
3. Insert the Greenspace Architects logo in Slide 1 as shown in Figure 5.20 by completing the following steps:
   a. Click Insert, point to Picture, and then click From File.
   b. At the Insert Picture dialog box, navigate to the Logos folder on the CD that accompanies this textbook, and then double-click the file named ***GrnspcLogo***.
   c. Size and move the logo so it is positioned on the slide as shown in Figure 5.20.
4. Add a chart to Slide 5 with the following specifications:
   a. Click the Insert Chart button in the content placeholder in the slide.
   b. Delete the data in the datasheet and then type the following:

	Court Bldg.	Rose Mall	East Hills	RW Const.
Contract	34.1	58.2	23.7	19.5

   c. Change the chart type to a pie.
   d. Remove the border from the perimeter of the pie. ***(Hint: To do this, position the mouse pointer anywhere on the line around the pie until*** Plot Area ***displays in a yellow box. Click the right mouse button and then click Format Plot Area at the shortcut menu. At the Format Plot Area dialog box, click*** None ***in the*** Border ***section, and then click OK.)***
   e. Insert data labels around the pie chart that will display the percentages.
   f. Resize the chart as large as possible to fill the slide.
5. Add a table to Slide 6 with the following specifications:
   a. Create a table with two columns and five rows.
   b. Type the following data in the cells:

Course Title	Participating Division
Telecommunications	Mechanical Engineering
Air Particle Analysis	Environmental Group
Wireless Networks	Technical Support
Security Online	Security Engineers

c. Bold the text in the first row.
d. Change all of the border lines to *3 pt* and change the border color to match one of the design colors.

6. Create a new Slide 7 with the Blank slide layout and include the following objects:
   a. Create the words *Thank you* as WordArt. Size and position the WordArt text so it fills most of the slide.
   b. Insert the sound file named **Greenspace** located in the SoundandVideo folder on the CD that accompanies this textbook and specify that the sound begin automatically when the slide displays. Position the sound icon in the lower right corner of the slide.
7. Apply an animation scheme of your choosing to all slides in the presentation. (The animation scheme will not apply to Slide 7 because the slide contains only WordArt.)
8. Run the presentation beginning with Slide 1.
9. Print the presentation as handouts with all seven slides on one page.
10. Save and then close the presentation.

FIGURE 5.20 ***Slide 1, Assessment 2***

Assessment 3

1. Open **sppc5sc02**.
2. Display Slide 5 and then double-click the pie chart.
3. Use the Microsoft Graph Help feature to learn how to pull out a slice of the pie chart.
4. Pull the pie slice representing the Court Bldg. contract away from the pie approximately .25 inch.
5. Print only Slide 5.
6. Save the presentation with the same name (**sppc5sc02**) and then close the presentation.

CHAPTER challenge

You are a sales representative for Safe and Secure Insurance Company. Part of your job responsibilities includes selling insurance policies for home, health, auto, and life. To reach more people, you have decided to conduct weekly presentations for individuals who are interested in obtaining more information about each type of policy. Create a PowerPoint presentation with at least seven slides containing information about the importance of insurance, the benefits, and any other details you feel necessary. Include an organizational chart, table, sound or video effects, and at least one other new feature learned in Chapter 5. Save the presentation as **SafeandSecure**.

During the weekly presentations, you would like to be able to quickly jump to various Web sites during the PowerPoint presentation. Use the Help feature to learn about hyperlinks and how to insert them into a presentation. Add at least one hyperlink to the presentation created in the first part of the Chapter Challenge. Save the presentation again.

After reviewing the presentation, you realize that it might be beneficial to show how Safe and Secure's rates compare to rates with other companies. Create a chart in Excel that would show this information and save the chart as **Comparisons**. Then import and link the Excel chart to the **SafeandSecure** presentation created in the first part of the Chapter Challenge. Be sure the slide with the chart is arranged so that it flows logically with the rest of the presentation. Save the presentation again.

CHAPTER 6

SHARING AND CONNECTING DATA

PERFORMANCE OBJECTIVES

Upon successful completion of Chapter 6, you will be able to:

- **Copy an Excel chart to a slide and then modify the chart**
- **Copy text from Word to a slide**
- **Import text from Word**
- **Copy and paste text using the Clipboard task pane**
- **Export an outline to Word**
- **Save a presentation as an Outline/RTF**
- **Add action buttons connecting slides within a presentation**
- **Add action buttons connecting to a Web site and another presentation**
- **Insert hyperlinks in slides connecting to a Web site**
- **Rehearse and set timings for each slide in a presentation**
- **Create a summary slide**

Chapter06S PowerPoint

A variety of methods are available for sharing data between PowerPoint and other Office programs. You can copy data in one program and then paste it in another. You can also copy and then embed or copy and then link data. In this chapter you will learn how to use the Copy and Paste buttons on the Standard toolbar and you will also learn commands for importing and exporting data. In the next chapter, you will learn how to copy and embed and copy and link objects between programs.

Use action buttons in a slide to connect to slides within the same presentation, connect to another presentation, connect to a Web site, or connect to a file in another program. You can also use the Insert Hyperlink dialog box to create a hyperlink in a slide to a Web site or file.

If you are preparing a self-running presentation, consider using the Rehearse Timings feature in PowerPoint. With this feature you can rehearse running the presentation and determine how much time each slide should remain on the screen.

Copying and Pasting Data

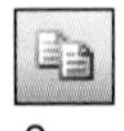
Copy

Paste

Use the Copy and Paste buttons on the Standard toolbar to copy data such as text or an object from one program and then paste it into another program within the Microsoft Office suite. For example, in Exercise 1, you will copy an Excel chart and then paste it into a PowerPoint slide. A copied object, such as a chart, can be moved and sized like any other object. You can also edit a copied object by double-clicking the object.

exercise 1

COPYING AN EXCEL CHART TO A SLIDE AND THEN MODIFYING THE CHART

1. Open **TravelPresentation**.
2. Save the presentation with Save As and name it **sppc6x01**.
3. Insert an Excel chart on Slide 2 as shown in Figure 6.1 by completing the following steps:
   a. Display Slide 2 in the Slide pane.
   b. Open Microsoft Excel.
   c. Open the file named **Top5Tours** from the PowerPointChapter06S folder on your disk.
   d. Click the chart to select it. (Click near the outside of the chart. Make sure you select the entire chart and not an element inside the chart.)
   e. Click the Copy button on the Standard toolbar.
   f. Close **Top5Tours**. (If a message displays asking if you want to save the file, click No.)
   g. Exit Microsoft Excel.
   h. In PowerPoint, click the Paste button on the Standard toolbar. (This inserts the chart in Slide 2.)
   i. Resize and move the chart so it displays in the slide as shown in Figure 6.1.
4. Modify the chart by removing the border and changing the title by completing the following steps:
   a. Double-click the chart.
   b. Position the mouse pointer on the single-line border until *Chart Area* displays in a yellow box.
   c. Click the *right* mouse button and then click Format Chart Area at the shortcut menu.
   d. At the Format Chart Area dialog box, click the Patterns tab.
   e. At the Format Chart Area dialog box with the Patterns tab selected, click *None* in the *Border* section.
   f. Click OK.
   g. Click the chart title to select it.

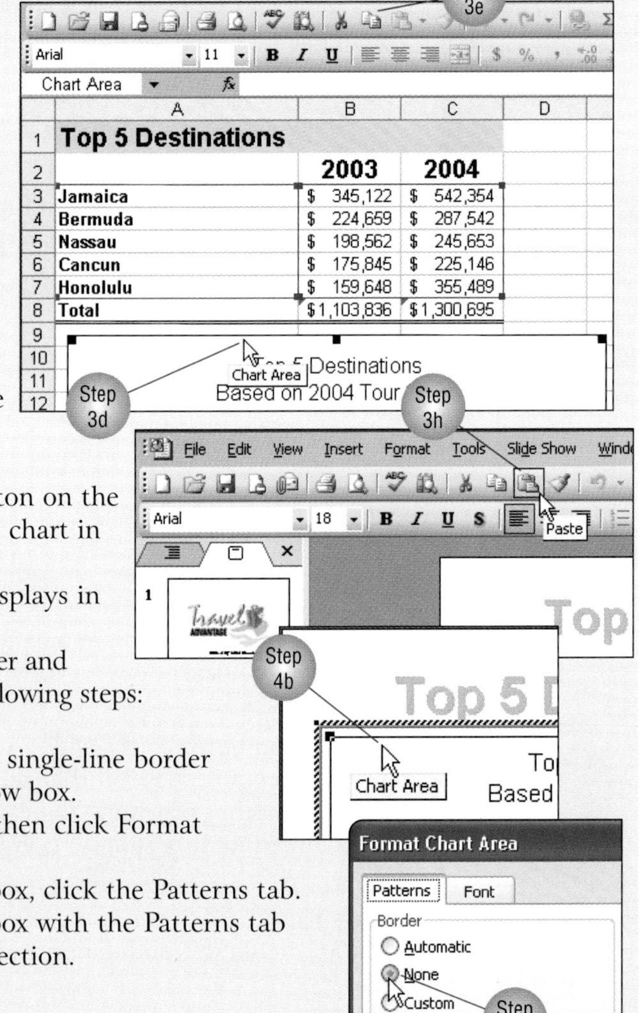

h. Click inside the chart title.
i. Delete the first line of the title, *Top 5 Destinations*.
j. Deselect the chart by clicking in the slide but outside the chart.
5. Display Slide 1 in the Slide pane and then run the presentation.
6. Print only Slide 2.
7. Save and then close the presentation.

FIGURE 6.1 ***Slide 2, Exercise 1***

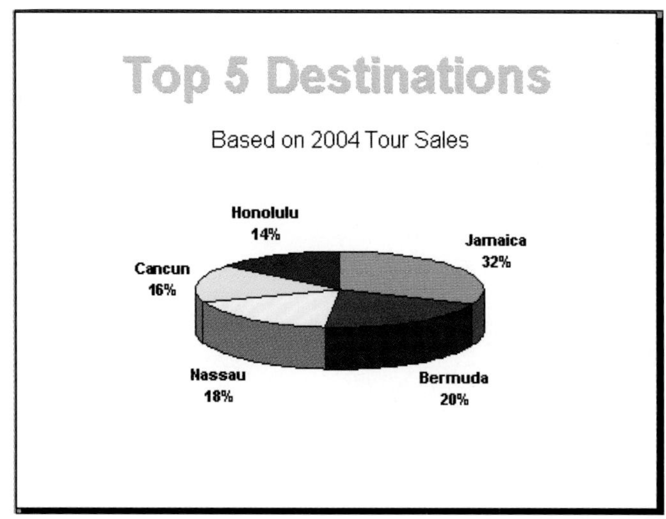

Copying and Pasting Word Text

You can copy text from a Word document and paste the text in a PowerPoint slide. To specify the area on the slide where you want the text inserted, draw a text box. To do this, click the Text Box button on the Drawing toolbar and then drag in the slide to create the box. With the insertion point positioned inside the text box, click the Paste button on the Standard toolbar to insert the copied text.

Text Box

exercise 2 COPYING TEXT FROM WORD TO A SLIDE

1. Open **sppc6x01**.
2. Save the presentation with Save As and name it **sppc6x02**.
3. Copy text in a Word document and paste it in Slide 3 as shown in Figure 6.2 by completing the following steps:
   a. Display Slide 3 in the Slide pane.
   b. Click the Text Box button on the Drawing toolbar.
   c. Drag in the slide to create a text box approximately the size shown at the right.
   d. Open Microsoft Word.

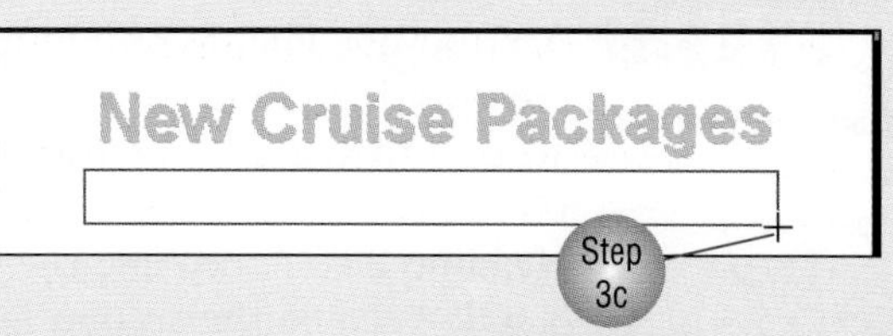

e. Open the file named **NewCruises** from the PowerPointChapter06S folder on your disk.
f. Select the text from the heading *Worldwide Cruises* through the paragraph in the *Somerset Cruises* section (see figure at the right).
g. Click the Copy button on the Standard toolbar.
h. Close the **NewCruises** file.
i. Exit Microsoft Word.
j. In PowerPoint, click the Paste button on the Standard toolbar.
k. Click at the beginning of the heading *Somerset Cruises* and then press the Enter key.
l. Select the text inside the placeholder and then change the font size to 20.
m. If necessary, move the text box so it is positioned as shown in Figure 6.2.

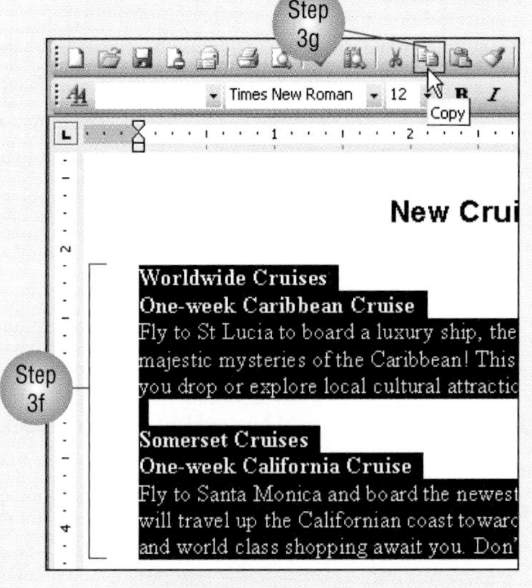

4. Display Slide 1 in the Slide pane and then run the presentation.
5. Print only Slide 3.
6. Save and then close the presentation.

FIGURE 6.2 ***Slide 3, Exercise 2***

New Cruise Packages

Worldwide Cruises
One-week Caribbean Cruise
Fly to St Lucia to board a luxury ship, then relax and enjoy as the next 7 days unveil the majestic mysteries of the Caribbean! This cruise will stop at 5 ports so you can shop till you drop or explore local cultural attractions. Call us today to check availability.

Somerset Cruises
One-week California Cruise
Fly to Santa Monica and board the newest luxury ship in the Somerset fleet. This cruise will travel up the Californian coast towards San Francisco. Mystic sunsets, ocean breezes, and world class shopping await you. Don't delay -- this package will sell fast.

Importing Data

Import Word Data to PowerPoint
1. Open Word.
2. Open document.
3. Click File, Send To, Microsoft Office PowerPoint.

A Word document containing heading styles can be imported into a PowerPoint presentation. To do this, open the document in Word, click File, point to Send To, and then click Microsoft Office PowerPoint. Paragraphs formatted with a Heading 1 style become the title of a new slide. Paragraphs formatted with a Heading 2 style become the first level of text, paragraphs formatted as a Heading 3 style become the second level, and so on. PowerPoint creates a presentation with the imported text using the Blank Presentation template. After importing the text into PowerPoint, apply the desired formatting, or apply a design template.

Changing the Slide Layout

Text imported from Word into PowerPoint is inserted in a slide with a specific slide layout. In some cases, this slide layout is appropriate for the imported text. In other cases, you may need to change the layout. To do this, click Format on the Menu bar, and then click Slide Layout at the drop-down list. Click the desired layout at the Slide Layout task pane.

exercise 3

IMPORTING TEXT FROM WORD

1. Make sure PowerPoint is open and then open Microsoft Word.
2. With Word the active program, open **WordOutline01** (located in the PowerPointChapter06S folder on your disk).
3. Import the document (formatted with Heading 1 and Heading 2 styles) into PowerPoint by clicking File, pointing to Send To, and then clicking Microsoft Office PowerPoint.
4. With Slide 1 of the presentation displayed in PowerPoint, change the slide layout for Slide 1 by completing the following steps:
   a. Click Format and then Slide Layout.
   b. Click the Title Slide layout in the Slide Layout task pane.
5. Click the Slide Design button on the Formatting toolbar and then click the *Satellite Dish* design template in the *Apply a design template* list box at the Slide Design task pane. (You will need to scroll down the list to display this template.)
6. Make the following changes to the presentation:
   a. Increase the font size and/or line spacing of the bulleted text in Slides 2 through 4 so the bulleted lists are better spaced on the slides.
   b. Consider inserting an appropriate clip art image in one or two of the slides.
   c. Add a transition and sound of your choosing to each slide.
7. Save the presentation and name it **sppc6x03**.
8. Run the presentation.
9. Print the presentation as handouts with all four slides on the same page.
10. Save and then close the presentation.
11. Make Word the active program, close **WordOutline01**, and then exit Word.

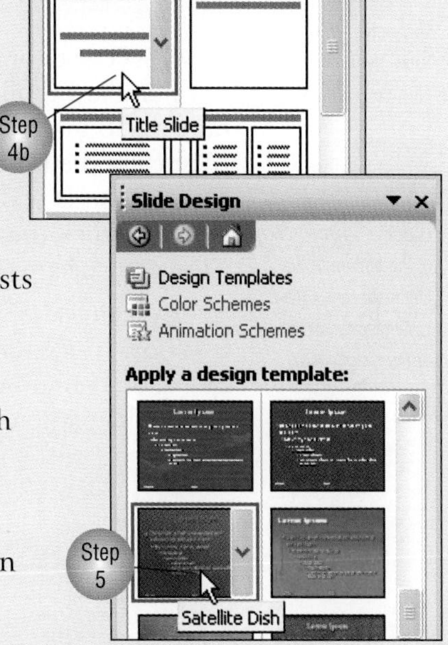

Using the Clipboard Task Pane

Use the Clipboard task pane to collect and paste multiple items. You can collect up to 24 different items and then paste them in various locations. Turn on the display of the Clipboard task pane by clicking Edit and then Office Clipboard or by clicking the Other task panes button (displays as a down-pointing arrow) located in the upper right corner of the current task pane, and then clicking Clipboard at the drop-down list. The Clipboard task pane displays at the right side of the screen in a manner similar to what you see in Figure 6.3.

HINT
To delete one item from the Clipboard task pane, point to the item, click the down-pointing arrow, and then click Delete.

FIGURE 6.3 *Clipboard Task Pane*

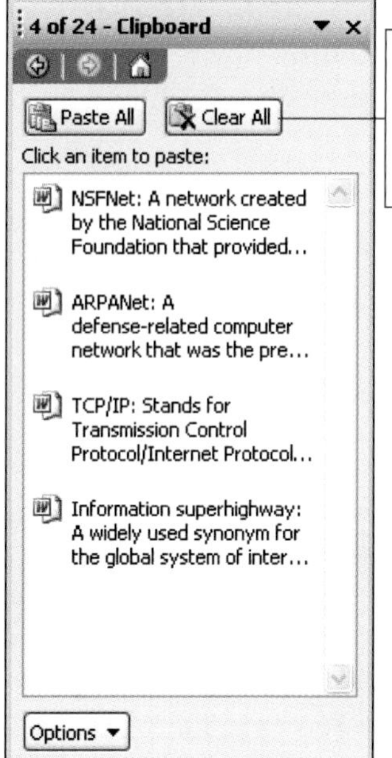

Click this button to clear all items from the Clipboard task pane.

Copy Item to Clipboard Task Pane
1. Click Edit, Office Clipboard.
2. Select item.
3. Click Copy button.

HINT
Click the Options button at the bottom of the Clipboard task pane to customize the display of the task pane.

Select data or an object you want to copy and then click the Copy button on the Standard toolbar. Continue selecting text or items and clicking the Copy button. To insert an item, position the insertion point in the desired location and then click the button in the Clipboard task pane representing the item. If the copied item is text, the first 50 characters display. When all desired items are inserted, click the Clear All button to remove any remaining items from the Clipboard task pane.

In Exercise 2, you drew a text box in a slide and then pasted text inside the text box. In Exercise 4, you will copy text in a Word document and then paste it in a slide containing a bulleted list placeholder. Since the slide contains a placeholder where you can insert the text, you do not need to draw a text box.

exercise 4 COLLECTING TEXT IN WORD AND PASTING IT IN A POWERPOINT SLIDE

1. In PowerPoint, open **sppc6x03**.
2. Save the presentation with Save As and name it **sppc6x04**.
3. Create a new Slide 5 by completing the following steps:
   a. Display Slide 4 and then click the New Slide button on the Formatting toolbar.
   b. Click the text *Click to add title* and then type **Internet Terminology**.
   c. Click the text *Click to add text* and then copy terms from Word and paste them into slides by completing the following steps:
      1) Open Word and then open **WordTerms**.
      2) Display the Clipboard task pane by clicking Edit and then Office Clipboard.
      3) If any data displays in the Clipboard task pane, click the Clear All button located toward the top of the task pane.

4) Select the first term *(Information superhighway)* and its definition by triple-clicking with the mouse.
5) With the term and definition selected, click the Copy button on the Standard toolbar. (Notice that the copied item displays in the Clipboard task pane.)
6) Select the second term *(TCP/IP)* and its definition and then click the Copy button.

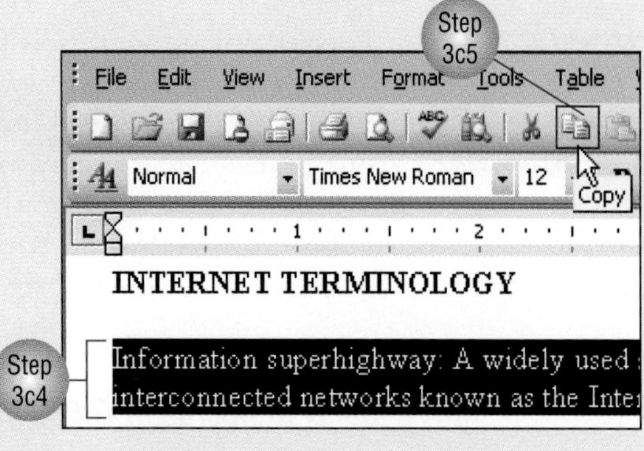

7) Select the third term *(ARPANet)* and its definition and then click the Copy button on the Clipboard toolbar.
8) Select the fourth term *(NSFNet)* and its definition and then click the Copy button on the Clipboard toolbar.
9) Click the button on the Taskbar representing **sppc6x04**.
10) Click Edit and then Office Clipboard to display the Clipboard task pane.
11) Make sure the insertion point is positioned in the bulleted list placeholder and then click the item on the Clipboard task pane representing the term *ARPANet*.
12) Press the Enter key.
13) Click the item on the Clipboard task pane representing the term *Information superhighway*.

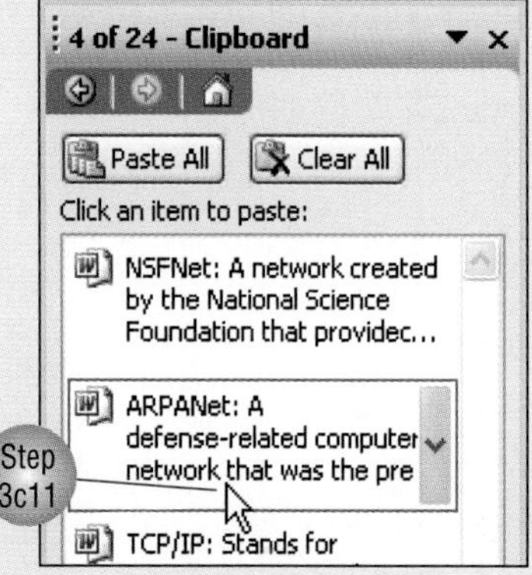

4. Create a new Slide 6 by completing the following steps:
   a. Click the New Slide button on the Standard toolbar.
   b. Click the text *Click to add title* and then type **Internet Terminology**.
   c. Click the text *Click to add text* and then paste terms in the slide by completing the following steps:
      1) Display the Clipboard task pane by clicking the Other Task Panes button (displays with the current task pane name and a down-pointing arrow) located towards the top of the task pane and then clicking *Clipboard* at the drop-down list.
      2) Make sure the insertion point is positioned in the bulleted list placeholder and then click the item on the Clipboard task pane representing the term *NFSNet*.
      3) Press the Enter key.
      4) Click the item on the Clipboard task pane representing the term *TCP/IP*.
5. Clear the Clipboard task pane by clicking the Clear All button located in the upper right corner of the task pane.
6. Close the Clipboard task pane by clicking the Close button (contains an *X*) located in the upper right corner of the task pane.
7. Make Slide 1 the active slide and then run the presentation.
8. Print the six slides on one page.
9. Save and then close the presentation.
10. Make Word the active program, close **WordTerms**, and then exit Word.

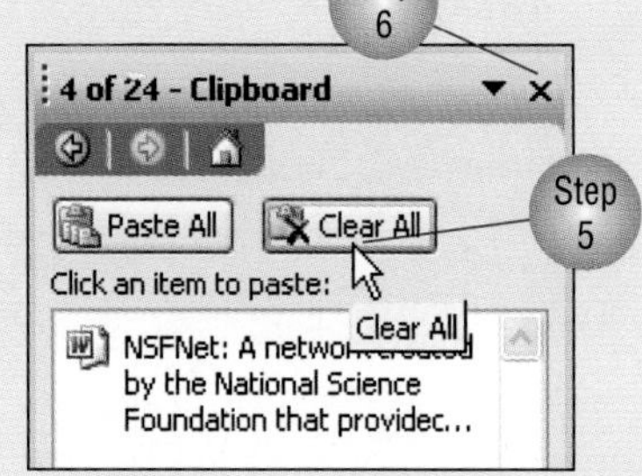

Exporting an Outline to Word

Export Outline to Word
1. Open presentation.
2. Click File, Send To, Microsoft Office Word.

A PowerPoint presentation can be exported to a Word document which can then be edited and formatted using Word's capabilities. You can print slides as handouts in PowerPoint; however, you may prefer to export the presentation to Word to have greater control over the formatting of the handouts. To export the presentation that is currently open, click File, point to Send To, and then click Microsoft Office Word. At the Send To Microsoft Office Word dialog box shown in Figure 6.4, select the page layout you want to use in Word, and then click OK.

FIGURE 6.4 **Send To Microsoft Office Word Dialog Box**

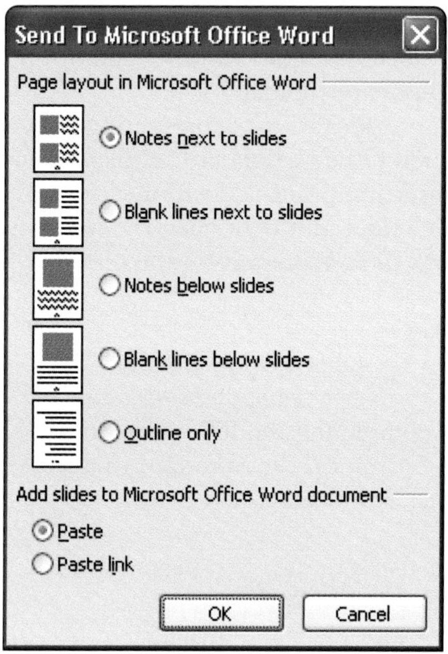

The first four page layout options will export slides as they appear in PowerPoint with lines to the right or below the slides. The last option will export the text only as an outline. If you select the *Paste link* option, the Word document will automatically be updated whenever changes are made to the PowerPoint presentation.

exercise 5

EXPORTING A PRESENTATION AS AN OUTLINE TO WORD

1. Open **PotentialPresentation**.
2. Create an outline in Word by completing the following steps:
   a. Click File, point to Send To, and then click Microsoft Office Word.
   b. At the Send To Microsoft Office Word dialog box, click the *Outline only* option.
   c. Click OK.
3. Save the Word document in the PowerPointChapter06S folder on your disk and name it **WordPotentialOutline**.
4. Click the Print button on the Standard toolbar to print **WordPotentialOutline**.
5. Close **WordPotentialOutline** and then exit Word.
6. In PowerPoint, close **PotentialPresentation**.

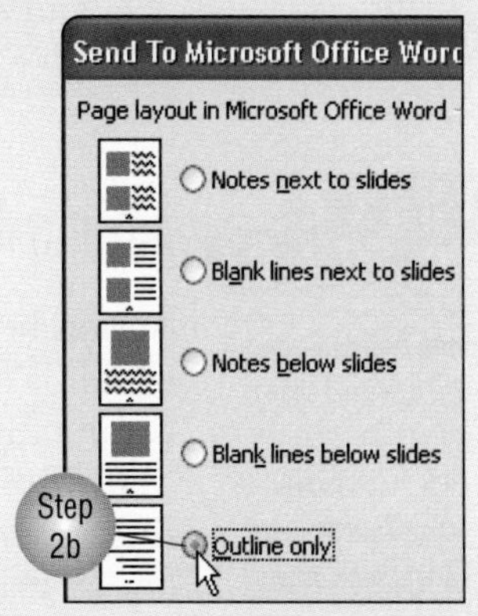

Saving a Presentation as an Outline/RTF

With the *Save as type* option at the Save As dialog box, you can save a presentation in a different format such as a Web page, a previous version of PowerPoint, a design template, and as an outline in rich text format (RTF). In Exercise 6, you will use the *Outline/RTF* option to save a PowerPoint presentation as an outline in Word in rich text format. In this format, the presentation loses graphical elements but retains the character formatting of the presentation.

Save Presentation as an Outline/RTF
1. Click File, Save As.
2. Type presentation name.
3. Click *Save as type* option.
4. Click *Outline/RTF*.

exercise 6

SAVING A PRESENTATION IN OUTLINE/RTF FORMAT

1. Open **DesignPresentation**.
2. Save the presentation as a Word outline in rich text format by completing the following steps:
   a. Click File and then Save As.
   b. At the Save As dialog box, type **DesignOutline** in the *File name* text box.
   c. Click the down-pointing arrow at the right side of the *Save as type* option box and then click *Outline/RTF* at the drop-down list. (You will need to scroll to the end of the list to display this option.)
   d. Change the *Save in* option to the *PowerPointChapter06S* folder on your disk.
   e. Click the Save button.
3. Close **DesignPresentation**.
4. Open and then close the **DesignOutline** document in Word by completing the following steps:
   a. Open Word.
   b. Click the Open button on the Standard toolbar.
   c. At the Open dialog box, change the *Look in* option to the *PowerPointChapter06S* folder on your disk.

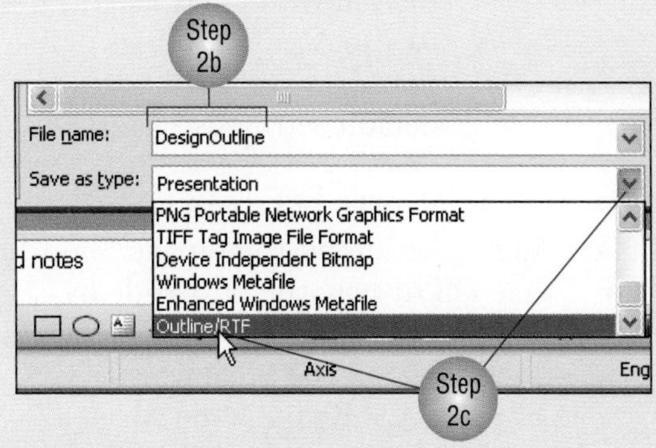

d. Double-click ***DesignOutline*** in the file list box.
e. With the **DesignOutline** document open, click the Print button on the Standard toolbar.
f. Click File and then Close to close the **DesignOutline** document.

5. Exit Word.

QUICK STEPS

Create Action Button

1. Make desired slide active.
2. Click AutoShapes, Action Buttons.
3. Click desired action button.
4. Drag in slide to create button.
5. Make desired change at Action Settings dialog box.

Adding Action Buttons

Action buttons are drawn objects on a slide that have a routine attached to them which is activated when the viewer or the speaker clicks the button. They contain commonly understood symbols. For example, you could include an action button that displays a specific Web page, a file in another program, or the next slide in the presentation. Creating an action button is a two-step process. The button is drawn using the AutoShapes button on the Drawing toolbar and then the action that will take place is defined in the Action Settings dialog box. Once an action button has been created it can be customized using the same techniques employed for customizing drawn objects. When the viewer or speaker moves the mouse over an action button during a presentation, the pointer changes to a hand with a finger pointing upward to indicate clicking will result in an action.

exercise 7

ADDING ACTION BUTTONS

1. Open **JobSearchPresentation.**
2. Save the presentation with Save As and name it **sppc6x07.**
3. Add an action button that will display the next slide on the title slide by completing the following steps:
   a. Make sure Slide 1 displays in the Slide pane.
   b. Draw an action button in the lower right corner of Slide 1 by completing the following steps:
      1) Click the AutoShapes button on the Drawing toolbar, point to Action Buttons, and then click Action Button: Forward or Next (second option from the left in the second row).
      2) Move the crosshair pointer to the lower right corner of Slide 1 and drag to create a button that is approximately .5 inch in width and height.
      3) At the Action Settings dialog box that displays, click OK. (The default setting is *Hyperlink to Next Slide.*)
      4) Deselect the action button.
4. Add an action button on the Slide Master that will display the next slide by completing the following steps:
   a. Change to the Slide Master view.
   b. Click the Radial Slide Master miniature in the Outline/Slides pane.

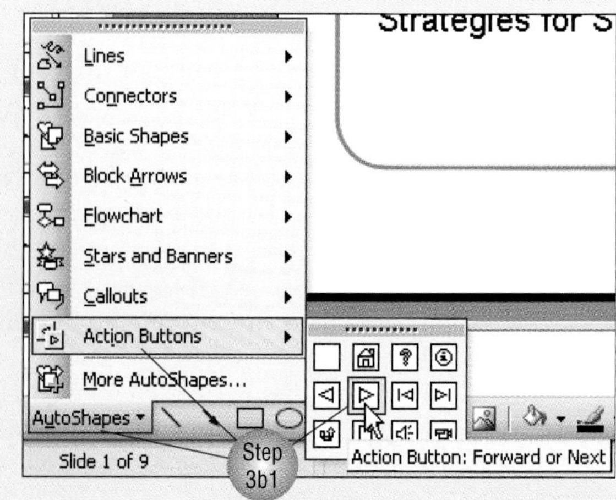

c. Click the AutoShapes button on the Drawing toolbar, point to Action Buttons, and then click Action Button: Forward or Next (second option from the left in the second row).
d. Move the crosshair pointer to the lower right corner of the Slide Master and drag to create a button that is approximately .5 inch in width and height. (The button will overlap the Number Area on the Slide Master. Creating the action button on the slide master means the button will automatically appear on all slides except the title slide.)
e. At the Action Settings dialog box, click OK. (The default setting is *Hyperlink to Next Slide*.)
f. Click the Normal View button on the View toolbar.
5. Click the Slide Show button on the View toolbar and then navigate through the slide show by clicking the action button. At the last slide, click in the slide (outside the action button).
6. Save and then close the presentation.

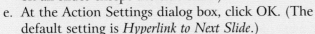

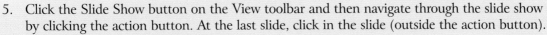

In Exercise 7, creating the action button on the Slide Master saved the work of drawing a button on each slide. However, the next slide action button on the last slide does not make sense since there is no next slide. In the next exercise you will create action buttons using the copy and paste routine, which will still be efficient but allows you to control to which slide a button is pasted.

8 COPYING AND PASTING ACTION BUTTONS

1. Open **PotentialPresentation**.
2. Save the presentation with Save As and name it **sppc6x08**.
3. Add an action button that will display the next slide on the title slide by completing the following steps:
   a. Make sure Slide 1 displays in the Slide pane.
   b. Draw an action button in the lower right corner of Slide 1 that will display the next slide by completing steps similar to those in Exercise 7, Step 3b (except do not deselect the action button).
   c. With the action button selected, click the down-pointing arrow at the right of the Fill Color button on the Drawing toolbar, and then click the green color.
   d. With the action button still selected, click the Copy button on the Standard toolbar.
   e. Display Slide 2 and then click the Paste button on the toolbar.
   f. Paste the action button to Slides 3 through 5.
4. Create an action button on the last slide that returns to the beginning of the presentation by completing the following steps:
   a. Display Slide 6 in the Slide pane.
   b. Click AutoShapes, point to Action Buttons, and then click Action Button: Home (second from the left in the first row).

c. Drag to create a button in the lower right corner of Slide 6 that is approximately .5 inch in width and height.
d. At the Action Settings dialog box with the *Hyperlink to First Slide* option selected, click OK.
e. With the button selected, click the Fill Color button on the Drawing toolbar. (This changes the color of the button to green.)
f. Deselect the button.

5. Display Slide 1 in the Slide pane and then run the presentation. Navigate through the slide show by clicking the action button. When you click the action button on the last slide the first slide displays. End the slide show by pressing the Esc key.
6. Print the presentation as handouts with all six slides on one page.
7. Save and then close the presentation.

Hyperlinks are active when running the presentation, not when creating it.

You can specify that an action button links to a Web site during a presentation. To do this, draw an Action button. At the Action Settings dialog box, click the *Hyperlink to* option, click the down-pointing arrow at the right side of the *Hyperlink to* option box, and then click URL at the drop-down list. At the Hyperlink To URL dialog box, type the Web address in the URL text box, and then click OK. Click OK to close the Action Settings dialog box.

Other actions you can link to using the *Hyperlink to* drop-down list include: Next Slide, Previous Slide, First Slide, Last Slide, Last Slide Viewed, End Show, Custom Show, Slide, Other PowerPoint Presentation, and Other File. The Action Settings dialog box can also be used to run another program when the action button is selected, run a macro, or activate an embedded object.

exercise 9 LINKING TO A WEB SITE AND ANOTHER PRESENTATION

1. Open **JobSearchPresentation**.
2. Save the presentation with Save As and name it **sppc6x09**.
3. Add an action button that will link to another presentation by completing the following steps:
   a. Display Slide 4 in the Slide pane.
   b. Click AutoShapes, point to Action Buttons, and then click Action Button: Help (third from the left in the top row).
   c. Draw the action button in the lower right corner of Slide 4. (You determine the size of the button.)
   d. At the Action Settings dialog box, click the *Hyperlink to* option.
   e. Click the down-pointing arrow at the right side of the *Hyperlink to* option box and then click *Other PowerPoint Presentation* at the drop-down list. (You will need to scroll down the list to display this option.)

f. At the Hyperlink to Other PowerPoint Presentation dialog box, navigate to the PowerPointChapter06S folder on your disk, and then double-click the presentation named ***ContactsPresentation***.

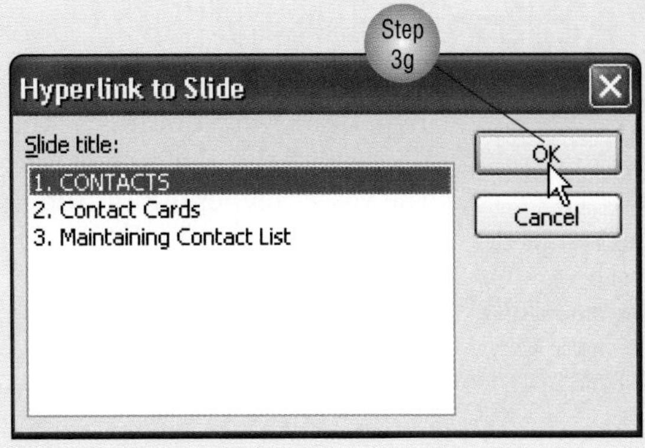

g. At the Hyperlink to Slide dialog box, click OK.
h. Click OK to close the Action Settings dialog box.
i. With the button selected, click the down-pointing arrow at the right side of the Fill Color button on the Drawing toolbar, and then click a color of your choosing that follows the color scheme of the design template.
j. Deselect the action button.

4. Add an action button that will link to a Web site address by completing the following steps:
   a. Display Slide 5 in the Slide pane.
   b. Click AutoShapes, point to Action Buttons, and then click Action Button: Information (fourth from the left in the top row).
   c. Draw the action button in the lower right corner of Slide 5.
   d. At the Action Settings dialog box, click the *Hyperlink to* option.
   e. Click the down-pointing arrow at the right of the *Hyperlink to* option box, and then click *URL* at the drop-down list.
   f. At the Hyperlink To URL dialog box, type **www.employment-resources.com** and then press Enter.
   g. Click OK to close the Action Settings dialog box.
   h. With the button selected, click the Fill Color button on the Drawing toolbar.
   i. Click outside the button to deselect it.
5. Run the presentation by completing the following steps:
   a. Make sure you are connected to the Internet.
   b. Display Slide 1 in the Slide pane.
   c. Click the Slide Show button on the View toolbar.
   d. Navigate through the slide show to Slide 4.
   e. Click the action button on Slide 4. (This displays Slide 1 of the **ContactsPresentation**.)
   f. Navigate through the three slides in the **ContactsPresentation**. Continue clicking the mouse button until you return to Slide 4 of the **sppc6x09** presentation.
   g. Display Slide 5 and then click the action button. (If you are connected to the Internet, the Employment Resources Web site displays.)
   h. Click a few links at the Employment Resources Web site.
   i. When you are finished with the site, close Internet Explorer (click File and then Close).
   j. Continue viewing the remainder of the presentation.
6. Print the presentation as handouts with all nine slides on one page.
7. Save and then close the presentation.

QUICK STEPS

Create Hyperlink
1. Make desired slide active.
2. Select text.
3. Click Insert Hyperlink button.
4. Type Web address or file name in *Address* text box.

Creating Hyperlinks

In Exercise 9, you created hyperlinks using action buttons. You can also create hyperlinks with options at the Insert Hyperlink dialog box shown in Figure 6.5. To display this dialog box, select a key word or phrase in a slide, and then click the Insert Hyperlink button on the Standard toolbar. At the Insert Hyperlink dialog box, type the Web address in the *Address* text box, and then click OK.

FIGURE 6.5 ***Insert Hyperlink Dialog Box***

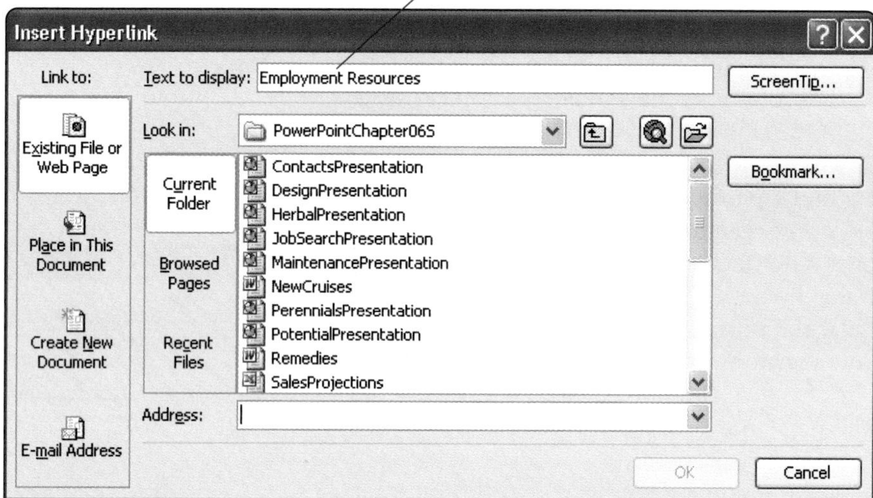

exercise 10

ADDING A SLIDE WITH HYPERLINKS

1. Open **JobSearchPresentation**.
2. Save the presentation with Save As and name it **sppc6x10**.
3. Add a new Slide 6 by completing the following steps:
   a. Display Slide 5 in the Slide pane.
   b. Click the New Slide button on the Formatting toolbar.
   c. Click the Title Slide layout in the Slide Layout task pane.
   d. Click the text *Click to add title* and then type **Internet Job Resources**.
   e. Click the text *Click to add subtitle* and then type **Employment Resources**, press Enter, and then type **America's Job Bank**.
4. Add a hyperlink to the Employment Resources site by completing the following steps:
   a. Select *Employment Resources* in Slide 6.
   b. Click the Insert Hyperlink button on the Standard toolbar.

c. At the Insert Hyperlink dialog box, type www.employment-resources.com in the *Address* text box. (PowerPoint automatically inserts *http://* at the beginning of the address.)
d. Click OK.

5. Add a hyperlink to the America's Job Bank site by completing the following steps:
   a. Select *America's Job Bank* in Slide 6.
   b. Click the Insert Hyperlink button on the Standard toolbar.
   c. At the Insert Hyperlink dialog box, type www.ajb.dni.us in the *Address* text box.
   d. Click OK.

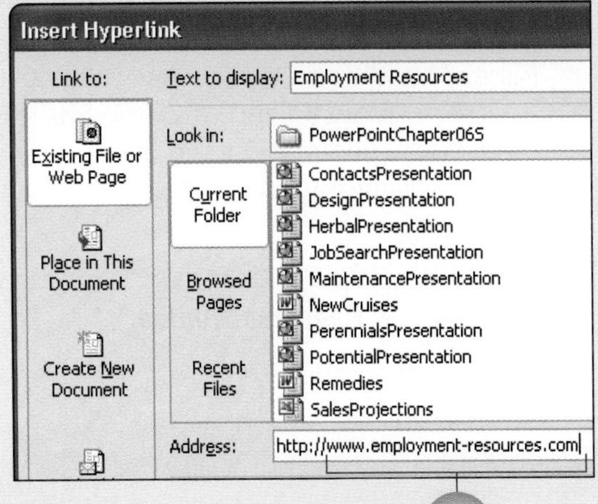

6. Run the presentation by completing the following steps:
   a. Make sure you are connected to the Internet.
   b. Display Slide 1 in the Slide pane.
   c. Click the Slide Show button on the View toolbar.
   d. Navigate through the slides. When you reach Slide 6, click the Employment Resources hyperlink.
   e. Scroll through the employment site and then close Internet Explorer.
   f. Click the America's Job Bank hyperlink.
   g. Scroll through the America's Job Bank site and then close Internet Explorer.
   h. Continue viewing the remainder of the presentation.
7. Print only Slide 6 of the presentation.
8. Save and then close the presentation.

Setting Automatic Times for Slides

Set Automatic Times for Slides
1. Display presentation in Slide Sorter view.
2. Click Rehearse Timings button.
3. Using Rehearsal toolbar, specify time for each slide.
4. Click Yes.

Rehearse Timings

The time a slide remains on the screen during a slide show can be manually set using the *Automatically after* option at the Slide Transition task pane. Type the number of seconds in the seconds text box and the time is applied to the current slide. If you want the time to apply to all slides in the presentation, click the Apply to All Slides button.

Applying the same time to all slides is not very practical unless the same amount of text occurs on every slide. In most cases, some slides should be left on the screen longer than others. Use the Rehearse Timings feature to help set the times for slides as you practice delivering the slide show.

To set times for slides using Rehearse Timings, click Slide Show and then Rehearse Timings or display the presentation in Slide Sorter view, and then click the Rehearse Timings button on the Slide Sorter toolbar. The first slide displays in Slide Show view and the Rehearsal toolbar displays on the slide. The buttons on the Rehearsal toolbar are identified in Figure 6.6.

Next

Pause

Repeat

When the slide displays on the screen, the timer on the Rehearsal toolbar begins. Click the Next button on the Rehearsal toolbar when the slide has displayed for the appropriate amount of time. If you want to stop the timer, click the Pause button. Click the Pause button again to resume the timer. Use the Repeat button on the Rehearsal toolbar if you get off track and want to reset the time for the current slide. Continue through the presentation until the slide show is complete. After the last slide, a message displays showing the total time for the presentation and asks if you want to record the new slide timings. At this message, click Yes to set the times for each slide recorded during the rehearsal.

FIGURE 6.6 **Rehearsal Toolbar**

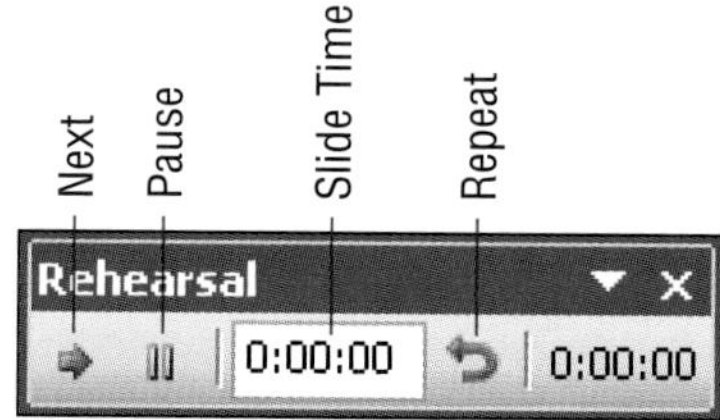

HINT

If your computer is equipped with a sound card, microphone, and speakers, you can record a voice narration for a presentation.

Use options at the Set Up Show dialog box shown in Figure 6.7 to control the slide show. Display this dialog box by clicking Slide Show and then Set Up Show. Use options in the *Show type* section to specify the type of slide show you want to display. If you want the presentation to be totally automatic and run continuously until you end the show, click the *Loop continuously until 'Esc'* check box to insert a check mark. In the *Advance slides* section, the *Using timings, if present* option should be selected by default. Select *Manually* if you want to advance the slides using the mouse during the slide show instead of the slides advancing using your preset times.

FIGURE 6.7 **Set Up Show Dialog Box**

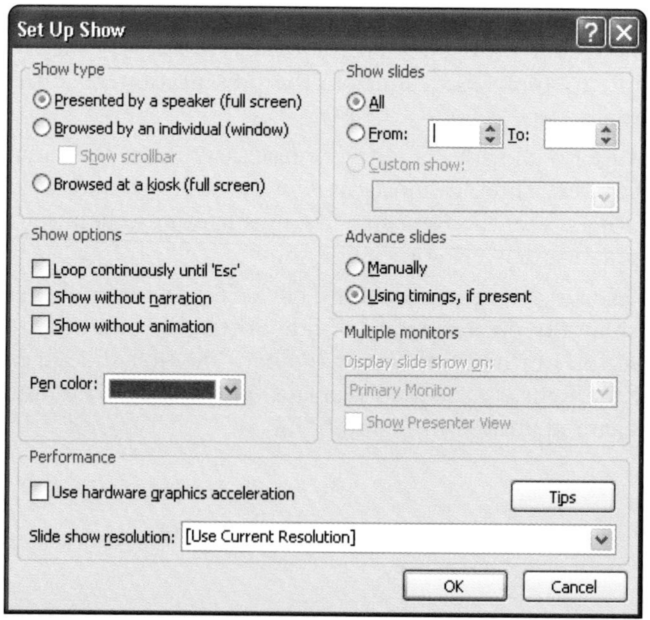

exercise 11

USING REHEARSE TIMINGS TO SET TIMES FOR SLIDES

1. Open **JobSearchPresentation**.
2. Save the presentation with Save As and name it **sppc6x11**.
3. Set times for the slides to display during a slide show by completing the following steps:
   a. Display the presentation in Slide Sorter view.
   b. Click the Rehearse Timings button on the Slide Sorter toolbar.
   c. The first slide displays in Slide Show view and the Rehearsal toolbar displays. Wait until the time displayed for the current slide reaches four seconds and then click Next. (If you miss the time, click the Repeat button to reset the clock back to zero for the current slide.)

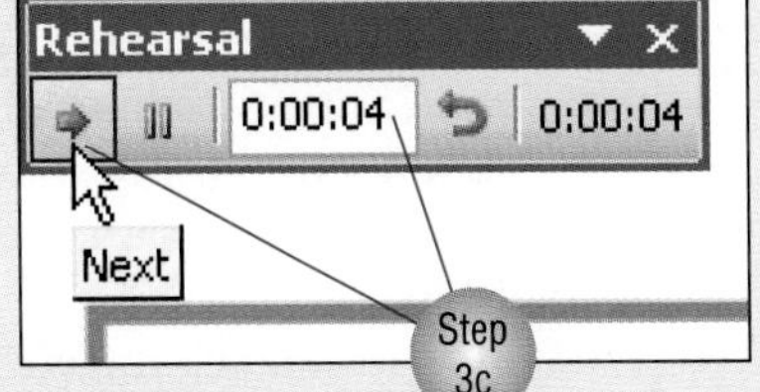

   d. Set the times for remaining slides as follows:
      Slide 2 8 seconds
      Slide 3 6 seconds
      Slide 4 8 seconds
      Slide 5 4 seconds
      Slide 6 6 seconds
      Slide 7 8 seconds
      Slide 8 8 seconds
      Slide 9 6 seconds
   e. After the last slide has displayed, click Yes at the message asking if you want to record the new slide timings.
4. Set up the slide show to run continuously by completing the following steps:
   a. Click Slide Show and then select Set Up Show.
   b. At the Set Up Show dialog box, click the *Loop continuously until 'Esc'* check box.
   c. Click OK to close the Set Up Show dialog box.

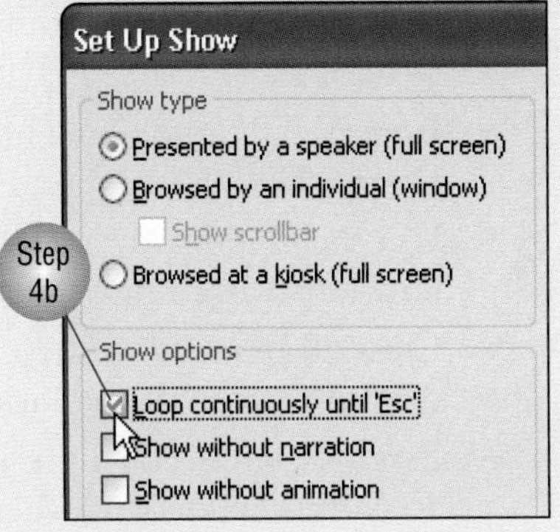

5. Click Slide 1 and then click the Slide Show button on the View toolbar. The slide show will start and run continuously. Watch the presentation until it has started for the second time and then end the show by pressing the Esc key.
6. Save and then close the presentation.

Creating a Summary Slide

A summary slide is a slide created by PowerPoint that lists the titles of the other slides in your presentation. Create a summary slide if you want to include a slide at the beginning of the presentation that outlines what topics will follow. To create a summary slide, change to the Slide Sorter view, click the slides you want included in the summary slide, and then click the Summary Slide button on the Slide Sorter toolbar. The Summary Slide is inserted immediately before the first selected slide and includes the titles from the selected slides in a bulleted list.

Create Summary Slide
1. Display presentation in Slide Sorter view.
2. Select specific slides.
3. Click Summary Slide button.

Summary Slide

exercise 12

CREATING A SUMMARY SLIDE

1. Open **JobSearchPresentation**.
2. Save the presentation with Save As and name it **sppc6x12**.
3. Create a summary slide between Slides 1 and 2 by completing the following steps:
   a. Display the presentation in Slide Sorter view.
   b. Click Slide 2 to select it, hold down the Shift key, and then click Slide 9. (This selects Slides 2 through 9.)
   c. Click the Summary Slide button on the Slide Sorter toolbar. (This creates a new Slide 2 containing the titles of Slides 2 through 9 in a bulleted list.)

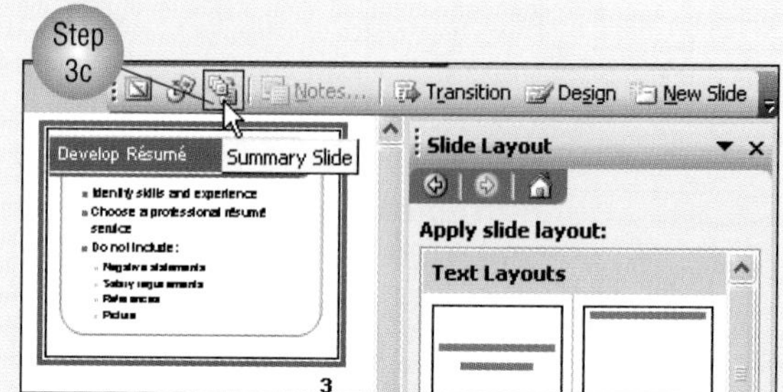

4. Display Slide 1 in Normal view.
5. Run the presentation. (Notice the new summary slide [Slide 2].)
6. Print only Slide 2.
7. Save and then close the presentation.

CHAPTER summary

- Use the Copy and Paste buttons on the Standard toolbar to copy data from one program to another.
- Import a Word document into a PowerPoint presentation by opening the document in Word, clicking File, pointing to Send To, and then clicking Microsoft Office PowerPoint.
- Use the Clipboard task pane to collect up to 24 different items and paste them in various locations within or between programs.
- Clear all items from the Clipboard task pane by clicking the Clear All button located toward the top of the task pane.
- Export a PowerPoint presentation to a Word document by clicking File, pointing to Send To, and then clicking Microsoft Office Word. Choose the desired page layout for the Word document at the Send To Microsoft Office Word dialog box.
- Save a presentation in a different format, such as Outline/RTF format, with the *Save as type* option at the Save As dialog box.
- Action buttons are drawn objects on a slide that have a routine attached, such as displaying the next slide, the first slide, a Web site, or another PowerPoint presentation.
- Create an action button by clicking the AutoShapes button on the Drawing toolbar, pointing to Action Buttons, and then clicking the desired button. Drag in the slide to create the button.
- Create a hyperlink in a document by selecting text in the slide and then clicking the Insert Hyperlink button on the Standard toolbar. At the Insert Hyperlink dialog box, type the Web site address or file location, and then click OK.

- Set times for slides by clicking Slide Show and then Rehearse Timings or displaying the presentation in Slide Sorter view and then clicking the Rehearse Timings button on the Slide Sorter toolbar. Use the timer and buttons on the Rehearsal toolbar to establish specific times for each slide.
- Use options at the Set Up Show dialog to control the slide show.
- A summary slide lists the titles of the other slides in a presentation. Create a summary slide by displaying the presentation in Slide Sorter view, clicking the slides to be included, and then clicking the Summary Slide button on the Slide Sorter toolbar.

FEATURES summary

FEATURE	BUTTON	MENU	KEYBOARD
Import Word document in PowerPoint presentation		File, Send To, Microsoft Office PowerPoint	
Display Clipboard task pane		Edit, Office Clipboard	
Export presentation to Word document		File, Send To, Microsoft Office Word	
Display action buttons		AutoShapes, Action Buttons	
Display Insert Hyperlink dialog box		Insert, Hyperlink	Ctrl + K
Display Rehearsal toolbar		Slide Show, Rehearse Timings	
Display Set Up Show dialog box		Slide Show, Set Up Show	
Create summary slide			

CONCEPTS check

Completion: On a blank sheet of paper, indicate the correct term, symbol, or command for each description.

1. Use the Copy and Paste buttons on this toolbar to copy data from one program to another.
2. To import a Word document into a PowerPoint presentation, click File on the Menu bar, point to this option, and then click Microsoft Office PowerPoint.
3. Using the Clipboard task pane, you can collect up to this number of items and then paste them in various locations.
4. Click Edit on the Menu bar and then click this option to display the Clipboard task pane.
5. Click this button in the Clipboard task pane to remove all items from the task pane.
6. With this option at the Save As dialog box, you can save a presentation in a different format.

7. Insert this action button in a slide to display the next slide in the presentation.
8. Insert this action button in a slide to display the first slide in the presentation.
9. Draw an action button in a slide and this dialog box displays.
10. To rehearse times for slides, display the presentation in Slide Sorter view, and then click this button on the Slide Sorter toolbar.
11. Click this button on the Rehearsal toolbar if you get off track and want to reset the time for the current slide.
12. This dialog box contains the *Loop continuously until 'Esc'* option.

SKILLS check

Assessment 1

1. Open **HerbalPresentation**.
2. Save the presentation with Save As and name it **sppc6sc01**.
3. Copy and paste an Excel chart to Slide 2 by completing the following steps:
   a. Display Slide 2 in the Slide pane.
   b. Open Excel and then open the workbook named **SalesProjections** (located in the PowerPointChapter06S folder).
   c. Copy the chart to Slide 2 in the presentation.
   d. Resize and move the chart so it fills most of the slide below the title.
   e. Display the **SalesProjections** workbook, close the workbook, and then exit Excel.
4. Copy and paste text from Word to Slide 4 and Slide 5 by completing the following steps:
   a. Display Slide 4 in the Slide pane.
   b. Draw a text box in the slide.
   c. Open Word and then open the document named **Remedies**.
   d. Copy the first three terms and paragraphs in the document to the text box in Slide 4.
   e. Add a blank line above *Chamomile* and above *Evening Primrose Oil*.
   f. Select the text in the placeholder and change the font size to 24 and turn on bold.
   g. Move and/or resize the placeholder so it fills most of the slide below the title.
5. Copy and paste the last two terms and paragraphs in the **Remedies** document to Slide 5 following steps similar to those in Step 4.
6. Apply an animation scheme of your choosing to the slides in the presentation. (The animation scheme will not apply to Slide 1 because the slide contains only WordArt.)
7. Run the presentation beginning with Slide 1.
8. Print the presentation as handouts with all six slides on one page.
9. Save and then close the presentation.

Assessment 2

1. Open **sppc6sc01**.
2. Export the presentation to Word as an outline.
3. Save the Word document in the PowerPointChapter06S folder on your disk and name it **WordHerbalOutline**.
4. Click the Print button on the Standard toolbar to print **WordHerbalOutline**.
5. Close **WordHerbalOutline** and then exit Word.
6. In PowerPoint, close the **sppc6sc01** presentation.

Assessment 3

1. Make sure PowerPoint is open and then open Word.
2. With Word the active program, open **WordOutline02** (located in the PowerPointChapter06S folder on your disk).
3. Import the document into PowerPoint.
4. Make the following changes to the presentation:
   a. With Slide 1 of the presentation displayed in PowerPoint, change the slide layout to Title Slide.
   b. Apply the Cascade slide design template to all slides in the presentation.
   c. Increase the font size and/or line spacing of the bulleted text in Slides 2 through 4 so the bulleted lists are better spaced in the slides.
   d. Consider inserting an appropriate clip art image in one or two of the slides.
   e. Apply an animation scheme of your choosing to all slides in the presentation.
5. Save the presentation and name it **sppc6sc03**.
6. Run the presentation.
7. Print the presentation as handouts with all four slides on the same page.
8. Save and then close the presentation.
9. Make Word the active program, close **WordOutline02**, and then exit Word.

Assessment 4

1. Open **PerennialsPresentation**.
2. Save the presentation with Save As and name it **sppc6sc04**.
3. Create the following action buttons:
   a. Insert an action button in the lower right corner of Slides 1 through 7 that displays the next slide (change to a fill color that matches the design template color scheme).
   b. Insert an action button in the lower right corner of Slide 8 that displays the first slide in the presentation.
   c. Insert a second action button in the lower right corner of Slide 2 that will link to another PowerPoint presentation named **MaintenancePresentation** (located in the PowerPointChapter06S folder).
4. Display Slide 8 and then create a hyperlink with the text *Better Homes and Gardens* that connects to the Web site www.bhg.com.
5. Make sure you are connected to the Internet and then run the presentation beginning with Slide 1. Navigate through the slide show by clicking the next action button and display the connected presentation by clicking the information action button. At Slide 8, click the Better Homes and Gardens hyperlink (if you are connected to the Internet). Scroll through the site and click a couple different hyperlinks that interest you. After viewing a few Web pages in the magazine, close your Web browser. When you click the action button on the last slide, the first slide displays. End the slide show by pressing the Esc key.
6. Print the presentation as handouts with all eight slides on one page.
7. Save and then close the presentation.

Assessment 5

1. Open **PerennialsPresentation**.
2. Save the presentation with Save As and name it **sppc6sc05**.
3. Create a summary slide between Slides 1 and 2 that includes topics for Slides 2 through 8.
4. Use the Rehearse Timings feature to set the following times for the slides to display during a slide show:

   Slide 1 = 3 seconds
   Slide 2 = 7 seconds
   Slide 3 = 4 seconds
   Slide 4 = 6 seconds
   Slide 5 = 5 seconds
   Slide 6 = 6 seconds
   Slide 7 = 6 seconds
   Slide 8 = 7 seconds
   Slide 9 = 4 seconds
5. Set up the slide show to run continuously.
6. Run the presentation beginning with Slide 1. Watch the slide show until the presentation has started for the second time and then end the show.
7. Print the presentation as handouts with all nine slides on one page.
8. Save and then close the presentation.

Assessment 6

1. In this chapter, you learned to insert a number of action buttons in a slide. Experiment with the other action buttons (click the AutoShapes button and then point to Action Buttons) and then prepare a PowerPoint presentation with the following specifications:
   a. The first slide should contain the title of your presentation.
   b. Create one slide each for nine of the available action buttons (you decide which nine). For visual appeal, consider inserting the specific action button on the slide (without linking it).
   c. Apply a design template of your choosing to the presentation.
2. Save the presentation and name it **sppc6sc06**.
3. Print the presentation as a handout.
4. Close the presentation.

CHAPTER challenge

You are the manager of Plenty O' Pets, a pet store located in your city. The owner has decided to set up a kiosk in the store that will provide information on how to choose the best pet, as well as what the responsibilities are of owning a pet. The owner has asked you to prepare the presentation that will be placed on the kiosk. The presentation should have at least five slides. Create a chart in Excel that can be used in the presentation. Save the chart in Excel, then copy the chart to a slide in the presentation. Add action buttons, a summary slide, and any other features that would improve the appearance of the presentation. Set appropriate timings on each of the slides and set the slide show to run by itself until Esc is pressed. The owner does not have PowerPoint on his computer, but would like to review the content of the presentation and add and delete to it as necessary. Save the presentation as a Word outline, as well as a PowerPoint presentation. Name both files **PetCare**.

To ensure that others do not modify and change the presentation, set a password to open the presentation. Use the Help feature to learn about protecting a presentation with a password. Then protect the presentation created in the first part of the Chapter Challenge with the password *P3t Car3.*

After reviewing the presentation, the owner believes that the information should be shared with customers via the Internet. Publish the **PetCare** presentation created in the first part of the Chapter Challenge as a Web Page so that it can be posted on Plenty O' Pets' Web site. Save the Web Page as **PetCare**.

CHAPTER 7

LINKING AND EMBEDDING OBJECTS AND FILES

PERFORMANCE OBJECTIVES

Upon successful completion of Chapter 7, you will be able to:

- **Embed a Word table in a PowerPoint presentation**
- **Embed and edit an Excel chart in a PowerPoint presentation**
- **Link a Word table in a PowerPoint presentation**
- **Link and edit an Excel chart in a PowerPoint presentation**
- **Break a link between a source and destination program**
- **Launch another program from a PowerPoint presentation**
- **Create a folder**
- **Select, copy, delete, and rename presentations**
- **Create, run, edit, and print a custom show**

Chapter07S

PowerPoint

Share objects between programs in the Microsoft Office suite by copying and pasting objects, copying and embedding objects, or copying and linking objects. In Chapter 6, you learned how to copy and paste data and objects. In this chapter you will learn how to copy and embed and copy and link objects between programs. You will also learn some basic file maintenance activities such as creating a folder and selecting, copying, deleting, and renaming presentations.

Linking and Embedding Objects

One of the reasons the Microsoft Office suite is used extensively in business is because it allows data from an individual program to seamlessly integrate into another program. For example, a chart depicting the sales projections created in Excel can easily be added to a slide in a presentation to the company board of directors on the new budget forecast.

Integration is the process of completing a file by adding parts to it from other sources. Duplicating data that already exist in another program should be a rare instance. In Chapter 6, you learned how to insert a chart from Excel and text from Word into slides in a PowerPoint presentation using the copy and paste method. The copy and paste method is fast and is used in situations where the content is not likely to change. If the content is dynamic, the copy and paste method becomes problematic and prone to error. To illustrate this point, assume one of the outcomes from the presentation to the board of directors is a revision to the sales projections. The chart that was originally created in Excel has to be updated to reflect the new projections. The existing chart in PowerPoint needs to be deleted and then the revised chart in Excel copied and pasted to the slide. Both Excel and PowerPoint need to be opened and edited to reflect this change in projection. In this case, copying and pasting the chart was not efficient.

In other situations, the source of the content may not be readily apparent, requiring the user to go searching for the program that was used for the original task. Individual programs may also be updated without the corresponding updates to other programs to which the data was copied, thus resulting in potential errors.

To eliminate the inefficiency of the copy and paste method, you can integrate data between programs using ***object linking and embedding (OLE)***. Object linking and embedding is the sharing of data from one program to another. An object can be text in a document, data in a table, a chart, a picture, a slide, or any combination of data that you would like to share between programs. The program that was used to create the object is called the ***source*** and the program the object is linked or embedded to is called the ***destination***.

HINT

Static data remains the same while dynamic data changes periodically or continually.

Embedding versus Linking

Embedding and linking are two methods that can be used to integrate data in addition to the copy and paste routine discussed in Chapter 6. When an object is embedded, the content in the object is stored in both the source and the destination programs. When you edit an embedded object in the destination program, the source program in which the program was created opens. If the content in the object is changed in the source program, the change is not reflected in the destination program and vice versa.

HINT

If you take a file containing an embedded object to another computer, make sure that computer contains the necessary program before trying to edit the object.

Linking inserts a code into the destination file connecting the destination to the name and location of the source object. The object itself is not stored within the destination file. If a change is made to the content in the source program, the destination program reflects the change automatically.

Your decision to integrate data by embedding or linking will depend on whether the data is dynamic or static. If the data is dynamic, then linking the object is the most efficient method of integration. Static data can be embedded or copied and pasted from the source to the destination program.

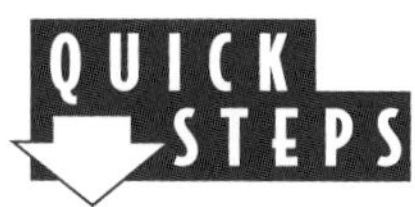

Embed an Object
1. Open source program.
2. Select desired object.
3. Click Copy button.
4. Open destination program.
5. Click Edit, Paste Special.
6. Click OK.

Embedding Objects

As previously discussed, an object that is embedded will be stored in both the source *and* the destination programs. The content of the object can be edited in *either* the source or the destination; however, a change made in one will not be reflected in the other. The difference between copying and pasting and embedding is that embedded objects can be edited with the source program's editing menus and toolbars. Figure 7.1 illustrates a table from Word embedded in a slide in PowerPoint that has been opened for editing. Notice the Word options on the menu and toolbars displayed in Figure 7.1, as well as the horizontal and vertical ruler bars from Word that are visible within the editing window.

FIGURE 7.1 *Editing a Word Table Embedded in PowerPoint*

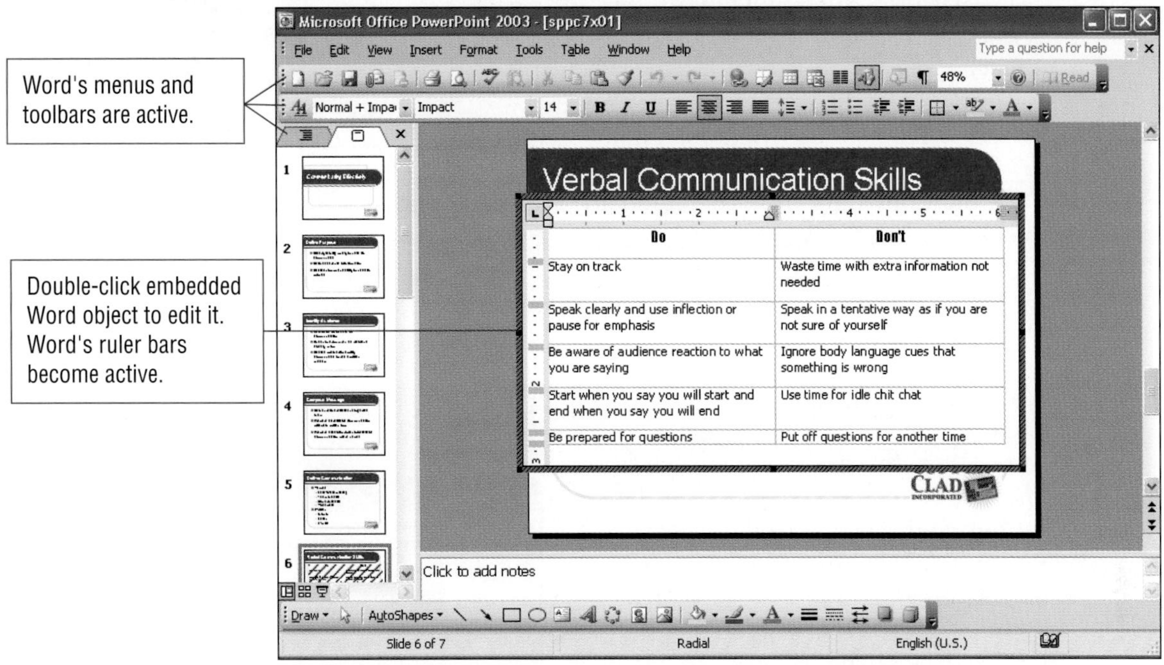

Since embedded objects are edited within the source program, the source program must reside on the computer when the presentation is opened for editing. If you are preparing a presentation that will be edited on another computer, you may want to check before embedding any objects to verify that the other computer has the same programs. You would complete the following basic steps to embed an object from one program to another:

1. Open both programs and open both files needed for the integration.
2. Activate the source program.
3. Select the desired object.
4. Copy the selected object using the Copy button on the Standard toolbar.
5. Activate the destination program.
6. Move to the location where you want the object inserted.
7. Click Edit and then Paste Special.
8. At the Paste Special dialog box, click the source of the object in the *As* list box, and then click OK.

exercise 1

EMBEDDING A WORD TABLE IN A POWERPOINT PRESENTATION

1. In PowerPoint, open **CommunicationPresentation** from the PowerPointChapter07S folder on your disk.
2. Save the presentation with Save As and name it **sppc7x01**.
3. Copy and embed a Word table in Slide 5 by completing the following steps:
   a. Open Microsoft Word.
   b. Open the **VerbalSkills** document from the PowerPointChapter07S folder on your disk.

c. Below the second paragraph is a two-column table set in a different font that begins with the title row *Do* and *Don't*. Select the table by completing the following steps:
   1) Click in any text below *Do* or *Don't*.
   2) Click Table on the Menu bar, point to Select, and then click Table.

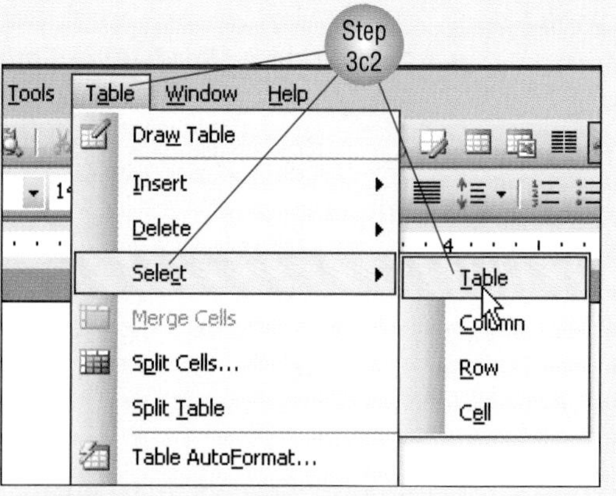

d. Click the Copy button on the Standard toolbar.
e. Click the button on the Taskbar representing PowerPoint.
f. Display Slide 5 in the Slide pane.
g. Click the New Slide button on the Formatting toolbar.
h. Click the Title Only slide layout in the Slide Layout task pane.
i. Click Edit and then Paste Special.
j. At the Paste Special dialog box, click *Microsoft Word Document Object* in the *As* list box, and then click OK.

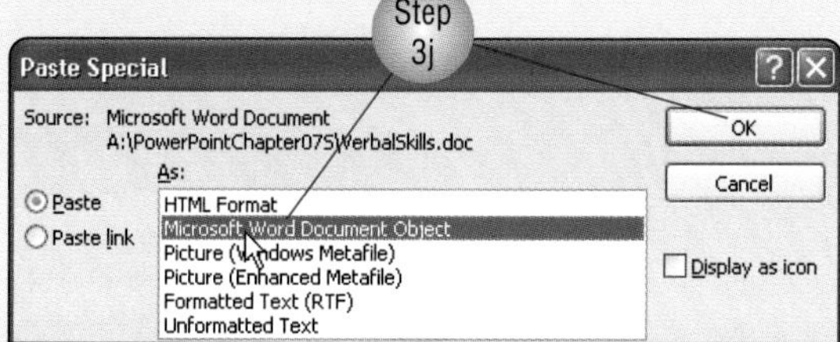

k. Resize the table as large as possible without overlapping the logo at the bottom right of the slide.
l. Deselect the table.
m. Click the text *Click to add title* and then type **Verbal Communication Skills**.

4. Display Slide 1 in the Slide pane and then run the presentation.
5. Print only Slide 6 (this is the new slide you created).
6. Save and then close the presentation.
7. Switch to Word, close **VerbalSkills**, and then exit Word.

Editing an Embedded Object

Once an object has been embedded it can be edited by double-clicking the object. When you double-click an embedded object, the object displays in an editing window with the source program's menu options and toolbars displayed in the current program (see Figure 7.1). Make any changes necessary using the normal editing features available in the source program and then click outside the object to exit the source program's editing tools.

Click to select an embedded object and then use the white sizing handles that appear around the object to move and/or size it. Embedded objects can also be animated or edited using the same techniques used in editing drawn objects discussed in Chapter 5.

exercise 2

EMBEDDING AND EDITING AN EXCEL CHART IN A SLIDE

1. In PowerPoint, open **sppc7x01**.
2. Save the presentation with Save As and name it **sppc7x02**.
3. Open Microsoft Excel.
4. Open the workbook named **NonverbalCues** from the PowerPointChapter07S folder on your disk.
5. Copy and embed the chart to a slide by completing the following steps:
   a. Click the chart to select it.
   b. Click the Copy button on the Standard toolbar.
   c. Click the button on the Taskbar representing PowerPoint.
   d. Display Slide 6 in the Slide pane.
   e. Click the New Slide button on the Formatting toolbar.
   f. Click the Title Only slide layout in the Slide Layout task pane.
   g. Click Edit and then Paste Special.
   h. At the Paste Special dialog box, make sure *Microsoft Office Excel Chart Object* is selected in the *As* list box, and then click OK.
6. Edit the chart in the slide by completing the following steps:
   a. Double-click the chart.
   b. Click Chart and then Chart Type.
   c. At the Chart Type dialog box, click *Bar* in the *Chart type* list box.
   d. Click the first sub-type in the second row in the *Chart sub-type* section.
   e. Click OK.
   f. Click Chart and then Chart Options.
   g. At the Chart Options dialog box, with the Titles tab selected, change the chart title to **Cues Causing a Response**.
   h. Click the Data Labels tab.
   i. At the Chart Options dialog box with the Data Labels tab selected, click the *Category name* option to remove the check mark and then click the *Value* option to remove the check mark.
   j. Click OK to close the Chart Options dialog box.
   k. Right-click one of the blue bars inside the chart and then click Format Data Series at the shortcut menu.
   l. At the Format Data Series dialog box with the Patterns tab selected, click a yellow color in the *Area* section that closely matches the yellow of the accent line in the slide.

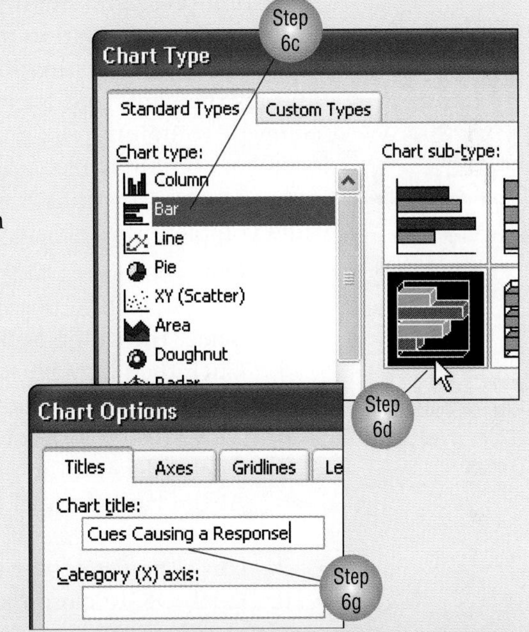

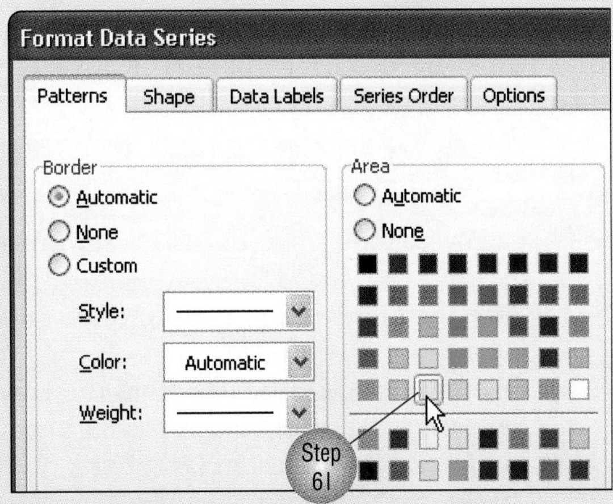

m. Click OK to close the Format Data Series dialog box.
n. Click outside the chart to exit editing in Excel.
o. Resize the chart so it fills the slide without overlapping the accent line or logo.
p. Type **Nonverbal Cues** as the title for the slide.

7. Display Slide 1 in the Slide pane and then run the presentation.
8. Print only Slide 7 (this is the new slide containing the chart).
9. Save and then close the presentation.
10. Switch to Excel, close **NonverbalCues**, and then exit Excel.

HINT

Linking does not increase the size of the file in the destination program. Link objects if file size is a consideration.

Link an Object
1. Open source program.
2. Select desired object.
3. Click Copy button.
4. Open destination program.
5. Click Edit, Paste Special.
6. Click *Paste link* option.
7. Click OK.

Linking Objects

If the content of the object that will be integrated between programs is likely to change, then the object should be linked from the source program to the destination program. Linking the object establishes a direct connection between the source and destination program. The object will be stored in the source program only. The destination program will have a code inserted into it that indicates the name and location of the source of the object. Whenever the document containing the link is opened, a message displays saying that the document contains links and the user is prompted to update the links. This process of updating links is referred to as ***Dynamic Data Exchange (DDE)***. You would complete these basic steps to link an object from one program to another:

1. Open both programs and open both files needed for the link.
2. Activate the source program.
3. Select the desired object.
4. Click the Copy button on the Standard toolbar.
5. Activate the destination program.
6. Move to the location where you want the object inserted.
7. Click Edit and then Paste Special.
8. At the Paste Special dialog box, click the source program for the object in the *As* list box.
9. Click the *Paste link* option located at the left side of the *As* list box.
10. Click OK to close the Paste Special dialog box.

exercise 3

LINKING EXCEL CHARTS TO A POWERPOINT PRESENTATION

1. In PowerPoint, open **FundsPresentation** from the PowerPointChapter07S folder on your disk.
2. Save the presentation with Save As and name it **sppc7x03**.
3. Open Microsoft Excel.
4. Open **ExcelWorkbook01** from the PowerPointChapter07S folder on your disk.
5. Save the workbook by completing the following steps:
   a. Click File and then Save As.
   b. At the Save As dialog box, type **FundsWorkbook01**.
   c. Click the Save button.

6. Copy and link the chart to a slide in the presentation by completing the following steps:
   a. Click the chart to select it.
   b. Click the Copy button on the Standard toolbar.
   c. Click the button on the Taskbar representing PowerPoint.
   d. Display Slide 2 in the Slide pane.
   e. Click Edit and then Paste Special.
   f. In the Paste Special dialog box, make sure *Microsoft Office Excel Chart Object* is selected in the *As* list box.
   g. Click the *Paste link* option.
   h. Click OK.
   i. Increase the size of the chart in the slide so it fills a good portion of the slide below the title. Move the chart so it appears balanced below the title.

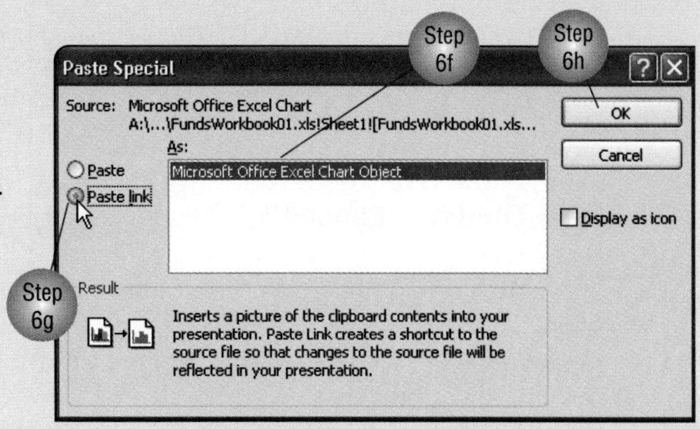

7. Click the button on the Taskbar representing Excel and then close **FundsWorkbook01**.
8. Open **ExcelWorkbook02**.
9. Save the workbook with Save As and name it **FundsWorkbook02**.
10. Link the chart in the workbook to Slide 3 by completing steps similar to those in Step 6.
11. In PowerPoint, print the presentation as handouts with all slides on one page (the fourth slide is blank, except for the title).
12. Display Slide 1 in the Slide pane and then run the presentation.
13. Save and then close **sppc7x03**.
14. Click the button on the Taskbar representing Excel, close **FundsWorkbook02**, and then exit Excel.

Editing Linked Objects

Linked objects are edited in the source program in which they were created. Open the document, workbook, or presentation in which the object was created, make the changes as required, and then save and close the file. If both the source and destination programs are open at the same time, the changed content is reflected immediately in both programs. In Exercise 4, you will make changes to information in the Excel charts, and this will update the charts in the PowerPoint presentation.

exercise 4 CHANGING DATA IN LINKED CHARTS

1. Open Excel and then open **FundsWorkbook01**.
2. Make the following changes to the data in the cells in the workbook:
   a. Change B2 from *18%* to *10%*.
   b. Change B3 from *28%* to *20%*.
3. Save the workbook again with the same name (**FundsWorkbook01**).
4. Close **FundsWorkbook01**.
5. Open **FundsWorkbook02**.

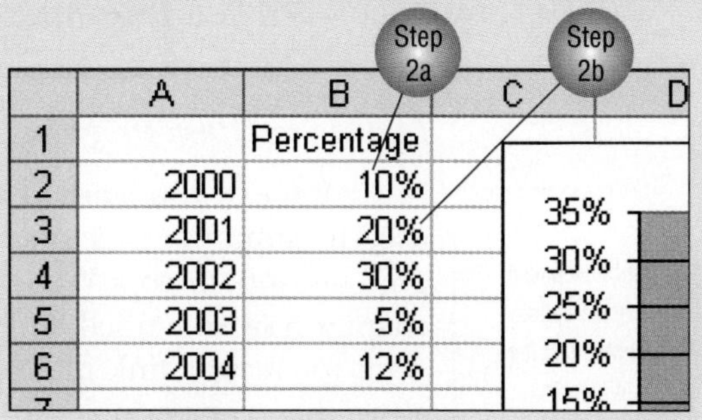

	A	B	C	D
1		Percentage		
2	2000	10%		
3	2001	20%		
4	2002	30%		
5	2003	5%		
6	2004	12%		

6. Make the following changes to the data in the cells in the worksheet:
   a. Change B2 from *13%* to *17%*.
   b. Change B3 from *9%* to *4%*.
   c. Change B6 from *15%* to *19%*.
7. Save the workbook again with the same name (**FundsWorkbook02**).
8. Close **FundsWorkbook02**.
9. Exit Excel.
10. With PowerPoint the active program, open **sppc7x03**.
11. At the message telling you that the presentation contains links to other files, click the Update Links button.
12. Print the presentation as handouts with all slides on one page. (The fourth slide will be blank, except for the title.)
13. Save and then close the presentation.

	A	B	C	D
1		Percentage		
2	2000	17%		
3	2001	4%		20%
4	2002	18%		
5	2003	4%		15%
6	2004	19%		
7				10%

Step 6a
Step 6b
Step 6c

Break a Link
1. Open destination file.
2. Click Edit, Links.
3. At Links dialog box, click desired linked object.
4. Click Break Link button.

Breaking a Link

If you linked an object from one program to another and then determine afterward that the data is not likely to change, you can break the link between the two files. Breaking the link does not remove the object from the destination program. It removes the direct connection between the source and the destination file. To do this, open the destination file, click Edit and then Links. At the Links dialog box as shown in Figure 7.2, click the linked object in the *Links* list box, and then click the Break Link button. The object becomes an embedded object in the destination file and will no longer be updated if changes occur to the source.

FIGURE 7.2 ***Links Dialog Box***

To break a link, click the desired object in this list box and then click the Break Link button.

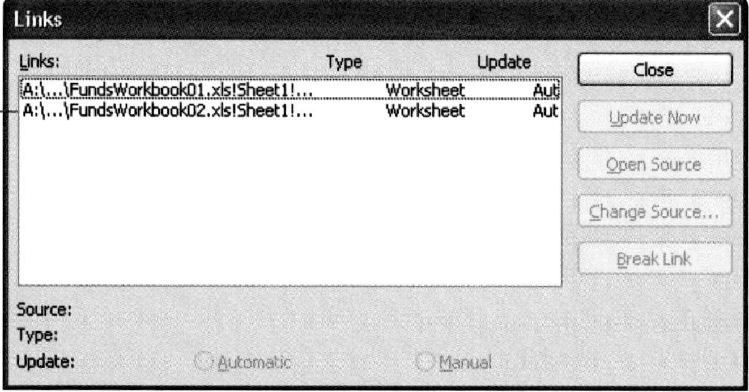

Linking to Other Programs

HINT
Control how linked objects are updated with options at the Links dialog box.

In Chapter 6, you learned how to create action buttons on slides that could be used to jump to other slides within the presentation, to another PowerPoint presentation, or to a Web site on the Internet. You have also learned in this chapter how to embed and link objects from other programs. Sometimes you may want to create a link in a presentation that will launch another program altogether. For example, in the previous exercises, you linked an Excel chart to a slide in a PowerPoint presentation. What if you wanted to launch Excel instead and have the worksheet and chart display side by side? To do this, you can create an action button on the slide as discussed in Chapter 6, or you can select a word in a slide, click Slide Show, and then click Action Settings. This displays the Action Settings dialog box where you can specify the file to which you want to create the hyperlink.

When a program is launched from a PowerPoint presentation, the other program is opened in its own window on top of the slide show. When the other program is exited, the presentation resumes from the slide where it was left.

exercise 5

LAUNCHING OTHER PROGRAMS FROM A POWERPOINT PRESENTATION

1. Open **CommunicationPresentation**.
2. Save the presentation with Save As and name it **sppc7x05**.
3. Create a link that will launch Excel from a slide in the presentation by completing the following steps:
   a. Display Slide 5 in the Slide pane.
   b. Select the word *Verbal* in the slide.
   c. Click Slide Show on the Menu bar and then click Action Settings at the drop-down menu.
   d. At the Action Settings dialog box, click the *Hyperlink to* option.
   e. Click the down-pointing arrow at the right of the *Hyperlink to* option box, and then click *Other File* at the drop-down list.
   f. At the Hyperlink to Other File dialog box, navigate to the PowerPointChapter07S folder on your disk, and then double-click the Excel workbook named ***NonverbalCues***.
   g. Click OK to close the Action Settings dialog box.

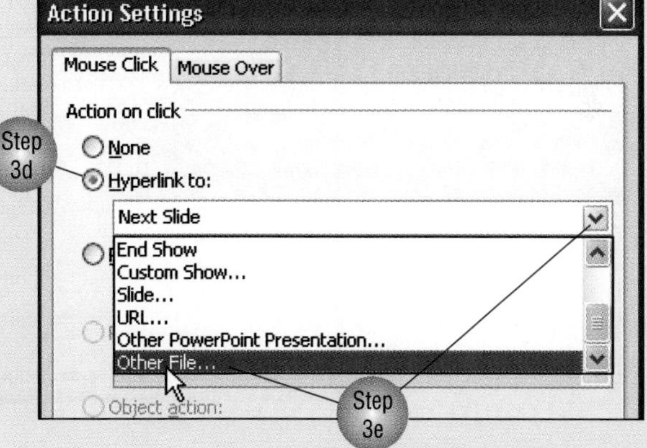

4. Select the word *Written* in the slide and then create a hyperlink to the Word document named **WrittenSkills** by completing steps similar to those in Steps 3c through 3g.
5. Apply a transition and sound of your choosing to all slides in the presentation.
6. Run the presentation beginning with Slide 1. At Slide 5, click the Verbal hyperlink. Look at the Excel workbook that displays and then close Excel by clicking the Close button (contains an *X*) located in the upper right corner of the screen. Click the Written hyperlink, look at the Word document that displays, and then click the Close button.
7. Print the presentation as handouts with all six slides on the same page.
8. Save and then close the presentation.

Maintaining Presentation Files

When you have been working with PowerPoint for a period of time, you will have accumulated a number of presentation files. These files should be organized into folders to facilitate fast retrieval of information. Occasionally you should perform file maintenance activities such as copying, moving, renaming, and deleting presentation files to ensure the presentations in your various folders are manageable.

Open

Many file management tasks can be completed at the Open dialog box (and some at the Save As dialog box). These tasks can include creating a new folder; copying, moving, printing, and renaming presentation files; and opening and closing multiple presentations. Display the Open dialog box, shown in Figure 7.3, by clicking the Open button on the Standard toolbar. Some file maintenance tasks such as creating a folder and deleting files are performed by using buttons on the Open dialog box toolbar. Figure 7.3 identifies the dialog box toolbar.

FIGURE 7.3 ***Open Dialog Box***

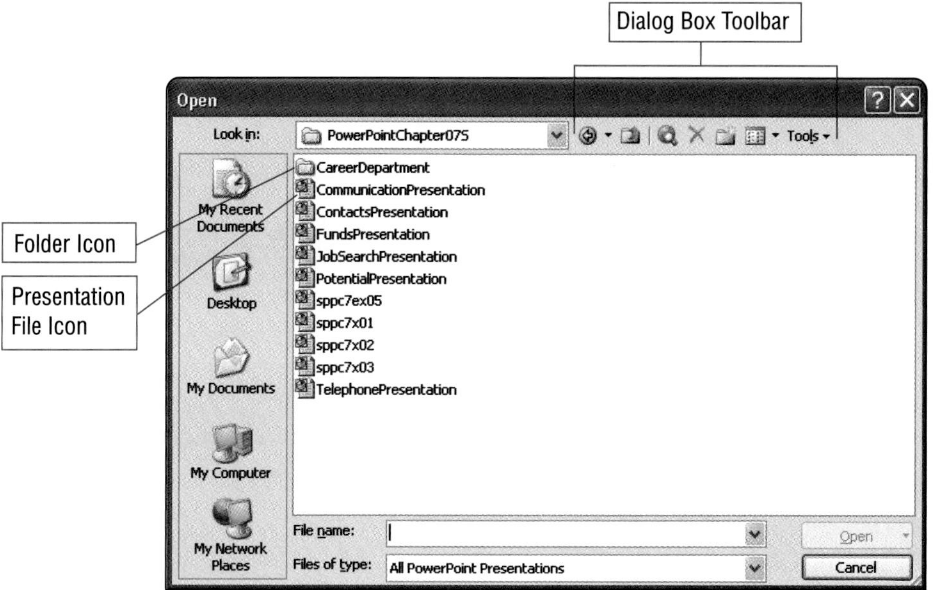

QUICK STEPS

Create a Folder
1. Click Open button.
2. Click Create New Folder button.
3. Type folder name.
4. Click OK.

Creating a Folder

In PowerPoint, presentations should be grouped logically and stored in folders. For example, all of the presentations related to one department within a company could be stored in one folder with the department name being the folder name. A folder can be created within a folder (called a ***subfolder***). If you create presentations for a department by individual, each individual could have a subfolder name within the department folder. The main folder on a disk or drive is called the ***root folder***. Additional folders are created as branches of this root folder.

HINT

Display all files in a folder by changing the *Files of type* option at the Open dialog box to *All Files*.

At the Open dialog box, presentation file names display in the list box preceded by a presentation icon and a folder name is preceded by a folder icon. The folder and presentation icons are identified in Figure 7.3.

Create a new folder by clicking the Create New Folder button located on the Open dialog box toolbar. At the New Folder dialog box shown in Figure 7.4, type a name for the folder in the *Name* text box, and then click OK or press Enter. The new folder becomes the active folder.

Create New Folder

FIGURE

7.4 ***New Folder Dialog Box***

If you want to make the previous folder the active folder, click the Up One Level button on the dialog box toolbar. Clicking this button changes to the folder that was up one level from the current folder. After clicking the Up One Level button, the Back button becomes active. Click this button and the previously active folder becomes active again. A folder name can contain a maximum of 255 characters.

Up One Level

Back

exercise 6

CREATING A FOLDER

1. Create a folder named *CareerDepartment* on your disk by completing the following steps:
   a. Display the Open dialog box with the PowerPointChapter07S folder on your disk the active folder.
   b. Click the Create New Folder button (located on the dialog box toolbar).
   c. At the New Folder dialog box, type CareerDepartment.
   d. Click OK or press Enter. (The CareerDepartment folder is now the active folder.)
   e. Change back to the PowerPointChapter07S folder by clicking the Up One Level button on the dialog box toolbar.
2. Click the Cancel button to close the Open dialog box.

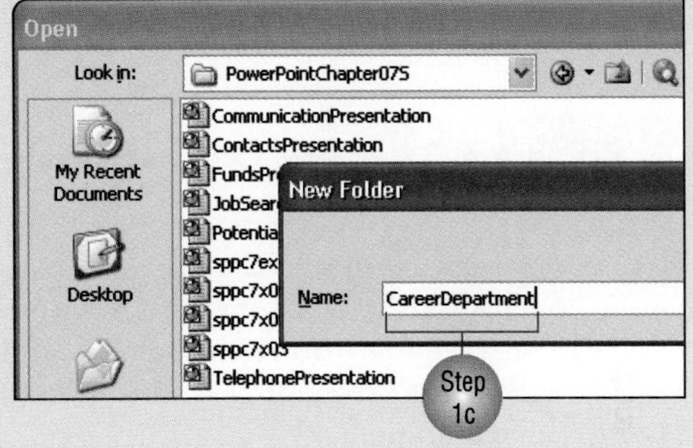

Selecting Files

File management tasks can be completed on one file or more than one selected file. For example, you can move one file to a different folder, or you can select several files and move them all in one operation. Selected files can be opened, deleted, copied, moved, or printed.

Select Adjacent Files
1. Click Open button.
2. Click first file name.
3. Hold down Shift key.
4. Click last file name.

QUICK STEPS

Select Nonadjacent Files
1. Click Open button.
2. Click first file name.
3. Hold down Ctrl key.
4. Click any other desired file names.

To select one file, display the Open dialog box, and then click the desired file in the file list. To select several adjacent files (files displayed next to each other), click the first file, hold down the Shift key, click the last file to be selected, and then release the Shift key.

You can also select files that are not adjacent in the Open dialog box. To do this, click the first file, hold down the Ctrl key, click each additional file to be selected, and then release the Ctrl key.

Copying Files

QUICK STEPS

Copy a File
1. Click Open button.
2. Right-click file name.
3. Click Copy at shortcut menu.
4. Navigate to desired folder.
5. Right-click white area in list box.
6. Click Paste at shortcut menu.

In this and previous chapters, you opened a file from the chapter folder on your data disk and saved it with a new name on the same disk. This process makes an exact copy of the file, leaving the original on the disk. You can also copy a file into another folder and use the file's original name, give it a different name, or select files at the Open dialog box and copy them to the same folder or into a different folder.

To copy a file into another folder, open the file, display the Save As dialog box, change to the desired folder, and then click the Save button. A file also can be copied to another folder without opening the file first. To do this, use the Copy and Paste options from a shortcut menu at the Open (or Save As) dialog box.

A file or selected files can be copied into the same folder. When you do this, PowerPoint names the duplicated file(s) "Copy of xxx" (where *xxx* is the current file name). You can copy one file or selected files into the same folder.

exercise 7

COPYING SELECTED FILES INTO A DIFFERENT FOLDER

1. Copy selected files to the CareerDepartment folder by completing the following steps:
   a. Display the Open dialog box with PowerPointChapter07S the active folder.
   b. Click ***JobSearchPresentation***, hold down the Ctrl key, and then click ***PotentialPresentation*** and ***ContactsPresentation***. (This selects the three, nonadjacent presentations.)
   c. Position the arrow pointer on one of the selected files, click the right mouse button, and then click Copy at the shortcut menu.
   d. Double-click the *Career Department* folder.
   e. Position the arrow pointer in any white area in the list box, click the right mouse button, and then click Paste at the shortcut menu.
   f. Click the Up One Level button to change back to the PowerPointChapter07S folder.
2. Close the Open dialog box.

Deleting Files and Folders

QUICK STEPS

Delete File/Folder
1. Click Open button.
2. Click file or folder name.
3. Click Delete button.
4. Click Yes.

At some point, you may want to delete certain files from your data disk or any other disk or folder in which you may be working. If you use PowerPoint on a regular basis, you should establish a periodic system for deleting files that are no longer used. The system you choose depends on the work you are doing and the amount of folder or disk space available. To delete a file, display the Open or Save As dialog box, select the file, and then click the Delete button on the dialog box toolbar. At the dialog box asking you to confirm the deletion, click Yes.

You can also delete a file by displaying the Open dialog box, selecting the file to be deleted, clicking the Tools button on the dialog box toolbar, and then clicking Delete at the drop-down menu. Another method for deleting a file is to display the Open dialog box, right-click the file to be deleted, and then click Delete at the shortcut menu. Delete a folder and all of its contents in the same manner as deleting a file or selected files.

Delete

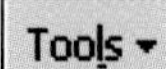

Tools

exercise 8 — DELETING A FILE

1. Display the Open dialog box with the PowerPointChapter07S folder active.
2. Double-click the CareerDepartment folder.
3. Delete **JobSearchPresentation** by completing the following steps:
   a. Right-click ***JobSearchPresentation*** in the list box.
   b. At the shortcut menu that displays, click Delete.
   c. At the message that displays, click the Yes button.
4. Click the Up One Level button to return to the PowerPointChapter07S folder.
5. Close the Open dialog box.

exercise 9 — DELETING A FOLDER

1. Display the Open dialog box with the PowerPointChapter07S folder active.
2. Delete the CareerDepartment folder by completing the following steps:
   a. Right-click the *CareerDepartment* folder in the list box.
   b. At the shortcut menu that displays, click Delete.
   c. At the message asking if you are sure you want to remove the folder and all of its contents, click Yes.
   d. If a message displays telling you that the presentation is a read-only file, click the Yes to All button.
3. Close the Open dialog box.

Renaming Files

At the Open dialog box, use the Rename option from the Tools drop-down menu or the shortcut menu to give a file a different name. The Rename option changes the name of the file and keeps it in the same folder. To use Rename, display the Open dialog box, click once on the file to be renamed, click the Tools button on the dialog box toolbar, and then click Rename. This causes a thin black border to surround the file name and the name to be selected. Type the new name and then press Enter.

You can also rename a file by right-clicking the file name at the Open dialog box and then clicking Rename at the shortcut menu. Type the new name for the file and then press the Enter key.

Rename File
1. Click Open button.
2. Right-click file name.
3. Click Rename at shortcut menu.
4. Type new name.
5. Press Enter.

exercise 10

RENAMING A FILE

1. Display the Open dialog box with the PowerPointChapter07S folder active.
2. Rename a file by completing the following steps:
   a. Click once on ***sppc7x01***.
   b. Click the Tools button on the dialog box toolbar.
   c. At the drop-down menu that displays, click Rename.
   d. Type **sppc7x10** and then press the Enter key.
3. Close the Open dialog box.

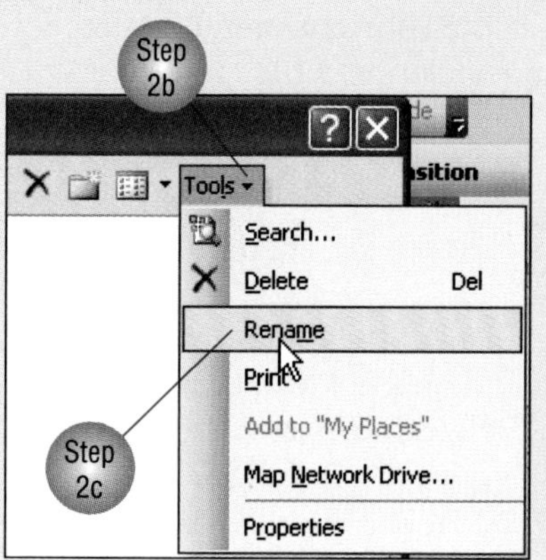

QUICK STEPS

Create a Custom Show

1. Click Slide Show, Custom Shows.
2. Click New button.
3. Type custom show name.
4. Add desired slides to *Slides in custom show* list box.
5. Click OK.
6. Click Close.

Creating a Custom Show

Specific slides within a presentation can be selected to create a presentation within a presentation. This might be useful in situations where you want to show only a select number of slides to a particular audience. To create a custom show, open the presentation, click Slide Show, and then click Custom Shows. At the Custom Shows dialog box, click the New button and the Define Custom Show dialog box displays similar to what you see in Figure 7.5.

FIGURE 7.5 ***Define Custom Show Dialog Box***

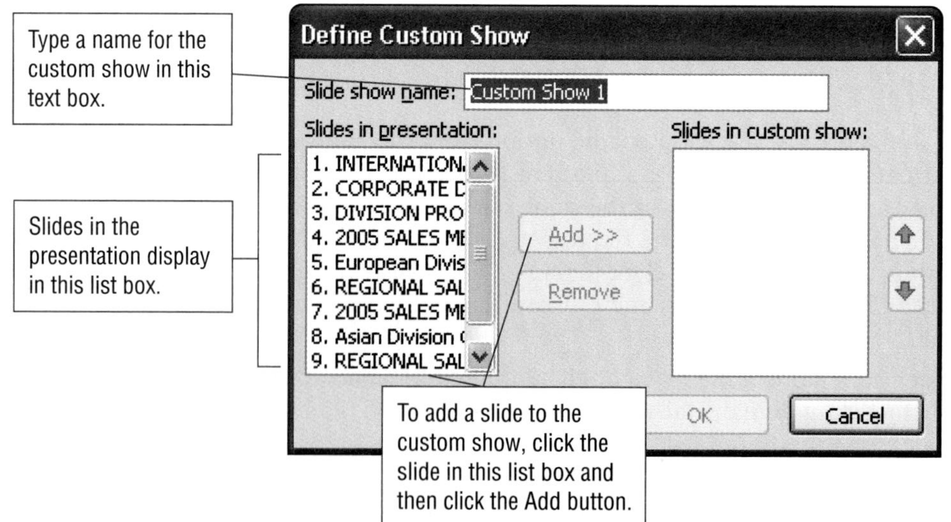

At the Define Custom Show dialog box, type a name for the custom presentation in the *Slide show name* text box. To insert a slide in the custom show, click the slide in the *Slides in presentation* list box and then click the Add button. This inserts the slide in the *Slides in custom show* list box. Continue in this manner until all desired slides are added to the custom show. If you want to change the order of the slides in the *Slides in custom show* list box, click one of the arrow keys to move the selected slide up or down in the list box. When the desired slides are inserted in the *Slides in custom show* list box and in the desired order, click OK. You can create more than one custom show in a presentation.

HINT

Preview a custom show by clicking the show name in the Custom Shows dialog box and then clicking the Show button.

Running a Custom Show

To run a custom show within a presentation, open the presentation, click Slide Show, and then click Set Up Show. This displays the Set Up Show dialog box shown in Figure 7.6. If the presentation contains only one custom show, click the *Custom show* option button. If the presentation contains more than one custom show, click the down-pointing arrow at the right of the *Custom show* option, and then click the show name at the drop-down list. Click OK to close the Set Up Show dialog box and then run the custom show by clicking the Slide Show button on the View toolbar (or any other method you choose for running a presentation).

QUICK STEPS

Run a Custom Show
1. Click Slide Show, Set Up Show.
2. Click *Custom show* option button.
3. Click OK.
4. Click Slide Show button.

FIGURE 7.6 **Set Up Show Dialog Box**

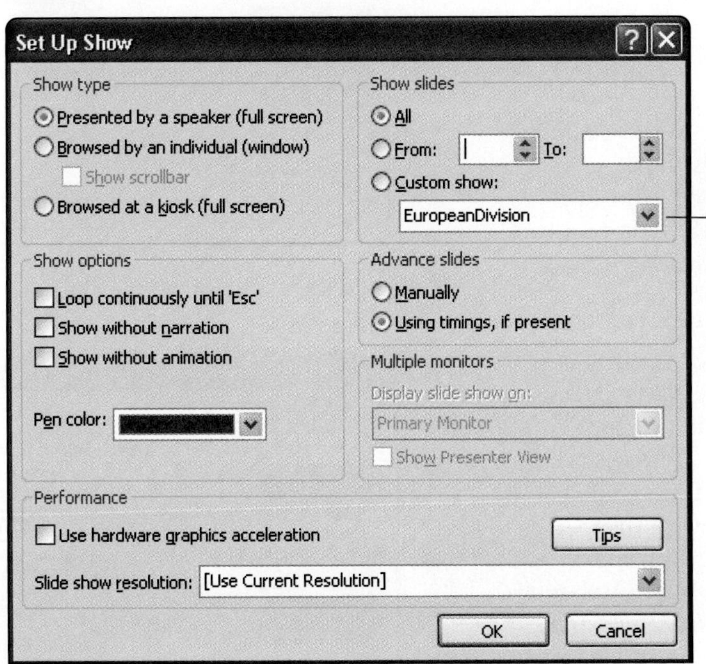

Click this down-pointing arrow to display a drop-down list of any custom shows created in the presentation.

Editing a Custom Show

A custom show is saved with the presentation and can be edited. To edit a custom show, open the presentation, click Slide Show, and then click Custom Shows. At the Custom Shows dialog box, click the name of the custom show you want to edit, and then click the Edit button. At the Define Custom Show dialog box, make the desired changes to the custom show such as adding or removing slides or changing the order of slides. When all changes have been made, click the OK button.

QUICK STEPS

Edit a Custom Show
1. Click Slide Show, Custom Shows.
2. Click custom show name.
3. Click Edit button.
4. Make desired changes.
5. Click OK.
6. Click Close.

QUICK STEPS

Print a Custom Show
1. Click File, Print.
2. Click *Custom show* option.
3. Click OK.

Printing a Custom Show

You can print a custom show with the *Custom Show* option in the Print dialog box. To do this, click File and then Print. At the Print dialog box, click the down-pointing arrow at the right of the *Custom Show* option located in the *Print range* section, click the desired show at the drop-down list, and then click OK.

exercise 11

CREATING, EDITING, AND RUNNING CUSTOM SHOWS

1. Open **ISPresentation**.
2. Save the presentation with Save As and name it **sppc7x11**.
3. Create two custom shows by completing the following steps:
   a. Click Slide Show and then Custom Shows.
   b. At the Custom Shows dialog box, click the New button.
   c. At the Define Custom Show dialog box, type **EuropeanDivision** in the *Slide show name* text box.
   d. Add Slides 1 through 6 to the *Slides in custom show* list box by completing the following steps:
      1) Click Slide 1 in the *Slides in presentation* list box.
      2) Hold down the Shift key and then click Slide 6 in the *Slides in presentation* list box.
      3) Click the Add button.
   e. Scroll down the *Slides in presentation* list box until Slide 10 is visible, click Slide 10, and then click the Add button.
   f. Click OK.
   g. At the Custom Shows dialog box, click the New button.
   h. At the Define Custom Show dialog box, type **AsianDivision** in the *Slide show name* text box.
   i. Add slides to the *Slides in custom show* list box by completing the following steps:
      1) Click Slide 1 in the *Slides in presentation* list box.
      2) Hold down the Ctrl key and then click each of the following slides: Slide 2, Slide 3, Slide 7, Slide 8, Slide 9, and Slide 10.
      3) Click the Add button.

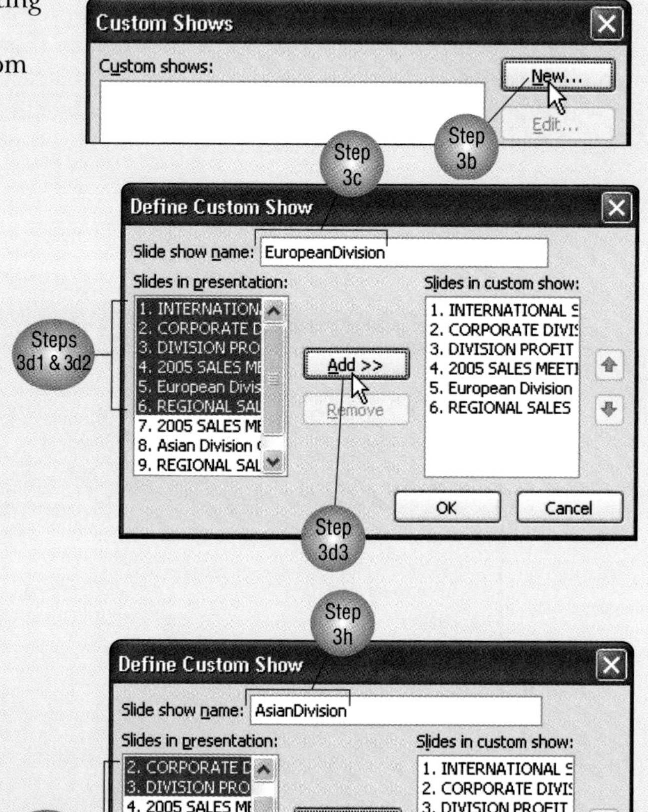

j. Click OK to close the Define Custom Shows dialog box.
k. At the Custom Shows dialog box, click the Close button.

4. Run the EuropeanDivision custom show by completing the following steps:
   a. Click Slide Show and then Set Up Show.
   b. At the Set Up Show dialog box, click the *Custom show* option located in the *Show slides* section.
   c. Make sure *EuropeanDivision* displays in the *Custom show* option box. If not, click the down-pointing arrow at the right of the *Custom show* option and then click *EuropeanDivision* at the drop-down list.
   d. Click OK to close the Set Up Show dialog box.
   e. Click the Slide Show button located in the View toolbar to begin the EuropeanDivision custom show.
   f. Advance through the seven slides of the custom show.
5. After running the EuropeanDivision custom show, run the AsianDivision custom show by completing the following steps:
   a. Click Slide Show and then Set Up Show.
   b. At the Set Up Show dialog box, click the down-pointing arrow at the right of the *Custom show* option and then click *AsianDivision* at the drop-down list.
   c. Click OK to close the Set Up Show dialog box.
   d. Click the Slide Show button located in the View toolbar to begin the AsianDivision custom show.
   e. Advance through the seven slides of the custom show.
6. After viewing the two custom shows, you decide to make some changes to each show. To do this, complete the following steps:
   a. Click Slide Show and then Custom Shows.
   b. At the Custom Shows dialog box, click *EuropeanDivision* in the *Custom shows* list box, and then click the Edit button.
   c. At the Define Custom Show dialog box, remove Slide 3 by clicking Slide 3 in the *Slides in custom show* list box and then clicking the Remove button.

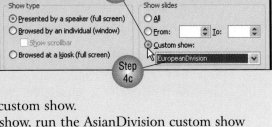

   d. Move Slide 6 above Slide 3 by completing the following steps:
      1) Click Slide 6 in the *Slides in custom show* list box.
      2) Click the up arrow button at the right of the *Slides in custom show* list box three times.
      3) Click OK.
   e. At the Custom Shows dialog box, click *AsianDivision* in the *Custom shows* list box, and then click the Edit button.
   f. At the Define Custom Show dialog box, remove Slide 2 from the *Slides in custom show* list box.
   g. Click OK.

h. At the Custom Shows dialog box, click the Close button.
7. Run the EuropeanDivision custom show.
8. Run the AsianDivision custom show.
9. Print the AsianDivision custom show by completing the following steps:
   a. Click File and then Print.
   b. At the Print dialog box, click the down-pointing arrow at the right of the *Custom Show* option in the *Print range* section, and then click *AsianDivision*.
   c. Change the *Print what* option to *Handouts*.
   d. Make sure the *Slides per page* option is set at *6*.
   e. Click OK.

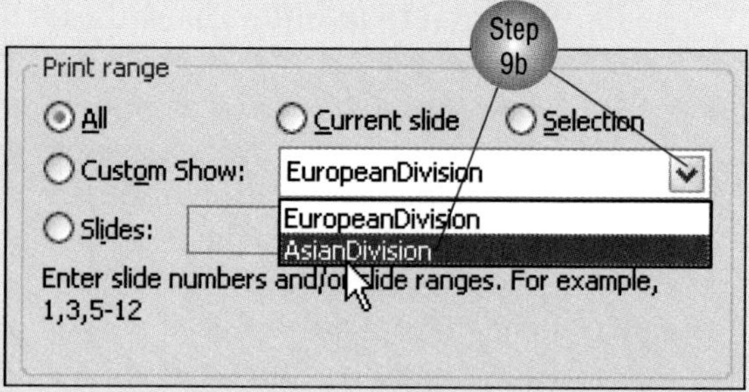

10. Print the EuropeanDivision custom show.
11. Save and then close the **sppc7x11** presentation.

CHAPTER summary

- Integration is the process of completing a file by adding parts to it from other sources.
- An object created in one program of the Microsoft Office suite can be copied, linked, or embedded to another program in the suite.
- The program containing the original object is called the source and the program the object is pasted to is called the destination.
- An embedded object is stored in both the source and the destination programs.
- Edit an embedded object by double-clicking it to open the source program's menus and toolbars.
- An object should be linked if the content in the object is subject to change. Linking will ensure that the content in the destination always reflects the current content in the source.
- A linked object is stored in the source program only. The destination program contains a code indicating the name and location of the source.
- The content in a link is edited by opening the document containing the linked object in the source program, making the required changes, and then saving and closing the file.
- When you open a document containing links, a message displays asking if you want to update the links.
- A link can be broken between the source and the destination program if there is no longer any need to update the destination program.
- Another program such as Word or Excel can be launched within a PowerPoint presentation by creating a hyperlink to a Word or Excel file.
- When another program is launched from a slide show, the application is opened in its own window on top of the slide show.

- Perform file management tasks such as creating a new folder and copying, deleting, and renaming files at the Open dialog box.
- Presentation files should be grouped logically and stored in folders. A folder can be created within a folder (a subfolder). The main folder on a disk or drive is called the root folder. Additional folders are created as a branch of this root folder.
- Create a new folder by clicking the Create New Folder button located on the Open dialog box toolbar.
- Use the Shift key while selecting files to select multiple adjacent files and use the Ctrl key to select multiple nonadjacent files.
- Use the Copy and Paste options from the shortcut menu at the Open dialog box to copy a file from one folder to another folder or drive.
- When you copy a file into the same folder, PowerPoint names the duplicated file(s) "Copy of xxx" (where *xxx* is the original file name).
- To delete a file, select the file and then click the Delete button on the dialog box toolbar; click Tools, and then click Delete at the drop-down menu; or right-click the file to be deleted, and then click Delete at the shortcut menu.
- You can create a custom show with specific slides in a presentation with options at the Custom Shows dialog box. To create a new show, click the New button at the Custom Shows dialog box. At the Define Custom Show dialog box, name the custom show, and then insert specific slides in the *Slides in custom show* list box.
- Run a custom show by choosing the specific custom show from the *Custom show* option at the Set Up Show dialog box and then running the show in the normal manner.
- Edit a custom show by displaying the Custom Shows dialog box, selecting the specific show, and then clicking the Edit button. At the Define Custom Show dialog box, make the desired changes and then click OK.
- Print a custom show by clicking the *Custom show* option in the Print dialog box.

FEATURES summary

FEATURE	BUTTON	MENU	KEYBOARD
Paste Special dialog box		Edit, Paste Special	
Links dialog box		Edit, Links	
Action Settings dialog box		Slide Show, Action Settings	
Open dialog box		File, Open	Ctrl + O
Custom Shows dialog box		Slide Show, Custom Shows	
Set Up Show dialog box		Slide Show, Set Up Show	

CONCEPTS check

Completion: On a blank sheet of paper, indicate the correct term, symbol, or command for each description.

1. The process of completing a document by adding parts from other sources is referred to as this.
2. To link or embed an object, open this dialog box in the destination program after copying the source object.
3. An object can be duplicated in a destination program by embedding, linking, or this.
4. Do this with the mouse to open an object in an editing window with the source program's menus and toolbars.
5. If an object has been linked from a Word document to a PowerPoint presentation, you would open this program to edit the content of the link.
6. Display this dialog box to disconnect the source program link from the destination object.
7. A file from another program can be opened from a PowerPoint presentation by creating a hyperlink at this dialog box.
8. File management tasks such as copying or deleting files can be performed at this dialog box.
9. Select multiple adjacent files by clicking the first file, holding down this key, and then clicking the last file.
10. Select multiple nonadjacent files by holding down this key while clicking each file name.
11. Click the New button at the Custom Shows dialog box and this dialog box displays.
12. To run a custom show, select the custom show with the *Custom show* option at this dialog box.

SKILLS check

Assessment 1

1. In PowerPoint, open **TelephonePresentation** (located in the PowerPointChapter07S folder on your disk).
2. Save the presentation with Save As and name it **sppc7sc01**.
3. Create a new Slide 6 with the following specifications:
   a. Use the Title Only slide layout.
   b. Insert the title *Placing Calls with Voice Mail.*
   c. Open Word and then open the document named **VoiceMailEtiquette** located in the PowerPointChapter07S folder on your disk.
   d. Copy and embed the bulleted list from the Word document to Slide 6. ***(Hint: The bulleted list is not in a table. You will need to select all of the bulleted items.)***
   e. Double-click the embedded object, press Ctrl + A to select all of the text in the object, and then change the font size to 16 points.
   f. Click outside the text to remove the Word editing tools.
   g. With the text object selected, resize and move the text object so it fills most of the slide below the title.

h. Click the button on the Taskbar representing Word, close the **VoiceMailEtiquette** document, and then exit Word.

4. Create a new Slide 3 with the following specifications:
   a. Apply the Title Only slide layout to the new Slide 3.
   b. Type **Average Time by Region** as the slide title.
   c. Open Excel and then open the workbook named **CallsWorkbook** from the PowerPointChapter07S folder on your disk.
   d. Select the chart and then copy and embed it in Slide 3 in the **sppc7sc01** presentation.
   e. Resize the chart as large as possible.
5. Print only Slide 3 of the presentation.
6. Double-click the chart and then change the chart type to Column.
7. Run the presentation beginning with Slide 1.
8. Print the presentation as handouts with all slides on one page.
9. Save and then close the presentation.
10. Click the button on the Taskbar representing Excel, close the **CallsWorkbook**, and then exit Excel.

Assessment 2

1. In PowerPoint, open **sppc7sc01**.
2. Save the presentation with Save As and name it **sppc7sc02**.
3. Display Slide 2 in the Slide pane, select the title text *Answering Calls,* and then hyperlink the text to the Word document named **VerbalSkills**.
4. Apply an animation scheme of your choosing to all slides in the presentation.
5. Run the presentation beginning with Slide 1. At Slide 2, click the hyperlink to view the Word document **VerbalSkills**.
6. Review the **VerbalSkills** document and then exit Word.
7. Navigate through the remainder of the slide show.
8. Save and then close the presentation.

Assessment 3

1. In PowerPoint, open **sppc7x03**. (You edited this presentation in Exercise 3. If you did not complete Exercise 3, open **FundsPresentation**.)
2. At the message telling you that the presentation contains links to other files, click the Update Links button.
3. Open Microsoft Excel and then open **ExcelWorkbook03** from the PowerPointChapter07S folder on your disk.
4. Save the workbook with Save As and name it **FundsWorkbook03**.
5. Copy and link the chart to Slide 4 in the presentation.
6. Increase the size of the chart in the slide so it fills a good portion of the slide below the title.
7. Print only Slide 4.
8. Save the presentation with Save As and name it **sppc7sc03**.
9. Close **sppc7sc03**.
10. Click the button on the Taskbar representing Excel.
11. Close **FundsWorkbook03** and then exit Excel.

Assessment 4

1. Open Excel and then open **FundsWorkbook03**.
2. Make the following changes to the data in cells in **FundsWorkbook03**:
   a. Change B2 from *5%* to *12%*.
   b. Change B4 from *10%* to *15%*.
   c. Change B6 from *8%* to *17%*.
3. Save the workbook again with the same name (**FundsWorkbook03**).
4. Close **FundsWorkbook03** and then exit Excel.
5. With PowerPoint the active program, open **sppc7sc03**. At the message telling you that the presentation contains links to the other files, click the Update Links button.
6. Add an animation scheme of your choosing to all slides in the presentation.
7. Run the presentation beginning with Slide 1.
8. Print the presentation as handouts with all slides on one page.
9. Save and then close the presentation.

Assessment 5

1. Open **JobSearchPresentation**.
2. Save the presentation with Save As and name it **sppc7sc05**.
3. Create a custom show named *Interview* that contains Slides 1, 3, 6, 7, and 9. ***(Hint: For help, refer to Exercise 11.)***
4. Run the Interview custom show.
5. Print the Interview custom show.
6. Edit the Interview custom show by removing Slide 2.
7. Print the Interview custom show again.
8. Save and then close **sppc7sc05**.

Assessment 6

1. Use PowerPoint's Help feature to learn how to copy slides with the Slide Finder feature.
2. After reading the information, insert slides from one presentation into another by completing the following these basic steps:
   a. Open **CommunicationPresentation**.
   b. Display Slide 6 in the Slide pane.
   c. Using the information you learned in the Help files, insert all of the slides in the **TelephonePresentation** into the current presentation. ***(Hint: Make sure you use the Slide Finder feature to do this.)***
   d. Check the inserted slides and make any minor adjustments necessary.
3. Save the presentation with Save As and name it **sppc7sc06**.
4. Run the presentation beginning with Slide 1.
5. Print the presentation as handouts with six slides per page (the second page will contain five slides).
6. Save and then close the presentation.

CHAPTER challenge

You are the computer trainer at Computer Corner, a computer store specializing not only in computer software and hardware, but also computer training. You have been asked to conduct a seminar on "How to Purchase a Computer." Create a PowerPoint presentation consisting of 10 slides. Include a Word table and an Excel chart. The presentation should be visually appealing with features such as clip art/pictures, transitions, custom animation, video/sound, and so on. Create a folder on your disk named *Training* and save the presentation as **ComputerPurchase** in that folder. Copy the presentation (within the folder Training) and rename it **ComputerPurchaseBackup**.

Since you are not sure what computer lab you will be using when conducting this presentation, you would like to ensure that the fonts (assuming you used TrueType fonts) in the presentation will display correctly on any computer. Use the Help feature to learn about embedding TrueType fonts in a presentation. Save the presentation created in the first part of the Chapter Challenge again (as **ComputerPurchase**) and embed the TrueType fonts (embed characters in use only).

Your supervisor would like to review the presentation prior to the seminar. E-mail the presentation to your supervisor (your professor) for review.

CHAPTER 8

SHARING PRESENTATIONS

PERFORMANCE OBJECTIVES

- **Upon successful completion of Chapter 8, you will be able to:**
- **Send a presentation for review**
- **Edit a presentation sent for review**
- **Accept/reject changes from reviewers**
- **Insert comments in a presentation**
- **Print comments**
- **Save a presentation for use on another computer using the Package for CD feature**
- **Save a presentation as a Web page**
- **Preview a Web page**
- **Format a Web page**
- **Broadcast a presentation online**

If you want to share your presentation with others, send the presentation for review and then merge the changes in the original presentation. The process for merging changes into the original presentation varies depending on whether you are using Outlook or another e-mail program. In this chapter, you will learn about the review cycle, and the steps to merge changes to a presentation using the Compare and Merge Presentations feature. You can insert a comment in a presentation that you are sending out for review.

Use the Package for CD feature to save a PowerPoint presentation for use on another computer that does not have PowerPoint installed. Slides can be converted to HTML for viewing as Web pages. Along with on-screen slide shows, presentations can be delivered by broadcasting them online.

Sending a Presentation for Review

Some employees in a company may be part of a *workgroup,* which is a networked collection of computers sharing files, printers, and other resources. In a workgroup, you generally make your files available to your colleagues. With the Windows

Send a Presentation for Review
1. Open presentation.
2. Click File, Save As.
3. Type new name.
4. Click Save as type option box.
5. Click *Presentation for Review.*
6. Click Save.

operating system and Office applications, you can share and distribute your files quickly and easily to members of your workgroup from your desktop computer.

If you are part of a workgroup, you may want to send a copy of a PowerPoint presentation to other members of the workgroup for review. To do this, you would set up a review cycle for reviewing the presentation. This cycle consists of the following general steps:

1. Using Microsoft Outlook or another e-mail program, send a separate copy of the presentation to each person who is to review the presentation.
2. Each reviewer makes changes to his or her own copy of the presentation.
3. Each reviewer sends his or her own edited presentation back to you.
4. You compare each edited presentation with the original presentation and determine if you want to accept or reject changes.

If you are using Microsoft Outlook to send the presentation, click File, point to Send To, and then click Mail Recipient (for Review). Specify to whom you want the presentation sent and then click the Send button. If you are using an e-mail program other than Outlook, you would complete these general steps to send a presentation for review:

1. Open the presentation.
2. Click File and then Save As.
3. At the Save As dialog box, type a new name for the presentation in the *File name* text box.
4. Click the down-pointing arrow at the right side of the *Save as type* option box and then click *Presentation for Review* at the drop-down list.
5. Click the Save button.
6. Close the presentation.

exercise 1

SENDING A PRESENTATION FOR REVIEW

1. Open **JobSearchPresentation** (located in the PowerPointChapter08S folder on your disk).
2. Save the presentation with Save As and name it **sppc8x01**.
3. Save the presentation for review by Suzanne Nelson by completing the following steps:
   a. Click File and then Save As.
   b. At the Save As dialog box, type sppc8x01SN in the *File name* text box.
   c. Make sure the PowerPointChapter08S folder on your disk is the active folder.
   d. Click the down-pointing arrow at the right of the *Save as type* option box and then click *Presentation for Review* in the drop-down list.
   e. Click the Save button.

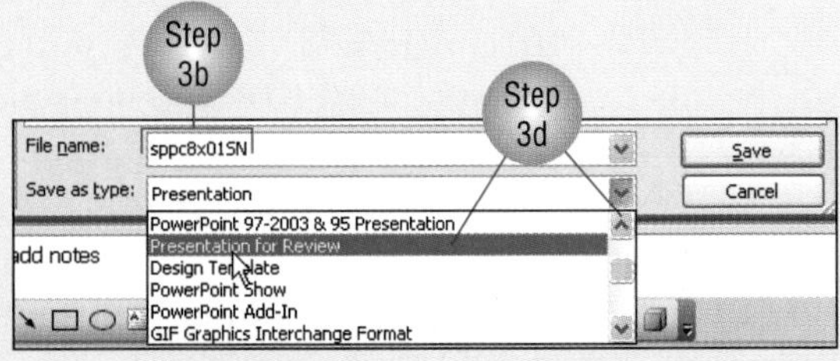

4. Save the presentation for review by Michael Ramsey by completing Steps 3a through 3e, except save the presentation with the name **sppc8x01MR** in Step 3b.
5. Close **sppc8x01**.

Editing a Presentation Sent for Review

When a presentation is saved as a presentation for review, PowerPoint inserts a link in the copy of the presentation back to the original presentation. When you open the copy of the presentation, a message displays asking if you want to merge changes to the copy of the presentation back into the original presentation. Click Yes if you want changes you make to the copy of the presentation to apply to the original. Click No if you do not want the original presentation to reflect the changes you make to the copy. Make the desired changes to the presentation and then save it in the normal manner.

In Exercise 3, you will be reviewing changes made by two reviewers to two different copies of the job search presentation. PowerPoint uses different colors to identify reviewers. In Exercise 2, you will specify a user name at the Options dialog box with the General tab selected and then make changes to a copy of the job search presentation. You will then change the user name at the Options dialog box and make changes to another copy of the presentation.

To change the user name, click Tools and then Options. At the Options dialog box, click the General tab. At the Options dialog box with the General tab selected, select the name in the *Name* text box and then type the new name. Select the initials in the *Initials* text box and then type the new initials. Click OK to close the dialog box.

exercise 2

EDITING PRESENTATIONS SENT FOR REVIEW

1. At the blank PowerPoint screen, change the user name and initials by completing the following steps:
   a. Click Tools and then Options.
   b. At the Options dialog box, click the General tab. (Make a note of the current name and initials. You will reenter this information later in this exercise.)
   c. At the Options dialog box with the General tab selected, select the name in the *Name* text box and then type Suzanne Nelson.
   d. Select the initials in the *Initials* text box and then type SN.
   e. Click OK to close the dialog box.

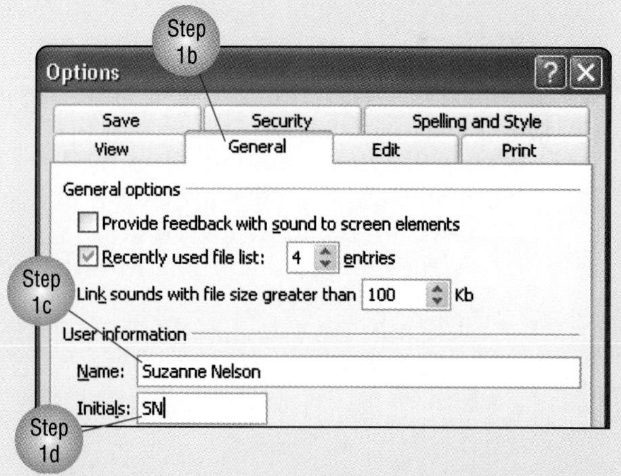

2. Edit the job search presentation as Suzanne Nelson by completing the following steps:
   a. Open the **sppc8x01SN** presentation.
   b. At the message asking if you want to merge changes in **sppc8x01SN** back into **sppc8x01**, click No.
   c. Make the following changes:
      1) Edit the title in Slide 1 so it reads *JOB SEARCH* (instead of *JOB SEARCH IN THE NEW MILLENNIUM*).

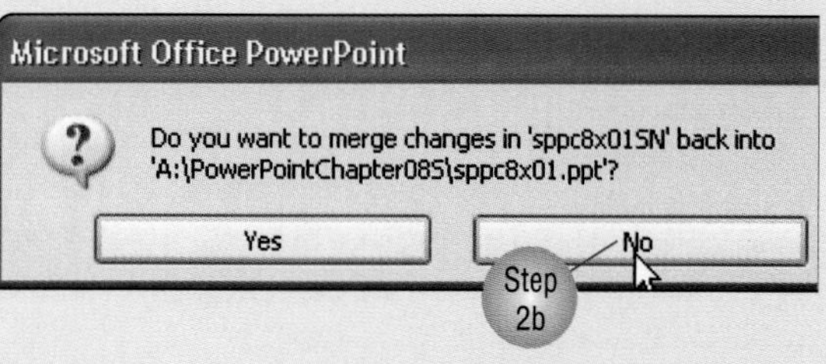

2) Display Slide 3 and then insert the text *Include any volunteer experience* between the first and second bulleted items.
3) Display Slide 5 and then edit the second bulleted item so it reads *Locate newspaper ads*.
4) Display Slide 6 and then edit the fourth bulleted item so it reads *Bring at least three references*.

3. Print the presentation as handouts with all nine slides on one page.
4. Save the presentation with the same name (**sppc8x01SN**) and then close **sppc8x01SN**.
5. At the blank PowerPoint screen, change the user name and initials by completing the following steps:
   a. Click Tools and then Options.
   b. At the Options dialog box, click the General tab.
   c. At the Options dialog box with the General tab selected, select the name in the *Name* text box and then type Michael Ramsey.
   d. Select the initials in the *Initials* text box and then type MR.
   e. Click OK to close the dialog box.
6. Edit the job search presentation as Michael Ramsey by completing the following steps:
   a. Open the **sppc8x01MR** presentation located in the PowerPointChapter08S folder on your disk.
   b. At the message asking if you want to merge changes in **sppc8x01MR** back into **sppc8x01**, click No.
   c. Make the following changes:
      1) Edit the subtitle in Slide 1 so it reads *Strategies for Employment Search*.
      2) Display Slide 5 and then edit the last bulleted item so it reads *Locate resources on the Internet*.
      3) Display Slide 6 and then edit the second bulleted item so it reads *Be on time for the interview*.
      4) Display Slide 9 and then edit the last bulleted item so it reads *Establish personal work goals*.
7. Print the presentation as handouts with all nine slides on the same page.
8. Save the presentation with the same name (**sppc8x01MR**) and then close **sppc8x01MR**.
9. Change the name and initials in the User information back to the original information by completing the following steps:
   a. Click Tools and then Options.
   b. At the Options dialog box with the General tab selected, type the original name in the *Name* text box.
   c. Press the Tab key and then type the original initials in the *Initials* text box.
   d. Click OK to close the dialog box.

HINT

PowerPoint identifies reviewer changes that conflict. You decide what changes to make when a conflict exists.

Accepting/Rejecting Changes from Reviewers

When you open a presentation saved as a presentation for review, a message displays asking if you want to merge changes to the copy of the presentation back into the original presentation. If you click Yes, the changes made to the copy are automatically made to the original (this is because of the link established between the presentations). If you want control over what changes are made to the original presentation, click No (this is what you did in Exercise 2).

If you used Outlook to distribute presentations for review, combine the review by double-clicking the attached reviewed presentation. At the dialog box that displays, click Yes and PowerPoint will automatically combine the reviewed presentation with the original presentation.

If you used another e-mail program to distribute presentations for review, use PowerPoint's Compare and Merge Presentations feature to combine changes. To use this feature, open the original presentation, click Tools, and then click Compare and Merge Presentations. At the Choose Files to Merge with Current Presentation dialog box, click to select all reviewed presentations, and then click the Merge button. This displays the original presentation with change markers identifying changes made by each reviewer. The Revisions Pane also displays at the right side of the PowerPoint screen as shown in Figure 8.1 along with the Reviewing toolbar, which displays immediately below the Formatting toolbar.

Accepting/Rejecting Changes to Presentation Sent for Review

1. Open original presentation.
2. Click Tools, Compare and Merge Presentations.
3. Click to select all reviewed presentations.
4. Click Merge button.
5. Accept or reject changes.

FIGURE 8.1 ***Original Presentation Merged with Reviewed Presentations***

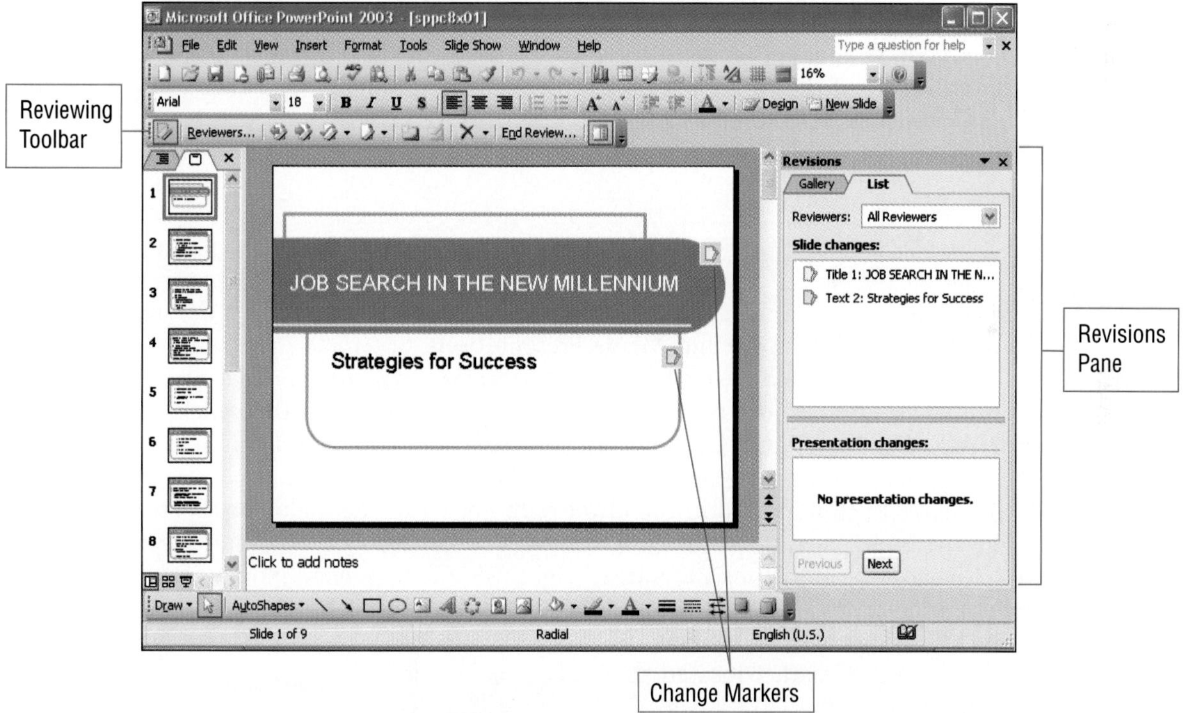

Changes made by each reviewer display in a change marker in the original presentation. Change markers for each reviewer display in a different color. This helps you identify who suggested what change.

The Revisions Pane contains two tabs—Gallery and List. The Revisions Pane with the List tab selected displays changes in the *Slide changes* list box. You can also display a list of reviewers by clicking the down-pointing arrow at the right side of the *Reviewers* option box. By default, all reviewers are selected. If you do not want to view changes made by a specific reviewer, remove the check mark by the reviewer's name.

HINT

Click the End Review button on the Reviewing toolbar to end a review and permanently end the ability to combine reviewed presentations with the original.

Click the Gallery tab and the Revisions Pane displays the current slide as slide miniatures for each reviewer showing the changes made by the reviewer. Above each pane is the reviewer's name preceded by a check box. Click this check box to accept all changes to the slide made by that specific reviewer.

Apply

Next Item

To accept a change to a slide, click the change marker and a box displays containing a check box followed by a description of the change. Move the mouse pointer over the description and the location of the change is identified in the slide by red marks. Accept the change by clicking the check box located in the change marker box to insert a check mark. You can also accept a change by clicking the Apply button on the Reviewing toolbar. Move to the next change by clicking the Next button located toward the bottom of the Revisions Pane or click the Next Item button on the Reviewing toolbar.

To accept all changes made to a slide, click the down-pointing arrow at the right side of the Apply button on the Reviewing toolbar, and then click *Apply All Changes to the Current Slide* at the drop-down list. To accept all changes made by one reviewer on one slide, click the Gallery tab at the Revisions Pane. Click the check box that displays for the specific reviewer above the slide miniature. You can also point to a slide miniature of the reviewer whose changes you want to accept, click the down-pointing arrow that displays at the right side of the miniature, and then click *Apply Changes By This Reviewer* at the drop-down list. To accept all changes made to the presentation, click the down-pointing arrow at the right side of the Apply button on the Reviewing toolbar, and then click *Apply All Changes to the Presentation*.

exercise 3 — COMPARING AND MERGING CHANGES INTO THE ORIGINAL PRESENTATION

1. Open **sppc8x01**.
2. Click Tools and then Compare and Merge Presentations.
3. At the Choose Files to Merge with Current Presentation dialog box, make sure the PowerPointChapter08S folder on your disk is the active folder and then click ***sppc8x01MR***. Hold down the Ctrl key and then click ***sppc8x01SN***. (This selects both presentations.)
4. Click the Merge button located in the lower right corner of the dialog box. (This displays Slide 1 in the Slide pane, displays the Reviewing toolbar below the Formatting toolbar, and also displays the Revisions Pane at the right side of the screen. Notice the two change markers [in two different colors] that display in Slide 1.)
5. Make the following changes to Slide 1:
   a. Click the change marker located at the right side of the Slide 1 title. (This displays a description of the change followed by the reviewer's name *Suzanne Nelson*.)
   b. You do not want to make this change, so click in the slide outside the change description box.
   c. Click the change marker located at the right side of the Slide 1 subtitle.
   d. Accept the changes to the subtitle by clicking the check box preceding the text *All changes to Text 2*.

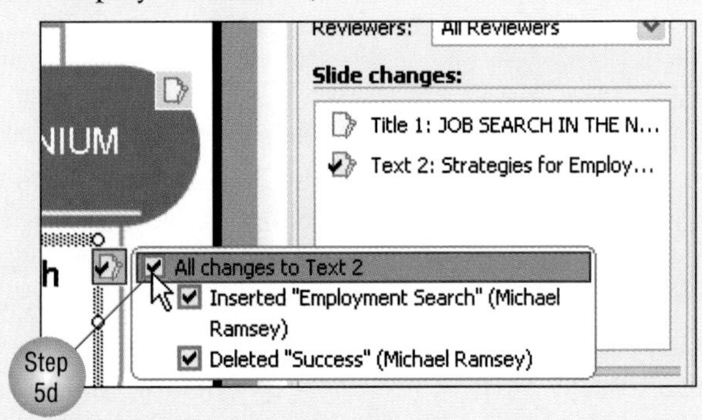

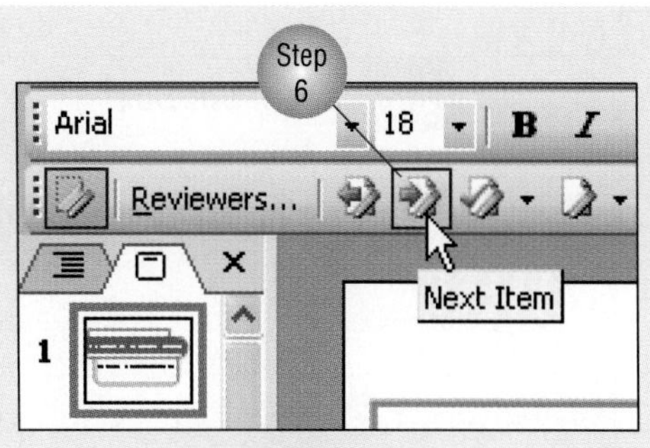

6. Click the Next Item button on the Reviewing toolbar to display the next change (located on Slide 3).
7. Accept all changes to Slide 3 by clicking the check box preceding the text *All changes to Text 2*.
8. Click the Next Item button on the Reviewing toolbar. (This displays Slide 5.)
9. Accept the changes by completing the following steps:
   a. Click the Gallery tab at the Revisions Pane. (This displays slide miniatures in the pane showing changes made by each reviewer.)
   b. Accept the changes made to Slide 5 by Michael Ramsey by clicking in the check box that displays above the top slide miniature.
   c. Accept the changes made to Slide 5 by Suzanne Nelson by clicking in the check box that displays above the bottom slide miniature.

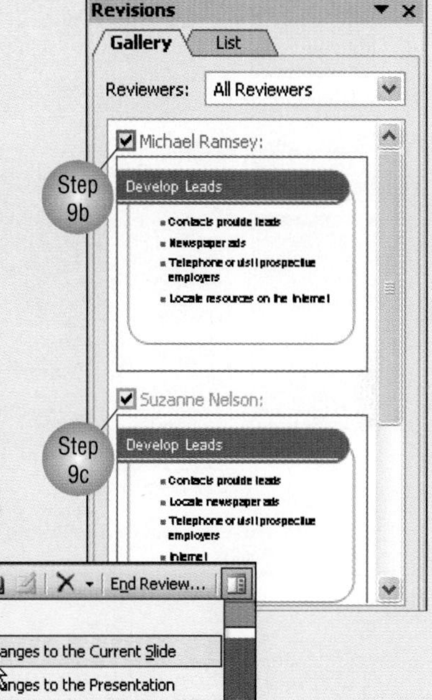

10. Click the Next Item button on the Reviewing toolbar. (This displays Slide 6.)
11. Accept all changes made to Slide 6 by clicking the down-pointing arrow at the right side of the Apply button on the Reviewing toolbar and then click *Apply All Changes to the Current Slide* at the drop-down list.
12. Click the Next Item button on the Reviewing toolbar. (This displays Slide 9.)
13. Accept the change to Slide 9 by clicking the Apply button on the Reviewing toolbar.
14. Display Slide 1 and then run the presentation.
15. Save the presentation with Save As and name it **sppc8x03**.
16. Print the presentation as handouts with all nine slides on one page.
17. Save and then close **sppc8x03**.

Inserting Comments

Insert a Comment
1. Click Insert, Comment.
2. Type comment text.

If you are sending out a presentation for review and want to ask reviewers specific questions or provide information about slides in a presentation, insert comments. To insert a comment, display the desired slide and then position the insertion point where you want the comment to appear. Click Insert on the Menu bar and then click Comment and a comment box displays similar to the one shown in Figure 8.2. You can also insert a comment by clicking the Insert Comment button on the Reviewing toolbar. Display this toolbar by clicking View, pointing to Toolbars, and then clicking Reviewing.

Insert Comment

FIGURE

8.2 **Comment Box**

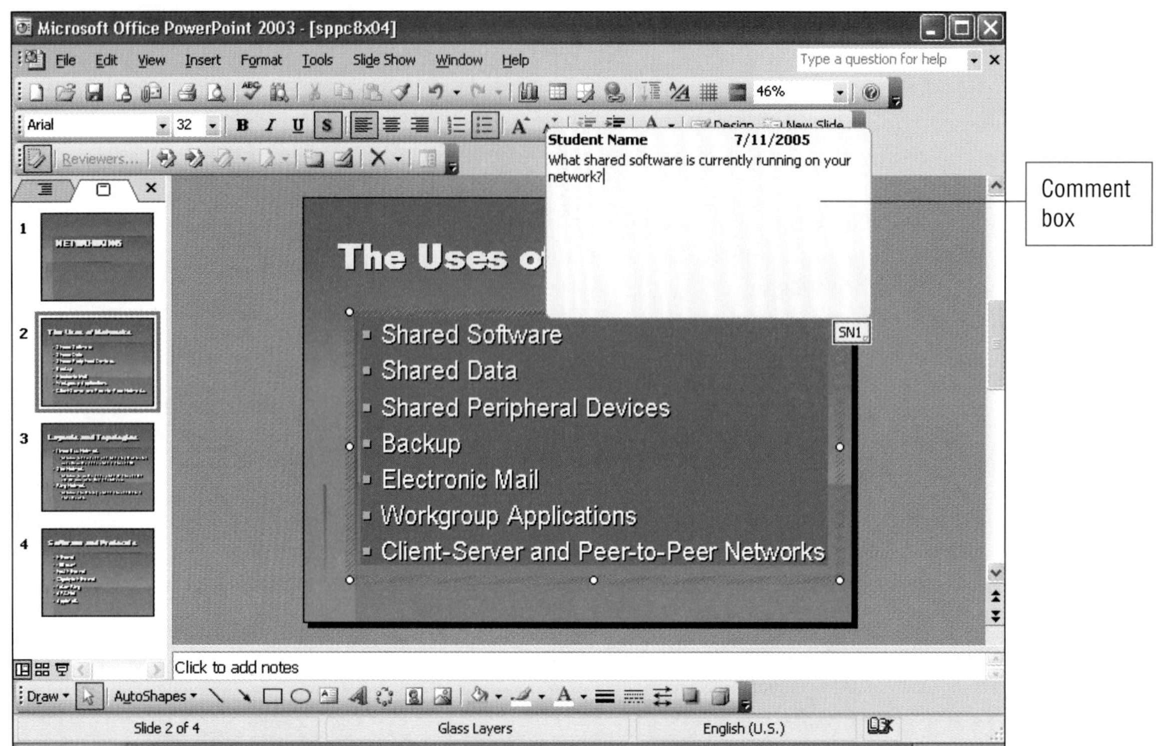

Delete Comment

HINT

Move a comment by selecting the comment box and then dragging it to the desired location.

HINT

Turn on or off the display of comment boxes with the Show/Hide Markup button on the Reviewing toolbar.

After typing the desired comment, click outside the comment box. A small yellow box displays at the right side of the slide aligned horizontally with the position where the comment was inserted. The user's initials display in the yellow box followed by a number. Comments by individual users are numbered sequentially beginning with 1.

To edit a comment, double-click the comment box, make the desired changes, and then click outside the box. To delete a comment from a slide, click the small box containing the user's initials and comment number and then click the Delete Comment button on the Reviewing toolbar. You can also right-click the box containing the initials and then click Delete at the shortcut menu.

To print comments, display the Print dialog box, choose how you want slides printed with the *Print what* option, and then insert a check mark in the *Include comments page* check box. Comments print on a separate page after the presentation is printed.

exercise 4 INSERTING AND PRINTING COMMENTS

1. Open **NetworkingPresentation**.
2. Save the presentation with Save As and name it **sppc8x04**.
3. Insert comments by completing the following steps:
   a. Display Slide 2 in the Slide pane.
   b. Turn on the Reviewing toolbar by clicking View, pointing to Toolbars, and then clicking Reviewing.
   c. Click immediately right of *Shared Software* (the first bulleted item). This moves the insertion point immediately right of *Software*.
   d. Click the Insert Comment button on the Reviewing toolbar.
   e. Type the following in the comment box: **What shared software is currently running on your network?**
   f. Display Slide 3 in the Slide pane.
   g. Click immediately right of *Star Network* (the second bulleted item).
   h. Click the Insert Comment button on the Reviewing toolbar.
   i. Type the following in the comment box: **Please include examples of star networks with which you have experience.**
   j. Click outside the comment box to deselect it.
4. Print the presentation and comments by completing the following steps:
   a. Click File and then Print.
   b. At the Print dialog box, click the down-pointing arrow at the right side of *Print what* and then click *Handouts*.
   c. Make sure *6* displays in the *Slides per page* option box.
   d. Make sure the *Print comments and ink markup* check box contains a check mark.
   e. Click OK.
5. Run the presentation beginning with Slide 1.
6. Save and then close the presentation.

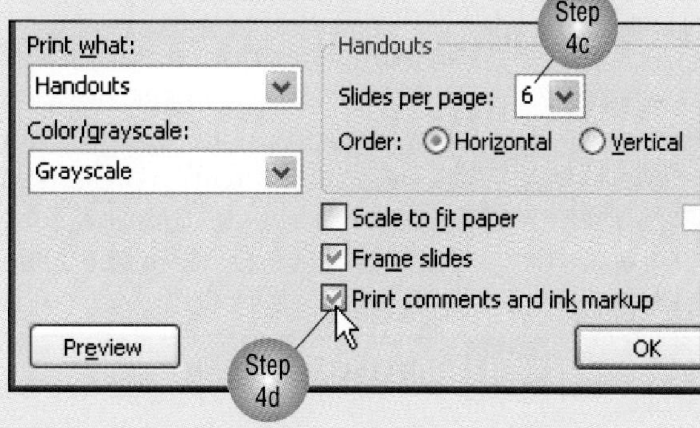

Saving a Presentation to Use on Another Computer

The safest way to transport a PowerPoint presentation to another computer is to use the Package for CD feature. With this feature, you can copy a presentation including all of the linked files, fonts used, and the PowerPoint Viewer program (in case the destination computer does not have PowerPoint installed on it) onto a CD or to a folder or network location. To use the Package for CD feature, click File and then Package for CD. This displays the Package for CD dialog box shown in Figure 8.3.

HINT
Include the Microsoft PowerPoint Viewer when packaging a presentation if you plan to run the presentation on a computer without PowerPoint.

FIGURE

8.3 ***Package for CD Dialog Box***

Click this button to copy the presentation and all related files to a specific folder.

Click this button to copy the presentation and all related files to a CD.

Package for CD

Copy PowerPoint presentations to a CD that will play on computers running Microsoft Windows, even without PowerPoint.

Name the CD: PresentationCD

Files to be copied:

ContactsPresentation.ppt

Add Files...

Linked files and the PowerPoint Viewer are included by default. To change this, click Options.

Options...

Copy to Folder... | Copy to CD | Close

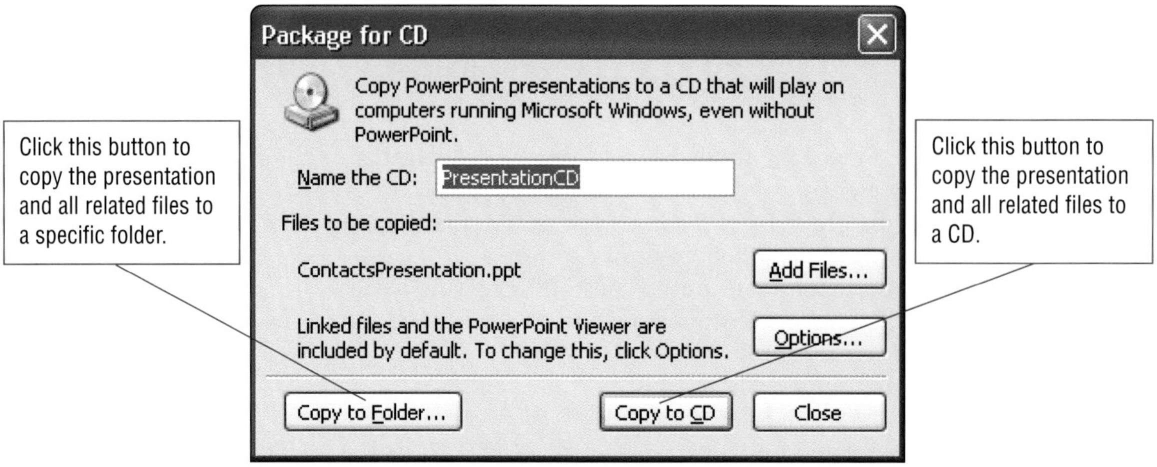

QUICK STEPS

Save Presentation to Use on Another Computer

1. Open presentation.
2. Click File, Package for CD.
3. Type name.
4. Click Copy to CD button or click Copy to Folder button.

At the Package for CD dialog box, type a name in the *Name the CD* text box, and then click the Copy to CD button. If you want to copy the presentation to a specific folder (instead of a CD), click the Copy to Folder button.

Click the Options button at the Package for CD dialog box and the Options dialog box displays as shown in Figure 8.4. Insert a check mark in the check box for those features you want to be included on the CD or in the folder or remove the check mark from those you do not want to include. If the computer you will be using does not contain the PowerPoint program, insert a check mark in the *PowerPoint Viewer* check box. The PowerPoint Viewer allows you to run a presentation on a computer that does not contain PowerPoint. If charts or other files are linked to the presentation, insert a check mark in the *Linked files* check box and, if the destination computer does not have the same fonts installed, insert a check mark in the *Embedded TrueType fonts* check box.

FIGURE

8.4 ***Options Dialog Box***

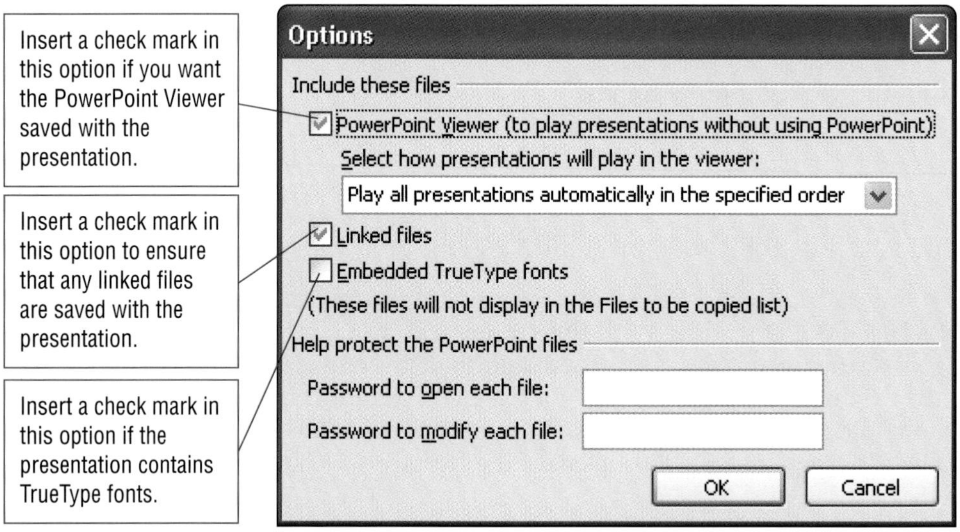

Insert a check mark in this option if you want the PowerPoint Viewer saved with the presentation.

Insert a check mark in this option to ensure that any linked files are saved with the presentation.

Insert a check mark in this option if the presentation contains TrueType fonts.

Options

Include these files

PowerPoint Viewer (to play presentations without using PowerPoint)

Select how presentations will play in the viewer:

Play all presentations automatically in the specified order

Linked files

Embedded TrueType fonts

(These files will not display in the Files to be copied list)

Help protect the PowerPoint files

Password to open each file:

Password to modify each file:

OK | Cancel

exercise 5

USING THE PACKAGE FOR CD FEATURE

1. Open **E-commercePresentation** from the PowerPointChapter08S folder on your disk.
2. Use the Package for CD feature by completing the following steps:
   a. Click File and then Package for CD.
   b. At the Package for CD dialog box, type **sppc8x05** in the *Name the CD* text box.
   c. Click the Options button.
   d. At the Options dialog box, remove the check mark from the *PowerPoint Viewer* check box.
   e. Make sure the *Linked files* option contains a check mark.
   f. Insert a check mark in the *Embedded TrueType fonts* check box.
   g. Click OK to close the Options dialog box.

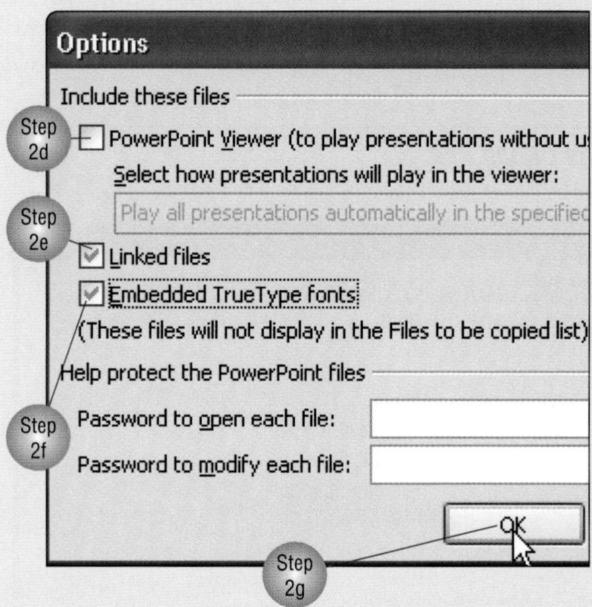

   h. At the Package for CD dialog box, click the Copy to Folder button.
   i. At the Copy to Folder dialog box, click the Browse button.
   j. Navigate to Drive A (or the drive where your disk is located).
   k. Click the Select button.
   l. At the Copy to Folder dialog box, click OK.
   m. After the presentation is saved, close the Package for CD dialog box by clicking the Close button.
3. Close **E-commercePresentation**.

Saving a Presentation as a Web Page

QUICK STEPS

Save Presentation as Web Page

1. Open presentation.
2. Click File, Save as Web Page.
3. Type file name.
4. Click Save.

The Internet is fast becoming a preferred choice as a presentation medium. Once a presentation has been published to the Internet, anyone around the world with Internet access can view your presentation. If you are traveling to several remote locations to deliver a presentation you can access the slides from any computer with Internet access instead of transporting disks or portable computers.

You can save a presentation as a Web page as a folder with an HTML file and all supporting files or you can save a presentation as a Web page as a single file with all supporting files. ***HTML*** is an acronym for Hypertext Markup Language, which is the programming language used to code pages to display graphically on the World Wide Web. HTML is a collection of instructions that include ***tags*** applied to text and graphics to instruct the Web browser software how to properly display the page.

HINT

Publish your presentation to the Web to make it available to colleagues for viewing.

Fortunately, PowerPoint will translate the slides into Web pages for you so you can publish presentations to the Internet without having to learn HTML programming statements. To do this, open the presentation you want to save as a Web page, click File, and then click Save as Web Page. At the Save As dialog box shown in Figure 8.5, the name in the *File name* text box will default to the presentation file name and the *Save as type* option will default to *Single File Web Page* (which saves the presentation with a *.mht* file extension). This default can be changed to *Web Page*, which will save the presentation with the file extension *.htm*.

FIGURE 8.5 ***Save As Dialog Box***

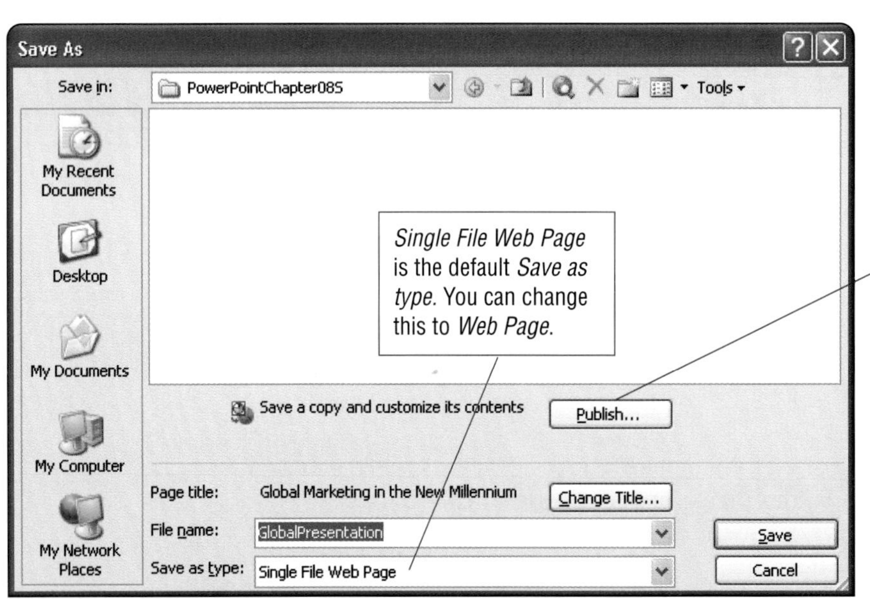

At the Save As dialog box, click the Publish button and the Publish as Web Page dialog box displays as shown in Figure 8.6. If you do not want to convert all of the slides in the presentation, specify the starting slide number in the *Slide number* text box and the ending slide number in the *through* text box in the *Publish what?* section. You can convert to specific versions of Web browser software with the options in the *Browser support* section as shown in Figure 8.6. Click the Web Options button to display the Web Options dialog box displayed in Figure 8.7.

FIGURE

8.6 *Publish as Web Page Dialog Box*

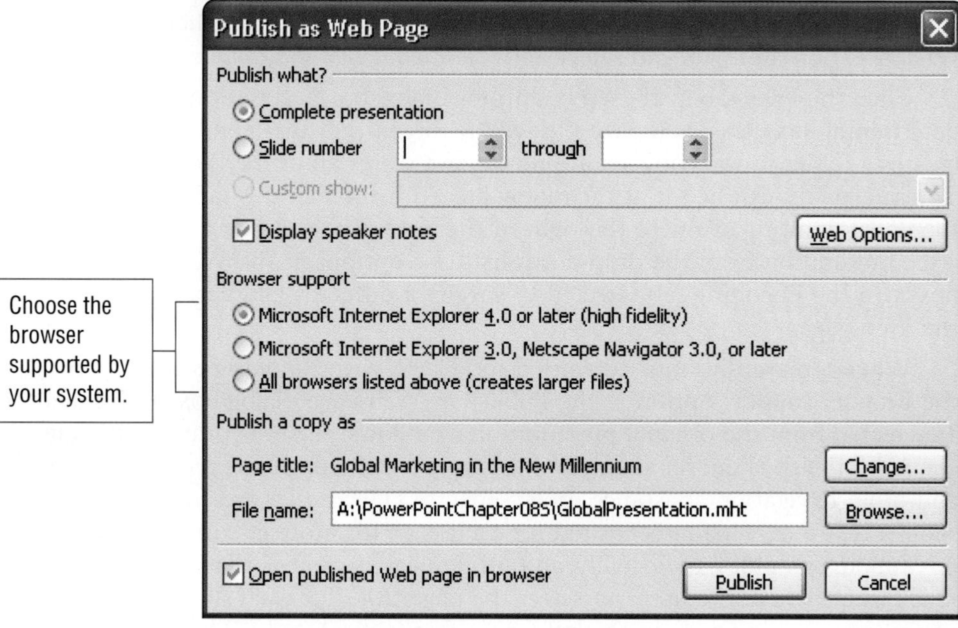

FIGURE

8.7 *Web Options Dialog Box*

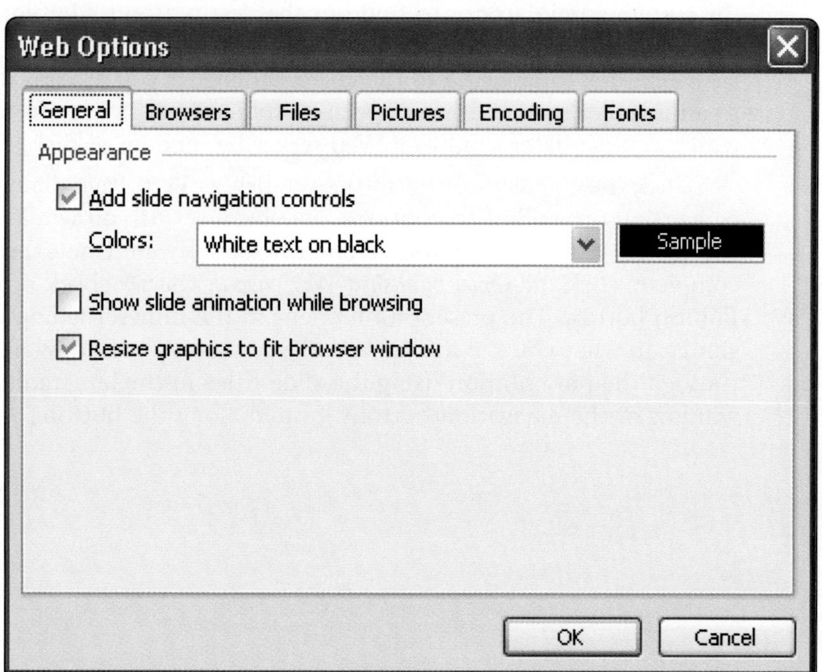

When PowerPoint converts the presentation to HTML format, navigation buttons are created for users to navigate through the slides in the Web browser. The default colors for the navigation buttons are *White text on black*. You can select different color schemes with the *Colors* option at the Web Options dialog box with the General tab selected. If the target browser is Microsoft Internet Explorer version 4.0 or later, you can select *Show slide animation while browsing*.

Click the Files tab at the Web Options dialog box and options display for determining how the Web page files will be organized. By default, PowerPoint creates a folder in the conversion process and stores all of the files in the folder. The screen size can be set at the dialog box with the Pictures tab selected. Click the down-pointing arrow to the right of the *Screen size* text box and then click a screen resolution from the drop-down list. Use options at the Web Options dialog box with the Encoding tab selected to specify a different language code for saving the Web page.

When a presentation is converted to HTML with *All browsers listed above* as the Browser support option at the Publish as Web Page dialog box, additional files are created from the original presentation as follows: separate graphic files are created for each slide; separate graphic files are created for the navigation buttons and other navigation assistance tools; separate HTML files are created for each slide; a text-only version is created for each page for browser software that does not support graphics; and finally, an outline page is created that becomes the index frame where the user can select the page titles for each slide. The outline page is the opening page in the left frame that is displayed in the Web browser. A single presentation file can result in several files being created after conversion to Web pages.

If you are directly connected to a company intranet or Web server, contact the system administrator to find out the destination folder you need to specify in the *Publish a copy as File name* text box. Use the Browse button next to the *File name* text box to navigate to the correct folder. If you are not directly connected to an intranet or Web server, specify a folder on your system to copy the files to which you can later send to a Web server by modem or disk.

Click the Publish button in the Publish as Web Page dialog box to begin the conversion once all of the options have been set. If you would like to view the completed Web pages in your Web browser software when the conversion is complete, click the *Open published Web page in browser* check box before clicking the Publish button. The presentation opens in the browser window in a manner similar to what you see in Figure 8.8 (your browser window may vary). Navigate through the presentation using the slide titles in the left frame of the browser window or the navigation buttons located along the bottom of the window.

FIGURE 8.8 ***Presentation in Web Browser Window***

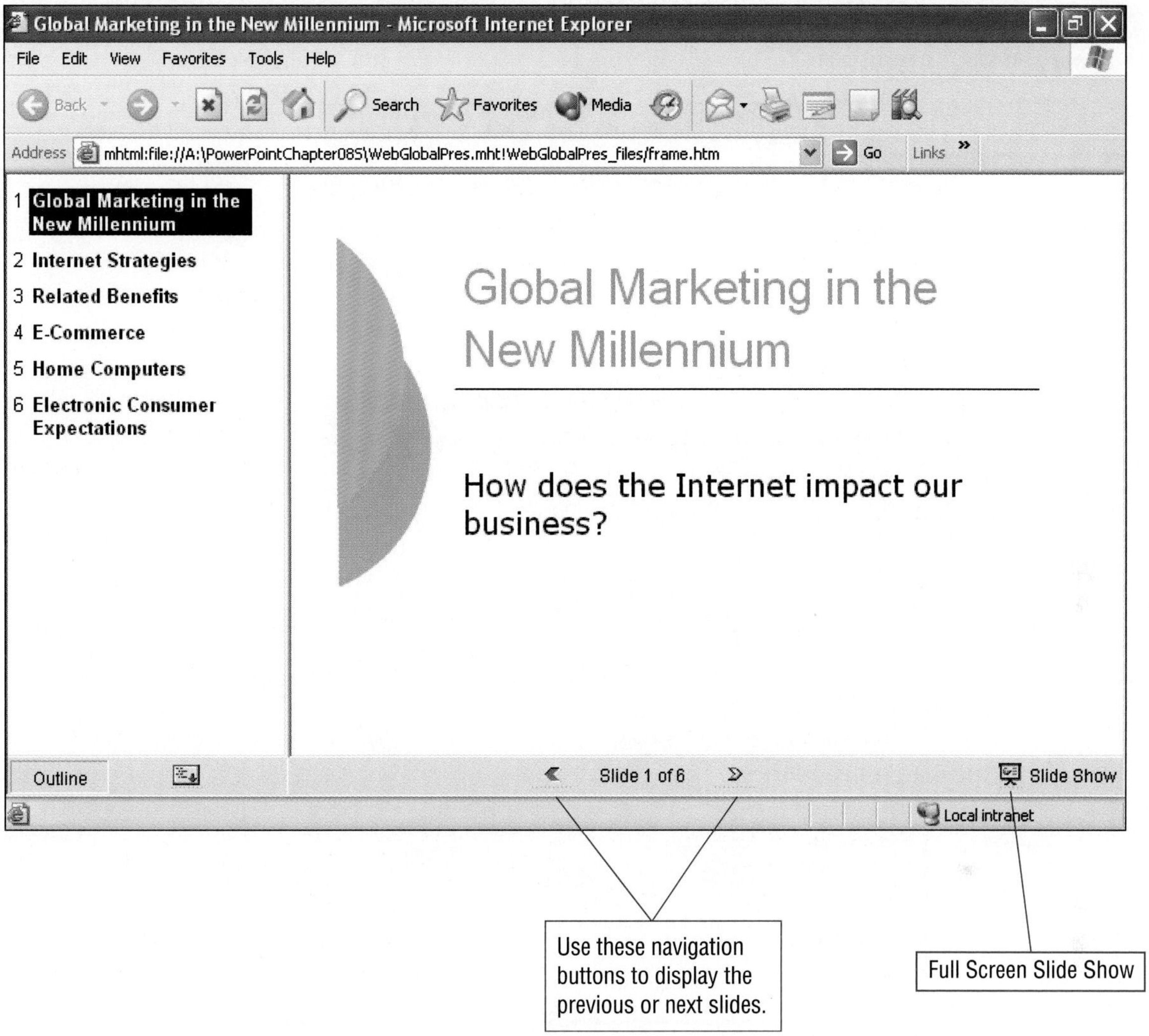

Use these navigation buttons to display the previous or next slides.

Full Screen Slide Show

exercise 6

SAVING A PRESENTATION AS A WEB PAGE AS A SINGLE FILE

1. Open **GlobalPresentation** from the PowerPointChapter08S folder on your disk.
2. Save the presentation as a Web page as a single file by completing the following steps:
   a. Click File and then Save as Web Page.
   b. At the Save As dialog box, type **WebGlobalPres**.
   c. Make sure the *Save as type* option is set at *Single File Web Page*.
   d. Click the Publish button.

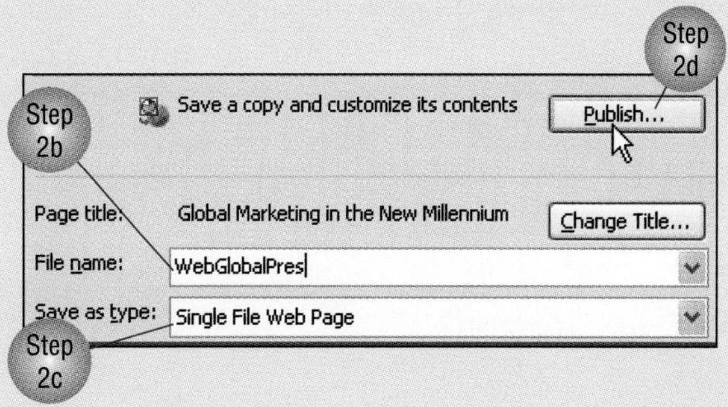

e. At the Publish as Web Page dialog box, click the Web Options button in the *Publish what?* section.

f. At the Web Options dialog box with the General tab selected, click the down-pointing arrow next to the *Colors* option box, and then click *Black text on white* at the drop-down list.

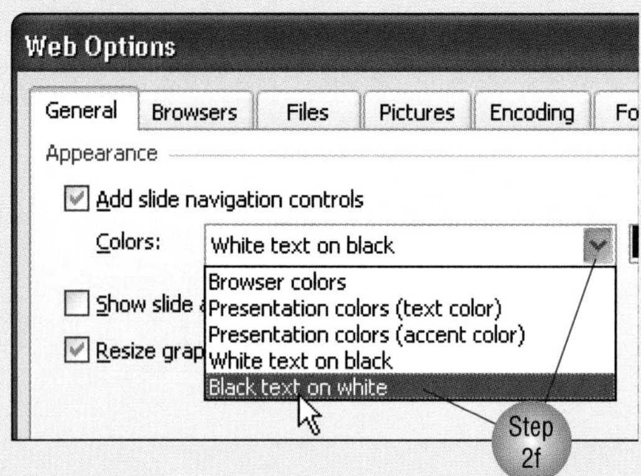

g. Click OK to close the Web Options dialog box.

h. At the Publish as Web Page dialog box, choose the target browser in the *Browser support* section that applies to your school. Check with your instructor if you are not sure which target browser you should be using. The default selection is *Microsoft Internet Explorer 4.0 or later*.

i. Click the Browse button next to the *File name* text box, make sure the correct folder is displayed for storing the presentation, and then click OK.

j. Click the *Open published Web page in browser* check box to insert a check mark.

k. Click the Publish button.

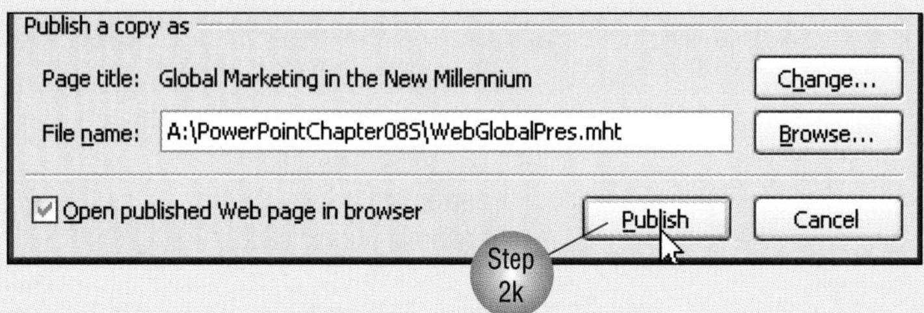

l. In a few moments, the conversion will be complete and the Microsoft Internet Explorer or other default browser window will open with the opening page of the presentation displayed.

3. Navigate through the presentation by clicking the slide titles along the left frame, or using the Next Slide and Previous Slide navigation buttons along the bottom of the window. (Refer to Figure 8.8.) When you have finished viewing all of the slides, close the Internet Explorer or other browser window.
4. Close **GlobalPresentation** without saving the changes.

exercise 7

SAVING A PRESENTATION AS A WEB PAGE AS A FOLDER WITH SUPPORTING FILES

1. In PowerPoint, open **JobSearchPresentation**.
2. Save the presentation as a Web page as a folder with supporting files by completing the following steps:
   a. Click File and then Save as Web Page.
   b. At the Save As dialog box, type **WebJobSearchPres** in the *File name* text box.
   c. Click the down-pointing arrow at the right of the *Save as type* option and then click *Web Page*.
   d. Click the Publish button.
   e. At the Publish as Web Page dialog box, choose the target browser in the *Browser support* section that applies to your school. Check with your instructor if you are not sure which target browser you should be using. The default selection is *Microsoft Internet Explorer 4.0 or later*.
   f. Click the Browse button next to the *File name* text box, make sure the correct folder is displayed for storing the presentation, and then click OK.
   g. Make sure the *Open published Web page in browser* check box contains a check mark.
   h. Click the Publish button.
   i. In a few moments, the conversion will be complete and the Microsoft Internet Explorer or other default browser window will open with the opening page of the presentation displayed.
3. Navigate through the presentation by clicking the slide titles along the left frame, or using the Next Slide and Previous Slide navigation buttons along the bottom of the window. (Refer to Figure 8.8.) When you have finished viewing all of the slides, close the Internet Explorer or other browser window.
4. Close **JobSearchPresentation** without saving the changes.
5. Display the Open dialog box with the PowerPointChapter08S folder active.
6. Double-click the *WebJobSearchPres_files* folder in the list box and then look at the HTML files saved in the folder.
7. Click the down-pointing arrow at the right side of the Views button on the Open dialog box toolbar and then click Details. Scroll through and look at the file types and names for the files that were created in the conversion process.
8. Click the down-pointing arrow at the right side of the Views button and then click List.
9. Click the Up One Level button to display the PowerPointChapter08S folder contents.
10. Close the Open dialog box.

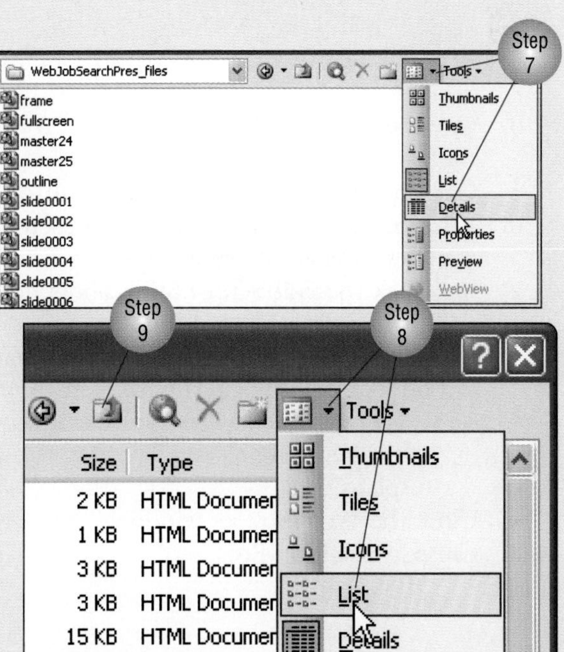

To make a presentation available to others on the Internet, the HTML files need to be copied to a ***Web server***. A Web server is a computer connected to the Internet that is set up to store Web pages that can be accessed by other Internet users by referencing an address such as www.microsoft.com. The system administrator for the Web server would provide you with instructions on where and how to copy the HTML files. You may be assigned an account name and password for the Web server by the administrator and will probably use File Transfer Protocol (FTP) to send the files to the server.

QUICK STEPS

Preview a Web Page

1. Open presentation Web file.
2. Click File, Web Page Preview.

Previewing a Web Page

If you want to see how the presentation displays in your Web browser, view the presentation in Web Page Preview. To do this, open the presentation you have saved as a Web page, click File, and then click Web Page Preview. This displays the first slide in the Web browser as shown in Figure 8.8.

When you first display the presentation in Web Page Preview, you may need to click the Maximize button located in the upper right corner of the Web browser window. Scroll through the slides in the presentation by clicking the Next Slide button located toward the bottom of the browser window (see Figure 8.8). Click the Previous Slide button to view the previous slide. The Outline pane displays at the left side of the browser. Move to various slides in the presentation by clicking the title of the desired slide in the Outline pane. If you want the slide to fill the entire screen, click the Full Screen Slide Show button located in the lower right corner of the browser window. Run the presentation as you would any other presentation.

HINT

Preview your presentation in Web Page Preview before publishing it to the Web to determine if changes need to be made to the presentation.

exercise 8

VIEWING A PRESENTATION IN WEB PAGE PREVIEW

1. Open **WebGlobalPres**.
2. Click File and then Web Page Preview.
3. At the browser window, click the slide title *2 Internet Strategies* to display the next slide in the presentation.

4. Click the Next Slide button located toward the bottom of the window to display Slide 3.
5. Click twice on the Previous Slide button to display Slide 1.
6. With Slide 1 displayed, run the presentation by completing the following steps:
   a. Click the Full Screen Slide Show button located in the lower right corner of the window.
   b. When Slide 1 fills the screen, navigate through the presentation by clicking the left mouse button.
   c. Continue clicking the mouse button until the Web browser window displays.
7. Close the Web browser window.
8. Close **WebGlobalPres**.

Formatting Web Pages

A presentation that has been converted to HTML can be edited in PowerPoint by opening the original presentation file, editing and/or formatting the presentation, and then saving it as a Web page to republish the Web pages. You can also directly open the HTML presentation, edit as required, and then use the regular Save command to update the Web pages. However, you should use the first method described to ensure the original source file and the HTML files have the same content.

exercise 9 — EDITING AND FORMATTING WEB PAGES

1. Open **GlobalPresentation** from the PowerPointChapter08S folder on your disk.
2. Edit the content and format the presentation by completing the following steps:
   a. Apply the Network design template to the presentation.
   b. Change to the Slide Master view and then make the following changes:
      1) Make sure the Network Title Master miniature is selected.
      2) Click the text *Click to edit Master title style*.
      3) Change the font to 40-point Tahoma bold.
      4) Click the Network Slide Master miniature.
      5) Click the text *Click to edit Master title style* and then change the font to 32-point Tahoma bold.
   c. Change back to the Normal view.
   d. Delete Slide 5. (To do this, click Slide 5 in the Outline/Slides pane with the Slides tab selected, and then press the Delete key.)
3. Update the revised HTML files by completing the following steps:
   a. Click File and then Save as Web Page.
   b. At the Save As dialog box, type **WebGlobalPres** in the *File name* text box.
   c. Click the Publish button.
   d. At the Publish as Web Page dialog box, click the Publish button.
   e. At the message asking if you want to replace the existing Web page, click Yes.
4. View the revised Web pages in the Internet Explorer window or other browser software window.
5. Close the Internet Explorer or other browser window.
6. Close **GlobalPresentation** without saving the changes.

Broadcasting a Presentation Online

A slide show can be delivered to audience members in remote locations or dispersed to more than one conference room by broadcasting it using the Web. The presentation can be recorded and saved for viewing later, scheduled for a live viewing at a preset day and time, or a live viewing can be started instantaneously. Video and/or audio can be included if the host computer has a video camera and/or microphone connected. PowerPoint initiates invitations to the broadcast via a meeting request message through Microsoft Outlook. Before broadcasting a presentation, you need to download the feature. You can do this at the Microsoft Office Online Web site.

HINT Broadcasting a presentation is live and publishing it to the Web is static.

HINT Rehearse your presentation before broadcasting it.

The presentation is saved in HTML format, so that the audience members can view the presentation in their Web browser software. The online broadcast feature requires that members have Internet Explorer version 5.1 or later and access to the server where the broadcast files are stored. You would complete the following basic steps to set up and schedule a live broadcast:

1. Open the presentation that you want to broadcast.
2. Click Slide Show, point to Online Broadcast, and then click Schedule a Live Broadcast.
3. At the Schedule Presentation Broadcast dialog box, type the welcome message that you want displayed on the lobby page for the broadcast in the *Description* text box, the name of the presenter in the *Speaker* text box, and the contact person's e-mail address in the *Email* text box.
4. Click the Settings button to display the Broadcast Settings dialog box with the Presenter tab selected.
5. Type the server name and folder name for the broadcast files in the *Save broadcast files in* text box in the *File location* section, or, click the Browse button and navigate to the server and folder name in the Choose Directory dialog box. The file location must be a shared folder that can be accessed by the audience participants.
6. If necessary, change the Audio/Video settings, change *Slide show mode* from Full Screen to Resizable Screen, or, click the *Display speaker notes with the presentation* check box in the Presentation options section.
7. Click OK.
8. Click the Schedule button in the Schedule Presentation Broadcast dialog box to start Microsoft Outlook and set up a meeting request to identify the broadcast participants, message, and the start and end times.

When you are ready to begin the broadcast, open the presentation, click Slide Show, point to Online Broadcast, and then click Start Live Broadcast Now. If you are a participant in the broadcast, a reminder message will appear in Outlook when the presentation is to begin. If Outlook is not your e-mail program, open the invitation e-mail message and then click the URL for the broadcast.

OPTIONAL exercise

STEPS TO SET UP AND SCHEDULE AN ONLINE BROADCAST

(Note: Before completing this exercise, check with your instructor for further details on the online broadcast. Either you will be given a server name and folder name location for the broadcast HTML files and a list of whom to invite to the broadcast or you will be instructed to complete the steps up to Step2e only and then click Cancel to return to the PowerPoint screen.)

1. Open **E-commercePresentation**.
2. Set up and schedule an online broadcast by completing the following steps:
   a. Click Slide Show, point to Online Broadcast, and then click Schedule a Live Broadcast.
   b. Click in the *Description* text box and then type the following text:
      Welcome to Global Marketing in the New Millennium.
   c. Press Tab and then type your first and last names in the *Speaker* text box.
   d. Press Tab three times and then type your e-mail address in the *Email* text box.
   e. Click the Settings button.

f. At the Broadcast Settings dialog box, type the server and folder location that you were given by your instructor in the *Save broadcast files in* text box. (The file location name should be in the format *||servername|foldername*.)
g. Click OK to close the Broadcast Settings dialog box.
h. At the Schedule Presentation Broadcast dialog box, click the Schedule button.
i. Microsoft Outlook will open with a meeting request message window open. Enter the e-mail addresses of the audience participants in the *To. . .* text box.
j. Type a description for the meeting in the *Subject* text box.
k. Click the *This is an online meeting using* check box and then click *Windows Media Services* in the drop-down list.
l. Enter the start time, end time, and reminder information as per instructions from your instructor.
m. Click Send.

3. If you will be viewing a broadcast, your instructor will provide instructions on how to participate.
4. Close **E-commercePresentation**.

This feature works for an online broadcast to 10 or fewer audience members at a time. To broadcast to a larger audience, a Windows Media Server that supports streaming media (such as video and audio) is required.

CHAPTER summary

- If you want to share a presentation with others, send the presentation for review and then merge the changes in the original presentation. The process for merging changes varies depending on whether you are using Outlook or another e-mail program.
- One method for sending a presentation for review is to display the Save As dialog box, type a name for the presentation, change the *Save as type* option to *Presentation for Review*, and then click the Save button.
- PowerPoint inserts a link in a presentation saved as a presentation for review that links back to the original presentation. When you open a presentation sent for review, you can choose whether or not you want changes reflected in the original presentation.
- One method for merging reviewers' changes is to use the Compare and Merge Presentations feature. To use this feature, open the original presentation, click Tools, and then click Compare and Merge Presentations. At the Choose Files to Merge with Current Presentation dialog box, select all reviewed presentations, and then click the Merge button.
- Changes made by each reviewer display in a change marker in the original presentation.
- Use the change markers, buttons on the Reviewing toolbar, or options at the Revisions Pane to accept and/or reject reviewer changes.

- Insert a comment in a slide by clicking the Insert Comment button on the Reviewing toolbar or by clicking Insert and then Comment. Type the comment text in the comment box that displays.
- To print comments, display the Print dialog box, choose how you want slides printed, and then insert a check mark in the *Include comments page* check box. Comments print on a separate page after the presentation is printed.
- Use the Package for CD feature to save a presentation for use on another computer. Fonts used in a presentation can be embedded within the presentation file.
- Save a presentation as a Web page as a single file by clicking File and then Save as Web Page. At the Save As dialog box, click the Publish button to display the Publish as Web Page dialog box where you specify what you want published and identify the supported browser.
- Save a presentation as a Web page as a folder with all supporting files by clicking File and then Save as Web Page. At the Save As dialog box, change the *Save as type* option to *Web Page*.
- Preview a presentation in the default Web browser by clicking File and then Web Page Preview.
- Format Web pages directly in PowerPoint using the regular features you would use to format slides.
- You can broadcast a presentation using the Web to an audience in remote locations or dispersed to more than one conference room. The online broadcast feature requires that audience members are using Internet Explorer 5.1 or later and have access to the server where the broadcast files are stored.
- Schedule an online broadcast with options at the Schedule Presentation Broadcast dialog box. Specify broadcast settings with options at the Broadcast Settings dialog box.
- To begin the broadcast, open the presentation, click Slide Show, point to Online Broadcast, and then click Start Live Broadcast Now.

FEATURES summary

FEATURE	BUTTON	MENU
Choose Files to Merge with Current Presentation dialog box		Tools, Compare and Merge Presentations
Insert comment		Insert, Comment
Reviewing toolbar		View, Toolbars, Reviewing
Package for CD dialog box		File, Package for CD
Save as Web page		File, Save as Web Page
Preview Web page		File, Web Page Preview
Schedule Presentation Broadcast dialog box		Slide Show, Online Broadcast, Schedule a Live Broadcast

CONCEPTS check

Completion: On a blank sheet of paper, indicate the correct term, symbol, or command for each description.

1. To send a presentation out for review, display the Save As dialog box, type a name for the presentation, change the *Save as type* option to this, and then click the Save button.
2. Change user's information at this dialog box with the General tab selected.
3. To display the Choose Files to Merge with Current Presentation dialog box, click Tools and then click this option.
4. Accept or reject reviewers' changes with buttons on the Reviewing toolbar or with options at this pane.
5. Accept a reviewer's change, click the change marker, and then click this button on the Reviewing toolbar.
6. Move to the next change in a presentation by clicking this button on the Reviewing toolbar.
7. Insert a comment in a presentation by clicking Insert and then Comment or by clicking the Insert Comment button on this toolbar.
8. To print comments, display the Print dialog box, specify how you want the presentation printed, and insert a check mark in this option check box.
9. Use this feature to transport a PowerPoint presentation to another computer.
10. *HTML* is an acronym for this, which is the programming language used to code pages to display graphically on the World Wide Web.
11. To begin the process of saving a presentation as a Web page, click File on the Menu bar and then click this option at the drop-down menu.
12. Click File on the Menu bar and then click this option to see how a presentation displays in your Web browser.

SKILLS check

Assessment 1

1. Open **CommunicationPresentation**.
2. Save the presentation with Save As and name it **sppc8sc01**.
3. Save the presentation for review by Jennifer Riley with the name **sppc8sc01JR**. *(Hint: Change the* **Save as type** *option at the Save As dialog box to* **Presentation for Review.***)*
4. Save the presentation for review by Greg Lui with the name **sppc8sc01GL**.
5. Close **sppc8sc01**.
6. At the blank PowerPoint screen, display the Options dialog box with the General tab selected, type Jennifer Riley in the *Name* text box, type JR in the *Initials* text box, and then close the dialog box.

7. Edit the communication presentation as Jennifer Riley by completing the following steps:
   a. Open the **sppc8sc01JR** presentation located in the PowerPointChapter08S folder on your disk.
   b. At the message asking if you want to merge changes in **sppc8sc01JR** back into **sppc8sc01**, click No.
   c. Make the following changes:
      1) Display Slide 2 and then edit the first bulleted item so it reads *Clearly identify to the audience what you need to communicate.*
      2) Display Slide 3 and then edit the third bulleted item so it reads *Decide whether to communicate verbally or in writing.*
      3) Display Slide 4 and then edit the first bulleted item so it reads *Gather and organize relevant facts.*
8. Print the presentation as handouts with all six slides on one page.
9. Save and then close **sppc8sc01JR.**
10. At the blank PowerPoint screen, display the Options dialog box with the General tab selected, type **Greg Lui** in the *Name* text box, type **GL** in the *Initials* text box, and then close the dialog box.
11. Edit the communication presentation as Greg Lui by completing the following steps:
    a. Open the **sppc8sc01GL** presentation located in the PowerPointChapter08S folder on your disk.
    b. At the message asking if you want to merge changes in **sppc8sc01GL**, back into **sppc8sc01**, click No.
    c. Make the following changes:
       1) Display Slide 2 and then insert a new bulleted item at the beginning of the bulleted list that reads *Identify the intended audience.*
       2) Display Slide 3 and then edit the second bulleted item so it reads *Determine what the audience already knows.*
       3) Display Slide 5 and delete *Voice mail* in the *Verbal* section.
12. Print the presentation as handouts with all six slides on one page.
13. Save and then close **sppc8sc01GL**.
14. Display the Options dialog box with the General tab selected, change the name and initials in the *User information* section back to the original information, and then close the dialog box.

Assessment 2

1. Open **sppc8sc01**.
2. Display the Choose Files to Merge with Current Presentation dialog box, select ***sppc8sc01GL***, select ***sppc8sc01JR***, and then click the Merge button.
3. Apply the following changes to slides:

Slide 2	=	Apply change made by Jennifer Riley
		Do not apply change by Greg Lui
Slide 3	=	Apply all changes
Slide 4	=	Apply all changes
Slide 5	=	Do not apply changes

4. Apply an animation scheme of your choosing to all slides in the presentation.
5. Run the presentation beginning with Slide 1.
6. Save the presentation with Save As and name it **sppc8sc02**.
7. Print the presentation as handouts with all six slides on one page.
8. Close the presentation.

Assessment 3

1. Open **GlobalPresentation**.
2. Save the presentation with Save As and name it **sppc8sc03**.
3. Insert the following comments:

   Slide 1 = Click immediately right of the subtitle *How does the Internet impact our business?* and then insert the comment **Change this from a question to a statement.**

   Slide 2 = Click immediately right of the bulleted item *Think "global"* and then insert the comment **Define global markets.**

   Slide 4 = Click immediately right of the bulleted item *Netscape and Microsoft* and then insert the comment **Include browser versions.**
4. Print the presentation as handouts with all five slides on one page and also print the comments page.
5. Save and then close the presentation.

Assessment 4

1. Open **SkillsPresentation**.
2. Save the presentation file as a Web page as a single file. Name the presentation **WebSkillsPres** and select the option to display the Web page in the Web browser window when the conversion is complete.
3. View the entire presentation in the Web browser window.
4. Close the Web browser window.
5. Close **SkillsPresentation**.

Assessment 5

1. Open **SkillsPresentation**.
2. Save the presentation with Save As and name it **sppc8sc05**.
3. Apply a different color scheme of your choosing to the presentation.
4. Delete Slide 8.
5. Save the presentation as a Web page as a folder with all supporting files. Name the presentation **SkillsPresWebPages**, change the *Save as type* option to *Web Page*, and select the option to display the Web page in the Web browser window when the conversion is complete.
6. Close the Web browser window.
7. Print the presentation as handouts with all seven slides on one page.
8. Save and then close **sppc8sc05**.

Assessment 6

1. In this and previous chapters, you have learned how to save presentations in different file formats. Use PowerPoint's Help feature to learn about the various file formats for saving presentations. Learn specifically about the Windows Metafile format.
2. Open **GlobalPresentation** and then save only Slide 5 in the Windows Metafile format in the PowerPointChapter08S folder on your disk and name the slide file **HomeComputers**.
3. Open Word and then open the document named **GlobalMarketing** located in the PowerPointChapter08S folder on your disk.

4. Position the insertion point at the beginning of the third paragraph (begins with *Call Global Marketing today...*).
5. Click the Insert Picture button on the Drawing toolbar.
6. At the Insert Picture dialog box, navigate to the PowerPointChapter08S folder on your disk and then double-click ***HomeComputers***.
7. Print the document by clicking the Print button on the Standard toolbar.
8. Save the document with the same name (**GlobalMarketing**).
9. Close **GlobalMarketing** and then exit Word.
10. Close ***Global Presentation*** without saving changes.

CHAPTER challenge

You work with the Marketing/Sales Director at Get Fit Athletic Club, a fitness club in your city. The Director has asked you to prepare a presentation for potential members who are interested in joining the club. The presentation should provide information on activities available at the club, incentive programs, and any other additional information you feel necessary. The presentation should include at least 10 slides. Use any of the features learned in the previous chapters that would make the presentation visually appealing. Insert at least two comments in the presentation and then send it to the Director (your professor) for review. Save the presentation as **GetFitAthleticClub.** Also, save the presentation (with the same name) as a Web page so that it can be posted to the club's Web site.

You would like to include pictures of individuals who are employed at the club, as well as pictures of the actual facility. Use the Help feature to learn about inserting pictures from a scanner or camera, and then insert at least one picture from a scanner or digital camera into the presentation created in the first part of the Chapter Challenge. Save the presentation again.

Create an Excel worksheet showing times that the club is being used by members and then create a chart based on the information. The chart should show the peak times and times when the facility is less utilized. Using the presentation, created and used in the first two parts of the Chapter Challenge, import the Excel chart into the presentation. Strategically position the slide, so that it logically flows in the presentation. Save the presentation again.

WORKPLACE Ready

Customizing and Enhancing PowerPoint Presentations

ASSESSING proficiency

In this unit, you have learned to add visual elements to presentations such as WordArt, organizational charts, diagrams, charts, tables, and sound and video clips. You also learned methods for sharing objects and files such as copying and pasting, copying and embedding, copying and linking, using action buttons, and creating hyperlinks. Techniques for sending presentations for review and then merging reviewers' comments were introduced as well as information on how to insert and print comments in a presentation and save a presentation as a Web page.

Assessment 1

1. Open **TelecomPresentation** (located in the PowerPointUnit02S folder on your disk).
2. Save the presentation with Save As and name it **sppu2pa01**.
3. Create a new Slide 7 (with the Title and Text slide layout) with the following specifications:
   a. Click the text *Click to add title* and then type APPLICATIONS.
   b. Click the text *Click to add text* and then copy text from Word and paste it into Slide 7 by completing the following steps:
      1) Open Word and then open **WordConcepts01**.
      2) Display the Clipboard task pane by clicking Edit and then Office Clipboard. (Make sure the Clipboard task pane is empty. If not, click the Clear All button.)
      3) Select *RECEIVING* and the paragraph below it and then click the Copy button.
      4) Select *STORING* and the paragraph below it and then click the Copy button.
      5) Select *TRANSMITTING* and the paragraph below it and then click the Copy button.
      6) Click the button on the Taskbar representing PowerPoint.
      7) Display the Clipboard task pane by clicking Edit and then Office Clipboard.
      8) Make sure the insertion point is positioned in the bulleted list placeholder in Slide 7 and then click the *TRANSMITTING* item in the Clipboard task pane.
      9) Press the Enter key and then click the *RECEIVING* item in the Clipboard task pane.

10) Clear the Clipboard task pane by clicking the Clear All button located in the upper right corner of the task pane.
11) Close the Clipboard task pane.
12) If necessary, make adjustments to the inserted text in the placeholder.

4. Apply an animation scheme of your choosing to all slides in the presentation.
5. Print the presentation as handouts with all seven slides on one page.
6. Run the presentation beginning with Slide 1.
7. Save and then close the presentation.
8. Make Word the active program, close the Clipboard task pane, close **WordConcepts01**, and then exit Word.

Assessment 2

1. Make sure PowerPoint is open and then open Word.
2. With Word the active program, open **WordOutline03**.
3. Import the text into PowerPoint.
4. Make PowerPoint the active program.
5. Make the following changes to the presentation:
   a. Change the slide layout for Slide 2 to Title Slide.
   b. Change the slide layout for Slide 3 to Title Slide.
   c. Change the slide layout for Slide 6 to Title Slide.
   d. Apply a design template of your choosing.
   e. Insert a clip art image related to "software" in Slide 5. If necessary, recolor the image to follow the color scheme of the design template.
   f. Check each slide and make any formatting changes to enhance the slide.
   g. Create the following hyperlinks for the text in Slide 6:

      Apple Computer = www.apple.com
      Microsoft Corporation = www.microsoft.com

   h. Insert the action button named Action Button: Home (links to first slide) at the bottom of Slide 3, Slide 4, and Slide 5.
   i. Insert the action button named Action Button: Return (links back to last slide viewed) at the bottom of Slide 1.
6. Apply a transition and sound of your choosing to all slides in the presentation.
7. Save the presentation and name it **sppu2pa02**.
8. Run the presentation beginning with Slide 1. (When Slide 3 displays, click the Home action button. After viewing Slide 1, click the Return action button. Continue in this manner with Slide 4 and Slide 5. If you are connected to the Internet, click the Apple Computer hyperlink in Slide 6. At the Apple Computer Web site, click a few hyperlinks that interest you and then close the Web browser. Click the Microsoft Corporation hyperlink in Slide 6. At the Microsoft Corporation Web site, click a few hyperlinks that interest you and then close the Web browser.)
9. Print all six slides on one page.
10. Save and then close the presentation.
11. Make Word active, close **WordOutline03**, and then exit Word.

Assessment 3

1. Create a presentation with the following specifications:
   a. Use a design template of your choosing.
   b. Create the first slide with the following specifications:
      1) Choose the Blank slide layout.
      2) Use WordArt to create the text *International Securities*. (You determine the shape and formatting of the WordArt text.)
   c. Create the second slide with the following specifications:
      1) Choose the Title Slide layout.
      2) Type **2005 SALES MEETING** as the title.
      3) Type **European Division** as the subtitle.
   d. Create the third slide with the following specifications:
      1) Choose the Title Only slide layout.
      2) Type **REGIONAL SALES** as the title.
      3) Open Excel and then open **ExcelWorkbook04**.
      4) Save the workbook with Save As and name it **SalesWorkbook**.
      5) Select cells A1 through D5 (the cells containing data) and then copy and embed the cells in Slide 3.
      6) Increase the size of the cells so they better fill the slide.
   e. Create the fourth slide with the following specifications:
      1) Make sure the slide contains the Title and Text slide layout.
      2) Type **2005 GOALS** as the title.
      3) Type the following as the bulleted items:

         Increase product sales by 15 percent.
         Open a branch office in Spain.
         Hire one manager and two additional account managers.
         Decrease production costs by 6 percent.
   f. Create the fifth slide with the following specifications:
      1) Choose the Title and Content slide layout.
      2) Type **HIRING TIMELINE** as the title.
      3) Click the Insert Table button in the content placeholder and then create a table with two columns and five rows.
      4) Type the following text in the cells in the table. (You determine the formatting of the cells.)

Task	*Date*
Advertise positions	**03/01/05 – 04/30/05**
Review resumes	**05/15/05 – 06/01/05**
Conduct interviews	**06/15/05 – 07/15/05**
Hire personnel	**08/01/05**

   g. Create the sixth slide with the following specifications:
      1) Choose the Title Only slide layout.
      2) Type **PRODUCTION EXPENSES** as the title.
      3) Make Excel the active program and then close **SalesWorkbook**.
      4) Open **ExcelWorkbook05**.
      5) Save the workbook with Save As and name it **ExpensesWorkbook**.
      6) Copy and then link the pie chart in **ExpensesWorkbook** to Slide 6.

7) Increase the size of the pie chart so it better fills the slide. (Be sure to maintain the integrity of the chart.)
8) Make Excel active, close **ExpensesWorkbook**, and then exit Excel.

h. Create the seventh slide with the following specifications:
1) Choose the Title and Content slide layout.
2) Type **OFFICE STRUCTURE** as the title.
3) Click the Insert Diagram or Organization Chart button in the content placeholder and then create an organizational chart with the following text:

	Ricardo Miraflores Manager	
Audrina Chorrillos Account Manager	Hector Palencia Account Manager	Jules Verde Account Manager

4) Apply an autoformat of your choosing to the organizational chart.

2. Save the presentation and name it **sppu2pa03**.
3. Add an animation scheme of your choosing to the slides in the presentation. (The animation scheme will not apply to Slide 1 because the slide contains only WordArt.)
4. Run the presentation beginning with Slide 1.
5. Print the slides as a handout with all slides on one page.
6. Save and then close the presentation.

Assessment 4

1. Open Excel and then open **ExpensesWorkbook**.
2. Make the following changes:
   a. B2: Change *38% to 41%*.
   b. B3: Change *35% to 32%*.
   c. B4: Change *18%* to *21%*.
   d. B5: Change *9%* to *6%*.
3. Save the workbook again with the same name (**ExpensesWorkbook**).
4. Print and then close **ExpensesWorkbook**.
5. Exit Excel.
6. With PowerPoint the active program, open **sppu2pa03**. (At the message that displays, click the Update Links button.)
7. Display Slide 3, double-click the cells to display Excel editing tools, and then make the following changes to the data in the embedded cells:
   a. C2: Change *2,678,450* to *2,857,300*.
   b. C3: Change *1,753,405* to *1,598,970*.
   c. C5: Change *2,315,600* to *2,095,170*.
8. Print the slides as a handout with all slides on one page.
9. Save and then close the presentation.

Assessment 5

1. Open **TelecomPresentation**.
2. Save the presentation with Save As and name it **sppu2pa05**.

3. Save the presentation for review by Marcus Cook with the name **sppu2pa05MC**. ***(Hint: Change the*** **Save as type** ***option at the Save As dialog box to*** **Presentation for Review.*)***
4. Save the presentation for review by Naomi Holden with the name **sppu2pa05NH**.
5. Close **sppu2pa05**.
6. At the blank PowerPoint screen, display the Options dialog box with the General tab selected, type **Marcus Cook** in the *Name* text box, type **MC** in the *Initials* text box, and then close the dialog box.
7. Edit the presentation as Marcus Cook by completing the following steps:
   a. Open **sppu2pa05MC**.
   b. At the message asking if you want to merge changes in **sppu2pa05NH** back into **sppu2pa05**, click No.
   c. Make the following changes:
      1) Edit Slide 1 so the subtitle reads *Technology Concepts*.
      2) Display Slide 2 and then edit the second bulleted item so it reads *Digital Camera* (instead of *35mm Camera*).
      3) Display Slide 5 and then add a new bulleted item at the end of the list that reads *Amplifier*.
8. Print the presentation as handouts with all six slides on one page.
9. Save and then close **sppu2pa05MC**.
10. At the blank PowerPoint screen, display the Options dialog box with the General tab selected, type **Naomi Holden** in the *Name* text box, type **NH** in the *Initials* text box, and then close the dialog box.
11. Edit the communication presentation as Naomi Holden by completing the following steps:
    a. Open **sppu2pa05NH**.
    b. At the message asking if you want to merge changes in **sppu2pa05NH** back into **sppu2pa05**, click No.
    c. Make the following changes:
       1) Display Slide 2 and then edit the fourth bulleted item so it displays as *Pointing Devices* (rather than *Mouse*) and add a new bulleted item at the end of the list that reads *Keyboard*.
       2) Display Slide 3 and then delete the second bulleted item *Telephone* and then insert a new bulleted item at the end of the list that reads *Monitoring Systems*.
       3) Display Slide 4 and then insert a new bulleted item between the third and fourth items that reads *Twisted-Pair and Coaxial Cable*.
12. Print the presentation as handouts with all six slides on one page.
13. Save and then close **sppu2pa05NH**.
14. Display the Options dialog box with the General tab selected, change the name and initials in the *User information* section back to the original information, and then close the dialog box.

Assessment 6

1. Open **sppu2pa05**.
2. Display the Choose Files to Merge with Current Presentation dialog box, select ***sppu2pa05MC***, select ***sppu2pa05NH***, and then click the Merge button.

3. Apply the following changes to slides:
   Slide 1 = Do not apply changes
   Slide 2 = Apply change made by Marcus Cook
   Do not apply change by Naomi Holden
   Slide 3 = Apply all changes
   Slide 4 = Do not apply changes
   Slide 5 = Apply all changes
4. Save the presentation with Save As and name it **sppu2pa06**.
5. Apply a transition and sound of your choosing to all slides in the presentation.
6. Print the presentation as handouts with all six slides on one page.
7. Use the Rehearse Timings feature to set the following times for the slides to display during a slide show:
   Slide 1 = 3 seconds
   Slide 2 = 4 seconds
   Slide 3 = 5 seconds
   Slide 4 = 5 seconds
   Slide 5 = 6 seconds
   Slide 6 = 5 seconds
8. Set up the slide show to run continuously.
9. Run the presentation beginning with Slide 1. Watch the slide show until the presentation has started for the second time and then end the show.
10. Save and then close the presentation.

Assessment 7

1. Open **sppu2pa02**.
2. Save the presentation with Save As and name it **sppu2pa07**.
3. Insert the following comments:
   Slide 4 = Click immediately right of the third bulleted item and then insert the comment **Include specific timeline on hiring new personnel.**
   Slide 5 = Click immediately right of the last bulleted item and then insert the comment **Specify the percentage of business for each category.**
4. Print the presentation as handouts with all six slides on one page and also print the comments page.
5. Save and then close the presentation.

Assessment 8

1. Open **TelecomPresentation**.
2. Save the presentation file as a Web page as a single file. Name the presentation **WebTelecomPres** and select the option to display the Web page in the Web browser window.
3. View the entire presentation in the Web browser window.
4. Close the Web browser window.
5. Close **TelecomPresentation** without saving the changes.

WRITING activities

The following activities give you the opportunity to practice your writing skills along with demonstrating an understanding of some of the important PowerPoint features you have mastered in this unit. Use correct grammar, appropriate word choices, and clear sentence structure.

Activity 1

Using PowerPoint's Help feature, learn more about file formats for saving and importing in presentations and then prepare a PowerPoint presentation with the information by completing the following steps:

1. Use the PowerPoint Help feature to look up and then print information on the following topics:
   - File formats for saving presentations
   - File formats PowerPoint can import as charts
   - Graphic file types and filters
2. Read the information you printed on file formats and then prepare a PowerPoint presentation that includes *at least* the following information:
   - Slide containing the title of presentation and your name
   - Two slides containing available file formats for saving presentations including the file format type, extension, and what it is used to save
   - Slide containing information on what file formats PowerPoint can import
   - Slide containing information on graphic file types and filters
3. Apply an animation scheme of your choosing to all slides in the presentation.
4. Save the completed presentation and name it **sppu2act01**.
5. Run the presentation.
6. Print the presentation as handouts with all slides on one page (if possible).
7. Close the presentation.

Activity 2

1. Open Word and then open and print **TravelVacations**. Close **TravelVacations** and then exit Word. Looking at the printing of this document, create a presentation in PowerPoint that presents the main points of the document. Apply an animation scheme of your choosing to all slides in the presentation.
2. Save the presentation and name it **sppu2act02**.
3. Run the presentation.
4. Print the slides as handouts with six slides per page.
5. Close the presentation.

INTERNET activity

Presenting Office 2003

Make sure you are connected to the Internet and then explore the Microsoft Web site at www.microsoft.com. Browse the various categories and links on the Web site to familiarize yourself with how information has been organized.

Create a PowerPoint presentation that could be delivered to someone who has just purchased Office 2003 and wants to know how to find more information about the software from the Microsoft Web site. Include points or tips on where to find product release information and technical support. Include hyperlinks to important pages at the Microsoft Web site. Add formatting and enhancements to make the presentation as dynamic as possible. Save the presentation and name it **MicrosoftPresentation**. View the slide show. Print the presentation as handouts with all slides on one page (if possible). Close **MicrosoftPresentation**.

JOB study

Creating a Skills Presentation

Your manager has asked you to prepare a PowerPoint presentation explaining to a group of new employees the skills they will be trained in as they begin a position with your company. Your presentation should include at least one table (use **JobSkillsTable** in the PowerPointUnit02S folder on the CD that accompanies this text), one hyperlink to a Web site, one hyperlink to a file, and one linked or embedded object that can be updated automatically from within the presentation.

Create at least 10 slides, as well as a summary slide, for a total of at least 11 slides. Insert action buttons to move to the next page for the first slide through the second from the end. On your final slide, create an action button to return to the first slide.

Save and then run the presentation. Print the slides as handouts with six slides per page. Send your presentation to Microsoft Word and then save and print an outline of your presentation.

INDEX

OFFICE 2003

INTEGRATED PROJECT

Now that you have completed the chapters in this textbook, you have learned to create documents in Word, build worksheets in Excel, organize data in Access, and design presentations in PowerPoint. To learn the various programs in the Microsoft Office 2003 suite, you have completed a variety of exercises, assessments, and activities. This integrated project is a final assignment that allows you to apply the knowledge you have gained about the programs in the Office suite to produce a variety of documents and files.

Situation

You are the vice president of Classique Coffees, a gourmet coffee company. Your company operates two retail stores that sell gourmet coffee and related products to the public. One retail store is located in Seattle, Washington, the other in Tacoma. The company is three years old and has seen approximately a 15- to 30-percent growth in profit each year. Your duties as the vice president of the company include researching the coffee market, studying coffee buying trends, designing and implementing new projects, and supervising the marketing, sales, and personnel managers.

Activity 1: Writing Persuasively

Using Word, compose a memo to the president of Classique Coffees, Leslie Steiner, detailing your research and recommendations:

- Research has shown a 20-percent growth in the iced coffee market.
- The target population for iced coffees is people from ages 18 to 35.
- Market analysis indicates that only three local retail companies sell iced coffees in the greater Seattle-Tacoma area.
- The recommendation is that Classique Coffees develop a suite of iced coffees for market consumption by early next year. (Be as persuasive as possible.)

Save the completed memo and name it **ProjectAct01**. Print and then close **ProjectAct01**.

Activity 2: Designing a Letterhead

You are not satisfied with the current letterhead used by your company. Design a new letterhead for Classique Coffees using Word and include the following information:

- Use a clip art image in the letterhead. (Consider downloading a clip art image from the Microsoft Office Online Clip Art and Media Web site.)
- Include the company name—Classique Coffees.
- Include the company address—355 Pioneer Square, Seattle, WA 98211.
- Include the company telephone number—(206) 555-6690.
- Include the company e-mail address—ccoffees@gourmet.emcp.net.
- Create a slogan that will help your business contacts remember your company.
- Add any other information or elements that you feel are appropriate.

When the letterhead is completed, save it and name it **ProjectAct02**. Print and then close **ProjectAct02**.

Activity 3: Preparing a Notice

Using Word, prepare a notice about an upcoming marketing seminar. Include the following information in the notice:

- Name of the seminar—Marketing to the Coffee Gourmet
- Location of the seminar—Conference room at the corporate office, 355 Pioneer Square, Seattle, WA 98211
- Date and time of seminar—Friday, October 14, 2005, 9:00 a.m. to 2:30 p.m.
- Topics that will be covered at the seminar:
    - > identifying coffee-drinking trends
    - > assessing the current gourmet coffee market
    - > developing new products
    - > analyzing the typical Classique Coffees customer
    - > marketing a new product line
- Consider including a clip art image in the notice. (You determine an appropriate clip art image.)

When the notice is completed, save it and name it **ProjectAct03**. Print and then close **ProjectAct03**.

Activity 4: Designing a Web Page

At a recent corporate meeting, a decision was made to create a Web site home page for Classique Coffees. You have been asked to design a preliminary Web page. Create the Web page in Word and include the following:

- Company name, address, and e-mail address
- Brief explanation of the company (see the "Situation" section at the beginning of this project)
- List the types of coffees sold (see Activity 7 for the list of coffees).
- Add that iced coffees will be introduced soon.
- Include some hyperlinks to interesting gourmet coffee sites (search the Web for sites, find two or three interesting sites, and then include the URL for each site as a hyperlink in your Web page).

When the Web page is completed, save it and name it **CCHomePage**. Print and then close **CCHomePage**.

Activity 5: Building a Budget Worksheet

Using Excel, prepare a worksheet with the following information:

Annual Budget: $1,450,000

Department	**Percent of Budget**	**Total**
Administration	10%	
Purchasing	24%	
Sales	21%	
Marketing	23%	
Personnel	12%	
Training	10%	

Insert formulas that will calculate the total amount for each budget based on the specified percentage of the annual budget. When the worksheet is completed, save it and name it **ProjectAct05** and then print **ProjectAct05**.

Determine the impact of a 10-percent increase in the annual budget on the total amount for each department. With the amounts displayed for a 10-percent increase, save and then print **ProjectAct05**.

Activity 6: Determining Sales Quota Increases

The Marketing Department for Classique Coffees employs seven employees who market the company products to customers. These employees are given a quota for yearly sales that they are to meet. You have determined that the quota needs to be raised for the upcoming year. You are not sure whether the quotas should be increased 5 percent or 10 percent. Using Excel, prepare a worksheet with the following information:

CLASSIQUES COFFEES

Sales Quotas

Employee	**Current Quota**	**Projected Quota**
Berenstein	$125,000	
Evans	$100,000	
Grayson	$110,000	
Lueke	$135,000	
Nasson	$125,000	
Phillips	$150,000	
Samuels	$175,000	

Insert a formula to determine the projected quotas at 5 percent more than the current quota. Save the worksheet and name it **ProjectAct06A** and then print **ProjectAct06A**. Determine the projected quotas at 10 percent more than the current quota. Save the worksheet and name it **ProjectAct06B** and then print **ProjectAct06B**.

Activity 7: Building a Sales Worksheet and Creating a Chart

Using Excel, prepare a worksheet with the following information:

Type of Coffee	Percent of Sales
Regular blend	22%
Espresso blend	12%
Regular blend decaf	17%
Espresso blend decaf	10%
Flavored blend	25%
Flavored blend decaf	14%

Save the completed worksheet and name it **ProjectAct07** and then print **ProjectAct07**. With the worksheet still displayed, create a pie chart as a new sheet with the data in the worksheet. Title the pie chart *2005 Percentage of Sales*. When the chart is completed, save the worksheet (now two sheets) with the same name (**ProjectAct07**). Print only the sheet containing the pie chart and then close **ProjectAct07**.

Activity 8: Building a Projected Sales Worksheet and Creating a Chart

Using Excel, prepare a worksheet with the following information:

Type of Coffee	Percent of Sales
Regular blend	21%
Espresso blend	10%
Regular blend decaf	16%
Espresso blend decaf	8%
Flavored blend	24%
Flavored blend decaf	13%
Iced	5%
Iced decaf	3%

Create a pie chart as a new sheet with the data in the worksheet. Title the pie chart *Year 2006 Projected Percentage of Sales*. When the chart is completed, save the worksheet (two sheets) and name it **ProjectAct08**. Print and then close **ProjectAct08**.

Analyze the sales data by comparing and contrasting the pie charts created in ProjectAct07 and ProjectAct08. What areas in the projected sales percentages have changed? What do these changes indicate? Assume that the projected 2006 annual income for Classique Coffees is $2,200,000. What amount of that income will come from iced coffees (including decaf iced coffees)? Does this amount warrant marketing this new product? Prepare a memo in Word to Leslie Steiner that includes your analysis. Add any other interpretations you can make from analyzing the pie charts. Save the memo and name it **WordProject08**. Print and then close **WordProject08**.

Activity 9: Designing and Creating a Presentation

Using PowerPoint, prepare a marketing slide presentation. Include the following information in the presentation:

- Classique Coffees 2006 Marketing Plan (title)
- Company reorganization (create an organizational chart)

President

Vice President

Marketing Manager	**Sales Manager**	**Personnel Manager**
Marketing Assistants	**Sales Associates**	**Assistant Manager**

- 2005 sales percentages (insert into the slide the pie chart that is part of the ProjectAct07 worksheet)
- 2006 projected sales percentages (insert into the slide the pie chart that is part of the ProjectAct08 worksheet)
- Iced coffee marketing strategy
    > target customer
    > analysis of competition
    > wholesale resources
    > pricing
    > volume
- Product placement
    > stocking strategies
    > shelf allocation
    > stock rotation schedule
    > seasonal display

When preparing the slide presentation, you determine the presentation design and the autolayouts. Include any clip art images that might be appropriate and apply an animation scheme to all slides. When the presentation is completed, save it and name it **ProjectAct09**. Run the presentation and then print the presentation with six slides on a page.

Activity 10: Creating a Database File and Organizing Data

Use Access to create a database for Classique Coffees that contains information on suppliers and products. Include the following fields in the Suppliers table and the Products table (you determine the specific field names):

Suppliers table:
- Supplier #
- Supplier Name
- Address
- City
- State
- ZIP Code
- E-mail Address

Products table:
- Product #
- Product
- Supplier #

Type the following data in the Suppliers table:

Supplier #	=	24
Supplier Name	=	Gourmet Blends
Address	=	109 South Madison
City	=	Seattle
State	=	WA
ZIP Code	=	98032
E-mail Address	=	gblends@coffee.emcp.net

Supplier #	=	36
Supplier Name	=	Jannsen Company
Address	=	4122 South Sprague
City	=	Tacoma
State	=	WA
ZIP Code	=	98402
E-mail Address	=	jannsen@coffee.emcp.net

Supplier #	=	62
Supplier Name	=	Sure Shot Supplies
Address	=	291 Pacific Avenue
City	=	Tacoma
State	=	WA
ZIP Code	=	98418
E-mail Address	=	sssupplies@coffee.emcp.net

Supplier #	=	41
Supplier Name	=	Bertolino's
Address	=	11711 Meridian East
City	=	Seattle
State	=	WA
ZIP Code	=	98109
E-mail Address	=	bertolino@coffee.emcp.net

Type the following data in the Products table:

Product #	= 12A-0		Product #	= 59R-1	
Product	= Premium blend		Product	= Vanilla syrup	
Supplier #	= 24		Supplier #	= 62	
Product #	= 12A-1		Product #	= 59R-2	
Product	= Cappuccino blend		Product	= Raspberry syrup	
Supplier #	= 24		Supplier #	= 62	
Product #	= 12A-2		Product #	= 59R-3	
Product	= Hazelnut blend		Product	= Chocolate syrup	
Supplier #	= 24		Supplier #	= 62	
Product #	= 21B-2		Product #	= 89T-3	
Product	= 12-oz cup		Product	= Napkins, 500 ct	
Supplier #	= 36		Supplier #	= 41	
Product #	= 21B-3		Product #	= 89T-4	
Product	= 16-oz cup		Product	= 6-inch stir stick	
Supplier #	= 36		Supplier #	= 41	

Print both the Suppliers table and the Products table in landscape orientation. Prepare a report with the following information: Supplier name, Supplier #, Supplier e-mail, and Product.

Merge the records of those suppliers that are located in Tacoma to a blank Word screen. You determine the fields to use in the inside address and an appropriate salutation. Compose a business letter that will be sent to the contacts in Tacoma that includes the following information:

- Explain that Classique Coffees is interested in selling iced coffees in the greater Seattle/Tacoma area.
- Ask if the company offers any iced coffee products.
- If the company does not currently offer any iced coffee products, will these products be available in the future?

- Ask the company to send any materials on current products and specifically on iced coffees.
- Ask someone at the company to contact you at the Classique Coffees address, by telephone at (206) 555-6690, or e-mail at ccoffees@gourmet.emcp.net.
- Include any other information you think appropriate to the topic.

Merge to a new document and then save the document with the name **ProjectAct10**. Print and then close **ProjectAct10**. Save the main document as **IcedCoffeeLetter** and then close **IcedCoffeeLetter**.

Activity 11: Assessing Your Work

Review the documents you developed and assess your own work in writing. In order to develop an objective perspective of your work, openly solicit constructive criticism from your teacher, peers, and contacts outside of school. Your self-assessment document should specify the weaknesses and strengths of each piece and your specific recommendations for revision and improvement.